Modeling the Dynamics of Life

Calculus for Life Scientists

Custom Edition

Frederick R. Adler

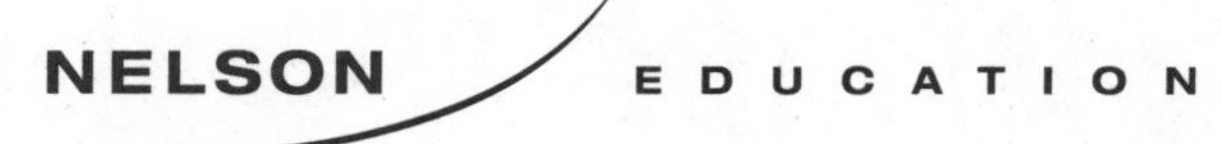

Printed and bound in Canada
4 5 11 10 09

For more information contact
Nelson Education Limited
1120 Birchmount Road,
Scarborough, Ontario, M1K 5G4.
Or you can visit our internet site at
http://www.nelson.com

This textbook is a Nelson custom publication. Because your instructor has chosen to produce a custom publication, you pay only for material that you will use in your course.

ISBN-13: 978-0-17-647634-2
ISBN-10: 0-17-647634-2

Consists of:

Modeling the Dynamics of Life, Second Edition
Frederick R. Adler
ISBN-13: 978-0-534-40486-4
ISBN-10: 0-534-40486-3 , © 2005

Algebra

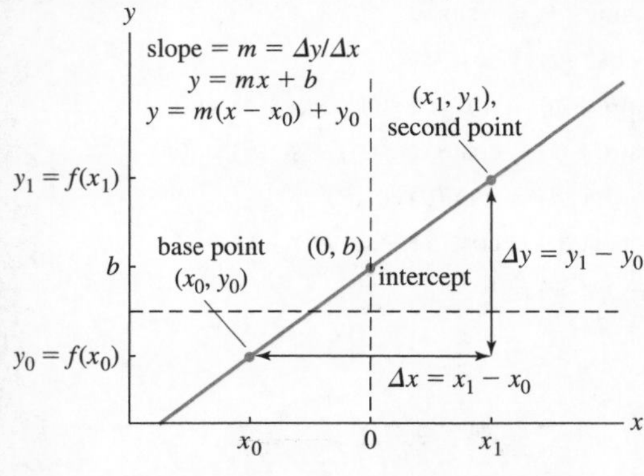

Formulas for a Line

Slope-intercept form: The line passing through the point $(0, b)$ with slope m has formula $y = mx + b$.

Point-slope form: The line passing through the point (x_0, y_0) with slope m has formula $y = m(x - x_0) + y_0$.

Solving Equations

Solving a linear equation for x:

$ax + b = 0$	Original equation
$ax = -b$	Subtract b from both sides
$x = -\frac{b}{a}$	Divide both sides by a

Solving a quadratic equation for x: The solutions of $ax^2 + bx + c = 0$ are

$$x = \frac{-b \pm \sqrt{b^2 - 4ac}}{2a}$$

Geometry

Area of circle of radius $r = \pi r^2$ Volume of sphere of radius $r = \frac{4}{3}\pi r^3$

Circumference of circle $= 2\pi r$ Surface area of sphere $= 4\pi r^2$

Trigonometry

Definitions of Trigonometric Functions

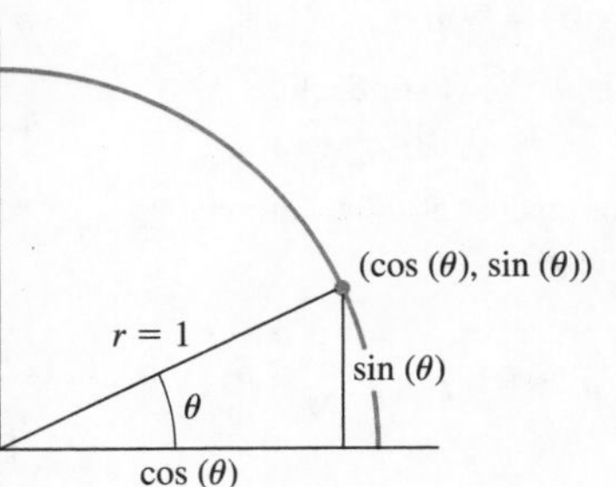

Sine	$\sin(\theta)$	vertical coordinate of a point on the unit circle making an angle θ with the horizontal axis
Cosine	$\cos(\theta)$	horizontal coordinate of a point on the unit circle making an angle θ with the horizontal axis
Tangent	$\tan(\theta)$	$\frac{\sin(\theta)}{\cos(\theta)}$
Cotangent	$\cot(\theta)$	$\frac{\cos(\theta)}{\sin(\theta)}$
Secant	$\sec(\theta)$	$\frac{1}{\cos(\theta)}$
Cosecant	$\csc(\theta)$	$\frac{1}{\sin(\theta)}$

Trigonometric Identities

Symmetry	$\sin(-\theta) = -\sin(\theta)$
	$\cos(-\theta) = \cos(\theta)$
Angle addition	$\sin(\theta + \phi) = \sin(\theta)\cos(\phi) + \cos(\theta)\sin(\phi)$
	$\cos(\theta + \phi) = \cos(\theta)\cos(\phi) - \sin(\theta)\sin(\phi)$
Double angle	$\sin(2\theta) = 2\sin(\theta)\cos(\theta)$
	$\cos(2\theta) = \cos^2(\theta) - \sin^2(\theta)$
Basic Identity	$\sin^2(\theta) + \cos^2(\theta) = 1$

Basic Discrete-Time Dynamical Systems

Description	Updating Function	Solution or Behavior
Population of size b_t with constant per capita production r	$b_{t+1} = rb_t$	Exponential growth or decay $b_t = r^t b_0$
Quantity h_t with constant growth by amount c	$h_{t+1} = h_t + c$	Linear growth or decline $h_t = h_0 + ct$
Concentration c_t with lung with fraction $q < 1$ exchanged and ambient concentration γ	$c_{t+1} = (1-q)c_t + q\gamma$	Approaches equilibrium at $c^* = \gamma$
Selection model: Fraction of mutants p_t where mutant per capita production is s and wild-type per capita production is r	$p_{t+1} = \dfrac{sp_t}{sp_t + r(1-p_t)}$	Approaches $p^* = 1$ if $s > r$ and $p^* = 0$ if $s < r$
Logistic model: Population, relative to a maximum of 1, of size x_t with per capita production r	$x_{t+1} = rx_t(1-x_t)$	Approaches $x^* = 0$ if $r \le 1$ Approaches positive stable equilibrium if $1 < r \le 3$ No stable equilibrium if $3 < r \le 4$

Basic Autonomous Differential Equations

Description	Equation	Solution or Behavior
Population of size $b(t)$ with constant per capita production rate λ	$\dfrac{db}{dt} = \lambda b$	Exponential growth or decay $b(t) = b(0)e^{\lambda t}$
Quantity $V(t)$ with constant increase or decrease at rate c	$\dfrac{dV}{dt} = c$	Linear growth or decline $V(t) = V(0) + ct$
Newton's Law of Cooling: The temperature $H(t)$ of an object with cooling rate α and ambient temperature A	$\dfrac{dH}{dt} = \alpha(A - H)$	Approaches equilibrium at $H^* = A$
Selection model: The proportion of mutants $p(t)$ where mutant per capita production rate is μ and wild-type per capita production rate is λ	$\dfrac{dp}{dt} = (\mu - \lambda)p(1-p)$	Approaches $p^* = 1$ if $\mu > \lambda$ $p^* = 0$ if $\mu < \lambda$

Basic Theorems of Calculus

Intermediate Value Theorem: A continuous function f defined for $a \leq x \leq b$ takes on each value c between $f(a)$ and $f(b)$ at least once.

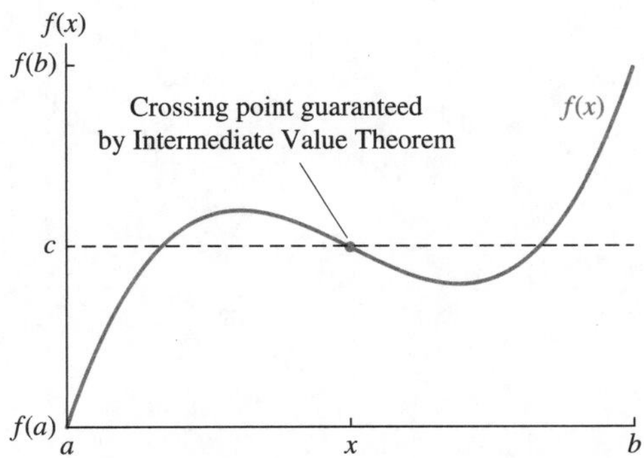

Extreme Value Theorem: A continuous function f defined for $a \leq x \leq b$ takes on its global maximum and minimum.

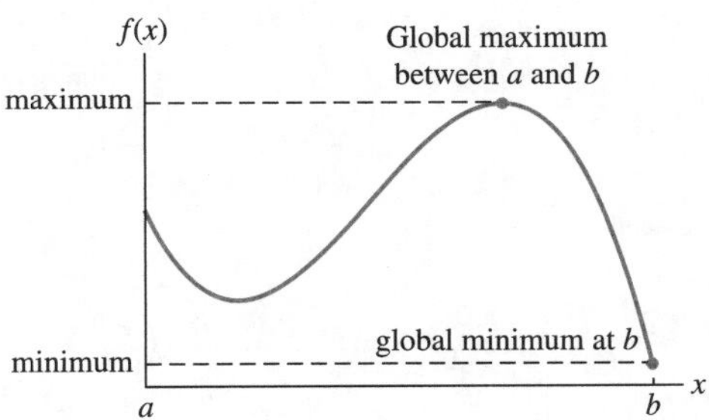

Mean Value Theorem: A differentiable function f defined for $a \leq x \leq b$ has a point c where $f'(c)$ is equal to the slope of the secant line connecting $(a, f(a))$ and $(b, f(b))$.

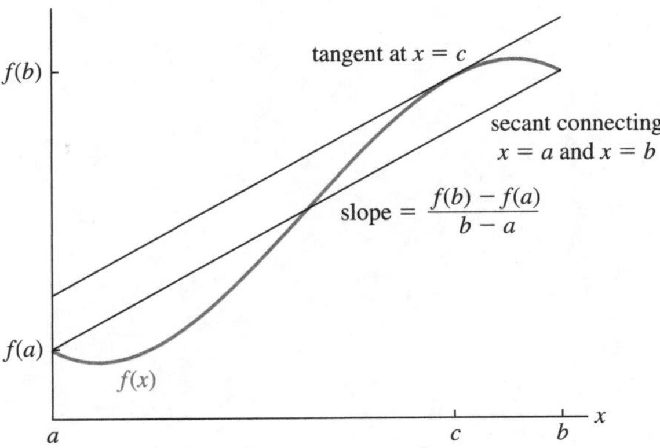

Fundamental Theorem of Calculus: If $F(x) = \int f(x)dx$ then $\int_a^b f(x)dx = F(b) - F(a) = F(x)|_a^b$.

Contents

Preface

Modeling the Dynamics of Life teaches calculus, with additional chapters on probability and statistics, as a way of introducing freshman and sophomore life science majors to the insights mathematics can provide into biology. Why should there be a special book for this audience? Although the importance of quantitative skills in the life sciences is much discussed, current realities tend to conceal their vital role. Too often, biology is the natural science of last resort for students who believe "they aren't cut out for math." Most colleges and universities require little calculus for their biology majors, and those that require a full calculus course doubt its worth when students emerge unable to apply even precalculus mathematics in new contexts. Students are left with similar doubts when the techniques they learned for tests vanish as swiftly from the curriculum as from their memories. Students, biology faculty, and administrators see that biology is burgeoning as a science and as a major, apparently unhindered by pervasive mathematical illiteracy.

In fact, mathematics has played an important if underappreciated role in biology, providing the impetus for breakthroughs in areas including epidemiology, genetics, statistics, and physiology. As a theoretical biologist who uses mathematics to make sense of complex biological systems, I see this role expanding, not contracting. Although a great deal of biology can be done without any mathematics, the powerful new technologies that are transforming fields of biology—from genetics and physiology to ecology—are increasingly quantitative, as are many of the questions at the frontiers of knowledge. Along with genetics, mathematics is one of two unifying factors in the life sciences. And as biology becomes more important in society, mathematical literacy becomes as vital for doctors, business people, lawyers, and art historians as for researchers.

Modeling

The central goal of this book is simple: to teach biology majors the mathematical ideas I use every day in my own research and in collaborations with colleagues engaged in more empirical activities. These ideas are not specific techniques such as differentiation, but concepts of modeling. The skills include describing a system, translating appropriate aspects into equations, and interpreting the results in terms of the original problem. In this process, the science is central, and solving the equations is in some ways the least important step.

Even students who will do little modeling on their own will be confronted by the models of others. This book teaches students how to **read** models. Like computers, mathematical models have an aura of authority to those who cannot understand them. As a modeler myself, I want my work to be read, understood, and challenged by knowledgeable scientists. This book aims to give students the skills and confidence to do so.

The Dynamics of Life

Mathematics helps unify biology by identifying dynamical principles that underlie a remarkable diversity of biological processes. This book follows three themes throughout: **growth, diffusion,** and **selection.** Each theme is studied in turn with three kinds of model: discrete-time dynamical systems (Chapters 1–3), differential equations

(Chapters 4–5), and stochastic processes (Chapters 6–8). The concept of diffusion is treated as a discrete-time dynamical system describing a lung (Section 1.9), as a differential equation describing movement of a chemical across a membrane (Section 5.1), and as a Markov chain describing the random behavior of an individual molecule (Section 6.2). Addressing these themes in different ways shows students how different mathematical ideas describe and explain different facets of a biological process.

The Contents

These three themes provide a logical context to teach the standard material of a calculus text, and more. First, students review the basic functional building blocks of applied mathematics in the context of dynamics. For example, exponential functions are studied as the solutions of linear discrete-time dynamical systems (Section 1.7). Because dynamics motivates the book from the beginning, differentiation arises naturally as a way to describe instantaneous rates of change (Section 2.1). The dynamical models provide an array of functions for which differentiation is more than an algebraic exercise (Section 2.8). Integration is introduced via its most important application, solving differential equations (Sections 4.2 and 5.4).

Additional topics, which are often covered in less detail in traditional texts, fit naturally within the framework created by modeling and dynamics. Just as students need an intuitive understanding of basic measurements, such as distance and temperature, they need an intuitive understanding of the functions that express relationships between these measurements. The book emphasizes "reasoning about functions" and includes extensive sections devoted to applications of such general theorems as the Intermediate Value Theorem (Section 3.4), sketching graphs using the method of leading behavior (Section 3.6), and approximating functions with the tangent line or Taylor polynomials (Section 3.7). These skills translate into the ability to reason about the stability of discrete-time dynamical systems (Sections 3.1 and 3.2) and differential equations (Section 5.2). Dynamics provides a natural context to derive and explain Newton's method (Section 3.8) and the meaning of the second derivative (Section 2.7).

Teaching probability without using calculus is like studying biology without using genetics. The final three chapters teach probability and statistics from the dynamical perspective, using discrete-time dynamical systems (Section 6.2) and differential equations (Section 7.6) to model fundamental stochastic processes such as Markov chains (Section 6.1) and the Poisson process (Section 7.7). The integral and the Fundamental Theorem of Calculus have one of their most important applications in the theory of probability density functions (Section 6.6), reinforcing these foundational calculus concepts.

In the minds of some, statistics is the only quantitative skill that life scientists need. *Modeling the Dynamics of Life* stresses that it is impossible to use statistics correctly and flexibly without understanding the underlying probabilistic models, such as Markov chains and the Poisson process. The book emphasizes the links between models of those processes and the fundamental statistical notions of likelihood (Section 8.1), confidence limits (Section 8.2), and hypothesis testing (Section 8.4). Students learn the **principles** of statistics and emerge with a set of tools that encourage understanding statistics rather than merely choosing the correct recipe.

Graphical Methods

The focus on reasoning about what models **mean** favors graphical and computer techniques, the methods professionals use when equations cannot be solved. Understanding a discrete-time dynamical system with cobwebbing (Section 1.6) makes visual sense of such advanced topics as stability (Section 3.1) and chaos (Section 3.2). The phase line (Section 5.2) provides a visual presentation that summarizes the meaning of an autonomous differential equation, just as the phase plane (Section 5.6) summarizes a system of coupled differential equations and describes one mechanism of biological oscillation (Section 5.8). Approximation methods essential in more advanced applied mathematics are introduced through the method of leading behavior (Section 3.6) and its graphical interpretation.

Algorithms

There are many crucial logical procedures that students will use again and again to solve problems. These are set out as approximately 30 algorithms, including

- Finding equilibria for discrete-time dynamical systems (Section 1.6)
- Applying the chain rule (Section 2.9)
- Finding global maxima and minima (Section 3.3)
- Applying integration by substitution (Section 4.3)
- Using the method of separation of variables (Section 5.4)
- Computing descriptive statistics such as the mean, median, and mode (Section 6.8)
- Applying the standard normal distribution (Section 7.9)
- Finding the value of r^2 from a linear regression (Section 8.9).

In-Depth Explorations of Particular Models

The book includes several extended explorations. Early on, the power of cobwebbing is put to work to study the phenomenon of AV block in the heart (Section 1.11). The application of maximization methods to fisheries, along with their interaction with dynamics, is presented in Section 3.3. These methods are used to analyze fully an extension of the basic lung model to study optimal breathing patterns (Section 3.9). Phase-plane methods are used to analyze the Fitzhugh-Nagumo equations describing a neuron (Section 5.8). These extended developments show students how to combine a set of processes into a coherent whole and how to use models to clarify hypotheses and answer specific questions.

Problems

In addition to more routine skills problems at the end of each section, each section includes a wide variety of modeling problems to emphasize consistently the importance of interpretation. Examples include

- Harvesting (introduced in Section 1.5, Exercises 57–58 and revisited in Sections 1.9, 3.1, 3.3, and 5.2)
- Mutation (Section 1.10, Exercises 25–32, returned to in Section 6.2, Exercises 53–56)
- Consequences of non-linear medication dynamics (introduced in Section 1.10, Exercises 39–42 and explored further in Section 3.1, Exercises 32–33 and Section 3.8, Exercises 27–28).

Each chapter includes supplementary problems drawn from previous tests and practice tests. These introduce a variety of new applications and can be used for review and practice sessions.

Complete Solutions Manual

A complete solutions manual is available. It contains solutions to all odd- and even-numbered problems and to the supplementary problems (excluding computer problems and projects).

Computer Problems

The book includes well over 100 exercises designed to be explored via computer or graphing calculator. These exercises emphasize visualization, experimentation, and simulation. Examples include

- Simulation of a simple linear discrete-time dynamical system describing harvesting and observation of threshold behavior to motivate the later discussion of unstable equilibria in Section 3.1 (Section 1.6, Exercise 47)
- Exploration of the power of Fourier series through seeing how cosine functions can sum to an approximate square wave (Section 1.8, Exercise 55)
- Experimentation with the approximate rate of change to motivate the subsequent derivation of the derivative of cosine (Section 2.1, Exercise 45)
- Simulation of a mutation process to show how different individual samples can be from averages (Section 6.2, Exercise 59).

The computer lab is an effective alternative learning environment for students who communicate well with machines, and it is an excellent place for students to work with one another and with instructors.

Projects

Each chapter includes projects. These are recommended for individual or group exploration. Examples include

- Modeling the balance between selection and mutation (project 1.1)
- Study of periodic hematopoiesis with a discrete-time dynamical system (project 2.1)
- Experimentation with different numerical schemes for solving differential equations (project 4.1)
- Careful study of models of adaptation by cells (project 5.1)
- Development of the famous Luria-Delbruck fluctuation test (project 7.2).

Teaching

Although the book is designed for a full-year, introductory-level course, there are many other ways in which it can be used.

- One-semester calculus course: Chapters 1–4 (with the possible omission of the extended models in Sections 1.11 and 3.9)
- One-quarter calculus course: Chapters 1–4 (with the possible omission of Sections 1.11, 3.1, 3.2, 3.6, 3.7, 3.8, 3.9, and 4.7)
- One-semester probability course for students who have had calculus: Chapters 6–8 (with background on discrete-time dynamical systems from Sections 1.5–1.7, and a short review of differential equations as in Section 5.1)
- One-quarter probability course for students who have had calculus: Chapters 6–8 (like the one-semester course, but must be taken at a rather rapid pace; can be made to work by eliminating the final three sections)
- One-quarter or one-semester graduate modeling course: The entire book, with an emphasis on the main modeling ideas. Introduce discrete-time dynamical systems (Sections 1.2, 1.5–1.10, and 3.1–3.2), reasoning about functions (Sections 3.3–3.8), one-dimensional differential equations (Sections 4.1, 4.2,

and 5.1–5.3), two-dimensional differential equations (Sections 5.4–5.7), stochastic processes (Sections 6.1–6.3, and 6.6), probability models (Sections 7.3–7.8), and statistics (Sections 8.1–8.4). Such a course should emphasize the extended modeling sections (Sections 1.11, 3.9, and 5.8) and the projects.

Why Bother?

What are the benefits of this approach? The modeling approach is naturally a **problem-solving** approach. All instructors know that students will not remember every technique they have learned. This book emphasizes understanding what a model *is* and recognizing what models *say*. To be able to **recognize** a differential equation, **interpret** the terms, and **use** the solution is far more important than knowing how to **find** the solution. These reasoning skills, in addition to familiarity with models in general, are what stay with the motivated student and are what matter most in the end.

Most important, the course is fun to teach. Leading students through an integrated course for a full year removes the pressure for instant instructor gratification. ("All of my students could take the derivatives of polynomials.") Instead, one can allow understanding to develop as concepts come up for the second or third time. Students find this unsettling and yearn for instant gratification too. But with time, they accept the challenge of thinking. When they begin to apply their new powers to their own problems, when they solve a problem on the computer without being told to, and when they teach me something about biology in the context of a mathematical idea, delayed gratification starts to feel like the best possible kind.

Preface to the Second Edition

Modeling the Dynamics of Life teaches calculus, with additional chapters on probability and statistics, as a way of introducing freshman and sophomore life science majors to the insights mathematics can provide into biology. This second edition maintains the philosophy of the first edition: an emphasis on modeling, interpretation of results, basic biological processes, and the integration of calculus with probability and statistics.

I have made extensive changes to make the text work better in the classroom. Most important, the number of problems has been more than tripled, and these problems have been divided into "Mathematical Techniques," "Applications," and "Computer Exercises." The well over 3000 problems included will give students ample practice in the mechanics of calculations as well as explorations of the art of modeling. To help students with the exercises, I have included many more worked examples in the text and have set them apart graphically for easy reference.

The contents of the book have been slightly rearranged and expanded for clarity. In particular, the first chapter now opens with a review of functions, units, and linear functions before launching into the new topic of discrete-time dynamical systems. It introduces the basic methods for analysis of discrete-time dynamical systems before developing the more detailed models of the lung, natural selection, and the heart. The difficult section "Power Functions and Allometry" has been removed. Finally, I added a section to Chapter 8 describing the fundamentals of contigency table analysis.

Acknowledgments

This book would never have been written without the support of a Hughes Foundation Grant to the University of Utah, which included as part of its mission an attempt to more effectively teach mathematics to biology majors. The grant was fathered by Gordon Lark, who has been a colleague, a mentor, and a mensch throughout this project. The grant brought together a committee of faculty to guide creation of this book and course: Aaron Fogelson, David Goldenberg, Jim Keener, Mark Lewis, David Mason, Larry Okun, Hans Othmer, Jon Seger, and Ryk Ward. Each added much to this work, generously providing ideas and corrections. Particular thanks to Jon "Preface" Seger and Mark "reasoning about functions" Lewis for discussion and ideas. Frank Wattenberg, Lou Gross, and Simon Levin looked over the book and delivered much-needed advice early in the writing process. Alan Rogers let me use his exercise style and Nelson Beebe helped smooth over many technical problems.

Thanks to Gary Ostedt for getting this project started, Bob Pirtle for carrying on with the Second Edition, Tom Novack for skillfully shepherding the speedy production process, Cheryll Linthicum for handling all the crises, Katherine Cook for editorial assistance, Connie Day for copyediting, Edgar Diaz and Angie Marchant for answer-checking, and Kathleen Kerr for, well, helping. Thanks to Vernon Boes for cover design, Cheryl Carrington for the elegant cover layout, and Anna Campbell Bliss for allowing me to use the beautiful image she created for the building where I am fortunate to work. I am particularly grateful to Professor Jerry Grossman for both teaching and humbling me with his amazing job of fact-checking, with his eagle eye for everything from details of layout and grammar, through consistency of terminology, to mathematical rigor and precision.

Many reviewers were instrumental in making this book comprehensible. Particular thanks to the class testers: Joe Mahaffy, Kathleen Crowe, Rollie Lamberson, Daniel Bentil, and the student reviewers at San Diego State. The following reviewers were honest in their criticism and generous with their expertise, and constantly provided needed perspective and ideas: Sharon Brown, Humboldt State University; Dwight A. Duffus, Emory University; Tyler J. Evans, Humboldt State University; Brian M. Loft, University of Oregon; Bori Mazzag, Humboldt State University; and Jennifer Lynn Mueller, Colorado State University. I only failed to follow their advice when blinded by over-weaning pride, misguided philosophy, or general sloth. The remaining errors and oversights are entirely my own.

In addition to her extraordinary sartorial advice and culinary support, I thank Anne Collopy for her inspirational example of writing with clear transitions, extended metaphors, and elegant sentence structure. And for filling the work-free interstices of life with the same. Thanks to Claire and Frank for their joy in life and the many much-needed hugs and distractions. All of them bring to life Nietzsche's words: "A musician who *loves* the slow tempo will take the same pieces slower and slower. Thus there is no standstill in any love."

Frederick R. Adler
Salt Lake City, Utah

Chapter 1

Introduction to Discrete-Time Dynamical Systems

This chapter introduces the main tools needed to use mathematics to study biology: **functions** and **modeling.** Biological phenomena are described by **measurements,** a set of numerical values with units (like degrees or centimeters). Many **relations** between measurements are described by functions, which take one value as an input and return another as an output. We review the important functions used to describe biological systems: linear, trigonometric, power, logarithmic, and exponential functions.

Modeling is the art of taking a description of a biological phenomenon and converting it into mathematical form. Living things are characterized by change. One goal of modeling is to quantify these **dynamics** with an appropriate function. By using our understanding of the system and carefully following how a set of basic measurements change step by step, we will learn to derive an **updating function** that models the change in a **discrete-time dynamical system.** We will follow this process to derive models of bacterial population growth, gas exchange in the lung, and genetic change in a population of competing bacteria. We will develop a set of algebraic and graphical tools to deduce the dynamics that result from a particular discrete-time dynamical system.

Throughout this chapter, keep the following questions in mind:

- What biological process are we trying to describe?
- What biological questions do we seek to answer?
- What are the basic measurements and their units?
- What are the relationships between the basic measurements?
- What do results mean biologically?

1.1 Biology and Dynamics

Living systems, from cells to organisms to ecosystems, are characterized by change and dynamics. Living things grow, maintain themselves, and reproduce.Even remaining the same requires dynamical responses to a changing environment. Understanding the mechanisms behind these dynamics and deducing their consequences is crucial to understanding biology. This book uses a dynamical approach to address questions about biology.

This dynamical approach is necessarily mathematical because describing dynamics requires quantifying measurements. What is changing? How fast is it changing? What is it changing into?

In this book, we use the language of mathematics to describe quantitatively the working of living systems and develop the mathematical tools needed to compute how they change. From measurements describing the initial state of a system and a set of rules describing how change occurs, we will attempt to predict what will

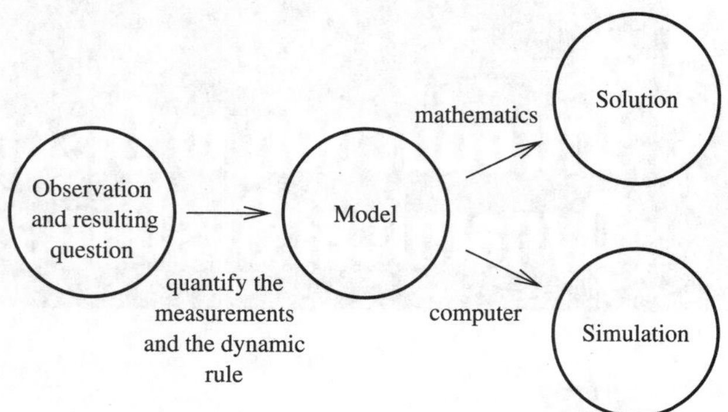

FIGURE 1.1.1

The workings of applied mathematics: the use of mathematics to answer scientific questions

happen to the system. For example, using the position and velocity of a planet (the initial state) and the laws of gravitation and inertia (the set of rules), Isaac Newton invented the mathematical methods of calculus to predict the planet's position at any future time. This example illustrates the approach of **applied mathematics,** *the use of mathematics to answer scientific questions* (Figure 1.1.1). Applied mathematics begins with scientific observations and questions, perhaps about the position of a planet, which are then quantified into a **model.** When possible, mathematical methods are developed to answer the question. In other cases, computers are used to **simulate** the process and find answers in particular cases.

The steps in applied mathematics

Step	Definition
Quantify the basic measurements.	The numerical values that describe the system
Describe a **dynamical rule.**	A description of how the basic measurements change
Develop a **model.**	A mathematical translation of the observations
Find a **solution.**	Use of mathematical methods to predict behavior
Write a **simulation.**	Use of a computer to predict behavior

This book is organized around three basic biological processes: **growth, maintenance,** and **replication.** Mathematical methods have contributed significantly to the understanding of each of these three processes. After briefly describing these contributions, we will outline the different types of models and mathematics to be used in this book.

Growth: Models of Malaria

Early in this century, Sir Ronald Ross discovered that malaria is transmitted by certain types of mosquitos. Because the disease was (and remains) difficult to treat, one promising strategy for control seemed to be reduction of the number of mosquitos. Many people thought that all the mosquitos would have to be killed to eradicate the disease. Because killing every single mosquito was impossible, it was feared that malaria might be impossible to control in this way.

Ross decided to use mathematics to convince people that mosquito control could be effective. The problem can be formulated dynamically as a problem in population growth. His first step was to **quantify the basic measurements**—in this case, the numbers of people and mosquitos with and without malaria. The **dynamical rule** describes how these numbers change. Ross knew that an uninfected person can become infected upon being bitten by an infected mosquito and that an uninfected mosquito can

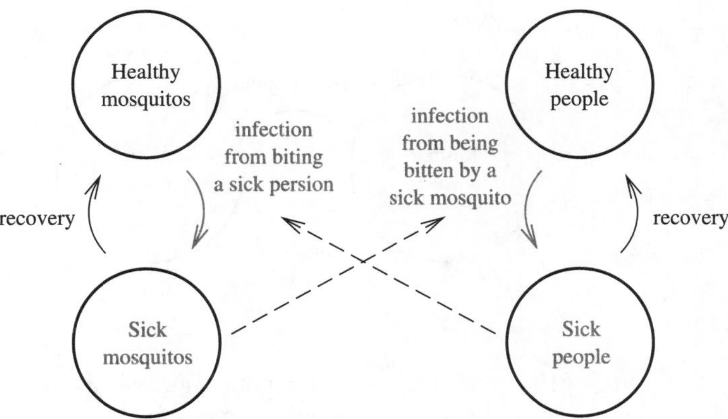

FIGURE 1.1.2
The dynamics of malaria

be infected when it bites an infected person (Figure 1.1.2). From these assumptions, he built a **mathematical model** describing the population dynamics of malaria. With this model he proved that the disease *could* be eradicated without killing every single mosquito (we will study a simple version of this model in Section 5.5). We see evidence of this today in the United States, where malaria has been virtually eliminated even though the mosquitos capable of transmitting the disease persist in many regions.

Many dynamical biological processes besides population dynamics are forms of growth. Growth in size is ubiquitous. One might use measurements of size (such as weight, height, or stomach volume) and a rule describing change in size (increase in weight due to large stomach volume) to predict the size of an organism over time. For example, one organism might add a constant amount to its weight every day, and another might add a constant fraction to its weight every day.

Organisms can also grow in complexity. For example, a tree can add branches as well as increase in size. The quantitative description of the system might include the number of branches and their ages, sizes, and pattern. The dynamical rule might give the number of new branches produced each day, the probability that a given branch divides during the next month, or the rate at which new branches are formed. From the description and rule, we could compute the number of branches as a function of age.

Maintenance: Models of Neurons

Neurons are cells that transmit information throughout the brain and body. Even the simplest neuron faces a challenging task. It must be able to amplify an appropriate incoming stimulus, transmit it to neighboring neurons, and then turn off and be ready for the next stimulus. This task is not as simple as it might seem. If we imagine the stimulus to be an input of electrical charge, a plausible sounding rule is "If electrical charge is raised above a certain level, increase it further." Such a rule works well for the first stimulus but provides no way for the cell to turn itself off. How does a neuron maintain functionality?

In the early 1950s, Hodgkin and Huxley used their own measurements of neurons to develop a mathematical model of dynamics to explain the behavior of neurons. The idea, explained in detail in Section 5.8, is that the neuron has fast and slow mechanisms to open and close specialized ion channels in response to electrical charge (Figure 1.1.3). Hodgkin and Huxley measured the dynamical behavior of these channels and showed mathematically that their mechanism explained many aspects of the functioning of neurons. They received the Nobel Prize in physiology or medicine for this work in

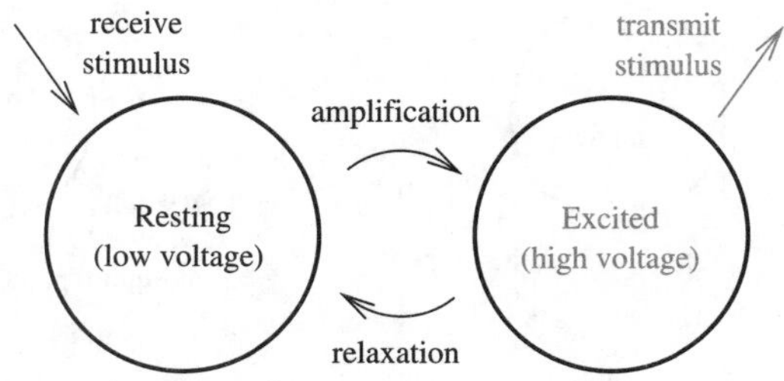

FIGURE 1.1.3
The dynamics of a neuron

1963 and, perhaps even more impressively, developed a model that is still used today to study neurons and other types of cells.

In general, maintenance of biological systems depends on preserving the distinction between inside and outside while maintaining flows of necessary materials from outside to inside, and vice versa. The neuron maintains itself at a different electrical potential from the surrounding tissue in order to be able to respond, while remaining ready to exchange ions with the outside to create the response. As applied mathematicians, we **quantify the basic measurements,** the concentrations of various substances inside and outside the cell. The **dynamical rules** express how concentrations change, generally as a function of properties of the cell membrane. Most commonly, the rule describes the process of **diffusion,** movement of materials from regions of high concentration to regions of low concentration.

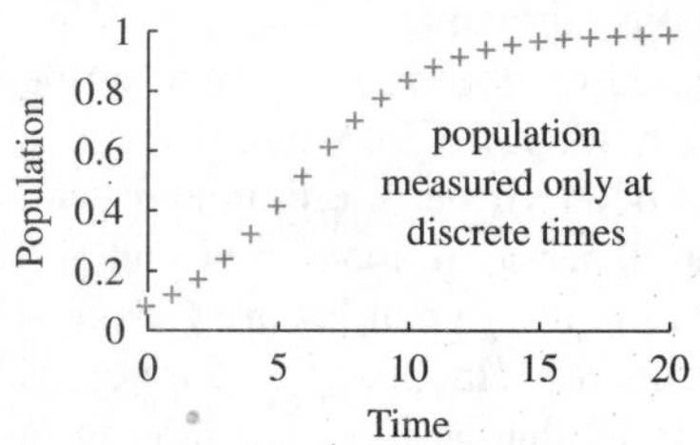

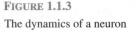

FIGURE 1.1.4
Measurements described by a discrete-time dynamical system

Replication: Models of Genetics

Although Mendel's work on genetics from the 1860s had been rediscovered around 1900, many biologists in the following decades remained unconvinced of his proposed mechanism of genetic transmission. In particular, it was unclear whether Darwin's theory of evolution by natural selection was consistent with this, or any other, proposed mechanism.

Working independently, biologists R. A. Fisher, J. B. S. Haldane, and Sewall Wright developed mathematical models of the dynamics of evolution in natural populations. These scientists **quantified the basic measurement**—in this case, the number of individuals with a particular allele (a version of a gene). Their **dynamical rules** described how many individuals in a subsequent generation would have a particular allele as a function of numerous factors, including **selection** (differential success of particular types in reproducing) and **drift** (the workings of chance). They showed that Mendel's ideas were indeed consistent with observations of evolution. This work led to the development of methods of genetic analysis used to analyze DNA sequences today. We study a simple model of selection in Section 1.10 and examine some of the consequences of Mendel's laws in Section 6.2.

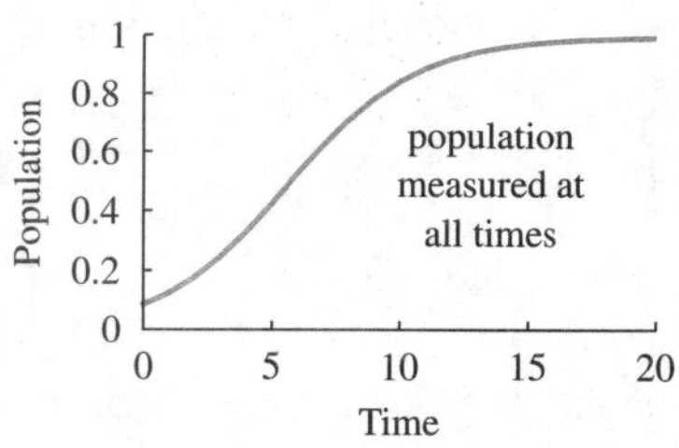

FIGURE 1.1.5
Measurements described by a continuous-time dynamical system

Types of Dynamical Systems

We will study each of the three processes—growth, maintenance, and replication—with three types of dynamical systems: discrete-time, continuous-time, and probabilistic systems. The first two types are **deterministic,** meaning that the dynamics include no chance factors. In this case, the values of the basic measurements can be predicted exactly at all future times. Probabilistic dynamical systems include chance factors, and values can be predicted only on average.

Discrete-Time Dynamical Systems

Discrete-time dynamical systems describe a sequence of measurements made at equally spaced intervals (Figure 1.1.4). These dynamical systems are described mathematically by a rule that gives the value at one time as a function of the value at the previous time.

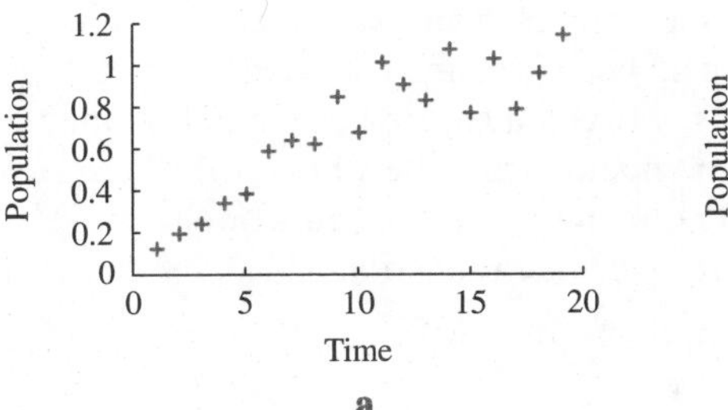

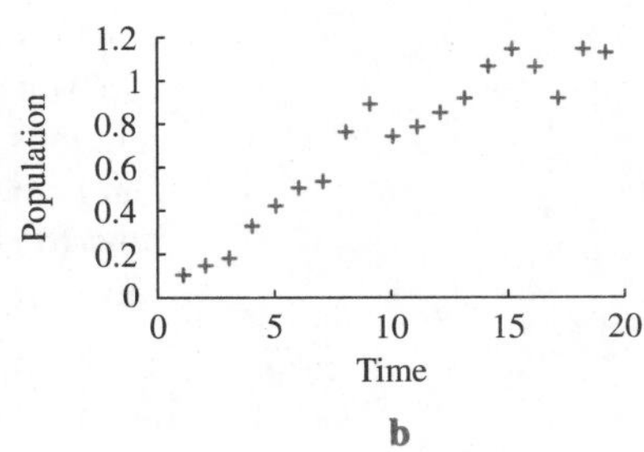

FIGURE 1.1.6

Two set of measurements described by the same probabilistic dynamical system (discrete-time case)

For example, a discrete-time dynamical system describing population growth is a rule that gives the population in one year as a function of the population in the previous year. A discrete-time dynamical system describing the concentration of oxygen in the lung is a rule that gives the concentration of oxygen in a lung after one breath as a function of the concentration after the previous breath. A discrete-time dynamical system describing the spread of a mutant allele is a rule that gives the number of mutant alleles in one generation as a function of the number in the previous generation. Mathematical analysis of the rule can make scientific predictions, such as the maximum population size, the average concentration of oxygen in the lung, or the final number of mutant alleles. The study of these systems requires the mathematical methods of modeling (Chapter 1) and **differential calculus** (Chapters 2 and 3).

Continuous-Time Dynamical Systems

Continuous-time dynamical systems, usually known as **differential equations,** describe measurements that are collected continuously (Figure 1.1.5). A differential equation consists of a rule that gives the **instantaneous rate of change** of a set of measurements. The beauty of differential equations is that information about a system at one time is sufficient to predict the state of a system at all future times. For example, a continuous-time dynamical system describing the growth of a population is a rule that gives the rate of change of population size as a function of the population size itself. The study of these systems requires the mathematical methods of **integral calculus** (Chapters 4 and 5).

Probabilistic Dynamical Systems

Probabilistic dynamical systems describe measurements, in either discrete or continuous time, that are affected by random factors. In the discrete time case, data are collected at equally spaced time intervals (Figure 1.1.6). The rule indicating how the measurements at one time depend on measurements at the previous time includes random factors. Rather than knowing the next measurements with certainty, we know only a set of possible outcomes and their associated probabilities and can therefore predict the outcome only in a probabilistic or statistical sense. For example, a probabilistic dynamical system describing population growth is a rule that gives the **probability** that a population has a particular size in one year as a function of the population in the previous year. The study of such systems requires the mathematical methods of **probability theory** (Chapters 6 and 7).

1.2 Variables, Parameters, and Functions in Biology

Quantitative science is built upon measurements. Mathematics provides the notation for describing and thinking about measurements and relations between them. In fact, the development of clear notation for measurements and relations was essential for the progress of modern science. In this section, we develop the algebraic notation needed to describe measurements, introducing **variables** to describe measurements that change *during* the course of an experiment and **parameters** that remain constant during an experiment but can change *between* different experiments. The most important types of relations between measurements are described with **functions**, where the value of one can be computed from the value of the other. We will review how to graph functions, how to combine them with **addition, multiplication,** and **composition,** and how to recognize whether a function has an **inverse** and how to compute it.

Describing Measurements with Variables, Parameters, and Graphs

Algebra uses letters or other symbols to represent numerical quantities.

Definition 1.1 A **variable** is a symbol that represents a measurement that can change during the course of an experiment.

A simple experiment measures how the population of bacteria in a culture changes over time. Because two changing quantities are being measured (time and bacterial population), we need two variables to represent them. In applied mathematics, we choose variables that remind us of the measurements they represent. In this case, we can use t to represent time and b to represent the population of bacteria. Because there are fewer letters than quantities to be measured, the same letter can be used to represent different quantities in different problems. Always define variables explicitly when writing a model, and be sure to check their definitions when reading one.

Example 1.2.1 Describing Bacterial Population Growth

t	b
0.0	1.00
1.0	1.24
2.0	1.95
3.0	3.14
4.0	4.81
5.0	6.95
6.0	9.57

The table lists measurements of bacterial population size (in millions), denoted by the variable b, at different times t after the beginning of an experiment.

Thinking about data is often easier with a graph. Graphs are drawn on the **Cartesian coordinate** plane—that is, by using two perpendicular number lines called **axes** to describe two numbers (Figure 1.2.7). The input is placed on the horizontal axis (sometimes called the x-axis) and the output is placed on the vertical axis (sometimes called the y-axis). The crossing point of the two axes is the **origin.** The axes are labeled with the variable name, the measurement it represents, and often the units of measurement (Section 1.3). **Never draw a graph without labeling the axes.**

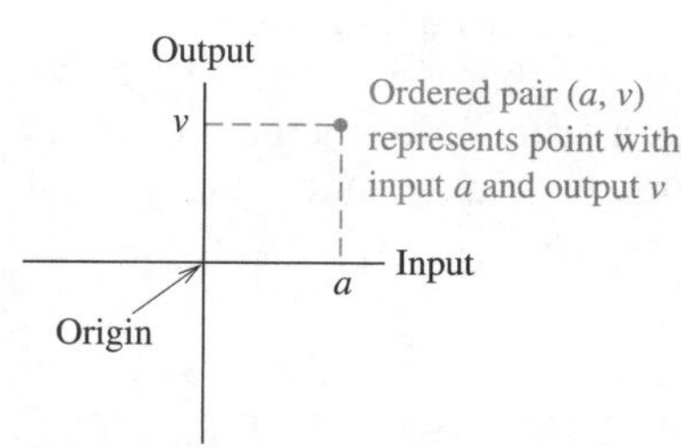

FIGURE 1.2.7
The components of a graph using Cartesian coordinates

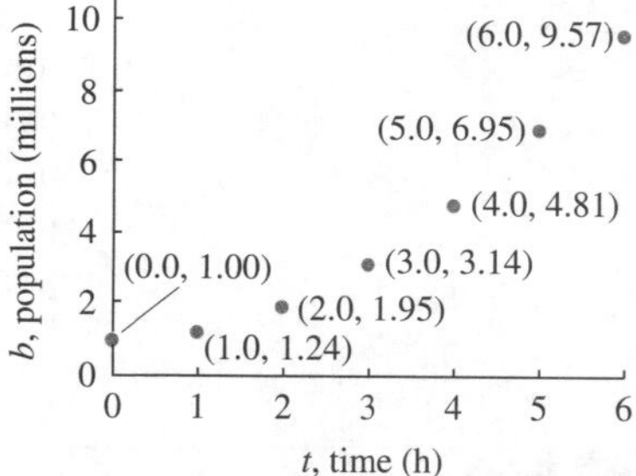

FIGURE 1.2.8
Results of bacterial growth experiment: Cartesian coordinates

Example 1.2.2 Graphing Data Describing Bacterial Population Growth

To graph the six data points in Example 1.2.1, plot each point by moving a distance t to the right of the origin along the horizontal axis and a distance b up from the origin along the vertical axis (Figure 1.2.8). For example, the data point at $t = 4.0$ is graphed by moving a distance 4.0 to the right of the origin on the horizontal axis and a distance 4.81 up from the origin on the vertical axis.

Example 1.2.3 Describing the Dynamics of a Bacterial Population

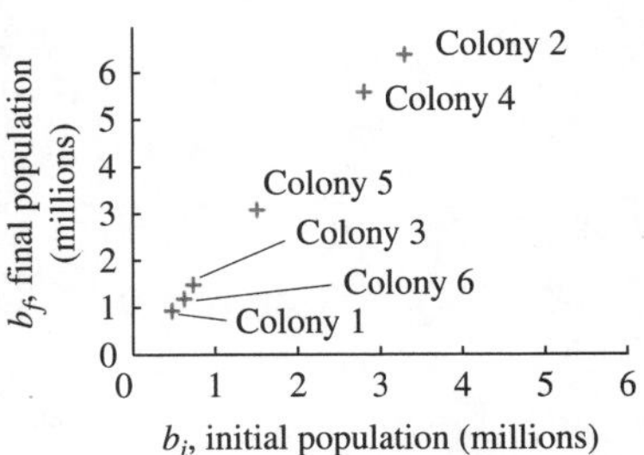

FIGURE 1.2.9
Results of alternative bacterial growth experiment

Suppose several bacterial cultures with different initial population sizes are grown in controlled conditions for one hour and then carefully counted. The population size acts as the basic measurement at both times. We must use different variables to represent these values, and we choose to use **subscripts** to distinguish them. In particular, we let b_i (for the **initial** population) represent the population at the beginning of the experiment, and we let b_f (for the **final** population) represent the population at the end. The following table and Figure 1.2.9 present the results for six colonies.

Colony	Initial Population, b_i	Final Population, b_f
1	0.47	0.94
2	3.30	6.60
3	0.73	1.46
4	2.80	5.60
5	1.50	3.00
6	0.62	1.24

Experiments of this sort form the basis of discrete-time dynamical systems (Section 1.5) and are the central topic of this chapter.

Experiments are done in a particular set of controlled conditions that remain constant during the experiment. However, these conditions might differ between experiments.

Definition 1.2 A **parameter** is a symbol that represents a measurement that does not change during the course of an experiment.

Different experiments tracking the growth of bacterial populations over time might take place at temperatures that are constant during an experiment but differ between experiments. The temperature, in this case, is represented by a parameter. Parameters, like variables, are represented by symbols that recall the measurement. We can use T to represent temperature. In applied mathematics, capital letters (like T) and small letters (like t) are often used in the same problem to represent different quantities.

Example 1.2.4 Variables and Parameters

Suppose a biologist measures growing bacterial populations at three different temperatures. During the course of each experiment, the temperature is held constant, while the population changes.

t	b when $T = 25°C$	b when $T = 35°C$	b when $T = 45°C$
0.0	1.00	1.00	1.00
1.0	1.14	1.45	0.93
2.0	1.30	2.10	0.87
3.0	1.48	3.03	0.81
4.0	1.68	4.39	0.76
5.0	1.92	6.36	0.70
6.0	2.18	9.21	0.66

Figure 1.2.10 compares the population sizes of the three populations. The population grows most quickly at the intermediate temperature of 35°C and declines at the high temperature of 45°C.

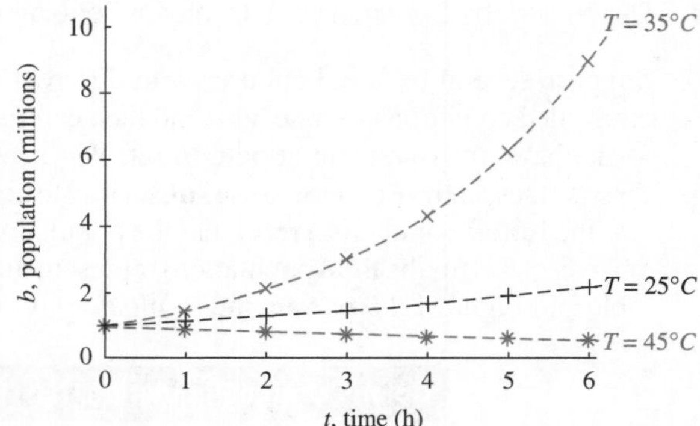

FIGURE 1.2.10

Results of bacterial growth experiment at three temperatures

Describing Relations Between Measurements with Functions

Numbers describe measurements, and **functions** describe **relations** between measurements. For example, bacterial population growth relates two measurements, denoted by the variables t and b. In general, a **relation** between two variables is the set of all pairs of values that occur.

Example 1.2.5 A Relation Between Temperature and Population Size

T	P
25.0	2.18
25.0	2.45
25.0	2.10
25.0	3.03
35.0	9.21
35.0	7.39
35.0	6.36
45.0	0.66
45.0	0.93

Suppose the temperature T and final population size P are measured for 9 populations, with the results shown in the table and Figure 1.2.11. These values could result from repeating the experiment in Example 1.2.4 several times and measuring the population at $t = 6.0$.

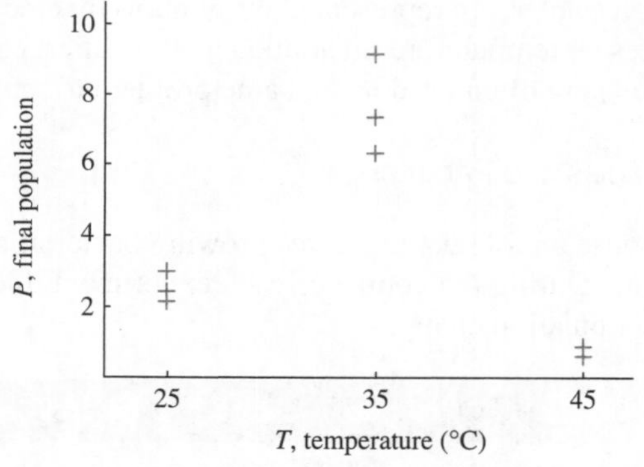

FIGURE 1.2.11

Final population size at three temperatures

Different values of the population P are related to each temperature, perhaps, because of differences in experimental conditions.

A **function** describes a specific, and important, type of relation. A function is a mathematical object that takes something (such as a number) as input, performs an operation on it, and returns a unique new object (such as another number) as output. The input is called the **argument** (or the **independent variable**) and the output is called the **value** (or the **dependent variable**) (Figure 1.2.12). The set of all possible things that a function can accept as inputs is called the **domain.** The set of all possible things that a function *can* return as outputs is called the **codomain,** and the set of all things the function *does* return as outputs is called the **range.**

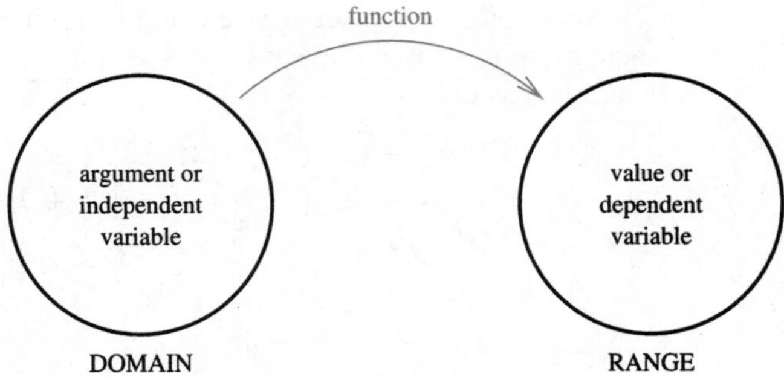

FIGURE 1.2.12
The basic terminology for describing a function

Example 1.2.6 Data That Can Be Described by a Function

The data in Example 1.2.1 can be described by a function. Each value of the input t is associated with only a single value of the output b.

Example 1.2.7 Graphing a Function from its Formula

To graph a function from a formula, it is easiest to start by plugging in some representative arguments. Suppose we wish to graph the function $f(x) = 4 + x - x^2$ for $x \geq 0$ (restricting the domain to positive numbers and zero). Evaluating the function at the arguments 0, 1, 2 and 3, we find

$$f(0) = 4 + 0 - 0^2 = 4$$
$$f(1) = 4 + 1 - 1^2 = 4$$
$$f(2) = 4 + 2 - 2^2 = 2$$
$$f(3) = 4 + 3 - 3^2 = -2$$

We plot the four ordered pairs (0, 4), (1, 4), (2, 2) and (3, −2), and connect them with a smooth curve (Figure 1.2.13). This is precisely the method that calculators and computers use to plot functions, except that they generally use 20 or more points to make a graph.

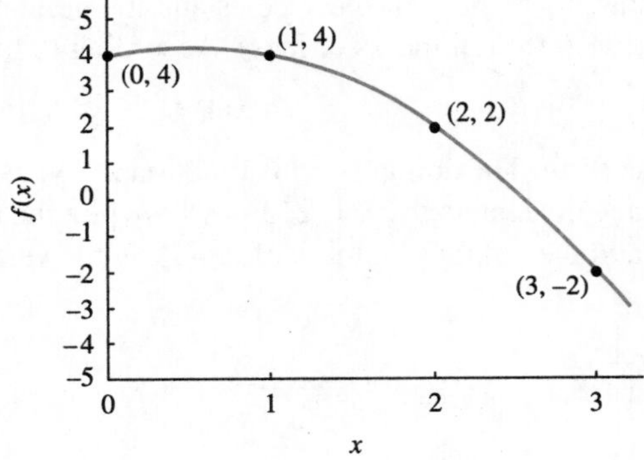

FIGURE 1.2.13
Plotting a function from its formula

One of the great advantages of functional notation is that functions can be evaluated at arguments that consist of parameters and variables (combinations of letters). To do so, replace the basic variable in the formula with the new argument, however complicated.

Example 1.2.8 Evaluating a Function at a Complicated Argument

To evaluate the function $f(x) = 4 + x - x^2$ (Example 1.2.7) at the more complicated argument $2z + 3$, replace all occurrences of x in the formula with the new argument $2z + 3$, obtaining

$$f(2z + 3) = 4 + (2z + 3) - (2z + 3)^2$$

To avoid confusion, place the new argument in parentheses wherever it appears. Although doing so is not always necessary, this expression can be multiplied out and simplified as follows:

$$\begin{aligned} f(2z+3) &= 4 + (2z+3) - (2z+3)^2 && \text{original expression} \\ &= 4 + (2z+3) - \left(4z^2 + 12z + 9\right) && \text{expand the square} \\ &= 4 + 2z + 3 - 4z^2 - 12z - 9 && \text{multiply negative sign through} \\ &= 4 + 3 - 9 + 2z - 12z - 4z^2 && \text{group like terms} \\ &= -2 - 10z - 4z^2 && \text{combine like terms} \end{aligned}$$

Example 1.2.9 A Function Describing Bacterial Population Growth

The population in Examples 1.2.1 and 1.2.2 obeys the formula

$$b(t) = \frac{t^2}{4.2} + 1.0$$

The population size b is a function of the time t. The **argument** of the function b is t, the time after the beginning of the experiment. The **value** of the function is the population of bacteria. The formula summarizes the relation between these two measurements: The output is found by squaring the input, dividing by 4.2, and then adding 1.0.

The function b takes time after the beginning of the experiment as its input. Because negative time does not make sense in this case, the **domain** of this function consists of all positive numbers and zero. We write that

$$b \text{ is defined on the domain } t \geq 0$$

Because the function b returns population sizes as output, the **codomain** of b also consists of all positive numbers and zero. We write that

$$b \text{ has codomain } b \geq 0$$

The **range** is $b \geq 1$.

Example 1.2.10 A Function with Non-Numerical Domain

Animal	Number of Legs
Ant	6
Crab	10
Duck	2
Fish	0
Human	2
Mouse	4
Spider	8

Consider the adjacent table of data. These data describe a relation between two observations: the identity of the species and the number of legs. We can express this as the function L (to remind us of legs). According to the table,

$$L(\text{Ant}) = 6, \quad L(\text{Crab}) = 10$$

and so forth. The domain of this function is "types of animals," and the codomain is the non-negative integers (0, 1, 2, 3, ...). We plot the input ("animal") along the horizontal axis and the output ("number of legs") on the vertical axis (Figure 1.2.14).

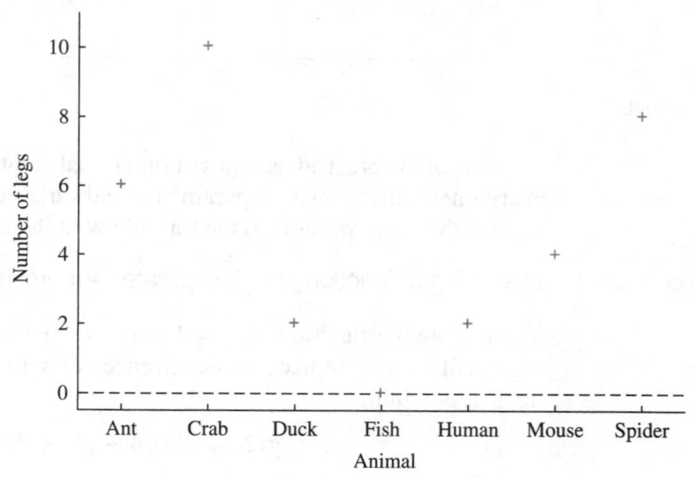

FIGURE 1.2.14

Numbers of legs on various organisms, plotted on a graph

It is important to realize that the graph of a function is *not* the function, just as the spot labeled 2 on the number line is not the number 2 and a photograph of a dog is not a dog. The graph is a depiction of the function.

Functions can be described in four ways: (1) numerically (by means of a table), (2) algebraically (as a formula), (3) pictorially (as a graph), and (4) verbally. Biologists or applied mathematicians need to learn to use all four methods and to translate fluently between them. In particular, we must know how to translate graphical information into words that communicate key observations to colleagues and the public.

Example 1.2.11 Describing Results in Graphs and Words

Time	Population Size
0	0.86
2	1.69
4	2.98
6	4.49
8	5.69
10	6.17
12	5.95
14	5.29
16	4.41
18	3.50
20	2.67
22	1.96
24	1.41

A more complicated pattern of change in population size is presented in the adjacent table.

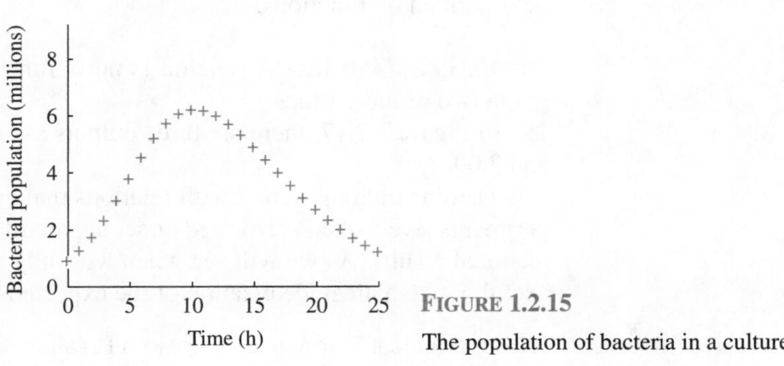

FIGURE 1.2.15

The population of bacteria in a culture

We can see (more easily from the graph, Figure 1.2.15, than from the table) that the bacterial population grew during the first ten hours and declined thereafter. The population reached a maximum at time 10. This graph and its description can be used to understand the results even without a mathematical formula.

Example 1.2.12 Sketching a Graph from a Verbal Description

Conversely, it can be useful to sketch a graph of a function from a verbal description. Suppose we are told that a population increases between time 0 and time 5, decreases nearly to 0 by time 12, increases to a higher maximum at time 20, and goes extinct at time 30. A graph (Figure 1.2.16) translates this information into pictorial form. Because we

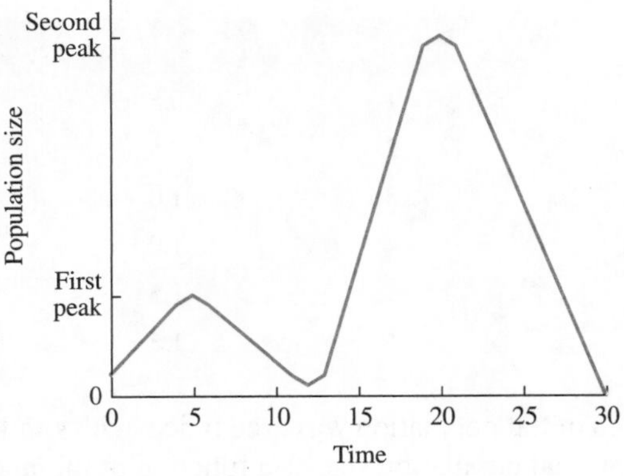

FIGURE 1.2.16

A bacterial population plotted from a verbal description

were not given exact values, the graph is not exact. It instead gives a **qualitative** picture of the results.

Not all relations are described by functions. A function must give a unique output for a given input. Relations between measurements can be more complicated.

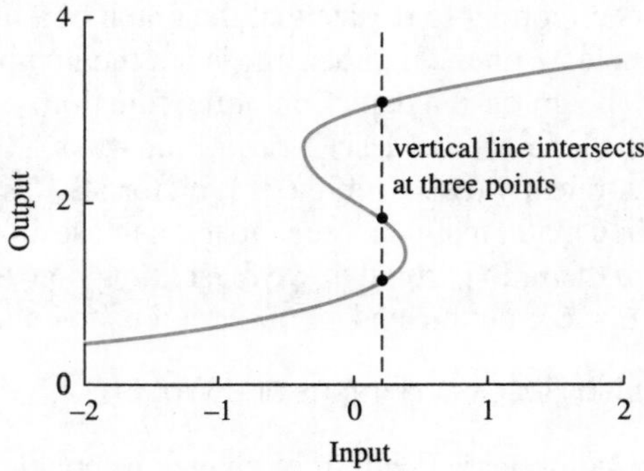

FIGURE 1.2.17
The vertical line test

The **vertical line test** provides a graphical method to recognize relations that cannot be described by functions.

The Vertical Line Test A relation is not a function if some vertical line crosses the graph two or more times.

In Figure 1.2.17, there are three outputs associated with the input 0.2: 1.12, 1.79, and 3.09.

There is nothing wrong with relations that cannot be described by functions. Experiments, even when performed under apparently identical conditions, rarely produce identical results. As we will see when we study statistics (Chapter 8), functions are a useful mathematical idealization of the expected or average result of an experiment.

Example 1.2.13 A Mathematical Formula Describing a Relation That Is Not a Function

The set of solutions for x and y satisfying the equation

$$x^2 + y^2 = 1$$

is the circle of radius 1 centered at the origin (Figure 1.2.18). Each value of x between $x = -1$ and $x = 1$ is associated with two different values of y. For example, the value $x = 0.6$ is associated with both $y = 0.8$ and $y = -0.8$.

Example 1.2.14 A Relation That Is Not a Function

Suppose several bacterial cultures with different initial population sizes are grown in controlled conditions for 1 hour, as in Example 1.2.3, with the results shown in the accompanying table and in Figure 1.2.19.

Colony	Initial Population, b_i	Final Population, b_f
1	0.5	0.9
2	0.5	1.0
3	1.0	2.2
4	1.0	1.9
5	1.5	3.0
6	1.5	2.8

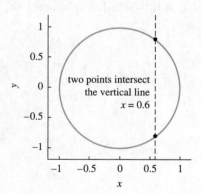

FIGURE 1.2.18
The circle describes a relation that is not a function

Each initial population was used twice, with similar but not identical results. We cannot treat final population size as a function of initial population size.

Combining Functions

Mathematics makes complicated problems simpler by building complicated structures from simple pieces. Understanding each of the simple pieces and the rules for

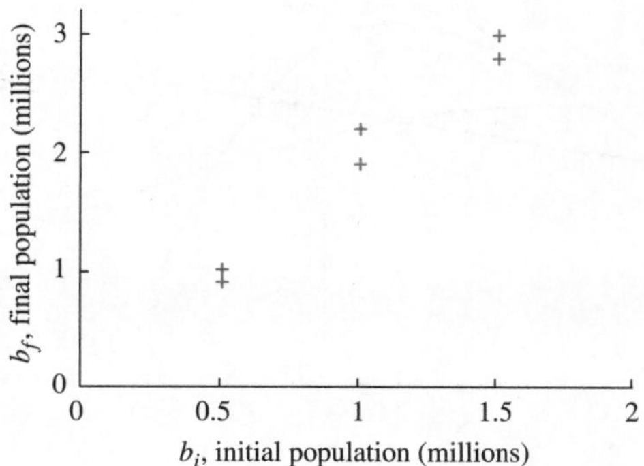

FIGURE 1.2.19
Bacterial growth experiment where results are not a function

combining them makes it possible to analyze and understand a huge array of complicated relations. The most important ways to combine functions are as **sums, products,** and **compositions.**

Adding Functions The height of the graph of the sum of two functions is the height of the first plus the height of the second. Geometrically, we can graph each of the pieces and add them together point by point.

Algebraically, the value of the function $f + g$ is computed as the sum of the values of the functions f and g.

Definition 1.3 The sum $f + g$ of the functions f and g is the function defined by

$$(f + g)(x) = f(x) + g(x)$$

Multiplying Functions The value of the product $f \cdot g$ is computed as the product of the values of the functions f and g.

Definition 1.4 The product $f \cdot g$ of the functions f and g is the function defined by

$$(f \cdot g)(x) = f(x) \cdot g(x)$$

We use the dot $\cdot$ rather than the times sign $\times$ to indicate multiplication to avoid confusing the latter with the variable x.

Example 1.2.15 Adding and Multiplying Functions

Consider the functions $f(x)$ and $g(x)$ with formulas

$$f(x) = 4 + x - x^2$$
$$g(x) = 2x$$

graphed in Figures 1.2.20 and 1.2.21. The table on p. 14 computes the values of $f + g$ and $f \cdot g$ at several points.

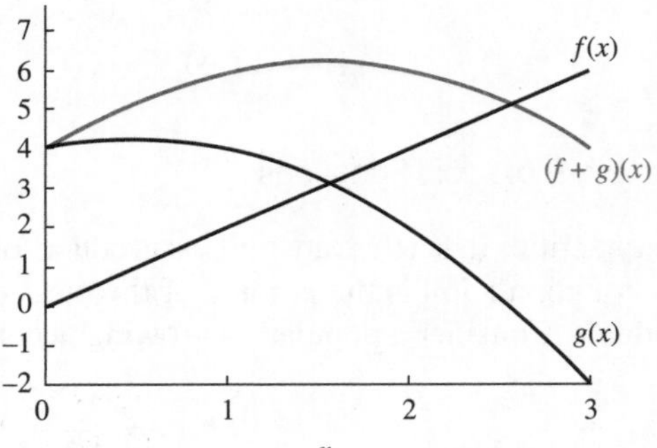

FIGURE 1.2.20
Adding functions

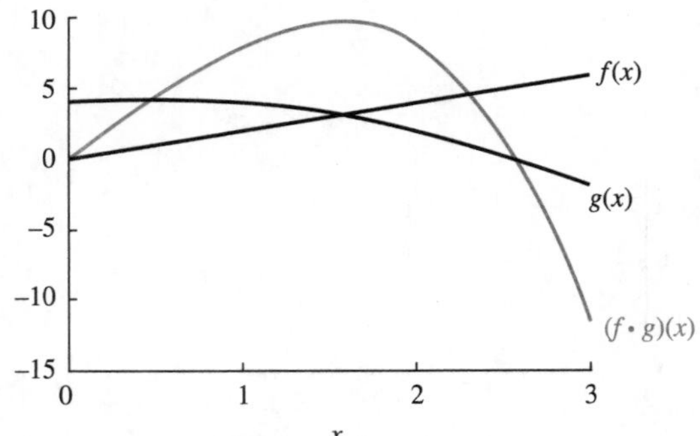

FIGURE 1.2.21
Multiplying functions

x	$f(x)$	$g(x)$	$(f+g)(x)$	$(f \cdot g)(x)$
0	4	0	4	0
0.5	4.25	1	5.25	4.25
1	4	2	6	8
1.5	3.25	3	6.25	9.75
2	2	4	6	8
2.5	0.25	5	5.25	1.25
3	−2	6	4	−12

Example 1.2.16 Adding Biological Functions

If two bacterial populations are separately counted, the total population is the sum of the two individual populations. Suppose a growing population is described by the function

$$b_1(t) = t^2 + 1$$

and a declining population is described by the function

$$b_2(t) = \frac{5}{1+2t}$$

The individual population sizes and their sum are computed in the following table and graphed in Figure 1.2.22.

t	$b_1(t)$	$b_2(t)$	$(b_1+b_2)(t)$
0.00	1.00	5.00	6.00
0.50	1.25	2.50	3.75
1.00	2.00	1.67	3.67
1.50	3.25	1.25	4.50
2.00	5.00	1.00	6.00
2.50	7.25	0.83	8.08
3.00	10.00	0.71	10.71

Example 1.2.17 Multiplying Biological Functions

Many quantities in science are built as products of simpler quantities. For example, the mass of a population is the product of the mass of each individual and the number of individuals. Consider a population growing according to

$$b(t) = \frac{t^2}{4.2} + 1.0$$

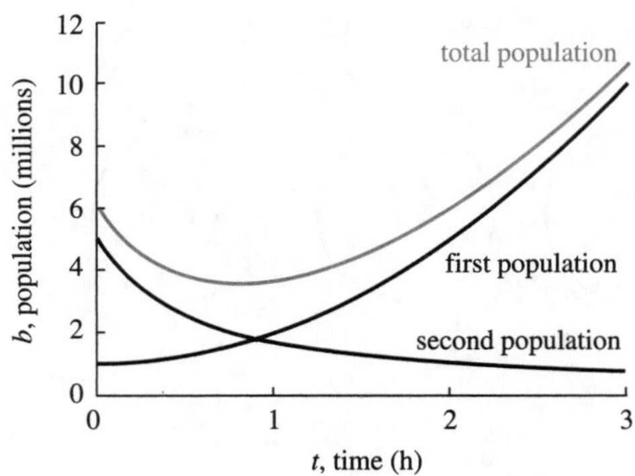

FIGURE 1.2.22
Adding biological functions

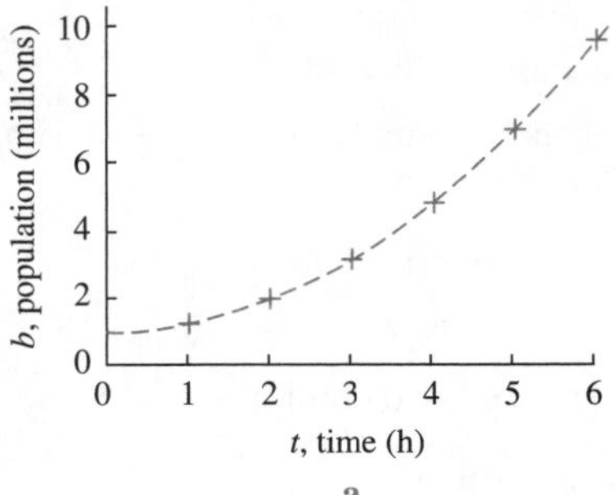

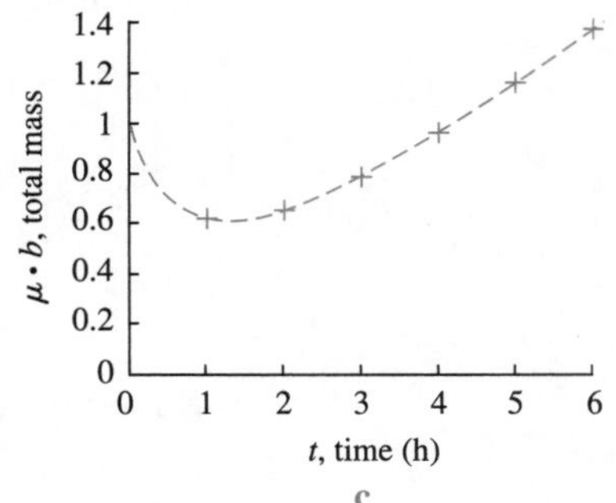

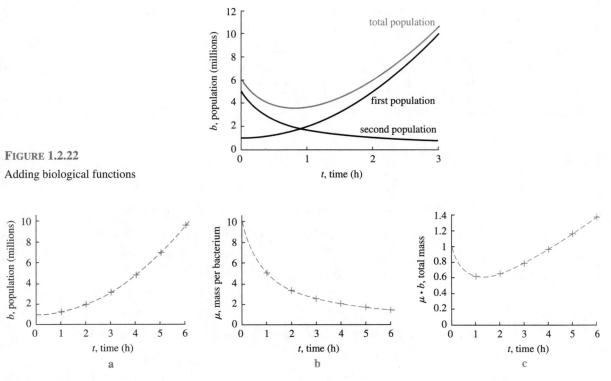

FIGURE 1.2.23
Multiplying biological functions

t	b	μ	$\mu \cdot b$
0.0	1.00	1.00	1.00
1.0	1.24	0.50	0.62
2.0	1.95	0.33	0.65
3.0	3.14	0.25	0.79
4.0	4.81	0.20	0.96
5.0	6.95	0.17	1.16
6.0	9.57	0.14	1.37

(Example 1.2.9). Suppose that as the population gets larger, the individuals become smaller. Let $\mu(t)$ (the Greek letter mu)[1] represent the mass of an individual at time t, and suppose that

$$\mu(t) = \frac{1}{1+t}$$

We can find the total mass by multiplying the mass per individual by the number of individuals, as in the table. (See also Figure 1.2.23.)

The total mass of this population initially declines and then increases after about 2 hours.

Composition of Functions The most important way to combine functions is through **composition,** where the output of one function acts as the input of another.

Definition 1.5 The composition $f \circ g$ of functions f and g is the function defined by

$$(f \circ g)(x) = f(g(x)) \tag{1.2.1}$$

We say "f composed with g evaluated at x" or "f of g of x." The function f is called the **outer function,** and g is called the **inner function.** See Figure 1.2.24.

Example 1.2.18 Computing the Value of a Functional Composition

Consider the functions $f(x)$ and $g(x)$ from Example 1.2.15,

$$f(x) = 4 + x - x^2$$
$$g(x) = 2x$$

[1] Applied mathematicians often use Greek letters to represent variables and parameters. The Greek alphabet, along with pronunciations of the letters, is given on the inside back cover.

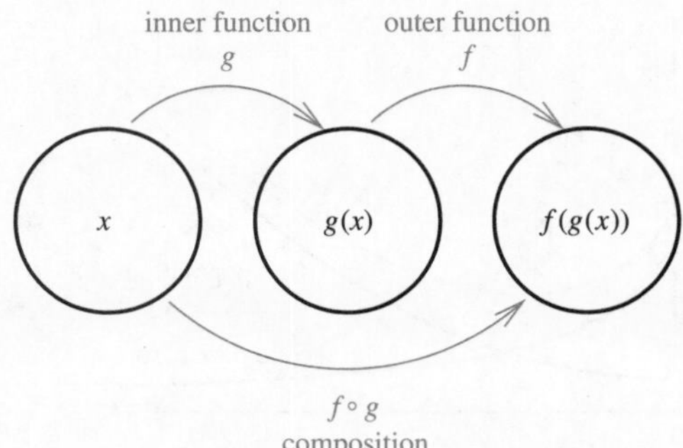

FIGURE 1.2.24
Composition of functions

To find the value of the composition $f \circ g$ at $x = 2$, we compute

$$
\begin{aligned}
(f \circ g)(2) &= f(g(2)) && \text{definition of composition} \\
&= f(2 \cdot 2) && \text{substitute 2 for } x \text{ in the formula for } g(x) \\
&= f(4) && \text{compute } 2 \cdot 2 = 4 \\
&= 4 + 4 - 4^2 && \text{substitute 4 for } x \text{ in the formula for } f(x) \\
&= -8 && \text{compute the numerical answer}
\end{aligned}
$$

Similarly, to find the value of the composition $g \circ f$ at $x = 2$, we compute

$$
\begin{aligned}
(g \circ f)(2) &= g(f(2)) && \text{definition of composition} \\
&= g(4 + 2 - 2^2) && \text{substitute 2 for } x \text{ in the formula for } f(x) \\
&= g(2) && \text{compute } 4 + 2 - 2^2 = 2 \\
&= 2 \cdot 2 && \text{substitute 2 for } x \text{ in the formula for } g(x) \\
&= 4 && \text{compute the numerical answer}
\end{aligned}
$$

Example 1.2.19 Computing the Formula of a Functional Composition

Consider again the functions $f(x)$ and $g(x)$ from Example 1.2.18,

$$
\begin{aligned}
f(x) &= 4 + x - x^2 \\
g(x) &= 2x
\end{aligned}
$$

with domains consisting of all numbers. To find the composition $f \circ g$, plug the definition of the **inner function** g into the formula for the **outer function** f, or

$$
\begin{aligned}
(f \circ g)(x) &= f(g(x)) && \text{the definition} \\
&= f(2x) && \text{write out the formula for the inner function } g(x) \\
&= 4 + (2x) - (2x)^2 && \text{plug the formula for } g(x) \text{ into the outer function } f \\
&= 4 + 2x - 4x^2 && \text{expand the square}
\end{aligned}
$$

This is the same procedure we used to compute the value of the function $f(x)$ at a complicated argument in Example 1.2.8. In Example 1.2.18 we computed that $(f \circ g)(2) = -8$. If we evaluate by substituting into the formula $(f \circ g)(x) = 4 + 2x - 4x^2$, we find

$$(f \circ g)(2) = 4 + 2 \cdot 2 - 4 \cdot 2^2 = -8$$

matching our earlier result.

We find the composition $g \circ f$ by following the same steps, or

$$
\begin{aligned}
(g \circ f)(x) &= g(f(x)) && \text{the definition} \\
&= g(4 + x - x^2) && \text{write out the formula for the inner function } f(x) \\
&= 2(4 + x - x^2) && \text{plug the formula for } f(x) \text{ into the outer function } g \\
&= 8 + 2x - 2x^2 && \text{multiply through}
\end{aligned}
$$

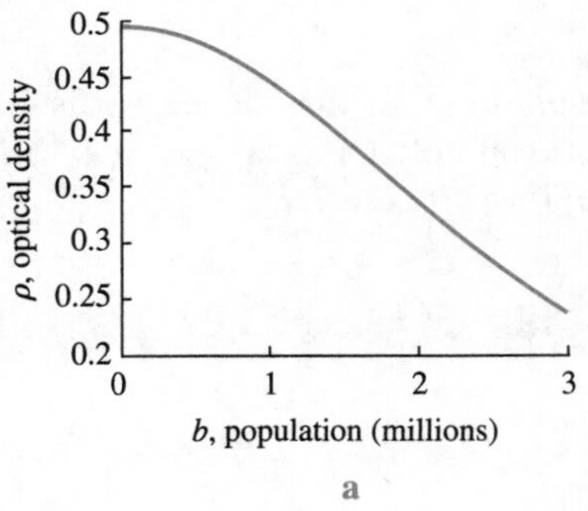

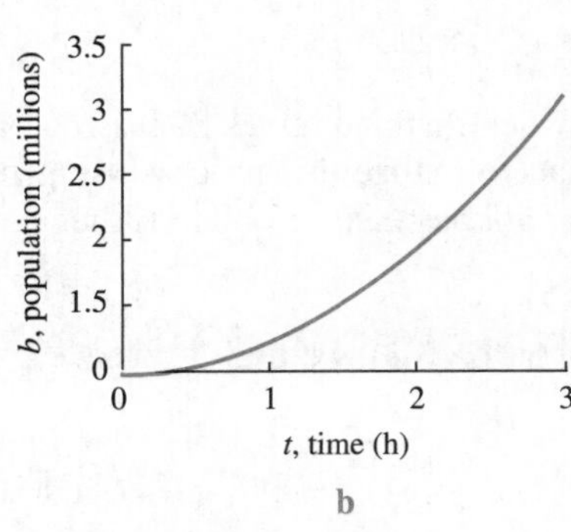

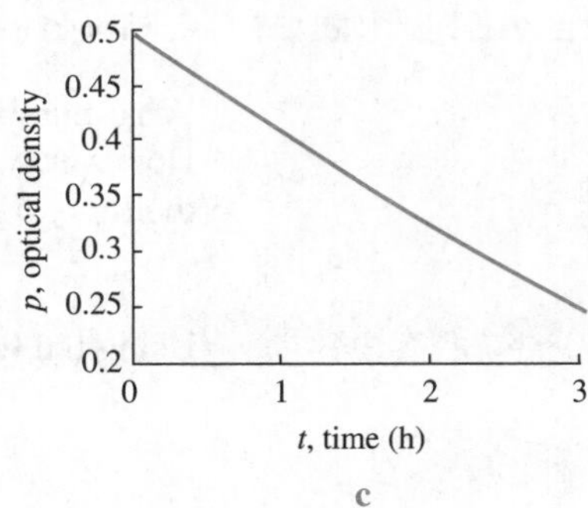

FIGURE 1.2.25
Composing biological functions

The key step is substituting the output of the inner function into the outer function. In Example 1.2.18 we computed that $(g \circ f)(2) = 4$. If we evaluate by substituting into the formula $(g \circ f)(x) = 8 + 2x - 2x^2$, we find

$$(g \circ f)(2) = 8 + 2 \cdot 2 - 2 \cdot 2^2 = 4$$

again matching our earlier result.

Example 1.2.19 illustrates an important point about the composition of functions: the answer is generally different when the functions are composed in a different order. If $f \circ g = g \circ f$, we say that the two functions **commute.** When the two compositions do not match, we say that the two functions do not commute. Without a good reason, never assume that two functions commute. If you think of functions as operations, this should make sense. Sterilizing the scalpel and then making an incision produces a quite different result from making an incision and then sterilizing the scalpel.

Example 1.2.20 Composition of Functions in Biology

Numbers of bacteria are usually measured indirectly, by measuring the optical density of the medium. Water allows through less light as the population becomes larger. Suppose that the optical density ρ is a function of the bacterial population size b with formula

$$\rho(b) = \frac{1}{1 + b}$$

illustrated in Figure 1.2.25a. Then the optical density as a function of time is the composition of the function $\rho(b)$ with the function $b(t)$. Suppose that $b(t) = \frac{t^2}{4.2} + 1.0$ as in Example 1.2.9 (Figure 1.2.25b). Then

$$\rho(b(t)) = \rho\left(\frac{t^2}{4.2} + 1.0\right) = \frac{1}{1 + \frac{t^2}{4.2} + 1.0}$$

t	$b(t)$	$\rho(b(t))$
0.00	1.00	0.500
0.50	1.06	0.486
1.00	1.24	0.447
1.50	1.54	0.394
2.00	1.95	0.339
2.50	2.49	0.287
3.00	3.14	0.241

with values given in the table and graphed in Figure 1.2.25c.

The composition $b \circ \rho$ is not merely different from the composition $\rho \circ b$, it does not even make sense. The function b accepts as input only the time t, not the optical density returned as output by the function ρ. We will study this issue more carefully in Section 1.3.

Finding Inverse Functions

A function describes the relation between two measurements and gives us a way to compute the output from a given input. Sometimes we wish to reverse the process and figure out which input produced a given output. The **inverse function,** when it exists, provides a way to do this.

Example 1.2.21 A Simple Inverse Operation

What number, when doubled, gives 8? It is not difficult to guess that the answer is 4. However, we can formalize this process using functional notation. Let $f(x) = 2x$ be the function that doubles. Our problem is then solving

$$f(x) = 8$$

Using the formula for $f(x)$, we find

$$\begin{aligned} 2x &= 8 && \text{the equation to be solved} \\ x &= 4 && \text{divide both sides by 2} \end{aligned}$$

Example 1.2.22 A Simple Inverse Function

Example 1.2.21 undoes the act of multiplying by 2. What function does this in general? If we set $y = f(x)$, we would like to know what value of x produces a given y in general, without picking a particular value such as $y = 8$. We follow the same steps,

$$\begin{aligned} 2x &= y && \text{the equation to be solved} \\ x &= \frac{y}{2} && \text{divide both sides by 2} \end{aligned}$$

The function f^{-1}, which is read "f inverse" and defined by

$$f^{-1}(y) = \frac{y}{2}$$

is the **inverse** of f; the function that undoes what f did in the first place. Whereas f takes a number as input and returns double that number as output, f^{-1} takes the doubled number as input and returns the initial number as output.

We can use this inverse like any other function, finding that

$$f^{-1}(8) = \frac{8}{2} = 4$$

as we found in Example 1.2.21.

The definition of an inverse function in general states precisely that the inverse undoes the action of the original function.

Definition 1.6 The function f^{-1} is the inverse of f if

$$f(f^{-1}(x)) = x$$

and

$$f^{-1}(f(x)) = x$$

Each of f and f^{-1} undoes the action of the other (Figure 1.2.26).

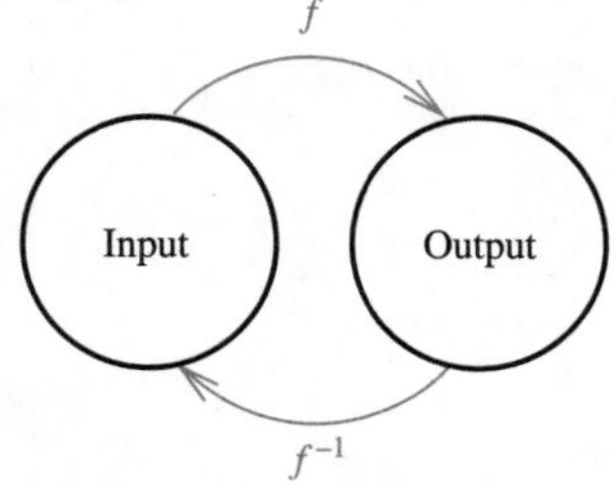

FIGURE 1.2.26
The action of a function and its inverse

The steps for computing the inverse of a function can be summarize in an **algorithm,** which can be thought of as a recipe. This book contains many algorithms for solving particular problems. As with a recipe, following an algorithm without thinking about the steps can lead to disaster. Unlike most algorithms in this book, this one is not guaranteed to work.

Algorithm 1.1 Finding the Inverse of a Function

1. Write the equation $y = f(x)$.
2. Solve for x in terms of y.
3. The inverse function is the operation done to y.

It may look odd to have a function defined in terms of y. Do *not* change the letters around to make it look normal. In applied mathematics, different letters stand for different things and resent having their names switched as much as we do.

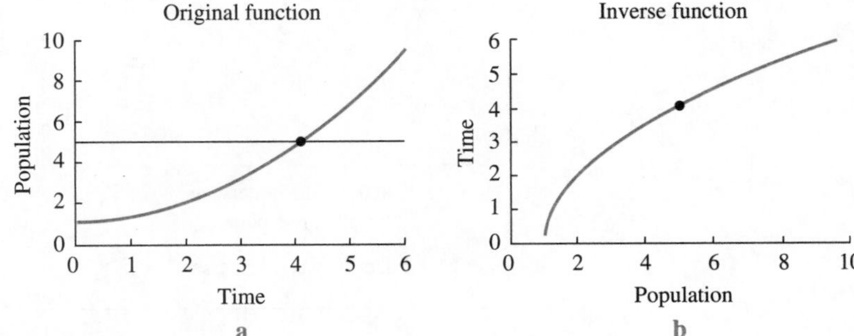

FIGURE 1.2.27

Going backwards with the inverse function

This algorithm may fail in two different ways: a function might not have an inverse, or the inverse might be impossible to compute. There is a useful way to recognize a function that fails to have an inverse. An operation can be undone only if you can deduce the input from the output. If any particular output is associated with more than one input, there is no way to tell where you started solely on the basis of where you ended up.

Example 1.2.23 Finding a More Complicated Inverse

Consider the population that changes in accordance with the equation

$$b(t) = \frac{t^2}{4.2} + 1.0$$

(Example 1.2.9 and Figure 1.2.27a). If we wish to find the time t from the population b, we must solve for t.

$$\frac{t^2}{4.2} + 1.0 = b \quad \text{the equation to be solved for } t$$

$$\frac{t^2}{4.2} = b - 1.0 \quad \text{subtract 1.0 from both sides}$$

$$t^2 = 4.2(b - 1.0) \quad \text{multiply both sides by 4.2}$$

$$t = \sqrt{4.2(b - 1.0)} \quad \text{take the positive square root of both sides because } t \geq 0$$

This function is graphed in Figure 1.2.27b. The last step requires that $b \geq 1.0$ because we cannot take the square root of a negative number. For example, the time associated with a population of 5.0 is

$$t = \sqrt{4.2(5.0 - 1.0)} \approx 4.1$$

▲

Example 1.2.24 A Relation That Cannot Be Inverted

Consider the data in the following table.

Initial Mass (g)	Final Mass (g)	Initial Mass (g)	Final Mass (g)
1.0	7.0	9.0	20.0
2.0	12.0	10.0	18.0
3.0	16.0	11.0	15.0
4.0	19.0	12.0	12.0
5.0	22.0	13.0	9.0
6.0	23.0	14.0	6.0
7.0	23.0	15.0	3.0
8.0	22.0	16.0	1.0

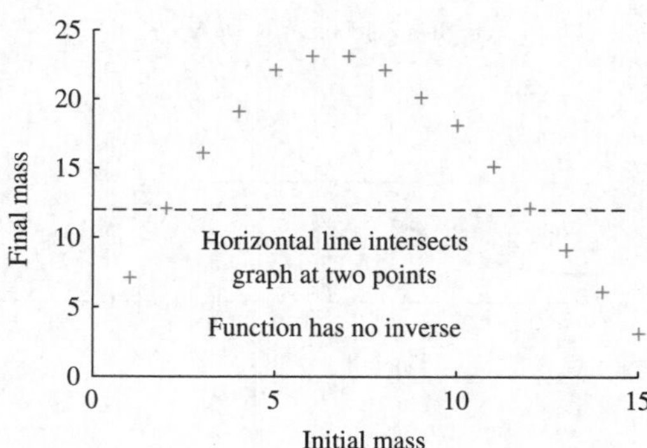

FIGURE 1.2.28
A relation with no inverse

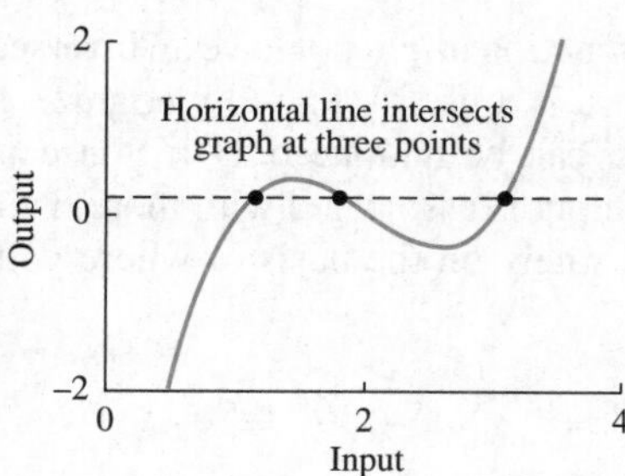

FIGURE 1.2.29
The horizontal line test

Suppose you were told that the mass at the end of the experiment was 12.0 grams. Initial masses of 2.0 and 12.0 grams both produce a final mass of 12.0 grams. You cannot tell whether the input was 2.0 or 12.0. This function has no inverse (Figure 1.2.28).

This reasoning leads to a useful graphical test for whether a function has an inverse.

The Horizontal Line Test A function has no inverse if it takes on the same value twice. This can be established by graphing the function and checking whether the graph intersects any horizontal line two or more times (Figure 1.2.29).

One can think of functions without inverses as losing information over the course of the experiment: things that started out different ended up the same.

Example 1.2.25 A Function That Has an Inverse on Part of Its Domain

Consider the function $g(x) = x^2$ defined for $x \geq 0$ (Figure 1.2.30). We find the inverse $f^{-1}(y)$ by solving $y = x^2$ for x.

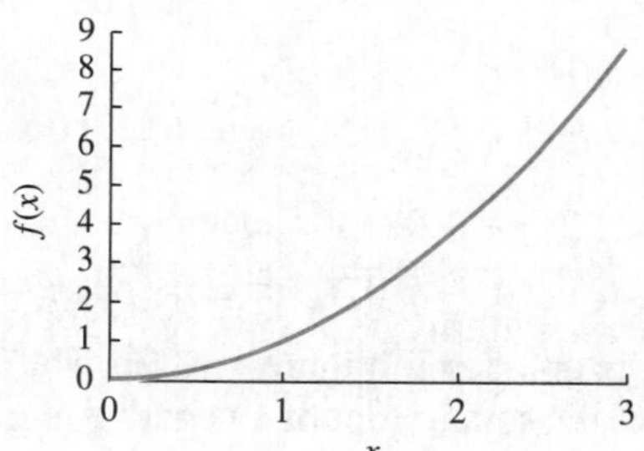

FIGURE 1.2.30
The inverse of x^2 is defined when $x \geq 0$

1. Set $y = x^2$.
2. Then $x = \sqrt{y}$ because $x \geq 0$.
3. $f^{-1}(y) = \sqrt{y}$.

Example 1.2.26 A Function Without an Inverse

Consider the function $f(x) = 4 + x - x^2$ (used in Example 1.2.7). We found that the inputs $x = 0$ and $x = 1$ both produce the same output of $f(x) = 4$ (Figure 1.2.31). If the

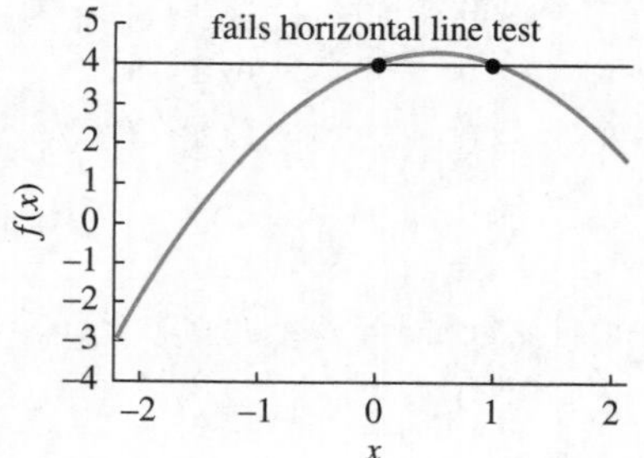

FIGURE 1.2.31
A function with no inverse

output is 4, it is impossible to tell which was the input. A graph shows that this function fails the horizontal line test at almost all values in its range.

In addition, Algorithm 1.1 might fail because the algebra is impossible. Step 2 requires solving an equation. Many equations cannot be solved algebraically.

Example 1.2.27 A Function with an Inverse That Is Impossible to Compute Algebraically

Consider the function

$$f(x) = x^5 + x + 1$$

The graph satisfies the horizontal line test (see Figure 1.2.32). We try to find the inverse $f^{-1}(y)$ as follows:

1. Set $y = x^5 + x + 1$.
2. Try to solve for x. Even with the cleverest algebraic tricks, this is impossible (a remarkable theorem, proved by the French mathematician Evariste Galois when he was just 20 years old, assures us that there is no formula for the solution of a general polynomial with degree greater than 4).
3. Give up.

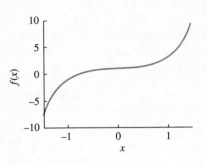

FIGURE 1.2.32
A function with an inverse that is impossible to compute

In mathematical modeling, however, it is often more important to know that something exists (such as the inverse in this case) than to be able to write down a formula. We will later learn a method to compute this inverse numerically, with a computer (Section 3.8).

Summary Quantitative science is built upon measurements, and mathematics provides the methods for describing and thinking about measurements and relations between them. **Variables** describe measurements that change during the course of an experiment, and **parameters** describe measurements that remain constant during an experiment but might change between different experiments. **Functions** describe relations between different measurements when a single ouput is associated with each input; they can be recognized graphically with the **vertical line test.** New functions are built by combining functions through **addition, multiplication,** and **composition.** In functional composition, the output of the **inner function** is used as the input of the **outer function.** Many functions do not **commute,** meaning that composing the functions in a different order gives a different result. Finally, we can use the **horizontal line test** to check whether a functions has an **inverse.** If it does, the inverse can be used to compute the input from the output.

1.2 Exercises

Mathematical Techniques

1–2 ▪ Give mathematical names to the measurements in the following situations, and identify the variables and parameters.

1. A scientist measures the density of wombats at three altitudes: 500 m, 750 m, and 1000 m. He repeats the experiment in 3 different years, with rainfall of 30 cm in the first year, 50 cm in the second, and 60 cm in the third.

2. A scientist measures the density of bandicoots at three altitudes: 500 m, 750 m, and 1000 m. She repeats the experiment in three different years that have different densities of wombats, which compete with bandicoots. The density is 10 wombats per square kilometer in the first year, 20 wombats per square kilometer in the second, and 15 wombats per square kilometer in the third.

3–6 ▪ Compute the values of the following functions at the points indicated and sketch a graph.

3. $f(x) = x + 5$ at $x = 0$, $x = 1$, and $x = 4$
4. $g(y) = 5y$ at $y = 0$, $y = 1$, and $y = 4$
5. $h(z) = \frac{1}{5z}$ at $z = 1$, $z = 2$, and $z = 4$
6. $F(r) = r^2 + 5$ at $r = 0$, $r = 1$, and $r = 4$

7–10 ▪ Graph the given points and say which point does not seem to fall on the graph of a simple function that describes the other four.

7. (0, −1), (1, 1), (2, 2), (3, 5), (4, 7)
8. (0, 8), (1, 10), (2, 8), (3, 6), (4, 4)
9. (0, 2), (1, 3), (2, 6), (3, 11), (4, 12)
10. (0, 30), (1, 25), (2, 15), (3, 12), (4, 10)

11–14 ▪ Evaluate the following functions at the given algebraic arguments.

11. $f(x) = x + 5$ at $x = a$, $x = a + 1$, and $x = 4a$
12. $g(y) = 5y$ at $y = x^2$, $y = 2x + 1$, and $y = 2 - x$
13. $h(z) = \frac{1}{5z}$ at $z = \frac{c}{5}$, $z = \frac{5}{c}$, and $z = c + 1$
14. $F(r) = r^2 + 5$ at $r = x + 1$, $r = 3x$, and $r = \frac{1}{x}$

15–16 ▪ Sketch graphs of the following relations. Is there a more convenient order for the arguments?

15. A function whose argument is the name of a state and whose value is the highest altitude in that state.

State	Highest Altitude (ft)
California	14,491
Idaho	12,662
Nevada	13,143
Oregon	11,239
Utah	13,528
Washington	14,410

16. A function whose argument is the name of a bird and whose value is the average length of that bird.

Bird	Length (cm)
Cooper's hawk	50
Goshawk	66
Sharp-shinned hawk	35

17–20 ▪ For each of the following pairs of functions, graph each component piece. Compute the value of the sum at $x = -2$, $x = -1$, $x = 0$, $x = 1$, and $x = 2$ and plot the result.

17. $f(x) = 2x + 3$ and $g(x) = 3x - 5$
18. $f(x) = 2x + 3$ and $h(x) = -3x - 12$
19. $F(x) = x^2 + 1$ and $G(x) = x + 1$
20. $F(x) = x^2 + 1$ and $H(x) = -x + 1$

21–24 ▪ For each of the following pairs of functions, graph each component piece. Compute the value of the product at $x = -2$, $x = -1$, $x = 0$, $x = 1$, and $x = 2$ and graph the result.

21. $f(x) = 2x + 3$ and $g(x) = 3x - 5$
22. $f(x) = 2x + 3$ and $h(x) = -3x - 12$
23. $F(x) = x^2 + 1$ and $G(x) = x + 1$
24. $F(x) = x^2 + 1$ and $H(x) = -x + 1$

25–28 ▪ Find the inverse of each of the following functions when an inverse exists. In each case, compute the output at an input of 1.0, and show that the inverse undoes the action of the function.

25. $f(x) = 2x + 3$
26. $g(x) = 3x - 5$
27. $F(y) = y^2 + 1$
28. $F(y) = y^2 + 1$ for $y \geq 0$

29–32 ▪ Graph each of the following functions and its inverse if it exists. Mark the given point on the graph of each function.

29. $f(x) = 2x + 3$. Mark the point $(1, f(1))$ on the graphs of f and the corresponding point on f^{-1} (based on Exercise 25).
30. $g(x) = 3x - 5$. Mark the point $(1, g(1))$ on the graphs of g and the corresponding point on g^{-1} (based on Exercise 26).
31. $F(y) = y^2 + 1$. Mark the point $(1, F(1))$ on the graphs of F and the corresponding point on F^{-1} (based on Exercise 27).
32. $F(y) = y^2 + 1$ for $y \geq 0$. Mark the point $(1, F(1))$ on the graphs of F and the corresponding point on F^{-1} (based on Exercise 28).

33–36 ▪ Find the compositions of the given functions. Which pairs of functions commute?

33. $f(x) = 2x + 3$ and $g(x) = 3x - 5$
34. $f(x) = 2x + 3$ and $h(x) = -3x - 12$
35. $F(x) = x^2 + 1$ and $G(x) = x + 1$
36. $F(x) = x^2 + 1$ and $H(x) = -x + 1$

Applications

37–40 ▪ Describe what is happening in the graphs shown.

37. A plot of cell volume against time in days.

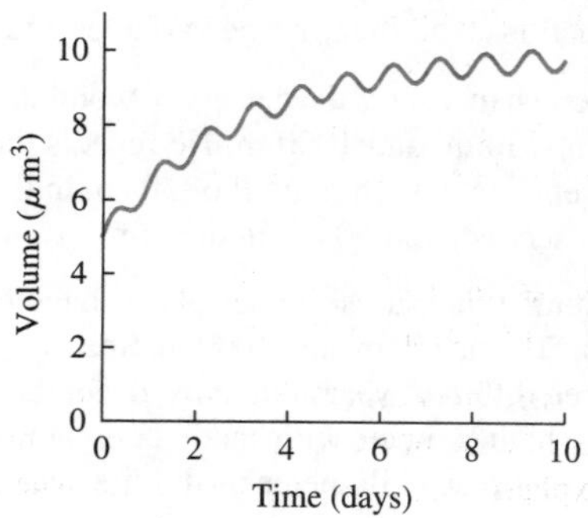

38. A plot of a Pacific salmon population against time in years.

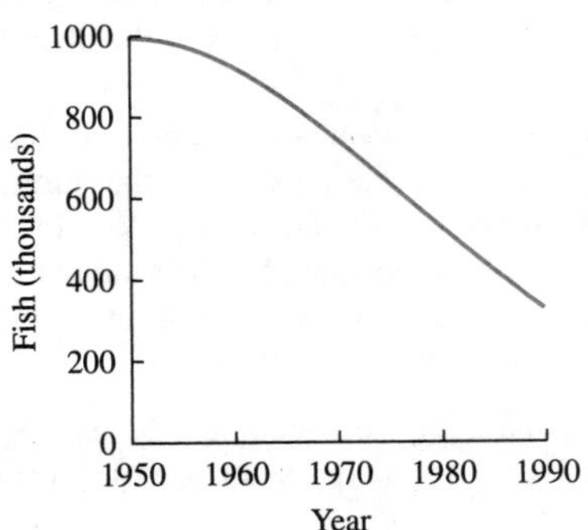

39. A plot of the average height of a population of trees plotted against age in years.

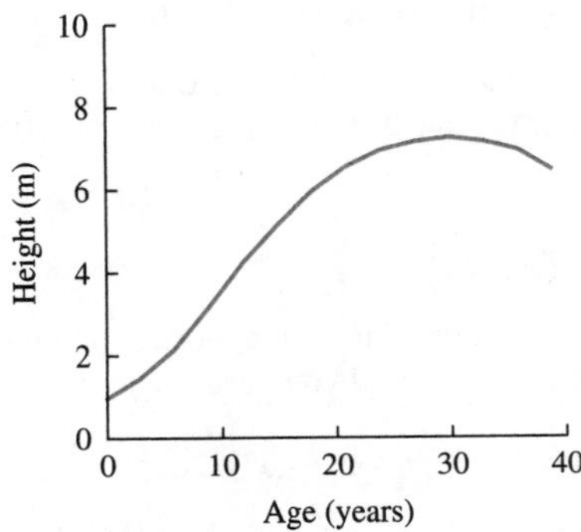

40. A plot of an Internet stock price against time.

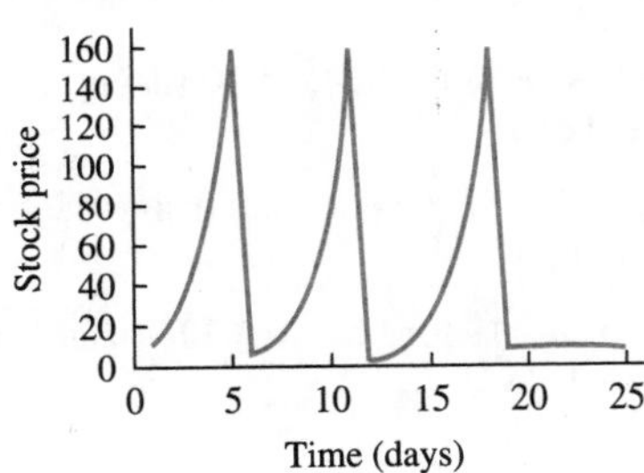

41–44 ▪ Draw graphs based on the following descriptions.

41. A population of birds begins at a large value, decreases to a tiny value, and then increases again to an intermediate value.

42. The amount of DNA in an experiment increases rapidly from a very small value and then levels out at a large value before declining rapidly to 0.

43. Body temperature oscillates between high values during the day and low values at night.

44. Soil is wet at dawn, quickly dries out and stays dry during the day, and then becomes gradually wetter again during the night.

45–48 ▪ Evaluate the following functions over the suggested range, sketch a graph of the function, and answer the biological question.

45. The number of bees b found on a plant is given by $b = 2f + 1$ where f is the number of flowers, ranging from 0 to about 20. Explain what might be happening when $f = 0$.

46. The number of cancerous cells c as a function of radiation dose r (measured in rads) is

$$c = r - 4$$

for r greater than or equal to 5, and is zero for r less than 5. Suppose r ranges from 0 to 10. What is happening at $r = 5$ rads?

47. Insect development time A (in days) obeys $A = 40 - \frac{T}{2}$ where T represents temperature in °C for $10 \leq T \leq 40$. Which temperature leads to the most rapid development?

48. Tree height h (in meters) follows the formula

$$h = \frac{100a}{100 + a}$$

where a represents the age of the tree in years. The formula is valid for any positive value of a, which ranges from 0 to 1000. How tall would this tree get if it lived forever?

49–52 ▪ Consider the following data describing the growth of an tadpole.

Age, a (days)	Length, L (cm)	Tail Length, T (cm)	Mass M (g)
0.5	1.5	1.0	1.5
1.0	3.0	0.9	3.0
1.5	4.5	0.8	6.0
2.0	6.0	0.7	12.0
2.5	7.5	0.6	24.0
3.0	9.0	0.5	48.0

49. Graph length as a function of age.

50. Graph tail length as a function of age.

51. Graph tail length as a function of length.

52. Graph mass as a function of length, and then graph length as a function of mass. How do the two graphs compare?

53–56 ▪ The following series of functional compositions describe connections between several measurements.

53. The number of mosquitos (M) that end up in a room is a function of how much the window is open (W, in square centimeters) according to $M(W) = 5W + 2$. The number of bites (B) depends on the number of mosquitos according to $B(M) = 0.5M$. Find the number of bites as a function of how much the window is open. How many bites would you get if the window were 10 cm^2 open?

54. The temperature of a room (T, in degrees Celsius) is a function of how much the window is open (W, in square centimeters) according to $T(W) = 40 - 0.2W$. How long you sleep (S, measured in hours) is a function of the temperature according to $S(T) = 14 - \frac{T}{5}$. Find how long you sleep as a function of how much the window is open. How long would you sleep if the window were 10 cm^2 open?

55. The number of viruses (V, measured in trillions) that infect a person is a function of the degree of immunosuppression (I, the fraction of the immune system that is turned off by medication) according to $V(I) = 5I^2$. The fever (F, measured in °C) associated with an infection is a function of the number of viruses according to $F(V) = 37 + 0.4V$. Find fever as a function of immunosuppression. How high will the fever be if immunosuppression is complete ($I = 1$)?

56. The length of an insect (L, in millimeters) is a function of the temperature during development (T, measured in °C) according to $L(T) = 10 + \frac{T}{10}$. The volume of the insect (V, in cubic millimeters) is a function of the length according to $V(L) = 2L^3$. The mass (M in milligrams) depends on volume according to $M(V) = 1.3V$. Find mass as a function of temperature. How much would an insect weigh that developed at 25°C? Would you be frightened to meet this insect?

57–58 ▪ Each of the following measurements is the sum of two components. Find the formula for the sum. Sketch a graph of each component and the total as functions of time for $0 \le t \le 3$. Describe each component and the sum in words.

57. A population of bacteria consists of two types, a and b. The first follows $a(t) = 1 + t^2$, and the second follows $b(t) = 1 - 2t + t^2$ where populations are measured in millions and time is measured in hours. The total population is $P(t) = a(t) + b(t)$.

58. The above-ground volume (stem and leaves) of a plant is $V_a(t) = 3.0t + 20.0 + \frac{t^2}{2}$ and the below-ground volume (roots) is $V_b(t) = -1.0t + 40.0$ where t is measured in days after seed germination and volumes are measured in cm^3. The domain is $0 \le t \le 40$. The total volume is $V(t) = V_a(t) + V_b(t)$.

59–62 ▪ Consider the following data describing a plant.

Age, a (days)	Mass, M (g)	Volume, V (cm^3)	Glucose production, G (mg)
0.5	1.5	5.1	0.0
1.0	3.0	6.2	3.4
1.5	4.3	7.2	6.8
2.0	5.1	8.1	8.2
2.5	5.6	8.9	9.4
3.0	5.6	9.6	8.2

59. Graph M as a function of a. Does this function have an inverse? Could we use mass to figure out the age of the plant?

60. Graph V as a function of a. Does this function have an inverse? Could we use volume to figure out the age of the plant?

61. Graph G as a function of a. Does this function have an inverse? Could we use glucose production to figure out the age of the plant?

62. Graph G as a function of M. Does this function have an inverse? What is strange about it? Could we use glucose production to figure out the mass of the plant?

63–66 ▪ The total mass of a population (in kg) as a function of the number of years, t, is the product of the number of individuals, $P(t)$, and the mass per person, $W(t)$ (in kg). In each of the following exercises, find the formula for the total mass, sketch graphs of $P(t)$, $W(t)$, and the total mass as functions of time for $0 \le t \le 100$, and describe the results as words.

63. The population of people P is $P(t) = 2.0 \times 10^6 + 2.0 \times 10^4 t$, and the mass per person $W(t)$ (in kg) is $W(t) = 80 - 0.5t$.

64. The population P is $P(t) = 2.0 \times 10^6 - 2.0 \times 10^4 t$, and the mass per person $W(t)$ is $W(t) = 80 + 0.5t$.

65. The population P is $P(t) = 2.0 \times 10^6 + 1000t^2$, and the mass per person $W(t)$ is $W(t) = 80 - 0.5t$.

66. The population P is $P(t) = 2.0 \times 10^6 + 2.0 \times 10^4 t$, and the mass per person $W(t)$ is $W(t) = 80 - 0.005t^2$.

Computer Exercises

67–70 ▪ Have your graphics calculator or computer plot the following functions. How would you describe them in words?

67. a. $f(x) = x^2 e^{-x}$ for $0 \le x \le 20$

b. $g(x) = 1.5 + e^{-0.1x}\sin(x)$ for $0 \le x \le 20$

c. $h(x) = \sin(5x) - \cos(7x)$ for $0 \le x \le 20$ for x measured in radians

d. $f(x) + h(x)$ for $0 \le x \le 20$ (using the functions in parts a and c)

e. $g(x) \cdot h(x)$ for $0 \le x \le 20$ (using the functions in parts b and c)

f. $h(x) \cdot h(x)$ for $0 \le x \le 20$ (using the function in part c)

68. Have your computer plot the function

$$h(x) = e^{-x^2} - e^{-1000(x-0.13)^2} - 0.2$$

for values of x between -10 and 10.

a. How would you describe the result in words?

b. Blow up the graph by changing the range to find all points where the value of the function is 0. For example, one such value is between 1 and 2. Plot the function again for x between 1 and 2 to zoom in

c. If you found only two points where $h(x) = 0$, blow up the region between 0 and 1 to try to find two more

69. Use your computer to find and plot the following functional compositions.

a. $(f \circ g)(x)$ and $(g \circ f)(x)$ if $f(x) = \sin(x)$ and $g(x) = x^2$

b. $(f \circ g)(x)$ and $(g \circ f)(x)$ if $f(x) = e^x$ and $g(x) = x^2$

c. $(f \circ g)(x)$ and $(g \circ f)(x)$ if $f(x) = e^x$ and $g(x) = \sin(x)$

70. Have your graphics calculator or computer plot the following functions for $-2 \leq x \leq 2$. Do they have inverses?

a. $h_1(x) = x + 2x$

b. $h_2(x) = x^2 + 2x$

c. $h_3(x) = x^3 + 2x$

d. $h_4(x) = x^4 + 2x$

e. $h_5(x) = x^5 + 2x$

Have your computer try to find the formula for the inverses of these functions and plot the results. Does the machine always succeed in finding an inverse when there is one? Does it sometimes find an inverse when there is none?

1.3 The Units and Dimensions of Measurements and Functions

Unlike the numbers and functions studied in many mathematics courses, the measurements and relations used by scientists and applied mathematicians have **units** and **dimensions.** Measurements of number, mass, height, and volume are fundamentally different from each other and are said to have different **dimensions.** Measurements of height in inches or in centimeters describe the same quantity but are presented in different **units.** In this section, we learn how to work with the units and dimensions of both measurements and functions. When we wish to express a measurement or relation in different units, we must use appropriate **conversion factors.** Changing the units of a function corresponds to **scaling** or **shifting** the graph of the function. When we wish to express a function in different dimensions, we must **translate** with a **fundamental relation.**

Converting Between Units

The equation

$$2 + 2 = 2$$

looks hopelessly wrong. But

$$2\ \mathrm{Na}^+ + 2\ \mathrm{Cl}^- = 2\ \mathrm{NaCl}$$

is a standard formula from chemistry. The difference is that the terms in the second equation have explicit units: ions of sodium, ions of chlorine, and molecules of salt. Similarly, although it is absurd to write

$$1 = 2.54$$

it is true that

$$1\ \text{in.} = 2.54\ \text{cm}$$

(This is the official definition of 1 in.) Numbers with units behave very differently from pure numbers.

Often, data are presented with more than one unit. To compare measurements, we must be able to convert between different units.

Example 1.3.1 Converting Miles to Centimeters

Suppose we want to know how many centimeters make up a mile. We can do this in steps, first changing miles to feet, then feet to inches, and then inches to centimeters. To convert between units, we first **write down the basic identities**

$$5280\ \text{ft} = 1\ \text{mile}$$

$$12\ \text{in.} = 1\ \text{ft}$$

$$2.54\ \text{cm} = 1\ \text{in.}$$

These define how many centimeters are in an inch, how many inches are in a foot, and so on. We next **divide** to find three **conversion factors**

$$1 = 5280 \frac{\text{ft}}{\text{mile}}$$

$$1 = 12 \frac{\text{in.}}{\text{ft}}$$

$$1 = 2.54 \frac{\text{cm}}{\text{in.}}$$

Units are manipulated exactly like the numerators and denominators of fractions. We next **multiply** the original measurement by the conversion factors (which are just fancy ways to write the number 1), finding

$$\begin{aligned} 1 \text{ mile} &= 1 \text{ mile} \times 1 \times 1 \times 1 \\ &= 1 \text{ mile} \times 5280 \frac{\text{ft}}{\text{mile}} \times 12 \frac{\text{in.}}{\text{ft}} \times 2.54 \frac{\text{cm}}{\text{in.}} \\ &\approx 160{,}934.4 \text{ cm} \end{aligned}$$

The units cancel just like the numerators and denominators of fractions. This method is often called the "factor-label" method in chemistry.

Algorithm 1.2 The Procedure for Converting Between Units

1. Write down the basic identities that relate the original units to the new units.
2. Divide the basic identities to create conversion factors equal to 1, placing unwanted units where they will cancel.
3. Multiply the original measurement by the appropriate conversion factors.

Example 1.3.2 Using the Algorithm to Change Units of Area

Suppose a house has an area of 2030 square feet. What is this in square meters? The basic identity relating the new unit to the original unit is

$$0.3048 \text{ m} = 1 \text{ ft}$$

We want to place feet in the denominator, so we divide to find the conversion factor

$$1 = 0.3048 \frac{\text{m}}{\text{ft}}$$

Square feet are feet times feet, so we can find

$$\begin{aligned} 2030 \text{ ft}^2 &= 1 \times 1 \times 2030 \text{ ft}^2 \\ &= 0.3048 \frac{\text{m}}{\text{ft}} \times 0.3048 \frac{\text{m}}{\text{ft}} \times 2030 \text{ ft}^2 \\ &\approx 188.6 \text{ m}^2 \end{aligned}$$

Alternatively, we can create a single conversion factor for changing square feet to square meters

$$1 \approx 0.3048^2 \frac{\text{m}^2}{\text{ft}^2} \approx 0.0929 \frac{\text{m}^2}{\text{ft}^2}$$

Then

$$\begin{aligned} 2030 \text{ ft}^2 &= 1 \times 2030 \text{ ft}^2 \\ &= 0.0929 \frac{\text{m}^2}{\text{ft}^2} \times 2030 \text{ ft}^2 \\ &\approx 188.6 \text{ m}^2 \end{aligned}$$

Example 1.3.3 Results of Mixing up Numerator and Denominator

In Example 1.3.1, it would be equally true that

$$1 = \frac{1}{5280}\,\frac{\text{mile}}{\text{ft}}$$

$$1 = \frac{1}{12}\,\frac{\text{ft}}{\text{in.}}$$

$$1 = \frac{1}{2.54}\,\frac{\text{in.}}{\text{cm}}$$

Multiplying by these conversion factors yields

$$\begin{aligned}1\text{ mile} &= 1\text{ mile} \times 1 \times 1 \times 1\\ &= 1\text{ mile} \times \frac{1}{5280}\,\frac{\text{mile}}{\text{ft}} \times \frac{1}{12}\,\frac{\text{ft}}{\text{in.}} \times \frac{1}{2.54}\,\frac{\text{in.}}{\text{cm}}\\ &\approx \frac{1}{160934}\,\frac{\text{mile}^2}{\text{cm}}\end{aligned}$$

The units did not cancel. Even though the result is true, miles and centimeters are left over in a rather inconvenient way. The trick to getting unit conversions to work is making sure that unwanted units in the numerator are canceled by using conversion factors with those same units in the denominator, and vice versa.

Translating Between Dimensions

Miles and centimeters measure the same quantity—length—with different rulers. Miles and grams measure completely different quantities—length and mass. **Dimensions** describe the underlying quantities. **Units** are a particular standard for measurement. Measurements in miles and centimeters share the same dimension and can be **converted** into one another. Measurements with different dimensions cannot. The dimensions and the units commonly used for some common biological measurements are listed in Table 1.3.1.

Suppose we want to measure a bacterial population in grams (mass) rather than numbers or to measure the size of a water droplet in cubic centimeters (volume) rather than centimeters (length of radius). We cannot apply a series of identities like 1 in. = 2.54 cm because we are translating between dimensions rather than converting between units. Instead of **identities,** we use **fundamental relations** among measurements with different dimensions (Table 1.3.2).

Table 1.3.1 Some quantities, their dimensions, and sample units

Quantity	Dimensions	Sample Units
length	length	meter, micron, inch
duration	time	second, minute, day
mass	mass	gram, kilogram
area	length^2	square meter, acre
volume	length^3	liter, cubic meter, gallon
speed	length/time	meters/second, mph
acceleration	length/time^2	meters/second^2
force	$\text{mass} \times \text{length/time}^2$	dynes, pounds
density	mass/length^3	grams/liter

Table 1.3.2 Important fundamental relations in biology

Relation	Variables	Formula
Geometric Relations		
Volume of a sphere	$V=$ volume $r=$ radius	$V=\frac{4\pi}{3}r^3$
Surface area of a sphere	$S=$ surface area $r=$ radius	$S=4\pi r^2$
Area of a circle	$A=$ area $r=$ radius	$A=\pi r^2$
Perimeter of a circle	$P=$ perimeter $r=$ radius	$P=2\pi r$
Volume, area, and thickness	$V=$ volume $A=$ area $T=$ thickness	$V=AT$
Relations Involving Mass		
Total number and mass	$m=$ total mass $\mu=$ mass per individual $b=$ number of individuals	$m=\mu b$
Mass, density, and volume	$M=$ mass $\rho=$ density $V=$ volume	$M=\rho V$

Example 1.3.4 Translating Between Number and Total Mass

μ = mass per bacterium

b = number of bacteria

total mass = mass per bacterium × number of bacteria $m=\mu b$

FIGURE 1.3.33
Fundamental relation between mass and number

The fundamental relation between number and total mass is

$$\text{total mass} = \text{mass per bacterium} \times \text{number of bacteria}$$

Let m represent the total mass, μ the mass per bacterium, and b the number of bacteria (Figure 1.3.33). The fundamental relation can be rewritten in mathematical symbols as

$$m=\mu b$$

Like numbers, variables representing measurements have both dimensions and units. The variable m has units of grams, μ has units of grams, and b has units of number of bacteria. If

$$b=2.0\times 10^5 \text{ and } \mu=3.1\times 10^{-9}\text{ g}$$

then

$$m=\left(3.1\times 10^{-9}\text{ g}\right)\cdot\left(2.0\times 10^5\right)=6.2\times 10^{-4}\text{ g}$$

Example 1.3.5 Computing the Volume of a Spherical Droplet from Its Radius

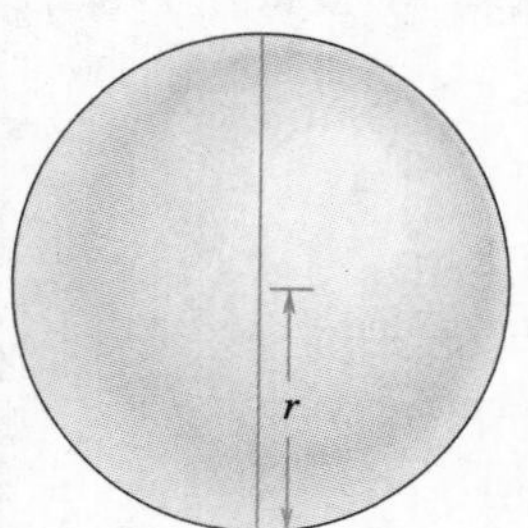

FIGURE 1.3.34
Volume and radius of a spherical droplet

Computing the volume of a droplet requires a fundamental relation between radius and volume, which depends on the **shape** of the droplet. Suppose that droplets are perfect spheres. The fundamental relation between radius and volume comes from geometry. The volume V of a sphere with radius r is

$$V=\frac{4\pi}{3}r^3$$

where r has units of centimeters and V has units of cubic centimeters, or cm^3 (Figure 1.3.34). If a droplet has radius 0.23 cm, the volume is

$$V=\frac{4\pi}{3}0.23^3\approx 0.051\text{ cm}^3$$

Example 1.3.6 Computing the Mass from the Volume

To compute the mass of the droplet in Example 1.3.5 from its volume, we use the fundamental relation

$$\text{mass} = \text{density} \times \text{volume}$$

If we denote the density by ρ and the mass by M, the fundamental relation can be rewritten in mathematical symbols as

$$M = \rho V$$

Suppose that the droplet is made of mercury, which has density of 13.58 g/cm^3. The mass M of a droplet with radius 0.23 cm is

$$M \approx 13.58 \frac{\text{g}}{\text{cm}^3} \cdot 0.051 \text{ cm}^3 \approx 0.693 \text{ g}$$

It is crucial to check the dimensions and units in any unfamiliar equation you encounter. In the equation

$$M = \rho V$$

the dimensions of M are mass, the dimensions of V are length^3, and the dimensions of ρ are $\text{mass}/\text{length}^3$. Rewriting this equation in dimensions yields

$$\text{mass} = \frac{\text{mass}}{\text{length}^3} \times \text{length}^3$$

The length^3 terms cancel and the dimensions of the two sides match, as they must. This procedure is called **dimensional analysis.** Many errors can be nipped in the bud by checking the dimensions. An equation with inconsistent dimensions is not merely incorrect, it is nonsensical.

Functions and Units: Composition, Scaling, and Shifting

Because functions describe relations between measurements, both their inputs and their outputs have units and dimensions. Care must be taken to ensure that functions are composed only when their units and dimensions match.

Example 1.3.7 Composing Functions with Dimensions

Suppose that F takes the radius r of a sphere as input and returns the volume of the sphere as output (as with the spherical droplet in Example 1.3.5). Then F has the formula

$$F(r) = \frac{4\pi}{3} r^3$$

Suppose G takes a volume V as input and returns the mass of an object with that volume as output according to mass = density × volume, or

$$G(V) = 13.58V$$

using the density $\rho = 13.58 \text{ g/cm}^3$. The composition $G \circ F$ takes radius as input and returns mass as output in a single step (Figure 1.3.35). The composition is

$$\begin{aligned}(G \circ F)(r) &= G(F(r)) \\ &= G\left(\frac{4\pi}{3} r^3\right) \\ &= 13.58 \frac{4\pi}{3} r^3 \approx 56.88 r^3\end{aligned}$$

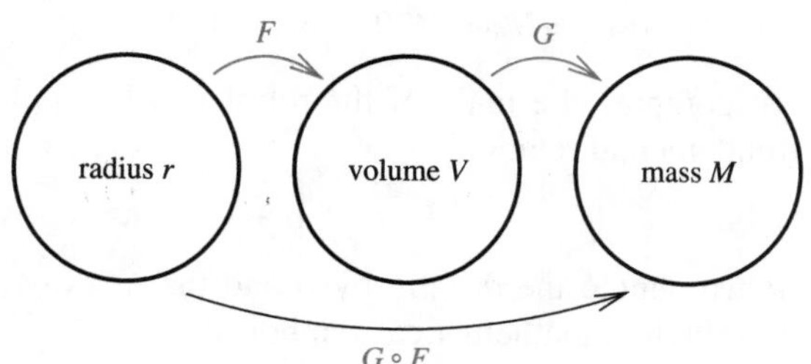

FIGURE 1.3.35
The composition of two functions with units

We could find the mass of a droplet with radius 0.23 cm in two steps by finding the volume and then the mass with the steps

$$V = F(0.23 \text{ cm}) = \frac{4\pi}{3} 0.23 \text{ cm}^3 \approx 0.051 \text{ cm}^3$$

$$M = G(0.051 \text{ cm}^3) = 13.58 \text{ g/cm}^3 \cdot 0.051 \text{ cm}^3 \approx 0.693 \text{ g}$$

Alternatively, we could find the mass in a single step by composing the functions G and F,

$$M = (G \circ F)(0.23 \text{ cm}) = 13.58 \text{ g/cm}^3 \frac{4\pi}{3} 0.23 \text{ cm}^3 \approx 0.692 \text{ g}$$

with the slight discrepancy caused by round-off error.

The function F accepts inputs with dimensions of length and returns outputs with dimensions of volume. G accepts inputs with dimensions of volume and returns outputs with dimensions of mass. Because G takes as input precisely what F provides as output, the composition makes sense.

What if we tried to compute $F \circ G$? F cannot accept an input with dimensions of mass, and such outputs are the only outputs that G can return. It is impossible to compute the volume of a sphere with a radius of 4.3 grams. This composition is nonsense.

Changing the units of a measurement that acts as the input or output of a function corresponds to **scaling** or **shifting** the graph of the function. In most cases, the measurement corresponding to a value of zero is the same in different units, and graphs of the function are scaled by changes in units. When units differ in the value corresponding to zero (as with temperature), then the graph of the function is shifted.

Example 1.3.8 Scaling Functions on the Vertical Axis by Changing Units of the Output

Consider the following function describing the growth of a bacterial population:

$$b(t) = 2.0t$$

where t is measured in hours and $b(t)$ is in millions of bacteria.

If bacteria are measured instead in thousands of bacteria, we choose a different variable to represent the new measurement, such as B. The relation becomes

$$\begin{aligned} B(t) &= 2.0t \, \frac{\text{million bacteria}}{\text{hr}} \times \frac{1000 \text{ thousand bacteria}}{\text{one million bacteria}} \\ &= 2000.0t \, \frac{\text{thousand bacteria}}{\text{hr}} \end{aligned}$$

(Figure 1.3.36). The graph has been changed by **scaling** the vertical axis. It looks the same, except that the numbers that appear on the axis are 1000 times larger.

Example 1.3.9 Scaling Functions on the Horizontal Axis by Changing Units of the Input

Suppose again that $b(t) = 2.0t$ where b is measured in millions and t is measured in hours. If time is measured in minutes instead of hours, we must define a new variable

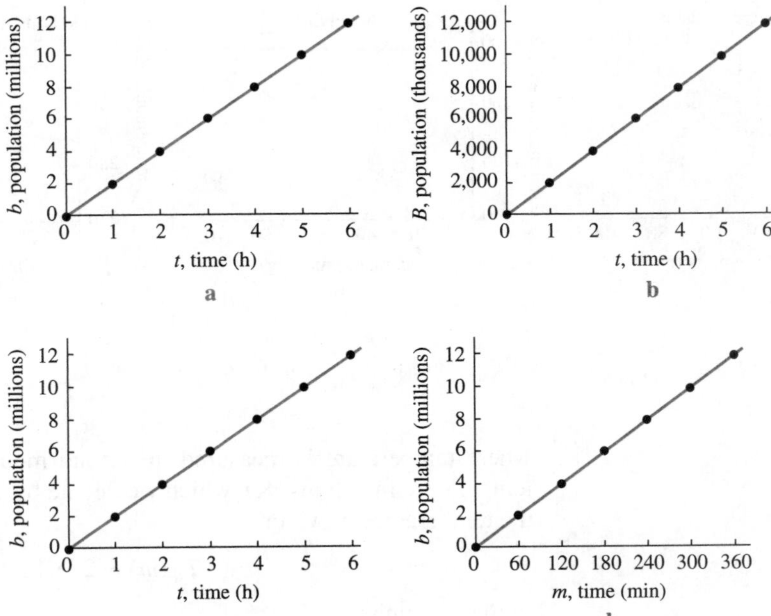

FIGURE 1.3.36
A growing bacterial population: new units on vertical axis

FIGURE 1.3.37
A growing bacterial population: new units on horizontal axis

for time, perhaps m. The relation becomes

$$\begin{aligned} b(m) &= 2.0m \, \frac{\text{million bacteria}}{\text{hr}} \times \frac{1 \text{ hr}}{60 \text{ min}} \\ &= \frac{1.0}{30.0} m \, \frac{\text{million bacteria}}{\text{min}} \\ &\approx 0.0333m \, \frac{\text{million bacteria}}{\text{min}} \end{aligned}$$

(Figure 1.3.37).

The graph has been changed by **scaling** the horizontal axis. Again, it looks the same, except that the numbers labeling the horizontal axis are 60 times larger. The data point (1, 2) that indicated that there were 2.0 million bacteria after 1 hour becomes the point (60, 2), indicating 2.0 million bacteria after 60 minutes.

t (h)	m (min)	b (millions)	B (thousands)
0	0	0	0
1	60	2	2,000
2	120	4	4,000
3	180	6	6,000
4	240	8	8,000
5	300	10	10,000
6	360	12	12,000

Example 1.3.10 Shifting Functions Vertically by Changing Units

Temperatures can be measured on scales with different values of zero (Figure 1.3.38a). For example, 0°C corresponds to 273.15 K. (The units of temperature on the Kelvin scale are referred to as kelvins, rather than as degrees, and no degree symbol is used.) Suppose that the temperature of a snake after digesting a mouse with mass m obeys the equation

$$T(m) = 10 + 0.06m$$

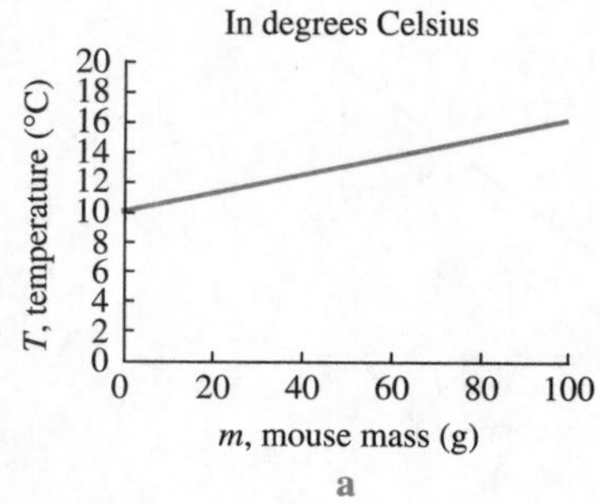

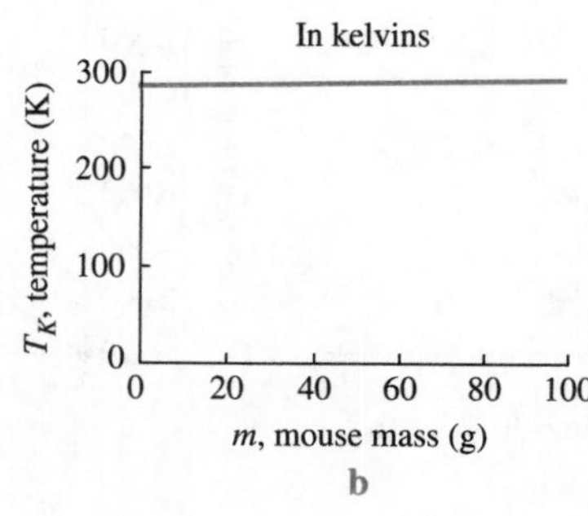

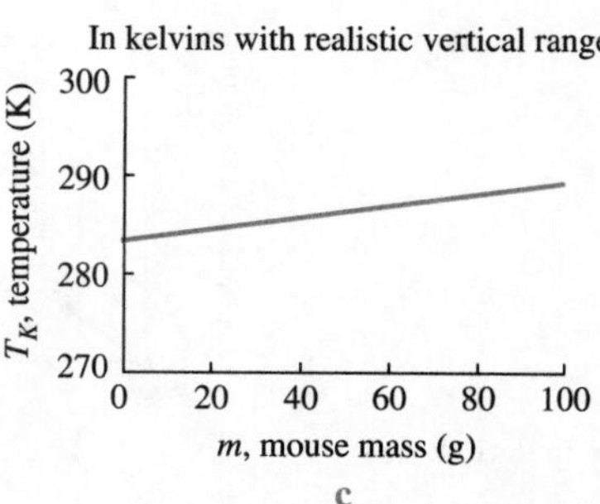

FIGURE 1.3.38
Snake temperature in different units

where temperature is measured in °C and mouse mass is measured in grams. The temperature in kelvins (K), which we denote by T_K, can be found by adding 273.15 to the temperature in °C, or

$$T_K(m) = 273.15 + T(m)$$

In the new units,

$$T_K(m) = 283.15 + 0.06m$$

(Figure 1.3.38b). The graph has been **shifted** vertically. It looks different because 0 K is so far from the temperatures measured. A graph with the horizontal axis set at 270 K is more informative (Figure 1.3.38c).

Example 1.3.11 Shifting Functions Horizontally by Changing Units

Suppose that the sprint speed of a snake is a function of temperature according to the equation

$$s(T) = 4 + 0.1T$$

where temperature is measured in °C and speed is measured in m/sec (Figure 1.3.39a). Temperature in K can be found by adding 273.15 to temperature in °C, or $T_K = T + 273.15$. To write the equation in the new units, we solve for $T = T_K - 273.15$, giving

$$s(T_K) = 4 + 0.1(T_K - 273.15)$$

(Figure 1.3.39b). The graph has been **shifted** horizontally. However, by including extremely cold temperatures, the function predicts impossible negative speeds. A graph showing only the vertical range from 275 K to 325 K is more informative (Figure 1.3.39c).

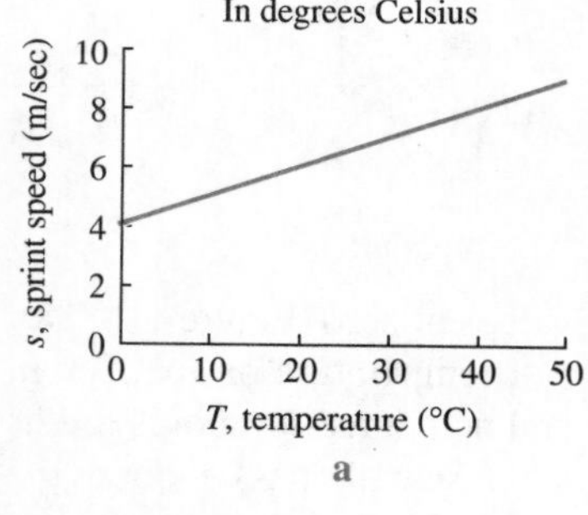

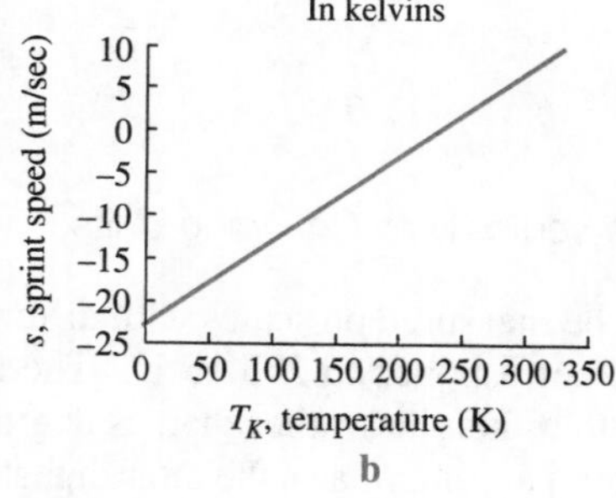

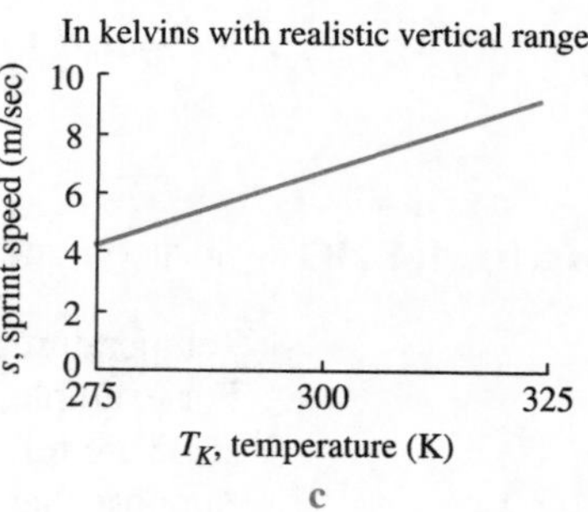

FIGURE 1.3.39
Snake speed in different units

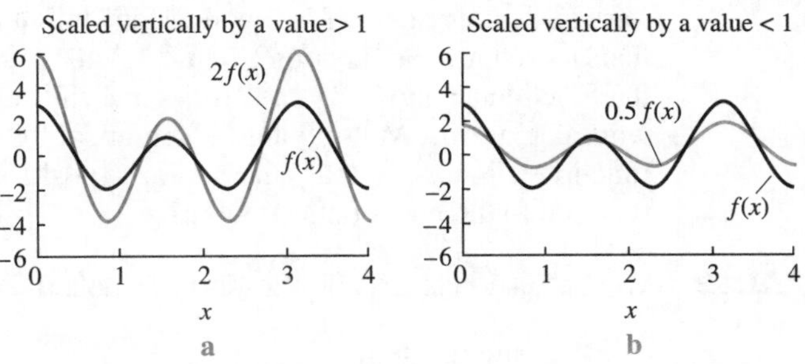

FIGURE 1.3.40
Vertically scaling a function

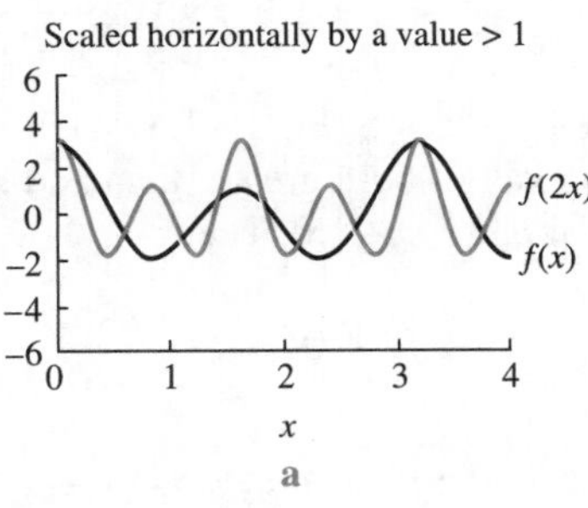

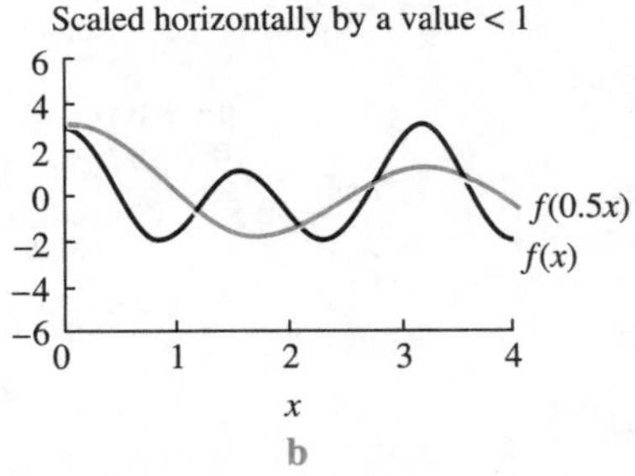

FIGURE 1.3.41
Horizontally scaling a function

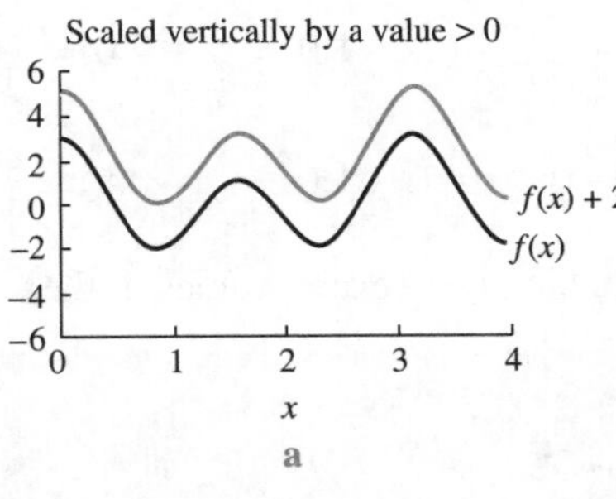

FIGURE 1.3.42
Vertically shifting a function

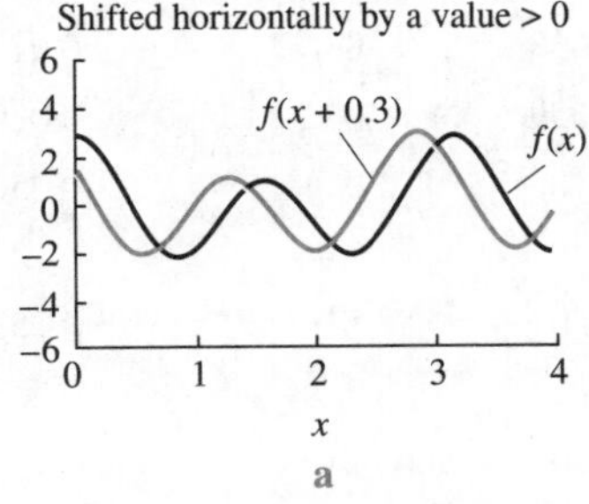

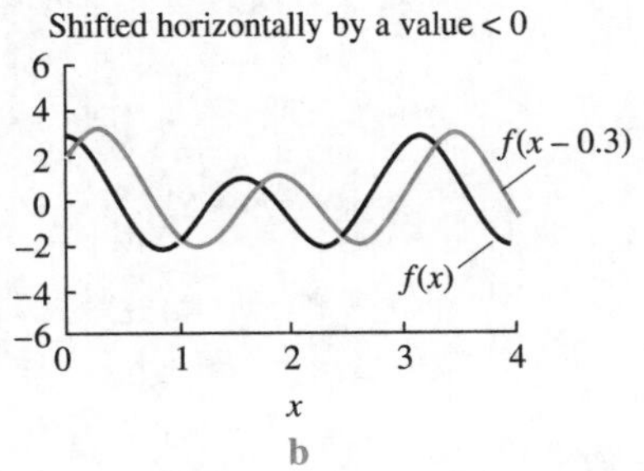

FIGURE 1.3.43
Horizontally shifting a function

Mathematically, scaling corresponds to multiplying the value or the argument of a function by a constant, whereas shifting corresponds to adding a constant to the value or argument. In particular, the function $f(x)$ can be scaled or shifted as follows:

- **Vertical Scaling** Multiply the value by the constant a to make the new function $af(x)$ (Figure 1.3.40).
- **Horizontal Scaling** Multiply the argument by the constant a to make the new function $f(ax)$ (Figure 1.3.41).
- **Vertical Shifting** Add the constant a to the value to make the new function $f(x) + a$. (Figure 1.3.42).
- **Horizontal Shifting** Add the constant a to the argument to make the new function $f(x + a)$ (Figure 1.3.43).

Vertical scaling and shifting work as one might expect: multiplying by a value greater than 1 stretches the function (Figure 1.3.40a), and adding a value greater than 0 raises the function (Figure 1.3.42a). Horizontal shifting and scaling, however, might seem to work backwards. Multiplying the argument by a value greater than 1 compresses the function (Figure 1.3.41a), and adding a positive constant to the argument moves the function to the left (Figure 1.3.43a).

Example 1.3.12 Vertically and Horizontally Scaling a Function

Consider the function

$$f(x) = \frac{1}{1+x^2}$$

shown plotted for $-5 \leq x \leq 5$ (Figure 1.3.44). We will scale the value and the argument of this function by values both greater than and less than 1.

Consider the input $x = -1.0$. Then

$$2f(-1.0) = 2 \cdot \frac{1}{1+(-1.0)^2} = 1.0$$

$$0.5f(-1.0) = 0.5 \cdot \frac{1}{1+(-1.0)^2} = 0.25$$

$$f(2 \cdot -1.0) = f(-2.0) = \frac{1}{1+(-2.0)^2} = 0.2$$

$$f(0.5 \cdot -1.0) = f(-0.5) = \frac{1}{1+(-0.5)^2} = 0.8$$

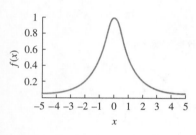

FIGURE 1.3.44
The original function

The following table gives several values of the scaled functions.

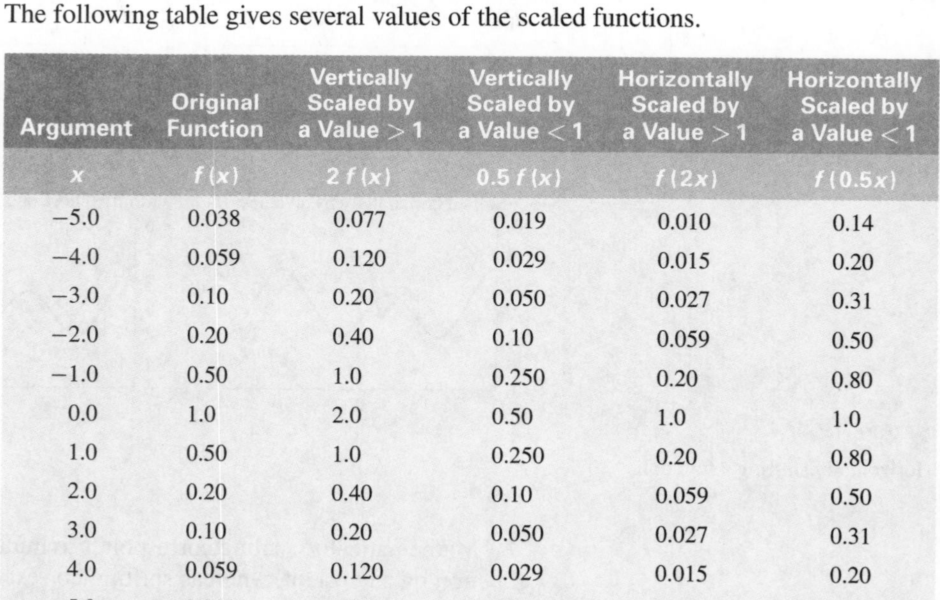

Argument	Original Function	Vertically Scaled by a Value > 1	Vertically Scaled by a Value < 1	Horizontally Scaled by a Value > 1	Horizontally Scaled by a Value < 1
x	$f(x)$	$2f(x)$	$0.5f(x)$	$f(2x)$	$f(0.5x)$
−5.0	0.038	0.077	0.019	0.010	0.14
−4.0	0.059	0.120	0.029	0.015	0.20
−3.0	0.10	0.20	0.050	0.027	0.31
−2.0	0.20	0.40	0.10	0.059	0.50
−1.0	0.50	1.0	0.250	0.20	0.80
0.0	1.0	2.0	0.50	1.0	1.0
1.0	0.50	1.0	0.250	0.20	0.80
2.0	0.20	0.40	0.10	0.059	0.50
3.0	0.10	0.20	0.050	0.027	0.31
4.0	0.059	0.120	0.029	0.015	0.20
5.0	0.038	0.077	0.019	0.010	0.14

Scaling vertically makes the graph of the function taller if it is scaled by a value greater than 1 or shorter if it is scaled by a value less than 1. Scaling horizontally makes the graph of the function thinner if it is scaled by a value greater than 1 or wider if it is scaled by a value less than 1.

Example 1.3.13 Vertically and Horizontally Shifting a Function

Consider again the function in Example 1.3.12 (Figure 1.3.44). We will shift the value and the argument of this function by values both greater than and less than 0.

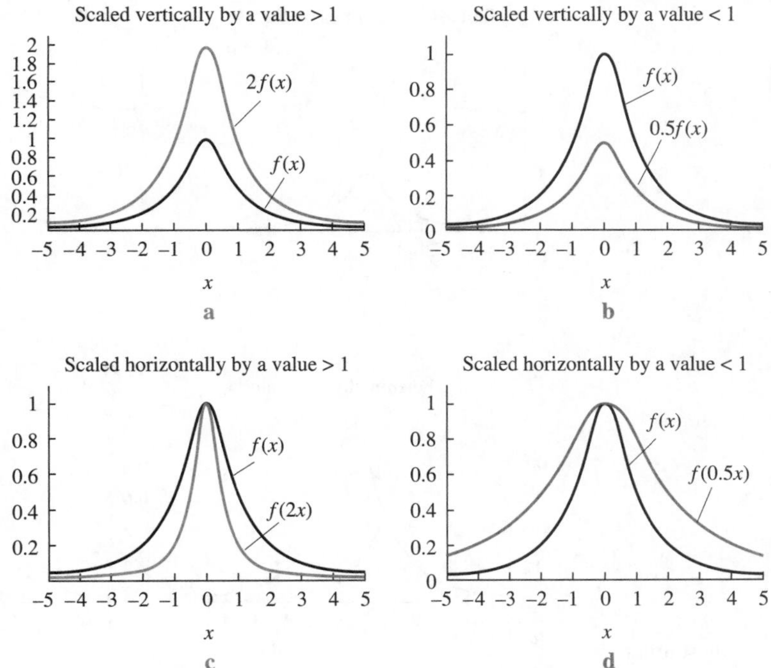

FIGURE 1.3.45
Vertically and horizontally scaling a function

Shifting the function vertically corresponds to adding a constant to f.

Argument	Original Function	Vertically Shifted by a Value > 0	Vertically Shifted by a Value < 0	Horizontally Shifted by a Value > 0	Horizontally Shifted by a Value < 0
x	$f(x)$	$f(x)+2$	$f(x)-2$	$f(x+2)$	$f(x-2)$
−5	0.038	2.04	−1.96	0.10	0.020
−4	0.059	2.06	−1.94	0.20	0.027
−3	0.10	2.1	−1.9	0.50	0.038
−2	0.20	2.2	−1.8	1.0	0.059
−1	0.50	2.5	−1.5	0.50	0.10
0	1.0	3.0	−1.0	0.20	0.20
1	0.50	2.5	−1.5	0.10	0.50
2	0.20	2.2	−1.8	0.059	1.0
3	0.10	2.1	−1.9	0.038	0.50
4	0.059	2.06	−1.94	0.027	0.20
5	0.038	2.04	−1.96	0.020	0.10

Shifting vertically moves the function up if it is shifted by a value greater than 0 or down if it is shifted by a value less than 0. Shifting horizontally moves the function to the right if it is shifted by a value greater than 0 or to the left if it is shifted by a value less than 0.

Checking: Dimensions and Estimation

Just as it is essential to check the dimensions and units of equations, it is essential to check the plausibility of the numerical results of calculations. Suppose you wanted to figure out how many tons all the people in the United States weigh. Each person (counting children) weighs on average about 100 pounds, or 1/20 of a ton per person. If there are about 300 million people, they should weigh a net amount of around 15 million

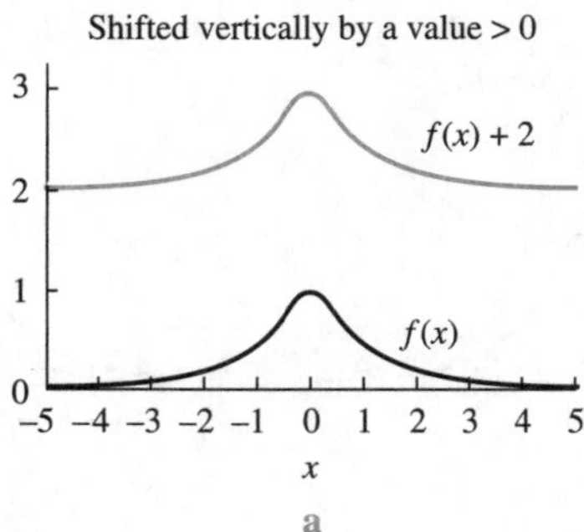

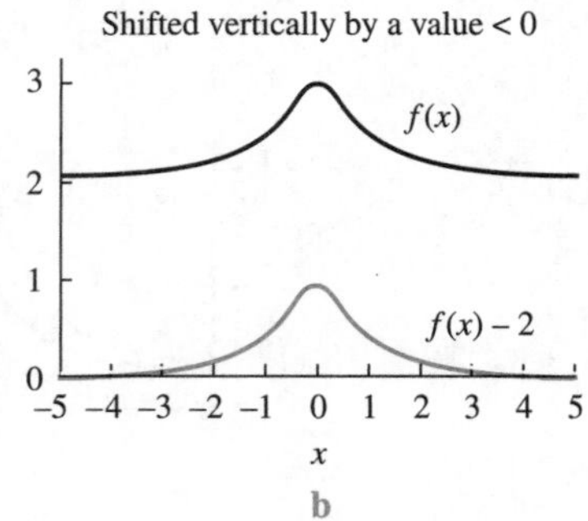

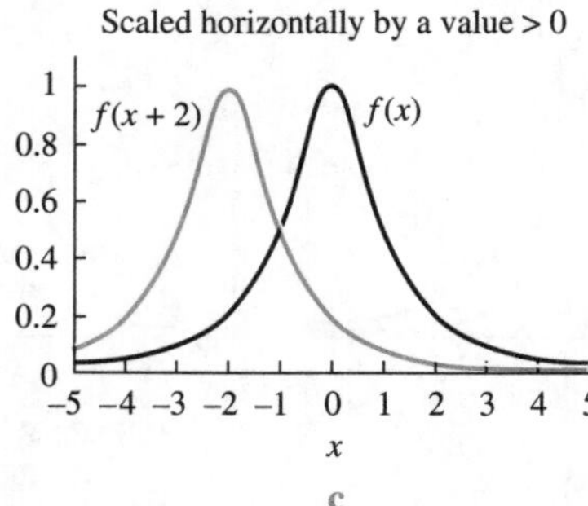

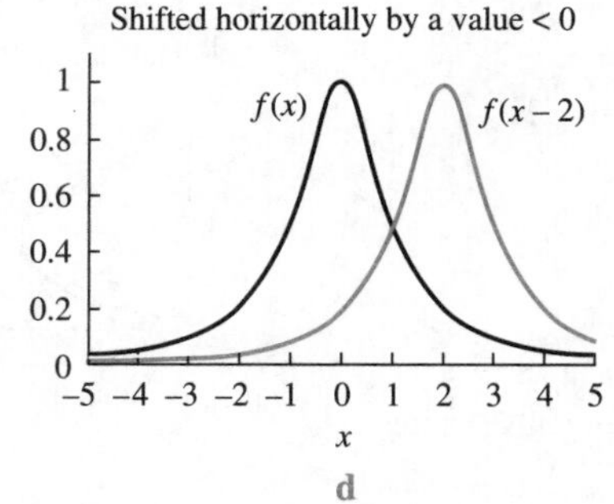

FIGURE 1.3.46
Vertically and horizontally shifting a function

tons (using the fundamental relation that total mass is equal to mass per individual times the number of individuals). If you had worked this out with a more complicated set of measurements and found a more precise answer of 14.7 million tons, everything is probably all right. If the complicated method gave an answer of 1.47 million tons, it needs to be checked.

Example 1.3.14 Estimating the Area of a Bacterial Colony

How much area does a colony of 2.0×10^5 bacteria take up on a Petri dish (Figure 1.3.47)? One method is to use our computation of the mass (6.2×10^{-4} g in Example 1.3.4), convert to volume, and then to find the area by dividing by the thickness. If we assume that bacteria have approximately the density of water (which is 1 g/cm^3), the volume is

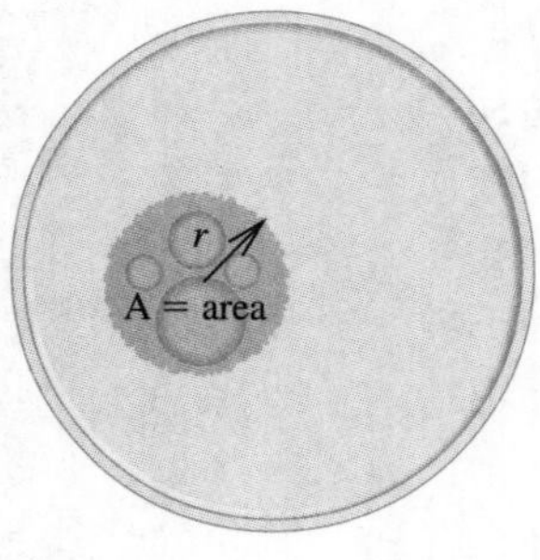

FIGURE 1.3.47
A bacterial colony on a Petri dish

$$V = \frac{M}{\rho} = \frac{6.2 \times 10^{-4}\ \text{g}}{1.0 \times 10^{-12}\ \text{g}/\mu\text{m}^3} = 6.2 \times 10^8\ \mu\text{m}^3$$

Here we used the fact that $1.0\,\mu\text{m}^3 = 10^{-12}\ \text{cm}^3$ to find density in $\text{g}/\mu\text{m}^3$. The next **fundamental relation** translates between volume and area and is

$$\text{volume} = \text{area} \times \text{thickness}$$

so that

$$\text{area} = \frac{\text{volume}}{\text{thickness}}$$

If we estimate the thickness of the colony to be about 20 μm (roughly the thickness of a cell),

$$\text{area} \approx \frac{6.2 \times 10^8\ \mu\text{m}^3}{20\ \mu\text{m}} \approx 3 \times 10^7\ \mu\text{m}^2$$

This sounds rather large. To convert to square centimeters, we use the basic identity

$$1\ \mu\text{m} = 10^{-4}\ \text{cm}$$

so that the conversion factor is

$$1 = 10^{-4}\ \text{cm}/\mu\text{m}$$

Multiplying yields

$$\begin{aligned} 3 \times 10^{7}\ \mu\text{m}^2 &= 3 \times 10^{7}\ \mu\text{m}^2 \times 10^{-4}\ \text{cm}/\mu\text{m} \times 10^{-4}\ \text{cm}/\mu\text{m} \\ &= 0.3\ \text{cm}^2 \end{aligned}$$

To find the radius, we use the **fundamental geometric relation** between the area A and radius r for a circle,

$$A = \pi r^2$$

The radius r of this colony satisfies

$$\pi r^2 \approx 0.3\ \text{cm}^2$$

Solving for r yields

$$r \approx \sqrt{\frac{0.3\ \text{cm}^2}{\pi}} \approx 0.3\ \text{cm}$$

This colony is actually quite small, but large enough to be seen.

Example 1.3.15 Fermi's Piano Tuner Problem

The great physicist Enrico Fermi emphasized our ability to combine educated guesses of ordinary quantities to estimate more complicated quantities. For example, we can estimate the number of piano tuners in Salt Lake City and vicinity knowing only that the population is about 1,000,000 people. First, we estimate the number of pianos. If the average family contains four members, the number of families is about 250,000. As a rough guess, suppose that one in five families owns a piano. There will then be 50,000 pianos. If the average piano tuner tunes 4 pianos every day and works for 250 days per year (50 weeks of 5 days), she will tune 1000 pianos per year. If each piano is tuned once in 2 years (another very rough guess), there will be 25,000 pianos tuned per year, requiring 25 piano tuners. A quick check of the phone book indicates that there are in fact about 30 piano tuners. Like all mathematical models, this method requires us to **analyze** the problem by breaking it into component parts. If our estimate proved to be extremely inaccurate, we could check each of our assumptions to find the source of the error.

Summary Understanding scientific equations and formulas requires understanding the **units** and **dimensions** of the measurements and variables. **Dimensions** describe the underlying quantities and tell what sort of thing is being measured. **Units** express numerical values based on a particular scale. Converting between units can be done by starting with **basic identities,** deriving **conversion factors,** and multiplying. Unit conversions correspond to **scaling** or **shifting** the graphs of functions describing the measurements. Translating between measurements with different dimensions requires using **fundamental relations,** such as those between mass and volume or between volume and radius. All such relations, and every scientific formula, should be checked for consistency with **dimensional analysis.** Using basic identities and fundamental relations, we can compute useful estimates of quantities, often without using a calculator. Checking results for plausibility can help locate mistakes.

1.3 Exercises

Mathematical Techniques

1–6 ▪ Convert the following into the new units.

1. Find 3.4 pounds in grams (1 oz is 28.35 g and 1 lb is 16 oz).
2. Find one yard in millimeters (1 in. is 25.4 mm and 1 yd is 36 in.).
3. Find 60 years in hours (1.0 year $\approx$ 365.25 days).
4. Find 65 miles per hour in centimeters per second (using information in Example 1.3.1).
5. Find 2.3 grams per cubic centimeter in pounds per cubic foot (using conversion factors in Exercises 1 and 2).
6. Find 9.807 $\mathrm{m/sec^2}$ (the acceleration due to gravity) in miles per hour per second.

7–10 ▪ Compute the answers by adding the given quantities.

7. A boy who is 1.34 m tall grows 2.3 cm. How tall is he then?
8. After waiting for 1.2 hr for a plane flight, you are told you will have to wait another 17 min. What is the total wait?
9. You purchase 6 apples that weigh 145 gm each, and 7 oranges that weigh 123 gm each. What is the total weight if you add the apples to the oranges?
10. The density of the apples in the previous problem is 0.8 $\mathrm{g/cm^3}$ and the density of the oranges is 0.95 $\mathrm{g/cm^3}$. What is the total volume if you add the apples to the oranges?

11–14 ▪ Figure out which is larger.

11. The area of a square with side length 1.7 cm or of a disk with radius 1.0 cm.
12. The perimeter of a square with side length 1.7 cm or of a circle with radius 1.0 cm.
13. The volume of a sphere with radius 100 m or of a lake 50 cm deep with an area of 3.0 $\mathrm{km^2}$.
14. The surface area of a sphere with radius 100 m or the surface area of a lake with area 3.0 $\mathrm{km^2}$.

15–18 ▪ Find the dimensions of the following quantities.

15. Pressure (force per unit area).
16. Energy (force times distance).
17. The rate of change of the area of a colony of bacteria growing on a plate.
18. The force of gravity between two objects is equal to Gm_1m_2/r^2 where m_1 and m_2 are the masses of the two objects, and r is the distance between them. What are the dimensions of the gravitational constant G?

19–22 ▪ Check whether the following formulas are dimensionally consistent.

19. Distance = rate times time
20. Velocity = acceleration times time
21. Force = mass times acceleration
22. Energy = 1/2 mass times the square of velocity (see Exercise 16 for the units of energy)

23–26 ▪ Using the graph of the function $g(x)$, sketch a graph of the shifted or scaled function, say which kind of shift or scale it is, and compare with the original function.

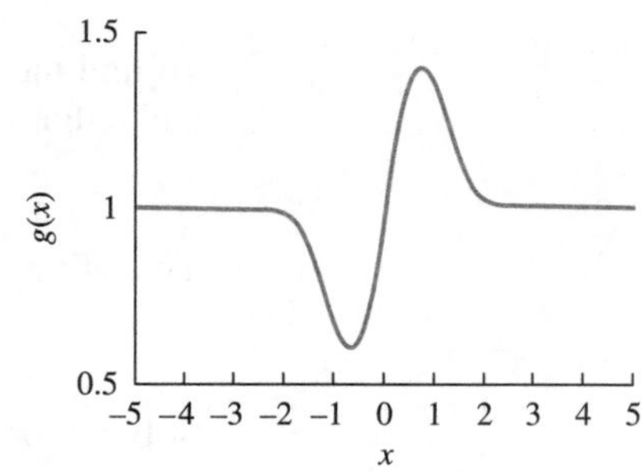

23. $4g(x)$
24. $g(x) - 1$
25. $g(x/3)$
26. $g(x+1)$

Applications

27–30 ▪ Find the volumes of the following cartoon trees (drawing a sketch can help), assuming first that the height is 23.1 m and then that the height is 24.1 m. What is the ratio of the volume of the larger tree to that of the smaller tree?

27. A tree is a perfect cylinder with radius 0.5 m no matter what the height (the volume of a cylinder with height h and radius r is πhr^2).
28. A tree is a perfect cylinder with radius equal to 0.1 times the height.
29. A tree looks like the tree in Exercise 27, but with half the height in the cylindrical trunk and the other half in a spherical blob on top.
30. A tree looks like the tree in Exercise 27, but with 90% of the height in the cylindrical trunk and the remaining 10% in a spherical blob on top.

31–34 ▪ Find the masses in kilograms of the following objects (the density of water is 1.0 $\mathrm{g/cm^3}$).

31. A water bed that is 2 meters long, 20 cm thick, and 1.5 m wide.
32. A spherical cow with diameter 1.3 m and density 1.3 times that of water.
33. A coral colony consisting of 3200 individuals each weighing 0.45 g.
34. A circular colony of mold with diameter of 4.8 cm and density of 0.0023 $\mathrm{g/cm^2}$.

35–38 ▪ Change the units in the following functions, and compare a graph in the new units with that in the original units.

35. (Based on Section 1.2, Exercise 45) The number of bees b on a plant is given by $b = 2f + 1$ where f is the number of flowers. Suppose each flower has 4 petals. Graph the number of bees as a function of the number of petals.

36. The number of cancerous cells c as a function of radiation dose r is

$$c = r - 4$$

for r (measured in rads) greater than or equal to 5, and is zero for r less than 5 (as in Section 1.2, Exercise 46). Suppose that radiation is instead measured in millirads (1 rad = 1000 millirads).

37. Insect development time A (in days) obeys $A = 40 - \frac{T}{2}$ where T represents temperature in °C for C between 10 and 40 (as in Section 1.2, Exercise 47). Suppose that development time is measured in hours.

38. Tree height h (in meters) follows the formula

$$h = \frac{100a}{100 + a}$$

where a represents the age of the tree in years (as in Section 1.2, Exercise 48). Suppose that tree age is measured instead in decades.

39–44 ▪ Estimate the following.

39. The speed of light in centimeters per nanosecond (1 ns = 10^{-9} sec). (The speed of light is about 186,000 miles/s). A fast computer takes about 0.3 ns per operation. How far does light travel in the time required by one computer operation?

40. The speed that your hair grows in miles per hour (this problem was borrowed from the book *Innumeracy*).

41. The weight of the earth in kilograms. The earth is approximately a sphere with radius 6500 km and density five times that of water.

42. Suppose a person eats 2000 kCal per day. Using the facts that 1 kCal is approximately 4.2 kJ (a kilojoule is a unit of energy equal to 1000 joules) and 1 watt is one joule per second (a unit of power), about how many watts does a person use?

43. If a movie is about 2 hours long, how many movies could you watch if you spent half your time watching movies for 60 years?

44. The volume of all the people on earth in cubic kilometers. If a large mine is about 3 km across and 1 km deep, would they all fit?

45–48 ▪ The following problems give several ways to estimate the size or number of cells in your body. A cell is roughly a sphere 10 μm in radius, where 1 μm is 10^{-6} m.

45. Using the fact that the density of a cell is approximately the density of water, and that water weighs 1 g/cm^3, estimate the number of cells in your body.

46. Estimate your volume in cubic meters by pretending you are shaped like a board. Pretending that cells are cubes 20 μm on a side, what do you estimate the number of cells to be by this method?

47. The brain weighs about 1.3 kg, and it is estimated to have about 100 billion neurons and 10 to 50 times as many other cells (glial cells). Is this consistent with our previous estimates in Exercises 45 and 46?

48. The nematode *C. elegans* is a cylinder about 1 mm long and 0.1 mm in diameter, consisting of about 1000 cells. Are these cells about the same size as the ones in your body?

49–50 ▪ The following problems involve tying string around or gift-wrapping our planet, which can be thought of as a sphere with radius 6500 km.

49. How long would a piece of string have to be to go around the equator? If the string were made 1.0 m longer and stretched out all the way around, how high would it be above the surface? Does the result surprise you?

50. How large a piece of wrapping paper would be required to cover the entire planet? If the wrap were increased in area by 1.0 m^2 and stretched out all around, how high would it be above the surface? Why do you think the result is so different from that in the previous problem? (Working this out takes a lot of decimal places.)

1.4 Linear Functions and Their Graphs

Complicated models are built from simple pieces. Throughout the sciences, the simplest building blocks for mathematical models are **linear** functions, functions that have lines as their graphs. In this section, we derive formulas for linear functions, including the **point-slope formula** and the **slope-intercept formula.** Because linear functions are simple to work with algebraically, we use them to review methods for solving linear equations to answer scientific questions. In particular, we **interpolate** between known values to make predictions about the results of additional experiments.

Proportional Relations

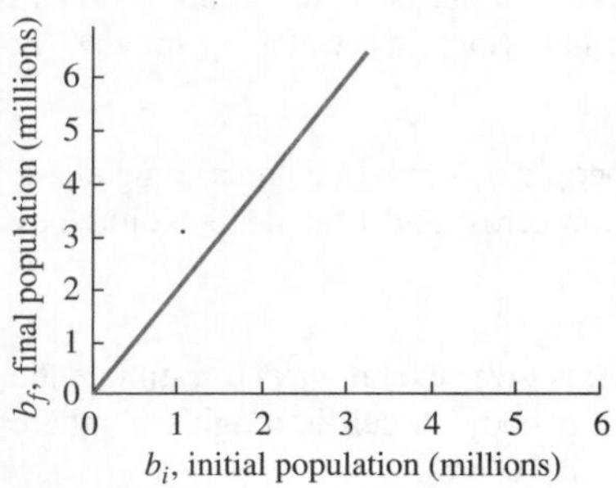

FIGURE 1.4.48
A proportional relation: bacterial populations

The simplest relations are **proportional** relations, meaning that the output is **proportional** to the input. Mathematically, this means that the ratio of the output to the input is a constant. The general formula for a proportional relation is

$$f(x) = ax$$

where a is some constant value. The ratio of the output ax to the input x is

$$\frac{\text{output}}{\text{input}} = \frac{ax}{x} = a$$

as long as $x \neq 0$. When the ratio is constant, the value a is called the **constant of proportionality.** Constants of proportionality, like all measurements, have units and dimensions.

Example 1.4.1 A Proportional Relation Between Population Sizes

The function describing the relation

$$b_f = 2.0 b_i$$

(Example 1.2.3) multiplies its input by 2.0 to produce the output. The ratio of the output population to the input population is

$$\frac{b_f}{b_i} = 2.0$$

a constant value. The graph of this proportional relation, as Figure 1.4.48 shows, is a line.

Example 1.4.2 A Proportional Relation Between Mass and Volume

In the fundamental relation between mass and volume $M = \rho V$ (Table 1.3.2), mass is found by multiplying volume by the constant value ρ. The ratio of mass to volume is

$$\frac{\text{mass}}{\text{volume}} = \text{density} = \rho$$

again a constant. As it must, the constant of proportionality, ρ, has the dimensions of density (mass per unit volume).

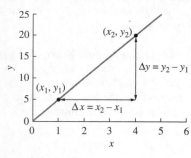

FIGURE 1.4.49
Slope and Δ notation

The proportion in a proportional relation is the **slope** of the graph. Slope is often defined as "rise over run," but we replace these archaic terms with more scientifically meaningful synonyms.

Definition 1.7 **Slope of a Line**

$$\text{slope} = \frac{\text{change in output}}{\text{change in input}}$$

The "change" is the change between two data points. Suppose we denote two points on the graph by (x_1, y_1) and (x_2, y_2) (Figure 1.4.49). Then

$$\text{slope} = \frac{\text{change in output}}{\text{change in input}} = \frac{y_2 - y_1}{x_2 - x_1} \tag{1.4.1}$$

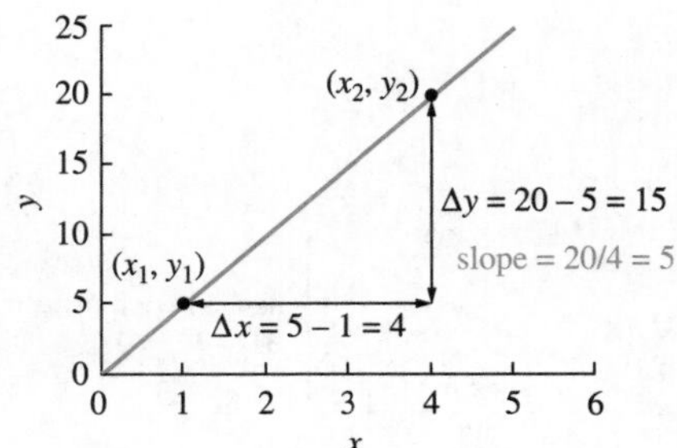

FIGURE 1.4.50
Finding the slope

Example 1.4.3 Finding the Slope Between Two Data Points

In Figure 1.4.49, the data points are $(x_1, y_1) = (1, 5)$ and $(x_2, y_2) = (4, 20)$. The slope (see Figure 1.4.50) is

$$\text{slope} = \frac{\text{change in output}}{\text{change in input}} = \frac{y_2 - y_1}{x_2 - x_1} = \frac{20 - 5}{4 - 1} = \frac{15}{3} = 5$$

The changes in the input x and the output y are often written with the shorthand

$$\Delta x = x_2 - x_1$$
$$\Delta y = y_2 - y_1$$

where Δ (the Greek letter Delta) means "change in." The slope is Δy divided by Δx, or

$$\text{slope} = \frac{\Delta y}{\Delta x} \tag{1.4.2}$$

This notation will prove very useful when we study derivatives later in this book.

Example 1.4.4 The Slope of a Proportional Relation Between Populations

Recall the data in Example 1.2.3, graphed in Figure 1.4.51.

Colony	Initial Population, b_i	Final Population, b_f
1	0.47	0.94
2	3.30	6.60
3	0.73	1.46
4	2.80	5.60
5	1.50	3.00
6	0.62	1.24

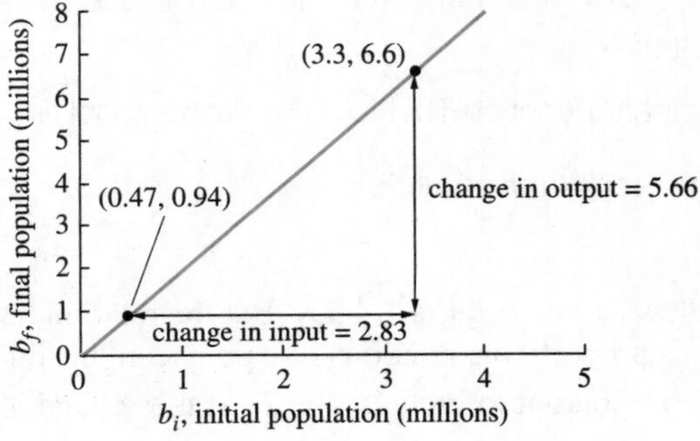

FIGURE 1.4.51
The slope of the proportional relation between bacterial populations

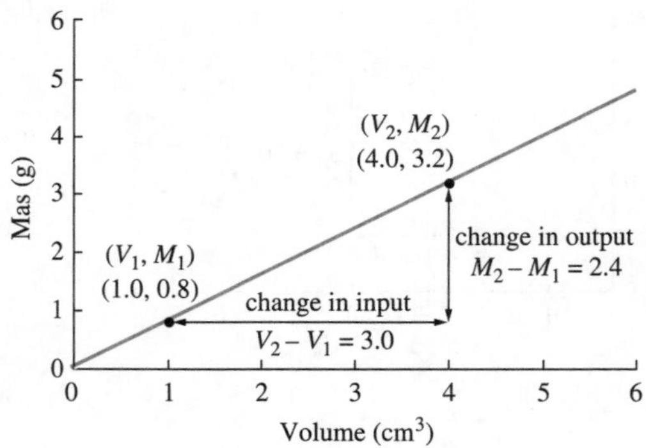

FIGURE 1.4.52

The slope of the proportional relation between mass and volume

The first two data points are (0.47, 0.94) and (3.30, 6.60). Then

$$\Delta b_i = 3.30 - 0.47 = 2.83$$
$$\Delta b_f = 6.60 - 0.94 = 5.66$$

The slope is

$$\text{slope} = \frac{\text{change in output}}{\text{change in input}} = \frac{\Delta b_f}{\Delta b_i} = \frac{6.60 - 0.94}{3.30 - 0.47} = \frac{5.66}{2.83} = 2.0$$

The slope is equal to the constant of proportionality.

Example 1.4.5 The Slope of a Proportional Relation Between Mass and Volume

Suppose that $\rho = 0.8\ \frac{\text{g}}{\text{cm}^3}$. A first object with volume $V_1 = 1.0\ \text{cm}^3$ has mass $M_1 = 0.8$ g. A second object with volume $V_2 = 4.0\ \text{cm}^3$ has mass $M_2 = 3.2$ g (Figure 1.4.52). We then find

$$\text{change in output} = \Delta M = 3.2 - 0.8 = 2.4\ \text{g}$$
$$\text{change in input} = \Delta V = 4.0 - 1.0 = 3.0\ \text{cm}^3$$

The slope is then

$$\text{slope} = \frac{\text{change in output}}{\text{change in input}} = \frac{\Delta M}{\Delta V} = \frac{2.4\ \text{g}}{3.0\ \text{cm}^3} = 0.8\ \frac{\text{g}}{\text{cm}^3}$$

Again, the slope is equal to the constant of proportionality, complete with the units of density.

Linear Functions and the Equation of a Line

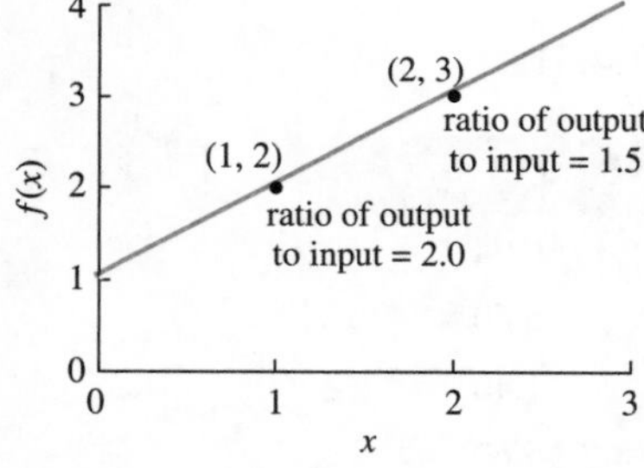

FIGURE 1.4.53

A linear function that is not a proportional relation

Proportional relations are described by functions that perform a single operation on their input: multiplication by a constant. The graphs of such functions are lines with slope equal to the constant of proportionality. Furthermore, these lines pass through the point (0, 0) because an input of 0 produces an output of 0.

Many functions other than those describing proportional relations have linear graphs.

Example 1.4.6 A Linear Function That Is not a Proportional Relation

The graph of the function

$$y = f(x) = x + 1$$

follows a line (Figure 1.4.53). But the relation between the input x and the output y is *not* a proportional relation. Two points on this line are (1, 2) and (2, 3). At the first, the ratio of output to input is $\frac{2}{1} = 2$. At the second, the ratio of output to input is $\frac{3}{2} = 1.5$. The ratio of output to input is not constant.

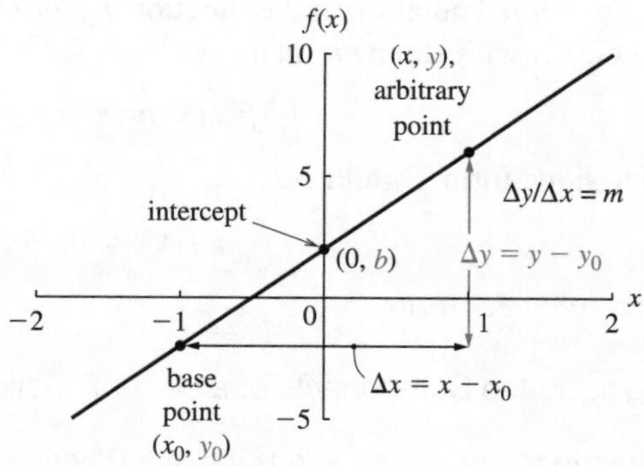

FIGURE 1.4.54
The elements of the general linear graph

For linear functions, it is the ratio of the **change in output** to the **change in input** that is constant. Suppose we start at the point (0, 1) on the graph. The ratio of change in output to change in input between this point and (1, 2) is

$$\frac{\text{change in output}}{\text{change in input}} = \frac{2-1}{1-0} = \frac{1}{1} = 1$$

The ratio of change in output to change in input between (0, 1) and (2, 3) is

$$\frac{\text{change in output}}{\text{change in input}} = \frac{3-1}{2-0} = \frac{2}{2} = 1$$

In general, a **line** is characterized by a **constant slope,** like a constant grade on a road. We use this fact to find a formula for a line. First, choose any point that lies on the graph of the function and call it the **base point** (Figure 1.4.54). If the base point has coordinates (x_0, y_0), the slope between it and an arbitrary point (x, y) on the line is

$$\text{slope} = \frac{\Delta y}{\Delta x} = \frac{y - y_0}{x - x_0}$$

Because the slope between any two points on the graph is constant,

$$\frac{y - y_0}{x - x_0} = m$$

for some fixed value of m. Multiplying both sides by $(x - x_0)$, we find

$$y - y_0 = m(x - x_0)$$

After solving for y by adding y_0 to both sides, we find the following form.

Definition 1.8 **The Point-Slope Form for a Line**

A line passing through the point (x_0, y_0) with slope m has formula

$$y = m(x - x_0) + y_0$$

Alternatively, we can multiply out the terms on the right-hand side of the point-slope form, finding

$$y = mx + (y_0 - mx_0)$$

We can combine the constants y_0, m, and x_0 into a single new parameter $b = y_0 - mx_0$. The letter b represents the point where the graph crosses the y-axis and is called the **y-intercept.**

Definition 1.9 **The Slope-Intercept Form for a Line**

A line with slope m and y-intercept b has formula

$$y = mx + b$$

In functional notation, if the function f has a linear graph passing through the base point (x_0, y_0) with slope m, then

$$f(x) = m(x - x_0) + y_0$$

in point-slope form. Similarly,

$$f(x) = mx + b$$

in slope-intercept form.

Example 1.4.7 Recognizing the Components of a Linear Function: Slope-Intercept Form

The function $f(x) = -4x + 5$ is a linear function in slope-intercept form. The slope is the factor multiplying the input x, or $m = -4$. The intercept is $b = 5$.

Example 1.4.8 Recognizing the Components of a Linear Function: Point-Slope Form

The function $f(x) = 3(x + 2) + 7$ is a linear function in point-slope form. To find x_0, we must write $x + 2$ as $x - (-2)$. This is in the form $x - x_0$ with $x_0 = -2$. The y-coordinate of the point is the added value, so $y_0 = 7$. Thus the base point is $(x_0, y_0) = (-2, 7)$. The slope is the factor multiplying the variable x, so $m = 3$.

Example 1.4.9 Recognizing the Components of a Biological Linear Function

The function describing the relation between initial and final bacterial populations in (Example 1.4.1),

$$b_f = f(b_i) = 2.0b_i$$

is a linear function with a slope of 2.0 and a y-intercept of 0 (and is therefore a proportional relation). In applications, inputs and outputs are rarely called x and y. Nonetheless, we recognize linear functions by the operations done to the input variable. If the formula involves only adding, subtracting, and multiplying by constants, the equation describes a linear function.

Example 1.4.10 Recognizing a Nonlinear Function

The function

$$b(t) = \frac{5.0}{1 + 2t}$$

is not a linear function because the input variable t appears in the the denominator. The function

$$b(t) = t^2 + 3t + 2$$

is not linear because the input variable t is squared.

Example 1.4.11 The Linear Relation Between Fahrenheit and Celsius

A once important linear function converts temperature in degrees Fahrenheit into temperature in degrees Celsius (Figure 1.4.55). Recall that

$$F = 1.8C + 32 \tag{1.4.3}$$

where C represents temperature in degrees Celsius and F represents temperature in degrees Fahrenheit. Unlike almost all unit conversions, this formula does not express a proportional relation. The F-intercept of 32 indicates that 0°C corresponds to 32°F rather than 0°F. The slope, nonetheless, describes the number of degrees Fahrenheit per degree Celsius as in an ordinary conversion. To check the slope, we compute ΔF and ΔC between the points with $C = 0$ and $C = 20$. Because 20°C corresponds to 68°F, the

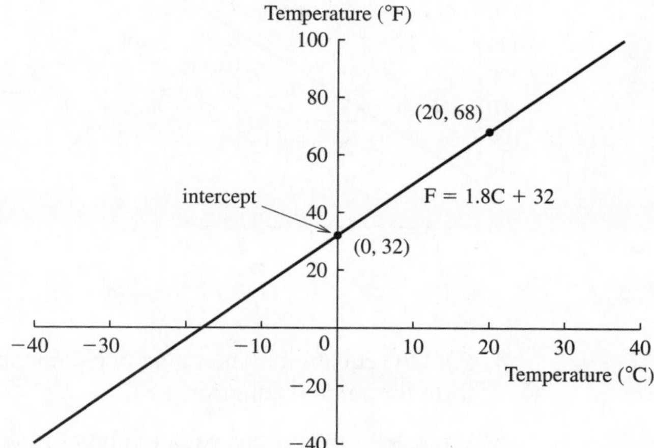

FIGURE 1.4.55
The relation between Fahrenheit and Celsius temperatures

change in °F (the output) is

$$\Delta F = 68°\text{F} - 32°\text{F} = 36°\text{F}$$

and the change in °C (the input) is

$$\Delta C = 20°\text{C} - 0°\text{C} = 20°\text{C}$$

Therefore

$$\text{slope} = \frac{36°\text{F}}{20°\text{C}} = 1.8\,\frac{°\text{F}}{°\text{C}}$$

It takes 1.8°F to make up 1.0°C.

Finding Equations and Graphing Lines

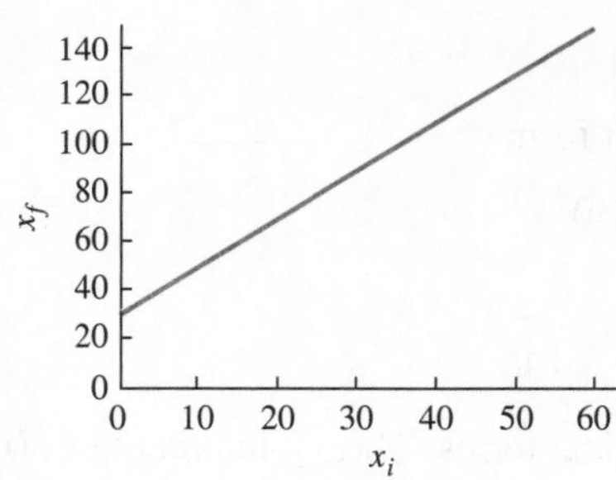

FIGURE 1.4.56
Graph describing a changing mite population

Pet store owners can be plagued by parasites. Suppose the employees spend a week observing populations of mites on several lizards and collect the following data, plotted in Figure 1.4.56.

Initial Number, x_i	Final Number, x_f
20	70
30	90
40	110
50	130

Here x_i is the initial number of mites and x_f is the final number. Suppose we wish to estimate the number of mites we would find after a week on a lizard that has 45 mites today. To do so, we must first find an equation for the function relating x_f and x_i and then evaluate it at $x_i = 45$.

We can find the equation with the following steps.

Algorithm 1.3 Finding the Equation of a Line from Data

1. Graph the data and check that the points lie on a line.
2. Pick two data points.
3. Find the slope as the change in output divided by the change in input.

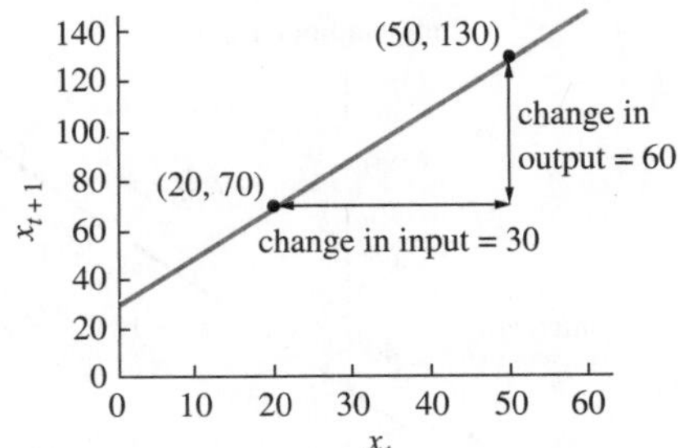

FIGURE 1.4.57
Finding the equation of the function describing mites

4. Find the equation by plugging one point and the slope into the point-slope form for a line (Definition 1.8).
5. If needed, convert this equation into the slope-intercept form.

Example 1.4.12 Finding the Equation of a Line from Data

We can follow this algorithm to find the equation of the function describing our data.

1. The graph in Figure 1.4.56 looks like a line.
2. Pick the first and last data points (any others could be chosen as long as the data lie on a line (Figure 1.4.57)).
3. The slope m is
$$m = \frac{\Delta x_f}{\Delta x_i} = \frac{130 - 70}{50 - 20} = \frac{60}{30} = 2.0$$
4. If we choose the point (20, 70) as (x_0, y_0) in the point-slope form for a line, the equation is
$$\begin{aligned} x_f &= m(x_i - (x_i)_0) + (x_f)_0 \\ &= 2.0(x_i - 20) + 70 \end{aligned}$$
5. We can expand this to find the slope-intercept form
$$x_f = 2.0x_i + 30$$
This defines a function $h(x_i)$ with formula
$$x_f = h(x_i) = 2.0x_i + 30$$

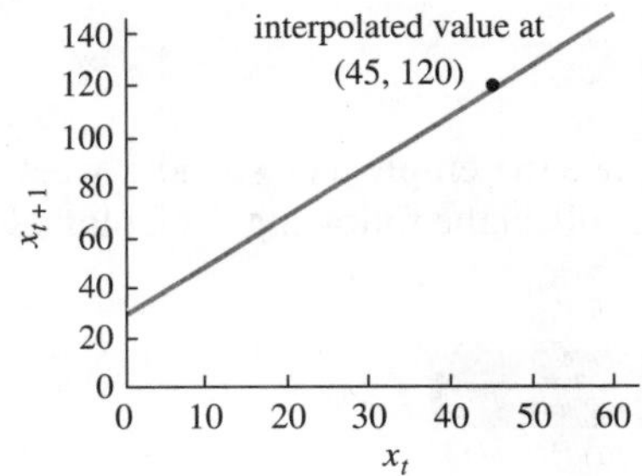

FIGURE 1.4.58
Interpolating a value

This function $h(x_i)$ can be interpreted in biological terms. The x_f-intercept of 30 is the number of mites we would find on a lizard that started out with no mites. These mites probably arrived from other lizards. The slope of 2.0 is the number of additional mites we would find after a week if we added one mite at the beginning. For example, $h(1) = 32$, two more than $h(0) = 30$. The one additional mite left two offspring.

Example 1.4.13 Using a Linear Function to Interpolate

To predict the number of mites we will find after a week on a lizard that has 45 mites today, we substitute $x_i = 45$ into the function $h(x_i) = 2.0x_i + 30$, finding
$$x_f = h(x_i) = 2.0 \cdot 45 + 30 = 120$$
(See Figure 1.4.58.) We have used the formula for the function to **interpolate** a prediction between known values.

In this example, we used a set of numerical data to plot a graph and derive an algebraic formula. In other cases, we are given a formula and need to produce a graph. The easiest way to graph a linear function from its formula is to plug two reasonable values of the input into the equation, graph the points, and connect them with a line.

Example 1.4.14 Plotting a Line from an Equation

Suppose we wish to plot the linear function $F(x)$ given by

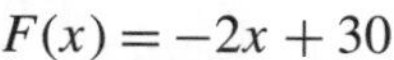

$$F(x) = -2x + 30$$

Plugging in $x = 0$ gives $F(0) = 30$, and $x = 10$ gives $F(10) = 10$ (Figure 1.4.59). The graph of the line connects the points (0, 30) and (10, 10). This line goes down with a negative slope of -2.

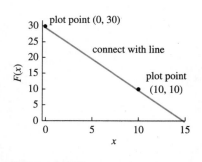

FIGURE 1.4.59
Graphing a line from its equation

When the graph goes down when read from left to right (as in Example 1.4.14), we say that the function is a **decreasing function.** A larger input produces a smaller output. Linear functions with negative slopes are decreasing functions. In contrast, a positive slope corresponds to an **increasing function.** Larger inputs produce larger outputs. A slope of exactly 0 corresponds to a function with equation

$$f(x) = 0 \cdot x + b = b$$

Such a function always takes on the constant value b, the y-intercept, and has as its graph a horizontal line.

Slope	Graph	Function
positive	goes up	increasing
negative	goes down	decreasing
zero	flat	constant

An example of each type is shown in Figure 1.4.60.

Solving Equations Involving Lines

Answering questions about linear relations requires solving **linear equations,** which are among the simplest equations to solve.

Example 1.4.15 Solving a Linear Equation

Suppose we wish to find where the line

$$y = 3x + 1$$

takes on the value $y = 7$ (Figure 1.4.61).

$7 = 3x + 1$	substitute the value of y
$6 = 3x$	subtract 1 from both sides
$2 = x$	divide both sides by 3

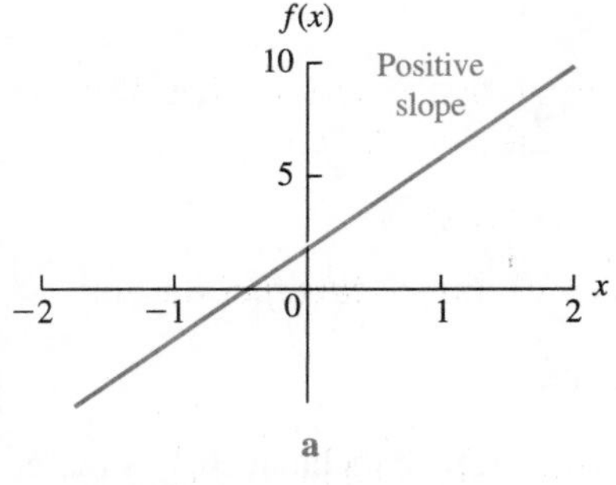

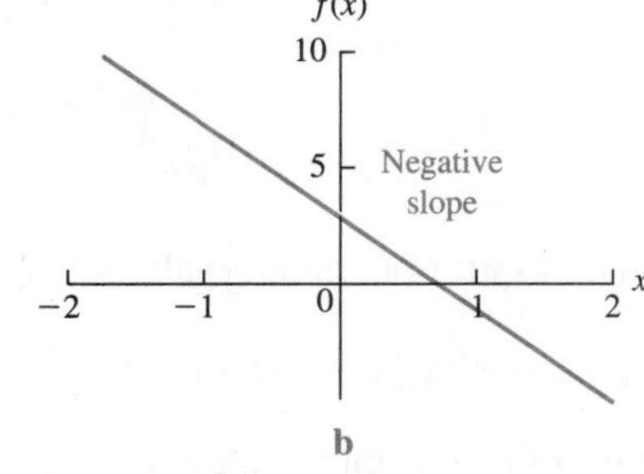

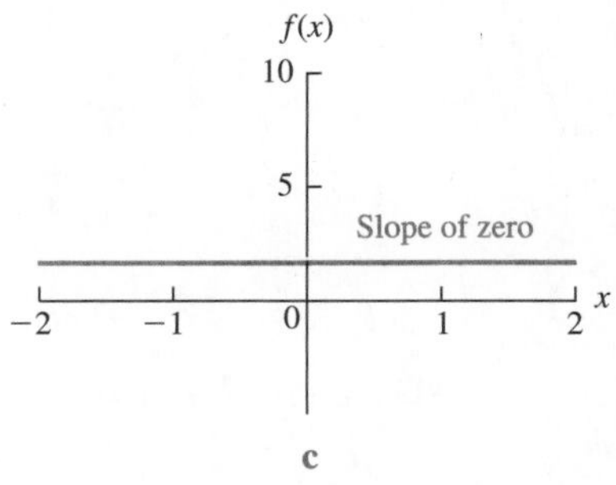

FIGURE 1.4.60
Linear functions with positive, negative, and zero slopes

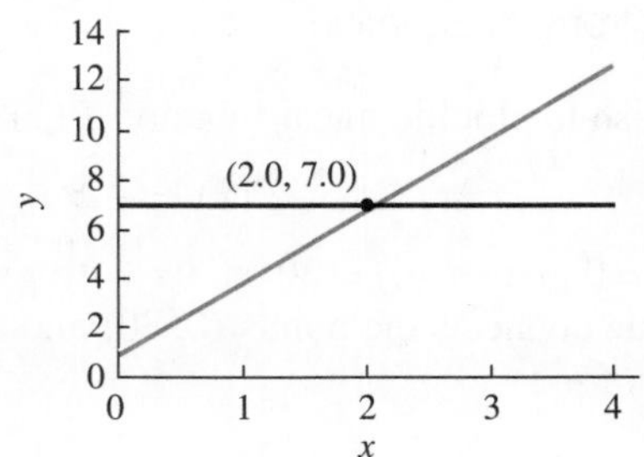

FIGURE 1.4.61
Solving an equation involving a linear function

Graphically, this equation corresponds to finding where the line $y = 3x + 1$ crosses the horizontal line that represents $y = 7$.

Example 1.4.16 Solving a Linear Equation Involving a Parameter

Suppose we wish to find where the line

$$y = mx + 1$$

takes on the value $y = 7$ for any value of the slope m.

$$7 = mx + 1 \quad \text{substitute the value of } y$$
$$6 = mx \quad \text{subtract 1 from both sides}$$
$$\frac{6}{m} = x \quad \text{divide both sides by } m$$

This solution makes sense for any value of $m \neq 0$.

Example 1.4.17 Finding the Intersection of Two Lines

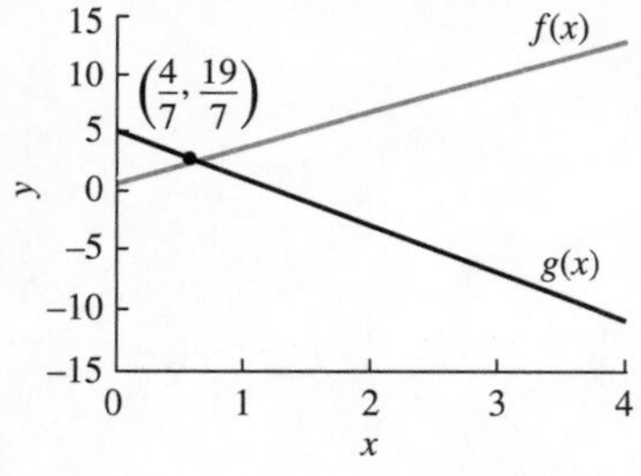

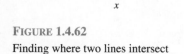

FIGURE 1.4.62
Finding where two lines intersect

Suppose we wish to find where the lines $f(x) = 3x + 1$ and $g(x) = -4x + 5$ intersect (Figure 1.4.62). We set the two values equal, and solve for x as follows:

$$3x + 1 = -4x + 5 \quad \text{set the two formulas equal to each other}$$
$$7x + 1 = 5 \quad \text{add } 4x \text{ to both sides}$$
$$7x = 4 \quad \text{subtract 1 from both sides}$$
$$x = \frac{4}{7} \quad \text{divide both sides by 7}$$

This gives the value of x where the two intersect. The value of y can be found by substituting $x = \frac{4}{7}$ into either function, or

$$f\left(\frac{4}{7}\right) = 3 \cdot \frac{4}{7} + 1 = \frac{19}{7}$$
$$g\left(\frac{4}{7}\right) = -4 \cdot \frac{4}{7} + 5 = \frac{19}{7}$$

Both functions give the same result, as they must.

Example 1.4.18 Solving a Classic Word Problem with Linear Equations

Little Billy's father is three times as old as Billy in 2001. Ten years later, Billy's father will be only twice as old as Billy. What year was Billy born, and how old was his dad

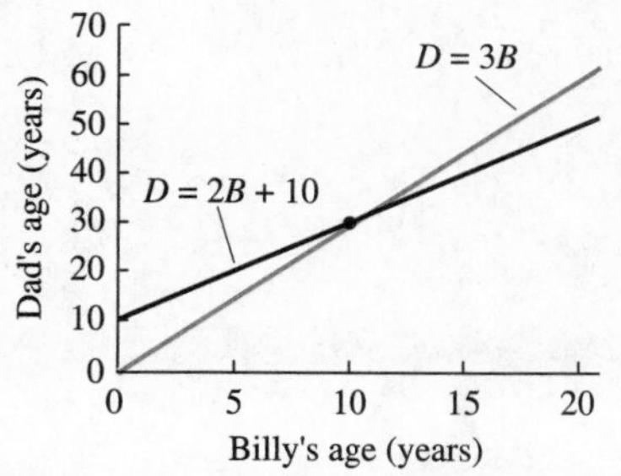

FIGURE 1.4.63
Graphical method to find ages

at that time? Let B represent Billy's age in 2001, and D his dad's age. Then

$$D = 3B$$

Ten years later, Billy is $B + 10$ and his dad is $D + 10$. Because his dad is then twice as old,

$$D + 10 = 2(B + 10)$$

We can rewrite this (in slope-intercept form) to find that

$$D = 2B + 10$$

This gives two equations for D (Figure 1.4.63). Setting the right-hand sides equal gives the single linear equation

$$3B = 2B + 10$$

Subtracting $2B$ from both sides gives $B = 10$, Billy's age in 2001. His dad was three times as old, or 30. Thus Billy was born in 1991, when his dad was 20. Ten years later, in 2011, Billy will be 20, exactly half as old as his 40-year-old father.

Example 1.4.19 A Linear Equation with No Solution

Suppose we are given the following variant of the classic word problem. Little Billy's father is three times as old as Billy in 2001. Ten years later, Billy's father will be 10 years less than three times Billy's age. What year was Billy born, and how old was his dad at that time? Let B represent Billy's age in 2001, and D his dad's age. Then

$$D = 3B$$

Ten years later, Billy is $B + 10$ and his dad is $D + 10$. Because his dad is then 10 years less than three times as old,

$$D + 10 = 3(B + 10) - 10$$

Subtracting 10 from both sides and solving for D gives

$$D = 3B + 10$$

Setting these two equations for D equal gives

$$3B = 3B + 10$$

Subtracting $3B$ from both sides gives $0 = 10$, which is impossible. The original problem has no solution. Graphically, this corresponds to trying to find the intersection of two parallel lines (Figure 1.4.64).

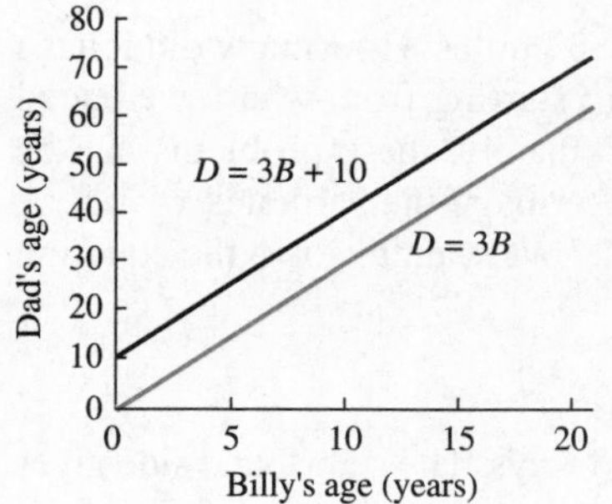

FIGURE 1.4.64
Failure of graphical method to find ages

Example 1.4.20 A Linear Equation with Many Solutions

Suppose we are given yet another variant of the classic word problem. Little Billy's father is three times as old as Billy in 2001. Ten years later, Billy's father will be 20 years less than three times Billy's age. What year was Billy born, and how old was his dad at that time? Then

$$D = 3B$$

Ten years later, Billy is $B + 10$ and his dad is $D + 10$. Because his dad is then 20 years less than three times as old,

$$D + 10 = 3(B + 10) - 20$$

Solving for D, we find

$$D = 3B$$

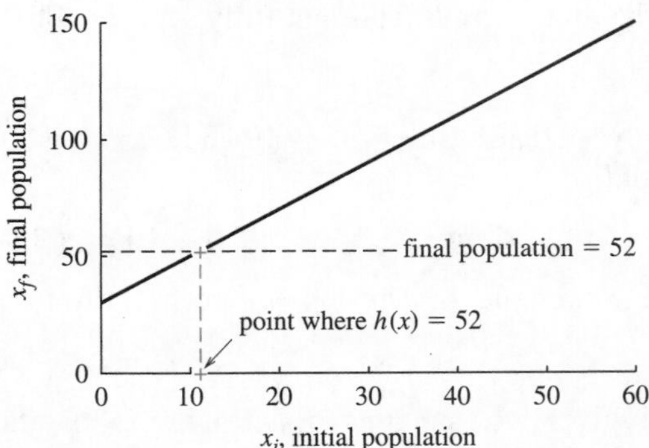

FIGURE 1.4.65
Going backwards with the mite population

This matches our original equation and works for any value of B. For example, if Billy was born in 1988, and consequently was 13 in 2001, his dad was three times as old in 2001, or 39. Ten years later, Billy would be 23, and his dad would be 49, exactly 20 years less than 3 times 23. But if Billy had been born in 1992, he would have been 9 in 2001, and his dad would have been 27. Ten years later, Billy would be 19, and dad would be 37, again exactly 20 years less than 3 times 19. ▲

Example 1.4.21 Solving Another Word Problem with Linear Equations

Recall the lizards with mites obeying the equation

$$x_f = 2.0x_i + 30$$

(Example 1.4.12). Suppose a lizard ends up with $x_f = 52$ mites. How many did it have the week before? This is a kind of "inverse" problem; starting from where we ended up, we want to try to end up where we started. Fortunately, these problems can be expressed more clearly in equations than in words. In terms of the variables x_i and x_f, our question can be rephrased. What was x_i if x_f is 52? We want to solve the equation $h(x_i) = 52$ for x_i, or

$$2.0x_i + 30 = 52$$

The two sides of the equation say the same thing in two ways. The right-hand side gives our measured value 52. The left-hand side gives the measured value as a function of the unknown x_i. We can solve for x_i

$$2.0x_i = 52 - 30 = 22 \quad \text{subtract 30 from both sides}$$

$$x_i = \frac{22}{2.0} = 11 \quad \text{divide both sides by 2}$$

We can check this answer by plugging in, finding

$$h(11) = 2 \cdot 11 + 30 = 52$$

(Figure 1.4.65). ▲

Summary The graphs of many important functions in biology are lines. We derived the link between lines and **linear functions.** A **proportional relation** is a special type of linear function in which the ratio of the output to the input is always the same. This constant ratio is the **slope** of the graph of the relation. Lines other than proportional relations can be expressed in **point-slope form** or **slope-intercept form.** The slope can be found as the change in output divided by the change in input. Equations of linear functions can be used to **interpolate**—that is, to estimate outputs from untested inputs.

1.4 Exercises

Mathematical Techniques

1–4 ▪ For the following lines, find the slope between the two given points by finding the change in output divided by the change in input. What is the ratio of the output to the input at each of the points? Which are proportional relations? Which are increasing and which are decreasing? Sketch a graph.

1. $y = 2x + 3$, using points with $x = 1$ and $x = 3$
2. $z = -5w$, using points with $w = 1$ and $w = 3$
3. $z = 5(w - 2) + 8$, using points with $w = 1$ and $w = 3$
4. $y - 5 = -3(x + 2) - 6$, using points with $x = 1$ and $x = 3$

5–6 ▪ Check that the point indicated lies on the line and find the equation of the line in point-slope form using the given point. Multiply out to check that the point-slope form matches the original equation.

5. The line $f(x) = 2x + 3$ and the point (2, 7).
6. The line $g(y) = -2y + 7$ and the point (3, 1).

7–12 ▪ Find equations in slope-intercept form for the following lines. Sketch a graph indicating the original point from the point-slope form.

7. The line $f(x) = 2(x - 1) + 3$.
8. The line $g(z) = -3(z + 1) - 3$.
9. A line passing through the point (1, 6) with slope −2.
10. A line passing through the point (−1, 6) with slope 4.
11. A line passing through the points (1, 6) and (4, 3).
12. A line passing through the points (6, 1) and (3, 4).

13–16 ▪ Check whether the following are linear functions.

13. $h(z) = \frac{1}{5z}$
14. $F(r) = r^2 + 5$
15. $P(q) = 8(3q + 2) - 6$
16. $Q(w) = 8(3w + 2) - 6(w + 4)$

17–18 ▪ Check that the following curves do not have constant slope by computing the slopes between the points indicated. Compare with the graphs in Section 1.2, Exercises 5 and 6.

17. $h(z) = \frac{1}{5z}$ at $z = 1$, $z = 2$, and $z = 4$, as in Section 1.2, Exercise 5. Find the slope between $z = 1$ and $z = 2$, and the slope between $z = 2$ and $z = 4$.
18. $F(r) = r^2 + 5$ at $r = 0$, $r = 1$, and $r = 4$, as in Section 1.2, Exercise 6. Find the slope between $r = 0$ and $r = 1$, and the slope between $r = 1$ and $r = 4$.

19–24 ▪ Solve the following equations. Check your answer by plugging in the value you found.

19. $2x + 3 = 7$
20. $\frac{1}{2}z - 3 = 7$
21. $2x + 3 = 3x + 7$
22. $-3y + 5 = 8 + 2y$
23. $2(5(x - 1) + 3) = 5(2(x - 2) + 5)$
24. $2(4(x - 1) + 3) = 5(2(x - 2) + 5)$

25–28 ▪ Solve the following equations for the given variable, treating the other letters as constant parameters.

25. Solve $2x + b = 7$ for x.
26. Solve $mx + 3 = 7$ for x.
27. Solve $2x + b = mx + 7$ for x. Are there any values of b or m for which this has no solution?
28. Solve $mx + b = 3x + 7$ for x. Are there any values of b or m for which this has no solution?

29–32 ▪ Most unit conversions are proportional relations. Find the slope and graph the relations between the following units.

29. Place inches on the horizontal axis and centimeters on the vertical axis. Use the fact that 1 in. = 2.54 cm. Mark the point corresponding to 1 in. on your graph.
30. Place centimeters on the horizontal axis and inches on the vertical axis. Use the fact that 1 in. = 2.54 cm. Mark the point corresponding to 1 in. on your graph.
31. Place grams on the horizontal axis and pounds on the vertical axis. Use the identity 1 lb ≈ 453.6 g. Mark the point corresponding to 1 lb on your graph.
32. Place pounds on the horizontal axis and grams on the vertical axis. Use the identity 1 lb ≈ 453.6 g. Mark the point corresponding to 1 lb on your graph.

33–34 ▪ Not very many functions commute with each other (Section 1.2). The following problems ask you to find all linear functions that commute with the given linear function.

33. Find all functions of the form $g(x) = mx + b$ that commute with the function $f(x) = x + 1$. Can you explain your answer in words?
34. Find all functions of the form $g(x) = mx + b$ that commute with the function $f(x) = 2x$. Can you explain your answer in words?

Applications

35–38 ▪ Many fundamental relations express a proportional relation between two measurements with different dimensions. Find the slopes and the equations of the relations between the following quantities.

35. Volume = area × thickness. Find the volume V as a function of the area A if the thickness is 1.0 cm.
36. Volume = area × thickness. Find the volume V as a function of thickness T if the area is 7.0 cm^2.

37. Total mass = mass per bacterium × number of bacteria. Find the total mass M as a function of the number of bacteria b if the mass per bacterium is 5.0×10^{-9} g.

38. Total mass = mass per bacterium × number of bacteria. Find the total mass M as a function of mass per bacterium m if the number of bacteria is 10^6.

39–42 ▪ A ski slope has a slope of −0.2. You start at an altitude of 10,000 feet.

39. Write the equation giving altitude a as a function of horizontal distance moved d.

40. Write the equation of the line in meters.

41. What will be your altitude when you have gone 2000 feet horizontally?

42. The ski run ends at an altitude of 8000 feet. How far will you have gone horizontally?

43–46 ▪ The following data give the elevation of the surface of the Great Salt Lake in Utah.

Year, y	Elevation, E (ft)
1965	4193
1970	4196
1975	4199
1980	4199
1985	4206
1990	4203
1995	4200

43. Graph these data.

44. During which periods is the surface elevation changing linearly?

45. What was the slope between 1965 and 1975? What would the surface elevation have been in 1990 if things had continued as they began? How different is this from the actual elevation?

46. What was the slope during the period between 1985 and 1995? What would the surface elevation have been in 1965 if things had always followed this trend? How different is this from the actual elevation?

47–50 ▪ Graph the following relations between measurements of a growing plant, checking that the points lie on a line. Find the equations in both point-slope and slope-intercept form. What do the y-intercepts mean?

Age, a (days)	Mass, M (g)	Volume, V (cm³)	Glucose Production, G (mg)
0.5	2.5	5.1	0.0
1.0	4.0	6.2	3.4
1.5	5.5	7.3	6.8
2.0	7.0	8.4	10.2
2.5	8.5	9.5	13.6
3.0	10.0	10.6	17.0

47. Mass as a function of age. Find the mass on day 1.75.

48. Volume as a function of age. Find the volume on day 2.75.

49. Glucose production as a function of mass. Estimate glucose production when the mass reaches 20.0 g.

50. Volume as a function of mass. Estimate the volume when the mass reaches 30.0 g. How will the density at that time compare with the density when $a = 0.5$?

51–54 ▪ Consider the data in the following table (adapted from *Parasitoids* by H. C. F. Godfray), describing the number of wasps that can develop inside caterpillars of different weights.

Weight of Caterpillar (g)	Number of Wasps
0.5	80
1.0	115
1.5	150
2.0	175

51. Graph these data. Which point does not lie on the line?

52. Find the equation of the line connecting the first two points.

53. How many wasps does the function predict would develop in a caterpillar weighing 0.72 g?

54. How many wasps does the function predict would develop in a caterpillar weighing 0.0 g? Does this make sense? How many would you really expect?

55–58 ▪ The world record times for various races are decreasing at roughly linear rates (adapted from *Guinness Book of Records*, 1990).

55. The men's Olympic record for the 1500 meters was 3:36.8 (3 minutes and 36.8 seconds) in 1972 and was 3:35.9 in 1988. Find and graph the line connecting these. (Don't forget to convert everything into seconds.)

56. The women's Olympic record for the 1500 meters was 4:01.4 in 1972 and was 3:53.9 in 1988. Find and graph the line connecting these.

57. If things continue at this rate, when will women finish the race in exactly no time? (Set the time equal to 0 and solve for the date.) What might happen before that date?

58. If things continue at this rate, when will women be running this race faster than men? (Set the two speeds equal and solve for the date.)

Computer Exercises

59. Try Exercise 58 on the computer. Compute the year when the times will reach 0. Give your best guess of the times in the year 1900.

60. Graph the ratio of temperature measured in Fahrenheit to temperature measured in Celsius for $-273 \le C < 200$. What happens near $C = 0$? What happens for large and small values of C? How would the results differ if the zero for Fahrenheit were changed to match that of Celsius?

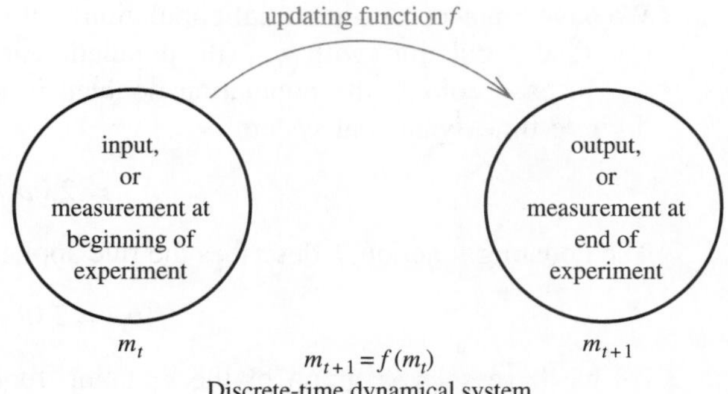

FIGURE 1.5.66
Notation for a discrete-time dynamical system

1.5 Discrete-Time Dynamical Systems

Suppose we collect data on how much several bacterial cultures grow in one hour or on how much trees grow in one year. How can we predict what will happen in the long run? In this section, we begin addressing these dynamical problems, which form the theme of this chapter and indeed of much of this book. We follow the basic steps of applied mathematics: **quantifying the basic measurement** and describing the **dynamical rule.** We will learn how to summarize the rule with a **discrete-time dynamical system** or an **updating function** that describes change. From the discrete-time dynamical system and a starting point, called an **initial condition,** we will compute a **solution** that gives the values of the measurement as a function of time.

Discrete-Time Dynamical Systems and Updating Functions

A discrete-time dynamical system describes the relation between a quantity measured at the beginning and the end of an experiment or a time interval. If the measurement is represented by the variable m, we will use the notation m_t to denote the measurement at the beginning of the experiment and m_{t+1} to denote the measurement at the end of the experiment (Figure 1.5.66). Think of t as the current time and of $t+1$ as the time one step into the future. The relation between the initial measurement m_t and the final measurement m_{t+1} is given by the **discrete-time dynamical system**

$$m_{t+1} = f(m_t) \tag{1.5.1}$$

The **updating function** f accepts the initial value m_t as input and returns the final value m_{t+1} as output.

We will begin by applying this notation to several examples of discrete-time dynamical systems.

Example 1.5.1 A Discrete-Time Dynamical System for a Bacterial Population

Recall the data introduced in Example 1.2.3. Several bacterial cultures with different initial population sizes are grown in controlled conditions for 1 hour and then carefully measured.

Colony	Initial Population, b_t	Final Population, b_{t+1}
1	0.47	0.94
2	3.3	6.6
3	0.73	1.46
4	2.8	5.6
5	1.5	3.0
6	0.62	1.24

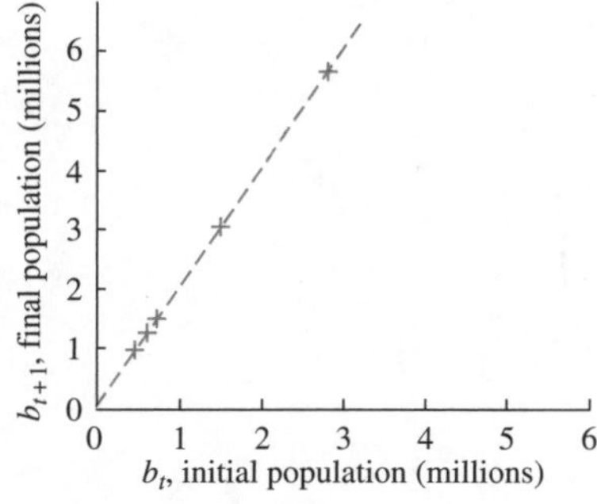

FIGURE 1.5.67

Graph of the updating function for a bacterial population

We have replaced b_i (the initial population) with b_t (the population at time t) and b_f (the final population) with b_{t+1} (the population at time $t+1$).

In each colony, the population doubled in size. We can describe this with the discrete-time dynamical system

$$b_{t+1} = 2.0b_t$$

The updating function f describes the rule applied to the initial population,

$$f(b_t) = 2.0b_t$$

As we have seen, a graph of the updating function plots the initial measurement b_t on the horizontal axis and the final measurement b_{t+1} on the vertical axis (Figure 1.5.67).

Example 1.5.2 A Discrete-Time Dynamical System for Tree Growth

Suppose you measure the heights of several trees in one year and then again the next year. Denoting the initial height by h_t and the final height by h_{t+1}, you might find the data in the following table (all expressed in meters).

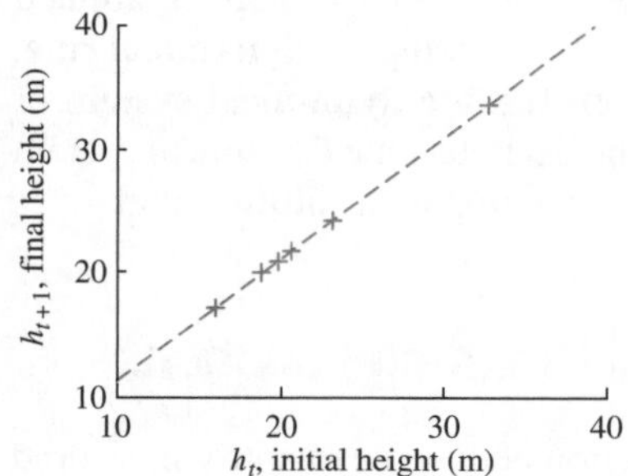

FIGURE 1.5.68

Data describing the growth of six trees

Tree	Initial Height, h_t	Final Height, h_{t+1}	Change in Height
1	23.1	24.1	1.0
2	18.7	19.8	1.1
3	20.6	21.5	0.9
4	16.0	17.0	1.0
5	32.5	33.6	1.1
6	19.8	20.6	0.8

The trees increase in height by about 1.0 m per year (Figure 1.5.68).

If we approximate this by assuming that trees grow exactly 1.0 m per year, then the discrete-time dynamical system that expresses this relation is

$$h_{t+1} = h_t + 1.0$$

The updating function, which we can denote by g, has formula

$$g(h_t) = h_t + 1.0$$

For example, for a tree beginning with height 12.2 m, the discrete-time dynamical system predicts a final height of

$$h_{t+1} = g(12.2) = 12.2 + 1.0 = 13.2\,\text{m}$$

In this example, the data points do not exactly match the discrete-time dynamical system. The updating function captures the major trend in the data while ignoring the noise. Including only the trend corresponds to the use of a **deterministic** dynamical system to describe the behavior. To include the noise, we must use a **probabilistic** dynamical system (Chapter 6). We will specifically address the problem of **finding** an updating function that captures the major trends in the data when we study the technique of data-fitting called linear regression (Section 8.9).

Example 1.5.3 Discrete-Time Dynamical System for Mites

Recall the lizards infested by mites (Example 1.4.12). The final number of mites x_{t+1} is related to the initial number of mites x_t by the formula

$$x_{t+1} = 2x_t + 30$$

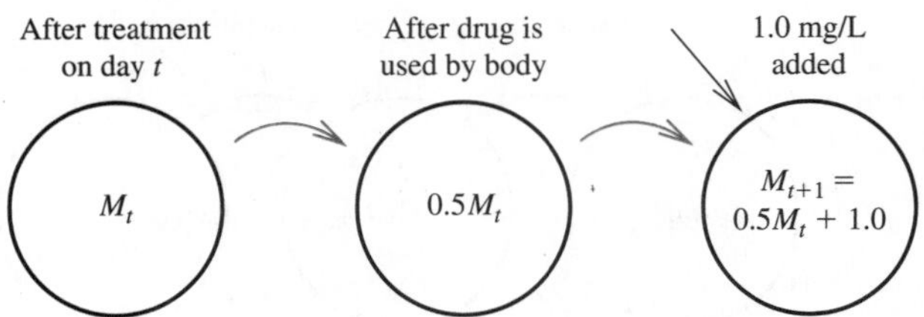

FIGURE 1.5.69

The dynamics of medication concentration in the blood

This is the discrete-time dynamical system for this population. The updating function is

$$h(x_t) = 2x_t + 30$$

The discrete-time dynamical systems for bacterial populations, tree height, and mite number were all derived from data. Often, dynamical rules can instead be derived directly from the principles governing a system.

Example 1.5.4 A Discrete-Time Dynamical System for Medication Concentration

Suppose we know the following facts about the dynamics of medication. Each day, a patient uses up half of the medication in his bloodstream. However, he is given a new dose sufficient to raise the concentration in the bloodstream by 1.0 milligram per liter (Figure 1.5.69). Let M_t denote the concentration at time t. The discrete-time dynamical system is

$$M_{t+1} = 0.5M_t + 1.0$$

The term $0.5M_t$ indicates that only half of the initial medication **remains** the next day. The factor 0.5 is the slope of this linear function. The second term, the intercept, indicates that 1.0 milligram per liter of medication is added each day. We can graph this linear function by substituting two reasonable values for M_t. If $M_t = 0$, then $M_{t+1} = 1$, the vertical intercept of this line. If $M_t = 1$, then $M_{t+1} = 1.5$ (Figure 1.5.70).

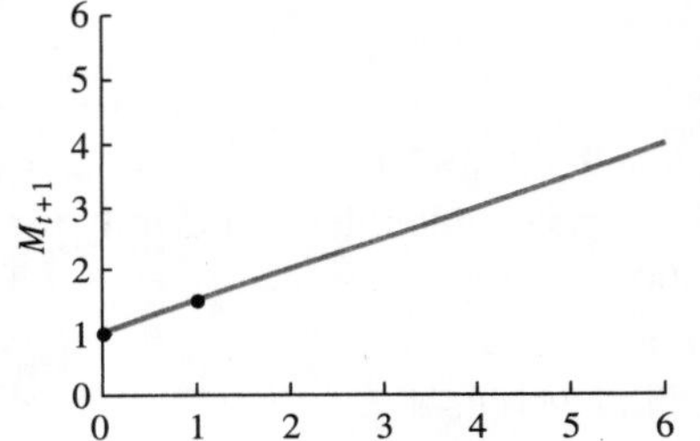

FIGURE 1.5.70

A graph of the updating function for medication concentration

Manipulating Updating Functions

All of the operations that can be applied to ordinary functions can be applied to updating functions, but with special interpretations. We will study **composition** of an updating function with itself, find the **inverse** of an updating function, and **convert the units** or **translate the dimensions** of a discrete-time dynamical system.

Composition Consider the discrete-time dynamical system

$$m_{t+1} = f(m_t)$$

with updating function f. What does the composition $f \circ f$ mean? The updating function **updates** the measurement by one time step. Then

$$\begin{aligned}(f \circ f)(m_t) &= f(f(m_t)) && \text{definition of composition}\\ &= f(m_{t+1}) && \text{definition of updating function}\\ &= m_{t+2} && \text{updating function applied to } m_{t+1}\end{aligned}$$

Therefore,

$$(f \circ f)(m_t) = m_{t+2}$$

The composition of an updating function with itself corresponds to a two-step updating function (Figure 1.5.71).

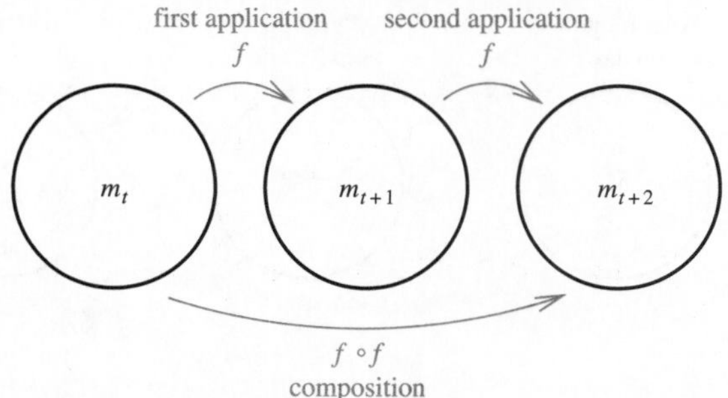

FIGURE 1.5.71
Composition of an updating function with itself

Example 1.5.5 Composition of the Bacterial Population Updating Function with Itself

The bacterial updating function is $f(b_t) = 2b_t$. The function $f \circ f$ takes the population size at time t as input and returns the population size 2 hours later, at time $t + 2$, as output. We can compute $f \circ f$ with the steps

$$\begin{aligned}(f \circ f)(b_t) &= f(f(b_t))\\ &= f(2.0b_t)\\ &= 2.0 \times 2.0b_t\\ &= 4.0b_t\end{aligned}$$

After two hours, the population is four times larger, having doubled twice. In this case, composition of f with itself looks like multiplication. This simple rules works **only** for an updating function expressing a proportional relation.

Example 1.5.6 Composition of the Mite Population Updating Function with Itself

The composition of the mite population updating function $h(x_t) = 2x_t + 30$ with itself gives

$$\begin{aligned}(h \circ h)(x_t) &= h(h(x_t))\\ &= h(2x_t + 30)\\ &= 2(2x_t + 30) + 30\\ &= 4x_t + 90\end{aligned}$$

Suppose we started with $x_t = 10$ mites. After 1 week, we would find $h(10) = 2 \cdot 10 + 30 = 50$ mites. After a second week, we would find $h(50) = 2 \cdot 50 + 30 = 130$ mites. Using the composition of the updating function with itself, we can compute the number of mites after 2 weeks, skipping over the intermediate value of 50 mites after 1 week, finding

$$(h \circ h)(10) = 4 \cdot 10 + 90 = 130$$

Inverses Consider again the general discrete-time dynamical system

$$m_{t+1} = f(m_t)$$

with updating function f. What does the inverse f^{-1} mean? The updating function updates the measurement by one time step, and the inverse function undoes the action of the updating function. Therefore,

$$f^{-1}(m_{t+1}) = m_t$$

The inverse of an updating function corresponds to an "updating" function that goes **backwards** in time (Figure 1.5.72).

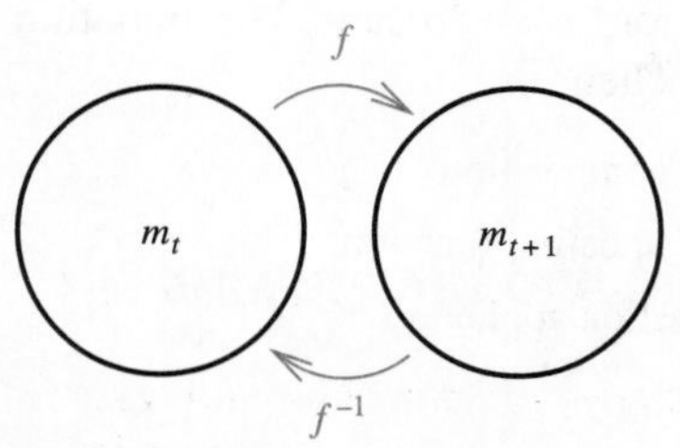

FIGURE 1.5.72
Inverse of an updating function

Example 1.5.7 Inverse of the Bacterial Population Updating Function

The bacterial population updating function is $f(b_t) = 2b_t$. We find the inverse by writing the discrete-time dynamical system

$$b_{t+1} = 2.0b_t$$

and solving for the input variable b_t (Algorithm 1.1). In this case, dividing both sides by 2.0 gives

$$b_t = \frac{b_{t+1}}{2.0}$$

The inverse function is

$$f^{-1}(b_{t+1}) = \frac{b_{t+1}}{2.0}$$

If **multiplying** by 2.0 describes how the population changes forward in time, **dividing** by 2.0 describes how it changes backwards in time.

If $b_t = 3.0$, then $b_{t+1} = 2.0b_t = 2.0 \cdot 3.0 = 6.0$. If we go backwards from $b_{t+1} = 6.0$ using the inverse of the updating function, we find

$$b_t = f^{-1}(6.0) = \frac{6.0}{3.0} = 3.0$$

exactly where we started. ▲

Example 1.5.8 Inverse of the Mite Population Updating Function

To find the inverse of the mite population updating function $h(x_t) = 2.0x_t + 30$, we use Algorithm 1.1

$$2.0x_t + 30 = x_{t+1} \quad \text{the original equation}$$

$$2.0x_t = x_{t+1} - 30 \quad \text{subtract 30 from both sides}$$

$$x_t = \frac{x_{t+1} - 30}{2.0} \quad \text{divide both sides by 2.0}$$

Therefore,

$$x_t = h^{-1}(x_{t+1}) = \frac{x_{t+1} - 30}{2.0} = 0.5x_{t+1} - 15$$

Suppose we started with $x_t = 10$ mites. After one week, we would find

$$h(10) = 2 \cdot 10 + 30 = 50$$

Applying the inverse, we find

$$h^{-1}(50) = 0.5 \cdot 50 - 15 = 10$$

The inverse function takes us back to where we started. ▲

Discrete-Time Dynamical Systems: Units and Dimensions

The updating function $f(b_t) = 2.0b_t$ accepts as input positive numbers with units of bacteria. If we measure this quantity in different units, we must convert the updating function itself into the new units. If we measure a different quantity, such as total mass or volume, we can translate the updating function into different dimensions.

Example 1.5.9 Describing the Dynamics of Tree Height in Centimeters

Suppose we wish to study tree height (Example 1.5.2) in units of centimeters rather than meters. In meters, the discrete-time dynamical system is

$$g(h_t) = h_t + 1.0\,\text{m}$$

First, we define a new variable to represent the measurement in the new units. Let H_t be tree height measured in centimeters rather than meters. Then $H_t = 100h_t$, because there are 100 centimeters in a meter. We wish to find a discrete-time dynamical system that gives a formula for H_{t+1} in terms of H_t (Figure 1.5.73).

$$\begin{aligned} H_{t+1} &= 100h_{t+1} && \text{definition of } H_{t+1} \\ &= 100(h_t + 1.0) && \text{discrete-time dynamical system for } h_{t+1} \\ &= 100h_t + 100 && \text{multiply through by 100} \\ &= H_t + 100 && \text{definition of } H_t \end{aligned}$$

The discrete-time dynamical system in the new units corresponds to adding 100 centimeters to the height, which is equivalent to adding 1 meter. Although the underlying process is the same, the discrete-time dynamical system and the corresponding updating function are different, just as the numerical values of measurements are different in different units.

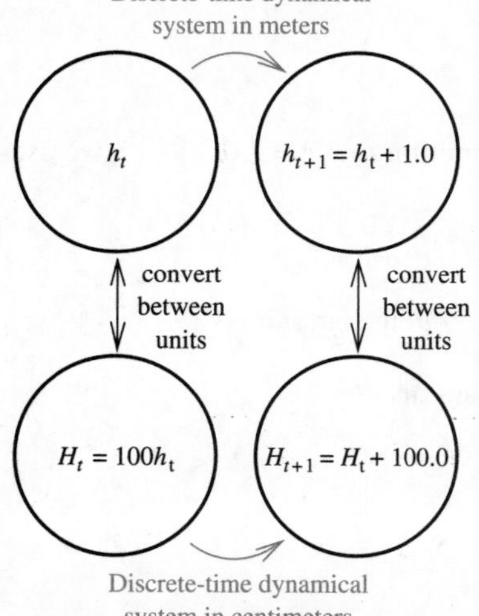

FIGURE 1.5.73
Finding the discrete-time dynamical system for trees in centimeters

Example 1.5.10 Describing the Dynamics of Bacterial Mass

Suppose we wish to study the bacterial population in terms of mass rather than number. At the beginning, the mass, denoted by m_t, is

$$m_t = \mu b_t$$

where μ is the mass per bacterium (as in Example 1.3.4). The updated mass m_{t+1} is

$$\begin{aligned} m_{t+1} &= \mu b_{t+1} && \text{definition of } m_{t+1} \\ &= \mu \cdot 2.0b_t && \text{substitute the original updating function} \\ &= 2.0\mu b_t && \text{rearrange the terms by the associative and commutative laws} \\ &= 2.0m_t && \text{recognize that } m_t = \mu b_t \end{aligned}$$

This new discrete-time dynamical system doubles its input just as the original discrete-time dynamical system did, but it takes mass as its input rather than numbers of bacteria (Figure 1.5.74).

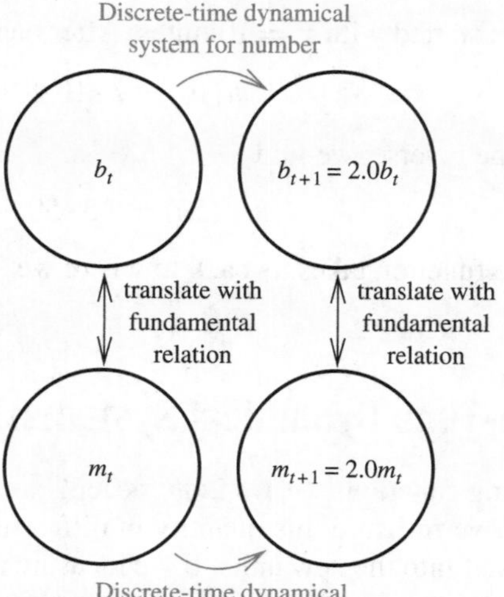

FIGURE 1.5.74
Finding the discrete-time dynamical system for bacteria in terms of mass

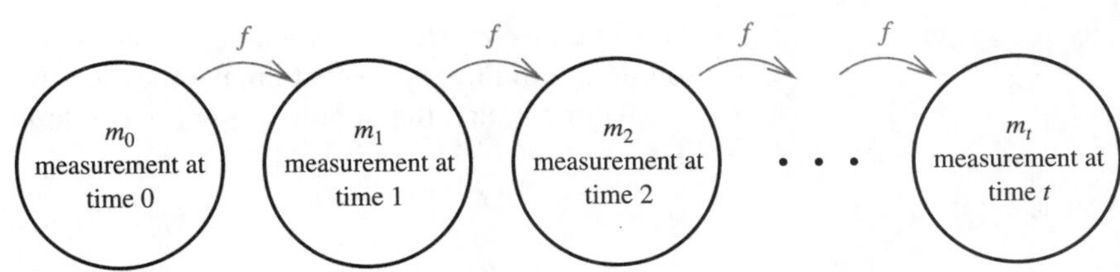

FIGURE 1.5.75

The repeated action of an updating function

Solutions

A discrete-time dynamical system describes some quantity at the end of an experiment as a function of that same quantity at the beginning. What if we were to continue the experiment? A bacterial population growing according to $b_{t+1} = 2.0b_t$ would double again and again. A tree growing according to $h_{t+1} = h_t + 1.0$ would add more and more meters to its height. An infested lizard would become even more heavily infested.

To describe a situation where a dynamical process is repeated many times, we let m_0 represent the measurement at the beginning, m_1 the measurement after one time step, m_2 the measurement after two time steps, and so forth (Figure 1.5.75). In general, we define

$$m_t = \text{measurement } t \text{ hours after the beginning of the experiment.}$$

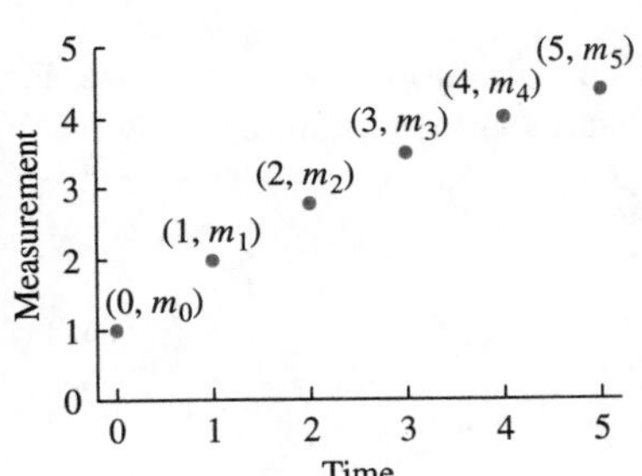

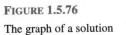

FIGURE 1.5.76

The graph of a solution

Our goal is to find the values of m_t for all values of t. Before we can do so, however, we must know where we **started.** Without knowing where you started, it is impossible to answer a question such as "Where are you after driving 5 miles south?" The starting value is known as the **initial condition.**

Definition 1.10 The sequence of values of m_t for $t = 0, 1, 2, \ldots$ is the **solution** of the discrete-time dynamical system $m_{t+1} = f(m_t)$ starting from the **initial condition** m_0.

The graph of a solution is a discrete set of points with the time t on the horizontal axis and the measurement m_t on the vertical axis. The initial point has coordinates $(0, m_0)$ to describe the initial condition. The next point, with coordinates $(1, m_1)$, describes the measurement at $t = 1$, and so forth (Figure 1.5.76). It is possible to find a formula for the solution for simple discrete-time dynamical systems, but not in many more complicated cases.

Example 1.5.11 A Solution of the Bacterial Discrete-time Dynamical System

Suppose we begin with one million bacteria, which corresponds to an initial condition of $b_0 = 1.0$ (with bacterial population measured in millions). If the bacteria obey the discrete-time dynamical system $b_{t+1} = 2.0b_t$, then

$$b_1 = 2.0b_0 = 2.0 \cdot 1.0 = 2.0$$
$$b_2 = 2.0b_1 = 2.0 \cdot 2.0 = 4.0$$
$$b_3 = 2.0b_2 = 2.0 \cdot 4.0 = 8.0$$

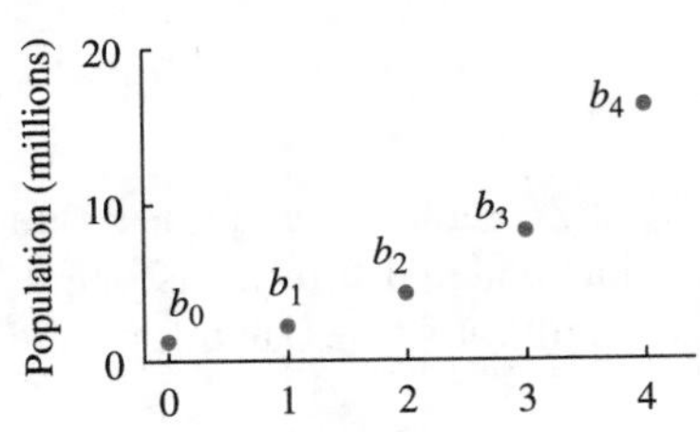

FIGURE 1.5.77

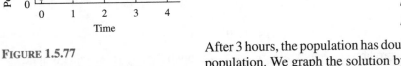

A solution: Bacterial population size as a function of time

Examining these results, we notice that

$$b_1 = 2.0 \cdot 1.0$$
$$b_2 = 2.0^2 \cdot 1.0$$
$$b_3 = 2.0^3 \cdot 1.0$$

After 3 hours, the population has doubled three times and is $2.0^3 = 8.0$ times the original population. We graph the solution by plotting the time t on the horizontal axis and the number of bacteria after t hours (b_t) on the vertical axis (Figure 1.5.77). The graph consists only of a discrete set of points describing the hourly measurements—hence the name *discrete-time dynamical system.* Sometimes, we will connect the points in a solution with line segments to make the pattern easier to see.

After t hours, the population will have doubled t times and will have reached the size

$$b_t = 2.0^t \cdot 1.0 \tag{1.5.2}$$

This formula describes the solution of the discrete-time dynamical system with initial condition $b_0 = 1.0$. It predicts the population after t hours of reproduction for any value of t. For example, we can compute

$$b_8 = 2.0^8 \cdot 1.0 = 256.0$$

without ever computing b_1, b_2, or other intermediate values.

Example 1.5.12 A Solution with a Different Initial Condition

Suppose we started the system with a different initial condition of $b_0 = 0.3$. We can find subsequent values by repeatedly applying the discrete-time dynamical system,

$$b_1 = 2.0 \cdot 0.3 = 0.6$$
$$b_2 = 2.0 \cdot 0.6 = 1.2$$
$$b_3 = 2.0 \cdot 1.2 = 2.4$$

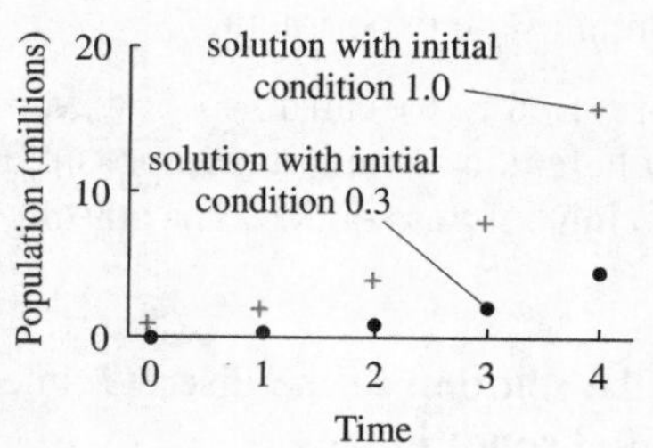

FIGURE 1.5.78
Solutions starting from two different initial conditions

If we look for the pattern in this case,

$$b_1 = 2.0 \cdot 0.3$$
$$b_2 = 2.0^2 \cdot 0.3$$
$$b_3 = 2.0^3 \cdot 0.3$$

After t hours, the population will have doubled t times, as before, and will have reached the size

$$b_t = 2.0^t \cdot 0.3 \text{ million bacteria}$$

The solution is **different** from the one found in Example 1.5.11 with a different initial condition (Figure 1.5.78). Although the two solutions get further and further apart, the ratio always remains the same (see Exercise 55, page 66).

Example 1.5.13 Two Solutions of the Tree Height Discrete-time Dynamical System

Tree height obeys the discrete-time dynamical system

$$h_{t+1} = h_t + 1.0$$

(Example 1.5.2). Suppose the tree begins with a height of $h_0 = 10.0$ m. Then

$$h_1 = h_0 + 1.0 = 11.0 \text{ m}$$
$$h_2 = h_1 + 1.0 = 12.0 \text{ m}$$
$$h_3 = h_2 + 1.0 = 13.0 \text{ m}$$

Each year, the height of the tree increases by 1.0 m. After 3 years, the height is 3.0 m greater than the original height. After t years the tree has added 1.0 m to its height t times, meaning that the height will have increased by a total of t m. Therefore, the solution is

$$h_t = 10.0 + t \text{ m}$$

This formula predicts the height after t years of growth for any t. We can compute

$$h_8 = 10.0 + 8.0 = 18.0 \text{ m}$$

without computing h_1, h_2, or other intermediate values (Figure 1.5.79).

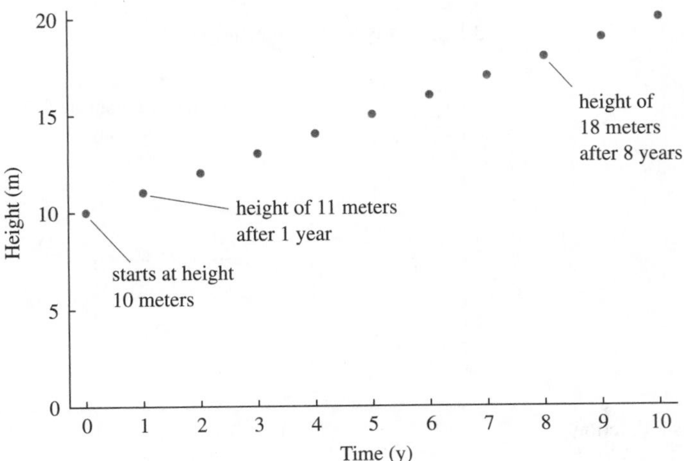

FIGURE 1.5.79
A solution: tree height as a function of time

If the tree began at the smaller size of 2.0 m, the size for the first few years would be

$$h_1 = h_0 + 1.0 = 3.0 \text{ m}$$
$$h_2 = h_1 + 1.0 = 4.0 \text{ m}$$
$$h_3 = h_2 + 1.0 = 5.0 \text{ m}$$

Again, the tree adds t m of height in t years, so the height is

$$h_t = 2.0 + t \text{ m}$$

The solution with this smaller initial condition is always exactly 8.0 m less than the solution found before (Figure 1.5.80).

Is it always possible to guess the formula for a solution in this way? We will next see some cases where computing the solution step by step is straightforward but finding a formula for the solution is tricky. Remarkably, there are simple discrete-time dynamical systems for which it is *impossible* to write a formula for a solution. For example, **chaotic** dynamical systems have solutions so unpredictable that no formula can describe them. (See "Analysis of the Logistic Dynamical System," p. 257–261, in Section 3.2.)

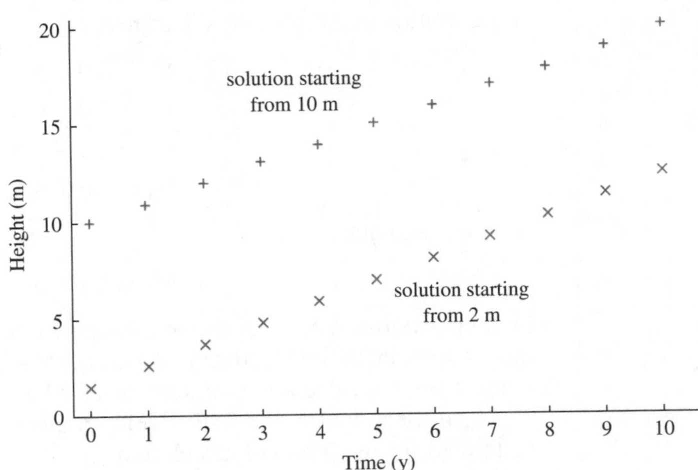

FIGURE 1.5.80
Two solutions for tree height as functions of time

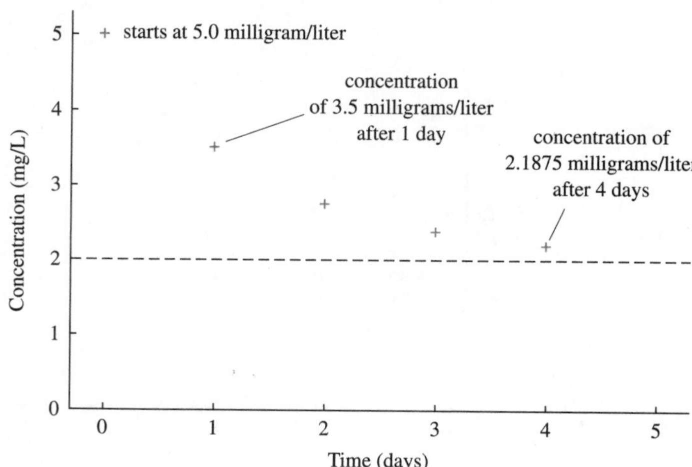

FIGURE 1.5.81

Medication concentration as a function of time

Example 1.5.14 Finding a Solution of the Medication Discrete-time Dynamical System

Consider the discrete-time dynamical system for medication (Example 1.5.4) given by

$$M_{t+1} = 0.5M_t + 1.0$$

Suppose we begin from an initial condition of $M_0 = 5.0$ milligrams per liter. Then

$$M_1 = 0.5 \cdot 5.0 + 1.0 = 3.5$$
$$M_2 = 0.5 \cdot 3.5 + 1.0 = 2.75$$
$$M_3 = 0.5 \cdot 2.75 + 1.0 = 2.375$$
$$M_4 = 0.5 \cdot 2.375 + 1.0 = 2.1875$$

The values are getting closer and closer to 2.0 (Figure 1.5.81). More careful examination indicates that the results move exactly **halfway** toward 2.0 each step. In particular, we find that the difference between the measured rate and 2.0 is

$$M_0 - 2.0 = 5.0 - 2.0 = 3.0$$
$$M_1 - 2.0 = 3.5 - 2.0 = 1.5 = 0.5 \cdot 3.0$$
$$M_2 - 2.0 = 2.75 - 2.0 = 0.75 = 0.5 \cdot 1.5$$
$$M_3 - 2.0 = 2.375 - 2.0 = 0.375 = 0.5 \cdot 0.75$$
$$M_4 - 2.0 = 2.1875 - 2.0 = 0.1875 = 0.5 \cdot 0.375$$

Can we convert these observations into the formula for a solution? If we write the concentration as 2.0 plus the difference,

$$M_0 = 2.0 + 3.0$$
$$M_1 = 2.0 + 0.5 \cdot 3.0$$
$$M_2 = 2.0 + 0.5^2 \cdot 3.0$$
$$M_3 = 2.0 + 0.5^3 \cdot 3.0$$

we might see that

$$M_t = 2.0 + 0.5^t \cdot 3.0$$

Finding patterns in this way and translating them into formulas can be tricky. It is much more important to be able to *describe* the behavior of solutions with a graph or in words. In this case, our calculations quickly revealed that the solution moved closer and closer to 2.0. In Section 1.6, we will develop a powerful graphical method to deduce this pattern with a minimum of calculation.

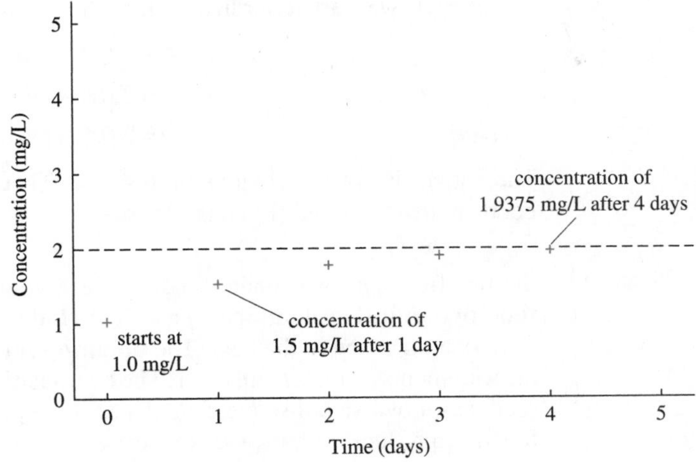

FIGURE 1.5.82
Another solution of medication concentration as a function of time

Example 1.5.15 A Second Solution of the Medication Discrete-time Dynamical System

If we begin with an initial concentration of $M_0 = 1.0$ milligrams per liter, then

$$M_1 = 0.5 \cdot 1.0 + 1.0 = 1.5$$
$$M_2 = 0.5 \cdot 1.5 + 1.0 = 1.75$$
$$M_3 = 0.5 \cdot 1.75 + 1.0 = 1.875$$
$$M_4 = 0.5 \cdot 1.875 + 1.0 = 1.9375$$

(See Figure 1.5.82.) Unlike graphs of bacterial populations (Example 1.5.12) and tree size (Example 1.5.13), the graphs of solutions starting from different initial conditions look completely different.

However, the values still get closer and closer to 2.0, and the difference from 2.0 is reduced by a factor of 2 each day:

$$M_0 - 2.0 = 1.0 - 2.0 = -1.0$$
$$M_1 - 2.0 = 1.5 - 2.0 = -0.5$$
$$M_2 - 2.0 = 1.75 - 2.0 = -0.25$$
$$M_3 - 2.0 = 1.875 - 2.0 = -0.125$$
$$M_4 - 2.0 = 1.9375 - 2.0 = -0.0625$$

We can find the formula using the same idea as before. If we write

$$M_0 = 2.0 - 1.0$$
$$M_1 = 2.0 - 0.5 \cdot 1.0$$
$$M_2 = 2.0 - 0.5^2 \cdot 1.0$$
$$M_3 = 2.0 - 0.5^3 \cdot 1.0$$

we can see that

$$M_t = 2.0 - 0.5^t \cdot 1.0$$

In Section 2.2, we will use the fundamental idea of the **limit** to study more carefully what it means for the sequence of values that define a solution to get closer and closer to 2.0.

Example 1.5.16 A Solution of the Mite Population Discrete-time Dynamical System

Recall the discrete-time dynamical system

$$x_{t+1} = 2x_t + 30$$

for mites. If we started our lizard off with $x_0 = 10$ mites, we compute

$$x_1 = 2.0x_0 + 30 = 50$$
$$x_2 = 2.0x_1 + 30 = 130$$
$$x_3 = 2.0x_2 + 30 = 290$$

The pattern is not too obvious in this case. There is a pattern, however, which it is a good challenge to find (Exercise 35, p. 65).

Summary Starting from data or an understanding of a biological process, we can derive a **discrete-time dynamical system,** the **dynamical rule** that tells how a measurement changes from one time step to the next. The **updating function** describes the relation between measurements at times t and $t + 1$. The **composition** of the updating function with itself produces a two-step discrete-time dynamical system, and the **inverse** of the updating function produces a backwards discrete-time dynamical system. Like all biological relations, a discrete-time dynamical system can be described in different units and dimensions. Repeated application of a discrete-time dynamical system starting from an **initial condition** generates a **solution,** the value of the measurement as a function of time. With the proper combination of diligence, cleverness, and luck, it is sometimes possible to find a formula for the solution.

1.5 Exercises

Mathematical Techniques

1–4 ▪ Write the updating function associated with each of the following discrete-time dynamical systems and evaluate it at the given arguments. Which are linear?

1. $p_{t+1} = p_t - 2$, evaluate at $p_t = 5$, $p_t = 10$, and $p_t = 15$.

2. $\psi_{t+1} = \frac{\psi_t}{2}$, evaluate at $\psi_t = 4$, $\psi_t = 8$, and $\psi_t = 12$.

3. $x_{t+1} = x_t^2 + 2$, evaluate at $x_t = 0$, $x_t = 2$, and $x_t = 4$.

4. $Q_{t+1} = \frac{1}{Q_t + 1}$, evaluate at $Q_t = 0$, $Q_t = 1$, and $Q_t = 2$.

5–8 ▪ Compose with itself the updating function associated with each discrete-time dynamical system. Find the two-step discrete-time dynamical system. Check that the result of applying the original discrete-time dynamical system to the given initial condition twice matches the result of applying the new discrete-time dynamical system to the given initial condition once.

5. Volume follows $v_{t+1} = 1.5v_t$, starting from $v_0 = 1220\,\mu\text{m}^3$.

6. Length obeys $l_{t+1} = l_t - 1.7$, starting from $l_0 = 13.1$ cm.

7. Population size follows $n_{t+1} = 0.5n_t$, starting from $n_0 = 1200$.

8. Medication concentration obeys $M_{t+1} = 0.75M_t + 2.0$ starting from the initial condition $M_0 = 16.0$.

9–12 ▪ Find the backwards discrete-time dynamical system associated with each discrete-time dynamical system. Use it to find the value at the previous time.

9. $v_{t+1} = 1.5v_t$. Find v_0 if $v_1 = 1220\,\mu\text{m}^3$.

10. $l_{t+1} = l_t - 1.7$. Find l_0 if $l_1 = 13.1$ cm.

11. $n_{t+1} = 0.5n_t$. Find n_0 if $n_1 = 1200$.

12. $M_{t+1} = 0.75M_t + 2.0$. Find M_0 if $M_1 = 16.0$.

13–14 ▪ Find the composition of each of the following mathematically elegant updating functions with itself, and find the inverse function.

13. The updating function $f(x) = \frac{x}{1+x}$. Remember to put things over a common denominator to simplify the composition.

14. The updating function $h(x) = \frac{x}{x-1}$. Remember to put things over a common denominator to simplify the composition.

15–18 ▪ Find and graph the first five values of the following discrete-time dynamical systems, starting from the given initial condition. Compare the graph of the solution with the graph of the updating function.

15. $v_{t+1} = 1.5v_t$, starting from $v_0 = 1220\,\mu\text{m}^3$.

16. $l_{t+1} = l_t - 1.7$, starting from $l_0 = 13.1$ cm.

17. $n_{t+1} = 0.5n_t$, starting from $n_0 = 1200$.

18. $M_{t+1} = 0.75M_t + 2.0$ starting from the initial condition $M_0 = 16.0$.

19–22 ▪ Using a formula for the solution, you can project far into the future without computing all the intermediate values. Find the following, and indicate whether the results are reasonable.

19. From the solution found in Exercise 15, find the volume at $t = 20$.

20. From the solution found in Exercise 16, find the length at $t = 20$.

21. From the solution found in Exercise 17, find the number at $t = 20$.

22. From the solution found in Exercise 18, find the concentration at $t = 20$.

23–26 ▪ Experiment with the following mathematically elegant updating functions and try to find the solution.

23. Consider the updating function

$$f(x) = \frac{x}{1+x}$$

from Exercise 13. Starting from an initial condition of $x_0 = 1$, compute x_1, x_2, x_3, and x_4, and try to spot the pattern.

24. Use the updating function in Exercise 23, but start from the initial condition $x_0 = 2$.

25. Consider the updating function

$$g(x) = 4 - x$$

Start from initial condition of $x_0 = 1$, and try to spot the pattern. Experiment with a couple of other initial conditions. How would you describe your results in words?

26. Consider the updating function

$$h(x) = \frac{x}{x-1}$$

from Exercise 14. Start from initial condition of $x_0 = 3$, and try to spot the pattern. Experiment with a couple of other initial conditions. How would you describe your results in words?

Applications

27–30 ▪ Consider the following actions. Which of them commute (produce the same answer when done in either order)?

27. A population doubles in size; 10 individuals are removed from a population. Try starting with 100 individuals, and then try to figure out what happens in general.

28. A population doubles in size; population size is divided by 4. Try starting with 100 individuals, and then try to figure out what happens in general.

29. An organism grows by 2.0 cm; an organism shrinks by 1.0 cm.

30. A person loses half her money. A person gains $10.

31–34 ▪ Use the formula for the solution to find the following, and indicate whether the results are reasonable.

31. Using the solution for tree height $h_t = 10.0 + t$ (Example 1.5.13), find the tree height after 20 years.

32. Using the solution for tree height $h_t = 10.0 + t$ (Example 1.5.13), find the tree height after 100 years.

33. Using the solution for bacterial population number $b_t = 2.0^t \cdot 1.0$ (Equation 1.5.2), find the bacterial population after 20 hours. If an individual bacterium weighs about 10^{-12} g, how much will the whole population weigh?

34. Using the solution for bacterial population number $b_t = 2.0^t \cdot 1.0$ (Equation 1.5.2), find the bacterial population after 40 hours.

35–36 ▪ Try to find a formula for the solution of the given discrete-time dynamical system.

35. Find the pattern in the number of mites on a lizard, starting with $x_0 = 10$ and following the discrete-time dynamical system $x_{t+1} = 2x_t + 30$. (*Hint:* add 30 to the number of mites.)

36. Try to find the pattern in the number of mites on a lizard, starting with $x_0 = 10$ and following the discrete-time dynamical system $x_{t+1} = 2x_t + 20$.

37–40 ▪ The following tables display data from four experiments:

1. Cell volume after 10 minutes in a watery bath
2. Fish length after 1 week in a chilly tank
3. Gnat population size after 3 days without food
4. Yield (in bushels) of several varieties of soybeans before and one month after fertilization.

For each, graph the new value as a function of the initial value, find a simple discrete-time dynamical system, and fill in the missing value in the table.

37.

Cell Volume (μm^3)	
Initial, v_t	Final, v_t
1220	1830
1860	2790
1080	1620
1640	2460
1540	2310
1420	??

38.

Fish Mass (g)	
Initial, m_t	Final, m_{t+1}
13.1	11.4
18.2	16.5
17.3	15.6
16.0	14.3
20.5	18.8
1.5	??

39.

Gnat Number	
Initial, n_t	Final, n_{t+1}
1.2×10^3	6.0×10^2
2.4×10^3	1.2×10^3
1.6×10^3	8.0×10^2
2.0×10^3	1.0×10^3
1.4×10^3	7.0×10^2
8.0×10^2	??

40.

Soybean Yield Per Acre (bushels)	
Initial, Y_t	Final, Y_{t+1}
100	210
50	110
200	410
75	160
95	200
250	??

41–44 ▪ Recall the data used for Section 1.2, Exercises 49–52.

Age, *a* (days)	Length, *L* (cm)	Tail Length, *T* (cm)	Mass, *M* (g)
0.5	1.5	1.0	1.5
1.0	3.0	0.9	3.0
1.5	4.5	0.8	6.0
2.0	6.0	0.7	12.0
2.5	7.5	0.6	24.0
3.0	9.0	0.5	48.0

These data define several discrete-time dynamical systems. For example, between the first measurement (on day 0.5) and the second (on day 1.0), the length increases by 1.5 cm. Between the second measurement (on day 1.0) and the third (on day 1.5), the length again increases by 1.5 cm.

41. Graph the length at the second measurement as a function of length at the first, the length at the third measurement as a function of length at the second, and so on. Find the discrete-time dynamical system that reproduces the results.

42. Find and graph the discrete-time dynamical system for tail length.

43. Find and graph the discrete-time dynamical system for mass.

44. Find and graph the discrete-time dynamical system for age.

45–48 ▪ Suppose students are permitted to take a test again and again until they get a perfect score of 100. We wish to write a discrete-time dynamical system describing these dynamics.

45. In words, what is the argument of the updating function? What is the value?

46. What are the domain and range of the updating function? What value do you expect if the argument is 100?

47. Sketch a possible graph of the updating function.

48. On the basis of your graph, how would a student do on her second try if she scored 20 on her first try?

49–50 ▪ Consider the discrete-time dynamical system $b_{t+1} = 2.0b_t$ for a bacterial population (Example 1.5.1).

49. Write a discrete-time dynamical system for the total volume of bacteria (suppose each bacterium takes up 10^4 μm^3).

50. Write a discrete-time dynamical system for the total area taken up by the bacteria (suppose the thickness is 20 μm).

51–52 ▪ Recall the equation $h_{t+1} = h_t + 1.0$ for tree height.

51. Write a discrete-time dynamical system for the total volume of the cylindrical trees in Section 1.3, Exercise 27.

52. Write a discrete-time dynamical system for the total volume of a spherical tree (this is kind of tricky).

53–54 ▪ Consider the following data describing the levels of a medication in the blood of two patients over the course of several days (measured in milligrams per liter).

Day	Medication level in patient 1 (mg/L)	Medication level in patient 2 (mg/L)
0	20.0	0.0
1	16.0	2.0
2	13.0	3.2
3	10.75	3.92

53. Graph three points on the updating function for the first patient. Find a linear discrete-time dynamical system for the first patient.

54. Graph three points on the updating function for the second patient, and find a linear discrete-time dynamical system.

55–56 ▪ For the following discrete-time dynamical systems, compute solutions starting from each of the given initial conditions. Then find the difference between the solutions as a function of time, and the ratio of the solutions as a function of time. In which cases is the difference constant, and in which cases is the ratio constant? Can you explain why?

55. Two bacterial populations follow the discrete-time dynamical system $b_{t+1} = 2.0b_t$, but the first starts with initial condition $b_0 = 1.0 \times 10^6$ and the second starts with initial condition $b_0 = 3.0 \times 10^5$ (in millions of bacteria).

56. Two trees follow the discrete-time dynamical system $h_{t+1} = h_t + 1.0$, but the first starts with initial condition $h_0 = 10.0$ m and the second starts with initial condition $h_0 = 2.0$ m.

57–60 ▪ Derive and analyze discrete-time dynamical systems that describe the following contrasting situations.

57. A population of bacteria doubles every hour, but 1.0×10^6 individuals are removed after reproduction to be converted into valuable biological by-products. The population begins with $b_0 = 3.0 \times 10^6$ bacteria.

a. Find the population after 1, 2, and 3 hours.

b. How many bacteria were harvested?

c. Write the discrete-time dynamical system.

d. Suppose you waited to harvest bacteria until the end of 3 hours. How many could you remove and still match the population b_3 found in part **a**? Where did all the extra bacteria come from?

58. Suppose that a population of bacteria doubles every hour but that 1.0×10^6 individuals are removed **before** reproduction to be converted into valuable biological by-products. Suppose the population begins with $b_0 = 3.0 \times 10^6$ bacteria.

a. Find the population after 1, 2, and 3 hours.

b. Write the discrete-time dynamical system.

c. How does the population compare with that in the previous problem? Why is it doing worse?

59. Suppose the fraction of individuals with some superior gene increases by 10% each generation.

a. Write the discrete-time dynamical system for the fraction of organisms with the gene (denote the fraction at time t by f_t and figure out the formula for f_{t+1}).

b. Write the solution, starting from an initial condition of $f_0 = 0.0001$.

c. Will the fraction reach 1.0? Does the discrete-time dynamical system make sense for all values of f_t?

60. The Weber-Fechner law describes how human beings perceive differences. Suppose, for example, that a person first hears a tone with a frequency of 400 hertz (cycles per second). He is then tested with higher tones until he can hear the difference. The ratio between these values describes how well this person can hear differences.

a. Suppose the next tone he can distinguish has a frequency of 404 hertz. What is the ratio?

b. According to the Weber-Fechner law, the next higher tone will be greater than 404 by the same ratio. Find this tone.

c. Write the discrete-time dynamical system for this person. Find the fifth tone he can distinguish.

d. Suppose the experiment is repeated on a musician, and she manages to distinguish 400.5 hertz from 400 hertz. What is the fifth tone she can distinguish?

61–62 ▪ The total mass of a population of bacteria will change if the number of bacteria changes, if the mass per bacterium changes, or if both of these variables change. Try to derive a discrete-time dynamical system for the total mass in the following situations.

61. The number of bacteria doubles each hour, and the mass of each bacterium triples during the same time.

62. The number of bacteria doubles each hour, and the mass of each bacterium increases by 1.0×10^{-9} g. What seems to go wrong with this calculation? Can you explain why?

1.6 Analysis of Discrete-Time Dynamical Systems

We have defined discrete-time dynamical systems that describe what happens during a single time step and have defined the solution as the sequence of values taken on over many time steps. Often enough, finding a formula for the solution is difficult or impossible. Nonetheless, we can often deduce the behavior of the solution with simpler methods. This section introduces two such methods. **Cobwebbing** is a graphical technique that makes it possible to sketch solutions without computing anything. Algebraically, we will learn how to solve for **equilibria,** points where the discrete-time dynamical system leaves the value unchanged.

Cobwebbing: A Graphical Solution Technique

Suppose we have a general discrete-time dynamical system

$$m_{t+1} = f(m_t)$$

with updating function graphed in Figure 1.6.83. By adding the diagonal (the line $m_{t+1} = m_t$) to the graph, we can find the behavior of solutions graphically. The technique is called **cobwebbing.**

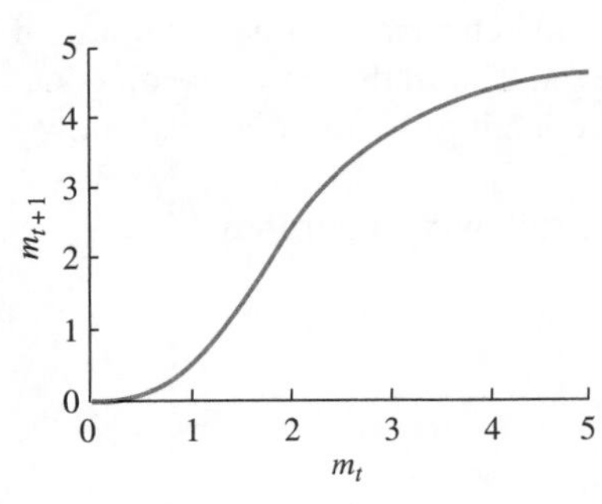

FIGURE 1.6.83
Graph of the updating function

Suppose we are given some initial condition m_0. To find m_1, we must remember the meaning of the updating function,

$$m_1 = f(m_0)$$

Graphically, m_1 is the coordinate of the vertical point on the graph of the updating function directly above m_0 (Figure 1.6.84a). Similarly, m_2 is the coordinate of the vertical point on the graph of the updating function directly above m_1, and so on.

The missing step is moving m_1 from the vertical axis onto the horizontal axis. The trick is to **reflect** it off the diagonal line that has equation $m_{t+1} = m_t$. Move the point (m_0, m_1) horizontally until it intersects the diagonal. Moving a point horizontally does

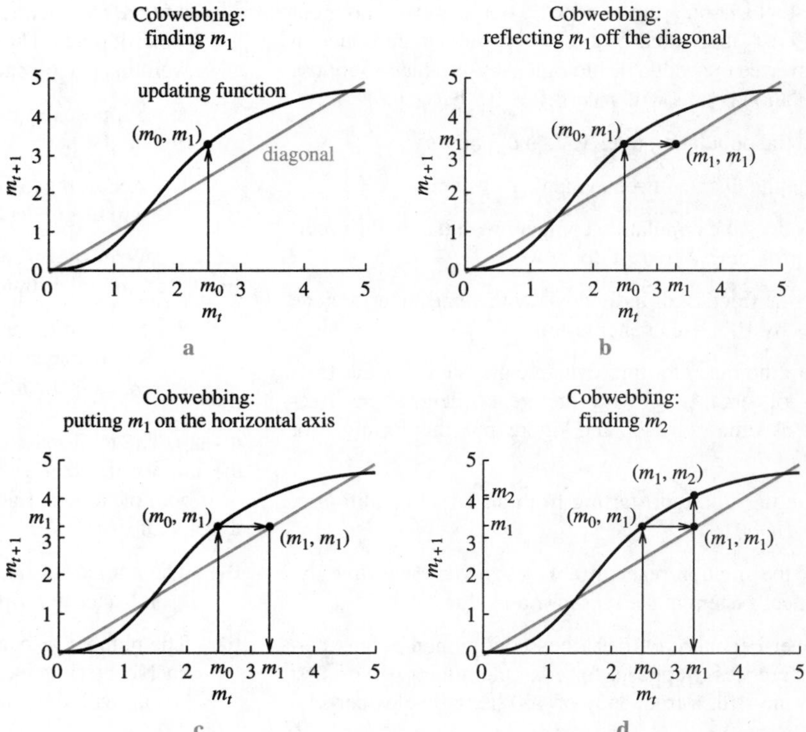

FIGURE 1.6.84
Cobwebbing: The first steps

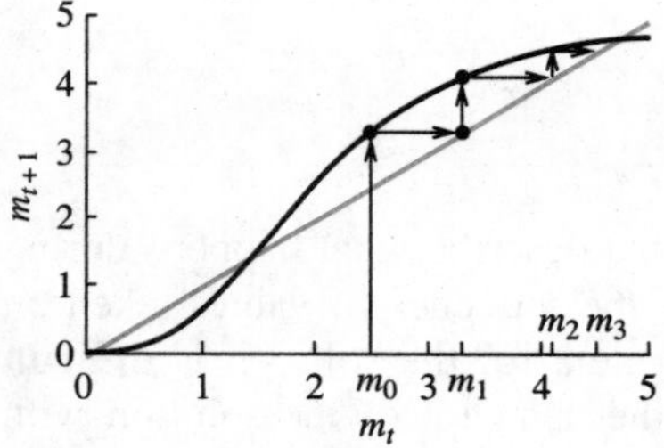

FIGURE 1.6.85
Cobwebbing

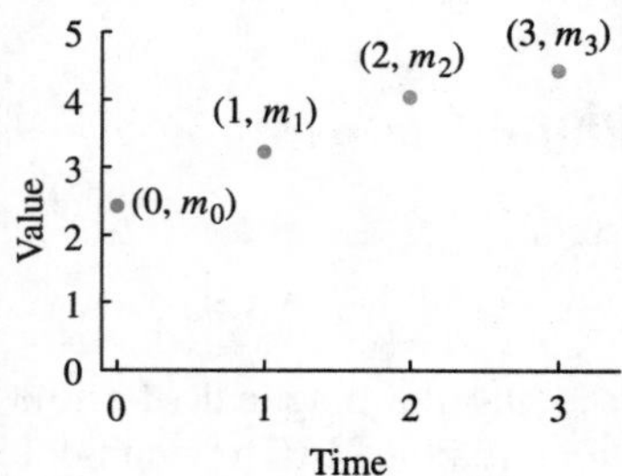

FIGURE 1.6.86
The solution derived from a cobweb diagram

not change the vertical coordinate. The intersection with the diagonal occurs at the point (m_1, m_1) (Figure 1.6.84b). The point $(m_1, 0)$ lies directly below (Figure 1.6.84c).

What have we done? Starting from the initial value m_0, plotted on the horizontal axis, we used the updating function to find m_1 on the vertical axis and the reflecting trick to project m_1 onto the horizontal axis. We then can find m_2 by moving vertically to the graph of the updating function (Figure 1.6.84d). To find m_3, we move horizontally to the diagonal to reach the point (m_2, m_2), and then vertically to the point (m_2, m_3). Because the lines reaching all the way to the horizontal axis are unnecessary, they are generally omitted to make the diagram more readable (Figure 1.6.85).

Having found m_1, m_2, and m_3 on our cobwebbing graph, we can sketch a graph of the solution that shows the measurement as a function of time. In Figure 1.6.84, we began at $m_0 = 2.5$. This is plotted as the point $(0, m_0) = (0, 2.5)$ in the solution (Figure 1.6.86). The value m_1 is approximately 3.2 and is plotted as the point $(1, m_1)$ in the solution. The values of m_2 and m_3 increase more slowly and are plotted thus on the graph. Without plugging numbers into the formula, we have used the graph of the updating function to figure out the behavior of a solution starting from a given initial condition.

Similarly, we can find how the concentration would behave over time if we started from the different initial condition $m_0 = 1.2$ (Figure 1.6.87). In this case, the diagonal lies below the graph of the updating function, so reflecting off the diagonal moves points to the left. Therefore, the solution decreases.

The steps for cobwebbing are summarized in the following algorithm.

Algorithm 1.4 Using Cobwebbing to Find a Solution

1. Graph the updating function and the diagonal.
2. Starting from the initial condition on the horizontal axis, go "up to the updating function and over to the diagonal."

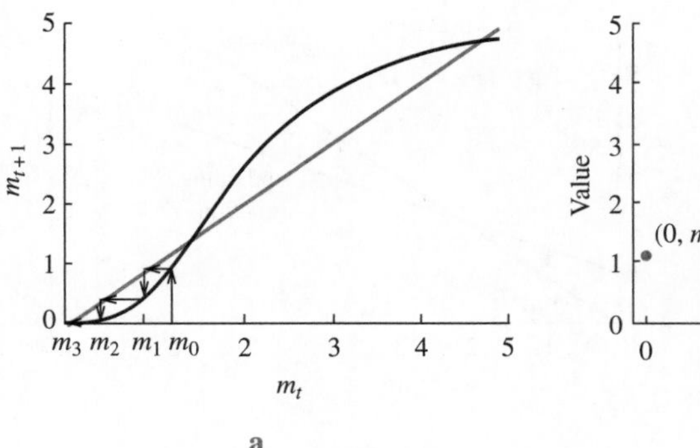

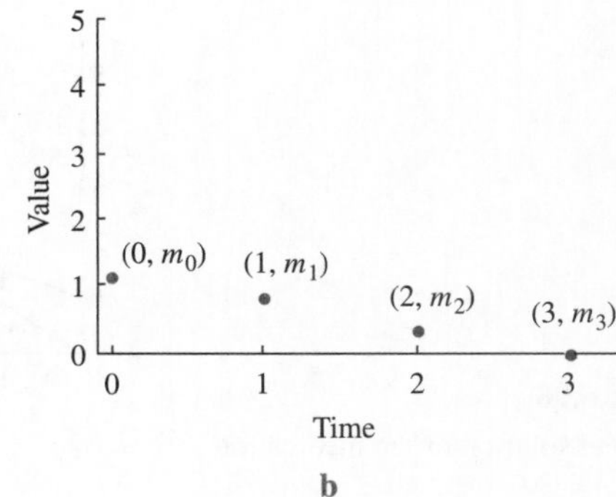

FIGURE 1.6.87
Cobweb and solution with a different initial condition

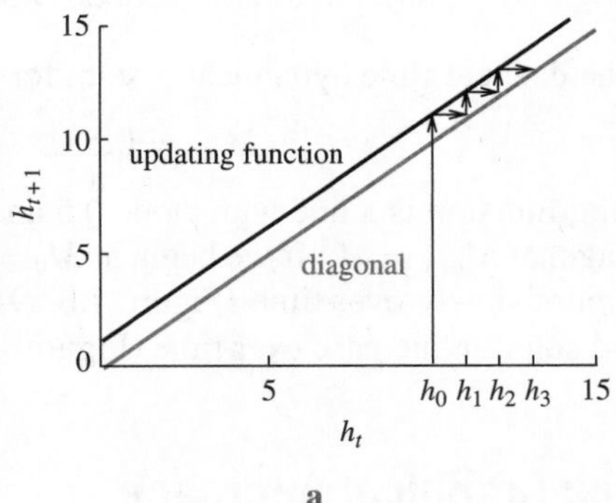

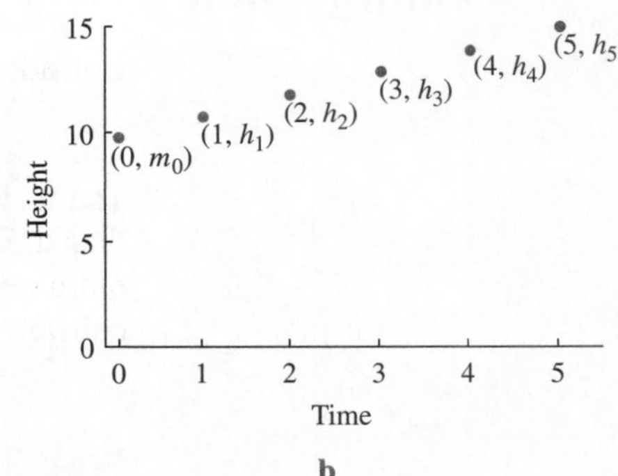

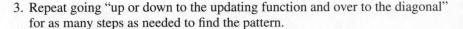

FIGURE 1.6.88
Cobweb and solution of tree growth model

3. Repeat going "up or down to the updating function and over to the diagonal" for as many steps as needed to find the pattern.
4. Sketch the solution at times 0, 1, 2, and so forth as the consecutive horizontal coordinates of intersections with the diagonal.

Example 1.6.1 Cobwebbing and Solution of the Tree Growth Model

Consider the discrete-time dynamical system for a growing tree (Example 1.5.2)

$$h_{t+1} = h_t + 1.0$$

The updating function $g(h_t) = h_t + 1.0$ is a line with slope 1 and intercept 1.0, and thus it is parallel to the diagonal $h_{t+1} = h_t$ (Figure 1.6.88). Starting from an initial condition of 10.0, the cobweb moves up steadily, as does the solution (Figure 1.6.89). The graphical solution is consistent with the exact solution $h_t = 10.0 + t$ (Example 1.5.13), although it does not provide exact **quantitative** predictions.

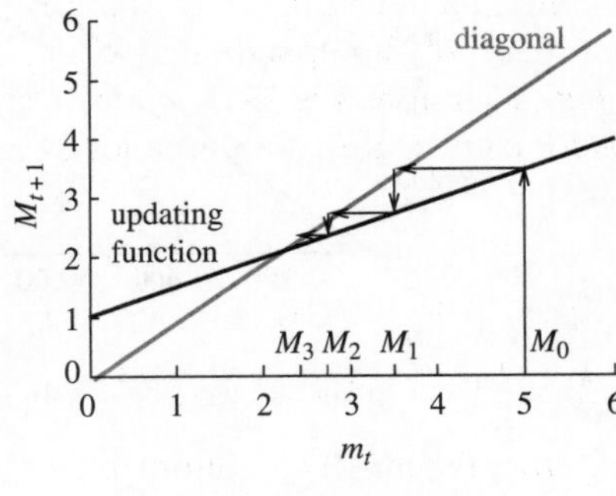

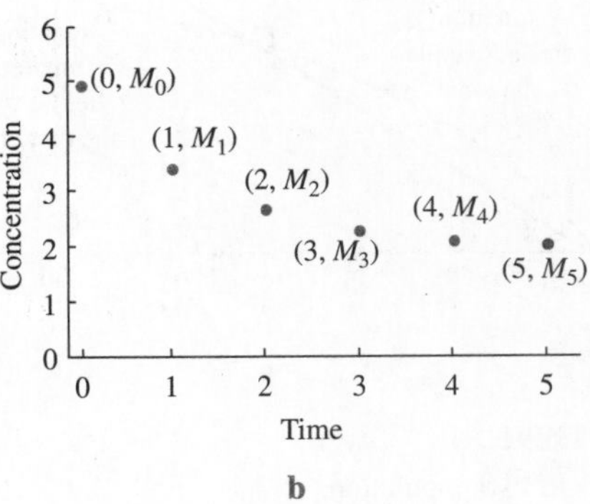

FIGURE 1.6.89
Cobweb and solution of the medication model: $M_0 = 5.0$

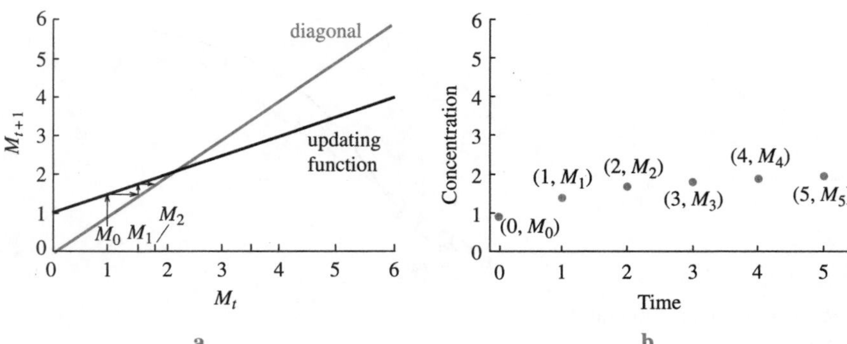

FIGURE 1.6.90
Cobweb and solution of the medication model: $M_0 = 1.0$

Example 1.6.2 Cobwebbing and Solution of the Medication Model

Consider the discrete-time dynamical system for medication (Example 1.5.4)

$$M_{t+1} = 0.5M_t + 1.0$$

The updating function is a line with slope 0.5 and intercept 1, and thus it is less steep than the diagonal $M_{t+1} = M_t$. If we begin at $M_0 = 5$, the cobweb and solution decrease more and more slowly over time (Figure 1.6.89). If we begin instead at $M_0 = 1$, the cobweb and solution increase over time (Figure 1.6.90).

Equilibria: Graphical Approach

The points where the graph of the updating function intersects the diagonal play a special role in cobweb diagrams. These points also play an essential role in understanding the behavior of discrete-time dynamical systems. Consider the discrete-time dynamical systems plotted in Figure 1.6.91. The first describes a population of plants (denoted by P_t at time t) and the second a population of birds (denoted by B_t at time t). Each graph includes the diagonal line used in cobwebbing.

If we begin cobwebbing from an initial condition where the graph of the updating function lies *above* the diagonal, the population increases (Figure 1.6.92a). In contrast, if we begin cobwebbing from an initial condition where the graph of the updating function lies *below* the diagonal, the population decreases (Figure 1.6.92b). The plant population will thus increase if the initial condition lies below the crossing point, but it will decrease if it lies above.

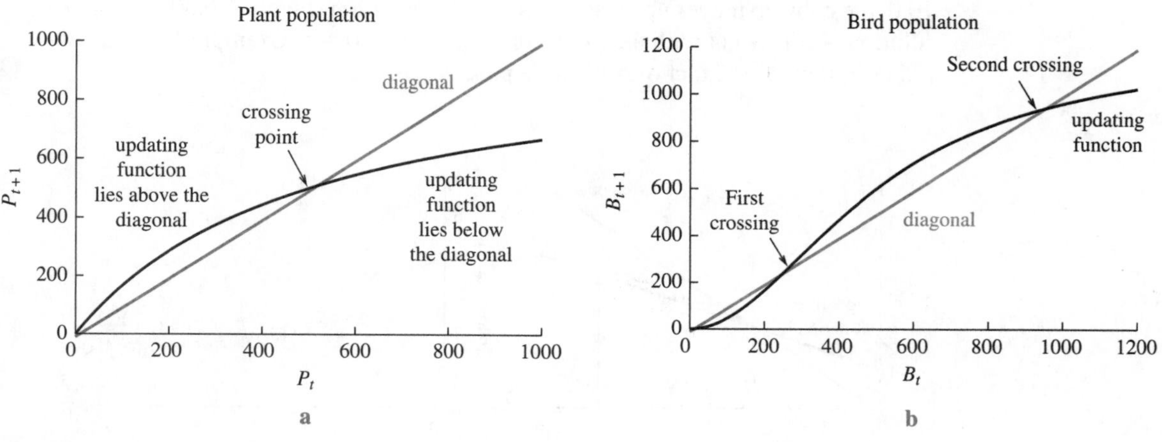

FIGURE 1.6.91
Dynamics of two populations

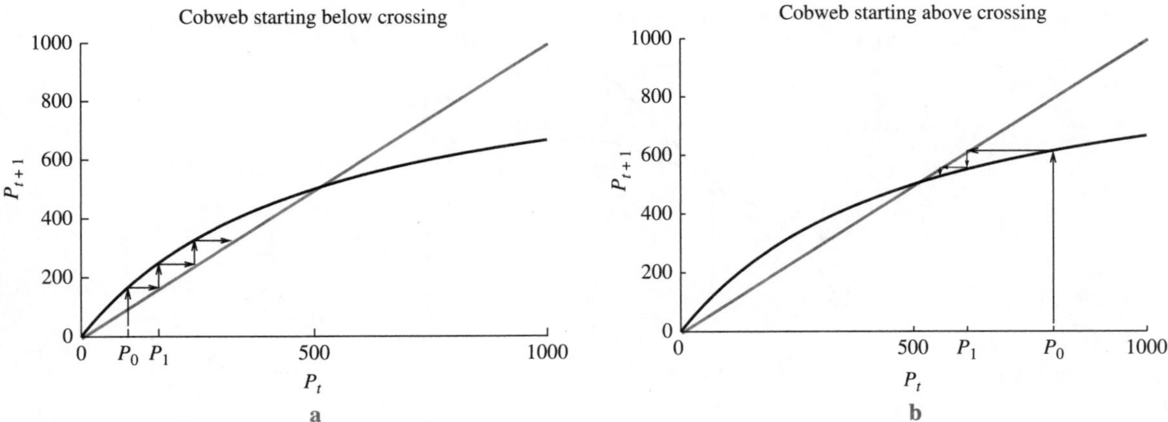

FIGURE 1.6.92
Behavior of plant population starting from two initial conditions

Similarly, the updating function for the bird population lies below the diagonal for initial conditions less than the first crossing, and the population decreases (Figure 1.6.93a). The updating function is above the diagonal for initial conditions between the crossings, and the population increases (Figure 1.6.93b). Finally, the updating function is again below the diagonal for initial conditions greater than the second crossing, and the population decreases (Figure 1.6.93c).

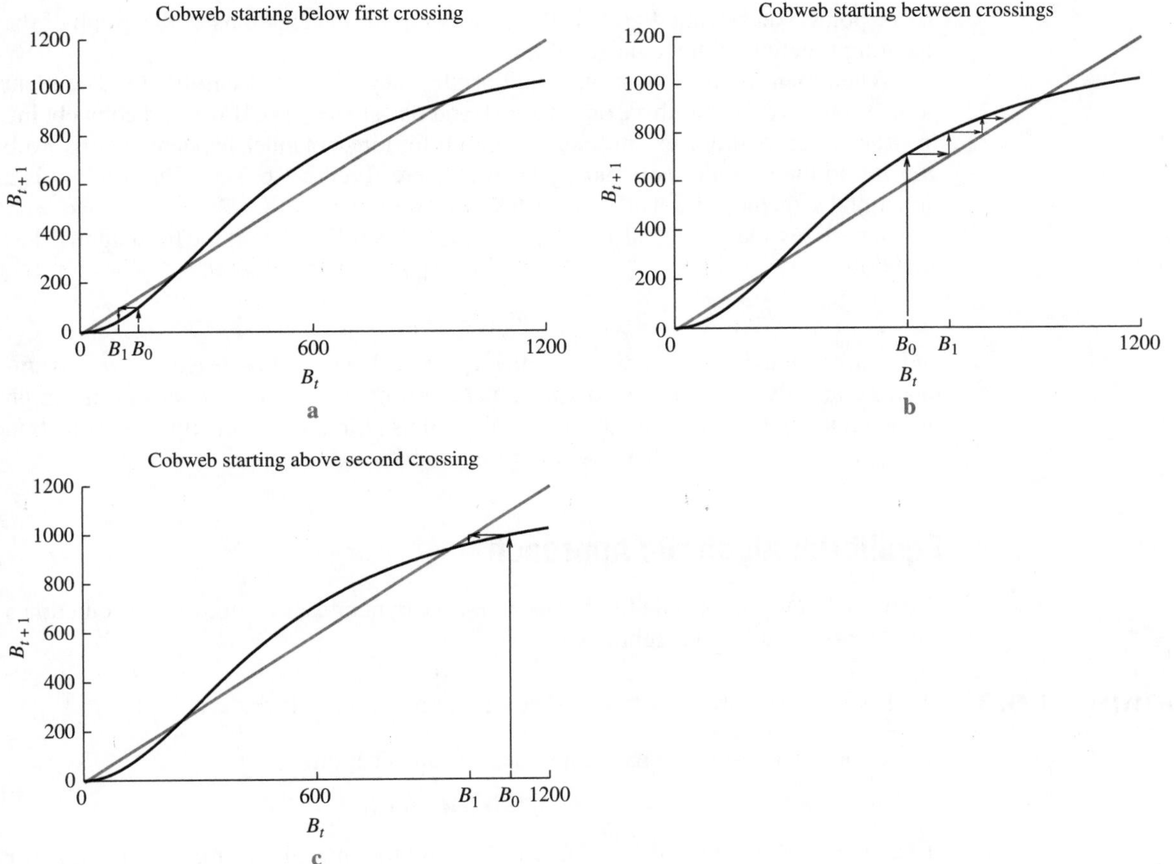

FIGURE 1.6.93
Behavior of bird population starting from three initial conditions

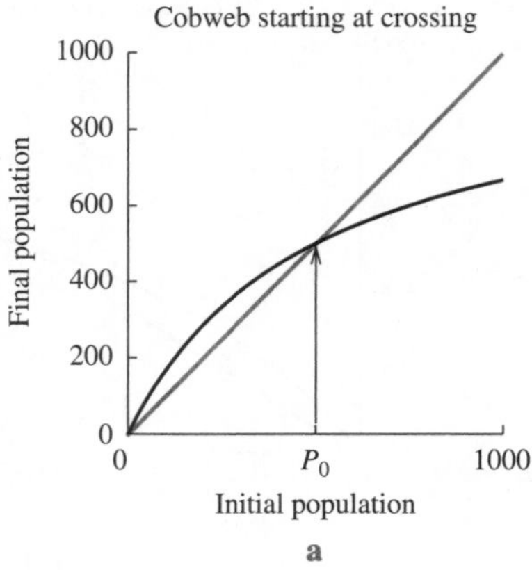

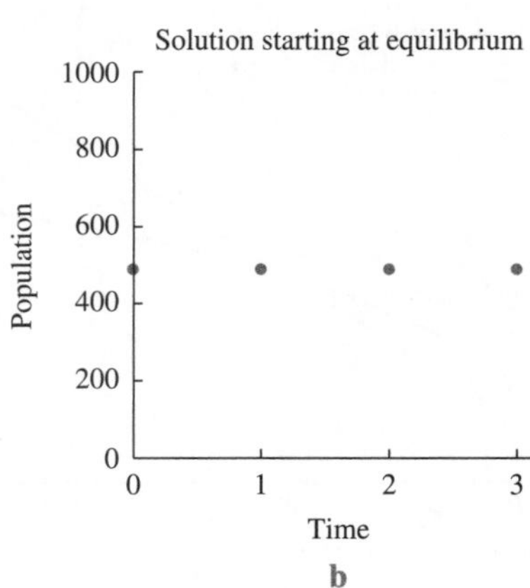

FIGURE 1.6.94
Behavior of plant population starting from an equilibrium

What happens where the updating function crosses the diagonal? At these points, the population neither increases nor decreases and thus remains the same. Such a point is called an **equilibrium.**

Definition 1.11 A point m^* is called an equilibrium of the discrete-time dynamical system

$$m_{t+1} = f(m_t)$$

if $f(m^*) = m^*$.

This definition says that the discrete-time dynamical system leaves m^* unchanged. These points can be found graphically by looking for intersections of the graph of the updating function with the diagonal line.

When there is more than one equilibrium, they are called **equilibria**. The plant population has two equilibria, one at $P = 0$ and one at $P = 500$. If we start cobwebbing from an initial condition exactly equal to an equilibrium, not much happens. The cobweb goes up to the crossing point and gets stuck there (Figure 1.6.94a). The solution is a horizontal sequence of dots (Figure 1.6.94b).

Why does the graphical method for finding equilibria work? The diagonal has equation

$$m_{t+1} = m_t$$

and can be thought of as a discrete-time dynamical system that leaves *all* inputs unchanged and always returns an output equal to its input. The intersections of the graph of the updating function with the diagonal are thus points where the updating function leaves its input unchanged. These are the equilibria.

Equilibria: Algebraic Approach

When we know the formula for the discrete-time dynamical system, we can sometimes solve for the equilibria algebraically.

Example 1.6.3 The Equilibrium of the Medication Discrete-time Dynamical System

Recall the discrete-time dynamical system for medication

$$M_{t+1} = 0.5M_t + 1.0$$

(Example 1.5.4 and Figure 1.6.95). Let M^* stand for an equilibrium. The equation for equilibrium says that M^* is unchanged by the discrete-time dynamical system, or

$$M^* = 0.5M^* + 1.0$$

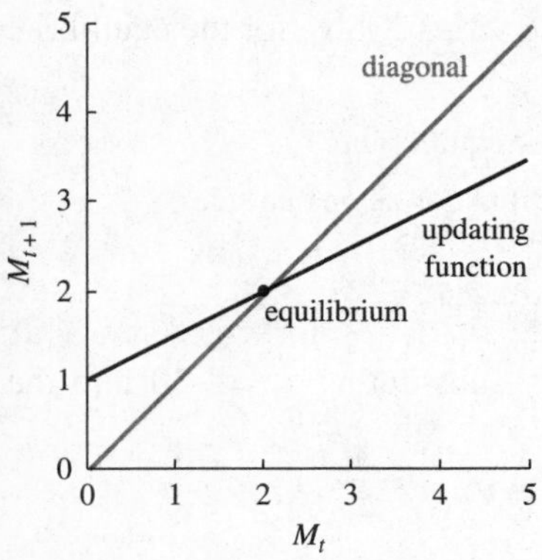

FIGURE 1.6.95

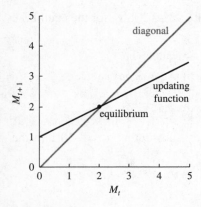

Equilibrium of the medication discrete-time dynamical system

We can solve this linear equation.

$$M^* = 0.5M^* + 1.0 \quad \text{the original equation}$$
$$M^* - 0.5M^* = 1.0 \quad \text{subtract } 0.5M^* \text{ to get unknowns on one side}$$
$$0.5M^* = 1.0 \quad \text{do the subtraction}$$
$$M^* = \frac{1.0}{0.5} = 2.0 \quad \text{divide by 0.5}$$

The equilibrium value is 2.0 mg/l. We can check this by plugging $M_t = 2.0$ into the discrete-time dynamical system, finding that

$$M_{t+1} = 0.5 \cdot 2.0 + 1.0 = 2.0$$

A concentration of 2.0 is indeed unchanged over a course of days. Furthermore, we have seen that solutions tend to approach the equilibrium (Examples 1.5.14 and 1.5.15).

Example 1.6.4 The Equilibrium of the Bacterial Discrete-time Dynamical System

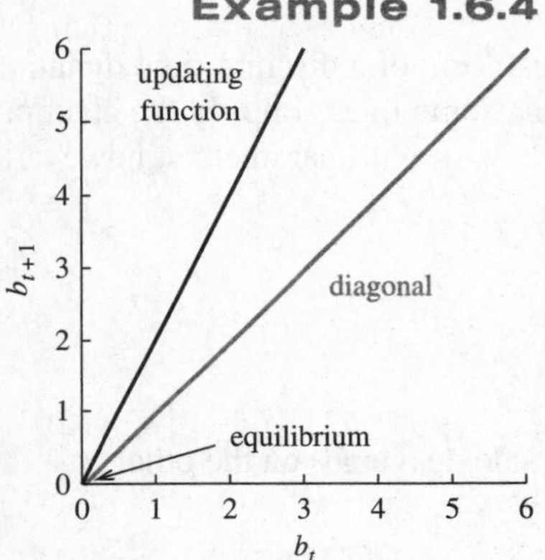

FIGURE 1.6.96

Equilibrium of the bacterial discrete-time dynamical system

To find the equilibria for the bacterial population discrete-time dynamical system

$$b_{t+1} = 2b_t$$

(Example 1.5.1 and Figure 1.6.96), we write the equation for equilibria,

$$b^* = 2b^*$$

We then solve this equation

$$b^* = 2b^* \quad \text{the original equation}$$
$$b^* - b^* = 2b^* - b^* \quad \text{subtract } b^* \text{ from both sides}$$
$$0 = b^* \quad \text{do the subtraction}$$

Consistent with our picture, the only equilibrium is at $b_t = 0$. The only number that remains the same after doubling is 0.

Example 1.6.5 A Discrete-time Dynamical System with No Equilibrium

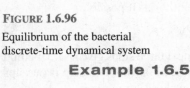

FIGURE 1.6.97

A discrete-time dynamical system for mites

The updating function for a growing tree (Example 1.5.2) following the discrete-time dynamical system

$$h_{t+1} = h_t + 1.0$$

has a graph that is parallel to the diagonal Figure 1.6.97. To solve for the equilibria, we try

$$h^* = h^* + 1 \quad \text{the equation for the equilibrium}$$
$$h^* - h^* = 1 \quad \text{subtract } h^* \text{ to get unknowns on one side}$$
$$0 = 1 \quad \text{do the subtraction}$$

This looks bad. The graph of the updating function and the graph of the diagonal do not intersect because they are parallel lines. Something that grows 1.0 m per year cannot remain unchanged.

Example 1.6.6 A Biologically Unrealistic Equilibrium

The graph of the updating function associated with a mite population (Example 1.5.3) that follows the discrete-time dynamical system

$$x_{t+1} = 2x_t + 30$$

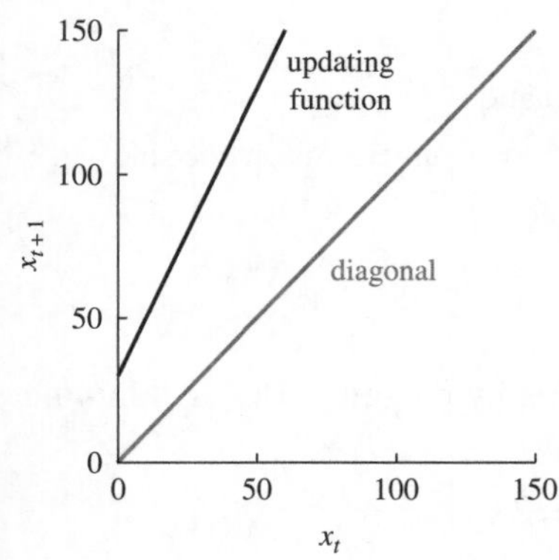

FIGURE 1.6.98

The discrete-time dynamical system for mites

lies above the diagonal for all values of x_t (Figure 1.6.98). To solve for the equilibria, try

$$
\begin{aligned}
x^* &= 2x^* + 30 && \text{the equation for the equilibrium} \\
x^* - 2x^* &= 30 && \text{subtract } 2x^* \text{ to get unknowns on one side} \\
-x^* &= 30 && \text{do the subtraction} \\
x^* &= -30 && \text{divide both sides by } -1
\end{aligned}
$$

This looks like nonsense. However, if we check by substituting $x_t = -30$ into the discrete-time dynamical system, we find

$$x_{t+1} = 2 \cdot (-30) + 30 = -30$$

which is indeed equal to x_t.

Although there is a **mathematical** equilibrium, there is no **biological** equilibrium. If we extend the graph to include biologically meaningless negative values, we see that the graph of the updating function does intersect the diagonal (Figure 1.6.99).

Algebra Involving Parameters Studying the general form of a discrete-time dynamical system, using parameters instead of numbers, can sometimes simplify the algebra and make the results easier to understand. When we work with parameters, however, we must be more careful with the algebra.

Algorithm 1.5 Solving for Equilibria

1. Write the equation for the equilibrium.
2. Use subtraction to move all the terms to one side, leaving 0 on the other.
3. Factor (if possible).
4. Set each factor equal to 0 and solve for the equilibria (if possible).
5. Think about the results.

As always, we begin by setting up the problem. The next three steps give a safe method to do the algebra (although the algebra may be impossible). The final step is perhaps the most important. A result is worthwhile only if it makes sense.

Example 1.6.7 Finding Equilibria of the Bacterial Model in General

Consider the bacterial discrete-time dynamical system where the factor of 2.0 has been replaced with a general **per capita production** of r,

$$b_{t+1} = rb_t$$

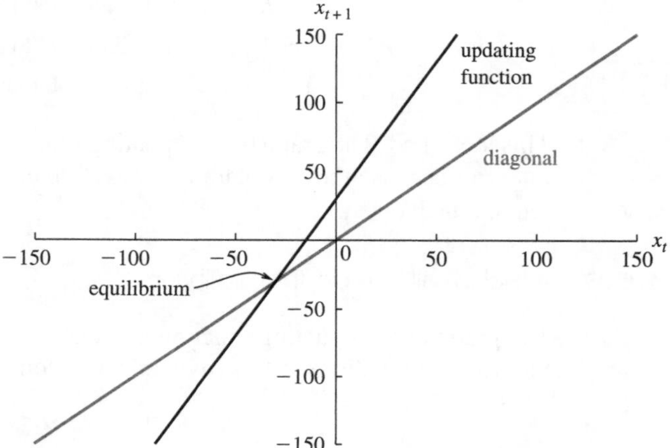

FIGURE 1.6.99

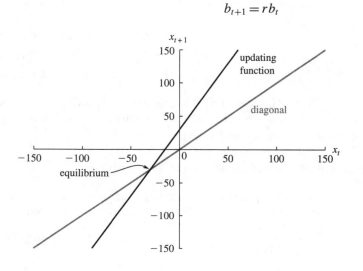

Extending the discrete-time dynamical system for mites to include a negative domain

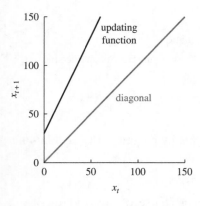

We will study this form in more detail in Section 1.7. The factor r describes how much the population grows (or declines) in 1 hour. Applying Algorithm 1.5 gives

$$\begin{aligned} b^* &= rb^* && \text{the equation for the equilibrium} \\ b^* - rb^* &= 0 && \text{move everything to one side} \\ b^*(1-r) &= 0 && \text{factor out the common factor of } b^* \\ b^* = 0 &\text{ or } 1 - r = 0 && \text{set both factors to 0} \\ b^* = 0 &\text{ or } r = 1 && \text{solve each equation} \end{aligned}$$

There are two possibilities. The first matches what we found earlier; a population of 0 is at equilibrium. This makes sense because an extinct population remains extinct. The second is new. If the per capita production r is exactly 1, every value of b_t is an equilibrium. In this case, each bacterium exactly replaces itself. The population size will remain the same no matter what its size, even though the individual bacteria are reproducing and dying.

Example 1.6.8 Equilibria of the Medication Model with a Dosage Parameter

Consider the medication discrete-time dynamical system with the parameter S,

$$M_{t+1} = 0.5M_t + S$$

where S represents the daily dosage. The algorithm for finding equilibria gives

$$\begin{aligned} M^* &= 0.5M^* + S && \text{the equation for the equilibrium} \\ M^* - 0.5M^* - S &= 0 && \text{move everything to one side} \\ 0.5M^* - S &= 0 && \text{simplify} \\ M^* &= 2.0S && \text{nothing to factor, solve for } M^* \end{aligned}$$

The equilibrium value is proportional to S, the daily dosage.

Example 1.6.9 Equilibria of the Medication Model with Absorption

Consider the medication discrete-time dynamical system with parameter α,

$$M_{t+1} = (1-\alpha)M_t + 1.0$$

where the parameter α represents the fraction of existing medication absorbed by the body during a given day. For example, if $\alpha = 0.1$, 10% of the medication is absorbed by the body and 90% remains.

$$\begin{aligned} M^* &= (1-\alpha)M^* + 1.0 && \text{the equation for the equilibrium} \\ M^* - (1-\alpha)M^* - 1.0 &= 0 && \text{move everything to one side} \\ M^* - M^* + \alpha M^* - 1.0 &= 0 && \text{distribute negative sign through quantity} \\ \alpha M^* - 1.0 &= 0 && \text{cancel } M^* - M^* \\ M^* &= \frac{1.0}{\alpha} && \text{solve for } M^* \end{aligned}$$

The equilibrium value is proportional to the reciprocal of α and thus is smaller when the fraction absorbed is larger. If $\alpha = 0.1$, the equilibrium is

$$M^* = \frac{1.0}{0.1} = 10.0$$

In contrast, if the body absorbs 50% of the medication each day, leading to a larger value of $\alpha = 0.5$, then

$$M^* = \frac{1.0}{0.5} = 2.0$$

The body that absorbs more reaches a lower equilibrium.

Example 1.6.10 Equilibria of the Medication Model with Two Parameters

Consider the medication discrete-time dynamical system with both parameters from Examples 1.6.8 and 1.6.9,

$$M_{t+1} = (1 - \alpha)M_t + S$$

The algorithm for finding equilibria gives

$$\begin{aligned} M^* &= (1-\alpha)M^* + S && \text{the equation for the equilibrium} \\ M^* - (1-\alpha)M^* - S &= 0 && \text{move everything to one side} \\ M^* - M^* + \alpha M^* - S &= 0 && \text{distribute negative sign through quantity} \\ \alpha M^* - S &= 0 && \text{cancel } M^* - M^* \\ M^* &= \frac{S}{\alpha} && \text{solve for } M^* \end{aligned}$$

The equilibrium value is larger if S is larger or if α is smaller. This makes sense because the equilibrium concentration can be increased in two ways: by increasing the dosage or by decreasing the fraction absorbed.

Summary We have developed a graphical technique called cobwebbing to estimate solutions. By examining the diagrams used for cobwebbing, we found that intersections of the graph of the updating function with the diagonal line play a special role. These **equilibria** are points that are unchanged by the discrete-time dynamical system. Algebraically, we find equilibria by solving the equation that describes such points. With a little extra care, we can often solve for equilibria in general, without substituting numerical values for the parameters. Solving the equations in this way can help clarify the underlying biological process.

1.6 Exercises

Mathematical Techniques

1–2 ▪ The following steps are used to build a cobweb diagram. Follow them for the given discrete-time dynamical systems based on bacterial populations.

a. Graph the updating function.

b. Use your graph of the updating function to find the point (b_0, b_1).

c. Reflect it off the diagonal to find the point (b_1, b_1).

d. Use the graph of the updating function to find (b_1, b_2).

e. Reflect off the diagonal to find the point (b_2, b_2).

f. Use the graph of the updating function to find (b_2, b_3).

g. Sketch the solution as a function of time.

1. The discrete-time dynamical system $b_{t+1} = 2.0b_t$ with $b_0 = 1.0$.

2. The discrete-time dynamical system $n_{t+1} = 0.5n_t$ with $n_0 = 1.0$.

3–6 ▪ Cobweb the following discrete-time dynamical systems for three steps, starting from the given initial condition. Compare with the solution found earlier.

3. $v_{t+1} = 1.5v_t$, starting from $v_0 = 1220\ \mu\text{m}^3$ (as in Section 1.5, Exercise 5).

4. $l_{t+1} = l_t - 1.7$, starting from $l_0 = 13.1$ cm (as in Section 1.5, Exercise 6).

5. $n_{t+1} = 0.5n_t$, starting from $n_0 = 1200$ (as in Section 1.5, Exercise 7).

6. $M_{t+1} = 0.75M_t + 2.0$ starting from $M_0 = 16.0$ mg/l (as in Section 1.5, Exercise 8).

7–12 ▪ Graph the updating functions associated with the following discrete-time dynamical systems, and cobweb for five steps, starting from the given initial condition.

7. $x_{t+1} = 2x_t - 1$, starting from $x_0 = 2$.

8. $z_{t+1} = 0.9z_t + 1$, starting from $z_0 = 3$.

9. $w_{t+1} = -0.5w_t + 3$, starting from $w_0 = 0$.

10. $x_{t+1} = 4 - x_t$, starting from $x_0 = 1$ (as in Section 1.5, Exercise 25).

11. $x_{t+1} = \dfrac{x_t}{1 + x_t}$, starting from $x_0 = 1$ (as in Section 1.5, Exercise 23).

12. $x_{t+1} = \dfrac{x_t}{x_t - 1}$, starting from $x_0 = 3$ (as in Section 1.5, Exercise 26). Graph for $x_t > 1$.

13–16 ▪ Find the equilibria of the following discrete-time dynamical system from the graphs of their updating functions. Label the coordinates of the equilibria.

13.

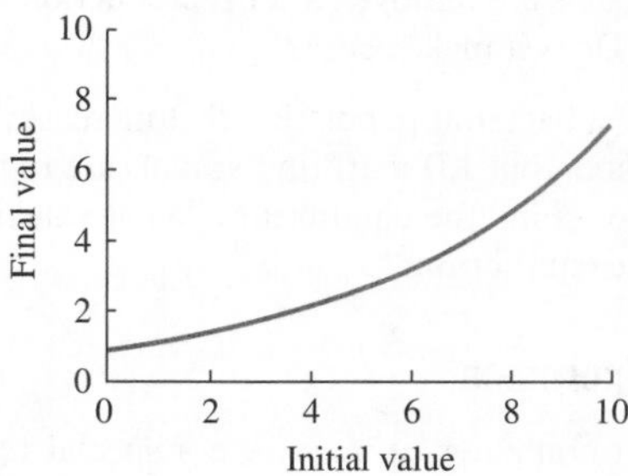

14.

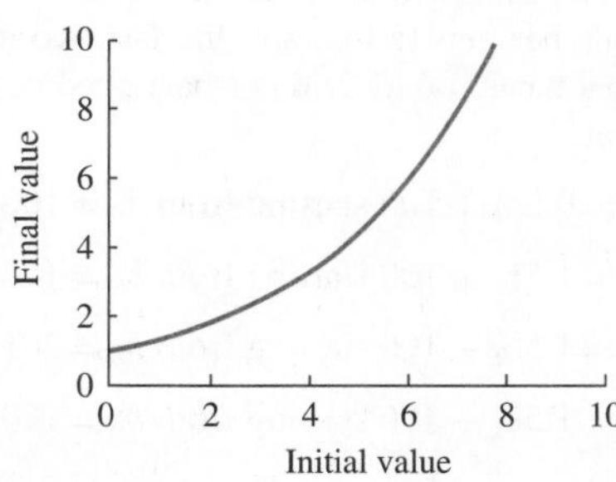

15.

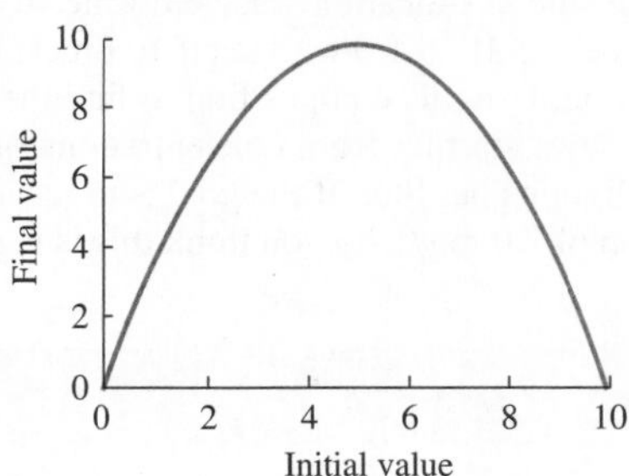

16.

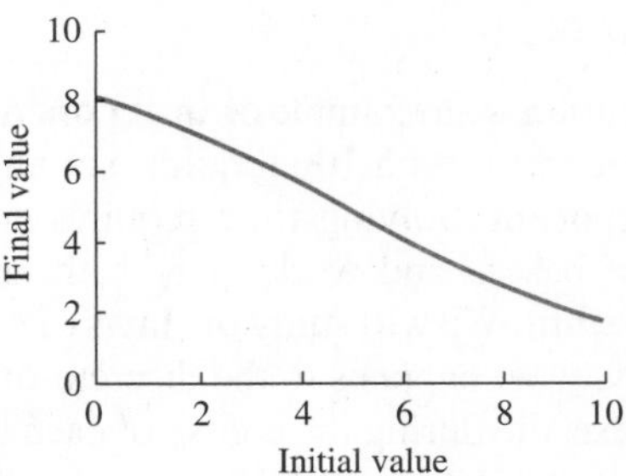

17–18 ▪ Sketch graphs of the following updating functions over the given range, and mark the equilibria. Find the equilibria algebraically if possible.

17. $f(x) = x^2$ for $0 \le x \le 2$

18. $g(y) = y^2 - 1$ for $0 \le y \le 2$

19–22 ▪ Graph the following discrete-time dynamical systems. Solve for the equilibria algebraically, and identify equilibria and the regions where the updating function lies above the diagonal on your graph.

19. $c_{t+1} = 0.5c_t + 8.0$, for $0 \le c_t \le 30$

20. $b_{t+1} = 3b_t$, for $0 \le b_t \le 10$

21. $b_{t+1} = 0.3b_t$, for $0 \le b_t \le 10$

22. $b_{t+1} = 2.0b_t - 5.0$, for $0 \le b_t \le 10$

23–30 ▪ Find the equilibria of the following discrete-time dynamical systems. Compare with the results of your cobweb diagram from the earlier problem.

23. $v_{t+1} = 1.5v_t$ (as in Section 1.5, Exercise 5)

24. $l_{t+1} = l_t - 1.7$ (as in Section 1.5, Exercise 6)

25. $x_{t+1} = 2x_t - 1$ (as in Section 1.6, Exercise 7)

26. $z_{t+1} = 0.9z_t + 1$ (as in Section 1.6, Exercise 8)

27. $w_{t+1} = -0.5w_t + 3$ (as in Section 1.6, Exercise 9)

28. $x_{t+1} = 4 - x_t$ (as in Section 1.6, Exercise 10)

29. $x_{t+1} = \dfrac{x_t}{1 + x_t}$ (as in Section 1.6, Exercise 11)

30. $x_{t+1} = \dfrac{x_t}{x_t - 1}$ for $x_t > 1$ (as in Section 1.6, Exercise 12)

31–34 ▪ Find the equilibria of the following discrete-time dynamical systems that include parameters. Identify values of the parameter for which there is no equilibrium, for which the equilibrium is negative, and for which there is more than one equilibrium.

31. $w_{t+1} = aw_t + 3$

32. $x_{t+1} = b - x_t$

33. $x_{t+1} = \dfrac{ax_t}{1 + x_t}$

34. $x_{t+1} = \dfrac{x_t}{x_t - K}$

Applications

35–40 ▪ Cobweb the following discrete-time dynamical systems for five steps, starting from the given initial condition.

35. An alternative tree growth discrete-time dynamical system with form $h_{t+1} = h_t + 5.0$ with initial condition $h_0 = 10$.

36. The mite population discrete-time dynamical system (Example 1.6.6) $x_{t+1} = 2x_t + 30$ with initial condition $x_0 = 0$.

37. The model defined in Section 1.5, Exercise 37, starting from an initial volume of 1420.

38. The model defined in Section 1.5, Exercise 38, starting from an initial length of 13.1.

39. The model defined in Section 1.5, Exercise 39, starting from an initial population of 800.

40. The model defined in Section 1.5, Exercise 40, starting from an initial yield of 20.

41–42 ■ Reconsider the data describing the levels of a medication in the blood of two patients over the course of several days (measured in milligrams per liter), used in Section 1.5, Exercises 53 and 54.

Day	Medication Level in Patient 1 (mg/L)	Medication Level in Patient 2 (mg/L)
0	20.0	0.0
1	16.0	2.0
2	13.0	3.2
3	10.75	3.92

41. For the first patient, graph the updating function, and cobweb starting from the initial condition on day 0. Find the equilibrium.

42. For the second patient, graph the updating function, and cobweb starting from the initial condition on day 0. Find the equilibrium.

43–44 ■ Cobweb and find the equilibrium of the following discrete-time dynamical systems.

43. Consider a bacterial population that doubles every hour, but 1.0×10^6 individuals are removed after reproduction (Section 1.5, Exercise 57). Cobweb starting from $b_0 = 3.0 \times 10^6$ bacteria. Is the result consistent with the result of Exercise 57?

44. Consider a bacterial population that doubles every hour, but 1.0×10^6 individuals are removed before reproduction (Section 1.5, Exercise 58). Cobweb starting from $b_0 = 3.0 \times 10^6$ bacteria. Is the result consistent with the result of Exercise 58?

45–46 ■ Consider the following general models for bacterial populations with harvest.

45. Consider a bacterial population that doubles every hour, but h individuals are removed after reproduction. Find the equilibrium. Does it make sense?

46. Consider a bacterial population that increases by a factor of r every hour, but 1.0×10^6 individuals are removed after reproduction. Find the equilibrium. What values of r produce a positive equilibrium?

Computer Exercises

47. Use your computer (it may have a special feature for this) to find and graph the first 10 points on the solutions of the following discrete-time dynamical systems. The first two describe populations with reproduction and immigration of 100 individuals per generation, and the last two describe populations that have 100 individuals harvested or removed each generation.
    a. $b_{t+1} = 0.5b_t + 100$ starting from $b_0 = 100$
    b. $b_{t+1} = 1.5b_t + 100$ starting from $b_0 = 100$
    c. $b_{t+1} = 1.5b_t - 100$ starting from $b_0 = 201$
    d. $b_{t+1} = 1.5b_t - 100$ starting from $b_0 = 199$
    e. What happens if you run the last one (part d) for 15 steps? What is wrong with the model?

48. Compose the medication discrete-time dynamical system $M_{t+1} = 0.5M_t + 1.0$ with itself 10 times. Plot the resulting function. Use this composition to find the concentration after 10 days, starting from concentrations of 1.0, 5.0, and 18.0 milligrams per liter. If the goal is to reach a stable concentration of 2.0 mg/l, do you think this is a good therapy?

1.7 Expressing Solutions with Exponential Functions

The solution associated with the bacterial discrete-time dynamical system given by $b_{t+1} = 2.0b_t$ is

$$b_t = 2.0^t$$

when $b_0 = 1.0$. As a function of t, the solution is an example of an **exponential function.** To find how long it will take the population to reach 100 requires solving an equation where the variable t appears in the exponent. Solving for t requires converting this function into a standard form with the base e and working with the inverse of the exponential function, the **natural logarithm.** We will study the **laws of exponents** and the **laws of logarithms.** More generally, what happens to the discrete-time dynamical system and solution if some of the bacteria die during the course of each hour? We will see that the solution is again an exponential function, with base equal to the **per capita production** of the bacteria.

Bacterial Population Growth in General

The bacteria studied hitherto have doubled in number each hour. Each bacterium divided once and both "daughter" bacteria survived. Suppose instead that only a fraction σ (sigma) of the daughters survive. Instead of 2.0 offspring per bacteria, we find an average of 2σ offspring (Figure 1.7.100). For example, if only 75% of offspring survived

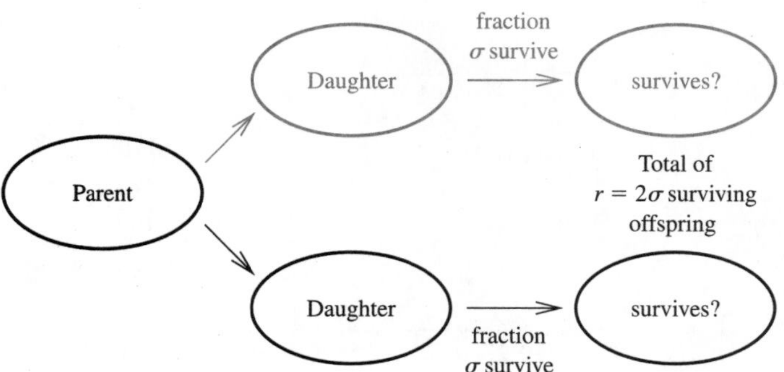

FIGURE 1.7.100
Bacterial population growth with reproduction and mortality

($\sigma = 0.75$), there are an average of only 1.5 surviving offspring per parent. Let

$$r = 2\sigma$$

The new parameter r represents the number of new bacteria produced per bacterium and is called the **per capita production.**

In terms of the parameter r, the discrete-time dynamical system is

$$b_{t+1} = rb_t$$

This fundamental equation of population biology says that the population at time $t+1$ is equal to the per capita production (the number of new bacteria per old bacterium) times the population at time t (the number of old bacteria), or

$$\text{new population} = \text{per capita production} \times \text{old population}$$

Example 1.7.1 Discrete-time Dynamical System if Most Offspring Survive

If $\sigma = 0.75$, then $r = 2 \cdot 0.75 = 1.5$. The discrete-time dynamical system is

$$b_{t+1} = 1.5b_t$$

If $b_0 = 100$, then $b_1 = 1.5 \cdot 100 = 150$. The population increases by 50% each hour.

Example 1.7.2 Discrete-time Dynamical System if Few Offspring Survive

If $\sigma = 0.25$, then $r = 2 \cdot 0.25 = 0.5$. The discrete-time dynamical system is

$$b_{t+1} = 0.5b_t$$

If $b_0 = 100$, then $b_1 = 0.5 \cdot 100 = 50$. Because the value of the survival σ is so small, this population decreases by 50% each hour.

Starting from a population with b_0 bacteria, we can apply the discrete-time dynamical system repeatedly to derive a solution, much as we did in Example 1.5.11 with the particular value $r = 2$ (Figure 1.7.101). We find

$$b_1 = rb_0$$
$$b_2 = rb_1 = r^2 b_0$$
$$b_3 = rb_2 = r^3 b_0$$

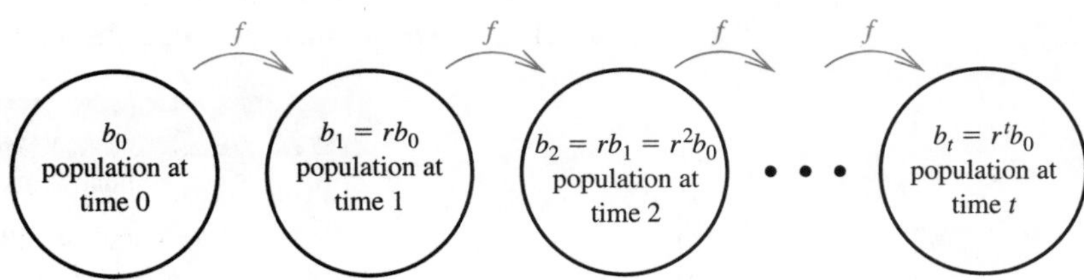

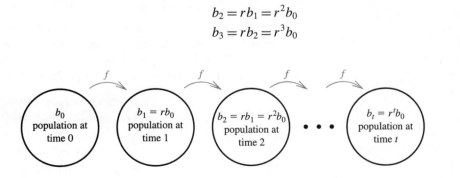

FIGURE 1.7.101
Bacterial population growth

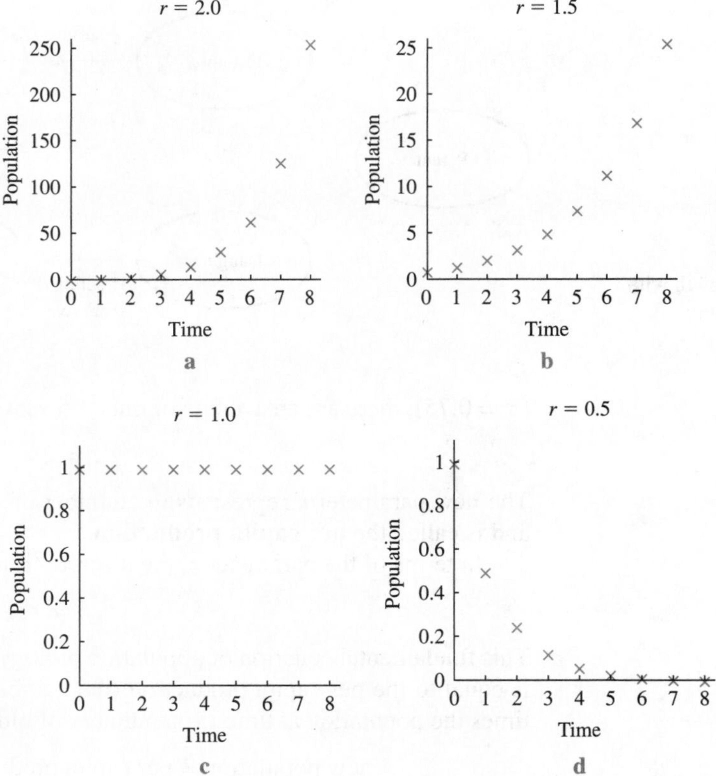

FIGURE 1.7.102
Growing and declining bacterial populations

Each hour, the initial population b_0 is multiplied by the per capita production r. After t hours, the initial population b_0 has been multiplied by t factors of r. Therefore,

$$b_t = r^t b_0$$

How do these solutions behave for different values of the per capita production r? Results with four values of r starting from $b_0 = 1.0$ are given in the following table.

t	$r = 2.0$	$r = 1.5$	$r = 1.0$	$r = 0.5$
0	1.0	1.0	1.0	1.0
1	2.0	1.5	1.0	0.5
2	4.0	2.25	1.0	0.25
3	8.0	3.37	1.0	0.125
4	16.0	5.06	1.0	0.0625
5	32.0	7.59	1.0	0.0312
6	64.0	11.4	1.0	0.0156
7	128.0	17.1	1.0	0.00781
8	256.0	25.6	1.0	0.00391

In the first two columns, $r > 1$ and the population increases each hour (Figure 1.7.102a and b). In the third column, $r = 1$ and the population remains the same hour after hour (Figure 1.7.102c). In the final column, $r < 1$ and the population decreases each hour (Figure 1.7.102d). We summarize these observations in the following table.

Value of r	Behavior of Population
$r > 1$	population increases
$r = 1$	population remains constant
$r < 1$	population decreases

A population with $r = 1$ exactly replaces itself each generation and retains a constant size, even though the individuals in the population change. This is consistent with our finding that any value of b is an equilibrium when $r = 1$ (Example 1.6.7).

Laws of Exponents and Logs

In the solution $b_t = r^t b_0$, the variable t appears in the exponent, in contrast to a function such as $f(t) = t^3$ where the variable t is raised to a power. For any positive number a, the **exponential function to the base a** is written

$$f(x) = a^x$$

and is read "a to the xth power." This function takes x as input and returns x factors of a multiplied together. The notation generalizes that used in equations such as

$$a^2 = a \cdot a$$

The key to using exponential functions is knowing the **laws of exponents**, summarized in the following table. This table also includes examples using $a = 2$ that can help in remembering when to add and when to multiply.

Laws of exponents

	General Formula	Example with $a=2$, $x=2$, and $y=3$
Law 1	$a^x \cdot a^y = a^{x+y}$	$2^2 \cdot 2^3 = 2^5 = 32$
Law 2	$(a^x)^y = a^{xy}$	$(2^2)^3 = 2^6 = 64$
Law 3	$a^{-x} = \frac{1}{a^x}$	$2^{-2} = \frac{1}{2^2} = \frac{1}{4}$
Law 4	$\frac{a^y}{a^x} = a^{y-x}$	$\frac{2^3}{2^2} = 2^{3-2} = 2$
Law 5	$a^1 = a$	$2^1 = 2$
Law 6	$a^0 = 1$	$2^0 = 1$

The exponential function is defined for all values of x, including negative numbers and fractions. What does it mean to multiply half an a or -3 a's together? These expressions must be computed with the laws of exponents.

Example 1.7.3 Negative Powers

To compute a^{-3}, apply law 3 to find

$$a^{-3} = \frac{1}{a^3}$$

For example,

$$2^{-3} = \frac{1}{2^3} = \frac{1}{8} = 0.125$$

Negative powers in the numerator are positive in the denominator. ▲

Example 1.7.4 Fractional Powers

To compute $a^{0.5}$, we raise this unknown quantity to the 2nd power (square it) and use law 2 to find

$$\left(a^{0.5}\right)^2 = a^{0.5 \cdot 2} = a^1 = a$$

Therefore, a to the 0.5 power is the number that, when squared, gives back a. In other words, a to the 0.5 power is the square root of a. For example

$$2^{0.5} = \sqrt{2} \approx 1.41421$$ ▲

For reasons that will make sense only with a bit of calculus (Section 2.8), the base most commonly used throughout the sciences is the irrational number

$$e = 2.718281828459\ldots.$$

The function

$$f(x) = e^x$$

which is read "e to the x," is called the **exponential function** to the base e, or simply the **exponential function** (Figure 1.7.103). Calculators and computers often abbreviate this as exp. The domain of this function consists of all numbers, and the range is all **positive** numbers.

Example 1.7.5 The Laws of Exponents for the Base e

- $e^3 \cdot e^4 = e^{3+4} = e^7$ (law 1).
- $e^3 + e^4$ cannot be simplified with a law of exponents.
- $(e^3)^4 = e^{3\cdot 4} = e^{12}$ (law 2).
- $e^{-2} = \frac{1}{e^2}$ (law 3).
- $\frac{e^4}{e^3} = e^{4-3} = e^1 = e$ (laws 4 and 5).
- $e^0 = 1$ (law 6).

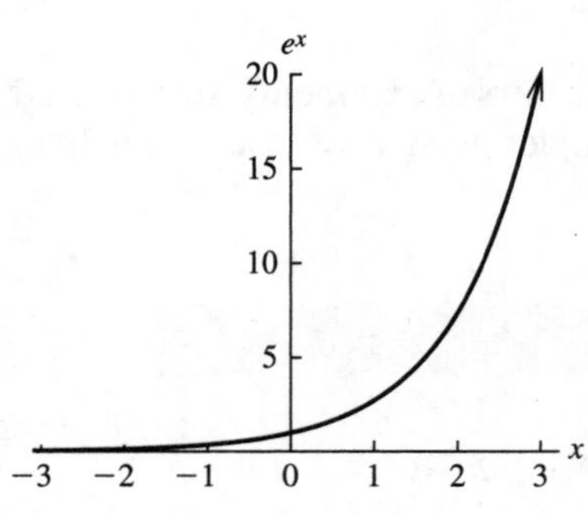

FIGURE 1.7.103
Graph of the exponential function

The graph of the exponential function crosses every positive horizontal line only once and thus passes the horizontal line test for having an inverse (see "Finding Inverse-Functions," Section 1.2, p. 17). The inverse is the natural log.

Definition 1.12 The inverse function of the exponential function e^x is called the **natural logarithm** (or natural log). The natural log of x is written $\ln(x)$. The natural logarithm has a domain consisting of all positive numbers.

From the definition of the inverse (Definition 1.6),

$$\ln(e^x) = x$$
$$e^{\ln(x)} = x$$

The graph of the natural logarithm increases from "negative infinity" near $x = 0$ through 0 at $x = 1$ and rises more and more slowly as x becomes larger (Figure 1.7.105). It is impossible to compute the natural log of a negative number (although more advanced fields of mathematics define these quantities using *complex numbers*).

Example 1.7.6 Exponential and Logarithmic Functions

- If $\ln(100) \approx 4.605$, then $e^{4.605} \approx 100$.
- If $e^5 \approx 148.41$, then $\ln(148.41) \approx 5$.
- If $\ln(0.1) \approx -2.303$, then $e^{-2.303} \approx 0.1$.
- If $e^{-3} \approx 0.04979$, then $\ln(0.04979) \approx -3$.

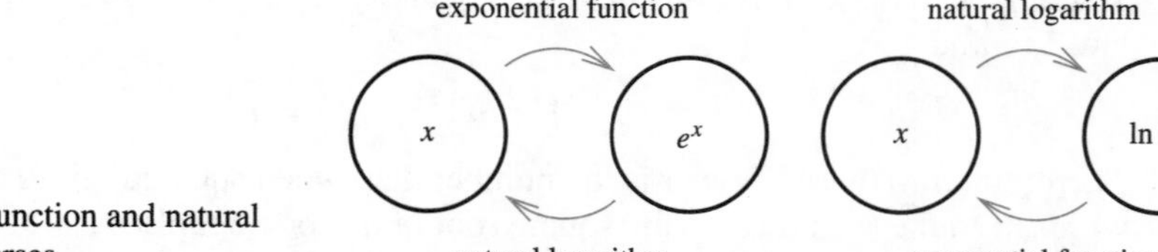

FIGURE 1.7.104
The exponential function and natural logarithm are inverses

The key to understanding natural logarithms is knowing the laws of logs, presented in the accompanying table, which are the laws of exponents in reverse.

The laws of logs (for x, $y > 0$, and any number p)

Law 1	$\ln(xy) = \ln(x) + \ln(y)$
Law 2	$\ln(x^p) = p\ln(x)$
Law 3	$\ln(1/x) = -\ln(x)$
Law 4	$\ln(x/y) = \ln(x) - \ln(y)$
Law 5	$\ln(e) = 1$
Law 6	$\ln(1) = 0$

Example 1.7.7 The Laws of Logs in Action

- $\ln(3) + \ln(4) = \ln(3 \cdot 4) = \ln(12)$, using law 1.
- $\ln(3) \cdot \ln(4)$ cannot be simplified with a law of logs.
- $\ln(3^4) = 4\ln(3)$, using law 2.
- $\ln(1/3) = -\ln(3)$, using law 3.
- $\ln(4/3) = \ln(4) - \ln(3)$, using law 4.

In some disciplines, people use the **exponential function with base 10,** or

$$f(x) = 10^x$$

Its inverse is the **logarithm to the base 10,** which is written

$$\log_{10} x$$

and is read "log base 10 of x." Just as $\ln(x) = y$ implies that $x = e^y$,

$$\log_{10} x = y$$

implies that

$$x = 10^y$$

For example, if $\log_{10} x = 2.3$, then $x = 10^{2.3} \approx 199.5$. In most ways, the exponential function with base 10 and the log base 10 work much like the exponential function with base e and the natural logarithm. All laws of exponents and logs are the same except law 5, which becomes

$$\text{Law 5 of exponents:} \quad 10^1 = 10$$
$$\text{Law 5 of logs:} \quad \log_{10}(10) = 1$$

The base e is more convenient for studying dynamics with calculus.

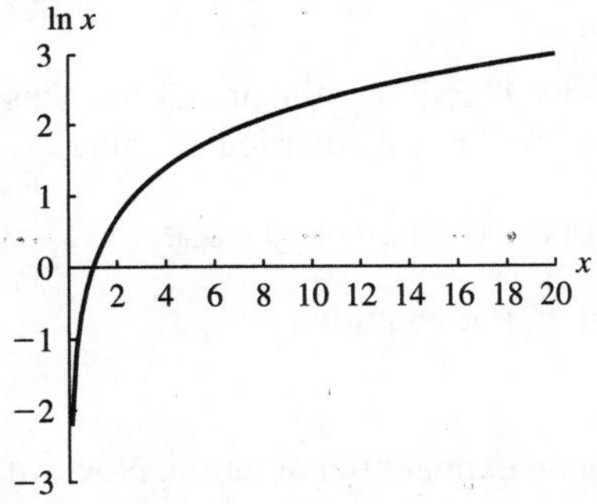

ln x
3
2
1
0
−1
−2
−3
2 4 6 8 10 12 14 16 18 20 x

FIGURE 1.7.105

Graph of the natural logarithm

Example 1.7.8 Converting Logarithms in Base 10 to Natural Logs

Suppose $\log_{10}(x) = y$. How can we find $\ln(x)$? By the definition of $\log_{10}$,

$$x = 10^y$$

Then

$$\begin{aligned} \ln(x) &= \ln(10^y) && \text{take the natural log of both sides} \\ &= y\ln(10) && \text{law 2 of logs} \\ &\approx 2.303y && \text{because } \ln(10) \approx 2.303 \end{aligned}$$

Rewriting in terms of $\log_{10}$, we find that

$$\ln(x) \approx 2.303 \log_{10}(x)$$

For instance, $\log_{10}(100) = 2$, so $\ln(100) \approx 2.303 \cdot 2 = 4.606$.

Expressing Results with Exponentials

We can use the laws of exponentials and logs to express

$$b_t = r^t b_0$$

in terms of the exponential function with base e. Because the exponential function and the natural logarithm are inverses, we can rewrite r as

$$r = e^{\ln(r)}$$

Then, using law 2 of exponents,

$$\begin{aligned} r^t &= \left(e^{\ln(r)}\right)^t \\ &= e^{\ln(r)t} \end{aligned}$$

Therefore, the **general solution** for the discrete-time dynamical system

$$b_{t+1} = r b_t$$

with initial condition b_0 can be written in exponential notation as

$$b_t = b_0 e^{\ln(r)t}$$

Example 1.7.9 Expressing a Solution with the Exponential Function

Consider the case $r = 2.0$ and $b_0 = 1.0$. Because $\ln(2.0) \approx 0.6931$, the solution is

$$b_t = 1.0e^{\ln(2.0)t} \approx 1.0e^{(0.6931)t}$$

What is the value of rewriting the solution in this way? Exponential notation makes it easier to answer questions about when a population will reach a particular value.

Example 1.7.10 Using a Solution Expressed with the Exponential Function: Increasing Case

When will the population described in the introduction, with solution

$$b_t = 2.0^t$$

reach 100.0? In Example 1.7.9 we wrote this solution in exponential notation. Now we can set $b_t = 100.0$ and solve for t with the steps

$$\begin{aligned} e^{\ln(2.0)t} &= 100.0 && \text{equation for } t \\ \ln(2.0)t &= \ln(100.0) && \text{take the natural log of both sides} \\ t &= \frac{\ln(100.0)}{\ln(2.0)} \approx 6.64 && \text{solve for } t \end{aligned}$$

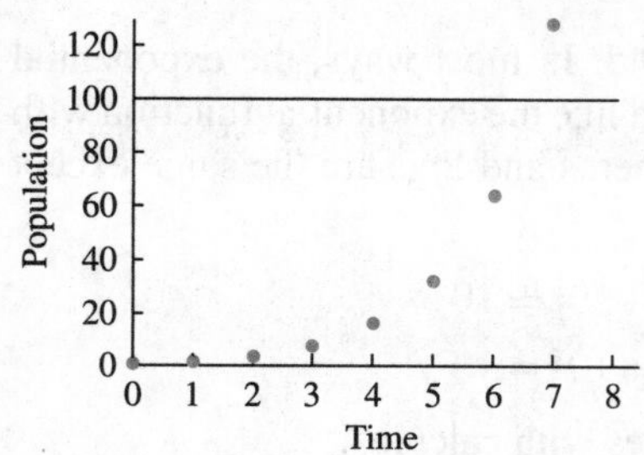

FIGURE 1.7.106
Using solutions to find times

The population will pass 100 million between hours 6 and 7 (Figure 1.7.106). The key step uses the natural log, the inverse of the exponential function, to remove the variable t from the exponent.

Example 1.7.11 Using a Solution Expressed with the Exponential Function: Decreasing Case

How long it will take a population with $r < 1$ to decrease to some specified value? Suppose $r = 0.7$ and $b_0 = 100$. The population decreases because $r < 1$. When will it reach $b_t = 2$? In exponential notation,

$$b_t = 100.0e^{\ln(0.7)t}$$

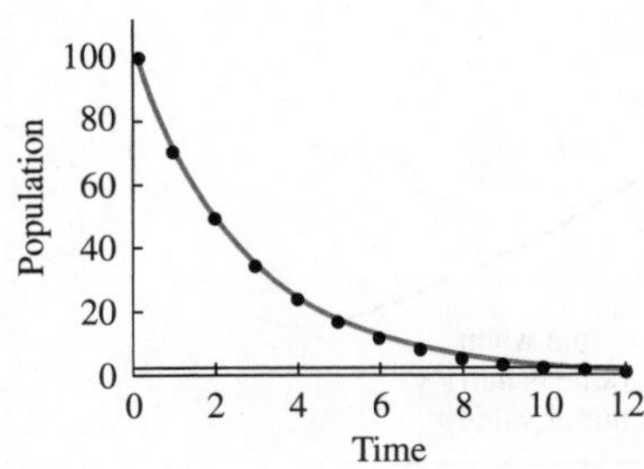

FIGURE 1.7.107

Using solutions to find times

Then $b_t = 2.0$ can be solved

$$100.0e^{\ln(0.7)t} = 2.0 \quad \text{equation for } t$$

$$e^{\ln(0.7)t} = 0.02 \quad \text{divide both sides by 100}$$

$$\ln(0.7)t = \ln(0.02) \quad \text{take the natural log}$$

$$t = \frac{\ln(0.02)}{\ln(0.7)} \approx 10.97 \quad \text{solve for } t$$

This population will pass 2.0 just before hour 11 (Figure 1.7.107).

Throughout the sciences, many measurements other than population sizes are described by exponential functions. In such cases, we write the measurement S as a function of t as

$$S(t) = S(0)e^{\alpha t}$$

The parameter $S(0)$ represents the value of the measurement at time $t = 0$. The parameter α describes how the measurement changes; α has dimensions of 1/time. When $\alpha > 0$, the function is increasing (Figure 1.7.108a and b). When $\alpha < 0$, the function is decreasing (Figure 1.7.108c and d). The function increases most quickly with large positive values of α, and it decreases most quickly with large negative values of α.

One important number describing such measurements is the **doubling time.** When $\alpha > 0$, the measurement is increasing. A convenient measure of the speed of increase is the time it takes the initial value to double.

Example 1.7.12 Computing a Doubling Time from Scratch

Suppose

$$S(t) = 150.0e^{1.2t}$$

with t measured in hours. This measurement starts at $S(0) = 150.0$ and doubles when

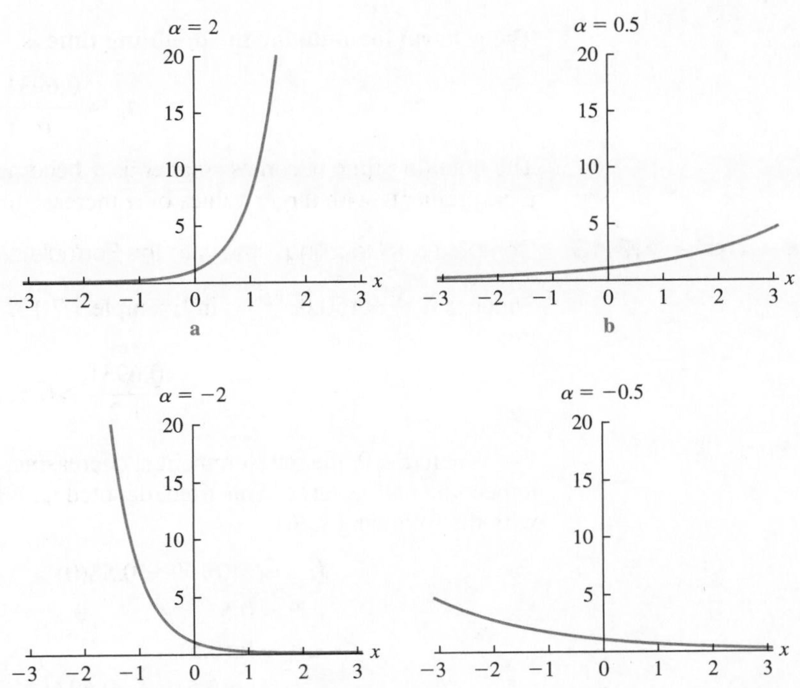

FIGURE 1.7.108

The exponential function with different parameter values in the exponent

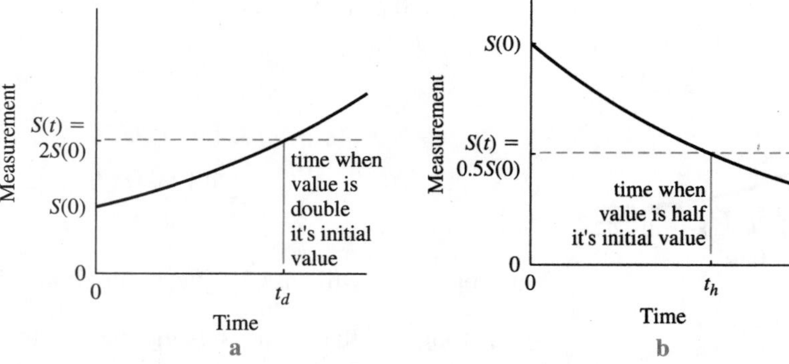

FIGURE 1.7.109
Doubling times and half-lives

$S(t) = 300.0$, or

$$\begin{aligned} 150.0e^{1.2t} &= 300.0 \\ e^{1.2t} &= 2.0 \\ 1.2t &= \ln(2.0) \\ t &= \frac{\ln(2.0)}{1.2} \approx 0.5776 \end{aligned}$$

As a check, we compute

$$S(0.5776) = 150.0e^{1.2 \cdot 0.5776} \approx 300.0$$

We can solve for the doubling time for a measurement following $S(t) = S(0)e^{\alpha t}$ by finding the time t_d when $S(t_d) = 2S(0)$,

$$\begin{aligned} S(t_d) &= S(0)e^{\alpha t_d} = 2S(0) && \text{equation for } t_d \\ e^{\alpha t_d} &= 2 && \text{divide by } S(0) \\ \alpha t_d &= \ln(2) && \text{take the natural log} \\ t_d &= \frac{\ln(2)}{\alpha} \approx \frac{0.6931}{\alpha} && \text{solve for } t_d \end{aligned}$$

The **general formula for the doubling time** is

$$t_d \approx \frac{0.6931}{\alpha}$$

The doubling time becomes smaller as α becomes larger, consistent with the fact that measurements with larger values of α increase more quickly.

Example 1.7.13 Computing a Doubling Time with the Formula

Suppose $S(t) = 150.0e^{1.2t}$ as in Example 1.7.13. Then $\alpha = 1.2$/hour, and the doubling time is

$$t_d \approx \frac{0.6931}{1.2} \approx 0.5776 \text{ hour}$$

When $\alpha < 0$, the measurement is decreasing, and we can ask how long it will take to become half as large. This time, denoted t_h, is called the **half-life** and can be found with the following steps.

$$\begin{aligned} S(t_h) &= S(0)e^{\alpha t_h} = 0.5S(0) && \text{equation for } t_h \\ e^{\alpha t_h} &= 0.5 && \text{divide by } S(0) \\ \alpha t_h &= \ln(0.5) && \text{take the natural log} \\ t_h &= \frac{\ln(0.5)}{\alpha} \approx -\frac{0.6931}{\alpha} && \text{solve for } t_h \end{aligned}$$

Therefore, the **general formula for the half-life** is

$$t_h \approx -\frac{0.6931}{\alpha}$$

The half-life becomes smaller when α grows larger in absolute value. Remember to apply this equation only when $\alpha < 0$.

Example 1.7.14 Computing the Half-Life

If a measurement follows the equation

$$M(t) = 240.0e^{-2.3t}$$

with t measured in seconds, then $\alpha = -2.3$/second and the half-life is

$$t_h \approx \frac{-0.6931}{-2.3} \approx 0.3013 \text{ second}$$

Example 1.7.15 Thinking in Half-Lives

Consider the measurement $M(t)$ given in Example 1.7.14, with a half-life of 0.3014 second. To figure out how much the value will have decreased in 2.0 seconds, we could plug into the original formula, finding

$$M(2.0) = 240.0e^{-2.3 \cdot 2.0} \approx 2.41$$

The value decreased by a factor of nearly 100. Alternatively, 2.0 seconds is

$$\frac{2.0}{0.3013} \approx 6.636$$

half-lives. After this many half-lives, the value will have decreased by a factor of $2^{6.636} \approx 99.46$, so that $M(2.0) \approx \frac{240.0}{99.46} \cong 2.41$. We can think of using half-lives as converting the exponential to base 2.

Conversely, if we are told the initial value and the doubling time or half-life of some measurement, we can find the formula. Instead of solving for the doubling time, we solve for the parameter α.

Example 1.7.16 Finding the Formula from the Doubling Time

Suppose $t_d = 26{,}200$ years for some measurement m. Because

$$t_d \approx \frac{0.6931}{\alpha}$$

we can solve for α as

$$\alpha \approx \frac{0.6931}{t_h} = \frac{0.6931}{26{,}200} = 2.645 \times 10^{-5}$$

If $m(0) = 0.031$, then the formula for $m(t)$ is

$$m(t) = 0.031e^{2.645 \times 10^{-5} t}$$

Example 1.7.17 Finding the Formula from the Half-Life

Suppose $t_h = 6.8$ years for some measurement V. Because

$$t_h \approx -\frac{0.6931}{\alpha}$$

we can solve for α as

$$\alpha \approx -\frac{0.6931}{t_h} = -\frac{0.6931}{6.8} \approx -0.1019$$

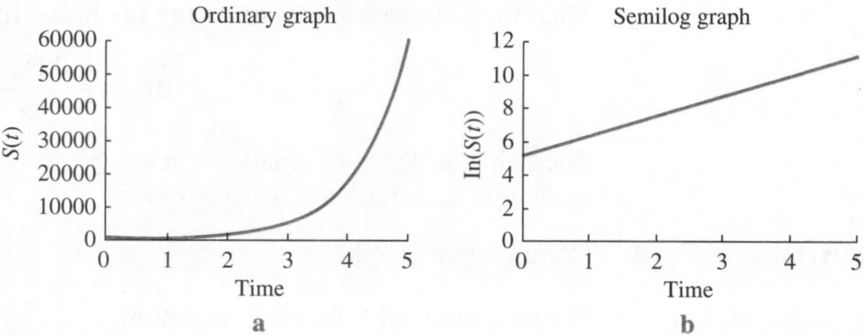

FIGURE 1.7.110
Original graph and semilog graph

If $V(0) = 23.1$, then the formula for $V(t)$ is

$$V(t) = 23.1e^{-0.1019t}$$

When a measurement follows an exponential function, the results are often plotted on a **semilog graph.**

Definition 1.13 A semilog graph plots the logarithm of the output against the input.

Example 1.7.18 A Semilog Graph of a Growing Value

Suppose

$$S(t) = 150.0e^{1.2t}$$

with t measured in hours (Example 1.7.13 and Figure 1.7.110a). To plot a semilog graph of $S(t)$ against t, we find the natural logarithm of $S(t)$.

$$\begin{aligned} \ln(S(t)) &= \ln\left(150.0e^{1.2t}\right) && \text{the natural logarithm of } S(t) \\ &= \ln(150.0) + \ln\left(e^{1.2t}\right) && \text{break up with law 2 of logs} \\ &\approx 5.01 + 1.2t && \text{evaluate } \ln(150.0) \text{ and cancel ln and exponent} \end{aligned}$$

Therefore, the semilog graph is a line with intercept 5.01 and slope 1.2 (Figure 1.7.110b) and transforms a curve into a line.

Example 1.7.19 A Semilog Graph of Some Data

Suppose we are to graph the following data.

Time	Value
0	120.12
1	24.34
2	2.19
3	0.89
4	0.056
5	0.078
6	0.125
7	0.346
8	1.128

The graph of the original data is difficult to read because the large vertical scale makes the small values almost indistinguishable (Figure 1.7.111a). If we take the logarithm of the data, however, the values are much easier to compare (Figure 1.7.111b).

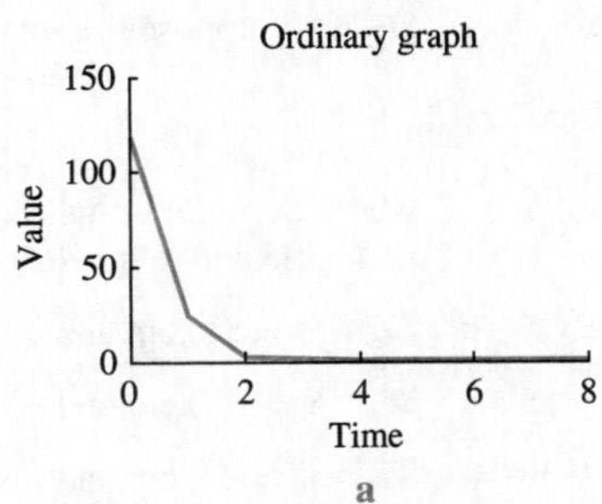

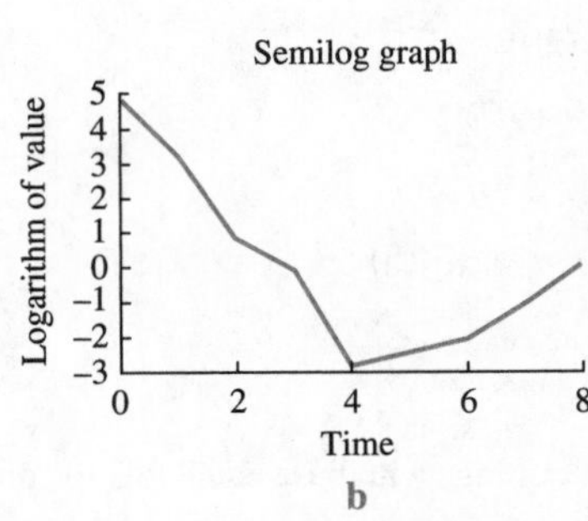

FIGURE 1.7.111
Original graph and semilog graph

Time	Value	Logarithm of Value
0	120.12	4.79
1	24.34	3.19
2	2.19	0.78
3	0.89	−0.12
4	0.056	−2.88
5	0.078	−2.55
6	0.125	−2.08
7	0.346	−1.06
8	1.128	0.12

We can see that the value reached a minimum at time 4 and increased steadily after that. ▲

Summary We generalized the discrete-time dynamical system for bacterial population growth to compute when populations would reach particular values. If some offspring die, the discrete-time dynamical system can be written in terms of the **per capita production** r. A population grows if $r > 1$ and declines if $r < 1$. The solution can be expressed as an **exponential function to the base *r*.** For convenience, exponential functions are often expressed to the base e, often called the **exponential function.** Using the laws of exponents, any exponential function can be expressed to the base e. The inverse of the exponential function is the **natural logarithm** or natural log. This function can be used to solve equations involving the exponential function, including finding **doubling times** and **half-lives.** Measurements that cover a large range of positive values can be conveniently displayed on a **semilog graph,** which reduces the range and which produces a linear graph if the measurements follow an exponential function.

1.7 Exercises

Mathematical Techniques

1–10 ▪ Use the laws of exponents to rewrite the following, if possible. If no law of exponents applies, say so.

1. 43.2^0
2. 43.2^1
3. 43.2^{-1}
4. $43.2^{-0.5} + 43.2^{0.5}$
5. $43.2^{7.2}/43.2^{6.2}$
6. $43.2^{0.23} \cdot 43.2^{0.77}$
7. $(3^4)^{0.5}$
8. $(43.2^{-1/8})^{16}$
9. $2^{2^3} \cdot 2^{2^2}$
10. $4^2 \cdot 2^4$

11–20 ▪ Use the laws of logs to rewrite the following, if possible. If no law of logs applies or the quantity is not defined, say so.

11. $\ln(1)$
12. $\ln(-6.5)$
13. $\log_{43.2} 43.2$
14. $\log_{10}(3.5 + 6.5)$

15. $\log_{10}(5) + \log_{10}(20)$

16. $\log_{10}(0.5) + \log_{10}(0.2)$

17. $\log_{10}(500) - \log_{10}(50)$

18. $\log_{43.2}(5 \cdot 43.2^2) - \log_{43.2}(5)$

19. $\log_{43.2}(43.2^7)$

20. $\log_{43.2}(43.2^7)^4$

21–22 ▪ Apply the laws of logs with base equal to 7 to compute the following.

21. Using the fact that $\log_7 43.2 \approx 1.935$, find $\log_7\left(\frac{1}{43.2}\right)$.

22. Using the fact that $\log_7 43.2 \approx 1.935$, find $\log_7[(43.2)^3]$.

23–26 ▪ Solve the following equations for x. Plug in your answer to check.

23. $7e^{3x} = 21$

24. $4e^{2x+1} = 20$

25. $4e^{-2x+1} = 7e^{3x}$

26. $4e^{2x+3} = 7e^{3x-2}$

27–30 ▪ Sketch graphs of the following exponential functions. For each, find the value of x where the function is equal to 7.0. For the increasing functions, find the doubling time, and for the decreasing functions, find the half-life. For what value of x is the value of the function 3.5? For what value of x is the value of the function 14.0?

27. e^{2x}

28. e^{-3x}

29. $5e^{0.2x}$

30. $0.1e^{-0.2x}$

31–32 ▪ Sketch graphs of the following updating functions over the given range, and mark the equilibria.

31. $h(z) = e^{-z}$ for $0 \le z \le 2$

32. $F(x) = \ln(x) + 1$ for $0 \le x \le 2$. (Although the equilibria cannot be found algebraically, you can guess the answer.)

Applications

33–36 ▪ Find the solution of each discrete-time dynamical system, express it in exponential notation, and solve for the time when the value reaches the given target. Sketch a graph of the solution.

33. A population follows the discrete-time dynamical system $b_{t+1} = rb_t$ with $r = 1.5$ and $b_0 = 1.0 \times 10^6$. When will the population reach 1.0×10^7?

34. A population follows the discrete-time dynamical system $b_{t+1} = rb_t$ with $r = 0.7$ and $b_0 = 5.0 \times 10^5$. When will the population reach 1.0×10^5?

35. Cell volume follows the discrete-time dynamical system $v_{t+1} = 1.5v_t$ with initial volume of 1350 μm^3 (as in Section 1.5, Exercise 37). When will the volume reach 3250 μm^3?

36. Gnat number follows the discrete-time dynamical system $n_{t+1} = 0.5n_t$ with an initial population of 5.5×10^4. When will the population reach 1.5×10^3?

37–40 ▪ Suppose the size of an organism at time t is given by

$$S(t) = S_0 e^{\alpha t}$$

where S_0 is the initial size. Find the time it takes for the organism to double and to quadruple in size in the following circumstances.

37. $S_0 = 1.0$ cm and $\alpha = 1.0$/day

38. $S_0 = 2.0$ cm and $\alpha = 1.0$/day

39. $S_0 = 2.0$ cm and $\alpha = 0.1$/hour

40. $S_0 = 2.0$ cm and $\alpha = 0.0$/hour

41–42 ▪ Suppose the size of an organism at time t is given by

$$S(t) = S_0 10^{\alpha t}$$

where S_0 is the initial size and t is measured in days. Find the time it takes for the organism to double in size by converting to base e. How long will it take to increase by a factor of 10?

41. $S_0 = 2.34$ and $\alpha = 0.5$

42. $S_0 = 2.34$ and $\alpha = 0.693$

43–46 ▪ The amount of carbon-14 (C^{14}) left t years after the death of an organism is given by

$$Q(t) = Q_0 e^{-0.000122t}$$

where Q_0 is the amount left at the time of death. Suppose $Q_0 = 6.0 \times 10^{10}$ C^{14} atoms.

43. How much is left after 50,000 years? What fraction is this of the original amount?

44. How much is left after 100,000 years? What fraction is this of the original amount?

45. Find the half-life of C^{14}.

46. About how many half-lives will occur in 50,000 years? Roughly what fraction will be left? How does this compare with the answer to Exercise 43?

47–50 ▪ Suppose a population has a doubling time of 24 years and an initial size of 500.

47. What is the population in 48 years?

48. What is the population in 12 years?

49. Find the equation for population size $P(t)$ as a function of time.

50. Find the 1-year discrete-time dynamical system for this population (figure out the factor multiplying the population in 1 year).

51–54 ▪ Suppose a population is dying with a half-life of 43 years. The initial size is 1600.

51. How long will it take to reach 200?

52. Find the population in 86 years.

53. Find the equation for population size $P(t)$ as a function of time.

54. Find the 1-year discrete-time dynamical system for this population (figure out the factor multiplying the population in 1 year).

55–58 ■ Plot semilog graphs of the values from the earlier problems.

55. The growing organism in Exercise 37 for $0 \le t \le 10$. Mark where the organism has doubled in size and where it has quadrupled in size.

56. The carbon-14 in Exercise 43 for $0 \le t \le 20000$. Mark where the amount of carbon has gone down by half.

57. The population in Exercise 47 for $0 \le t \le 100$. Mark where the population has doubled.

58. The population in Exercise 51 for $0 \le t \le 100$. Mark where the population has gone down by half.

Computer Exercises

59. Use your computer to find the following. Plot the graphs to check.
    a. The doubling time of $S_1(t) = 3.4e^{0.2t}$.
    b. The doubling time of $S_2(t) = 0.2e^{3.4t}$.
    c. The half-life of $H_1(t) = 3.4e^{-0.2t}$.
    d. The half-life of $H_2(t) = 0.2e^{-3.4t}$.

60. Have your computer solve for the times when the following hold. Plot the graphs to check your answers.
    a. $S_1(t) = S_2(t)$ with S_1 and S_2 from the previous problem.
    b. $H_1(t) = 2H_2(t)$ with H_1 and H_2 from the previous problem.
    c. $H_1(t) = 0.5H_2(t)$ with H_1 and H_2 from the previous problem.

61. Use your computer to plot the following functions.
    a. $\ln(x)$ for $10 \le x \le 100{,}000$
    b. $\ln(\ln(x))$ for $10 \le x \le 100{,}000$
    c. $\ln(\ln(\ln(x)))$ for $10 \le x \le 100{,}000$
    d. e^x for $0 \le x \le 2$
    e. e^{e^x} for $0 \le x \le 2$
    f. $e^{e^{e^x}}$ for $0 \le x \le 2$. Will your machine let you do it? Can you compute the value of $e^{e^{e^2}}$?

62. Use your computer to compute the following. Does this give you any idea why e is special?
    a. $2^{0.001}$
    b. $10^{0.001}$
    c. $0.5^{0.001}$
    d. $e^{0.001}$

1.8 Oscillations and Trigonometry

We have used linear and exponential functions to describe several types of relations between measurements. Important as they are, these functions cannot describe **oscillations,** processes that repeat in cycles. Heartbeats and breathing are examples of biological oscillations. In addition, the daily and seasonal cycles imposed by the movements of the earth drive sleep-wake cycles, seasonal population cycles, and the tides. In this section, we will use **trigonometric functions** to describe simple oscillations. Four numbers are needed to describe such oscillations with the **cosine** function: the **average,** the **amplitude,** the **period,** and the **phase.**

Sine and Cosine: A Review

Like many functions, the trigonometric functions have two interpretations: geometric and dynamical. Geometrically, the trigonometric functions are used to compute angles and distances. After briefly reviewing the geometry behind the **sine** and **cosine** functions, we will use them to study the dynamics of biological oscillations.

In applied mathematics, angles are measured in **radians.** For an angle with vertex at the center of a circle of radius 1, its measure in radians is equal to the length of the arc of the circle subtended (lying inside) the angle (Figure 1.8.112). Because the full circumference of a circle with radius 1 is 2π, 2π radians corresponds to 360°, or one complete revolution. There is thus a **basic identity** between radians and degrees given by

$$2\pi \text{ radians} = 360^\circ$$

From this, we derive the **conversion factors**

$$1 = \frac{2\pi \text{ radians}}{360^\circ} = \frac{\pi \text{ radians}}{180^\circ}$$

$$1 = \frac{360^\circ}{2\pi \text{ radians}} = \frac{180^\circ}{\pi \text{ radians}}$$

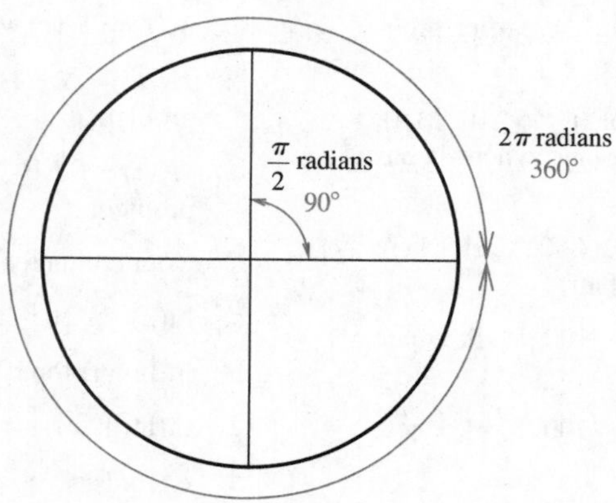

FIGURE 1.8.112
Degrees and radians

Example 1.8.1 Converting Degrees to Radians

To find 60° in radians, we convert

$$60^\circ = 60^\circ \times \frac{\pi \text{ radians}}{180^\circ} = \frac{\pi}{3}\text{radians}$$

Example 1.8.2 Converting Radians to Degrees

Similarly, to find 1.0 radians in degrees, we convert

$$1.0\,\text{radians} = 1.0\,\text{radians} \times \frac{180^\circ}{\pi \text{ radians}} \approx 57.3^\circ$$

The **sine function** and the **cosine function** take angles as inputs and return numbers between -1 and 1 as outputs. We write $\sin(\theta)$ and $\cos(\theta)$ to denote these functions, where the Greek letter θ (theta) is often used for angles. The sine and cosine give the Cartesian coordinates of points on the circle (Figure 1.8.113).

Definition 1.14 The Cartesian coordinates of the point on the unit circle an angle θ measured counterclockwise from (1, 0) are $(\cos(\theta), \sin(\theta))$.

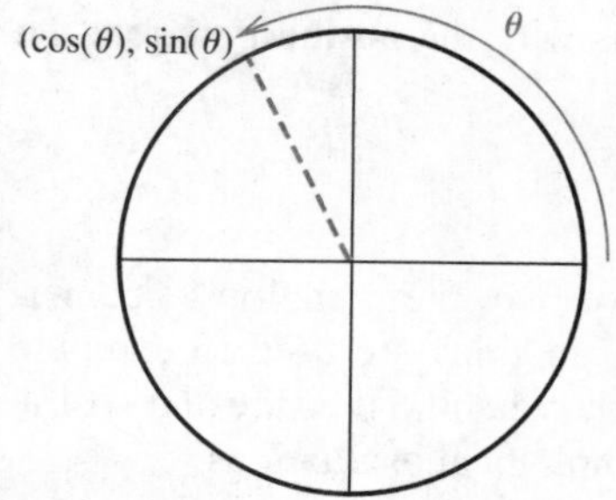

FIGURE 1.8.113
The definition of $\sin(\theta)$ and $\cos(\theta)$

Values of these functions for representative inputs are given in the following table.

Radians	Degrees	$\cos(\theta)$	$\sin(\theta)$	Radians	Degrees	$\cos(\theta)$	$\sin(\theta)$
0	0°	1	0	π	180°	-1	0
$\frac{\pi}{6}$	30°	$\frac{\sqrt{3}}{2}$	$\frac{1}{2}$	$\frac{7\pi}{6}$	210°	$-\frac{\sqrt{3}}{2}$	$-\frac{1}{2}$
$\frac{\pi}{4}$	45°	$\frac{\sqrt{2}}{2}$	$\frac{\sqrt{2}}{2}$	$\frac{5\pi}{4}$	225°	$-\frac{\sqrt{2}}{2}$	$-\frac{\sqrt{2}}{2}$
$\frac{\pi}{3}$	60°	$\frac{1}{2}$	$\frac{\sqrt{3}}{2}$	$\frac{4\pi}{3}$	240°	$-\frac{1}{2}$	$-\frac{\sqrt{3}}{2}$
$\frac{\pi}{2}$	90°	0	1	$\frac{3\pi}{2}$	270°	0	-1
$\frac{2\pi}{3}$	120°	$-\frac{1}{2}$	$\frac{\sqrt{3}}{2}$	$\frac{5\pi}{3}$	300°	$\frac{1}{2}$	$-\frac{\sqrt{3}}{2}$
$\frac{3\pi}{4}$	135°	$-\frac{\sqrt{2}}{2}$	$\frac{\sqrt{2}}{2}$	$\frac{7\pi}{4}$	315°	$\frac{\sqrt{2}}{2}$	$-\frac{\sqrt{2}}{2}$
$\frac{5\pi}{6}$	150°	$-\frac{\sqrt{3}}{2}$	$\frac{1}{2}$	$\frac{11\pi}{6}$	330°	$\frac{\sqrt{3}}{2}$	$-\frac{1}{2}$
π	180°	-1	0	2π	360°	1	0

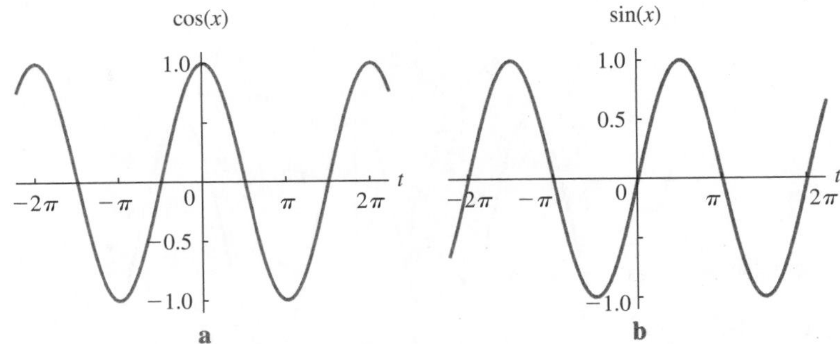

FIGURE 1.8.114
Graphs of the cosine and sine functions

Both the sine and cosine functions repeat every 2π radians (Figure 1.8.114). The value 2π is called the **period** of the oscillation. This means that adding (or subtracting) multiples of 2π to (or from) the argument does not change the value, so

$$\cos(\theta) = \cos(\theta + 2\pi) = \cos(\theta + 4\pi) = \cos(\theta + 2n\pi)$$
$$\cos(\theta) = \cos(\theta - 2\pi) = \cos(\theta - 4\pi) = \cos(\theta - 2n\pi)$$

for any value of θ and any integer n and similarly for the sine function.

Example 1.8.3 Periodicity of the Cosine Function

$$\cos\left(\frac{\pi}{4}\right) = \cos\left(\frac{\pi}{4} + 2\pi\right) = \cos\left(\frac{\pi}{4} + 4\pi\right) = \frac{\sqrt{2}}{2}$$
$$\cos\left(\frac{\pi}{4}\right) = \cos\left(\frac{\pi}{4} - 2\pi\right) = \cos\left(\frac{\pi}{4} - 4\pi\right) = \frac{\sqrt{2}}{2}$$

The graphs of sine and cosine have the same shape but are **shifted** from each other by $\pi/2$ rad (Figure 1.8.114). In equations,

$$\sin(\theta) = \cos\left(\theta - \frac{\pi}{2}\right)$$

Example 1.8.4 Relation Between Sine and Cosine

$$\sin\left(\frac{2\pi}{3}\right) = \cos\left(\frac{2\pi}{3} - \frac{\pi}{2}\right) = \cos\left(\frac{\pi}{6}\right) = \frac{\sqrt{3}}{2}$$

Because we can compute the sine function in terms of the cosine function, we will use cosine to describe oscillations.

Describing Oscillations with the Cosine

A measurement is said to **oscillate** as a function of time if the values vary regularly between high and low values. Oscillations that are shaped like the graph of the sine or cosine function are called **sinusoidal.** There are four numbers needed to describe an oscillation with the cosine function: the **average,** the **amplitude,** the **period,** and the **phase** (Figure 1.8.115).

- The **amplitude** is the difference between the maximum and the average (or the average and the minimum).
- The **average** lies halfway between the minimum and maximum values.
- The **period** is the time between successive peaks.
- The **phase** is the time of the first peak.

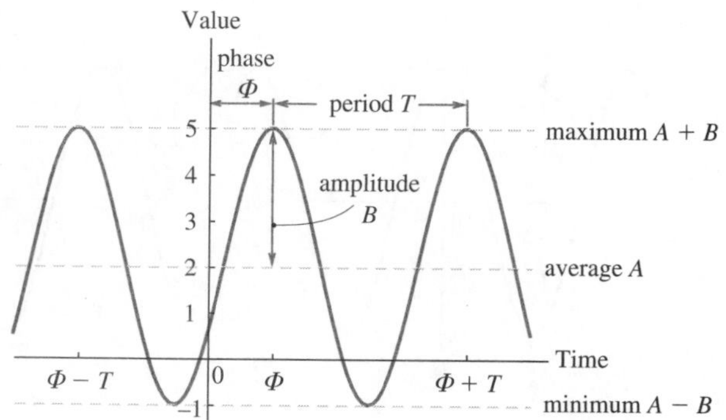

FIGURE 1.8.115
The four numbers that describe a sinusoidal oscillation

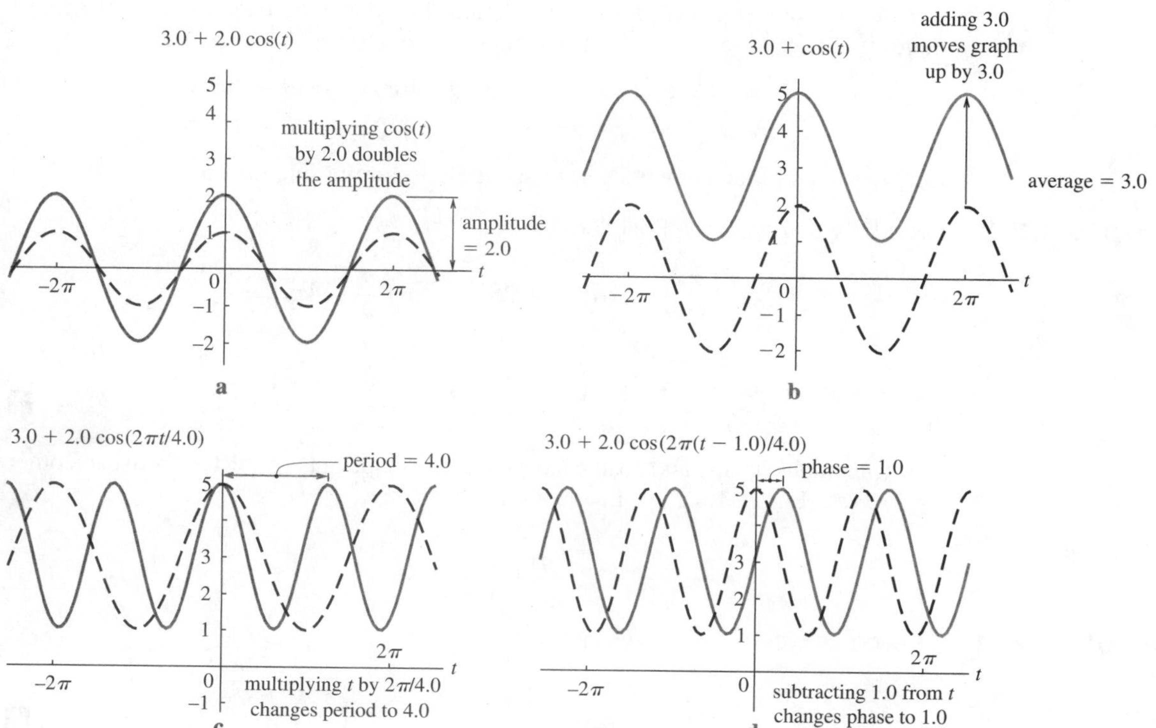

FIGURE 1.8.116
Building a function with different average, amplitude, period, and phase

We can build the oscillation shown in Figure 1.8.115 from the cosine function by **shifting** and **scaling** both vertically and horizontally (Section 1.3).

Example 1.8.5 Building an Oscillation by Shifting and Scaling the Cosine Function

Suppose we wish to build a function with an amplitude of 2.0, an average of 3.0, a period of 4.0, and a phase of 1.0. We can construct the formula in steps.

1. To increase the amplitude by a factor of 2.0, we scale vertically by **multiplying** the cosine by 2.0 (Figure 1.8.116a). The function is now

$$f(t) = 2.0\cos(t)$$

2. To raise the **average** from 0 to 3.0, we vertically shift the function by **adding** 3.0 to the function (Figure 1.8.116b), making

$$f(t) = 3.0 + 2.0\cos(t)$$

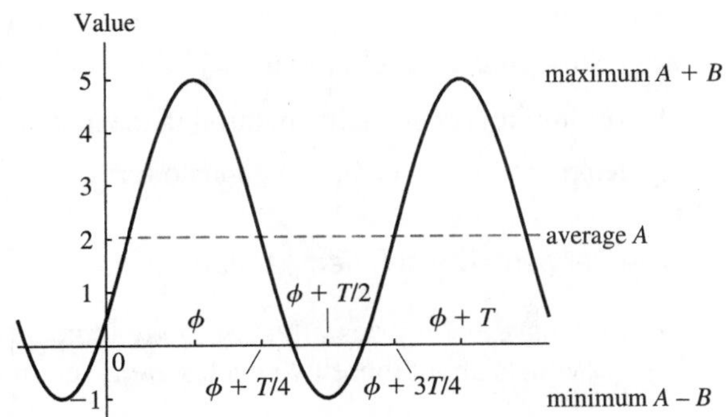

FIGURE 1.8.117
The guideposts for plotting $f(t) = A + B\cos\left(\frac{2\pi}{T}(t - \phi)\right)$

3. Next, we wish to decrease the period from 2π to 4.0. We do this by scaling horizontally by a factor of $\frac{2\pi}{4}$, or by **multiplying** the t inside the cosine by $\frac{2\pi}{4.0}$ (Figure 1.8.116c). Our function is now

$$f(t) = 3.0 + 2.0\cos\left(\frac{2\pi}{4.0}t\right)$$

4. Finally, we shift the curve horizontally so that the first peak is at 1.0 instead of 0.0. We do this by **subtracting** 1.0 from t (Figure 1.8.116d), arriving at the final answer of

$$f(t) = 3.0 + 2.0\cos\left(\frac{2\pi}{4.0}(t - 1.0)\right)$$

In general, a sinusoidal oscillation with amplitude B, average A, period T, and phase ϕ (phi) can be described as a function of time t with the formula

$$f(t) = A + B\cos\left(\frac{2\pi}{T}(t - \phi)\right) \tag{1.8.1}$$

This function has a maximum at $t = \phi$, has a minimum at $t = \phi + \frac{T}{2}$, and takes on its average value at $t = \phi + \frac{T}{4}$ and $t = \phi + \frac{3T}{4}$. Thereafter, it repeats every T (Figure 1.8.117).

Example 1.8.6 Plotting a Sinusoidal Function from its Equation

Suppose we wish to plot

$$f(t) = 2.0 + 0.4\cos\left(\frac{2\pi}{10.0}(t - 7.0)\right)$$

The amplitude is 0.4, and the average is 2.0, the period is 10.0, and the phase is 7.0 (Figure 1.8.118). The maximum is the sum of the average and amplitude, or $2.0 + 0.4 = 2.4$, and the minimum is the average minus the amplitude, or $2.0 - 0.4 = 1.6$. The first

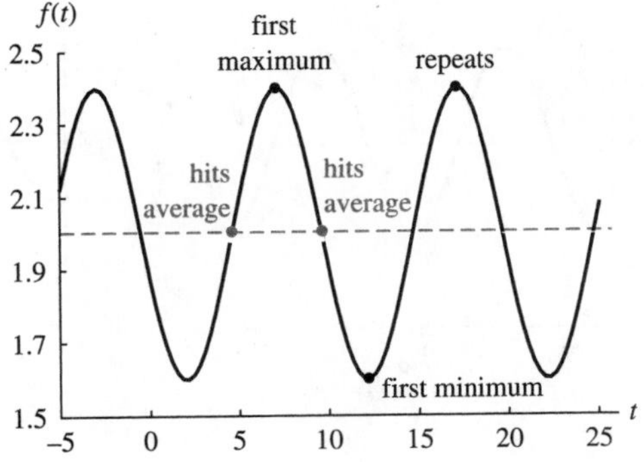

FIGURE 1.8.118
Graphing a sinusoidal oscillation from its equation

maximum occurs at the phase, or at $t = 7.0$. The average occurs 1/4 and 3/4 of the way through each cycle, or at $t = 7.0 + \frac{1}{4}(10.0) = 9.5$ and $t = 7.0 + \frac{3}{4}(10.0) = 14.5$. The minimum occurs halfway through the first period at $t = 7.0 + \frac{1}{2}(10.0) = 12.0$. The cycle repeats at $t = 17.0$, 27.0, and so forth. ▲

Example 1.8.7 The Daily and Monthly Temperature Cycles

Women have two cycles affecting body temperature: a daily and a monthly rhythm. The key facts about these two cycles are given in the following table.

	Minimum	Maximum	Average	Time of Maximum	Period
Daily cycle	36.5	37.1	36.8	2:00 P.M.	24 hours
Monthly cycle	36.6	37.0	36.8	Day 16	28 days

Assuming that these cycles are sinusoidal, we can use this information to describe these cycles with the cosine function.

The amplitude of a cycle is

$$\text{amplitude} = \text{maximum} - \text{average}$$

For the daily cycle, the amplitude is

$$\text{daily cycle amplitude} = 37.1 - 36.8 = 0.3$$

For the monthly cycle, the amplitude is

$$\text{monthly cycle amplitude} = 37.0 - 36.8 = 0.2$$

The phase depends on the time chosen as the starting time. We define the daily cycle to begin at midnight and the monthly cycle to begin at menstruation. The maximum of the daily cycle occurs 14 hours after the start, and that of the monthly cycle 16 days after the start. The oscillations can be described by the fundamental formula (Equation 1.8.1). For the daily cycle, with t measured in hours, the formula $P_d(t)$ is

$$P_d(t) = 36.8 + 0.3\cos\left(\frac{2\pi(t-14)}{24}\right)$$

(Figure 1.8.119a.) For the monthly cycle, with t measured in days, the formula $P_m(t)$ is

$$P_m(t) = 36.8 + 0.2\cos\left(\frac{2\pi(t-16)}{28}\right)$$

(Figure 1.8.119b.) ▲

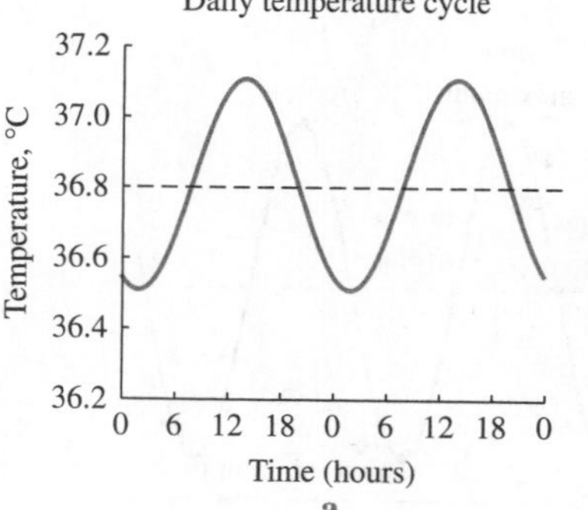

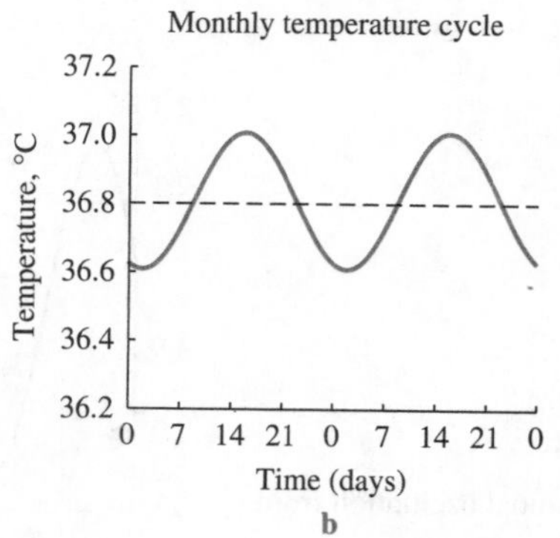

FIGURE 1.8.119

The daily and monthly temperature cycles

More Complicated Shapes

Real oscillations are not perfectly sinusoidal. Nonetheless, the cosine function is useful for describing more complicated oscillations. A powerful theory beyond the scope of this book, called **Fourier series,** shows how almost any oscillation can be written as the sum of many cosine functions with different amplitudes, periods, and phases (see Exercise 55).

As an illustration, we will combine the daily and monthly temperature cycles. To do so, we must write both cycles in the same time units, days. In days, the period of the daily cycle is 1.0 day and the phase (the time of the maximum) is

$$\text{phase in days} = 14 \text{ hours} \cdot \frac{1.0 \text{ days}}{24 \text{ hours}} \approx 0.583 \text{ day}$$

The equation for the daily cycle, with t measured in days, is

$$P_d(t) = 36.8 + 0.3\cos(2\pi(t - 0.583))$$

To figure out how the daily and monthly cycles combine, we cannot simply add them together, because

$$\begin{aligned} P_d(t) + P_m(t) &= 36.8 + 0.3\cos(2\pi(t - 0.583)) + 36.8 + 0.2\cos\left(\frac{2\pi(t-16)}{28}\right) \\ &= 73.6 + 0.3\cos(2\pi(t - 0.583)) + 0.2\cos\left(\frac{2\pi(t-16)}{28}\right) \end{aligned}$$

which has an average of 73.6.

To keep the average at the appropriate value of 36.8, we add only the two cosine terms to the average, getting a formula for the combined cycle of

$$P_t(t) = 36.8 + 0.2\cos\left(\frac{2\pi(t-16)}{28}\right) + 0.3\cos(2\pi(t - 0.583))$$

(Figure 1.8.120). In the course of one month, there is a single slow cycle, with 28 daily cycles superimposed. The maximum possible temperature can be found by adding the sum of the amplitudes of the daily and monthly cycles to the overall average. That is,

$$\text{maximum possible temperature} = 36.8 + (0.2 + 0.3) = 37.3$$

This maximum occurs only if each cycle takes on its maximum at the same time, which does not happen exactly in this case. It is closest at 2:00 P.M. on the 16th day of the cycle.

The minimum possible temperature can be found by subtracting the sum of the amplitudes of the daily and monthly cycles from the overall average, or

$$\text{minimum possible temperature} = 36.8 - (0.2 + 0.3) = 36.3$$

This minimum occurs only if each cycle takes on its minimum at the same time, which also does not happen exactly. It is closest at 2:00 A.M. on the 2nd day of the cycle.

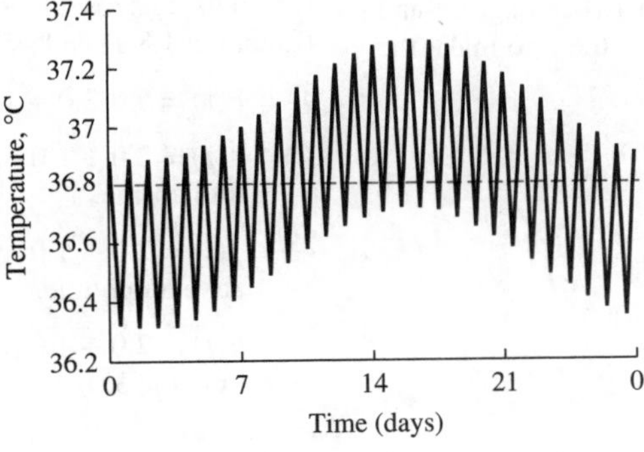

FIGURE 1.8.120

The combined effect of the daily and monthly temperature cycles

Summary **Sinusoidal** oscillations can be described mathematically with the **cosine** function. Four factors change the shape of the graph: the **amplitude** (the distance from the middle to the minimum or maximum), the **average** (the middle value), the **period** (the time between successive maxima), and the **phase** (the time of the first maximum). Functions with these parameters can be created by **shifting** and **scaling** the cosine function vertically and horizontally. Oscillations with more complicated shapes can be described by adding together appropriate cosine functions.

1.8 Exercises

Mathematical Techniques

1–6 ▪ Use a table or a calculator to find the values of sine and cosine for the following inputs (all in radians), and plot them **a.** on a graph of $\sin(\theta)$, **b.** on a graph of $\cos(\theta)$, **c.** as the coordinates of a point on the circle.

1. $\theta = \pi/2$
2. $\theta = 3\pi/4$
3. $\theta = \pi/9$
4. $\theta = 5.0$
5. $\theta = -2.0$
6. $\theta = 3.2$

7–14 ▪ Convert the following angles from degrees to radians, or vice versa.

7. $30°$
8. $330°$
9. $1°$
10. $-30°$
11. 2.0 radians
12. $\pi/5$ radians
13. $-\pi/5$ radians
14. 30 radians

15–20 ▪ There are 360° in a full circle because the ancient Babylonians were fond of the number 60 and its multiples (as an approximation to the 365 days in a year). In the 1790s, the French introduced another system for measuring angles called "grads," where 400 grads make up a full circle (or 100 grads make up 90°). Although they are found on many calculators, these units are almost never used. Write the basic identities between degrees and grads, and between radians and grads, and use them to make the following conversions.

15. 180° into grads
16. 60° into grads
17. $\pi/4$ radians into grads
18. 3.0 radians into grads
19. 150 grads into degrees
20. 250 grads into radians

21–26 ▪ The other trigonometric functions (tangent, cotangent, secant, and cosecant) are defined in terms of sin and cos by

$$\tan(x) = \frac{\sin(x)}{\cos(x)}, \quad \cot(x) = \frac{\cos(x)}{\sin(x)}$$

$$\sec(x) = \frac{1}{\cos(x)}, \quad \csc(x) = \frac{1}{\sin(x)}$$

Calculate the value of each of these functions at the following angles (all in radians). Plot the points on a graph of each function.

21. $\pi/2$
22. $3\pi/4$
23. $\pi/9$
24. 5.0
25. -2.0
26. 3.2

27–32 ▪ The following are some of the most important trigonometric identities. Check each of them at the points **a.** $\theta = 0$, **b.** $\theta = \pi/4$, **c.** $\theta = \pi/2$, **d.** $\theta = \pi$.

27. $\cos\left(\frac{\theta}{2}\right) = \sqrt{\frac{1+\cos(\theta)}{2}}$ for $0 \le \theta \le \pi$ (using the positive square root). Check only at points **a**, **c**, and **d**.
28. $\sin^2(\theta) + \cos^2(\theta) = 1$
29. $\cos(\theta - \pi) = -\cos(\theta)$
30. $\cos\left(\theta - \frac{\pi}{2}\right) = \sin(\theta)$
31. $\cos(2\theta) = \cos^2(\theta) - \sin^2(\theta)$
32. $\sin(2\theta) = 2\sin(\theta)\cos(\theta)$

33–36 ▪ The following are alternative ways to write formulas for sinusoidal oscillations. Convert them to the standard form (Equation 1.8.1) and sketch a graph.

33. $r(t) = 5.0(2.0 + 1.0\cos(2\pi t))$
34. $g(t) = 2.0 + 1.0\sin(t)$. Use Exercise 30 to change the sine into cosine.
35. $f(t) = 2.0 - 1.0\cos(t)$. Use Exercise 29 to get rid of the negative amplitude.
36. $h(t) = 2.0 + 1.0\cos(2\pi t - 3.0)$ (the factor 2π does not multiply the 3.0).

Applications

37–40 ▪ Find the average, minimum, maximum, amplitude, period, and phase from the graphs of the following oscillations.

37.

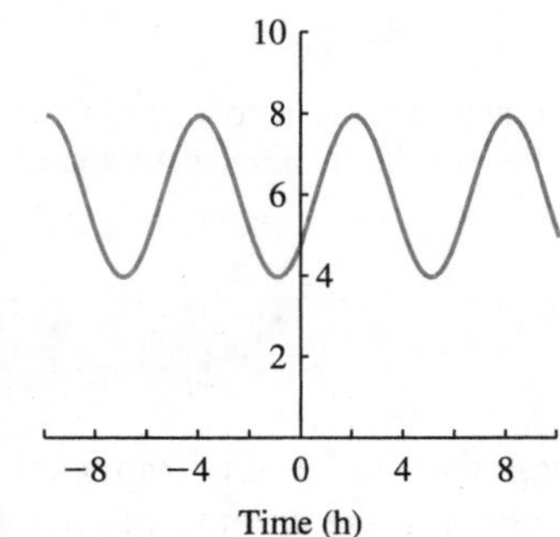

38.

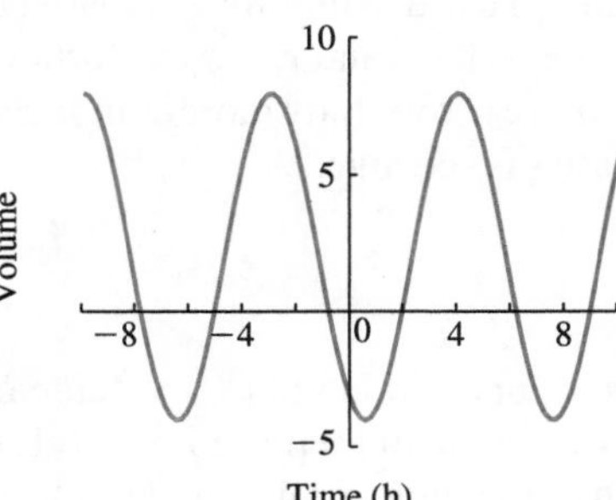

39.

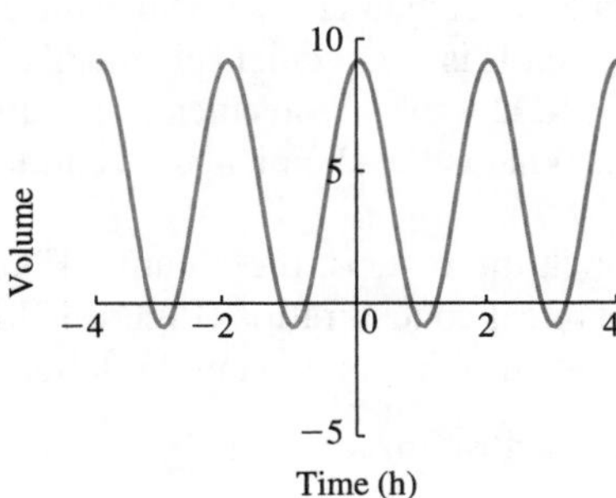

40.

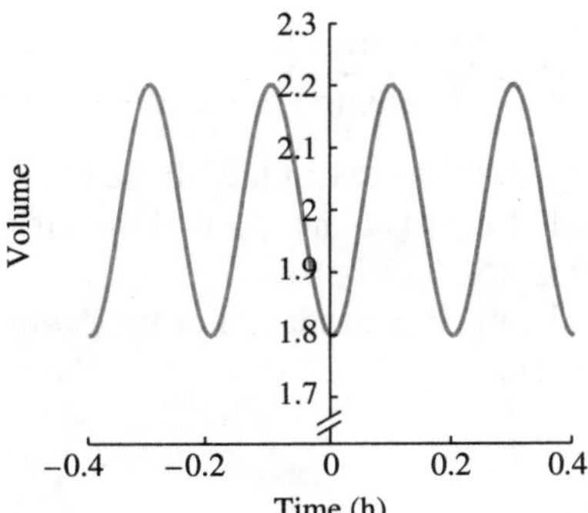

41–44 ▪ Graph the following functions. Give the average, maximum, minimum, amplitude, period, and phase of each and mark them on your graph.

41. $f(x) = 3.0 + 4.0\cos\left(2\pi \frac{x - 1.0}{5.0}\right)$

42. $g(t) = 4.0 + 3.0\cos(2\pi(t - 5.0))$

43. $h(z) = 1.0 + 5.0\cos\left(2\pi \frac{z - 3.0}{4.0}\right)$

44. $W(y) = -2.0 + 3.0\cos\left(2\pi \frac{y + 0.1}{0.2}\right)$

45–50 ▪ Oscillations are often combined with growth or decay. Plot graphs of the following functions, and describe in words what you see. Make up a biological process that might have produced the result.

45. $f(t) = 1 + t + \cos(2\pi t)$ for $0 < t < 4$, where t is measured in days.

46. $h(t) = t + 0.2\sin(2\pi t)$ for $0 < t < 4$, where t is measured in days.

47. $g(t) = e^t \cos(2\pi t)$ for $0 < t < 3$, where t is measured in years.

48. $W(t) = e^{-t}\cos(2\pi t)$ for $0 < t < 3$, where t is measured in years.

49. $H(t) = \cos(e^t)$ for $0 < t < 3$, where t is measured in years.

50. $b(t) = \cos(e^{-t})$ for $0 < t < 3$, where t is measured in years.

51–54 ▪ Sleepiness has two cycles, a circadian rhythm with a period of approximately 24 hours and an ultradian rhythm with a period of approximately 4 hours. Both have phase 0 and average 0, but the amplitude of the circadian rhythm is 1.0 sleepiness unit, and that of the ultradian is 0.4 sleepiness unit.

51. Find the formula and sketch the graph of sleepiness over the course of a day due to the circadian rhythm.

52. Find the formula and sketch the graph of sleepiness over the course of a day due to the ultradian rhythm.

53. Sketch the graph of the two cycles combined.

54. At what time of day are you sleepiest? At what time of day are you least sleepy?

Computer Exercises

55. Consider the following functions.

$$f_1(x) = \cos\left(x - \frac{\pi}{2}\right)$$

$$f_3(x) = \frac{\cos\left(3x - \frac{\pi}{2}\right)}{3}$$

$$f_5(x) = \frac{\cos\left(5x - \frac{\pi}{2}\right)}{5}$$

$$f_7(x) = \frac{\cos\left(7x - \frac{\pi}{2}\right)}{7}$$

a. Plot them all on one graph.

b. Plot the sum $f_1(x) + f_3(x)$.

c. Plot the sum $f_1(x) + f_3(x) + f_5(x)$.

d. Plot the sum $f_1(x) + f_3(x) + f_5(x) + f_7(x)$.

e. What does this sum look like?

f. Try to guess the pattern, and add on $f_9(x)$ and $f_{11}(x)$. This is an example of a **Fourier series,** a sum of cosine functions that add up to a **square wave** that jumps between values of -1 and 1.

56. Use a computer to graph solutions of the following discrete-time dynamical systems. Try three different initial conditions for each. Can you make any sense of what happens? Why don't the solutions follow a sinusoidal oscillation?

a. $x_{t+1} = \cos(x_t)$

b. $y_{t+1} = \sin(y_t)$

c. $z_{t+1} = \sin(z_t) + \cos(z_t)$

57. Plot the function $f(x) = \cos(2\pi \cdot 440x) + \cos(2\pi \cdot 441x)$. Describe the result. If these were sounds, what might you hear?

1.9 A Model of Gas Exchange in the Lung

The exchange of materials between an organism and its environment is one of the most fundamental biological processes. By following the amount of chemical step by step through the breathing process, we can derive a discrete-time dynamical system that models this process for a simplified lung. This discrete-time dynamical system describes how the outside air mixes with internal air, and takes the form of a **weighted average.** This model provides a framework we use to study more complicated biological processes such as the absorption or release of a chemical.

A Model of the Lungs

Consider a simplified breathing process. Suppose a lung has a volume of 3.0 L when full. With each breath, 0.6 L of the air is exhaled and replaced by 0.6 L of outside (or **ambient**) air. After exhaling, the volume of the lung is 2.4 L, and it returns to 3.0 liters after inhaling (Figure 1.9.121).

Suppose further that the lung contains a particular chemical with concentration 2.0 millimoles per liter before exhaling. (A mole is a convenient chemical unit indicating 6.02×10^{23} molecules, and a millimole is 6.02×10^{20} molecules). The ambient air has a chemical concentration of 5.0 mmol/L. What is the chemical concentration after one breath?

We must track three quantities through these steps: the volume (Figure 1.9.121), the total amount of chemical, and the chemical concentration (Figure 1.9.122). To find the total amount from the concentration, we use the fundamental relation

$$\text{total amount} = \text{concentration} \times \text{volume}$$

Conversely, to find the concentration from the total amount, rearrange the fundamental relation to

$$\text{concentration} = \frac{\text{total amount}}{\text{volume}}$$

One basic biological assumption underlies our reasoning: that air breathed out has a concentration equal to that of the whole lung. This means that the air in the lung is completely mixed at each breath, which is not exactly true.

Assuming also that neither air nor chemical is produced or used while breathing, we can track through the process step by step.

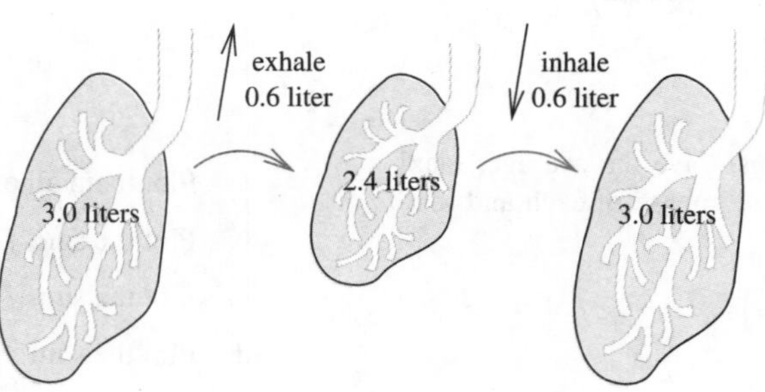

FIGURE 1.9.121
Gas exchange in the lung: the volume

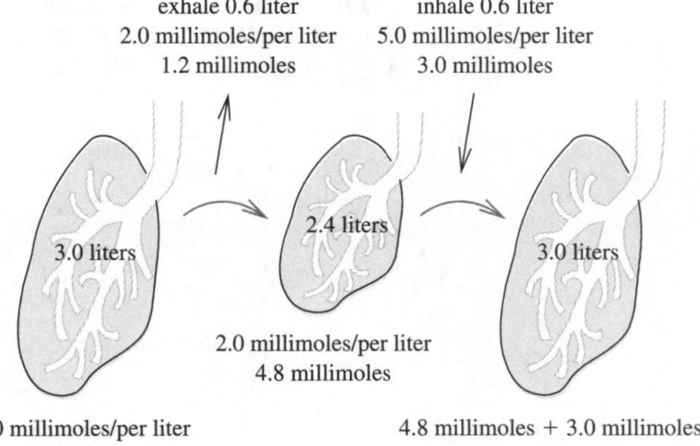

FIGURE 1.9.122
Gas exchange in the lung: the concentration

Step	Volume (L)	Total Chemical (mmol)	Concentration (mmol/L)	What We did
Air in lung before breath	3.0	6.0	2.0	Multiplied volume of lung (3.0) by concentration (2.0) to get 6.0.
Air exhaled	0.6	1.2	2.0	Multiplied volume exhaled (0.6) by concentration (2.0) to get 1.2.
Air in lung after exhalation	2.4	4.8	2.0	Multiplied volume remaining (2.4) by concentration (2.0) to get 4.8.
Air inhaled	0.6	3.0	5.0	Multiplied volume inhaled (0.6) by ambient concentration (5.0) to get 3.0.
Air in lung after breath	3.0	7.8	2.6	Found total by adding $4.8 + 3.0 = 7.8$ and divided by volume (3.0) to get 2.6.

Breathing creates a discrete-time dynamical system. The original concentration of 2.0 mmol/L is updated to 2.6 mmol/L after a breath. To write the discrete-time dynamical system, we must figure out the concentration after a breath, c_{t+1}, as a function of the concentration before the breath, c_t. We follow the same steps but replace 2.0 with c_t (Figure 1.9.123).

Step	Volume (L)	Total Chemical (mmol)	Concentration (mmol/L)	What We did
Air in lung before breath	3.0	$3.0c_t$	c_t	Multiplied volume of lung (3.0) by concentration (c_t) to get $3.0c_t$.
Air exhaled	0.6	$0.6c_t$	c_t	Multiplied volume exhaled (0.6) by concentration (c_t) to get $0.6c_t$.
Air in lung after exhalation	2.4	$2.4c_t$	c_t	Multiplied volume remaining (2.4) by concentration (c_t) to get $2.4c_t$.
Air inhaled	0.6	3.0	5.0	Multiplied volume inhaled (0.6) by ambient concentration (5.0) to get 7.5.
Air in lung after breath	3.0	$3.0 + 2.4c_t$	$1.0 + 0.8c_t$	Found total by adding $3.0 + 2.4c_t$ and divided by volume (3.0) to get $1.0 + 0.8c_t$.

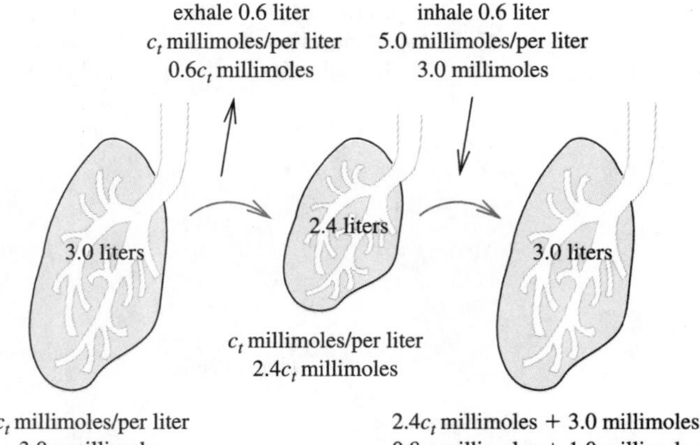

FIGURE 1.9.123
Gas exchange in the lung: finding the discrete-time dynamical system

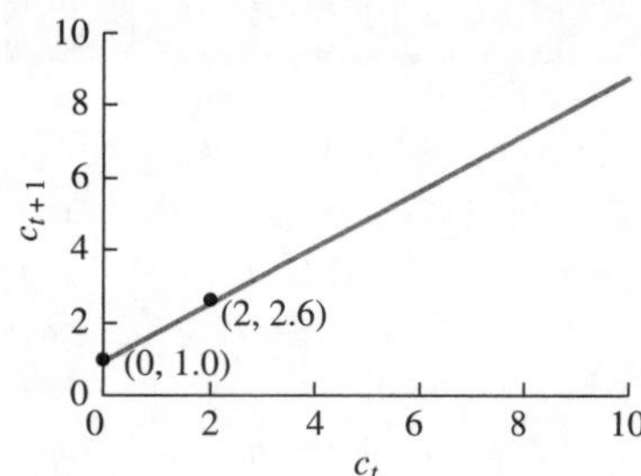

FIGURE 1.9.124
Updating function for the lung model

The discrete-time dynamical system is therefore

$$c_{t+1} = 1.0 + 0.8c_t$$

Checking, we find that an input of $c_t = 2.0$ gives

$$c_{t+1} = 1.0 + 0.8 \cdot 2.0 = 2.6$$

as found above. The graph of the updating function is a line with y-intercept 1.0 and slope 0.8 (Figure 1.9.124). We graph it by connecting the y-intercept (0, 1.0) with another point, such as (2.0, 2.6).

We can solve for equilibria and use cobwebbing to better understand this discrete-time dynamical system. Let the new variable c^* stand for an equilibrium. The equation for equilibrium says that an input of c^* is unchanged by the discrete-time dynamical system, or

$$c^* = 1.0 + 0.8c^*$$

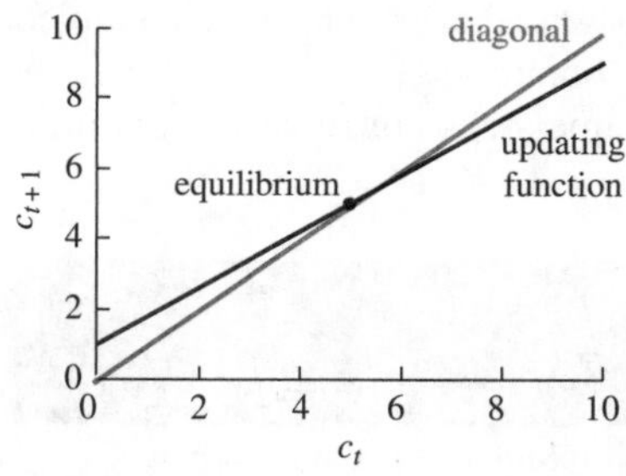

FIGURE 1.9.125
Equilibrium of the lung discrete-time dynamical system

The solutions of this equation are equilibria (Figure 1.9.125). To solve,

$c^* = 1.0 + 0.8c^*$	the original equation
$c^* - 0.8c^* = 1.0$	subtract $0.8c^*$ to get unknowns on one side
$0.2c^* = 1.0$	do the subtraction
$c^* = \frac{1.0}{0.2} = 5.0$	divide by 0.2

The equilibrium value is 5.0 mmol/L. We can check this by plugging $c_t = 5.0$ into the discrete-time dynamical system, finding

$$c_{t+1} = 1.0 + 0.8 \cdot 5.0 = 5.0$$

A concentration of 5.0 is indeed unchanged by the breathing process.

We can use cobwebbing to check whether solutions move toward or away from this equilibrium. Recall that cobwebbing is a graphical procedure for finding approximate solutions (Section 1.6), with steps summarized in the phrase "up to the updating function and over to the diagonal." Both the cobweb starting from $c_0 = 10.0$ (Figure 1.9.126) and the one starting from $c_0 = 0.0$ (Figure 1.9.127) produce solutions that approach the equilibrium at $c^* = 5.0$.

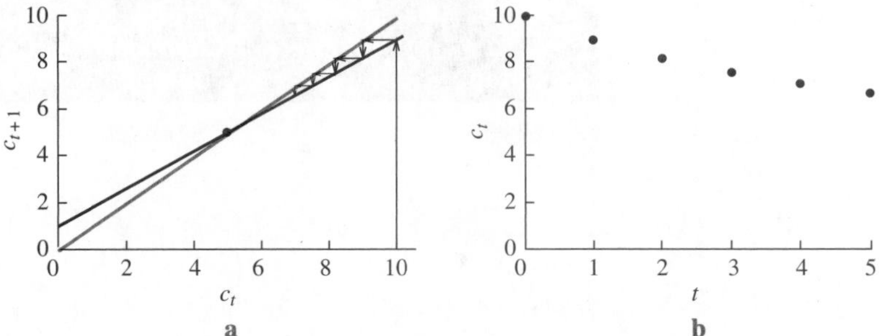

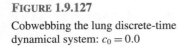

FIGURE 1.9.126
Cobwebbing the lung discrete-time dynamical system: $c_0 = 10.0$

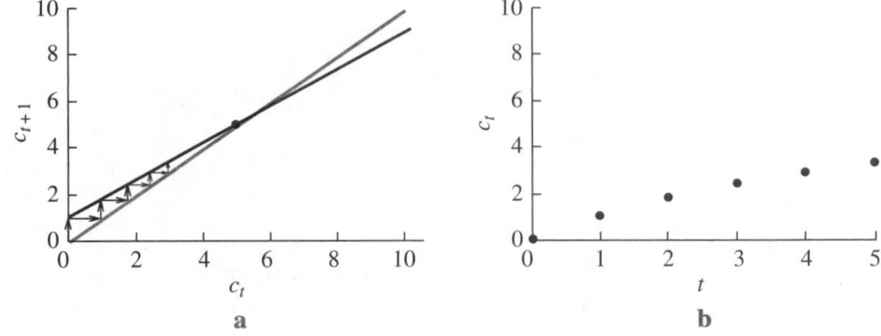

FIGURE 1.9.127
Cobwebbing the lung discrete-time dynamical system: $c_0 = 0.0$

The Lung System in General

In the previous subsection, we assumed that the lung had a volume of 2.0 L, that 1.5 L of air was exhaled and inhaled, and that the ambient concentration of chemical was 5.0 mmol/L. Suppose, more generally, that the lung has a volume of V L, that W L of air is exhaled and inhaled at each breath, and that the ambient concentration of chemical is γ (gamma). Our goal is to find the discrete-time dynamical system giving c_{t+1} as a function of c_t, which we can do by again following the breathing process step by step (Figure 1.9.128).

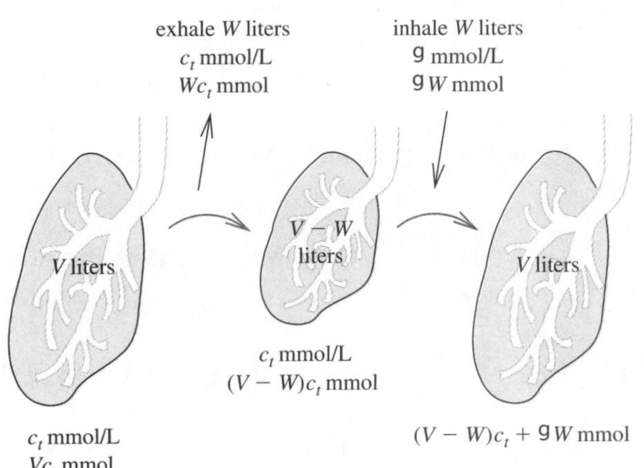

FIGURE 1.9.128
Gas exchange in the lung: general case

Step	Volume (L)	Total Chemical (mmol)	Concentration (mmol/L)	What We did
Air in lung before breath	V	$c_t V$	c_t	Multiplied volume of lung (V) by concentration (c_t) to get $c_t V$.
Air exhaled	W	$c_t W$	c_t	Multiplied volume exhaled (W) by concentration (c_t) to get $c_t W$.
Air in lung after exhalation	$V - W$	$c_t(V - W)$	c_t	Multiplied volume remaining ($V - W$) by concentration (c_t) to get $c_t(V - W)$.
Air inhaled	W	γW	γ	Multiplied volume inhaled (W) by ambient concentration (γ) to get γW.
Air in lung after breath	V	$c_t(V - W) + \gamma W$	$\frac{c_t(V - W) + \gamma W}{V}$	Found total by adding $c_t(V - W)$ to γW and divided by volume (V).

The new concentration appears at the end of the last line of the table, giving the discrete-time dynamical system

$$c_{t+1} = \frac{c_t(V - W) + \gamma W}{V}$$

This equation can be simplified by multiplying out the first term and dividing out the V,

$$\begin{aligned} c_{t+1} &= \frac{c_t(V - W) + \gamma W}{V} \\ &= \frac{c_t V - c_t W + \gamma W}{V} \\ &= c_t - c_t \frac{W}{V} + \gamma \frac{W}{V} \end{aligned}$$

The two values W and V appear only as the ratio $\frac{W}{V}$, which is the fraction of the total volume exchanged at each breath. For example, when $W = 0.6$ L and $V = 3.0$ L, $\frac{W}{V} = 0.2$, which means that 20% of air is exhaled each breath. We define a new parameter

$$q = \frac{W}{V} = \text{fraction of air exchanged}$$

to represent this quantity. We can then write the discrete-time dynamical system as

$$c_{t+1} = c_t - c_t q + \gamma q$$

or, after combining terms with c_t, as **the general lung discrete-time dynamical system,**

$$c_{t+1} = (1 - q)c_t + q\gamma \tag{1.9.1}$$

Example 1.9.1 Finding the Discrete-time Dynamical System with Specific Parameter Values

In the original example, $W = 0.6$ and $V = 3.0$, giving $q = \frac{W}{V} = 0.2$. Using $\gamma = 5.0$, the general equation matches our original discrete-time dynamical system because

$$c_{t+1} = (1 - 0.2)c_t + 0.2 \cdot 5.0 = 0.8c_t + 1.0$$

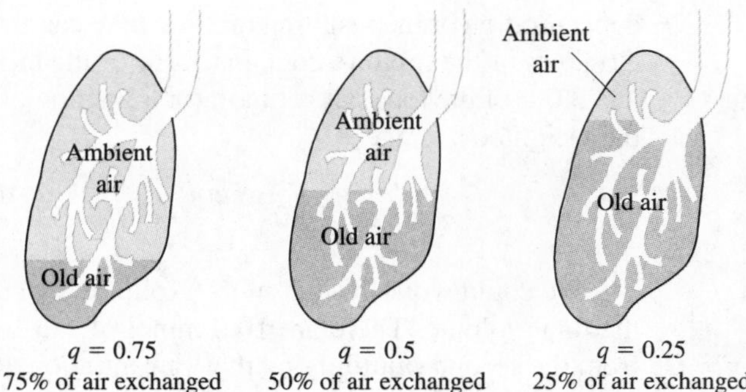

FIGURE 1.9.129
Effects of different values of q

After a breath, the air in the lung is a mix of old air and ambient air (Figure 1.9.129). The fraction $1-q$ is old air that remains in the lung, and the remaining fraction q is ambient air. If $q=0.5$, half of the air in the lung after a breath came from outside, and c_{t+1} is the average of the previous concentration and the ambient concentration. If q is small, little of the internal air is replaced with ambient air, and c_{t+1} is close to c_t. If q is near 1, most of the internal air is replaced with ambient air. The air in the lung then resembles ambient air, and c_{t+1} is close to the ambient concentration γ.

The right-hand side of this equation is a **weighted average.**

Definition 1.15 A weighted average of two values x and y is a sum of the form $qx+(1-q)y$ for some value of q between 0 and 1.

When $q=1/2$, the weighted average is the ordinary average. The concentration in the lung after breathing is a weighted average: a fraction $1-q$ of air is left over from the previous breath, and a fraction q is ambient air.

Example 1.9.2 A Weighted Average

Suppose $x=2$ and $y=5$. Then the weighted average that places a weight $q=0.8$ on x and a weight $1-q=0.2$ on y is

$$qx+(1-q)y=0.8\cdot 2+0.2\cdot 5=2.6$$

Less weight is placed on y, and the weighted average is closer to x.

Example 1.9.3 A Contrasting Weighted Average

Suppose $x=2$ and $y=5$, as in Example 1.9.2. The weighted average that places a weight $q=0.2$ on x and a weight $1-q=0.8$ on y is

$$qx+(1-q)y=0.2\cdot 2+0.8\cdot 5=4.4$$

More weight is placed on y, and the weighted average is closer to y.

Example 1.9.4 An Ordinary Average

Suppose $x=2$ and $y=5$, as in Examples 1.9.2 and 1.9.3. The ordinary average places equal weight $q=0.5$ on x and $1-q=0.5$ on y, and is equal to

$$qx+(1-q)y=0.5\cdot 2+0.5\cdot 5=3.5$$

This value is exactly in the middle between x and y.

Example 1.9.5 The Weighted Average Applied to Liquids

Suppose 1.0 L of liquid with a concentration of 10.0 mmol/L of salt are mixed with 3.0 liters of liquid with a concentration of 5.0 mmol/L of salt (Figure 1.9.130). What is the concentration of the resulting mixture? We can think of this as a weighted average. The 4.0 liters of the mixture contains 1.0 L of the high-salt solution (or a fraction of 0.25) and 3.0 L of the low-salt solution (or a fraction of 0.75). The resulting concentration is the weighted average

$$0.25 \cdot 10.0 \frac{\text{mmol}}{\text{L}} + 0.75 \cdot 5.0 \frac{\text{mmol}}{\text{L}} = 6.25 \frac{\text{mmol}}{\text{L}}$$

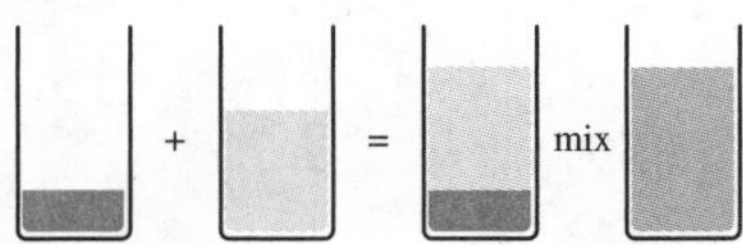

FIGURE 1.9.130
Mixing liquids as a weighted average

We could work this out more explicitly by computing the total amount of salt and the total volume. There are 10.0 mmol of salt from the first solution and 15.0 mmol from the second (multiplying the concentration of 5.0 mmol/L by the volume of 3.0 l), for a total of 25.0 mmol in 4 L. The concentration is

$$\frac{25.0 \text{ mmol}}{4.0 \text{ L}} = 6.25 \text{ mmol/L}$$

The weighted average provides a simpler way to find this answer.

Example 1.9.6 A Weighted Average with More Than Two Components

Weighted averages also work when more than two solutions are mixed. Suppose 1.0 L of liquid with a concentration of 10.0 mmol/L of salt is mixed with 3.0 L of liquid with a concentration of 5.0 mmol/L of salt and 1.0 L of liquid with a concentration of 2.0 mmol/L of salt. What is the concentration of the resulting mixture? In this case, the 5.0 L of the mixture is composed of 20% (or 0.20) of the high-salt solution, 60% (or 0.60) of the medium-salt solution, and 20% (or 0.20) of the low-salt solution. The resulting concentration is the weighted average

$$0.20 \cdot 10.0 \text{ mmol/L} + 0.60 \cdot 5.0 \text{ mmol/L} + 0.20 \cdot 2.0 \text{ mmol/L} = 5.4 \text{ mmol/L}$$

If we work this out explicitly, there is a total of 10.0 mmol from the first solution, 15.0 mmol from the second, and 2.0 from the last, for a total of 27.0 mmol in the 5.0 L of the mixture. The concentration is

$$\frac{27.0 \text{ mmol}}{5.0 \text{ L}} = 5.4 \text{ mmol/L}$$

The Equilibrium of the Lung Discrete-time Dynamical System The general discrete-time dynamical system for the lung model is

$$c_{t+1} = (1-q)c_t + q\gamma$$

Following the steps for finding equilibria gives

$$\begin{aligned} c^* &= (1-q)c^* + q\gamma && \text{the equation for the equilibrium} \\ c^* - (1-q)c^* - q\gamma &= 0 && \text{move everything to one side} \\ c^* - c^* + qc^* - q\gamma &= 0 && \text{multiply } c^* \text{ through } (1-q) \\ qc^* - q\gamma &= 0 && \text{do the subtraction} \\ q(c^* - \gamma) &= 0 && \text{factor out the } q \\ q = 0 \text{ or } c^* - \gamma &= 0 && \text{set both factors to 0} \\ q = 0 \text{ or } c^* &= \gamma && \text{solve each term} \end{aligned}$$

The key algebraic step comes after factoring. Remember that the product of two terms (such as q and $c^* - \gamma$) can equal 0 only if one of the terms is equal to 0.

What do these results mean? The first case, $q = 0$, occurs when no air is exchanged. Because there is no expression for c^* in this case, **any** value of c_t is an equilibrium. This make sense because a lung that is exchanging no air is, in fact, at equilibrium. The second case is more interesting. It says that the equilibrium value of the concentration is equal to the ambient concentration. Exchanging air with the outside world has no effect when the inside and the outside match. Doing the calculation in general explains

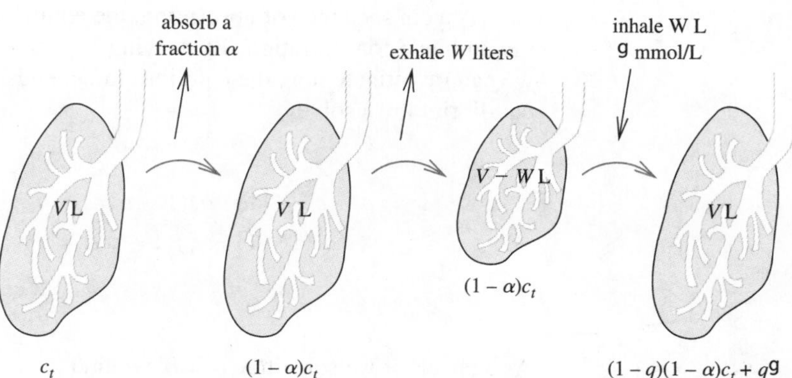

FIGURE 1.9.131
Dynamics of a lung with absorption

why the equilibrium of 5.0 mmol/L found in "A Model of the Lungs," Section 1.9, must match the ambient concentration of 5.0 mmol/L.

Lung Dynamics with Absorption

Our model of chemical dynamics in the lung ignored any absorption of the chemical by the body. We can now consider the dynamics of oxygen, which is in fact absorbed by blood. How will this change the discrete-time dynamical system and the resulting solution and equilibrium?

We can use the weighted average to derive the discrete-time dynamical system describing absorption. Suppose that a fraction q of air is exchanged each breath, that ambient air has a concentration of γ, and that a fraction α of chemical is absorbed before breathing out (Figure 1.9.131). After absorption, the concentration in the lung is $(1-\alpha)c_t$. Mixing produces a weighted average with a fraction $1-q$ of this old air and a fraction q of ambient air, giving the discrete-time dynamical system

$$c_{t+1} = (1-q)(1-\alpha)c_t + q\gamma$$

If $\alpha = 0$, this reduces to the original model of a lung without absorption.

Example 1.9.7 Absorption of Oxygen by the Lung

Consider again a lung that has a volume of 3.0 L and that replaces 0.6 L at each breath with ambient air (as in Figure 1.9.122). Suppose now that we are tracking oxygen, with an ambient concentration of 21%. Assume that 30% of the oxygen in the lung is absorbed at each breath. We then have

$$q = 0.2$$
$$\alpha = 0.3$$
$$\gamma = 0.21$$

The discrete-time dynamical system is then

$$c_{t+1} = 0.8 \cdot 0.7c_t + 0.2 \cdot 0.21 = 0.56c_t + 0.042$$

The equilibrium concentration in the lung solves

$$c^* = 0.56c^* + 0.042$$
$$0.44c^* = 0.042$$
$$c^* \approx 0.095$$

The equilibrium concentration of oxygen in the lung, which is equal to the concentration of oxygen in the air breathed out, would be about 9.5%, or less than half the ambient concentration.

As a consequence of absorption, the equilibrium concentration will be lower than the ambient concentration. By solving for the equilibrium of the system in general, we can investigate how the equilibrium depends on the fraction absorbed. To find the equilibrium, we solve

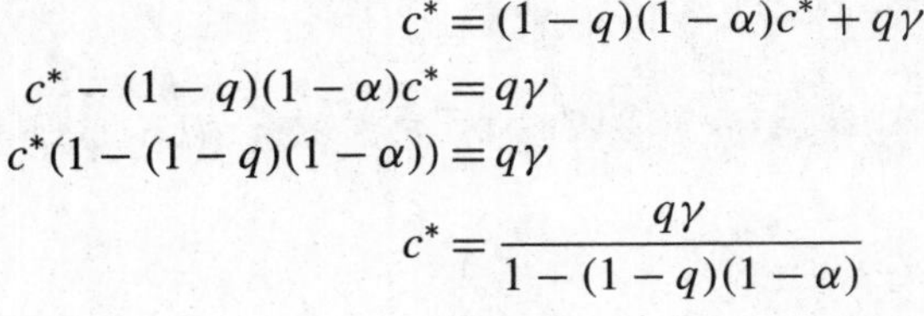

$$\begin{aligned} c^* &= (1-q)(1-\alpha)c^* + q\gamma \\ c^* - (1-q)(1-\alpha)c^* &= q\gamma \\ c^*(1-(1-q)(1-\alpha)) &= q\gamma \\ c^* &= \frac{q\gamma}{1-(1-q)(1-\alpha)} \end{aligned}$$

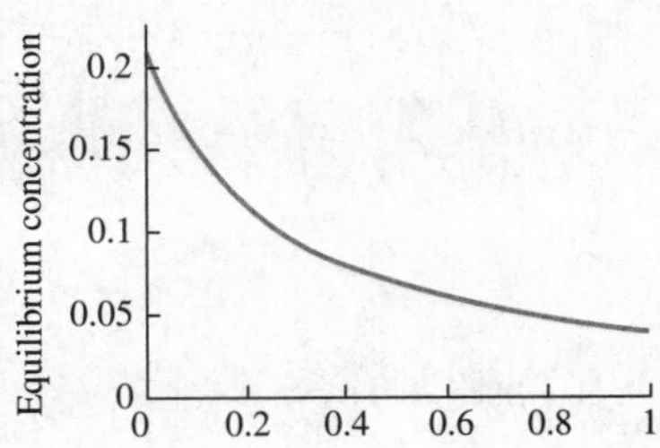

FIGURE 1.9.132
Equilibrium as a function of α

As a check, if we substitute $\alpha = 0$, we find

$$c^* = \frac{q\gamma}{1-(1-q)} = \frac{q\gamma}{q} = \gamma$$

matching the result without absorption.

Example 1.9.8 The Equilibrium Concentration of Oxygen As a Function of α

With the parameter values $q = 0.2$ and $\gamma = 0.21$, we find

$$c^* = \frac{0.2 \cdot 0.21}{1-0.8(1-\alpha)} = \frac{0.042}{1-0.8(1-\alpha)}$$

By substituting values of α ranging from $\alpha = 0$ to $\alpha = 1$, we can plot the equilibrium concentration as a function of absorption (Figure 1.9.132).

Example 1.9.9 Finding α from the Equilibrium Concentration of Oxygen

The actual oxygen concentration in exhaled air is approximately 15%. What fraction of oxygen is in fact absorbed? We can find this by solving for the value of α that produces $c^* = 0.15$.

$$\begin{aligned} 0.15 &= \frac{0.042}{1-0.8(1-\alpha)} \\ 0.15(1-0.8(1-\alpha)) &= 0.042 \\ 0.15(0.2+0.8\alpha) &= 0.042 \\ 0.2+0.8\alpha &= \frac{0.042}{0.15} = 0.28 \\ 0.8\alpha &= 0.08 \\ \alpha &= 0.1 \end{aligned}$$

Rather surprisingly, the lung absorbs only about 10% of the available oxygen, leading to exhaled air that has nearly 30% less oxygen than ambient air.

Summary This section develops a mathematical model of chemical concentration in the lung. Starting from an understanding of how a lung exchanges air, we derived a discrete-time dynamical system for the chemical concentration. The discrete-time dynamical system can be described as a **weighted average** of the internal concentration and the **ambient concentration.** The equilibrium is equal to the ambient concentration, and cobwebbing diagrams indicate that solutions approach this equilibrium. Including absorption produces a slightly more complicated model, with an equilibrium that is less than the ambient concentration. We used this model to investigate the dynamics of oxygen in the lung.

1.9 Exercises

Mathematical Techniques

1–4 ▪ Use the idea of the weighted average to find the following.

1. 1.0 L of water at 30°C is mixed with 2.0 L of water at 100°C. What is the temperature of the resulting mixture?
2. 2.0 ml of water with a salt concentration of 0.85 moles/L is mixed with 5.0 ml of water with a salt concentration of 0.70 moles/L. What is the concentration of the mixture?
3. In a class of 52 students, 20 scored 50 on a test, 18 scored 75, and the rest scored 100. What was the average score?
4. In a class of 100 students, 10 score at 20, 20 score at 40, 30 score at 60, and 40 score at 80. What is the average score in the class?

5–8 ▪ Express the following weighted averages in terms of the given variables.

5. 1.0 L of water at temperature T_1 is mixed with 2.0 L of water at temperature T_2. What is the temperature of the resulting mixture? Set $T_1 = 30$ and $T_2 = 100$, and compare with the result of Exercise 1.
6. V_1 L of water at 30°C is mixed with V_2 L of water at 100°C. What is the temperature of the resulting mixture? Set $V_1 = 1.0$ and $V_2 = 2.0$, and compare with the result of Exercise 1.
7. V_1 L of water at temperature T_1 is mixed with V_2 L of water at temperature T_2. What is the temperature of the resulting mixture?
8. V_1 L of water at temperature T_1 is mixed with V_2 L of water at temperature T_2 and V_3 L of water at temperature T_3. What is the temperature of the resulting mixture?

9–12 ▪ The following are similar to examples of weighted averages with absorption.

9. 1.0 L of water at 30°C is to be mixed with 2.0 L of water at 100°C, as in Exercise 1. Before mixing, however, the temperate of each moves halfway to 0°C (so the 30°C water cools to 15°C). What is the temperature of the resulting mixture? Is this half the temperature of the result in Exercise 1?
10. 2.0 ml of water with a salt concentration of 0.85 moles/L is to be mixed with 5.0 ml of water with a salt concentration of 0.70 moles/L, as in Exercise 2. Before mixing, however, evaporation leads the concentration of each component to double. What is the concentration of the mixture? Is it exactly twice the concentration found in Exercise 2?
11. In a class of 52 students, 20 scored 50 on a test, 18 scored 75, and the rest scored 100. The professor suspects cheating, however, and deducts 10 from each score. What is the average score after the deduction? Is it exactly 10 less than the average found in Exercise 3?
12. In a class of 100 students, 10 score at 20, 20 score at 40, 30 score at 60, and 40 score at 80, as in Exercise 4. Because students did so poorly, the professor moves each score halfway up toward 100 (so the students with 20 are moved up to 60). What is the average score in the class? Is the new average the old average moved halfway to 100?

Applications

13–16 ▪ Suppose that the volume of the lung is V, the amount breathed in and out is W, and the ambient concentration is γ mmol/L. For each of the given sets of parameter values and the given initial condition, find the following:

a. The amount of chemical in the lung before breathing
b. The amount of chemical breathed out
c. The amount of chemical in the lung after breathing out
d. The amount of chemical breathed in
e. The amount of chemical in the lung after breathing in
f. The concentration of chemical in the lung after breathing in
g. Compare this result with the result of using the general lung discrete-time dynamical system (Equation 1.9.1). Remember that $q = W/V$.

13. $V = 2.0$ L, $W = 0.5$ L, $\gamma = 5.0$ mmol/L, $c_0 = 1.0$ mmol/L
14. $V = 1.0$ L, $W = 0.1$ L, $\gamma = 8.0$ mmol/L, $c_0 = 4.0$ mmol/L
15. $V = 1.0$ L, $W = 0.9$ L, $\gamma = 5.0$ mmol/L, $c_0 = 9.0$ mmol/L
16. $V = 10.0$ L, $W = 0.2$ L, $\gamma = 1.0$ mmol/L, $c_0 = 9.0$ mmol/L

17–20 ▪ Find and graph the updating function in the following cases. Cobweb for three steps, starting from the points indicated in the earlier problems. Sketch the solutions.

17. The situation in Exercise 13.
18. The situation in Exercise 14.
19. The situation in Exercise 15.
20. The situation in Exercise 16.

21–24 ▪ Find the lung discrete-time dynamical system with the following parameter values, and compute the equilibrium. Check that it matches the formula $c^* = \gamma$.

21. $V = 2.0$ L, $W = 0.5$ L, $\gamma = 5.0$ mmol/L, $c_0 = 1.0$ mmol/L (as in Exercise 13).
22. $V = 1.0$ L, $W = 0.1$ L, $\gamma = 8.0$ mmol/L, $c_0 = 4.0$ mmol/L (as in Exercise 14).
23. $V = 1.0$ L, $W = 0.9$ L, $\gamma = 5.0$ mmol/L, $c_0 = 9.0$ mmol/L (as in Exercise 15).
24. $V = 10.0$ L, $W = 0.2$ L, $\gamma = 1.0$ mmol/L, $c_0 = 9.0$ mmol/L (as in Exercise 16).

25–26 ▪ The following problems investigate what happens if the breathing rate changes in the models of absorption examined in "Lung Dynamics with Absorption," Section 1.9. Use an external concentration of $\gamma = 0.21$, as before.

25. Find the equilibrium oxygen concentration if the fraction of air exchanged is $q = 0.4$ and the fraction absorbed is $\alpha = 0.1$.

Can you explain why the concentration becomes higher even though the person is breathing more?

26. Find the equilibrium oxygen concentration if the fraction of air exchanged decreases to $q = 0.1$ and the fraction absorbed decreases to $\alpha = 0.05$. Think of this as a person gasping for breath. Why is the concentration nearly the same as the value found in Example 1.9.9? Does this mean that gasping for breath is OK?

27–30 ▪ The following problems investigate absorption that is not proportional to the concentration in the lung, as in "Lung Dynamics with Absorption," Section 1.9. Assume an external concentration of $\gamma = 0.21$ and $q = 0.2$.

27. Suppose that the oxygen concentration is reduced by 2% at each breath. Find the discrete-time dynamical system and the equilibrium. Are there values of c_t for which the system does not make sense?

28. Suppose that the oxygen concentration is reduced by 3% at each breath. Find the discrete-time dynamical system and the equilibrium. Are there values of c_t for which the system does not make sense?

29. Suppose that the amount absorbed is $0.2(c_t - 0.05)$ if $c_t \geq 0.05$. This models a case where the only oxygen available is that in excess of the concentration in the blood, which corresponds roughly to 5%.

30. Consider a case like Exercise 29, but suppose that the amount absorbed is $0.1(c_t - 0.05)$ if $c_t \geq 0.05$. Why is the concentration different from that found in Example 1.9.9?

31–32 ▪ On the basis of the problems investigating absorption that is not proportional to the concentration in the lung (Exercises 27–30), find the value of the parameter that produces an exhaled concentration of exactly 0.15. Assume $\gamma = 0.21$ and $q = 0.2$.

31. Suppose that the concentration is reduced by an amount A (generalizing the case in Exercises 27 and 28). Does the amount of oxygen absorbed match that found in Example 1.9.9?

32. Suppose that the amount absorbed is $\alpha(c_t - 0.05)$ (generalizing the case where only available oxygen is absorbed in Exercises 29 and 30). Does the amount of oxygen absorbed match that found in Example 1.9.9?

33–34 ▪ The following problems investigate production of carbon dioxide by the lung. Suppose that the concentration increases by an amount S before the air is exchanged. Assume an external concentration of carbon dioxide of $\gamma = 0.0004$ and $q = 0.2$.

33. Suppose $S = 0.001$. Write the discrete-time dynamical system and find its equilibrium. Compare the equilibrium with the external concentration.

34. The actual concentration of carbon dioxide in exhaled air is about 0.04, or 100 times the external concentration. Find the value of S that gives this as the equilibrium.

35–36 ▪ A bacterial population that has per capita production $r < 1$ but which is supplemented each generation follows a discrete-time dynamical system much like that of the lung. Use the following steps to build the discrete-time dynamical system in the two given cases.

a. Starting from 3.0×10^6 bacteria, find the number after reproduction.

b. Find the number after the new bacteria are added.

c. Find the discrete-time dynamical system.

35. A population of bacteria has per capita production $r = 0.6$, and 1.0×10^6 bacteria are added each generation.

36. A population of bacteria has per capita production $r = 0.2$, and 5.0×10^6 bacteria are added each generation.

37–40 ▪ Find the equilibrium population of bacteria in the following cases with supplementation.

37. A population of bacteria has per capita production $r = 0.6$, and 1.0×10^6 bacteria are added each generation (as in Exercise 35).

38. A population of bacteria has per capita production $r = 0.2$, and 5.0×10^6 bacteria are added each generation (as in Exercise 36).

39. A population of bacteria has per capita production $r = 0.5$, and S bacteria are added each generation. What happens to the equilibrium when S is large? Does this make biological sense?

40. A population of bacteria has per capita production $r < 1$, and 1.0×10^6 bacteria are added each generation. What happens to the equilibrium if $r = 0$? What happens if r is close to 1? Do these results make biological sense?

41–44 ▪ Lakes receive water from streams each year and lose water to outflowing streams and evaporation. The following values are based on the Great Salt Lake in Utah. The lake receives 3.0×10^6 m^3 of water per year with salinity of 1 part per thousand (concentration 0.001). The lake contains 3.3×10^7 m^3 of water and starts with no salinity. Assume that the water that flows out is well mixed, having a concentration equal to that of the entire lake. Compute the discrete-time dynamical system by finding (a) the total salt before the inflow, (b) total water, (c) total salt and salt concentration after inflow, and (d) total water, total salt, and salt concentration after outflow or evaporation,

41. There is no evaporation, and 3.0×10^6 m^3 of water flows out each year.

42. 1.5×10^6 m^3 of water flows out each year, and 1.5×10^6 m^3 evaporates. No salt is lost through evaporation.

43. A total of 3.0×10^6 m^3 of water evaporates, and there is no outflow.

44. Assume instead that 2.0×10^6m^3 of water evaporates and that there is no outflow. The volume of this lake is increasing.

45–48 ▪ Find the equilibrium concentration of salt in a lake in the following cases. Describe the result in words by comparing the equilibrium salt level with the salt level of the water flowing in.

45. The situation described in Exercise 41.

46. The situation described in Exercise 42.

47. The situation described in Exercise 43.

48. The situation described in Exercise 44.

49–50 ▪ A lab is growing and harvesting a culture of valuable bacteria described by the discrete-time dynamical system

$$b_{t+1} = rb_t - h$$

The bacteria have per capita production r, and h are harvested each generation.

49. Suppose that $r = 1.5$ and $h = 1.0 \times 10^6$ bacteria. Sketch the updating function, and find the equilibrium both algebraically and graphically.

50. Without setting r and h to particular values, find the equilibrium algebraically. Does the equilibrium get larger when h gets larger? Does it get larger when r gets larger? If the answers seem odd (as they should), look at a cobweb diagram to try to figure out why.

Computer Exercises

51. Use your computer to graph the trigonometric discrete-time dynamical systems from Section 1.8, Exercise 56.

a. $x_{t+1} = \cos(x_t)$

b. $y_{t+1} = \sin(y_t)$

c. $z_{t+1} = \sin(z_t) + \cos(z_t)$

Find the equilibria of each, and produce cobweb diagrams starting from three different initial conditions (as in Section 1.8, Exercise 56). Do the new diagrams help make sense of the solutions?

52. Consider the discrete-time dynamical system

$$x_{t+1} = e^{ax_t}$$

for the following values of the parameter a. Use your computer to graph the function and the diagonal to look for equilibria. Cobweb starting from $x_0 = 1$ in each case.

a. $a = 0.3$

b. $a = 0.4$

c. $a = 1/e$

1.10 An Example of Nonlinear Dynamics

The discrete-time dynamical systems we have studied in detail (for bacterial populations, tree height, mite populations, and the lung) are said to be **linear** because the updating function is linear. We now derive a model of two competing bacterial populations that leads naturally to a discrete-time dynamical system that is not linear. **Nonlinear dynamical systems** can have much more complicated behavior than a linear system. For example, they may have more than one equilibrium. By comparing the two equilibria in this model of selection, we will catch a glimpse of an important theme of this book, the **stability** of equilibria.

A Model of Selection

Our original model of bacterial growth followed the population of a single type of bacterium, denoted by b_t at time t. Suppose that a mutant type with population m_t appears and begins competing. If the original type (or **wild type**) has a per capita production of 1.5 and the mutant type has a per capita production of 2.0 (Figure 1.10.133), the two populations will follow the discrete-time dynamical systems

$$\begin{aligned} b_{t+1} &= 1.5b_t && \text{discrete-time dynamical system for wild type} \\ m_{t+1} &= 2.0m_t && \text{discrete-time dynamical system for mutants} \end{aligned} \quad \textbf{(1.10.1)}$$

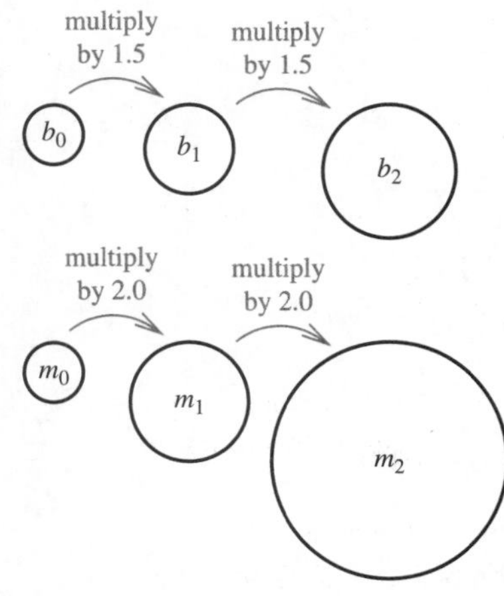

FIGURE 1.10.133
An invasion by mutant bacteria

The per capita production of the mutant type is greater than that of the wild type, perhaps because it is better able to survive in a particular laboratory. Over time, we would expect the population to include a larger and larger proportion of mutant bacteria. The establishment of this mutant is an example of **selection**. Selection occurs when the frequency of a genetic type changes over time.

Imagine observing this mixed population for many hours. Counting all of the bacteria each hour would be impossible. Nonetheless, we could track the mutant invasion by taking a sample and measuring the fraction of the mutant type by counting or using a specific stain. If this fraction became larger and larger, we would know that the mutant type was taking over.

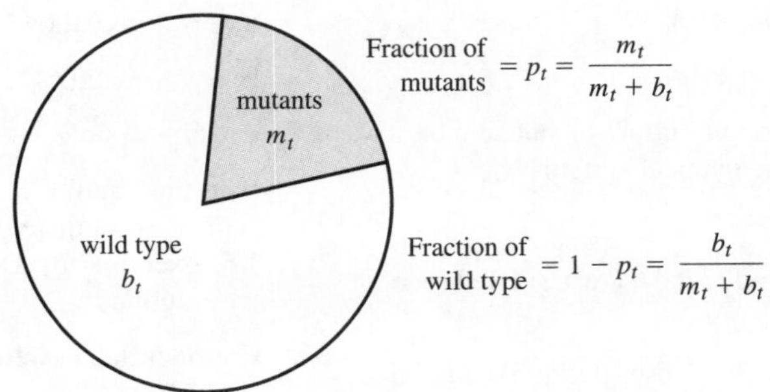

FIGURE 1.10.134
The fraction of mutants and wild type

How can we model the dynamics of the fraction? The vital first step is to **define a new variable.** In this case, we set p_t to be the fraction of mutants at time t. Then

$$\begin{aligned} p_t &= \frac{\text{number of mutants}}{\text{total number}} \\ &= \frac{\text{number of mutants}}{\text{number of mutants} + \text{number of wild type}} \\ &= \frac{m_t}{m_t + b_t} \end{aligned} \tag{1.10.2}$$

Example 1.10.1 Finding the Fraction of Mutants

If $m_t = 2.0 \times 10^5$ and $b_t = 3.0 \times 10^6$, there are a total of 3.2×10^6 bacteria. The fraction of the mutant type is

$$p_t = \frac{2.0 \times 10^5}{2.0 \times 10^5 + 3.0 \times 10^6} = \frac{2.0 \times 10^5}{3.2 \times 10^6} = 0.0625$$

What is the fraction of the wild type? It is the number of wild type divided by the total number of bacteria, or

$$\begin{aligned} \text{fraction of wild type} &= \frac{\text{number of wild type}}{\text{total number}} \\ &= \frac{\text{number of wild type}}{\text{number of mutants} + \text{number of wild type}} \\ &= \frac{b_t}{m_t + b_t} \end{aligned}$$

(Figure 1.10.134).

Example 1.10.2 Finding the Fraction of Wild Type

If $m_t = 2.0 \times 10^5$ and $b_t = 3.0 \times 10^6$ (as in Example 1.10.1), then

$$\begin{aligned} \text{fraction of wild type} &= \frac{3.0 \times 10^6}{2.0 \times 10^5 + 3.0 \times 10^6} \\ &= \frac{3.0 \times 10^6}{3.2 \times 10^6} = 0.9375 \end{aligned}$$

We do not need to give a new name to this fraction because we know that

$$\text{fraction of mutants} + \text{fraction of wild type} = 1$$

Because all bacteria are of these two types, the fractions must add up to 1.

Example 1.10.3 The Fraction of Mutants and the Fraction of Wild Type

In Examples 1.10.1 and 1.10.2, the fraction of mutants is 0.0625 and that of wild type is 0.9375. These two fractions do indeed add up to $0.0625 + 0.9375 = 1$, as they must.

Solving for the fraction of wild type,

$$\begin{aligned}\text{fraction of wild type} &= 1 - \text{fraction of mutants}\\ &= 1 - p_t\end{aligned}$$

Putting this together with our original calculation, we find

$$\frac{b_t}{m_t + b_t} = 1 - p_t \tag{1.10.3}$$

Our goal is to find p_{t+1}, the fraction of the mutant type after one hour.

Example 1.10.4 Finding the Updated Fraction

If $m_t = 2.0 \times 10^5$ and $b_t = 3.0 \times 10^6$ (Example 1.10.1), the updated populations are

$$\begin{aligned}m_{t+1} &= 2.0m_t = 4.0 \times 10^5\\ b_{t+1} &= 1.5b_t = 4.5 \times 10^6\end{aligned}$$

The updated fraction of the mutant type, p_{t+1}, is

$$p_{t+1} = \frac{4.0 \times 10^5}{4.0 \times 10^5 + 4.5 \times 10^6} \approx 0.0816$$

As expected, the fraction has increased. We might expect that the the fraction of mutants would increase by a factor equal to the ratio $\frac{2.0}{1.5} \approx 1.333$ of the per capita production of the two types. In fact,

$$\frac{p_{t+1}}{p_t} = \frac{0.0816}{0.0625} \approx 1.3056$$

which is slightly less. We will soon see why the mutant increases more slowly than we might at first expect.

We can follow these same steps to find the discrete-time dynamical system for p_t. By definition,

$$p_{t+1} = \frac{m_{t+1}}{m_{t+1} + b_{t+1}}$$

Using the discrete-time dynamical systems for the two types (Equation 1.10.1), we find

$$p_{t+1} = \frac{2.0m_t}{2.0m_t + 1.5b_t} \tag{1.10.4}$$

Although mathematically correct, this is not a satisfactory discrete-time dynamical system. We have supposed that the actual values of m_t and b_t are impossible to measure. The discrete-time dynamical system must give the new fraction p_{t+1} in terms of the old fraction p_t, which we can measure by sampling.

We can do this by using an algebraic trick: dividing the numerator and denominator by the same thing. Because the definition of p_t has the total population $m_t + b_t$ in the denominator, we divide it into the numerator and denominator, finding

$$p_{t+1} = \frac{2.0\dfrac{m_t}{m_t + b_t}}{2.0\dfrac{m_t}{m_t + b_t} + 1.5\dfrac{b_t}{m_t + b_t}}$$

We can simplify by substituting

$$p_t = \frac{m_t}{m_t + b_t}$$

(Equation 1.10.2) and

$$1 - p_t = \frac{b_t}{m_t + b_t}$$

(Equation 1.10.3), finding

$$p_{t+1} = \frac{2.0p_t}{2.0p_t + 1.5(1 - p_t)} \tag{1.10.5}$$

This is the discrete-time dynamical system we sought, giving a formula for the fraction at time $t + 1$ in terms of the fraction at time t.

Example 1.10.5 Using the Discrete-time Dynamical System to Find the Updated Fraction

If $p_t = 0.0625$, as in Example 1.10.1, the discrete-time dynamical system tells us that

$$p_{t+1} = \frac{2.0 \cdot 0.0625}{2.0 \cdot 0.0625 + 1.5(1 - 0.0625)} \approx 0.0816$$

This matches the answer we found before but is based only on *measurable quantities.*

This calculation illustrates one of the great strengths of mathematical modeling. Our *derivation* of this measurable discrete-time dynamical system used the values m_t and b_t, which are impossible to measure. But just because things cannot be measured in practice does not mean they cannot be measured in principle. These values do exist, and they can be worked with mathematically. One can think of mathematical models as a way to "see the invisible."

The discrete-time dynamical system for the fraction (Equation 1.10.5) is not linear because it involves division. The graph of the function is curved (Figure 1.10.135). We plotted it by substituting in representative values for a fraction, which must lie between 0 and 1. The points (0, 0), (0.5, 0.57), and (1, 1) lie on the graph, and we connected them with a smooth curve.

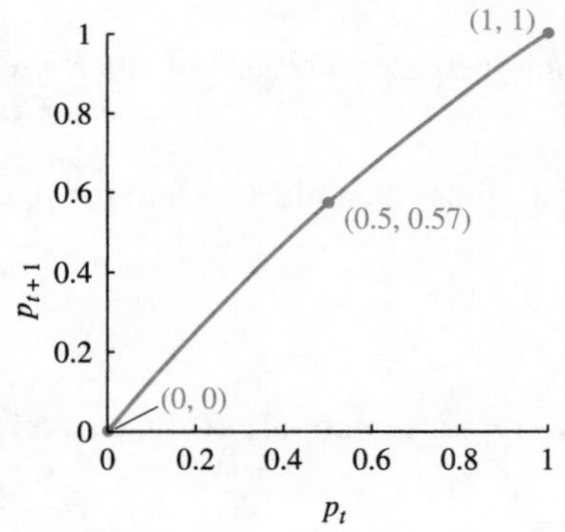

FIGURE 1.10.135
Graph of updating function from the selection model

The equilibria of this discrete-time dynamical system are found by solving

$p^* = \dfrac{2.0p^*}{2.0p^* + 1.5(1 - p^*)}$	the equation for the equilibrium
$p^*(2.0p^* + 1.5(1 - p^*)) = 2.0p^*$	multiply through by the denominator
$p^*(2.0p^* + 1.5(1 - p^*)) - 2.0p^* = 0$	move everything to one side
$p^*(2.0p^* + 1.5(1 - p^*) - 2.0) = 0$	factor out p^*
$p^*(2.0p^* + 1.5 - 1.5p^* - 2.0) = 0$	multiply out terms in parentheses
$p^*(0.5p^* - 0.5) = 0$	simplify

Therefore, $p^* = 0$, or $0.5p^* - 0.5 = 0$, which has solution $p^* = 1$. These equilibria correspond to extinction of the mutant (at $p^* = 0$) and extinction of the wild type (at $p^* = 1$).

The Discrete-time Dynamical System and Equilibria

We can gain a better understanding of this process by studying the general case. Suppose that the mutant type has per capita production s and the wild type has per capita

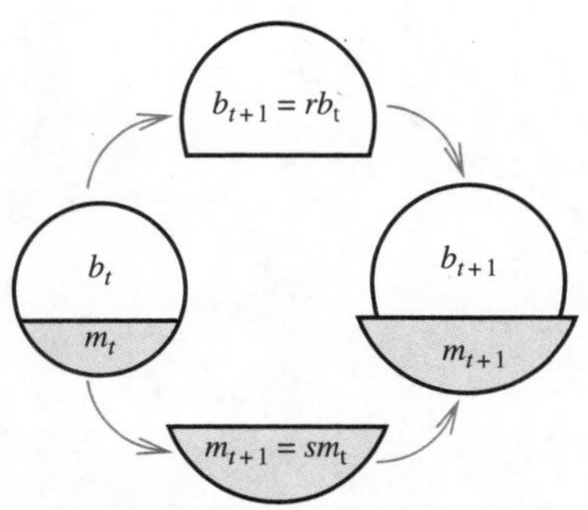

FIGURE 1.10.136
The general case

production r (Figure 1.10.136). The populations follow

$$\begin{aligned} m_{t+1} &= sm_t \\ b_{t+1} &= rb_t \end{aligned} \tag{1.10.6}$$

We can follow the steps above to derive the discrete-time dynamical system for the fraction.

$$\begin{aligned} p_{t+1} &= \frac{m_{t+1}}{m_{t+1} + b_{t+1}} \\ &= \frac{sm_t}{sm_t + rb_t} \\ &= \frac{s\dfrac{m_t}{m_t + b_t}}{s\dfrac{m_t}{m_t + b_t} + r\dfrac{b_t}{m_t + b_t}} \\ &= \frac{sp_t}{sp_t + r(1 - p_t)} \end{aligned}$$

This gives the general form

$$p_{t+1} = \frac{sp_t}{sp_t + r(1 - p_t)} \tag{1.10.7}$$

Example 1.10.6 Substituting Parameters into the General Discrete-time Dynamical System

The derivation in the previous subsection considered the case $s = 2.0$ and $r = 1.5$. Substituting these parameter values into the general form for bacterial selection gives

$$p_{t+1} = \frac{2.0p_t}{2.0p_t + 1.5(1 - p_t)}$$

matching what we found before.

When $s > r$, the graph of the updating function lies above the diagonal except at the intersection points $p_t = 0$ and $p_t = 1$ (Figure 1.10.137a). This means that any

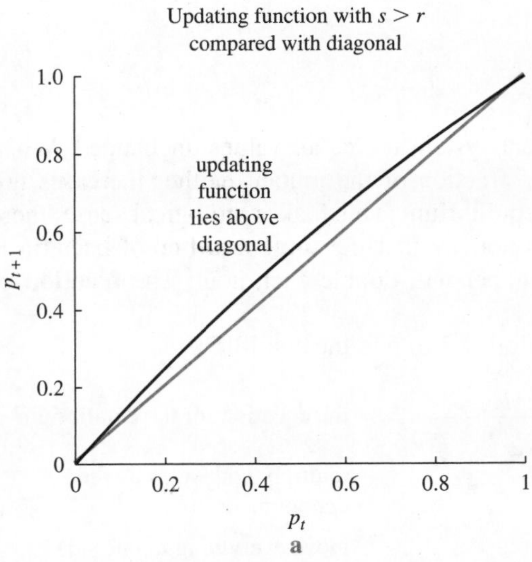

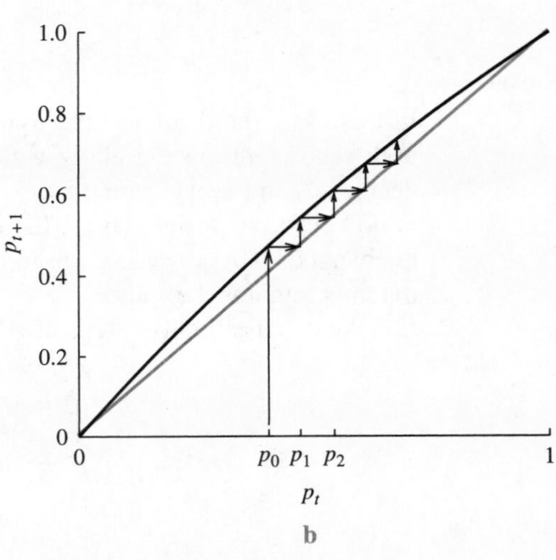

FIGURE 1.10.137
Dynamics when mutants reproduce more quickly

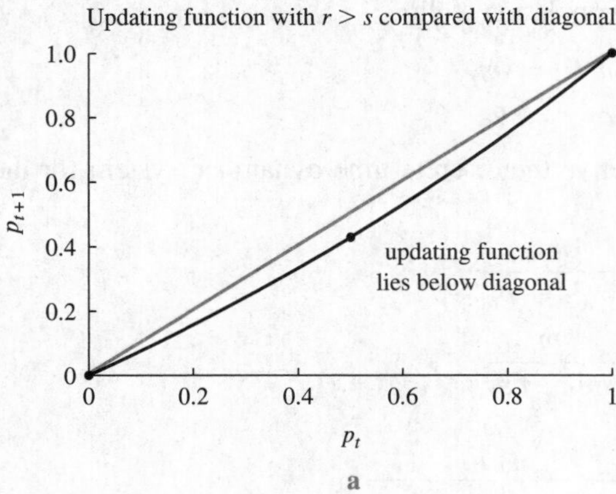

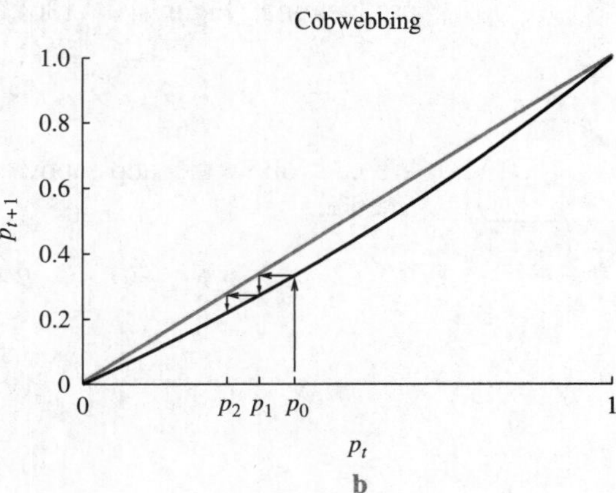

FIGURE 1.10.138
Dynamics when wild type reproduces more quickly

value of p_t between 0 and 1 will be increased by the discrete-time dynamical system, consistent with the higher per capita production of the mutants. The cobwebbing moves up, indicating this increase (Figure 1.10.137b).

What happens if the per capita production of the wild type exceeds that of the mutants? With $r = 2.0$ and $s = 1.5$, the discrete-time dynamical system is

$$p_{t+1} = \frac{1.5p_t}{1.5p_t + 2.0(1 - p_t)}$$

The three points (0, 0), (0.5, 0.43), and (1, 1) lie on the graph, which itself lies below the diagonal (Figure 1.10.138a). Values of p_t between 0 and 1 are decreased by the discrete-time dynamical system, as shown by the decreasing cobweb (Figure 1.10.138b). This is consistent with the lower production of the mutants.

Finally, what happens if the two types have equal per capita production? If $r = s$, the discrete-time dynamical system simplifies

$$\begin{aligned} p_{t+1} &= \frac{sp_t}{sp_t + s\,(1 - p_t)} \\ &= \frac{sp_t}{sp_t + s - sp_t} \\ &= \frac{sp_t}{s} \\ &= p_t \end{aligned}$$

In this case, the discrete-time dynamical system leaves all values unchanged. When both types reproduce equally well, the fraction of the mutant neither increases nor decreases, and every value of p_t is an equilibrium. This makes biological sense; there is no selection in this case. This does not say that the **total number** of bacteria is unchanged; if $r = s = 2.0$, the total number will double each hour. The **fraction** of mutants remains the same.

We can use the five steps of Algorithm 1.5 to find the equilibria.

$$p^* = \frac{sp^*}{sp^* + r(1 - p^*)}.$$ the equation for the equilibrium

$$(sp^* + r(1 - p^*))p^* = sp^*$$ multiply both sides by the denominator

$$(sp^* + r(1 - p^*))p^* - sp^* = 0$$ move everything to one side

$$(sp^* + r - rp^*)p^* - sp^* = 0$$ multiply out inner term

$$sp^{*2} + rp^* - rp^{*2} - sp^* = 0$$ multiply out all terms

$$sp^{*2} - sp^* + rp^* - rp^{*2} = 0 \qquad \text{collect like terms}$$
$$(s - r)p^*(p^* - 1) = 0 \qquad \text{factor}$$
$$s - r = 0 \text{ or } p^* = 0 \text{ or } p^* = 1 \qquad \text{set each factor to 0}$$
$$s = r \text{ or } p^* = 0 \text{ or } p^* = 1 \qquad \text{solve each term}$$

Factoring involves some tricky algebra, which is worth checking.

What do these three equilibria mean? If $s = r$, the discrete-time dynamical system leaves all values unchanged, and every value of p_t is an equilibrium. Otherwise, the equilibria are $p_t = 0$ and $p_t = 1$. When $p_t = 0$, the population consists entirely of the wild type. Because our model includes no mutation or immigration, there is nowhere for the mutant type to arise. Similarly, when $p_t = 1$ the population consists entirely of the mutant type, and the wild type will never arise. These equilibria correspond to the extinction equilibrium for a population of one type of bacteria: at $p_t = 0$ the mutants are extinct, and at $p_t = 1$ the wild type are extinct.

Stable and Unstable Equilibria

Figure 1.10.139 shows many steps of cobwebbing with $s = 2.0$ and $r = 1.5$, starting near the equilibrium $p^* = 0$. The solution moves slowly away from 0, moves swiftly through the halfway point at $p_t = 0.5$, and then slowly approaches the other equilibrium at $p_t = 1$.

If we started *exactly* at $p_0 = 0$, the solution would remain at $p_t = 0$ for all times t. Similarly, if we started *exactly* at $p_t = 1$, the solution would remain at $p_t = 1$ for all times t. The two equilibria behave quite differently, however, if our starting point is nearby. A solution starting *near* $p_0 = 0$ moves steadily *away from* the equilibrium (Figure 1.10.139). A solution starting *near* $p_0 = 1$ moves *toward* the equilibrium (Figure 1.10.140).

This situation is analogous to keeping a ball from rolling around on a surface. If we place it at the bottom of a small depression, it will remain at an equilibrium (Figure 1.10.141a). If it is moved slightly away from this equilibrium, it will come back, much like the solution that starts near the equilibrium $p^* = 1$ (Figure 1.10.140). We call an equilibrium with this property **stable.** Similarly, if we place it exactly on top of a small hill, it will remain there (Figure 1.10.141b). However, if it is moved even slightly away from this equilibrium, it will roll farther and farther away, much like the solution that starts near the equilibrium $p^* = 0$ (Figure 1.10.139). We call an equilibrium with this property **unstable.**

This leads us to an informal definition of stable and unstable equilibria.

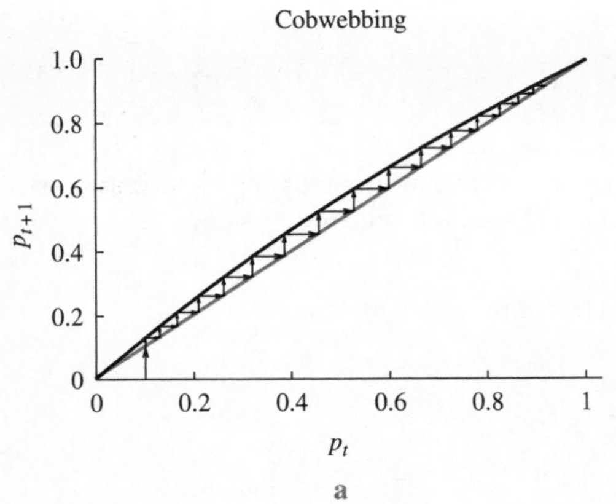

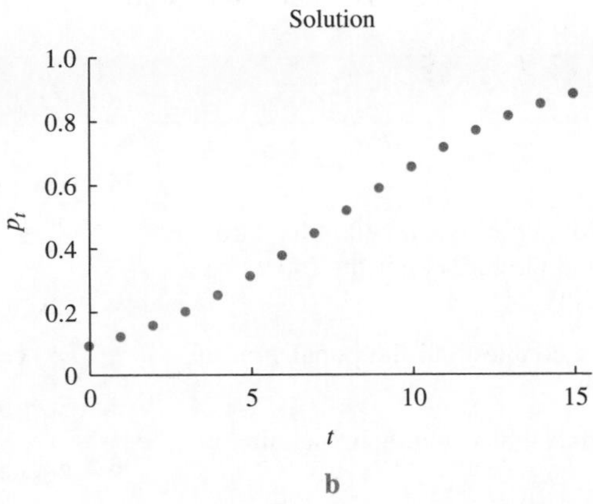

FIGURE 1.10.139
Solution of the selection model starting near $p_0 = 0$

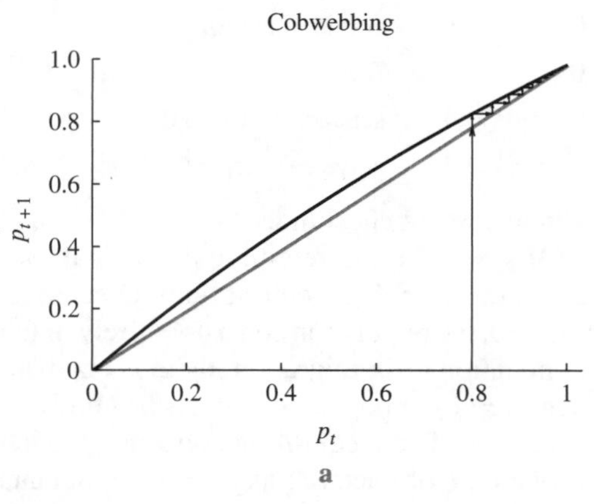

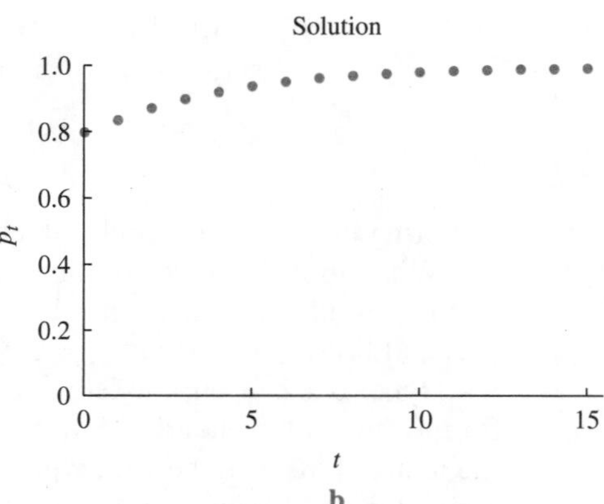

FIGURE 1.10.140
Solution of the selection model starting near $p_0 = 1$

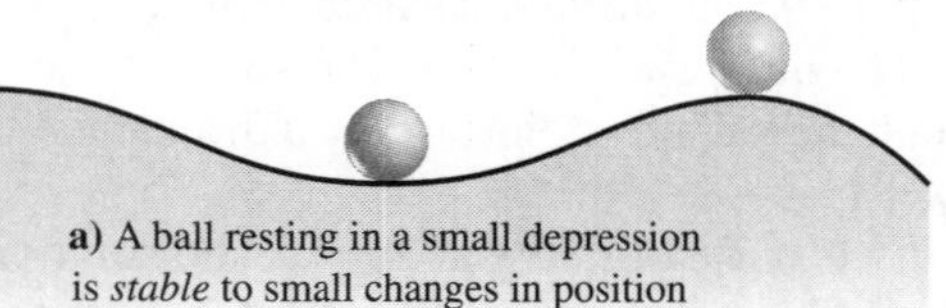

b) A ball resting on a small hill is *unstable* to small changes in position
a) A ball resting in a small depression is *stable* to small changes in position

FIGURE 1.10.141
Stable and unstable resting points for a ball

Definition 1.16 An equilibrium is **stable** if solutions that begin near that equilibrium stay near or approach that equilibrium. An equilibrium is **unstable** if solutions which begin near that equilibrium move away from that equilibrium.

In Section 3.1, we will derive powerful methods to analyze discrete-time dynamical systems and determine whether their equilibria are stable or unstable. Because these techniques require the **derivative,** a central idea from calculus, we must first study the foundational notions of limits and rate of change.

Summary As an example of a **nonlinear dynamical system,** a discrete-time dynamical system with a curved graph, we derived the equation for the fraction of mutants invading a population of wild type bacteria. This dynamical system, unlike the linear ones studied hitherto, has two equilibria. One of these equilibria is **unstable;** solutions starting nearby move farther and farther away. The other is **stable;** solutions starting nearby move closer and closer to the equilibrium.

1.10 Exercises

Mathematical Techniques

1–4 ▪ A population consists of 200 red birds and 800 blue birds. Find the fraction of red birds and blue birds after the following. Check that the fractions add up to 1.

1. The population of red birds doubles and the population of blue birds remains the same.
2. The population of blue birds doubles and the population of red birds remains the same.
3. The population of red birds is multiplied by a factor of r and the population of blue birds remains the same.
4. The population of blue birds is multiplied by a factor of s and the population of red birds remains the same.

5–6 ▪ Sketch graphs of the following functions.

5. $f(x) = \dfrac{x}{x+1}$ for $0 \le x \le 2$ (the updating function in Section 1.5, Exercise 23).
6. $g(x) = \dfrac{3x}{2x+1}$ for $0 \le x \le 2$

7–10 ▪ Using the discrete-time dynamical system and the derivation of Equation 1.10.7, find p_t, m_{t+1}, b_{t+1}, and p_{t+1} in the following situations.

7. $s = 1.2, r = 2.0, m_t = 1.2 \times 10^5, b_t = 3.5 \times 10^6$

8. $s = 1.2, r = 2.0, m_t = 1.2 \times 10^5, b_t = 1.5 \times 10^6$

9. $s = 0.3, r = 0.5, m_t = 1.2 \times 10^5, b_t = 3.5 \times 10^6$

10. $s = 1.8, r = 1.8, m_t = 1.2 \times 10^5, b_t = 3.5 \times 10^6$

11–12 ▪ Solve for the equilibria of the following discrete-time dynamical systems.

11. $p_{t+1} = \dfrac{p_t}{p_t + 2.0(1 - p_t)}$

12. $p_{t+1} = \dfrac{4.0p_t}{4.0p_t + 0.5(1 - p_t)}$

13–14 ▪ Find all non-negative equilibria of the following mathematically elegant discrete-time dynamical systems.

13. $x_{t+1} = \dfrac{x_t}{1 + ax_t}$ where a is a positive parameter. What happens to this system if $a = 0$?

14. $x_{t+1} = \dfrac{x_t}{a + x_t}$ where a is a positive parameter. What happens to this system if $a = 0$?

15–18 ▪ Identify stable and unstable equilibria on the following graphs of updating functions.

15.

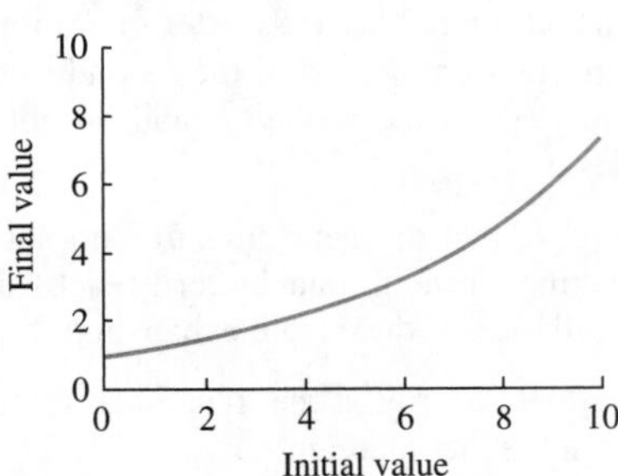

16.

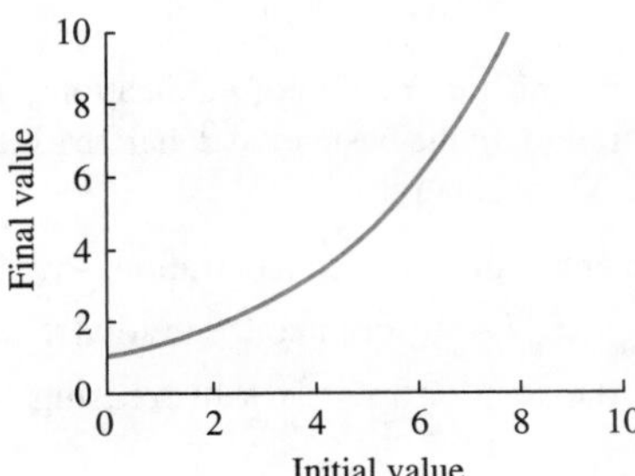

17.

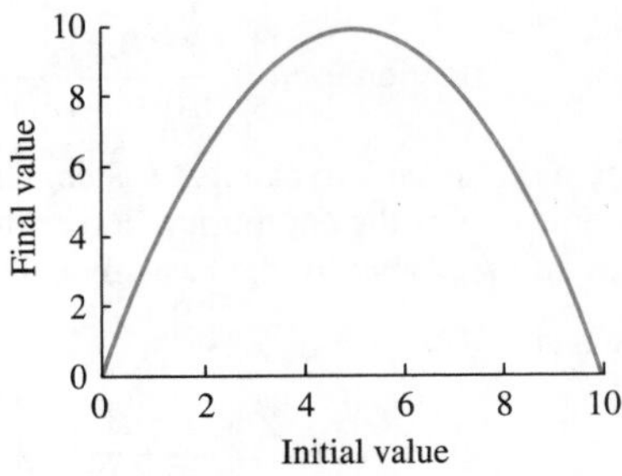

18.

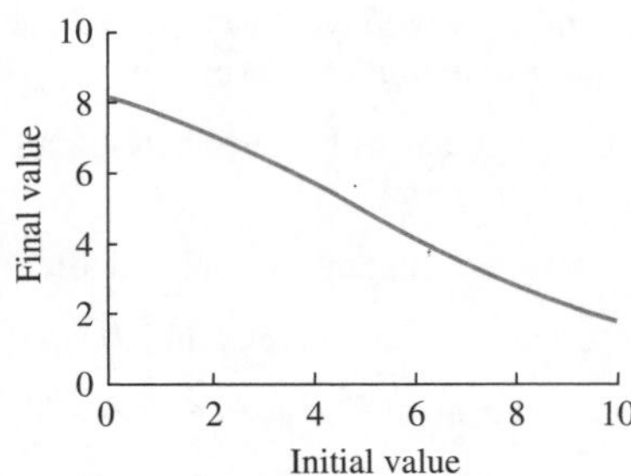

Applications

19–22 ▪ Find and graph the updating functions for the following cases of the selection model (Equation 1.10.7). Cobweb starting from $p_0 = 0.1$ and $p_0 = 0.9$. Which equilibria seem to be stable in each case?

19. $s = 1.2, r = 2.0$

20. $s = 1.8, r = 0.8$

21. $s = 0.3, r = 0.5$. Compare with the result of Exercise 19

22. $s = 1.8, r = 1.8$

23–24 ▪ For each of the following discrete-time dynamical systems, indicate which of the equilibria are stable and which are unstable.

23.

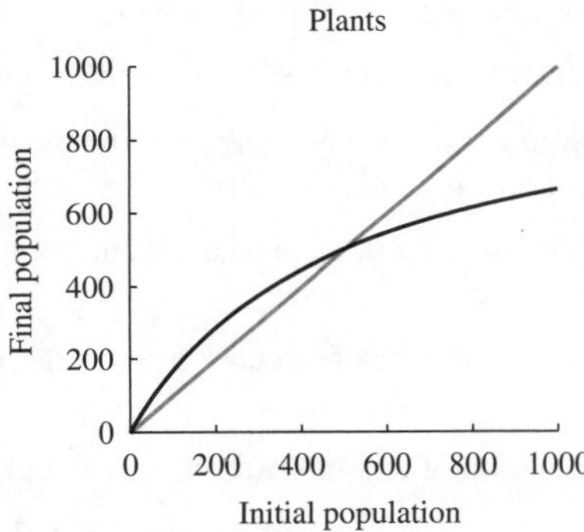

24.

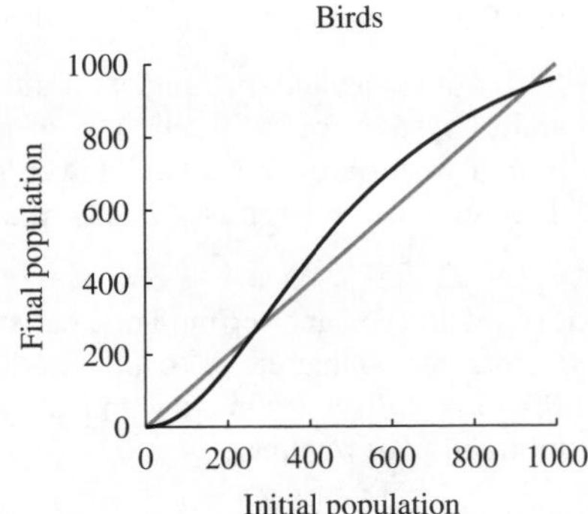

25–28 ▪ This section ignores the important evolutionary force of mutation. This series of problems builds models that consider mutation without reproduction. Suppose that 20% of wild type bacteria transform into mutants and that 10% of mutants transform back into wild type ("revert"). In each case, find the following.

a. The number of wild type bacteria that mutate and the number of mutants that revert.

b. The number of wild type bacteria and the number of mutants after mutation and reversion.

c. The total number of bacteria before and after mutation. Why is it the same?

d. The fraction of mutants before and after mutation.

25. Begin with 1.0×10^6 wild type and 1.0×10^5 mutants.

26. Begin with 1.0×10^5 wild type and 1.0×10^6 mutants.

27. Begin with b_t wild type and m_t mutants. Find the discrete-time dynamical system for the fraction p_t of mutants (divide m_{t+1} by $b_{t+1} + m_{t+1}$ to find p_{t+1} and use the fact that $b_{t+1} + m_{t+1} = b_t + m_t$). Find the equilibrium fraction of mutants. Cobweb starting from the initial condition in Exercise 25. Is the equilibrium stable?

28. Begin with b_t wild type and m_t mutants, but suppose that a fraction 0.1 mutate and a fraction 0.2 revert. Find the discrete-time dynamical system and the equilibrium fraction of mutants.

29–32 ▪ This series of problems combines mutation with selection. In one simple scenario, mutations occur in only one direction (wild type turn into mutants but not vice versa), but wild type and mutants have different per capita production. Suppose that a fraction 0.1 of wild type mutate each generation but that each wild type individual produces 2.0 offspring while each mutant produces only 1.5 offspring. In each case, find the following.

a. The number of wild type bacteria that mutate.

b. The number of wild type bacteria and the number of mutants after mutation.

c. The number of wild type bacteria and the number of mutants after reproduction.

d. The total number of bacteria after mutation and reproduction.

e. The fraction of mutants after mutation and reproduction.

29. Begin with 1.0×10^6 wild type and 1.0×10^5 mutants.

30. Begin with 1.0×10^5 wild type and 1.0×10^6 mutants.

31. Begin with b_t wild type and m_t mutants. Find the discrete-time dynamical system for the fraction p_t of mutants. Find the equilibrium fraction of mutants. Cobweb starting from the initial condition in Exercise 29. Is the equilibrium stable?

32. Begin with b_t wild type and m_t mutants, but suppose that a fraction 0.2 mutate and that the per capita production of mutants is 1.0. Find the discrete-time dynamical system and the equilibrium fraction of mutants.

33–36 ▪ The model of selection studied in this section is similar in many ways to a model of migration. Suppose two nearby islands have populations of butterflies, with x_t on the first island and y_t on the second. Each year, 20% of the butterflies from the first island fly to the second and 30% of the butterflies from the second island fly to the first.

33. Suppose there are 100 butterflies on each island at time $t = 0$. How many are on each island at $t = 1$? At $t = 2$?

34. Suppose there are 200 butterflies on the first island and none on the second at time $t = 0$. How many are on each island at $t = 1$? At $t = 2$?

35. Find equations for x_{t+1} and y_{t+1} in terms of x_t and y_t.

36. Divide both sides of the discrete-time dynamical system for x_t by $x_{t+1} + y_{t+1}$ to find a discrete-time dynamical system for the fraction p_t on the first island. What is the equilibrium fraction?

37–38 ▪ The following two problems extend the migration models to include some reproduction. Each year, 20% of the butterflies from the first island fly to the second and 30% of the butterflies from the second island fly to the first. Again, x_t represents the number of butterflies on the first island, y_t represents the number of butterflies on the second island, and p_t represents the fraction of butterflies on the first island. In each case:

a. Start with 100 butterflies on each island and find the number after migration and after reproduction.

b. Find equations for x_{t+1} and y_{t+1} in terms of x_t and y_t.

c. Find the discrete-time dynamical system for p_{t+1} in terms of p_t.

d. Find the equilibrium p^*.

e. Sketch a graph and cobweb from a reasonable initial condition.

37. Each butterfly that begins the year on the first island produces one additional butterfly after migration (whether they find themselves on the first or the second island). Those that begin the year on the second island do not reproduce. No butterflies die.

38. Now suppose that the butterflies that do not migrate reproduce (making one additional butterfly each) and those that do migrate fail to reproduce from exhaustion. No butterflies die.

39–42 ▪ The model describing the dynamics of the concentration of medication in the bloodstream,

$$M_{t+1} = 0.5M_t + 1.0$$

becomes nonlinear if the fraction of medication used is a function of the concentration. In the basic model, half is used no matter how much there is. More generally,

$$\begin{aligned} \text{new concentration} &= \text{old concentration} - \text{fraction used} \\ &\quad \times \text{old concentration} + \text{supplement} \end{aligned}$$

Suppose that the fraction used is a **decreasing function** of the concentration.

39. Suppose that

$$\text{fraction used} = \frac{0.5}{1.0 + 0.1M_t}$$

Write the discrete-time dynamical system and solve for the equilibrium. Why is the equilibrium larger than the value of $M^* = 2.0$ that we found for the basic model?

40. Suppose that

$$\text{fraction used} = \frac{0.5}{1.0 + 0.4M_t}$$

Write the discrete-time dynamical system and solve for the equilibrium. Why is the equilibrium larger than the value of $M^* = 2.0$ that we found for the basic model?

41. Suppose that

$$\text{fraction used} = \frac{\beta}{1.0 + 0.1M_t}$$

for some parameter $\beta \le 1$. Write the discrete-time dynamical system and solve for the equilibrium. Sketch a graph of the equilibrium as a function of β. Cobweb starting from $M_0 = 1.0$ in the cases $\beta = 0.05$ and $\beta = 0.5$.

42. Suppose that

$$\text{fraction used} = \frac{0.5}{1.0 + \alpha M_t}$$

for some parameter α. Write the discrete-time dynamical system and solve for the equilibrium. Sketch a graph of the equilibrium as a function of α. What happens when $\alpha > 0.5$? Can you explain this in biological terms? Cobweb starting from $M_0 = 1.0$ in the cases $\alpha = 0.1$ and $\alpha = 1.0$.

43–46 ▪ Our models of bacterial population growth neglect the fact that bacteria produce fewer offspring in large populations. The following problems introduce two important models of this process, having the form

$$b_{t+1} = r(b_t)b_t$$

where the per capita production r is a function of the population size b_t. In each case:

a. Graph the per capita production as a function of population size.

b. Write the discrete-time dynamical system and graph the updating function.

c. Find the equilibria.

d. Cobweb and indicate whether the equilibrium seems to be stable.

43. One widely used nonlinear model of competition is the "logistic" model, where per capita production is a linearly decreasing function of population size. Suppose that the per capita production is $r(b) = 2\left(1 - \frac{b}{1.0 \times 10^6}\right)$.

44. In an alternative model, the per capita production decreases as the reciprocal of a linear function. Suppose that the per capita production is $r(b) = \dfrac{2}{1 + \dfrac{b}{1.0 \times 10^6}}$.

45. In another alternative model, called the Ricker model, the per capita production decreases exponentially. Suppose that per capita production is $r(b) = 2e^{-\frac{b}{1.0 \times 10^6}}$.

46. In a model with an **Allee effect,** organisms reproduce poorly when the population is small. In one case, per capita production follows $r(b) = \dfrac{4b}{1 + b^2}$.

Computer Exercises

47. Consider the discrete-time dynamical system

$$x_{t+1} = rx_t(1 - x_t)$$

similar to the form in Exercise 43. Plot the updating function and have your computer find solutions for 50 steps starting from $x_0 = 0.3$ for the following values of r:

a. Some value of r between 0 and 1. What is the only equilibrium?

b. Some value of r between 1 and 2. Where are the equilibria? Which one seems to be stable?

c. Some value of r between 2 and 3. Where are the equilibria? Which one seems to be stable?

d. Try several values of r between 3 and 4. What is happening to the solution? Is there any stable equilibrium?

e. The solution is **chaotic** when $r = 4$. One property of chaos is **sensitive dependence on initial conditions.** Compare a solution starting from $x_0 = 0.3$ with one starting at $x_0 = 0.30001$. Even though they start off very close, they soon separate and become completely different. Why might this be a problem for a scientific experiment?

48. Consider the equation describing the dynamics of selection (Equation 1.10.7),

$$p_{t+1} = \frac{sp_t}{sp_t + r(1 - p_t)}$$

Suppose you have two cultures 1 and 2. In 1, the mutant does better than the wild type, and in 2 the wild type does better. In particular, suppose that $s = 2.0$ and $r = 0.3$ in culture 1 and that $s = 0.6$ and $r = 2.0$ in culture 2. Define discrete-time dynamical systems f_1 and f_2 to describe the dynamics in the two cultures.

a. Graph the functions f_1 and f_2 along with the identity function. Find the first five values of solutions, starting from $p_0 = 0.02$ and $p_0 = 0.98$ in each culture. Explain in words what each solution is doing and why.

b. Suppose you change the experiment. Begin by taking a population with a fraction p_0 of mutants. Split this population in half, and place one half in culture 1 and the other half in culture 2. Let the bacteria reproduce once in each culture, and then mix them together. Split the mix in half and repeat the process. The updating function is

$$f(p) = \frac{f_1(p) + f_2(p)}{2}$$

Can you derive this? Plot this updating function along with the diagonal. Have your computer find the equilibria and label them on your graph. Do they make sense?

c. Use cobwebbing to figure out which equilibria are stable.

d. Find one solution starting from $p_0 = 0.001$ and another starting from $p_0 = 0.999$. Are these results consistent with the stability of the equilibria? Explain in words why the solutions do what they do. Why don't they move toward $p = 0.5$?

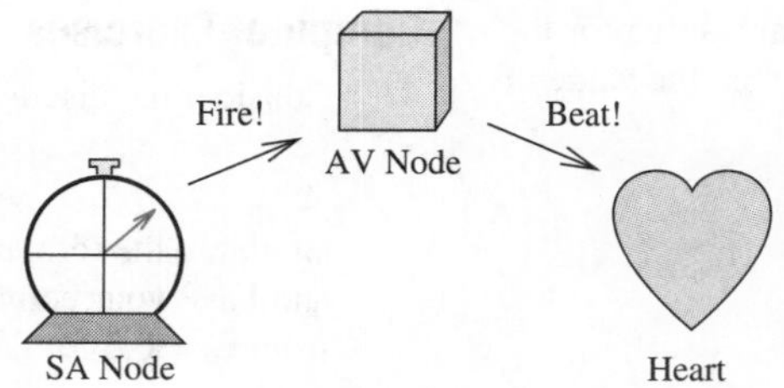

FIGURE 1.11.142
A mathematician's version of the heart

1.11 Excitable Systems I: The Heart

We can use the methods of cobwebbing and equilibria to study a simplified model of the heart. Our goal is to understand how simple changes in the parameters of a heart can produce heartbeat patterns called **second-degree block.** With these syndromes, people's hearts either beat half as often as they should or beat normally for a while, skip a beat, and return to beating. These conditions are solutions for the same model that describes a normal heartbeat, but with different parameter values.

A Simple Heart

Figure 1.11.142 shows the basic apparatus for beating in the heart. The sinoatrial node (SA node) is the pacemaker, sending regular signals to the atrioventricular node (AV node). The AV node then tells the heart to beat if conditions are suitable.

The AV node can be thought of as keeping track of the condition of the heart with an electrical potential. Denote the potential after responding to a signal from the SA node as V_t. Two processes go into updating this potential. During the time τ between signals from the SA node, the electrical potential of the AV node decays exponentially at rate α. Setting $\hat{V}_t$ to be the potential of the AV node just before receiving the next signal from the SA node,

$$\hat{V}_t = e^{-\alpha\tau} V_t$$

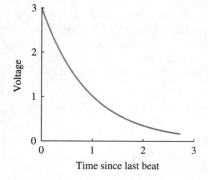

FIGURE 1.11.143
The exponential decay of voltage between beats

(Figure 1.11.143). Whether the heart beats depends on the response of the AV node when a signal arrives. If the potential $\hat{V}_t$ is too high, the heart has not had enough time to recover from the last beat, and the AV node ignores the signal. Otherwise, the AV node accepts the signal, tells the heart to beat, and increases its potential by u (Figure 1.144).

Let V_c be the threshold potential. If $\hat{V}_t > V_c$, the heart is not ready to beat and

$$V_{t+1} = \hat{V}_t \quad \text{if } \hat{V}_t > V_c$$

If $\hat{V}_t \le V_c$, the AV node responds and tells the heart to beat, and

$$V_{t+1} = \hat{V}_t + u \quad \text{if } \hat{V}_t \le V_c$$

To translate this description into a discrete-time dynamical system, we must write V_{t+1} entirely in terms of V_t, eliminating the $\hat{V}_t$ terms. Because $\hat{V}_t = e^{-\alpha\tau} V_t$, the two cases can be summarized as

$$V_{t+1} = \begin{cases} e^{-\alpha\tau} V_t & \text{if } e^{-\alpha\tau} V_t > V_c \\ e^{-\alpha\tau} V_t + u & \text{if } e^{-\alpha\tau} V_t \le V_c \end{cases}$$

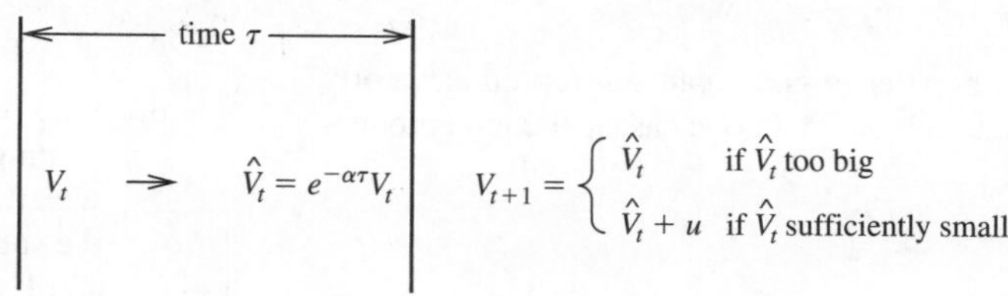

time τ
V_t
$\hat{V}_t = e^{-\alpha\tau} V_t$
$V_{t+1} = \begin{cases} \hat{V}_t & \text{if } \hat{V}_t \text{ too big} \\ \hat{V}_t + u & \text{if } \hat{V}_t \text{ sufficiently small} \end{cases}$
Signal from SA node
Next signal from SA node

FIGURE 1.11.144
Schematic diagram of the potential of the AV node

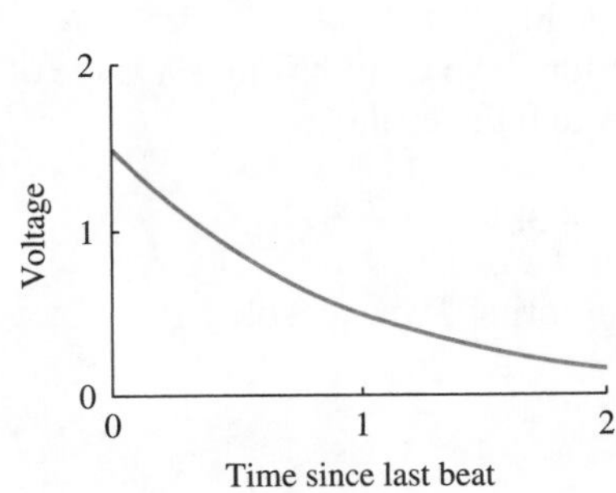

FIGURE 1.11.145
Graph of the potential of the AV node without beating

FIGURE 1.11.146
The updating function for the potential of the AV node

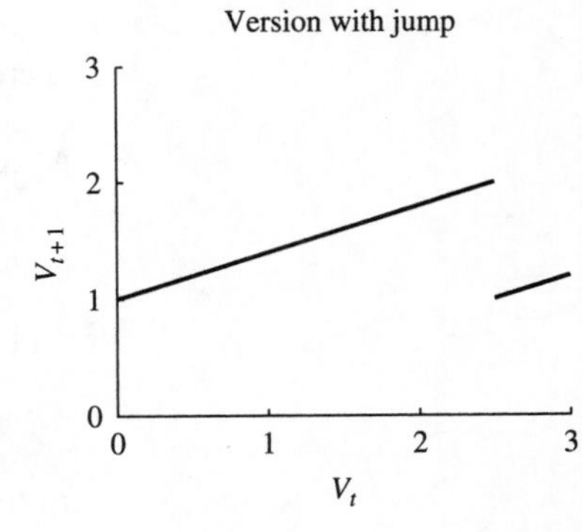

For convenience we substitute the new parameter c for $e^{-\alpha\tau}$. A value of c near 1 means that the potential decays very little, and a value of c near 0 means that the potential decays a great deal (Figure 1.11.145).

Example 1.11.1 The Relation Between c, α, and τ

If $\tau = 1$ and $\alpha = \ln(3) \approx 1.099$, then $c = e^{-\alpha\tau} = 1/3$. The potential decays to $1/3$ of its initial value between beats.

Example 1.11.2 The Relation Between c, α, and τ

If $\tau = 1$ and $\alpha = \ln(1.5) \approx 0.405$, then $c = e^{-\alpha\tau} = 2/3$. The potential decays less, to $2/3$ of its initial value between beats, because α is smaller.

Version without jump

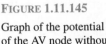

FIGURE 1.11.147
A smoothed updating function for the potential of the AV node

Using this new notation,

$$V_{t+1} = \begin{cases} cV_t & \text{if } cV_t > V_c \\ cV_t + u & \text{if } cV_t \le V_c \end{cases}$$

This updating function is graphed with $u = 1$, $c = 0.4$, and $V_c = 1$ in Figure 1.11.146.

This function, unlike those we have studied hitherto, has a jump (where $cV_t = V_c$). This jump reflects the sharp response threshold. In the real heart, the threshold is not precise, and the two branches of the updating function are connected (Figure 1.11.147).

We can use the graphical method for finding equilibria as intersections with the diagonal to study this discrete-time dynamical system. Each piece of the updating function is a line with slope $c < 1$. There are two possible pictures. Either the upper branch of the updating function crosses the diagonal at an equilibrium (Figure 1.11.148a), or the diagonal sneaks through the gap between the two branches and there is no equilibrium at all (Figure 1.11.148b).

What does this equilibrium mean? An equilibrium is a point where different processes balance. In the present case, an equilibrium represents a value of the potential

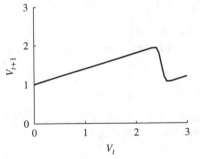

FIGURE 1.11.148
The heart updating function with and without an equilibrium: $u = 1$, $V_c = 1$.

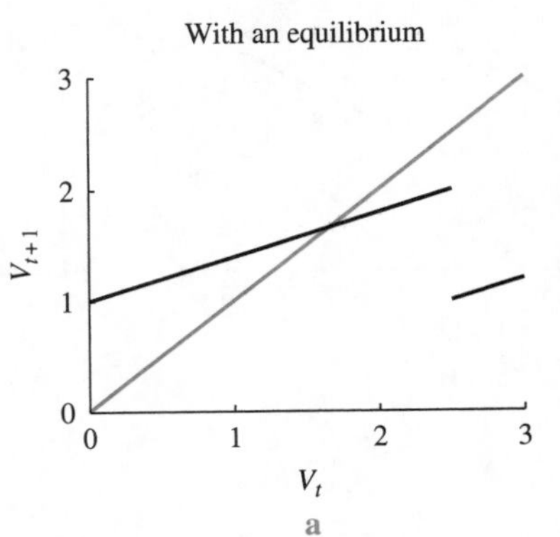

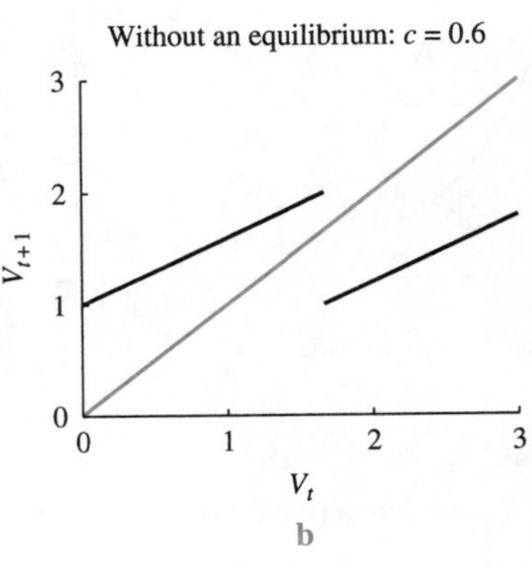

where the decay (by a factor of c) is exactly balanced by the response to the signal (an increase of u). This means that the heart will beat steadily.

What are the algebraic conditions for an equilibrium? An equilibrium is a value of V_t that solves $V_{t+1} = V_t$. The heart must proceed through the cycle

$$V_t \xrightarrow{\text{decay}} \hat{V}_t = cV_t \xrightarrow{\text{beat}} cV_t + u = V_t$$

and end up where it started. Setting V^* to be the equilibrium, we can solve

$$V^* = cV_t + u$$

to find

$$V^* = \frac{u}{1-c} \tag{1.11.1}$$

This equilibrium exists only if the heart is indeed ready to beat when the next signal comes, or if

$$cV^* = c\frac{u}{1-c} \leq V_c \tag{1.11.2}$$

Example 1.11.3 Case Where Heart Beats with Every Signal

Suppose that $u = 1$, $V_c = 1$, $\tau = 1$, and $\alpha = \ln(3) \approx 1.099$. We found in Example 1.11.1 that $c = e^{-\alpha\tau} = 1/3$. The equilibrium is

$$V^* = \frac{1}{1-c} = \frac{1}{1-1/3} = 1.5$$

This equilibrium exists only if $cV^* = 0.5$ is less than $V_c = 1$. Because it is, the heart will beat every time, with voltage decaying from 1.5 to 0.5 between beats and increasing back to 1.5 on the beat (Figure 1.11.149a).

Example 1.11.4 Case Where Heart Fails to Beat with Every Signal

What happens if α, the recovery rate, becomes smaller? We found in Example 1.11.2 that with $\alpha = \ln(1.5) \approx 0.405$, then $c = e^{-\alpha\tau} = 2/3$. The equilibrium is

$$V^* = \frac{1}{1-2/3} = 3.0$$

This equilibrium exists only if $cV^* = 2.0$ is less than $V_c = 1.0$. Because it is not, the heart cannot beat every time. If α is too small, the AV node recovers too slowly from

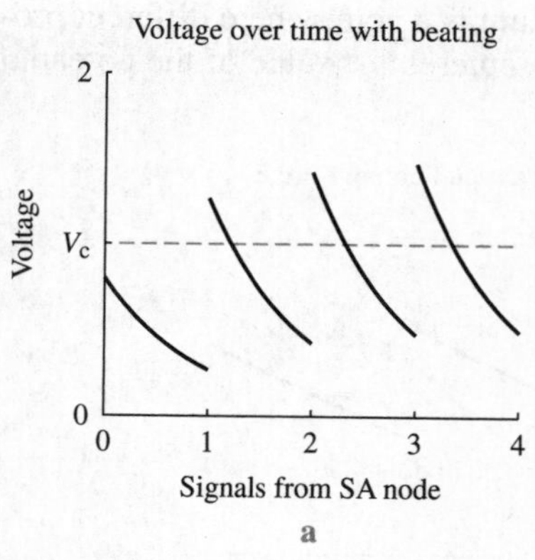

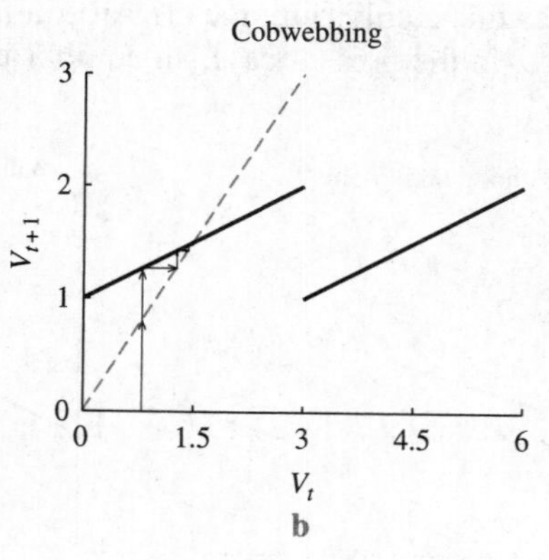

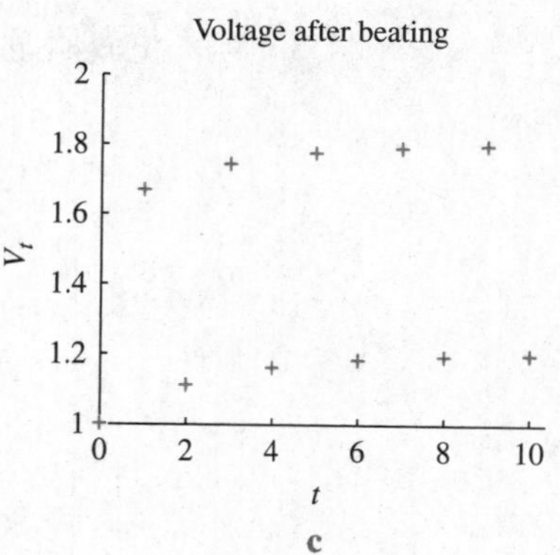

FIGURE 1.11.149
The behavior of a heart with an equilibrium

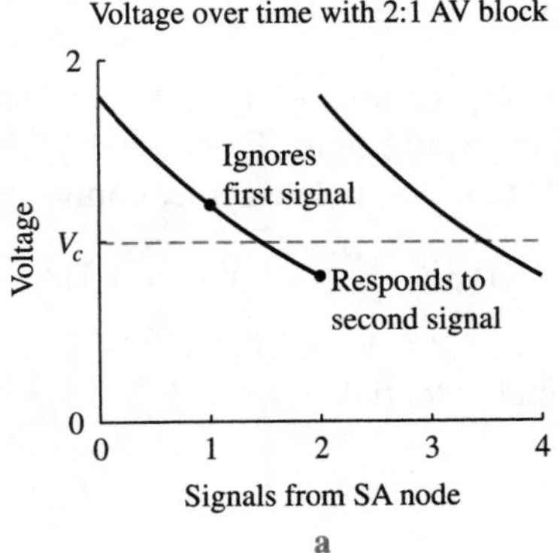

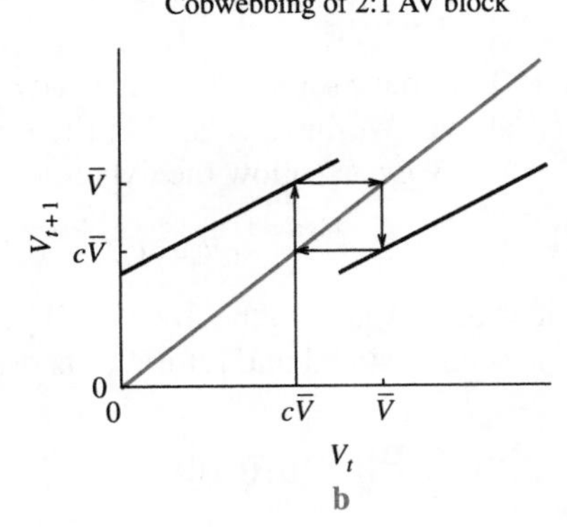

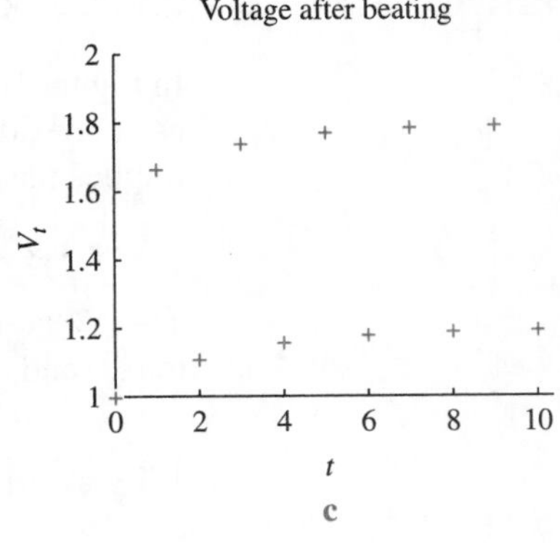

FIGURE 1.11.150
The dynamics of 2:1 AV block

one signal to be ready to respond to the next. Similarly, if the time τ between beats is decreased by too much, the heart might not have time to recover, and there will be no equilibrium. The AV node cannot respond to every signal when signals from the SA node arrive too frequently. The more complicated dynamics that result are our next topic.

2:1 AV Block

When the heart fails to beat in response to every signal from the SA node, the condition is called **second-degree block.** In one type, called **2:1 AV block,** the heart beats only with every other stimulus. In another, called the **Wenckebach phenomenon,** the heart beats normally for a while, skips a beat, and then resumes normal beating and repeats the cycle. Our model of the heart can help us understand these two conditions.

Graphically, 2:1 AV block corresponds to the situation in Figure 1.11.150. There is no equilibrium. The potential of the AV node alternates between a high value and a low value. When high, the potential does not decay sufficiently to respond to the next signal. After another cycle (time τ), however, the potential has reached a low enough value to respond.

To find the conditions for 2:1 AV block, we use techniques similar to those used to find an equilibrium. Suppose the potential is V_t just after beating (Figure 1.11.150). If the node responds to the second signal but not to the first

$$V_t \xrightarrow{\text{decay}} cV_t \xrightarrow{\text{signal ignored}} cV_t \xrightarrow{\text{decay}} c^2V_t \xrightarrow{\text{signal obeyed}} c^2V_t + u \tag{1.11.3}$$

If the potential after these two full cycles comes back exactly to where it started, the heart beats with every other signal, producing 2:1 AV block. The updated potential after two cycles matches the original potential if V_t is equal to some value $\overline{V}$ that satisfies the following system of equations:

$$\begin{aligned} c^2\overline{V} + u &= \overline{V} \\ c\overline{V} &> V_c \\ c^2\overline{V} &< V_c \end{aligned} \tag{1.11.4}$$

which has solution

$$\overline{V} = \frac{u}{1-c^2} \tag{1.11.5}$$

if the inequalities are satisfied. Note the similarity to the equation for an equilibrium for this model (Equation 1.11.1).

Example 1.11.5 2:1 AV Block

In Figure 1.11.150, we have set $u = V_c = 1.0$ and $c = 2/3$, corresponding to the second case considered above. We have seen that there is no equilibrium. Equation 1.11.5 implies that $\overline{V} = 1.8$. We can follow the dynamics through a complete cycle, finding

$$\overline{V} = 1.8 \xrightarrow{\text{decay}} c\overline{V} = 1.2 \xrightarrow{\text{signal ignored}} c\overline{V} = 1.2 \xrightarrow{\text{decay}} c^2\overline{V} = 0.8 \xrightarrow{\text{signal obeyed}} c^2\overline{V} + u = 1.8$$

The AV node does not respond to the first signal because $1.2 > V_c = 1.0$, but it is ready to respond to the second signal and return to its original potential.

The Wenckebach Phenomenon

With the parameter values $u = V_c = 1$, we can compute the conditions on c for the existence of an equilibrium. The equation for an equilibrium is

$$V^* = \frac{1}{1-c}$$

requiring that $cV^* \leq 1$ (Equation 1.11.2). The equilibrium at V^* exists only if

$$\frac{c}{1-c} \leq 1$$

We can solve for c, finding

$$\begin{aligned} c &\leq 1 - c \\ 2c &\leq 1 \\ c &\leq 0.5 \end{aligned}$$

The value $c = 1/3$ that produced an equilibrium and normal beating (Figure 1.11.149) is well below this value. The value $c = 2/3$ that produced 2:1 AV block (Figure 1.11.150) is well above this value. What happens if c is only slightly above 0.5 and the heart can nearly recover?

Figure 1.11.151 shows the behavior of the system when $c = 0.5001$, a hair above the threshold for existence of an equilibrium. The heart beats 12 times, building up to a higher and higher potential. Eventually, the potential becomes too high, the AV node cannot recover, and the heart fails to beat. After this rest, the potential drops, and the process begins again. This is the Wenckebach phenomenon.

Actual measurements of the Wenckebach phenomenon correspond in part to this model but show that the heart beats a bit more slowly before missing a beat. Why might this be the case? Our model assumes that the SA node sends out precise pulses at precise times. If the signals from the SA node take a little while to build up, an AV

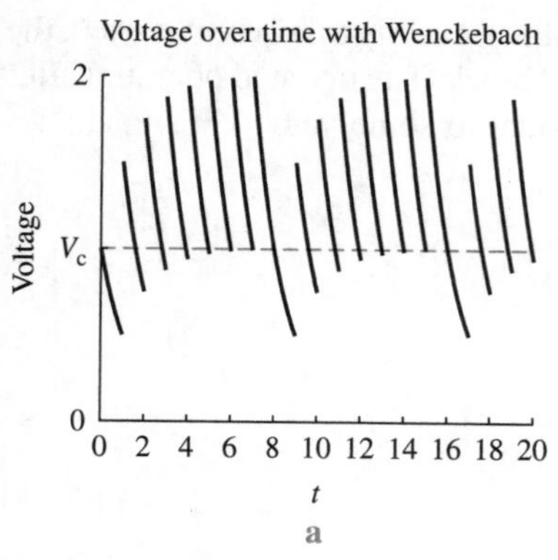

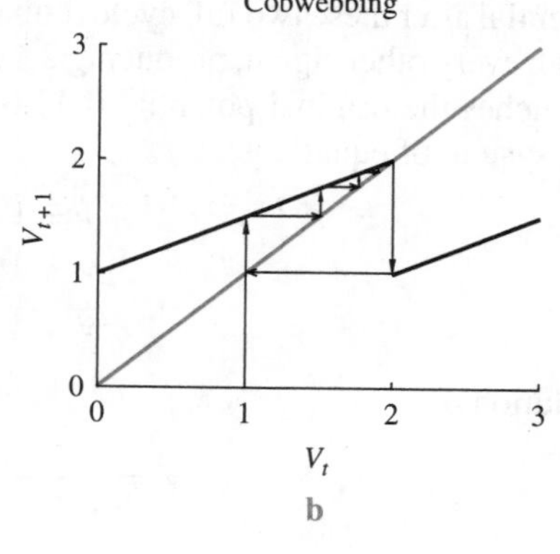

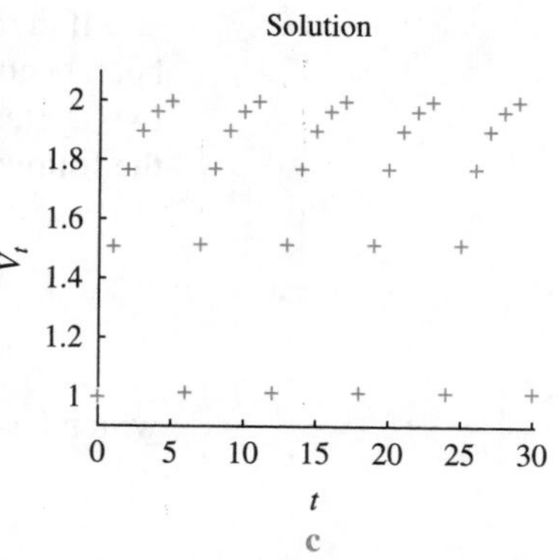

FIGURE 1.11.151
The Wenckebach phenomenon

node at low potential will respond right at the beginning of a signal from the SA node. An AV node close to the threshold will be slower and might respond near the end of the signal from the SA node, delaying the heart beat slightly. This slowing indicates that the AV node will soon exceed the threshold and that the heart will miss a beat.

Summary A simplified model of the heart includes two phases: decay of potential in the AV node (recovery from the last beat) and response to a rhythmic signal from the SA node. We derived conditions for the heart to beat properly with each signal and showed that if the recovery time is not long enough, two types of **second-degree block** can result. In the first, **2:1 AV block**, the heart beats with every other signal. In the second, the **Wenckebach phenomenon,** the heart misses a beat only occasionally.

1.11 Exercises

Applications

1–4 ▪ In the following circumstances, compute $\hat{V}_t$ and V_{t+1} and state whether the heart will beat.

1. $V_c = 20.0$ mV, $u = 10.0$ mV, $c = 0.5$, $V_t = 30.0$ mV
2. $V_c = 20.0$ mV, $u = 10.0$ mV, $c = 0.6$, $V_t = 30.0$ mV
3. $V_c = 20.0$ mV, $u = 10.0$ mV, $c = 0.7$, $V_t = 30.0$ mV
4. $V_c = 20.0$ mV, $u = 10.0$ mV, $c = 0.8$, $V_t = 30.0$ mV

5–8 ▪ Describe the long-term dynamics in each of the given cases. Find which ones will beat every time, which display 2:1 AV block, and which show some sort of Wenckebach phenomenon.

5. The case in Exercise 1.
6. The case in Exercise 2.
7. The case in Exercise 3.
8. The case in Exercise 4.

9–12 ▪ Use the parameter values in Exercise 1 (except for the values of c), and state whether the heart would beat every time with the given values of α and τ.

9. $\alpha = 1.0$, $\tau = 1.0$
10. $\alpha = 1.0$, $\tau = 0.5$
11. $\alpha = 2.0$, $\tau = 0.5$
12. $\alpha = 0.5$, $\tau = 0.5$

13–14 ▪ Consider the following continuous system that approximates the discontinuous model studied in this chapter.

$$V_{t+1} = cV_t + u(V_t)$$

where

$$u(V_t) = \frac{2(1-c)}{1+V_t^n}$$

for the following values of n. Sketch a graph and cobweb in the given cases.

13. Suppose $n = 2$. Show that $V_t = 1$ is an equilibrium. Sketch a graph and cobweb with $c = 1/4$. Does the equilibrium seem to be stable?
14. Suppose $n = 4$. Show that $V_t = 1$ is an equilibrium. Sketch a graph and cobweb with $c = 1/4$. Does the equilibrium seem to be stable?

15–18 ▪ Population models with thresholds can also have unusual behavior. Evaluate the following models where individuals emigrate when the population is overly crowded. In particular, suppose h individuals leave if the population is larger than some critical value N_c,

$$N_{t+1} = \begin{cases} rN_t - h & \text{if } N_t > N_c \\ rN_t & \text{if } N_t \le N_c \end{cases}$$

15. Suppose $h = 1000$, $N_c = 1000$, and $r = 1.5$. Investigate some solutions starting with different values of $N_0 < 1000$. What is happening?
16. Find the equilibrium when $h = 1000$, $N_c = 1000$, and $r = 1.5$. What would happen to solutions starting with values greater than the equilibrium? Use this information, and that in the previous problem, to sketch a cobweb diagram.
17. Redo Exercise 15 with $r = 1.65$. How do the solutions differ from those in Exercise 15?
18. Find the equilibrium when $h = 1000$, $N_c = 1000$, and $r = 1.65$. Can you explain why solutions that start below the equilibrium can shoot off to infinity?

Computer Exercises

19. Study the dynamics of the previous problem for values of c ranging from 0.4 up to 1.0. Are there any cases where the behavior is neither 2:1 AV block or the Wenckebach phenomenon? How would you describe these behaviors?
20. What happens to the dynamics of the example illustrated in Figure 1.11.151 if c is made even closer to 0.5? What does it look like on a cobwebbing diagram? If $c = 0.5000000000001$, do you think it would be possible to distinguish the Wenckebach phenomenon from normal beating? Is it?

Supplementary Problems

1. Suppose you have a culture of bacteria, where the density of each bacterium is 2.0 g/cm^3.
   a. If each bacterium is 5 μm × 5 μm × 20 μm in size, find the number of bacteria if their total mass is 30 grams. Recall that 1 μm = 10^{-6} meters.
   b. Suppose that you learn that the sizes of bacteria range from 4 μm × 5 μm × 15 μm to 5 μm × 6 μm × 25 μm. What is the range of the possible number of bacteria making up the total mass of 30 grams?
2. Suppose the number of bacteria in culture is a linear function of time.
   a. If there are 2.0×10^8 bacteria in your lab at 5 P.M. on Tuesday, and 5.0×10^8 bacteria the next morning at 9 A.M., find the equation of the line describing the number of bacteria in your culture as a function of time.
   b. At what time will your culture have 1.1×10^9 bacteria?
   c. The lab across the hall also has a bacterial culture where the number of bacteria is a linear function of time. If they have 2.0×10^8 bacteria at 5 P.M. on Tuesday, and 3.4×10^8 bacteria the next morning at 9 A.M., when will your culture have twice as many bacteria as theirs?
3. Consider the functions $f(x) = e^{-2x}$ and $g(x) = x^3 + 1$.
   a. Find the inverses of f and g, and use these to find when $f(x) = 2$ and when $g(x) = 2$.
   b. Find $f \circ g$ and $g \circ f$ and evaluate each at $x = 2$.
   c. Find the inverse of $g \circ f$. What is the domain of this function?
4. A lab has a culture of a new kind of bacteria where each individual takes 2 hours to split into three bacteria. Suppose that these bacteria never die and that all offspring are OK.
   a. Write an updating function describing this system.
   b. Suppose there are 2.0×10^7 bacteria at 9 A.M. How many will there be at 5 P.M.?
   c. Write an equation for how many bacteria there are as a function of how long the culture has been running.
   d. When will this population reach 10^9?
5. The number of bacteria (in millions) in a lab are

Time, t (h)	Number, b_t (h)
0.0 hour	1.5
1.0 hours	3.0
2.0 hours	4.5
3.0 hours	5.0
4.0 hours	7.5
5.0 hours	9.0

   a. Graph these points.
   b. Find the line connecting them and the time t at which the value does not lie on the line.
   c. Find the equation of the line, and use it to find what the value at t would have to be to lie on the line.
   d. How many bacteria would you expect at time 7.0 h?
6. The number of bacteria in another lab follows the discrete-time dynamical system

$$b_{t+1} = \begin{cases} 2.0b_t & b_t \le 1.0 \\ -0.5(b_t - 1.0) + 2.0 & b_t > 1.0 \end{cases}$$

   where t is measured in hours and b_t in millions of bacteria.
   a. Graph the updating function. For what values of b_t does it make sense?
   b. Find the equilibrium.
   c. Cobweb starting from $b_0 = 0.4$ million bacteria. What do you think happens to this population?
7. Convert the following angles from degrees to radians, and find the sine and cosine of each. Plot the related point both on a circle and on a graph of the sine or cosine.
   a. $\theta = 60°$
   b. $\theta = -60°$
   c. $\theta = 110°$
   d. $\theta = -190°$
   e. $\theta = 1160°$
8. Suppose the temperature H of a bird follows the equation

$$H = 38.0 + 3.0\cos\left(\frac{2\pi(t - 0.4)}{1.2}\right)$$

   where t is measured in days and H is measured in degrees C.
   a. Sketch a graph of the temperature of this bird.
   b. Write the equation if the period changes to 1.1 days. Sketch a graph.
   c. Write the equation if the amplitude increases to 3.5 degrees. Sketch a graph.
   d. Write the equation if the average decreases to 37.5 degrees. Sketch a graph.
9. The butterflies on a particular island are not doing too well. Each autumn, every butterfly produces on average 1.2 eggs and then dies. Half of these eggs survive the winter and produce new butterflies by late summer. At this time, 1000 butterflies arrive from the mainland to escape overcrowding.
   a. Write a discrete-time dynamical system for the population on this island.

b. Graph the updating function and cobweb starting from 1000.

c. Find the equilibrium number of butterflies.

10. A culture of bacteria has mass 3.0×10^{-3} g and consists of spherical cells of mass 2.0×10^{-10} g and density 1.5 g/cm^3.

a. How many bacteria are in the culture?

b. What is the radius of each bacterium?

c. If the bacteria were mashed into mush, how much volume would they take up?

11. A person develops a small liver tumor. It grows according to

$$S(t) = S(0)e^{\alpha t}$$

where $S(0) = 1.0$ g and $\alpha = 0.1$/day. At time $t = 30$ days, the tumor is detected and treatment begins. The size of the tumor then decreases linearly with slope of -0.4 g/day.

a. Write the equation for tumor size at $t = 30$.

b. Sketch a graph of the size of the tumor over time.

c. When will the tumor disappear completely?

12. Two similar objects are left to cool for 1 hour. One starts at 80°C and cools to 70°C, and the other starts at 60°C and cools to 55°C. Suppose the discrete-time dynamical system for cooling objects is linear.

a. Find the discrete-time dynamical system. Find the temperature of the first object after 2 hours. Find the temperature after 1 hour of an object starting at 20°C.

b. Graph the updating function, and cobweb starting from 80°C.

c. Find the equilibrium. Explain in words what the equilibrium means.

13. A culture of bacteria increases in area by 10% each hour. Suppose the area is 2.0 cm^2 at 2:00 P.M.

a. What will the area be at 5:00 P.M.?

b. Write the relevant discrete-time dynamical system, and cobweb starting from 2.0.

c. What was the area at 1:00 P.M.?

d. If all bacteria are the same size and each adult produces two offspring each hour, what fraction of offspring must survive?

e. If the culture medium is only 10 cm^2 in size, when will it be full?

14. Candidates Dewey and Howe are competing for fickle voters. Exactly 100,000 people are registered to vote in the election, and each will vote for one of these two candidates. Each week, some voters switch their allegiance. Twenty percent of Dewey's supporters switch to Howe each week. Howe's supporters are more likely to switch when Dewey is doing well: the fraction switching from Howe to Dewey is proportional to Dewey's percentage of the vote—none switch if Dewey commands 0% of the vote, and 50% switch if Dewey commands 100% of the vote. Suppose Howe starts with 90% of the vote.

a. Find the number of votes Dewey and Howe have after a week.

b. Find Dewey's percentage after a week.

c. Find the discrete-time dynamical system describing Dewey's percentage.

d. Graph the updating function and find the equilibrium or equilibria.

e. Who will win the election?

15. A certain bacterial population has the following odd behavior. If the population is less than 1.5×10^8 in a given generation, each bacterium produces two offspring. If the population is greater than or equal to 1.5×10^8 in a given generation, it will be exactly 1.0×10^8 in the next.

a. Cobweb starting from an initial population of 10^7.

b. Graph a solution starting from an initial population of 10^7.

c. Find the equilibrium or equilibria of this population.

16. An organism is breathing a chemical that modifies the depth of its breaths. In particular, suppose that the fraction q of air exchanged is given by

$$q = \frac{c_t}{c_t + \gamma}$$

where γ is the ambient concentration and c_t is the concentration in the lung. After a breath, a fraction q of the air came from outside, and a fraction $1 - q$ remained from inside. Suppose $\gamma = 0.5$ moles/liter.

a. Describe in words the breathing of this organism.

b. Find the discrete-time dynamical system for the concentration in the lung.

c. Find the equilibrium or equilibria.

17. Lint is building up in a dryer. With each use, the old amount of lint x_t is divided by $1 + x_t$, and 0.5 linton (the units of lint) are added.

a. Find the discrete-time dynamical system and graph the updating function.

b. Cobweb starting from $x_0 = 0$. Graph the associated solution.

c. Find the equilibrium or equilibria.

18. Suppose people in a bank are waiting in two separate lines. Each minute several things happen: some people are served, some people join the lines, and some people switch lines. In particular, suppose that $1/10$ of the people in the first line are served, and $3/10$ of the people in the second line are served. Suppose that the number of people who join each line is equal to $1/10$ of the total number of people in both lines and that $1/10$ of the people in each line switch to the other.

a. Suppose there are 100 people in each line at the beginning of a minute. Find how many people are in each line at the end of the minute.

b. Write a discrete-time dynamical system for the number of people in the first line and another discrete-time dynamical system for the number of people in the second.

c. Write a discrete-time dynamical system for the fraction of people in the first line.

19. A gambler faces off against a small casino. She begins with \$1000, and the casino starts with \$11,000. In each round, the gambler loses 10% of her current funds to the casino, and the casino loses 2% of its current funds to the gambler.

a. Find the amount of money each has after one round.

b. Find a discrete-time dynamical system for the amount of money the gambler has and another for the amount of money the casino has.

c. Find the discrete-time dynamical system for the fraction p of money the gambler has.

d. Find the equilibrium fraction of the money held by the gambler.

e. Using the fact that the total amount of money is constant, find the equilibrium amount of money held by the gambler.

20. Let V represent the volume of a lung and c the concentration of some chemical inside. Suppose the internal surface area is proportional to volume, and a lung with volume 400 cm^3 has a surface area of 100 cm^2. The lung absorbs the chemical at a rate per unit surface area of

$$R = \alpha \frac{c}{4.0 \times 10^{-2} + c}$$

Time is measured in seconds, surface area in cm^2 and volume in cm^3. The parameter α takes on the value 6.0 in the appropriate units.

a. Find surface area as a function of volume. Make sure your dimensions make sense.

b. What are the units of R? What must be the units of α?

c. Suppose that $c = 1.0 \times 10^{-2}$ $V = 400$. Find the total amount of chemical absorbed.

d. Suppose that $c = 1.0 \times 10^{-2}$. Find the total chemical absorbed as a function of V.

21. Suppose a person's head diameter D and height H grow according to

$$D(t) = 10.0e^{0.03t}$$
$$H(t) = 50.0e^{0.09t}$$

during the first 15 years of life.

a. Find D and H at $t = 0$, $t = 7.5$, and $t = 15$.

b. Sketch graphs of these two measurements as functions of time.

c. Sketch semilog graphs of these two measurements as functions of time.

d. Find the doubling time of each measurement.

22. On another planet, people have three hands and like to compute tripling times instead of doubling times.

a. Suppose a population follows the equation $b(t) = 3.0 \times 10^3 e^{0.333t}$ where t is measured in hours. Find the tripling time.

b. Suppose a population has a tripling time of 33 hours. Find the equation for population size $b(t)$ if $b(0) = 3.0 \times 10^3$.

23. A Texas millionaire (with \$1,000,001 in assets in 1995) got rich by clever investments. She managed to earn 10% interest per year for the last 20 years, and she plans to do the same in the future.

a. How much did she have in 1975?

b. When will she have \$5,000,001?

c. Write the discrete-time dynamical system and graph the updating function.

d. Write and graph the solution.

24. A major university hires a famous Texas millionaire to manage its endowment. The millionaire decides to follow this plan each year:

- Spend 25% of all funds above \$100 million on university operations.
- Invest the remainder at 10% interest.
- Collect \$50 million in donations from wealthy alumni.

a. Suppose the endowment has \$340 million to start. How much will it have after spending on university operations? After collecting interest on the remainder? After the donations roll in?

b. Find the discrete-time dynamical system.

c. Graph the updating function, and cobweb starting from \$340 million.

25. Another major university hires a different famous Texas millionaire to manage its endowment. This millionaire starts with \$340 million, brings back \$355 million the next year, and claims to be able to guarantee a linear increase in funds thereafter.

a. How much money will this university have after 8 years?

b. Graph the endowment as a function of time.

c. Write the discrete-time dynamical system, graph, and cobweb starting from \$340 million.

d. Which university do you think will do better in the long run? Which Texan would you hire?

26. A heart receives a signal to beat every second. If the voltage when the signal arrives is below 50 microvolts, the heart beats and increases its voltage by 30 microvolts. If the voltage when the signal arrives is greater than 50 microvolts, the heart does not beat and the voltage does not change. The voltage of the heart decreases by 25% between beats in either case.

a. Suppose the voltage of the heart is 40 microvolts right after one signal arrives. What is the voltage before the next signal and will the heart beat?

b. Graph the updating function for the voltage of this heart.

c. Will this heart exhibit normal beating or some sort of AV block?

27. Suppose vehicles are moving at 72 kph (kilometers per hour). Each car carries an average of 1.5 people, and all are carefully keeping a 2-second following distance (getting no closer than the distance a car travels in 2 seconds) on a three-lane highway.

a. How far is it between vehicles?

b. How many vehicles per kilometer are there?

c. How many people will pass a given point in an hour?

d. If commuter number oscillates between this maximum (at 8:00 A.M.) and a minimum that is one-third as large (at 8:00 P.M.) on a 24-hour cycle, give a formula for the number of people passing the given point as a function of time of day.

28. Suppose traffic volume on a particular road has been as shown in the following table.

Year	Vehicles
1970	40,000
1980	60,000
1990	90,000
2000	135,000

a. Sketch a graph of traffic over time.

b. Find the discrete-time dynamical system that describes this traffic.

c. What was the traffic volume in 1960?

d. Give a formula for the predicted traffic in the year 2050.

e. Find the half-life or doubling time of traffic.

29. In order to improve both the economy and the quality of life, policies are designed to encourage growth and decrease traffic flow. In particular, the number of cars is encouraged to increase by a factor of 1.6 over each 10-year period, but the commuters from 10,000 cars are to choose to ride comfortable new trains instead of driving.

a. If there were 40,000 people commuting by car in 1970, how many would there be in 1980?

b. Find the discrete-time dynamical system describing the number of people commuting by car.

c. Find the equilibrium.

d. Graph the updating function, and cobweb starting from an initial number of 40,000.

e. In the long run, will there be more or less traffic with this policy than with the policy that led to the data in the previous problem? Why?

Projects

1. Combine the model of selection from the chapter with the models of mutation and reversion. Assume that wild type have per capita production r, mutants have per capita production s, a fraction μ of the offspring of the wild type mutate into the mutant type, and a fraction ν of the offspring of the mutant type revert. First set $b_t = 4.0 \times 10^6$, $m_t = 2.0 \times 10^5$, $\mu = 0.2$, $\nu = 0.1$, $r = 1.5$, and $s = 2.0$.

a. How many of the wild type individuals will there be after production and before mutation? How many of these will mutate? How many will remain the wild type?

b. How many mutant individuals will there be after production and before mutation? How many of these will revert? How many will not?

c. Find the total number of wild type after reproduction, mutation, and reversion.

d. Find the total number of mutants after reproduction, mutation, and reversion.

e. Find the total number of bacteria after reproduction, mutation, and reversion. Why is it different from the initial number?

f. Find the fraction of mutants to begin with and the fraction after reproduction, mutation, and reversion.

Now, treat b_t and m_t as variables. The following steps will help you find the updating function.

a. Use the above steps to find m_{t+1} in terms of b_t and m_t.

b. Find the total number of bacteria, $b_{t+1} + m_{t+1}$, in terms of b_t and m_t.

c. Divide your equation for m_{t+1} by $b_{t+1} + m_{t+1}$ to find an expression for p_{t+1} in terms of b_t and m_t.

d. Divide the numerator and denominator by $m_t + b_t$ as in the derivation of Equation 1.10.5, and write the updating function in terms of p_t.

e. Find the equilibrium of this updating function.

Finally, we can do this in general by treating r, s, μ, and ν as parameters. Do exactly the above steps to find the updating function. After doing so, study the following special cases. In each case, explain your answer.

a. $r = s$ (no selection) and mutation in only one direction ($\mu = 0.0$ and $\nu > 0$). Find the updating function and the equilibrium. What does this mean?

b. $r = s$ and $\mu = \nu$. Find the updating function and the equilibrium. What does this mean?

c. $r > s$, $\nu = 0$, and $\mu > 0$. This means that the wild type has a reproductive advantage but keeps mutating. Find the updating function and the equilibrium. The result is called mutation-selection balance. Can you guess why?

2. Suppose a measurement follows

$$f(t) = \cos\left(\frac{2\pi t}{r}\right)$$

where the period r is an unknown number. You guess that the period is 1.0 and figure you can get a good fix on the behavior of the measurement by checking every 1.0 time step (once per period). Try the following for these values of r: 1.0, 0.6, 0.601, 0.602, 0.603, and 0.618. Experimenting with other values of r is highly recommended.

a. Graph the actual data as a continuous function of time $0 \le t \le 100$.

b. Graph what you find by plotting data points every 1.0 time unit.

c. Would you be able to figure out what was going on?

Chapter 2

Limits and Derivatives

Discrete-time dynamical systems describe biological change when measurements are made at discrete intervals. We now develop methods to describe a value that changes **continuously.** This description requires the two central ideas of differential calculus: the **limit** and the **instantaneous rate of change,** or **derivative.** We will find a **geometric** interpretation of the derivative as the **slope of the tangent line,** which will help us to graph and analyze complicated functions.

Achieving these goals requires both understanding the idea of the derivative and having the tools to compute the derivatives of a wide range of functions. Complicated functions are built by combining simple pieces, and their derivatives are computed with a set of rules for combining the derivatives of sums, powers, products, quotients, and compositions. Starting with the derivatives of linear, exponential, logarithmic, and trigonometric functions, we will be able to differentiate pretty much any function we can write down. The ability to compute the derivative, combined with its dual interpretation as the instantaneous rate of change and as the slope, opens up a dazzling array of applications.

2.1 Introduction to Derivatives

Discrete-time dynamical systems are a powerful tool for describing the dynamics of biological systems when change can be accurately described by measurements made at **discrete times.** In order for us to understand other systems fully, however, measurements must be made at all times, or **continuously.** We have only to think of the growth of a plant or the motion of an animal to realize that some change is best described by a continuous set of measurements.

In this chapter, we will develop the tools needed to describe measurements that change continuously. We will switch from thinking about what *happens* to thinking about what *is happening* to a measurement. The central idea is the **instantaneous rate of change,** or the **derivative.** Graphically, the derivative is equal to the slope of the **tangent line** to a curve.

These two ideas of the derivative, as the instantaneous rate of change of a measurement and as the slope of a curve, are the keys to appreciating the many applications of **calculus.** Understanding that the derivative must be computed as a **limit** is the key to using calculus correctly.

The Average Rate of Change

Suppose we measure a bacterial population continuously and find that the population size $b(t)$ (in millions) follows the equation

$$b(t) = 2.0^t$$

where t is measured in hours (Figure 2.1.1). How can we completely describe the growth of this population?

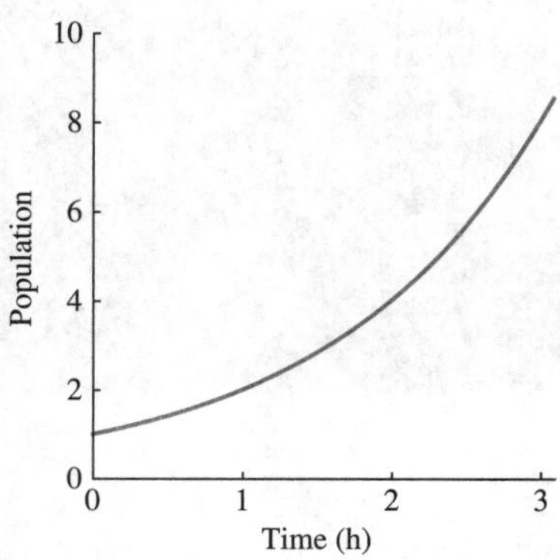

FIGURE 2.1.1
A bacterial population measured continuously

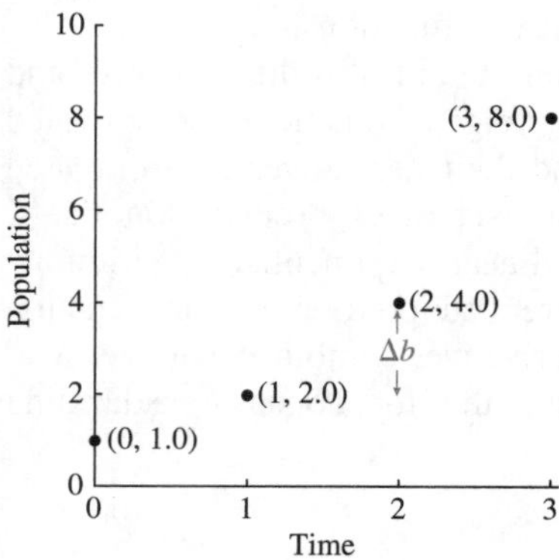

FIGURE 2.1.2
Hourly measurement of a bacterial population

Table 2.1.1

t (h)	$b(t)$ (millions)	Change, $\Delta b = b(t) - b(t-1)$
0	1.0	—
1	2.0	1.0
2	4.0	2.0
3	8.0	4.0
4	16.0	8.0
5	32.0	16.0

If we checked the population size every hour, we would find the following data (Figure 2.1.2).

If this were the whole story, we could describe it with the discrete-time dynamical system

$$b_{t+1} = 2.0b_t$$

To begin working toward a description of how the population *is changing* at any given time, we have added a column Δb, denoting the change in the population between times $t-1$ and t. Recall that Δ (the Greek capital letter Delta) means "change in" (Section 1.4 Proportional Relations, p. 41). For example, the bacterial population increased by 2.0 million between $t = 1.0$ and $t = 2.0$. The change in population is not defined at $t = 0$ because there was no previous measurement.

For more accuracy, we could check the population every half-hour (Figure 2.1.3). We have added another column to the table, indicating the **average rate of change** of the population, defined as

$$\text{average rate of change} = \frac{\text{change in population}}{\text{change in time}} = \frac{\Delta b}{\Delta t}$$

The average rate of change is an indication of how rapidly the population is changing.

Table 2.1.2

t (h)	$b(t)$ (millions)	Change, $\Delta b = b(t) - b(t-0.5)$	Average Rate of Change, $\frac{\Delta b}{\Delta t} = \frac{b(t) - b(t-0.5)}{0.5}$
0.0	1.0000	—	—
0.5	1.4142	0.4142	0.8284
1.0	2.0000	0.5858	1.1716
1.5	2.8284	0.8284	1.6568
2.0	4.0000	1.1716	2.3431
2.5	5.6569	1.6569	3.3137
3.0	8.0000	2.3431	4.6863

Example 2.1.1 Computing the Average Rate of Change

Between $t = 1.0$ and $t = 1.5$, the population grew by 0.8284 million. Because this change took only $\Delta t = 0.5$ h,

$$\text{average rate of change} = \frac{\Delta b}{\Delta t} = \frac{0.8284}{0.5} \approx 1.6568$$

in units of million bacteria per hour.

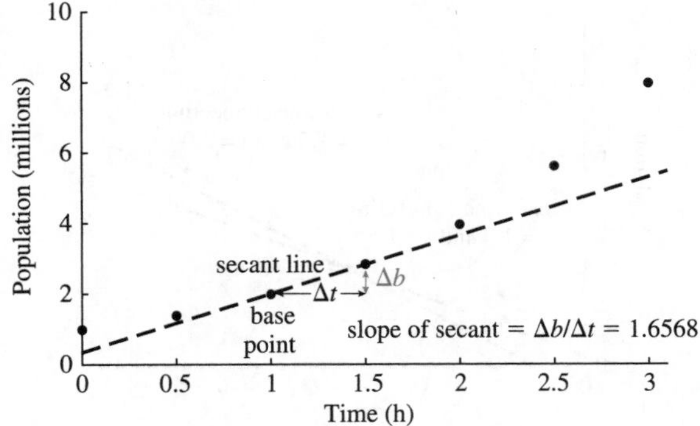

FIGURE 2.1.3
Half-hourly measurement of a bacterial population

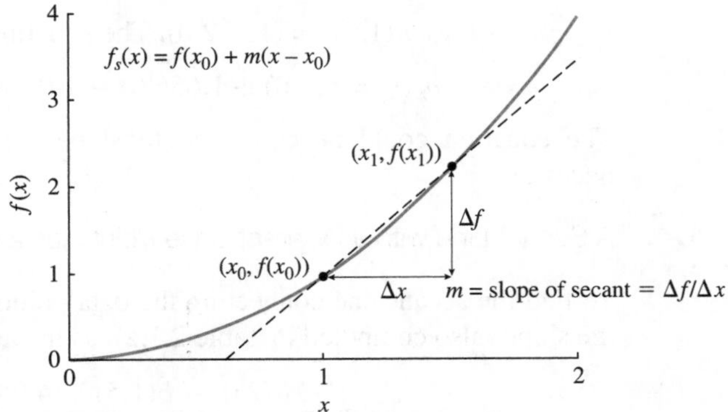

FIGURE 2.1.4
The secant line, its slope, and its equation

There is an important graphical interpretation of the average rate of change, as the slope of the line connecting the two points on a graph.

Definition 2.1 **Secant Line**

A line connecting two points on the graph of a function is called a **secant line.**

We will often single out one of the two points as a **base point** to focus on for more detailed study.

Example 2.1.2 The Slope of a Secant Line

Suppose we choose (1, 2.0) as the base point. The average rate of change between $t = 1.0$ and $t = 1.5$, found to be 1.6568 in Example 2.1.1, is equal to the slope of the secant line connecting the data points at these two times (see Figure 2.1.3).

The **equation** of a secant line can be found using the point-slope form for a line (Definition 1.8). Suppose we are given a base point $(x_0, f(x_0))$ on the graph of a function $f(x)$. If the second point is $(x_1, f(x_1))$, the slope is

$$m = \frac{\Delta f}{\Delta x} = \frac{f(x_1) - f(x_0)}{x_1 - x_0}$$

The equation of the secant line, which we will represent by the function $f_s(x)$, is

$$f_s(x) = f(x_0) + m(x - x_0),$$

where we used $(x_0, f(x_0))$ as the base point and m as the slope (Figure 2.1.4).

Example 2.1.3 The Equation of a Secant Line

In Example 2.1.2, we computed the slope of the line connecting the data points at $t = 1.0$ and $t = 1.5$ to be 1.6568. To use point-slope form, we identify the base point

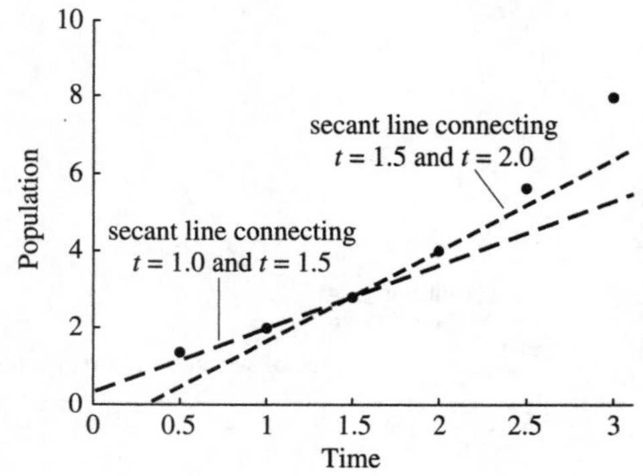

FIGURE 2.1.5
A different secant line to the same data

(x_0, y_0) as $(1.0, b(1.0)) = (1.0, 2.0)$. The equation of the secant line is then

$$b_s(t) = b(1.0) + 1.6568(t - 1.0) = 2.0 + 1.6568(t - 1.0)$$

The equation could be converted to slope-intercept form, but this is usually not necessary.

Example 2.1.4 A Secant Line with a Different Base Point Has a Different Equation

To find the secant line connecting the data points at $t = 1.5$ and $t = 2.0$, we first find the slope (also computed in Table 2.1.2), as the average rate of change, or

$$\text{slope} = \frac{b(2.0) - b(1.5)}{2.0 - 1.5} = \frac{4.0 - 2.8284}{0.5} \approx 2.3431$$

The base point (x_0, y_0) is $(2.0, b(2.0)) = (2.0, 4.0)$. The equation of the secant line is then

$$b_s(t) = b(2.0) + 2.3431(t - 2.0) = 4.0 + 2.3431(t - 2.0)$$

As shown in Figure 2.1.5, this secant line has a different slope and base point than the secant line in Example 2.1.3 because we are connecting different points on the graph.

To find an accurate estimate of the rate of change right at $t = 1.0$, we should look only at the change near that point. The following table shows the results when measurements are taken every 0.1 h.

Table 2.1.3

t	$b(t)$	Change, $\Delta b = b(t) - b(t - 0.1)$	Average Rate of Change, $\frac{\Delta b}{\Delta t}$
0.7000	1.6245	0.1088	1.0879
0.8000	1.7411	0.1166	1.1660
0.9000	1.8661	0.1250	1.2496
1.0000	2.0000	0.1339	1.3393
1.1000	2.1435	0.1435	1.4355
1.2000	2.2974	0.1538	1.5385
1.3000	2.4623	0.1649	1.6489

The measurements over this shorter interval of time appear nearly to follow a line (Figure 2.1.6). This is the key observation in calculus: Over short intervals, curves look like lines. The art of calculus is finding the *slope* of the line that most closely matches the curve.

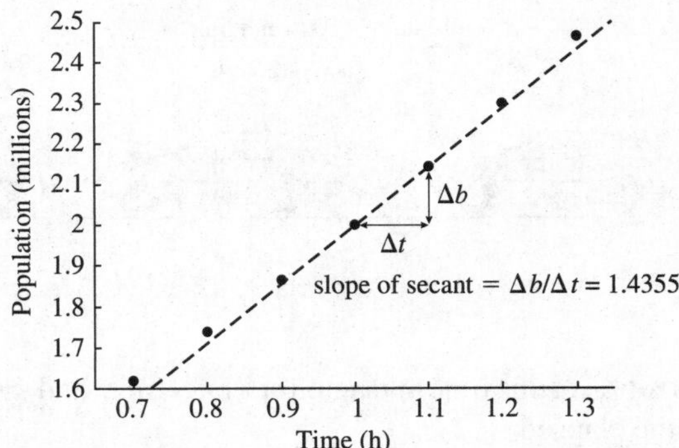

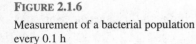

FIGURE 2.1.6
Measurement of a bacterial population every 0.1 h

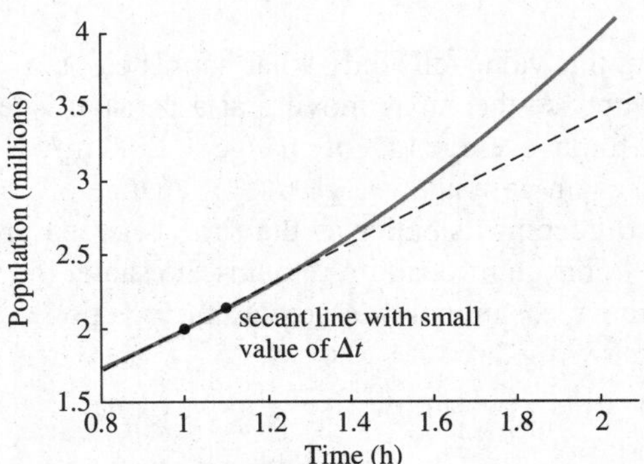

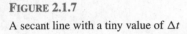

FIGURE 2.1.7
A secant line with a tiny value of Δt

Instantaneous Rates of Change

As the time Δt between measurements becomes smaller, the average rate of change between times $t = 1.0$ and $t = 1.0 + \Delta t$ becomes a better and better description of what is happening exactly at $t = 1.0$ (Figure 2.1.7). Average rates of change over smaller and smaller intervals are computed in the following table.

Table 2.1.4

Δt	$1.0 + \Delta t$	$b(1.0 + \Delta t)$	Δb	$\frac{\Delta b}{\Delta t}$
1.0	2.0	4.0000	2.0000	2.0000
0.5	1.5	2.8284	0.8284	1.6568
0.1	1.1	2.1435	0.1435	1.4354
0.01	1.01	2.0139	0.0139	1.3911
0.001	1.001	2.00139	0.00139	1.3868
0.0001	1.0001	2.000139	0.000139	1.3863

As Δt becomes smaller, there is less and less time for anything to happen, and the **change** in population Δb also becomes small. However, the average *rate* of change does not become tiny because the change takes place over shorter and shorter time intervals. In fact, the average rate of change approaches a value of about 1.386. We would like to define this value as the **instantaneous rate of change,** the rate of change *exactly* at $t = 1.0$.

What do we mean by instantaneous rate of change? The most familiar instantaneous rate of change is speed, the rate of change of position, as measured by a speedometer. But how does a speedometer *measure* this rate? In fact, most speedometers directly measure the speed by converting rotation of the drive shaft into a magnetic field. However, for an organism without wheels, speed must be estimated by measuring

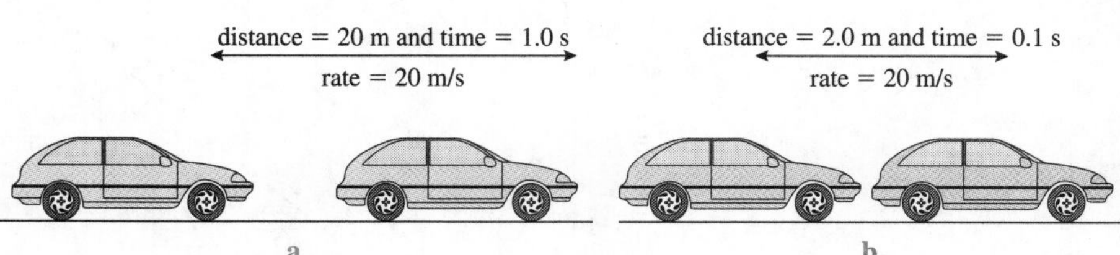

FIGURE 2.1.8

A car moving at constant speed travels a shorter distance in a shorter time

position at one time and again at a later time, and then dividing the distance moved by the time elapsed:

$$\text{average rate of change} = \frac{\text{change in position}}{\text{change in time}}$$

Again, this value tells only what happened on **average** during the interval.

Suppose the car is moving at a constant speed of 20.0 m/s. It moves 20.0 m in 1.0 s, for an average rate of change of 20.0 m/s (Figure 2.1.8a). It moves only 2.0 m in 0.1 s, again with an average rate of change of 20.0 m/s (Figure 2.1.8b). The distance moved becomes smaller as the time between checks becomes smaller. The average rate of change of position remains the same. If we continued to make more and more accurate measurements, assessing the position of the car every Δt s, we would collect the following data:

Table 2.1.5

Δt	Distance Moved	Average Rate of Change
1.0	20.0	20.0
0.1	2.0	20.0
0.01	0.2	20.0
0.001	0.02	20.0

The average rate of change is always 20.0 because the car is moving at a constant speed. This constant speed must be the instantaneous rate of change.

With the bacterial population, it is not as easy to guess the instantaneous rate of change. Ideally, we would compute the instantaneous rate of change by picking $\Delta t = 0$, the smallest possible value, resulting in

Δt	$1.0 + \Delta t$	$b(1.0 + \Delta t)$	Δb	$\frac{\Delta b}{\Delta t}$
0.0	1.0	2.0	0.0	$\frac{0.0}{0.0}$ = undefined!

Dividing by 0 is a mathematical misdemeanor. Dividing 0 by 0 is a mathematical felony. Not only have we failed to find the answer but we have also violated a major mathematical law.

Gradually choosing a smaller and smaller value of Δt corresponds to picking the second point on the curve closer and closer to the base point (Figure 2.1.9). With $\Delta t = 0$, the second point lies right on top of the base point. It is impossible to draw a unique line through a single point. In fact, there are an infinite number of possible lines through this point (Figure 2.1.10). Only one of these lines is close to the secant lines in Figure 2.1.9. This **tangent line** does touch the curve in only a single point, but it does so by just kissing the side of it rather than rudely crossing straight through. In fact, as we zoom in on the tangent line, it looks more and more similar to the curve (Figure 2.1.11).

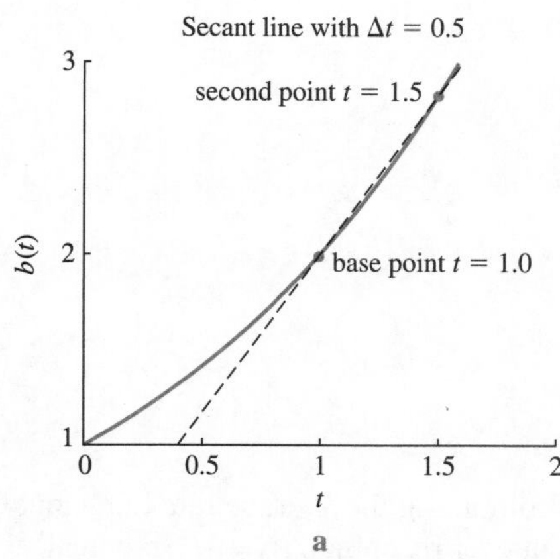

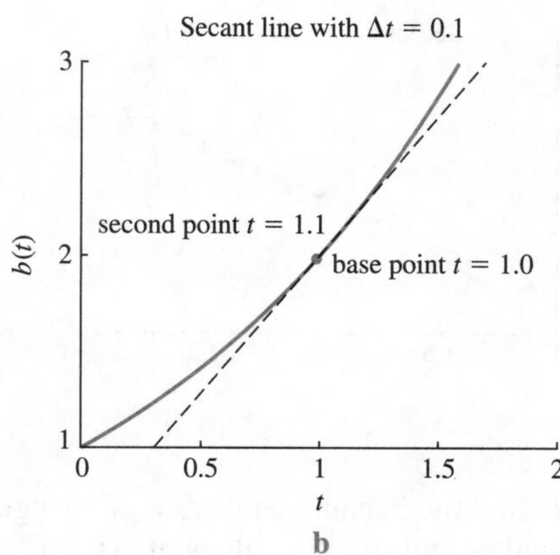

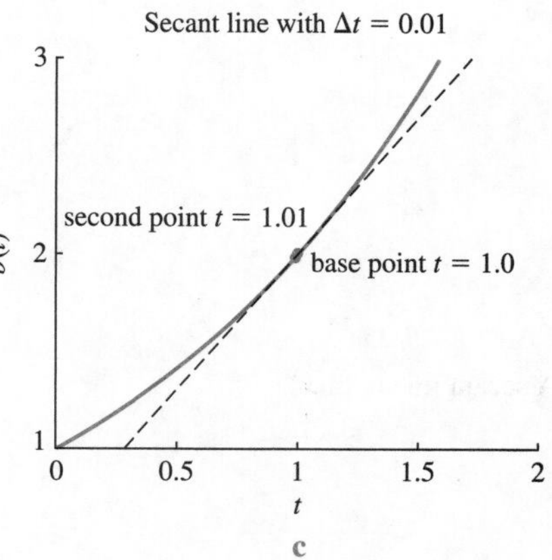

FIGURE 2.1.9
Some secant lines

Example 2.1.5 Finding a Tangent Line

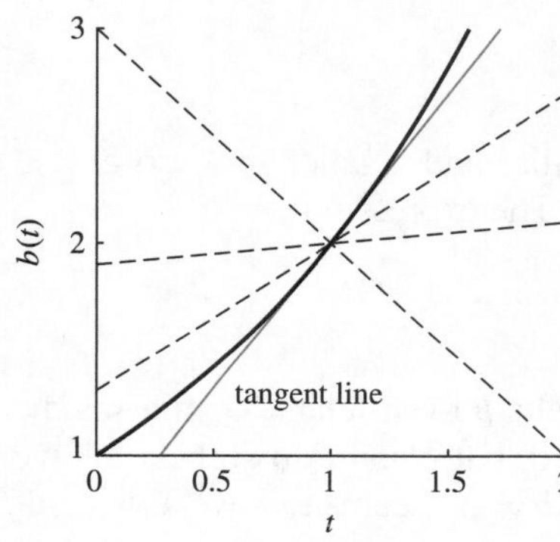

FIGURE 2.1.10

Some of the infinite number of lines through a single point

Suppose we wish to find the slope of the tangent line to the function $f(x) = \ln(x)$ at $x = 2$. See Figure 2.1.12. We can evaluate the slope of the tangent as a function of Δx for both positive and negative values of Δx.

Table 2.1.6

Δx	$2.0 + \Delta x$	$f(2.0 + \Delta x)$	Δf	$\frac{\Delta f}{\Delta x}$
1.00000	3.00000	1.09861	0.40547	0.40547
0.50000	2.50000	0.91629	0.22314	0.44629
0.10000	2.10000	0.74194	0.04879	0.48790
0.01000	2.01000	0.69813	0.00499	0.49875
0.00100	2.00100	0.69365	0.00050	0.49988
−1.00000	1.00000	0.00000	−0.69315	0.69315
−0.50000	1.50000	0.40547	−0.28768	0.57536
−0.10000	1.90000	0.64185	−0.05129	0.51293
−0.01000	1.99000	0.68813	−0.00501	0.50125
−0.00100	1.99900	0.69265	−0.00050	0.50013

As Δx becomes small, the slope of the secant gets close to 0.5. ▲

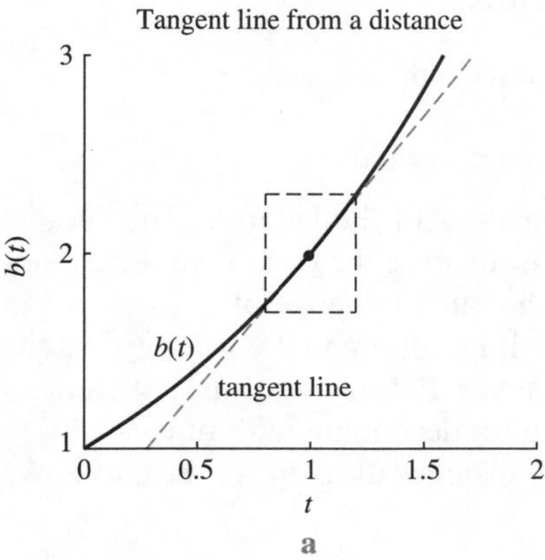

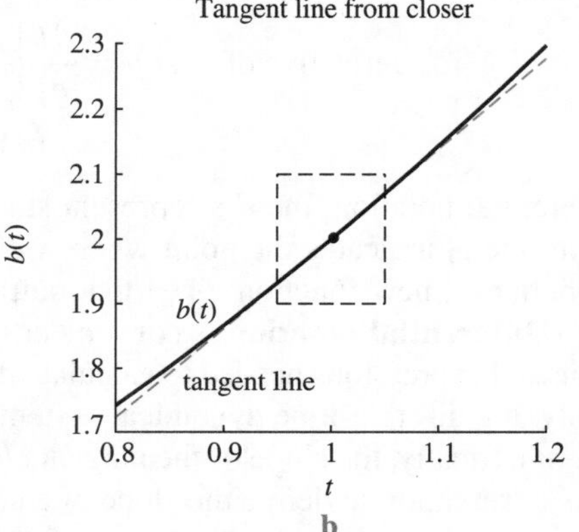

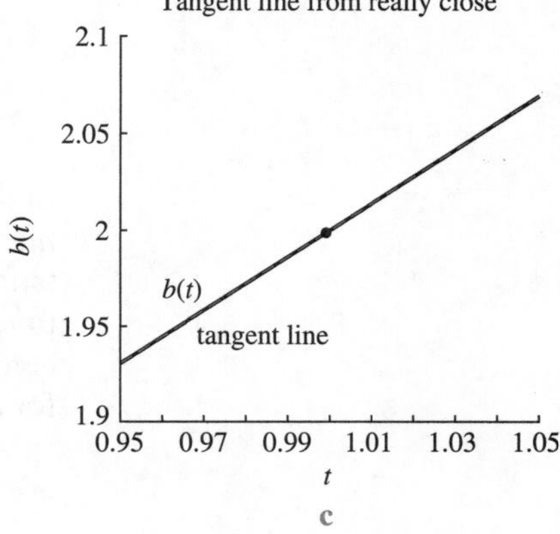

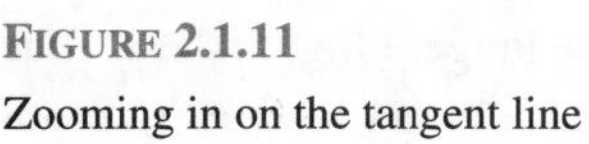

FIGURE 2.1.11

Zooming in on the tangent line

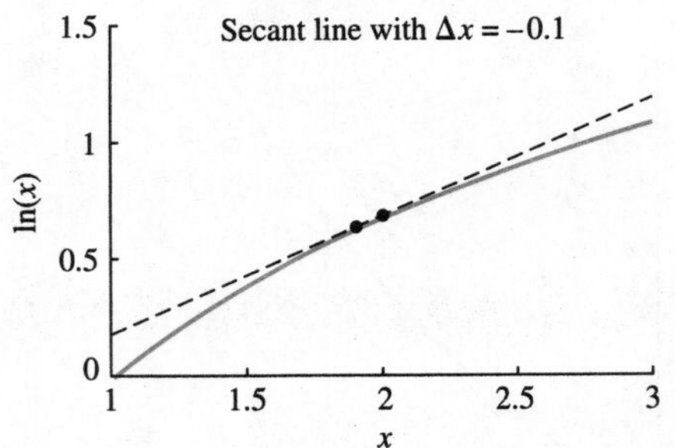

FIGURE 2.1.12
A secant line to $\ln(x)$

We find the instantaneous rate of change by computing the average rate of change with smaller and smaller values of Δt, but without ever reaching $\Delta t = 0$. Graphically, this corresponds to moving the second point closer and closer to the base point and seeing that the secant line gets closer and closer to the tangent line. Just as the slope of the secant line is equal to the average rate of change, the slope of the tangent line is equal to the instantaneous rate of change.

Limits and Derivatives

We now need a way to work with the idea of "smaller and smaller" or "closer and closer." This mathematical notion is called the **limit.** The expression

$$\lim_{\Delta t \to 0} \frac{\Delta b}{\Delta t}$$

which is read "the limit as delta t approaches 0 of delta b over delta t," expresses the idea that we *would like to* get by plugging in $\Delta t = 0$, but *cannot* do so because we cannot divide 0 by 0. Near $t = 1.0$, we found that $\Delta b \neq \Delta t$ seems to have a value of about 1.386, so we define that value to be the limit.

Using the limit, we can define the derivative.

Definition 2.2 The instantaneous rate of change of a function $f(t)$ at $t = t_0$ is called the **derivative of** f and is computed as

$$\lim_{\Delta t \to 0} \frac{\Delta f}{\Delta t}$$

where $\Delta f = f(t_0 + \Delta t) - f(t_0)$.

The derivative measures how rapidly a measurement is changing at a particular instant.

There are two different notations for the derivative:

$$\text{derivative of } f \text{ at } t_0 = \left.\frac{df}{dt}\right|_{t_0} \qquad \text{differential notation}$$
$$= f'(t_0) \qquad \text{prime notation}$$

In differential notation, the d's represent small versions of the letter Δ. The vertical line with the t_0 indicates the point where we are evaluating the derivative. Prime notation defines a new function $f'(t_0)$ that outputs the rate of change of f at any input time t_0. **Differential notation** is convenient for writing differential equations and the complicated expressions needed to calculate derivatives. **Prime notation** is convenient for analyzing discrete-time dynamical systems and for describing rates of change.

Geometrically, the slope of the tangent closely matches the slope of the curve. We use this observation to define the slope of a curve.

Definition 2.3 The slope of the graph of a function is equal to the slope of the tangent line to the graph, which is itself equal to the derivative of the function.

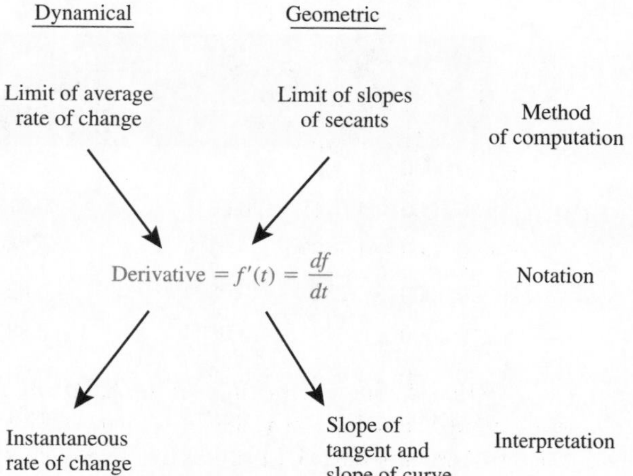

FIGURE 2.1.13
The interrelated meanings of the derivative

These two ways of thinking about the derivative are linked in Figure 2.1.13.

The tangent line is a good approximation because it lies so close to the curve (Figure 2.1.11). The central trick in calculus is realizing that from up close, a smooth curve looks like its tangent line and that the slope of the tangent can be computed with the derivative. We will soon see examples of curves that are not smooth and have no well-defined tangent line.

Differential Equations: A Preview

Using the derivative, we can find the instantaneous rate of change of the bacterial population at $t = 1.0$, or indeed at any time. However, this description does not tell us the **rule** followed by the population. We can use the derivative along with our intuition about the behavior of growing populations to derive such a rule. Instead of finding a discrete-time dynamical system, a formula for the new population as a function of the old population, we will derive a **differential equation,** a formula for the **rate of change** of the population.

The following table illustrates how we estimate the instantaneous rate of change via the average rate of change by using a fairly small value of $\Delta t = 0.1$. In other words, we estimate that the derivative $\frac{db}{dt}$ at each time t is approximately

$$\frac{db}{dt} \approx \frac{\Delta b}{\Delta t} = \frac{b(t) - b(t - 0.1)}{0.1}$$

We have another new column to the table, the **per capita rate of change,** defined as

$$\text{per capita rate of change} = \frac{\text{instantaneous rate of change}}{\text{population}}$$

When studying the discrete-time dynamical system for a growing bacterial population, we found that the **per capita production** provided a useful description. Similarly, the per capita rate of change, or per capita **rate** of production, provides a useful description of a continuous set of measurements of population size.

Mathematically,

$$\text{per capita rate of production} = \frac{\frac{db}{dt}}{b(t)} \approx 0.6697$$

Solving for the derivative $\frac{db}{dt}$ yields

$$\frac{db}{dt} = 0.6697b(t) \tag{2.1.1}$$

Table 2.1.7

t	$b(t)$	Change, Δb	Average Rate of Change, $\frac{\Delta b}{\Delta t} \approx \frac{db}{dt}$	Per Capita Rate of Change, $\frac{db/dt}{b(t)}$
0.0000	1.0000	—	—	—
0.1000	1.0718	0.0718	0.7177	0.6697
0.2000	1.1487	0.0769	0.7692	0.6697
0.3000	1.2311	0.0824	0.8245	0.6697
0.4000	1.3195	0.0884	0.8836	0.6697
0.5000	1.4142	0.0947	0.9471	0.6697
0.6000	1.5157	0.1015	1.0150	0.6697
0.7000	1.6245	0.1088	1.0879	0.6697
0.8000	1.7411	0.1166	1.1660	0.6697
0.9000	1.8661	0.1250	1.2496	0.6697
1.0000	2.0000	0.1339	1.3393	0.6697
1.1000	2.1435	0.1435	1.4355	0.6697
1.2000	2.2974	0.1538	1.5385	0.6697
1.3000	2.4623	0.1649	1.6489	0.6697
1.4000	2.6390	0.1767	1.7673	0.6697
1.5000	2.8284	0.1894	1.8941	0.6697
1.6000	3.0314	0.2030	2.0301	0.6697
1.7000	3.2490	0.2176	2.1758	0.6697
1.8000	3.4822	0.2332	2.3319	0.6697
1.9000	3.7321	0.2499	2.4993	0.6697
2.0000	4.0000	0.2679	2.6787	0.6697

This is a **differential equation.** A differential equation sets the derivative of some function (usually written in differential notation) equal to some combination of measurements not involving derivatives. In this case, the rate of change of the population is proportional to the population size itself. Of course, this differential equation is not exactly correct, because we estimated the instantaneous rate of change as the average rate of change with $\Delta t = 0.1$. Exercises 31 through 34 follow the same steps to find more accurate differential equations by using smaller values of Δt.

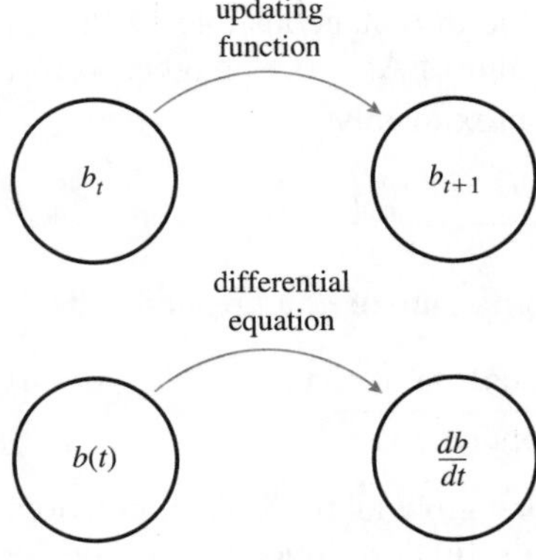

FIGURE 2.1.14
The difference between discrete-time dynamical systems and differential equations

Differential equations and discrete-time dynamical systems are two types of rules describing how a measurement changes. How do they differ? A discrete-time dynamical system, such as $b_{t+1} = 2.0b_t$, gives the new value of the population (at time $t+1$) as a function of the previous value (at time t). A differential equation instead gives the **rate of change** of the population as a function of the population. Unlike a discrete-time dynamical system, it does not involve the population at two different times (such as b_{t+1} and b_t). The differential equation instead relates two different pieces of information about the population at one time: here, the population size $b(t)$ and the rate of change $\frac{db}{dt}$ (Figure 2.1.14).

Consider again the car moving at a constant speed of 20.0 m/s. The instantaneous rate of change of position, or derivative, is equal to 20.0 m/s. If we denote the position at time t by $P(t)$, we can describe the car with the differential equation

$$\frac{dP}{dt} = 20.0$$

This differential equation says mathematically that the rate of change of position is exactly 20.0 m/s at all times.

Differential equations are the single most powerful tool in applied mathematics. Their discovery by Sir Isaac Newton, the great English physicist, is one of the greatest insights in the history of science. If differential equations seem hard to understand, remember that it took hundreds of years of work by the world's leading mathematicians and scientists to realize their importance. The detailed study of differential equations in this book begins in Chapter 4, after we learn how to compute and apply derivatives in other circumstances.

Summary To describe how a measurement changes, we defined the **average rate of change** of the population, the change in population divided by the change in time. The average rate of change corresponds graphically to the slope of the **secant line** connecting two data points. To find the **instantaneous rate of change,** or **derivative,** we estimated the average rate of change over shorter and shorter intervals. Because it is impossible to use an interval of length zero, we found the **limit** as the interval approaches zero. Graphically, the instantaneous rate of change corresponds to the slope of the **tangent line,** which is defined to be equal to the slope of the curve itself. In some cases, we can write a **differential equation,** a formula for the derivative.

2.1 Exercises

Mathematical Techniques

1–6 ▪ For each of the following functions, find the average rate of change between the given base point t_0 and times $t_0 + \Delta t$ for the four following values of Δt: $\Delta t = 1.0$, $\Delta t = 0.5$, $\Delta t = 0.1$, and $\Delta t = 0.01$.

1. $f(t) = 2 + 3t$ with base point $t_0 = 1.0$
2. $g(t) = 2 - 3t$ with base point $t_0 = 0.0$
3. $h(t) = 2t^2$ with base point $t_0 = 1.0$
4. $h(t) = t^2 + 1$ with base point $t_0 = 0.0$
5. $G(t) = e^{2t}$ with base point $t_0 = 0.0$
6. $G(t) = e^{-t}$ with base point $t_0 = 0.0$

7–12 ▪ For each of the following functions, find the equation of the secant line connecting the given base point t_0 and times $t_0 + \Delta t$ for $\Delta t = 1.0$, $\Delta t = 0.5$, $\Delta t = 0.1$, and $\Delta t = 0.01$. Sketch the function and each of the secant lines.

7. $f(t) = 2 + 3t$ with base point $t_0 = 1.0$ (based on Exercise 1).
8. $g(t) = 2 - 3t$ with base point $t_0 = 0.0$ (based on Exercise 2).
9. $h(t) = 2t^2$ with base point $t_0 = 1.0$ (based on Exercise 3).
10. $h(t) = t^2 + 1$ with base point $t_0 = 0.0$ (based on Exercise 4).
11. $G(t) = e^{2t}$ with base point $t_0 = 0.0$ (based on Exercise 5).
12. $G(t) = e^{-t}$ with base point $t_0 = 0.0$ (based on Exercise 6).

13–18 ▪ Using the results in Exercises 1–6, take a guess at the limit of the slopes of the secants, and find the slope and equation of the tangent line.

13. $f(t) = 2 + 3t$ with base point $t_0 = 1.0$. Call the tangent line function $\hat{f}(t)$ (based on Exercise 1).
14. $g(t) = 2 - 3t$ with base point $t_0 = 0.0$. Call the tangent line function $\hat{g}(t)$ (based on Exercise 2).
15. $h(t) = 2t^2$ with base point $t_0 = 1.0$. Call the tangent line function $\hat{h}(t)$ (based on Exercise 3).
16. $h(t) = t^2 + 1$ with base point $t_0 = 0.0$. Call the tangent line function $\hat{h}(t)$ (based on Exercise 4).
17. $G(t) = e^{2t}$ with base point $t_0 = 0.0$. Call the tangent line function $\hat{G}(t)$ (based on Exercise 5).
18. $G(t) = e^{-t}$ with base point $t_0 = 0.0$. Call the tangent line function $\hat{G}(t)$ (based on Exercise 6).

19–20 ▪ Important concepts have many names and formulas. The following problems ask you to recall them.

19. Give two other names for the instantaneous rate of change of the function $g(t)$.
20. Give three different notations for the instantaneous rate of change of a function $g(t)$.

Applications

21–22 ▪ For each equation for population size, find the following and illustrate on a graph.

a. The population at times 0, 1, and 2.
b. The average rate of change between times 0 and 1.
c. The average rate of change between times 1 and 2.

21. A population of bacteria described by the formula $b(t) = 1.5^t$ where the time t is measured in hours.
22. A population of bacteria described by the formula $b(t) = 1.2^t$ where the time t is measured in hours.

23–26 ▪ For each equation for population size, find the following.

a. The average rate of change between times 0 and 1.0.
b. The average rate of change between times 0 and 0.1.
c. The average rate of change between times 0 and 0.01.
d. The average rate of change between times 0 and 0.001.
e. What do you think the limit is?
f. Graph the tangent line.

23. A population following $b(t) = 1.5^t$.

24. A population following $b(t) = 2.0^t$.

25. A population following $h(t) = 5.0t^2$.

26. A bacterial population following $b(t) = (1.0 + 2.0t)^3$.

27–30 ▪ For the following bacterial populations, find the average rate of change during the first hour and during the first and second half-hours. Graph the data and the secant lines associated with the average rates of change. Which populations change more rapidly during the first half-hour?

27. $b(t) = 3.0(2.0^t)$

28. $b(t) = e^{0.5t}$

29. $b(t) = 2.0e^{-0.5t}$

30. $b(t) = 3.0(0.5^t)$

31–34 ▪ Follow the steps in the text used to derive the approximate differential equation 2.1.1,

$$\frac{db}{dt} = 0.6697b(t)$$

with the following values of Δt. This requires computing the value of the function $b(t) = 2.0^t$ at times separated by Δt and finding the average rate of change between those times.

31. $\Delta t = 1.0$

32. $\Delta t = 0.5$

33. $\Delta t = 0.01$

34. $\Delta t = 0.001$

35–36 ▪ Consider the following data on a tree.

Age	Height (m)	Mass (Metric Tons)
0	10.11	30.0
1	11.18	39.1
2	12.40	50.6
3	13.74	65.8
4	15.01	85.9
5	16.61	111.6
6	18.27	144.2
7	20.17	187.7
8	22.01	244.1
9	24.45	319.2
10	26.85	414.2

For each of the measurements:

a. Estimate the rate of change at each age.

b. Graph the rate of change as a function of age.

c. Find and graph the rate of change divided by the value as a function of age.

d. Use these results to describe the growth of this tree with a differential equation.

35. The height.

36. The mass.

37–43 ▪ The procedure that banks use to compute continuously compounded interest is similar to the process we used to derive a differential equation. Suppose that several banks claim to be giving 5% annual interest and that you have \$1000 to deposit.

37. How much would you have after a year from a bank that has no compounding?

38. A bank that compounds twice yearly really gives 2.5% interest twice. How much would you have after a year from this bank? How much better is this than your outcome with a bank that has no compounding?

39. A bank that compounds monthly really gives 5/12% interest each month. How much would you have after a year from this bank?

40. How much would you have after a year from a bank that compounded daily?

41. Write down a limit that expresses the amount of money you would get from a bank that compounded continuously, and try to guess the answer.

42. Follow the steps in Exercises 37, 39, and 40 to compare yearly, monthly, and daily compounding for a bank giving 20% interest.

43. Follow the steps in Exercise 42 to compare yearly, monthly, and daily compounding for a bank giving 100% interest (in a time of severe inflation). Why do you think compound interest makes a bigger difference when the interest rate is higher?

Computer Exercises

44. Consider the function

$$f(x) = \sqrt{1 - x^2}$$

defined for $-1 \le x \le 1$. This is the equation for a semicircle. The tangent line at the base point $(\sqrt{2}/2, \sqrt{2}/2)$ has slope -1. Graph this tangent line. Now zoom in on the base point. Does the circle look more and more like the tangent line? How far do you need to go before the circle looks flat? Would a tiny insect be able to tell that his world was curved?

45. Suppose a bacterial population oscillates with the formula

$$b(t) = 2.0 + \cos(t)$$

a. Graph this function.

b. Find and graph the function that gives the rate of change between times t and $t + 1$ as a function of t for $0 \le t \le 10$.

c. Find and graph the function that gives the rate of change between times t and $t + 0.1$ as a function of t for $0 \le t \le 10$.

d. Try the same with smaller values of Δt. Do you have any idea what the limit might be?

46. Repeat the steps in Exercise 45 for a bacterial population that follows the formula

$$b(t) = e^{-0.1t}(2.0 + \cos(t))$$

2.2 Limits

The derivative, the mathematical version of the instantaneous rate of change and the slope of a curve, includes a **limit** in its definition. We will now study the mathematical and scientific basis of this fundamental idea. By understanding the useful properties of limits, we will be able to calculate limits of polynomials and rational functions. We will also define **left-hand limits** and **right-hand limits** for functions that make sense on only one side and **infinite limits** for quantities or functions that become extremely large.

Limits of Functions

We begin by formalizing the steps we used to compute the instantaneous rate of change of our population following the law

$$b(t) = 2.0^t$$

at $t = 1.0$. First, we found the change in the population, Δb, between times 1.0 and $1.0 + \Delta t$ as

$$\begin{aligned}\Delta b &= b(1.0 + \Delta t) - b(1.0)\\ &= 2^{1.0+\Delta t} - 2.0\end{aligned}$$

The average rate of change, the change in the population divided by the change in time, is then

$$\frac{\Delta b}{\Delta t} = \frac{2^{1.0+\Delta t} - 2.0}{\Delta t}$$

The instantaneous rate of change (or derivative) at $t = 1.0$ is

$$\frac{db}{dt} = b'(1.0) = \lim_{\Delta t \to 0} \frac{2^{1.0+\Delta t} - 2.0}{\Delta t}$$

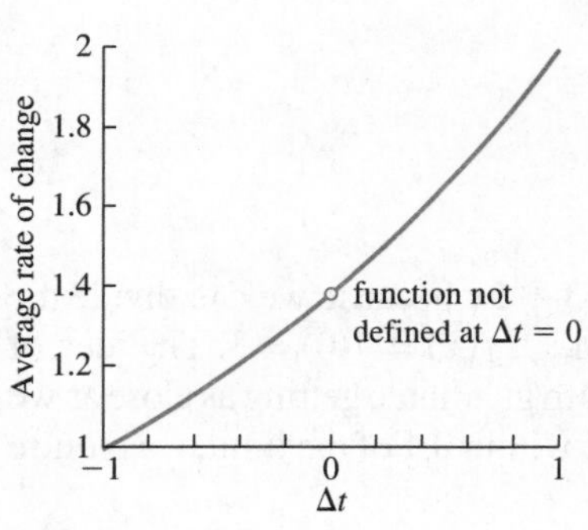

FIGURE 2.2.15
The limit of the average rate of change

As Δt becomes smaller and smaller, the average rate of change gets closer and closer to a value near 1.386. We could not take the smallest possible value, $\Delta t = 0$, because that would have led to division of zero by zero.

We can think of the average rate of change

$$\frac{\Delta b}{\Delta t} = \frac{2^{1.0+\Delta t} - 2.0}{\Delta t}$$

as a **function** of Δt that is defined at all points except $\Delta t = 0$ (Figure 2.2.15). We guessed that the limit is 1.386 because values get closer and closer to 1.386. But what does it mean for a function to get "closer and closer" to a "limit"? What, indeed, does it mean to be "close"?

As is often the case, this mathematical question can be understood by thinking of it **scientifically.** What does it mean scientifically for two quantities to be close to one another?

> Two quantities are close when they are too similar to distinguish with a precise measuring device.

Consider the measurement of temperature. With a crude measuring device, such as waving your hand around in the air, it might be difficult to distinguish between temperatures of 20°C and 21°C. Without a more precise device, the two temperatures are effectively the same. With an ordinary thermometer, we can distinguish between 20°C and 21°C, but we may not be able to distinguish between 20°C and 20.1°C. Two temperatures are **exactly** equal if no thermometer, no matter how precise, can distinguish between them.

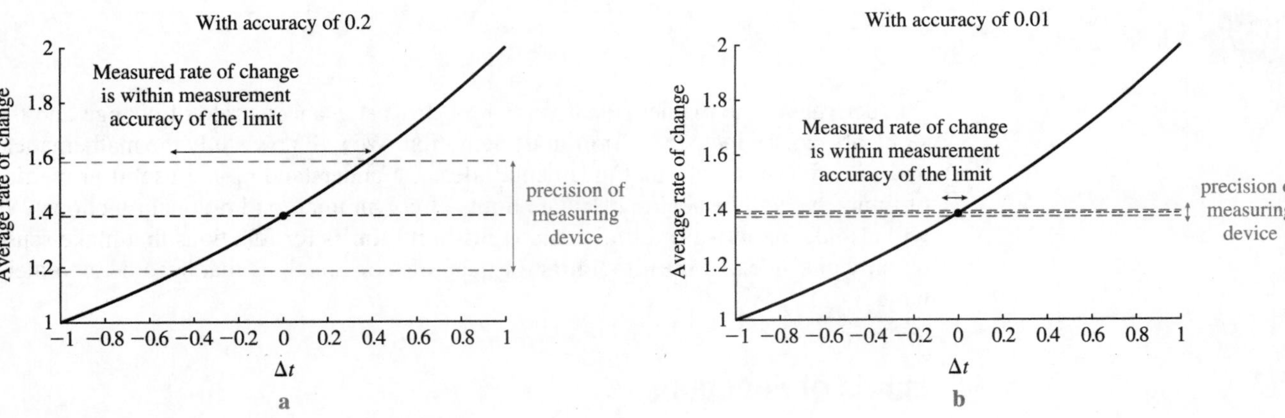

FIGURE 2.2.16
An experimental output approaching a limit

We can translate this scientific idea into the mathematical idea of a limit. The average rate of change is a function of Δt (Figure 2.2.15). If we can measure the rate of change with an accuracy of only 0.1, we do not need a very small value of Δt to be within 0.1 of the limit (Figure 2.2.16a). For a more precise measurement of the average rate of change with an accuracy of 0.01, we need a much smaller Δt to be within measurement accuracy of the limit (Figure 2.2.16b). No matter how precisely we can measure rate of change, however, we can always pick a sufficiently small Δt to be within measurement accuracy of the limit.

Example 2.2.1 How Close Must the Input Be?

Consider the function

$$f(x) = \frac{3x + 2x^2}{x}$$

which is not defined at $x = 0$. For any $x \neq 0$, $f(x) = 3 + 2x$ because we can divide the numerator through by x. We will soon show that $\lim_{x\to 0} f(x) = f(0) = 3$. The idea of the limit says we can pick values of x close enough to 0 to guarantee getting as close as we might wish to this limit. For example, if we wish to be within 0.1 of the limit, we require

$$\begin{aligned} 2.9 &< f(x) < 3.1 \\ 2.9 &< 3 + 2x < 3.1 \\ -0.1 &< 2x < 0.1 \\ -0.05 &< x < 0.05 \end{aligned}$$

Graphically, the inputs on the horizontal axis must lie within the region that produces outputs within the range on the vertical axis (Figure 2.2.17). If we wish to be within

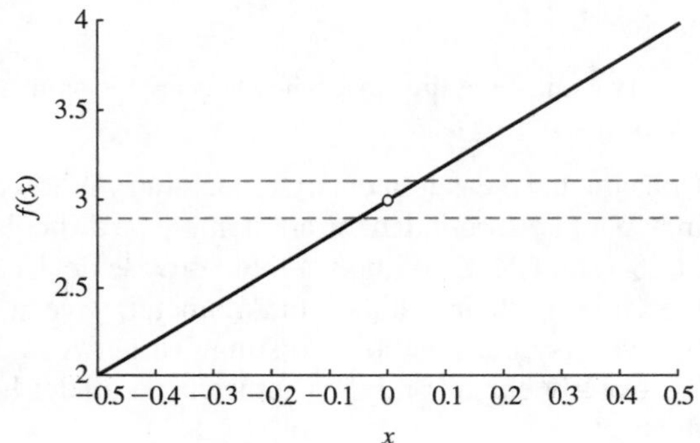

FIGURE 2.2.17
Finding how close the input must be

0.01 of the limit, we require

$$2.99 < f(x) < 3.01$$
$$2.99 < 3 + 2x < 3.01$$
$$-0.01 < 2x < 0.01$$
$$-0.005 < x < 0.005$$

Getting closer to the limit requires inputs that are closer to 0.

Example 2.2.2 Finding the Limit of the Average Rate of Change Algebraically

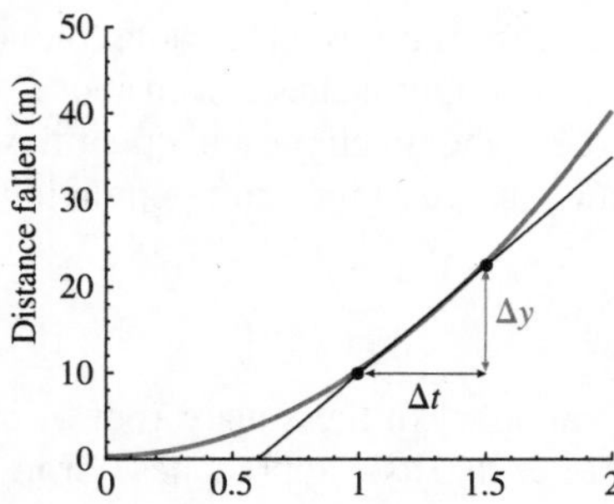

FIGURE 2.2.18

The distance traveled by a falling rock and the average rate of change

Consider finding the instantaneous rate of change of distance traveled by a falling rock, which follows the quadratic function (approximately the value on earth)

$$y(t) = 10.0t^2$$

where t is measured in seconds and y is measured in meters fallen (Figure 2.2.18). We wish to find the rate of change at $t = 1.0$. The change Δy between times 1.0 and $1.0 + \Delta t$ is

$$\begin{aligned}\Delta y &= y(1.0 + \Delta t) - y(1.0)\\ &= 10.0(1.0 + \Delta t)^2 - 10.0\\ &= 10.0\left(1.0 + 2.0\Delta t + \Delta t^2\right) - 10.0\\ &= 20.0\Delta t + 10.0\Delta t^2\end{aligned}$$

Then

$$\begin{aligned}\text{average rate of change} &= \frac{\Delta y}{\Delta t}\\ &= \frac{20.0\Delta t + 10.0\Delta t^2}{\Delta t}\end{aligned}$$

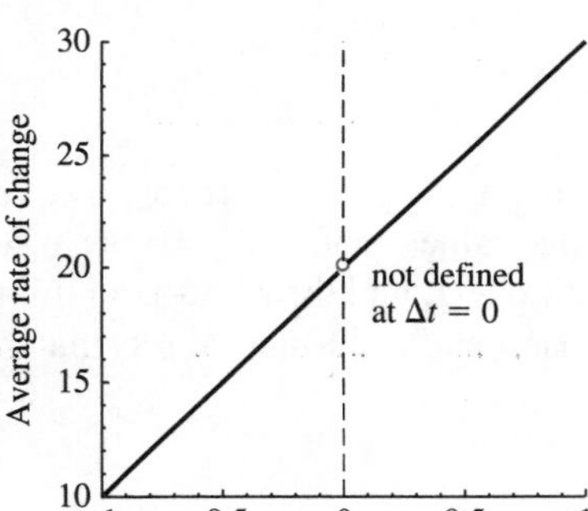

FIGURE 2.2.19

The average rate of change of distance for the falling rock

(Figure 2.2.19). As long as $\Delta t \neq 0$, we can divide out the Δt, so that

$$\text{average rate of change} = 20.0 + 10.0\Delta t$$

To find the exact rate of change, we must take the limit as $\Delta t \to 0$. For small values of Δt, the average rate of change gets as close as we might wish to 20.0. The limit is exactly 20.0.

Left-Hand and Right-Hand Limits

Sometimes a function is defined only on one side of a point. For example, the value of the function shown in Figure 2.2.20a seems to get closer and closer to 2.0 as x approaches 1 even though it is defined only for $x < 1$. If we wish to find the limit as x

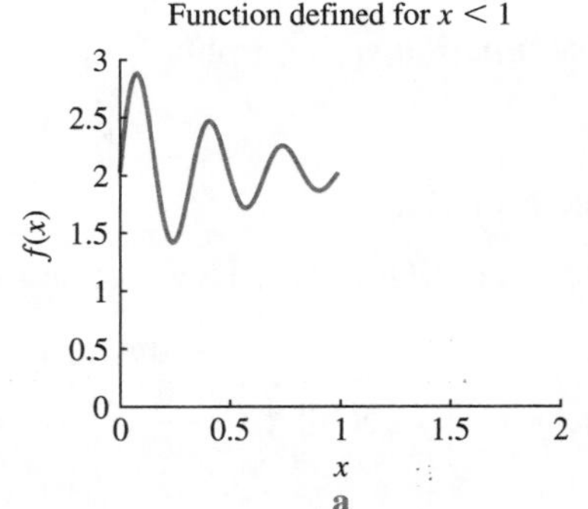

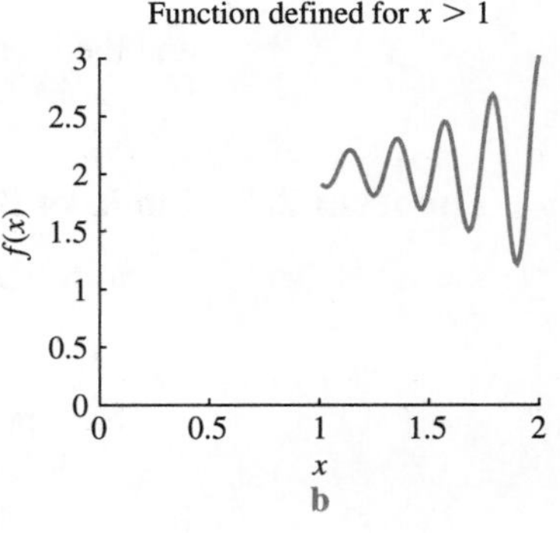

FIGURE 2.2.20

Functions with left-hand and right-hand limits

approaches 1, we must consider only values of x that lie in the domain. We write

$$\lim_{x \to 1^-} f(x) = 2$$

where the minus sign above the 1 indicates that x approaches 1 from *below*. This notation is called the **left-hand limit** and is read "the limit of $f(x)$ as x approaches 1 from below."

Similarly, if the domain of f contains only values of $x > 1$ (Figure 2.2.20b), we write

$$\lim_{x \to 1^+} f(x) = 2$$

The plus sign above the 1 indicates that x approaches 1 from *above*. This notation is called the **right-hand limit** and is read "the limit of $f(x)$ as x approaches 1 from above."

Left- and right-hand limits are most often used to describe functions and quantities that have only positive numbers in their domains, such as $\sqrt{x}$, $\ln(x)$ and population sizes. Suppose we are asked to find

$$\lim_{x \to 0^+} \sqrt{x}$$

We must compute the right-hand limit because we cannot take the square root of a negative number. Because the graph gets closer and closer to 0 as x approaches 0 from above, the limit is 0.

Example 2.2.3 A Function with Unequal Left-Hand and Right-Hand Limits

Consider the **signum** function, defined by

$$\begin{cases} \text{signum}(x) = -1 & \text{if } x < 0 \\ \text{signum}(x) = 0 & \text{if } x = 0 \\ \text{signum}(x) = 1 & \text{if } x > 0 \end{cases}$$

This function gives the "sign" of a number, telling whether it is negative, zero, or positive (Figure 2.2.21). The limit as x approaches 0 is not the value $\text{signum}(0) = 0$ because the function does not get close to 0. The left-hand limit is -1, and the right-hand limit is 1. This is an example of a function where the left-hand and right-hand limits match neither each other nor the value of the function.

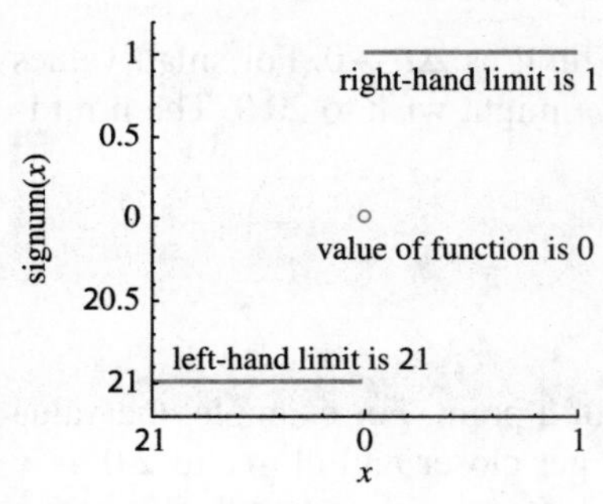

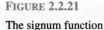

FIGURE 2.2.21
The signum function

Properties of Limits

Limits have many properties that simplify their computation. The basic idea is an important one; we first find the limits of some simple functions and then build limits of more complicated functions by combining these simple pieces with rules that tell how limits add, multiply, and divide.

The simple functions we begin with are constant functions, with formula

$$f(x) = c$$

and the **identity function** with formula

$$f(x) = x$$

Theorem 2.1 Limits of Basic Functions

a. Suppose $f(x) = c$ for all x. Then, for any value of a,

$$\lim_{x \to a} f(x) = c$$

b. Suppose $f(x) = x$ for all x. Then, for any value of a,

$$\lim_{x \to a} f(x) = a$$

Example 2.2.4 Finding the Limit of a Constant

Suppose the function $h(x)=5$, a constant. See Figure 2.2.22. Then Theorem 2.1 implies that

$$\lim_{x\to 7} h(x)=5$$

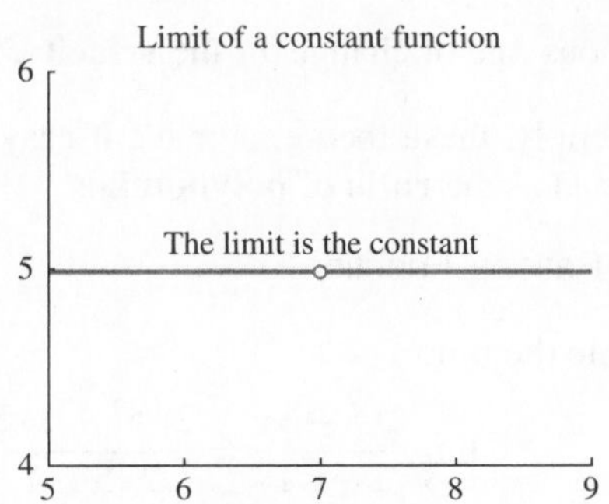

FIGURE 2.2.22
Limit of a constant function

Example 2.2.5 Finding the Limit of the Identity Function

Suppose the function $g(x)=x$, the identity function. See Figure 2.2.23. Then Theorem 2.1 implies that

$$\lim_{x\to 7} g(x)=7$$

Second, we can combine limits by adding, multiplying, and dividing (as long as we avoid dividing by 0).

Theorem 2.2 Rules for Combining Limits

Suppose $f(x)$ and $g(x)$ are functions with well-defined limits at $x=a$.

a. The limit of the sum is the sum of the limits, or

$$\lim_{x\to a}[f(x)+g(x)]=\lim_{x\to a} f(x)+\lim_{x\to a} g(x)$$

b. The limit of the product is the product of the limits, or

$$\lim_{x\to a} f(x)g(x)=[\lim_{x\to a} f(x)]\cdot[\lim_{x\to a} g(x)]$$

c. The limit of the product of a constant and a function is the product of the constant and the limit of the function, or

$$\lim_{x\to a}[cf(x)]=c\cdot \lim_{x\to a} f(x)$$

d. Suppose $\lim_{x\to a} g(x)\neq 0$. Then the limit of the quotient is the quotient of the limits, or

$$\lim_{x\to a}\left[\frac{f(x)}{g(x)}\right]=\frac{\lim_{x\to a} f(x)}{\lim_{x\to a} g(x)}$$

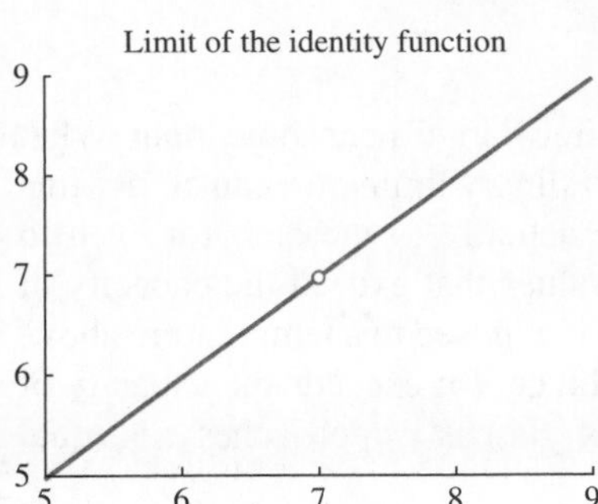

FIGURE 2.2.23
Limit of the identity function

Together, these theorems imply that we can find the limit of any **polynomial** by **plugging in the value.** Remember that a polynomial is a function that can be written as a sum of constants multiplied by powers of the argument.

Example 2.2.6 Finding the Limit of a Polynomial

The function $f(x)=2x^2+3x$ is a polynomial. We can find the limit by substituting the value. For example,

$$\lim_{x\to 5} 2x^2+3x=2\cdot 5^2+3\cdot 5=65$$

Example 2.2.7 Finding the Instantaneous Rate of Change of Distance Fallen of a Rock

In Example 2.2.2, we found the average rate of change of distance fallen of a rock to be $20.0 + 10.0\Delta t$ as a function of the interval Δt. Because this is a polynomial, we can find the limit by substituting the value $\Delta t = 0$:

$$\lim_{\Delta t\to 0} 20.0 + 10.0\Delta t = 20.0 + 10.0 \cdot 0 = 20.0$$

The instantaneous rate of change, or the **velocity,** is indeed 20.0 m/s.

More generally, these theorems make it easy to compute the limit of a **rational function,** defined as the **ratio of polynomials.**

Example 2.2.8 The Limit of a Rational Function

We can compute the limit

$$\lim_{x\to 5} \frac{2x^2 + 3x}{2x + 1} = \frac{2 \cdot 5^2 + 3 \cdot 5}{2 \cdot 5 + 1} = \frac{65}{11} \approx 5.91$$

by plugging in $x = 5$ because the denominator is not equal to 0 at $x = 5$.

Left- and right-hand limits share the properties of ordinary limits summarized in Theorems 2.1 and 2.2: They add, multiply, and divide.

Example 2.2.9 Combining Right-Hand Limits

We can use the rules for combining limits to find

$$\begin{aligned} \lim_{x\to 0^+} (3\sqrt{x} + 2) &= \lim_{x\to 0^+} 3\sqrt{x} + \lim_{x\to 0^+} 2 && \text{limit of sum} \\ &= 3\lim_{x\to 0^+} \sqrt{x} + \lim_{x\to 0^+} 2 && \text{constant comes out} \\ &= 3 \cdot 0 + 2 = 2 && \text{substitute} \end{aligned}$$

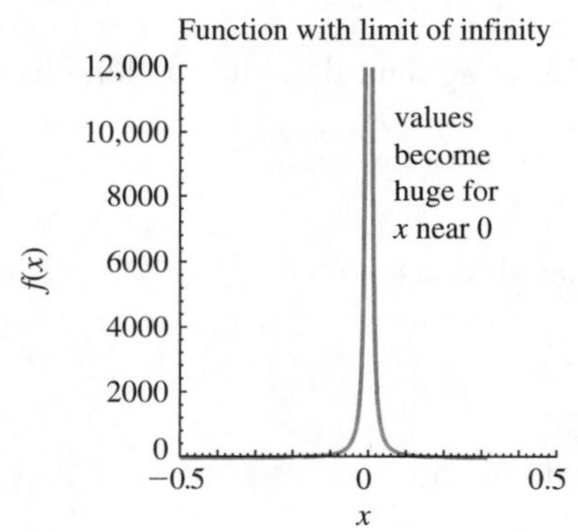

FIGURE 2.2.24
A function with a limit of infinity

Infinite Limits

One sometimes hears it said that a function gets "infinitely large" near some input. What might such a statement mean scientifically? As with ordinary limits, we can clarify this idea by thinking of measurements. It is impossible actually to measure (or even to imagine) a value of infinity. Instead, we encounter values that exceed the capacity of our measuring device. A thermometer would explode if exposed to a temperature above its capacity. A value can be thought of as **infinitely large** if it exceeds the capacity of *every possible* measuring device. We say "the limit of $f(x)$ as x approaches a is equal to infinity" and write

$$\lim_{x\to a} f(x) = \infty$$

Example 2.2.10 A Function with a Limit of Infinity

x	$f(x)$
1.0	1.0
0.1	100.0
0.01	10000.0
0.001	1.0×10^6
−1.0	1.0
−0.1	100.0
−0.01	10000.0
−0.001	1.0×10^6

Consider the function

$$f(x) = \frac{1}{x^2}$$

(Figure 2.2.24). If we plug in values of x closer and closer to 0, $f(x)$ becomes larger and larger.

In fact, almost any calculator will give an "error" if x is too small (although some calculators are smart enough to say "infinity"). In this case,

$$\lim_{x\to 0} f(x) = \infty$$

Similarly, a limit is equal to **negative infinity,** which is written $-\infty$, when the output becomes smaller than every possible value. We write

$$\lim_{x \to a} f(x) = -\infty$$

Example 2.2.11 A Function with a Limit of Negative Infinity

The function

$$g(x) = \frac{-1}{x^2}$$

has a limit of negative infinity as x approaches 0 (Figure 2.2.25).

x	$g(x)$
1.0	−1.0
0.1	−100.0
0.01	−10000.0
0.001	-1.0×10^6
−1.0	−1.0
−0.1	−100.0
−0.01	−10000.0
−0.001	-1.0×10^6

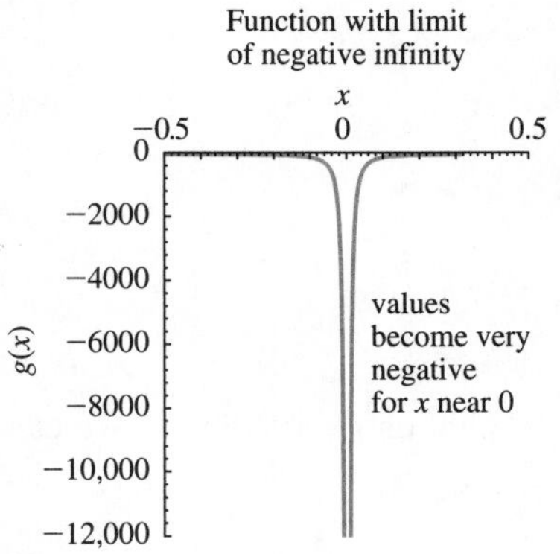

FIGURE 2.2.25

A function with a limit of negative infinity

Example 2.2.12 A Function with Different, but Infinite, Left-Hand and Right-Hand Limits

Consider the function

$$h(x) = \frac{1}{x}$$

(Figure 2.2.26). Suppose we wish to find the limit as x approaches 0. This function increases to positive infinity for $x > 0$ and to negative infinity for $x < 0$.

x	$h(x)$
1.0	1.0
0.1	10.0
0.01	100.0
0.001	1000.0
−1.0	−1.0
−0.1	−10.0
−0.01	−100.0
−0.001	−1000.0

The left-hand and right-hand limits help us to separate out these two types of behavior. As we move toward 0 from the left (negative x), the values of the function get smaller and smaller. As we move toward 0 from the right (positive x), the values of the function get larger and larger. In mathematical notation, $\lim_{x \to 0^-} h(x) = -\infty$ and $\lim_{x \to 0^+} h(x) = \infty$.

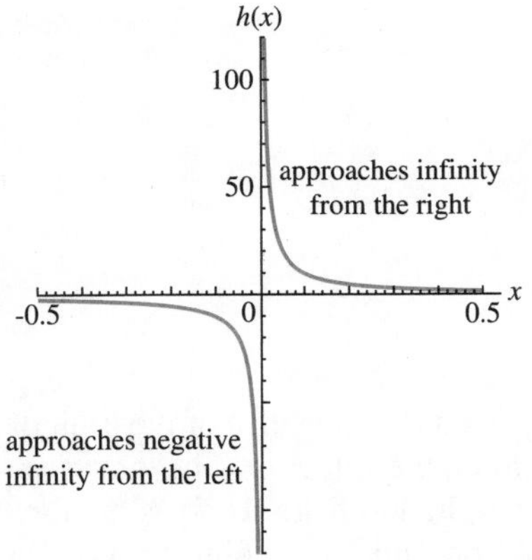

FIGURE 2.2.26

A function with a left-hand limit of $-\infty$ and a right-hand limit of ∞

Example 2.2.13 The Limit of $\ln(x)$ as $x \to 0^+$

During our study of the natural logarithm, we indicated that $\ln(x)$ is not defined for 0 or negative values of x and that the graph of $\ln(x)$ rises from negative infinity near $x = 0$ (Figure 2.2.27).

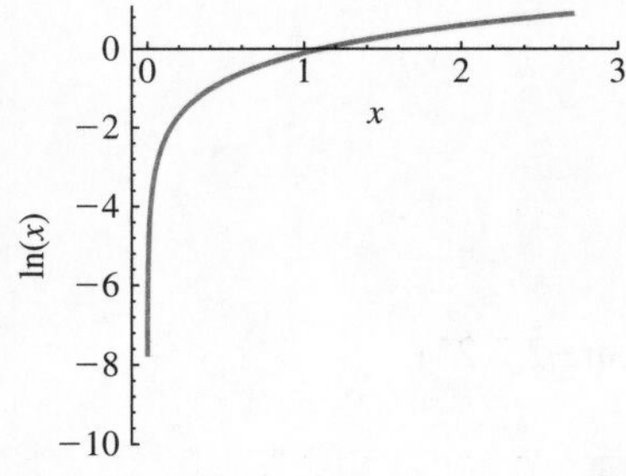

FIGURE 2.2.27
The natural logarithm approaching negative infinity

x	$\ln(x)$
1.0	0.0
0.1	−2.30
0.01	−4.61
0.001	−6.91
1.0×10^{-6}	−13.82
1.0×10^{-9}	−20.72

The value of $\ln(x)$ becomes more and more negative, although very slowly. We can now describe this in terms of the limit as

$$\lim_{x \to 0^+} \ln(x) = -\infty$$

Example 2.2.14 How Close Must the Input Be?

Consider the function $\ln(x)$. If the limit as $x \to 0^+$ is indeed negative infinity, we should be able to choose inputs x so small that the output is less than −10, or −100, or any large negative number. When is $\ln(x) < -10$? Solving yields

$$\ln(x) < -10$$
$$x < e^{-10} = 4.5 \times 10^{-5}$$

Graphically, the inputs on the horizontal axis must lie close enough to zero for the output to be below the horizontal line (Figure 2.2.28). A tiny input is required to get an output even this small. We will later think of this as meaning that $\ln(x)$ approaches negative infinity "slowly."

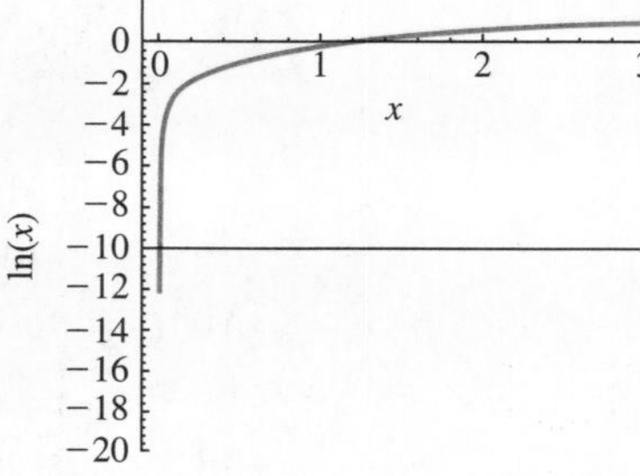

FIGURE 2.2.28
Finding how small the input must be

Summary On the basis of scientific reasoning, we have developed an intuitive idea of the limit of a function. A function $f(x)$ approaches a particular limit if the values of f become very close to that limit. We defined **left-hand limits** and **right-hand limits** for situations where functions or quantities are meaningful on only one side of a point. Limits can be added, multiplied, and divided. Finally, we defined limits of **infinity** and **negative infinity** on the basis of the idea that a quantity is effectively infinite when it exceeds the capacity of any measuring device.

2.2 Exercises

Mathematical Techniques

1–8 ▪ Using a computer or calculator, estimate the following limits. Sketch the function.

1. $\lim_{x\to 0}(1+x)^{1/x}$
2. $\lim_{x\to 0}\dfrac{\sin(x)}{x}$
3. $\lim_{x\to 0}\dfrac{1-\cos(x)}{x}$
4. $\lim_{x\to 0^+} x^x$ (the function is defined only for positive values of x)
5. $\lim_{x\to 0^+} x\ln(x)$
6. $\lim_{x\to 0}\dfrac{e^{2x}-1}{x}$
7. $\lim_{x\to 1^-}\dfrac{\ln(1-x)}{x}$
8. $\lim_{x\to 1^+}\sqrt{\ln(x)}$

9–12 ▪ Using the results from the earlier problems, find the combined limits using Theorem 2.2. Indicate how the new function was built.

9. $\lim_{x\to 0} 5(1+x)^{1/x}$ (based on Exercise 1).
10. $\lim_{x\to 0} 3\dfrac{\sin(x)}{x}+4$ (based on Exercise 2).
11. $\lim_{x\to 0}(1+x)^{1/x}\left(\dfrac{1-\cos(x)}{x}\right)$ (based on Exercises 1 and 3).
12. $\lim_{x\to 0^+}\dfrac{(1+x)^{1/x}}{x^x}$ (based on Exercises 1 and 4).

13–16 ▪ The given functions all have limits of 0 as $x \to 0^+$. For each function, find how close the input must be to 0 for the output to be a) within 0.1 of 0, and b) within 0.01 of the limit. Sketch a graph of each function for $x < 1$, and indicate which functions approach 0 quickly and which approach 0 slowly.

13. $f_1(x)=\sqrt{x}$
14. $f_2(x)=x$
15. $f_3(x)=x^2$
16. $f_4(x)=x^4$

17–20 ▪ The given functions all have limits of ∞ as $x \to 0^+$. For each function, find how close the input must be to 0 for the output to be a) greater than 10, and b) greater than 100. Sketch a graph of each function for $x < 1$, and indicate which functions approach infinity quickly and which approach infinity slowly.

17. $g_1(x)=\dfrac{1}{\sqrt{x}}$
18. $g_2(x)=\dfrac{1}{x}$
19. $g_3(x)=\dfrac{1}{x^2}$
20. $g_4(x)=\dfrac{1}{x^4}$

21–24 ▪ From the following pictures, find the left-hand and right-hand limits as x approaches 1.

21.

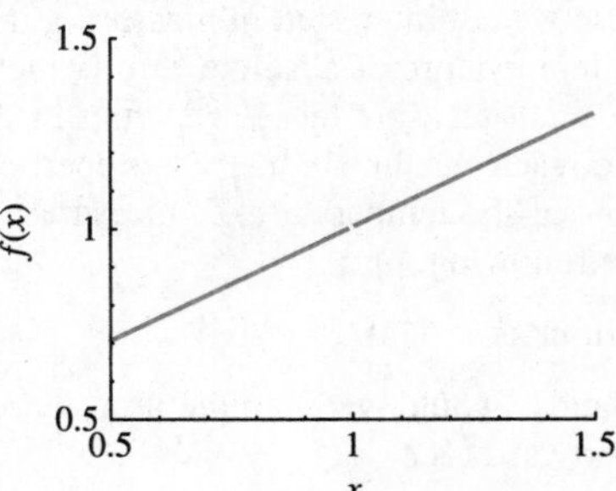

22.

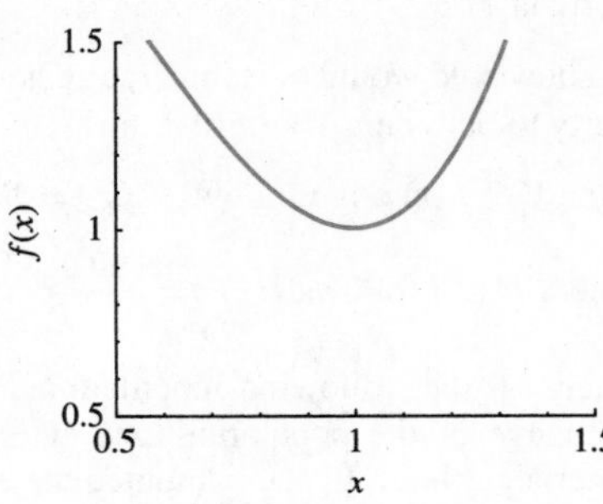

23.

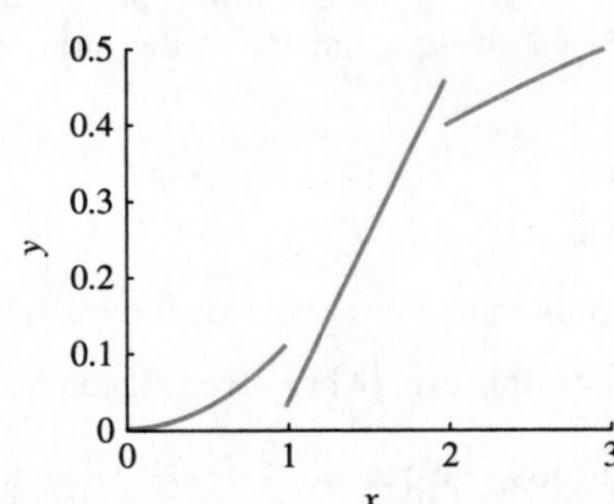

24.

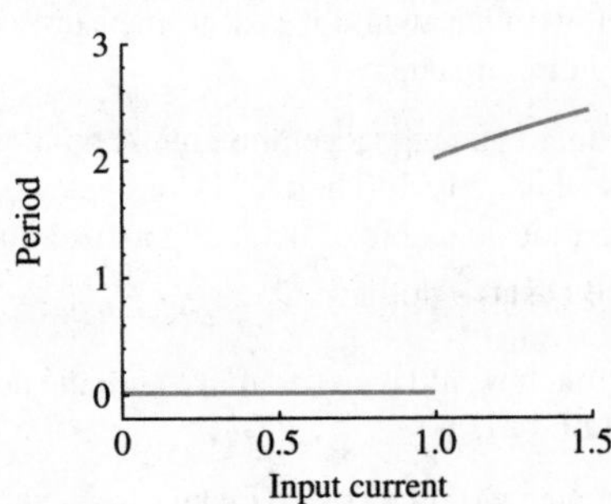

25–30 ▪ Find the average rate of change of the following functions as a function of Δx, and find the limit as $\Delta x \to 0$. Graph the function and indicate the rate of change on your graph.

25. $f(x)=5x+7$ near $x=0$.
26. $f(x)=5x+7$ near $x=1$.
27. $f(x)=5x^2$ near $x=0$.
28. $f(x)=5x^2$ near $x=1$.

29. $f(x) = 5x^2 + 7x + 3$ near $x = 1$.

30. $f(x) = 5x^2 + 7x + 3$ near $x = 2$.

Applications

31–32 ▪ Suppose we are interested in measuring the properties of a substance at temperature of absolute zero (which is 0 kelvins). However, we cannot measure these properties directly because it is impossible to reach absolute 0. Instead, properties are measured for small values of the temperature T, measured in kelvins (K). For each of the following, find

a. The limit as $T \to 0^+$.

b. How close would we be to the limit if we measured the property at 2 °K?

c. How close would we be to the limit if we measured the property at 1 °K?

d. About how cold would the temperature have to be for the property to be within 1% of its limit?

31. The volume $V(T)$ (in cm^3) follows $V(T) = 1 + T^2$.

32. The hardness $H(T)$ follows $H(T) = \dfrac{10.0}{1+T}$.

33–36 ▪ For each of the following populations, the instantaneous rate of change of the population size at $t = 0$ is exactly 1.0 million bacteria per hour. If you computed the average rate of change between $t = 0$ and $t = \Delta t$, how small would Δt have to be before your value was within 1% of the instantaneous rate of change?

33. $b(t) = t + t^2$

34. $b(t) = t + 0.1t^2$

35. $b(t) = e^t$ (this cannot be solved algebraically).

36. $b(t) = \sin(t)$ (this cannot be solved algebraically).

37–40 ▪ Scientifically, two quantities are close if it requires an accurate measuring device to detect the difference. In real life, accuracy costs money. How much would it cost to measure the differences in the following circumstances?

37. A piano tuner is trying to get the note A on a piano to have a frequency of exactly 440 hertz (H), or cycles per second. An electronic tuner capable of detecting a difference of x cycles per second costs $\dfrac{5}{x}$ dollars.

a. How much would it cost to make sure the note was within 1.0 H of 440?

b. How much would it cost to make sure the note was within 0.1 H of 440?

c. How much would it cost to make sure the note was within 0.01 H of 440?

38. The army is developing satellite-based targeting systems. A system that can send a missile within y m of its target costs $\dfrac{1}{y^2}$ million dollars.

a. How much would it cost to hit within 10 m?

b. How much would it cost to hit within 1 m?

c. How much would it cost to hit within 1 cm?

39. Suppose a body has temperature B and is cooling toward room temperature of 20°C according to the function $B(t) = 20 + 17e^{-t}$ where t is measured in hours. A $10 thermocouple can detect a difference of 0.1°C, a $100 thermocouple can detect a difference of 0.01°C, and so forth.

a. How much would it cost to detect the difference after 1 h?

b. How much would it cost to detect the difference after 5 h?

c. How much would it cost to detect the difference after 10 h?

40. Some dangerously radioactive and toxic radium was dumped in the desert in 1950. It has a half-life of 50 years, and the initial level of radioactivity was $r = 10.0$ rads. Nobody remembers where it was. How much will it cost to find it in the following years if detecting radioactivity at level r costs $\dfrac{5}{r}$ thousand dollars?

a. How much will it cost to find in the year 2000?

b. How much will it cost to find in the year 2050?

c. How much will it cost to find in the year 2130?

41–42 ▪ Scientifically, a quantity is large if it requires a tough measuring device to assess. In real life, toughness costs money. How much would it cost to measure the value in the following circumstances?

41. We are interested in measuring the pressure at different depths below the surface of the ocean. Pressure increases by approximately 1 atmosphere (atm) for every 10 m of depth below the surface (for example, at a depth of 20 m, there are approximately 3 atm of pressure: 2 atm due to the ocean and 1 atm due to the atmosphere itself). Measuring a pressure of x atm without crushing the device costs x^2 dollars.

a. How much would it cost to measure the pressure 100 m down?

b. How much would it cost to measure the pressure 1000 m down?

c. How much would it cost to measure the pressure 5000 m down?

42. Solar scientists want to measure the temperature inside the sun by sending in probes. Imagine that temperature increases by 1 million °C for every 10,000 km below the surface. A probe that can handle a temperature of x million °C costs x^3 million dollars.

a. How much would it cost to measure the temperature 10,000 km down?

b. How much would it cost to measure the temperature 100,000 km down?

c. How much would it cost to measure the temperature 200,000 km down?

Computer Exercise

43. There are various ways to find the smallest and largest numbers your calculator or computer can handle.

    a. Try doubling some number until you get an overflow.

    b. Try halving some number until you get an underflow.

    c. Compute $1.0 + \epsilon$ for smaller and smaller values of ϵ. At what point does your calculator return 1.0 as the answer?

    d. Compare the answers of parts **b** and **c**.

2.3 Continuity

Even with their useful properties, computing limits can be rather slow. When we are finding the limit of some function $f(x)$ as x approaches a, we would like simply to compute $f(a)$. In this section, we will learn the conditions under which this method works. The chief new tool is the **continuous function,** the mathematically precise definition of a function without "jumps." The definition of continuous function depends on the concept of limit, and continuous functions share the useful properties of limits. Scientifically, continuous functions represent relations between measurements where a small change in the input produces a small change in the output. Functions that are not continuous do occur in biological systems, and can generate novel phenomena, such as **hysteresis.**

Continuous Functions

We can find

$$\lim_{x\to 0} 2x + 1 = 1$$

in two ways. We can plug in values of x close to 0 and see that the results gets close to 1. Alternatively, we could break the function into component parts and use the properties of limits. But why not simply compute $2 \cdot 0 + 1 = 1$ to find the limit?

We can do just this when the function is **continuous.** What is a continuous function? Our intuitive notion of "continuous" is that the graph is "connected," without jumps. Figure 2.3.29 illustrates a function without jumps and a function with jumps. The graph of a continuous function can be drawn without lifting one's pencil.

The mathematical definition is supposed to capture this intuitive idea.

Definition 2.4 A function f is **continuous** at a point a if

$$\lim_{x\to a} f(x) = f(a)$$

Otherwise, we say the function is **discontinuous** at the point a.

This definition requires that the left- and right-hand limits are equal. As the graph approaches a particular point in the domain, the value of a continuous function gets closer and closer to the value of the function at that point. Otherwise, the graph would have a jump and could not be drawn without lifting a pencil.

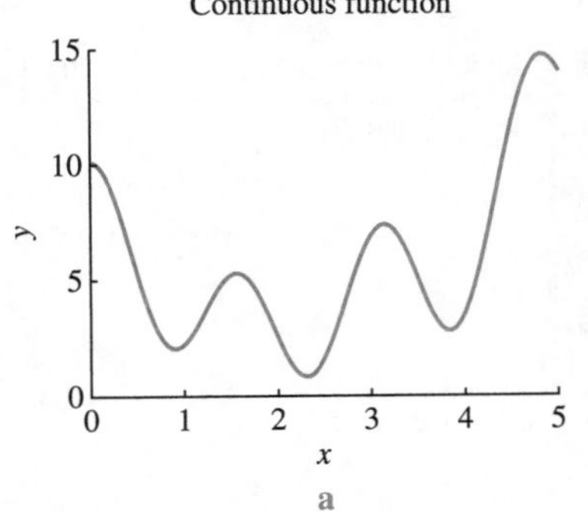

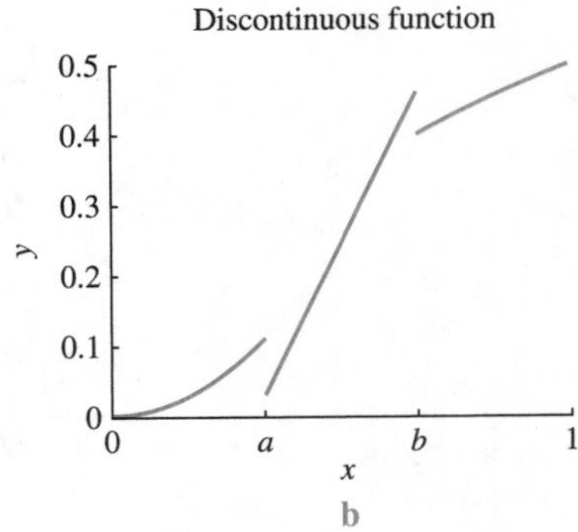

FIGURE 2.3.29
Continuous and discontinuous functions

Continuity is defined at *points*. A function can be continuous at some points and discontinuous at others. The points a and b are points of discontinuity of the function in Figure 2.3.29b; the function is continuous at all other points. When we say that a function is continuous without specifying a particular point, we mean that the function is continuous at *all* points of its domain.

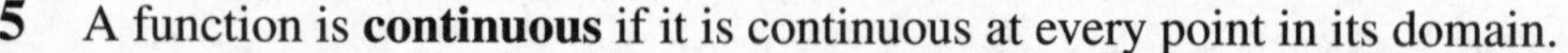

Definition 2.5 A function is **continuous** if it is continuous at every point in its domain.

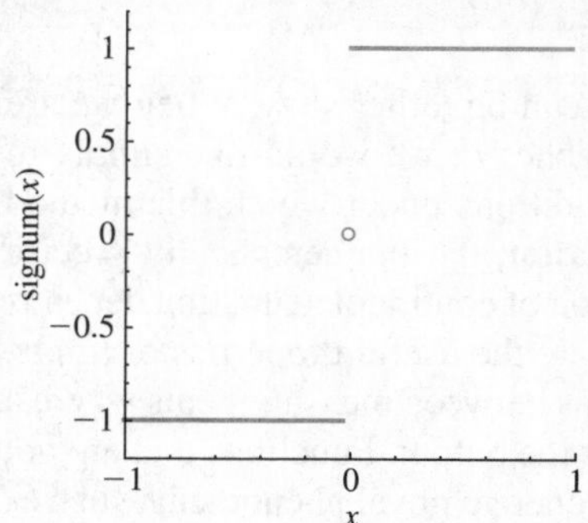

FIGURE 2.3.30

The signum function is not continuous at 0

What sorts of functions are not continuous? We have met examples of several types. Some functions have jumps—for example, the signum function, which is equal to -1 for negative arguments, to 0 when the argument is 0, and to 1 for positive arguments (Figure 2.3.30). At the point $x=0$, the value of the function is 0, the left-hand limit is -1, and the right-hand limit is 1. Because the left-hand limit and the right-hand limit do not match, the limit does not exist. Furthermore, neither of these limits matches the value of the function.

Second, functions with limits of infinity or negative infinity cannot be graphed without a jump (strictly speaking, these functions can be continuous at all points in their domain). In Figure 2.3.31a, the limit is infinity from both below and above. However, the function cannot be evaluated at $x=0$ and has a jump. In Figure 2.3.31b, the limit is negative infinity from below and positive infinity from above. This function has an infinitely large jump.

Continuous functions are useful because we can find limits by plugging in. How can we recognize a continuous function? Like limits, continuous functions can be combined in many useful ways, including addition, multiplication, division, and composition. Mathematically, we build the edifice of continuous functions on a stable foundation of two theorems, one giving the basic continuous functions and the other saying how they can be combined.

Theorem 2.3 **The Basic Continuous Functions**

a. The constant function $f(x)=c$ is continuous.

b. The identity function $f(x)=x$ is continuous.

c. The exponential function $f(x)=e^x$ is continuous.

d. The logarithmic function $f(x)=\ln(x)$ is continuous for $x>0$.

e. The cosine function $f(x)=\cos(x)$ is continuous.

Theorem 2.4 **Combining Continuous Functions**

Suppose $g(x)$ is continuous at $x=a$.

a. If $f(x)$ is continuous at $x=a$, the sum $f(x)+g(x)$ is continuous at $x=a$.

b. If $f(x)$ is continuous at $x=a$, the product $f(x)g(x)$ is continuous at $x=a$.

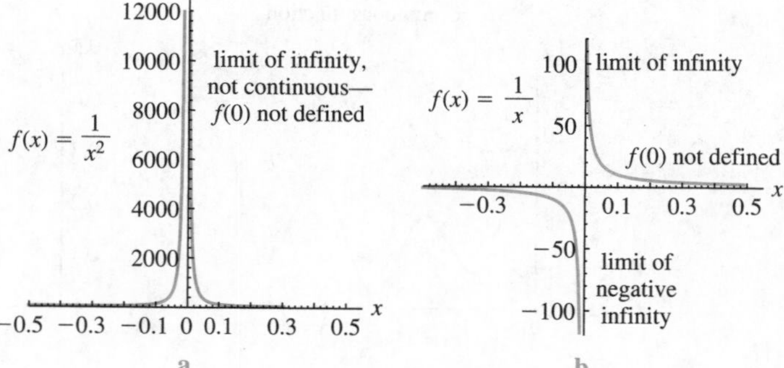

FIGURE 2.3.31

Two functions that are not defined at $x=0$

c. If $f(x)$ is continuous at $x = a$, the quotient $\frac{f(x)}{g(x)}$ is continuous at $x = a$ if $g(a) \neq 0$.

d. If $f(x)$ is continuous at $x = g(a)$, then the composition $(f \circ g)(x)$ is continuous at $x = a$.

The rules for recognizing continuous functions can be summarized in three tables: the basic continuous functions (Table 2.3.1), the rules for combining (Table 2.3.2), and the three trouble signs (Table 2.3.3).

Table 2.3.1 Basic continuous functions

Type of Function	Example	Where Continuous
Linear	$f(x) = mx + b$	All x
Polynomial	$f(x) = ax^3 + bx^2 + cx + d$	All x
Exponential	$f(x) = e^{\alpha x}$	All x
Cosine	$f(x) = \cos(x)$	All x
Logarithm	$f(x) = \ln(x)$	$x > 0$

Table 2.3.2 Continuous combinations of continuous functions $f(x)$ and $g(x)$

Type of Combination	Formula	Where Continuous	Example
Sum	$f(x) + g(x)$	where defined	$2x + 1 + e^x$
Product	$f(x)g(x)$	where defined	$(2x + 1)e^x$
Quotient	$\frac{f(x)}{g(x)}$	where $g(x) \neq 0$	$\frac{e^x}{2x+1}$ if $2x + 1 \neq 0$
Composition	$(f \circ g)(x)$	where defined	e^{2x+1}

Table 2.3.3 The three trouble signs: points where a function may be undefined or discontinuous

Division by 0
Logs of 0
Points where the definition of the function changes

Example 2.3.1 Recognizing a Discontinuous Function

The function $f(x) = \sin\left(\frac{1}{x}\right)$ oscillates faster and faster as x approaches zero. See Figure 2.3.32. There is no limit as $x \to 0$. No matter what value we assign to $f(0)$, we

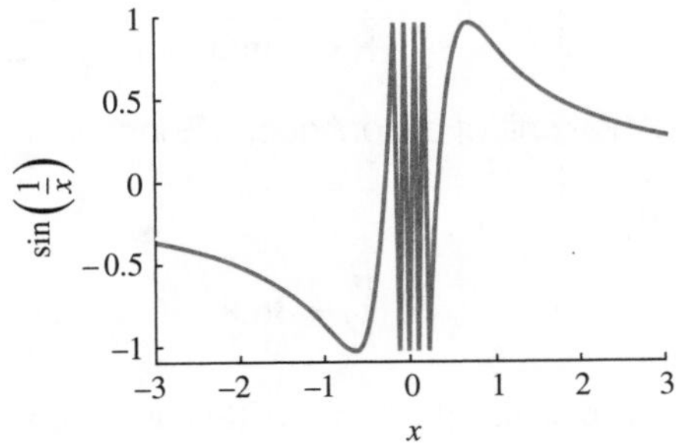

FIGURE 2.3.32
The function $f(x) = \sin(1/x)$

recognize that there might be a point of discontinuity at $x = 0$ because this composition of functions involves division by x if $x = 0$.

Example 2.3.2 Recognizing a Cryptic Discontinuous Function

The function $f(x) = \tan(x)$ does not have any obvious trouble signs. See Figure 2.3.33. But if we recall that

$$\tan(x) = \frac{\sin(x)}{\cos(x)}$$

we note that there is division by 0 when $\cos(x) = 0$. This occurs at $x = \frac{-\pi}{2}$, $x = \frac{\pi}{2}$ and so forth. These are points where the function is not defined.

Example 2.3.3 Evaluating the Limit of a Continuous Function I

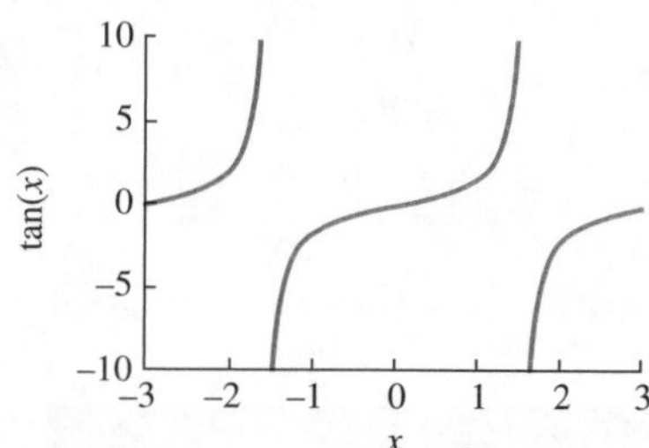

FIGURE 2.3.33
The function $f(x) = \tan(x)$

We can find

$$\lim_{x \to 0} f(x)$$

where

$$f(x) = e^{x^2+3}$$

by evaluating $f(0)$ if f is continuous at $x = 0$. This function is built up as a **composition** of the polynomial function $x^2 + 3$ and the exponential function. Both of the pieces are continuous (Table 2.3.1). The composition of these pieces is also continuous (Table 2.3.2). Therefore,

$$\lim_{x \to 0} e^{x^2+3} = e^{0^2+3} = e^3 \approx 20.09$$

Example 2.3.4 Evaluating the Limit of a Continuous Function II

If we wish to find

$$\lim_{x \to 0} g(x)$$

where

$$g(x) = \frac{f(x)}{h(x)} = \frac{e^{x^2+3}}{2 + x + \ln(x+1)}$$

we must take more care in taking apart the function. First, it is the quotient of the previous function $f(x) = e^{x^2+3}$, which is continuous, and a new function $h(x) = 2 + x + \ln(x+1)$. $h(x)$ is the sum of a continuous linear function $2 + x$ and the natural log, which is continuous when its argument is positive. The quotient will then be continuous at 0 as long as $h(0) \neq 0$. But

$$h(0) = 2 + 0 + \ln(0+1) = 2 + 0 + 0 = 2 \neq 0$$

Therefore, $h(x)$ is continuous and

$$\lim_{x \to 0} \frac{e^{x^2+3}}{2 + x + \ln(x+1)} = \frac{e^{0^2+3}}{2} = \frac{e^3}{2} \approx 10.04$$

Example 2.3.5 Evaluating the Limit of a Continuous Function III

The function

$$P_d(t) = 36.8 + 0.3\cos\left(\frac{2\pi(t-14)}{24}\right)$$

is continuous because it can be written as the composition

$$P_d(t) = g(\cos(h(t)))$$

where

$$g(x) = 36.8 + 0.3x$$
$$h(t) = \frac{2\pi(t - 14)}{24}$$

Both g and h are continuous linear functions, whereas cos is one of the basic continuous functions.

Example 2.3.6 Recognizing Disguised Division by 0

Division by 0 can be disguised. Suppose we are asked to find

$$\lim_{x\to 1^-} F(x) = \lim_{x\to 1^-} (1 - x)^{-3}$$

Negative exponents can be written in the denominator (law of exponents 3, p. 82), so

$$F(x) = \frac{1}{(1 - x)^3}$$

Because the denominator is equal to 0 at $x = 1$, this function may not be continuous. If we try to evaluate $F(1)$, we find ourselves dividing by 0. The limit is in fact equal to infinity.

Example 2.3.7 A Discontinuous Function that Is Defined in Pieces

Functions defined in pieces look like the signum function (Figure 2.3.30) or the functions used to describe the heart (Section 1.11). An example is the discrete-time dynamical system

$$V_{t+1} = \begin{cases} 3.0V_t & \text{if } V_t > 2.0 \\ 2.0V_t + 1.0 & \text{if } V_t \le 2.0 \end{cases}$$

The only way to check whether the updating function is continuous is to check whether the two parts match up at $V_t = 2.0$, the point where the definition changes. See Figure 2.3.34. The value at $V_t = 2.0$, jumps from 6.0 to 5.0. These do not match and the function is not continuous.

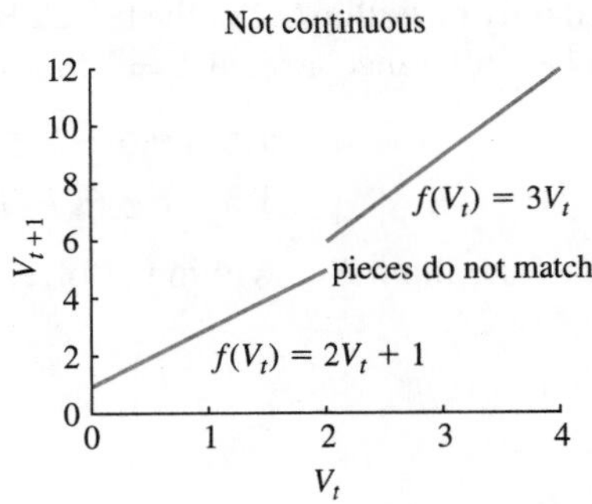

FIGURE 2.3.34
A discontinuous function that is defined in pieces

Example 2.3.8 A Continuous Function that Is Defined in Pieces

In contrast, the function

$$V_{t+1} = \begin{cases} 3.0V_t & \text{if } V_t > 2.0 \\ 2.0V_t + 2.0 & \text{if } V_t \le 2.0 \end{cases}$$

shown in Figure 2.3.35, is continuous because the two pieces match up, each taking the value $V_{t+1} = 6.0$ at $V_t = 2.0$.

Input and Output Tolerances

In applied mathematics, functions describe relationships between measurements. Continuous functions represent a special sort of relationship between measurements where a small change in the input produces only a small change in the output.

Example 2.3.9 Input and Output Tolerances for a Continuous Function I

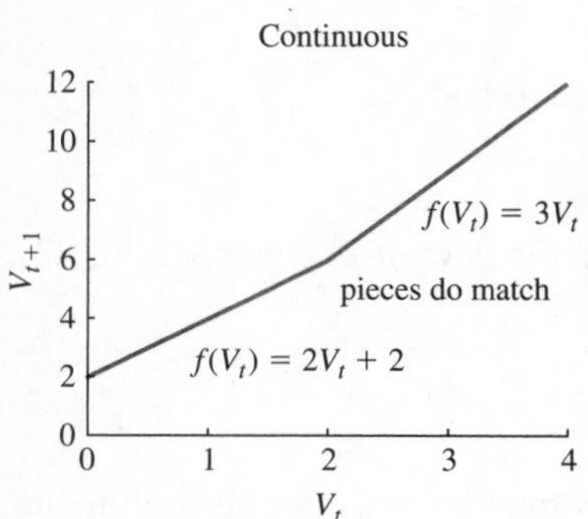

FIGURE 2.3.35

A continuous function that is defined in pieces

Recall the discrete-time dynamical system

$$b_{t+1} = 2.0b_t$$

describing a bacterial population (Example 1.5.1). Suppose we want a population of 2.0×10^6 at time $t = 1$. To hit 2.0×10^6 exactly, we require $b_0 = 1.0 \times 10^6$. How close must b_0 be to 1.0×10^6 for b_1 to be within 0.1×10^6 of our target (Figure 2.3.36)? We require

$$1.9 \times 10^6 \le b_1 \le 2.1 \times 10^6$$
$$1.9 \times 10^6 \le 2.0b_0 \le 2.1 \times 10^6$$
$$0.95 \times 10^6 \le b_0 \le 1.05 \times 10^6$$

As long as we can guarantee that b_0 is within 0.05×10^6 of 1.0×10^6, the output is within our tolerance. A small error in the input produces a small (but somewhat larger) error in the output. In other words, the output tolerance of 0.1×10^6 translates into an input tolerance of 0.05×10^6.

Example 2.3.10 Input and Output Tolerances for a Continuous Function II

Consider the discrete-time dynamical system

$$M_{t+1} = 0.5M_t + S$$

for the concentration of medication in the blood (Example 1.5.4), modified so that the dosage is a variable S rather than the constant 1.0. Suppose the concentration on day t is $M_t = 1.0$ and we wish to hit $M_t = 2.0$. What value of S should be used? The value of M_{t+1} is

$$M_{t+1} = 0.5 \cdot 1.0 + S = 0.5 + S$$

Therefore, to hit $M_{t+1} = 2.0$ exactly, we require $S = 1.5$. Nothing in biology is exact, and perhaps we need only be within 0.2 of the target. Because M_{t+1} is a continuous function of S, there will be a tolerance around $S = 1.5$. For M_{t+1} to be between 1.8 and 2.2,

$$1.8 \le 0.5 + S \le 2.2$$
$$1.3 \le S \le 1.7$$

(Figure 2.3.37). If the input S is within 0.2 of 1.5, the output M_{t+1} will be within the desired tolerance of 2.0.

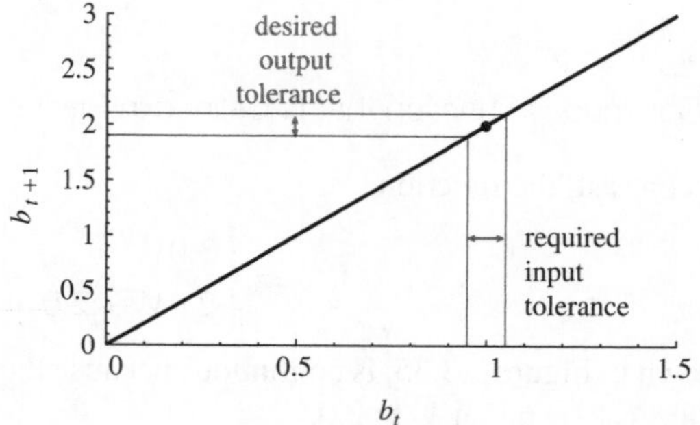

FIGURE 2.3.36

Tolerances and continuous functions

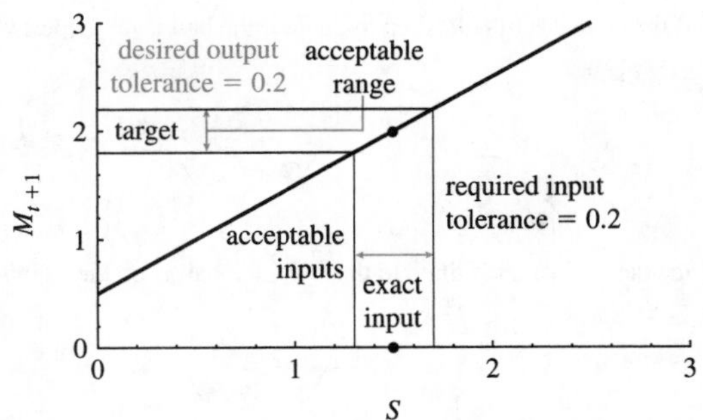

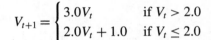

FIGURE 2.3.37
Tolerances and continuous functions

Example 2.3.11 Failure to Find Input Tolerance of a Discontinuous Function

In contrast, if the updating function is discontinuous, a tiny change in the input can produce a huge change in the output. Suppose we wish to have a voltage $V_1 = 5.0$ from the discrete-time dynamical system

$$V_{t+1} = \begin{cases} 3.0V_t & \text{if } V_t > 2.0 \\ 2.0V_t + 1.0 & \text{if } V_t \leq 2.0 \end{cases}$$

(Example 2.3.7). We could hit $V_1 = 5.0$ exactly with $V_0 = 2.0$. But if the input is even a tiny bit too high, the output will be different. If $V_0 = 2.001$, then $V_1 = 6.003$ (Figure 2.3.38). If the output tolerance was 0.1, meaning that values between 4.9 and 5.1 were satisfactory, there is no input tolerance at all.

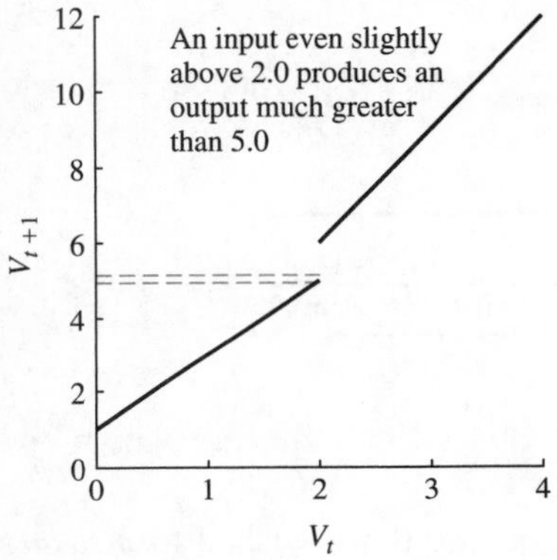

An input even slightly above 2.0 produces an output much greater than 5.0

FIGURE 2.3.38
A discontinuous function with no input tolerance

Relations that are described by functions that are not continuous are difficult to deal with experimentally. Because no measurement can be controlled exactly, we hope that small errors in one measurement will not result in large errors in another. Systems with threshold behavior, or which display hysteresis (as in the next section), can include discontinuous relations and must be treated with caution.

Hysteresis

Different left-hand and right-hand limits arise in biological systems with **hysteresis** (Figure 2.3.39). In the experiment shown, a neuron is stimulated with different levels of electric current. Low levels of current generally have no effect, whereas large levels tend to induce an oscillation. If the current is started at a low level and is steadily increased, the neuron switches from no oscillation (designated as period 0 on the graph) to an oscillation with period 2.0 when the input current crosses 3.0. If the current is instead started at a high value and steadily decreased, the neuron switches from an oscillation of period 1 to no oscillation when the input current crosses 2.0. In both cases, the jump indicates that the left-hand and right-hand limits do not match.

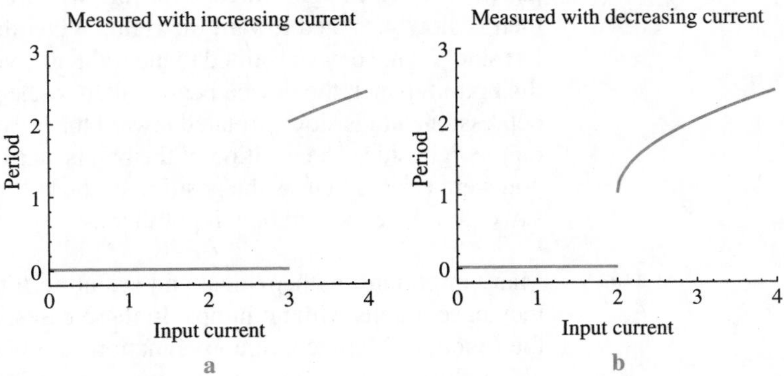

FIGURE 2.3.39
Hysteresis

If the device starts off tilted to the left, the ball is on the left when device is flat

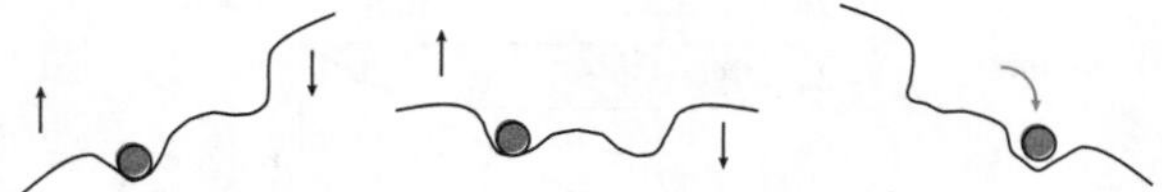

If the device starts off tilted to the right, the ball is on the right when device is flat

FIGURE 2.3.40
Hysteresis and stability

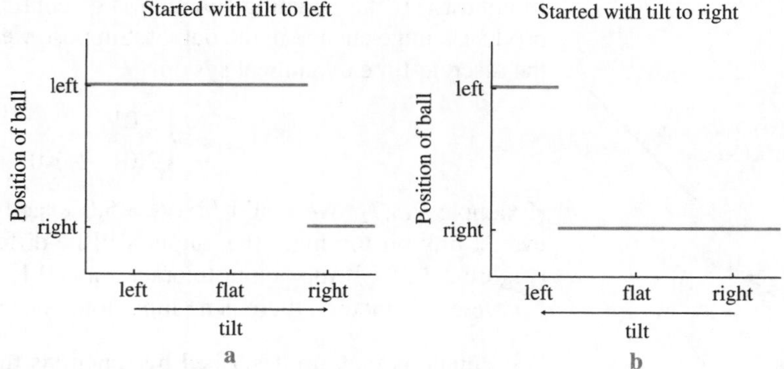

FIGURE 2.3.41
The position of a ball as a function of tilt

More oddly, the two graphs jump at different points. If we wished to *measure* the left-hand limit, we would slowly increase the current toward the jump, finding the results in Figure 2.3.39a. If we wished to measure the right-hand limit, we would slowly decrease the current toward the jump, finding the results in Figure 2.3.39b. However, both the position and the size of the jump depend on which way we change the current.

Why do they fail to match? The explanation is related to the idea of equilibria. When the current increases, the equilibrium without an oscillation eventually becomes **unstable** and the cell begins to oscillate. When the current decreases, the oscillation itself becomes unstable and the cell stops oscillating. For input currents between 2.0 and 3.0, *both* the oscillation and the lack of oscillation are stable, and the behavior of the neuron depends on what it was last doing. Hysteresis is a simple form of memory, because knowing the input current at one time is insufficient to describe the behavior of the system.

Hysteresis can be pictured with a physical device. Figure 2.3.40 compares two experiments on a device with two possible stable resting places for a ball. In the top panel, the device begins tilted to the left, with the ball resting in the left depression, and then is slowly rotated toward the right. When the device is flat, the ball is still on the left side. As the device is tilted to the right, the ball will roll into the right depression. In the bottom panel, the device begins tilted to the right, with the ball resting in the right depression, and is slowly rotated toward the left. When the device is flat, the ball is still on the right side. The position of the ball is an example of hysteresis (Figure 2.3.41). If you were asked to guess the position of the ball when the device is flat, you could only say that it depended on how it got there.

Summary Many important mathematical and scientific functions are **continuous,** meaning that they have graphs with no jumps. In these cases, limits can be computed by evaluating the function. Many continuous functions are built from four basic pieces: polynomials (including linear functions), exponentials, logarithms, and cosines, combined with addition, multiplication, division (except by zero), and functional composition. Most functions encountered in biology are continuous unless they exhibit one of the three warning flags: division by zero, taking the log of zero, or being defined in pieces. Continuous functions describe scientific measurements when small changes in the input produce only small changes in the output. With a discontinuous function, even a tiny error in the input can produce a large jump in the output. We examined discontinuous functions created by **hysteresis,** where the results of an experiment depend on the order in which conditions are tested.

2.3 Exercises

Mathematical Techniques

1–10 ■ Describe how the following functions are built out of the basic continuous functions. Identify points where they might not be continuous.

1. $l(t) = 5t + 6$
2. $p(x) = x^5 + 6x^3 + 7$
3. $f(x) = \dfrac{e^x}{x+1}$
4. $h(y) = y^2 \ln(y - 1)$ for $y > 1$
5. $g(z) = \dfrac{\ln(z-1)}{z^2}$ for $z > 1$
6. $F(t) = \cos(e^{t^2})$
7. $\sin(x)\left(\text{recall that } \sin(x) = \cos\left(x - \frac{\pi}{2}\right)\right)$
8. $a(t) = t^2$ if $t > 0$ and 0 if $t \le 0$
9. $r(w) = (1 - w)^{-4}$
10. $q(z) = (1 + z^2)^{-2}$

11–20 ■ Using the given functions, find the limits by plugging in (if possible). Indicate whether the limit is infinity or negative infinity. Compute the value of the function 0.1 and 0.01 above and below the limiting argument as a test of whether your answer is correct.

11. $\lim_{t\to 5} l(t)$ where $l(t) = 5t + 6$ (based on Exercise 1).
12. $\lim_{x\to 2} p(x)$ where $p(x) = x^5 + 6x^3 + 7$ (based on Exercise 2).
13. $\lim_{x\to 0} f(x)$ where $f(x) = \dfrac{e^x}{x+1}$ (based on Exercise 3).
14. $\lim_{y\to 1^+} h(y)$ where $h(y) = y^2 \ln(y-1)$ for $y > 1$ (based on Exercise 4).
15. $\lim_{z\to 2} g(z)$ where $g(z) = \dfrac{\ln(z-1)}{z^2}$ for $z > 1$ (based on Exercise 5).
16. $\lim_{y\to 2} h(y)$ where $h(y) = y^2 \ln(y-1)$ for $y > 1$ (based on Exercise 4).
17. $\lim_{z\to 1^+} g(z)$ where $g(z) = \dfrac{\ln(z-1)}{z^2}$ for $z > 1$ (based on Exercise 5).
18. $\lim_{t\to 2} F(t)$ where $F(t) = \cos(e^{t^2})$ (based on Exercise 6).
19. $\lim_{w\to 1} r(w)$ where $r(w) = (1-w)^{-4}$ (based on Exercise 9).
20. $\lim_{t\to 0} a(t)$ where $a(t) = t^2$ if $t > 0$ and 0 if $t \le 0$ (based on Exercise 8).

21–24 ■ For the following functions, find the input tolerance necessary to achieve the given output tolerance.

21. How close must the input be to $x = 0$ for $f(x) = x + 2$ to be within 0.1 of 2?
22. How close must the input be to $x = 1$ for $f(x) = 2x + 1$ to be within 0.1 of 3?
23. How close must the input be to $x = 1$ for $f(x) = x^2$ to be within 0.1 of 1?
24. How close must the input be to $x = 2$ for $f(x) = 5x^2$ to be within 0.1 of 20?

25–26 ■ Consider the Heaviside function, defined by

$$\begin{cases} H(x) = 0 & \text{if } x < 0 \\ H(x) = 1 & \text{if } x \ge 0 \end{cases}$$

25. How close must the input be to $x = 1$ for $H(x)$ to be within 0.1 of 1?
26. How close must the input be to $x = 0$ for $H(x)$ to be within 0.1 of 0?

27–28 ■ We can build different continuous approximations of signum (the function giving the sign of a number) as follows. For each case,

a. Graph the continuous function.
b. Find the formula.
c. Indicate how close the input would have to be to 0 for the output to be within 0.1 of 0.

27. A continuous function that is -1 for $x \le -0.1$, 1 for $x \ge 0.1$, and is linear for $-0.1 < x < 0.1$.
28. A continuous function that is -1 for $x \le -0.01$, 1 for $x \ge 0.01$, and is linear for $-0.01 < x < 0.01$.

Applications

29–32 ■ Find the accuracy of input necessary to achieve the desired output accuracy.

29. Suppose the mass of an object as a function of volume is given by $M = \rho V$. If $\rho = 2.0\ \text{g/cm}^3$, how close must V be to $2.5\ \text{cm}^3$ for M to be within 0.2 g of 5.0 g?

30. The area of a disk as a function of radius is given by $A = \pi r^2$. How close must r be to 2.0 cm to guarantee an area within 0.5 cm^2 of 4π?

31. The flow rate F through a vessel is proportional to the fourth power of the radius, or

$$F(r) = ar^4$$

Suppose $a = 1.0$/cm sec. How close must r be to 1.0 cm to guarantee a flow within 5% of 1 cm^3/s?

32. Consider an organism growing according to $S(t) = S(0)e^{\alpha t}$. Suppose $\alpha = 0.001$/s, and $S(0) = 1.0$ mm. At time 1000 s, $S(t) = 2.71828$ mm. How close must t be to 1000 s to guarantee a size within 0.1 mm of 2.71828 mm?

33–36 ▪ Suppose a population of bacteria follows the discrete-time dynamical system

$$b_{t+1} = 2.0b_t$$

and we wish to have a population within 1.0×10^8 of 1.0×10^9 at $t = 10$.

33. What values of b_9 produce a result within the desired tolerance? What is the input tolerance?

34. What values of b_5 produce a result within the desired tolerance? What is the input tolerance? Why is it harder to hit the target from here?

35. What values of b_0 produce a result within the desired tolerance? What is the input tolerance?

36. How would your answers differ if the discrete-time dynamical system were $b_{t+1} = 5.0b_t$? Would the tolerances be larger or smaller? Why?

37–40 ▪ Suppose the amount of toxin in a culture declines according to $T_{t+1} = 0.5T_t$ and we wish to have a concentration within 0.02 of 0.5 g/L at $t = 10$.

37. What values of T_9 produce a result within the desired tolerance? What is the input tolerance?

38. What values of T_5 produce a result within the desired tolerance? What is the input tolerance?

39. What values of T_0 produce a result within the desired tolerance? What is the input tolerance?

40. How would your answers differ if the discrete-time dynamical system were $T_{t+1} = 0.1T_t$? Would the tolerances be larger or smaller? Why?

41–44 ▪ Suppose a neuron has the following response to inputs. If it receives a voltage input V greater than or equal to a threshold of V_0, it outputs a voltage of kV for some constant k. If it receives an input less than the threshold value of V_0, it outputs a fixed voltage V^*.

41. Suppose that $k = 2.0$, $V_0 = 50$, and $V^* = 80$. Write and graph the function giving output in terms of input as a function defined in pieces.

42. Suppose that $k = 1.5$, $V_0 = 60$, and $V^* = 100$. Write and graph the function giving output in terms of input as a function defined in pieces.

43. If $k = 2.0$ and $V_0 = 50$, what would V^* have to be for the function to be continuous? Graph the resulting function.

44. If $V_0 = 50$ and $V^* = 80$, what would k have to be to make the function continuous? Graph the resulting function.

45–46 ▪ The following questions are based on examples of hysteresis involving children.

45. A child outside is swinging on a swing that makes a horrible screeching noise. Starting from when the swing is furthest back, the pitch of the screeching noise increases as it swings forward and then decreases as it swings back.

   a. Draw a graph of the pitch as a function of position without hysteresis.

   b. Draw a graph with hysteresis. Which graph seems more likely?

   c. Imagine what each noise sounds like. Which is more irritating?

46. Little Billy walks due east to school but must cross from the south side to the north side of the street. Because he is a very careful child, he crosses quickly at the first possible opportunity.

   a. Graph little Billy's latitude as a function of distance from home on the way to school.

   b. Graph little Billy's latitude as a function of distance from home on the way home.

   c. Is this an example of hysteresis?

Computer Exercise

47. Graph the function $f(x) = \sin\left(\frac{1}{x}\right)$. What happens near $x = 0$?

2.4 Computing Derivatives: Linear and Quadratic Functions

We learned about continuous functions and limits as a means to compute a particular, and particularly important, limit: the limit of the average rate of change. When it exists, this limit is the **instantaneous rate of change,** or the **derivative.** First, we ask whether every function has a derivative, finding examples of functions that do not. Those that do are called **differentiable functions.** We then use the definition of the derivative to compute the derivatives of two simple functions, a **linear function** and a

quadratic function. Along the way, we will see that the derivative, thought of as the slope of a graph, can help us reason more effectively about the measurements that graphs depict. We can tell whether a function is increasing or decreasing simply by checking whether the derivative is positive or negative.

Differentiable Functions

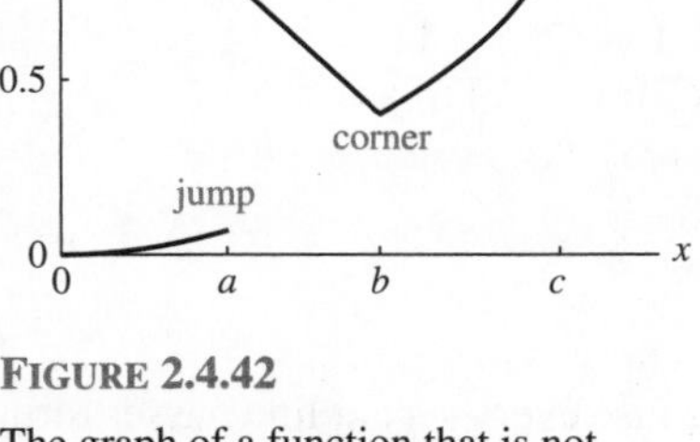

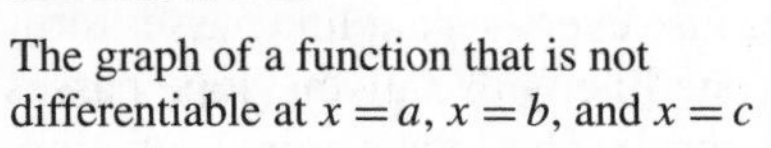

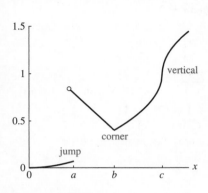

FIGURE 2.4.42
The graph of a function that is not differentiable at $x = a$, $x = b$, and $x = c$

Recall the two ways to interpret the derivative: dynamically as the instantaneous rate of change and graphically as the slope of the tangent line. Do all functions (thought of as measured quantities that depend on time in this case) have a well-defined instantaneous rate of change and a well-defined tangent line?

The function shown in Figure 2.4.42 is not differentiable at three points in three different ways. At **a,** the function is not continuous. There is no way to draw a tangent. At **b,** there is a corner. No line can hug the curve at this point. At **c,** the tangent line is vertical. The tangent line, although it can be drawn, is not a function and has no slope.

If Figure 2.4.42 represents a graph of position against time, the derivative is the velocity. At a point of discontinuity (such as point **a**) the object jumped instantly from one place to another. The idea of speed or instantaneous rate of change makes no sense. At a corner (such as point **b**), the object has instantly changed direction and has no well-defined velocity. At a point with a vertical tangent line (such as point **c**), the tangent line has "infinite slope," meaning that the object has "infinite" speed at this time.

The Three Ways a Function Can Fail to Be Differentiable
The graph has a jump.
The graph has a corner.
The graph is vertical.

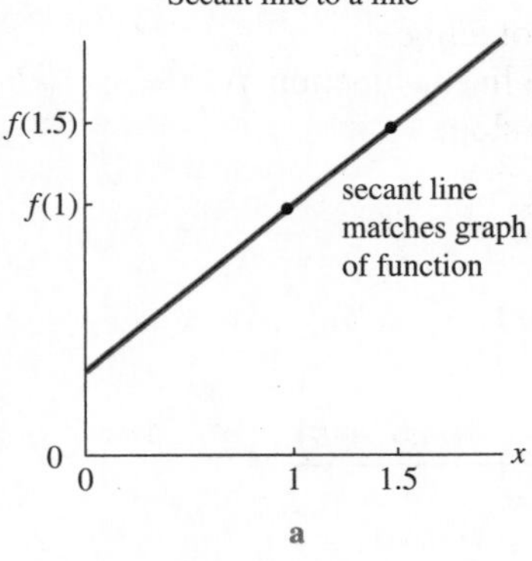

a

Tangent line to a line

b

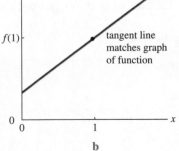

FIGURE 2.4.43
The secant and tangent line for a line

Differentiability, like continuity, is a property of a function at a point. If a function has a well-defined tangent line with finite slope at some point, the function is said to be **differentiable** at that point. If we say that a function is differentiable without mentioning a particular point, the function is differentiable on its entire domain. The function shown in Figure 2.4.42 is differentiable everywhere except at **a, b** and **c.** Points where a function fails to have a derivative are one type of **critical point.** We define the second type in the next subsection.

The Derivative of a Linear Function

What is the slope of the graph of the function $f(x) = 2x + 1$ at $x = 1$? We now have two ways to answer this question. Because f is a linear function, we know that the slope is the factor 2 multiplying x. Alternatively, we could compute the slope by computing the derivative, which requires finding the slope of a secant line and taking the limit as Δx approaches 0. These two methods should give the same answer.

The secant line to $f(x) = 2x + 1$ connects two points on the graph of the function. Because the graph of the function is a line, the graph of the secant line matches the graph of the function (Figure 2.4.43). For example, with base point $x_0 = 1.0$ and $\Delta x = 0.5$,

$$\begin{aligned}\text{slope of secant} &= \frac{\Delta f}{\Delta x}\\ &= \frac{f(x_0 + \Delta x) - f(x_0)}{\Delta x}\\ &= \frac{f(1.0 + 0.5) - f(1.0)}{0.5}\end{aligned}$$

$$= \frac{f(1.5) - f(1.0)}{0.5}$$
$$= \frac{4.0 - 3.0}{0.5}$$
$$= 2.0$$

The slope of the secant matches the slope of the function.

In general, with base point x_0 and second point $x_0 + \Delta x$,

$$\text{slope of secant} = \frac{\Delta f}{\Delta x}$$
$$= \frac{f(x_0 + \Delta x) - f(x_0)}{\Delta x}$$
$$= \frac{2\,(x_0 + \Delta x) + 1 - (2x_0 + 1)}{\Delta x}$$
$$= \frac{2\Delta x}{\Delta x}$$
$$= 2$$

as long as $\Delta x \neq 0$. Every secant line has slope 2. Because every secant line passes through a base point on a given line, and because only one line with a given slope passes through that point, the secant coincides exactly with the graph of the original function.

The slope of the tangent is the limit as Δx approaches 0 of the slope of the secant. The slope of the secant is the **constant** function 2 (except that it is not defined for $\Delta x = 0$). This function is **continuous** (Theorem 2.3a), and we can find the limit by evaluating the function at $\Delta x = 0$, so

$$\text{slope of tangent} = \lim_{\Delta x \to 0} 2 = 2$$

The derivative does match the usual idea of the slope of a line.

In general, we can follow the same steps with the linear function $f(x) = mx + b$. The secant line connecting points x_0 and $x_0 + \Delta x$ has slope

$$\text{slope of secant} = \frac{\Delta f}{\Delta x}$$
$$= \frac{f(x_0 + \Delta x) - f(x_0)}{\Delta x}$$
$$= \frac{(m\,(x_0 + \Delta x) + b) - (mx_0 + b)}{\Delta x}$$
$$= \frac{m\Delta x}{\Delta x}$$
$$= m$$

as long as $\Delta x \neq 0$. The derivative of a linear function, the limit of m as Δx approaches 0, is equal to the slope m of the line.

In differential and prime notation, if $f(x) = mx + b$, then

$$\frac{df}{dx} = m \qquad \text{differential notation}$$
$$f'(x_0) = m \qquad \text{prime notation}$$

Sometimes we use a different version of differential notation and write

$$\frac{d(mx + b)}{dx} = m$$

or

$$\frac{d}{dx}(mx + b) = m$$

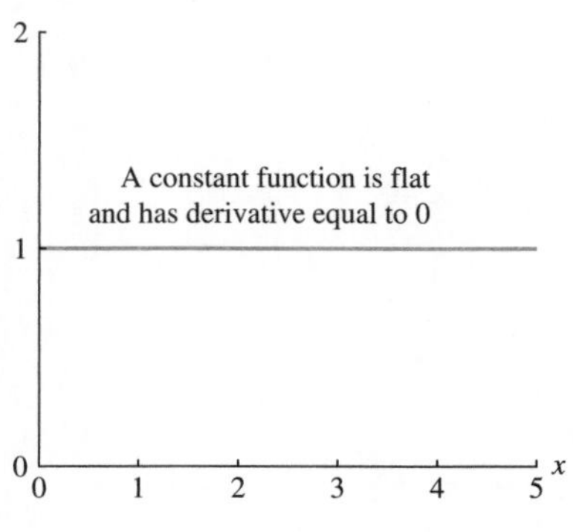

FIGURE 2.4.44

The slope of a constant function is 0

One special case is worthy of note. The function

$$f(x) = b$$

the constant function, is a linear function with slope 0. According to the general formula for the derivative of a linear function,

$$\frac{df}{dx} = 0$$

when $f(x)$ is constant. The rate of change of something that does not change is 0 (Figure 2.4.44).

Lines can have positive, negative, or zero slope, corresponding to increasing, decreasing, and constant functions (Section 1.4). Because the derivative is equal to the slope, this same correspondence holds in general. If the derivative is positive, the rate of change of the function is positive and the function is **increasing** (Figure 2.4.45a). If the derivative is negative, the function is **decreasing** (Figure 2.4.45b). If the derivative is exactly zero, the function is neither increasing nor decreasing (Figure 2.4.45c) at that point.

Points where the derivative is zero are the other type of **critical point** and will prove extremely useful for finding maxima and minima of functions (Section 3.3). The definition combines the two types of critical points.

Definition 2.6 A function f has a **critical point** at x in the domain of f if $f'(x) = 0$ or if the derivative is not defined at x.

The derivative encodes more information than simply whether the function is increasing or decreasing. We know that lines with large slopes are steep. Large values of the derivative are thus associated with points where the graph of the function is steep.

Example 2.4.1 Graphing and Interpreting the Derivative

The derivative of the function plotted in Figure 2.4.46a is shown in Figure 2.4.46b. Steep increasing portions of the graph correspond to large positive values of the derivative.

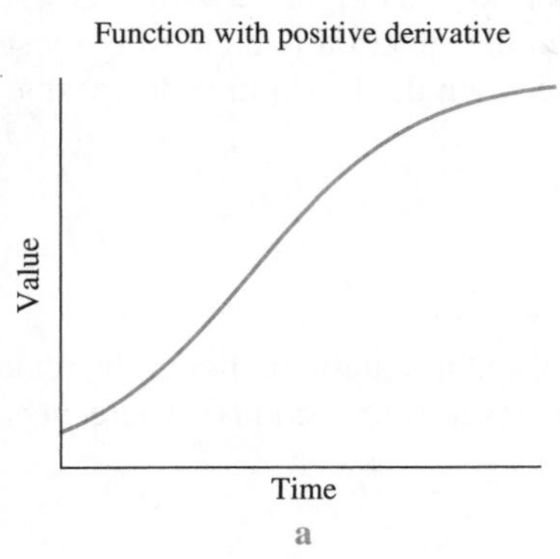

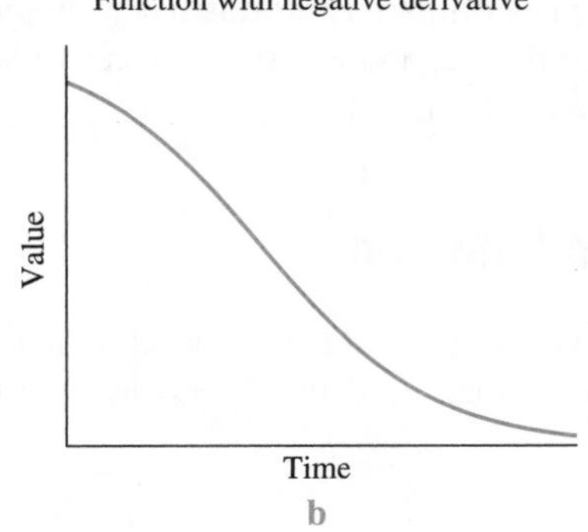

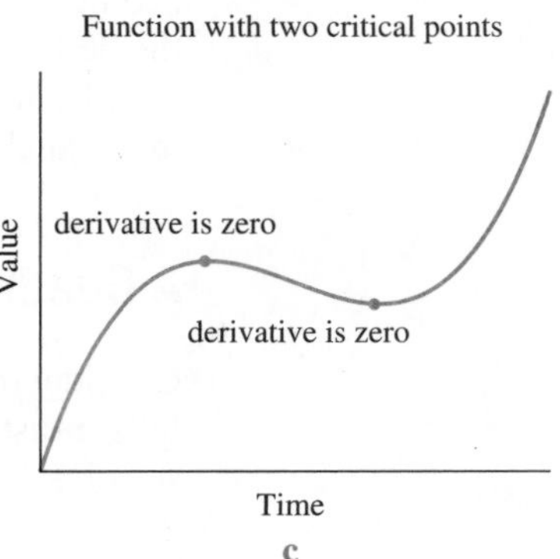

FIGURE 2.4.45

Functions with positive and negative derivatives

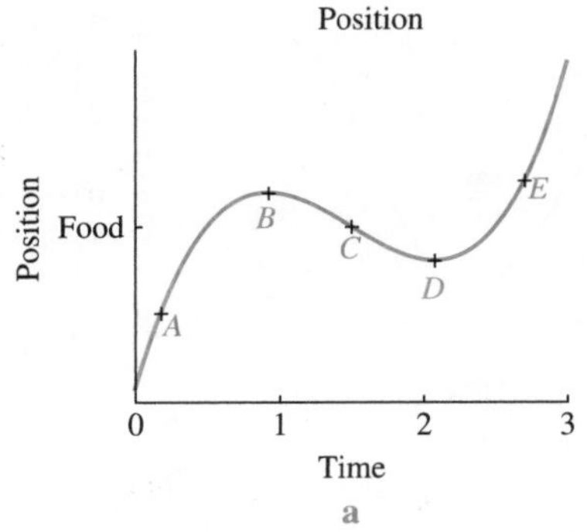

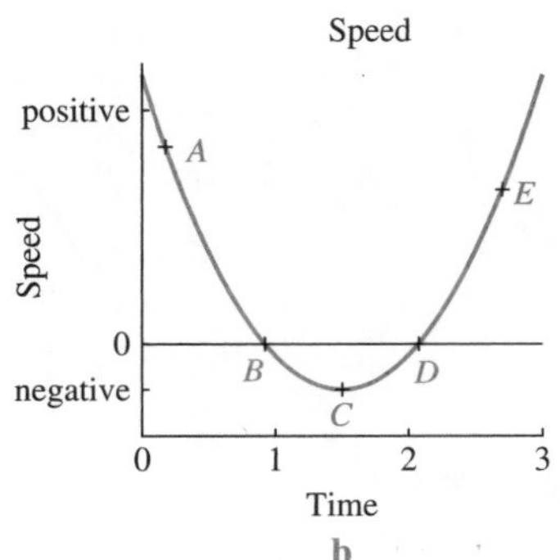

FIGURE 2.4.46

A function and its derivative

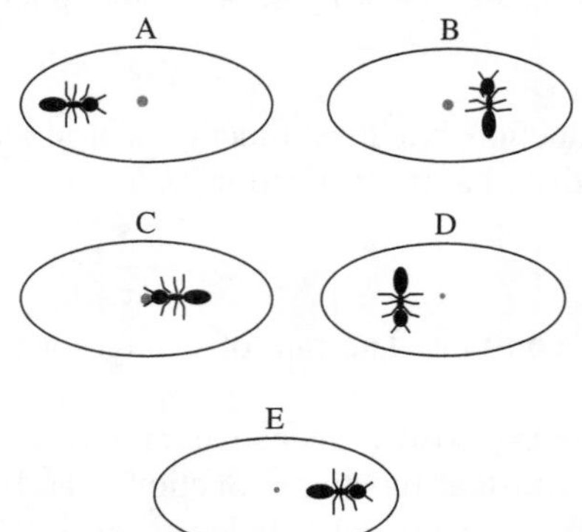

FIGURE 2.4.47
The experiences of an ant

Steep decreasing portions of the graph correspond to large negative values of the derivative. The derivative passes through zero wherever the graph is flat.

Suppose Figure 2.4.46a represents the position of an ant as a function of time. There is a bit of food at the position marked **C.** At the point marked **A** the ant is moving forward quickly toward the food. At **B,** the ant has overshot the food and stopped. At **C** the ant is walking slowly through the food in a reverse direction, eating as it goes. By **D** the ant has passed the food and stopped, preparatory to turning around and walking quickly away at **E** (Figure 2.4.47).

Example 2.4.2 Identifying Regions with Positive and Negative Rates of Change

Suppose the volume of a cell is given graphically (Figure 2.4.48a). The volume is increasing when the graph is increasing, or between times 0 and about 0.6, and again between times 1.5 and about 2.6. It is decreasing between times 0.6 and 1.5, and again after time 2.6. The graph of the derivative is positive when the function is increasing and negative when the function is decreasing. Furthermore, as Figure 2.4.48b shows, the derivative takes on its largest positive value when the function is increasing most steeply, at about time 2, and its largest negative value when the function is decreasing most quickly, at about time 1.

A Quadratic Function

Consider now a rock dropped from a building in a constant gravitational field. The rock falls a distance y (measured in meters) in time t (measured in seconds) where $y(t)$ satisfies

$$y(t) = 5t^2$$

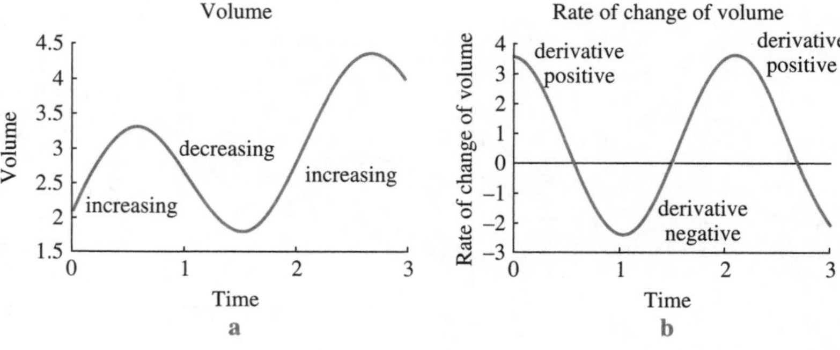

FIGURE 2.4.48
The changing volume of a cell

What is the velocity of the rock after 1.0 s? The velocity is the rate of change of position. The average velocity between $t = 1.0$ and $t = 1.0 + \Delta t$ is found by dividing the distance traveled by the elapsed time, or

$$\begin{aligned}
\text{average velocity} &= \frac{\text{distance}}{\text{time}} \\
&= \frac{\Delta y}{\Delta t} \\
&= \frac{y(1.0 + \Delta t) - y(1.0)}{\Delta t} \\
&= \frac{5(1.0 + \Delta t)^2 - 5}{\Delta t} \\
&= \frac{(5 + 10\Delta t + 5\Delta t^2) - 5}{\Delta t} \\
&= \frac{10\Delta t + 5\Delta t^2}{\Delta t} \\
&= 10 + 5\Delta t
\end{aligned}$$

as long as $\Delta t \neq 0$. To compute the derivative, we must take the limit of this function as Δt approaches 0. The average velocity is a linear function of Δt and is therefore continuous (Table 2.1). We can thus find the limit by evaluating at $\Delta t = 0$,

$$\begin{aligned}
\text{velocity} &= \lim_{\Delta t \to 0} (10 + 5\Delta t) \\
&= 10 + 5 \cdot 0 = 10
\end{aligned}$$

What are the units of the velocity? The change in distance Δy is measured in meters, and the change in time Δt is measured in seconds. The velocity at $t = 1.0$ is therefore 10 m/s.

We can follow this procedure to find the exact velocity at any time t. The velocity is a function of time because it is constantly changing (Figure 2.4.49). The average velocity between times t and $t + \Delta t$ is

$$\begin{aligned}
\text{average velocity} &= \frac{\Delta y}{\Delta t} \\
&= \frac{y(t + \Delta t) - y(t)}{\Delta t} \\
&= \frac{5(t + \Delta t)^2 - 5t^2}{\Delta t} \\
&= \frac{5\left(t^2 + 2t\Delta t + \Delta t^2\right) - 5t^2}{\Delta t} \\
&= \frac{(5t^2 + 10t\Delta t + 5\Delta t^2) - 5t^2}{\Delta t} \\
&= \frac{10t\Delta t + 5\Delta t^2}{\Delta t} \\
&= 10t + 5\Delta t
\end{aligned}$$

as long as $\Delta t \neq 0$. Taking the limit by evaluating this continuous function at $\Delta t = 0$, we find

$$\begin{aligned}
\text{velocity} &= \lim_{\Delta t \to 0} 10t + 5\Delta t \\
&= 10t + 5 \cdot 0 = 10t
\end{aligned}$$

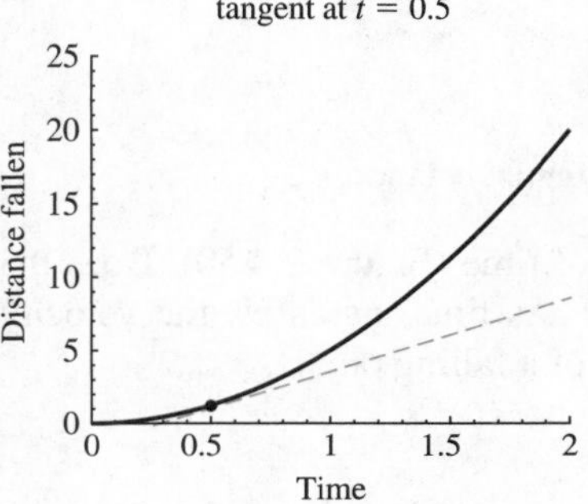

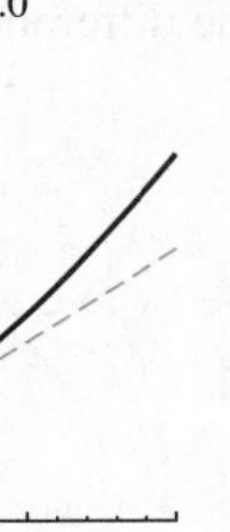

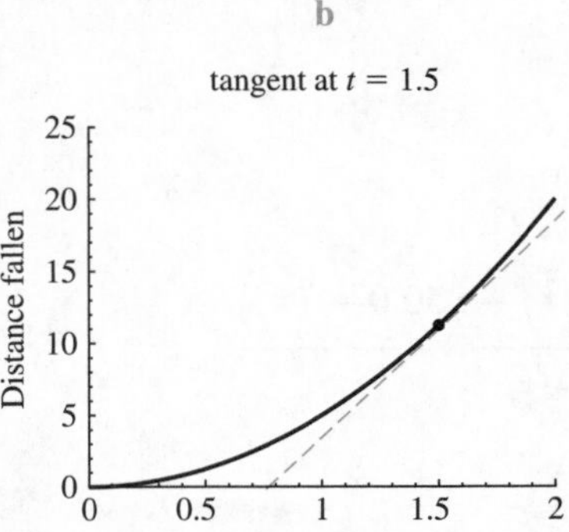

FIGURE 2.4.49
The slope of a quadratic function is constantly changing

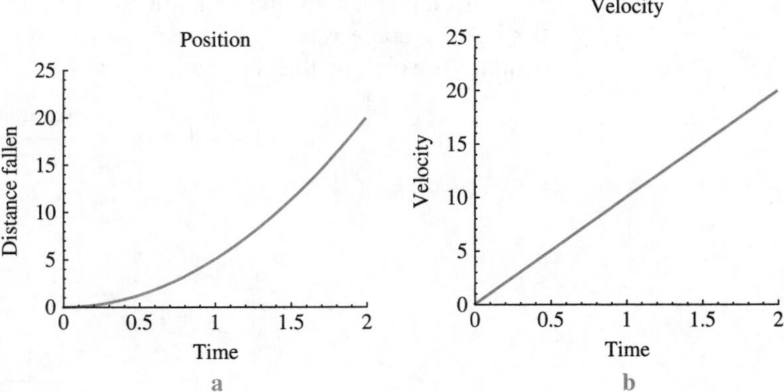

FIGURE 2.4.50
Position and velocity as functions of time

In differential and prime notation, if $y(t) = 5t^2$, we have

$$\frac{dy}{dt} = 10t \quad \text{differential notation}$$

$$y'(t) = 10t \quad \text{prime notation}$$

$$\frac{d}{dt}\left(5t^2\right) = 10t \quad \text{alternative differential notation.}$$

The function $y'(t)$ gives the velocity as a function of time (Figure 2.4.50). Does the result make sense? At time $t = 0$, the velocity is 0. As time increases, the velocity increases linearly, as is consistent with the behavior of a falling object.

When written in differential notation, the equation

$$\frac{dy}{dt} = 10t$$

is a **differential equation,** giving a formula for the rate of change as a function of time. In this case, we know the **solution** $y(t) = 5t^2$ of the differential equation because we began with a formula for $y(t)$ itself.

Example 2.4.3 The Behavior of a Falling Object

An object dropped from a height of 50 m on a planet where gravity has acceleration a has distance above the ground of

$$M(t) = 50.0 - \frac{a}{2}t^2$$

We can use the derivative to find the velocity of the object as a function of time. To find the velocity, we compute the derivative as

$$\begin{aligned}
\text{average velocity} &= \frac{\Delta M}{\Delta t} \\
&= \frac{M(t+\Delta t) - M(t)}{\Delta t} \\
&= \frac{\left(50.0 - \frac{a}{2}(t+\Delta t)^2\right) - \left(50.0 - \frac{a}{2}t^2\right)}{\Delta t} \\
&= \frac{-\frac{a}{2}(t+\Delta t)^2 + \frac{a}{2}t^2}{\Delta t} \\
&= \frac{-\frac{a}{2}\left((t+\Delta t)^2 - t^2\right)}{\Delta t} \\
&= \frac{-\frac{a}{2}\left(t^2 + 2t\Delta t + \Delta t^2 - t^2\right)}{\Delta t}
\end{aligned}$$

$$= \frac{-\frac{a}{2}\left(2t\Delta t + \Delta t^2\right)}{\Delta t}$$

$$= -\frac{a}{2}(2t + \Delta t)$$

as long as $\Delta t \neq 0$. The limit of this continuous function can be found by plugging in $\Delta t = 0$, giving an instantaneous velocity of

$$v(t) = -\frac{a}{2}(2t + 0) = -at$$

The speed (the absolute value of velocity) increases linearly with time.

Example 2.4.4 How Fast Does a Falling Object Hit the Ground?

On earth, the accelaration of gravity is 9.8 m/s^2. We can use this to find the velocity of this object when it hits the ground. To find the time when it hits the ground, we solve $M(t) = 0$ for t,

$$50.0 - 4.9t^2 = 0$$

$$50.0 = 4.9t^2$$

$$\frac{50.0}{4.9} = t^2$$

$$10.2 = t^2$$

$$t = \sqrt{10.2} \approx 3.19$$

The velocity is $v(3.19) = -9.8 \cdot 3.19 \approx 31.3$ m/s.

Summary A function might fail to have a derivative at a particular point in three ways: if the graph has a jump, a corner, or is vertical. The graphs of linear and quadratic functions have none of these problems, and we can compute their derivatives directly from the definition. The derivative of a linear function is equal to the usual slope. The derivative is positive when the function is increasing and negative when the function is decreasing. **Critical points** are points where the derivative either is zero or is not defined. Finally, we studied a quadratic function describing the position of an object in a constant gravitational field, finding that the deriviative (the **velocity**) is a linear function of time.

2.4 Exercises

Mathematical Techniques

1–4 ▪ Expand the following binomials.

1. $(x + \Delta x)^2$

2. $(x + 2\Delta x)^2$

3. $(3x + 2\Delta x)^2$

4. $\left(2x + \frac{\Delta x}{2}\right)^2$

5–6 ▪ On the following graphs, identify:

a. Points where the function is not continuous.

b. Points where the function is not differentiable (and say why).

c. Points where the derivative is zero.

5.

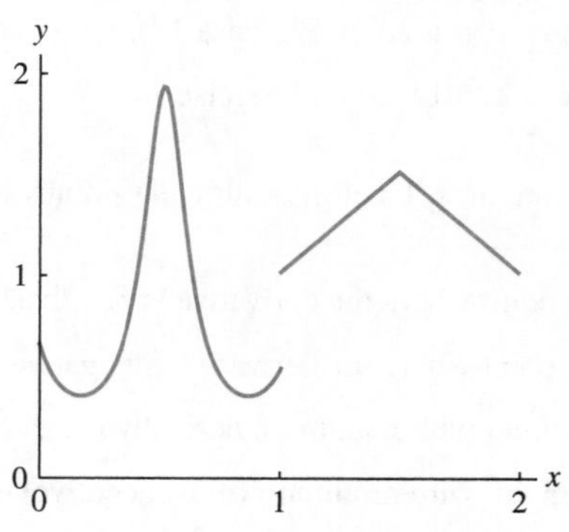

6.

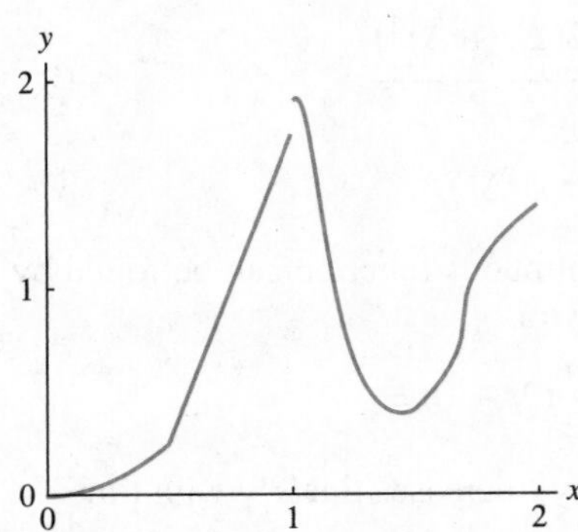

7–10 ▪ Find the derivatives of the following functions. Write your answers in both differential and prime notation. Which functions are increasing and which are decreasing?

7. $M(x) = 0.5x + 2$
8. $L(t) = 2t + 30$
9. $g(y) = -3y + 5$
10. $Q(z) = -3.5 \times 10^8$

11–12 ▪ For each of the following quadratic functions, find the slope of the secant line connecting $x = 1$ and $x = 1 + \Delta x$, and the slope of the tangent line at $x = 1$ by taking the limit.

11. $f(x) = 4 - x^2$
12. $g(x) = x + 2x^2$

13–14 ▪ For each of the following quadratic functions, find the slope of the secant line connecting x and $x + \Delta x$, and the slope of the tangent line as a function of x. Write your result in both differential and prime notation.

13. $f(x) = 4 - x^2$ (based on Exercise 11).
14. $g(x) = x + 2x^2$ (based on Exercise 12).

15–16 ▪ For each of the following quadratic functions, graph the function and the derivative. Identify critical points, points where the function is increasing, and points where the function is decreasing.

15. $f(x) = 4 - x^2$ (based on Exercise 13).
16. $g(x) = x + 2x^2$ (based on Exercise 14).

17–18 ▪ On the figures, label the following points and sketch the derivative.

a. One point where the derivative is positive.
b. One point where the derivative is negative.
c. The point with maximum derivative.
d. The point with minimum (most negative) derivative.
e. Points with derivative of zero (critical points).

17.

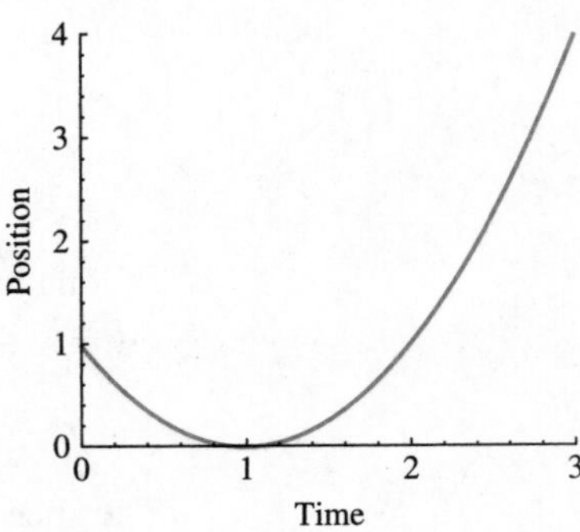

18.

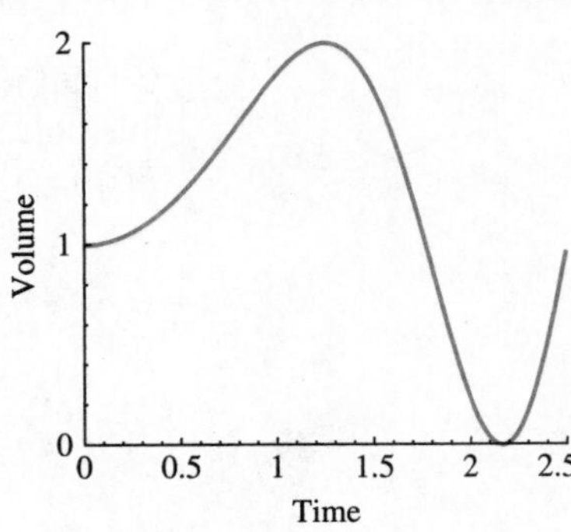

19–22 ▪ On the figures, identify which of the curves is a graph of the derivative of the other.

19.

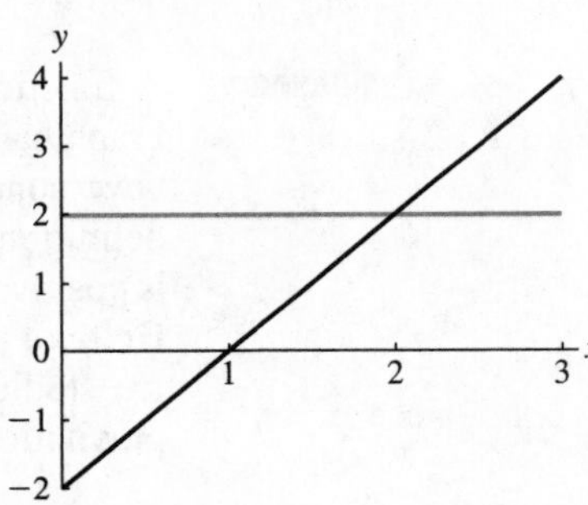

20.

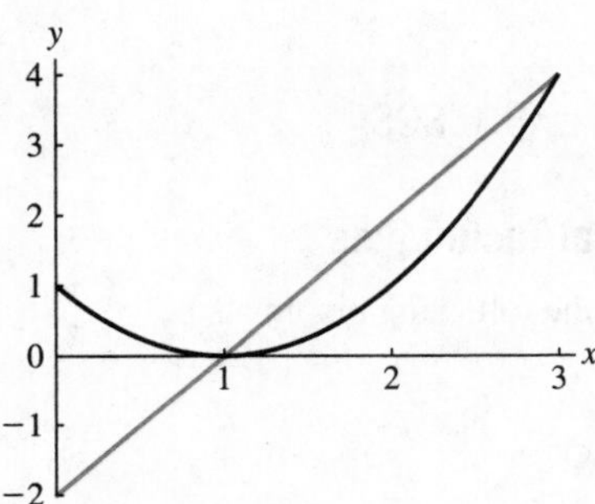

21.

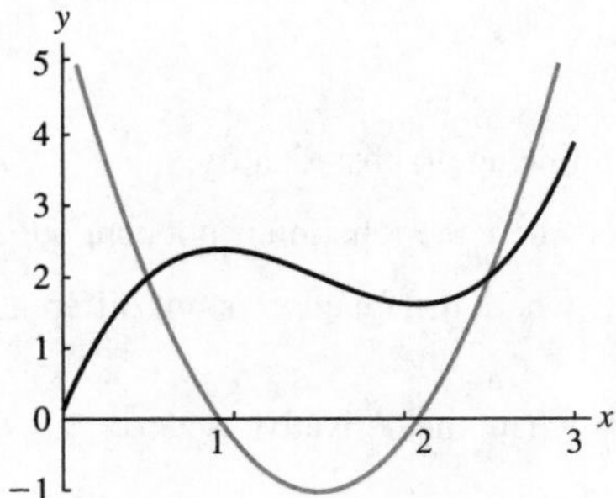

22.

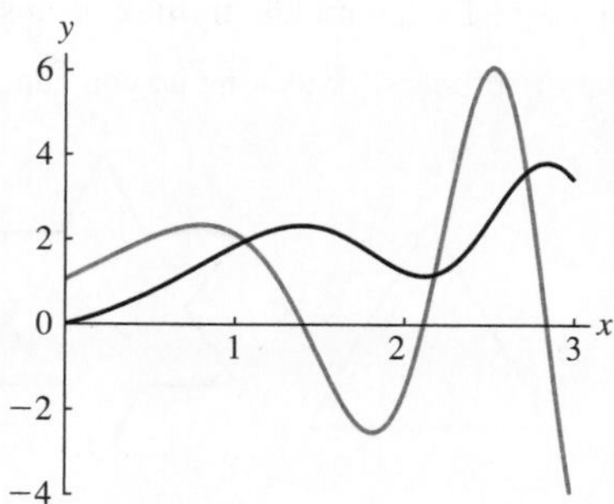

23–26 ▪ The following functions all fail to be differentiable at $x = 0$. In each case, graph the function, see what happens when you try to compute the derivative as the limit of the slopes of secant lines, and say something about the tangent line.

23. The absolute value function $f(x) = |x|$.

24. The square root function $f(x) = \sqrt{x}$. (Because this function is defined only for $x \geq 0$, you can only use $\Delta x > 0$.)

25. The Heaviside function (Section 2.3, Exercise 25), defined by

$$\begin{cases} H(x) = 0 & \text{if } x < 0 \\ H(x) = 1 & \text{if } x \geq 0 \end{cases}$$

26. The signum function, defined by

$$\begin{cases} S(x) = -1 & \text{if } x < 0 \\ S(x) = 0 & \text{if } x = 0 \\ S(x) = 1 & \text{if } x \geq 0 \end{cases}$$

Applications

27–30 ▪ The following graphs show the temperature of different solutions with chemical reactions as functions of time. Graph the rate of change of temperature in each case, and indicate when the solution is warming up and when it is cooling down.

27.

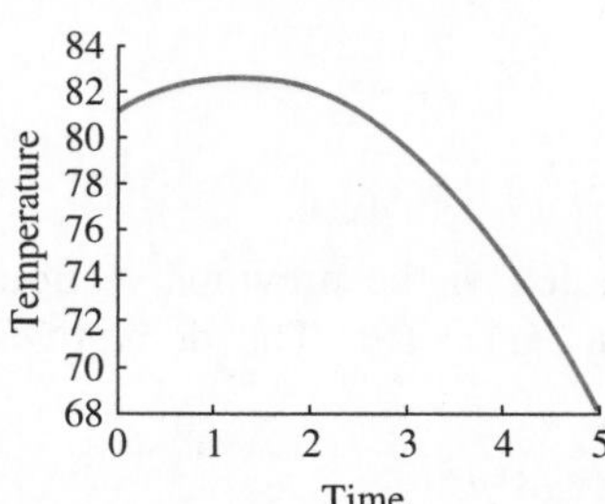

28.

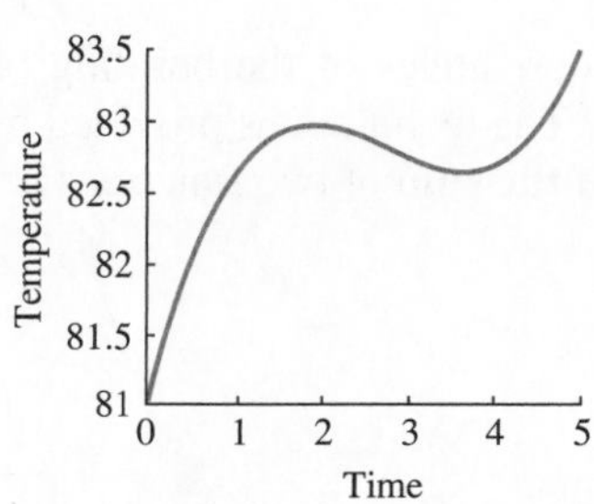

29.

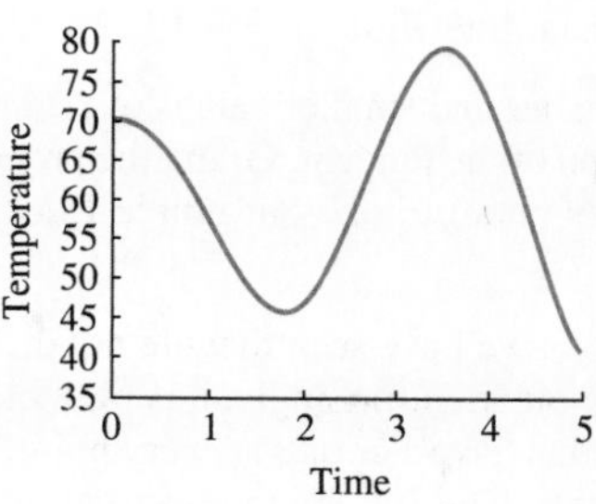

30.

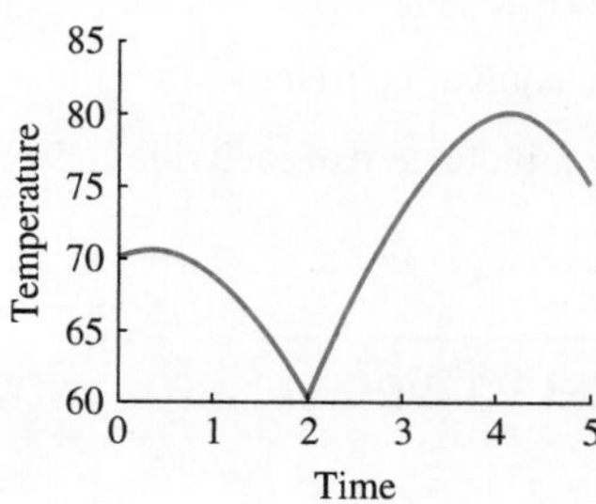

31–34 ▪ A bear sets off in pursuit of a hiker. Graph the position of the bear and that of the hiker as functions of time from the following descriptions.

31. Both move at constant speed, but the bear is faster and eventually catches the hiker.

32. Both increase speed until the bear catches the hiker.

33. The bear increases speed and the hiker steadily slows down until the bear catches the hiker.

34. The bear runs at constant speed, the hiker steadily runs faster until the bear gives up and stops. The hiker slows down and stops soon after that.

35–38 ▪ An object dropped from a height of 100 m has distance above the ground of

$$M(t) = 100 - \frac{a}{2}t^2$$

where a is the acceleration of gravity. For each of the following celestial bodies and with the given acceleration, find the time when the object hits the ground and the speed of the object at that time.

35. On Earth, where $a = 9.78$ m/s^2.

36. On the moon, where $a = 1.62$ m/s^2.

37. On Jupiter, where $a = 22.88$ m/s^2.

38. On Mars's moon Deimos, where $a = 2.15 \times 10^{-3}$ m/s^2.

Computer Exercises

39. On a graph of the function

$$y(t) = 10t^{2.5}$$

have your computer plot the following (use base point $t = 1$).

a. The secant line with $\Delta t = 1$.

b. The secant line with $\Delta t = -1$.

c. The secant line with $\Delta t = 0.1$.

d. The secant line with $\Delta t = -0.1$.

e. Use smaller and smaller values of Δt and try to estimate the slope of the tangent. Graph the proposed tangent line and then zoom in on your graph. Does the tangent look right?

40. The functions we have seen that are not differentiable fail at only a few points. Surprisingly, it is possible to find continuous curves that have a corner at every point. These curves are called fractals. The following construction creates a fractal called Koch's snowflake.

a. Draw an equilateral triangle.

b. Take the middle third of each side and expand it as shown.

c. Do the same for the middle third of each straight piece.

d. Repeat the process for as long as you can.

If this process is continued for an infinite number of steps, the resulting curve has a corner at every point.

2.5 Derivatives of Sums, Powers, and Polynomials

In the previous section, we used the definition of the derivative and the limit to compute some derivatives. Derivatives of complicated functions can be computed easily when the functions have been built from simpler component parts. If we have one set of rules for computing derivatives of these components, and another set for putting these derivatives together, we will be able to find the derivative of almost any function. The following sections are dedicated to finding these rules. We will derive ways to compute derivatives of the most important components used to build biological functions: power functions, exponential functions and trigonometric functions. We will then combine these with the **sum rule, product rule, quotient rule,** and **chain rule** (for computing derivatives when functions have been combined with functional composition).

This section presents three rules for putting derivatives together. First, **the sum rule** says that the derivative of the sum is the sum of the derivatives. Second, the **power rule** gives a formula for the derivative of a power function. Third, the **constant product rule** states that multiplying a function by a constant multiplies the derivative by that same constant. With these tools, we can compute the derivative of any **polynomial.**

The Sum Rule

Consider the function

$$s(t) = 5t^2 + 15t$$

This is the sum of two functions we studied in the previous section: the quadratic function $y(t) = 5t^2$ and a linear function $l(t) = 15t$. The derivatives of the pieces are

$$y'(t) = 10t$$
$$l'(t) = 15$$

How can we use our knowledge of the derivatives of the building blocks $y(t)$ and $l(t)$ to find the derivative of the sum $s(t)$? The technique is provided by the following theorem, which says that **the derivative of the sum** of two functions is **the sum of the derivatives.**

Theorem 2.5 The Sum Rule for Derivatives

Suppose

$$s(x) = f(x) + g(x)$$

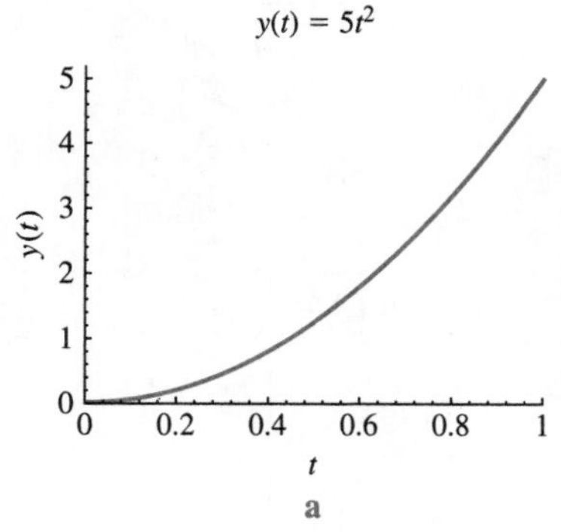

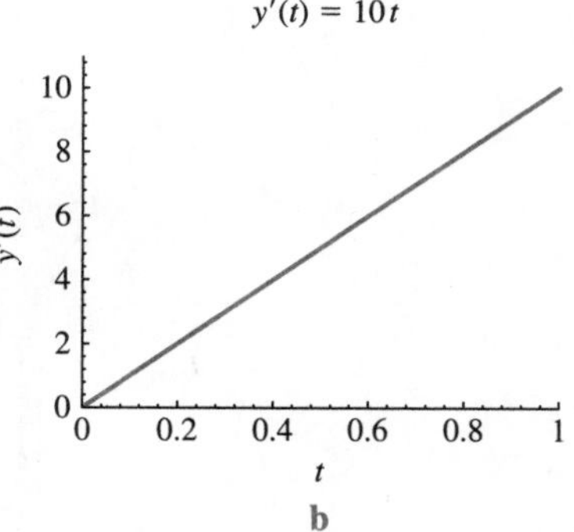

FIGURE 2.5.51
Graph and derivative of $y(t)$

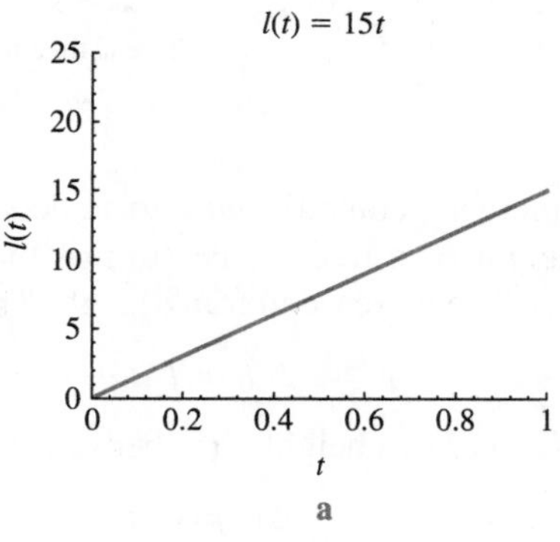

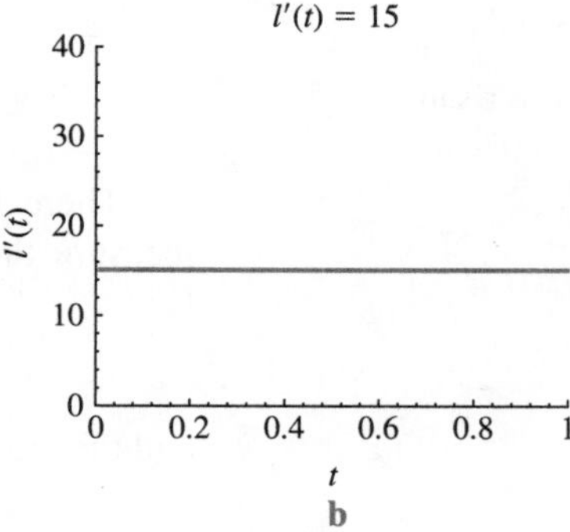

FIGURE 2.5.52
Graph and derivative of $l(t)$

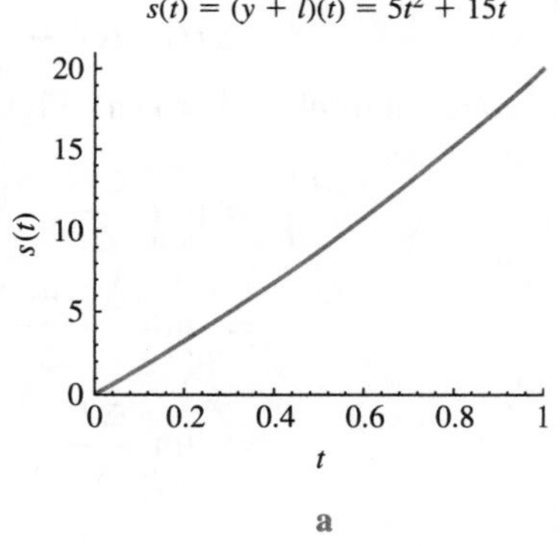

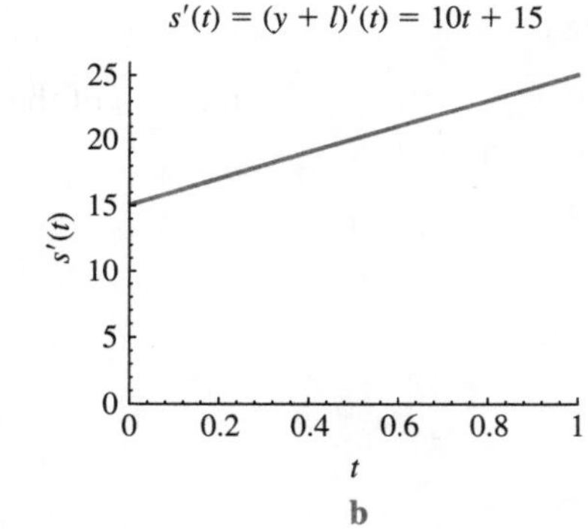

FIGURE 2.5.53
Graph and derivative of $s(t) = y(t) + l(t)$

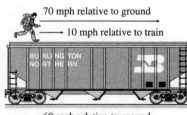

where f and g are both differentiable functions. Then

$$s'(x) = f'(x) + g'(x) \qquad \text{prime notation}$$

$$\frac{ds}{dx} = \frac{df}{dx} + \frac{dg}{dx} \qquad \text{differential notation}$$

Applying the sum rule to our example with $y(t) = 5t^2$ and $l(t) = 15t$, we get

$$s'(t) = y'(t) + l'(t) = 10t + 15$$

The functions and their derivatives are shown in Figures 2.5.51, 2.5.52, and 2.5.53.

Why does the sum rule work? In one interpretation, the derivative of position is the velocity of a moving object. Suppose a train has a speed of 60 mph and a person is running forward on the train at a speed of 10 mph. Relative to the ground, the person is moving at $60 + 10 = 70$ mph, the sum of the two velocities (Figure 2.5.54). Similarly, if the person is running backwards on the train at a speed of 10 mph, her velocity relative to the ground will be $60 - 10 = 50$ mph. Velocities add (and subtract). Derivatives, the mathematical version of velocity, also add.

70 mph relative to ground
10 mph relative to train
BURLINGTON NORTHERN
60 mph relative to ground

FIGURE 2.5.54
Velocities add

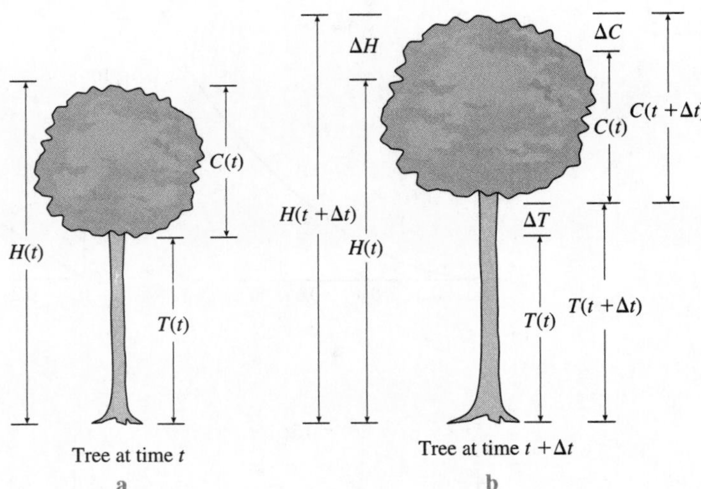

FIGURE 2.5.55
The height of a tree as a sum

There is another geometric way to understand the sum rule. Suppose that we measure the height of a tree as the sum of the trunk length and the crown height (Figure 2.5.55a). The increase in trunk height $T(t)$ between times t and $t+\Delta t$ is

$$\Delta T = T(t+\Delta t) - T(t)$$

and the increase in crown height $C(t)$ between times t and $t+\Delta t$ is

$$\Delta C = C(t+\Delta t) - C(t)$$

The total increase in height $H(t)$ is

$$\Delta H = \Delta T + \Delta C$$

the sum of the changes in trunk and crown. (Figure 2.5.55b). Therefore,

$$\begin{aligned}
\frac{dH}{dt} &= \lim_{\Delta t\to 0}\frac{\Delta H}{\Delta t} \\
&= \lim_{\Delta t\to 0}\frac{\Delta T+\Delta C}{\Delta t} \\
&= \lim_{\Delta t\to 0}\frac{\Delta T}{\Delta t} + \lim_{\Delta t\to 0}\frac{\Delta C}{\Delta t} \\
&= \frac{dT}{dt} + \frac{dC}{dt}
\end{aligned}$$

The total rate of change of height is the sum of the rate of change of trunk height and the rate of change of crown height.

Example 2.5.1 Applying the Sum Rule

Consider the function

$$p(t) = 5t^2 - 8t$$

In differential notation,

$$\begin{aligned}
\frac{dp}{dt} &= \frac{d}{dt}(5t^2 - 8) \\
&= \frac{d\,(5t^2)}{dt} - \frac{d}{dt}(8t) \\
&= 10t - 8
\end{aligned}$$

because the derivative of the linear function $-8t$ is the constant -8. ▲

Example 2.5.2 The Constant Sum Rule

We measured the position of our falling rock from the point where we dropped it, finding

$$y(t) = 5t^2$$

Suppose we measured the position of the rock from a point 2 m higher instead. The distance fallen would be

$$s(t) = 5t^2 + 2$$

(Figure 2.5.56a). In differential notation, the velocity of the rock is

$$\begin{aligned}\frac{ds}{dt} &= \frac{d}{dt}(5t^2 + 2)\\ &= \frac{d\left(5t^2\right)}{dt} + \frac{d}{dt}2\\ &= 10t + 0 = 10t\end{aligned}$$

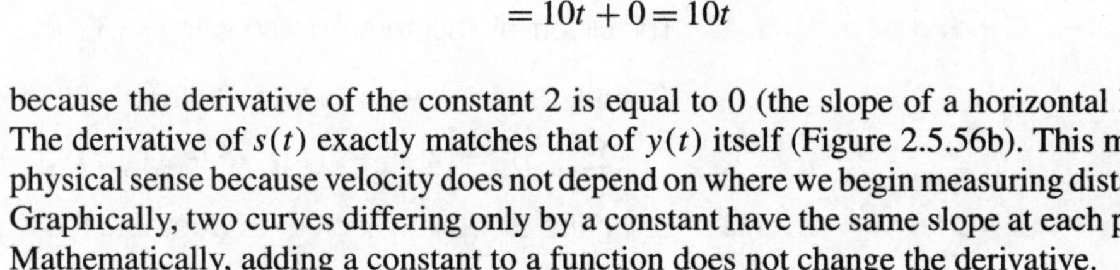

because the derivative of the constant 2 is equal to 0 (the slope of a horizontal line). The derivative of $s(t)$ exactly matches that of $y(t)$ itself (Figure 2.5.56b). This makes physical sense because velocity does not depend on where we begin measuring distance. Graphically, two curves differing only by a constant have the same slope at each point. Mathematically, adding a constant to a function does not change the derivative. ▲

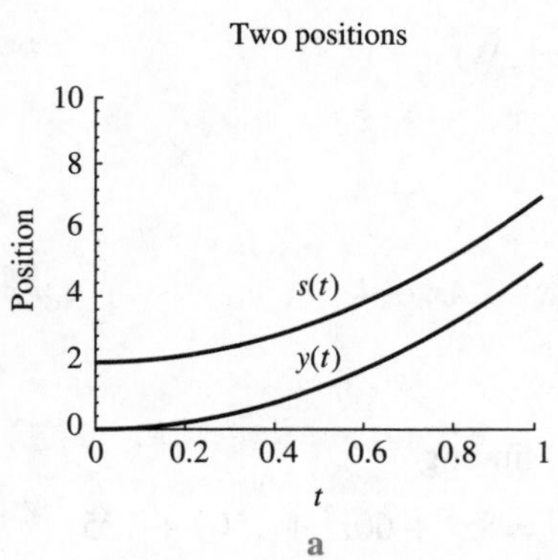

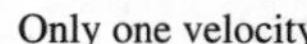

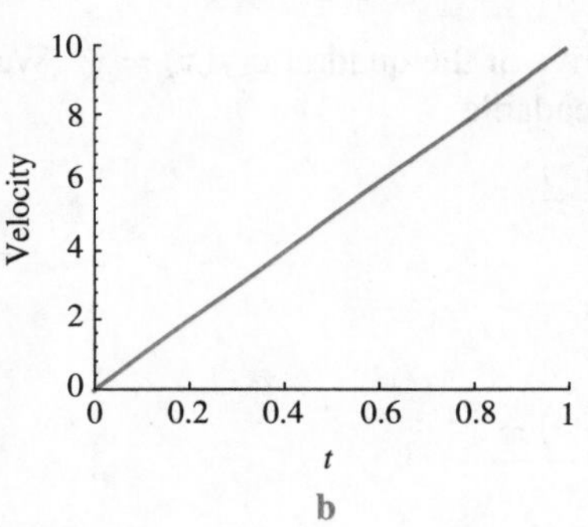

FIGURE 2.5.56
Two functions with the same derivative

We summarize the sum rule, along with the special cases involving constants, in the following tables.

Prime notation

Rule	Function	Derivative
Sum rule	$f(x) + g(x)$	$f'(x) + g'(x)$
Constant sum rule	$f(x) + c$	$f'(x)$

Differential notation

Rule	Function	Derivative
Sum rule	$f(x) + g(x)$	$\frac{df}{dx} + \frac{dg}{dx}$
Constant sum rule	$f(x) + c$	$\frac{df}{dx}$

Derivatives of Power Functions

Power functions take the form

$$f(x) = x^p$$

for some power p. We begin by finding the derivatives of the simplest power functions

$$f(x) = x^n$$

where n is a positive integer (1, 2, 3, . . .).

There are two ways to compute the derivative of $f(x) = x^n$. One uses the **binomial theorem** and the other uses **mathematical induction.** We use the binomial theorem to derive the result in the text, leaving mathematical induction to the exercises (see Section 2.6, Exercises 19–22). The binomial theorem gives a formula for computing powers of sums.

Theorem 2.6 The Binomial Theorem (Simplified Version)

The expansion of $(x+y)^n$ is a polynomial of degree n in x, with expansion

$$(x+y)^n = x^n + nx^{n-1}y + \cdots$$

The dots represent terms with smaller powers of x and larger powers of y. For small values of n,

$$(x+y)^2 = x^2 + 2xy + y^2$$
$$(x+y)^3 = x^3 + 3x^2y + 3xy^2 + y^3$$
$$(x+y)^4 = x^4 + 4x^3y + 6x^2y^2 + 4xy^3 + y^4$$

Example 2.5.3 The Binomial Theorem Applied with $n=2$

To find $(x+2)^2$, we substitute 2 for y, finding

$$(x+2)^2 = x^2 + 2x\cdot 2 + 2^2 = x^2 + 4x + 4$$

Example 2.5.4 The Binomial Theorem Applied with $n=3$

To find $(2z+5)^3$, we substitute $2z$ for x and 5 for y, finding

$$(2z+5)^3 = (2z)^3 + 3(2z)^2\cdot 5 + 3\cdot(2z)\cdot 5^2 + 5^3 = 8z^3 + 60z^2 + 150z + 125$$

Example 2.5.5 Using the Binomial Theorem to Compute the Derivative of x^2

We can use the binomial theorem to find the derivative of the quadratic $f(x)=x^2$. We use h instead of Δx to make the calculation more readable.

$$\begin{aligned}\frac{dx^2}{dx} &= \lim_{h\to 0}\frac{f(x+h)-f(x)}{h}\\ &= \lim_{h\to 0}\frac{(x+h)^2-x^2}{h}\\ &= \lim_{h\to 0}\frac{\left(x^2+2xh+h^2\right)-x^2}{h}\\ &= \lim_{h\to 0}\frac{2xh+h^2}{h}\\ &= \lim_{h\to 0} 2x+h\\ &= 2x\end{aligned}$$

We computed the limit by evaluating the continuous function $2x+h$ at $h=0$.

Example 2.5.6 Using the Binomial Theorem to Compute the Derivative of x^3

When $n=3$, we expand $(x+h)^3$, finding

$$\begin{aligned}\frac{dx^3}{dx} &= \lim_{h\to 0}\frac{(x+h)^3-x^3}{h}\\ &= \lim_{h\to 0}\frac{\left(x^3+3x^2h+3xh^2+h^3\right)-x^3}{h}\\ &= \lim_{h\to 0}\frac{3x^2h+3xh^2+h^3}{h}\\ &= \lim_{h\to 0} 3x^2+3xh+h^2\\ &= 3x^2\end{aligned}$$

We used the expansion

$$(x+h)^3 = x^3 + 3x^2h + 3xh^2 + h^3$$

finding that the only term that appears in the derivative is the second. The first term canceled when we subtracted $f(x) = x^3$, and the terms with h^2 and h^3 disappear because they approach 0 even after being divided by h.

Now consider the function $f(x) = x^n$. Using the binomial theorem to expand the term $f(x+h)$ in the definition of the derivative gives

$$\begin{aligned}\frac{df}{dx} &= \lim_{h\to 0} \frac{(x+h)^n - x^n}{h} \\ &= \lim_{h\to 0} \frac{\left(x^n + nx^{n-1}h + Eh^2\right) - x^n}{h} \\ &= \lim_{h\to 0} \frac{nx^{n-1}h + Eh^2}{h} \\ &= \lim_{h\to 0} nx^{n-1} + Eh \\ &= nx^{n-1}\end{aligned}$$

where E is the expression (a polynomial in x and h) that multiplies h^2 in the additional terms in the binomial theorem.

We have derived the **power rule:**

Theorem 2.7 **The Power Rule for Derivatives: Positive Integer Powers**

Suppose

$$f(x) = x^n$$

when n is a positive integer. Then

$$f'(x) = nx^{n-1} \quad \text{prime notation}$$

$$\frac{df}{dx} = nx^{n-1} \quad \text{differential notation}$$

For the first few values of n, derivatives are given in the following table.

Function	Derivative
x^1	1
x^2	$2x$
x^3	$3x^2$
x^4	$4x^3$

In words, to find the derivative of a power function, multiply by the power out front and then decrease the power by 1.

Example 2.5.7 The Power Rule in Action

With $n = 1$, the graph of the power function is a line with constant slope of 1 (Figure 2.5.57a). With $n = 2$, the graph of the power function is a parabola. The graph of the derivative is a line with slope 2 (Figure 2.5.57b). The function changes from decreasing to increasing at $x = 0$, indicated by the derivative crossing from negative to positive values. With $n = 3$, the power function is always increasing but has a critical point at $x = 0$ (Figure 2.5.57c).

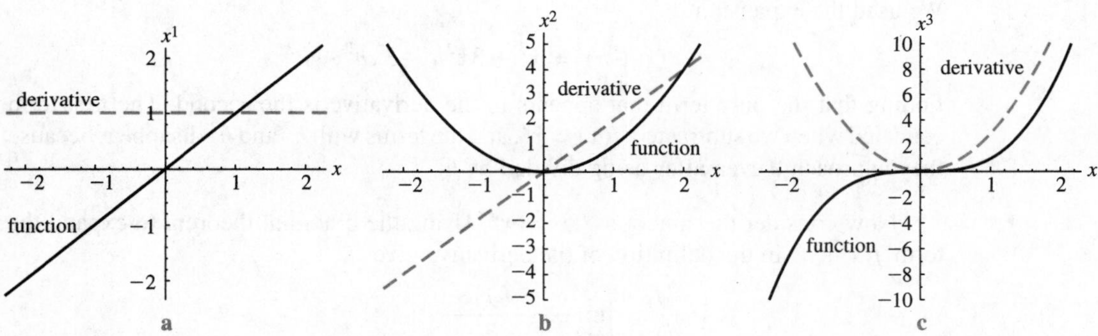

FIGURE 2.5.57

The first few power functions and their derivatives

Negative and Fractional Powers The power rule also works for negative and fractional powers. One derivative uses an extension of the binomial theorem, and another, presented in Section 2.9, Exercises 23–24, uses rules for finding the derivatives of exponential functions and functional compositions.

Theorem 2.8 **The Power Rule for Derivatives**

Suppose

$$f(x) = x^p$$

defined for $x > 0$. Then

$$f'(x) = px^{p-1} \quad \text{prime notation}$$

$$\frac{df}{dx} = px^{p-1} \quad \text{differential notation}$$

Example 2.5.8 The Power Rule Applied to Negative Powers

For the first few negative powers, derivatives are given in the following table.

Function	Derivative
x^{-1}	$-x^{-2}$
x^{-2}	$-2x^{-3}$
x^{-3}	$-3x^{-4}$

To find the derivative, multiply out front by the power and decrease the power by 1. Be careful to **subtract** 1 from the power even when it is negative. The function and derivative with power equal to −1 are shown in Figure 2.5.58. The derivative is always negative, indicating that the function is decreasing (except at $x = 0$ where it is not defined). Near $x = 0$, the slope approaches negative infinity.

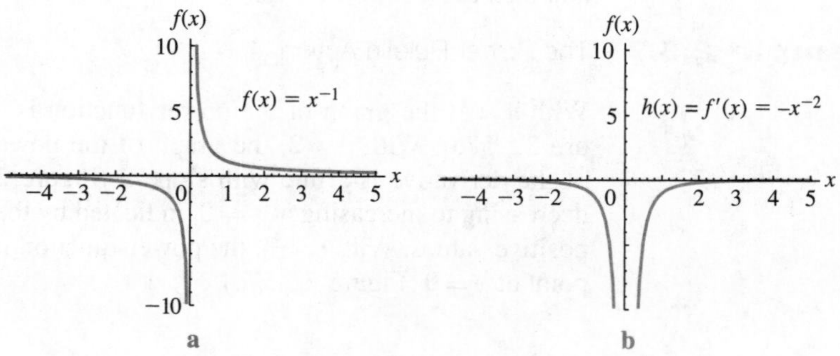

FIGURE 2.5.58

Power function with a negative power and its derivative

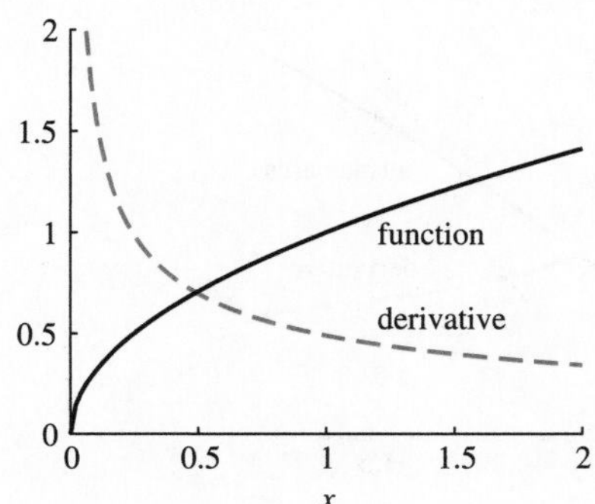

FIGURE 2.5.59
The square root function and its derivative

Example 2.5.9 The Power Rule Applied to the Square Root

The power rule can be used to find the derivative of $\sqrt{x} = x^{1/2}$.

$$\begin{aligned}\frac{d}{dx}x^{1/2} &= \frac{1}{2}x^{1/2-1}\\ &= \frac{1}{2}x^{-1/2}\\ &= \frac{1}{2\sqrt{x}}\end{aligned}$$

Near $x = 0$, the slope becomes infinite. For large x, the slope becomes small (Figure 2.5.59).

Example 2.5.10 Using the Power Rule Along with the Sum Rule

Consider the function

$$g(z) = z^{-2} + z^4 + 3.$$

We find the derivative with the following steps

$$\begin{aligned}\frac{dg}{dz} &= \frac{d\left(z^{-2}\right)}{dz} + \frac{d\left(z^4\right)}{dz} + \frac{d3}{dz} && \text{sum rule}\\ &= \frac{d\left(z^{-2}\right)}{dz} + \frac{d\left(z^4\right)}{dz} && \text{constant sum rule}\\ &= -2z^{-3} + 4z^3 && \text{power rule}\end{aligned}$$

Derivatives of Polynomials

A **polynomial** is a function built from power functions with nonnegative integer powers that are multiplied by constants and added up. For example, the function

$$p(x) = 2x^3 - 5x^2 + 7x - 8$$

is a polynomial constructed by multiplying x^3 by 2, subtracting 5 times x^2, adding 7 times x^1, and subtracting 8. The **degree** of a polynomial is the highest power that appears in the formula—in this case, 3. Using the power rule, the sum rule, and a new rule, the **constant product rule,** we can find the derivative of any polynomial.

Theorem 2.9 **The Constant Product Rule for Derivatives**

If c is a constant and $f(x)$ is a differentiable function, then

$$\frac{d}{dx}cf(x) = c\frac{d}{dx}f(x).$$

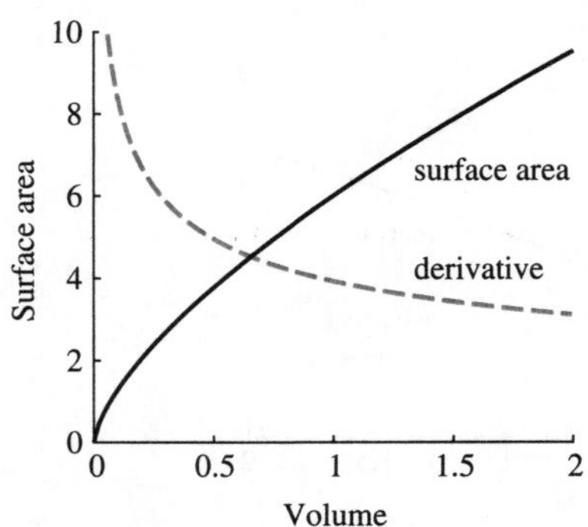

FIGURE 2.5.60
The derivative of the power relations between surface area and volume

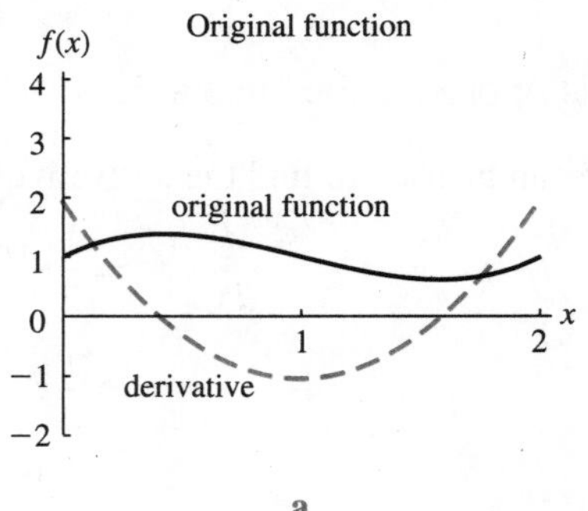

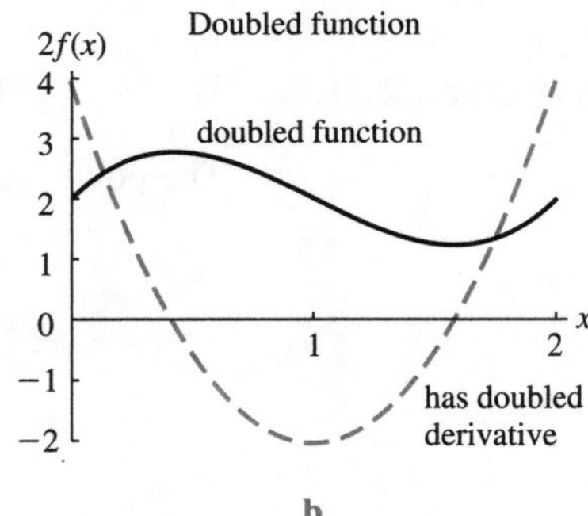

FIGURE 2.5.61
The constant product rule for derivatives

The constant product rule says constants come "outside" of derivatives. For example, doubling a function doubles the derivative (Figure 2.5.61).

Example 2.5.11 The Power Rule Applied to Comparing Surface Area and Volume

We can use the generalized power rule to interpret power relations between measurements. The surface area S of an object is proportional to the volume V raised to the $2/3$ power, or

$$S = cV^{2/3}$$

where the constant c depends on the shape of the object. If we imagine increasing the volume of an object without changing its shape, the surface area will increase, with

$$\frac{dS}{dV} = \frac{2}{3}cV^{-1/3}$$

Surface area does increase, but at a **decreasing rate** (Figure 2.5.60). In words, as an object gets larger, the ratio of surface area to volume decreases.

Example 2.5.12 Finding the Derivative of a Power Function

The derivative of the function $8t^4$ is

$$\begin{aligned} \frac{d(8t^4)}{dt} &= 8\frac{d(t^4)}{dt} && \text{constant product rule} \\ &= 8 \cdot 4t^3 && \text{power rule} \\ &= 32t^3 && \text{multiply constants} \end{aligned}$$

Example 2.5.13 Finding the Derivative of a Complicated Polynomial

Using the power rule, the constant product rule, and the sum rule, we can find the derivative of the polynomial $p(x)$,

$$p(x) = 2x^3 - 7x^2 + 7x + 1$$

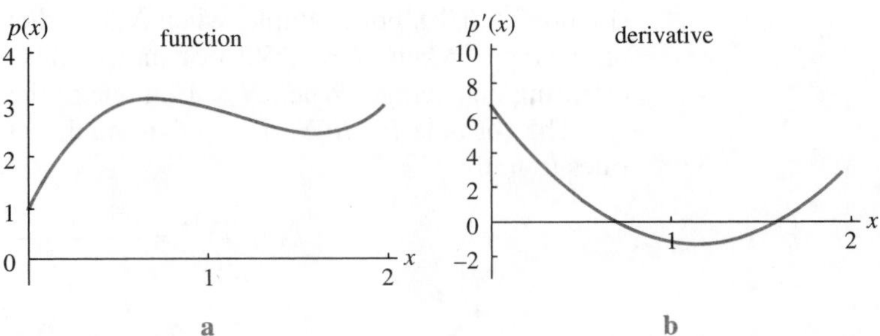

FIGURE 2.5.62
The polynomial $p(x)$ with its derivative

by breaking it into component parts as follows.

$$\begin{aligned}\frac{dp}{dx} &= \frac{d\left(2x^3\right)}{dx} + \frac{d\left(-7x^2\right)}{dx} + \frac{d(7x)}{dx} + \frac{d(1)}{dx} && \text{sum rule}\\ &= 2\frac{d\left(x^3\right)}{dx} - 7\frac{d\left(x^2\right)}{dx} + 7\frac{d(x)}{dx} + 1\frac{d(1)}{dx} && \text{constant product rule}\\ &= 2 \cdot 3x^2 - 7 \cdot 2x + 7 \cdot 1 && \text{power rule and constant sum rule}\\ &= 6x^2 - 14x + 7 && \text{multiply out}\end{aligned}$$

The derivative of a polynomial is always another polynomial. Because the power rule reduces the power by 1, the degree of the derivative is always 1 less than the degree of the original polynomial. The function and its derivative are plotted in Figure 2.5.62.

Example 2.5.14 Using Polynomials to Describe Bird Reproduction

Polynomials are convenient to work with mathematically and describe many biological processes. Consider the following model of offspring production. Let N be the number of eggs a bird lays. Suppose that each chick survives with probability

$$P(N) = 1 - 0.1N$$

(Figure 2.5.63a). The more offspring a parent has, the smaller chance each offspring has to survive. If the bird lays 1 egg, the chick has a 90% chance of surviving. If the bird lays 5 eggs, each chick has only a 50% chance of surviving. If the bird lays 10 eggs, none of the chicks survive. Mathematically, the total number of offspring that are likely to survive, $S(N)$, is the product of the number of eggs N and the probability of survival for each $P(N)$, or

$$S(N) = N \cdot P(N) = N(1 - 0.1N) = N - 0.1N^2$$

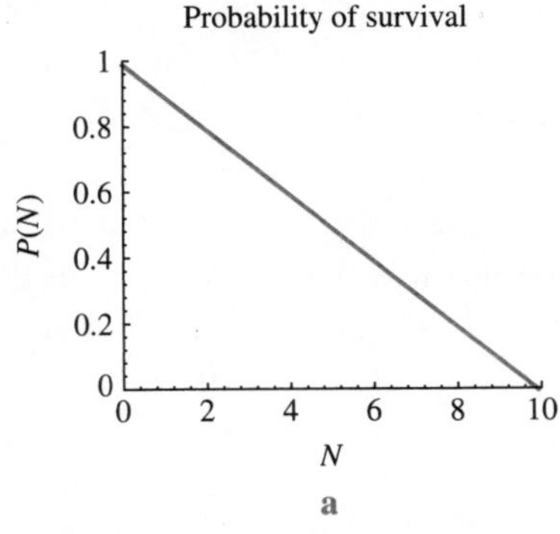

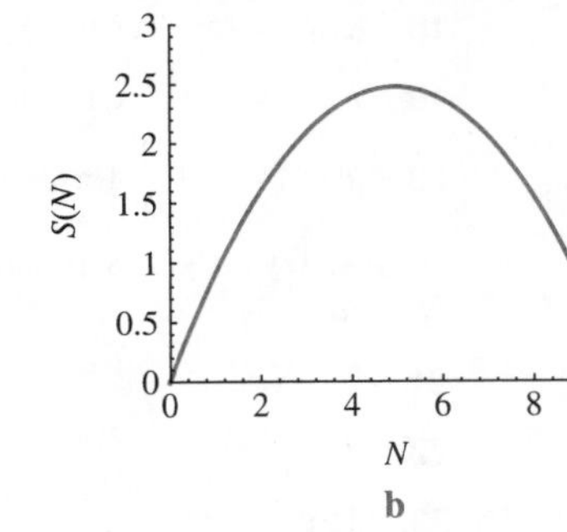

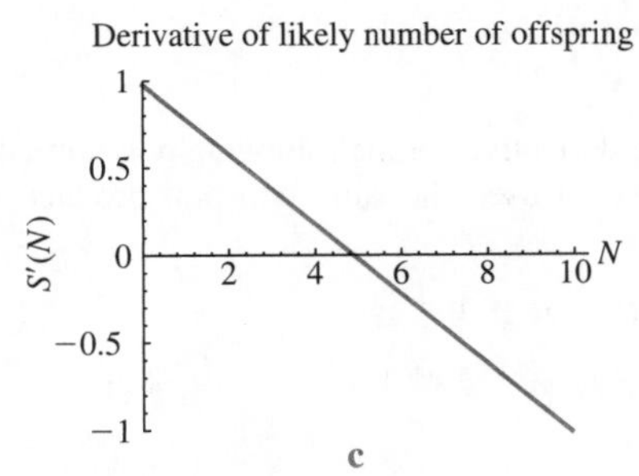

FIGURE 2.5.63
A model of offspring number and survival

(Figure 2.5.63b). For example, when $N = 1$, then $1 - 0.1 \times 1^2 = 0.9$ offspring survive on average. When $N = 5$, 50% of the 5 chicks are likely to survive, producing 2.5 offspring on average. When $N = 10$, none of the chicks survive.

The formula for $S(N)$ is a polynomial. We use the constant product and power rules to find

$$\begin{aligned}\frac{dS}{dN} &= \frac{d\left(N - 0.1N^2\right)}{dN}\\ &= \frac{dN}{dN} - 0.1\frac{d\left(N^2\right)}{dN}\\ &= 1 - 0.1(2N)\\ &= 1 - 0.2N\end{aligned}$$

At $N = 0$, the derivative is positive (Figure 2.5.63c) meaning that a higher value of N will likely produce more surviving offspring. At $N = 5$ the derivative is zero. For $N > 5$, the derivative is negative. The negative derivative indicates that the number of surviving offspring is likely to **decrease** when the number of eggs becomes too large.

Summary By combining three rules, the **sum rule,** the **power rule,** and the **constant product rule,** we can find the derivative of any polynomial. The **sum rule** states that the derivative of the sum of two functions is equal to the sum of the derivatives. This corresponds to the physical fact that velocities add. As a special case, we found the **constant sum rule,** which states that adding a constant to a function does not change the derivative. The **power rule** gives the formula for the derivative of the power function x^p as px^{p-1} for any power. The **constant product rule** says that constants come "outside" the derivative; multiplying a function by a constant multiplies the derivative by that same constant.

2.5 Exercises

Mathematical Techniques

1–8 ▪ Find the derivatives of the following power functions.

1. x^5
2. x^{-5}
3. $x^{0.2}$
4. $x^{-0.2}$
5. x^e
6. x^{-e}
7. $x^{1/e}$
8. $x^{-1/e}$

9–12 ▪ Find the derivatives of the following polynomial functions. Indicate where you used the sum, constant product, and power rules.

9. $f(x) = 3x^2 + 3x + 1$
10. $s(x) = 1 - x + x^2 - x^3 + x^4$
11. $g(z) = 3z^3 + 2z^2$
12. $p(x) = 1 + x + \frac{x^2}{2} + \frac{x^3}{6} + \frac{x^4}{24}$

13–16 ▪ Use the binomial theorem to compute the following.

13. $(x + 1)^3$
14. $(x + 2)^3$
15. $(2x + 1)^3$
16. $(x + 1)^4$

17–20 ▪ Use the derivative to sketch a graph of each of the following functions.

17. $f(x) = 1 - 2x + x^2$ for $0 \le x \le 2$
18. $g(x) = 4x - x^2$ for $0 \le x \le 5$
19. $h(x) = x^3 - 3x$ for $0 \le x \le 2$
20. $F(x) = x + \frac{1}{x}$ for $0 < x \le 2$

21–26 ▪ Try to guess functions that have the following as their derivatives.

21. 2
22. $2x$
23. $15x^{14}$
24. x^{14}

25. $-x^{-2}$

26. $3x^{-4}$

Applications

27–30 ▪ Find the derivatives of the following functions.

27. In the early phase of the epidemic, the number of AIDS cases in the United States grew approximately according to a cubic equation, $A(t) = 175t^3$ where t is measured in years since the beginning of the epidemic in 1972. Find and interpret the derivative.

28. Let $F(r) = 1.5r^4$, where F represents the flow in cubic centimeters per second through a pipe of radius r. If $r = 1$, how much will a small increase in radius change the flow (try it with $\Delta r = 0.1$)? If $r = 2$, how will a small increase in radius change the flow?

29. The area of a circle as a function of radius is $A(r) = \pi r^2$, with area measured in square centimeters and radius measured in centimeters. Find the derivative of area with respect to radius. On a geometric diagram, illustrate the area corresponding to $\Delta A = A(r + \Delta r) - A(r)$. What is a geometric interpretation of the derivative? Do the units make sense?

30. The volume of a sphere as a function of radius is $V(r) = \frac{4}{3}\pi r^3$. Find the derivative of volume with respect to radius. On a geometric diagram, illustrate the volume corresponding to $\Delta V = V(r + \Delta r) - V(r)$. What is a geometric interpretation of this derivative? Do the units make sense?

31–32 ▪ One car is towing another using a rigid 50-ft pole. Sketch the positions and speeds of the two cars as functions of time in the following circumstances.

31. The car starts from a stop, slowly speeds up, cruises for a while, and then abruptly stops.

32. The car starts from a stop, goes slowly in reverse for a short time, stops, goes forward slowly, and then goes forward more quickly.

33–36 ▪ A passenger is traveling on a luxury train that is moving west at 80 mph.

33. The passenger starts running east at 10 mph. What is her velocity relative to the ground?

34. While running, the passenger flips a dinner roll over her shoulder (west) at 25 mph. What is the velocity of the roll relative to the train? What is the velocity of the roll relative to the ground?

35. A roll weevil jumps east off the roll at 5 mph. What is the velocity of the roll relative to the passenger? What is the velocity of the roll relative to the train? What is the velocity of the roll relative to the ground?

36. A roll weevil flea jumps west off the roll weevil at 15 mph. What is the velocity of the roll weevil flea relative to the roll? What is the velocity of the roll weevil flea relative to the passenger? What is the velocity of the roll weevil flea relative to the train? What is the velocity of the roll weevil flea relative to the ground?

37–38 ▪ Each of the following measurements is the sum of two components.

a. Find the formula for the sum.

b. Find the derivative of each component. What are the units?

c. Find the derivative of the sum, and check that the sum rule worked.

d. Describe in words what is happening.

e. Sketch a graph of each component and the total as functions of time.

37. A population of bacteria consists of two types, a and b. The first follows $a(t) = 1 + t^2$, and the second follows $b(t) = 1 - 2t + t^2$ where populations are measured in millions and time is measured in hours. The total population is $P(t) = a(t) + b(t)$.

38. The above-ground volume (stem and leaves) of a plant is $V_a(t) = 3.0t + 20.0 + \frac{t^2}{2}$ and the below-ground volume (roots) is $V_b(t) = -1.0t + 40.0$ where t is measured in days and volumes are measured in cubic centimeters. The total volume is $V(t) = V_a(t) + V_b(t)$.

39–42 ▪ An object tossed upward at 10 m/s from a height of 100 m has distance above the ground of

$$M(t) = 100 + 10t - \frac{a}{2}t^2$$

where a is the acceleration of gravity. For each of the following celestial bodies, with the given acceleration, find the time when the object reaches a critical point, how high it gets, the time when it hits the ground, and the speed of the object at that time. Sketch the position of the object as a function of time.

39. On Earth, where $a = 9.78\ \text{m/s}^2$.

40. On the moon, where $a = 1.62\ \text{m/s}^2$.

41. On Jupiter, where $a = 22.88\ \text{m/s}^2$.

42. On Mars's moon Deimos, where $a = 2.15 \times 10^{-3}\ \text{m/s}^2$.

43–46 ▪ Try different power functions of the form t^n to guess a solution for each of the following differential equations describing the size of an organism, measured in kg. Find the size at $t = 1$ and $t = 2$. Can you explain why some grow so much faster than others?

43. $\frac{dS}{dt} = 6t$

44. $\frac{dS}{dt} = 6t^2$

45. $\frac{dS}{dt} = 6\frac{S(t)}{t}$

46. $\frac{dS}{dt} = 12\frac{S(t)}{t}$

Computer Exercise

47. Consider the polynomials

$$p_0(x) = 1$$
$$p_1(x) = 1 + x$$
$$p_2(x) = 1 + x + \frac{x^2}{2}$$
$$p_3(x) = 1 + x + \frac{x^2}{2} + \frac{x^3}{6}$$

To find the fourth polynomial in the series, add a term equal to the last term of $p_3(x)$ multiplied by $\frac{x}{4}$. To find the fifth polynomial in the series, add a term equal to the last term of $p_4(x)$ multiplied by $\frac{x}{5}$ and so forth.

a. Find the first six polynomials in this series.

b. Plot them all for $-3 \le x \le 3$.

c. Take the derivative of $p_6(x)$. What is it equal to? Compare the graph of $p_6(x)$ with the graph of its derivative.

d. Can you guess what function these polynomials are approaching?

2.6 Derivatives of Products and Quotients

The previous section derived the three rules needed to find the derivative of a polynomial. The next two ways to combine functions are multiplication and division. In this section, we learn how to compute the derivatives of products and quotients of known functions by deriving the **product rule** and **quotient rule.** These two rules enable us to study the derivatives of **rational functions,** functions that are the ratios of two polynomials.

The Product Rule

Tempting as it might sound, the derivative of the product is *not* the product of the derivatives (see Exercises 2.6.15 and 2.6.16). Finding the derivative of a product is a bit more complicated. But as for the derivative of the sum, there is a useful geometric argument to help us derive and understand the formula.

Suppose the density $\rho(t)$ (Greek letter "rho") and the volume $V(t)$ of an object are functions of time. The mass $M(t)$, the product of the density and volume, is also a function of time and has the formula

$$M(t) = \rho(t)V(t)$$

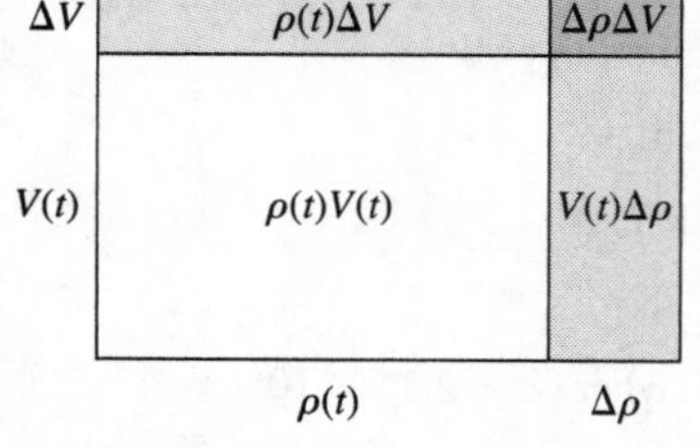

FIGURE 2.6.64
The product rule

What is the derivative of the mass? For example, if both the density and volume are increasing, the mass is also increasing. But if the density increases while the volume decreases, we cannot tell whether mass increases without more information.

$M(t)$ can be represented geometrically as the area of a rectangle with base $\rho(t)$ and height $V(t)$ (Figure 2.6.64). Between times t and $t + \Delta t$, the density changes from $\rho(t)$ to $\rho(t) + \Delta\rho$ and the volume changes from $V(t)$ to $V(t) + \Delta V$. The mass at time $t + \Delta t$ is then

$$\begin{aligned} M(t + \Delta t) &= (\rho(t) + \Delta\rho)(V(t) + \Delta V) \\ &= \rho(t)V(t) + \rho(t)\Delta V + V(t)\Delta\rho + \Delta\rho\Delta V \\ &= M(t) + \rho(t)\Delta V + V(t)\Delta\rho + \Delta\rho\Delta V \end{aligned}$$

The change in mass ΔM is

$$\begin{aligned} \Delta M &= M(t + \Delta t) - M(t) \\ &= \rho(t)\Delta V + V(t)\Delta\rho + \Delta\rho\Delta V \end{aligned}$$

Each component of ΔM corresponds to one of the shaded regions in Figure 2.6.64.

How does this help us compute the derivative of the product? To find the derivative of M with respect to t, we divide ΔM by Δt and take the limit. ΔM divided by Δt is

$$\begin{aligned} \frac{\Delta M}{\Delta t} &= \frac{\rho(t)\Delta V + V(t)\Delta\rho + \Delta\rho\Delta V}{\Delta t} \\ &= \rho(t)\frac{\Delta V}{\Delta t} + V(t)\frac{\Delta\rho}{\Delta t} + \frac{\Delta\rho\Delta V}{\Delta t} \end{aligned}$$

Taking the limit, we get

$$\lim_{\Delta t \to 0} \frac{\Delta M}{\Delta t} = \rho(t) \lim_{\Delta t \to 0} \frac{\Delta V}{\Delta t} + V(t) \lim_{\Delta t \to 0} \frac{\Delta \rho}{\Delta t} + \lim_{\Delta t \to 0} \frac{\Delta \rho \Delta V}{\Delta t}$$

where we used the properties of limits (Theorems 2.1 and 2.2) to break up the sum and take constants outside the limits. The first two pieces are

$$\rho(t) \lim_{\Delta t \to 0} \frac{\Delta V}{\Delta t} = \rho(t) V'(t)$$

$$V(t) \lim_{\Delta t \to 0} \frac{\Delta \rho}{\Delta t} = V(t) \rho'(t)$$

by the definition of the derivative. The final piece can be analyzed as a product,

$$\lim_{\Delta t \to 0} \frac{\Delta \rho \Delta V}{\Delta t} = \lim_{\Delta t \to 0} \Delta \rho \lim_{\Delta t \to 0} \frac{\Delta V}{\Delta t}$$

However,

$$\lim_{\Delta t \to 0} \Delta \rho = 0$$

because ρ is a continuous function. Therefore,

$$\lim_{\Delta t \to 0} \frac{\Delta \rho \Delta V}{\Delta t} = 0 \cdot V'(t) = 0$$

Geometrically, the region labeled $\Delta\rho\Delta V$ becomes very small as Δt approaches 0 and disappears in the limit. We summarize this calculation in the following theorem.

Theorem 2.10 The Product Rule for Derivatives

Suppose

$$p(x) = f(x)g(x)$$

where f and g are both differentiable. Then

$$p'(x) = f(x)g'(x) + g(x)f'(x) \quad \text{prime notation}$$

$$\frac{dp}{dx} = f(x)\frac{dg}{dx} + g(x)\frac{df}{dx} \quad \text{differential notation}$$

Special Cases and Examples

The constant product rule is a special case of the product rule. If we measure distance fallen in centimeters rather than meters, the distance fallen will be 100 times the original distance $y(t)$, or

$$p(t) = 100y(t)$$

This function is a product of the constant function 100 and the function $y(t)$. The velocity is then

$$\begin{aligned} \frac{dp}{dt} &= \frac{d(100y)}{dt} && \text{definition of } p(t) \\ &= 100\frac{dy}{dt} + y(t)\frac{d(100)}{dt} && \text{the product rule} \\ &= 100\frac{dy}{dt} + y(t) \cdot 0 = 100\frac{dy}{dt} && \text{the derivative of the constant 100 is 0} \end{aligned}$$

In centimeters per second, the velocity is 100 times the velocity in meters per second. Mathematically, multiplying a function by a constant multiplies the derivative by that same constant.

We summarize these rules in the following tables.

Prime notation

Rule	Function	Derivative
Product rule	$f(x)g(x)$	$f(x)g'(x) + g(x)f'(x)$
Constant product rule	$cf(x)$	$cf'(x)$

Differential notation

Rule	Function	Derivative
Product rule	$\frac{d(fg)}{dx}$	$f(x)\frac{dg}{dx} + g(x)\frac{df}{dx}$
Constant product rule	$\frac{d(cf)}{dx}$	$c\frac{df}{dx}$

Example 2.6.1 Using the Product Rule

To find the derivative of

$$p(x) = (x - 1)(x + 1)$$

think of $p(x)$ as the product of $f(x) = x - 1$ and $g(x) = x + 1$. Both $f(x)$ and $g(x)$ are linear functions with slope 1, so

$$f'(x) = 1$$
$$g'(x) = 1$$

Then, by the product rule,

$$p'(x) = (x - 1) \cdot 1 + (x + 1) \cdot 1 = 2x$$

To check, we can multiply the function out, finding

$$p(x) = x^2 - 1$$

Using the power and constant sum rules yields

$$p'(x) = 2x + 0 = 2x$$

which matches the result found with the product rule. ▲

Example 2.6.2 Applying the Product Rule

Suppose the volume V of a plant is increasing according to

$$V(t) = 100.0 + 12.0t$$

where t is measured in days and V is measured in cubic centimeters, and that the density is decreasing according to

$$\rho(t) = 0.8 - 0.05t$$

where ρ is measured in grams per cubic centimeter. Is the mass increasing or decreasing? We can use the product rule to find out.

$$\begin{aligned} M'(t) &= \rho(t)V'(t) + V(t)\rho'(t) \\ &= (0.8 - 0.05t)12.0 + (100.0 + 12.0t)(-0.05) \\ &= 9.6 - 0.6t - 5.0 - 0.6t \\ &= 4.6 - 1.2t \end{aligned}$$

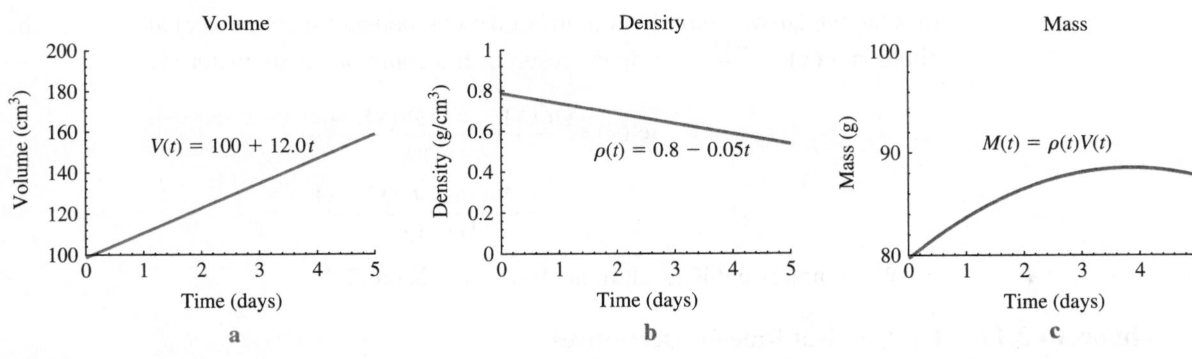

FIGURE 2.6.65
The volume, density, and mass of a plant

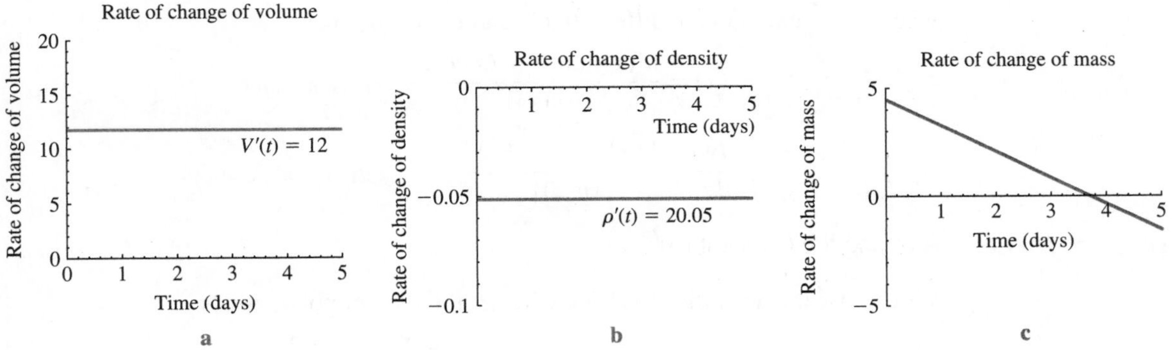

FIGURE 2.6.66
The rates of change of volume, density, and mass of a plant

At $t = 0$, the derivative is positive and the mass is increasing. By $t = 4$ the decrease in density has overwhelmed the increase in volume, and the mass is decreasing (Figures 2.6.65 and 2.6.66). ▲

The Quotient Rule

Suppose we are interested in finding the derivative of a function $w(x)$ defined as the quotient of $u(x)$ and $v(x)$:

$$w(x) = \frac{u(x)}{v(x)}$$

With a bit of a trick, we can find $w'(x)$ from the product rule. First, multiply both sides by $v(x)$.

$$v(x)w(x) = u(x)$$

Now take the derivative of both sides using the product rule,

$$v(x)w'(x) + v'(x)w(x) = u'(x)$$

This can be thought of as an equation for $w'(x)$, the derivative of the quotient, and can be solved for $w'(x)$ as follows:

$$v(x)w'(x) = u'(x) - v'(x)w(x)$$

$$w'(x) = \frac{u'(x) - v'(x)w(x)}{v(x)}$$

To write the answer entirely in terms of the component functions $u(x)$ and $v(x)$, substitute in $w(x)=\frac{u(x)}{v(x)}$. Putting the result over a common denominator gives

$$\begin{aligned} w'(x) &= \frac{u'(x) - v'(x)u(x)/v(x)}{v(x)} \\ &= \frac{u'(x)v(x) - v'(x)u(x)}{[v(x)]^2} \end{aligned}$$

We summarize this result in the following theorem.

Theorem 2.11 **The Quotient Rule for Derivatives**

Suppose

$$w(x) = \frac{u(x)}{v(x)}$$

where $u(x)$ and $v(x)$ are differentiable and $v(x) \neq 0$. Then

$$w'(x) = \frac{u'(x)v(x) - v'(x)u(x)}{[v(x)]^2} \quad \text{prime notation}$$

$$\frac{dw}{dx} = \frac{v(x)\frac{du}{dx} - \frac{dv}{dx}u(x)}{[v(x)]^2} \quad \text{differential notation}$$

Example 2.6.3 Applying the Quotient Rule

We can use the derivative to check whether the ratio of polynomials

$$f(x) = \frac{x^3 + 2x}{1 + x^2}$$

is an increasing function. We write

$$f(x) = \frac{u(x)}{v(x)}$$

where we define the numerator as $u(x) = x^3 + 2x$ and the denominator as $v(x) = 1 + x^2$. Then

$$u'(x) = 3x^2 + 2 \text{ and } v'(x) = 2x$$

The quotient rule says that

$$\begin{aligned} f'(x) &= \frac{u'(x)v(x) - v'(x)u(x)}{[v(x)]^2} \\ &= \frac{(3x^2+2)(1+x^2) - 2x(x^3+2x)}{(1+x^2)^2} \end{aligned}$$

This can be simplified as

$$\begin{aligned} f'(x) &= \frac{(3x^2+2)(1+x^2) - 2x(x^3+2x)}{(1+x^2)^2} \\ &= \frac{(3x^4+5x^2+2) - (2x^4+4x^2)}{(1+x^2)^2} \\ &= \frac{x^4+x^2+2}{(1+x^2)^2} \end{aligned}$$

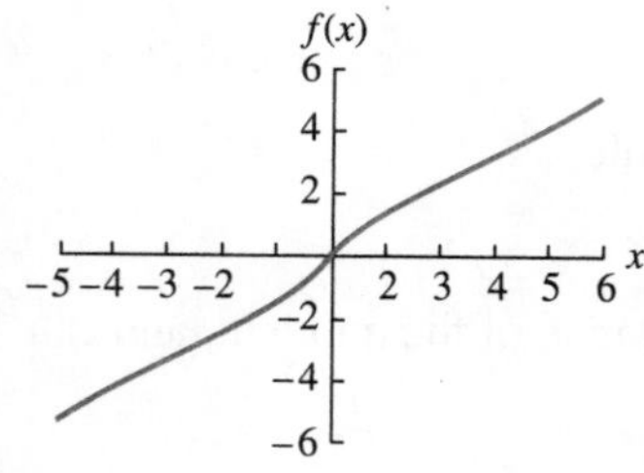

FIGURE 2.6.67

The increasing rational function $\frac{x^3+2x}{1+x^2}$

All the components of this expression are positive, meaning that the derivative is positive and this function is always increasing (Figure 2.6.67). This would be difficult to show simply by plotting points.

Example 2.6.4 Applying the Quotient Rule

Consider the discrete-time dynamical system for the fraction of invading mutants p_t

$$p_{t+1} = \frac{2.0p_t}{2.0p_t + 1.5(1 - p_t)}$$

(Section 1.10). The updating function is

$$f(p) = \frac{2.0p}{2.0p + 1.5(1 - p)}$$

The numerator is $u(p) = 2.0p$ and the denominator is $v(p) = 2.0p + 1.5(1 - p)$, with derivatives

$$\frac{du}{dp} = 2.0$$

$$\frac{dv}{dp} = 2.0 - 1.5 = 0.5$$

Therefore, the derivative is

$$\begin{aligned}\frac{df}{dp} &= \frac{v(p)\frac{du}{dp} - u(p)\frac{dv}{dp}}{v(p)^2}\\ &= \frac{[2.0p + 1.5(1 - p)]\frac{d(2.0p)}{dp} - 2.0p\frac{d[2.0p + 1.5(1 - p)]}{dp}}{[2.0p + 1.5(1 - p)]^2}\\ &= \frac{[2.0p + 1.5(1 - p)]2.0 - 2.0p \cdot 0.5}{[2.0p + 1.5(1 - p)]^2}\\ &= \frac{3.0}{2.0p + 1.5(1 - p)^2}\end{aligned}$$

At $p = 0$, the derivative is

$$\frac{3.0}{[2.0 \cdot 0 + 1.5(1 - 0)]^2} \approx 1.333$$

and at $p = 1$, the derivative is

$$\frac{3.0}{[2.0 \cdot 1 + 1.5(1 - 1)]^2} = 0.75$$

Compared to the diagonal line, which has slope 1, the graph of this function starts out steep and ends up rather flat (Figure 2.6.68).

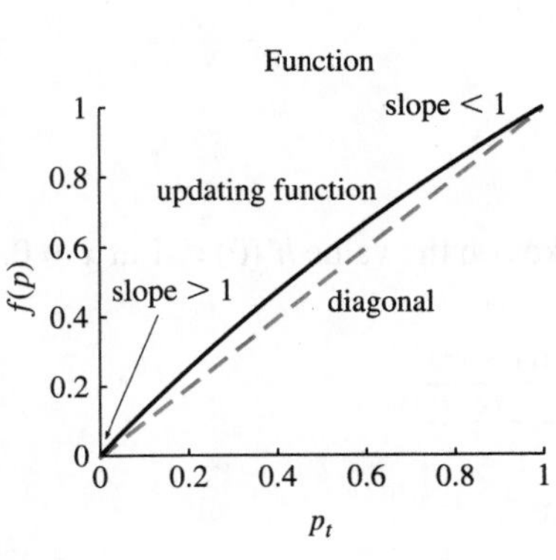

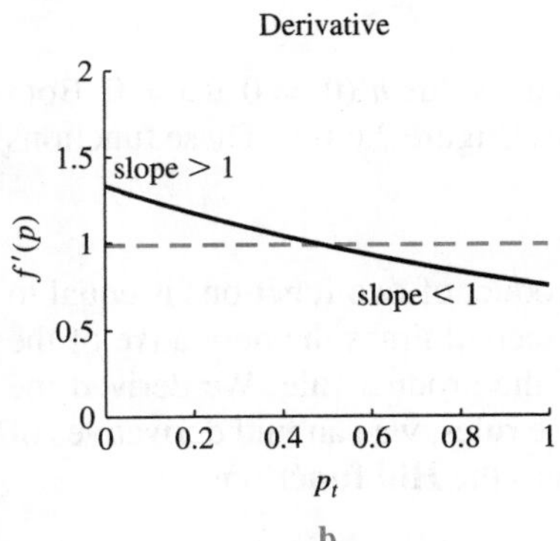

FIGURE 2.6.68
An updating function and its derivative

An important family of functions used to describe biological processes is the set of **Hill functions,** with the form

$$h(x) = \frac{x^n}{1 + x^n} \tag{2.6.1}$$

where n can be any positive number. We will compute the derivatives of these functions with $n = 1$ and $n = 2$.

Example 2.6.5 Computing the Derivatives of Hill Functions

With $n = 1$, $u(x) = x$, and $v(x) = 1 + x$, so

$$\frac{dh}{dx} = \frac{(1 + x)\frac{dx}{dx} - x\frac{d(1 + x)}{dx}}{(1 + x)^2}$$

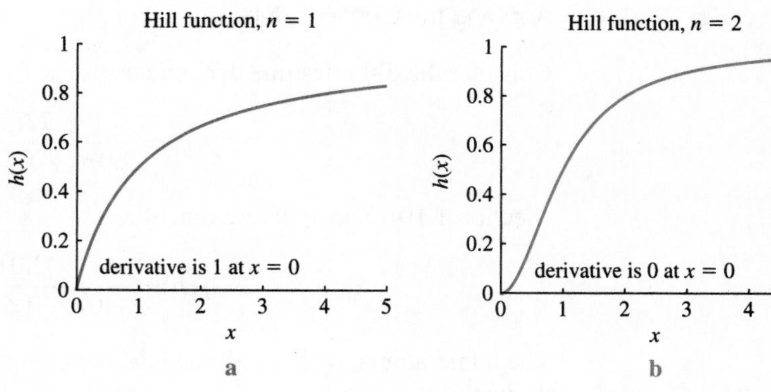

FIGURE 2.6.69
Two Hill functions

$$= \frac{(1+x) - x}{(1+x)^2}$$

$$= \frac{1}{(1+x)^2}$$

This derivative is always positive for $x > 0$, and it takes on the value $h'(0) = 1$ at $x = 0$.

When $n = 2$, $u(x) = x^2$ and $v(x) = 1 + x^2$, so

$$\frac{dh}{dx} = \frac{(1+x^2)\frac{d(x^2)}{dx} - x^2\frac{d(1+x^2)}{dx}}{(1+x^2)^2}$$

$$= \frac{(1+x^2)2x - x^2 \cdot 2x}{(1+x^2)^2}$$

$$= \frac{2x}{(1+x^2)^2}$$

This derivative too is always positive, but it takes on the value $h'(0) = 0$ at $x = 0$. Both Hill functions are increasing, but with different shapes (Figure 2.6.69). These functions are useful for describing the response to a stimulus. ▲

Summary The **product rule** states that the derivative of the product of two functions is equal to the first times the derivative of the second plus the second times the derivative of the first. The constant product rule is a special case of the product rule. We derived the **quotient rule** for differentiating quotients. With these rules, we can find derivatives of **rational functions** (the ratios of polynomials), such as the **Hill functions.**

2.6 Exercises

Mathematical Techniques

1–6 ▪ Find the derivatives of the following functions using the product rule.

1. $f(x) = (2x+3)(-3x+2)$
2. $g(z) = (5z-3)(z+2)$
3. $r(y) = (5y-3)(y^2-1)$
4. $s(t) = (t^2+2)(3t^2-1)$
5. $h(x) = (x+2)(2x+3)(-3x+2)$ (apply the product rule twice)
6. $F(w) = (w-1)(2w-1)(3w-1)$ (apply the product rule twice)

7–12 ▪ Find the derivatives of the following functions using the quotient rule.

7. $f(x) = \frac{1+x}{2+x}$
8. $f(x) = \frac{x^2}{1+2x^3}$
9. $g(z) = \frac{1+z^2}{1+2z^3}$
10. $h(z) = \frac{1+2z^3}{1+z^2}$

11. $F(x) = \dfrac{1+x}{(2+x)(3+x)}$ (apply the product rule to the denominator)

12. $G(x) = \dfrac{(1+x)(2+x)}{3+x}$ (apply the product rule to the numerator)

13–14 ▪ For the following functions, use base point $x_0 = 1.0$ and $\Delta x = 0.1$ to compute Δf and Δg. Find $\Delta(fg)$ (the change in the product) by computing $f(x_0 + \Delta x)g(x_0 + \Delta x) - f(x_0)g(x_0)$. Check that $\Delta(fg) = g(x_0)\Delta f + f(x_0)\Delta g + \Delta f \Delta g$. Try the same with $\Delta x = 0.01$ and see whether the term $\Delta f \Delta g$ becomes very small.

13. $f(x) = 2x + 3$ and $g(x) = -3x + 2$

14. $f(x) = x^2 + 2$ and $g(x) = 3x^2 - 1$

15–16 ▪ Suppose $p(x) = f(x)g(x)$. Test out the *incorrect* formula $p'(x) = f'(x)g'(x)$ on the following functions.

15. $f(x) = x$ and $g(x) = x^2$.

16. $f(x) = 1$ and $g(x) = x^3$

17–18 ▪ Suppose that $f(x)$ is a positive increasing function defined for all x.

17. Use the product rule to show that $f(x)^2$ is also increasing.

18. Use the quotient rule to show that $\dfrac{1}{f(x)}$ is decreasing.

19–22 ▪ For positive integer powers, it is possible to derive the power rule with **mathematical induction.** The idea is to show that a formula is true for $n = 1$ and then to show that whenever it is true for some particular n, it must also be true for $n + 1$.

19. Check that the power rule is true for $n = 1$.

20. Use the product rule on $x^2 = x \cdot x$ to check the power rule for $n = 2$ using only the power rule with $n = 1$.

21. Use the product rule on $x^3 = x^2 \cdot x$ to check the power rule for $n = 3$ using only the power rule with $n = 1$ and $n = 2$.

22. Assuming that the power rule is true for n, find $\dfrac{d(x^{n+1})}{dx}$ using the product rule, and check that it too satisfies the power rule.

Applications

23–26 ▪ The total mass of the population is the product of the number of individuals and the mass of each individual. In each case, time is measured in years, and mass is measured in kilograms.

a. Find the total mass as a function of time.

b. Compute the derivative.

c. Find the population, the mass of each individual, and the total mass at the time when the derivative is equal to zero.

d. Sketch a graph of the total mass over the next 100 years.

23. The population P is $P(t) = 2.0 \times 10^6 + 2.0 \times 10^4 t$ and the mass per person $W(t)$ is $W(t) = 80 - 0.5t$ (as in Section 1.2, Exercise 63).

24. The population P is $P(t) = 2.0 \times 10^6 - 2.0 \times 10^4 t$ and the mass per person $W(t)$ is $W(t) = 80 + 0.5t$ (as in Section 1.2, Exercise 64).

25. The population P is $P(t) = 2.0 \times 10^6 + 1000t^2$ and the mass per person $W(t)$ is $W(t) = 80 - 0.5t$ (as in Section 1.2, Exercise 65).

26. The population P is $P(t) = 2.0 \times 10^6 + 2.0 \times 10^4 t$ and the mass per person $W(t)$ is $W(t) = 80 - 0.005t^2$ (as in Section 1.2, Exercise 66).

27–28 ▪ In each of the following situations (extending Section 2.5, Exercise 38), the mass is the product of the density and the volume. In each case, time is measured in days and density is measured in grams per cubic centimeter.

a. Find the mass as a function of time.

b. Compute the derivative.

c. Sketch a graph of the mass over the first 30 days.

27. The above-ground volume is $V_a(t) = 3.0t + 20.0$ and the above-ground density is $\rho_a(t) = 1.2 - 0.01t$.

28. The below-ground volume is $V_b(t) = -1.0t + 40.0$ and the below-ground density is $\rho_b(t) = 1.8 + 0.02t$.

29–32 ▪ Suppose that the fraction of chicks that survive, $P(N)$, as a function of the number N of eggs laid is given by the following forms (variants of the model studied in Example 2.5.14). The total number of offspring that survive is $S(N) = N \cdot P(N)$. Find the expected number of surviving offspring when the bird lays 1, 5, or 10 eggs. Find $S'(N)$. Sketch a graph of $S(N)$. What do you think is the best strategy for each bird?

29. $P(N) = 1 - 0.08N$

30. $P(N) = 1 - 0.16N$. What seems strange if $N = 10$?

31. $P(N) = \dfrac{1}{1 + 0.5N}$

32. $P(N) = \dfrac{1}{1 + 0.1N^2}$

33–34 ▪ Find the derivative of the updating function from equation 1.51, $f(p) = \dfrac{sp}{sp + r(1-p)}$, with the following values of the parameters s and r.

33. $s = 1.2$, $r = 2.0$

34. $s = 1.8$, $r = 0.8$

35–36 ▪ Suppose that the mass $M(t)$ of an insect (in grams) and the volume $V(t)$ (in cubic centimeters) are known functions of time (in days).

a. Find the density $\rho(t)$ as a function of time.

b. Find the derivative of the density.

c. At what times is the density increasing?

d. Sketch a graph of the density over the first 5 days.

35. $M(t) = 1 + t^2$ and $V(t) = 1 + t$

36. $M(t) = 1 + t^2$ and $V(t) = 1 + 2t$

37–38 ▪ In a discrete-time dynamical system describing the growth of a population in the absence of immigration and emigration, the final population is the product of the initial population and the per capita production. Represent the initial population by b_t. In each case, find the final population as a function $f(b_t)$ of the initial population, find the derivative, and sketch the function.

37. Per capita production is $2.0(1 - \frac{b_t}{1000})$. Sketch $f(b_t)$ for $0 \le b_t \le 1000$.

38. Per capita production is $\frac{2.0}{1 + \frac{b_t}{1000}}$. Sketch $f(b_t)$ for $0 \le b_t \le 2000$.

39–40 ▪ The following steps should help you to figure out what happens to the Hill function $h_n(x) = \frac{x^n}{1+x^n}$ for large values of n.

a. Compute the value of the function at $x = 0$, $x = 1$, and $x = 2$.

b. Compute the derivative and evaluate at $x = 0$, $x = 1$, and $x = 2$.

c. Sketch a graph of $h_n(x)$ and $h_n'(x)$.

d. $h_n(x)$ can be thought of as representing a response to a stimulus of strength x. Would the response work as a good filter, giving a small output for inputs less than 1 and a large output for inputs greater than 1?

39. With $n = 3$

40. With $n = 10$

Computer Exercises

41. Consider the functions

$$g_n(x) = 1 + x + x^2 + \cdots + x^n$$

for various values of n. We will compare these functions with

$$g(x) = \frac{1}{1-x}$$

a. Plot $g_1(x)$, $g_3(x)$, $g_5(x)$, and $g(x)$ on the intervals $0 \le x \le 0.5$ and $0 \le x \le 0.9$.

b. Take the derivative of $g(x)$. Can you see how the derivative is related to $g(x)$ itself? In other words, what function could you apply to $g(x)$ to get $g'(x)$?

c. Apply the function found in part b to $g_1(x)$, $g_3(x)$, and $g_5(x)$. Can you see why these functions are good approximations to $g(x)$? Can you see why these approximations are best for small values of x? What happens to the approximations for x near 1?

42. Consider the function

$$r(x) = \frac{u(x)}{v(x)} = \frac{1+x}{2+x^2+x^3}$$

a. Make one graph of $u(x)$ and $v(x)$ for $0 \le x \le 1$, and another of $r(x)$. Could you have guessed the shape of $r(x)$ from looking at the graphs of $u(x)$ and $v(x)$?

b. What happens at the critical point?

c. Find the exact location of the critical point $x = x_c$.

d. Compare $\frac{u'(x_c)}{u(x_c)}$ with $\frac{v'(x_c)}{v(x_c)}$. Why are they equal?

2.7 The Second Derivative, Curvature, and Acceleration

A function with a positive derivative is increasing and one with a negative derivative is decreasing. In this section, we extend the graphical interpretation of the derivative by examining the derivative of the derivative, or the **second derivative.** In particular, we will see that the second derivative tells whether the graph of a function curves upward (**concave up**) or downward (**concave down**). Furthermore, just as the first derivative of position is the **velocity,** the second derivative of position is the **acceleration.**

The Second Derivative

Consider the two graphs in Figure 2.7.70. Both show functions that increase, but in different ways. In the first, the slope becomes steeper and steeper, indicating that the measurement is increasing faster and faster. In the second, the slope becomes smaller

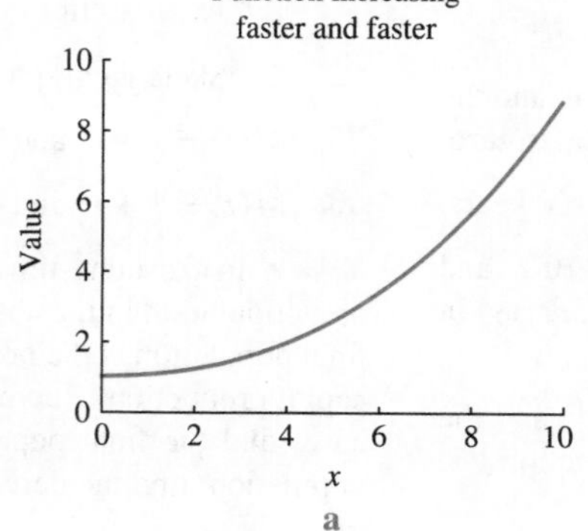

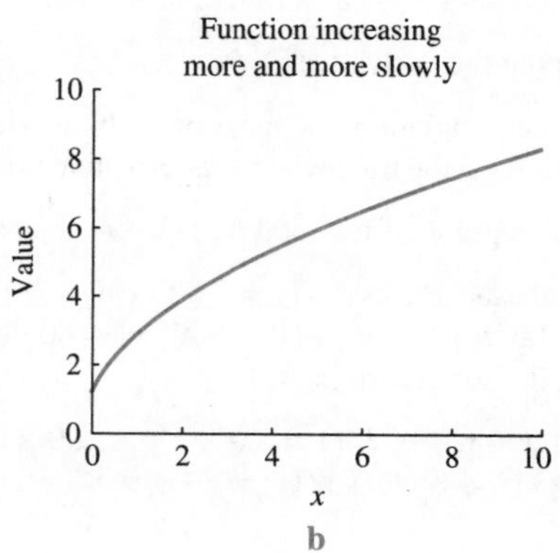

FIGURE 2.7.70
Two different increasing functions

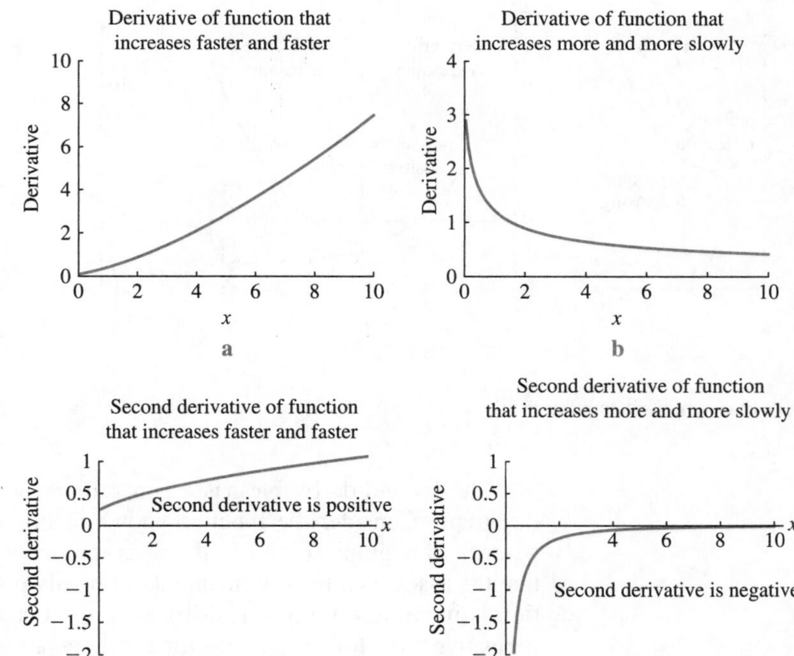

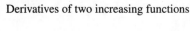

FIGURE 2.7.71
Derivatives of two increasing functions

FIGURE 2.7.72
Second derivatives of two increasing functions

and smaller. Although this measurement is increasing, it does so at a decreasing rate. These differences are clear on graphs of the derivatives of the two functions. Each derivative is **positive** because the functions are increasing. The derivative of the first function is **increasing** (Figure 2.7.71a) because the graph gets steeper and steeper. The derivative of the second function is decreasing (Figure 2.7.71b) because the graph becomes less and less steep.

The derivative of any function is positive when the function is increasing and is negative when the function is decreasing. We can apply this observation to the derivative itself. Because the **derivative** of the first function is increasing, the **derivative of the derivative** must be positive. Similarly, because the derivative of the second function is decreasing, the **derivative of the derivative** must be negative (Figure 2.7.72).

Definition 2.7 The Second Derivative

The derivative of the derivative is called the **second derivative.** We write the second derivative of f in prime notation as

$$\text{the second derivative of } f = f''(x) \tag{2.7.1}$$

In differential notation,

$$\text{the second derivative of } f = \frac{d^2 f}{dx^2} \tag{2.7.2}$$

For clarity, the derivative itself is often called the **first derivative.**

The differential notation for the second derivative may look odd. Think of the object $\frac{d}{dx}$ as a sort of function (called an **operator** by mathematicians) that takes one function as input and returns another function as output. This operator returns as output the derivative of its input. To find the second derivative, apply this operator twice. More generally, the result of taking n derivatives is written

$$\begin{aligned} \text{the } n\text{th derivative of } f &= f^{(n)}(x) && \text{prime notation} \\ &= \frac{d^n f}{dx^n} && \text{differential notation} \end{aligned}$$

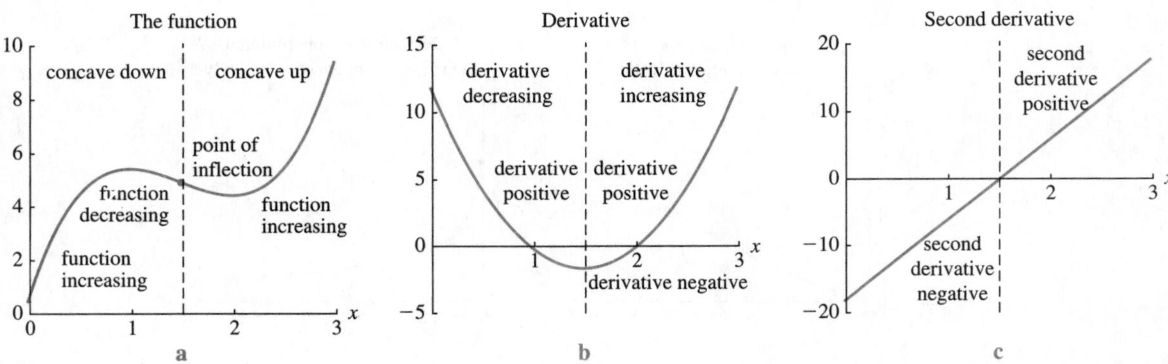

FIGURE 2.7.73
A function, its derivative, and its second derivative

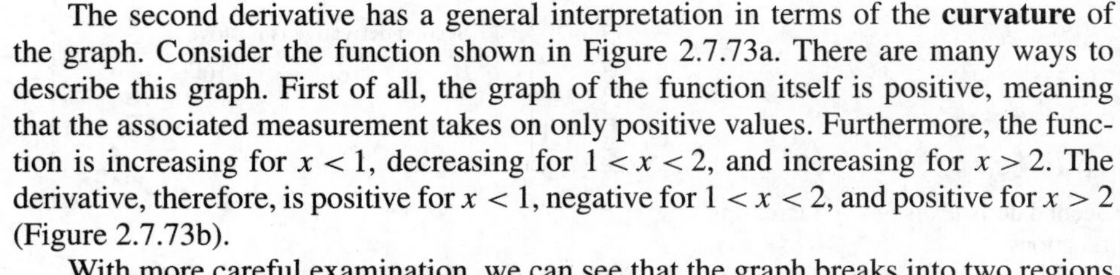

The second derivative has a general interpretation in terms of the **curvature** of the graph. Consider the function shown in Figure 2.7.73a. There are many ways to describe this graph. First of all, the graph of the function itself is positive, meaning that the associated measurement takes on only positive values. Furthermore, the function is increasing for $x < 1$, decreasing for $1 < x < 2$, and increasing for $x > 2$. The derivative, therefore, is positive for $x < 1$, negative for $1 < x < 2$, and positive for $x > 2$ (Figure 2.7.73b).

With more careful examination, we can see that the graph breaks into two regions of **curvature.** Between $x = 0$ and $x = 1.5$, the graph curves downward. This portion of the graph is said to be **concave down.** The slope of the curve is a **decreasing** function in this region (Figure 2.7.73b), implying that the **second derivative is negative** (Figure 2.7.73c). Between $x = 1.5$ and $x = 3$, the graph curves upward, like a bowl. This portion of the graph is said to be **concave up.** In this region, the slope of the curve becomes steeper and steeper, the derivative is increasing, and the **second derivative is positive** (Figure 2.7.73c).

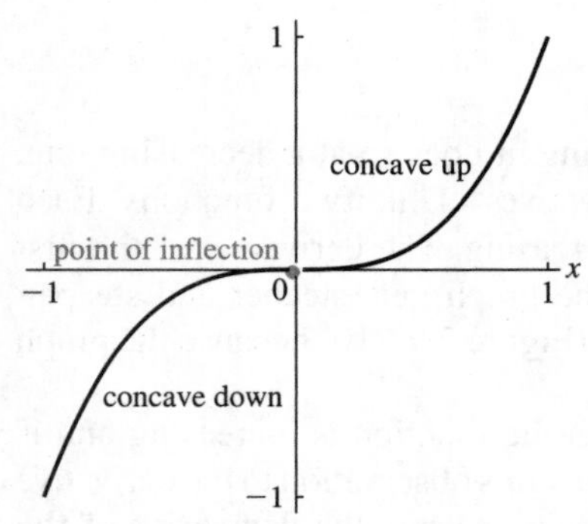

FIGURE 2.7.74
The function $C(x) = x^3$ has a point of inflection at a critical point

At a point where the **second derivative** is zero, the curvature of the graph can change. If the second derivative changes sign (from positive to negative or from negative to positive), such a point is called a **point of inflection.** In Figure 2.7.73a, the graph has a point of inflection at $x = 1.5$, where the function switches from concave down to concave up and the second derivative switches from negative to positive. Neither the function itself nor the derivative changes sign at this point. Points of inflection can occur when the derivative is positive, negative, or zero.

Example 2.7.1 Graphing a Power Function with the Second Derivative

Consider the power function $C(x) = x^3$ (Figure 2.7.74). Using the power rule, $C'(x) = 3x^2$ and $C''(x) = 6x$. Therefore, this function has both derivative and second derivative equal to 0 at the same point, $x = 0$. Furthermore, the second derivative changes from negative for $x < 0$ to positive for $x > 0$, meaning that it has both a critical point and a point of inflection at $x = 0$.

Example 2.7.2 A Point with Second Derivative Equal to Zero that Is Not a Point of Inflection

Consider the power function $Q(x) = x^4$ (Figure 2.7.75). Using the power rule, $Q'(x) = 4x^3$ and $Q''(x) = 12x^2$. This function has both derivative and second derivative equal to 0 at $x = 0$. However, the second derivative is positive for $x < 0$ and for $x > 0$. Because the function is concave up on both sides of $x = 0$, this is not a point of inflection.

Using the Second Derivative for Graphing

When we can compute the derivative and second derivative of a function, we can use these tools to sketch graphs quickly.

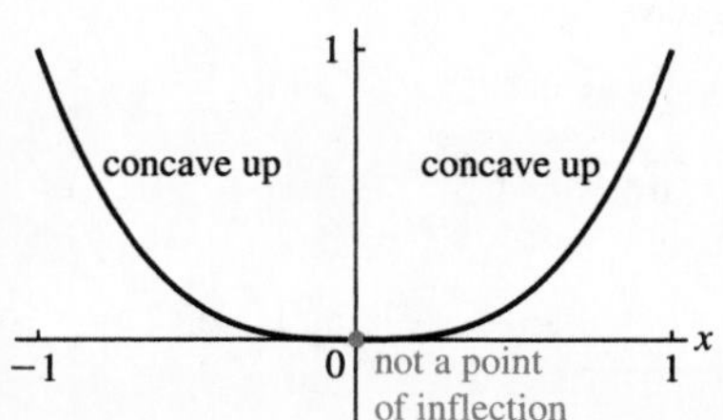

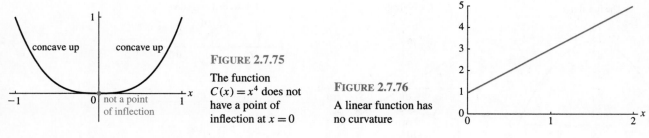

FIGURE 2.7.75
The function $C(x) = x^4$ does not have a point of inflection at $x = 0$

FIGURE 2.7.76
A linear function has no curvature

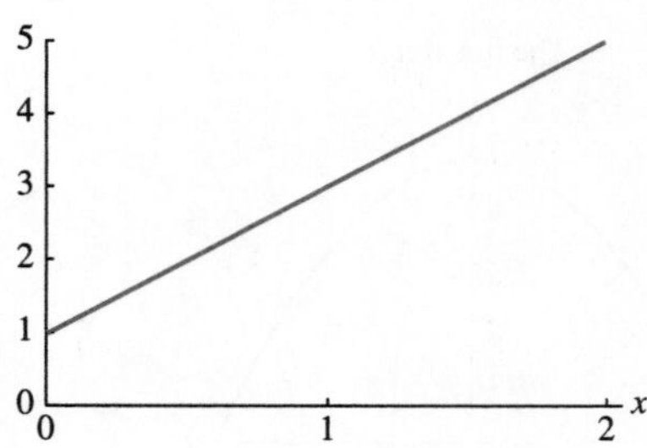

Example 2.7.3 The Second Derivative of a Linear Function

As a test, we check the second derivative of a linear function

$$f(x) = 2x + 1$$

The first derivative is $f'(x) = 2$, a constant, implying that the second derivative is 0, which is consistent with the fact that a line is straight and has no curvature (Figure 2.7.76).

Example 2.7.4 A Quadratic Function that Is Concave Up

Consider now the quadratic function

$$y(t) = 5t^2$$

The first derivative is $y'(t) = 10t$, which we find by applying the constant product and power rules. Because $y'(t)$ is a linear function, the second derivative is $y''(t) = 10$, which is a positive constant (Figure 2.7.77).

Example 2.7.5 A Quadratic Function that Is Concave Down

The quadratic function

$$z(t) = 5 - 5t^2$$

has first derivative $z'(t) = -10t$ and second derivative $z''(t) = -10$, a negative constant (Figure 2.7.78).

A quadratic function with a *positive* coefficient on the quadratic term has a positive second derivative and is concave up at all points. A quadratic function with a *negative* coefficient on the quadratic term has a negative second derivative and is concave down at all points.

Example 2.7.6 Graphing a Quadratic Function with the Second Derivative

The quadratic function

$$f(x) = 3x^2 - 6x + 5$$

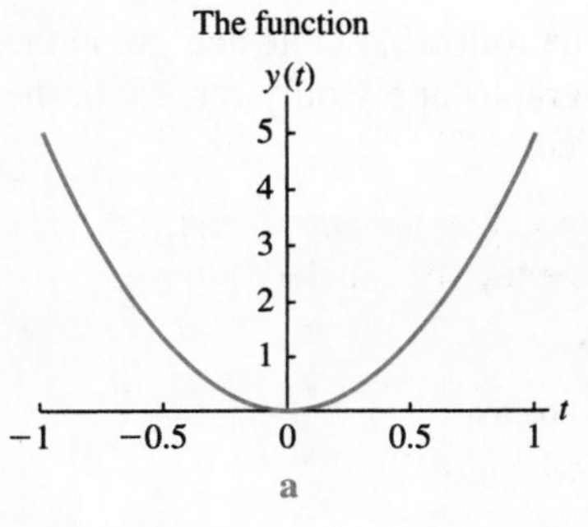

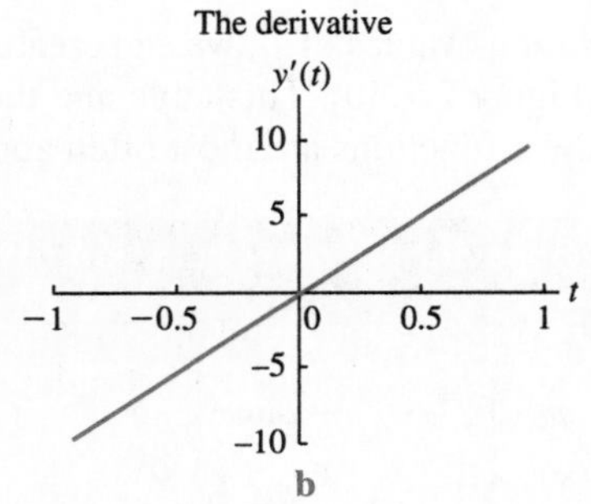

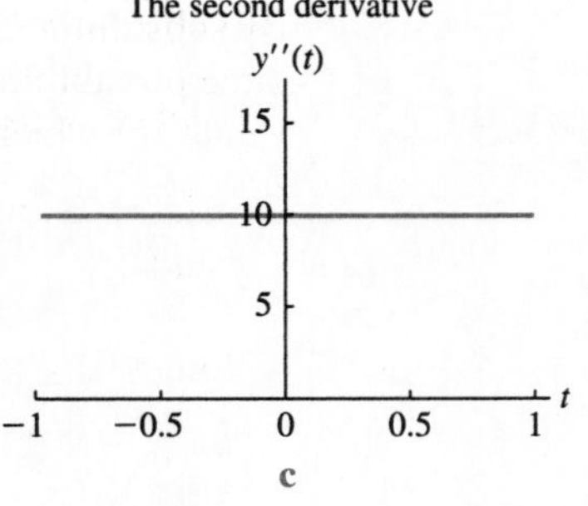

FIGURE 2.7.77
Concave up quadratic function

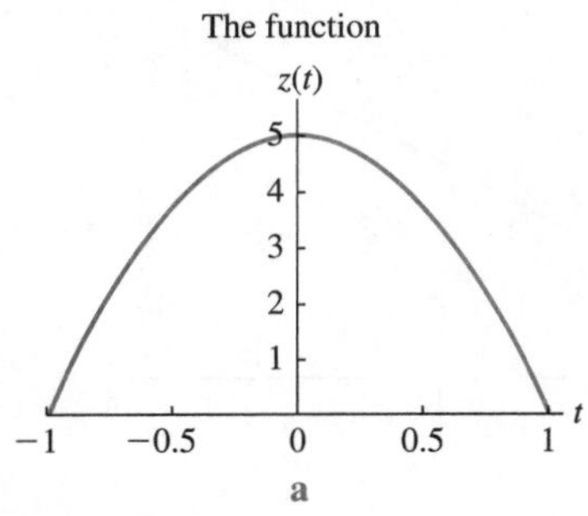

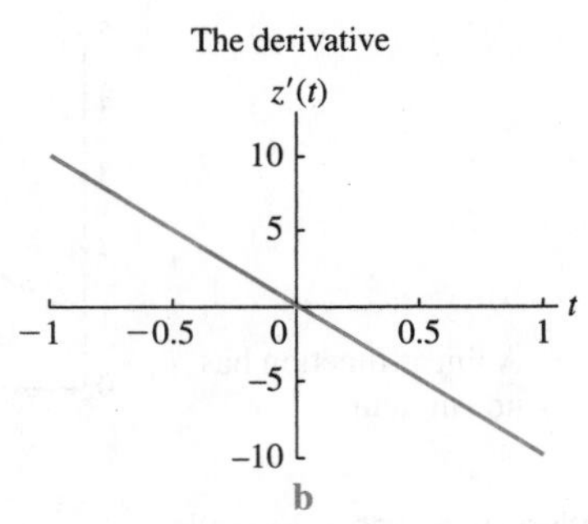

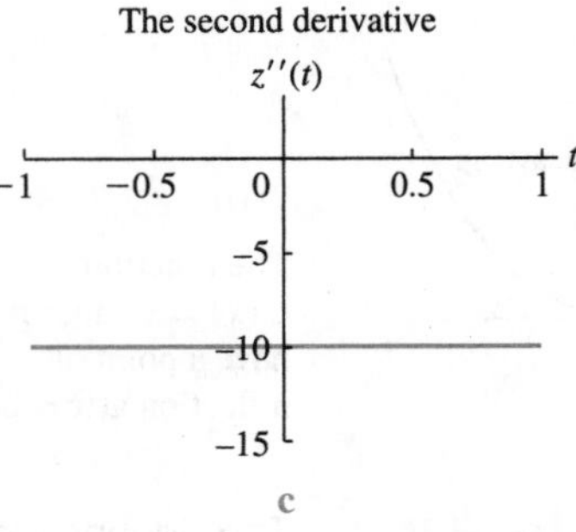

FIGURE 2.7.78
Concave down quadratic function

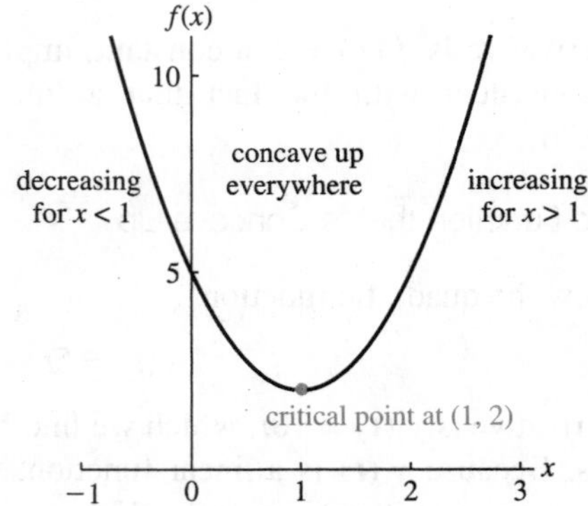

FIGURE 2.7.79
Graphing a quadratic using the first and second derivatives

has a positive coefficient 3 in front of x^2 and therefore must be concave up. The derivative is

$$f'(x) = 6x - 6$$

Solving for $f'(x) = 0$ gives a critical point at $x = 1$. Because the graph of this function is an upward-pointing parabola, this critical point must be the bottom of the bowl. Using the fact that $f(1) = 2$, we can easily sketch a graph of this function (Figure 2.7.79).

The second derivative helps to categorize all **power functions.** Consider the power function

$$g(x) = x^p$$

According to the power rule, the first and second derivatives are

$$g'(x) = px^{p-1}$$
$$g''(x) = p(p-1)x^{p-2}$$

By substituting in various values of p, we can create the following table and graph the three possibilities (Figure 2.7.80). This table and the graphs apply only for $x > 0$, the values for which power functions are most often applied.

Behavior of Power Function $g(x) = x^p$ for $x > 0$

Power	First Derivative	Second Derivative
$p > 1$	Positive	Positive
$0 < p < 1$	Positive	Negative
$p < 0$	Negative	Positive

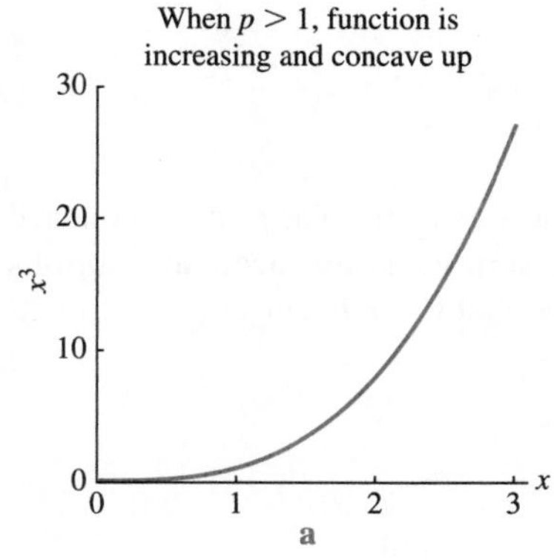

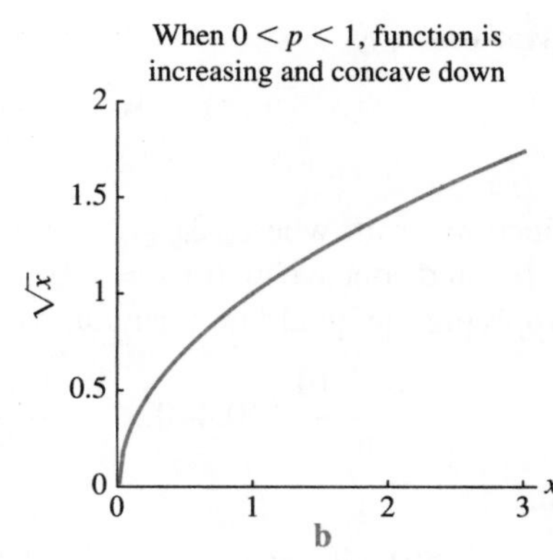

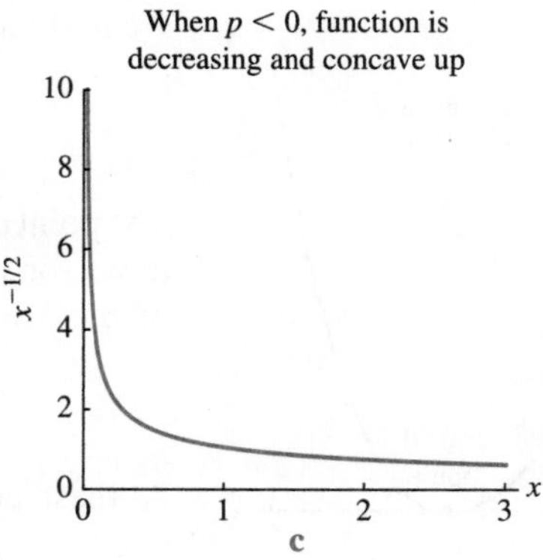

FIGURE 2.7.80

Graphs of the basic power functions

Example 2.7.7 The Cubic Function Revisited

The cubic power function $g(x) = x^3$ has first derivative $g'(x) = 3x^2$ and second derivative $g''(x) = 6x$. For $x > 0$, both are positive (Figure 2.7.80a). This function is increasing and concave up on this domain, which is consistent with the fact that the power is greater than 1.

Example 2.7.8 Graphing the Square Root Function

The square root function $g(x) = \sqrt{x}$ is the power function

$$g(x) = x^{1/2}$$

The first and second derivatives are

$$g'(x) = \frac{1}{2}x^{-1/2}$$
$$g''(x) = -\frac{1}{2} \cdot \frac{1}{2}x^{-3/2} = -\frac{1}{4}x^{-3/2}$$

In accordance with the table, the second derivative is negative and the function is concave down (Figure 2.7.80b).

Example 2.7.9 Graphing the Reciprocal of the Square Root Function

The function

$$g(x) = x^{-1/2}$$

has first and second derivatives

$$g'(x) = -\frac{1}{2}x^{-3/2}$$
$$g''(x) = \left(-\frac{3}{2}\right)\left(-\frac{1}{2}\right)x^{-5/2} = \frac{3}{4}x^{-5/2}$$

This decreasing function is concave up (Figure 2.7.80c).

Example 2.7.10 Graphing a Cubic Polynomial

Suppose we wish to study the polynomial

$$p(x) = 2x^3 - 7x^2 + 5x + 2$$

What does the graph look like? Does $p(x)$ take on negative values for $x > 0$? To begin,

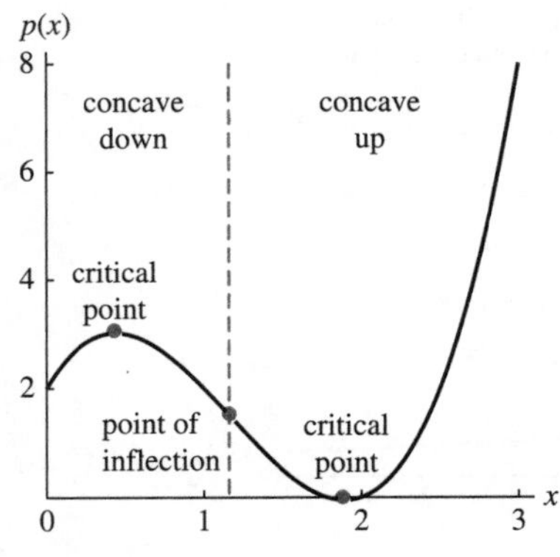

FIGURE 2.7.81

Using the first and second derivatives to graph a polynomial

we find the derivatives

$$p'(x) = 6x^2 - 14x + 5$$
$$p''(x) = 12x - 14$$

The point of inflection occurs where $12x - 14 = 0$, or at $x \approx 1.167$. The graph is concave down for $x < 1.167$ and concave up for $x > 1.167$. The critical points occur at solutions of $p'(x) = 0$. Applying the quadratic formula, we find that these occur at

$$\frac{7-\sqrt{19}}{6} \approx 0.440, \qquad \frac{7+\sqrt{19}}{6} \approx 1.893$$

At these points,

$$p(0.440) \approx 3.105, \qquad p(1.893) \approx -0.052$$

Figure 2.7.81 combines this information in a single graph. This function does indeed take on negative values, but only right near the critical point at $x \approx 1.893$. ▲

The guideposts for reading and interpreting a graph are summarized in the following table.

What the Graph Does	What the Derivative Does
Jump	Function discontinuous, derivative not defined
Corner	Derivative not defined
Graph vertical	Derivative not defined (infinite)
Graph increasing	Derivative positive
Graph decreasing	Derivative negative
Graph horizontal	Derivative equal to zero
Graph concave up	Second derivative positive
Graph concave down	Second derivative negative
Graph switches curvature	Point of inflection, second derivative zero

Acceleration

When we consider position as a function of time, the second derivative has an important physical interpretation as the **acceleration.** Suppose the position of an object is $y(t)$. The derivative $\frac{dy}{dt}$ is the velocity, and the second derivative is the rate of change of velocity. Formally,

$$\frac{d^2y}{dt^2} = \text{acceleration} \tag{2.7.3}$$

(Differential notation is generally used in physical applications.) A positive acceleration indicates that an object is speeding up, a negative acceleration that it is slowing down.

Equation 2.7.3 is a special case of a fundamental type of differential equation studied in physics. It says that acceleration is proportional to force. In fact, we can rewrite Newton's famous law

$$F = ma$$

where F is the force, m the mass of the object, and a the resulting acceleration, as

$$a = \frac{d^2y}{dt^2} = \frac{F}{m}$$

If we know the force F and the mass m, we have a differential equation for the position y.

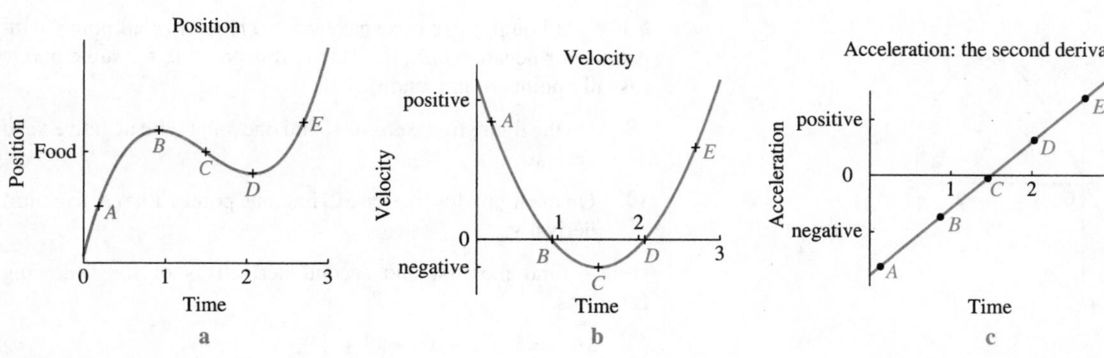

FIGURE 2.7.82
The acceleration of an ant

Example 2.7.11 A Falling Rock

A rock that has fallen a distance

$$y(t) = 5.0t^2$$

in time t has second derivative, and acceleration, of

$$\frac{d^2y}{dt^2} = 10.0$$

This acceleration is positive because we are measuring how far the rock has fallen, and the downward speed is increasing.

Example 2.7.12 Acceleration of an Ant

Consider again the ant pictured in Figures 2.4.46 and 2.4.47. The position, velocity, and acceleration are shown in Figure 2.7.82. This ant is slowing down, or decelerating, until point C, and then it speeds up. Deceleration includes both slowing down in the forward direction and speeding up in the negative direction. Physically, the ant acts as though there is a force pushing it to the left before it reaches C. After that time, the ant accelerates. Acceleration includes any change that tends to move the ant more toward the right.

Summary The **second derivative,** defined as the derivative of the derivative, is positive when the graph of a function is **concave up** and is negative when the graph of a function is **concave down.** A point where a function changes curvature is called a **point of inflection.** Using the second derivative, we can graph quadratic functions, power functions, and complicated polynomials. Physically, the second derivative of the position is the **acceleration,** the quantity used to write physical laws as differential equations.

2.7 Exercises

Mathematical Techniques

1–4 ▪ On the figures, label:

a. One critical point.

b. One point with a positive derivative.

c. One point with a negative derivative.

d. One point with a positive second derivative.

e. One point with a negative second derivative.

f. One point of inflection.

1.

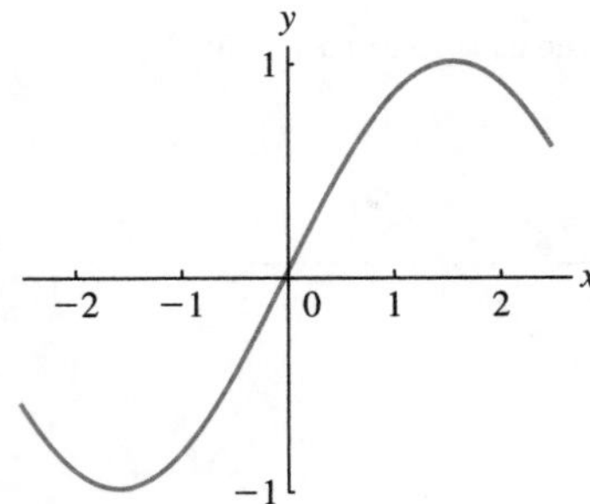

2.

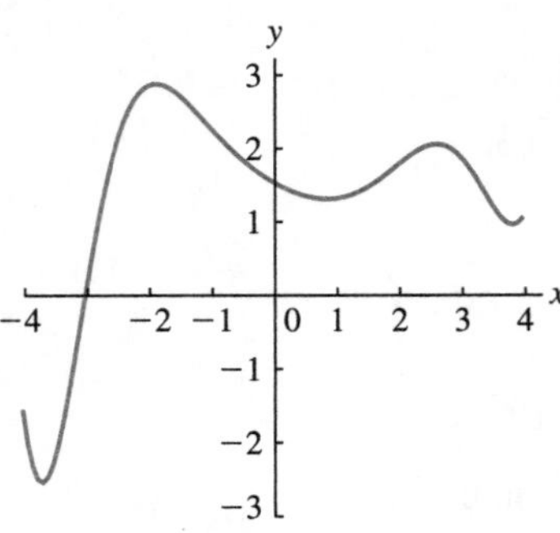

3.

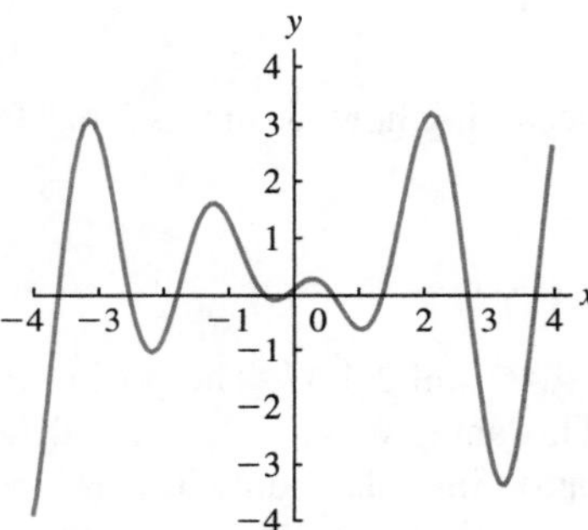

4.

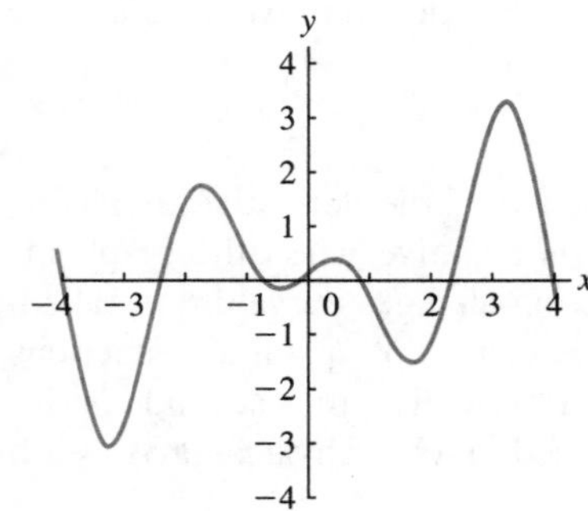

5–8 ▪ Draw graphs of functions with the following properties.

5. A function with a positive, increasing derivative.

6. A function with a positive, decreasing derivative.

7. A function with a negative, increasing (becoming less negative) derivative.

8. A function with a negative, decreasing (becoming more negative) derivative.

9–10 ▪ Although there is no easy way to recognize all points with positive or negative *third* derivative, it is possible for some points (usually points of inflection).

9. On the figure for Exercise 1, find one point with negative *third* derivative.

10. On the figure for Exercise 2, find one point with positive third derivative.

11–18 ▪ Find the first and second derivatives of the following functions.

11. $s(x) = 1 - x + x^2 - x^3 + x^4$

12. $g(z) = 3z^3 + 2z^2$

13. $h(y) = y^{10} - y^9$

14. $p(x) = 1 + x + \frac{x^2}{2} + \frac{x^3}{6} + \frac{x^4}{24}$

15. $F(z) = z(1+z)(2+z)$

16. $R(s) = (1+s^2)(2+s)$

17. $f(x) = \frac{3+x}{2x}$

18. $G(y) = \frac{2+y}{y^2}$

19–26 ▪ Find the first and second derivatives of the following functions and use them to sketch a graph.

19. $f(x) = x^{-3}$ for $x > 0$

20. $g(z) = z + \frac{1}{z}$ for $z > 0$

21. $h(x) = (1-x)(2-x)(3-x)$

22. $M(t) = \frac{t}{1+t}$ for $t > 0$

23. $f(x) = 2x^3 + 1$ for $-5 \le x \le 5$

24. $f(x) = \frac{1}{x^2}$ for $0 < x \le 2$

25. $f(x) = 10x^2 - 50x$ for $-5 \le x \le 5$

26. $f(x) = x - x^2$ for $0 \le x \le 1$

27–30 ▪ Some higher derivatives can be found without a lot of calculation.

27. Find the tenth derivative of x^9.

28. Describe the graph of the fifth derivative of x^5.

29. Is the eighth derivative of $p(x) = 7x^8 - 8x^7 - 5x^6 + 6x^5 - 4x^3$ positive or negative?

30. Find the fifth derivative of $x(1+x)(2+x)(3+x)(4+x)$.

31–32 ▪ We can approximate a function with the tangent line, which matches the value of the function and its first derivative. A better approximation uses a parabola that matches the value of the function, and its first and second derivatives. For each of the following functions:

a. Find the tangent line at $x = 1$.

b. Add a quadratic term to the formula of your tangent line to match the second derivative at $x = 1$.

c. Sketch a graph of the function, its tangent line, and the approximating quadratic for $0.5 < x < 1.5$.

31. $f(x) = x^{-3}$

32. $g(x) = x + \frac{1}{x}$

Applications

33–36 ▪ The following equations give the positions as functions of time of objects tossed from towers in various exotic solar system locations. For each,

a. Find the velocity and the acceleration of this object.

b. Sketch a graph of the position for $0 \le t \le 3$.

c. How high was the tower? Which way was the object thrown? How does the acceleration compare with that on Earth ($9.8\ \text{m/s}^2$)?

33. An object on Saturn that follows $p(t) = -5.2t^2 - 2.0t + 50.0$.

34. An object on the sun that follows $p(t) = -137t^2 + 20.0t + 500.0$.

35. An object on Pluto that follows $p(t) = -0.325t^2 - 20.0t + 500.0$.

36. An object on Mercury that follows $p(t) = -1.85t^2 + 20.0t$.

37–40 ▪ The total mass is the product of the following functions for mass and number as functions of time in years (Section 2.6, Exercises 23–26). Find the second derivative of each and check your graph.

37. The population P is $P(t) = 2.0 \times 10^6 + 2.0 \times 10^4 t$ and the mass in kg per person $W(t)$ is $W(t) = 80 - 0.5t$ (based on Section 2.6, Exercise 23).

38. The population P is $P(t) = 2.0 \times 10^6 - 2.0 \times 10^4 t$ and the mass in kg per person $W(t)$ is $W(t) = 80 + 0.5t$ (based on Section 2.6, Exercise 24).

39. The population P is $P(t) = 2.0 \times 10^6 + 1000t^2$ and the mass in kg per person $W(t)$ is $W(t) = 80 - 0.5t$ (based on Section 2.6, Exercise 25).

40. The population P is $P(t) = 2.0 \times 10^6 + 2.0 \times 10^4 t$ and the mass in kg per person $W(t)$ is $W(t) = 80 - 0.005t^2$ (based on Section 2.6, Exercise 26).

41–42 ▪ The following graphs show the horizontal distance traveled by a roller coaster as a function of time. When is the roller coaster going most quickly? When is it accelerating most quickly? When is it decelerating most quickly?

41.

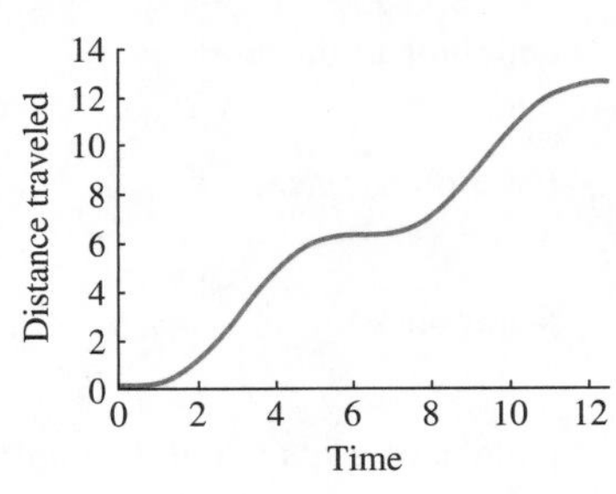

42.

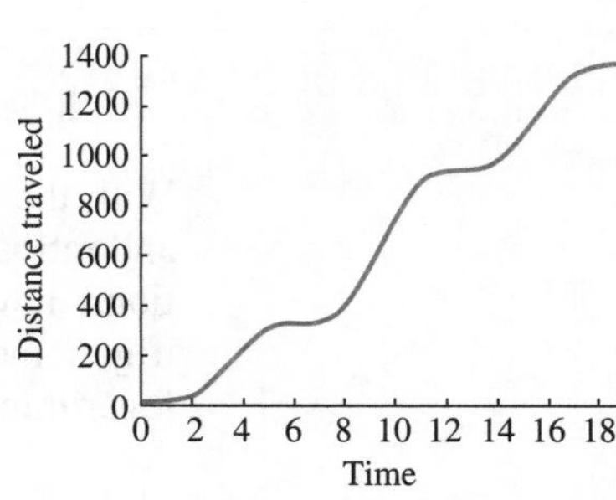

43–44 ▪ In a model of a growing population, we find the new population by multiplying the old population by the per capita production. For each case, find the second derivative of the new population as a function of the old population and sketch a graph.

43. Per capita production is $2.0\left(1 - \frac{b_t}{1000}\right)$. Consider values of b_t less than 1000.

44. Per capita production is $2.0b_t\left(1 - \frac{b_t}{1000}\right)$. Consider values of b_t less than 1000.

45–46 ▪ We can use the second derivative to study Hill functions $h_n(x) = \frac{x^n}{1 + x^n}$ for $x > 0$.

45. Find the second derivative of the Hill function with $n = 1$ and describe the curvature of the graph.

46. Find the second derivative of the Hill function with $n = 2$ and describe the curvature of the graph.

Computer Exercises

47. In the current universe, acceleration due to gravity is constant, so position follows a differential equation rather like

$$\frac{d^2 p}{dt^2} = -g$$

when g points in the downward direction. One can imagine a universe where gravity changed over time, making objects accelerate according to

$$\frac{d^2 p}{dt^2} = -gt^n$$

for some power n. Set $g = 10\ \text{m/s}^{n+2}$.

a. Find a solution of the normal differential equation.

b. Find solutions of the modified differential equation for different values of n. Would objects fall faster or slower in such an imagined universe?

48. Have your computer find all critical points and points of inflection of the function

$$P(x) = 8x^5 - 18x^4 - x^3 + 18x^2 - 7x$$

Show that these match what you see on a graph.

2.8 Derivatives of Exponential and Logarithmic Functions

With the sum, product, power, and quotient rules, we can differentiate polynomials and ratios of polynomials. To be able to differentiate all biologically important functions, however, we need three more building blocks: exponential, logarithmic, and trigonometric functions. We here find and apply the derivatives of the exponential and logarithmic functions.

The Exponential Function

Suppose we wish to find the derivative of the function $b(t) = 2^t$. None of our rules tells us how to find a formula for the derivative. The power rule looks promising, but it applies only to functions of the form t^n, not when t is in the exponent. The best way to find the derivative of an unfamiliar function is to return to the definition of the derivative (Definition 2.2),

$$\frac{db}{dt} = \lim_{h\to 0} \frac{b(t+h) - b(t)}{h}$$

The derivative of the function 2^t is

$$\begin{aligned}
\frac{d(2^t)}{dt} &= \lim_{h\to 0} \frac{2^{t+h} - 2^t}{h} && \text{definition of the derivative}\\
&= \lim_{h\to 0} \frac{2^t 2^h - 2^t}{h} && \text{law 1 of exponents}\\
&= \lim_{h\to 0} \frac{2^t\left(2^h - 1\right)}{h} && \text{factor out } 2^t\\
&= 2^t\left(\lim_{h\to 0} \frac{2^h - 1}{h}\right) && \text{pull the constant out of the limit}
\end{aligned}$$

The quantity 2^t acts as a constant because the limit depends on h, not on t. The derivative is the product of two factors, the function 2^t and the *number*

$$\lim_{h\to 0} \frac{2^h - 1}{h}$$

This is related to a limit we studied in Section 2.1. Exercise 34 in Section 2.1 investigated a small value of h, finding a result of approximately 0.693. We will finally learn how to compute this number exactly in Section 2.9. On the basis of our best estimate, the derivative is

$$\frac{db}{dt} \approx (0.693)2^t = 0.693b(t)$$

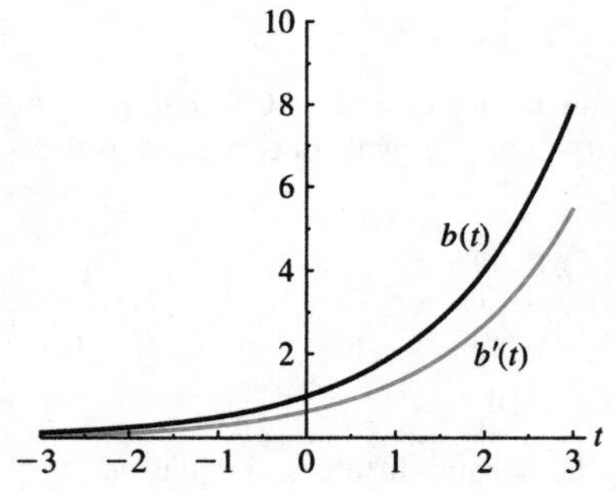

FIGURE 2.8.83
The function 2^t and its derivative

The derivative of this function is 0.693 times the function itself (Figure 2.8.83). The graph of the derivative looks like the graph of the function but is scaled down by a constant factor.

What happens when we try to find the derivative of the exponential function itself? We can follow the same steps to compute

$$\begin{aligned}
\frac{d(e^x)}{dx} &= \lim_{h\to 0} \frac{e^{x+h} - e^x}{h} && \text{definition of the derivative}\\
&= \lim_{h\to 0} \frac{e^x e^h - e^x}{h} && \text{law 1 of exponents}\\
&= \lim_{h\to 0} \frac{e^x\left(e^h - 1\right)}{h} && \text{factor out } e^x\\
&= e^x \lim_{h\to 0} \frac{e^h - 1}{h} && \text{pull the constant out of the limit}
\end{aligned}$$

Again, we can factor out e^x, leaving the limit

$$\lim_{h\to 0} \frac{e^h - 1}{h}$$

We can guess the limit by evaluating the function for smaller and smaller values of h.

h	e^h	$e^h - 1$	$\frac{e^h - 1}{h}$
1.0	2.718	1.718	1.718
0.1	1.105	0.105	1.052
0.01	1.010	0.010	1.005
0.001	1.001	0.001	1.0005

The limit seems to be 1.0. In fact, the number e is **defined** to be the number for which the limit is 1. Mathematically,

Definition 2.8 The number e is the number for which

$$\lim_{h\to 0} \frac{e^h - 1}{h} = 1$$

The number e is the irrational number 2.7182818284590 . . . , rather than some familiar number such as 2 or 3.

Therefore,

$$\frac{d(e^x)}{dx} = e^x$$

The exponential function is its own derivative. At every point on the graph, the slope of the curve is equal to the height of the curve (Figure 2.8.84).

Example 2.8.1 A Related Function that Is Its Own Derivative

Are there any other functions with this remarkable property? The function $g(x) = 2e^x$ has the derivative

$$\frac{d}{dx}(2e^x) = 2\frac{d(e^x)}{dx} \quad \text{the constant product rule}$$

$$= 2e^x \quad \text{derivative of the exponential function}$$

In general, any constant multiple of the exponential function is its own derivative, but these are the **only** functions with this property. Therefore, functions of the form $b(t) = Ke^t$ are solutions of the differential equation

$$\frac{db}{dt} = b$$

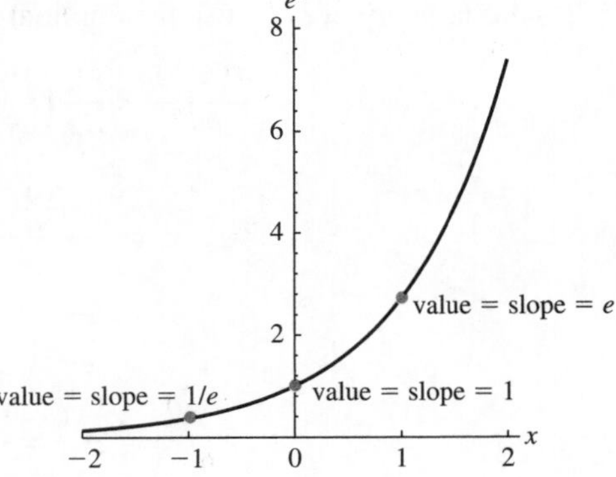

FIGURE 2.8.84
The function e^x and its derivative

which says that the rate of change of the population is equal to the population size. When we study differential equations in more detail, we will find that the constant K appearing in front of the exponential depends on the **initial condition,** just as in the solution of a discrete-time dynamical system.

Example 2.8.2 Computing the Derivative of e^{3t} from the Definition

How does including a constant in the exponent change the derivative?

$$\begin{aligned}\frac{d(e^{3t})}{dt} &= \lim_{h\to 0}\frac{e^{3(t+h)}-e^{3t}}{h} && \text{definition of the derivative}\\ &= \lim_{h\to 0}\frac{e^{3t}e^{3h}-e^{3t}}{h} && \text{law 1 of exponents}\\ &= \lim_{h\to 0}\frac{e^{3t}\left(e^{3h}-1\right)}{h} && \text{factor out } e^{3t}\\ &= e^{3t}\lim_{h\to 0}\frac{e^{3h}-1}{h} && \text{pull the constant outside the limit}\end{aligned}$$

Factoring out e^{3t} leaves the limit

$$\lim_{h\to 0}\frac{e^{3h}-1}{h}$$

We can find this limit with a clever trick, changing to a new variable $h' = 3h$. If we replace every appearance of h with $\frac{h'}{3}$ and note that $h' \to 0$ if $h \to 0$, we find

$$\begin{aligned}\lim_{h\to 0}\frac{e^{3h}-1}{h} &= \lim_{h'\to 0}\frac{e^{h'}-1}{h'/3} && \text{substitute } h'/3 \text{ for } h\\ &= \lim_{h'\to 0} 3\frac{e^{h'}-1}{h'} && \text{move the 3 to the numerator}\\ &= 3\lim_{h'\to 0}\frac{e^{h'}-1}{h'} && \text{pull constant outside limit}\\ &= 3 && \text{recognize that limit is equal to 1 from definition of } e\end{aligned}$$

Therefore,

$$\frac{d(e^{3t})}{dt} = 3e^{3t}$$

The derivative of this function is 3 times the original function, meaning that it is a solution of

$$\frac{db}{dt} = 3b$$

Example 2.8.3 Finding the Derivative of e^{-x}

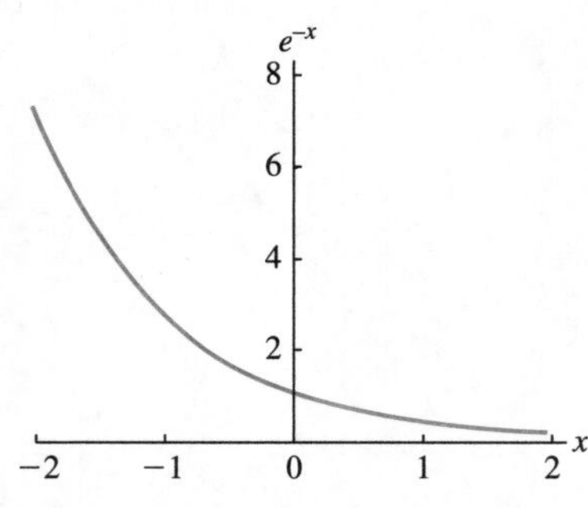

FIGURE 2.8.85
The function $F(x) = e^{-x}$

We could find the derivative of e^{-x} (Figure 2.8.85) using the same trick as in Example 2.8.2. Alternatively, we can use the quotient rule to find

$$\begin{aligned}\frac{d(e^{-x})}{dx} &= \frac{d}{dx}\left(\frac{1}{e^x}\right)\\ &= \frac{e^x\frac{d(1)}{dx} - 1\frac{d(e^x)}{dx}}{e^{2x}}\\ &= \frac{-e^x}{e^{2x}}\\ &= \frac{-1}{e^x} = -e^{-x}\end{aligned}$$

The derivative of this function is the negative of the original function. It is a solution of

$$\frac{db}{dt} = -b$$

Furthermore,

$$\begin{aligned} \frac{d^2(e^{-x})}{dx^2} &= \frac{d}{dx}\left(-e^{-x}\right) && \text{the derivative we just found} \\ &= -\frac{d}{dx}\left(e^{-x}\right) && \text{pull out negative sign using the constant product rule} \\ &= -\left(-e^{x}\right) = e^{-x} && \text{the derivative we just found and canceling negative signs} \end{aligned}$$

This function is its own second derivative. Because the exponential function takes on only positive values, this function has a negative first derivative and a positive second derivative everywhere.

Example 2.8.4 Graphing a Combined Exponential and Polynomial Function

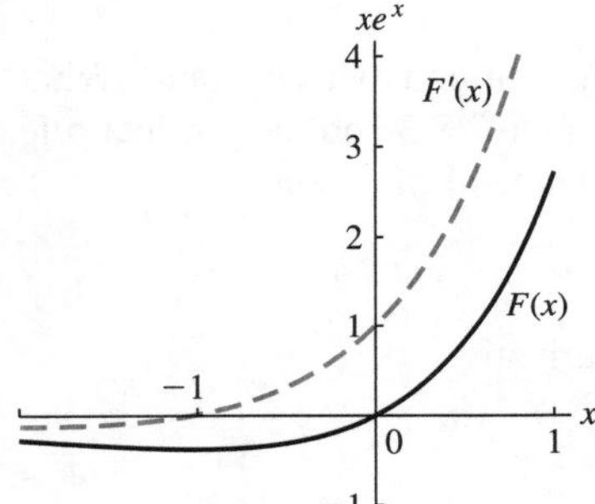

FIGURE 2.8.86
The function $F(x) = xe^x$ and its derivative

Using the derivative of the exponential function and the basic rules for differentiation, we can find the derivatives of more complicated functions. Consider the function $F(x) = xe^x$. This is a **product** of a power function and the exponential function. Therefore,

$$\begin{aligned} \frac{dF}{dx} &= x\frac{de^x}{dx} + e^x\frac{dx}{dx} && \text{product rule} \\ &= xe^x + e^x && \text{derivative of exponential and power rule} \\ &= (1+x)e^x && \text{factoring} \end{aligned}$$

This derivative is negative when $x < -1$, zero at $x = -1$, and positive when $x > -1$ (Figure 2.8.86).

The Natural Logarithm

The formula for the derivative of the inverse of the exponential function, the natural logarithm, is also simple:

$$\frac{d(\ln(x))}{dx} = \frac{1}{x}$$

We will use the fact that the natural log and exponential functions are inverses to derive this formula in Example 2.9.5. Because $\ln(x)$ is defined only for $x > 0$, the derivative is also defined only on this domain. The derivative of the natural logarithm is a power function with a power of -1. We can therefore find the second derivative with the power rule, computing

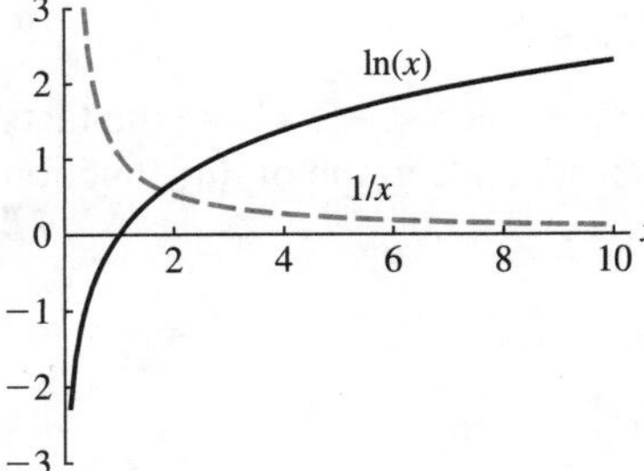

FIGURE 2.8.87
The natural logarithm and its derivative

$$\frac{d^2(\ln(x))}{dx^2} = -\frac{1}{x^2}$$

The graph of the natural logarithm is concave down, increasing more and more slowly. See Figure 2.8.87.

Example 2.8.5 The Derivative of $x\ln(x)$

The derivative of the function $g(x) = x\ln(x)$ is

$$\begin{aligned} \frac{dg}{dx} &= x\frac{d(\ln(x))}{dx} + \ln(x)\frac{dx}{dx} && \text{product rule} \\ &= x \cdot \frac{1}{x} + \ln(x)\cdot 1 && \text{derivative of log and power rule} \\ &= 1 + \ln(x) && \text{simplifying} \end{aligned}$$

Example 2.8.6 Finding the Derivative Using a Law of Logs

We can find the derivative of the function $\ln(2x)$ using law 1 of logs, which states that $\ln(2x) = \ln(2) + \ln(x)$.

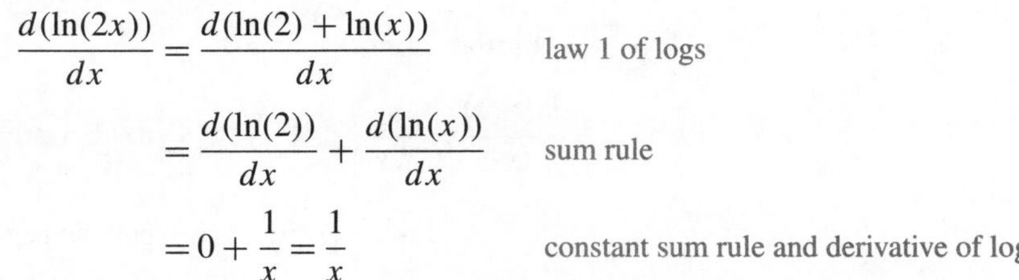

$$\frac{d(\ln(2x))}{dx} = \frac{d(\ln(2)+\ln(x))}{dx} \qquad \text{law 1 of logs}$$

$$= \frac{d(\ln(2))}{dx} + \frac{d(\ln(x))}{dx} \qquad \text{sum rule}$$

$$= 0 + \frac{1}{x} = \frac{1}{x} \qquad \text{constant sum rule and derivative of log}$$

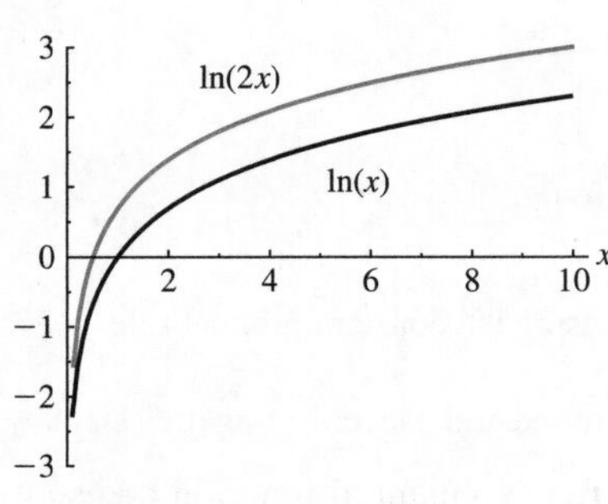

FIGURE 2.8.88
The functions $\ln(x)$ and $\ln(2x)$ have the same derivative

The derivative of $\ln(2x)$ matches the derivative of $\ln(x)$ because the graphs of the two functions differ only by a constant (Figure 2.8.88).

Applications

The gamma distributions are an important family of functions often used in probability theory. They are defined by formulas

$$g(x) = x^n e^{-x}$$

for various powers n (the real gamma distributions are multiplied by a constant). What do their graphs look like? We can use the result in Example 2.8.3 and the product rule to find the first and second derivatives and deduce the shape of the graph.

Example 2.8.7 The Gamma Distribution with $n = 1$

With $n = 1$, the gamma distribution $g(x) = xe^{-x}$ has derivative

$$g'(x) = \frac{dx}{dx}e^{-x} + x\frac{d\left(e^{-x}\right)}{dx}$$
$$= e^{-x} - xe^{-x} = (1-x)e^{-x}$$

This derivative is positive for $x < 1$ and negative for $x > 1$. Furthermore,

$$g''(x) = \frac{d(1-x)}{dx}e^{-x} + (1-x)\frac{d\left(e^{-x}\right)}{dx}$$
$$= -e^{-x} - (1-x)e^{-x} = (x-2)e^{-x}$$

The second derivative is negative when $x < 2$ and positive when $x > 2$. Using the facts that $g(0) = 0$ and $g(x) > 0$ when $x > 0$, we can draw an accurate graph of this function (Figure 2.8.89).

Example 2.8.8 The Gamma Distribution with $n = 2$

With $n = 2$, the gamma distribution is proportional to

$$g(x) = x^2 e^{-x}$$

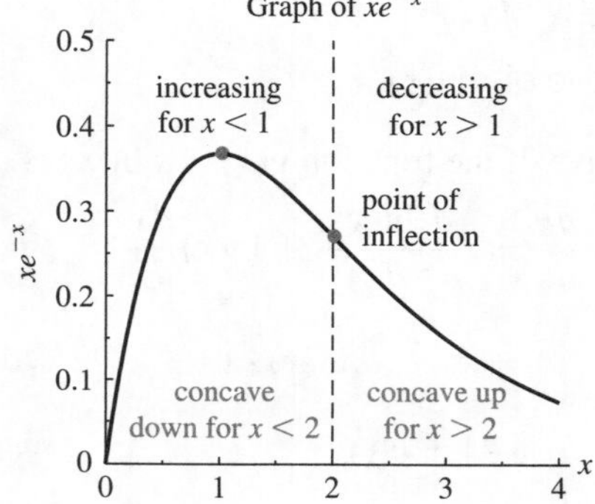

FIGURE 2.8.89
Graph of the gamma distribution with $n = 1$

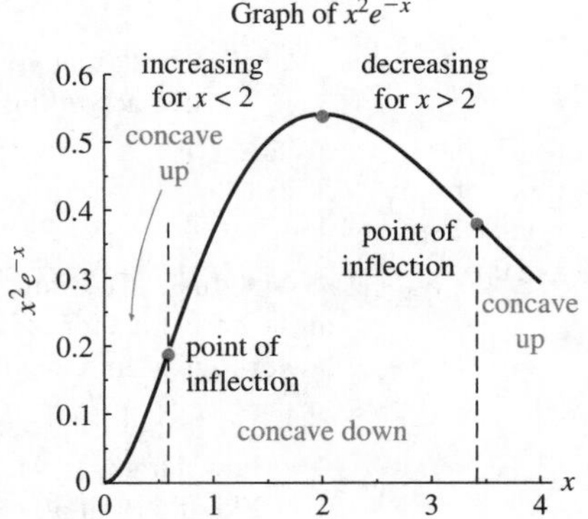

FIGURE 2.8.90
Graph of x^2e^{-x} with $n = 2$

(Figure 2.8.90). The derivative and second derivative are

$$\begin{aligned} g'(x) &= \frac{d(x^2)}{dx}e^{-x} + x^2\frac{d(e^{-x})}{dx} \\ &= 2xe^{-x} - x^2e^{-x} = (2x - x^2)\,e^{-x} \\ g''(x) &= \frac{d\,(2x - x^2)}{dx}e^{-x} + (2x - x^2)\,\frac{d(e^{-x})}{dx} \\ &= (2 - 2x)e^{-x} - (2x - x^2)\,e^{-x} = (x^2 - 4x + 2)\,e^{-x} \end{aligned}$$

The derivative is positive for $x < 2$ and negative for $x > 2$. There are two points of inflection, found by solving

$$x^2 - 4x + 2 = 0$$

for the roots

$$x = 2 - \sqrt{2} \approx 0.586, \quad x = 2 + \sqrt{2} \approx 3.414$$

The second derivative is negative between these roots.

Summary We added the derivatives of the exponential function and the natural log to our collection of building blocks. With these pieces and the basic rules for derivatives, we can find derivatives of many more complicated functions, including the gamma distributions.

2.8 Exercises

Mathematical Techniques

1–18 ▪ Compute the first and second derivatives of the following functions.

1. $F(x) = x^2 + 4e^x$
2. $V(y) = 1 + y + 2y^2 + 3y^3 - 4e^y$
3. $f(x) = x^2e^x$
4. $h(x) = (2 - x^2)e^x$
5. $g(x) = \dfrac{e^x}{x}$
6. $G(z) = \dfrac{e^z}{z^2}$
7. $f(x) = \dfrac{1+x}{e^x}$
8. $H(t) = \dfrac{1+t^2}{e^t}$
9. $f(x) = x + 4\ln(x)$
10. $h(x) = 2x^2 - 2\ln(x)$
11. $g(z) = (z + 4)\ln(z)$
12. $f(x) = x^2\ln(x)$
13. $F(w) = e^w\ln(w)$
14. $F(y) = \dfrac{\ln(y)}{e^y}$
15. $s(x) = \ln(x^2)$ (use a law of logs)
16. $r(x) = \ln(x^2e^x)$ (use a law of logs)

17. $F(z) = \dfrac{1+e^{-z}}{1+e^{x}}$

18. $p(x) = \dfrac{1-e^{x}}{1+e^{x}}$

19–24 ▪ Use the first and second derivatives to sketch graphs of the following functions on the given domains. Identify regions where the function is increasing and regions where it is concave up.

19. $f(x) = (1-x)e^x$ for $-2 \le x \le 1$

20. $g(x) = (2-x)e^x$ for $-2 \le x \le 1$

21. $G(z) = \dfrac{e^z}{z^2}$ for $1 \le z \le 3$

22. $F(z) = \dfrac{z^3}{e^z}$ for $0 \le z \le 5$

23. $L(x) = \dfrac{x}{2} - \ln(x)$ for $1 \le x \le 3$

24. $M(x) = (x+2)\ln(x)$ for $1 \le x \le 3$

25–26 ▪ We can return to the definition to find derivatives of other exponential functions. For each of the following functions:

a. Write down the definition of the derivative of this function.

b. Simplify with a law of exponents and factor.

c. Estimate the limit by plugging in small values of h.

d. Exponentiate the limit to figure out what it is.

e. Find the derivative.

25. $f(x) = 5^x$

26. $g(x) = e^{2x}$. After following the steps, use the fact that $g(x) = e^x \cdot e^x$ to find the derivative with the product rule.

27–30 ▪ Polynomials form a useful set of functions in part because the derivative of a polynomial is another polynomial. Another set of functions with this useful property is the set of **generalized polynomials,** formed as products and sums of polynomials and exponential functions. One simple group of generalized polynomials consists of the products of linear functions with the exponential function, taking the form

$$h(x) = (ax+b)e^x$$

for various values of a and b. We will call these **generalized first-order polynomials.**

27. Set $a = 1$ and $b = 1$. Find the first and second derivatives of $h(x)$.

28. Use the results of Exercise 27 to guess the tenth derivative of $h(x)$ when $a = 1$ and $b = 1$.

29. Find a generalized first-order polynomial such that $h(1) = 0$. Where is the critical point? Where is the point of inflection?

30. Let x^* be the solution of the equation $h(x^*) = 0$. Show that the critical point of a generalized first-order polynomial is $x^* - 1$ and the point of inflection is $x^* - 2$.

31–32 ▪ We can return to the definition to figure out the derivative of the natural log. We will first find the derivative at different values of x. For each value of x:

a. Write down the definition of the derivative for $\ln(x)$.

b. Plug in some small values of h to guess the limit.

c. Check that your answer matches the value of the derivative according to the formula.

31. $x = 1$

32. $x = 2$

33–34 ▪ Instead of plugging different values of x into the definition of the derivative for $\ln(x)$, as in Exercises 31 and 32, we can use a law of logs to find the derivative in general.

33. Write down the definition of the derivative at $x = 2$, and use a law of logs to try to convert the limit into something that looks like the limit at $x = 1$, as in Exercise 31. (*Hint*: Substitute a new variable for $h/2$.)

34. Write down the definition of the derivative for general x, and use a law of logs to try to convert the limit into something that looks like the limit at $x = 1$, as in Exercise 31. (*Hint*: Substitute a new variable for h/x.)

Applications

35–38 ▪ Suppose a population of bacteria grows according to $P(t) = 10e^t$. Find the first and second derivative to graph the total mass when the mass per individual $m(t)$ has the following forms. Is the total mass ever greater than it is at $t = 0$? When does the total mass reach zero?

35. $m(t) = 1 - \dfrac{t}{2}$

36. $m(t) = 1 - t$

37. $m(t) = 1 - t^2$

38. $m(t) = 1 - \dfrac{t^2}{4}$

39–40 ▪ Find the first and second derivatives of the following functions (related to the gamma distribution) and sketch graphs for $0 \le x \le 2$.

39. $G(x) = \sqrt{x}e^{-x}$

40. $G(x) = \dfrac{1}{\sqrt{x}}e^{-x}$

41–44 ▪ The following are differential equations that could describe a bacterial population. For each, describe in words what the equation says and check that the given solution works. Indicate whether the solution is an increasing or a decreasing function.

41. $\dfrac{db}{dt} = e^t$ has solution $b(t) = e^t$

42. $\dfrac{db}{dt} = b(t)$ has solution $b(t) = e^t$

43. $\dfrac{db}{dt} = -b(t)$ has solution $b(t) = e^{-t}$

44. $\dfrac{db}{dt} = e^{-b(t)}$ has solution $b(t) = \ln(t)$

Computer Exercises

45. Consider again the function

$$g(x) = x^n e^{-x}$$

describing the gamma distribution.

a. Find the critical point which is proportional to the gamma distribution.

b. Find the point or points of inflection. What happens when $n < 1$?

c. Graph this function for $n = 0.5$, $n = 2$, and $n = 5$. What happens for very large values of n?

46. Consider the generalized polynomial

$$R(x) = x^4 + \left(88x^3 - 76x^2 - 65x + 25\right) e^x$$

As defined in Exercise 27, a generalized polynomial is formed by multiplying and adding polynomials and exponential functions.

a. Find all critical points and points of inflection of $R(x)$ for $-1 \le x \le 1$.

b. Find the fifth derivative of $R(x)$. Does it look any simpler than $R(x)$ itself? Compare with what happens when you take many derivatives of a polynomial or of the exponential function.

2.9 The Chain Rule

Composition is perhaps the most important way to combine functions. If we know the derivatives of the components parts, the **chain rule** gives the formula for the derivative of the composition. Using the chain rule (along with the sum, product, power, and quotient rules and the derivatives of special functions), we can find the derivative of *any* function that can be built from polynomial, exponential, and trigonometric functions. We can also apply the chain rule to compute the derivatives of **inverse functions.**

The Derivative of a Composite Function

Consider the function

$$F(x) = e^{-x^2}$$

that we will use later to describe the **normal distribution.** This function is the **composition** of the exponential function $f(g) = e^g$ with the quadratic function $g(x) = -x^2$, or

$$F(x) = (f \circ g)(x)$$

(Figure 2.9.91) where $f \circ g$ is the notation for composition introduced in Section 1.2 (Definition 1.5).

Example 2.9.1 Another Functional Composition

The function

$$H(y) = \frac{1}{1 + y^2}$$

(Figure 2.9.92) is the composition of the reciprocal function $r(p) = \dfrac{1}{p}$ and the polynomial $p(y) = 1 + y^2$, or

$$H(y) = (r \circ p)(y)$$

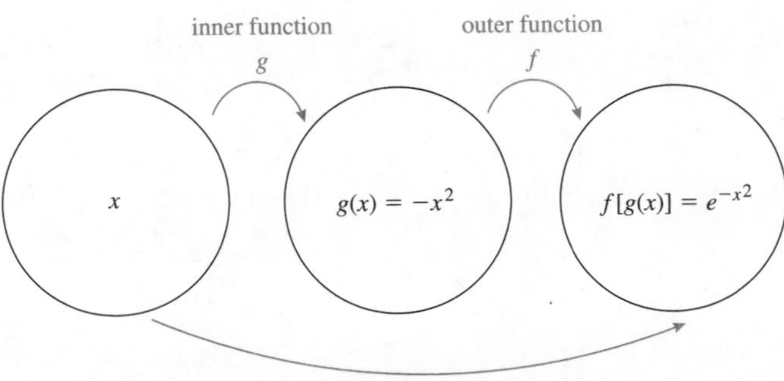

FIGURE 2.9.91
$F(x)$ written as a composition of functions

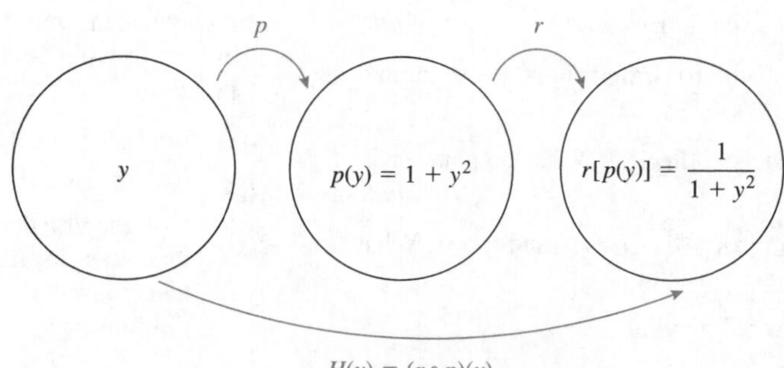

FIGURE 2.9.92
$H(y)$ written as a composition of functions

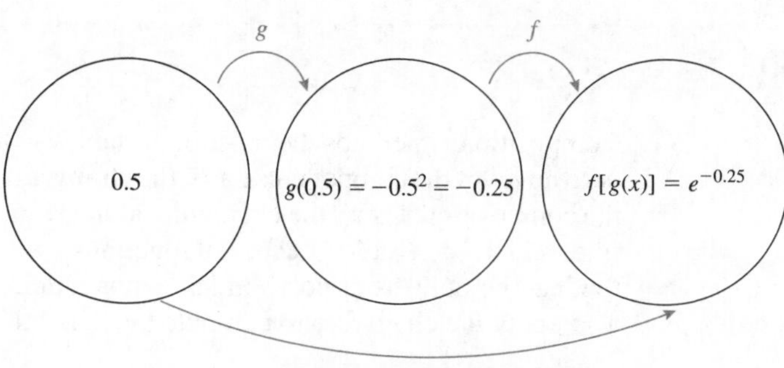

FIGURE 2.9.93
Computing $F(0.5)$

In each case, we know the derivative of the component functions. Can we use this information to find the derivative of the composition?

First, we need to recognize a function as a composition. To figure out how a function was built, think about computing the value on a calculator. To calculate $F(0.5)$, first find the negative of the square of 0.5 (the **inner function** g) as $g(0.5) = -0.5^2 = -0.25$, and then exponentiate that (the **outer function** f) to find the result $f(-0.25) = e^{-0.25} \approx 0.779$ (Figure 2.9.93).

Example 2.9.2 Calculating $H(1)$

To calculate $H(1)$ using the function in Example 2.9.1, first evaluate the polynomial $1 + y^2$ at $y = 1$ (the inner function p) to find $p(1) = 1 + 1^2 = 2$, and then take the reciprocal of that (the outer function r) to find the $r(2) = \frac{1}{2} = 0.5$ (Figure 2.9.94). ▲

The chain rule tells us how to compute the derivative by combining information about the inner and outer functions and their derivatives.

Theorem 2.12 The Chain Rule for Derivatives

Suppose

$$F(x) = (f \circ g)(x)$$

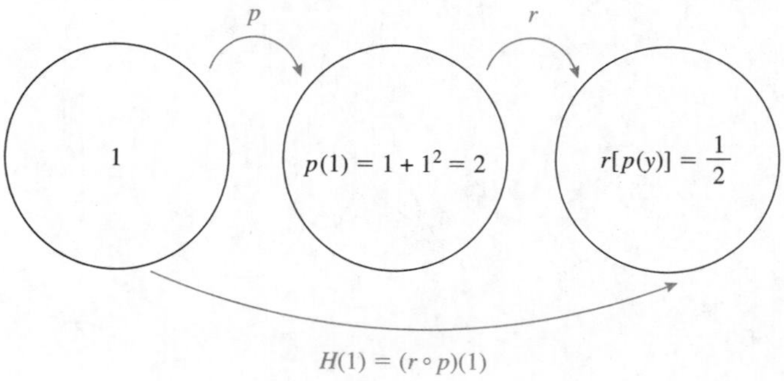

p
r
1
$p(1) = 1 + 1^2 = 2$
$r[p(y)] = \frac{1}{2}$
$H(1) = (r \circ p)(1)$

FIGURE 2.9.94
Computing $H(1)$

where f and g are both differentiable functions. Then

$$F'(x) = f'[g(x)]g'(x) \qquad \text{prime notation}$$

$$\frac{dF}{dx} = \frac{df}{dg}\frac{dg}{dx} \qquad \text{differential notation}$$

Proof: We know that

$$f'(y) = \lim_{\Delta y \to 0} \frac{f(y + \Delta y) - f(y)}{\Delta y}$$

at every point y. If we choose $y = g(x)$ and $\Delta y = \Delta g = g(x + \Delta x) - g(x)$, then

$$\begin{aligned}
f'[g(x)] &= \lim_{\Delta g \to 0} \frac{f[g(x) + \Delta g] - f[g(x)]}{\Delta g} && \text{substitute in for } y \text{ and } \Delta y \\
&= \lim_{\Delta x \to 0} \frac{f[g(x + \Delta x)] - f[g(x)]}{g(x + \Delta x) - g(x)} && \text{expand } \Delta g \text{ and use fact that } \Delta x \to 0 \text{ if } \Delta g \to 0 \\
&= \lim_{\Delta x \to 0} \frac{\dfrac{f[g(x + \Delta x)] - f[g(x)]}{\Delta x}}{\dfrac{g(x + \Delta x) - g(x)}{\Delta x}} && \text{divide top and bottom by } \Delta x \\
&= \frac{(f \circ g)'(x)}{g'(x)} && \text{apply the definition of derivative to top and bottom} \\
&= \frac{F(x)}{g'(x)}
\end{aligned}$$

Multiplying both sides by $g'(x)$ gives the chain rule. ■

The expression $f'[g(x)]$ means the derivative of the function f evaluated at the point $g(x)$. The expression

$$\frac{df}{dg}$$

refers to the same quantity, but it means the derivative of f thought of as a function of g, again evaluated at the point $g(x)$.

How do we *use* the chain rule? The following algorithm gives the necessary steps.

▸▸ Algorithm 2.1 Using the Chain Rule

1. Write the function as a composition.
2. Take the derivatives of the component pieces.
3. Multiply the derivatives together.
4. Put everything in terms of the original variable. ▲

We apply this method to the two functions F and H defined above. To find the derivative of $F(x)$:

1. Write $F(x) = f(g(x))$ where

$$f(g) = e^g$$
$$g(x) = -x^2$$

2. Find the derivative of each component function.

$$f'(g) = e^g$$
$$g'(x) = -2x$$

3. The derivative is the product

$$F'(x) = e^g \cdot (-2x)$$

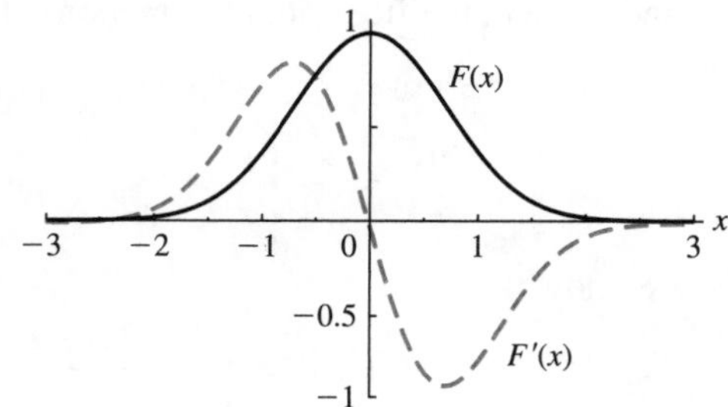

FIGURE 2.9.95
The function $F(x) = e^{-x^2}$ and its derivative

4. Substitute the definition of the inner function $g(x)$ to write the answer in terms of x.

$$F'(x) = e^g \cdot (-2x) = e^{-x^2} \cdot (-2x) = -2xe^{-x^2}$$

This derivative is positive for $x < 0$ and negative for $x > 0$ (Figure 2.9.95).

This information is organized in the following table.

The derivative of $F(x) = (f \circ g)(x) = e^{-x^2}$

Function	Derivative (Prime Notation)	Derivative (Differential Notation)
$g(x) = -x^2$	$g'(x) = -2x$	$\frac{dg}{dx} = -2x$
$f(g) = e^g$	$f'(g) = e^g$	$\frac{df}{dg} = e^g$
$F(x) = f(g(x))$	$F'(x) = -2xe^g = -2xe^{-x^2}$	$\frac{dF}{dx} = -2xe^g = -2xe^{-x^2}$

Example 2.9.3 Finding the Derivative of $H(y)$

To find the derivative of the function $H(y)$ defined by

$$H(y) = \frac{1}{1 + y^2}$$

in Example 2.9.1, we follow Algorithm 2.1.

1. Write $H(y) = (r \circ p)(y)$ where $p(y) = 1 + y^2$ and $r(p) = \frac{1}{p}$.
2. Find the derivatives of r and p.

$$p'(y) = 2y$$
$$r'(p) = -\frac{1}{p^2}$$

3. The derivative is the product

$$H'(y) = -\left(\frac{1}{p^2}\right) 2y$$

4. Substitute the definition of the inner function p to write the answer in terms of y.

$$H'(y) = -\frac{2y}{\left(1 + y^2\right)^2}$$

This derivative is positive for $y < 0$ and negative for $y > 0$, leading to a graph quite similar to that of $F(x) = e^{-x^2}$ (Figure 2.9.96).

As a table, written only in prime notation,

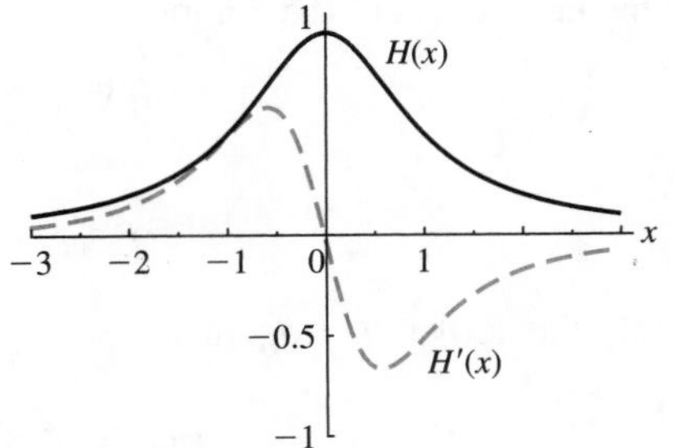

FIGURE 2.9.96
The function $H(y) = \frac{1}{1+y^2}$ and its derivative

The derivative of $H(y) = (r \circ p)(y) = \dfrac{1}{1+y^2}$

Function	Derivative
$p(y) = 1 + y^2$	$p'(y) = 2y$
$r(p) = \dfrac{1}{p}$	$r'(p) = -\dfrac{1}{p^2}$
$H(y) = r[p(y)]$	$H'(y) = -\dfrac{2y}{p^2} = -\dfrac{2y}{(1+y^2)^2}$

For more complicated functions, the chain rule can be applied several times. Some functions must be broken down into three or more component pieces. The version of the chain rule for triple compositions is

$$(f \circ g \circ h)'(x) = f'\{g[h(x)]\}g'[h(x)]h'(x) \tag{2.9.1}$$

or, in differential notation,

$$\frac{d(f \circ g \circ h)}{dx} = \frac{df}{dg}\frac{dg}{dh}\frac{dh}{dx} \tag{2.9.2}$$

As in the case with two functions, the derivative of the composition is found by multiplying the derivatives of the component functions.

Example 2.9.4 Using the Chain Rule on a Triple Composition

Consider the function

$$F(x) = \ln[(1-x)^4 + 1]$$

1. Write as the composition $F(x) = f\{g[h(x)]\}$ where

$$h(x) = 1 - x$$
$$g(h) = h^4 + 1$$
$$f(g) = \ln(g)$$

(Figure 2.9.97).

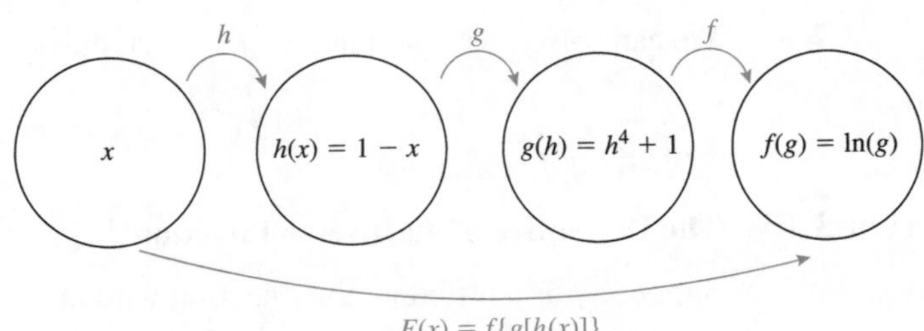

FIGURE 2.9.97
The function $F(x) = \ln((1-x)^4 + 1)$ written as a composition

2. Take the derivatives of the components.

$$h'(x) = -1$$
$$g'(h) = 4h^3$$
$$f'(g) = \frac{1}{g}$$

3. Multiply the derivatives together.

$$F'(x) = \frac{1}{g} \cdot 4h^3 \cdot (-1)$$

4. Substitute the definitions of the functions $h(x)$ and $g(h)$ to write the answer in terms of x.

$$\begin{aligned} F'(x) &= \frac{1}{h^4+1} \cdot 4h^3 \cdot (-1) \\ &= \frac{1}{(1-x)^4+1} \cdot 4(1-x)^3 \cdot (-1) \\ &= -4\frac{1}{(1-x)^4+1}(1-x)^3 \end{aligned}$$

This information can also be given in tabular form:

The derivative of $F(x) = f\{g[h(x)]\} = \ln[(1-x)^4+1]$

Function	Derivative
$h(x) = 1 - x$	$h'(x) = -1$
$g(h) = h^4 + 1$	$g'(h) = 4h^3$
$f(g) = \ln(g)$	$f'(g) = \frac{1}{g}$
$F(x) = f\{g[h(x)]\}$	$F'(x) = -1 \cdot 4h^3 \frac{1}{g} = -4(1-x)^3 \frac{1}{(1-x)^4+1}$

Derivatives of Inverse Functions

Many important functions, such as the natural logarithm, are defined as the **inverses** of other functions. The inverse f^{-1} of the function $f(x)$ is defined in terms of functional composition as

$$\left(f \circ f^{-1}\right)(x) = x$$

(Definition 1.6). We can use the chain rule to find the derivative. However, in this case we will use the derivative of the composition (which has the simple formula x) to find the derivative of the component part f^{-1}.

We can take the derivatives of both sides, finding

$$\left(f \circ f^{-1}\right)'(x) = f'\left[f^{-1}(x)\right]\left(f^{-1}\right)'(x) = 1$$

because

$$\frac{d}{dx}(x) = 1$$

We can solve this equation for $(f^{-1})'(x)$, the derivative of the inverse, finding

$$\left(f^{-1}\right)'(x) = \frac{1}{f'\left[f^{-1}(x)\right]}$$

Theorem 2.13 The Derivative of an Inverse Function

Suppose f is a differentiable function with inverse f^{-1} and that

$$f'\left[f^{-1}(x)\right] \neq 0$$

Then

$$\left(f^{-1}\right)'(x) = \frac{1}{f'\left[f^{-1}(x)\right]}$$

Example 2.9.5 Checking the Derivative of $\ln(x)$

We can use this theorem to check the derivative of $\ln(x)$. Setting $f(x) = e^x$, we have

$$f'(x) = e^x$$
$$f^{-1}(x) = \ln(x)$$

Therefore,

$$\begin{aligned}\left(f^{-1}\right)'(x) &= \frac{1}{f'\left[f^{-1}(x)\right]}\\ &= \frac{1}{e^{f^{-1}(x)}}\\ &= \frac{1}{e^{\ln(x)}}\\ &= \frac{1}{x}\end{aligned}$$

The simple formula for the derivative of the natural logarithm can be found from the simple formula for the derivative of the exponential function.

Example 2.9.6 Checking the Derivative of $\sqrt{x}$

We can also check the derivative of $\sqrt{x}$. Setting $S(x) = x^2$, we have

$$S'(x) = 2x$$
$$S^{-1}(x) = \sqrt{x}$$

Therefore,

$$\begin{aligned}\left(f^{-1}\right)'(x) &= \frac{1}{f'\left[f^{-1}(x)\right]}\\ &= \frac{1}{2f^{-1}(x)}\\ &= \frac{1}{2\sqrt{x}}\end{aligned}$$

matching the power rule for fractional powers (Theorem 2.8).

The formula for the derivative of the inverse has a nice geometric interpretation (Figure 2.9.98). The graph of the inverse function is the mirror image, through the

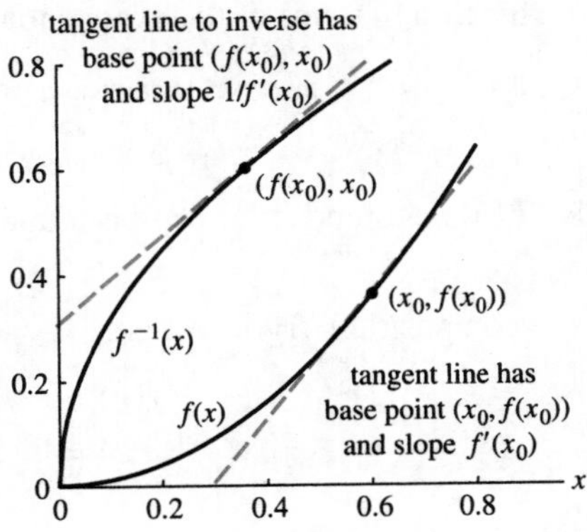

FIGURE 2.9.98

The tangent lines to a function and its inverse

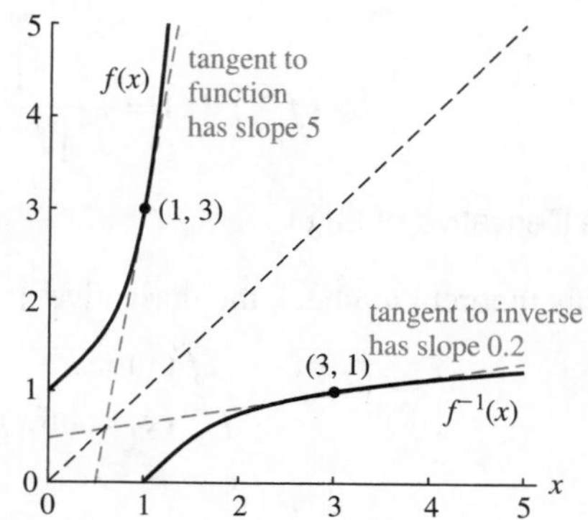

FIGURE 2.9.99

The tangent lines to an uncomputable inverse

line $y = x$, of the graph of the function itself. Therefore, the tangent line to the inverse function is the mirror image of the tangent line to the function. The tangent to the inverse at the point $(f(x_0), x_0)$, the reflection of the point $(x_0, f(x_0))$, will have slope

$$\text{slope of tangent to inverse at } (f(x_0), x_0) = \frac{1}{\text{slope of tangent to function at } (x_0, f(x_0))}$$

Therefore,

$$\left(f^{-1}\right)'[f(x_0)] = \frac{1}{f'(x_0)}$$

Example 2.9.7 Sketching the Derivative that Cannot Be Computed

With this geometric interpretation, we can find the slope of a curve for which we have no formula. When studying the inverse in Section 1.2, we found that the function

$$f(x) = x^5 + x + 1$$

has an inverse even though we cannot find a formula (Example 1.2.27). Suppose, nonetheless, that we wish to find the slope of the inverse at the point (3, 1). This point lies on the inverse because $f(1) = 3$. Furthermore,

$$f'(x) = 5x^4 + 1$$

so $f'(1) = 5$. Therefore, the slope of the inverse is the reciprocal, or

$$\left(f^{-1}\right)'(3) = \frac{1}{5}$$

(Figure 2.9.99.)

Applications

We can use the chain rule to find the derivative of $b(t) = 2.0^t$, the function we first studied in Section 2.1. We will finally be able to explain that factor of 0.693. The trick is to write the function in terms of the exponential function as

$$\begin{aligned} 2.0^t &= \left(e^{\ln(2.0)}\right)^t && \text{exponential and natural log are inverses} \\ &= e^{\ln(2.0)t} && \text{law 2 of exponents} \end{aligned}$$

The derivative of this composition can be found by following the chain rule, Algorithm 2.1.

1. $b(t)$ is a composition $f(g(t))$ where

$$f(g) = e^g$$
$$g(t) = \ln(2.0)t$$

2. The derivatives of the components are

$$f'(g) = e^g$$
$$g'(t) = \ln(2.0)$$

3. Using the chain rule, we find that the derivative of b is

$$b'(t) = e^g \ln(2.0)$$

4. Putting back in terms of t, we get

$$\begin{aligned} b'(t) &= e^{\ln(2.0)t} \ln(2.0) && \text{substitute the definition of } g \\ &= \left(e^{\ln(2.0)}\right)^t \ln(2.0) && \text{law 2 of exponents} \\ &= 2.0^t \ln(2.0) && \text{exponential and log are inverses} \\ &= \ln(2.0)2.0^t \approx 0.693 \cdot 2.0^t && \text{reorder and evaluate} \end{aligned}$$

The mysterious factor 0.693 that cropped up in Section 2.1 is the natural logarithm of 2.0. Perhaps better than any other calculation, this shows the pivotal role of the number e and the exponential function. Although the function 2.0^t does not contain any reference to e, a natural log is spontaneously generated by the derivative.

Exponential measurements are generally written in the form

$$M(t) = M(0)e^{\alpha t}$$

(Section 1.7). The constant $M(0)$ represents the value of the measurement at $t = 0$. The parameter α determines whether and how fast the measurement is increasing as a function of time. If α is negative, the measurement is decreasing, and it decreases faster the more negative α is. If α is positive, the measurement is increasing, and it increases faster the larger α is.

We can find the derivative of $M(t)$ with the chain rule.

1. $M(t)$ is the composition $f(g(t))$ where

$$f(g) = M(0)e^g$$
$$g(t) = \alpha t$$

2. The derivatives of the components are

$$f'(g) = M(0)e^g$$
$$g'(t) = \alpha$$

3. Using the chain rule, we find that the derivative of M is

$$M'(t) = M(0)e^g\alpha$$

4. Putting back in terms of t, we get

$$\begin{aligned} M'(t) &= M(0)e^{\alpha t}\alpha && \text{plug in definition of } g \\ &= \alpha M(0)e^{\alpha t} && \text{reorder} \\ &= \alpha M(t) && \text{rewrite in terms of } M(t) \end{aligned}$$

The derivative of the general exponential function can be found by multiplying the original function by the parameter α that appears in the exponent.

Example 2.9.8 Finding the Derivative of e^{3t}

In Example 2.8.2, we used the definition of the derivative to find that

$$\frac{d\left(e^{3t}\right)}{dt} = 3e^{3t}$$

We now see that this is one case of the general rule. The derivative of an exponential function is found by multiplying the original function e^{3t} by the parameter 3 that appears in the exponent.

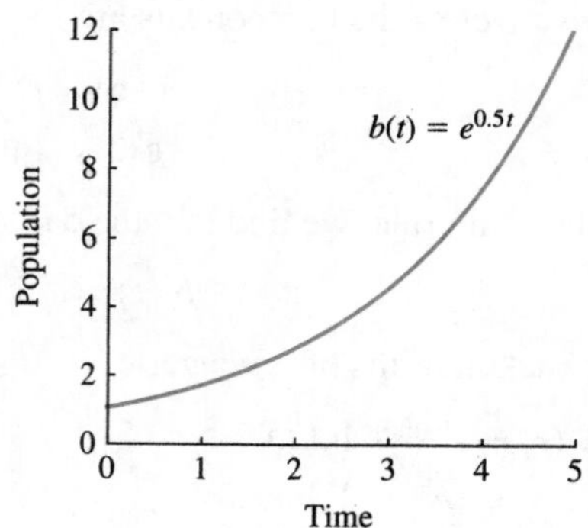

FIGURE 2.9.100
The growth of a population obeying $\frac{db}{dt} = 0.5b$

Example 2.9.9 Finding the Solution of a Differential Equation

We can use this rule to find a solution of the differential equation

$$\frac{db}{dt} = 0.5b$$

which says that the rate of change of the population is 0.5 times the population size. One solution is

$$b(t) = e^{0.5t}$$

because this function has parameter $\alpha = 0.5$ in the exponent (Figure 2.9.100).

Summary We derived the **chain rule** for differentiating the composition of two functions. Almost any complicated function can be differentiated in four steps: (1) breaking the function into components, (2) taking the derivative of each component, (3) multiplying the derivatives together, and (4) rewriting in terms of the original variable. The same technique works for compositions of more than two functions. The chain rule can be used to derive the formula for the derivatives of inverse functions and provides a useful tool for finding derivatives of general exponential functions.

2.9 Exercises

Mathematical Techniques

1–16 ▪ Compute the following derivatives using the chain rule.

1. $g(x) = (1 + 3x)^2$
2. $h(x) = (1 + 2x)^3$
3. $f_1(t) = (1 + 3t)^{30}$
4. $f_2(t) = (1 + 2t^2)^{15}$
5. $r(x) = \frac{(1 + 3x)^2}{(1 + 2x)^3}$
6. $p(z) = (1 + 3z)^2(1 + 2z)^3$
7. $F(z) = \left(1 + \frac{2}{1 + z}\right)^3$
8. $G(w) = \left[\left(2 - \frac{3}{1 - w}\right)^2 + 1\right]^2$
9. $f(x) = e^{-3x}$
10. $h(x) = 2^x 3^x$
11. $g(y) = \ln(1 + y)$
12. $A(z) = \ln(1 + e^z)$
13. $G(x) = 8e^{x^2}$
14. $s(w) = 4.2\sqrt{1 + e^w}$
15. $L(x) = \ln[\ln(x)]$
16. $q(y) = y^y$ (*Hint*: Rewrite with the exponential function)

17–24 ▪ Compute the derivative of each of the following functions in the two ways given.

17. $F(x) = \frac{1}{1 + e^x}$, first using the quotient rule and then using the chain rule.
18. $H(y) = \frac{1}{1 + y^3}$ first using the quotient rule and then using the chain rule.
19. $g(x) = \ln(3x)$ first using a law of logs and then using the chain rule.
20. $h(x) = \ln(x^3)$ first using a law of logs and then using the chain rule.

21. $F(x) = (1 + 2x)^2$ first by expanding the binomial and taking the derivative of the polynomial, and then with the chain rule.

22. $F(x) = (1 + 2x)^3$ first by expanding the binomial and taking the derivative of the polynomial, and then with the chain rule.

23. $F(x) = x^3$ first with the power rule and then by writing $F(x)$ using the exponential function and using the chain rule.

24. $F(x) = x^{-5}$ first with the power rule and then by writing $F(x)$ using the exponential function and using the chain rule.

25–30 ▪ Find the derivatives of the inverses of the following functions in two ways: first by finding the inverse and taking its derivative directly, and then by using Theorem 2.13 (the formula for the derivative of the inverse).

25. $f(x) = 3x + 1$

26. $g(x) = -x + 3$

27. $h(x) = 2 + x^3$

28. $F(x) = 1 - e^{-x}$

29. $q(x) = x + x^2$ for $x \geq 0$

30. $N(x) = e^{x^2}$ for $x \geq 0$

31–32 ▪ We can use laws of exponents and the chain rule to check the power rule.

31. Write $f(x) = x^n$ using the exponential function.

32. Take the derivative and then rewrite as a power function.

33–34 ▪ The equation for the top half of the unit circle is $f(x) = \sqrt{1 - x^2}$. We can find the slope of the tangent with the chain rule, or we can find it geometrically.

33. Find the derivative of $f(x)$ with the chain rule.

34. Find the slope of the ray connecting the center of the circle at (0, 0) to the point $(x, f(x))$ on the circle. Then use the fact that the tangent to a circle is perpendicular to the ray to find the slope of the tangent. Check that it matches the result with the chain rule.

Applications

35–38 ▪ The following functional compositions describe connections between measurements (as in Section 1.2, Exercises 53–56, page 23). Find the derivative of the composition using the chain rule.

35. The number of mosquitos (M) that end up in a room is a function of how far the window is open (W, in square centimeters) according to $M(W) = 5W + 2$. The number of bites (B) depends on the number of mosquitos according to $B(M) = 0.5M$. Find the derivative of B as a function of W.

36. The temperature of a room (T) in °C is a function of how far the window is open (W) according to $T(W) = 40 - 0.2W$. How long you sleep (S, measured in hours) is a function of the temperature according to $S(T) = 14 - T/5$. Find the derivative of S as a function of W.

37. The number of viruses (V, measured in trillions) that infect a person is a function of the degree of immunosuppression (I, the fraction of the immune system that is turned off by medication) according to $V(I) = 5I^2$. The fever (F, measured in degrees Celsius) associated with an infection is a function of the number of viruses according to $F(V) = 37 + 0.4V$. Find the derivative of F as a function of I.

38. The length of an insect (L, in millimeters) is a function of the temperature during development (T, measured in degrees Celsius) according to $L(T) = 10 + T/10$. The volume of the bug (V, in cubic millimeters) is a function of the length according to $V(L) = 2L^3$. The mass (M, in milligrams) depends on volume according to $M(V) = 1.3V$. Find the derivative of M as a function of T.

39–40 ▪ The amount of carbon-14 (C^{14}) per gram left t years after the death of an organism is given by

$$Q(t) = Q_0 e^{-0.000122t}$$

where Q_0 is the amount left per gram at the time of death. Suppose $Q_0 = 6.0 \times 10^{10}$ C^{14} atoms/g.

39. Find the derivative of $Q(t)$.

40. If C^{14} were lost at a constant rate equal to the rate at $t = 0$, how long would it take for half of the C^{14} to disappear? How does this compare with the half-life of C^{14}? Why are the results different?

41–44 ▪ Check the given solutions to the following differential equations. Which solutions are increasing and which are decreasing?

41. $\dfrac{db}{dt} = 3b(t)$ has solution $b(t) = 100e^{3t}$ if $b(0) = 100$.

42. $\dfrac{db}{dt} = -2b(t)$ has solution $b(t) = 10e^{-2t}$ if $b(0) = 10$.

43. $\dfrac{db}{dt} = 1 + 2b(t)$ has solution $b(t) = 3e^{2t} - 0.5$ if $b(0) = 2.5$.

44. $\dfrac{db}{dt} = 10 - 2b(t)$ has solution $b(t) = 5 + 20e^{-2t}$ if $b(0) = 25$.

2.10 Derivatives of Trigonometric Functions

The last group of special functions important in biology consists of the trigonometric functions. We here compute the derivatives of these special functions. Like the exponential function, the derivatives of sine and cosine have special properties that link them to solutions of important differential equations.

Deriving the Derivatives of Sine and Cosine

Because the functions sine and cosine cannot be built out of polynomials and exponential functions with products, sums, and quotients (except by using the more advanced topic of **complex numbers**), we must compute the derivative from its definition. For the sine and cosine functions,

$$\frac{d[\sin(x)]}{dx} = \lim_{h\to 0} \frac{\sin(x+h) - \sin(x)}{h}$$
$$\frac{d[\cos(x)]}{dx} = \lim_{h\to 0} \frac{\cos(x+h) - \cos(x)}{h}$$

These formulas do us little good unless we can expand the expressions for $\sin(x+h)$ and $\cos(x+h)$. When finding the derivative of the exponential function, we used a law of exponents to rewrite e^{x+h} as $e^x e^h$. Trigonometric functions have similarly useful sum laws, called the **angle addition formulas:**

$$\sin(x+h) = \sin(x)\cos(h) + \cos(x)\sin(h) \qquad \textbf{(2.10.1)}$$
$$\cos(x+h) = \cos(x)\cos(h) - \sin(x)\sin(h) \qquad \textbf{(2.10.2)}$$

We will use the sum law for sine to try to find the derivative.

$$\lim_{h\to 0} \frac{\sin(x+h) - \sin(x)}{h}$$
$$= \lim_{h\to 0} \frac{\sin(x)\cos(h) + \cos(x)\sin(h) - \sin(x)}{h} \qquad \text{apply the sum law for sine}$$
$$= \lim_{h\to 0} \frac{\sin(x)[\cos(h) - 1] + \cos(x)\sin(h)}{h} \qquad \text{combine terms involving } \sin(x)$$
$$= \lim_{h\to 0} \frac{\sin(x)[\cos(h) - 1]}{h} + \lim_{h\to 0} \frac{\cos(x)\sin(h)}{h} \qquad \text{break up the limit}$$
$$= \sin(x) \lim_{h\to 0} \frac{\cos(h) - 1}{h} + \cos(x) \lim_{h\to 0} \frac{\sin(h)}{h} \qquad \text{pull out terms without } h\text{'s}$$

Although this might not look much better than the limit we started with, it has an important simplification, much like that found with the exponential function. All terms involving x have come outside the limits. If we could figure out the numerical values of

$$\lim_{h\to 0} \frac{\cos(h) - 1}{h}$$

and

$$\lim_{h\to 0} \frac{\sin(h)}{h}$$

we would be finished.

In Derivation of the Key Limits, p. 232 we derive that

$$\lim_{h\to 0} \frac{\cos(h) - 1}{h} = 0$$
$$\lim_{h\to 0} \frac{\sin(h)}{h} = 1$$

Substituting these values into the formulas, we have found that

$$\frac{d[\sin(x)]}{dx} = \sin(x) \lim_{h\to 0} \frac{\cos(h) - 1}{h} + \cos(x) \lim_{h\to 0} \frac{\sin(h)}{h}$$
$$= \sin(x)\cdot 0 + \cos(x)\cdot 1 = \cos(x)$$

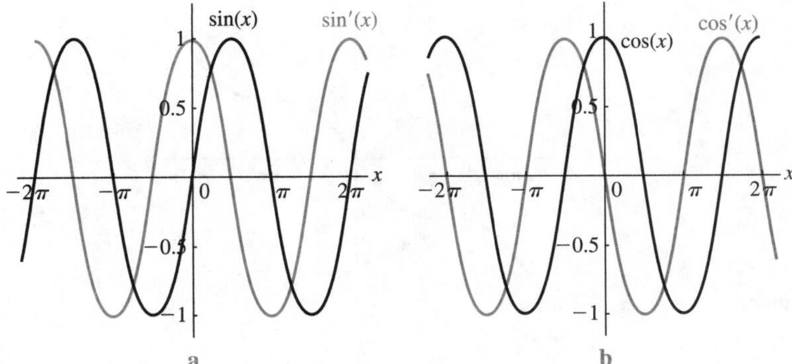

FIGURE 2.10.101
The graphs and derivatives of sine and cosine

Similarly, the derivative of $\cos(x)$ is

$$\begin{aligned}
&\lim_{h\to 0}\frac{\cos(x+h)-\cos(x)}{h}\\
&=\lim_{h\to 0}\frac{\cos(x)\cos(h)-\sin(x)\sin(h)-\cos(x)}{h} && \text{apply the sum law for cosine}\\
&=\lim_{h\to 0}\frac{\cos(x)[\cos(h)-1]-\sin(x)\sin(h)}{h} && \text{combine terms involving } \cos(x)\\
&=\lim_{h\to 0}\frac{\cos(x)[\cos(h)-1]}{h}-\lim_{h\to 0}\frac{\sin(x)\sin(h)}{h} && \text{break up the limit}\\
&=\cos(x)\lim_{h\to 0}\frac{[\cos(h)-1]}{h}-\sin(x)\lim_{h\to 0}\frac{\sin(h)}{h} && \text{pull out terms without } h\text{'s}\\
&=\cos(x)\cdot 0-\sin(x)\cdot 1 && \text{use the limits found earlier}\\
&=-\sin(x) && \text{multiply out}
\end{aligned}$$

In summary,

$$\frac{d[\sin(x)]}{dx}=\cos(x)$$
$$\frac{d[\cos(x)]}{dx}=-\sin(x)$$

To recall where the negative sign goes, remember the graphs of sine and cosine. At $x=0$, the cosine is flat but beginning to decrease, meaning that the derivative must begin at 0 and become negative. At $x=0$, the sine is increasing, meaning that the derivative should take on a positive value at that point (Figure 2.10.101a).

What is the second derivative of each of these functions?

$$\frac{d^2[\sin(x)]}{dx^2}=\frac{d[\cos(x)]}{dx}=-\sin(x)$$
$$\frac{d^2[\cos(x)]}{dx^2}=-\frac{d[\sin(x)]}{dx}=-\cos(x)$$

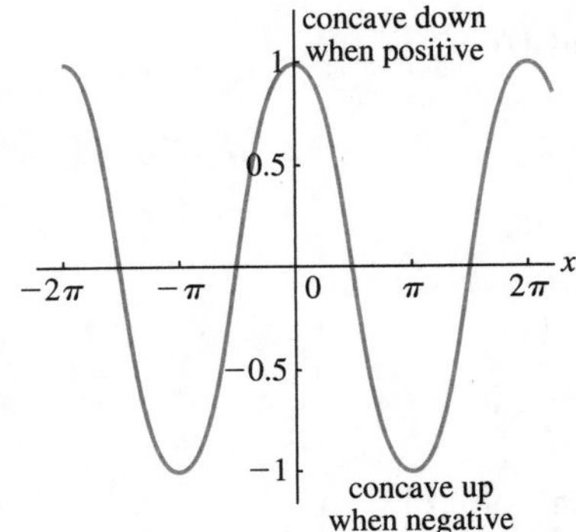

FIGURE 2.10.102
The concavity of cosine

Each of these functions has the remarkable property that it is equal to the *negative* of its second derivative. These functions are concave down when positive and are concave up when negative (Figure 2.10.102). Furthermore, both have points of inflection every time they cross zero. This property may remind you of the fact that the exponential function is its own derivative (and that e^{-x} is its own second derivative). There is a deep connection between these two types of functions that requires the more advanced topic of **complex numbers** to understand.

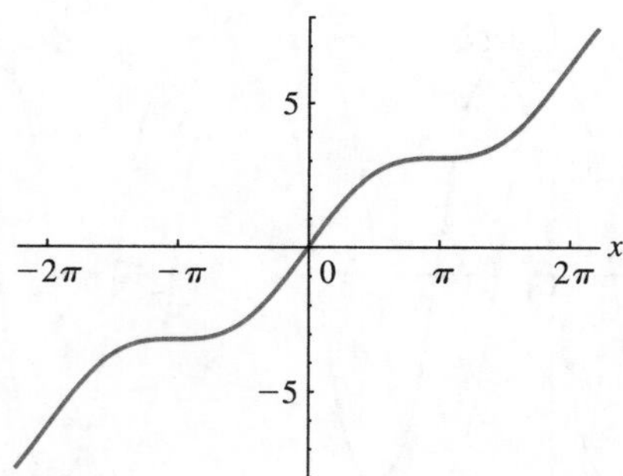

FIGURE 2.10.103
The graph of $x + \sin(x)$

Example 2.10.1 A Derivative Involving a Trigonometric Function

We can use rules for differentiation to find the derivatives of more complicated functions. For example, is the function

$$F(x) = x + \sin(x)$$

an increasing function? We can check by computing the derivative.

$$\begin{aligned} \frac{d(x + \sin(x))}{dx} &= \frac{dx}{dx} + \frac{d[\sin(x)]}{dx} && \text{sum rule} \\ &= 1 + \cos(x) && \text{power rule and derivative of sine} \end{aligned}$$

Because $\cos(x)$ is never smaller than -1, the derivative is never negative, and this function is increasing (Figure 2.10.103). The function has critical points where $\cos(x) = -1$, such as $x = -\pi$ and $x = \pi$.

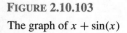

We have written sinusoidal oscillations as

$$f(t) = A + B\cos\left(\frac{2\pi}{T}(t - \phi)\right)$$

(Equation 1.8.1), where A is the average, B is the amplitude, T is the period, and ϕ is the phase. We can find the derivative of $f(t)$ with the chain rule.

1. $f(t)$ is the composition of $h[g(t)]$ where
$$\begin{aligned} h(g) &= A + B\cos(g) \\ g(t) &= \frac{2\pi}{T}(t - \phi) \end{aligned}$$
2. The derivatives of the components are
$$\begin{aligned} h'(g) &= -B\sin(g) \\ g'(t) &= \frac{2\pi}{T} \end{aligned}$$
3. Using the chain rule, the derivative of f is
$$f'(t) = \frac{2\pi B}{T}\sin(g)$$
4. Putting back in terms of t,
$$f'(t) = -\frac{2\pi B}{T}\sin\left[\frac{2\pi}{T}(t - \phi)\right]$$

This gives the derivative of the general function describing a sinusoidal oscillation.

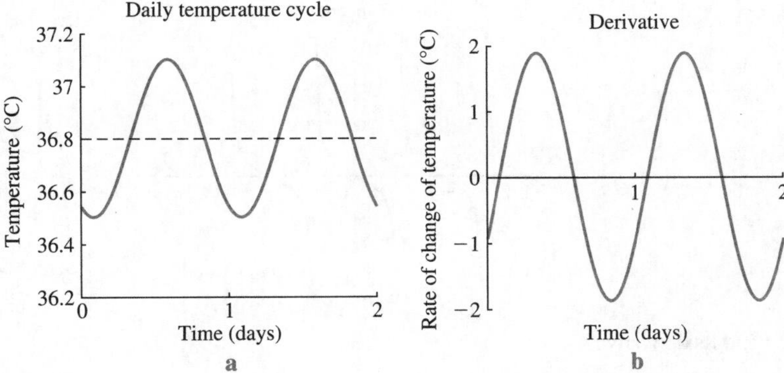

FIGURE 2.10.104

The daily temperature cycle and its derivative

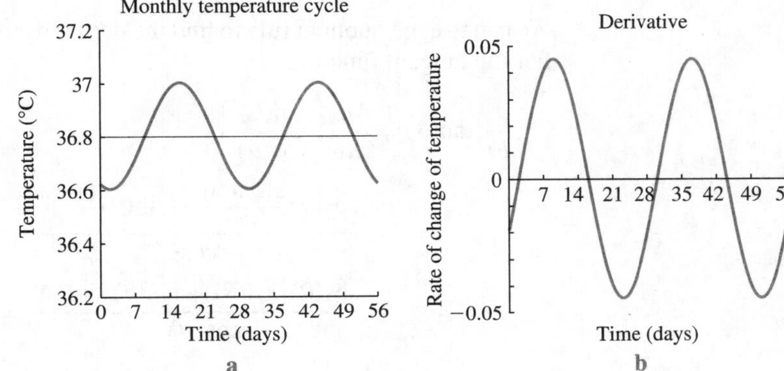

FIGURE 2.10.105

The monthly temperature cycle and its derivative

Example 2.10.2 Derivatives of Oscillations

The chain rule can be applied to find the derivatives of the daily and monthly temperature cycles introduced in Section 1.8 (written in units of days),

$$P_d(t) = 36.8 + 0.3\cos[2\pi(t - 0.583)]$$

$$P_m(t) = 36.8 + 0.2\cos\left[\frac{2\pi(t-16)}{28}\right]$$

Using the rule for finding the derivative of a general trigonometric function, along with the constant sum rule, we get

$$\begin{aligned}\frac{dP_d}{dt} &= 0.3\frac{d}{dt}\{\cos[2\pi(t - 0.583)]\}\\ &= -0.3\cdot 2\pi\sin[2\pi(t-0.583)]\\ \frac{dP_m}{dt} &= 0.2\frac{d}{dt}\left\{\cos\left[\frac{2\pi(t-16)}{28}\right]\right\}\\ &= -0.2\cdot\frac{2\pi}{28}\sin\left[\frac{2\pi(t-16)}{28}\right]\end{aligned}$$

The scales on the graphs of the two derivatives are very different (Figures 2.10.104 and 2.10.105). The daily oscillation has a much greater rate of change than the monthly one, nearly 2 degrees per day, with the other reaching only 0.05 degree per day. Biologically, this corresponds to the fact that the daily oscillation is much faster. Mathematically, this results from the factor of 28 dividing the amplitude of the derivative of the monthly rhythm.

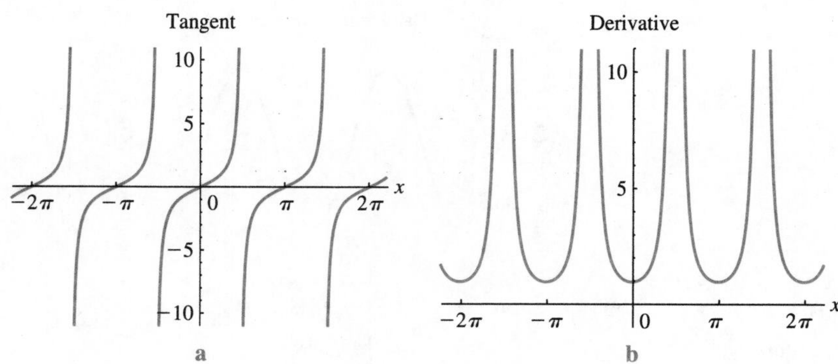

FIGURE 2.10.106
The tangent function and its derivative

Other Trigonometric Functions

We can use the quotient rule to find the derivatives of the other trigonometric functions. For the tangent function,

$$\begin{aligned}
\frac{d}{d\theta}[\tan(\theta)] &= \frac{d}{d\theta}\left[\frac{\sin(\theta)}{\cos(\theta)}\right] \\
&= \frac{\cos(\theta)\frac{d[\sin(\theta)]}{d\theta} - \sin(\theta)\frac{d[\cos(\theta)]}{d\theta}}{\cos^2\theta} && \text{quotient rule} \\
&= \frac{\cos(\theta)\cos(\theta) + \sin(\theta)\sin(\theta)}{\cos^2(\theta)} && \text{derivatives of sine and cosine} \\
&= \frac{1}{\cos^2\theta} && \sin^2(\theta) + \cos^2(\theta) = 1 \\
&= \sec^2\theta && \text{definition of the secant function}
\end{aligned}$$

On a graph of $\tan(\theta)$, the function has slope of 1 at $\theta = 0$ and is always increasing except at points where it is not defined (Figure 2.10.106).

Similarly (Exercises 9–12),

$$\frac{d}{dx}[\cot(x)] = -\csc^2(x)$$

$$\frac{d}{dx}[\sec(x)] = \tan(x)\sec(x)$$

$$\frac{d}{dx}[\csc(x)] = -\cot(x)\csc(x)$$

Although these functions also have simple derivatives, they do not have the remarkable properties of sine and cosine.

Applies no force when not stretched

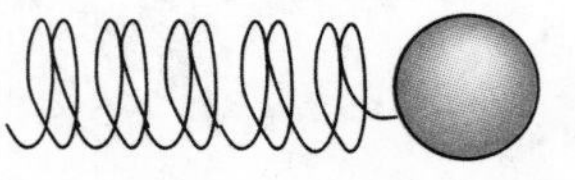

Applies outward force when compressed

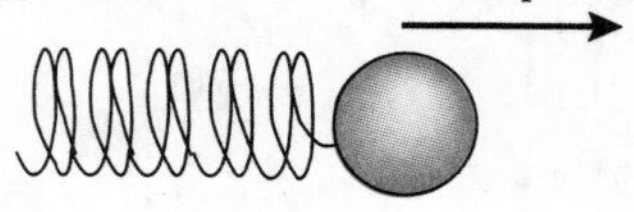

Applies inward force when stretched

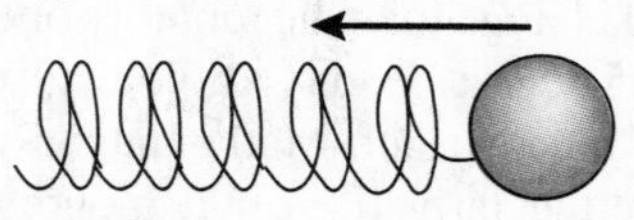

FIGURE 2.10.107
A perfect spring

Applications

We have studied the behavior of a rock falling in a constant gravitational field. Consider now an object attached to a perfect spring (Figure 2.10.107). The spring produces an outward force when compressed and an inward force when stretched. Assume that

$$\text{force} = -k(\text{amount of stretch})$$

The negative sign indicates that the force acts opposite the direction of stretch (Figure 2.10.107). If the spring is stretched to the right, it produces a force to the left, and if the spring is compressed to the left, it produces a force to the right. The constant k is the **spring constant,** with larger values indicating a stiffer spring.

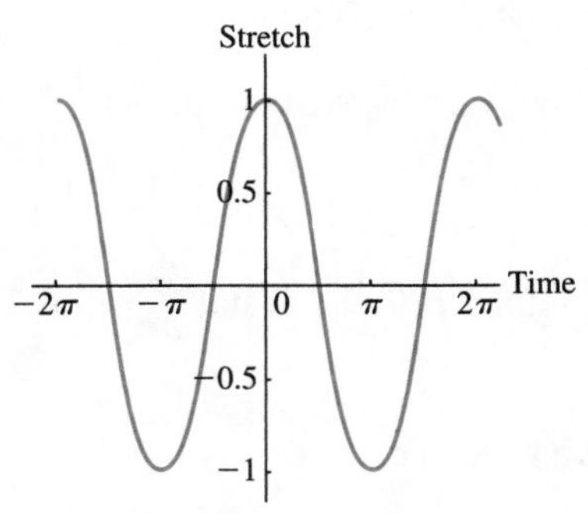

Solution starting from an outward stretch of 1

FIGURE 2.10.108
Solution of the spring equation with $p(0) = 1$

Newton's law says that acceleration, the second derivative of position, is proportional to force according to

$$F = ma$$

where m is the mass of the object.

Suppose first that both the mass of the object m and the spring constant k are equal to 1.0. Then, if the position (stretch) of the object is p,

$$a = \frac{d^2p}{dt^2} = -p$$

The solution of this differential equation is a function that has second derivative equal to the negative of itself. We have just met two such functions: sine and cosine. The position of an object attached to such an ideal spring (without friction) will follow exactly a sinusoidal oscillation. This spring is called the "simple harmonic oscillator" in physics and is one of the reasons why the sinusoidal functions are so important (in the same way that the simple differential equation $\frac{db}{dt} = b$ is one of the reasons why exponential functions are so important).

Example 2.10.3 A Solution of the Spring Equation: Stretched Initial Condition

Suppose the spring is stretched one unit and then the object is released. The subsequent movement follows the function

$$p(t) = \cos(t)$$

We can check that $p(0) = 1$ and that $\frac{dp}{dt} = -\sin(0) = 0$, meaning that the object does begin at rest at a position of 1. Furthermore,

$$\frac{d^2p}{dt^2} = -\cos(t) = -p(t)$$

This function solves the differential equation in the case $k = 1.0$ and $m = 1.0$, and it describes an oscillation with period $T = 2\pi$, the period of the cosine function itself (Figure 2.10.108).

Example 2.10.4 A Solution of the Spring Equation: Compressed Initial Condition

If the object is released when the spring is *compressed* by one unit, the solution is

$$p(t) = -\cos(t)$$

We can check that $p(0) = -1$ and that $\frac{dp}{dt} = -\sin(0) = 0$, so the object is at rest at time 0. Furthermore,

$$\frac{d^2p}{dt^2} = \cos(t) = -p(t)$$

(Figure 2.10.109).

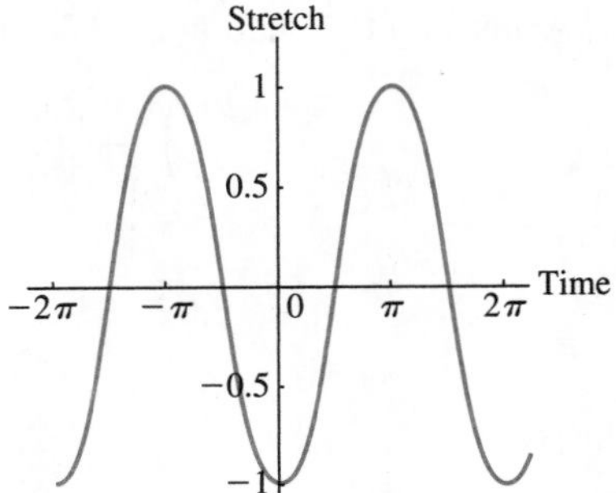

Solution starting from an inward stretch (compression) of 1

FIGURE 2.10.109
Solution of the spring equation with $p(0) = -1$

Example 2.10.5 A Solution of the Spring Equation: Slightly Stretched Initial Condition

If the object is released when the spring is stretched outward by 0.2 unit, the solution is

$$p(t) = 0.2\cos(t)$$

This is 0.2 times the solution in Example 2.10.3. Therefore, $p(0) = 0.2$ and $\frac{dp}{dt} = -0.2\sin(0) = 0$. See Figure 2.10.110.

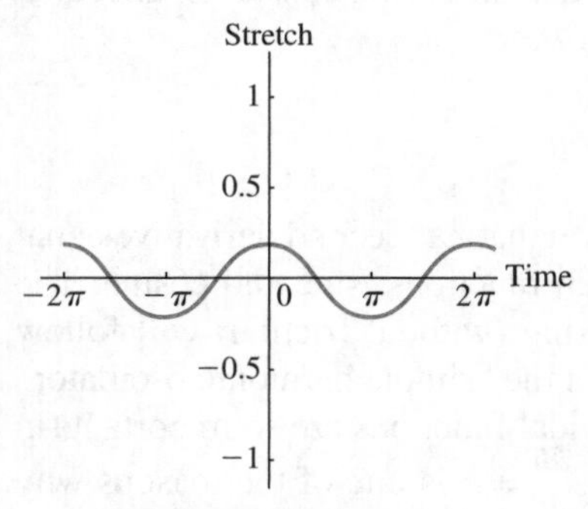

FIGURE 2.10.110

Solution of the spring equation with $p(0) = 0.2$

What happens if m and k are not exactly 1.0? We have that

$$\frac{d^2p}{dt^2} = \frac{F}{m} \quad F = ma \text{ solving for acceleration}$$

$$\frac{d^2p}{dt^2} = \frac{-kp}{m} \quad \text{substituting } F = -kp \text{ for the force}$$

The second derivative of position is no longer equal to its own negative but, rather, is equal to $-k/m$ times its negative.

Experience with springs shows that stiffer springs oscillate more quickly, with a smaller period. Perhaps a cosine function with a different period T will satisfy this equation. The function

$$p(t) = B\cos\left(\frac{2\pi}{T}t\right)$$

is a special case of the general sinusoidal oscillation (Section 1.8, Describing Oscillations with the Cosine, page 93) with period T and amplitude B, but with average and phase set to 0. Using the chain rule, we find

$$\frac{dp}{dt} = -B\frac{2\pi}{T}\sin\left(\frac{2\pi}{T}t\right)$$

$$\frac{d^2p}{dt^2} = B\left(\frac{2\pi}{T}\right)^2\cos\left(\frac{2\pi}{T}t\right)$$

$$= -\left(\frac{2\pi}{T}\right)^2 p(t).$$

This function is a solution of

$$\frac{dp}{dt^2} = \frac{-kp}{m}$$

if

$$\left(\frac{2\pi}{T}\right)^2 = \frac{k}{m} \tag{2.10.3}$$

Example 2.10.6 The Period of Oscillation When the Spring Is Strong

Suppose that $k = 2.0$, twice as strong as the spring in Example 2.10.3, but that the mass is still $m = 1.0$. According to equation 2.10.3, the period T must solve

$$\left(\frac{2\pi}{T}\right)^2 = \frac{2.0}{1.0} = 2.0$$

Isolating T gives

$$2.0T^2 = (2\pi)^2$$

$$T^2 = \frac{(2\pi)^2}{2.0}$$

$$T = \frac{2\pi}{\sqrt{2.0}}$$

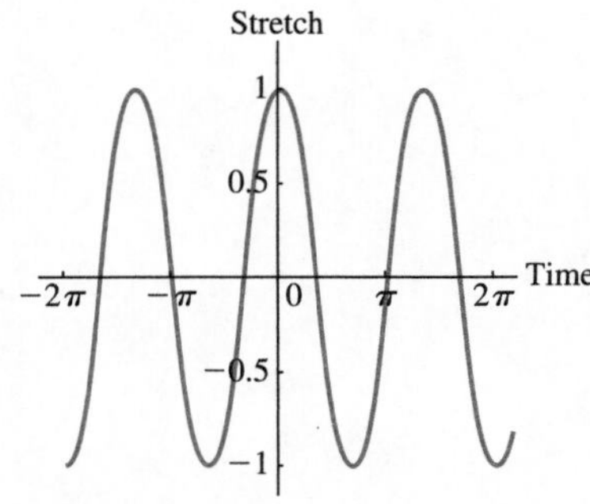

FIGURE 2.10.111
Solution of the spring equation with $p(0) = 1$ and $k = 2.0$

This period is smaller by a factor of $\sqrt{2.0}$ than the period $T = 2\pi$ of the spring with $k = 1.0$ (Figure 1.10.111).

Derivation of the Key Limits

Finding the derivatives of sine and cosine requires computing the following limits

$$\lim_{h \to 0} \frac{\cos(h) - 1}{h}$$

$$\lim_{h \to 0} \frac{\sin(h)}{h}$$

Testing with a calculator gives the following table. It seems as though the first limit is 0 and the second is 1.

h	$\frac{\cos(h)-1}{h}$	$\frac{\sin(h)}{h}$
1.0	−0.45970	0.84147
0.1	−0.04996	0.99833
0.01	−0.00500	0.99998
0.001	−0.00050	1.00000

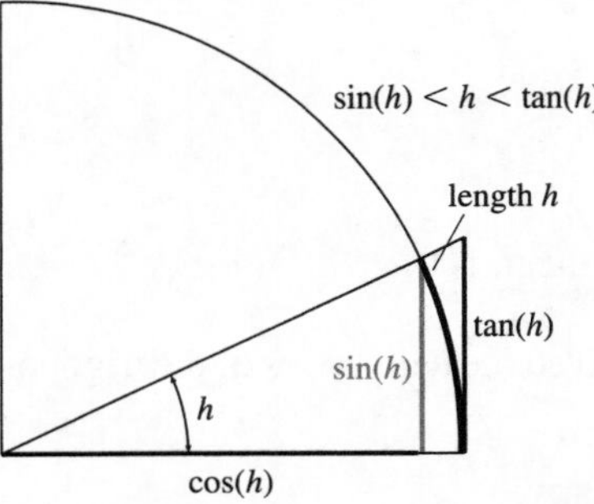

FIGURE 2.10.112
Geometric components of sine on the graph of the unit circle

We can see why this occurs from a geometric diagram of sine and cosine. First, we show that

$$\lim_{h \to 0} \frac{\sin(h)}{h} = 1$$

In Figure 2.10.112, the length of the arc is equal to the angle in radians and is greater than $\sin(h)$, the length of the vertical line segment. Therefore,

$$\frac{\sin(h)}{h} \le 1$$

Furthermore by similar triangles, the length of the line segment tangent to the circle is equal to $\tan(h)$, which is greater than the length of the arc, so $\tan(h) > h$, or

$$\frac{\sin(h)}{\cos(h)} > h$$

implying that

$$\frac{\sin(h)}{h} > \cos(h)$$

Therefore,

$$\lim_{h \to 0} \cos(h) \le \lim_{h \to 0} \frac{\sin(h)}{h} \le \lim_{h \to 0} 1$$

Because $\cos(h)$ is a continuous function, $\lim_{h \to 0} \cos(h) = \cos(0) = 1$. Furthermore, the limit of the constant 1 is also 1. Therefore,

$$1 \le \lim_{h \to 0} \frac{\sin(h)}{h} \le 1$$

implying that

$$\lim_{h \to 0} \frac{\sin(h)}{h} = 1$$

as found in the accompanying table and consistent with our calculator experiment.

To find the other limit,

$$\lim_{h \to 0} \frac{\cos(h) - 1}{h}$$

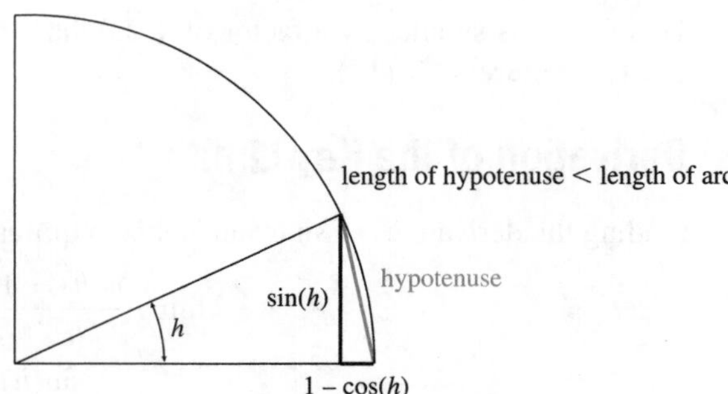

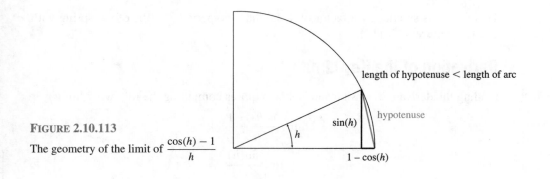

FIGURE 2.10.113
The geometry of the limit of $\frac{\cos(h) - 1}{h}$

we can use the fact that $\sin(h)$ and $1 - \cos(h)$ are two sides of a right triangle with hypotenuse of length less than the length of the arc (Figure 2.10.113). By the Pythagorean theorem, the square of the length of hypotenuse is the sum of the squares of the sides.

$$\sin^2(h) + [1 - \cos(h)]^2 < h^2 \quad \text{hypotenuse is shorter than arc}$$
$$\sin^2(h) + 1 - 2\cos(h) + \cos^2(h) < h^2 \quad \text{expand the quadratic}$$
$$2 - 2\cos(h) < h^2 \quad \text{use the fact that } \sin^2(h) + \cos^2(h) = 1$$
$$1 - \cos(h) < \frac{h^2}{2} \quad \text{divide by 2}$$

Thus

$$0 < \lim_{h\to 0} \frac{1 - \cos(h)}{h} < \lim_{h\to 0} \frac{h}{2} = 0.$$

This limit, again in accord with our calculator experiment, is 0.

Summary To complete our collection of building blocks, we derived the derivatives of the trigonometric functions.

Function	Derivative
$\sin(x)$	$\cos(x)$
$\cos(x)$	$-\sin(x)$
$\tan(x)$	$\sec^2(x)$
$\cot(x)$	$-\csc^2(x)$
$\sec(x)$	$\tan(x)\sec(x)$
$\csc(x)$	$-\cot(x)\csc(x)$

The sinusoidal functions provide the solutions of the differential equation describing a spring, the **simple harmonic oscillator.** They describe the position of an object that tends to move back to a resting state with force proportional to the displacement.

2.10 Exercises

Mathematical Techniques

1–8 ▪ Find the derivatives of the following functions.

1. $f(x) = x^2 \sin(x)$
2. $g(x) = x^2 \cos(x)$
3. $h(\theta) = \sin(\theta)\cos(\theta)$
4. $q(\theta) = \frac{\sin(\theta)}{1 + \cos(\theta)}$
5. $F(z) = 3 + \cos(2z - 1)$
6. $G(t) = 1 + 2\cos\left[\frac{2\pi}{5}(t - 3)\right]$
7. $f(x) = e^{\cos(x)}$
8. $f(x) = \cos(e^x)$

9–12 ▪ Use the definitions and the derivatives of $\sin(\theta)$ and $\cos(\theta)$ to check the derivatives of the other trigonometric functions and to find their second derivatives.

9. $\tan(\theta)$
10. $\cot(\theta)$
11. $\sec(\theta)$
12. $\csc(\theta)$

13–16 ▪ Use the angle addition formulas (Equations 2.10.1 and 2.10.2) to find the derivatives of the following. Compare the result with what you get with the chain rule.

13. $\cos(2\theta)$. Simplify the answer in terms of $\sin(2\theta)$.
14. $\sin(2\theta)$. Simplify the answer in terms of $\cos(2\theta)$.
15. Take the derivative of $\cos(\theta+\phi)$ with respect to θ, thinking of ϕ as a constant. Simplify the answer in terms of $\sin(\theta+\phi)$.
16. Take the derivative of $\sin(\theta+\phi)$ with respect to θ, thinking of ϕ as a constant. Simplify the answer in terms of $\cos(\theta+\phi)$.

17–22 ▪ Compute the derivatives of the following functions. Find the value of the function and the slope at 0, $\pi/2$, and π. Sketch a graph of the function on the given domain. How would you describe the behavior in words?

17. $a(x)=3x+\cos(x)$ for $0\le x\le 2\pi$
18. $b(y)=y^2+3\cos(y)$ for $0\le y\le 2\pi$
19. $c(z)=e^{-z}\sin(z)$ for $0\le z\le 2\pi$
20. $r(t)=t\cos(t)$ for $0\le t\le 4\pi$
21. $s(t)=e^{0.2t}\cos(t)$ for $0\le t\le 40$
22. $p(t)=e^t[1+0.2\cos(t)]$ for $0\le t\le 40$

23–26 ▪ We can use Theorem 2.13 to find the derivatives of the inverse trigonometric functions.

23. Find the derivative of $\sin^{-1}(x)$. If you use the identity $\cos^2(x)+\sin^2(x)=1$, you can write the answer without any trigonometric functions.
24. Find the derivative of $\cos^{-1}(x)$. Write the answer without any trigonometric functions.
25. Find the derivative of $\tan^{-1}(x)$. If you use the identity $1+\tan^2(x)=\sec^2(x)$, you can write the answer without any trigonometric functions.
26. Find the derivative of $\sec^{-1}(x)$. Write the answer without any trigonometric functions.

27–30 ▪ Show that the following are solutions of the given differential equation.

27. $\frac{ds}{dt}=\cos(t)$ has solution $s(t)=\sin(t)+4$.
28. $\frac{dy}{dt}=2t\sin(t)+t^2\cos(t)$ has solution $y(t)=t^2\sin(t)$.
29. $\frac{d^4g}{dt^4}=g(t)$ has solution $g(t)=\cos(t)+2\sin(t)-3e^t$.
30. $\frac{d^{40}h}{dt^{40}}=h(t)$ has solution $h(t)=\cos(t)+2\sin(t)-3e^t$.

Applications

31–34 ▪ Find the derivatives of the following functions (from Section 1.8, Exercises 41–44). Sketch a graph and check that your derivative has the correct sign when the argument is equal to 0.

31. $f(x)=3.0+4.0\cos\left(2\pi\frac{x-1.0}{5.0}\right)$
32. $g(t)=4.0+3.0\cos[2\pi(t-5.0)]$
33. $h(z)=1.0+5.0\cos\left(2\pi\frac{z-3.0}{4.0}\right)$
34. $W(y)=-2.0+3.0\cos\left(2\pi\frac{y+0.1}{0.2}\right)$

35–36 ▪ Consider the function $p(t)=\cos\left(\frac{2\pi t}{T}\right)$ where T is a constant.

35. Consider a spring with $k=0.1$ and $m=1.0$. Find the period T that produces a solution of the spring equation. Is this spring stronger or weaker than one with $k=1.0$, and does the oscillation have a larger or a smaller period?
36. Consider a spring with $k=1.0$ and $m=5.0$. Find the period T that produces a solution of the spring equation. Does a heavier object oscillate more slowly than a light one?

37–38 ▪ Consider the combination of the temperature cycles (Section 1.8.3, More Complicated Shapes)

$$P_d(t)=36.8+0.3\cos[2\pi(t-0.583)]$$
$$P_m(t)=36.8+0.2\cos\left[\frac{2\pi(t-16)}{28}\right]$$

given by

$$P_t(t)=36.8+0.2\cos\left[\frac{2\pi(t-16)}{28}\right]+0.3\cos[2\pi(t-0.583)]$$

37. Find the derivative of P_t.
38. Sketch a graph of the derivative over a month. If you measured only the derivative, which oscillation is easier to see?

39–40 ▪ The spring we studied had no friction. Friction acts as a force much like the spring itself, but it is proportional to velocity rather than displacement. One possible equation describing this is

$$\frac{d^2p}{dt^2}=-2p-2\frac{dp}{dt}$$

39. Explain each term in this equation and show that $p(t)=e^{-t}\cos(t)$ is a solution.
40. Graph the solution and explain what is going on. Is friction strong in this system?

41–46 ▪ Suppose a bacterial population follows the equation

$$\frac{db}{dt}=0.1[1+\cos(0.8t)]b(t)$$

41. Describe in words what is happening.
42. Show that $b(t)=e^{0.1t+0.125\sin(0.8t)}$ is a solution.
43. Graph this solution for $0\le t\le 20$.

44. Consider the more general equation

$$\frac{db}{dt} = 0.1[1 + A\cos(0.8t)]b(t)$$

where A is a constant. How does the constant A affect the population (compare small and large values)?

45. Show that $b(t) = e^{0.1t+0.125A\sin(0.8t)}$ is a solution.

46. Graph this solution for $A = 0$, $A = 0.5$, and $A = 2.0$.

47–48 ■ Use trigonometric derivatives to study the following.

47. In London, the number of hours of daylight follows roughly

$$L(t) = 12.0 - 4.5\cos(t)$$

where t represents time measured in units, 2π corresponds to 1 year, and the shortest day is December 21. A plant puts out leaves in the spring in response to the *change* in day length.

a. Find a value of t that produces the longest day. What day is this? How many hours of daylight does it have?

b. Find the smallest value of t that produces a day of average length. What day is this? How many hours of daylight does it have?

c. Find the rate of change of day length. When is this zero?

d. At what time of year would it be easiest for the plant to detect changes in day length?

48. Blood flow is pulsatile. Suppose the blood flow along the artery of a whale is

$$F(t) = 212.0\cos\left(\frac{2\pi t}{10}\right)$$

where F is measured in liters per second and t is measured in seconds.

a. Find the average flow and the amplitude.

b. Find the period of this flow. How many heartbeats does this whale have per minute?

c. When is the flow zero? What is happening at these times?

d. Find the rate of change of the flow. What does it mean when this is zero? What is the flow at these times?

Computer Exercises

49. This problem requires a computer program with a built-in ability to solve differential equations numerically. The spring equation

$$\frac{d^2y}{dt^2} = -y(t)$$

is only an approximation to the behavior of a pendulum, which is in fact better described by the equation

$$\frac{d^2y}{dt^2} = -\sin[y(t)]$$

It is impossible to write down an algebraic solution of this equation.

a. Starting from $y(0) = 0.1$ and $\frac{dy}{dt} = 0$ at $t = 0$, the solution of the spring equation is $y(t) = 0.1\cos(t)$. Compare this with the solution of the pendulum equation for one period (from $t = 0$ to $t = 2\pi$). Graph the two solutions.

b. Do the same starting from $y(0) = 0.2$.

c. Do the same starting from $y(0) = 0.5$.

d. Do the same starting from $y(0) = 1.0$.

e. Do the same starting from $y(0) = 1.5$.

f. How long does it take the pendulum to swing all the way back in each case? Does the period of a pendulum depend on the amplitude?

50. Consider the family of functions

$$h(t) = \cos(3.0t) + 1.5\cos(3.6t) + 2.0\cos(vt)$$

for various values of v ranging from 2.0 to 3.0. Graph them. Why do they look so weird? When do they look least weird?

51. Find the derivatives of the following functions. Where are the critical points and the points of inflection? What happens as more and more cosines are piled up? Explain this in terms of the discrete-time dynamical system

$$x_{t+1} = \cos(x_t)$$

a. $\cos[\cos(x)]$.

b. $\cos\{\cos[\cos(x)]\}$.

c. $\cos(\cos\{\cos[\cos(x)]\})$.

d. $\cos[\cos(\cos\{\cos[\cos(x)]\})]$.

52. An object attached to a spring with friction of strength α that oscillates with period T can have solution

$$p(t) = e^{-\alpha t}\cos\left(\frac{2\pi t}{T}\right)$$

a. Take the first and second derivatives.

b. Show that $p(t)$ is a solution of

$$\frac{d^2p}{dt^2} = -\left[\left(\frac{2\pi}{T}\right)^2 + \alpha^2\right]p - 2\alpha\frac{dp}{dt}$$

c. What is the strength of the spring?

d. Find two different values of spring strength and friction that produce the same period T.

Supplementary Problems

1–6 ▪ Find the limits of the following functions or explain why you can't.

1. $\lim_{x\to 0}(1+x^2)$
2. $\lim_{x\to -2}(1+x^2)$
3. $\lim_{x\to 1}\frac{1}{x^2-1}$
4. $\lim_{x\to 0}\frac{e^x}{1+e^{2x}}$
5. $\lim_{x\to 1^+}\frac{1}{x-1}$
6. $\lim_{x\to 1^-}\frac{1}{(x-1)}$

7–12 ▪ Find the derivatives of the following functions. Note any points where the derivative does not exist.

7. $F(y)=y^4+5y^2-1$
8. $a(x)=4x^7+7x^4-28$
9. $H(c)=\frac{c^2}{1+2c}$
10. $h(z)=\frac{z}{1+\ln(z^2)}$ for $z\geq 0$
11. For $y\geq 0$, $b(y)=\frac{1}{y^{0.75}}$
12. For $z\geq 0$, $c(z)=\frac{z}{(1+z)(2+z)}$

13–18 ▪ Find the derivatives of the following functions

13. $g(x)=(4+5x^2)^6$
14. $c(x)=\left(1+\frac{2}{x}\right)^5$
15. $s(t)=\ln(2t^3)$
16. $p(t)=t^2e^{2t}$
17. $s(x)=e^{-3x+1}+5\ln(3x)$
18. $g(y)=e^{3y^3+2y^2+y}$

19–22 ▪ Find the derivatives and other requested items for the following functions.

19. $f(t)=e^t\cos(t)$. Find one critical point.
20. $g(x)=\ln(1+x^2)$. Find one point where $g(x)$ is decreasing.
21. $h(y)=\frac{1-y}{(1+y)^3}$. Find all values where $h(x)$ is increasing.
22. $c(z)=\frac{e^{2z}-1}{z}$. What is $\lim_{z\to 0}c(z)$?

23–26 ▪ Find all critical points and points of inflection of the following. Sketch graphs.

23. $f(x)=e^{-x^3}$
24. $g(x)=e^{-x^4}$
25. $h(y)=\cos(y)+\frac{y}{2}$
26. $F(c)=e^{-2c}+e^c$

27–34 ▪ Solve the following.

27. A population of mosquitoes has size

$$N(t)=1000+10t^2$$

where t is measured in years.

a. What units should follow the 1000 and the 10?

b. Graph the population between $t=0$ and $t=10$.

c. Find the population after 7 yr and 8 yr. Find the approximate growth rate between these two times. Where does this approximate growth rate appear on your graph?

d. Find and graph the derivative $N'(t)$.

e. Find the per capita rate of growth. Is it increasing?

28. Suppose the volume of a cell is described by the function $V(t)=2-2t+t^2$ where t is measured in minutes and V is measured in thousands of cubic microns.

a. Graph the secant line from time $t=2$ to $t=2.5$.

b. Find the equation of this line.

c. Find the value of the derivative at $t=2$, and express it in both differential and prime notation. Don't forget the units.

d. What is happening to cell volume at time $t=2$?

e. Graph the derivative of V as a function of time.

29. Suppose a machine is invented to measure the amount of knowledge in a student's head in units called "factoids." One student is measured at $F(t)=t^3-6t^2+9t$ factoids at time t, where t is measured in weeks.

a. Find the rate at which the student is gaining (or losing) knowledge as a function of time (be sure to give the units).

b. During what time between $t=0$ and $t=11$ is the student losing knowledge?

c. Sketch a graph of the function $F(t)$.

30. The following measurements are made of a plant's height in centimeters and its rate of growth.

Day	Height	Growth Rate
1	8.0	5.2
2	15.0	9.4
3	28.0	17.8
4	53.0	34.6

a. Graph these data. Make sure to give units.

b. Write the equation of a secant line connecting two of these data points and use it to guess the height on day 5. Why did you pick the points you did?

c. Write the equation of a tangent line and use it to guess the height on day 5.

d. Which guess do you think is better?

e. How do you think the "growth rate" might have been measured?

31. Suppose the fraction of mutants in a population follows the discrete-time dynamical system

$$p_{t+1} = \frac{2.0p_t}{2.0p_t + 1.5(1 - p_t)}$$

Suppose you wish the fraction at time $t = 1$ to be close to $p_1 = 0.4$.

a. What would p_0 have to be to hit 0.4 exactly?

b. How close would p_0 have to be to this value to produce p_1 within 0.1 of the target?

c. What happens to the input tolerance as the output tolerance becomes smaller (as p_1 is required to be closer and closer to 0.4)?

32. Suppose the position of an object attached to a spring is

$$p(t) = 2.0\cos\left(\frac{2\pi t}{3.2}\right)$$

a. Find the derivative of $p(t)$. What does it mean physically?

b. Find the second derivative of $x(t)$. What does this mean physically?

c. What are the position and velocity at $t = 0$?

d. What are the position and velocity at $t = 1.6$?

e. What are the position and velocity at $t = 3.2$?

f. What differential equation does this object follow?

33. Suppose a system exhibits hysteresis. As the temperature T increases, the voltage response follows

$$V_i(T) = \begin{cases} T & \text{if } T \le 50 \\ 100 & \text{if } 50 < T \le 100 \end{cases}$$

As the temperature decreases, however, the voltage response follows

$$V_d(T) = \begin{cases} T & \text{if } T \le 20 \\ 100 & \text{if } 20 < T \le 100 \end{cases}$$

a. Graph these functions.

b. Find the left- and right-hand limits of V_i and V_d as T approaches 50.

c. Find the left- and right-hand limits of V_i and V_d as T approaches 20.

34. Suppose the total product in g generated by a chemical reaction is

$$P(t) = \frac{t}{1 + 2t}$$

where t is measured in hours.

a. Find the average rate of change between $t = 1$ and $t = 2$.

b. Find the equation of the secant line between these times.

c. Graph the secant line and the function $P(t)$.

d. Sketch a graph of the tangent line at $t = 2$. Judging from your graph, is the slope of the secant larger than, smaller than, or the same as the slope of the tangent?

e. Write the limit you would take to find the instantaneous rate of change at $t = 2$.

35–36 ▪ Each of the following graphs shows how far open, in square centimeters, a person's mouth while asleep is. Time is measured in hours after going to sleep at 10:00 P.M. In each case:

a. Label a point where the first derivative is positive and the second derivative is negative.

b. Label a point of inflection.

c. Sketch a graph of the rate of change.

d. Sketch a graph of the second derivative.

35.

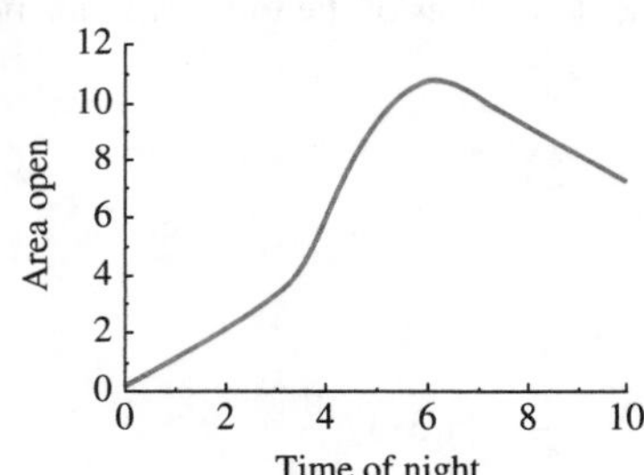

36.

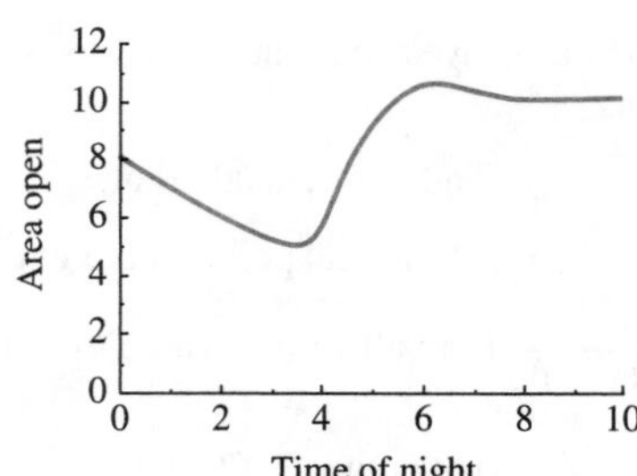

Projects

1. Periodic hematopoiesis is a disease characterized by large oscillations in the red blood cell count. Red blood cells are generated by a feedback mechanism that approximately obeys the following equation.

$$x_{t+1} = \frac{\tau}{1 + \gamma\tau} F(x_t) + \frac{1}{1 + \gamma\tau} x_t$$

The function $F(x_t)$ describes production as a function of number of cells and takes the form of a Hill function

$$F(x) = F_0 \frac{\theta^n}{\theta^n + x^n}$$

The terms are described as follows.

Parameter	Meaning	Normal Value
x_t	Number of cells at time t (in billions)	About 330
τ	Time for cell development	5.7 days
γ	Fraction of cells that die each day	0.0231
F_0	Maximum production of cells	76.2 billion
θ	Value where cell production is halved	247 billion
n	Shape parameter of Hill function	7.6

a. Graph and explain $F(x)$ with these parameter values. Does this sort of feedback system make sense?

b. Use a computer to find the equilibrium with normal parameters.

c. Graph and cobweb the updating function. If you start near the equilibrium, do values remain nearby? What would a solution look like?

d. Certain autoimmune diseases increase γ, the death rate of cells. Study what happens to the equilibrium and the solution as γ increases. Explain your results in biological terms.

e. Explore what would happen if the value of n were decreased. Does the equilibrium become more sensitive to small changes in γ?

M. C. Mackey. Mathematical models of hematopoietic cell replication and control. Pages 149–178 in H. G. Othmer, F. R. Adler, M. A. Lewis, and J. C. Dallon, editors, *Case Studies in Mathematical Modeling*. Prentice-Hall, Upper Saddle River, N.J., 1997.

Chapter 3

Applications of Derivatives and Dynamical Systems

We have developed techniques for computing derivatives of many functions and have interpreted the derivative as both the rate of change of a measurement and the slope of the graph of a function. The derivative has a remarkable range of applications for understanding the behavior of biological measurements, with the general theme of **reasoning about functions,** the mathematical version of reasoning about qualitative relationships between measurements. To begin, we will use the slope interpretation to find that the derivative of the updating function determines whether an equilibrium of a discrete-time dynamical system is **stable** or **unstable.** We will then use the derivative to find **maxima** and **minima** of functions. When combined with appropriate models of a biological process, these methods can be used to solve **optimization** problems.

Next, we will develop tools for reasoning about continuous and differentiable functions with a minimum of calculation. We will show, on the basis of the general properties of functions, that certain equations have solutions or that a maximum exists, and we will deduce more specific conclusions via a system of simple comparisons called the **method of leading behavior.** We will use the tangent line approximation to solve algebraically intractable equations with **Newton's method,** and we will extend the theme of approximating complicated functions with simple functions to **Taylor polynomials.**

3.1 Stability and the Derivative

In our initial study of discrete-time dynamical systems, we observed that equilibria can be **stable** or **unstable.** By examining the graph and cobweb of a discrete-time dynamical system, we will develop a method for evaluating the stability of an equilibrium by computing the **derivative of the updating function.** This method explains why some solutions, such as that for a growing bacterial population, move away from equilibrium, whereas others, like that of the lung model, move toward their equilibrium.

Motivation

Figures 3.1.1–3.1.5 review the cobwebbing diagrams for five of the discrete-time dynamical systems we have studied, and the following list reviews the terminology of discrete-time dynamical systems.

- A **discrete-time dynamical system** is a rule (described by its **updating function**) that takes a measurement at one time step as an input and returns the measurement at the next time step as an output (Section 1.5).
- **Cobwebbing** is a graphical method for finding solutions of discrete-time dynamical systems (Section 1.6).
- A **solution** gives the values of the measurement as a function of time (Section 1.5).
- An **equilibrium** is a point where the discrete-time dynamical system leaves the value unchanged (Definition 1.11 in Section 1.6). Graphically, an equilibrium is a point where the graph of the updating function crosses the diagonal line.

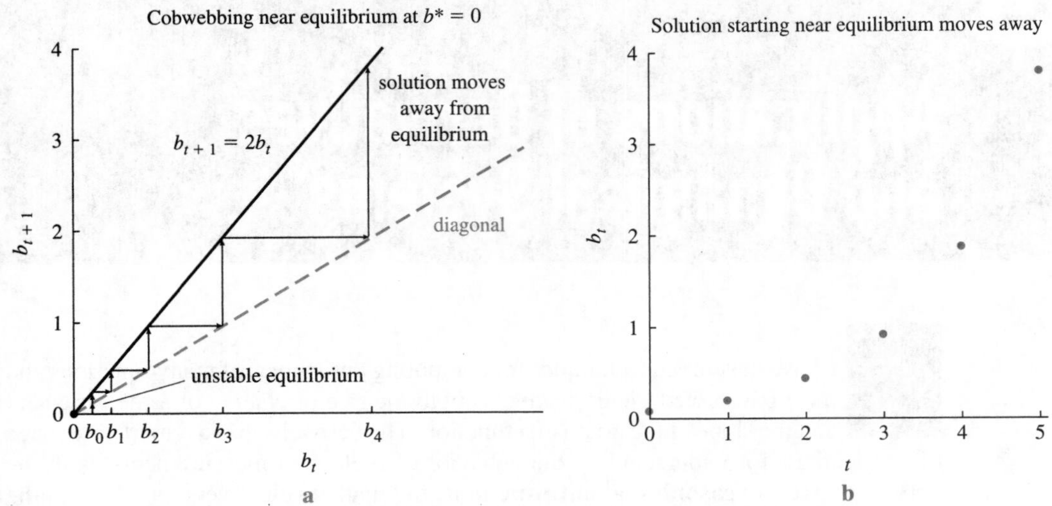

FIGURE 3.1.1
Bacterial population growth discrete-time dynamical system $b_{t+1} = 2b_t$

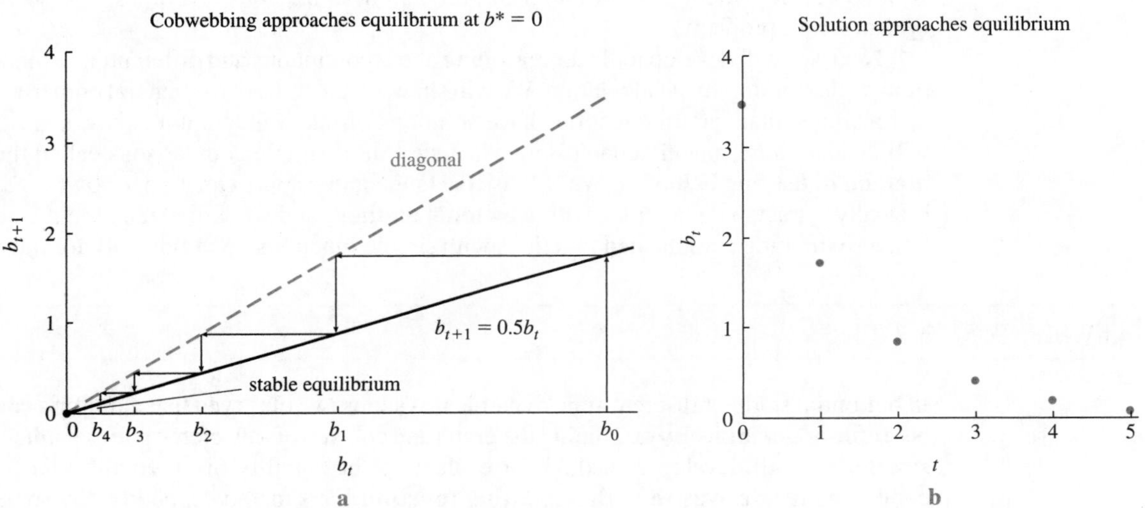

FIGURE 3.1.2
Bacterial population growth discrete-time dynamical system $b_{t+1} = 0.5b_t$

- An equilibrium is **stable** if solutions that start near the equilibrium move closer to the equilibrium. An equilibrium is **unstable** if solutions that start near the equilibrium move away from the equilibrium (Section 1.10).

The figures show four stable equilibria: $b^* = 0$ in Figure 3.1.2, $c^* = 5$ in Figure 3.1.3, $p^* = 1$ in Figure 3.1.4, and $p^* = 0$ in Figure 3.1.5. There are three unstable equilibria: $b^* = 0$ in Figure 3.1.1, $p^* = 0$ in Figure 3.1.4, and $p^* = 1$ in Figure 3.1.5. What is the pattern? How can we recognize which equilibria are stable?

Think about cobwebbing near a stable equilibrium, such as the one in Figure 3.1.3. If the initial condition is slightly less than the equilibrium, the solution *increases* because the graph of the updating function lies above the diagonal. Similarly, if we start slightly above the equilibrium, the solution *decreases* because the graph of the updating function lies below the diagonal. In other words, if the graph of the updating function crosses from above the diagonal to below the diagonal, the equilibrium is stable. Does this work for the other stable equilibria? It does if we imagine extending the graphs beyond

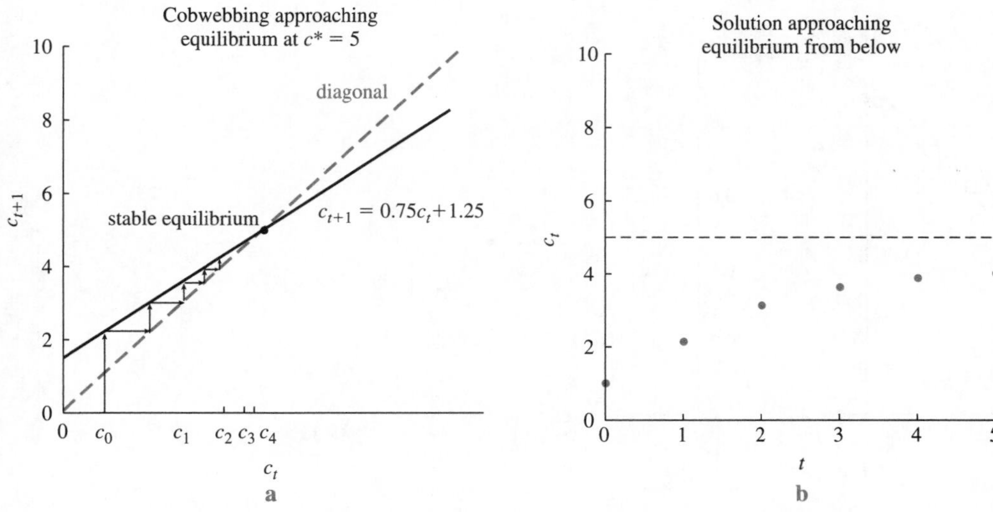

FIGURE 3.1.3

Lung discrete-time dynamical system $c_{t+1} = 0.75c_t + 1.25$

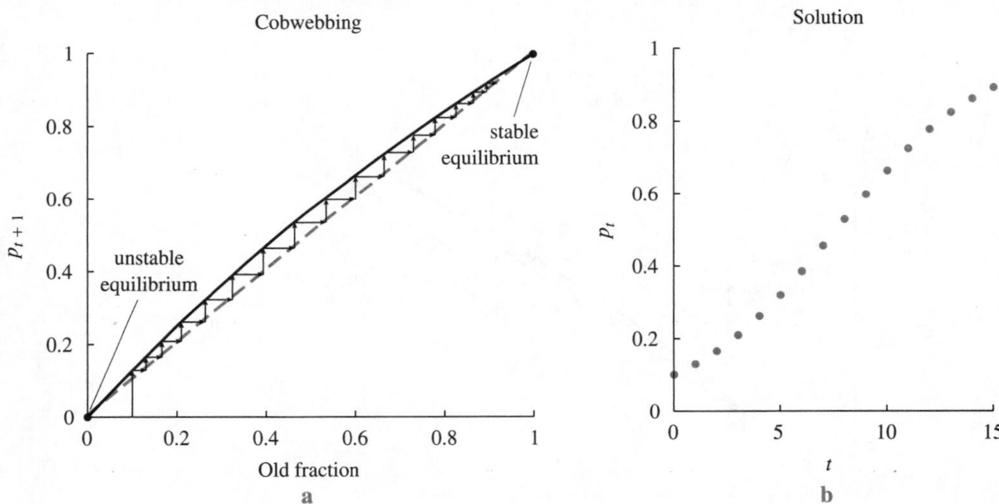

FIGURE 3.1.4

Bacterial selection discrete-time dynamical system $p_{t+1} = \dfrac{2.0p_t}{2.0p_t + 1.5(1 - p_t)}$

the biologically meaningful realm. For example, in Figure 3.1.4, the updating function intersects the diagonal from above near $p^* = 1$. If we extend the curve beyond $p^* = 1$, it crosses from above to below (Figure 3.1.6).

Unstable equilibria, in contrast, are points where the updating function crosses the diagonal from below to above. In this case, a solution that starts below the equilibrium will decrease further, moving away from the equilibrium. A solution that starts above the equilibrium will increase further, again moving away from the equilibrium. At the unstable equilibrium at $p^* = 0$ in Figure 3.1.4, the updating function crosses from below to above if we extend it below $p^* = 0$ (Figure 3.1.6).

We can summarize our observations with the following condition (Figure 3.1.7).

Graphical criterion for an equilibrium to be stable or unstable

- An equilibrium is stable if the graph of the updating function crosses the diagonal from above to below.
- An equilibrium is unstable if the graph of the updating function crosses the diagonal from below to above.

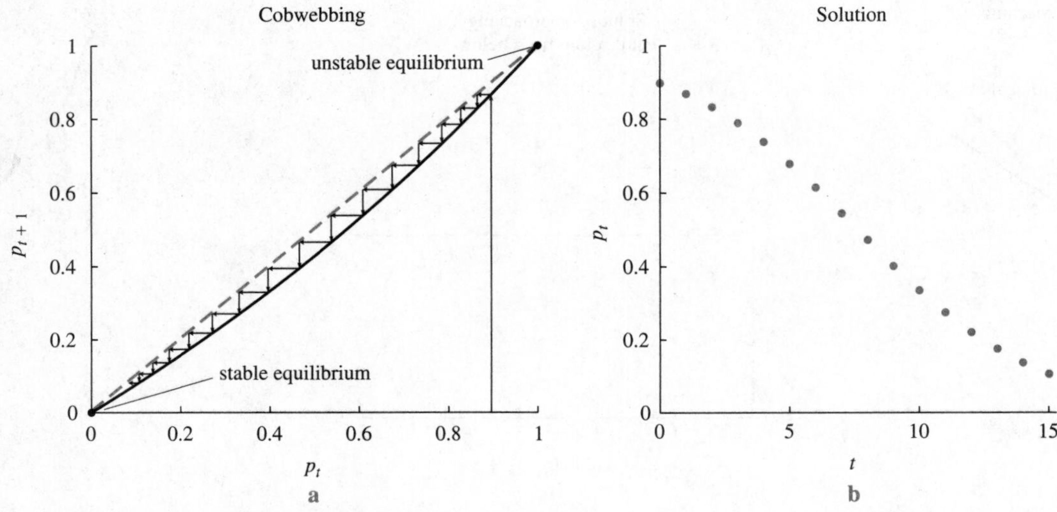

FIGURE 3.1.5

Bacterial selection discrete-time dynamical system $p_{t+1} = \dfrac{1.5p_t}{1.5p_t + 2.0(1 - p_t)}$

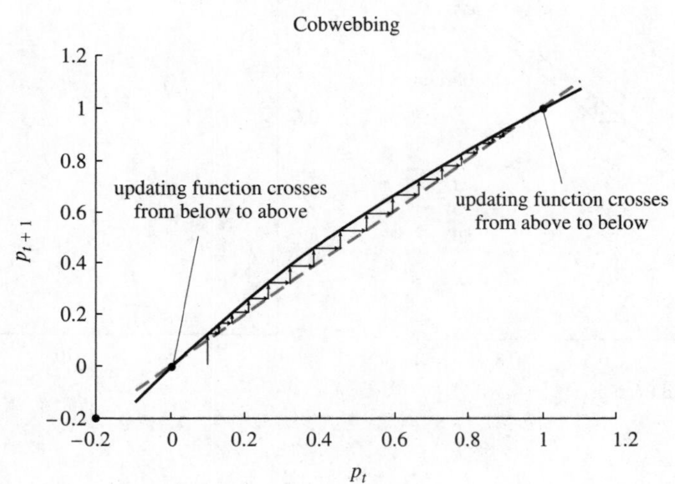

FIGURE 3.1.6

Bacterial selection discrete-time dynamical system with extended graph

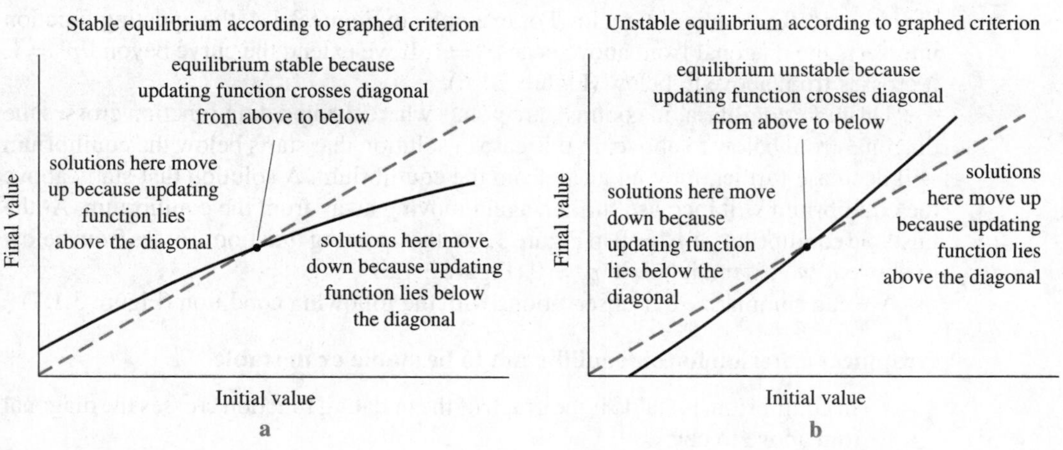

FIGURE 3.1.7

Graphical criterion for stability

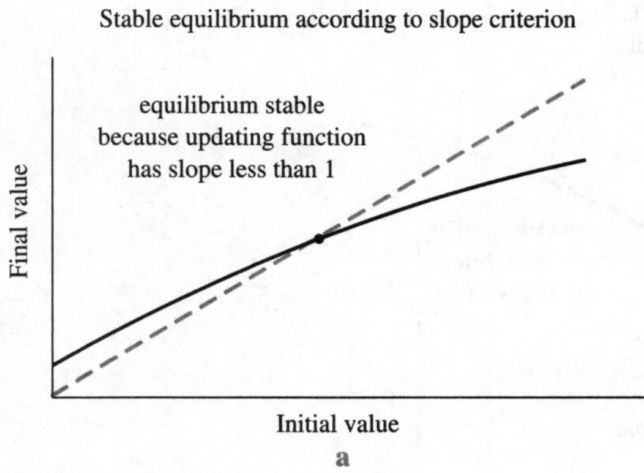

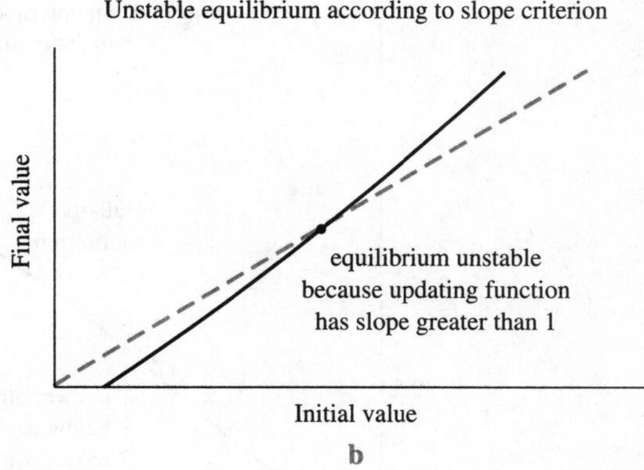

FIGURE 3.1.8
Slope criterion for stability

Stability and the Slope of the Updating Function

When does the updating function cross the diagonal from below to above? The diagonal is the graph of $y = x$, a line with a slope equal to 1. The graph of the updating function will cross from below to above when its slope is *greater than 1*. Conversely, a curve will cross from above to below when its slope is *less than 1*. We can therefore translate the Graphical Criterion for stability into a condition about the **derivative of the updating function,** because the derivative is equal to the slope (Figure 3.1.8).

Slope Criterion for an equilibrium to be stable or unstable

- An equilibrium is stable if the derivative of the updating function is less than 1 at the equilibrium.
- An equilibrium is unstable if the derivative of the updating function is greater than 1 at the equilibrium.

A nonlinear discrete-time dynamical system can have many equilibria. With the aid of the Graphical and Slope Criteria for stability, we can recognize stable and unstable equilibria by examining the slope of the updating function (Figure 3.1.9). We will see in the next section, however, that the dynamics can be much more complicated when the updating function has a negative slope.

The Slope Criterion for stability says nothing about what happens when the slope is exactly 1. Figure 3.1.10 shows an equilibrium where the updating function does not cross the diagonal but, rather, remains below the diagonal both to the left and to the right of the equilibrium. A solution that starts from any point below the equilibrium will decrease and move away from the equilibrium, as in the unstable case. A solution that starts from any point above the equilibrium will decrease and move toward the equilibrium, as in the stable case. This sort of half-stable equilibrium is possible because the diagonal is tangent to the updating function. It touches the curve but does not cross.

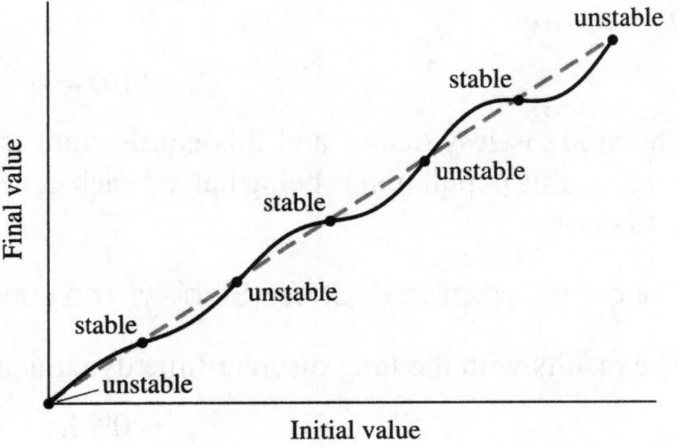

FIGURE 3.1.9
Recognizing the stability of a dynamical system with many equilibria

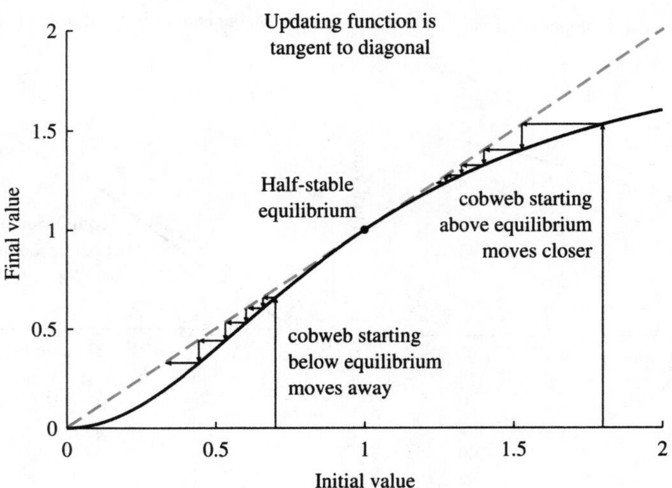

FIGURE 3.1.10
An unusual equilibrium

Evaluating Stability with the Derivative

We can test the Slope Criterion for stability by computing the derivatives of the discrete-time dynamical systems pictured in Figures 3.1.1–3.1.5.

Example 3.1.1 Using the Derivative to Check Stability: Bacterial Population Growth

In Figure 3.1.1, the discrete-time dynamical system is

$$b_{t+1} = 2.0b_t$$

with the updating function

$$f(b) = 2.0b$$

The only equilibrium is $b^* = 0$, corresponding to extinction. The updating function is a line with slope 2.0. More formally,

$$f'(b) = 2.0$$

Because this slope is greater than 1, the equilibrium is unstable. This makes biological sense because the population is doubling each generation and growing away from a population size of 0.

Example 3.1.2 Using the Derivative to Check Stability: Bacterial Population Decline

In Figure 3.1.2, the discrete-time dynamical system is

$$b_{t+1} = 0.5b_t$$

with the updating function

$$f(b) = 0.5b$$

Again, the only equilibrium is $b^* = 0$. This updating function, however, has a slope of 0.5 because

$$f'(b) = 0.5$$

The slope is less than 1 and this equilibrium is stable. This makes biological sense because this population is being halved each generation and hence is decreasing toward extinction.

Example 3.1.3 Using the Derivative to Check Stability: The Lung Model

The results with the lung discrete-time dynamical system

$$c_{t+1} = 0.75c_t + 1.25$$

are a little less obvious (Figure 3.1.3). If we designate the updating function $g(c) = 0.75c + 1.25$, we find

$$g'(c) = 0.75$$

because the updating function is linear with slope of 0.75. This slope is less than 1, implying that the single equilibrium is stable. In Section 1.9 we deduced that the equilibrium is always equal to the ambient concentration. Because the equilibrium is stable, we now know that the concentration in the lung (in the absence of absorption) gets closer and closer to the ambient concentration.

Example 3.1.4 Using the Derivative to Check Stability: The Selection Model

What happens when the discrete-time dynamical system is nonlinear? Figure 3.1.4 uses the bacterial selection discrete-time dynamical system

$$p_{t+1} = \frac{2.0p_t}{2.0p_t + 1.5(1 - p_t)}$$

where p_t represents the proportion of mutant bacteria at time t, 2.0 is the per capita production of mutant bacteria, and 1.5 is the per capita production of wild type bacteria. There are two equilibria, at $p^* = 0$ and $p^* = 1$ (Section 1.10). The first corresponds to extinction of the mutant and the second to extinction of the wild type.

By writing the updating function as

$$f(p) = \frac{2.0p}{2.0p + 1.5(1 - p)}$$

we computed the derivative in Example 2.6.4, finding

$$f'(p) = \frac{3.0}{[2.0p + 1.5(1 - p)]^2}$$

At the equilibrium $p^* = 0$,

$$f'(0) = \frac{3.0}{[2.0 \cdot 0 + 1.5(1 - 0)]^2} = \frac{3.0}{2.25} \approx 1.333$$

which is greater than 1. This equilibrium is unstable. At the equilibrium $p^* = 1$,

$$f'(1) = \frac{3.0}{[2.0 \cdot 1 + 1.5(1 - 1)]^2} = \frac{3.0}{4.0} = 0.75$$

which is less than 1. This equilibrium is stable (Figure 3.1.11). Biologically, any population that begins with a positive fraction of mutants will be taken over by mutants.

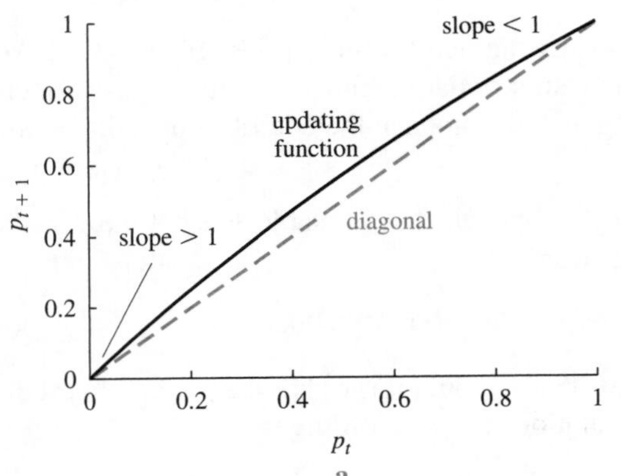

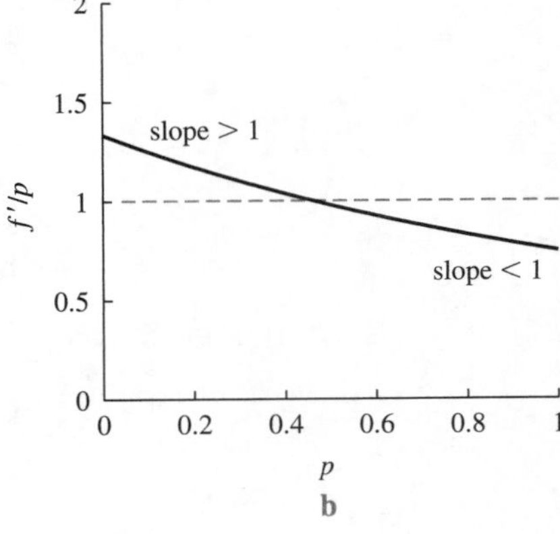

FIGURE 3.1.11
The discrete-time dynamical system for the fraction of mutants and its derivative

Example 3.1.5 Using the Derivative to Check Stability: The Selection Model with Inferior Mutants

In the case with $s = 1.5$ and $r = 2.0$, the updating function is

$$f(p) = \frac{1.5p}{1.5p + 2.0(1-p)}$$

The derivative (Example 2.6.4) is

$$f'(p) = \frac{3.0}{[1.5p + 2.0(1-p)]^2}$$

With these parameter values, $f'(0) = 0.75 < 1$ and $f'(1) = 1.333 > 1$. The $p^* = 0$ equilibrium is stable and the $p^* = 1$ equilibrium is unstable. When the wild type has an advantage ($r > s$), mutants cannot invade.

Example 3.1.6 Stability of the Medication Discrete-Time Dynamical System

Consider the discrete-time dynamical system for medication concentration in the bloodstream

$$M_{t+1} = 0.5M_t + 1.0$$

describing a patient who is administered 1.0 unit of medication each day but also, each day, uses up half of the previous amount (Example 1.5.4). The equilibrium concentration is 2.0. Because the updating function is linear with slope $0.5 < 1$, this equilibrium is stable (Figure 3.1.12).

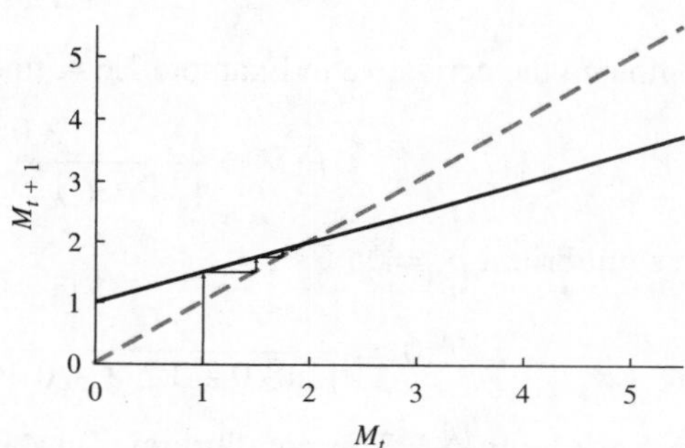

FIGURE 3.1.12
Stability of the medication discrete-time dynamical system

Example 3.1.7 Stability of the Medication Discrete-time Dynamical System if Run Backwards

What happens if we run this system backwards in time? The backwards discrete-time dynamical system can be found by solving for M_t as

$$M_t = 2.0(M_{t+1} - 1) = 2.0M_{t+1} - 2.0$$

The backwards updating function is

$$B(M) = 2.0M - 2.0$$

It shares the equilibrium at 2.0 (Figure 3.1.13). However, because the graph of the backwards updating function (the inverse function) is the mirror image across the diagonal, the slope at the equilibrium is the reciprocal of 0.5, or 2.0; in symbols,

$$B'(M) = 2.0$$

An equilibrium that is stable when time runs forward is *unstable* when time runs backwards.

Example 3.1.8 Stability of Limited Population

Consider a population where the per capita production is a decreasing function of the population size x according to

$$\text{per capita production} = \frac{2.0}{1 + 0.001x}$$

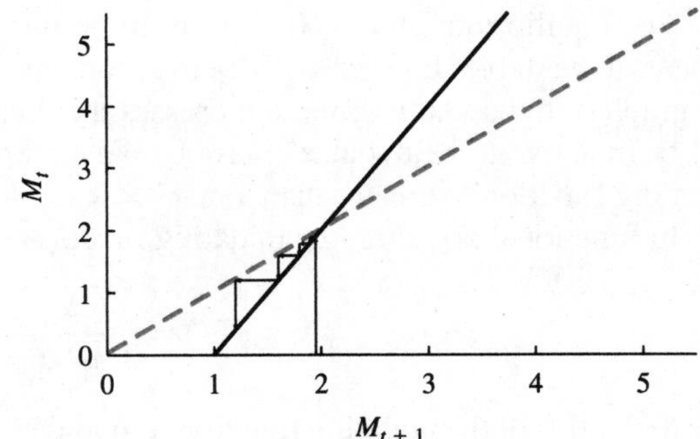

FIGURE 3.1.13

Stability of the medication discrete-time dynamical system if run backwards

The per capita production is 2.0 when $x=0$ and decreases as x becomes larger (Figure 3.1.14a). For example, when $x=500$,

$$\text{per capita production} = \frac{2.0}{1+0.001\cdot 500} \approx 1.333$$

Using the fact that the updated population is the per capita production (offspring per individual) times the old population (the number of individuals), the discrete-time

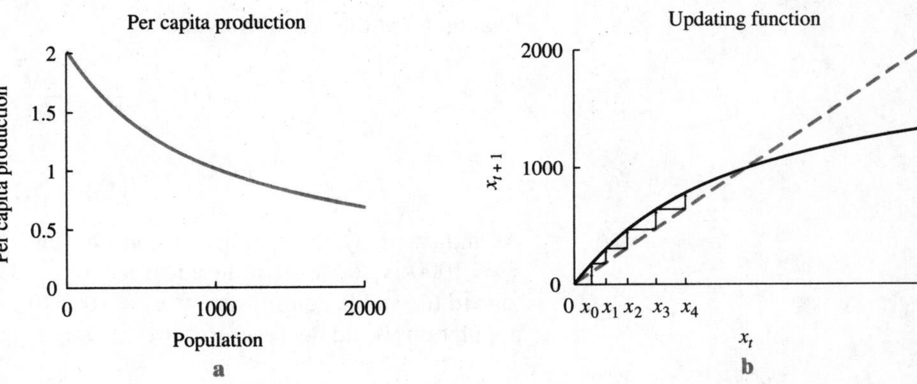

FIGURE 3.1.14

A discrete-time dynamical system describing competition

dynamical system for this population is

$$x_{t+1} = (\text{per capita production}) \cdot x_t$$

$$x_{t+1} = \frac{2.0x_t}{1+0.001x_t}$$

(Figure 3.1.14b).

To find the equilibria, we follow Algorithm 1.5.

$x^* = \dfrac{2.0x^*}{1+0.001x^*}$	the original equation
$x^* - \dfrac{2.0x^*}{1+0.001x^*} = 0$	subtract to get unknowns on one side
$(1+0.001x^*)x^* - 2.0x^* = 0$	multiply both sides by $1+0.001x^*$
$x^*(1+0.001x^* - 2.0) = 0$	factor
$x^* = 0$ or $1+0.001x^* - 2.0 = 0$	set both factors equal to 0
$x^* = 0$ or $0.001x^* = 1$	begin isolating x^*
$x^* = 0$ or $x^* = 1000$	solve the second equation

The equilibrium $x^*=0$ corresponds to extinction. The equilibrium $x^*=1000$ is the point where per capita production has been so reduced by crowding that the population can only break even.

The equilibrium at $x^* = 0$ appears to be unstable, and the equilibrium at $x^* = 1$ appears to be stable (Figure 3.1.14b). In accord with the Graphical Criterion for stability, the graph of the updating function crosses the diagonal from below to above at $x^* = 0$ and from above to below at $x^* = 1000$. We therefore expect that the derivative of the updating function is greater than 1 at $x^* = 0$ and less than 1 at $x^* = 1000$.

In functional notation, the updating function is

$$f(x) = \frac{2.0x}{1 + 0.001x}$$

The derivative of the updating function, found with the quotient rule (Subsection 2.6.3), is

$$\begin{aligned} f'(x) &= \frac{(1 + 0.001x)\frac{d(2.0x)}{dx} - 2.0x\frac{d(1 + 0.001x)}{dx}}{(1 + 0.001x)^2} \\ &= \frac{2.0(1 + 0.001x) - 2.0x \cdot 0.001}{(1 + 0.001x)^2} \\ &= \frac{2.0}{(1 + 0.001x)^2} \end{aligned}$$

Evaluating at the equilibria yields

$$\begin{aligned} f'(0) &= \frac{2.0}{(1 + 0.001 \cdot 0)^2} = 2.0 \\ f'(1000) &= \frac{2.0}{(1 + 0.001 \cdot 1000)^2} = 0.5 \end{aligned}$$

As indicated by the graph, the equilibrium $x^* = 0$ is unstable and the equilibrium $x^* = 1000$ is stable. If reduced to a low level, this population would increase back toward the stable equilibrium at $x^* = 1000$. If artificially increased to a high level, the population would decrease toward the stable equilibrium at $x^* = 1000$.

Example 3.1.9 Stability of Limited Population with Lower Production

Consider a variant of the model in Example 3.1.8 where the per capita production is a decreasing function of the population size x according to

$$\text{per capita production} = \frac{1.0}{1 + 0.001x}$$

The per capita production is 1.0 when $x = 0$ and decreases as x becomes larger (Figure 3.1.15a). The discrete-time dynamical system for this population is

$$\begin{aligned} x_{t+1} &= (\text{per capita production}) \cdot x_t \\ x_{t+1} &= \frac{x_t}{1 + 0.001x_t} \end{aligned}$$

(Figure 3.1.15b).

To find the equilibria, we follow Algorithm 1.5.

$x^* = \dfrac{x^*}{1 + 0.001x^*}$	the original equation
$x^* - \dfrac{x^*}{1 + 0.001x^*} = 0$	subtract to get unknowns on one side
$(1 + 0.001x^*)x^* - x^* = 0$	multiply both sides by $1 + 0.001x^*$
$x^*(1 + 0.001x^* - 1) = 0$	factor
$x^* \cdot 0.001x^* = 0$	simplify

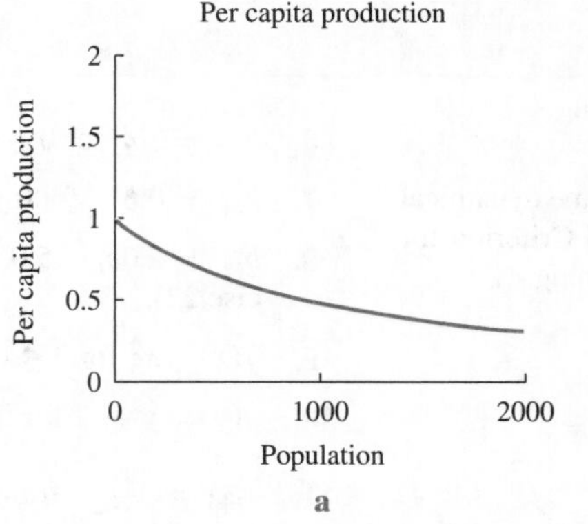

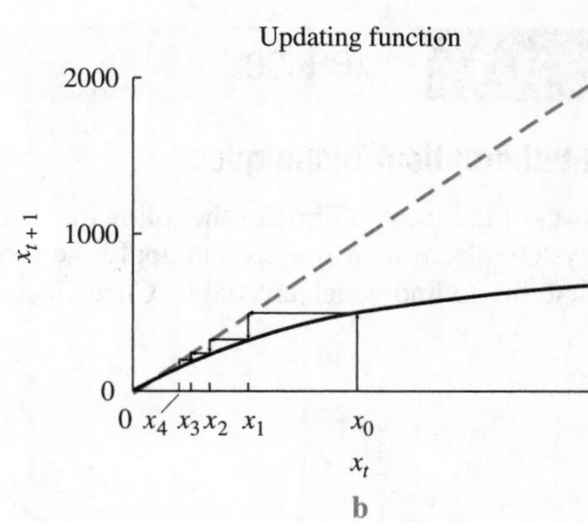

FIGURE 3.1.15
A discrete-time dynamical system with reduced per capita production

This has only a single equilibrium at $x^* = 0$ corresponding to extinction.

In functional notation, the updating function is

$$f(x) = \frac{x}{1 + 0.001x}$$

The derivative of the updating function, found with the quotient rule (see Section 2.6, pp. 186–194), is

$$\begin{aligned} f'(x) &= \frac{(1 + 0.001x)\frac{dx}{dx} - x\frac{d(1 + 0.001x)}{dx}}{(1 + 0.001x)^2} \\ &= \frac{(1 + 0.001x) - x \cdot 0.001}{(1 + 0.001x)^2} \\ &= \frac{1}{(1 + 0.001x)^2} \end{aligned}$$

Evaluating at the equilibrium yields

$$f'(0) = \frac{1}{(1 + 0.001 \cdot 0)^2} = 1.0$$

The updating function is tangent to the diagonal at the equilibrium $x^* = 0$, meaning that we cannot determine the stability from the slope criterion. By more carefully examining the function, we see that the graph of the updating function lies below the diagonal for $x > 0$. Algebraically,

$$f(x) = \frac{x}{1 + 0.001x} < x$$

because the denominator is greater than 1 for $x > 0$. Therefore, any positive population decreases, and the equilibrium $x^* = 0$ is stable.

Summary We used cobwebbing and logic to derive two criteria for the stability of equilibria. When the updating function crosses the diagonal from below to above, initial conditions both above and below the equilibrium are pushed away, making the equilibrium unstable (Graphical Criterion for stability). For the updating function to cross from below to above, the slope at the equilibrium must be greater than 1 (Slope Criterion for stability). The opposite occurs at stable equilibria, where the updating function crosses from above to below and has slope less than 1. In the special case that the slope is exactly equal to 1, the equilibrium might be neither stable nor unstable.

3.1 Exercises

Mathematical Techniques

1–4 ▪ Find the equilibria of the following discrete-time dynamical systems from their graphs and apply the Graphical Criterion for stability to find which are stable. Check by cobwebbing.

1.

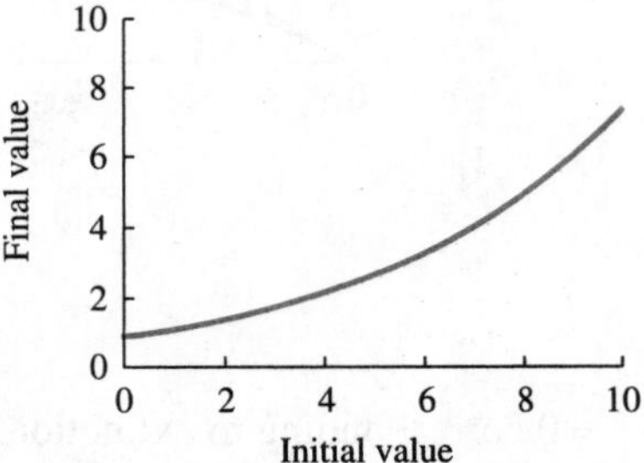

2.

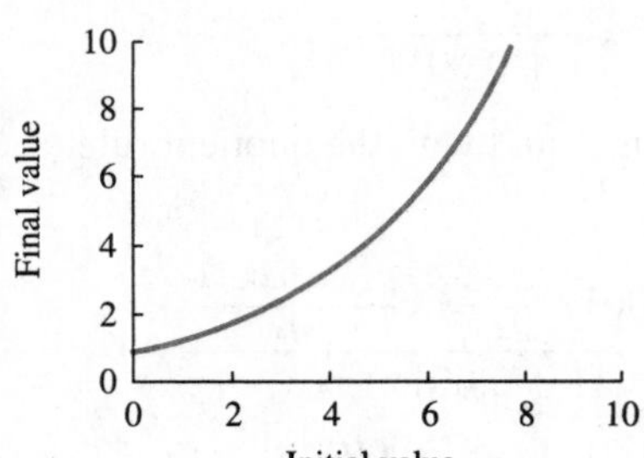

3.

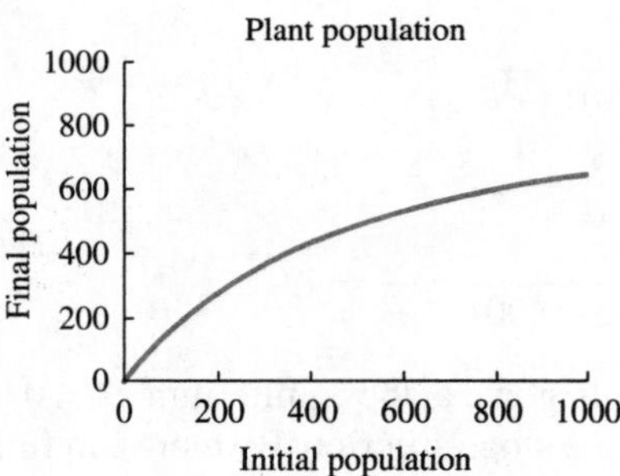

4.

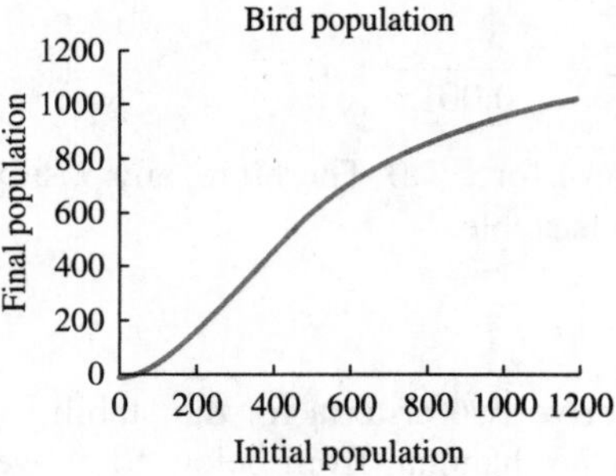

5–12 ▪ Graph the following discrete-time dynamical systems, find the equilibria algebraically, and check whether the stability derived from the Slope Criterion for stability matches that found with cobwebbing.

5. $c_{t+1} = 0.5c_t + 8.0$, for $0 \le c_t \le 30$ (from Section 1.6, Exercise 19).

6. $b_{t+1} = 3b_t$, for $0 \le b_t \le 10$ (from Section 1.6, Exercise 20).

7. $b_{t+1} = 0.3b_t$, for $0 \le b_t \le 10$ (from Section 1.6, Exercise 21).

8. $b_{t+1} = 2.0b_t - 5.0$, for $0 \le b_t \le 10$ (from Section 1.6, Exercise 22).

9. $f(x) = x^2$ for $0 \le x \le 2$ (from Section 1.6, Exercise 17).

10. $g(y) = y^2 - 1$ for $0 \le y \le 2$ (from Section 1.6, Exercise 18).

11. $x_{t+1} = \dfrac{x_t}{1 + x_t}$ (from Section 1.6, Exercise 29).

12. $x_{t+1} = -1 + 4x_t - 3x_t^2 + x_t^3$ (the only equilibrium is $x^* = 1$).

13–18 ▪ The unusual equilibrium in the text has an updating function that lies below the diagonal both to the left and to the right of the equilibrium. There are several other ways in which an updating function can intersect the diagonal at an equilibrium. In each case, cobweb starting from points to the left and to the right of the equilibrium, and describe the stability.

13. Graph an updating function that lies above the diagonal both to the left and to the right of an equilibrium.

14. Graph an updating function that is tangent to the diagonal at an equilibrium but crosses from below to above. Show by cobwebbing that the equilibrium is unstable. What is the second derivative at the equilibrium?

15. Graph an updating function that is tangent to the diagonal at an equilibrium but crosses from above to below. Show by cobwebbing that the equilibrium is stable. What is the second derivative at the equilibrium?

16. Sketch the graph of an updating function that has a corner at an equilibrium and is stable.

17. Sketch the graph of an updating function that has a corner at an equilibrium and is unstable.

18. Sketch the graph of an updating function that has a corner at an equilibrium and is neither stable nor unstable.

19–20 ▪ Another peculiarity of an updating function that is tangent to the diagonal at an equilibrium is that slight changes in the graph can produce big changes in the number of equilibria. The following exercises are based on Figure 3.1.10.

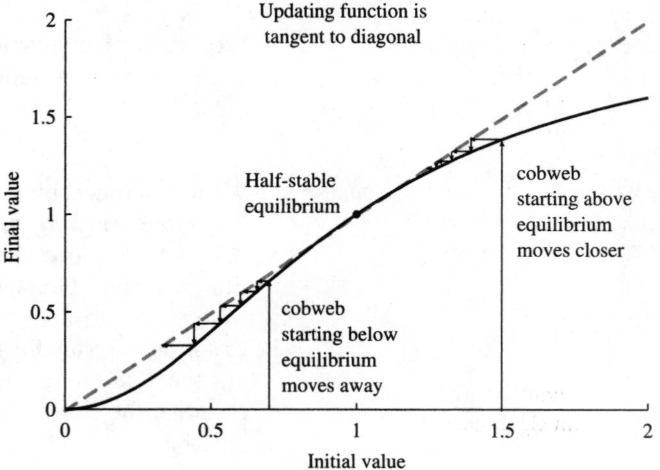

19. Move the curve slightly down (while keeping the diagonal in the same place). How many equilibria are there now? What happens when you cobweb starting from a point at the right-hand edge of the figure?

20. Move the curve slightly up (again keeping the diagonal in the same place). How many equilibria are there? Describe their stability.

21–22 ▪ Find the inverse of each of the following updating functions, and compute the slope of both the original updating function and the derivative at the equilibrium.

21. The updating function $f(x) = \frac{x}{1+x}$ (as in Exercise 11).

22. The updating function $f(x) = \frac{x}{x-1}$ (as in Section 1.6, Exercise 30).

Applications

23–26 ▪ Recall the updating function for the fraction p of mutant bacteria given by

$$f(p) = \frac{sp}{sp + r(1-p)}$$

where s is the per capita production of the mutant and r is the per capita production of the wild type. Find the derivative in the following cases, and evaluate at the equilibria $p^* = 0$ and $p^* = 1$. Are the equilibria stable?

23. $s = 1.2, r = 2.0$

24. $s = 3.0, r = 1.2$

25. $s = 1.5, r = 1.5$

26. In general (without substituting numerical values for s and r). Can both equilibria be stable? What happens if $r = s$?

27–28 ▪ Find the equilibrium population of bacteria in the following cases with supplementation. Graph the updating function for each, and use the Slope Criterion for stability to check the stability.

27. A population of bacteria has per capita production $r = 0.6$, and 1.0×10^6 bacteria are added each generation (as in Section 1.9, Exercise 35).

28. A population of bacteria has per capita production $r = 0.2$, and 5.0×10^6 bacteria are added each generation (as in Section 1.9, Exercise 36).

29–30 ▪ A lab is growing and harvesting a culture of valuable bacteria described by the discrete-time dynamical system

$$b_{t+1} = rb_t - h$$

The bacteria have per capita production r, and h are harvested each generation (as in Section 1.9, Exercises 49 and 50). Graph the updating function for each, and use the Slope Criterion for stability to check the stability.

29. Suppose that $r = 1.5$ and $h = 1.0 \times 10^6$.

30. Without setting r and h to particular values, find the equilibrium algebraically. When is the equilibrium stable?

31–32 ▪ The model describing the dynamics of the concentration of medication in the bloodstream,

$$M_{t+1} = 0.5M_t + 1.0$$

becomes nonlinear if the fraction of medication used is a function of the concentration (as in Section 1.10, Exercise 39). In each case, use the Slope Criterion for stability to check the stability of the equilibrium.

31. The nonlinear discrete-time dynamical system

$$M_{t+1} = M_t - \frac{0.5}{1.0 + 0.1M_t} M_t + 1.0$$

(studied in Section 1.10, Exercise 39).

32. The nonlinear discrete-time dynamical system

$$M_{t+1} = M_t - \frac{1.0}{1.0 + 0.1M_t} M_t + 1.0$$

How does this differ from the model in Exercise 31? Why is the equilibrium smaller?

33–36 ▪ An equilibrium that is stable when time goes forward should be unstable when time goes backwards. Find the inverses of the updating functions associated with the following discrete-time dynamical systems, and find the derivative at the equilibria.

33. $c_{t+1} = 0.5c_t + 8.0$, for $0 \le c_t \le 30$ (as in Exercise 5).

34. $b_{t+1} = 3b_t$ (as in Exercise 6).

35. $x_{t+1} = \frac{2x_t}{1 + 0.001x_t}$ (Example 3.1.8).

36. $p_{t+1} = \frac{2p_t}{2p_t + (1 - p_t)}$ (the selection system with $s = 2$ and $r = 1$).

37–38 ▪ Consider a population x_t with per capita production $r\frac{x_t}{1.0 + x_t^2}$. After writing the discrete-time dynamical system, do the following for the given values of the parameter r.

a. Find the equilibria.

b. Graph the updating function.

c. Indicate which equilibria are stable and which are unstable, and check via the Slope Criterion for stability.

d. Describe in words how the population would behave.

37. $r = 1.0$

38. $r = 2.5$

39–42 ▪ Consider the discrete-time dynamical system for a heart studied in Section 1.11.

$$V_{t+1} = \begin{cases} cV_t & \text{if } cV_t > V_c \\ cV_t + u & \text{if } cV_t \le V_c \end{cases}$$

where V is measured in millivolts. In each case, sketch the updating function. Why is the equilibrium stable when it exists?

39. $V_c = 20.0$ mV, $u = 10.0$ mV, $c = 0.5$

40. $V_c = 20.0$ mV, $u = 10.0$ mV, $c = 0.6$

41. $V_c = 20.0$ mV, $u = 10.0$ mV, $c = 0.7$

42. $V_c = 20.0$ mV, $u = 10.0$ mV, $c = 0.8$

Computer Exercises

43. Consider the discrete-time dynamical system found in Section 1.10, Exercise 48. In that exercise, there were two cultures, 1 and 2. In culture 1, the mutant does better than the wild type, and in culture 2, the wild type does better than the mutant. In particular, suppose that $s = 2.0$ and $r = 0.3$ in culture 1, and that $s = 0.6$ and $r = 2.0$ in culture 2. Define updating functions f_1 and f_2 to describe the dynamics in the two cultures. The overall updating function after mixing equal amounts from the two is

$$f(p) = \frac{f_1(p) + f_2(p)}{2}$$

a. Write the updating function explicitly.

b. Find the equilibria.

c. Find the derivative of the updating function.

d. Evaluate the stability of the equilibrium.

44. Consider again the following discrete-time dynamical systems (Section 1.9, Exercise 51). Check the stability of the equilibria.

a. $x_{t+1} = \cos(x_t)$

b. $y_{t+1} = \sin(y_t)$

c. $z_{t+1} = \sin(z_t) + \cos(z_t)$

45. Consider the discrete-time dynamical system

$$z_{t+1} = a^{z_t}$$

(thanks to Larry Okun). We will study this for different values of a.

a. Follow the dynamics starting from initial condition $z_0 = 1.0$ for $a = 1.0, 1.1, 1.2, 1.3, 1.4$. Keep running the system until it seems to reach an equilibrium.

b. Do the same, but increase a slowly past a critical value of about 1.4446679. Solutions should creep up for a while and then increase very quickly. Graph the updating function for values above and below the critical value and try to explain what is going on.

c. At the critical value, the slope of the updating function is 1 at the equilibrium. Show that this occurs with $a = e^{1/e}$. What is the equilibrium?

46. Consider a population with

$$\text{per capita production } = r\frac{x_t}{1.0 + x_t^2}$$

a. Write the discrete-time dynamical system.

b. Set $r = 3$ and $x_0 = 2$. Compute the solution until it gets close to an equilibrium and record this value.

c. Decrease r to 2.9. Use the equilibrium found with $r = 3$ as an initial condition and compute the solution until it approaches an equilibrium. Record this value.

d. Continue decreasing r down to $r = 1$, using the last equilibrium as the initial condition. What happens when r crosses 2?

e. If this were a real population and r were a measure of the quality of habitat, how would you interpret this behavior?

f. Follow the same procedure, but start with $r = 1$ and increase r to 3.

g. Can you explain what is going on?

3.2 More Complicated Dynamics

The derivative or slope of an updating function determines whether an equilibrium is stable or unstable. The Slope Criterion for stability tells how to assess stability by checking whether the slope is greater than or less than 1. We have yet, however, to consider cases where the slope of the updating function is **negative** at an equilibrium. By studying several such cases, we will see that rather exotic behaviors are possible. Using the idea of **qualitative dynamical systems,** where we approximate a nonlinear discrete-time dynamical system with its **tangent line approximation** at an equilibrium, we will find a general condition that includes these new cases.

The Logistic Dynamical System

In the previous section, we looked at a model where large population size reduced per capita production according to

$$\text{per capita production} = \frac{2.0}{1 + 0.001x}$$

(Example 3.1.8). Another widely studied model is the **logistic dynamical system** (introduced in Section 1.10, Exercise 43). In this model, the per capita production of a population decreases linearly with population size according to

$$\text{per capita production} = r\left(1 - \frac{N}{K}\right)$$

where N represents population size. The parameter r is the greatest possible production, and K is the maximum possible population. For populations greater than K, the per capita production is assumed to be 0. Using the fact that the new population is the per capita production times the old population, we find that the discrete-time dynamical system for the logistic dynamical system is

$$N_{t+1} = r\left(1 - \frac{N_t}{K}\right) N_t$$

To make the algebra simpler, we define the new variable

$$x_t = \frac{N_t}{K}$$

to represent the fraction of the maximum possible population. If K is 1000, a population of $N_t = 500$ corresponds to the fraction $x_t = 0.5$. We can write the discrete-time dynamical system for the x_t as

$$\begin{aligned} x_{t+1} &= \frac{N_{t+1}}{K} \\ &= \frac{r\left(1 - \frac{N_t}{K}\right) N_t}{K} \\ &= r(1 - x_t)x_t \end{aligned}$$

The factors on the right hand side are usually written in a different order, giving the logistic dynamical system

$$x_{t+1} = rx_t(1 - x_t) \tag{3.2.1}$$

To understand these diagrams, we begin by finding the equilibria by setting $x_t = x_{t+1} = x^*$ and solving with Algorithm 1.5.

$$\begin{aligned} x^* &= rx^*(1 - x^*) && \text{the original equation} \\ x^* - rx^*(1 - x^*) &= 0 && \text{place unknowns on one side} \\ x^*(1 - r(1 - x^*)) &= 0 && \text{factor} \\ x^* = 0 \quad &\text{or} \quad 1 - r(1 - x^*) = 0 && \text{set both factors equal to 0} \\ x^* = 0 \quad &\text{or} \quad x^* = 1 - \frac{1}{r} && \text{solve each piece} \end{aligned}$$

Do these solutions make sense? The first, $x^* = 0$, is the extinction equilibrium that shows up in all population models without immigration. The second equilibrium depends on the maximum per capita production r. If $r < 1$, this equilibrium is negative and biologically impossible. A population with a *maximum* per capita production less than 1 cannot replace itself and will go extinct. For larger values of r, the equilibrium becomes larger, a result consistent with the fact that a population with higher potential production grows to a larger value.

We will examine four cases: $r = 0.5$, $r = 1.5$, $r = 2.5$, and $r = 3.5$. The equilibria and their behavior as deduced from cobwebbing are summarized in the following table.

r	x^*	Stability
0.5	0	Stable
1.5	0	Unstable
1.5	$1-\frac{1}{1.5}\approx 0.333$	Stable
2.5	0	Unstable
2.5	$1-\frac{1}{2.5}=0.600$	Stable (oscillates)
3.5	0	Unstable
3.5	$1-\frac{1}{3.5}\approx 0.714$	Unstable (oscillates)

The results match the Graphical Criterion for stability pretty well until $r=3.5$ (Figure 3.2.16d). The updating function crosses the diagonal from above to below at the positive equilibrium, so we expect this equilibrium to be stable. However, a solution starting near the positive equilibrium $x^*\approx 0.714$ moves away, and it does so by jumping back and forth. Closer examination of the case with $r=2.5$ (Figure 3.2.16c) reveals that solutions jump back and forth as they approach the equilibrium at $x^*=0.6$. What is going on?

Qualitative Dynamical Systems

An equilibrium where the updating function has a positive slope is stable precisely when that slope is less than 1. These results match the behavior of the bacterial growth model

$$b_{t+1}=rb_t$$

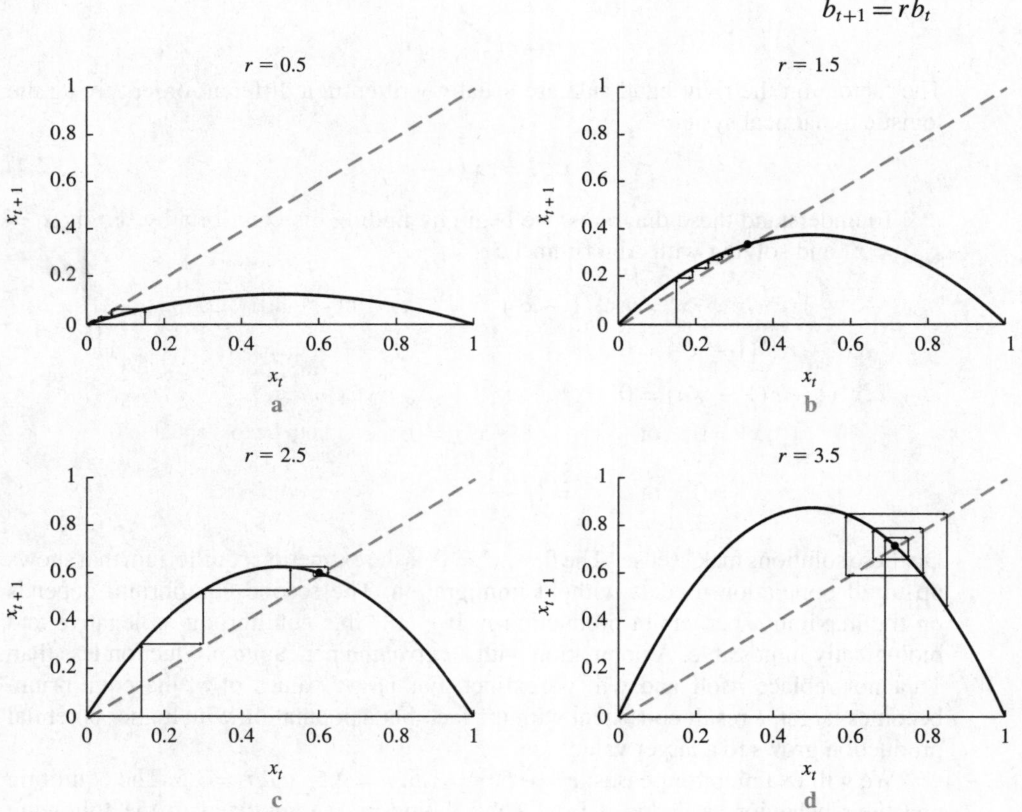

FIGURE 3.2.16
The behavior of the logistic dynamical system

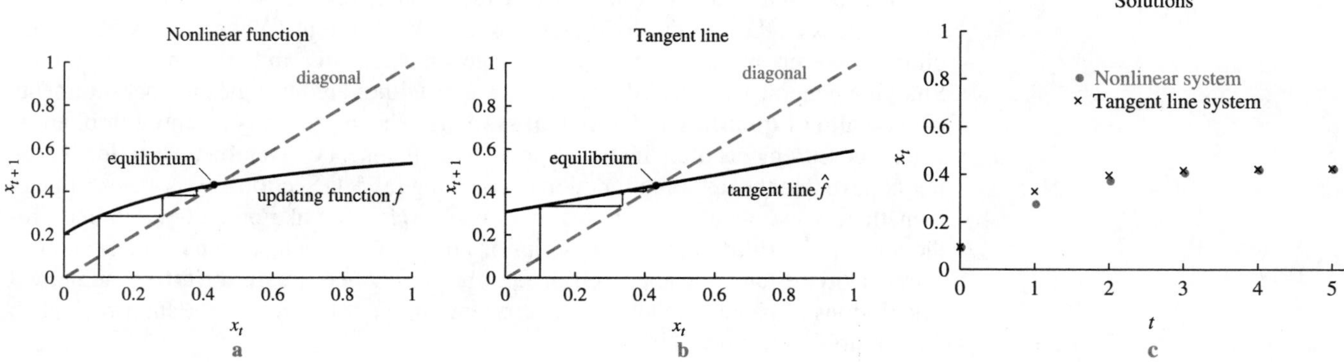

FIGURE 3.2.17
Comparing an updating function with its tangent line

at the $b^* = 0$ equilibrium. This linear system is stable precisely when the slope r is less than 1.

What happens if $r < 0$? Of course, this case does not make biological sense, but it will provide insight into what happens near equilibria with negative slopes, as found in Figure 3.2.16c and d. Why should this work? This is an example of the central idea in calculus: replacing problems about curves with simpler problems about lines.

Consider a nonlinear discrete-time dynamical system $x_{t+1} = f(x_t)$ and its tangent line $\hat{f}(x_t)$ at an equilibrium x^* (Figure 3.2.17). Because the graph of $\hat{f}(x_t)$ is the tangent line at the equilibrium x^* of the original system, the two systems share the equilibrium at x^* and have the same slope. Furthermore, solutions remain very close to each other (Figure 3.2.17c). According to the Slope Criterion for stability, the equilibrium of $\hat{f}$ should be stable precisely when the equilibrium of f is (Figure 3.2.17). Starting from a point near x^*, the solutions are nearly identical because the tangent line lies so close to the curve (Figure 3.2.18).

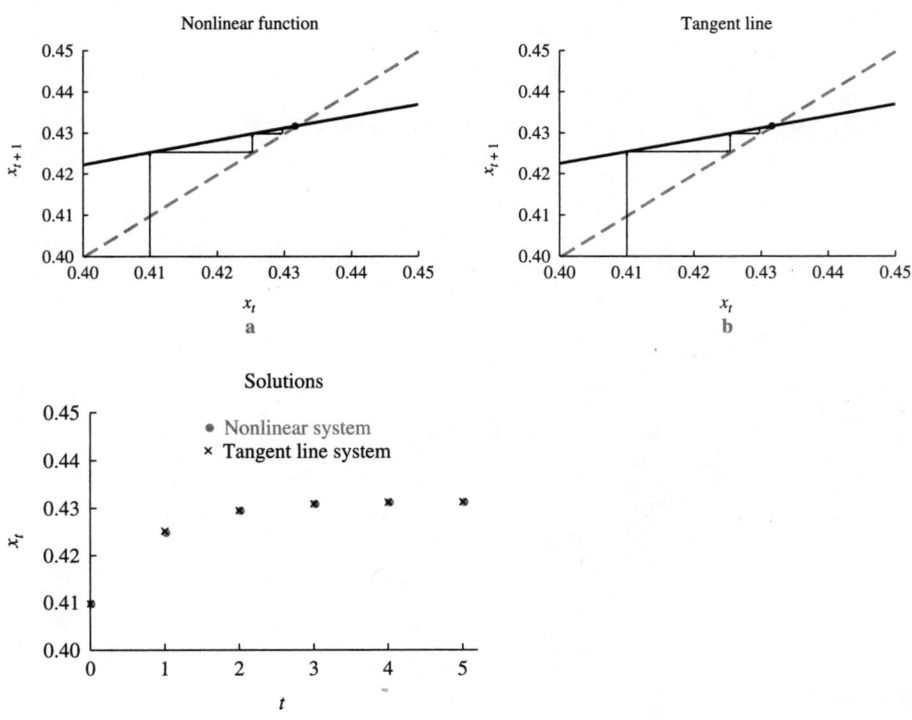

FIGURE 3.2.18
Zooming in on an updating function and its tangent line

The original updating function and the tangent line are not exactly equal. The exact values in the solution will therefore also be different. When we ask about stability, however, we are concerned with general behavior rather than exact values. Studying general aspects of dynamical systems without requiring exact measurements is the realm of **qualitative dynamical systems.** The approach is essential in biology, where measurements often include a great deal of noise. For example, we neither know nor believe that the updating function for the lung model (Section 1.9) is *exactly* linear. Nonetheless, we would like to use the linear model to make predictions. Some predictions are **qualitative,** verbal descriptions of behavior such as "the concentration of chemical in the lung will approach an equilibrium." Others are **quantitative,** numerical descriptions of behavior such as "the concentration of chemical in the lung will reach 5.23 mmol/L after seven breaths."

The qualitative theory of dynamical systems requires comparing the dynamics produced by similar discrete-time dynamical systems. If two nearly indistinguishable discrete-time dynamical systems produce qualitatively different dynamics, the underlying biological system might be highly sensitive to small changes in conditions. Such situations do occur. In this chapter, we restrict our attention to cases where similar discrete-time dynamical systems produce qualitatively similar dynamics. Other cases are treated in more advanced texts on **bifurcation theory.**

Using this philosophy, we can try to figure out what happens at an equilibrium where the slope is negative by studying the linear bacterial growth model

$$b_{t+1} = rb_t$$

with unrealistic negative values for the per capita production r.

Example 3.2.1 The Consequences of "Negative" Per Capita Production: $r = -0.5$

If $r = -0.5$, the discrete-time dynamical system is

$$b_{t+1} = -0.5b_t$$

Starting from an initial condition of $b_0 = 0.5$, we find that the solution is

$$b_1 = -0.25$$
$$b_2 = 0.125$$
$$b_3 = -0.0625$$
$$b_4 = 0.03125$$

The absolute value decreases while the sign switches back and forth (Figure 3.2.19).

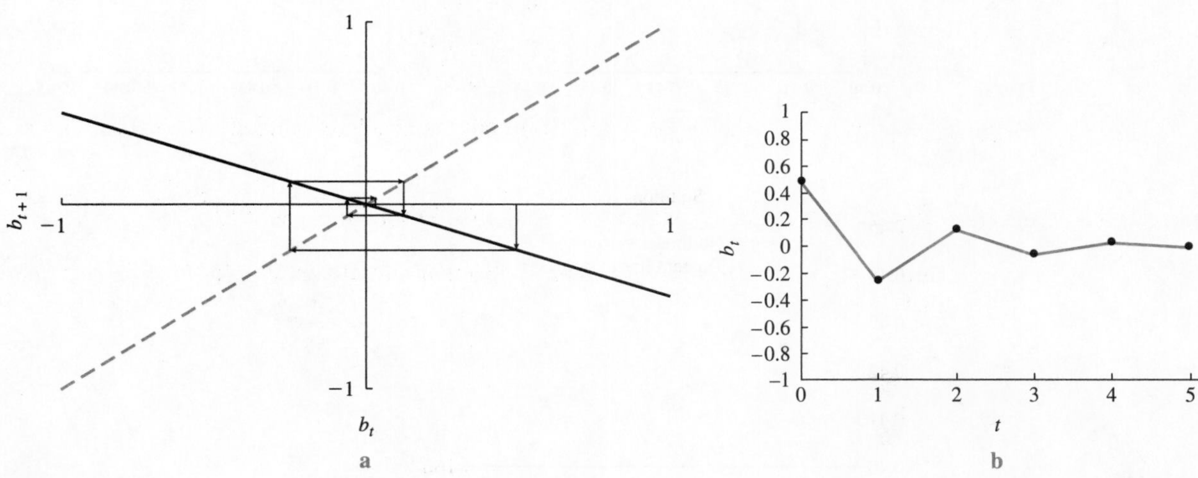

FIGURE 3.2.19
Cobwebbing and solutions with $r = -0.5$

Example 3.2.2 The Consequences of "Negative" Per Capita Production: $r = -0.9$

If $r = -0.9$, the discrete-time dynamical system is

$$b_{t+1} = -0.9b_t$$

Starting from an initial condition of $b_0 = 0.5$, we find that the solution is

$$b_1 = -0.45$$
$$b_2 = 0.405$$
$$b_3 = -0.3645$$
$$b_4 = 0.32805$$

The absolute value decreases slowly while the sign switches back and forth (Figure 3.2.20).

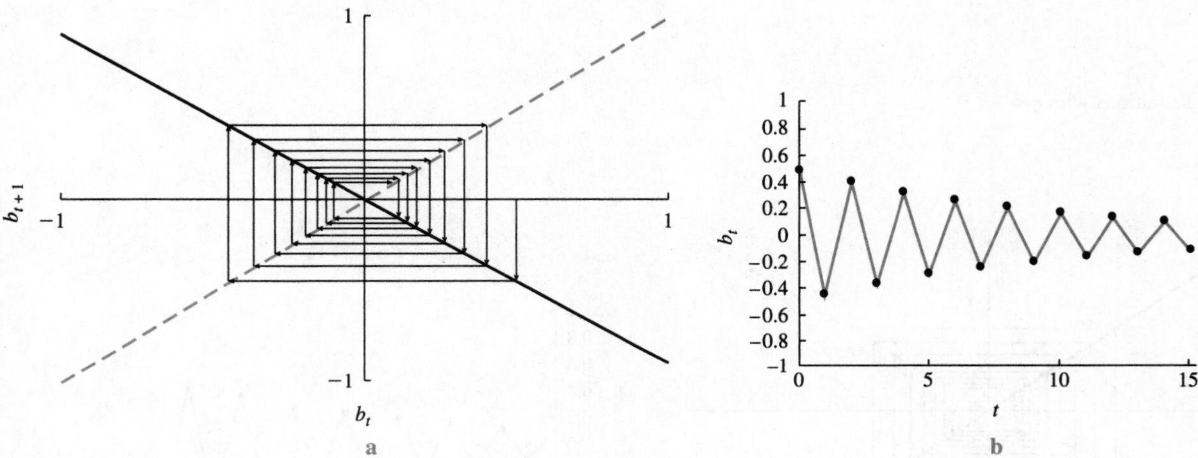

FIGURE 3.2.20
Cobwebbing and solutions with $r = -0.9$

Example 3.2.3 The Consequences of "Negative" Per Capita Production: $r = -2.0$

Suppose that $r = -2.0$. Starting from an initial condition of $b_0 = 0.02$, we find that the solution is

$$b_1 = -0.04$$
$$b_2 = 0.08$$
$$b_3 = -0.16$$
$$b_4 = 0.32$$

Again the sign switches back and forth, but the absolute value now increases (Figure 3.2.21).

Example 3.2.4 The Consequences of "Negative" Per Capita Production: $r = -1.1$

Finally, suppose that $r = -1.1$. Starting from an initial condition of $b_0 = 0.1$, we find that the solution is

$$b_1 = -0.11$$
$$b_2 = 0.121$$
$$b_3 = -0.1331$$
$$b_4 = 0.14641$$

The sign switches back and forth, and the absolute value increases slowly (Figure 3.2.22).

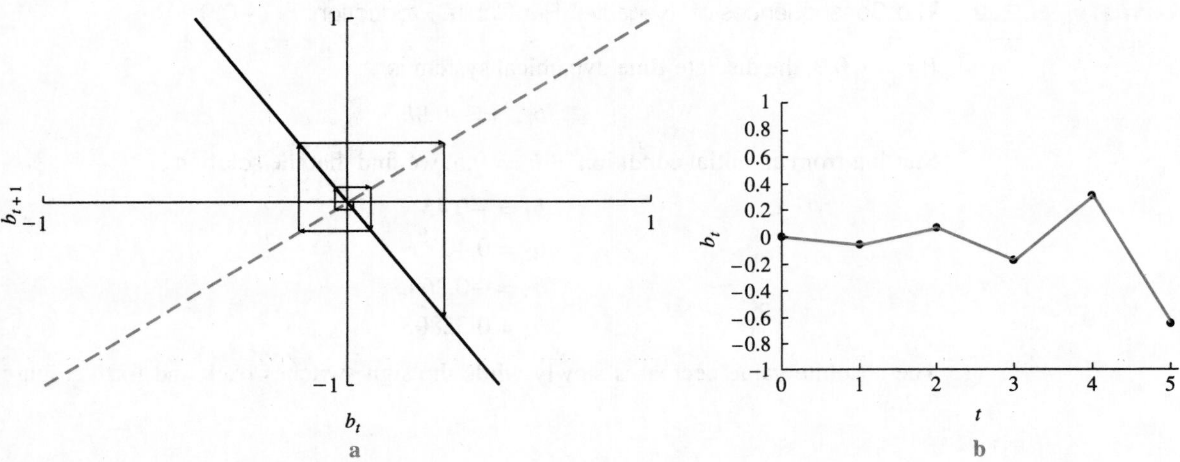

FIGURE 3.2.21

Cobwebbing and solutions with $r = -2.0$

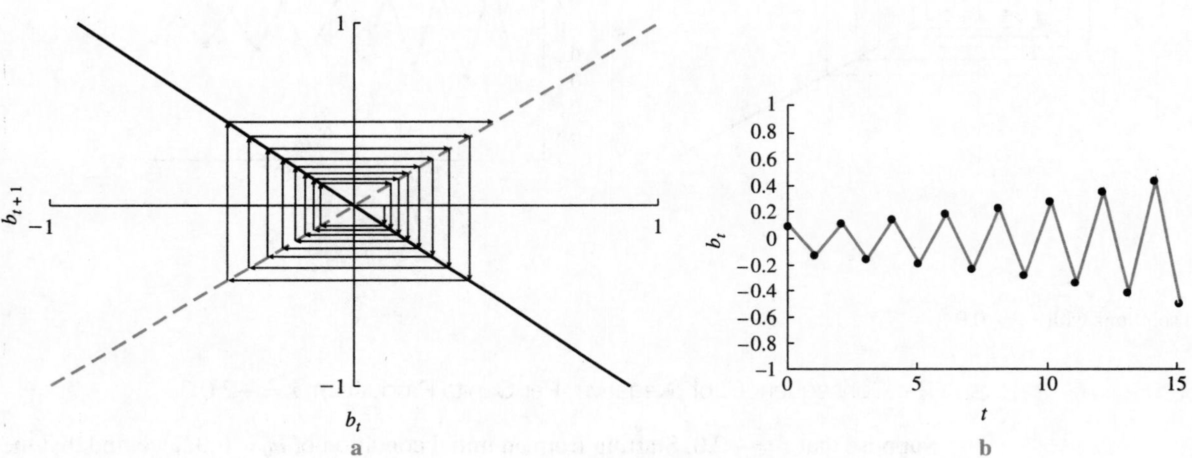

FIGURE 3.2.22

Cobwebbing and solutions with $r = -1.1$

With negative r, the system is stable when $r > -1$ and unstable when $r < -1$. Putting this together with the results with positive r gives

Behavior of solutions of $b_{t+1} = rb_t$

r	Stability	Behavior
$r > 1$	Unstable	Moves away from equilibrium
$0 < r < 1$	Stable	Moves toward equilibrium
$-1 < r < 0$	Stable	Oscillates toward equilibrium
$r < -1$	Unstable	Oscillates away from equilibrium

An equilibrium is stable if r is less than 1 in **absolute value,** or $|r| < 1$, and is unstable if r is greater than 1 in absolute value, or $|r| > 1$.

Because the behavior of a nonlinear dynamical system resembles that of its tangent line, we can extend these results to the following theorem.

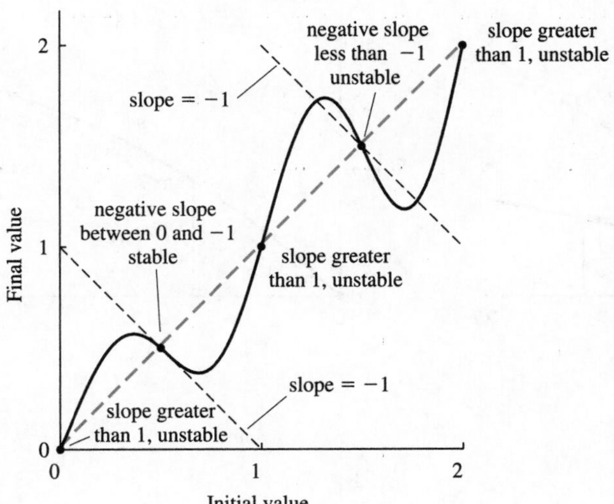

FIGURE 3.2.23

Applying the stability theorem for discrete-time dynamical systems

Theorem 3.1 Stability Theorem for Discrete-Time Dynamical Systems

Suppose that the discrete-time dynamical system

$$x_{t+1} = f(x_t)$$

has an equilibrium at x^*. Let $f'(x)$ be the derivative of f with respect to x. The equilibrium at x^* is stable if

$$|f'(x^*)| < 1$$

and is unstable if

$$|f'(x^*)| > 1$$

The proof depends on the Mean Value Theorem (Section 3.4).

Using this method, we can read off the stability of equilibria of more complicated discrete-time dynamical systems (Figure 3.2.23). By including lines with slope -1 on our graph in addition to the diagonal, we can see that the equilibrium at (0.5, 0.5) is stable because the slope is between 0 and -1, whereas the equilibrium at (1.5, 1.5) is unstable because the slope is less than -1.

Analysis of the Logistic Dynamical System

Do these results help make sense of the behavior of the logistic dynamical system? The derivative of the updating function is

$$
\begin{aligned}
f'(x) &= \frac{d}{dx} rx(1-x) && \text{derivative of updating function}\\
&= r\left[\frac{dx}{dx}(1-x) + \frac{d(1-x)}{dx}x\right] && \text{constant product rule and product rule}\\
&= r[(1-x) - x] && \text{evaluate derivatives of linear functions}\\
&= r(1-2x) && \text{combine terms}
\end{aligned}
$$

We next evaluate the derivative at the two equilibria. At $x^* = 0$,

$$f'(0) = r(1 - 2 \cdot 0) = r$$

According to the stability theorem for discrete-time dynamical systems, the equilibrium at 0 is stable if $r < 1$ and is unstable if $r > 1$. When $r > 1$, the derivative at the positive

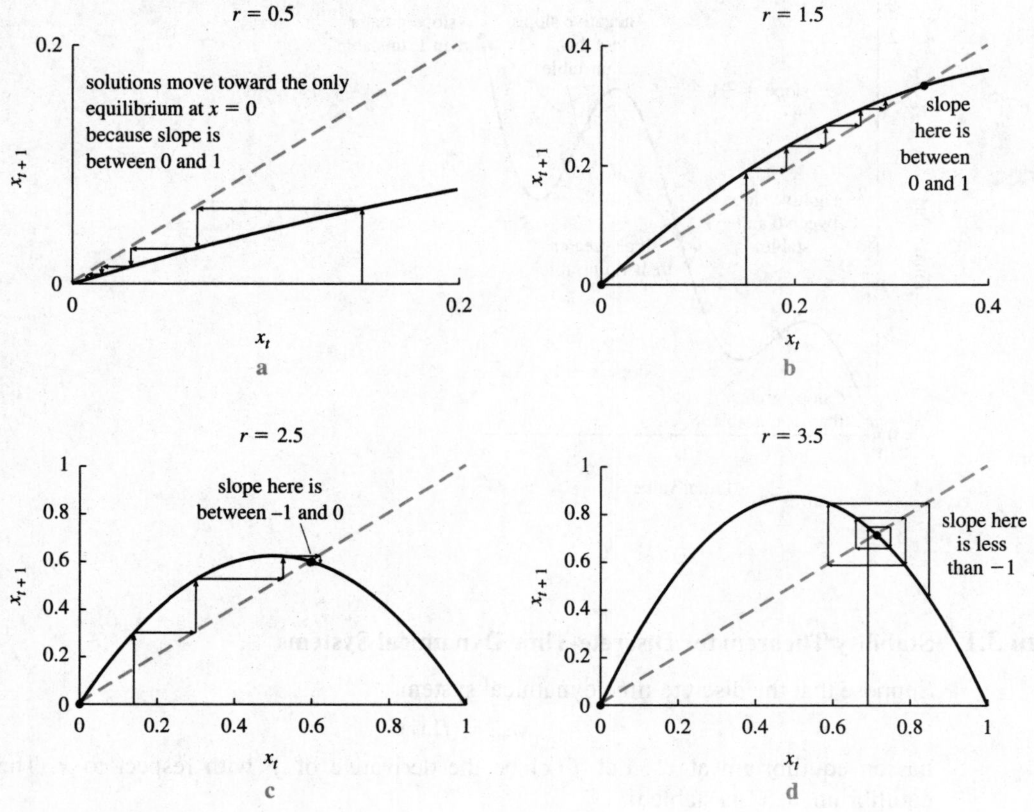

FIGURE 3.2.24
The behavior of the logistic dynamical system explained

equilibrium $x^* = 1 - \frac{1}{r}$ is

$$\begin{aligned} f'\left(1 - \frac{1}{r}\right) &= r\left[1 - 2\left(1 - \frac{1}{r}\right)\right] \\ &= r\left(1 - 2 + \frac{2}{r}\right) \\ &= r - 2r + \frac{2r}{r} \\ &= r - 2r + 2 \\ &= 2 - r \end{aligned}$$

The results are summarized in the following table and in Figure 3.2.24.

r	x^*	$f'(x^*)$	Stability
0.5	0	0.5	Stable
1.5	0	1.5	Unstable
1.5	0.333	0.5	Stable
2.5	0	2.5	Unstable
2.5	0.600	−0.5	Stable (oscillates)
3.5	0	3.5	Unstable
3.5	0.714	−1.5	Unstable (oscillates)

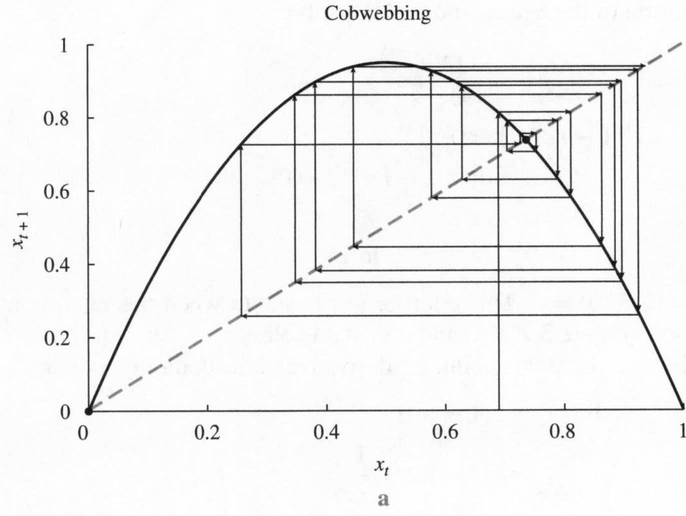

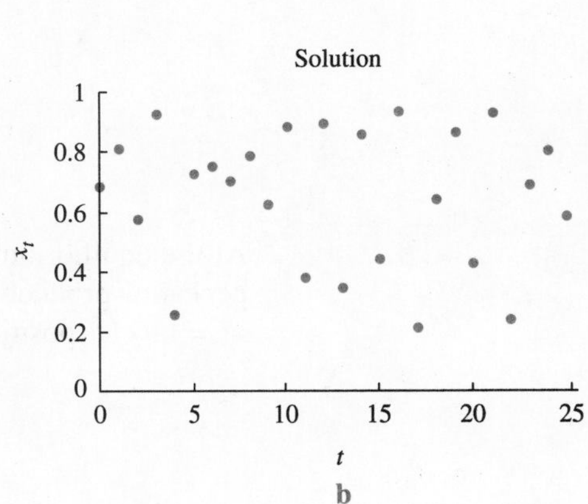

FIGURE 3.2.25
The long-term behavior of the logistic dynamical system with $r = 3.8$

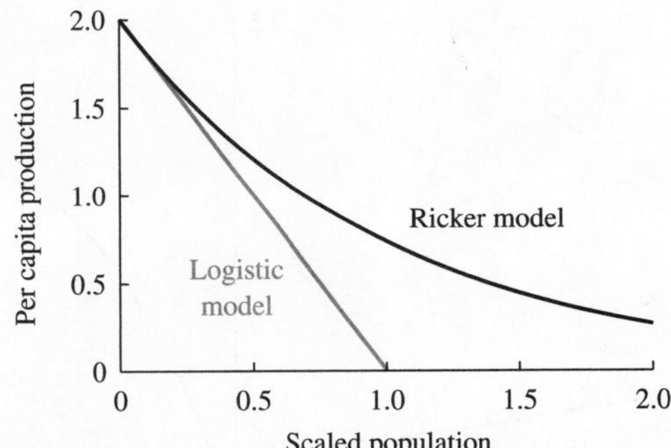

FIGURE 3.2.26
The per capita production in the Ricker and logistic models with $r = 2$

When $r = 3.5$, neither equilibrium is stable. This population has nowhere to settle down and will continue jumping around indefinitely. Some of the interesting dynamics that can result are shown in Figure 3.2.25. The solutions of this simple discrete-time dynamical system for $3.5 < r \leq 4$ are extremely complicated, including examples of **chaos** (Section 1.10, Exercise 47).

A commonly used model for reproduction in fisheries is the **Ricker model** defined by

$$x_{t+1} = r x_t e^{-x_t}$$

(introduced in Section 1.10, Exercise 45). The per capita production declines exponentially from a maximum of r as the population becomes larger. As in the logistic dynamical system, production decreases rapidly, but this model is a bit more realistic because per capita production never reaches zero (Figure 3.2.26). The updating function is the constant r multiplied by one of the gamma distributions we studied in "Applications," Section 2.8, p. 208 (Figure 3.2.27). If we write the updating function as

$$R(x) = r x e^{-x}$$

the first derivative is

$$R'(x) = r(1 - x)e^{-x}$$

(as in Example 2.8.7).

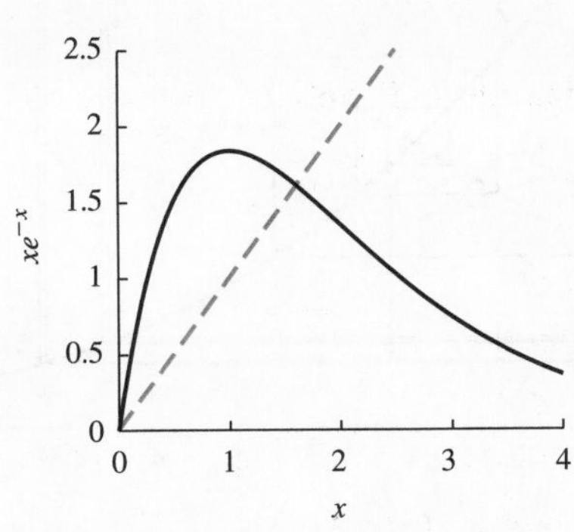

FIGURE 3.2.27
The Ricker discrete-time dynamical system with $r = 5.0$

Where are the equilibria of the Ricker model? We solve

$$
\begin{aligned}
x^* &= rx^*e^{-x^*} \\
x^* - rx^*e^{-x^*} &= 0 \\
x^*\left(1 - re^{-x^*}\right) &= 0 \\
x^* = 0 \quad &\text{or} \quad 1 - re^{-x^*} = 0 \\
x^* = 0 \quad &\text{or} \quad e^{x^*} = r \\
x^* = 0 \quad &\text{or} \quad x^* = \ln(r)
\end{aligned}
$$

At the equilibrium $x^* = 0$, $R'(0) = r$. This equilibrium is stable when the maximum per capita production $r < 1$ (Figure 3.2.28a) and is unstable otherwise. The equilibrium $x^* = \ln(r)$ is positive when $r > 1$. At this point, the derivative of the updating function is

$$
\begin{aligned}
R'(\ln(r)) &= r(1 - \ln(r))e^{-\ln(r)} \\
&= r(1 - \ln(r))\frac{1}{r} \\
&= 1 - \ln(r)
\end{aligned}
$$

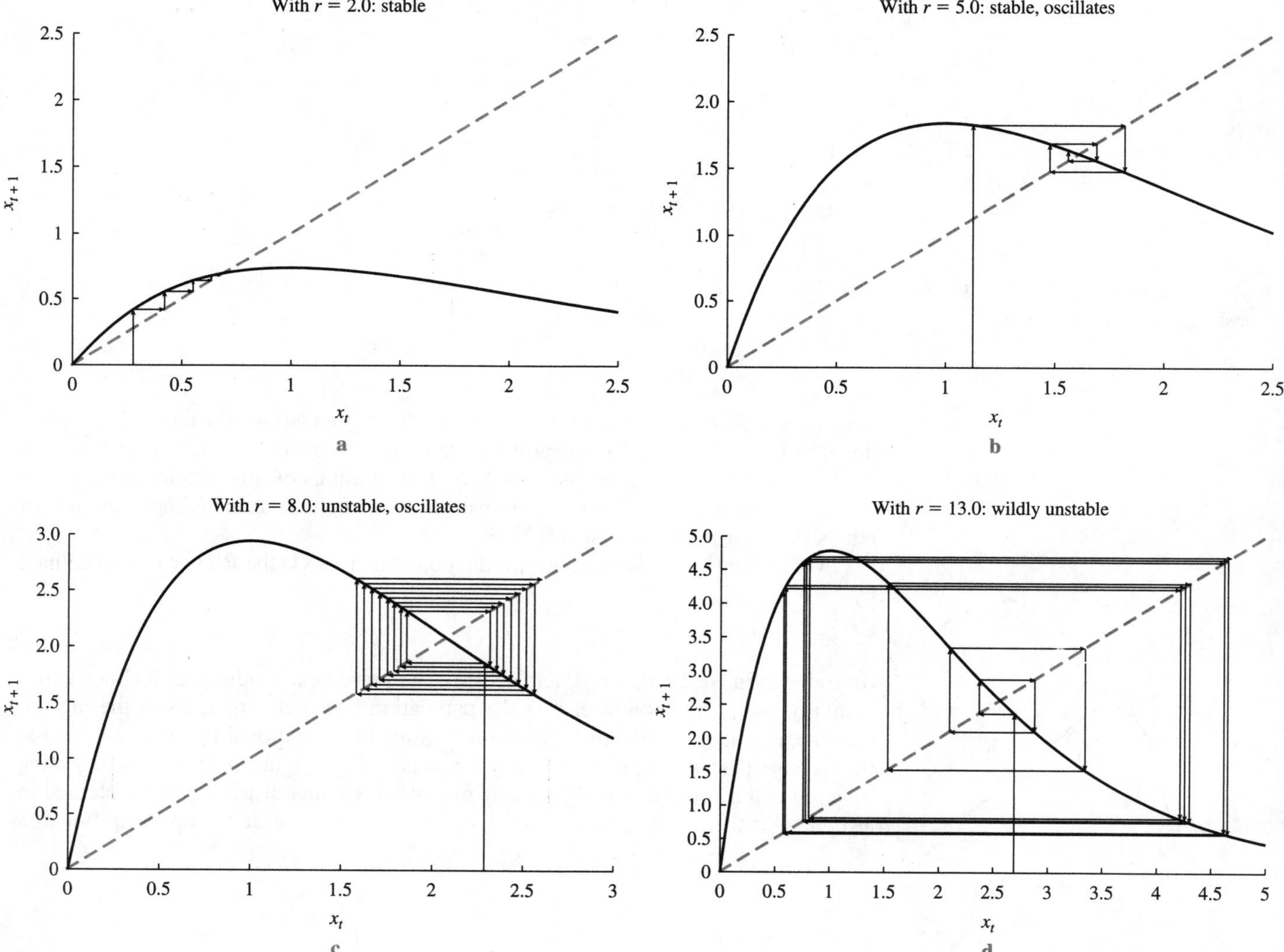

FIGURE 3.2.28
The dynamics of the Ricker model with various values of r

Results for various values of r are summarized in the following table.

r	x^*	$f'(x^*)$	Stability
0.5	0	0.5	Stable
2.0	0	2.0	Unstable
2.0	$\ln(2.0) \approx 0.693$	$1 - \ln(2.0) \approx 0.307$	Stable
4.0	0	4.0	Unstable
4.0	$\ln(4.0) \approx 1.386$	$1 - \ln(4.0) \approx -0.386$	Stable (oscillates)
8.0	0	8.0	Unstable
44.0	$\ln(8.0) \approx 2.079$	$1 - \ln(8.0) \approx -1.079$	Unstable (oscillates)
13.0	0	8.0	Unstable
13.0	$\ln(13.0) \approx 2.565$	$1 - \ln(13.0) \approx -1.565$	Unstable (oscillates)

As long as $\ln(r) < 2$, or $r < e^2 \approx 7.39$, the positive equilibrium is stable (Figure 3.2.28b). Like the logistic model, this discrete-time dynamical system produces unstable dynamics when the maximum possible per capita production is large (Figure 3.2.28c and d). In this case, fish can produce so many offspring that they destroy their resource base and induce a population crash in the following year.

Summary The approach of **qualitative dynamical systems** lets us think of behavior in general terms without depending on quantitative details about the discrete-time dynamical system. As an example, we compare the dynamics generated by a nonlinear discrete-time dynamical system with those generated by the tangent line at the equilibrium. Because stability of equilibria can be understood by studying linear discrete-time dynamical systems, we examined linear systems with negative slopes, finding that such systems oscillate. On the basis of these results, we stated the **stability theorem for discrete-time dynamical systems:** An equilibrium is stable if the *absolute value* of the slope is less than 1. We applied this condition to the **logistic dynamical system** and the **Ricker model** and found that there are parameter values with no stable equilibrium.

3.2 Exercises

Mathematical Techniques

1–4 ▪ Draw the tangent line approximating the given system at the specified equilibrium, and compare the cobweb diagrams. Use the stability theorem to check whether the equilibrium is stable.

1. The bacterial selection equation $p_{t+1} = \dfrac{1.5p_t}{1.5p_t + 2.0(1 - p_t)}$ at the equilibrium $p^* = 0$.
2. As in Exercise 1, but at the equilibrium $p^* = 1$.
3. $x_{t+1} = 1.5x_t(1 - x_t)$ at the equilibrium $x^* = 0$.
4. $x_{t+1} = 1.5x_t(1 - x_t)$ at the equilibrium $x^* = 1/3$.

5–8 ▪ Starting from the given initial condition, find the solution for five steps of each of the following.

5. $y_{t+1} = 1.2y_t$ with $y_0 = 2.0$. When will the value exceed 100?
6. $y_{t+1} = -1.2y_t$ with $y_0 = 2.0$. When will the value exceed 100?
7. $y_{t+1} = 0.8y_t$ with $y_0 = 2.0$. When will the value be less than 0.2?
8. $y_{t+1} = -0.8y_t$ with $y_0 = 2.0$. When will the value be between 0.0 and 0.2?

9–12 ▪ Consider the linear discrete-time dynamical system $y_{t+1} = 1.0 + m(y_t - 1.0)$. For each of the following values of m:

a. Find the equilibrium.

b. Graph and cobweb.

c. Compare your results with the stability condition.

9. $m = 0.9$

10. $m = 1.5$

11. $m = -0.5$

12. $m = -1.5$

13–16 ▪ The following discrete-time dynamical systems have slope of exactly -1 at the equilibrium. Check this, and then iterate the function for a few steps starting from near the equilibrium to see whether it is stable, unstable, or neither.

13. $x_{t+1} = 4 - x_t$ (as in Section 1.6, Exercise 10).

14. $x_{t+1} = \dfrac{x_t}{x_t - 1}$ for $x_t > 1$ (as in Section 1.6, Exercise 12).

15. $x_{t+1} = 3x_t(1 - x_t)$, the logistic system with $r = 3$.

16. $x_{t+1} = \dfrac{2}{1 + x_t^2}$ (the equilibrium is at $x^* = 1$).

17–18 ▪ Equilibria where the slope of the tangent line is exactly zero are also special. Show that the following systems satisfy this special relationship. What does this say about the stability of the equilibrium? (Think about a linear dynamical system with a slope of 0. How quickly do solutions approach the equilibrium?) Draw a cobweb diagram to illustrate these results.

17. The logistic dynamical system with $r = 2$.

18. The dynamical system $x_{t+1} = x_t e^{1-x_t}$ (equivalent to the Ricker model with $r = e$).

Applications

19–22 ▪ We have studied several systems where the fraction of medication absorbed depends on the concentration of medication in the bloodstream. These take the form

$$M_{t+1} = M_t - f(M_t)M_t + 1.0$$

where $f(M_t)$ is the fraction absorbed and 1.0 is the supplement. If the fraction absorbed increases, it seems possible that the equilibrium level will become unstable (high levels are rapidly reduced). For each of the following forms for $f(M_t)$, the equilibrium level is $M^* = 2$. Find the slope of the updating function at the equilibrium and check whether it is stable. In which cases does the solution oscillate?

19. $f(M_t) = \dfrac{M_t}{2 + M_t}$

20. $f(M_t) = \dfrac{M_t^2}{4 + M_t^2}$

21. $f(M_t) = \dfrac{M_t^4}{16 + M_t^4}$

22. $f(M_t) = \dfrac{M_t^8}{256 + M_t^8}$

23–26 ▪ Find values of r that satisfy the following conditions for the Ricker model. In each case, graph and cobweb.

23. The value of r where the positive equilibrium switches from having a positive to a negative slope.

24. One value of r between 1 and the value found in Exercise 23.

25. One value of r between the value found in Exercise 23 and $r = e^2$.

26. One value of r greater than $r = e^2$.

27–28 ▪ The logistic model quantifies a competitive interaction, where per capita production is a decreasing function of population size. In some situations, per capita production is enhanced by population size. For each of the following such cases:

a. Write the updating function.

b. Find the equilibria and their stability.

c. Graph the updating function and cobweb. Which equilibrium is stable?

d. Explain what this population is doing.

27. Per capita production $= 0.5 + 0.5b_t$.

28. Per capita production $= 0.5 + 0.5b_t^2$.

29–30 ▪ Consider a modified version of the logistic dynamical system $x_{t+1} = rx_t(1 - x_t^n)$. For the following values of n:

a. Sketch the updating function with $r = 2$.

b. Find the equilibria.

c. Find the derivative of the updating function at the equilibria.

d. For what values of r is the $x = 0$ equilibrium stable? For what values of r is the positive equilibrium stable?

29. $n = 2$

30. $n = 3$

31–32 ▪ Expanding oscillations can result from improperly tuned feedback systems. Suppose that a thermostat is supposed to keep a room at 20°C. Take the following steps to figure out what is happening in each of the given cases.

a. Suppose the temperature produced is a linear function of the temperature on the thermometer. Find this function.

b. You continue to respond to a temperature x°C above 20 by setting the thermostat to $(20 - x)$°C, and to a temperature x°C below 20° by setting the thermostat to $(20 + x)$°C. Find the temperature for the next few days.

c. Denote the temperature on day t by T_t. Find a formula for the thermostat setting z_t in response.

d. Use the answer to **a** to find T_{t+1}. Write the updating function.

e. Use the stability condition to describe what will happen in this room.

31. You come in one morning and find that the temperature is 21°C. To correct this, you move the thermostat down by 1°C to 19°C. But the next day the temperature has dropped to 18°C.

32. You come in one morning and find that the temperature is 21°C. To correct this, you move the thermostat down by 1°C

to 19°C. But the next day the temperature has dropped to 18.5°C.

33–34 ▪ The model of bacterial selection includes no **frequency-dependence,** meaning that the per capita production of the different types does not depend on the fraction of types in the population. Each of the following discrete-time dynamical systems for the number of mutants a_t and the number of wild type b_t depends on the fraction of mutants p_t. For each, explain in words how each type is affected by the frequency of the mutants, find the discrete-time dynamical system for p_t, find the equilibria, evaluate their stability, and plot a cobweb diagram. Do any of them oscillate?

33. $a_{t+1} = 2(1 - p_t)a_t$ and $b_{t+1} = (1 + p_t)b_t$

34. $a_{t+1} = 2(1 - p_t)^2 a_t$ and $b_{t+1} = (1 + p_t)b_t$

35–38 ▪ Crowded plants grow to smaller size. Smaller plants make fewer seeds. The following exercises describe the dynamics of a population described by n, the total number of seeds, and s, the size of the adult produced. Assume that adult plants die after producing seeds. In each case:

a. Start from $n = 20$ and find the total number of seeds for the next two years. (If the number of seeds per plant is a fraction, don't worry. Just think of it as an average).

b. Write the discrete-time dynamical system for the number of seeds.

c. Find the equilibrium number of seeds.

d. Graph the updating function and cobweb.

e. How is this result related to the stability condition?

35. If there are n seeds, each sprouts and grows to a size $s = \frac{100}{n}$. An adult of size s produces $s - 1$ seeds (because it must use 1 unit of energy to survive).

36. If there are n seeds, each sprouts and grows to a size $s = \frac{100}{n}$. An adult of size s produces $s - 0.5$ seeds.

37. If there are n seeds, each sprouts and grows to a size $s = \frac{100}{n}$. Suppose that an adult of size s produces $s - 2.0$ seeds.

38. If there are n seeds, each sprouts and grows to a size $s = \frac{100}{n+5}$. An adult of size s produces $s - 1$ seeds.

Computer Exercises

39. Study the behavior of the logistic dynamical system first for values of r near 3.0 and then for values between 3.5 and 4.0. Try the following with five values of r near 3.0 (such as 2.9, 2.99, 3.0, 3.01, and 3.1) and ten values of r between 3.5 and 4.0.

a. Use your computer to find solutions for 100 steps.

b. Look at the last 50 or so points on the solution and try to describe what is going on.

c. The case with $r = 4.0$ is rather famously chaotic. One of the properties of chaotic systems is "sensitivity to initial conditions." Run the system for 100 steps from one initial condition, and then run it again from an initial condition that is very close. If you compare your two solutions, they should be similar for a while but should eventually become completely different. What if a real system had this property?

40. Consider a population following

$$x_{t+1} = r x_t^2 e^{-x_t}$$

a. Graph the updating function for the following values of r: $r = 1$, $r = 2.6$, $r = e$, $r = 2.8$, $r = 3.6$, $r = \frac{e^2}{2}$, $r = 3.8$, $r = 6.6$, $r = \frac{e^3}{3}$, $r = 6.8$, and $r = 10.0$.

b. Find the equilibria for these values of r (the equation cannot be solved in general, but your computer should have a routine for solving, or just guess). Make sure you find them all.

c. Find the derivative of the updating function at each equilibrium.

d. Find which of the equilibria are stable.

e. When all of the positive equilibria are unstable, how might this model behave differently from the Ricker model with $r > e^2$? Can you explain why?

3.3 Maximization

A bee arrives at a flower. The more time she spends eating nectar, the more slowly the nectar comes out. But she knows that she must fly a long distance to find the next flower. When should she give up and leave? On a larger scale, a fisherman must decide how many fish to catch. The more he catches, the more he gets that year, but the more he depletes the fishery for next year. How many fish should he catch to catch the most fish in the long run? In fisheries jargon, what is the **maximum sustained yield** from the fish population?

Both of these are problems in **optimization,** finding the best solution to a problem. In this section, we will learn how to use the derivative to find **optima.** When the problem has been set up correctly, these best solutions are points where a function takes on a

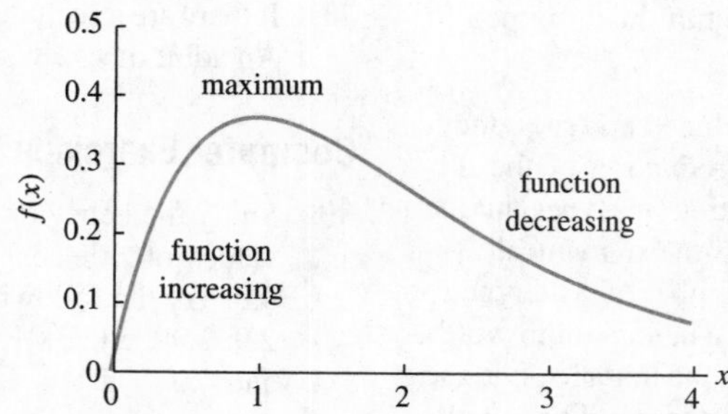

FIGURE 3.3.29
A function with a peak: $f(x) = xe^{-x}$

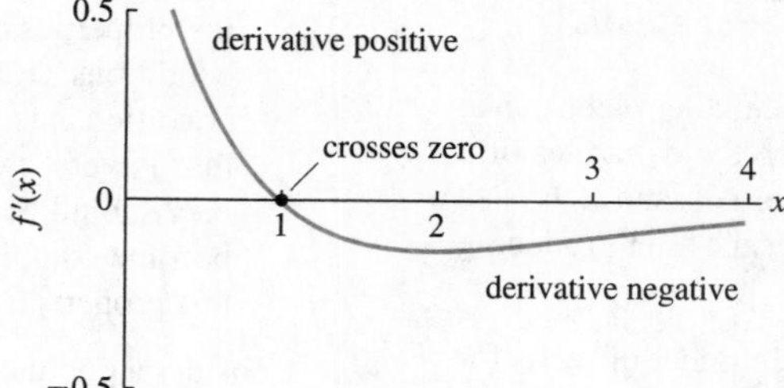

FIGURE 3.3.30
The derivative of a function with a peak: $f(x) = xe^{-x}$

minimum or **maximum** value. In particular, **critical points** (Definition 2.6) where the derivative is equal to zero or the derivative is not defined are candidates for being minima or maxima that can sometimes be distinguished with the **second derivative.** We will use these techniques to figure out the optimal behavior for the bee and the fisherman.

Minima and Maxima

The graph of the function

$$f(x) = xe^{-x}$$

rises to a peak known as a **maximum** of the function (Figure 3.3.29). How do we find where the maximum occurs? A function has a maximum where it switches from increasing to decreasing, just as a trail reaches a peak when it switches from ascending to descending. Mathematically, a maximum occurs when the derivative switches from positive to negative.

We have found the derivative of this function before (Example 2.8.7 and in Section 3.2),

$$\frac{df}{dx} = \frac{d}{dx}\left(xe^{-x}\right) = (1 - x)e^{-x}$$

(Figure 3.3.30). The derivative is positive for $x < 1$, negative for $x > 1$, and 0 for $x = 1$. The point where $f'(x) = 0$ is a **critical point** (Definition 2.6). Because the function switches from increasing to decreasing, the critical point at $x = 1$ is a maximum.

Example 3.3.1 A Quadratic Function with a Maximum

Similarly, the graph of

$$g(x) = x(1 - x)$$

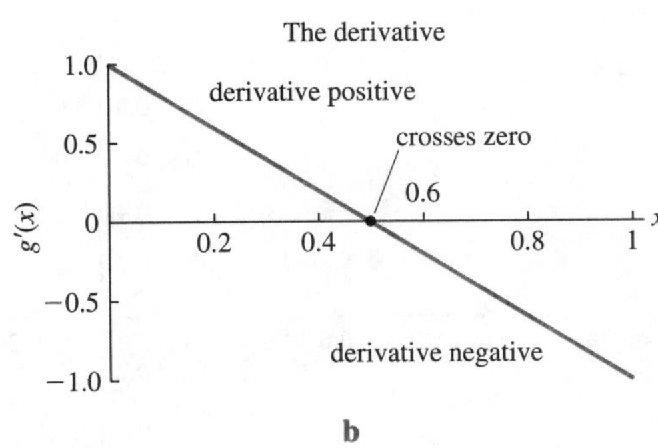

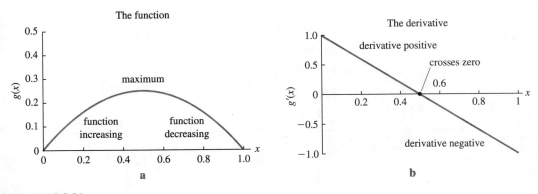

FIGURE 3.3.31
Another function with a peak: $g(x)=x(1-x)$

for $0 \leq x \leq 1$ rises to a peak for some value of x in this domain. The derivative is

$$\frac{dg}{dx}=\frac{d}{dx}\left(x-x^2\right)=1-2x$$

(Figure 3.3.31). The derivative is exactly zero when

$$1-2x=0$$
$$x=0.5$$

Because $f'(x)>0$ for $x<0.5$ and $f'(x)<0$ for $x>0.5$, the function switches from increasing to decreasing, this critical point is a maximum.

Example 3.3.2 Finding the Maximum of a Cubic Function

Consider the function

$$h(x)=x^3-x$$

for $-1<x<1$. Does this function have a maximum? To begin, take the derivative

$$\frac{dh}{dx}=3x^2-1$$

Next, set the derivative equal to 0 to find critical points

$$3x^2-1=0$$

Therefore,

$$3x^2=1$$
$$x^2=\frac{1}{3}$$
$$x=\pm\sqrt{\frac{1}{3}}$$

These points are candidates for where the function changes from increasing to decreasing. How can we tell what is happening at these points? One simple method is to evaluate the function, finding

$$h\left(\sqrt{\frac{1}{3}}\right)\approx -0.385$$

$$h\left(-\sqrt{\frac{1}{3}}\right)\approx 0.385$$

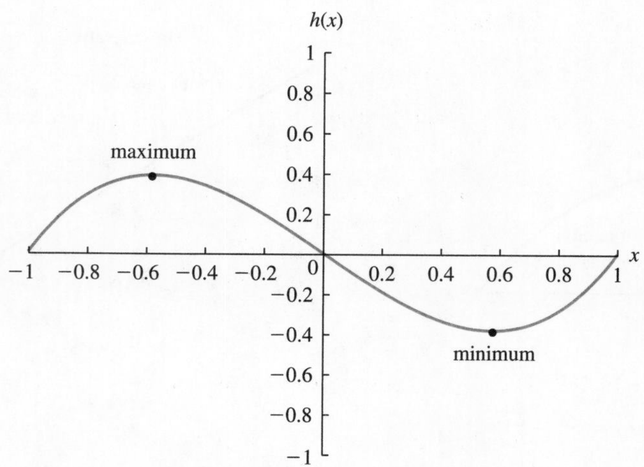

FIGURE 3.3.32

A function with a minimum and a maximum: $h(x) = x^3 - x$

The point $x = \sqrt{\frac{1}{3}}$ may be a minimum and the point $x = -\sqrt{\frac{1}{3}}$ may be a maximum (Figure 3.3.32).

To develop a general method for finding maxima and minima of functions, we must classify the types of maxima and minima. Maxima are classified as **global** or **local.** The global maximum of a function f is the largest value taken on by the function anywhere in its domain. Similarly, the global minimum is the smallest value taken on by the function. A local maximum is a "peak" where the function takes on its largest value in a region of the domain (Figure 3.3.33). The peak of the tallest mountain in Utah is a local maximum, but not a global one (Mt. Everest is taller). A function may have many local maxima with different values, just as a mountain range has many peaks with different heights. It may also have more than one input at which a global maximum occurs (if, for example, there were other mountains that were exactly as tall as Mt. Everest).

A special kind of maximum occurs at the boundary of the domain. The function in Figure 3.3.33 has a local maximum at the left-hand edge of its domain and a global minimum at the right. Maxima and minima at the boundaries can also be analyzed with the derivative. A function with negative derivative is decreasing and has a local maximum at the left-hand boundary and a local minimum at the right. The function in Figure 3.3.33 matches these criteria. A function with positive derivative is increasing and has a local minimum at the left-hand boundary and a local maximum at the right.

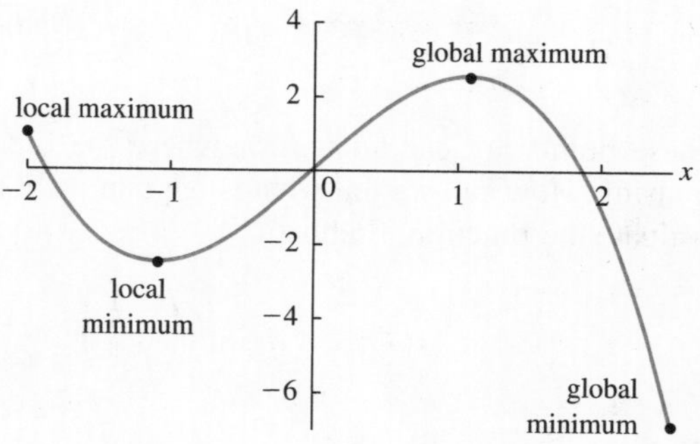

FIGURE 3.3.33

Local and global maxima

Algorithm 3.1 Finding Global Maxima and Minima

1. Compute the value of the function at the endpoints.
2. Find all critical points (points where the derivative is equal to zero or the function is not differentiable).
3. Compute the value of the function at all critical points.
4. The largest of the numbers found in steps 1 and 3 is the global maximum. The smallest of the numbers found in steps 1 and 3 is the global minimum.

Example 3.3.3 The Global Maximum and Minimum of a Function with a Corner

Consider the absolute value function $a(x) = |x|$ defined for $-2 \le x \le 3$ (Figure 3.3.34). Following the algorithm,

1. The endpoints are -2 and 3, where $a(-2) = |-2| = 2$ and $a(3) = |3| = 3$.
2. The function is not differentiable at $x = 0$ (because of the corner). For $x > 0$, we have that $a(x) = x$, so $a'(x) = 1$. For $x < 0$, we have that $a(x) = -x$, so $a'(x) = -1$. Thus $x = 0$ is the only critical point because the derivative is never 0.
3. The value at the critical point is $a(0) = |0| = 0$.
4. The largest of these values is 3, so the global maximum is at the right-hand endpoint. The smallest is 0, so $x = 0$ is the global minimum.

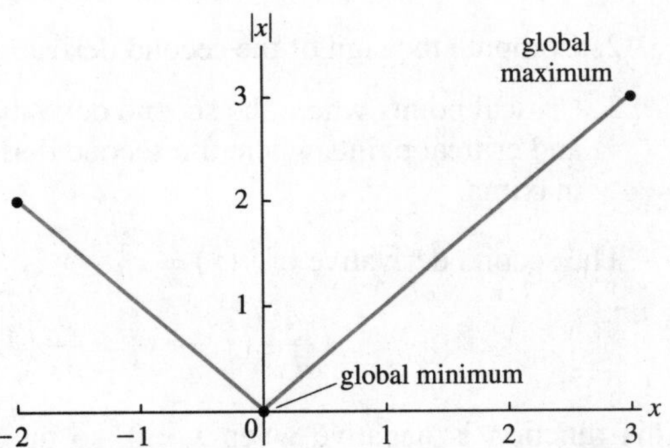

FIGURE 3.3.34
The maximum and minimum of the absolute value function

Example 3.3.4 The Global Maximum and Minimum of a Cubic Function

To find the global minimum and maximum of the differentiable function $h(x) = x^3 - x$ for $-1 \le x \le 1$ (Figure 3.3.32), we follow these steps:

1. $h(-1) = 0$ and $h(1) = 0$.
2. We found the critical points earlier to be at $x = \sqrt{\frac{1}{3}}$ and $x = -\sqrt{\frac{1}{3}}$.
3. $h\left(\sqrt{\frac{1}{3}}\right) = -0.385$ and $h\left(-\sqrt{\frac{1}{3}}\right) = 0.385$.
4. The largest of these values is 0.385, so the global maximum occurs at $x = -\sqrt{\frac{1}{3}}$. The smallest is -0.385, so the global minimum occurs at $x = \sqrt{\frac{1}{3}}$.

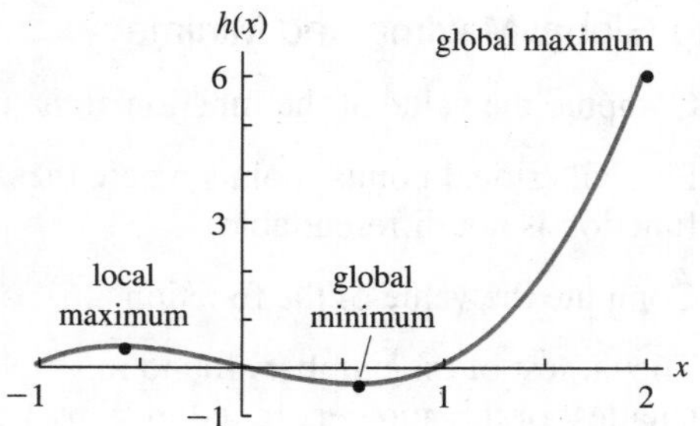

FIGURE 3.3.35

The global maximum of $h(x) = x^3 - x$ changes on an extended domain

Example 3.3.5 The Global Maximum and Minimum on a Different Domain

If we extended the domain of the function $h(x) = x^3 - x$ to include $-1 \leq x \leq 2$, the global maximum moves to $x = 2$. The critical point $x = -\sqrt{\frac{1}{3}}$ still yields still a **local maximum** (Figure 3.3.35).

The second derivative provides a method to check whether a critical point where the derivative is equal to 0 is a maximum or a minimum. On the graph of $h(x) = x^3 - x$, we can see that a critical point is a local maximum when the graph is **concave down** and is a local minimum when the graph is **concave up.**

We can formalize these observations into another algorithm.

Algorithm 3.2 Identifying Local Maxima and Minima with the Second Derivative

1. Find all critical points where the function is differentiable.
2. Compute the sign of the second derivative at these critical points.
3. Critical points where the second derivative is positive give local minima, and critical points where the second derivative is negative give to local maxima.

The second derivative of $h(x) = x^3 - x$ is

$$\frac{d^2}{dx^2}(x^3 - x) = \frac{d}{dx}(3x^2 - 1) = 6x$$

This function is negative when $x < 0$, so the critical point $x = -\sqrt{\frac{1}{3}}$ gives a local maximum, and the critical point $x = \sqrt{\frac{1}{3}}$ gives a local minimum (Figure 3.3.36c).

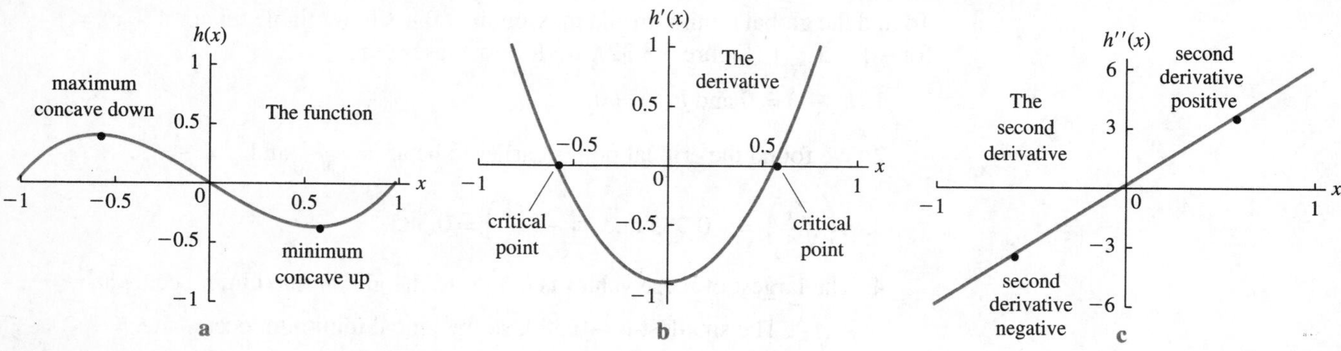

FIGURE 3.3.36

The function $h(x) = x^3 - x$, its derivative, and its second derivative

Example 3.3.6 Using the Second Derivative to Find Maxima

Consider again the function $f(x) = xe^{-x}$ with critical point at $x = 1$, studied in "Minima and Maxima," Section 3.3. The second derivative of $f(x) = xe^{-x}$ is

$$\begin{aligned} \frac{d^2 f}{dx^2} &= \frac{d}{dx}\left((1-x)e^{-x}\right) && \text{take derivative of derivative} \\ &= \frac{d(1-x)}{dx}e^{-x} + \frac{d\left(e^{-x}\right)}{dx}(1-x) && \text{product rule} \\ &= -e^{-x} + -e^{-x}(1-x) && \text{linear function and exponential rules} \\ &= (x-2)e^{-x} && \text{factoring} \end{aligned}$$

At the critical point $x = 1$,

$$f''(1) = (1-2)e^{-1} = -e^{-1} < 0$$

Because the second derivative is negative at the critical point, the function switches from increasing to decreasing at $x = 1$. There is a local maximum at $x = 1$.

Example 3.3.7 Using the Second Derivative to Identify Maxima of a Quadratic

The second derivative of $g(x) = x(1-x)$, studied in Example 3.3.1, is

$$\frac{d^2 g}{dx^2}(x(1-x)) = \frac{d}{dx}(1-2x) = -2$$

Because the second derivative is negative, the critical point at $x = 1/2$ gives a local maximum (Figure 3.3.31b).

If the second derivative is zero at a critical point, we cannot tell whether the critical point gives a local minimum, a local maximum, or neither.

Example 3.3.8 A Function with a Point of Inflection at a Critical Point

The function $C(x) = x^3$ has both a critical point and a point of inflection at $x = 0$ because

$$\begin{aligned} C'(x) &= 3x^2 \\ C''(x) &= 6x \end{aligned}$$

Because the derivative is positive for all values of $x \neq 0$, $C(x)$ is increasing everywhere. The critical point gives neither a minimum nor a maximum, but just an instantaneous pause (Figure 3.3.37).

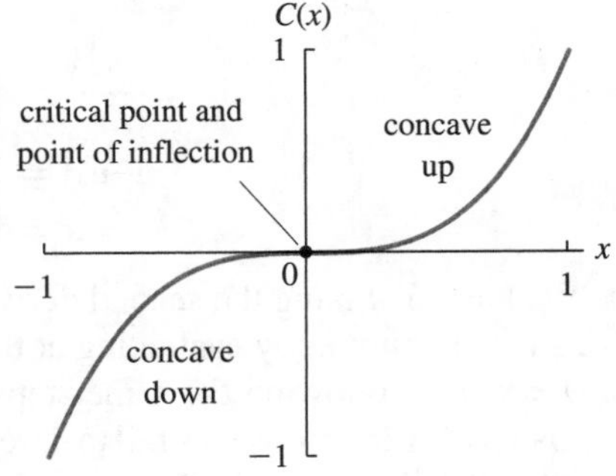

FIGURE 3.3.37
The function $C(x) = x^3$

Example 3.3.9 A Function with Second Derivative Equal to 0 at a Critical Point

The quartic function $Q(x) = x^4$ (considered in Example 2.7.2) has both a critical point and a point of inflection at $x = 0$ because

$$Q'(x) = 4x^3$$
$$Q''(x) = 12x^2$$

In this case, the second derivative is positive for all values of $x \neq 0$. Therefore, $Q(x)$ is concave up everywhere except at $x = 0$. The critical point gives a minimum (Figure 3.3.38).

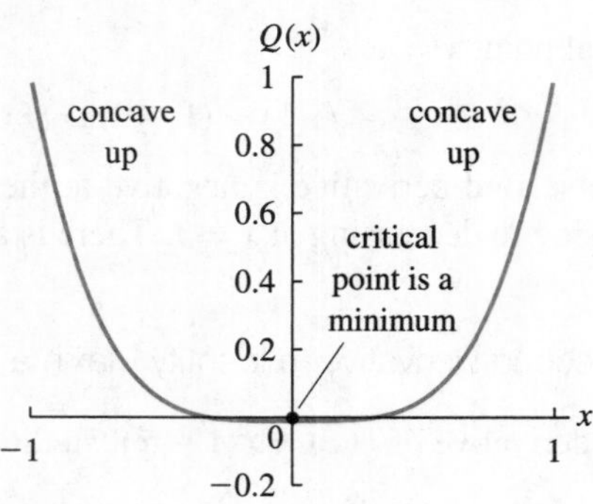

FIGURE 3.3.38
The function $Q(x) = x^4$

Example 3.3.10 The Tradeoff Between Medication and Side Effects

Suppose that a patient is given a dosage x of some medication, and the probability of a cure is

$$P(x) = \frac{\sqrt{x}}{1+x}$$

What dosage maximizes the probability of a cure? Taking the derivative, we find

$$P'(x) = \frac{(1+x)\frac{d}{dx}(\sqrt{x}) - \sqrt{x}\frac{d}{dx}(1+x)}{(1+x)^2} \quad \text{quotient rule}$$

$$= \frac{\frac{1+x}{2\sqrt{x}} - \sqrt{x}}{(1+x)^2} \quad \text{evaluate derivatives}$$

The derivative is zero when the numerator is zero, or when

$$\frac{1+x}{2\sqrt{x}} - \sqrt{x} = 0$$
$$\frac{1+x}{2\sqrt{x}} = \sqrt{x}$$
$$\frac{1+x}{2} = x$$
$$1 + x = 2x$$
$$x = 1$$

At this point, $P(1) = 0.5$. Taking the second derivative of this function is horrible. We can see that this is a maximum by evaluating at the endpoints. At $x = 0$, $P(0) = 0$ and $P'(x) > 0$ for $0 < x < 1$ (following the same steps with an inequality). Therefore, the optimal dosage is $x = 1$. Lower dosages fail to cure the disease, whereas a higher dosage causes side effects that also lead to failure. See Figure 3.3.39.

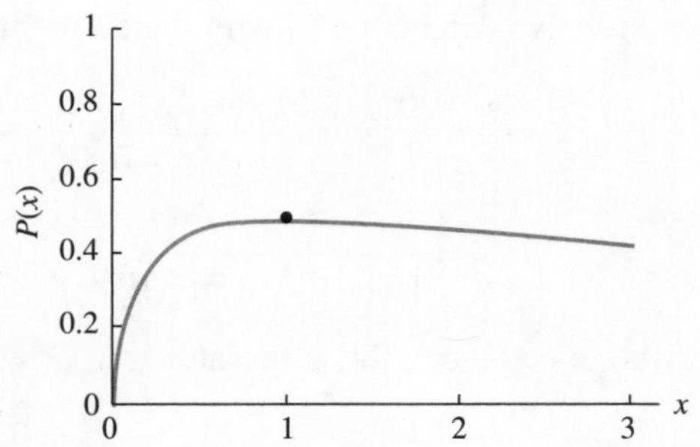

FIGURE 3.3.39
The tradeoff between treatment and side effects

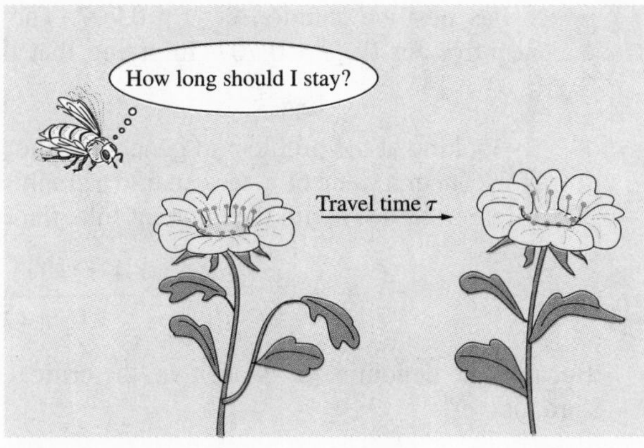

FIGURE 3.3.40
The bee's maximization problem

Maximizing Food Intake Rate

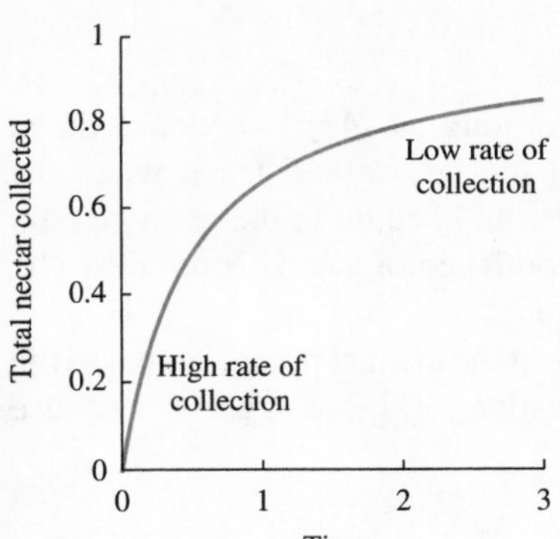

FIGURE 3.3.41
Nectar collected as a function of time

Consider the bee described in the introduction. After she finds a flower, she sucks up nectar at a slower and slower rate as the flower is depleted. However, she does not want to leave too soon because she must fly some distance to find the next flower. When should she give up and leave? If she stays a long time at each flower, she will get most of the nectar from that flower but will visit few flowers. If she stays a short time at each flower, she gets to skim the best nectar off the top but will spend most of her time flying to new flowers (Figure 3.3.40).

First, we must formulate this as a *maximization problem*. What is the bee trying to achieve? Her job is to bring back as much nectar as possible over the course of a day. To do so, she should maximize the *rate per visit,* which includes the travel time τ between flowers, measured in minutes. Suppose $F(t)$ is the amount of nectar collected by a bee that stays on a flower for time t (Figure 3.3.41). The rate $R(t)$ must take travel time into account.

$$\begin{aligned}\text{rate at which nectar is collected } R(t) &= \frac{\text{food per visit}}{\text{total time per visit}} \\ &= \frac{\text{food per visit}}{\text{time on flower + travel time}} \\ &= \frac{F(t)}{t+\tau}\end{aligned}$$

Example 3.3.11 Computing the Maximum with a Particular Parameter Value

As a particular case, assume that the travel time τ is equal to 1.0 min and that

$$F(t) = \frac{t}{t+0.5}$$

Then

$$R(t) = \frac{F(t)}{t+1.0} = \frac{t}{(t+0.5)(t+1.0)}$$

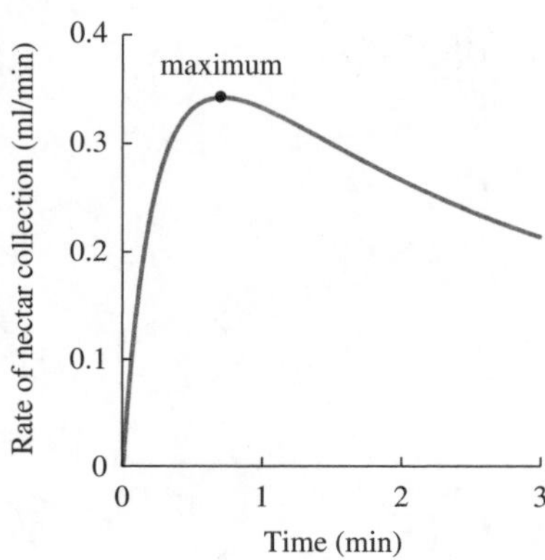

FIGURE 3.3.42
The average rate of return for the bee

The derivative can be found with the quotient rule and a lot of algebra to be

$$\frac{dR}{dt} = \frac{(t+0.5)(t+1.0) - t[(t+0.5)+(t+1.0)]}{[(t+0.5)(t+1.0)]^2}$$
$$= \frac{0.5 - t^2}{[(t+0.5)(t+1.0)]^2}$$

This derivative is 0 when the numerator is 0, or when

$$0.5 - t^2 = 0$$

which has positive solution $0 \le t \le 0.707$. The numerator is positive for $t < 0.707$ and negative for $0 \le t > 0.707$, implying that this value gives a maximum (Figure 3.3.42).

By looking at the problem in general, without substituting in a specific functional form for $F(t)$ or a value of τ, we can find a graphical method to solve the bee's problem. We differentiate $R(t)$ with the quotient rule, finding

$$\frac{dR}{dt} = \frac{(t+\tau)F'(t) - F(t)}{(t+\tau)^2}$$

Because the denominator is positive, the critical points occur where the numerator is zero, or

$$(t+\tau)F'(t) = F(t)$$

or

$$F'(t) = \frac{F(t)}{t+\tau} = R(t)$$

The solution of this equation is a local maximum as long as $F(t)$ is concave down (Exercise 40). This fundamental equation says that the bee should leave when the derivative of F, the instantaneous rate of food collection, is equal to the average rate. This **Marginal Value Theorem** is a powerful tool in both ecology and economics. The idea is simple: Leave when you can do better elsewhere.

Graphically, the slope of the food collection curve at the critical point is equal to the slope of line connecting that point with a point at negative τ (Figure 3.3.43a), because

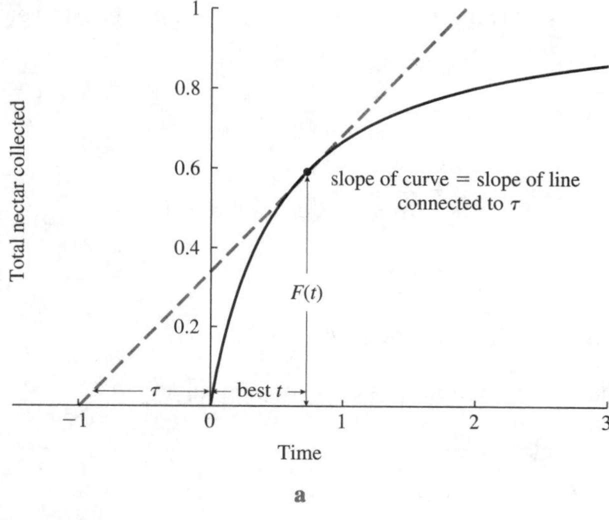

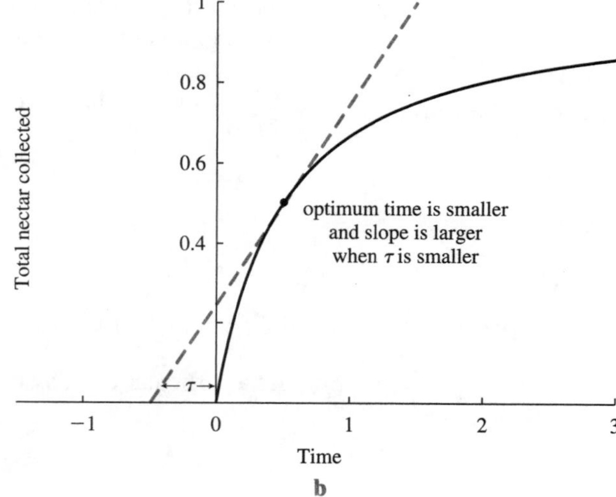

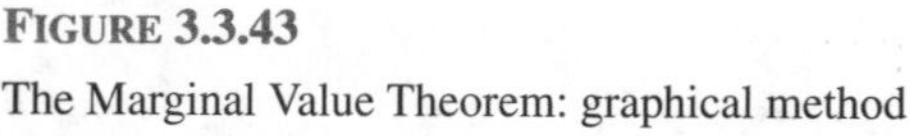
FIGURE 3.3.43
The Marginal Value Theorem: graphical method

that line has a "rise" of $F(t)$ and a "run" of $t+\tau$. The slope of the line is then

$$\frac{F(t)}{t+\tau} = R(t)$$

From the graph, we can see that the optimal time to remain becomes shorter when the travel time between flowers is shorter (Figure 3.3.43b).

Example 3.3.12 Using the Marginal Value Theorem to Solve a Maximization Problem

Consider the situation in Example 3.3.11 with the nectar collected as a function of time equal to

$$F(t) = \frac{t}{t+0.5}$$

and travel time of $\tau = 1.0$. In Example 3.3.11 we found that

$$R(t) = \frac{F(t)}{t+1.0} = \frac{t}{(t+0.5)(t+1.0)}$$

by writing down the formula for $R(t)$ and differentiating. Alternatively, we can find the maximum with the Marginal Value Theorem by solving for the time when $F'(t) = R(t)$. The derivative of $F(t)$ can be found with the quotient rule as

$$\begin{aligned} F'(t) &= \frac{(t+0.5)\frac{dt}{dt} - t\frac{d(t+0.5)}{dt}}{(t+0.5)^2} \\ &= \frac{(t+0.5)-t}{(t+0.5)^2} \\ &= \frac{0.5}{(t+0.5)^2} \end{aligned}$$

To find the maximum, we solve $F'(t) = R(t)$, or

$$\begin{aligned} \frac{0.5}{(t+0.5)^2} &= \frac{t}{(t+0.5)(t+1.0)} && \text{the original equation} \\ \frac{0.5}{t+0.5} &= \frac{t}{t+1.0} && \text{multiply both sides by } t+0.5 \\ 0.5(t+1.0) &= t(t+0.5) && \text{cross multiply} \\ 0.5t+0.5 &= t^2+0.5t && \text{multiply out} \\ 0.5 &= t^2 && \text{subtract } 0.5t \\ t &\approx 0.707 && \text{solve for } t \end{aligned}$$

This matches the result found by differentiating $R(t)$ directly. ▲

Example 3.3.13 The Effect of Increasing Travel Time

Suppose that the nectar collected as a function of time follows

$$F(t) = \frac{t}{t+0.5}$$

as in Example 3.3.12, but that the travel time is $\tau = 10.0$. Then

$$R(t) = \frac{F(t)}{t+10.0} = \frac{t}{(t+0.5)(t+10.0)}$$

The Marginal Value Theorem states that the optimal time for the bee to depart is when $F'(t) = R(t)$. We found the derivative of $F(t)$ in Example 3.3.12, so we can find the maximum by solving

$$\frac{0.5}{(t+0.5)^2} = \frac{t}{(t+0.5)(t+10.0)} \qquad \text{the equation } F'(t) = R(t)$$
$$\frac{0.5}{t+0.5} = \frac{t}{t+10.0} \qquad \text{multiply both sides by } t+0.5$$
$$0.5(t+10.0) = t(t+0.5) \qquad \text{cross multiply}$$
$$0.5t + 5.0 = t^2 + 0.5t \qquad \text{multiply out}$$
$$5.0 = t^2 \qquad \text{subtract } 0.5t$$
$$t \approx 2.236 \qquad \text{solve for } t$$

As expected, the optimal time to remain on the flower becomes longer when travel time becomes longer. Nonetheless, the bee still spends a smaller **fraction** of its time on flowers in this case. With $\tau = 10.0$, the fraction of time on flowers is

$$\text{fraction of time on flowers} = \frac{\text{time on flowers}}{\text{time on flowers} + \text{travel time}}$$
$$= \frac{2.236}{2.236 + 10.0} \approx 0.18$$

This bee is predicted to spend 18% of its time on flowers. The bee in Example 3.3.12, in contrast, is predicted to spend

$$\text{fraction of time on flowers} = \frac{0.707}{0.707 + 1.0} \approx 0.41$$

or 41% of its time.

Maximizing Fish Harvest

Consider a variant of the logistic dynamical system (Equation 3.2.1) that includes harvesting,

$$N_{t+1} = 2.5N_t(1 - N_t) - hN_t \tag{3.3.1}$$

(Figure 3.3.44). N_t denotes the population of fish at the beginning of one fishing season and N_{t+1} the population at the beginning of the next. The population is measured as the fraction of the maximum possible population size. The term $-hN_t$ is the harvest, where h is called the "harvesting effort." Harvesting effort depends on the number of ships, the number of fishing days, the quality of the fishing vessels, and many other factors. Total harvest is the product of harvesting effort and population size. In this case, the harvest is computed by subtracting a factor h times the number of fish before reproduction.

What harvesting effort brings in the maximum long-term harvest? Exerting no harvesting effort ($h = 0$) brings in nothing. An enormous harvesting effort might bring in many fish in the short term but end up depleting the population. We suspect that an intermediate harvesting effort will maximize the long-term harvest.

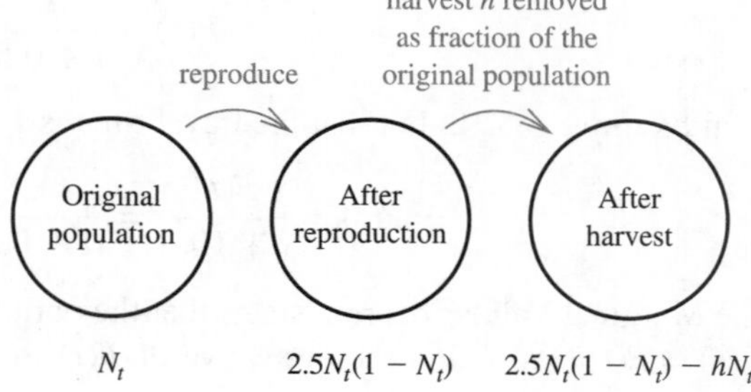

FIGURE 3.3.44
The dynamics of a simple fishery

The long-term behavior of this system is described by a stable equilibrium. What are the equilibria? The equilibrium value N^* can be found with Algorithm 1.5.

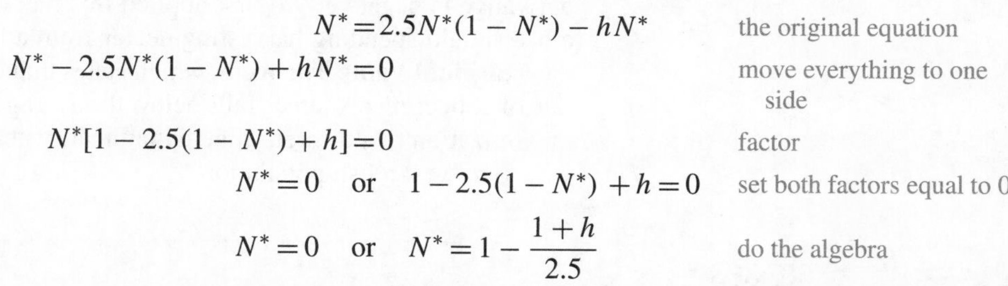

$$
\begin{aligned}
N^* &= 2.5N^*(1-N^*) - hN^* && \text{the original equation}\\
N^* - 2.5N^*(1-N^*) + hN^* &= 0 && \text{move everything to one side}\\
N^*[1-2.5(1-N^*)+h] &= 0 && \text{factor}\\
N^* = 0 \quad \text{or} \quad 1-2.5(1-N^*)+h &= 0 && \text{set both factors equal to 0}\\
N^* = 0 \quad \text{or} \quad N^* &= 1-\frac{1+h}{2.5} && \text{do the algebra}
\end{aligned}
$$

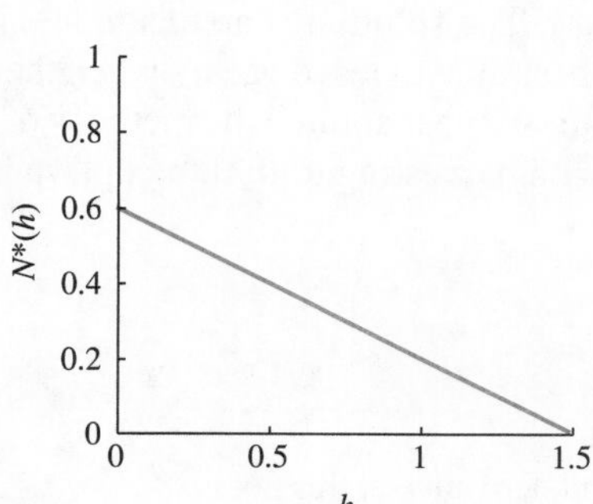

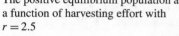

FIGURE 3.3.45

The positive equilibrium population as a function of harvesting effort with $r = 2.5$

(See Figure 3.3.45) We have the usual extinction equilibrium and a second equilibrium that is positive only if $\frac{1+h}{2.5} < 1$. If we choose h larger than 1.5, the only equilibrium is $N^* = 0$ and the population goes extinct. (The peculiar possibility that $h > 1$ occurs because our model measures the population before reproduction and collects the harvest after reproduction.)

Suppose that we have chosen a harvesting effort h and that the population has reached the positive equilibrium N^* (conditions for stability are derived in Exercise 47). The equilibrium harvest, denoted $P(h)$, is the product of the harvesting effort h and the population size N^*, so

$$P(h) = hN^* = h\left(1 - \frac{1+h}{2.5}\right) \tag{3.3.2}$$

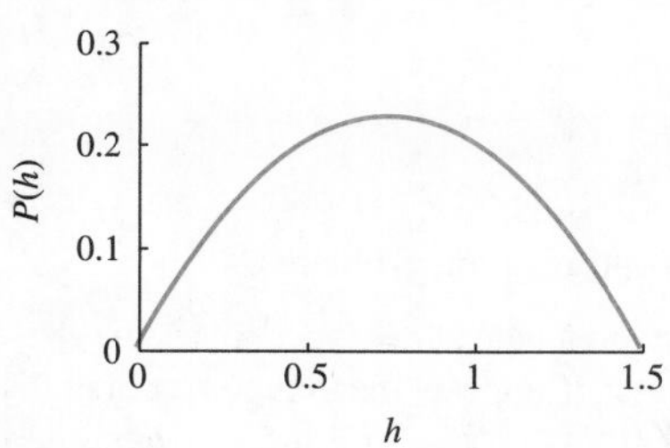

FIGURE 3.3.46

Long-term harvest as a function of harvesting effort with $r = 2.5$

(Figure 3.3.46). With Algorithm 3.1, we can find the value of h that maximizes harvest by checking the endpoints and locating critical points. The endpoints are $h = 0$ and $h = 1.5$ (above which the population goes extinct) where $P(0) = 0$ and $P(1.5) = 0$ as we suspected. To find critical points, we solve

$$P'(h) = 1 - \frac{1+2h}{2.5} = 0$$

for h, finding

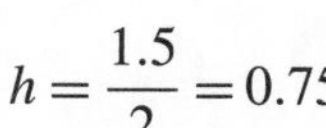

$$h = \frac{1.5}{2} = 0.75$$

This must be a maximum based on our knowledge of the graph of the function (Figure 3.3.46). We would do best by letting the fish reproduce and then collecting a harvest equal to 75% of the population before reproduction. The payoff $P(h)$ is

$$P(0.75) = 0.75\left(1 - \frac{1+0.75}{2.5}\right) = 0.225$$

A larger harvest would deplete the population. With $h = 1.0$,

$$P(1.0) = 1.0\left(1 - \frac{1+1.0}{2.5}\right) = 0.2$$

which is smaller because the equilibrium is only 0.2. In contrast, a smaller harvest is inefficient. With $h = 0.5$,

$$P(0.5) = 0.5\left(1 - \frac{1+0.5}{2.5}\right) = 0.2$$

which is smaller even though the equilibrium is larger.

Summary

We have seen how to use the derivative to find **maxima** and **minima** of functions by locating **critical points** where the derivative is either 0 or undefined. To find **global** maxima and minima, we must compare values at critical points with values at the endpoints, where maxima and minima often occur. When it is defined, the second derivative can be used to identify local minima and maxima. A critical point is a local minimum if the second derivative is positive, and a local maximum if the second derivative is negative. We first applied this method to find the optimal length of time a bee should spending harvesting nectar from a flower. The solution is an example of the **Marginal Value Theorem,** which states that the best time to leave occurs when the rate of collecting resources falls below the average rate. We next applied the methods of maximization to a discrete-time dynamical system with harvesting to find the optimal way to harvest a fish population.

3.3 Exercises

Mathematical Techniques

1–6 ▪ Find all critical points of the following functions.

1. $a(x) = \dfrac{x}{1+x}$
2. $f(x) = 1 + 2x - 2x^2$
3. $c(w) = w^3 - 3w$
4. $g(y) = \dfrac{y}{1+y^2}$
5. $h(z) = e^{z^2}$
6. $c(\theta) = \cos(2\pi\theta)$

7–12 ▪ Find the global minimum and the global maximum of the following functions on the interval given. Don't forget to check the endpoints.

7. $a(x) = \dfrac{x}{1+x}$ for $0 \le x \le 1$.
8. $f(x) = 1 + 2x - 2x^2$ for $0 \le x \le 2$.
9. $c(w) = w^3 - 3w$ for $-2 \le w \le 2$.
10. $g(y) = \dfrac{y}{1+y^2}$ for $0 \le y \le 2$.
11. $h(z) = e^{z^2}$ for $0 \le z \le 1$.
12. $F(x) = |1 - x|$ for $0 \le x \le 3$. (This function cannot be differentiated at $x = 1$.)

13–18 ▪ Find the second derivative at the critical points of the following functions. Classify the critical points as yielding local minima or local maxima. Use the second derivative to draw an accurate graph of the function for the given range.

13. $a(x) = \dfrac{x}{1+x}$ (as in Exercise 1) for $0 \le x \le 1$.
14. $f(x) = 1 + 2x - 2x^2$ (as in Exercise 2) for $0 \le x \le 2$.
15. $c(w) = w^3 - 3w$ (as in Exercise 3) for $-2 \le w \le 2$.
16. $g(y) = \dfrac{y}{1+y^2}$ (as in Exercise 4) for $0 \le y \le 2$.
17. $h(z) = e^{z^2}$ (as in Exercise 5) for $-1 \le z \le 1$.
18. $c(\theta) = \cos(2\pi\theta)$ (as in Exercise 6) for $-1 \le \theta \le 1$.

19–22 ▪ Suppose $f(x)$ is a positive function with a maximum at x^*. We can often find maxima and minima of other functions composed with $f(x)$. For each of the functions $h(x) = g[f(x)]$:

a. Show that h has a critical point at x^*.

b. Compute the second derivative at this point.

c. Check whether your function has a minimum or a maximum and explain.

d. Check your result using the function $f(x) = xe^{-x}$ for $x \ge 0$, which has a maximum at $x = 1$. Sketch a graph of $f(x)$ and $h(x)$ in this case.

19. $g(f) = \dfrac{1}{f}$
20. $g(f) = 1 - f$
21. $g(f) = \ln(f)$
22. $g(f) = f - f^2$

Applications

23–24 ▪ Solve the following optimization problems.

23. Organic waste deposited in a lake at $t = 0$ decreases the oxygen content of the water. Suppose the oxygen content is $C(t) = t^3 - 30t^2 + 6000$ for $0 \le t \le 25$. Find the maximum and minimum oxygen content during this time.

24. The size of a population of bacteria introduced to a nutrient grows according to

$$N(t) = 5000 + \frac{30000t}{100 + t^2}$$

Find the maximum size of this population for $t \ge 0$.

25–26 ▪ No calculus book is complete without optimization problems involving fences.

25. A farmer owns 1000 m of fence and wants to enclose the largest possible rectangular area. The region to be fenced has a straight canal on one side and a perpendicular and perfectly straight ancient stone wall on another. The area thus needs to be fenced on only two sides. What is the largest area she can enclose?

26. A farmer owns 1000 m of fence and wants to enclose the largest possible rectangular area. The region to be fenced has a straight canal on one side and thus needs to be fenced on only three sides. What is the largest area she can enclose?

27–30 ▪ Consider the bee confronted by the problem in "Maximizing Food Intake Rate," Section 3.3. Find the optimal strategy with the following travel times τ, and illustrate the graphical method of solution. For each particular value of τ, find the equation of the tangent line at the optimal t and show that it goes through the point $(-\tau, 0)$.

27. $\tau = 2.0$

28. $\tau = 0.5$

29. $\tau = 0.1$

30. Find the solution in general (without substituting a value for τ). What is the limit as τ approaches 0? Does this answer make sense?

31–34 ▪ Suppose that the total food collected by a bee follows

$$F(t) = \frac{t}{c + t}$$

where c is some parameter. If $\tau = 1.0$, find the optimal departure time in the following circumstances. When the value of c is given, sketch the plot via the graphical method in Figure 3.3.47.

31. $c = 2.0$

32. $c = 1.0$

33. $c = 0.1$

34. Find the solution in general (without substituting a value for c). What does the parameter c mean biologically (think about how long it takes the bee to collect half the nectar)? Explain in words why the bee leaves sooner when c is smaller.

35–38 ▪ Mathematical models can help us to estimate values that are difficult to measure. Consider again a bee sucking nectar from a flower, with

$$F(t) = \frac{t}{0.5 + t}$$

If the bee remains a length of time t on the flower, estimate the travel time τ, assuming that the bee understands the Marginal Value Theorem, for the following values of t.

35. $t = 1.0$

36. $t = 0.1$

37. $t = 4.0$

38. Find the solution in general (without substituting a value for t).

39–40 ▪ We never showed that the value found in computing the optimal t with the Marginal Value Theorem is in fact a maximum. For each of the following forms for the function $F(t)$, find the second derivative of $R(t)$ at the point where $F'(t) = \frac{F(t)}{t+\tau}$, and check whether the solution is a maximum.

39. Suppose $F(t) = \frac{t}{1+t}$ and travel time is $\tau = 1$.

40. Suppose $F(t)$ is any function with $F''(t) < 0$ and travel time is $\tau = 1$.

41–44 ▪ Animals must survive predation in addition to maximizing their rate of food intake. One theory assumes that they try to maximize the ratio of food collected to predation risk. Suppose that different flowers with nectar of quality n attract $P(n)$ predators. For example, flowers with higher-quality nectar (large values of n) might attract more predators (large value of $P(n)$). Bees must decide which flowers to use. For each of the following forms of $P(n)$, find the function the bees are trying to maximize, and find the optimal n.

41. Suppose that $P(n) = 1 + n^2$. Find the optimal n for the bees.

42. Suppose that $P(n) = 1 + n$. Find the optimal n for the bees and draw a graph like that for the Marginal Value Theorem. Does this make sense? Why is the result so different?

43. Find the condition for the maximum for a general function $P(n)$ by solving for $P'(n)$. Use this condition to find the optimal n for the cases $P(n) = 1 + n^2$ and $P(n) = 1 + n$.

44. Find a graphical interpretation of the condition in the previous problem, and test it on $P(n) = 1 + n^2$ and $P(n) = 1 + n$.

45–46 ▪ Find the maximum harvest from a population following the discrete-time dynamical system

$$N_{t+1} = rN_t(1 - N_t) - hN_t$$

for the given values of r.

a. Find the equilibrium population as a function of h. What is the largest h consistent with a positive equilibrium?

b. Find the equilibrium harvest as a function of h.

c. Find the harvesting effort that maximizes harvest.

d. Find the maximum harvest.

45. $r = 2.0$

46. $r = 1.5$

47–48 ▪ Find the conditions for stability of the equilibrium of

$$N_{t+1} = rN_t(1 - N_t) - hN_t$$

for the following values of r. Show that the equilibrium N^* is stable when h is set to the value that maximizes the long-term harvest. Graph the updating function and cobweb.

47. $r = 2.5$, as in the text.

48. $r = 1.5$, as in Exercise 46.

49–50 ▪ Calculate the maximum long-term harvest for an alternative model of competition that obeys the discrete-time dynamical system

$$N_{t+1} = \frac{rN_t}{1 + kN_t} - hN_t$$

Try the following steps for the given values of the parameters r and k.

a. Find the equilibrium as a function of h.

b. What is the largest value of h consistent with a positive equilibrium?

c. Find the harvest level giving the maximum long-term harvest.

d. Sketch a graph of $P(h)$ and compute the value at the maximum.

e. How do the results compare with those using the discrete-time dynamical system in the text?

49. With $r = 2.5$ and $k = 1$.

50. With $r = 1.5$ and $k = 1$.

51–54 ▪ The model of fish harvesting studied in the text includes nothing about harvesting cost. Suppose that the population follows

$$N_{t+1} = 2.5N_t(1 - N_t) - hN_t$$

as in the text, but that the payoff is

$$P(h) = hN^* - ch$$

where c is the cost per unit effort of harvesting. Find the optimal harvest for the following values of c, the associated equilibrium population N^*, and the associated payoff $P(h)$. Do your answers all make sense? What should the fisherman do if c becomes too large?

51. $c = 0.1$

52. $c = 0.2$

53. $c = 0.5$

54. $c = 1.0$

Computer Exercise

55. Suppose a population follows the updating function

$$N_{t+1} = 2.5N_t(1 - N_t) - hN_t$$

but can be harvested only every second year. This means that the harvest alternates between the chosen value h and 0.

a. Find the 2-yr updating function.

b. Find the optimal harvest.

c. Compare with the results in the text. Is it better to harvest less often?

3.4 Reasoning About Functions

Continuous and differentiable functions have many useful properties that can be employed to reason about the biological processes they describe without doing a great deal of algebra. In particular, we can make deductions about the solutions of equations, the existence of maxima and minima, or the values of the derivative. We will use the **Intermediate Value Theorem** to show, without solving any equations, that a discrete-time dynamical system has an equilibrium; the **Extreme Value Theorem** to show, without computing any derivatives, that a function has a maximum; and the **Mean Value Theorem** to find the value of a derivative without taking any limits.

Continuous Functions: The Intermediate Value Theorem

Consider a model for chemical concentration in the lung that includes absorption,

$$c_{t+1} = (1 - q)\left[1 - \alpha(c_t)\right]c_t + q\gamma \qquad (3.4.1)$$

In this discrete-time dynamical system, c_t represents the concentration before a breath, c_{t+1} the concentration before the next breath, q the fraction of air exchanged, γ the concentration of chemical in the ambient air, and $\alpha(c_t)$ the fraction of chemical *absorbed* as a function of the chemical concentration in the lung ("Lung Dynamics with Absorption," Section 1.9). Suppose that $\alpha(c_t)$ is

$$\alpha(c_t) = 0.5\left(1 - e^{-0.5c_t}\right)$$

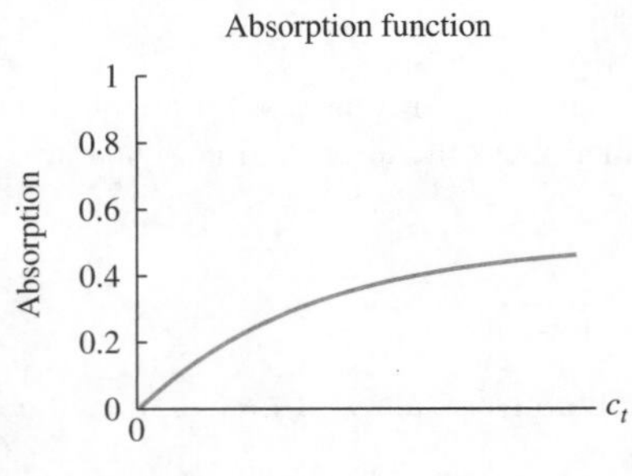

FIGURE 3.4.47
Dynamics of a lung with absorption

(Figure 3.4.47). Absorption is equal to 0 when $c_t = 0$ because there is nothing to absorb, and the fraction absorbed increases to 0.5 as the concentration becomes larger. What happens to the concentration in this lung? Does it still have an equilibrium?

We begin by trying to finding an equilibrium,

$$c^* = (1 - q)\left[1 - 0.5\left(1 - e^{-5c^*}\right)\right]c^* + q\gamma \qquad \text{the original equation}$$

$$0 = (1 - q)\left[1 - 0.5\left(1 - e^{-5c^*}\right)\right]c^* + q\gamma - c^* \qquad \text{place unknowns on one side}$$

This equation cannot be factored or solved. Is there any way to establish whether there is an equilibrium and to get some idea where it is?

We can answer these questions without further algebra by reasoning about the general process of breathing. One process, breathing in, adds chemical to the lungs,

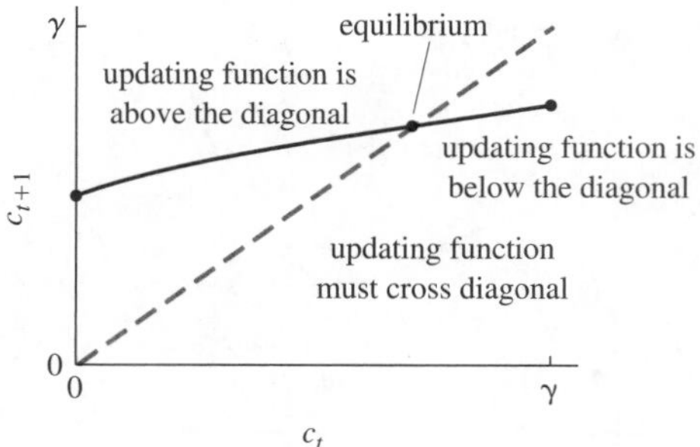

FIGURE 3.4.48

Reasoning about the equilibrium of the lung discrete-time dynamical system with absorption

and two processes, breathing out and absorption, remove chemical from the lungs. Without absorption, we found that the equilibrium concentration is γ, the ambient concentration. With absorption, then, we expect the equilibrium to be decreased below γ. We can test this intuition by reasoning about the updating function.

Suppose the lung starts out with $c_t = 0$, the lowest possible concentration. Then

$$c_{t+1} = (1-q)(1-\alpha(0)) \cdot 0 + q\gamma = q\gamma$$

As long as $q > 0$ (meaning that some air is exchanged) and $\gamma > 0$ (meaning that some chemical is available), $c_{t+1} = q\gamma > 0$. In other words, the amount of chemical has *increased*. Conversely, suppose the lung starts out with a concentration of $c_t = \gamma$. We expect that the concentration will decrease because of absorption. Substituting into the discrete-time dynamical system yields

$$\begin{aligned} c_{t+1} &= (1-q)[1-\alpha(\gamma)]\gamma + q\gamma && \text{discrete-time dynamical system with } c_t = \gamma \\ &= (1-q)\gamma + q\gamma - (1-q)\alpha(\gamma)\gamma && \text{separate out term with } \alpha \\ &= \gamma - (1-q)\alpha(\gamma)\gamma && \text{sum of first two terms is } \gamma \\ &< \gamma && \text{as long as } \alpha(\gamma) > 0 \text{ and } q < 1 \end{aligned}$$

Absorption reduces the concentration below the ambient concentration, the equilibrium value without absorption.

The graph of the updating function therefore lies above the diagonal at $c = 0$ and below at $c = \gamma$ (Figure 3.4.48). Furthermore, the updating function is *continuous* because it is built by combining continuous linear and exponential functions using only multiplication and composition (Section 2.3). The graph of a continuous function has no "jumps," meaning that it is impossible to draw a graph connecting these two points without crossing the diagonal. Such a crossing point is an equilibrium (Section 1.6, "Analysis of Discrete-Time Dynamical Systems").

We have found, without solving any equations, that this discrete-time dynamical system *must* have an equilibrium between 0 and γ, in accordance with our biological intuition. Furthermore, the updating function must cross the diagonal from above to below. However, we cannot be sure that the equilibrium is stable because the updating function could be decreasing steeply at the equilibrium (Section 3.4, Exercise 45).

How do we prove mathematically that the updating function must cross the diagonal? This result follows from the **Intermediate Value Theorem** for continuous functions.

Theorem 3.2 **Intermediate Value Theorem**

If $f(x)$ is continuous for $a \le x \le b$ and c is between $f(a)$ and $f(b)$, then there is some x between a and b such that $f(x) = c$.

The proof of this simple theorem is subtle, requiring deep facts about real numbers and continuity. The idea of the Intermediate Value Theorem is shown in Figure 3.4.49. The theorem guarantees that there is *at least* one crossing point, but there may be more.

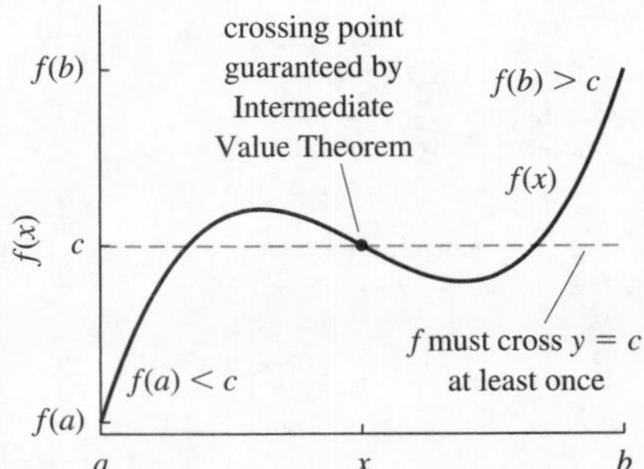

FIGURE 3.4.49
The Intermediate Value Theorem

Example 3.4.1 The Intermediate Value Theorem Applied to Height

Physically, the Intermediate Value Theorem says that if you grew from 2 ft to 6 ft in height, you must have been exactly 4 ft tall at some time (Figure 3.4.50).

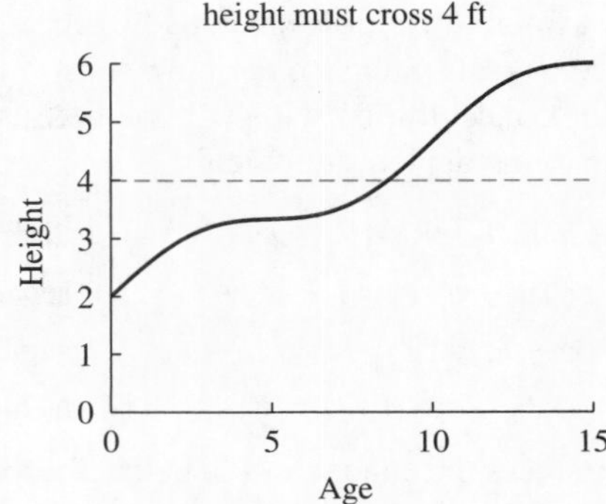

FIGURE 3.4.50
The Intermediate Value Theorem applied to height

Example 3.4.2 The Intermediate Value Theorem Applied to Velocity

If you accelerate from 0 to 60 mph, you must have been going exactly 31.4159 mph at some time (Figure 3.4.51).

Example 3.4.3 The Intermediate Value Theorem Applied to Solving an Equation

Suppose we wish to show there is a value of $x > 0$ that solves

$$e^x = 5x + 10$$

Define the function $f(x) = e^x - 5x - 10$. Then $f(x) = 0$ at any solution of the original equation. Checking $x = 0$ gives $f(0) = e^0 - 5 \cdot 0 - 10 = -9 < 0$. If we can find a positive value of x such that $f(x) > 0$, we will have guaranteed that a solution exists. Trying successive integers gives the values shown in the table.

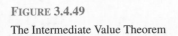

x	$f(x)$
1	$e^1 - 5 - 10 \approx -12.28 < 0$
2	$e^2 - 10 - 10 \approx -12.61 < 0$
3	$e^3 - 15 - 10 \approx -4.91 < 0$
4	$e^4 - 20 - 10 \approx 24.60 > 0$

There must be a solution for $3 < x < 4$ (Figure 3.4.52).

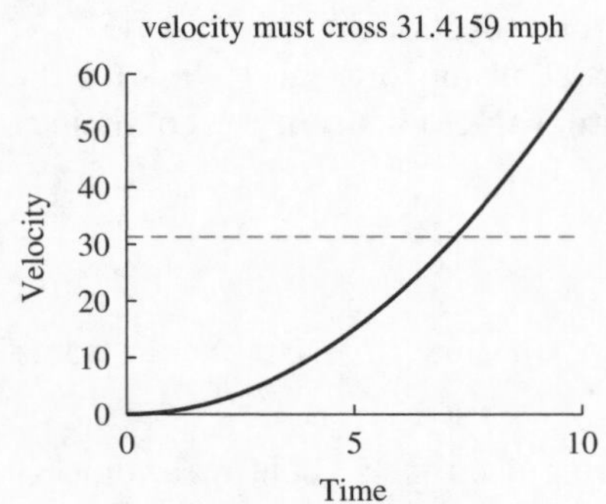

FIGURE 3.4.51
The Intermediate Value Theorem applied to velocity

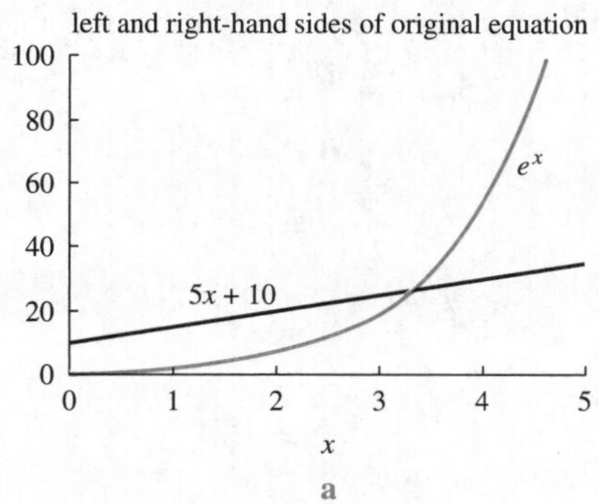

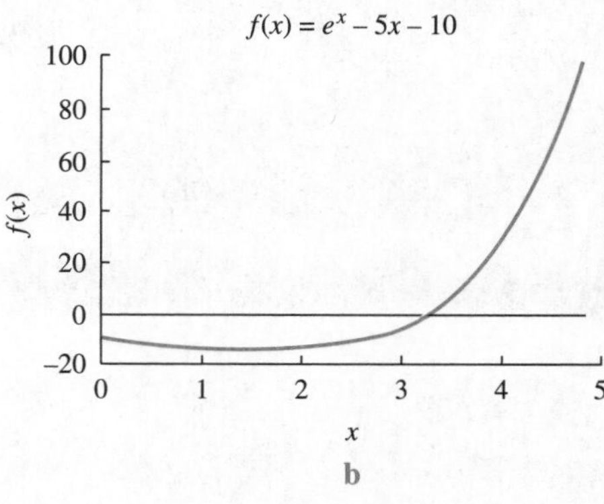

FIGURE 3.4.52
The Intermediate Value Theorem applied to solving an equation

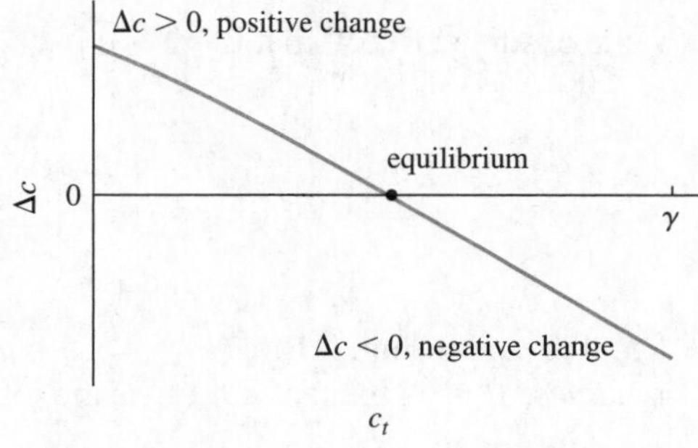

FIGURE 3.4.53
Reasoning about the equilibrium of the lung discrete-time dynamical system using the Intermediate Value Theorem

We need to make a transformation to apply this theorem to the equilibria of the lung discrete-time dynamical system with absorption. An equilibrium is a point where the **change in concentration** is equal to zero (Figure 3.4.53). The change in concentration Δc is

$$\Delta c = c_{t+1} - c_t$$

At $c_t = 0$, $c_{t+1} > c_t$ and $\Delta c > 0$. At $c_t = \gamma$, $c_{t+1} < \gamma$ and $\Delta c < 0$. The Intermediate Value Theorem guarantees that there must be some point where $\Delta c = 0$ (Figure 3.4.53). This point is the equilibrium.

Maximization: The Extreme Value Theorem

Suppose that the per capita production of a population of fish is

$$\text{per capita production} = 2.5e^{-N_t}$$

and that a factor h times the pre-productive population is harvested each year (modified from Equation 3.3.1 and Section 1.9, Exercise 50). The discrete-time dynamical system for the population is

$$N_{t+1} = 2.5N_t e^{-N_t} - hN_t \tag{3.4.2}$$

We want to find the harvesting effort h that maximizes long-term harvest. Recall the steps used in "Maximizing Fish Harvest," Section 3.3: First find the equilibrium N^* as a function of h, next find the fish harvested as $P(h) = hN^*$, and then compute the maximum of $P(h)$ by differentiating.

To find the equilibria, follow the usual steps.

$$N^* = 2.5N^* e^{-N^*} - hN^* \quad \text{the original equation}$$
$$N^* - 2.5N^* e^{-N^*} + hN^* = 0 \quad \text{move everything to one side}$$
$$N^*(1 - 2.5e^{-N^*} + h) = 0 \quad \text{factor}$$
$$N^* = 0 \quad \text{or} \quad 1 - 2.5e^{-N^*} + h = 0 \quad \text{set each piece equal to 0}$$

Solving the second part requires a bit of algebra.

$$\begin{aligned} 1 - 2.5e^{-N^*} + h &= 0 && \text{original equation} \\ 1 + h &= 2.5e^{-N^*} && \text{move unknowns to one side} \\ \frac{1+h}{2.5} &= e^{-N^*} && \text{divide by 2.5} \\ \ln\left(\frac{1+h}{2.5}\right) &= -N^* && \text{take the natural logarithm} \\ N^* &= -\ln\left(\frac{1+h}{2.5}\right) && \text{solve for } N^* \\ N^* &= \ln\left(\frac{2.5}{1+h}\right) && \text{use law 3 of logs} \end{aligned}$$

Is this value positive? Recall that $\ln(x) > 0$ if $x > 1$. Therefore, N^* is positive if

$$\begin{aligned} \frac{2.5}{1+h} &> 1 \\ 2.5 &> 1 + h \\ 1.5 &> h \end{aligned}$$

If $h = 1.5$, this equilibrium is 0.

The harvest $P(h)$ is the factor h times the total population N^*, so

$$P(h) = hN^* = h\ln\left(\frac{2.5}{1+h}\right)$$

Does this equation have a maximum? We have two algorithms for finding a maximum, and each requires that we find critical points by computing the derivative and finding where it is equal to zero. In this case,

$$P'(h) = \ln\left(\frac{2.5}{1+h}\right) - \frac{h}{1+h}$$

Finding critical points requires solving the equation $P'(h) = 0$. This equation cannot be solved algebraically.

Nonetheless, we can still prove that this function has a maximum. We know that $P(0) = 0$ (no harvesting) and that $P(1.5) = 0$ (no fish). Furthermore, $P(h) > 0$ if $0 < h < 1.5$ because both h and N^* are positive (Figure 3.4.54). A function which is 0 at its endpoints and positive in between must have a maximum. Mathematically, this result follows from the **Extreme Value Theorem.**

Theorem 3.3 Extreme Value Theorem

If $f(x)$ is continuous for $a \le x \le b$, then there is a point c_h, $a \le c_h \le b$, where $f(x)$ takes on its global maximum and a point c_l, $a \le c_l \le b$, where $f(x)$ takes on its global minimum.

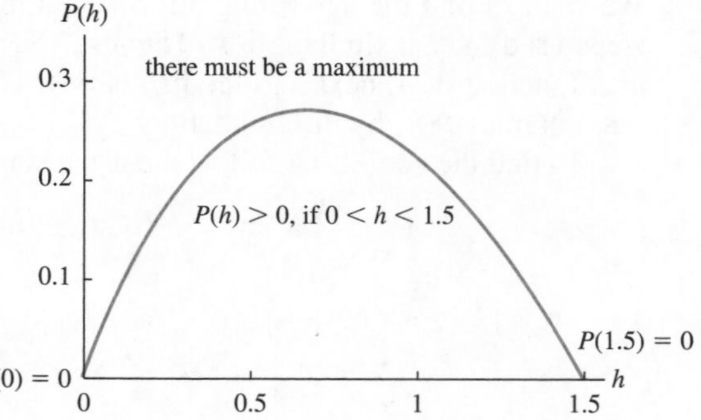

FIGURE 3.4.54

Reasoning about harvest: the Extreme Value Theorem

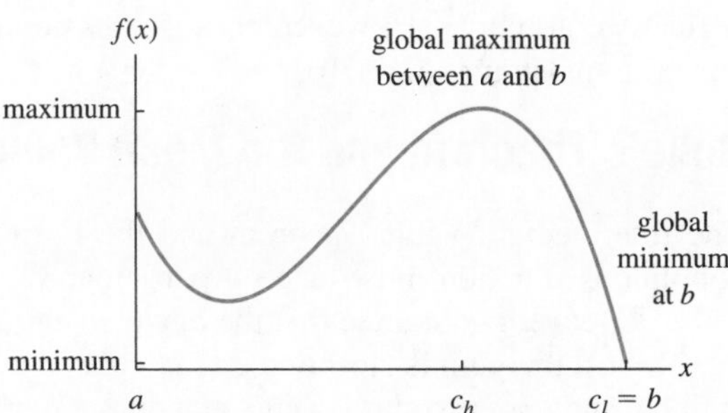

FIGURE 3.4.55
The Extreme Value Theorem

Again, the proof of this theorem in general is quite subtle. The conclusions are illustrated in Figure 3.4.55. The theorem does not guarantee that the maximum and minimum must occur strictly between a and b. Either might lie at one of the endpoints (the minimum in Figure 3.4.55 lies at the endpoint b).

Example 3.4.4 Applying the Extreme Value Theorem

Consider the function $f(x) = xe^{-x}$ (the gamma distribution with $n = 1$ studied in Example 2.8.7). The Extreme Value Theorem guarantees that the function has a maximum and a minimum on the interval $0 \leq x \leq 2$. In "Minima and Maxima," Section 3.3, we found that this function has a maximum at $x = 1$ and a minimum at $x = 0$ (Figure 3.4.56).

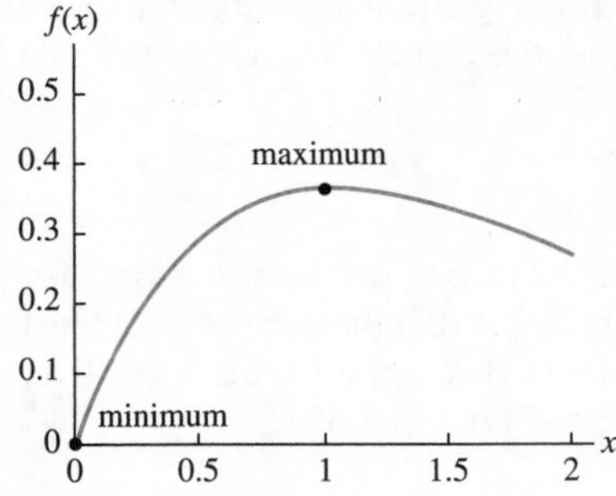

FIGURE 3.4.56
The function $f(x) = xe^{-x}$

The function $P(h)$ is continuous between $h = 0$ and $h = 1.5$ because it involves no division by or logs of zero. Therefore, the Extreme Value Theorem guarantees that it has a maximum. We know that the maximum does not lie at the endpoints because $P(h)$ takes on positive values, larger than the value at each endpoint, for all h between 0 and 1.5. The maximum guaranteed by the Extreme Value Theorem must occur for $0 < h < 1.5$. The minimum guaranteed by the Extreme Value Theorem is shared by the two endpoints.

Example 3.4.5 Failure of the Extreme Value Theorem When a Function Is Not Continuous

Why must the function in the Extreme Value Theorem be continuous? Consider the function $f(x) = \frac{1}{x}$ defined for x between -1 and 1 and with $f(0) = 0$ (Figure 3.4.57a). This function has a right-hand limit of infinity and a left-hand limit of negative infinity at $x = 0$, and it has neither a maximum nor a minimum value.

Even if we quarantine the trouble point $x = 0$ to the end of the interval, the Extreme Value Theorem breaks down. If we define the function only for $0 < x \leq 1$, $f(x)$ is

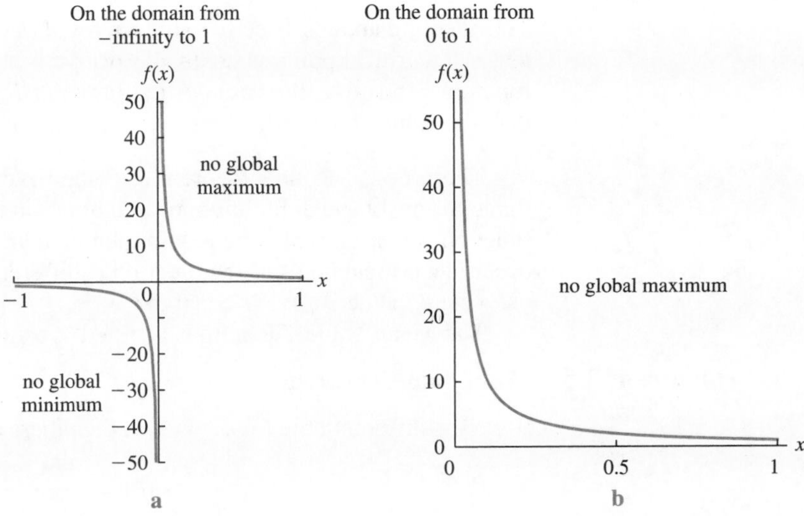

FIGURE 3.4.57
The function $f(x) = \frac{1}{x}$ fails to satisfy the conditions for the Extreme Value Theorem

perfectly continuous. However, because it is not defined at the endpoint, it fails to have a maximum (Figure 3.4.57b).

Rolle's Theorem and the Mean Value Theorem

The Intermediate Value Theorem and the Extreme Value Theorem guarantee that a continuous function must take on particular values. **Rolle's theorem** and the **Mean Value Theorem** guarantee that the *derivative* must take on particular values.

Rolle's theorem is closely related to the Extreme Value Theorem. If $P(h)$ is differentiable and the maximum occurs at a point other than an end point, then the derivative of $P(h)$ will be 0 at its maximum (Figure 3.4.54). Rolle's Theorem states that a differentiable function that takes on equal values at its endpoints must have a derivative equal to 0 at some point in between.

Theorem 3.4 Rolle's Theorem

If $f(x)$ is differentiable for all x with $a \le x \le b$, and $f(a) = f(b)$, then there exists some c such that $a < c < b$ and $f'(c) = 0$.

As with the Intermediate Value Theorem, this theorem guarantees only that there is at least one point at which the derivative is zero; there may be more than one (Figure 3.4.58).

Example 3.4.6 Application of Rolle's Theorem

The function $g(x) = x(1 - x)$ (studied in Example 3.3.1) takes on the value zero for both $x = 0$ and $x = 1$. Therefore, Rolle's theorem guarantees that there must be at least one point between 0 and 1 where the derivative is equal to 0. By computing the derivative, we found that there is only a single such point, $x = 0.5$ (Figure 3.4.59).

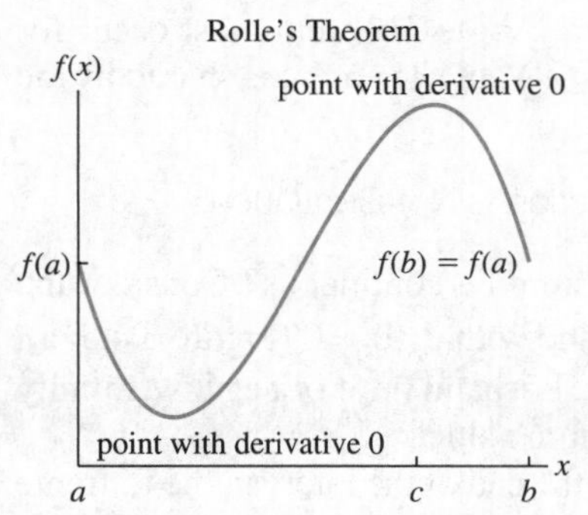

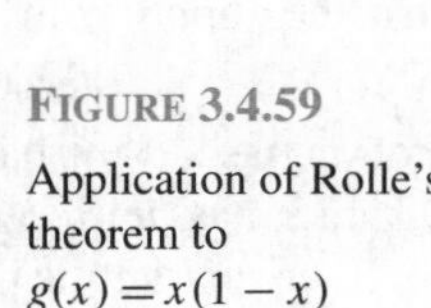

FIGURE 3.4.58
Rolle's theorem

FIGURE 3.4.59
Application of Rolle's theorem to $g(x) = x(1 - x)$

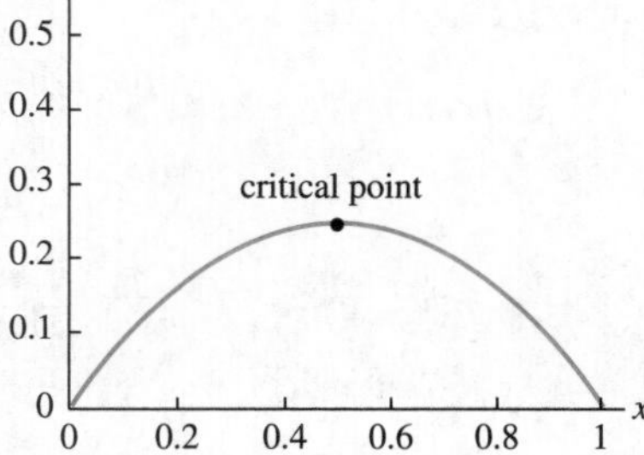

Example 3.4.7 Application of Rolle's Theorem to $P(h)$

This theorem applies directly to the harvest $P(h)$. Rolle's theorem guarantees the existence of a critical point where the derivative is equal to 0 for $0 < h < 1.5$. Because the function is positive, the value of the function P at the critical points must be greater than the value at the endpoints. The critical point must be a maximum.

The proof of Rolle's theorem uses the Extreme Value Theorem to show that the function must have a minimum or maximum in the interior of the interval (unless the function is constant) and the requirement that an interior minimum or maximum must occur at a critical point. If the function is differentiable, then the critical point must be one where the derivative is equal to 0.

The Mean Value Theorem is a "tilted" version of Rolle's theorem.

Theorem 3.5 Mean Value Theorem

If $f(x)$ is differentiable for $a \le x \le b$, then there exists some c such that $a < c < b$ and

$$f'(c) = \frac{f(b) - f(a)}{b - a}$$

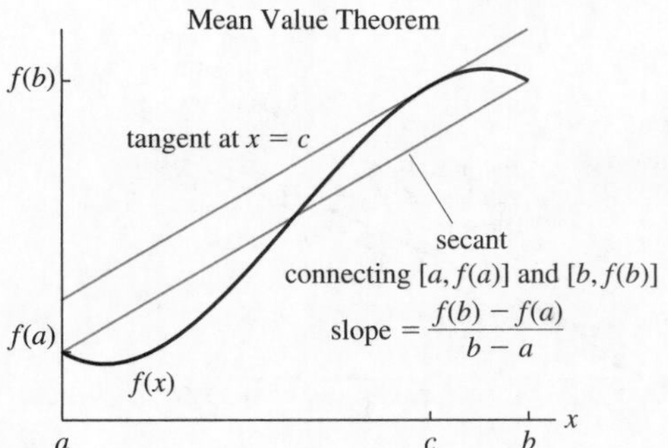

FIGURE 3.4.60

The Mean Value Theorem

This theorem says that the slope of the tangent line matches the slope of the secant at some point in the interval spanned by the secant (Figure 3.4.60). Alternatively, if the average rate of change during the interval from a to b is A, then there is a point in the interval when the instantaneous rate of change is equal to the A.

Example 3.4.8 Application of the Mean Value Theorem to Velocity

The most popular application of this theorem involves velocity. If a car travels 140 miles in 2 hrs, the average rate of change over this time is 70 mph. A graph of position versus time must pass through the two points (0, 0) and (2, 140), and the line connecting these is a secant line. The Mean Value Theorem guarantees that the instantaneous velocity (on the speedometer) must have been exactly 70 mph at some time (Figure 3.4.61).

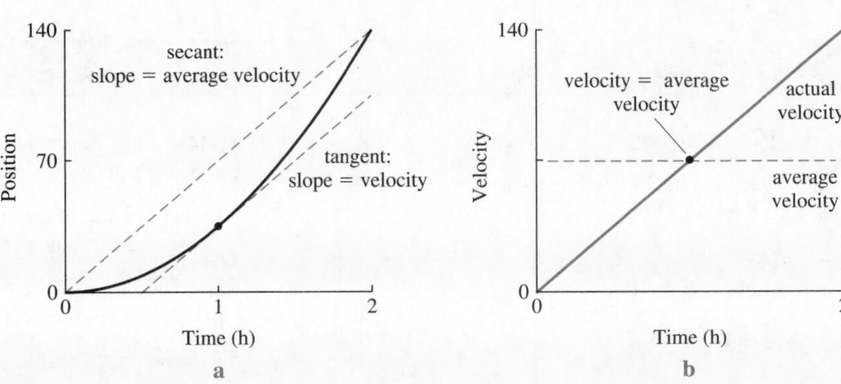

FIGURE 3.4.61

The Mean Value Theorem applied to velocity

Example 3.4.9 Finding the Point Guaranteed by the Mean Value Theorem

The Mean Value Theorem guarantees that for some x with $1 \le x \le 2$, the slope of $h(x) = \ln(x)$ must exactly match the slope of the secant connecting $(1, h(1))$ and $(2, h(2))$. The slope of the secant is

$$\text{slope of secant} = \frac{h(2) - h(1)}{2 - 1} = \frac{\ln(2) - \ln(1)}{1} = \ln(2)$$

Where is $h'(x) = \ln(2)$? We recall that

$$\frac{d}{dx}(\ln(x)) = \frac{1}{x}$$

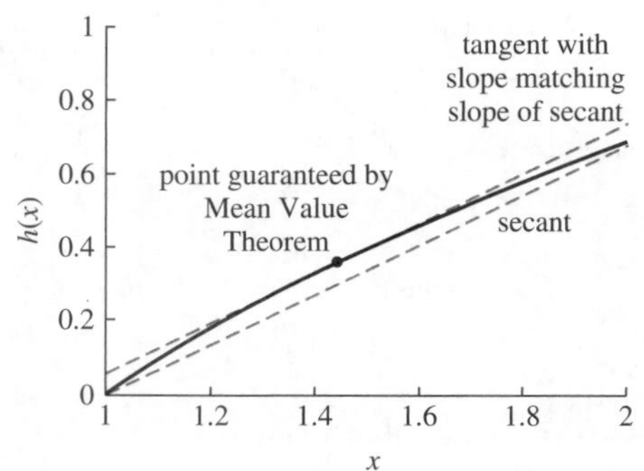

FIGURE 3.4.62
The Mean Value Theorem applied to $\ln(x)$

so the value is the solution of

$$h'(x) = \frac{1}{x} = \ln(2)$$

Therefore, $x = \frac{1}{\ln(2)} \approx 1.443$ (Figure 3.4.62).

Summary With a minimum of algebra, we can use theorems about continuous and differentiable functions to deduce mathematical conclusions. We began by showing that a version of the lung model with absorption must have an equilibrium by using the **Intermediate Value Theorem,** which guarantees that a continuous function takes on all values between those at its endpoints. We then argued that a new version of the harvesting model must take on a maximum value with the **Extreme Value Theorem,** which states that a continuous function that is defined on a domain including the endpoints must have a maximum and a minimum. We applied **Rolle's Theorem** to the same problem, arguing that a differentiable function that takes on equal values at its endpoints must have a critical point in between where the derivative is equal to 0. Its generalization, the **Mean Value Theorem,** states that the derivative of a differentiable function must at some point match the slope of the secant.

3.4 Exercises

Mathematical Techniques

1–6 ▪ Use the Intermediate Value Theorem to show that the following equations have solutions for $0 \le x \le 1$.

1. $e^x + x^2 - 2 = 0$
2. $e^x - 3x^2 = 0$
3. $e^x + x^2 - 2 = x$
4. $e^x + x^2 - 2 = \cos(2\pi x) - 1$
5. $xe^{-3(x-1)} - 2 = 0$ (you will need to check an intermediate point).
6. $x^3e^{-4(x-1)} - 1.1 = 0$ (you will need to check an intermediate point).

7–10 ▪ Show that each of the following functions has a positive maximum on the interval $0 \le x \le 1$.

7. $f(x) = x(x-1)e^x \le 0$
8. $f(x) = ex - xe^x$
9. $f(x) = 5x(1-x)(2-x) - 1$
10. $f(x) = 8x(1-x)^2 - 1$

11–14 ▪ Find the points guaranteed by the Mean Value Theorem and sketch the associated graph.

11. The graph of the function $f(x) = x^2$ must match the slope of the secant connecting $x = 0$ and $x = 1$.
12. The graph of the function $f(x) = x^2$ must match the slope of the secant connecting $x = 0$ and $x = 2$.
13. The graph of the function $g(x) = \sqrt{x}$ must match the slope of the secant connecting $x = 0$ and $x = 1$. (The mean value Theorem still applies even though $\sqrt{x}$ is not differentiable at $x = 0$.)
14. The graph of the function $g(x) = \sqrt{x}$ must match the slope of the secant connecting $x = 0$ and $x = 2$.

15–20 ▪ Draw graphs of functions with the following properties.

15. A function with a global minimum and a global maximum between the endpoints.
16. A function with a global maximum at the left endpoint and a global minimum between the endpoints.
17. A differentiable function with a global maximum at the left endpoint, a global minimum at the right endpoint, and no critical points.

18. A function with a global maximum at the left endpoint, a global minimum at the right endpoint, and at least one critical point.

19. A function with a global minimum and a global maximum between the endpoints, but no point with derivative equal to 0.

20. A function that never reaches a global maximum.

21–22 ▪ Check whether the conclusions of the Intermediate Value Theorem and the Mean Value Theorem fail in the following cases where the function is not continuous.

21. Consider the Heaviside function (Section 2.3, Exercise 25) defined by

$$\begin{cases} H(x) = 0 & \text{if } x < 0 \\ H(x) = 1 & \text{if } x \geq 0 \end{cases}$$

Show that there is no solution to the equation $H(x) = 1/2$ and that there is no tangent that matches the slope of the secant connecting $(-1, H(-1))$ and $(1, H(1))$.

22. Consider the absolute value function $g(x) = |x|$. Does this satisfy the conditions for the Intermediate Value Theorem? Show that there is no tangent whose slope matches the slope of the secant connecting $(-1, g(-1))$ and $(2, g(2))$.

23–24 ▪ There is a clever proof of the Mean Value Theorem from Rolle's theorem. The idea is to tilt the function f so that it takes on the same values at the endpoints a and b. In particular, we apply Rolle's theorem to the function

$$g(x) = f(x) - (x - a)\frac{f(b) - f(a)}{b - a}$$

For the following functions, show that $g(a) = g(b)$, apply Rolle's theorem to g, and find the derivative of f at a point where $g'(x) = 0$.

23. $f(x) = x^2$, $a = 1$ and $b = 2$.

24. In general, without assuming a particular form for $f(x)$ or values for a and b.

Applications

25–28 ▪ Try to apply the Intermediate Value Theorem to the following problems.

25. The price of gasoline rises from \$1.199 to \$1.279. Why is it not necessarily true that the price was exactly \$1.25 at some time?

26. A pot is dropped from the top of a 500-ft building exactly 200 ft above your office. Must it have fallen right past your office window?

27. A cell takes up 1.5×10^{-9} mL of water in the course of an hour. Must the cell have taken up exactly 1.0×10^{-9} mL at some time? Is it possible that the cell took up exactly 2.0×10^{-9} mL at some time?

28. The population of bears in Yellowstone Park has increased from 100 to 1000. Must it have been exactly 314 at some time? What additional assumption would guarantee this?

29–32 ▪ The Intermediate Value Theorem can often be used to prove that complicated discrete-time dynamical systems have equilibria.

29. Prove that the discrete-time dynamical system $x_{t+1} = \cos(x_t)$ has an equilibrium between 0 and $\pi/2$.

30. A lung follows the discrete-time dynamical system $c_{t+1} = 0.25e^{-3c_t}c_t + 0.75\gamma$ where $\gamma = 5.0$. Show that there is an equilibrium between 0 and γ.

31. A lung follows the discrete-time dynamical system $c_{t+1} = 0.75\alpha(c_t)c_t + 0.25\gamma$ where $\gamma = 5.0$ and the function $\alpha(c_t)$ is positive, decreasing, and $\alpha(0) = 1$. Show that there is an equilibrium between 0 and γ.

32. A lung follows the discrete-time dynamical system $c_{t+1} = f(c_t)$. We know only that neither c_{t+1} nor c_t can exceed 1 mol/L. Use the Intermediate Value Theorem to show that this discrete-time dynamical system must have an equilibrium.

33–34 ▪ The Intermediate Value Theorem has applications in agricultural transport.

33. A farmer sets off on Saturday morning at 6 A.M. to bring a crop to market, arriving in town at noon. On Sunday she sets off in the opposite direction at 6 A.M. and returns home along the same route, arriving once again at noon. Use the Intermediate Value Theorem to show that at some point along the path, her watch must have read exactly the same time on both of the two days.

34. Suppose instead that the farmer sets off one morning at 6 A.M. to bring a crop to market and arrives in town at noon. Having received a great price for her crop, she buys a new car and drives home the next day along the same route, leaving at 10 A.M. and arriving home at 11 A.M. Is it still true that at some point along the route her watch must read exactly the same time on both of the two days? If so, must that time occur between 10 and 11 A.M.?

35–38 ▪ An organism grows from 4.0 kg to 60 kg in 14 yr. Suppose that mass is a differentiable function of time.

35. Why must the mass have been exactly 10 kg at some time?

36. Why must the rate of increase have been exactly 4.0 kg/yr at some time?

37. Draw a graph of mass against time where the mass is increasing, is equal to 10.0 kg at 13 yr, and has a growth rate of exactly 4.0 kg/yr after 1 yr.

38. Draw a graph of mass against time where the organism reaches 10.0 kg at 1 yr and has a growth rate of exactly 4.0 kg/yr at 13 yr.

39–42 ▪ Draw the positions of cars from the following descriptions of 1-hr trips. What speed must the car achieve according to the Mean Value Theorem? What speeds must the car achieve according to the Intermediate Value Theorem?

39. A car starts at 60 mph and slows down to 0 mph. The average speed is 20 mph after 1 h.

40. A car starts at 60 mph, slows down to 20 mph, and then speeds up to 50 mph by the end of 1 h. The average speed over the whole time is 40 mph.

41. A car drives 60 miles in 1 h and never varies speed by more than 10 mph.

42. In a test, a car drives zero net distance in 1 h by switching from reverse to forward at some point. The test includes achieving the maximum possible reverse speed (20 mph) and the maximum possible forward speed (120 mph).

43–44 ▪ The Marginal Value Theorem states that the best time t to leave a patch (feeding location) is the solution t of the equation

$$F'(t) = \frac{F(t)}{t+\tau}$$

where τ is the travel time to the next patch and $F(t)$ is the total amount of food gathered in one location up to time t. Suppose that $\tau = 1$ and $F(t) = 1 - e^{-t}$.

43. Sketch the associated figure (as in Figure 3.3.61) and estimate the solution.

44. Use the Intermediate Value Theorem to prove that there is a solution.

Computer Exercise

45. Consider the model

$$c_{t+1} = (1-q)(1-\alpha(c_t))c_t + q\gamma$$

where

$$\alpha(c) = \frac{c^n}{1+c^n}$$

Study the behavior of the model for $n=1$, $n=5$, and $n=15$ and for values of q between 0 and 1 (you can pick any value of γ). When is the equilibrium stable? Can you explain in biological terms why the equilibrium is stable when $n=15$ and q is either near 0 or near 1?

3.5 Limits at Infinity

Models of biological systems sometimes lead to complicated functional forms. Reasoning about these functions often requires computing the behavior of the function at the endpoints of its domain. When there is no natural upper bound to the domain, we must figure out what happens to the function as its argument gets very large. To do so, we generalize the limit to include **limits at infinity** and study the behavior of the exponential, power, and logarithmic functions, finding which approach infinity, zero, or other values. Because many biological processes involve more than one basic function, we must be able to *compare* them. The key tool we will use is a way to formalize whether one function approaches infinity or zero **faster** or **slower** than another. The concept of limits at infinity can be used to study **limits of sequences,** the output of discrete-time dynamical systems with stable equilibria.

The Behavior of Functions at Infinity

Suppose the function

$$\alpha(c) = 0.5\left(1 - e^{-0.5c}\right)$$

describes the fraction of chemical absorbed by a lung during each breath. The total amount absorbed with each breath is

$$\begin{aligned}\text{amount absorbed} &= \alpha(c)cV \\ &= 0.5\left(1 - e^{-0.5c}\right)cV\end{aligned}$$

the product of the fraction absorbed, the concentration c, and the volume V. What does the graph of the function $\alpha(c)$ look like? What does the graph of the total amount absorbed look like?

The amount of a chemical or resource used as a function of the amount available is important throughout biology. For consumers, like predators, this relation is called the **functional response.** In chemical reactions, this relation is often described by **Michaelis-Menton** or **Monod** reaction kinetics.

Several possible absorption functions are given in Table 3.5.1 (see Figure 3.5.63 for graphs). Each describes the total amount of chemical absorbed as a function of the concentration c. The parameter A is a measure of efficiency, with small values producing low absorption and large values producing high absorption. The parameters k and β describe the shape of the function.

Table 3.5.1 Some Different Absorption Functions

Function of c	Description	Figure
Ac	Linear absorption	3.5.63a
$\frac{Ac}{k+c}$	Saturated absorption	3.5.63b
$\frac{Ac^2}{k+c^2}$	Saturated absorption with threshold	3.5.63c
$Ace^{-\beta c}$	Saturated absorption with overcompensation I	3.5.63d
$\frac{Ac}{k+c^2}$	Saturated absorption with overcompensation II	3.5.63e
$Ac(1+kc)$	Enhanced absorption	3.5.63f

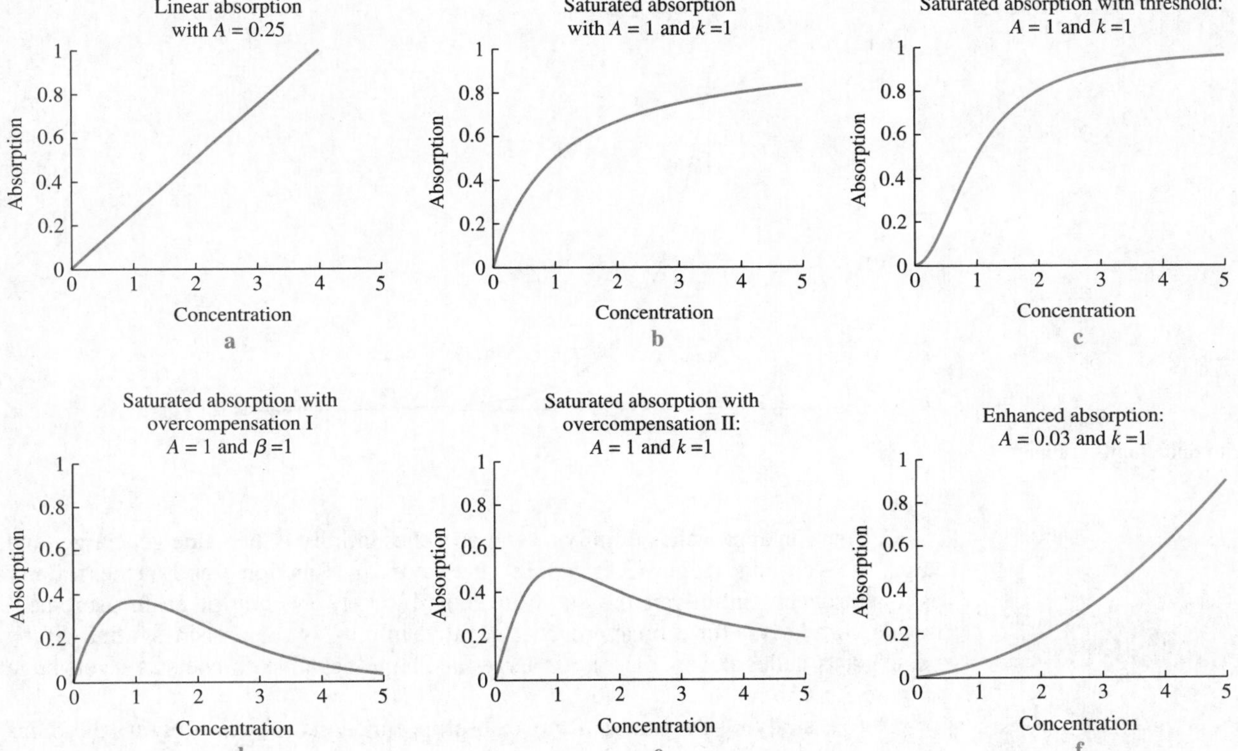

FIGURE 3.5.63
Various absorption functions

In each case, absorption is 0 when $c = 0$. The behavior of the absorption function for large values of c describes absorption at high concentrations. How do we compute and describe the functions as their arguments become large?

Recall that infinity is the mathematician's abstraction of the scientist's idea of "very large." Because infinity is not a number that we can substitute into equations, we can only *approach* it. The limit (Section 2.2) tells us how a function behaves as the argument approaches some finite value. We now extend this idea to find limits as the argument x becomes very large, or "approaches infinity."

To say that a function approaches a limit L as x approaches infinity means that the value gets closer and closer to L as x gets huge (Figure 3.5.64a). In other words, a function f approaches the limit L as x approaches infinity if the measurement eventually becomes indistinguishable from the limit.

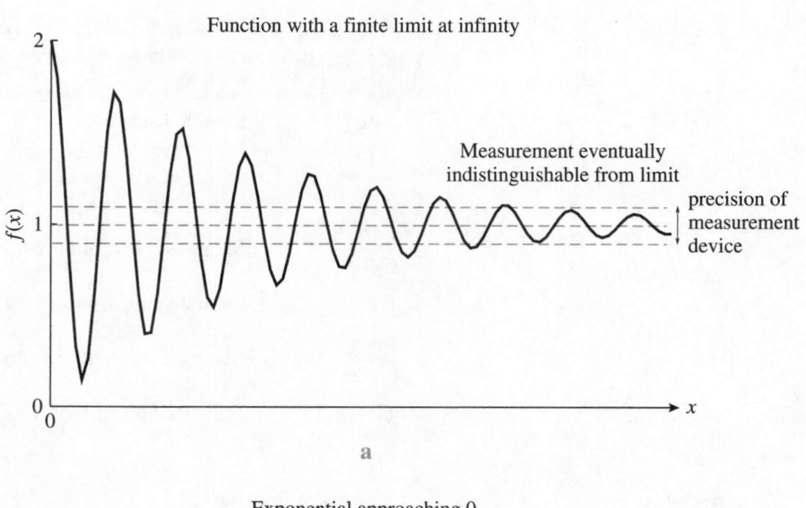

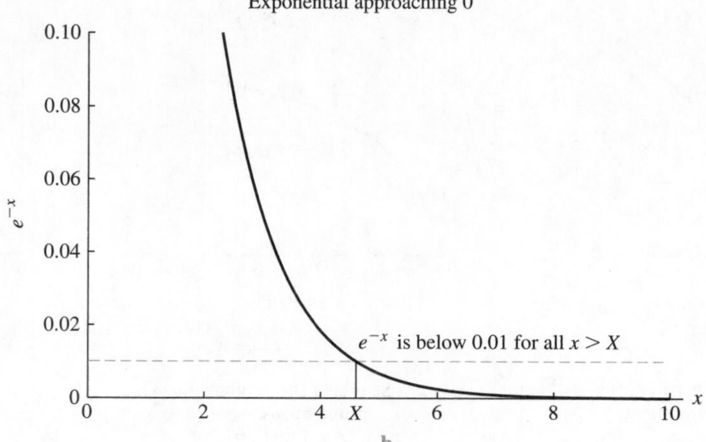

FIGURE 3.5.64
Functions with finite limits at infinity

A function approaches infinity as x approaches infinity if the value gets larger and larger as x gets huge (Figure 3.5.65a). In other words, the function f approaches infinity as x approaches infinity if the output eventually overflows any given measurement device. Similarly, a function approaches negative infinity as x approaches infinity if the value gets smaller and smaller (i.e., a large- and large-negative number) as x gets huge (Figure 3.5.65b).

Before studying the limits of the absorption functions shown in Figure 3.5.63 as c approaches infinity, we will learn how to compare the limits of power, logarithmic, and exponential functions.

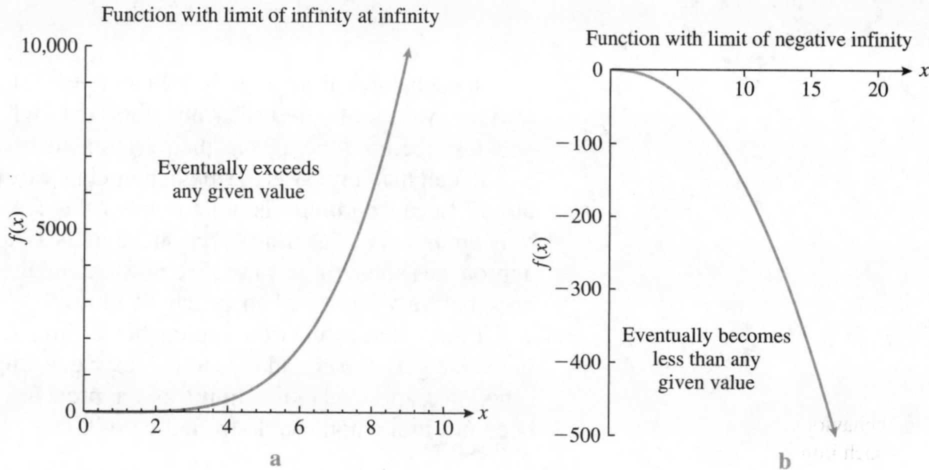

FIGURE 3.5.65
Functions with infinite limits at infinity

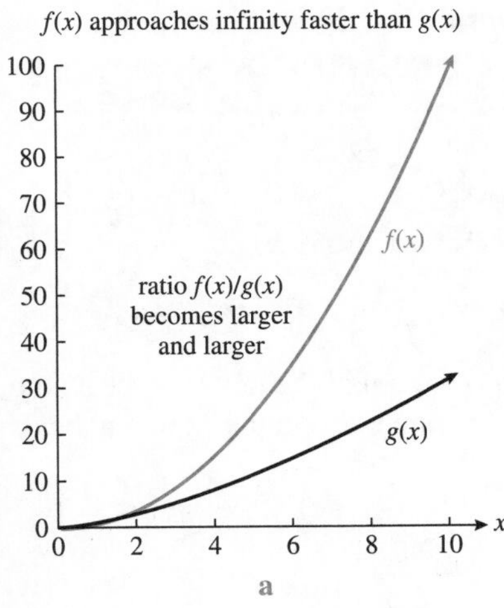

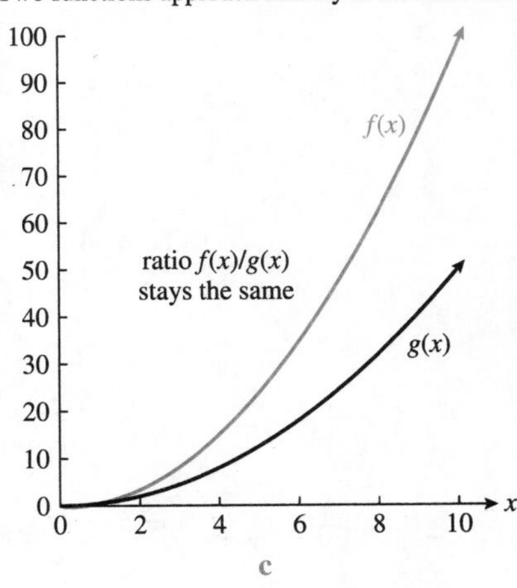

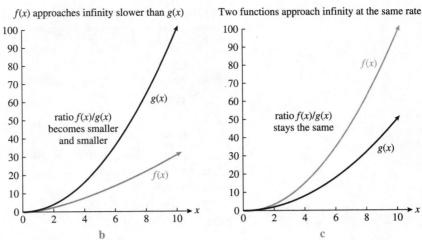

FIGURE 3.5.66
Comparing functions at infinity

Comparing Functions That Approach ∞ at ∞ Many of the fundamental functions of biology approach infinity at infinity, including the natural logarithm $\ln(x)$, the power function x^n with positive n, and the exponential function e^x.

To reason about more complicated functions, like those in Table 3.5.1, we must *compare* the behaviors of these basic functions. The graph of e^x increases very quickly, whereas that of $\ln(x)$ increases slowly. Is there a precise way in which the exponential function increases "faster" than the logarithmic function? What does it mean to approach infinity "faster" or "slower"? These relations are summarized in the following definition.

Definition 3.1 Suppose

$$\lim_{x\to\infty} f(x) = \infty$$
$$\lim_{x\to\infty} g(x) = \infty$$

1. The function $f(x)$ approaches infinity **faster** than $g(x)$ as x approaches infinity if

$$\lim_{x\to\infty} \frac{f(x)}{g(x)} = \infty$$

2. The function $f(x)$ approaches infinity **slower** than $g(x)$ if

$$\lim_{x\to\infty} \frac{f(x)}{g(x)} = 0$$

3. $f(x)$ and $g(x)$ approach infinity at the **same rate** if

$$\lim_{x\to\infty} \frac{f(x)}{g(x)} = L$$

where L is any finite number other than 0.

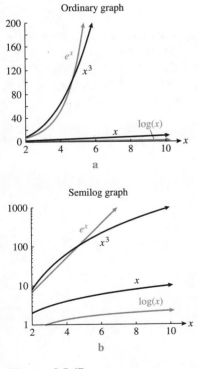

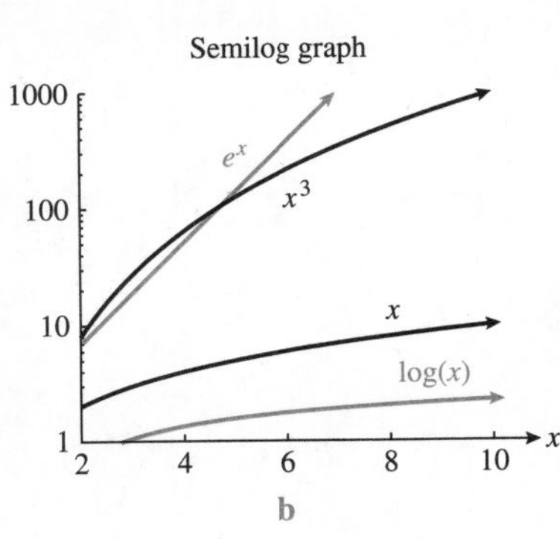

FIGURE 3.5.67
The behavior of the basic functions that approach infinity

When $f(x)$ approaches infinity faster than $g(x)$, $f(x)$ gets farther and farther ahead of $g(x)$ (Figure 3.5.66a). When $f(x)$ approaches infinity slower, $f(x)$ falls farther and farther behind $g(x)$ (Figure 3.5.66b). When the two functions approach infinity at the same rate, neither gets ahead or falls behind (Figure 3.5.66c). *Faster, slower,* and at *the same rate* act like *greater than, less than,* and *equal to* for numbers. They provide a way to compare the "sizes" of functions.

The basic functions are shown in increasing order in Table 3.5.2 and Figure 3.5.67. The constant a in front of each function can be any positive number and does not change

Table 3.5.2 The Basic Functions in Increasing Order of Speed

Function	Comments
$a\ln(x)$	Goes to infinity slowly
ax^n with $n > 0$	Approaches infinity faster for larger n
$ae^{\beta x}$ with $\beta > 0$	Approaches infinity faster for larger β

the order of the functions. Any power function, however small the power n, beats the logarithm. Any exponential function with a positive parameter β in the exponent beats any power function.

Example 3.5.1 Ordering a Set of Functions

To order the functions

$$0.1e^{2x},\ 4.5\ln(x),\ 23.2x^{0.5},\ 10.1e^{0.2x},\ 0.03x^4$$

in increasing order, first spot functions of the three types: logarithmic, power, and exponential. There is only one logarithmic function, which is therefore the slowest. There are two power functions, with $23.2x^{0.5}$ having the smaller power and $0.03x^4$ having the larger. There are two exponential functions, with $10.1e^{0.2x}$ having the smaller parameter (0.2) inside the exponent and the exponential function $0.1e^{2x}$ having the larger parameter (2) inside the exponent. In increasing order, these functions are $4.5\ln(x)$, $23.2x^{0.5}$, $0.03x^4$, $10.1e^{0.2x}$, $0.1e^{2x}$. The constants in front do not affect the ordering.

There are two cautions regarding this method. First, comparing functions that are not logarithmic, power, or exponential functions requires different techniques (Section 3.6). Second, these results hold only for very large values of x.

Example 3.5.2 Functions That Take a Long Time to Get into Order

The power function x^2 does eventually grow faster than $1000x$ because it has a larger power (Figure 3.5.68). However, $x^2 < 1000x$ for $x < 1000$. If x cannot realistically take on values greater than 1000, the comparison in Table 3.5.2 is not relevant. When a comparison includes a large or a small parameter (1000 in this case), we must first check whether the faster function becomes larger for biologically reasonable values of the argument.

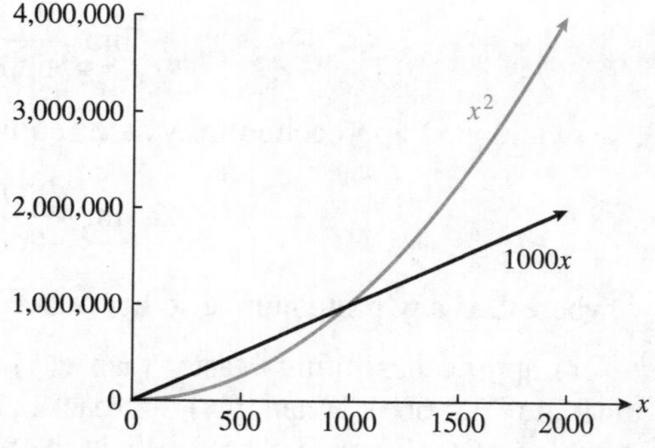

FIGURE 3.5.68
A faster function eventually overtaking a slower function

Functions Approaching 0 at ∞ We use a similar approach to compare the rate at which functions approach a limit of 0.

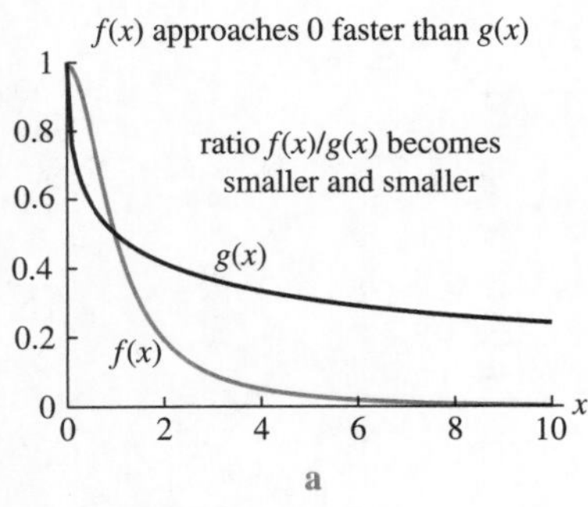

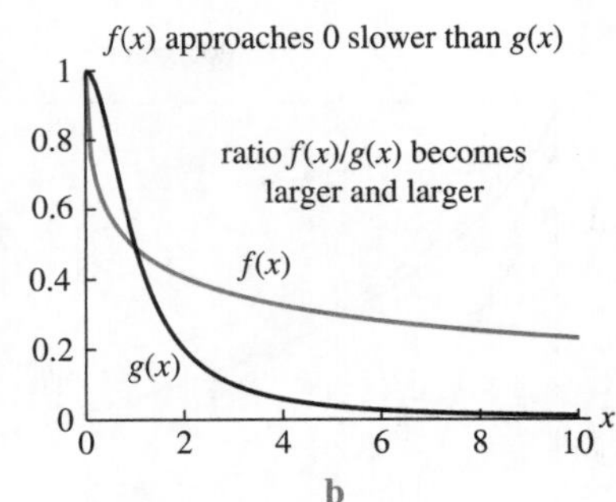

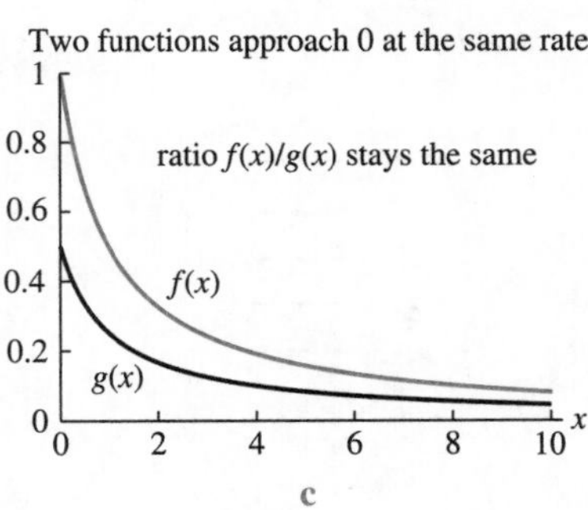

FIGURE 3.5.69
Comparing functions that approach a limit of zero at infinity

Definition 3.2 Suppose

$$\lim_{x \to \infty} f(x) = 0$$
$$\lim_{x \to \infty} g(x) = 0$$

1. The function $f(x)$ approaches 0 **faster** than $g(x)$ as x approaches infinity if

$$\lim_{x \to \infty} \frac{f(x)}{g(x)} = 0$$

2. The function $f(x)$ approaches 0 **slower** than $g(x)$ as x approaches infinity if

$$\lim_{x \to \infty} \frac{f(x)}{g(x)} = \infty$$

3. $f(x)$ approaches 0 at the same rate as $g(x)$ if

$$\lim_{x \to \infty} \frac{f(x)}{g(x)} = L$$

where L is any finite number other than 0.

Be careful not to confuse this with the definition for functions approaching infinity (Definition 3.1). The function $f(x)$ approaches 0 faster if it becomes *small* faster than $g(x)$ (Figure 3.5.69).

The basic examples are reciprocals of the functions in Table 3.5.2 (Table 3.5.3 and Figure 3.5.70). If $f(x)$ approaches *infinity* quickly, the reciprocal $\frac{1}{f(x)}$ approaches 0 quickly. Because these functions decrease so quickly, they are easier to distinguish on a semilog graph (Figure 3.5.70b). Again, the positive constant a does not change the ordering of the functions.

Example 3.5.3 Ordering Functions That Approach 0

To order the functions

$$0.1e^{-2x},\ 23.2x^{-0.5},\ 10.1e^{-0.2x},\ 0.03x^{-4}$$

from the one that approaches zero fastest to the one that approaches slowest, first identify the functions as exponential and power functions. The fastest is the exponential function

Table 3.5.3 The Basic Functions Approaching 0

Function	Comments
ax^{-n} with $n > 0$	Approaches 0 faster for larger n
$ae^{-\beta x}$ with $\beta > 0$	Approaches 0 faster for larger β
$ae^{-\beta x^2}$ with $\beta > 0$	Approaches 0 really fast

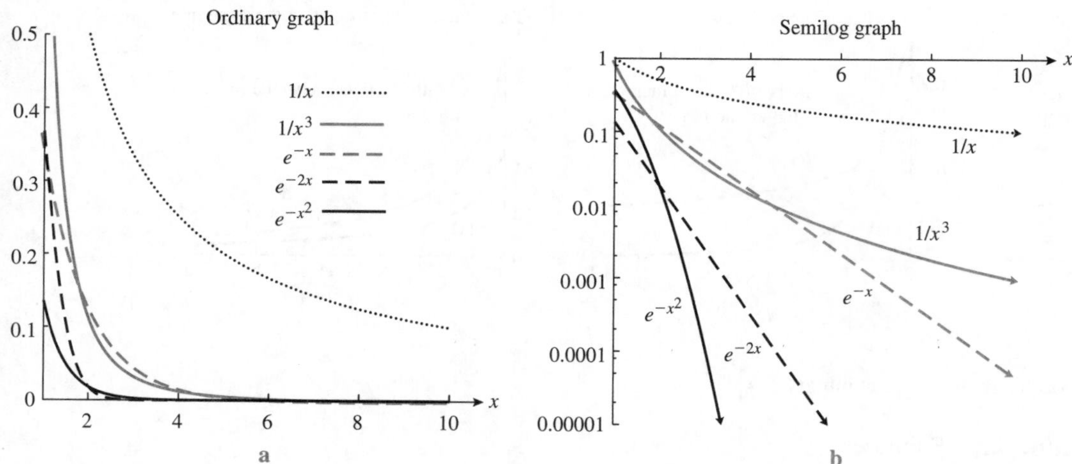

FIGURE 3.5.70
The behavior of the basic functions that approach 0

with the most negative parameter $0.1e^{-2x}$, followed by the exponential function with the less negative parameter $10.1e^{-0.2x}$, then the power function $0.03x^{-4}$ with the more negative power, and finally the power function $23.2x^{-0.5}$ with the less negative power. From fastest to slowest, they are $0.1e^{-2x}$, $10.1e^{-0.2x}$, $0.03x^{-4}$, $23.2x^{-0.5}$.

Application to Absorption Functions

How can we use these facts about the basic functions to understand the absorption functions in Table 3.5.1? The results are summarized in Table 3.5.4. We compare the numerator and denominator of the absorption function as functions of the concentration c. If the numerator grows faster than the denominator, absorption grows without bound as c gets large. If the numerator and denominator grow at the same rate, absorption approaches a constant as c gets large (Figure 3.5.63b and c). If the denominator grows faster than the numerator, absorption approaches zero as c gets large (Figure 3.5.63d and e).

With linear absorption (Figure 3.5.63a), absorption grows without bound (there is no denominator to balance the numerator). Because there are almost always limits to absorption, the saturated absorption functions (Figure 3.5.63b and c) provide more reasonable models.

The saturated absorption form represented in Figure 3.5.63b, a ratio of linear functions, is among the most important in biology and is known as the **Michaelis-Menton** or **Monod** equation. In the next section we will deduce the difference in shape between the forms shown in Figure 3.5.63b and c and formalize the calculation of the behavior at infinity with the **method of leading behavior.**

In the forms shown in Figure 3.5.63d and e, the denominator grows faster than the numerator (both exponential and quadratic functions grow faster than linear functions).

Table 3.5.4 Analyzing Absorption Functions

Number	Numerator	Denominator	Behavior at infinity
22.1a	Linear	None	Approaches infinity
22.1b	Linear	Linear	Approaches constant
22.1c	Quadratic	Quadratic	Approaches constant
22.1d	Linear	Exponential	Approaches zero
22.1e	Linear	Quadratic	Approaches zero

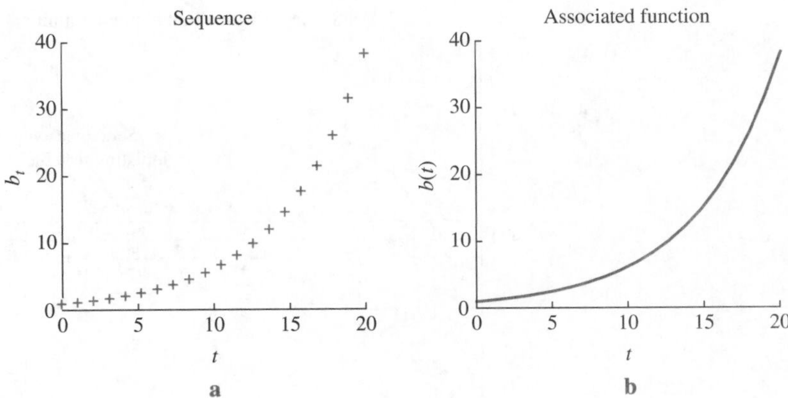

FIGURE 3.5.71
A sequence and its associated function

These functions begin at 0, increase to a maximum, and eventually decrease again to 0. This behavior is called **overcompensation** because absorption decreases when the concentration is too large.

Limits of Sequences

We use the same idea to define the limit of a solution of a discrete-time dynamical system. The solution of the bacterial discrete-time dynamical system $b_{t+1} = rb_t$ is

$$b_t = b_0 r^t = b_0 e^{\ln(r)t}$$

This differs from an ordinary function in that populations are defined only at integer values of t. The solution is a list of numbers known as a **sequence.**

To find the limit, define the **associated function** $b(t)$ as the exponential function

$$b(t) = b_0 e^{\ln(r)t}$$

defined for all values of t. This function fills in the gaps in the sequence (Figure 3.5.71). If the associated function has a limit, whether it is 0, infinity, or some other value, the sequence will share that limit. In this case, the associated function is an exponential function. If $r > 1$, the parameter in the exponent is positive, and the limit of the function—and therefore of the sequence—is infinity. If $r < 1$, the parameter in the exponent is negative, and the limit of the function—and therefore of the sequence—is zero. If $r = 1$, the function has the constant value b_0, and the function and sequence share the limit b_0.

This definition has an important connection with the idea of a **stable equilibrium.** If the sequence of points that represents a solution approaches a particular value as a limit, that limit is a stable equilibrium (Figure 3.5.72a).

Example 3.5.4 The Limit of a Solution of the Medication Discrete-time Dynamical System

In Example 1.5.14, we found the solution of the discrete-time dynamical system

$$M_{t+1} = 0.5M_t + 1.0$$

describing the concentration of medication in the bloodstream to be

$$M_t = 2.0 + 0.5^t \cdot 3.0$$

with initial condition $m(0) = 5.0$. The associated function $M(t)$ can be written as

$$M(t) = 2.0 + 3.0 \cdot e^{\ln(0.5)t}$$

The second term is an exponential function with a negative coefficient in the power ($\ln(0.5) \approx -0.693 < 0$), implying that this solution approaches 0 as the argument t approaches infinity. The whole associated function then approaches the value 2.0. The sequence of points that represents the solution also approaches 2.0. ▲

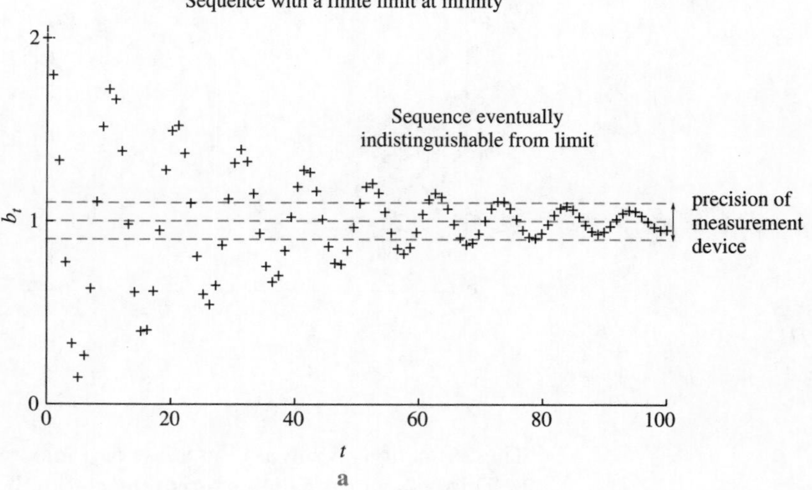

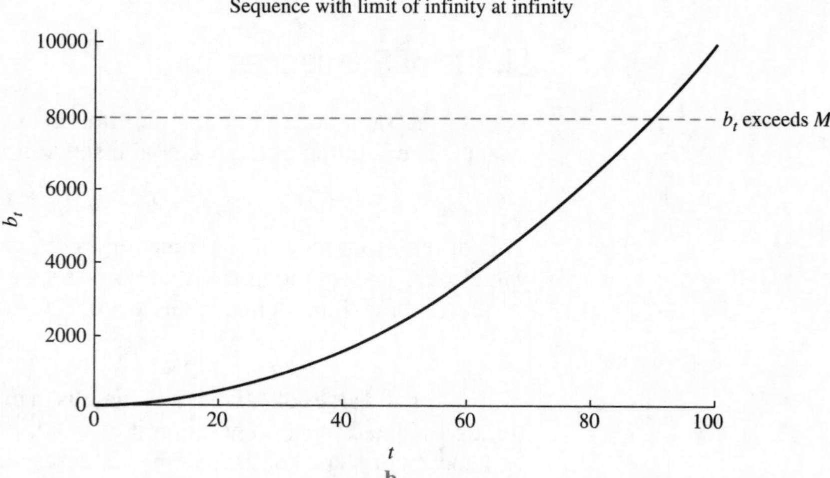

FIGURE 3.5.72
Limits of sequences at infinity

Example 3.5.5 A Case Where the Sequence and Associated Function Behave Differently

If the associated function has a limit, the sequence shares that limit. The sequence, however, may have a limit even when the associated function does not. Consider the sequence

$$a_t = \sin(2\pi t)$$

The associated function $a(t) = \sin(2\pi t)$ has no limit because it oscillates forever. The sequence, on the other hand, takes on only the value 0 and has the limit 0 (Figure 3.5.73).

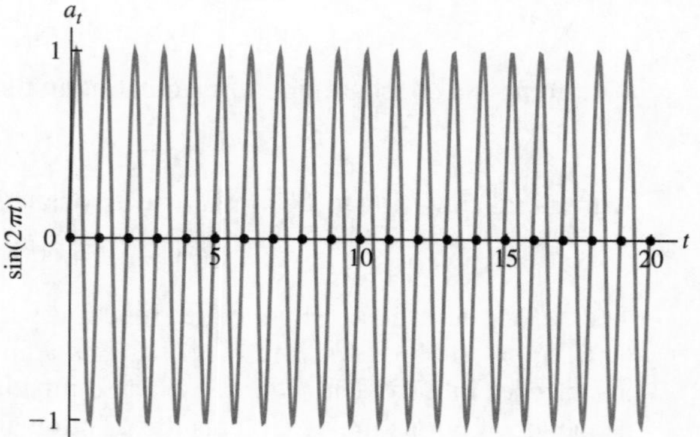

FIGURE 3.5.73
A sequence with a different limit from its associated function

Summary In order to reason about the behavior of functions with large inputs, we defined the **limit** of a function as its argument approaches infinity. As with ordinary limits, the limit formalizes the idea that the value gets closer and closer to some particular number (if the limit is finite) or larger than any given number (if the limit is infinite). One function approaches infinity **faster** than another if the limit of the ratio is infinity. Exponential functions approach infinity faster than power functions, which in turn approach infinity faster than the logarithmic functions. Conversely, one function approaches 0 faster than another if the limit of the ratio is 0. Exponential functions with negative parameters approach 0 faster than power functions with negative powers. Using limits at infinity, we analyzed the limits of **sequences,** lists of numbers generated as solutions of discrete-time dynamical systems, by studying the **associated function.**

3.5 Exercises

Mathematical Techniques

1–8 ▪ Find the following limits.

1. $\lim_{x\to\infty} x^{-0.25}$
2. $\lim_{x\to\infty} \ln(x/5)$
3. $\lim_{x\to\infty} 0.8^x$
4. $\lim_{x\to\infty} 1 - e^{-4x}$
5. $\lim_{x\to\infty} 1 + x^4$
6. $\lim_{x\to\infty} 1.2^{x+2}$
7. $\lim_{x\to\infty} e^{-x^2}$
8. $\lim_{x\to\infty} (x^2 + 2)^{0.25}$

9–14 ▪ For each pair of functions, say which approaches ∞ faster as x approaches infinity. Explain which rule you used to compare each pair. Compute the value of each function at $x = 1$, $x = 10$, and $x = 100$. How do these compare with the order of the functions in the limit? If they are different, how large would x have to be for the values to match the order in the limit?

9. x^2 and e^{2x}
10. x^3 and $1000x$
11. $x^{3.5}$ and $0.1x^{10}$
12. $5e^x$ and e^{5x}
13. $0.1x^{0.5}$ and $30\ln(x)$
14. $10x^{0.1}$ and $x^{0.5}$

15–20 ▪ For each pair of functions, say which approaches 0 more quickly as x approaches infinity. Explain which rule you used to compare each pair. Compute the value of each function at $x = 1$, $x = 10$, and $x = 100$. How do these compare with the order of the functions in the limit? If they are different, how large would x have to be for the values to match the order in the limit?

15. e^{-2x} and x^{-10}
16. $10e^{-x}$ and $0.1e^{-0.2x}$
17. $1000/x$ and $x^{-3.5}$
18. $x^{-0.1}$ and $25x^{-0.2}$
19. x^{-2} and $30/\ln(x)$
20. $1/\ln(x)$ and $30x^{-0.1}$

21–24 ▪ The following are possible absorption functions. What happens to each as c approaches infinity? Assume that all parameters take on positive values.

21. $\dfrac{\beta c^2}{1+e^c}$
22. $\dfrac{Ac}{\ln(1+c)}$
23. $\dfrac{\gamma(e^c-1)}{e^{2c}}$
24. $\dfrac{c^2}{1+10c}$

Applications

25–30 ▪ Find the derivatives of the following absorption functions (from Table 3.1 with particular values of the parameters). Compute the value at $c = 0$ and the limit of the derivative as c approaches infinity. Are your results consistent with the figures?

25. $\alpha(c) = 5c$
26. $\alpha(c) = \dfrac{5c}{1+c}$
27. $\alpha(c) = \dfrac{5c^2}{1+c^2}$
28. $\alpha(c) = \dfrac{5c}{e^{2c}}$
29. $\alpha(c) = \dfrac{5c}{1+c^2}$
30. $\alpha(c) = 5c(1+c)$.

31–34 ▪ A bacterial population that obeys the discrete-time dynamical system $b_{t+1} = rb_t$ with initial condition b_0 has solution $b_t = b_0 r^t$. For the following values of r and b_0, state which populations increase to infinity and which decrease to 0. For those increasing to infinity, find the time when the population will reach 10^{10}. For those decreasing to 0, find the time when the population will reach 10^3.

31. $b_0 = 10^8$ and $r = 1.1$
32. $b_0 = 10^8$ and $r = 1.5$

33. $b_0 = 10^8$ and $r = 0.5$

34. $b_0 = 10^8$, $r = 0.9$

35–36 ▪ In the polymerase chain reaction (PCR) used to amplify DNA, some sequences of DNA that are produced are too long and others are the right length. Denote the number of overly long pieces after t generations of the process by l_t and the number of pieces of the right length by r_t. The dynamics follow approximately

$$l_{t+1} = l_t + 2$$
$$r_{t+1} = 2r_t$$

because two new overly long pieces are produced each step while the number of good pieces doubles. Suppose that $l_0 = 0$ and $r_0 = 2$.

35. Find expressions for l_t and r_t, and compute the fraction of pieces that are too long after 1, 5, 10, and 20 generations of the process.

36. Find the ratio of the number of pieces that are too long to the total number of pieces as a function of time. What is the limit? How long would you have to wait to make sure that less than 1 in a million pieces are too long? (This can't be solved exactly, just plug in some numbers.)

37–40 ▪ Consider the discrete-time dynamical system for medication given by $M_{t+1} = 0.5M_t + 1.0$ with $M_0 = 3$.

37. Find the equilibrium.

38. The solution is $M_t = 2.0 + 0.5^t \cdot 3.0$. Find the limit as $t \to \infty$.

39. How long will the solution take to be within 1% of the equilibrium?

40. What are two ways to show that this equilibrium is stable?

41–46 ▪ As mentioned in the text, the amount of food a predator eats as a function of prey density is called the **functional response.** Functional response is often broken into three categories:

- Type I: Linear.
- Type II: Increasing, concave down, finite limit.
- Type III: Increasing with finite limit, concave up for small prey densities, concave down for large prey densities.

41. Sketch pictures of these three types. Which of the absorption functions do they resemble? What is the optimal prey density for a predator in each case?

42. Suppose that the number of prey that escape increases linearly with the number of prey (the prey join together and fight back). Let p be the number of prey and $F(p)$ be the functional response. The number of prey captured is then $F(p) - cp$. The constant c represents how effectively the prey can fight. Write the equation for the optimal prey density (the value giving the maximum rate of prey capture) in terms of $F'(p)$.

43. Draw a picture illustrating the optimal prey density in a case with a type II functional response.

44. Draw a picture illustrating the optimal prey density in a case with a type III functional response.

45. Find the optimal prey density if $F(p) = p$. Make sure to consider separately cases with $c < 1$ and $c > 1$.

46. Find the optimal prey density if $F(p) = \frac{p}{1+p}$. Make sure to consider separately cases with $c < 1$ and $c > 1$.

47–50 ▪ Try to think of a biological mechanism that could produce the following relations between the amount absorbed and the concentration of chemical.

47. Saturated absorption, but with an infinite limit as the concentration approaches infinity.

48. Saturated absorption with a finite limit as the concentration approaches infinity.

49. Overcompensation.

50. Enhanced absorption.

Computer Exercise

51. Use your computer to find out how large x must be before the faster function finally overtakes the slower function.

a. $e^{0.1x}$ catches up with x^3.

b. $0.1e^x$ catches up with x^3.

c. $0.1e^{0.1x}$ catches up with x^3.

d. $0.1x$ catches up with $\ln(x)$.

e. $x^{0.1}$ catches up with $\ln(x)$.

3.6 Leading Behavior and L'Hôpital's Rule

Finding limits at infinity gives general information about the behavior of functions. In particular, we learned how to compare the ratios of different functions by describing which increased to infinity or decreased to zero faster. We now study a much larger class of functions, **sums** of functions and the ratios of sums. The technique, called the **method of leading behavior,** consists of focusing on the largest piece of the function. By determining the leading behavior of a function at both infinity and zero, we can deduce a great deal about the *shape* of the function by using the technique of **matched leading behaviors.** When the method of leading behavior fails, **L'Hôpital's** rule provides an alternative way to compare the behavior of functions.

Leading Behavior of Functions at Infinity

Suppose we wish to describe how the sum of several functions, such as

$$f(x) = 5e^{2x} + 34e^{x} + 45x^{5} + 56\ln(x) + 10$$

behaves for large values of x. We might suspect that this function will be dominated by the fastest term, the one that increases faster than all the others in the sense of Definition 3.1. The **method of leading behavior** is based on this idea.

Definition 3.3 The **leading behavior** of a function at infinity is the term that is largest in absolute value as the argument approaches infinity. We write f_∞ to represent the leading behavior of the function f at infinity.

The largest term in the function $f(x)$ is $5e^{2x}$ because the exponential term with the largest parameter in the exponent grows to infinity most quickly. Therefore,

$$f_\infty(x) = 5e^{2x}$$

In what sense does the leading behavior describe a function? On a semilog plot, the graph of the leading behavior looks indistinguishable from the graph of the original function when x is large, even though the two functions are quite different for small x (Figure 3.6.74). More mathematically, if we divide a function by its leading behavior, the limit is 1 (they approach infinity at the same rate). For example,

$$\begin{aligned}\lim_{x\to\infty}\frac{f(x)}{f_\infty(x)} &= \lim_{x\to\infty}\frac{5e^{2x} + 34e^{x} + 45x^{5} + 56\ln(x) + 10}{5e^{2x}}\\ &= \lim_{x\to\infty} 1 + \frac{34e^{x}}{5e^{2x}} + \frac{45x^{5}}{5e^{2x}} + \frac{56\ln(x)}{5e^{2x}} + \frac{10}{5e^{2x}}\\ &= 1 + 0 + 0 + 0 + 0 = 1\end{aligned}$$

All terms after the first approach 0 because $5e^{2x}$ approaches infinity the fastest. Although these functions become similar relatively (their ratio approaches 1), they do not become similar absolutely (their difference does not approach 0).

Example 3.6.1 Comparing Functions with the Method of Leading Behavior

Complicated functions can be compared by comparing their leading behaviors. To find whether the function $f(x)$ increases to infinity faster than the function

$$g(x) = 23e^{2.5x} + 3e^{2x} + 2x^{6}$$

we need only compare the leading behavior of $f(x)$ with that of $g(x)$. The leading behavior of the function $g(x)$ is the first term, as the term with the largest parameter in the exponent, so

$$g_\infty(x) = 23e^{2.5x}$$

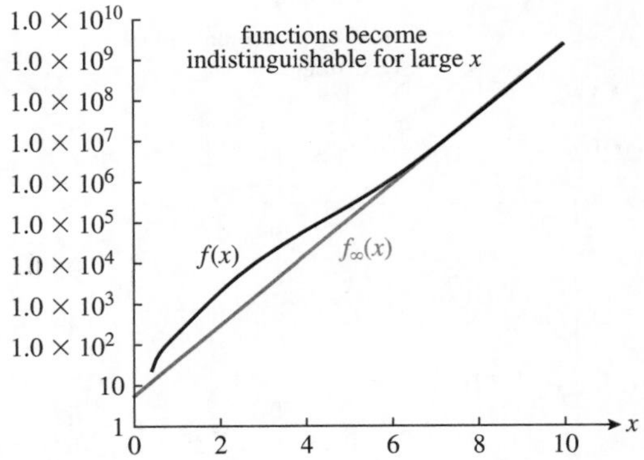

FIGURE 3.6.74
A comparison of a function and its leading behavior in a semilog plot

To see whether $f(x)$ approaches infinity faster than $g(x)$, we compute the limit of the ratio of the functions as x approaches infinity. Because each function is well represented by its leading behavior,

$$\begin{aligned}\lim_{x\to\infty}\frac{f(x)}{g(x)} &= \lim_{x\to\infty}\frac{f_\infty(x)}{g_\infty(x)}\\ &= \lim_{x\to\infty}\frac{5e^{2x}}{23e^{2.5x}}\\ &= 0\end{aligned}$$

because the exponential in the denominator has a larger parameter. The function $g(x)$ approaches infinity faster than $f(x)$.

However, the leading behavior gives more information than the limit. For large x,

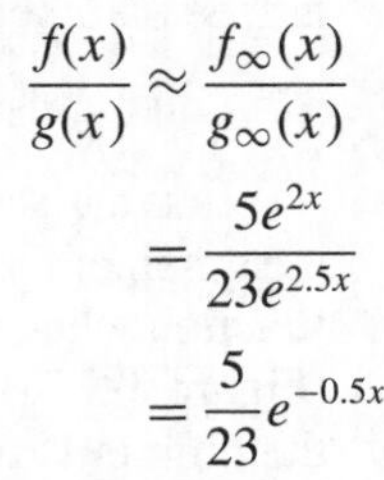

$$\begin{aligned}\frac{f(x)}{g(x)} &\approx \frac{f_\infty(x)}{g_\infty(x)}\\ &= \frac{5e^{2x}}{23e^{2.5x}}\\ &= \frac{5}{23}e^{-0.5x}\end{aligned}$$

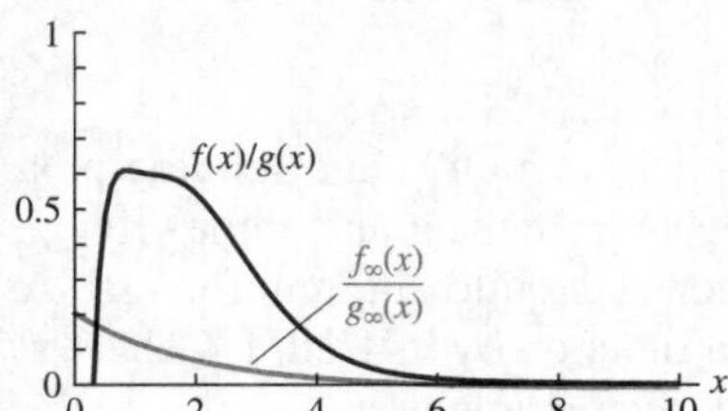

FIGURE 3.6.75
The ratio of two functions compared with the ratio of their leading behaviors

This computation tells us not only that $g(x)$ approaches infinity faster than $f(x)$ but also gives an idea of how much faster. The ratio of the functions behaves much like the ratio of the leading behaviors for large x (Figure 3.6.75).

The same definition of leading behavior works for sums of functions that approach 0. Remember that the largest term is the term approaching 0 the *most slowly*, in the sense of Definition 3.2.

Example 3.6.2 Computing the Leading Behavior of a Function That Approaches 0

The leading behavior of the function

$$h(x) = 5e^{-2x} + 34e^{-x} + 45x^{-5}$$

is the power term $45x^{-5}$ because it approaches 0 the most slowly and is therefore the largest for large x,

$$h_\infty(x) = 45x^{-5}$$

(Figure 3.6.76).

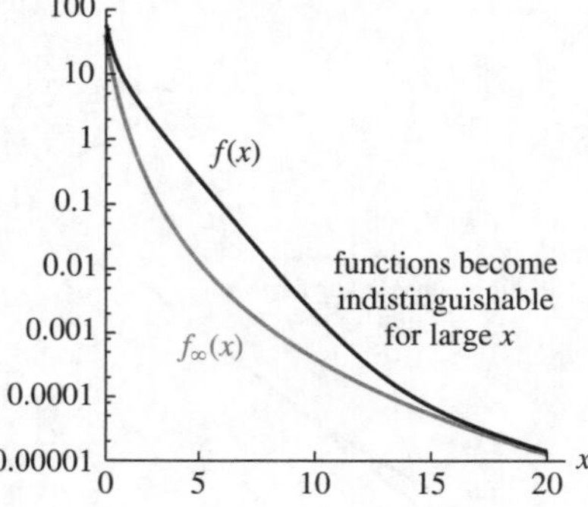

FIGURE 3.6.76
A function that approaches 0 and its leading behavior on a semilog plot

Example 3.6.3 The Leading Behavior of a Sum That Includes a Term That Does Not Approach 0

Similarly, the function

$$H(x) = 5e^{-2x} + 34e^{-x} + 45x^{-5} + 5$$

has leading behavior

$$H_\infty(x) = 5$$

because the constant 5 does not approach 0 and is therefore the largest (Figure 3.6.77).

Example 3.6.4 Application to the Absorption Function Shown in Figure 3.5.63b

We can apply the idea of leading behavior to supplement our reasoning about the absorption functions in Figure 3.5.63b. The absorption function with saturation has formula

$$\alpha(c) = \frac{Ac}{k + c}$$

where c is the concentration and A and k are constant parameters. Both numerator and denominator increase to infinity. The leading behavior of the denominator is c, the larger of the two terms. Replacing the denominator by the leading behavior, we have

$$\alpha_\infty(c) = \frac{Ac}{c} = A$$

for large values of c (Figure 3.6.78). In the figure, both k and A have been set to 1. Absorption saturates at A.

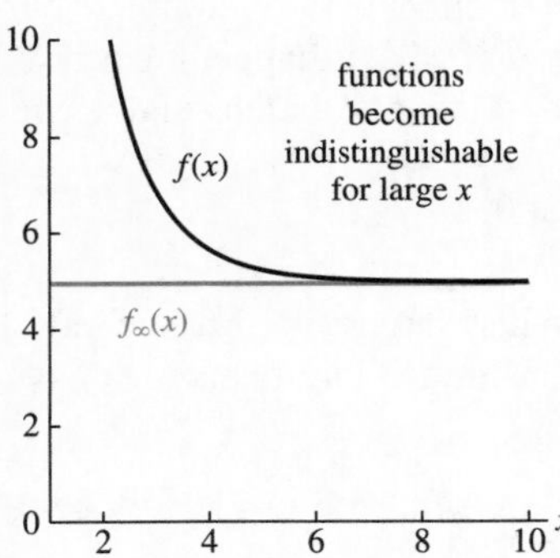

FIGURE 3.6.77
A function that approaches a finite value and its leading behavior

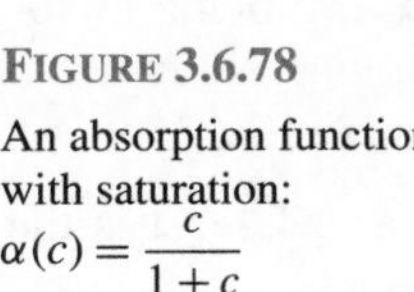

FIGURE 3.6.78
An absorption function with saturation: $\alpha(c) = \frac{c}{1 + c}$

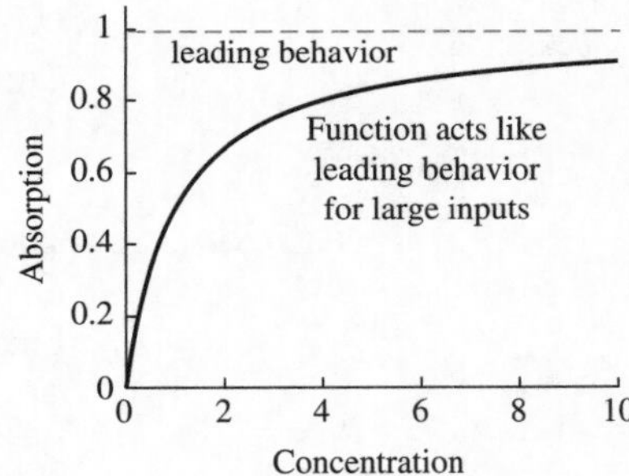

Example 3.6.5 Application to the Absorption Function Shown in Figure 3.5.63c

Similarly, the absorption function with saturation and a threshold (Figure 3.5.63c) has formula

$$\alpha(c) = \frac{Ac^2}{k + c^2}$$

The numerator is a single term, which is its own leading behavior. The leading behavior of the denominator is c^2 because it increases faster than the constant k. For large values of c,

$$\alpha_\infty(c) = \frac{Ac^2}{c^2} = A$$

This function also saturates at A (Figure 3.6.79). In the figure, the parameters k and A have been set to 1.

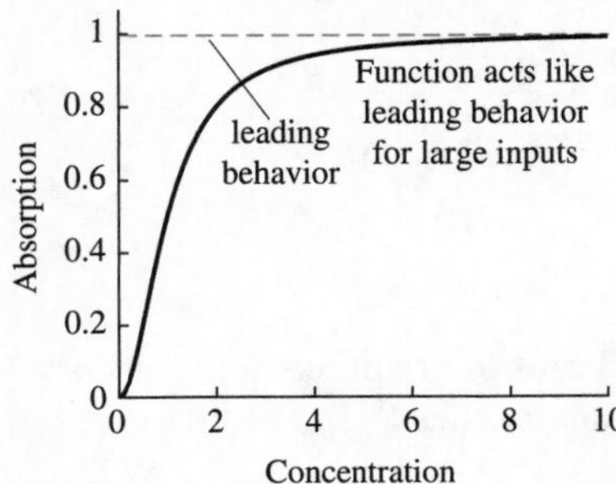

FIGURE 3.6.79
Another absorption function with saturation: $\alpha(c) = \frac{c^2}{1 + c^2}$

Example 3.6.6 Application to the Absorption Function Shown in Figure 3.5.63d

The method of leading behavior tells us nothing new about the absorption function

$$\alpha(c) = Ace^{-\beta c}$$

We can rewrite this function as a ratio by placing the negative power in the denominator, giving $\alpha(c) = \frac{Ac}{e^{\beta c}}$. The limit as c approaches infinity is 0 because an exponential function grows faster than a linear function. Because the numerator and denominator each have only a single term, we cannot simplify further.

Example 3.6.7 Application to the Absorption Function Shown in Figure 3.5.63e

The alternative absorption function with overcompensation (Figure 3.5.63e),

$$\alpha(c) = \frac{Ac}{k + c^2}$$

can be simplified with the method of leading behavior. In this case, the leading behavior of the denominator is again the quadratic term c^2, so

$$\alpha_\infty(c) = \frac{Ac}{c^2} = \frac{A}{c}$$

Absorption decreases to 0 and does so like the function $\frac{A}{c}$ (Figure 3.6.80).

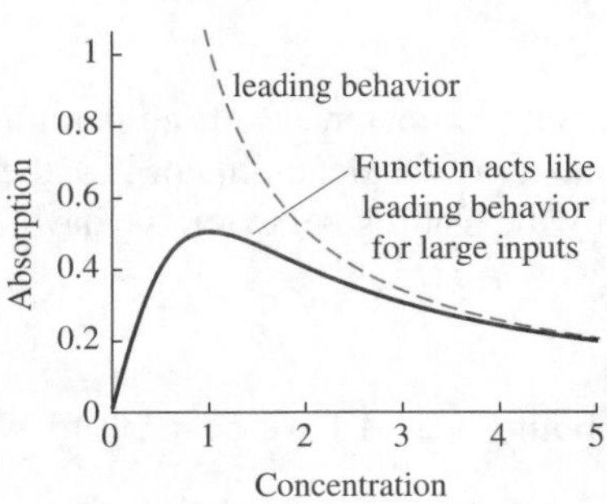

FIGURE 3.6.80
An absorption function with overcompensation

Leading Behavior of Functions at 0

In each comparison of an absorption function with its leading behavior, we have done well for large values of the concentration and poorly for small values. To complete our analysis of the absorption functions, we need a better sense of what is happening near 0. Once again, the method of leading behavior can be used to identify which small terms can be ignored.

First, we define the leading behavior of a function at 0.

Definition 3.4 The **leading behavior** of a function at 0 is the term that is largest in absolute value as the argument approaches 0. We write f_0 to represent the leading behavior of the function f at 0.

The idea of largest is the same at 0 and at infinity. It is formalized in the following definition.

Definition 3.5

1. The function $f(x)$ is **larger** than $g(x)$ as x approaches 0 if

$$\lim_{x\to 0} \frac{f(x)}{g(x)} = \infty$$

2. The function $f(x)$ is **smaller** than $g(x)$ as x approaches 0 if

$$\lim_{x\to 0} \frac{f(x)}{g(x)} = 0$$

This definition really includes two cases: $f(x)$ and $g(x)$ approach infinity as x approaches 0, and $f(x)$ and $g(x)$ approach 0 as x approaches 0. In the first case, all power functions of the form

$$f(x) = x^{-n}$$

with positive values of n approach infinity as x approaches 0 (from the right). The larger the value of n, the faster the function approaches infinity and thus the **larger** it is.

Example 3.6.8 The Leading Behavior with Negative Powers at 0

The sum

$$f(x) = x^{-1} + 5x^{-5}$$

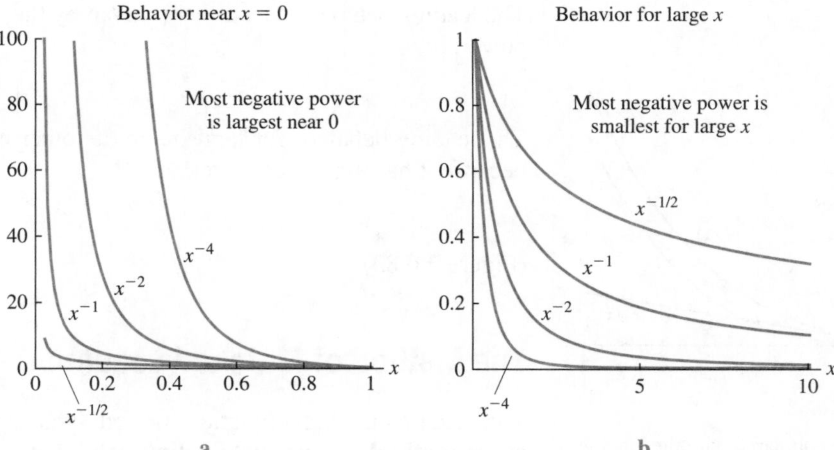

FIGURE 3.6.81
Power functions with negative powers

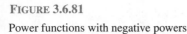

has leading behavior

$$f_0(x) = 5x^{-5}$$

because $5x^{-5}$ approaches infinity faster than x^{-1}. The limit of the ratio of the terms is

$$\lim_{x\to 0} \frac{5x^{-5}}{x^{-1}} = \lim_{x\to 0} 5x^{-4} = \infty$$

Power functions with large negative powers do everything fast, approaching ∞ quickly at 0, and 0 quickly at ∞, and are thus *largest* for small values of x and *smallest* for large values of x (Figure 3.6.81).

Similarly, if two functions $f(x)$ and $g(x)$ approach 0 as x approaches 0, the *larger* function approaches 0 more *slowly*. All power functions of the form

$$f(x) = x^n$$

for positive values of n approach 0 as x approaches 0. As before, power functions with large powers do everything quickly. The larger the power of n, the *faster* the function approaches 0 for x near 0 and the faster it approaches infinity as x approaches infinity (Figure 3.6.82). These functions are small for small x and large for large x.

Example 3.6.9 The Leading Behavior of a Polynomial at 0

Consider the function

$$F(x) = 4x + x^3$$

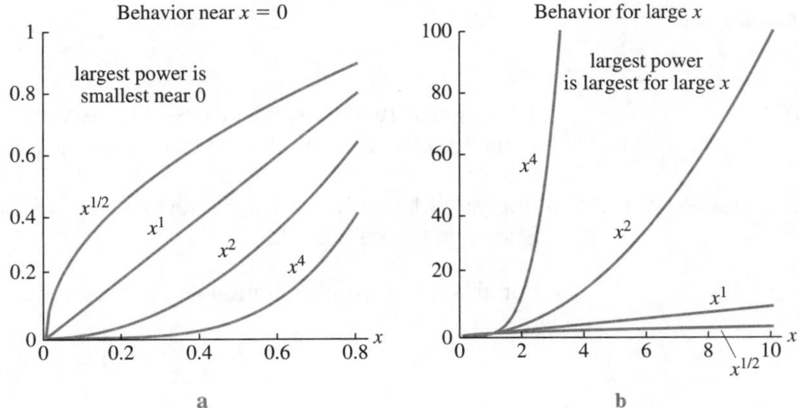

FIGURE 3.6.82
Power functions with positive powers

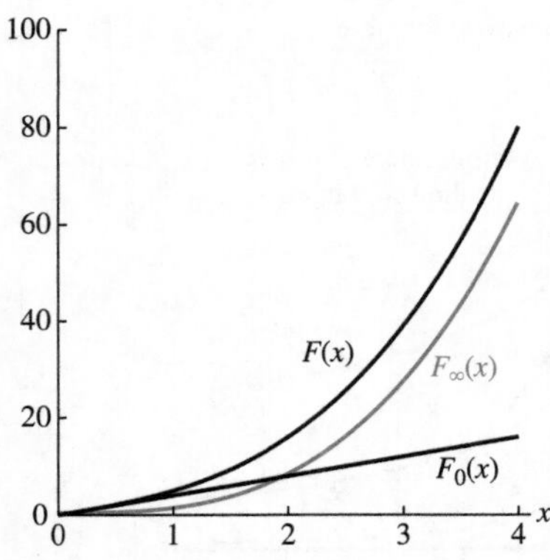

FIGURE 3.6.83

A function compared with the leading behavior at 0 and infinity

The leading behavior near $x = 0$ is given by the first term x because it has the smallest power, or

$$F_0(x) = 4x$$

The leading behavior for large x, on the other hand, is given by the second term $4x^3$ because it has the larger power, or

$$F_\infty(x) = x^3$$

(Figure 3.6.83).

The Method of Matched Leading Behaviors

The idea of studying a function for both large and small values of x can be formalized as the **method of matched leading behaviors.**

Algorithm 3.3 The Method of Matched Leading Behaviors

1. Find the leading behavior at 0 and at infinity.
2. Sketch graphs of each leading behavior.
3. Sketch a graph that matches the leading behavior at 0 and approaches the leading behavior at ∞.

Example 3.6.10 Applying Matched Leading Behaviors to the Absorption Function Shown in Figure 3.5.63b

Consider the absorption function with saturation (Example 3.6.4),

$$\alpha(c) = \frac{Ac}{k + c}$$

Near 0, we first simplify by finding the leading behavior of the denominator as

$$(k + c)_0 = k$$

because the constant value k is much *larger* than c for small c. Therefore,

$$\alpha_0(c) = \frac{Ac}{k}$$

For large values of c, the denominator becomes

$$(k + c)_\infty = c$$

because the constant value k is much *smaller* than c for large c. Therefore,

$$\alpha_\infty(c) = \frac{Ac}{c} = A$$

These linear functions can be easily approximated with a smooth curve, illustrated in Figure 3.6.84 with parameter values $A = 1$ and $k = 1$.

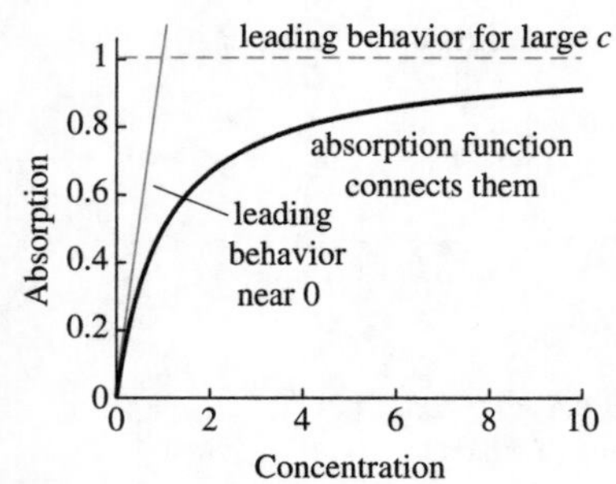

FIGURE 3.6.84

Saturated absorption

Example 3.6.11 Applying Matched Leading Behaviors to the Absorption Function Shown in Figure 3.5.63c

For absorption with saturation and a threshold

$$\alpha(c) = \frac{Ac^2}{k + c^2}$$

(Example 3.6.5), we can again use the method of matched leading behaviors to plot an accurate graph. For small values of c, the denominator has leading behavior

$$(k+c^2)_0 = k$$

because the constant value k is much larger than c^2 for small c. Therefore,

$$\alpha_0(c) = \frac{Ac^2}{k}$$

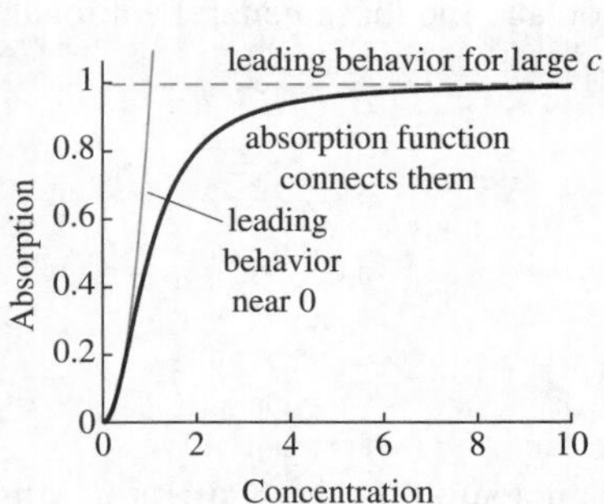

FIGURE 3.6.85

Saturated absorption with threshold

This part of the curve looks like a parabola. For large values of c, the denominator becomes

$$(k+c^2)_\infty = c^2$$

because the constant value k is much smaller than c^2 for large c. Therefore,

$$\alpha_\infty(c) = \frac{Ac^2}{c^2} = A$$

Approximating these portions of the graph with a smooth curve shows that the graph is concave up for small c and concave down for large c (sketched with parameter values $A = 1$ and $k = 1$ in Figure 3.6.85).

Example 3.6.12 Applying Matched Leading Behaviors to the Absorption Function Shown in Figure 3.5.63e

Saturated absorption with overcompensation II (Example 3.6.7),

$$\alpha(c) = \frac{Ac}{k+c^2}$$

has the same denominator as in Example 3.6.11, so

$$(k+c^2)_0 = k$$
$$(k+c^2)_\infty = c^2$$

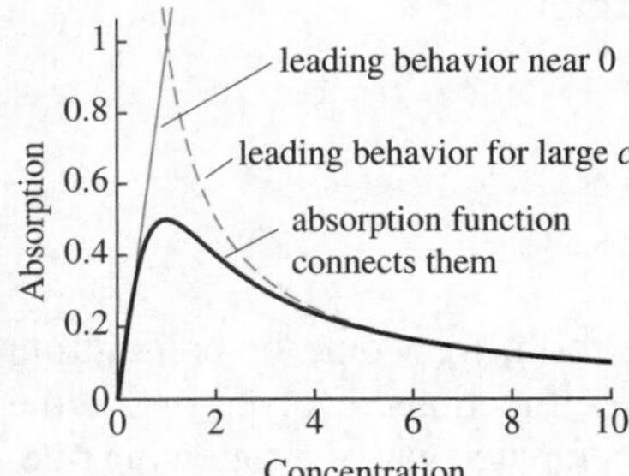

FIGURE 3.6.86

Saturated absorption with overcompensation II

Therefore,

$$\alpha_0(c) = \frac{Ac}{k}$$

$$\alpha_\infty(c) = \frac{Ac}{c^2} = \frac{A}{c}$$

This curve begins by increasing like a line with slope $\frac{A}{k}$ but eventually begins decreasing like $\frac{A}{c}$. As a consequence, this curve must have a maximum (Figure 3.6.86).

Example 3.6.13 Applying Matched Leading Behaviors to the Absorption Function Shown in Figure 3.5.63d

Finally, consider the function

$$\alpha(c) = \frac{Ac}{1+e^c}$$

For c near 0, both terms in the denominator have a limit of 1, and neither can be thrown out. All we can say is

$$\alpha_0(c) = \frac{Ac}{1+e^c} = \frac{Ac}{2}$$

However, for c large, the exponential term is dominant, so

$$\alpha_\infty(c) = \frac{Ac}{e^c}$$

When two terms have the same size, neither can be thrown out. To approximate functions in these circumstances, the tangent line approximation and the more general approach of Taylor series (Section 3.7) can be more effective.

L'Hôpital's Rule

Suppose we wish to find

$$\lim_{x\to 0} \frac{e^{2x} - 1}{x} \tag{3.6.1}$$

Both numerator and denominator approach 0. We cannot simplify the numerator with the method of leading behavior because both terms approach a limit of 1 rather than 0 or ∞.

There is a general and powerful rule for dealing with cases like this. Instead of comparing the functions, we compare their derivatives. This is known as L'Hôpital's rule. First, we define the cases where this rule can be applied, called indeterminate forms.

Definition 3.6 The limit of the ratio

$$\lim_{x\to a} \frac{f(x)}{g(x)}$$

(where a could be ∞) is called an **indeterminate form** if

$$\lim_{x\to a} f(x) = \lim_{x\to a} g(x) = 0$$

or

$$\lim_{x\to a} f(x) = \lim_{x\to a} g(x) = \infty$$

If we tried to substitute $x = a$ into an indeterminate form, we would be committing a mathematical felony. When we cannot recognize the functions involved or use the method of leading behavior, these limits can often be computed with the following rule.

Theorem 3.6 **L'Hôpital's Rule**

Suppose that f and g are differentiable functions and that

$$\lim_{x\to a} \frac{f(x)}{g(x)}$$

is an indeterminate form. If

$$\lim_{x\to a} \frac{f'(x)}{g'(x)} = L$$

then

$$\lim_{x\to a} \frac{f(x)}{g(x)} = L$$

In words, if the ratio of functions is an indeterminate form, the limit of the ratio of functions is equal to the limit of the ratio of their derivatives.

Example 3.6.14 Comparing Functions Using L'Hôpital's Rule

With this theorem we can prove that exponentials grow faster than power functions and that power functions grow faster than logarithms as x approaches infinity (Table 3.5.2).

L'Hôpital's rule says that

$$\lim_{x\to\infty} \frac{e^x}{x} = \lim_{x\to\infty} \frac{\frac{d(e^x)}{dx}}{\frac{dx}{dx}} \quad \text{take derivative of numerator and denominator because this is an indeterminate form}$$

$$= \lim_{x\to\infty} \frac{e^x}{1} \quad \text{compute derivatives}$$

$$= \infty \quad \text{the exponential function has a limit of infinity}$$

Example 3.6.15 Comparing the Logarithmic Function with a Linear Function

To compare the behavior of x and $\ln(x)$ at infinity using L'Hôpital's rule, we compute

$$\lim_{x\to\infty} \frac{x}{\ln(x)} = \lim_{x\to\infty} \frac{\frac{dx}{dx}}{\frac{d(\ln(x))}{dx}}$$

$$= \lim_{x\to\infty} \frac{1}{1/x}$$

$$= \lim_{x\to\infty} x$$

$$= \infty$$

If a single application of L'Hôpital's rule results in an another indeterminate form, a second or third application might make it possible to evaluate the limit.

Example 3.6.16 Case Requiring Multiple Applications of L'Hôpital's Rule

To show that e^x increases faster than x^3, we must take the derivative three times

$$\lim_{x\to\infty} \frac{e^x}{x^3} = \lim_{x\to\infty} \frac{e^x}{3x^2} \quad \text{indeterminate form, take derivatives}$$

$$= \lim_{x\to\infty} \frac{e^x}{6x} \quad \text{still indeterminate, take derivatives}$$

$$= \lim_{x\to\infty} \frac{e^x}{6} = \infty \quad \text{limit of the exponential function is infinity}$$

Example 3.6.17 L'Hôpital's Rule Can Succeed When the Method of Leading Behaviors Fails

L'Hôpital's rule is indispensable when the method of leading behaviors fails. We have seen that

$$\lim_{x\to 0} \frac{e^{2x} - 1}{x}$$

(Equation 3.6.1) is indeterminate. We apply L'Hôpital's rule, finding that

$$\lim_{x\to 0} \frac{e^{2x} - 1}{x} = \lim_{x\to 0} \frac{2e^{2x}}{1} = 2$$

Example 3.6.18 L'Hôpital's Rule Used Incorrectly

L'Hôpital's rule generally gives the wrong answer if applied to an expression that is not an indeterminate form. We can compute directly that

$$\lim_{x\to 0} \frac{e^{2x} - 1}{x + 1} = 0$$

because the numerator approaches 0 and the denominator approaches 1. If we mistakenly apply L'Hôpital's rule, we would have

$$\lim_{x\to 0} \frac{e^{2x}-1}{x+1} \text{ “=” } \lim_{x\to 0} \frac{2e^{2x}}{1} = 2$$

which is false. ▲

Why does L'Hôpital's rule work? Recall that the derivative can be used to approximate functions with the tangent line. The idea behind L'Hôpital's rule is to replace $f(x)$ by $\hat{f}(x)$ and replace $g(x)$ by $\hat{g}(x)$ and prove that

$$\lim_{x\to a} \frac{f(x)}{g(x)} = \lim_{x\to a} \frac{\hat{f}(x)}{\hat{g}(x)}$$

Remember that

$$\hat{f}(x) = f(a) + f'(a)(x-a)$$
$$\hat{g}(x) = g(a) + g'(a)(x-a)$$

If this is an indeterminate form of the $\frac{0}{0}$ type, it must be true that $f(a) = g(a) = 0$. Therefore,

$$\frac{\hat{f}(x)}{\hat{g}(x)} = \frac{f'(a)}{g'(a)}$$

if $x \neq a$.

Example 3.6.19 L'Hôpital's Rule Applied at $x = 0$

Consider the function

$$\lim_{x\to 0} \frac{e^{2x}-1}{x}$$

a ratio of the function $f(x) = e^{2x} - 1$ and $g(x) = x$. At $x = 0$, this is an indeterminate form. We can find the tangent line approximation of the numerator by computing the derivative, which gives $f'(x) = 2e^{2x}$ and $f'(0) = 2$. The tangent line approximation of f near $x = 0$ is then

$$\hat{f}(x) = f(0) + f'(0)x = 0 + 2x = 2x$$

Therefore,

$$\lim_{x\to 0} \frac{e^{2x}-1}{x} = \lim_{x\to 0} \frac{2x}{x} = 2$$

▲

In a way, this method recalls the idea of leading behavior. The tangent line $\hat{f}$ ignores the curvy parts of f as being smaller (Figure 3.6.87). Better approximations include some of the curve. This idea, called **Taylor series,** will be covered in Section 3.7.

Summary We have learned two ways to compute the behavior of complicated functions. The **method of leading behavior** is a way to examine sums of functions and determine which piece increases to infinity *fastest* or to zero *slowest*. For large values of the input, this piece is called the **leading behavior at infinity** and can be used to approximate the behavior of the function. For small values of the input, the largest piece is called the **leading behavior at zero** and can be used to approximate the behavior of the function. By graphing the leading behavior of functions at both 0 and infinity, we can use the **method of matched leading behaviors** to sketch an accurate graph. In other cases, we can evaluate **indeterminate forms** with **L'Hôpital's rule,** which says that a ratio of functions that both approach 0 or both approach infinity has the same limit as the ratio of their derivatives.

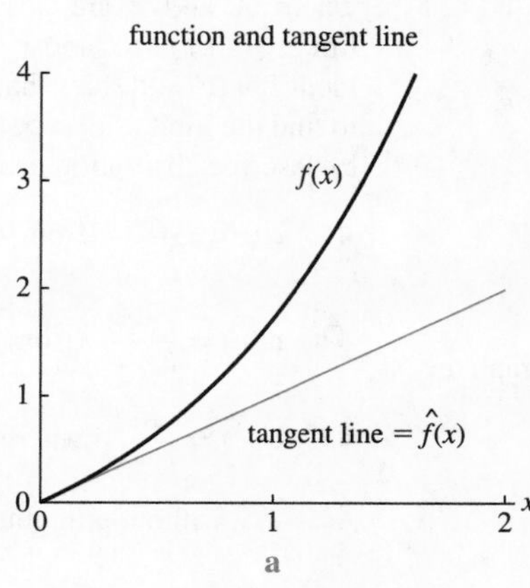

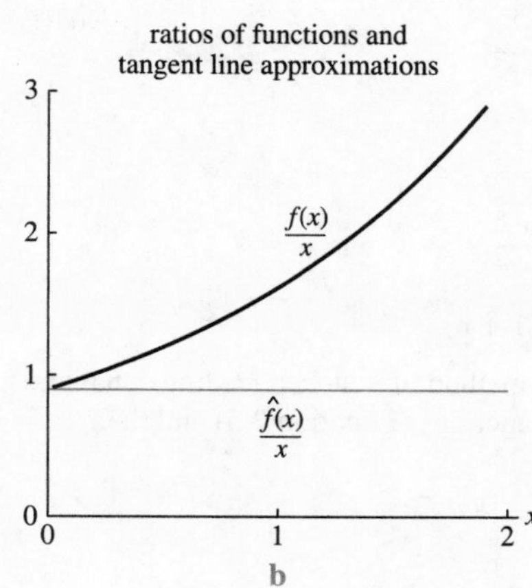

FIGURE 3.6.87
The tangent line as the leading behavior of a function

3.6 Exercises

Mathematical Techniques

1–6 ▪ Find the leading behavior of the following functions at 0 and ∞.

1. $f(x) = 1 + x$
2. $g(y) = y + y^3$
3. $h(z) = z + e^z$
4. $F(x) = 1 + 2x + 3e^x$
5. $m(a) = 100a + 30a^2 + \frac{1}{a}$
6. $G(c) = e^{-4c} + \frac{5}{c^2} + \frac{3}{c^5} + 10e^{-3c}$

7–16 ▪ For each pair of functions, use the basic functions (when possible) to say which approaches its limit more quickly, and then check with L'Hôpital's rule.

7. x^2 and e^{2x} as $x \to \infty$.
8. x^2 and $1000x$ as $x \to \infty$.
9. $0.1x^{0.5}$ and $30\ln(x)$ as $x \to \infty$.
10. x and $(\ln(x))^2$ as $x \to \infty$.
11. e^{-2x} and x^{-2} as $x \to \infty$.
12. $1/\ln(x)$ and $30x^{-0.1}$ as $x \to 0$.
13. x^{-1} and $-\ln(x)$ as $x \to 0$. Use your result to figure out $\lim_{x\to 0} x\ln(x)$.
14. x^{-1} and $\frac{1}{e^x - 1}$ as $x \to 0$.
15. x^2 and x^3 as $x \to 0$.
16. x^2 and $e^x - x - 1$ as $x \to 0$.

17–22 ▪ For each of the following functions, find the leading behavior of the numerator, the denominator, and the whole function at both 0 and ∞. Find the limit of the function at 0 and ∞ (and check with L'Hôpital's rule when appropriate). Use the method of matched leading behaviors to sketch a graph.

17. $\alpha(c) = \frac{2c^2}{1 + c}$
18. $\alpha(c) = \frac{c^2}{1 + 2c}$
19. $\alpha(c) = \frac{1 + c + c^2}{1 + c}$
20. $\alpha(c) = \frac{1 + c}{1 + c + c^2}$
21. $\alpha(c) = \frac{3c}{1 + \ln(1 + c)}$
22. $\alpha(c) = \frac{e^c + 1}{e^{2c} + 1}$

23–26 ▪ Write the tangent line approximation for the numerators and denominators of the following functions, and show that the result of applying L'Hôpital's rule matches that of comparing the linear approximations.

23. $f(x) = \frac{2x + x^2}{3x + 2x^2}$ at $x = 0$
24. $f(x) = \frac{\ln(1 + x)}{e^{2x} - 1}$ at $x = 0$
25. $f(x) = \frac{\ln(x)}{x^2 - 1}$ at $x = 1$
26. $f(x) = \frac{\cos(x) + 1}{\sin(x)}$ at $x = \pi$

Applications

27–32 ▪ Use the method of leading behavior, L'Hôpital's rule, and the method of matched leading behaviors to graph the following absorption functions.

27. $\alpha(c) = \frac{5c}{1 + c}$
28. $\alpha(c) = \frac{c}{5 + c}$

29. $\alpha(c)=\dfrac{5c^2}{1+c^2}$

30. $\alpha(c)=\dfrac{5c}{e^{2c}}$

31. $\alpha(c)=\dfrac{5c}{1+c^2}$

32. $\alpha(c)=5c(1+c)$

33–36 ▪ Use the method of matched leading behaviors to graph the following Hill functions (Equation 2.5) and their variants.

33. $h_3(x)=\dfrac{x^3}{1+x^3}$

34. $g_3(x)=\dfrac{x^3}{10+x^3}$

35. $h_{10}(x)=\dfrac{x^{10}}{1+x^{10}}$

36. $g_{10}(x)=\dfrac{x^{10}}{0.1+x^{10}}$

37–40 ▪ The following discrete-time dynamical systems describe the populations of two competing strains of bacteria.

$$a_{t+1}=sa_t$$
$$b_{t+1}=rb_t$$

For the following values of the initial conditions a_0 and b_0, and the per capita production s and r:

a. Find the number of each type as a function of time.

b. Find the fraction of type a as a function of time.

c. Use leading behavior or L'Hôpital's rule to find the limit of the fraction as $t\to\infty$.

d. Compute the fraction at $t=0$, 10, 20, and 50, and compare with your limit.

37. $a_0=10^4$, $b_0=10^6$, $s=2.0$, $r=1.5$

38. $a_0=10^4$, $b_0=10^6$, $s=1.5$, $r=2.0$

39. $a_0=10^4$, $b_0=10^5$, $s=0.8$, $r=1.2$

40. $a_0=10^4$, $b_0=10^5$, $s=0.5$, $r=0.3$

41–44 ▪ Many of our absorption equations are of the form

$$\alpha(c)=A\frac{r(c)}{k+r(c)}$$

where A and k are positive parameters, and where $r(0)=0$, $\lim_{c\to\infty}r(c)=\infty$, and $r'(c)>0$. In each of the following cases, identify $r(c)$ and show that $\alpha(c)$ is increasing. Use L'Hôpital's rule to find the limit as $c\to\infty$, and use the method of leading behavior to describe absorption near $c=0$ and $c=\infty$.

41. $\alpha(c)=\dfrac{Ac}{k+c}$ (from Table 3.1).

42. $\alpha(c)=\dfrac{Ac^2}{k+c^2}$ (from Table 3.1).

43. $\alpha(c)=\dfrac{Ac^n}{k+c^n}$ where n is a positive integer.

44. Try without plugging in a particular form for $r(c)$.

Computer Exercises

45. Consider the following functions

$$f(c)=\frac{c^2}{1+c^2}$$
$$g(c)=\frac{c}{1+c^2}$$

Find the leading behavior of each at 0 and infinity. Suppose we approximated each by a function defined in pieces

$$\breve{f}(c)=\begin{cases} f_0(c) & \text{if } f_0(c)<f_\infty(c)\\ f_\infty(c) & \text{if } f_0(c)>f_\infty(c)\end{cases}$$

and similarly for $\breve{g}(c)$. Plot this approximation in each case. Find and plot the ratios

$$\frac{\breve{f}(c)}{f(c)} \quad\text{and}\quad \frac{\breve{g}(c)}{g(c)}$$

When is the approximation best? When is it worst?

46. Consider the function

$$f(x)=\frac{1+x+x^2+x^3+x^4}{5+4x+3x^2+2x^3+x^4}$$

Find the leading behavior for large x. Next find a function that keeps both the largest and the second largest term from the numerator and denominator. How much better is this new approximation? How much improvement do you get by adding more and more terms?

3.7 Approximating Functions with Linear Functions and Polynomials

The method of leading behavior provides a way to *approximate* complicated functions with simpler functions. In this section, we extend the related idea of the **tangent line approximation** in several ways. First, we compare the tangent line approximation with the **secant line approximation,** showing that the tangent line is the *best* linear approximation to a curve near the point of tangency but that the secant line can be more useful over larger ranges.

The tangent line matches the value and derivative of a function at a point. More accurate approximations can be found by also matching the second, third, and higher derivatives. If we use **polynomials** to match these higher derivatives, the resulting approximation is called a **Taylor polynomial.**

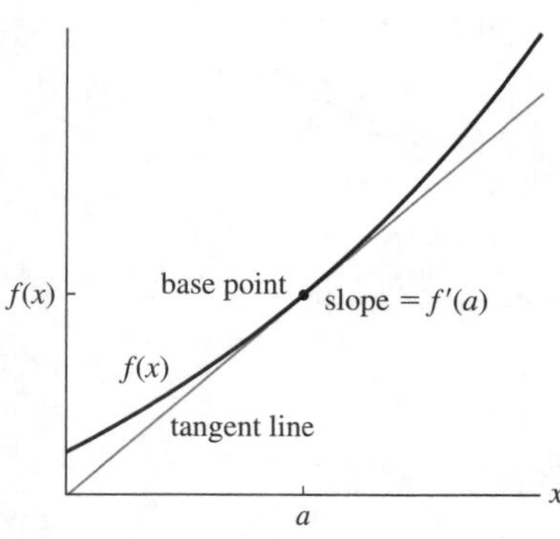

FIGURE 3.7.88

Approximating a function with the tangent line

The Tangent and Secant Lines

Suppose we wish to approximate the exponential function e^x near 0 with a line, perhaps in order to compare a complicated dynamical system with its linear approximation. The general formula for the tangent line, or tangent line approximation, to the function f at base point a is

$$\hat{f}(x) = f'(a)(x - a) + f(a)$$

(Figure 3.7.88). The function $\hat{f}(x)$ has as its graph the tangent line to $f(x)$ at a, and it matches both the value and the slope at the point of tangency.

Example 3.7.1 The Tangent Line to the Exponential Function

The tangent line to the graph of the exponential function

$$g(x) = e^x$$

at $x = 0$ matches the value $g(0) = e^0 = 1$ and the slope $g'(0) = e^0 = 1$. Hence

$$\hat{g}(x) = g(0) + g'(0)(x - 0) = 1 + x$$

(Figure 3.7.89). The graph of the tangent line hugs the curve near the point of tangency and provides a good way to approximate values. For example,

$$\hat{g}(0.1) = 1.1$$

which is close to the exact value $e^{0.1} \approx 1.10517$.

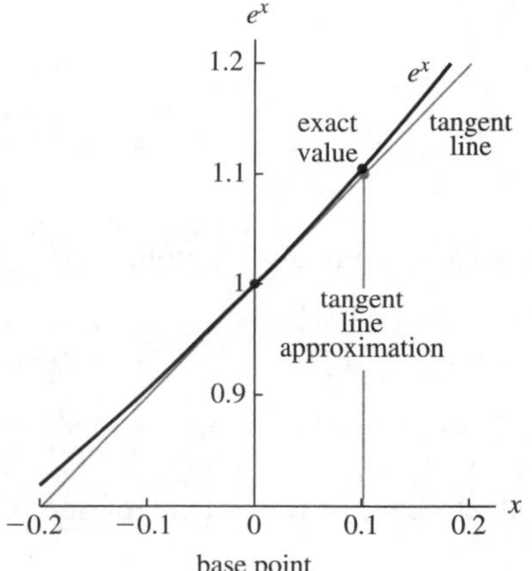

FIGURE 3.7.89

Approximating $e^{0.1}$ with the tangent line

Before the age of computers, this sort of approximation was indispensable. As we will soon see when we study Newton's method for solving equations (Section 3.8) and Euler's method for solving differential equations ("Euler's Method for Solving Differntial Equations," Section 4.1), the tangent line approximation remains necessary for more complicated problems.

Example 3.7.2 The Tangent Line to the Logarithmic Function

To estimate $\ln(0.9)$ without a calculator, note that the input value 0.9 is near 1.0. Because $\ln(1.0) = 0$, the answer is close to 0. To do better, we match both the value and the slope of the function $\ln(x)$ at $x = 1$. In this case,

$$\frac{d}{dx}(\ln(x)) = \frac{1}{x}$$

so the slope at $x = 1$ is 1. The tangent line is

$$\hat{\ln}(x) = 0 + 1(x - 1) = x - 1$$

Substituting in $x = 0.9$, we find an approximate value of -0.1, close to the exact value of $\ln(0.9) \approx -0.10536$ (Figure 3.7.90).

FIGURE 3.7.90

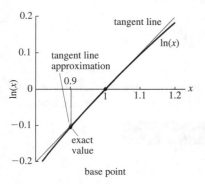

Approximating $\ln(0.9)$ with the tangent line

Recall the bacterial population growing according to

$$b(t) = 2.0^t$$

("The Average Rate of Change," Section 2.1). Can we find a good linear approximation to this function for times between 0 and 1? One method is to use the tangent line at

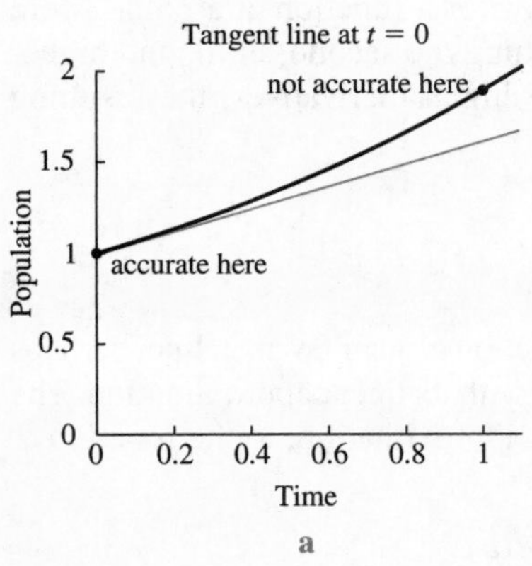

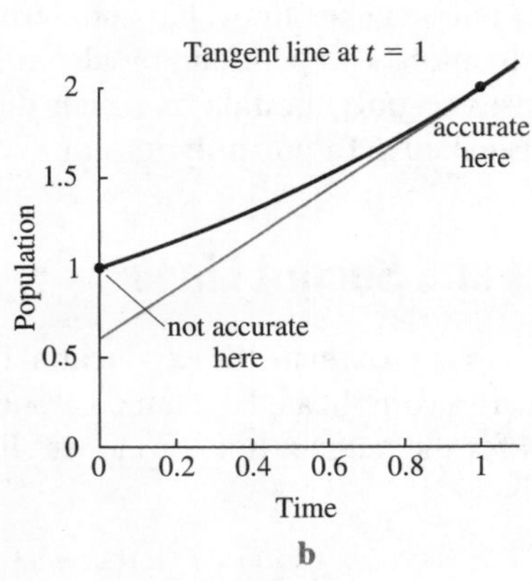

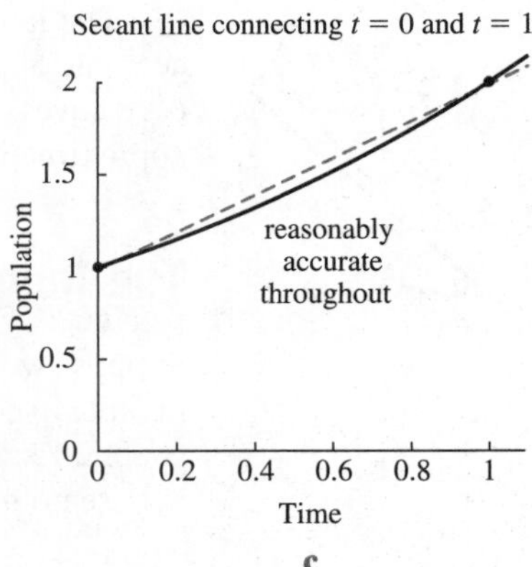

FIGURE 3.7.91
Two tangent lines and a secant line as approximations

$t = 0$. First, we find the derivative

$$\begin{aligned}\frac{db}{dt} &= \frac{d}{dt}(2.0^t) \\ &= \frac{d}{dt}(e^{\ln(2.0)t}) \\ &= \ln(2.0)e^{\ln(2.0)t}\end{aligned}$$

using the rule for finding derivatives of the general exponential function ("Applications," Section 2.9). The tangent line at $t = 0$ is therefore

$$\hat{b}_0(t) = b(0) + b'(0)(t - 0) = 1.0 + \ln(2.0)t$$

where the subscript 0 indicates the base point. If we are interested in approximating values near $t = 0$, the tangent line is accurate (Figure 3.7.91a).

If instead we are interested in approximating values near $t = 1$, this tangent line is quite inaccurate. At $t = 1$, the tangent line is

$$\hat{b}_1(t) = b(1) + b'(1)(t - 1) = 2.0 + 2.0\ln(2.0)(t - 1) \approx 2.0 + 1.386(t - 1)$$

because $b(1) = 2.0$ and $b'(1) = 2.0\ln(2.0)$. Near the base point $t = 1$, this tangent line provides an accurate approximation (Figure 3.7.91b).

Over the whole interval from $t = 0$ to $t = 1$, the secant line is reasonably good everywhere. The secant line has slope

$$\text{slope of secant} = \frac{\Delta b}{\Delta t} = \frac{b(1.0) - b(0.0)}{1.0 - 0.0} = 1.0$$

which lies between that of the two tangent lines, and has equation

$$\hat{b}_s(t) = b(0) + 1.0(t - 0) = 1 + t$$

How can we quantify the accuracy of these alternative approximations? Results near both endpoints and the middle of the interval are given in the following table.

t	$b(t)$	$\hat{b}_0(t)$	$\hat{b}_1(t)$	$\hat{b}_s(t)$
0.01	1.00696	1.00693	0.62757	1.01
0.10	1.07177	1.06931	0.75234	1.10
0.50	1.41421	1.34657	1.30685	1.50
0.90	1.86607	1.62383	1.86137	1.90
0.99	1.98618	1.68622	1.98614	1.99

Each tangent line is an excellent approximation near its point of tangency. The secant line is always fairly close. This is one of the two primary strengths of using the secant line, which is also called **linear interpolation.** The other is that the secant can be directly estimated from data, even when we do not know the underlying equation. We will see how this idea is used when solving equations (Section 3.8) and fitting data with lines (Section 8.9).

Nonetheless, the tangent line is the *best* possible approximation near the point of tangency. No other line is closer. Suppose we compare the tangent and secant lines near the base point 0. To quantify how close the estimates are to the exact values, define errors e_0 and e_s for the two lines as

$$e_0 = \hat{b}_0(t) - b(t)$$
$$e_s = \hat{b}_s(t) - b(t)$$

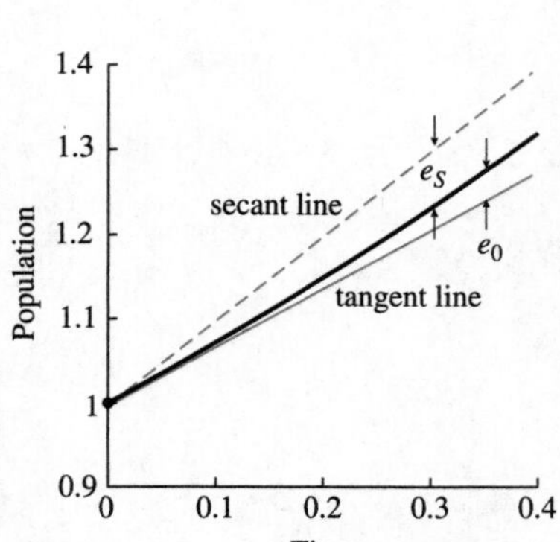

FIGURE 3.7.92
The errors associated with tangent and secant line approximations

To check how small these are for t near 0, we divide the errors e_0 and e_s by t.

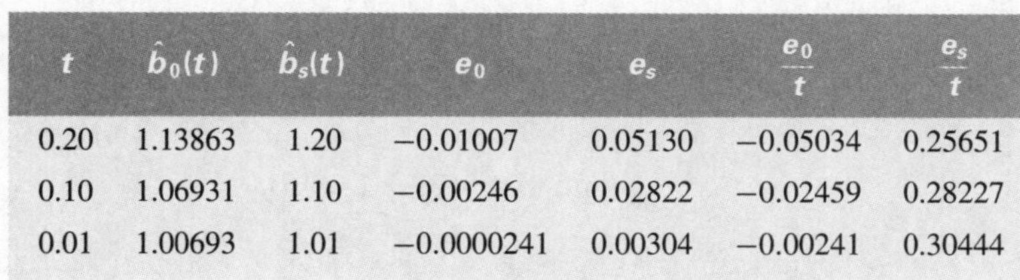

t	$\hat{b}_0(t)$	$\hat{b}_s(t)$	e_0	e_s	$\frac{e_0}{t}$	$\frac{e_s}{t}$
0.20	1.13863	1.20	−0.01007	0.05130	−0.05034	0.25651
0.10	1.06931	1.10	−0.00246	0.02822	−0.02459	0.28227
0.01	1.00693	1.01	−0.0000241	0.00304	−0.00241	0.30444

Both errors e_0 and e_s get smaller as t gets smaller. With the tangent line approximation, the *relative* error $\frac{e_0}{t}$ also gets smaller as t gets smaller. With the secant line approximation, the relative error $\frac{e_s}{t}$ remains roughly constant (Figure 3.7.92).

Quadratic Approximation

The tangent and secant lines provide ways to approximate curves with lines. We can do better by approximating curves with curves.

Example 3.7.3 Approximating the Exponential Function with a Quadratic

Suppose that we wish to approximate the exponential function near 0 with a quadratic function. Just as we can match the value of the function and the first derivative with the tangent line, we can match the function, the first derivative, and the *second derivative* with a quadratic. For the exponential function $g(x) = e^x$, $g'(x) = e^x$, and $g''(x) = e^x$. Therefore,

$$g(0) = 1$$
$$g'(0) = 1$$
$$g''(0) = 1$$

This does *not* mean that the quadratic approximation is $\hat{g}(x) = 1 + x + x^2$. We must be a bit more careful. The derivative is

$$\frac{d}{dx}(1 + x + x^2) = 1 + 2x$$

and the second derivative is

$$\frac{d^2}{dx^2}(1 + x + x^2) = 2$$

This is double what it should be. Thanks to the constant product rule for the derivatives, we can correct this by dividing the quadratic term by 2. We thus guess that

$$\hat{g}(x) = 1 + x + \frac{x^2}{2}$$

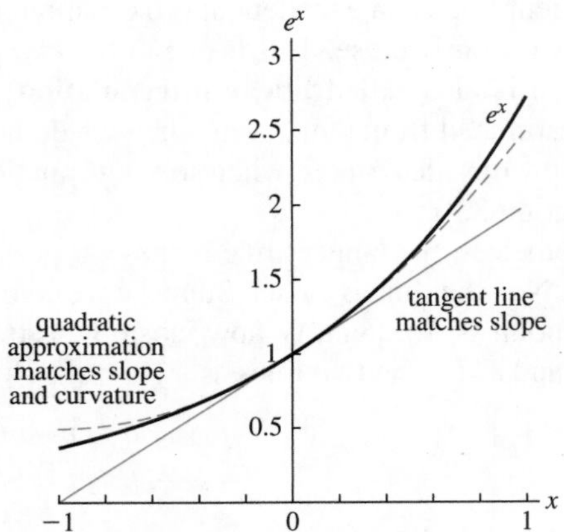

FIGURE 3.7.93

The linear and quadratic approximations of e^x

Checking, we find that

$$\frac{d}{dx}(\hat{g}(x)) = 1 + x$$

and that $\hat{g}(0) = 1$. Also,

$$\frac{d^2}{dx^2}(\hat{g}(x)) = 1$$

Therefore, the value, the first derivative, and the second derivative of this quadratic approximation match those of the exponential function (Figure 3.7.93). ◭

To find the quadratic approximation to a function $f(x)$ at the base point a in general, we match the value, the derivative, and the second derivative at the point a. To make the calculation easier, we write the quadratic in a version of point-slope form:

$$\hat{f}(x) = c_0 + c_1(x - a) + c_2(x - a)^2$$

We want to choose the values c_0, c_1, and c_2 so that

$$\hat{f}(a) = f(a)$$
$$\hat{f}'(a) = f'(a)$$
$$\hat{f}''(a) = f''(a)$$

Then

$$\hat{f}'(x) = c_1 + 2c_2(x - a)$$
$$\hat{f}''(x) = 2c_2$$

and

$$\hat{f}(a) = c_0 + c_1(a - a) + c_2(a - a)^2 = c_0$$
$$\hat{f}'(a) = c_1 + 2c_2(a - a) = c_1$$
$$\hat{f}''(a) = 2c_2$$

Therefore,

$$c_0 = f(a)$$
$$c_1 = f'(a)$$
$$2c_2 = f''(a) \quad \text{or} \quad c_2 = \frac{f''(a)}{2}$$

The approximating quadratic is therefore

$$\hat{f}(x) = f(a) + f'(a)(x - a) + \frac{f''(a)}{2}(x - a)^2$$

The first two terms in this approximate function exactly match the tangent line. The last term is an additional correction. Recall from the method of leading behavior that $(x-a)^2$ is smaller than $x-a$, as when $x-a$ itself is small. This new term has little effect near a. If the second derivative is equal to 0, this term vanishes and the best approximating quadratic is the tangent line itself.

Example 3.7.4 Approximating a Cubic with a Quadratic

Suppose we wish to approximate the function $g(x)=1+2x+x^2+3x^3$ with a quadratic function for x near 1. The derivative and second derivative of g are

$$g'(x)=2+2x+9x^2$$
$$g''(x)=2+18x$$

Therefore,

$$g(1)=1+2\cdot 1+1^2+3\cdot 1^3=7$$
$$g'(1)=2+2\cdot 1+9\cdot 1^2=13$$
$$g''(1)=2+18\cdot 1=20$$

Then

$$\hat{g}(x)=7+13(x-1)+10(x-1)^2$$

The approximating quadratic is *not* found by just ignoring the cubic term (except if the base point is 0; see Exercise 21).

Example 3.7.5 Approximating the Logarithmic Function with a Quadratic

In Example 3.7.2, we used the tangent line to estimate ln(0.9) by finding the tangent line to $\ln(x)$ at base point $x=1$. We can get a more accurate estimate by finding the quadratic approximation at this same base point. Denoting the function $\ln(x)$ by $f(x)$, we have that

$$f'(x)=\frac{d}{dx}(\ln(x))=\frac{1}{x}$$
$$f''(x)=\frac{d^2}{dx^2}(\ln(x))=-\frac{1}{x^2}$$

Evaluating at the point $x=1$,

$$f(1)=\ln(1)=0$$
$$f'(1)=\frac{1}{1}=1$$
$$f''(1)=-\frac{1}{1^2}=-1$$

Therefore, the approximating quadratic is

$$\hat{f}(x)=0+1(x-1)-\frac{1}{2}(x-1)^2=x-1-\frac{1}{2}(x-1)^2$$

Substituting in $x=0.9$, we find an approximate value of -0.105, very close to the exact value of $\ln(0.9)\approx -0.10536$. As we can see from Figure 3.7.94a, the approximation is nearly indistinguishable for x near 1. However, over a larger range, the function and the approximation diverge (Figure 3.7.94b).

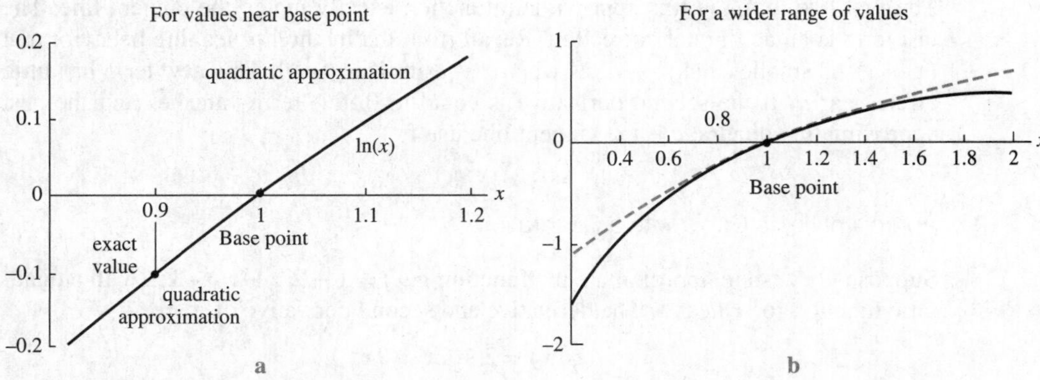

FIGURE 3.7.94

Approximating ln(0.9) with a quadratic

Example 3.7.6 Finding Approximating Quadratics at Three Points

The function

$$h(x) = xe^{-x}$$

has derivatives

$$h'(x) = (1 - x)e^{-x}$$
$$h''(x) = (x - 2)e^{-x}$$

(Example 2.8.7). This function has a critical point at $x = 1$ and a point of inflection at $x = 2$. Using the formula for the approximating quadratic at the three points $x = 0$, $x = 1$, and $x = 2$ we can find three different approximating quadratics that we denote $\hat{h}_0(x)$, $\hat{h}_1(x)$, and $\hat{h}_2(x)$, respectively.

$$\hat{h}_0(x) = h(0) + h'(0)x + \frac{h''(0)}{2}x^2 = x - x^2$$

$$\hat{h}_1(x) = h(1) + h'(1)(x - 1) + \frac{h''(1)}{2}(x - 1)^2 = \frac{1}{e} - \frac{1}{2e}(x - 1)^2$$

$$\hat{h}_2(x) = h(2) + h'(2)(x - 2) + \frac{h''(2)}{2}(x - 2)^2 = \frac{2}{e^2} - \frac{1}{e^2}(x - 2)$$

(Figure 3.7.95). At the critical point, the approximating quadratic has no $x - 1$ term because $h'(1) = 0$. At the point of inflection, the quadratic term drops out, leaving us with the tangent line.

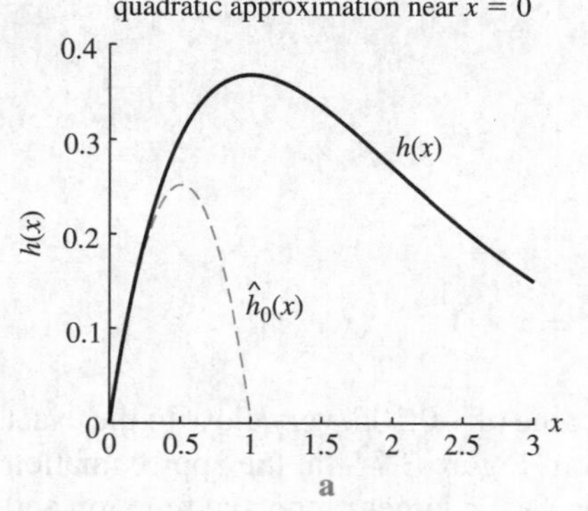

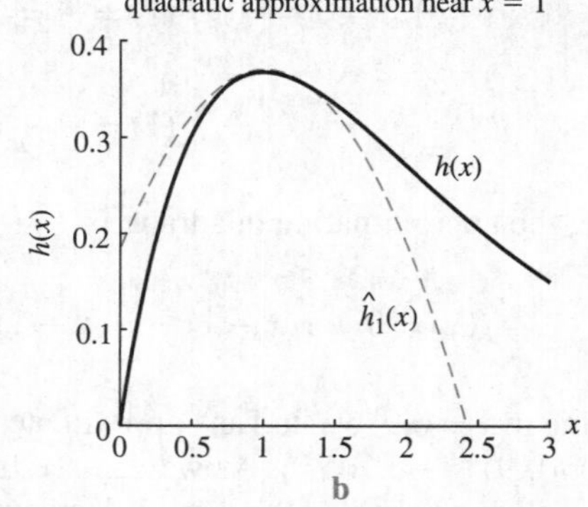

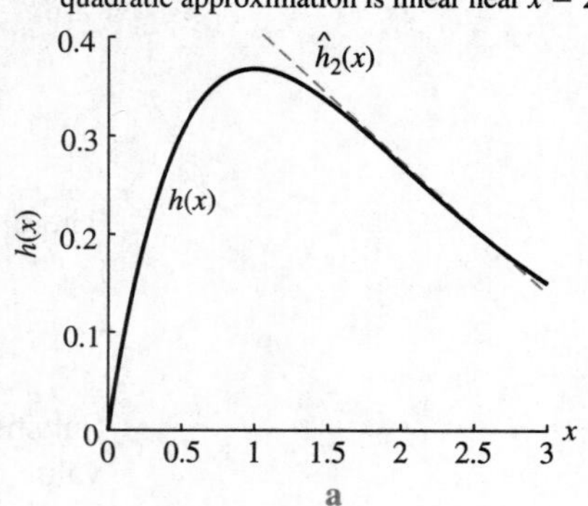

FIGURE 3.7.95

Three quadratic approximations to $h(x) = xe^{-x}$

Taylor Polynomials

The idea of matching derivatives can be extended to the third, fourth, and higher derivatives. With each added derivative, the approximation becomes more accurate but requires a polynomial of higher *degree* (largest power). The derivation of the following formula is the same as the derivation of the quadratic approximation. The approximating polynomial is called a **Taylor polynomial** of degree n.

Definition 3.7 The Taylor Polynomial

Suppose the first n derivatives of the function f are defined at $x = a$. Then the Taylor polynomial of degree n matching the values of the first n derivatives is

$$P_n(x) = f(a) + f'(a)(x-a) + \frac{f''(a)}{2}(x-a)^2 + \cdots + \frac{f^{(i)}(a)}{i!}(x-a)^i + \cdots + \frac{f^{(n)}(a)}{n!}(x-a)^n$$

We used two pieces of new notation in this definition. First, the notation

$$f^{(i)}(x)$$

indicates the ith derivative of f. For example, we could write

$$f^{(2)}(x) = f''(x)$$

for the second derivative. Second, the terms with exclamation points are called **factorials.** The value of $i!$ is the product of i and all positive integers smaller than i, or

$$i! = i \cdot (i-1) \cdot (i-2) + \cdot\cdot\cdot\cdot\cdot + 3 \cdot 2 \cdot 1$$

For example,

$$\begin{aligned} 2! &= 2 \cdot 1 = 2 \\ 3! &= 3 \cdot 2 \cdot 1 = 6 \\ 4! &= 4 \cdot 3 \cdot 2 \cdot 1 = 24 \\ 5! &= 5 \cdot 4 \cdot 3 \cdot 2 \cdot 1 = 120 \end{aligned}$$

The values of factorials increase very quickly, meaning that later terms in a Taylor polynomial become ever smaller.

Example 3.7.7 Approximating the Logarithmic Function with a Cubic

In Example 3.7.5, we used a quadratic to estimate $\ln(0.9)$. To find the cubic (third-order) approximation, we must also match the third derivative. Denoting the function $\ln(x)$ by $f(x)$, we have that

$$\begin{aligned} f'(x) &= \frac{d}{dx}(\ln(x)) = \frac{1}{x} \\ f''(x) &= \frac{d^2}{dx^2}(\ln(x)) = -\frac{1}{x^2} \\ f'''(x) &= \frac{d^3}{dx^3}(\ln(x)) = \frac{2}{x^3} \end{aligned}$$

Evaluating at the point $x = 1$ yields

$$\begin{aligned} f(1) &= \ln(1) = 0 \\ f'(1) &= \frac{1}{1} = 1 \end{aligned}$$

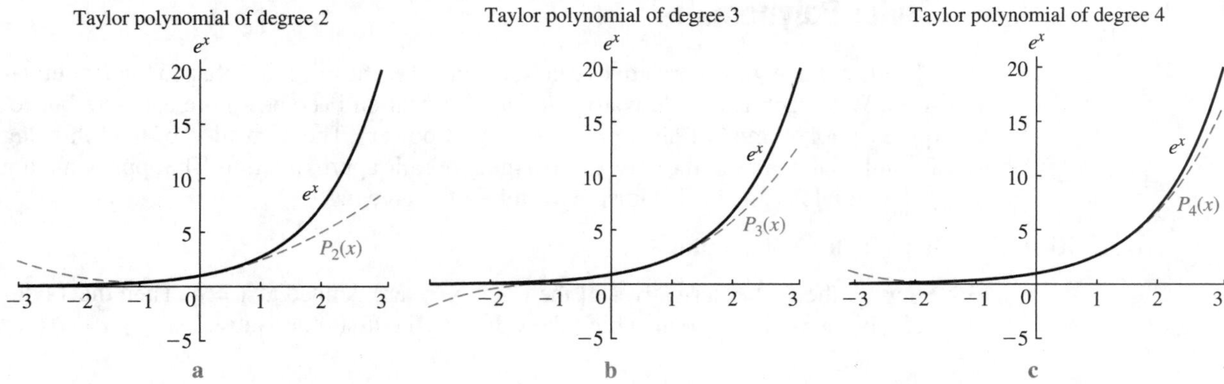

FIGURE 3.7.96
Three Taylor polynomial approximations to $g(x) = e^x$

$$f''(1) = -\frac{1}{1^2} = -1$$

$$f'''(1) = \frac{2}{1^3} = 2$$

Therefore, the approximating cubic is

$$\hat{f}(x) = 0 + 1(x-1) - \frac{1}{2}(x-1)^2 + \frac{2}{6}(x-1)^3$$

Substituting in $x = 0.9$, we find an approximate value of -0.10533, even closer to the exact value of $\ln(0.9) \approx -0.10536$.

Example 3.7.8 Taylor Polynomials for the Exponential Function

Consider again the exponential function $g(x) = e^x$. Using our new notation, we see that

$$g^{(i)}(x) = g(x)$$

because each derivative of the exponential function is equal to the function itself. For $a = 0$, then the Taylor polynomial of degree 4 is

$$P_4(x) = 1 + x + \frac{1}{2}x^2 + \frac{1}{6}x^3 + \frac{1}{24}x^4$$

See Figure 3.7.96. We estimate that

$$e^{0.1} \approx P_4(0.1) = 1 + 0.1 + \frac{1}{2}0.1^2 + \frac{1}{6}0.1^3 + \frac{1}{24}0.1^4 \approx 1.1051708$$

The correct value is $e^{0.1}$ to 7 decimal places is 1.1051709.

Summary Using lines to approximate curves is one of the central ideas in calculus. We have compared the tangent line with three other approximations. The secant line, or **linear interpolation,** has the joint virtues of using actual data and remaining fairly accurate over a broad domain. The tangent line is the **best linear approximation** near the base point. To do even better, we can use a quadratic polynomial to match both the first and second derivatives of the original function at the base point. This idea can be expanded to the **Taylor polynomial,** which is a polynomial of degree n that matches the first n derivatives of the function.

3.7 Exercises

Mathematical Techniques

1–6 ▪ Use the tangent line and secant line to estimate the following values. Be sure to identify the base point a used for the tangent line approximation and the second point used for the secant line approximation. Use a calculator to compare the estimates with the exact answer.

1. 2.02^3
2. 3.03^2
3. $\sqrt{4.01}$
4. $\sqrt{6}$
5. $\sin(0.02)$
6. $\cos(-0.02)$

7–12 ▪ Use the quadratic approximation to estimate the following values. Compare the estimates with the exact answer.

7. 2.02^3 (based on Exercise 1)
8. 3.03^2 (based on Exercise 2)
9. $\sqrt{4.01}$ (based on Exercise 3)
10. $\sqrt{6}$ (based on Exercise 4)
11. $\sin(0.02)$ (based on Exercise 5)
12. $\cos(-0.02)$ (based on Exercise 6)

13–16 ▪ Use the tangent line approximation to evaluate the following in two ways. First, find the tangent line to the whole function using the chain rule. Second, break the calculation into two pieces by writing the function as a composition, approximate the inner function with its tangent line, and use this value to substitute into the tangent line of the outer function. Do your answers match?

13. $(1+3\cdot 1.01)^2$
14. $\ln(\sqrt{0.98})$
15. $e^{\sin(0.02)}$
16. $\sin\left(\ln\left((1+0.1)^3\right)\right)$

17–20 ▪ For the following functions, find the tangent line approximation of the two values, and compare with the true value. Indicate which approximations are too high and which are too low. From graphs of the functions, try to explain what it is about the graph that causes this.

17. $e^{0.1}$ and $e^{-0.1}$
18. $\ln(1.1)$ and $\ln(0.9)$
19. 1.1^2 and 0.9^2
20. $\sqrt{1.1}$ and $\sqrt{0.9}$

21–26 ▪ Find the third-order Taylor polynomials for the following functions.

21. $f(x)=x^3+4x^2+3x+1$ for x near 0.
22. $g(x)=4x^4+x^3+4x^2+3x+1$ for x near 0.
23. $f(x)=4x^2+3x+1$ for x near 1.
24. $g(x)=4x^4+x^3+4x^2+3x+1$ for x near 1.
25. $h(x)=\ln(x)$ for x near 1.
26. $h(x)=\sin(x)$ for x near 0.

27–28 ▪ Taylor series can be used to sum some **infinite series** (sums with an infinite number of terms). Find the Taylor polynomials for the following functions, and use them to add up the series. Check by adding up the first terms in the series.

27. Find the Taylor polynomial of degree n for $f(x)=\dfrac{1}{1-x}$ with base point $x=0$. Use your result to find $1+\dfrac{1}{3}+\dfrac{1}{3^2}+\dfrac{1}{3^3}+\dfrac{1}{3^4}+\cdots$.
28. Find the Taylor polynomial of degree n for $f(x)=\ln(1+x)$ with base point $x=0$. Use your result to find $1-\dfrac{1}{2}+\dfrac{1}{3}-\dfrac{1}{4}+\dfrac{1}{5}-\cdots$.

Applications

29–34 ▪ Compare the tangent line approximation of the following absorption functions with the leading behavior at $c=0$. If they do not match, can you explain why?

29. $\alpha(c)=\dfrac{5c}{1+c}$ (as in Section 3.6, Exercise 27)
30. $\alpha(c)=\dfrac{c}{5+c}$ (as in Section 3.6, Exercise 28)
31. $\alpha(c)=\dfrac{5c^2}{1+c^2}$ (as in Section 3.6, Exercise 29)
32. $\alpha(c)=\dfrac{5c}{e^{2c}}$ (as in Section 3.6, Exercise 30)
33. $\alpha(c)=\dfrac{5c}{1+c^2}$ (as in Section 3.6, Exercise 31)
34. $\alpha(c)=5c(1+c)$ (as in Section 3.6, Exercise 32)

35–38 ▪ Consider a declining population following the formula

$$b(t)=\frac{1}{1+t}$$

(measured in millions). Approximate the population at each of the following times, using a) the tangent with base point $t=0$, b) the tangent with base point $t=1$, c) the secant connecting times $t=0$ and $t=1$. Graph each of the relevant tangents and secants. Which method is best for what?

35. $t=0.1$
36. $t=0.5$
37. $t=0.9$
38. $t=1.1$

39–40 ▪ Consider the following table giving mass as a function of age.

Age, a (days)	Mass M (g)
0.5	0.125
1.0	1.000
1.5	3.375
2.0	8.000

The data follow the equation $M(a) = a^3$. Estimate each of the following using the tangent line approximation and the secant line approximation. Which approximation is closer to the exact answer? Which method would be best if you did not know the formula for $M(a)$?

39. $M(1.25)$

40. $M(1.45)$

41–42 ▪ Consider the following table giving temperature as a function of time.

Time, t	Temperature, T (°C)
0.0	0.172
1.0	1.635
2.0	6.492
3.0	11.95
4.0	20.24

The data follow the equation $T(t) = t + t^2$, but there is some noise in each of the measurements, so the values are not exactly on the curve. Estimate each of the following using the tangent line approximation and the secant line approximation. Which method do you think deals best with the noise?

41. Estimate $T(1)$ using the values at $t = 0$ and $t = 2$.

42. Estimate $T(3)$ using the values at $t = 2$ and $t = 4$.

Computer Exercises

43. Find the Taylor polynomials for e^x, $\cos(x)$, and $\sin(x)$ with base point $x = 0$ up to degree 10. Can you see the pattern? Graph the function, P_2, P_5, and P_{10} on domains around 0 that get larger and larger. What happens to the approximation for values of x far from 0?

44. Find the Taylor polynomial for the function defined by

$$f(x) = \begin{cases} e^{-1 \neq x} & \text{if } x \neq 0 \\ 0 & \text{if } x = 0 \end{cases}$$

with base point $x = 0$ up to degree 10 (you will have to take the limit as $x \to 0$ to compute the derivatives). Can you see the pattern? Graph the function on the domain $-1 \leq x \leq 1$. What happens to the approximation for values of x far from 0? Do the Taylor polynomials make sense?

45. A simple equation that is impossible to solve algebraically is

$$e^x = x + 2$$

a. Graph the two sides and convince yourself there is a solution.

b. Replace e^x with its tangent line approximation at $x = 0$, and try to solve for the point where the tangent line approximation is equal to $x + 2$. This is an approximate solution. What goes wrong in this case?

c. Replace e^x with its quadratic approximation at $x = 0$, and solve for the point where the quadratic approximation is equal to $x + 2$.

d. Replace e^x with its tangent line at $x = 1$ and solve.

e. Replace e^x with its quadratic approximation at $x = 1$ and solve.

f. How close are these solutions to the exact answer?

3.8 Newton's Method

With powerful calculators and computers, it might seem unnecessary to approximate a function with a tangent line. On a calculator, exponentiation is no harder than multiplying or adding. But although computing specific functional values is easy, *solving equations* for specific values can be difficult. We have seen how to use the Intermediate Value Theorem to show that an equation *has* a solution. When we cannot solve the equation with algebraic methods, **Newton's method** can be implemented on a computer to find the exact value. The method replaces the original equation with the tangent line approximation and derives a discrete-time dynamical system that converges with remarkable speed to the solution.

Finding the Equilibrium of the Lung Model with Absorption

Suppose a lung is following

$$c_{t+1} = (1 - q)\left[1 - \alpha(c_t)\right] c_t + q\gamma$$

where

$$\alpha(c_t) = 0.5\left(1 - e^{-0.5c_t}\right)$$

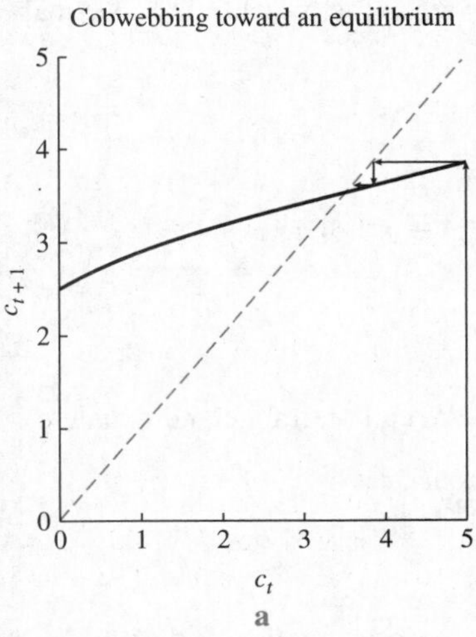

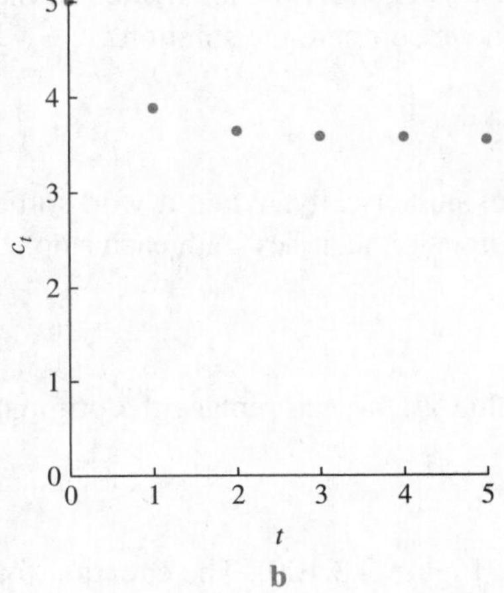

FIGURE 3.8.97
The iterative method of solving an equation

(Equation 3.4.1). In this discrete-time dynamical system, c_t represents the concentration, q the fraction of air exchanged, γ the concentration of chemical in the ambient air, and $\alpha(c_t)$ the fraction of chemical absorbed as a function of the chemical concentration in the lung. In Section 3.4, we used the Intermediate Value Theorem to show that this function has an equilibrium between 0 and γ. What if we wish to *compute* the exact value of the equilibrium with a particular set of parameter values?

If we set $q = 0.5$ and $\gamma = 5.0$, the discrete-time dynamical system is

$$c_{t+1} = 0.5\left[1 - 0.5\left(1 - e^{-0.5c_t}\right)\right] c_t + 2.5$$

It is impossible to set $c_{t+1} = c_t = c^*$ and algebraically solve the equation

$$c^* = 0.5\left[1 - 0.5\left(1 - e^{-0.5c^*}\right)\right] c^* + 2.5$$

for the equilibrium value, because equations involving both polynomial and exponential function cannot be solved except in unusual circumstances. How can we use a computer or calculator to find the value?

It looks as though the equilibrium we seek is stable (Figure 3.8.97a). A solution will approach the equilibrium (Figure 3.8.97b). This seems like a good way to get the computer to find the answer. The results of solving the discrete-time dynamical system starting from $c_0 = 5.0$ (the equilibrium $c^* = \gamma$ for the case without absorption) are given in the following table. The columns give the concentrations, the difference from the

Iteration	Concentration	Distance from Equilibrium	Factor by which Distance Decreased
0	5.0000000000	1.4654361738	—
1	3.8526062482	0.3180424220	0.2170291874
2	3.6034690548	0.0689052286	0.2166542067
3	3.5495215521	0.0149577259	0.2170767914
4	3.5378126599	0.0032488337	0.2172010455
5	3.5352695692	0.0007057430	0.2172296671
6	3.5347171389	0.0001533127	0.2172359626
7	3.5345971314	0.0000333052	0.2172373338
8	3.5345710613	0.0000072351	0.2172376315
9	3.5345653979	0.0000015717	0.2172376945
10	3.5345641676	0.0000003414	0.2172377007

true solution (which we do not really know yet), and the ratio of the distance on the current step to the distance in the previous step. For example, the factor in the second row is

$$\frac{0.3180424220}{1.4654361738} \approx 0.2170291874$$

After 10 steps, the first five digits have stopped changing, meaning that we have found the equilibrium to about 5 decimal places of accuracy. The factor in the final column is approximately equal to the slope of the tangent at the unknown equilibrium. Each step gets us almost five times closer to the answer, and we have a highly accurate answer in only 10 steps.

Example 3.8.1 Finding the Optimal Behavior for a Mathematically Sophisticated Bee

Suppose now we wish to find the optimal behavior for a bee (as in Section 3.3) but that the food intake follows the function

$$F(t) = 1 - e^{-t}$$

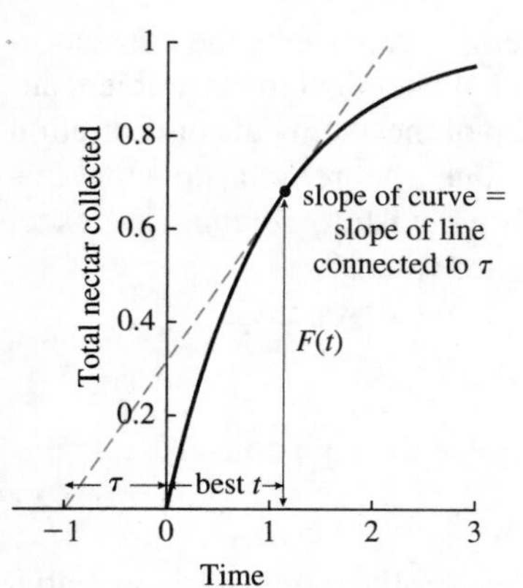

FIGURE 3.8.98

Applying the Marginal Value Theorem when $F(t) = 1 - e^{-t}$

We can see from Figure 3.8.98 that a solution exists when the travel time τ is equal to 1. To compute it, we must solve

$$F'(t) = \frac{F(t)}{t + \tau}$$

Substituting the equation for $F(t) = 1 - e^{-t}$ and $F'(t) = e^{-t}$ gives

$$e^{-t} = \frac{1 - e^{-t}}{t + 1}$$

We do not know how to solve an equation like this. We can rearrange and isolate e^t:

$$\begin{aligned} (t+1)e^{-t} &= 1 - e^{-t} && \text{multiply both sides by } t+1 \\ t + 1 &= e^t - 1 && \text{multiply both sides by } e^t \\ t + 2 &= e^t && \text{isolate } e^t \end{aligned}$$

This equation looks simple. At $t = 0$, the right-hand side is smaller, and at $t = 2$, the right-hand side is larger. The Intermediate Value Theorem (Theorem 3.2) guarantees that these two functions cross (Figure 3.8.99). But this equation is not written in the form of a discrete-time dynamical system. How can we compute the solution?

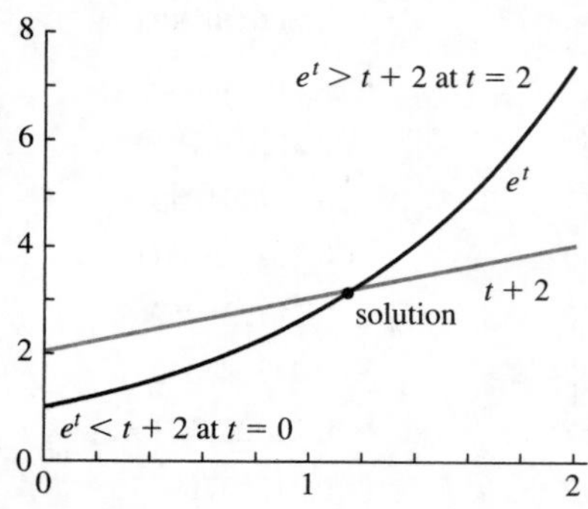

FIGURE 3.8.99

Finding the solution of an algebraically intractable equation

Newton's Method

Newton's method is a method for solving equations numerically. When it works, the method is incredibly fast, *doubling* the number of digits of accuracy with each step.

Suppose that we want to solve the equation

$$f(x) = 0$$

If we have some idea that a solution is near the value x_0, we can replace the original equation by the approximate equation

$$\hat{f}(x) = 0$$

where $\hat{f}(x)$ is the tangent line approximation at x_0 (Figure 3.8.100). The equation for the tangent line $\hat{f}(x)$ is

$$\hat{f}(x) = f(x_0) + f'(x_0)(x - x_0)$$

so our approximate equation $\hat{f}(x) = 0$ is

$$f(x_0) + f'(x_0)(x - x_0) = 0$$

As long as we can compute the derivative of $f(x)$, we can exactly solve this equation for x. Graphically, the solution of the original equation is the point where the curve intersects the horizontal axis. The solution of the approximate equation is the point where the tangent line intersects the horizontal axis.

Example 3.8.2 Computing a Square Root with Newton's Method: First Step

Suppose we wish to solve the equation

$$f(x) = x^2 - 3 = 0$$

FIGURE 3.8.100

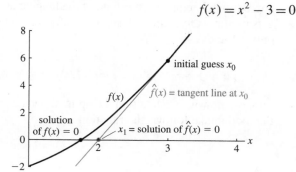

Newton's method: the first step

The solution of this equation is $\sqrt{3}$, a numerical value that is hard to compute by hand. The first step in Newton's method is to take a guess. We might begin with a rather poor guess of $x_0 = 3$. Next, we need to find the tangent line approximation by using the derivative

$$f'(x) = 2x$$

The tangent line approximation is

$$\begin{aligned}\hat{f}(x) &= f(3) + f'(3)(x-3)\\ &= (3^2 - 3) + 2\cdot 3(x-3)\\ &= 6 + 6(x-3)\end{aligned}$$

The approximate equation is

$$\hat{f}(x) = 6 + 6(x-3) = 0$$

which has can be solved as follows

$$\begin{aligned}6 + 6(x-3) &= 0\\ 6 + 6x - 18 &= 0\\ 6x &= 12\\ x &= 2\end{aligned}$$

This is closer to the right answer because 2^2 is much closer to 3.

We have replaced the difficult equation $f(x) = 0$ with the linear equation $\hat{f}(x) = 0$. It is possible to solve this linear equation for x (as long as $f'(x_0) \neq 0$). We find

$$\begin{aligned}f(x) &= 0 && \text{original equation}\\ f(x_0) + f'(x_0)(x - x_0) &= 0 && \text{substitute tangent line approximation}\\ f'(x_0)(x - x_0) &= -f(x_0) && \text{begin solving for } x\\ x - x_0 &= \frac{-f(x_0)}{f'(x_0)} && \text{divide by } f'(x_0)\\ x &= x_0 - \frac{f(x_0)}{f'(x_0)} && \text{solve for } x\end{aligned}$$

This value x is the point where the tangent line intersects the horizontal axis. Our hope is that this point is closer to the unknown exact answer than the original guess was. If so, we can use x as a new guess x_1, which we can compute with the formula

$$x_1 = x_0 - \frac{f(x_0)}{f'(x_0)} \tag{3.8.1}$$

Starting from the point x_1, we can follow the same steps to find the tangent line and solve for the intersection with the horizontal axis. The new guess, x_2, will have the same formula but with x_1 substituted for x_0, or

$$x_2 = x_1 - \frac{f(x_1)}{f'(x_1)}$$

Example 3.8.3 Computing a Square Root with Newton's Method: Second Step

In the example with $f(x) = x^2 - 3$, our first guess was $x_0 = 3$. By finding the tangent line and solving the equation, we found $x_1 = 2$. Alternatively, we could use Equation 3.8.1, with $f(3) = 6$ and $f'(3) = 6$, to find

$$\begin{aligned}x_1 &= 3 - \frac{f(3)}{f'(3)}\\ &= 3 - \frac{6}{6} = 2\end{aligned}$$

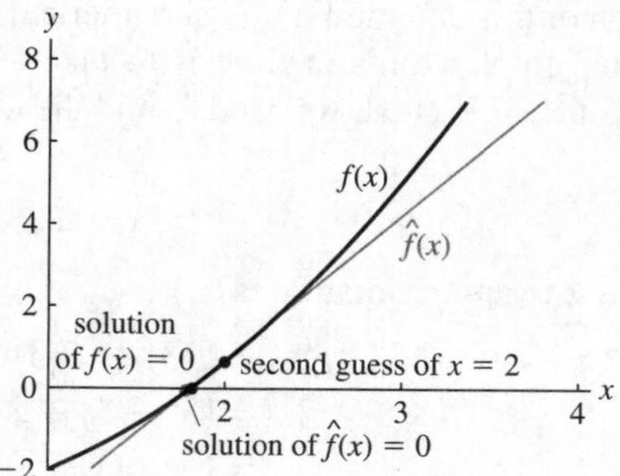

FIGURE 3.8.101
Newton's method: the second step

Starting from the new guess, $x_1 = 2$, we get

$$\begin{aligned} x_2 &= x_1 - \frac{f(x_1)}{f'(x_1)} \\ &= 2 - \frac{f(2)}{f'(2)} \\ &= 2 - \frac{2^2 - 3}{2 \cdot 2} \\ &= 2 - \frac{1}{4} = 1.75 \end{aligned}$$

(Figure 3.8.101). This is much closer to the exact answer because $1.75^2 = 3.0625$.

At each step, we applied the **Newton's method discrete-time dynamical system**

$$x_{t+1} = x_t - \frac{f(x_t)}{f'(x_t)}$$

This leads to the following algorithm.

Algorithm 3.4 Newton's Method for Solving a Nonlinear Equation

To solve the equation $f(x) = 0$:

1. Come up with a first guess called x_0.
2. Use the Newton's method discrete-time dynamical system

$$x_{t+1} = x_t - \frac{f(x_t)}{f'(x_t)}$$

to find x_1, x_2, and so forth until the answer converges.

When the sequence of points produced by Newton's method converge, why do they approach a point where $f(x_t) = 0$? If $f(x_t) = 0$, then the Newton's method discrete-time dynamical system gives

$$x_{t+1} = x_t - \frac{f(x_t)}{f'(x_t)} = x_t$$

Newton's method transforms the problem of solving the equation $f(x) = 0$ into the problem of finding the equilibrium of a discrete-time dynamical system. This problem we can solve by applying the discrete-time dynamical system starting with some initial guess and hoping that it converges.

Example 3.8.4 Computing a Square Root with Newton's Method

With the function $f(x) = x^2 - 3$, the Newton's method discrete-time dynamical system is

$$x_{t+1} = x_t - \frac{f(x_t)}{f'(x_t)}$$

$$= x_t - \frac{x_t^2 - 3}{2x_t}$$

The results of cobwebbing this equation and finding the solution are shown in Figure 3.8.102 and the following table.

Iteration	Value
0	3.0000000000
1	2.0000000000
2	1.7500000000
3	1.7321428571
4	1.7320508100

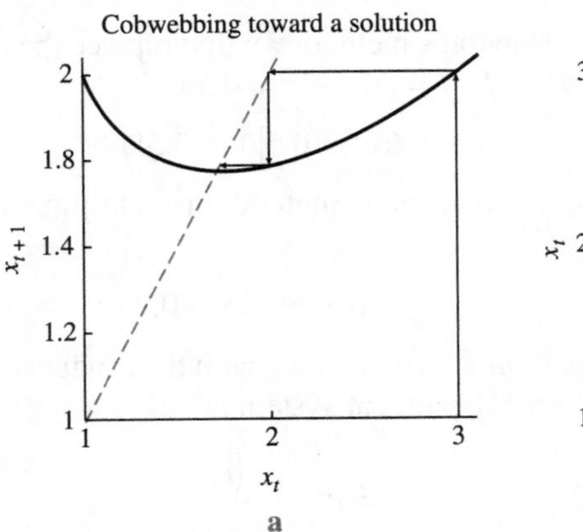

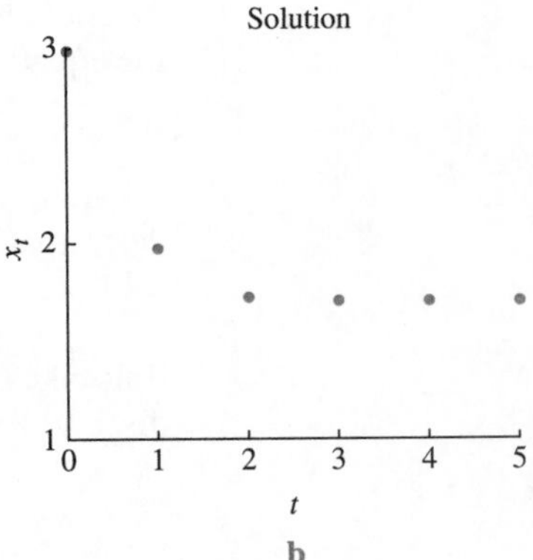

FIGURE 3.8.102
The Newton's method discrete-time dynamical system

Newton's method converges to the answer very quickly and is correct to eight decimal places after only four steps. And the calculation involved nothing more complicated than multiplication, subtraction, and division (enhanced by the awesome power of the derivative).

Example 3.8.5 Finding the Optimal Behavior of a Bee with Newton's Method

Now let us apply Newton's method to finding the optimal behavior of a bee, the solution of

$$e^t = t + 2$$

First we write the equation in the form $f(x) = 0$ as

$$f(x) = e^x - x - 2 = 0$$

Next we find $f'(x) = e^x - 1$. Therefore, the Newton's method discrete-time dynamical system is

$$x_{t+1} = x_t - \frac{e^{x_t} - x_t - 2}{e^{x_t} - 1}$$

To start the algorithm, we need a guess. From our graphs (Figures 3.8.98 and 3.8.99), it looks as though the solution is close to $x_0 = 1$. The results are

Iteration	Value
0	1.0
1	1.163953414
2	1.146421185
3	1.146193259
4	1.146193221

After only four steps, the values have converged to about seven decimal places, surely good enough for a bee!

Example 3.8.6 Finding an Equilibrium with Newton's Method

In our original problem of finding the equilibrium of a complicated lung discrete-time dynamical system, we already have a discrete-time dynamical system whose solution converges to the equilibrium. Do we gain anything by replacing the original discrete-time dynamical system with the Newton's method discrete-time dynamical system?

The original lung discrete-time dynamical system is

$$c_{t+1} = g(c_t) = 0.5\left[1 - 0.5\left(1 - e^{-0.5c_t}\right)\right] c_t + 2.5$$

To apply Newton's method, we first replace the equation for equilibrium $g(c) = c$ with the equation $f(c) = g(c) - c = 0$, or

$$f(c) = 0.5\left[1 - 0.5\left(1 - e^{-0.5c}\right)\right] c + 2.5 - c = 0$$

To find the Newton's method discrete-time dynamical system, we compute the derivative

$$f'(c) = 0.25 + 0.25e^{-0.5c} - 0.125ce^{-0.5c} - 1$$

(this takes some algebra along with the product and chain rules). The Newton's method discrete-time dynamical system is

$$\begin{aligned} c_{t+1} &= c_t - \frac{f(c_t)}{f'(c_t)} \\ &= c_t - \frac{0.5\left[1 - 0.5\left(1 - e^{-0.5c_t}\right)\right] c_t + 2.5 - c_t}{0.25 + 0.25e^{-0.5c_t} - 0.125c_te^{-0.5c_t} - 1} \end{aligned}$$

We have replaced the original, somewhat messy discrete-time dynamical system with a truly huge discrete-time dynamical system. Both share the equilibrium point we seek. Do we do better by repeatedly applying the Newton's method discrete-time dynamical system? Starting from the same initial guess, $c_0 = 5$, we find the date in the following table.

Iteration	Value	Distance from Equilibrium	Factor by which Distance Decreased
0	5.0000000000	1.4654361738	—
1	3.5304554457	−0.0041083804	−0.0028035205
2	3.5345638801	0.0000000539	−0.0000131336
3	3.5345638261	9.25×10^{-15}	1.712×10^{-10}

We have a full *16 decimal places* of accuracy after only three steps. The factor by which the distance decreases gets smaller and smaller, rather than remaining constant (as in

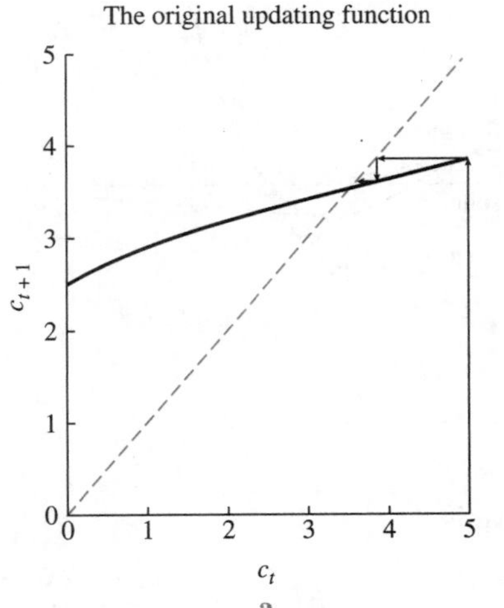

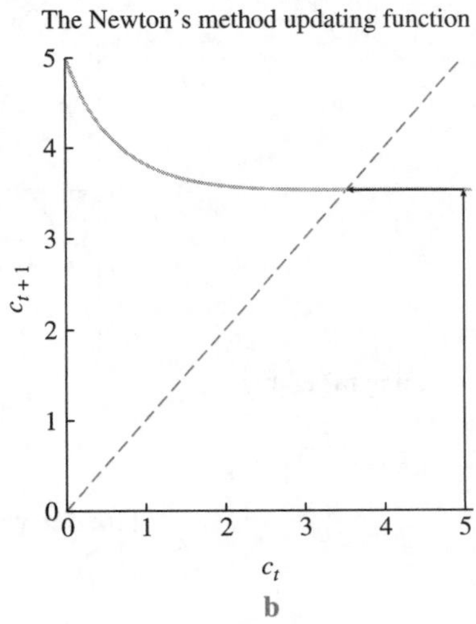

FIGURE 3.8.103
Comparison of discrete-time dynamical systems from original and Newton's methods

the table earlier in this section, p. 321). With a sufficiently accurate computer, we could *double* this number of digits with only one more step. It takes the ordinary discrete-time dynamical system dozens of steps to achieve this level of accuracy.

Why Newton's Method Works and When It Fails

Figure 3.8.103 indicates why Newton's method is so fast. The two discrete-time dynamical systems share the same equilibrium point, but the slope of the Newton's method discrete-time dynamical system is 0 at the equilibrium. The slope of the curve at an equilibrium determines stability. If the absolute value of the slope is less than 1, the distance from the equilibrium decreases and the solution moves toward the equilibrium. If the slope is very small (near 0), the distance decreases very quickly. If the slope of a discrete-time dynamical system is 0 at the equilibrium, the solution shoots right in toward the equilibrium (Figure 3.8.103b). An equilibrium where the slope is 0 is called **superstable.**

Is the slope of the updating function for Newton's method (Algorithm 3.4) really equal to 0 at the equilibrium? The derivative of the updating function for Newton's method,

$$h(x) = x - \frac{f(x)}{f'(x)}$$

can be computed with the quotient rule:

$$h'(x) = 1 - \frac{f'(x)f'(x) - f(x)f''(x)}{f'(x)^2} = \frac{f(x)f''(x)}{f'(x)^2}$$

The equilibrium of the updating function $h(x)$ is any point x^* where $f(x^*) = 0$. As long as $f'(x^*) \neq 0$,

$$h'(x^*) = \frac{f(x^*)f''(x^*)}{f'(x^*)^2} = 0$$

The equilibrium of the Newton's method discrete-time dynamical system is superstable.

Example 3.8.7 The Superstable Equilibrium for Newton's Method

When $f(x) = x^2 - 3$, the updating function for Newton's method is

$$h(x_t) = x_t - \frac{x_t^2 - 3}{2x_t}$$

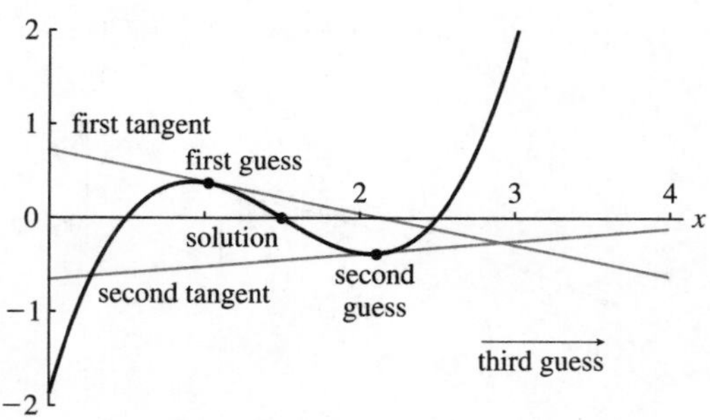

FIGURE 3.8.104
Newton's method failing miserably

The derivative is

$$h'(x_t) = 1 - \frac{2x_t \cdot 2x_t - 2 \cdot (x_t^2 - 3)}{4x_t^2}$$
$$= 1 - \left(1 - \frac{2 \cdot (x_t^2 - 3)}{4x_t^2}\right)$$
$$= \frac{2 \cdot (x_t^2 - 3)}{4x_t^2}$$

At any point where $x_t^2 - 3 = 0$, the derivative is indeed 0 (Figure 3.8.102).

As with many finely tuned machines, things can go drastically wrong with Newton's method. In Figure 3.8.104, our first guess was not too good and the solution eventually shot off to very large values. This picture shows geometrically why the slope $f'(x)$ must be different from 0. If we start at a point on the original curve where $f'(x) = 0$, the tangent never intersects the horizontal axis. The next step of Newton's method is not defined.

Furthermore, for functions with multiple solutions, Newton's method may not converge to the desired point. In Figure 3.8.104, Newton's method will eventually converge to the solution farthest to the right, which is not close to the first guess. To avoid these problems, computer algorithms usually start with the Intermediate Value Theorem to get close to a particular solution and then capitalize on the speed of Newton's method to gain accuracy.

Summary Solving equations for equilibria or other quantities is often impossible algebraically. Newton's method is a technique that can be implemented on the computer. By replacing the original equation with the tangent line approximation, we derived the **Newton's method discrete-time dynamical system,** which usually converges very quickly to the solution. The awesome speed of Newton's method results from the fact that the solution is a **superstable** equilibrium, where the slope of the graph of the updating function is 0 at the equilibrium.

3.8 Exercises

Mathematical Techniques

1–4 ▪ Try Newton's method graphically for two steps, starting from the given points on the figure.

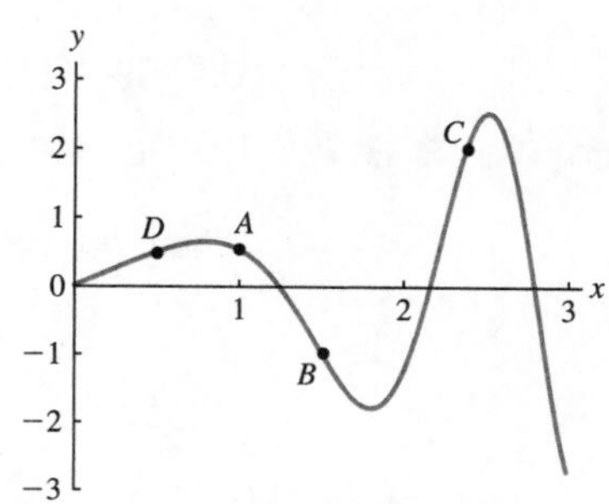

1. The point marked A.
2. The point marked B.
3. The point marked C.
4. The point marked D.

5–8 ▪ Use Newton's method for three steps to find the following. Find and sketch the tangent line for the first step, and then find the Newton's method discrete-time dynamical system to check your answer for the first step and compute the next two values.

5. $x^2 - 5x + 1 = 0$ (this can be solved exactly with the quadratic formula).
6. $\sqrt[3]{20}$ (solve $f(x) = x^3 - 20 = 0$).
7. A positive solution of $e^{x/2} = x + 1$ (solve $h(x) = e^{x/2} - x - 1 = 0$).
8. The point where $\cos(x) = x$ (in radians, of course).

9–12 ▪ Many equations can also be solved by repeatedly applying a discrete-time dynamical system. Compare the following discrete-time dynamical systems with the Newton's method discrete-time dynamical system. Show that each has the same equilibrium, and see how close you get in three steps with each method.

9. Use the discrete-time dynamical system $x_{t+1} = e^{x_t} - 2$ to solve $e^x = x + 2$ (as in the text).
10. Use the discrete-time dynamical system $x_{t+1} = x_t^3 + x_t - 20$ (based on Exercise 6).
11. Use the discrete-time dynamical system $x_{t+1} = e^{x_t/2} - 1$ (based on Exercise 7).
12. Use the discrete-time dynamical system $x_{t+1} = \cos(x_t)$ (based on Exercise 8).

13–14 ▪ Find the value of the parameter r for which the given discrete-time dynamical system will converge most rapidly to its positive equilibrium. Follow the system for four steps, starting from the given initial condition.

13. The logistic dynamical system $x_{t+1} = rx_t(1 - x_t)$. Start from $x_0 = 0.75$.
14. The Ricker dynamical system $x_{t+1} = rx_t e^{-x_t}$. Start from $x_0 = 0.75$.

15–18 ▪ As mentioned in the text, although Newton's method works incredibly well most of the time, it can fail or work less well in many circumstances. For each of the following exercises, graph the function to illustrate the failures.

15. Find all initial values from which Newton's method fails to solve $x(x-1)(x+1) = 0$. Which starting points converge to a negative solution?
16. Find two initial values from which Newton's method fails to solve $x^3 - 6x^2 + 9x - 1 = 0$. Graphically indicate a third such value.
17. Use Newton's method to solve $x^2 = 0$ (the solution is 0). Why does it approach the solution so slowly?
18. Use Newton's method to solve $\sqrt{|x|} = 0$ (the solution is 0). This is the square root of the absolute value of x. Why does the method fail?

19–20 ▪ Suppose we wish to solve the equation $f(x) = 0$ but cannot compute the derivative $f'(x)$. (This kind of problem arises when the function $f(x)$ must be evaluated with a complicated computer program.) An alternative approach approximates the derivative $f'(x)$ with $f(x+1) - f(x)$ (the secant line). For each of the following cases, write an approximate Newton's method discrete-time dynamical system, illustrate the procedure with a diagram, and try it for five steps to see how quickly it approaches the solution.

19. $f(x) = e^x - x - 2$ (from the text).
20. $f(x) = x^3 - 20$ (from Exercise 6).

21–22 ▪ There is an alternative way to approximate the slope of the function at the value x_t:

$$f'(x_t) \approx \frac{f(x_t) - f(x_{t-1})}{x_t - x_{t-1}}$$

For each of the following equations, use this estimate to write an approximate Newton's method discrete-time dynamical system and illustrate the idea with a diagram. How is it different from an ordinary discrete-time dynamical system? Run it for a few steps, starting from x_0 and x_1 from Problems 19–20. Does it converge faster than the earlier approximation? Why? How does it compare with Newton's method itself?

21. $f(x) = e^x - x - 2$ (from Exercise 19).
22. $f(x) = x^3 - 20$ (from Exercise 20).

Applications

23–24 ▪ Suppose the total amount of nectar that comes out of a flower after time t follows

$$F(t) = \frac{t^2}{1 + t^2}$$

After noting how this function differs from the forms studied in the text, write the equation used to find the optimal time to remain, and then solve it with Newton's method (or algebraically) if the travel time τ takes on the following values. Draw the associated Marginal Value Theorem diagram.

23. $\tau = 0$
24. $\tau = 1$

25–26 ▪ Suppose a fish population follows the discrete-time dynamical system

$$N_{t+1} = rN_t e^{-N_t} - hN_t$$

For the following values of r, find the equilibrium N^* as a function of h, write the equation for the critical point of the payoff function $P(h) = hN^*$, and use Newton's method to find the best h.

25. $r = 2.5$
26. $r = 1.5$

27–28 ▪ Consider a variant of the medication discrete-time dynamical system

$$M_t = p(M_t)M_t + 1.0$$

where the function $p(M_t)$ represents the fraction used (see Section 1.10, Exercise 39). Suppose that $p(M_t) = \alpha e^{-0.1M_t}$. For the following values of α, show that there is an equilibrium by using the Intermediate Value Theorem, follow the solution of the discrete-time dynamical system until it gets close to the equilibrium (about three decimal places), and find the equilibrium with Newton's method.

27. $\alpha = 0.5$

28. $\alpha = 0.9$

29–30 ▪ Thomas Malthus predicted doom for the human species when he argued that populations grow exponentially but their resources grow only linearly. Find the time when the population runs out of resources in the following cases.

29. The population grows according to $b(t) = 100e^{0.1t}$, and resources grow according to $R(t) = 400 + 100t$. The population starves when $b(t) = R(t)$.

30. The population grows according to $b(t) = 100e^{0.1t}$, and resources grow according to $R(t) = 4000 + 500t$. The population starves when $b(t) = R(t)$.

31–32 ▪ A lung follows the discrete-time dynamical system

$$c_{t+1} = 0.75\alpha(c_t)c_t + 0.25\gamma$$

where $\gamma = 5.0$, the function $\alpha(c_t)$ is positive and decreasing, and $\alpha(0) = 1$. We used the Intermediate Value Theorem (Exercise 30) to show that there is an equilibrium for any such function $\alpha(c)$. Use Newton's method to solve for the equilibrium for the following forms of $\alpha(c)$.

31. $\alpha(c) = e^{-c}$

32. $\alpha(c) = e^{-0.1c}$

Computer Exercises

33. An alternative method of solution, which is much slower but much safer, is called **bisection.** The method is based on the Intermediate Value Theorem. We will use it to solve $g(x) = e^x - x - 2 = 0$.
    a. We know there is a solution between $x = 0$ and $x = 2$. Show that there is a solution between $x = 1$ and $x = 2$.
    b. By computing $g(1.5)$, show that there is a solution between 1.0 and 1.5.
    c. Compute $g(1.25)$. There is a solution either between 1.0 and 1.25 or between 1.25 and 1.5. Which is it?
    d. Compute the value of g at the midpoint of the previous interval, and find an interval half as big that contains a solution.
    e. Continue **bisecting** the interval until your answer is right to three decimal places.
    f. About how many more steps would it take to reach six decimal places?

34. Solve the equation $e^x - x - 2 = 0$ by using the quadratic approximation (Section 3.7, p. 310) to the function and solving each step by using the quadratic formula. Compare how fast it converges with Newton's method. Which method do you think is better?

3.9 Panting and Deep Breathing

Why do some animals pant and others breathe slowly and deeply? Panting has the advantage of taking more breaths per second, but the breaths are shallower and leave the lung less time to absorb oxygen. Conversely, deep breathing has the advantage of giving the lung more time to absorb oxygen, but at the cost of taking fewer breaths per second. We will derive discrete-time dynamical systems describing a lung with absorption in order to generate hypotheses to explain these different breathing strategies. By writing a detailed model of the lung that includes absorption and different breathing rates, we can ask which kind of breathing maximizes the rate of oxygen absorption. We will find that the answer depends on the exact shape of the absorption function.

Breathing at Different Rates

Suppose lung expansion as a function of time behaves as shown in Figure 3.9.105. The lung receives a signal every T seconds to switch from exhaling to inhaling. The volume of air in the lung increases at a constant rate until the lung is full and then decreases at a constant rate until the next signal is received. In Figure 3.9.105a the signal arrives frequently and the animal breathes quickly and shallowly. In Figure 3.9.105b the signal arrives after a longer delay and the animal breathes slowly and deeply. In Figure 3.9.105c the signal does not arrive until the lung has nearly emptied and rested.

Suppose an animal is running and needs to gain oxygen as quickly as possible. Should it pant (breathe rapidly and shallowly) or should it breathe more slowly and deeply? The answer depends on how absorption depends on the internal concentration and the rate of breathing.

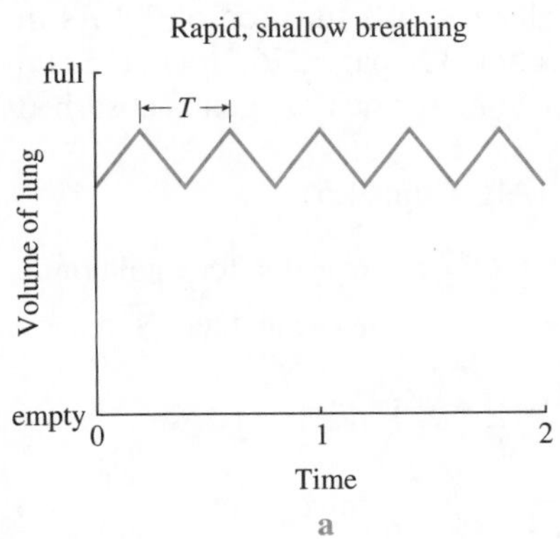

a

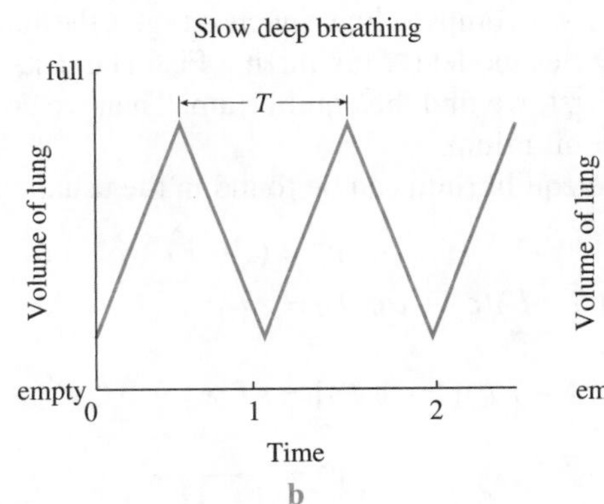

b

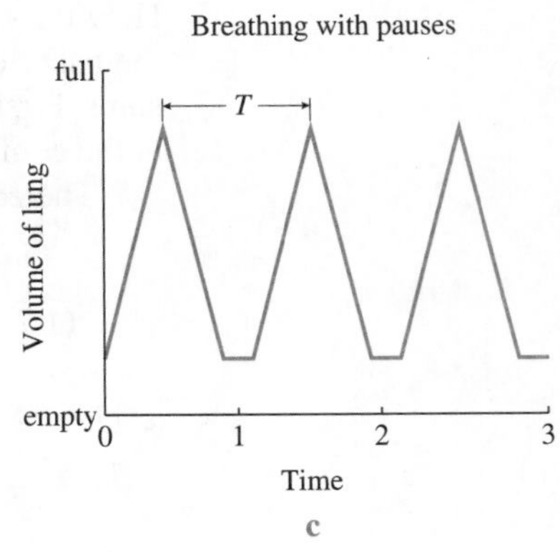

c

FIGURE 3.9.105
Three types of breathing

We can write a discrete-time dynamical system describing the concentration c_t of oxygen in the lung:

$$c_{t+1} = (1-q)\big(c_t - c_t A(T)\big) + q\gamma$$

As before, q represents the fraction of air exchanged and γ the ambient concentration. The function $A(T)$ denotes the fraction of oxygen absorbed as a function of time T between breaths. This is a different sort of absorption function from $\alpha(c)$, studied in Section 3.5, where absorption depended on the concentration rather than on the time. If $A(T) = 0$, there is no absorption and we recover the original lung discrete-time dynamical system (Equation 1.9.1).

In addition to changing the fraction of oxygen absorbed, changing the breathing rate changes the fraction of air exchanged. The fraction of air exchanged is proportional to the amount of time spent inhaling. We can therefore write

$$q = rT$$

for some value of r. Suppose that $T = 1.0$ represents maximum exhalation, or the longest possible time. If $r = 1.0$ and $T = 1.0$, all the air in the lung is exchanged. For most organisms, complete exchange is impossible. The value of r is the fraction of air exchanged if breathing totally exchanges air, and it must be less than or equal to 1.

The discrete-time dynamical system is then

$$c_{t+1} = (1 - rT)\big[c_t - c_t A(T)\big] + rT\gamma \tag{3.9.1}$$

If we knew the equation for $A(T)$, we could compare total absorption with different values of T.

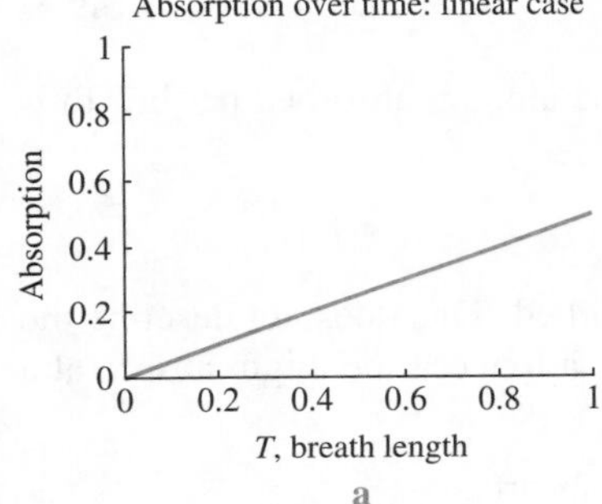

a

Absorption over time: saturation

Absorption

T, breath length

b

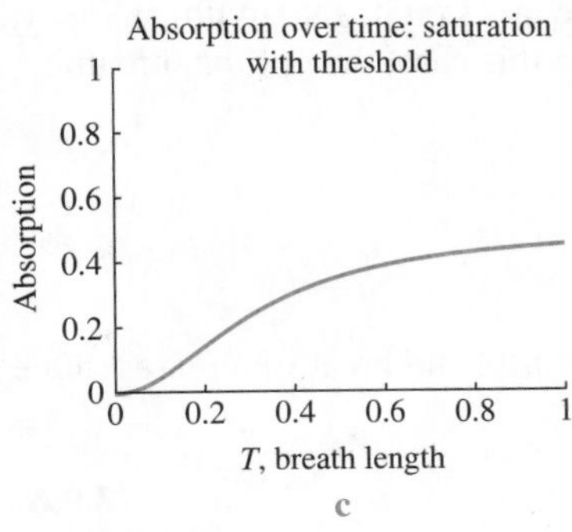

c

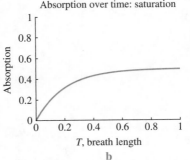

FIGURE 3.9.106
Three different absorption functions

Deep Breathing

It is simplest to assume that the fraction absorbed is proportional to T. If the lung has twice as much time to absorb oxygen, twice as much oxygen will be absorbed. If $A(T)$ is proportional to T, then

$$A(T) = \alpha T \tag{3.9.2}$$

for some value α (Figure 3.9.106a). If $\alpha = 1.0$ and $T = 1.0$ (maximum exchange), all of the oxygen is absorbed. Because complete absorption is impossible, the value of α must be less than 1.0.

Substituting $A(T) = \alpha T$ into the general discrete-time dynamical system (Equation 3.9.1) gives

$$c_{t+1} = (1 - rT)\big(c_t - \alpha c_t T\big) + rT\gamma \tag{3.9.3}$$

How do we compute how much oxygen the lung absorbs as a function of T? As in the fisheries model ("Maximizing Fish Harvest," Section 3.3, page 276), there are two steps. First, we find the equilibrium. Then we compute how much oxygen is absorbed at the equilibrium.

The equilibrium can be found in the usual way (Algorithm 1.5).

$$c^* = (1 - rT)(c^* - \alpha c^* T) + r\gamma T \quad \text{equation for equilibrium}$$

$$c^* - (1 - rT)(c^* - \alpha c^* T) = rT\gamma \quad \text{move all the } c^*\text{'s to one side}$$

$$c^*[1 - (1 - rT)(1 - \alpha T)] = rT\gamma \quad \text{factor out } c^*$$

$$c^* = \frac{rT\gamma}{1 - (1 - rT)(1 - \alpha T)} \quad \text{solve for } c^*$$

With a bit of algebra, we can cancel a T from the top and bottom, finding

$$\begin{aligned} c^* &= \frac{\gamma rT}{1 - \left(1 - rT - \alpha T + r\alpha T^2\right)} \\ &= \frac{\gamma rT}{rT + \alpha T - r\alpha T^2} \\ &= \frac{\gamma r}{r + \alpha - r\alpha T} \end{aligned} \tag{3.9.4}$$

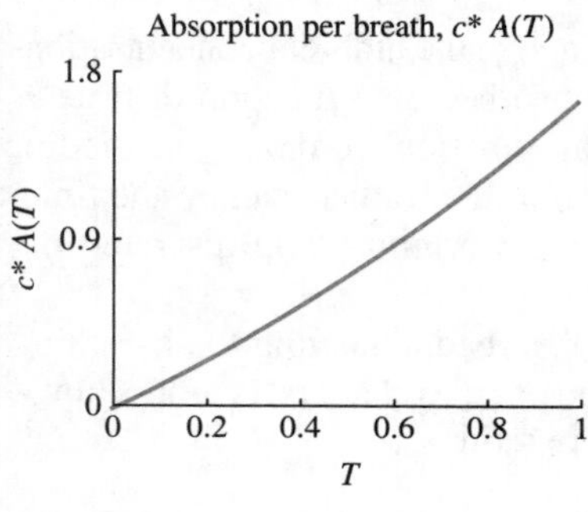

At what rate does this lung absorb chemical? The amount absorbed per breath is given by

$$\text{amount absorbed} = c^* A(T)$$

the equilibrium concentration times the fraction absorbed. This does not describe the *rate,* however. A lung that absorbs more oxygen over a longer time might absorb at a lower *rate*. The rate of absorption is

$$\begin{aligned} \text{rate of absorption} &= \frac{\text{amount absorbed}}{\text{time}} \\ &= \frac{c^* A(T)}{T} \end{aligned}$$

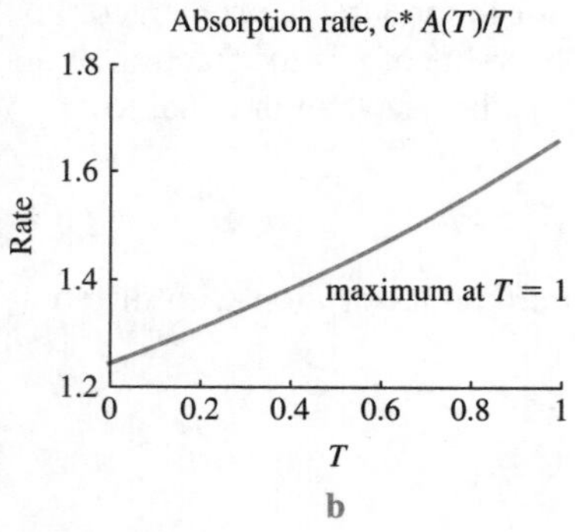

FIGURE 3.9.107
Absorption and rate of absorption at equilibrium as functions of T: linear case

Our goal is to maximize this rate. In this case,

$$\begin{aligned} \frac{c^* A(T)}{T} &= \frac{\alpha c^* T}{T} \\ &= \frac{\alpha\gamma r}{r + \alpha - r\alpha T} \end{aligned} \tag{3.9.5}$$

The only appearance of T in this formula is in the denominator, and the larger the value of T, the larger the function (see Exercise 4). This rate takes on its maximum at $T = 1$, the maximum possible value of T (Figure 3.9.107). In this case, the optimal breathing rate is slow, like a well-conditioned runner's.

Panting

What if absorption becomes less efficient as the length of the breath increases? One function describing saturation is

$$A(T) = \alpha\left(1 - e^{-kT}\right) \tag{3.9.6}$$

In this case, long breaths might not make sense because absorption becomes less and less efficient over time (Figure 3.9.106b).

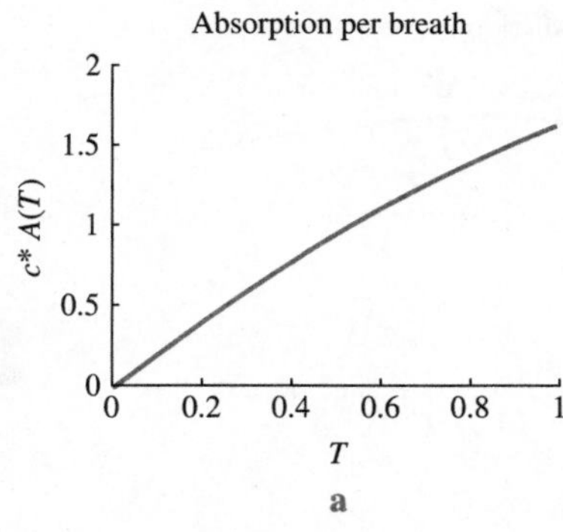

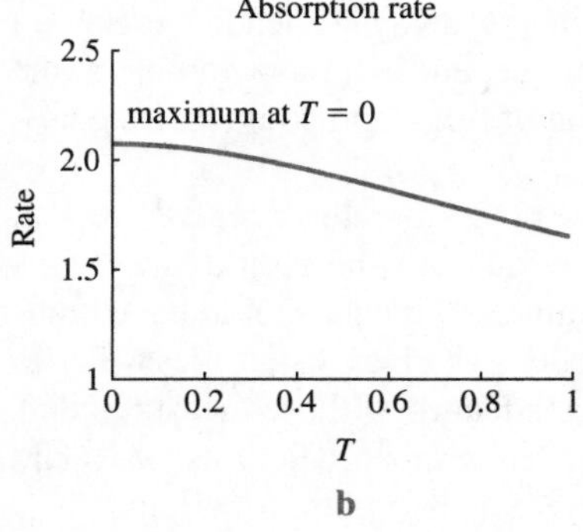

FIGURE 3.9.108

Absorption and rate of absorption as functions of T: saturating case

Substituting into the discrete-time dynamical system (Equation 3.9.1), we get

$$c_{t+1} = (1 - rT)\left[c_t - \alpha c_t\left(1 - e^{-kT}\right)\right] + rT\gamma \tag{3.9.7}$$

We can follow the same steps as before to find the equilibrium and maximize the rate of absorption. In this case,

$$c^* = \frac{\gamma r T}{1 - (1 - rT)\left[1 - \alpha\left(1 - e^{-kT}\right)\right]} \tag{3.9.8}$$

(Exercise 5). The absorption per breath is

$$\begin{aligned} c^* A(T) &= \alpha c^*\left(1 - e^{-kT}\right) \\ &= \frac{\alpha\gamma r T\left(1 - e^{-kT}\right)}{\left[1 - (1 - rT)1 - \alpha\left(1 - e^{-kT}\right)\right]} \end{aligned}$$

and the rate of absorption is

$$\frac{c^* A(T)}{T} = \frac{\alpha\gamma r\left(1 - e^{-kT}\right)}{1 - (1 - rT)\left(1 - \alpha\left[1 - e^{-kT}\right)\right]}$$

With the parameter values $\alpha = 0.5$, $r = 0.5$, $\gamma = 5$, and $k = 5$, the absorption and absorption rate are as shown in Figure 3.9.108. Although the amount of oxygen absorbed *per breath* increases with longer breaths, the absorption *rate* decreases. The optimal value of T is $T = 0$. This organism does best by breathing as fast as it can, like an overheated dog.

Intermediate Optimum

What if absorption takes a little time to get started? It might have a graph like that in Figure 3.9.106c. One function of T that produces this shape is

$$A(T) = \frac{\alpha T^2}{k + T^2} \tag{3.9.9}$$

(one of the Hill functions studied in Example 2.6.5). Two processes are involved: Absorption saturates for large T and takes some time to get started.

We follow the same steps to find the equilibrium and maximize the rate of absorption. The equilibrium is

$$c^* = \frac{\gamma r T}{1 - (1 - rT)\left(1 - \alpha\dfrac{T^2}{k + T^2}\right)} \tag{3.9.10}$$

(see Exercise 6). The absorption is

$$\begin{aligned} c^* A(T) &= \alpha c^* \frac{T^2}{k + T^2} \\ &= \frac{\alpha\gamma r T\dfrac{T^2}{k + T^2}}{1 - (1 - rT)\left(1 - \alpha\dfrac{T^2}{k + T^2}\right)} \end{aligned}$$

and the rate of absorption is

$$\frac{c^* A(T)}{T} = \frac{\alpha\gamma r\dfrac{T^2}{k + T^2}}{1 - (1 - rT)\left(1 - \alpha\dfrac{T^2}{k + T^2}\right)}$$

The absorption and rate of absorption with the parameter values $\alpha = 0.5$, $r = 0.5$, $\gamma = 5$, $k = 0.1$, are as plotted in Figure 3.9.109. Long breaths are not best because

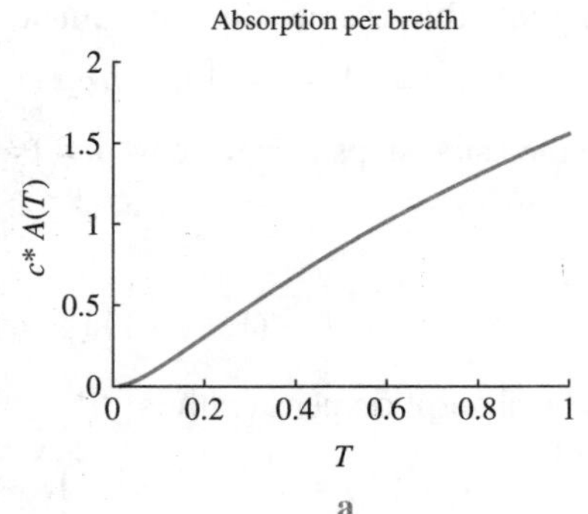

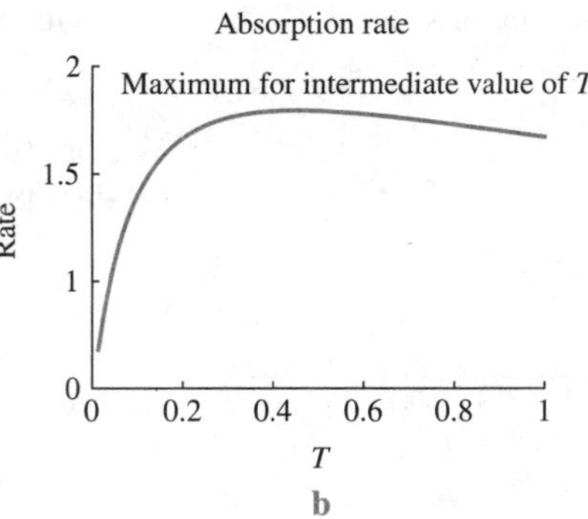

FIGURE 3.9.109
Absorption and rate of absorption as functions of T: case with saturation and threshold

of saturation, and panting is not optimal because of the delay. Instead, there is an intermediate maximum. The position of this maximum depends on the parameters (the detailed shape of the graph of absorption as a function of time) and could be longer or shorter, depending on the organism (see Exercise 8).

Have we explained why some animals pant and others breathe deeply? No, but these models provide a hypothesis: Animals that take long breaths should have lungs that do not saturate quickly (like $A(T) = \alpha T$), and animals that pant should have lungs that do saturate (like $A(T) = \alpha(1 - e^{-kT})$). The model has given us an idea what to measure next: oxygen absorption as a function of breath length. If those measurements seem to be consistent with the assumptions of the model and its predictions, we could attempt to discover the physiological basis of the different absorption functions.

Summary By incorporating explicit consideration of breath length into our model for the concentration of a chemical in the lung, we found optimal breathing rates. If absorption is a linear function of time, slow deep breaths maximize the rate of oxygen uptake. If absorption saturates with time, panting can be best. If absorption begins slowly, an intermediate breathing rate is best. This observation suggest a hypothesis to explain the different breathing behaviors of organisms.

3.9 Exercises

1–4 ▪ Show that the rate of absorption is maximized at $T = 1$ with the absorption function

$$A(T) = \alpha T$$

(Equation 3.9.2) for the following values of α, r, and γ.

1. With $\alpha = 0.5$, $r = 1$, and $\gamma = 5.0$.
2. With $\alpha = 0.5$, $r = 0.5$, and $\gamma = 5.0$. Why is the optimal absorption lower than in Exercise 1?
3. With $r = 1.0$ and $\gamma = 5.0$, but without picking a value for α. How does the optimal absorption depend on α?
4. In general, without picking values for any of the parameters.

5–6 ▪ Check the following formulas.

5. The equilibrium given in Equation 3.9.8.
6. The equilibrium given in Equation 3.9.10.

7–10 ▪ Find the value of T that maximizes the rate of absorption when the absorption function

$$A(T) = \alpha \frac{T^2}{k + T^2}$$

(Equation 3.9.9) for the following parameter values.

7. $\alpha = 0.5$, $r = 0.5$, $\gamma = 5.0$, and $k = 0.1$. You should get that the best T is $1/\sqrt{5.0} \approx 0.447$.
8. Check that $T = \sqrt{\frac{k}{1 - \alpha}}$ in general.
9. How does the optimal T change if r becomes larger?
10. How does the optimal T change if α becomes larger? Does this make sense?

11–12 ▪ Solve for the following without substituting in a particular functional form for $A(T)$.

11. The equilibrium concentration.
12. The equilibrium rate of absorption.

13–16 ▪ Substitute the following forms for $A(T)$ into the expressions found in Exercise 12 and compare with the results in the text.

13. With $A(T) = \alpha T$.
14. With $A(T) = \alpha(1 - e^{-kT})$.
15. With $A(T) = \dfrac{\alpha T^2}{k + T^2}$.

16. With $A(T) = \frac{\alpha T}{k+T}$ (a case not considered in the text).

17–21 ▪ Find

$$\lim_{T \to 0} \frac{c^* A(T)}{T}$$

for the following forms of $A(T)$. Do the results make sense?

17. With $A(T) = \alpha T$.

18. With $A(T) = \alpha(1 - e^{-kT})$.

19. With $A(T) = \alpha T^2$.

20. In general, assuming $A(0) = 0$.

21. Do a complete analysis of the case $A(T) = \frac{\alpha T}{k+T}$.

Computer Exercises

22. Use a computer to reproduce all the figures in this section.

23. Use a computer to experiment with the effects of the parameter α on the absorption function given in Equation 3.9.6. Set $r = 0.5$, $\gamma = 5.0$, and $k = 5$. Test values of α ranging from 0.1 to 1.0. Can you explain your results?

Supplementary Problems

1–2 ▪ For the functions shown:

a. Sketch the derivative.

b. Label local and global maxima.

c. Label local and global minima.

d. Find subsets of the domain with positive second derivative.

1.

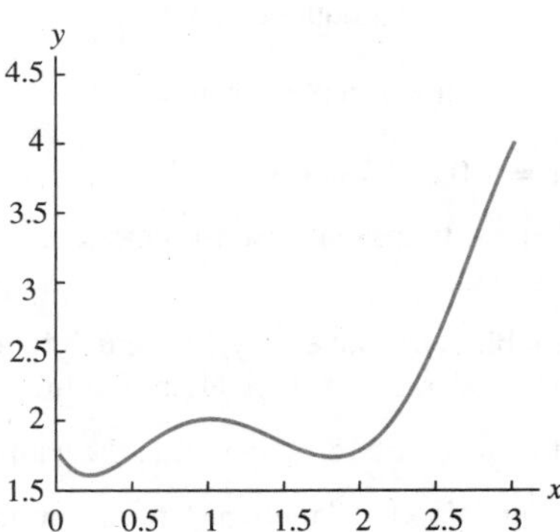

2.

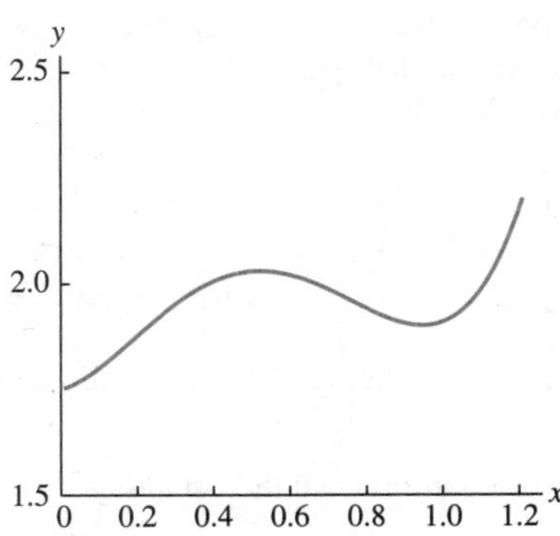

3–4 ▪ Use the tangent line and the quadratic Taylor polynomial to find approximate values of the following. Make sure to write down the function or functions you use and the equation of the tangent line. Check with your calculator.

3. $1/(3 + 1.01^2)$

4. $e^{3(1.02)^2 + 2(1.02)}$

5–6 ▪ Write down the tangent line approximation for the following functions, and estimate the requested values.

5. $f(x) = \frac{1+x}{1+e^{3x}}$. Estimate $f(-0.03)$.

6. $g(y) = (1 + 2y)^4 \ln(y)$. Estimate $g(1.02)$.

7–8 ▪ Sketch graphs of the following functions. Find all critical points, and state whether they are minima or maxima. Find the limit of the function as $x \to \infty$.

7. $(x^2 + 2x)e^{-x}$ for positive x.

8. $\ln(x)/(1 + x)$ for positive x. Do not solve for the maximum; just show that there must be one.

9–12 ▪ Find the Taylor polynomial of degree 2 approximating each of the following.

9. $f(x) = \frac{1+x}{1+x^2}$ for x near 0.

10. $f(x) = \frac{1+x}{1+x^2}$ for x near 1.

11. $g(x) = \frac{1+x}{1+e^x}$ for x near 0.

12. $h(x) = \frac{x}{2-e^x}$ for x near 0.

13–14 ▪ Combine the Taylor polynomials from the previous set of problems with the leading behavior of the functions for large x to sketch graphs

13. $g(x) = \frac{1+x}{1+e^x}$ (Problem 11)

14. $h(x) = \frac{x}{2-e^x}$ (Problem 12)

15. Between days 0 and 150 (measured from November 1), the snow at a certain ski resort is given by

$$S(t) = -\frac{1}{4}t^4 + 60t^3 - 4000t^2 + 96000t$$

where S is measured in microns (one micron, μm, is 10^{-4} cm).

a. A yeti tells you that this function has critical points at $t = 20$, $t = 40$, and $t = 120$. Confirm this assertion.

b. Find the global maximum and global minimum amounts of snow in feet. Remember that 1 in. = 2.54 cm.

c. Use the second derivative test to identify the critical points as local maxima and minima.

d. Sketch the function.

16. Let $r(x)$ be the function giving the per capita production as a function of population size x.

$$r(x) = \frac{4x}{1 + 3x^2}$$

a. Find the population size that produces the highest per capita production.

b. Find the highest per capita production.

c. Check with the second derivative test.

17. An organism is replacing 25% of the air in its lung with each breath, and the external concentration of a chemical is $\gamma = 5.0 \times 10^{-4}$ mol/L. Suppose the body uses a fraction α of the chemical just after breathing. That is, the chemical follows

$$c_t \overset{\text{absorption}}{\longrightarrow} (1-\alpha)c_t \overset{\text{breathing}}{\longrightarrow} \text{mix of 75\% used air and 25\% ambient air}$$

a. Write the updating function for this process.

b. Find the equilibrium level in the lung as a function of α.

c. Find the amount absorbed by the body with each breath at equilibrium as a function of α.

d. Find the value of α that maximizes the amount of chemical absorbed at equilibrium.

e. Explain your result in words.

18. An organism is replacing a fraction q of the air in its lung with each breath, and the external concentration of a chemical is $\gamma = 5.0 \times 10^{-4}$ mol/L. Suppose the body uses a fraction $\alpha = 1 - q$ of the chemical just after breathing. The chemical follows

$$c_t \overset{\text{absorption}}{\longrightarrow} (1-\alpha)c_t \overset{\text{breathing}}{\longrightarrow} \text{mix of used and ambient air}$$

a. Write the updating function for this process.

b. Find the equilibrium level in the lung as a function of q. Is it stable?

c. Find the amount absorbed by the body with each breath at equilibrium as a function of q.

d. Find the value of q that maximizes the amount of chemical absorbed at equilibrium.

e. Explain your result in words.

19. Suppose the volume of a plant cell follows $V(t) = 1000(1 - e^{-t})\ \mu\text{m}^3$ for t measured in days. Suppose the fraction of cell in a vacuole (a water-filled portion of the cell) is $H(t) = e^t/(1 + e^t)$.

a. Sketch a graph of the total size of the cell as a function of time.

b. Find the volume of cell outside the vacuole.

c. Find and interpret the derivative of this function. Don't forget the units.

d. Find when the volume of the cell outside the vacuole reaches a maximum.

20. Consider the function

$$F(t) = \frac{\ln(1 + t)}{t + t^2}$$

a. What is $\lim_{t \to 0} F(t)$?

b. What is $\lim_{t \to 0} F'(t)$?

c. What is $\lim_{t \to 0} F''(t)$?

d. Sketch a graph of this function.

21. During Thanksgiving dinner, the table is replenished with food every 5 min. Let F_t represent the fraction of the table laden with food.

$$F_{t+1} = F_t - \text{amount eaten} + \text{amount replenished}$$

Suppose that

$$\text{amount eaten} = \frac{bF_t}{1 + F_t}$$

$$\text{amount replenished} = a(1 - F_t)$$

and that $a = 1.0$ and $b = 1.5$.

a. Explain the terms that describe amount eaten and amount replenished.

b. If the table starts out empty, how much food is there after 5 min? How much is there after 10 min?

c. Use the quadratic formula to find the equilibria.

d. How much food will there be 5 min after the table is 60% full? Sketch the solution.

22. Let N_t represent the difference between the sodium concentration inside and that outside a cell at some time. After 1 s, the value of N_{t+1} is

$$\begin{cases} N_{t+1} = 0.5N_t & \text{if } N_t \le 2 \\ N_{t+1} = 4.0N_t - 7 & \text{if } 2 < N_t \le 4 \\ N_{t+1} = -0.25N_t + 10 & \text{if } 4 < N_t \end{cases}$$

a. Graph the updating function and show that it is continuous.

b. Find the equilibria and their stability.

c. Find all initial conditions for which solutions approach $N = 0$.

23. Consider the problem of finding a positive solution of the equation

$$e^x = 2x + 1$$

a. Draw a graph and pick a reasonable starting value.

b. Write down the Newton's method discrete-time dynamical system for this equation.

c. Find your next guess.

d. Show explicitly that the slope of the updating function for this iteration is 0 at the solution.

24. Consider the problem of solving the equation

$$\ln(x) = \frac{x}{3}$$

a. Convince yourself that there is indeed a solution and find a reasonable guess.

b. Use Newton's method to update your guess twice.

c. What would be a bad choice of an initial guess?

25. Suppose a bee gains an amount of energy

$$F(t) = \frac{3t}{1+t}$$

after it has been on a flower for time t but that it uses $2t$ energy units in that time (it has to struggle with the flower).

a. Find the net energy gain as a function of t.

b. Find when the net energy gain per flower is maximum.

c. Suppose the travel time between flowers is $\tau = 1$. Find the time spent on the flower that maximizes the rate of energy gain.

d. Draw a diagram illustrating the results of parts **b** and **c.** Why is the answer to part **c** smaller?

26. Consider the function for net energy gain from the previous problem.

a. Use the Extreme Value Theorem to show that there must be a maximum.

b. Use the Intermediate Value Theorem to show that there must be a residence time t that maximizes the rate of energy gain.

27. A peculiar variety of bacterium enhances its own per capita production. In particular, the number of offspring per bacterium increases according to the function

$$\text{per capita production} = r\left(1 + \frac{b_t}{K}\right)$$

Suppose that $r = 0.5$ and $K = 10^6$.

a. Graph per capita production as a function of population size.

b. Find and graph the updating function for this population.

c. Find the equilibria.

d. Find their stability.

28. A type of butterfly has two morphs, a and b. Each type reproduces annually after predation. Twenty percent of type a are eaten, and 10% of type b are eaten. Each type doubles its population when it reproduces. However, the types do not breed true. Only 90% of the offspring of type a are of type a, the rest being of type b. Only 80% of the offspring of type b are of type b, the rest being of type a.

a. Suppose there are 10,000 of each type before predation and reproduction. Find the number of each type after predation and reproduction.

b. Find the updating function for types a and b.

c. Find the updating function for the fraction p of type a.

d. Find the equilibria.

e. Find their stability.

29. A population of size x_t follows the rule

$$\text{per capita production} = \frac{4x_t}{1+3x_t^2}$$

a. Find the updating function for this population.

b. Find the equilibria.

c. What is the stability of each equilibrium?

d. Find the equation of the tangent line at each equilibrium.

e. What is the behavior of the approximate dynamical system defined by the tangent line at the middle equilibrium?

30. Consider a population following the updating function

$$N_{t+1} = \frac{rN_t}{1+N_t^2}$$

a. What is the per capita production?

b. Find the equilibrium as a function of r.

c. Find the stability of the equilibrium as a function of r.

d. Does this positive equilibrium become unstable as r becomes large?

Projects

1. Consider the following alternative version of the Ricker model for a fishery:

$$x_{t+1} = rx_te^{-x_{t-1}}$$

The idea is that the per capita production this year (year t) is a decreasing function of the population size last year (year $t-1$).

a. Discuss why this model might make more sense than the basic Ricker model.

b. Find the equilibrium of this equation (set $x_{t-1} = x_t = x_{t+1} = x^*$).

c. Use a computer to study the stability of the equilibrium. Do you have any idea why it might be different from that of the basic Ricker model?

d. Write a model in which the per capita production depends on the population size 2 years ago. Find the equilibrium and use a computer to test stability.

e. Subtract a harvest. Find the maximum sustained yield for different values of h. Is the equilibrium still stable?

f. Models with an extra delay are supposed to be simplified versions of models with two variables. The per capita production is an increasing function of the amount of food available in that year, whereas the amount of food available is a decreasing function of the number of fish the previous year. Try to write a pair of equations describing this situation. Try to find equilibria, and discuss whether your results make sense.

2. Many bees collect both pollen and nectar. Pollen is used for protein, and nectar is used for energy. Suppose the amount of nectar harvested during t s on a flower is

$$F(t) = \frac{t}{1+t}$$

and that the amount of pollen harvested during t s on a flower is

$$G(t) = \frac{t}{2+t}$$

The bee collects pollen and nectar simultaneously. Travel time between flowers is $\tau = 1.0$ sec.

a. What is the optimal time for the bee to leave one flower for the next in order to collect nectar at the maximum rate?

b. What is the optimal time for the bee to leave one flower for the next in order to collect pollen at the maximum rate? Why are the two times different?

c. Suppose that the bee values pollen twice as much as nectar. Find a single function $V(t)$ that gives the value of resources collected by time t. What is the optimal time for the bee to leave? (Solving the equation is easiest with Newton's method.)

d. Suppose that the bee values pollen k times as much as nectar. Compute the optimal time to leave, and graph it as a function of k. Do the values at $k = 0$ and the limit as k approaches infinity make sense?

e. Suppose that the bee first collects nectar and then switches to pollen. Assume it spends 1.0 s collecting nectar. How long should it spend on pollen?

f. Suppose again that the bee values pollen k times as much as nectar. Experiment to try to find a solution that is best when nectar and pollen are harvested sequentially.

3. We know enough to study the solutions of the logistic dynamical system for values of r between 3.0 and 3.5. Define the updating function to be

$$f(x) = rx(1-x)$$

a. Find the two-step updating function $g = f \circ f$.

b. Graph the function g along with the diagonal for values of r ranging from 2.8 to 3.6.

c. Write the equation for the equilibria of g.

d. Two of the equilibria, 0 and $x^* = 1 - \frac{1}{r}$, match those for f. Why?

e. The terms x and $x - x^*$ factor out of the equilibrium equation $g(x) - x = 0$. Why?

f. Factor $g(x) - x$ and find the other two equilibria, x_1 and x_2. For what values of r do they make sense? What do they mean? (Think about $f(x_1)$ and $f(x_2)$.)

g. For what values of r are x_1 and x_2 stable?

h. Describe the dynamics of f and g in these cases.

i. What happens for values of r just above the point where x_1 and x_2 become unstable?

Chapter

4

Differential Equations, Integrals, and Their Applications

Biological systems are constantly changing. Describing this change and deducing its consequences constitute the dynamical approach to the understanding of life. In the first three chapters of this book, we used discrete-time dynamical systems to study problems that could be treated in discrete time. Given the state of a system (such as a population size) at one time, the discrete-time dynamical system gives the state of the system at a later time. In the course of analyzing the behavior of discrete-time dynamical systems, we developed the idea of the derivative, which describes both the *slope* of a graph and the *instantaneous rate of change* of a measurement.

With the derivative, we can study a different kind of dynamical system, the **differential equation.** The instantaneous rate of change of a measurement takes the place of the discrete-time dynamical system and provides the information needed to deduce the future state of a system from its present state. Because the system can be measured at any time, these systems are a type of **continuous-time dynamical system.**

Differential equations were invented by Isaac Newton to study gravitation. They have proved to be the most powerful method for describing dynamics in all of the sciences. Like discrete-time dynamical systems, they can be applied to the three main areas of focus of this book (growth, maintenance, and replication), in addition to a wide range of other problems throughout biology.

4.1 Differential Equations

When we have a measurement, we can differentiate to find the rate of change (Figure 4.1.1). What if we know the rate of change and want to compute the measurement (Figure 4.1.2)? If we know, for example, that the velocity of an object is $v(t)$, a function of t, then the position p must satisfy the **differential equation**

$$\frac{dp}{dt} = v(t)$$

This equation relates two quantities, saying that one—the velocity, $v(t)$—is the derivative of the other—the position, $p(t)$. Until now, we have usually thought of ourselves as knowing the position and taking the derivative to find the velocity. With a differential equation, we know the velocity and wish to find the position.

When might we measure the rate of change of some quantity in this way? Two cases, position and cell sodium concentration, illustrate when this might occur. When you are lost, it is much easier to look at the speedometer to determine your speed than to locate landmarks and identify them on a map to determine your position (in the absence of a GPS device). In fact, the speedometer in a car directly measures the rate of rotation of the tires, and the odometer determines distance by adding up the number of rotations. Similarly, it might be easier to measure how many ions enter and leave a cell each second by measuring changes in electrical charge than to track down and count every sodium ion floating around in a cell.

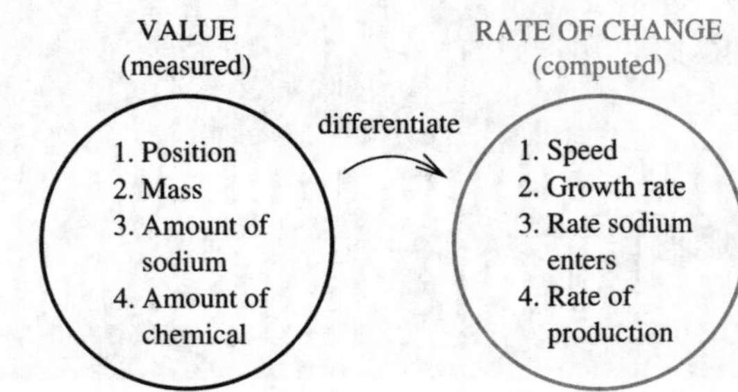

FIGURE 4.1.1
Finding the rate of change with the derivative

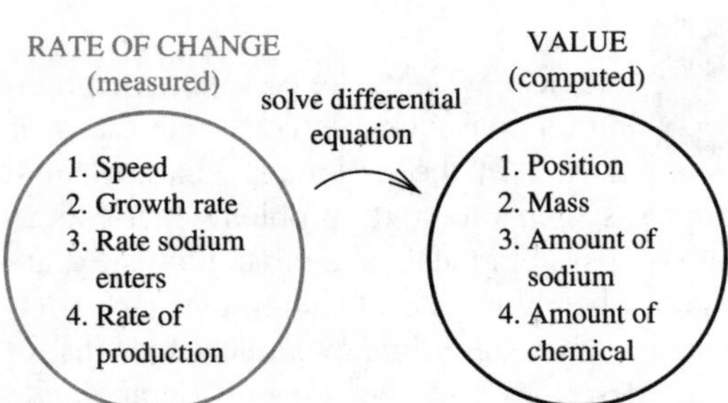

FIGURE 4.1.2
Finding a measurement from the rate of change

In cases in which we *measure* the rate of change, we can write down what is called a **pure-time differential equation,**

derivative of unknown measurement = measured rate of change

There is another way to arrive at a differential equation describing a measurement. On the basis of biological principles, we might know a *rule* describing how a measurement changes, just as we did when deriving discrete-time dynamical systems. For example, when resources are not limiting, the rate of population growth is proportional to population size. In these cases, we can write down an **autonomous differential equation,**

derivative of unknown quantity = some function of unknown quantity

Given that the unknown quantity appears on both sides of this equation, it is quite remarkable that it can be solved.

Our plan of attack in this chapter is to begin with a detailed study of pure-time differential equations, developing the method of **integration** to solve them. After studying several other applications of the integral, we return to autonomous differential equations in Chapter 5, where we show how to use both integration and graphical methods to analyze these important equations.

Differential Equations: Examples and Terminology

Suppose that 1.0 μm^3 of water enters a cell each second. The volume V of the cell is thus increasing by 1.0 $\mu m^3/s$. Mathematically, the rate of change of V is 1.0 $\mu m^3/s$, or

$$\frac{dV}{dt} = 1.0 \tag{4.1.1}$$

The quantity being differentiated (V in this case) is called the **state variable.** Because we *measured* the rate of change, this is a **pure-time differential equation.**

Our goal is to find the volume V of the cell as a function of time. Such a function is called a **solution,** just as with a discrete-time dynamical system. When it works, the best method for solving a differential equation is *guessing.* What function has a constant rate of change equal to 1.0? Geometrically, what function has a constant slope of 1.0? The answer is a line with slope 1. One such line is

$$V(t) = t$$

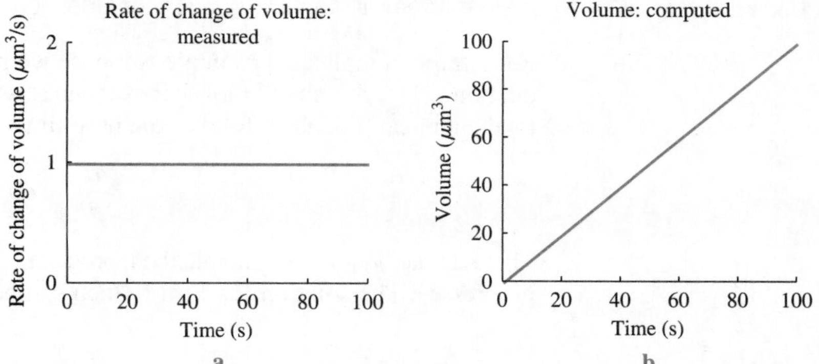

FIGURE 4.1.3
A function that solves the differential equation $\frac{dV}{dt} = 1$

(Figure 4.1.3). We can check whether this guess solves the differential equation by taking the derivative,

$$\frac{dV}{dt} = \frac{dt}{dt} = 1$$

Suppose we know that the volume of the cell at time $t = 0$ is 300 μm^3. Although the guess $V(t) = t$ is one solution of the differential equation, it does not match this **initial condition.** As with discrete-time dynamical systems, a solution also depends on where something starts. From our knowledge of lines, we realize that any function $V(t)$ with the form

$$V(t) = t + c$$

has a constant slope of 1 when c is a constant. In terms of the differential equation,

$$\frac{dV}{dt} = \frac{d}{dt}(t + c) = 1$$

The value of c can be chosen to match the initial condition. In this case, because

$$V(0) = 300 = 0 + c$$

we know that $c = 300$. The solution of the differential equation

$$\frac{dV}{dt} = 1$$

with the initial condition $V(0) = 300$ is

$$V(t) = t + 300$$

(Figure 4.1.4). From knowledge of the initial condition and a measurement of the rate of change, we have a formula giving the volume at any time. At $t = 50$, the volume is 350 μm^3.

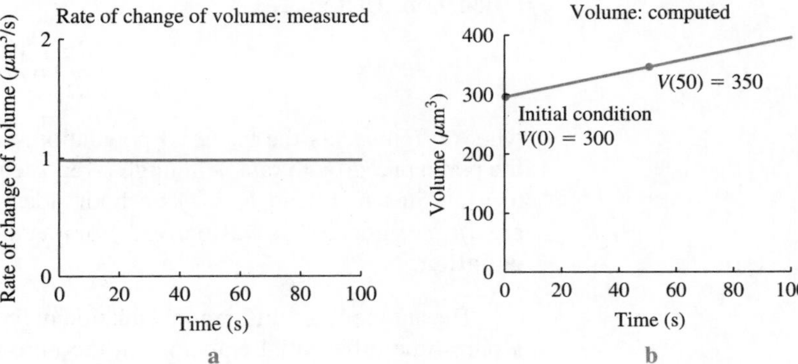

FIGURE 4.1.4
Volume as a function of time

Example 4.1.1 A Pure-Time Differential Equation for Chemical Production

For a more complicated example, suppose we measure that the rate of chemical production is e^{-t}, in units of moles per second (Figure 4.1.5a). The **state variable** P, the total chemical produced, follows the pure-time differential equation

$$\frac{dP}{dt} = e^{-t} \tag{4.1.2}$$

The rate at which the chemical is produced becomes slower and slower as time progresses. The solution for $P(t)$ (which can be found by guessing) can be sketched

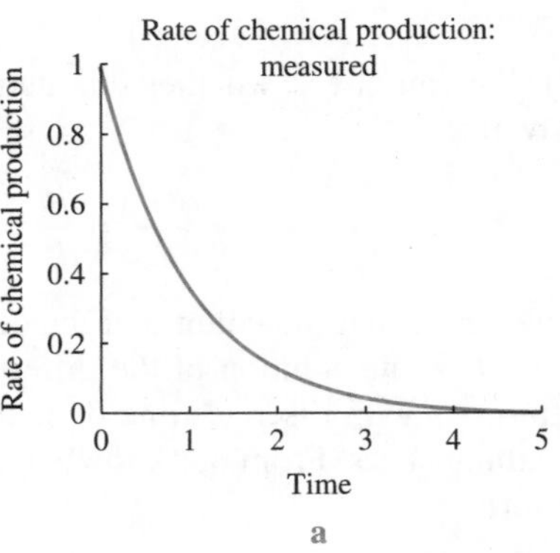

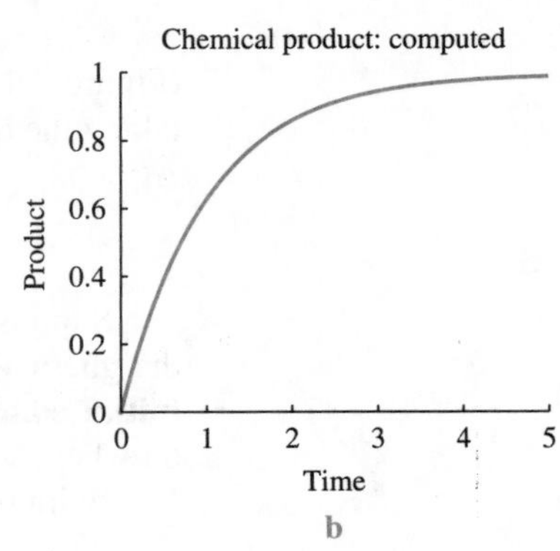

FIGURE 4.1.5
Product as a function of time

graphically. It must be a function that increases more and more slowly (Figure 4.1.5b). The solution sketched has initial condition $P(0) = 0$.

The differential equations for volume and chemical product (Equations 4.1.1 and 4.1.2) are pure-time differential equations because we *measured* the rate of change of the state variable. The equation for chemical production indicates the source for the name. The formula for the rate of change, e^{-t} in this case, depends *purely* on the time t.

Example 4.1.2 An Autonomous Differential Equation for Population Growth

Suppose instead we wish to describe a phenomenon with a differential equation derived from biological principles. For a population (of bacteria, say), the simplest rule is that the rate of production is proportional to the population size. The discrete-time dynamical system describing this process is

$$b_{t+1} = rb_t \tag{4.1.3}$$

where the parameter r is the per capita production (the number of offspring per bacterium). If population size can be measured *continuously* (at any time), the change in population is expressed as the *rate of change,* which in this case is equal to the rate of production. Therefore,

$$\frac{db}{dt} = \lambda b \tag{4.1.4}$$

where b represents the bacterial population, and the constant of proportionality λ is the per capita growth rate. Although b represents a function of time, it is conventional to write just b instead of $b(t)$ on both sides of the equation. The dimensions of λ are 1/time. Because it was derived from a rule, this is an **autonomous differential equation.**

The autonomous differential equation in Example 4.1.2 differs fundamentally from a pure-time differential equation. In the pure-time differential equations, the rate of change is a *measured* function of time. In an autonomous differential equation, the rate of change was derived from a *rule* and is a function of the state variable population size in this example.

Type of Differential Equation	Example	When Used
Pure-time differential equation	$\frac{dP}{dt} = e^{-t}$	When the rate of change is a measured function of time
Autonomous differential equation	$\frac{db}{dt} = 2b$	When a rule gives the rate of change as a function of the state variable

Example 4.1.3 Solving an Autonomous Differential Equation by Guessing

As before, we can often find the solution by guessing. Suppose that $\lambda = 2$ and that the population begins at $b(0) = 1.0 \times 10^6$. The differential equation is

$$\frac{db}{dt} = 2b$$

What function has a derivative equal to double itself? Remember that the derivative of the exponential function $b(t) = b_0 e^{\alpha t}$ is

$$\frac{db}{dt} = \alpha b_0 e^{\alpha t} = \alpha b(t)$$

("Applications," Section 2.9, pp. 218–220). The guess $b(t) = 1.0 \times 10^6 e^{2t}$ is a solution of the differential equation because

$$\begin{aligned}
\frac{db}{dt} &= \frac{d}{dt}(1.0 \times 10^6 e^{2t}) && \text{substituting into the formula} \\
&= 1.0 \times 10^6 \frac{d}{dt}(e^{2t}) && \text{constant product rule} \\
&= 1.0 \times 10^6 \cdot 2e^{2t} && \text{derivative of exponential} \\
&= 2 \cdot 1.0 \times 10^6 e^{2t} && \text{reorganizing} \\
&= 2b(t) && \text{recognizing the formula for } b(t)
\end{aligned}$$

Furthermore, this formula matches the initial condition because

$$b(0) = 1.0 \times 10^6 e^{2 \cdot 0} = 1.0 \times 10^6$$

Like a population described by the discrete-time dynamical system $b_{t+1} = rbt$, this population grows exponentially (Figure 4.1.6).

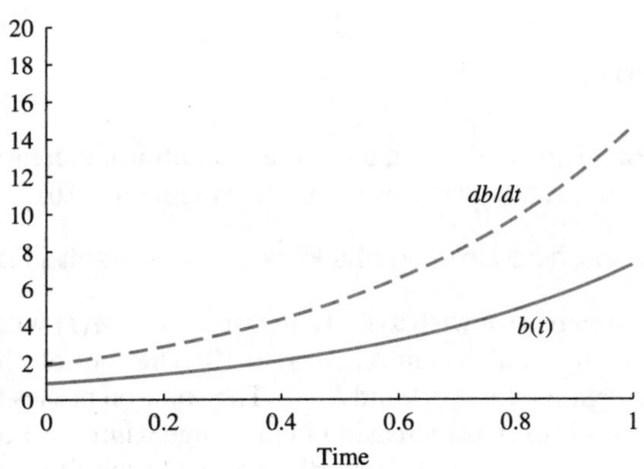

FIGURE 4.1.6
Exponential growth of a bacterial population

In Chapter 5 we will study methods to solve this equation without guessing, along with a variety of algebraic and graphical techniques to analyze the results.

Graphical Solution of Pure-Time Differential Equations

By checking whether the graph of a function is increasing or decreasing, we can sketch a graph of the derivative (Section 2.7, "The Second Derivative, Curvature, and Acceleration," pp. 194–201). Solving a pure-time differential equation reverses this process. From the graph of the derivative, we wish to sketch a graph of the function itself.

The guideposts for this process are the reverse of those for reading and interpreting a graph ("Using the Second Derivative for Graphing," Section 2.7, pp. 196–200), as summarized in the following table.

What the Derivatives Does	What the Graph Does
Derivative positive	Graph increasing
Derivative negative	Graph decreasing
Derivative zero	Graph horizontal

Example 4.1.4 Graphical Solution of a Pure-Time Differential Equation I

Suppose we wish to solve the pure-time differential equation

$$\frac{dG}{dt} = 4 - 2t$$

with initial condition $G(0) = 10$. The rate of change function $f(t) = 4 - 2t$ is positive for $t < 2$, is 0 at $t = 2$, and is negative for $t > 2$ (Figure 4.1.7a). The solution begins at $G(0) = 10$ (from the initial condition), increases until $t = 2$, has a derivative of 0 at $t = 2$, and decreases thereafter (Figure 4.1.7b).

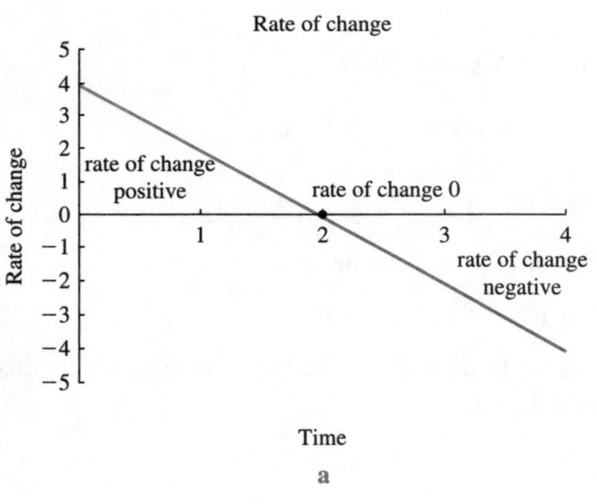

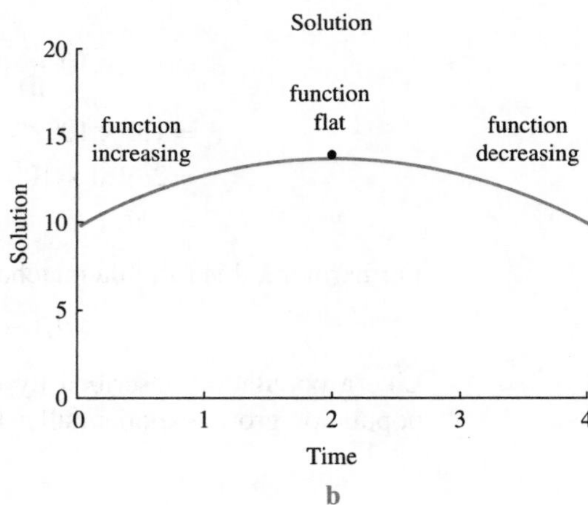

FIGURE 4.1.7
Graphical solution of a pure-time differential equation

Example 4.1.5 Graphical Solution of a Pure-Time Differential Equation II

Suppose we wish to find a measurement $M(t)$ with rate of change given in Figure 4.1.8a with initial condition $M(5) = 10$. The rate of change is positive for $1 < t < 7$ and is negative for $t < 1$ and $t > 7$. The solution passes through at $G(5) = 10$ (from the initial condition), is increasing in the range from $t = 1$ to $t = 7$, and is decreasing outside that range (Figure 4.1.8). Furthermore, the solution is increasing most rapidly when the rate

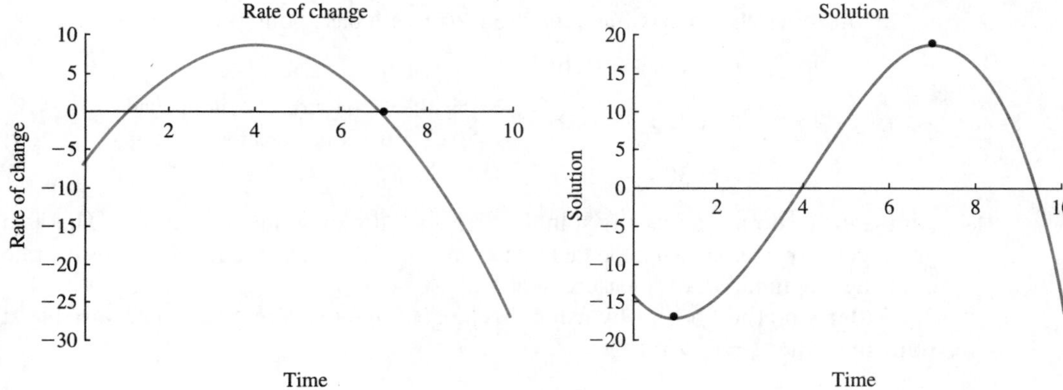

FIGURE 4.1.8
Finding a solution from a graph of the rate of change

of change is largest (at around $t = 4$) and is decreasing most rapidly when the rate of change is most negative (for t near 10).

Euler's Method for Solving Differential Equations

How do we solve a differential equation if the method of guessing does not work? We can sketch solutions of pure-time differential equations using our understanding of the derivative. In the next section, we will learn how to use **integration** to solve pure-time differential equations. Even that method, however, does not work for many equations. An alternative approach, called **Euler's method,** can be implemented on the computer. Like Newton's method for solving equations (Section 3.8), Euler's method works by converting the original problem into a problem about a discrete-time dynamical system. Also like Newton's method, Euler's method begins with the *tangent line approximation,* replacing a problem about *curves* with a problem about *lines.*

Example 4.1.6 Applying the Tangent Line Approximation to a Pure-Time Differential Equation

Consider again the pure-time differential describing the volume of a cell,

$$\frac{dV}{dt} = 1.0$$

(Equation 4.1.1) with initial condition $V(0) = 300$. How can we use this information to estimate the volume at time $t = 1$ if we fail to guess the solution? We have two pieces of information: the initial condition (a base point) and the differential equation (the derivative or slope). This is exactly the information we need to write down the tangent line approximation for $V(t)$ near the base point $t = 0$ (Figure 4.1.9).

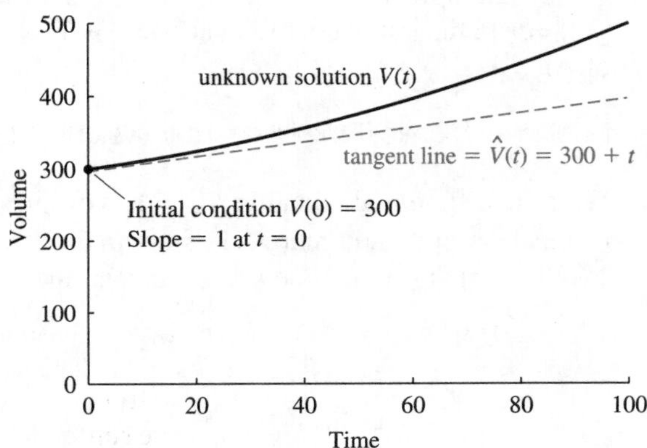

FIGURE 4.1.9
The tangent line approximation of a differential equation

In this case, the approximate function $\hat{V}(t)$ with base point 0 is

$$\begin{aligned}\hat{V}(0+\Delta t) &= V(0) + V'(0)\Delta t && \text{equation for tangent line}\\ &= 300 + 1\cdot\Delta t && V(0)=300 \text{ (initial condition) and } V'(0)=1 \text{ (differential equation)}\\ &= 300+\Delta t && \text{simplify}\end{aligned}$$

Although we do not know the solution $V(t)$, we do know its tangent line. This is a graphical way of expressing the fact that a pure-time differential equation gives the rate of change of an unknown measurement.

Euler's method begins by using this tangent line to estimate the state variable at some time after $t = 0$. With $\Delta t = 1$,

$$\hat{V}(1) = 300 + 1 = 301$$

To continue, we use this new information and the differential equation to estimate the volume at $t = 2$. The tangent line with base point $t = 1$ is

$$\begin{aligned}\hat{V}(1+\Delta t) &= V(1) + V'(1)\Delta t && \text{equation for tangent line}\\ &\approx \hat{V}(1) + V'(1)\Delta t && \text{substitute } \hat{V}(1) \text{ for unknown } V(1)\\ &= 301 + 1\cdot\Delta t && \hat{V}(1)=301 \text{ and } V'(1)=1 \text{ (from the differential equation)}\\ &= 301+\Delta t && \text{simplify}\end{aligned}$$

We estimate that

$$\hat{V}(1+1) = 301 + 1\cdot 1 = 302$$

Euler's method can be continued step-by-step to find approximate solutions for as long as we want. The method works as follows.

Algorithm 4.1 Euler's Method for Solving a Pure-Time Differential Equation

Suppose a measurement m obeys the pure-time differential equation

$$\frac{dm}{dt} = f(t)$$

with initial condition $m(t_0) = m_0$.

1. Choose a **time step** Δt (the length of time between estimated values).
2. Use the initial condition and the differential equation to find the tangent line $\hat{m}(t)$ with base point $t = t_0$, and use it to estimate $m(t_0 + \Delta t)$.
3. Use the estimate of $m(t_0 + \Delta t)$ and the differential equation to estimate the tangent line $\hat{m}(t)$ with base point $t_0 + \Delta t$, and estimate $m(t_0 + 2\Delta t)$.
4. Repeat as many times as needed.

In Example 4.1.6, the state variable is V, the rate of change obeys the function $f(t) = 1.0$, the initial condition at $t_0 = 0$ is $V(t_0) = V_0 = 300$, and we chose a time step of $\Delta t = 1$.

Example 4.1.7 Finding a Discrete-Time Dynamical System to Describe Euler's Method

With the differential equation $\frac{dV}{dt} = 1$, we can write down a simple discrete-time dynamical system to summarize the steps in Euler's method. Suppose we have an estimate $\hat{V}(t)$ for $V(t)$ at some time t. The tangent line approximation with base point t is

$$\begin{aligned}\hat{V}(t+\Delta t) &= V(t) + V'(t)\Delta t && \text{equation for tangent line}\\ &\approx \hat{V}(t) + V'(t)\Delta t && \text{substitute } \hat{V}(t) \text{ for unknown } V(t)\\ &= \hat{V}(t) + 1\cdot\Delta t && V'(1)=1 \text{ (from the differential equation)}\\ &= \hat{V}(t)+\Delta t && \text{simplify}\end{aligned}$$

Therefore,

$$\hat{V}(t+1) = \hat{V}(t) + 1$$

This discrete-time dynamical system says that approximately 1.0 μm^3 is added to the volume each second. We have seen this discrete-time dynamical system as a model for a growing tree (Example 1.5.2) with solution

$$\hat{V}(t) = 300 + t$$

Because the true solution is in fact a line, the results of Euler's method match the exact solution found by guessing.

Example 4.1.8 Applying Euler's Method to a Differential Equation for Chemical Production

The results are more interesting when we apply Euler's method to the differential equation for chemical production

$$\frac{dP}{dt} = e^{-t}$$

Suppose the initial condition is $P(0) = 0$. Following Algorithm 4.1, we perform these steps:

1. Pick a time step of $\Delta t = 1$ (we will next try a smaller step that should be more accurate).
2. The tangent line with base point $t = 0$ is

$$\begin{aligned}
\hat{P}(0+\Delta t) &= P(0) + P'(0)\Delta t && \text{equation for tangent line} \\
&= 0 + 1 \cdot \Delta t && P(0) = 0 \text{ (initial condition) and } P'(0) = e^{-0} = 1 \text{ (differential equation)} \\
&= \Delta t && \text{simplify}
\end{aligned}$$

We therefore estimate that

$$P(1) \approx \hat{P}(1) = 1$$

3. For the next step,

$$\begin{aligned}
\hat{P}(1+\Delta t) &= P(1) + P'(1)\Delta t && \text{equation for tangent line} \\
&\approx \hat{P}(1) + P'(1)\Delta t && \text{substitute } \hat{P}(1) \text{ for unknown } P(1) \\
&\approx 1 + 0.368\Delta t && \hat{P}(1) = 1 \text{ and } P'(1) = e^{-1} \approx 0.368
\end{aligned}$$

We therefore estimate that

$$P(2) \approx \hat{P}(2) \approx 1.0 + 0.368 \cdot 1.0 = 1.368$$

4. To find $\hat{P}(3)$, we calculate

$$\begin{aligned}
\hat{P}(2+\Delta t) &= P(2) + P'(2)\Delta t \\
&\approx \hat{P}(2) + P'(2)\Delta t \\
&\approx 1.368 + e^{-2} \cdot \Delta t \\
&\approx 1.368 + 0.135\Delta t \\
P(3) \approx \hat{P}(3) &\approx 1.503
\end{aligned}$$

To find $\hat{P}(4)$, we calculate

$$\begin{aligned}
\hat{P}(3+\Delta t) &= P(3) + P'(3)\Delta t \\
&\approx \hat{P}(3) + P'(3)\Delta t \\
&\approx 1.503 + e^{-3} \cdot \Delta t \\
&\approx 1.503 + 0.050\Delta t \\
P(4) \approx \hat{P}(4) &\approx 1.553
\end{aligned}$$

(Figure 4.1.10.)

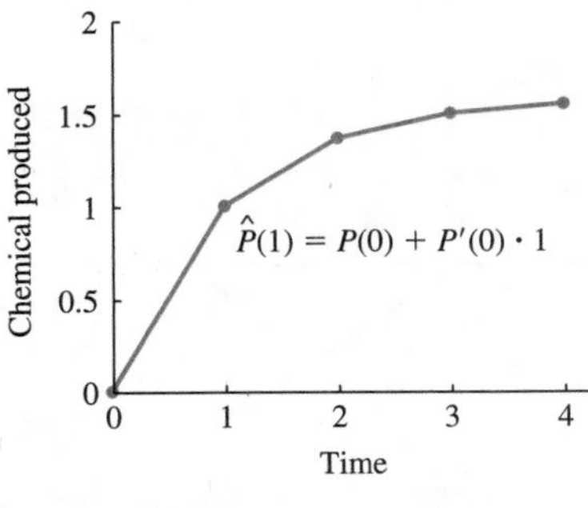

FIGURE 4.1.10
Euler's method applied to a pure-time differential equation, $\Delta t = 1$

Example 4.1.9 Euler's Method with a Smaller Time Step

If we try the same method with a smaller time step of $\Delta t = 0.5$, we get the data given in the accompanying table.

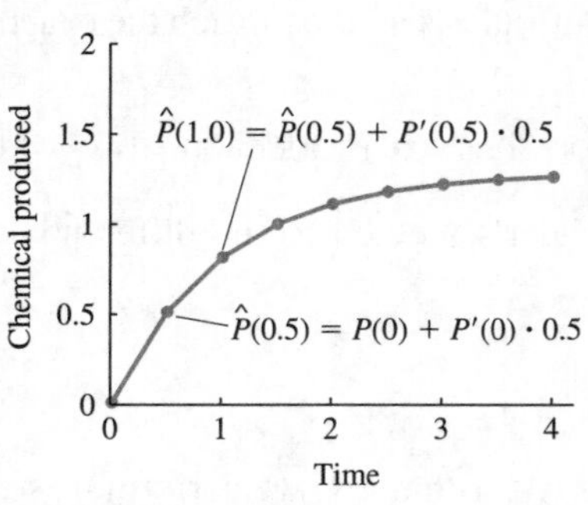

FIGURE 4.1.11

Euler's method applied to a pure-time differential equation, $\Delta t = 0.5$

t	$\hat{P}(t+\Delta t)$	$t+\Delta t$	$\hat{P}(t+\Delta t)$
0.0	$P(0) + P'(0)\Delta t = 0.0 + e^{-0}\Delta t$	0.5	0.5
0.5	$\hat{P}(0.5) + P'(0.5)\Delta t = 0.5 + e^{-0.5}\Delta t$	1.0	0.803
1.0	$\hat{P}(1.0) + P'(1.0)\Delta t \approx 0.803 + e^{-1.0}\Delta t$	1.5	0.987
1.5	$\hat{P}(1.5) + P'(1.5)\Delta t \approx 0.987 + e^{-1.5}\Delta t$	2.0	1.099
2.0	$\hat{P}(2.0) + P'(2.0)\Delta t \approx 1.099 + e^{-2.0}\Delta t$	2.5	1.167
2.5	$\hat{P}(2.5) + P'(2.5)\Delta t \approx 1.167 + e^{-2.5}\Delta t$	3.0	1.208
3.0	$\hat{P}(3.0) + P'(3.0)\Delta t \approx 1.208 + e^{-3.0}\Delta t$	3.5	1.233
3.5	$\hat{P}(3.5) + P'(3.5)\Delta t \approx 1.233 + e^{-3.5}\Delta t$	4.0	1.248

The smaller time step of $\Delta t = 0.5$ gives a more accurate answer but requires more calculation (Figure 4.1.11).

Euler's method applies equally well to autonomous differential equations, but we save that method for Section 5.1.

Summary A **differential equation** expresses the rate of change of a quantity, the **state variable,** as a function of time or of the state variable itself. If the rate of change has been measured as a function of time, the equation is a **pure-time differential equation.** If the rate of change has been derived from a rule, the equation is an **autonomous** differential equation. A **solution** gives the value of the state variable as a function of time. The solution also depends on the **initial condition,** the initial value of the state variable. When guessing fails, **Euler's method,** which is based on the tangent line approximation, can be used to convert a differential equation into a discrete-time dynamical system.

4.1 Exercises

Mathematical Techniques

1–4 ▪ Identify the following as pure-time differential equations or autonomous differential equations.

1. $\dfrac{dx}{dt} = t$

2. $\dfrac{dy}{dt} = 2y$

3. $\dfrac{dw}{dt} = \dfrac{2}{1+t}$

4. $\dfrac{dz}{dt} = 2\sqrt{z}$

5–8 ▪ Use the graph of the rate of change to sketch a graph of the function, starting from the given initial condition.

5. Start from $x(0) = 1$.

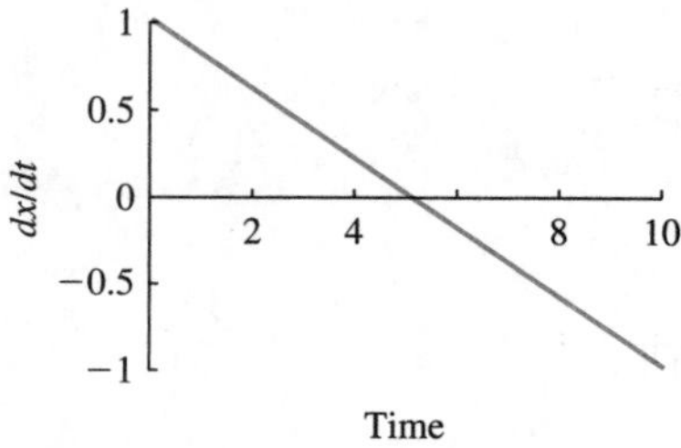

6. Start from $y(0) = -1$.

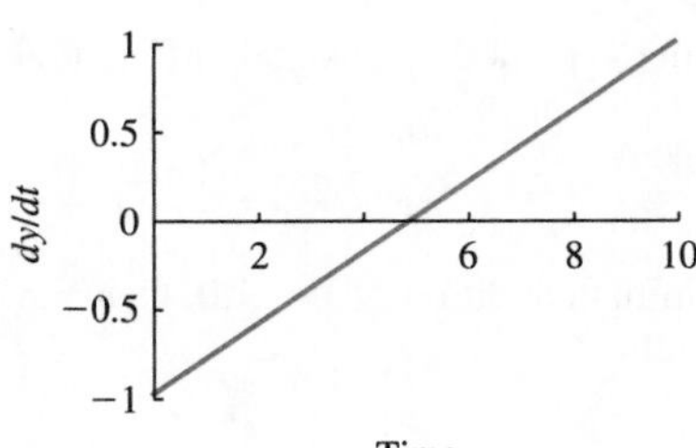

7. Start from $z(0) = 2$.

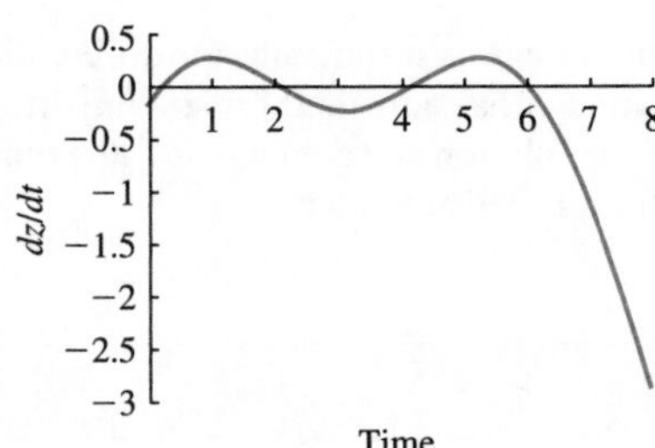

8. Start from $w(0) = 1$.

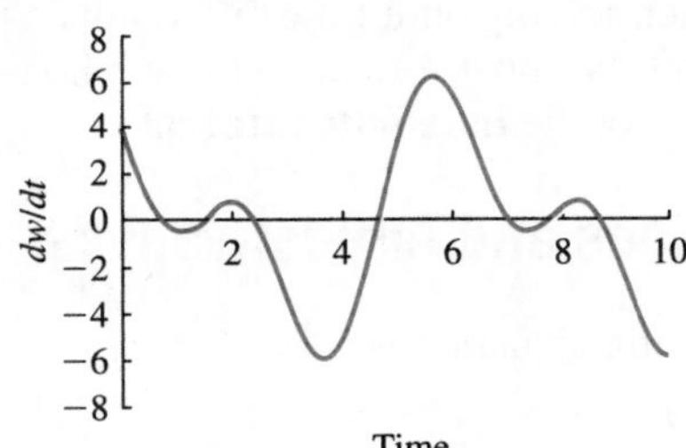

9-12 ▪ Check that the following are solutions of the given differential equation. What was the initial condition (the value of the state variable at $t = 0$)?

9. $\frac{dx}{dt} = t$ has solution $x(t) = 1 + \frac{t^2}{2}$.

10. $\frac{dw}{dt} = \frac{2}{1+t}$ has solution $w(t) = 2\ln(1+t) + 3$.

11. $\frac{dy}{dt} = 2y$ has solution $y(t) = 4e^{2t}$.

12. $\frac{dz}{dt} = 2\sqrt{z}$ has solution $z(t) = (t+2)^2$.

13-14 ▪ Apply Euler's method to the following differential equations to estimate the solution at $t = 1$ starting from the given initial condition. First use one step with $\Delta t = 1$, and then use two steps with $\Delta t = 0.5$. Compare with the exact result from the earlier problem.

13. $\frac{dx}{dt} = t$ with initial condition $x(0) = 1$ (as in Exercise 9).

14. $\frac{dw}{dt} = \frac{2}{1+t}$ with initial condition $w(0) = 3$ (as in Exercise 10).

Applications

15–18 ▪ For each of the following descriptions of the volume of a cell, write a differential equation, find and graph the solution, and indicate whether the solution makes sense for all time.

15. A cell starts at a volume of 600 μm^3 and loses volume at a rate of 2 $\mu\text{m}^3/\text{s}$.

16. A cell starts at a volume of 400 μm^3 and gains volume at a rate of 3 $\mu\text{m}^3/\text{s}$.

17. A cell starts at a volume of 900 μm^3 and loses volume at a rate of $2t$ $\mu\text{m}^3/\text{s}$.

18. A cell starts at a volume of 1000 μm^3 and loses volume at a rate of $3t^2$ $\mu\text{m}^3/\text{s}$.

19–20 ▪ The following describe the velocities of different animals. In each case:

a. Draw a graph of the velocity as a function of time.
b. Write a differential equation for the position.
c. Guess the solution of this equation.
d. Draw a graph of the position as a function of time.
e. How long will it take the animal to reach its goal?

19. A snail starts crawling across a sidewalk, trying to reach the other side, which is 50 cm away. The velocity of the snail t minutes after it starts is t cm/min.

20. A cheetah is standing 1 m from the edge of the jungle. It starts sprinting across the savanna to attack a zebra that is 200 m from the edge of the jungle. After t seconds, the velocity of the cheetah is e^t m/s.

21–26 ▪ Apply Euler's method with the given value of Δt to the differential equation. Compare the approximate result with the exact result from the earlier problem.

21. The cell in Exercise 15. Use a step size of $\Delta t = 10$ to estimate the volume at $t = 40$.

22. The cell in Exercise 16. Use a step size of $\Delta t = 5$ to estimate the volume at $t = 30$.

23. The cell in Exercise 17. Use a step size of $\Delta t = 10$ to estimate the volume at $t = 30$.

24. The cell in Exercise 18. Use a step size of $\Delta t = 2$ to estimate the volume at $t = 10$.

25. The snail in Exercise 19. Use a step size of $\Delta t = 2$ to estimate the position at $t = 10$.

26. The cheetah in Exercise 20. Use a step size of $\Delta t = 1$ to estimate the position at $t = 5$.

27–28 ▪ Use the hints to "guess" the solution of the following differential equations describing the rate of production of some chemical. In each case, check your solution, and graph the rate of change and the solution.

27. $\frac{dP}{dt} = e^{-t+1}$ with initial condition $P(0) = 0$. Start by finding the derivative of e^{-t+1}, correct it by multiplying by some constant, and then add an appropriate value to match the initial condition.

28. $\dfrac{dP}{dt} = e^{-2t}$ with initial condition $P(0) = 0$. Start by finding the derivative of e^{-2t}, correct it by multiplying by some constant, and then add an appropriate value to match the initial condition.

29–32 ▪ For each of the following measurements, give circumstances under which you could measure the following.

a. The value but not the rate of change.

b. The rate of change but not the value.

29. Position (rate of change is velocity).

30. Mass (rate of change is growth rate).

31. Sodium concentration (with rate of change equal to the rate at which sodium enters and leaves).

32. Total chemical (with rate of change equal to the chemical production rate).

Computer Exercise

33. Apply Euler's method to solve the differential equation

$$\frac{db}{dt} = \frac{e^t}{t+1} + t$$

with the initial condition $b(0) = 1.0$. Compare with the sum of the results of

$$\frac{db_1}{dt} = \frac{e^t}{t}$$

and

$$\frac{db_2}{dt} = t$$

Do you think there is a sum rule for differential equations? If your computer has a method for solving differential equations, find the solution and compare it with your approximate solution from Euler's method.

4.2 Solving Pure-Time Differential Equations

Pure-time differential equations describe situations where we have measured the rate of change of a quantity as a function of time and are interested in finding the quantity itself. We have seen two ways to approach solving pure-time differential equations: the method of guessing and Euler's method. We now formalize the method of guessing with a new tool, called an **antiderivative** or the **indefinite integral.**

Pure-Time Differential Equations and Antiderivatives

The general form of a pure-time differential equation is

$$\frac{dF}{dt} = f(t) \tag{4.2.1}$$

where $F(t)$ is the unknown state variable and $f(t)$ is the measured rate of change. The rate of change $f(t)$ depends only on the time t and not on the state variable F. We studied two pure-time differential equations in Section 4.1: an equation for volume with constant influx (Equation 4.1.1) and an equation for chemical product formation (Equation 4.1.2).

Pure-time differential equations are the easiest differential equations to solve—and even they are often impossible. Solving a pure-time differential equation for $F(t)$ requires finding a function that has derivative equal to $f(t)$. Because this process undoes taking the derivative, F is called an **antiderivative** of f.

Definition 4.1 An antiderivative of the function f is a function F with derivative equal to f, written

$$F(t) = \int f(t)dt$$

We say "$F(t)$ is equal to the integral of f of t dt." The curvy symbol is an **integral sign** and can be thought of as a kind of function that takes one function f as input and returns another function F as output. The function $f(t)$ is called the **integrand.** The dt is obligatory and indicates that t is the variable.

Every differentiable function has only one derivative. But every function has a whole family of antiderivatives. The two functions graphed in Figure 4.2.12b share the same derivative $f(t)$ (Figure 4.2.12a) and are *both* antiderivatives of f. All antiderivatives must share the same slope, however, and can differ from each other only by a constant. The set of all antiderivatives of f is known as the **indefinite integral** of f.

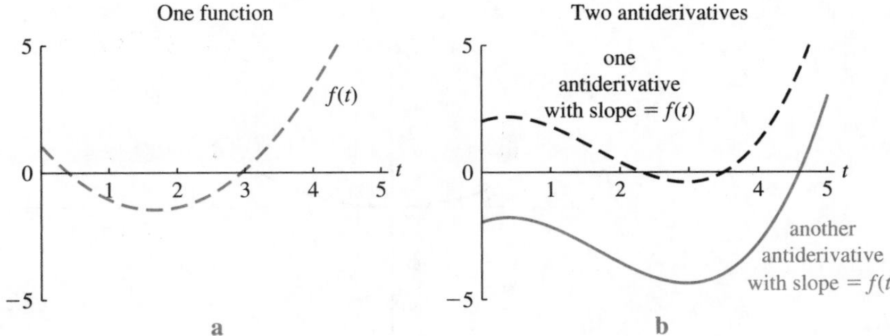

FIGURE 4.2.12
The function $f(t)$ and two antiderivatives

We write

$$\int f(t)dt = F(t) + c$$

to indicate that we can add any constant c to any particular antiderivative $F(t)$. The constant c is called an **arbitrary constant** because it can take on any value.

It might seem like a nuisance that we must include an arbitrary constant. It is not. Antiderivatives are the way to find the solutions of pure-time differential equations. A differential equation requires an initial condition to get the dynamics started, and the arbitrary constant allows us to find a solution that matches the initial condition.

Rules for Antiderivatives

To find the indefinite integrals (antiderivatives) of interesting functions, we begin by using three of the basic rules of differentiation: the power rule (Theorem 2.7), the constant product rule (Theorem 2.9, pp. 182–183), and the sum rule (Theorem 2.5).

The Power Rule for Integrals The power rule for derivatives says that

$$\frac{d(x^{n+1})}{dx} = (n+1)x^n$$

Dividing both sides by $n+1$, we get

$$\frac{d}{dx}\left(\frac{x^{n+1}}{n+1}\right) = x^n$$

We have found a function with derivative equal to x^n, which gives the **power rule** for indefinite integrals.

Theorem 4.1 The Power Rule for Integrals

Suppose $n \neq -1$. Then

$$\int x^n dx = \frac{x^{n+1}}{n+1} + c$$

We will address the case $n = -1$ in "Integrals of Special Functions," Section 4.3.1.

Example 4.2.1 Applying the Power Rule for Integrals to a Quadratic

Applying the power rule for integrals with $n = 2$, we see that the indefinite integral of x^2 is

$$\int x^2 dx = \frac{x^{2+1}}{2+1} + c = \frac{x^3}{3} + c$$

Graphically, the slope of the indefinite integral must match the original function. In Figure 4.2.13, the slope of the indefinite integral $F(x) = \frac{x^3}{3}$ is the original function

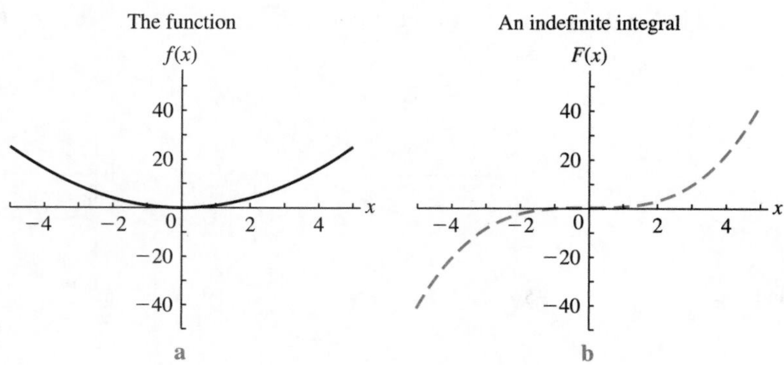

FIGURE 4.2.13

A quadratic function and its integral

$f(x) = x^2$. The indefinite integral here is always increasing because the original function is never negative, and it increases most steeply where $f(x)$ takes on its largest values.

Example 4.2.2 Applying the Power Rule for Integrals with a Negative Power

With $n = -2$, the indefinite integral of $g(x) = \frac{1}{x^2}$ is

$$g(x) = \int \frac{1}{x^2} dx = \int x^{-2} dx = \frac{x^{-2+1}}{-2+1} = -x^{-1} + c = -\frac{1}{x} + c$$

Example 4.2.3 Applying the Power Rule for Integrals with Fractional Powers

The power rule also works with fractional powers (Figure 4.2.14). When $n = 0.5$,

$$\int t^{0.5} dt = \frac{t^{0.5+1}}{0.5+1} + c = \frac{t^{1.5}}{1.5} + c$$

and when $n = -0.5$,

$$\int t^{-0.5} dt = \frac{t^{-0.5+1}}{-0.5+1} + c = \frac{t^{0.5}}{0.5} + c = 2.0t^{0.5} + c$$

The Constant Product Rule for Integrals The constant product rule for derivatives states that

$$\frac{d}{dx}[af(x)] = a\frac{df}{dx}$$

The derivative of a constant times a function is the constant times the derivative. Indefinite integrals work the same way.

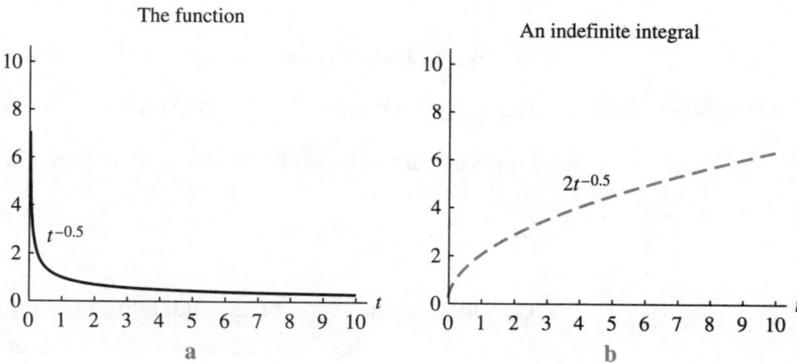

FIGURE 4.2.14

An indefinite integral of $t^{-0.5}$

Theorem 4.2 The Constant Product Rule for Integrals

Suppose

$$\int f(x)dx = F(x) + c$$

Then

$$\int af(x)dx = a\int f(x)dx = aF(x) + c$$

for any constant a.

We do not need to multiply the arbitrary constant c by the factor a, because the product ac is just another way to designate an arbitrary value.

Example 4.2.4 The Constant Product Rule for Integrals I

If we multiply the function $f(x) = x^2$ by 5, we multiply the indefinite integral by 5, so

$$\int 5x^2 dx = 5\int x^2 dx \qquad \text{pull constant 5 out front}$$

$$= 5\frac{x^3}{3} + c \quad \text{or} \quad \frac{5x^2}{3} + c \qquad \text{find integral with power rule, } n = 2$$

Example 4.2.5 The Constant Product Rule for Integrals II

Similarly,

$$\int \frac{-3}{x^2}dx = -3\int x^{-2}dx \qquad \text{pull constant } -3 \text{ outside}$$

$$= \frac{3}{x} + c \qquad \text{find integral with power rule, } n = -2$$

The Sum Rule for Integrals The sum rule for derivatives says that the derivative of the sum is the sum of the derivatives, or

$$\frac{d(f+g)}{dx} = \frac{df}{dx} + \frac{dg}{dx}$$

Again, indefinite integrals work the same way.

Theorem 4.3 The Sum Rule for Integrals

Suppose

$$\int f(x)dx = F(x) + c$$

$$\int g(x)dx = G(x) + c'$$

Then

$$\int [f(x) + g(x)]dx = \int f(x)dx + \int g(x)dx = F(x) + G(x) + c''$$

There is only a single arbitrary constant $c'' = c + c'$ added at the end.

Example 4.2.6 The Sum Rule Applied to Power Functions

We have found that

$$\int 5x^2 dx = \frac{5x^3}{3} + c$$

$$\int -3x^{-2} dx = \frac{3}{x} + c$$

Therefore,

$$\int (5x^2 - 3x^{-2})\, dx = \frac{5x^3}{3} + \frac{3}{x} + c$$

The power rule, constant product rule, and sum rule are summarized in the following table.

The power, constant product, and sum rules for integrals

Rule	Formula
Power rule	$\int x^n dx = \frac{x^{n+1}}{n+1} + c \text{ if } n \neq -1$
Constant product rule	$\int af(x)dx = a\int f(x)dx$
Sum rule	$\int [f(x) + g(x)]dx = \int f(x)dx + \int g(x)dx$

Solving Polynomial Differential Equations

With the power, constant product, and sum rules, we can find the indefinite integral of any polynomial and can therefore solve any pure-time differential equation where the rate of change is a polynomial function of time.

The simplest polynomial is a constant. We can solve the differential equation

$$\frac{dV}{dt} = 1.0$$

with the power rule because the rate of change is $1.0 = t^0$. Evaluating the indefinite integral, we get

$$\begin{aligned} V(t) &= \int 1.0\, dt \\ &= \int t^0 dt \\ &= \frac{t^{0+1}}{0+1} + c \\ &= t + c \end{aligned}$$

This is a solution for any value of c (Figure 4.2.15).

The constant c is determined by the initial conditions. Suppose the volume is 300 at time 0. This gives an equation for the arbitrary constant c,

$$V(0) = 0 + c = 300$$

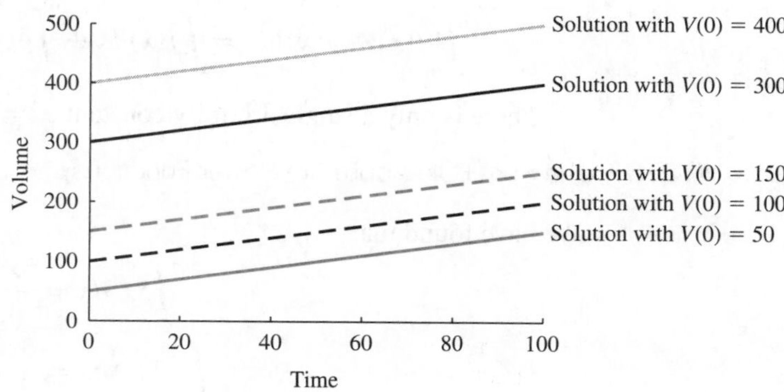

FIGURE 4.2.15
Several solutions of $\frac{dV}{dt} = 1.0$

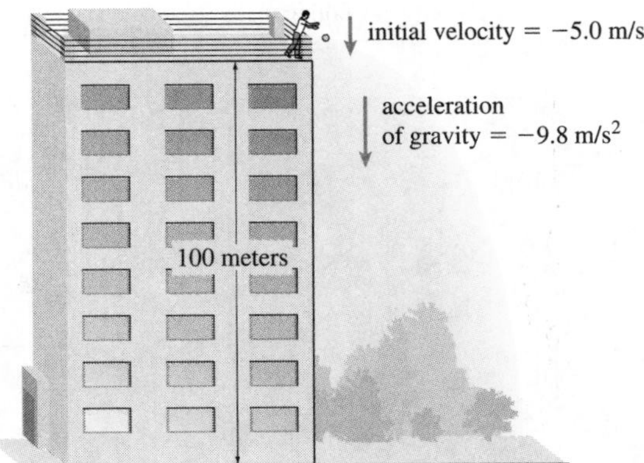

FIGURE 4.2.16
A falling rock

so $c = 300$. The solution of the pure-time differential equation

$$\frac{dV}{dt} = 1.0$$

with initial condition $V(0) = 300$ is therefore

$$V(t) = t + 300$$

Problems that involve finding the indefinite integrals of polynomials arise when we study the motion of objects with **constant acceleration.** Suppose we are told that a rock is thrown downward from a building 100 m tall with initial downward velocity of 5.0 m/s. The acceleration of gravity is about $-9.8\ \text{m/s}^2$ (Figure 4.2.16). How long will it take the rock to hit the ground? How fast will it be going?

Let a represent the acceleration, v the velocity, and p the position of the rock. The basic differential equations from physics are

$$\frac{dv}{dt} = a \qquad \text{acceleration is the rate of change of velocity}$$

$$\frac{dp}{dt} = v \qquad \text{velocity is the rate of change of position}$$

We can use these equations to solve for the position of the rock.

Example 4.2.7 The Physics of Constant Acceleration: Finding the Velocity

To find velocity, we know from physics that its rate of change, the acceleration, is $a = -9.8$. We are also given the initial condition $v(0) = -5.0$. Both values are negative because both are downward. We therefore have enough information to solve the differential equation

$$\frac{dv}{dt} = -9.8$$

with the initial condition $v(0) = -5.0$. As above, the rate of change is constant, so

$$v(t) = -9.8t + c$$

We find the constant c with the initial condition by solving

$$v(0) = -9.8 \cdot 0 + c = -5.0$$

so $c = -5.0$. Therefore, the equation for the velocity is

$$v(t) = -9.8t - 5.0$$

As time passes, the velocity becomes more and more negative as the rock falls faster and faster (Figure 4.2.17a).

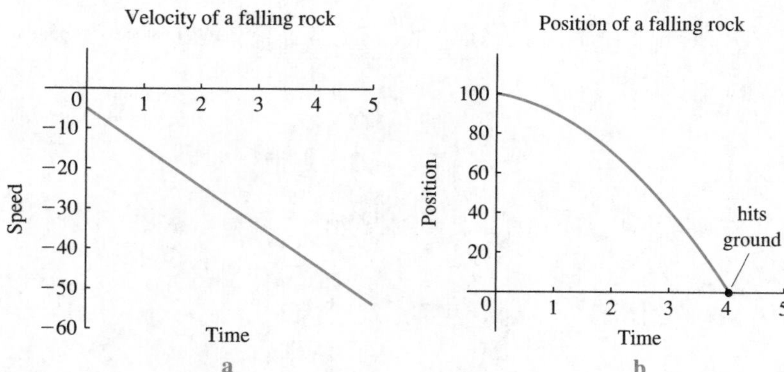

FIGURE 4.2.17
The velocity and position of a falling rock

Example 4.2.8 The Physics of Constant Acceleration: Finding the Position

We now have enough information to solve for the position p. We have the pure-time differential equation

$$\frac{dp}{dt} = -9.8t - 5.0$$

and the initial condition $p(0) = 100$. We first solve the differential equation with the indefinite integral, finding

$$p(t) = \int (-9.8t - 5.0)dt \qquad p(t) \text{ is the indefinite integral of } v(t)$$

$$= \int -9.8t dt - \int 5.0 dt \qquad \text{the sum rule}$$

$$= -9.8 \int t dt - 5.0 \int dt \qquad \text{the constant product rule}$$

$$= -9.8\frac{t^2}{2} - 5.0t + c = -4.9t^2 - 5.0t + c \qquad \text{the power rule}$$

We use the initial condition to find the constant c by solving

$$p(0) = -4.9 \cdot 0^2 - 5.0 \cdot 0 + c = 100.0$$

to obtain $c = 100.0$. Therefore, the equation for the position is

$$p(t) = -4.9t^2 - 5.0t + 100$$

(Figure 4.2.17b).

The solution tells when the rock will hit the ground and how fast it will be going. It hits the ground at the time when $p(t) = 0$, the solution of

$$-4.9t^2 - 5.0t + 100 = 0$$

For convenience, we multiply by -1, so

$$4.9t^2 + 5.0t - 100 = 0$$

With the quadratic formula, we get

$$t = \frac{-5.0 \pm \sqrt{5.0^2 - 4 \cdot 4.9 \cdot (-100)}}{2 \cdot 4.9}$$

$$= \frac{-5.0 \pm \sqrt{1985}}{9.8}$$

$$\approx \frac{-5.0 \pm 44.55}{9.8}$$

$$\approx 4.036 \text{ s} \quad \text{or} \quad -5.056$$

The positive solution is the one that makes sense. How fast will the rock be going when

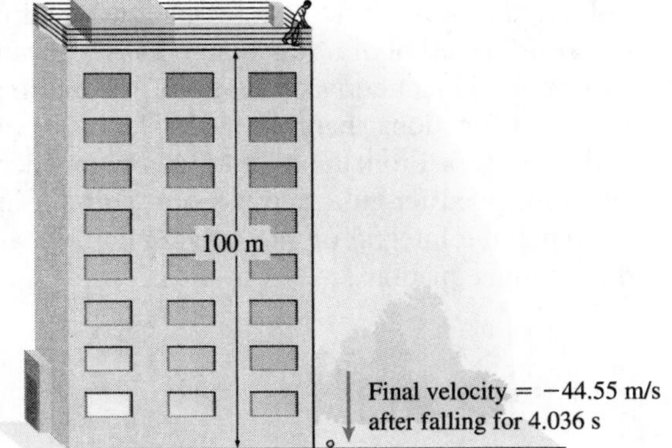

FIGURE 4.2.18
A falling rock hits the ground

it hits the ground? We use the formula for $v(t)$ to find

$$v(4.036) = -9.8 \cdot 4.036 - 5.0 \approx -44.55 \text{ m/s}.$$

(Figure 4.2.18).

Example 4.2.9 A Differential Equation for AIDS

Polynomial pure-time differential equations also arise in public health policy. During the early years of the AIDS epidemic, workers at the Centers for Disease Control (CDC) found that the number of new AIDS cases per year followed the formula

$$\text{rate at which new AIDS cases were reported} \approx 523.8t^2 \qquad (4.2.2)$$

where t is measured in years after the beginning of 1981. The CDC's formula for the number of AIDS cases $A(t)$ can be written as a polynomial pure-time differential equation:

$$\frac{dA}{dt} = 523.8t^2$$

To solve this equation for the total number of AIDS case, we require an initial condition. Surveys indicated that about 340 people had been infected at the beginning of 1981 ($t = 0$ in the model), so $A(0) = 340$. We can now solve for $A(t)$, finding

$$A(t) = \int 523.8t^2 dt = 523.8\frac{t^3}{3} = 174.6t^3 + c$$

The constant c is the solution of the equation

$$A(0) = 174.6 \cdot 0^3 + c = 340$$

so $c = 340$. The solution is

$$A(t) = 174.6t^3 + 340$$

(Figure 4.2.19).

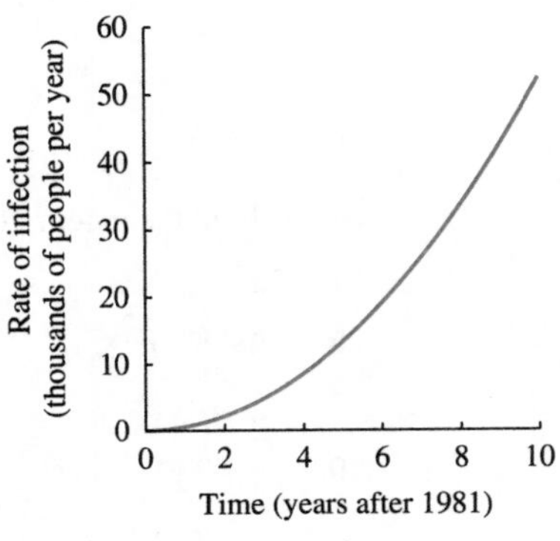

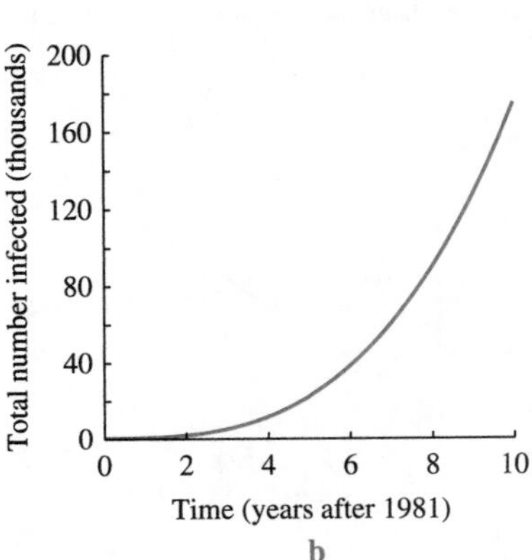

FIGURE 4.2.19
The early course of the AIDS epidemic in the United States

Summary Solving pure-time differential equations requires undoing the derivative. We defined the **antiderivative** of a function f as any function whose derivative is f. Unlike the derivative, the antiderivative includes an **arbitrary constant** to indicate that a whole family of functions share the same slope. The **indefinite integral** is the whole set of antiderivatives. From the rules for computing derivatives, we found the **power rule,** the **constant product rule,** and the **sum rule** for integrals. With these rules, we can find the indefinite integral of any polynomial. We applied this method to solve pure-time differential equations.

4.2 Exercises

Mathematical Techniques

1–6 ▪ From the graphs, sketch an antiderivative of the function that passes through the given point.

1. An antiderivative that passes through the point (0, 500).

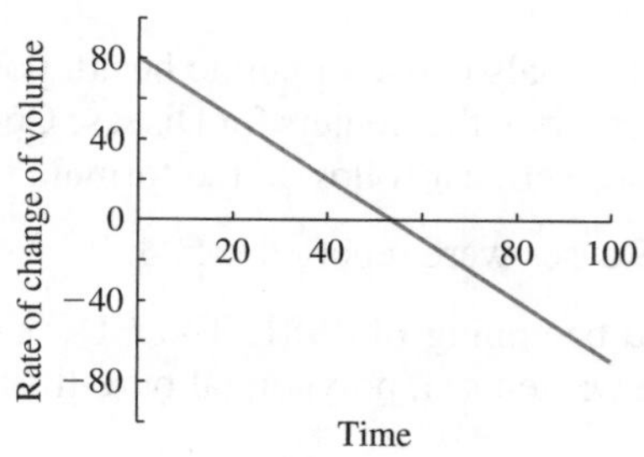

2. An antiderivative that passes through the point (50, 5000).

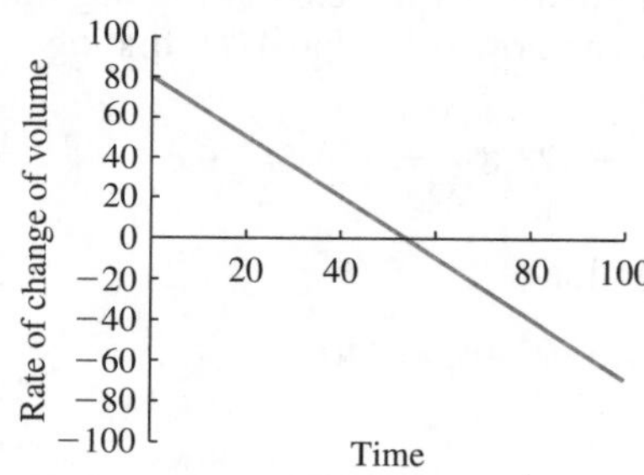

3. An antiderivative that passes through the point (100, 3000).

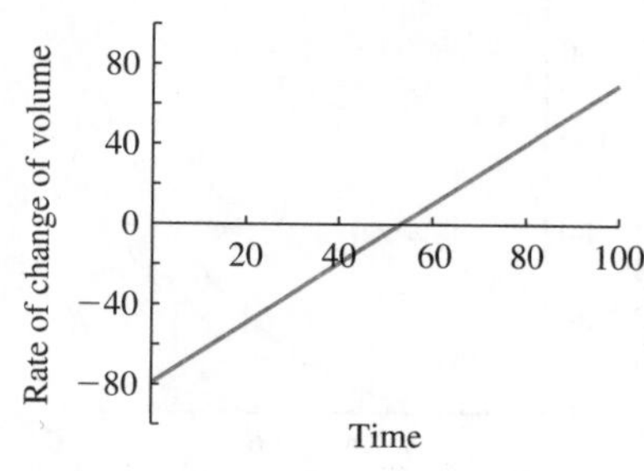

4. An antiderivative that passes through the point (0, 2500).

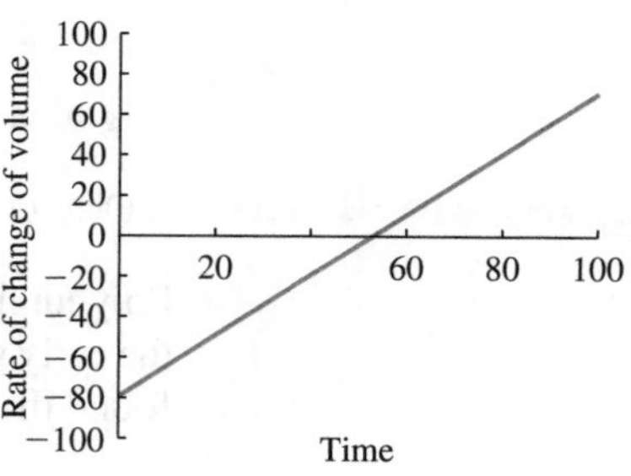

5. An antiderivative that passes through the point (100, 1000).

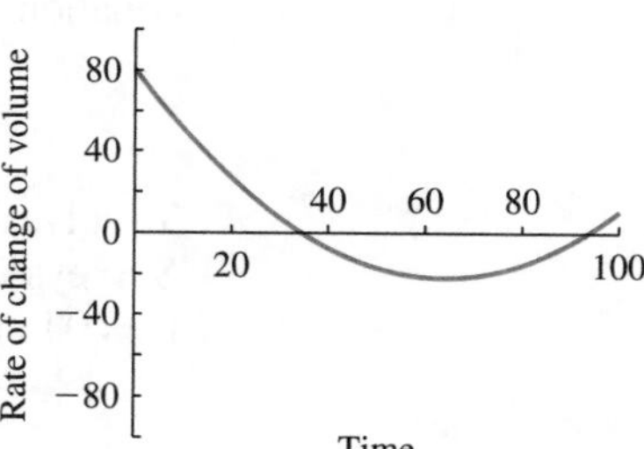

6. An antiderivative that passes through the point (0, 1000).

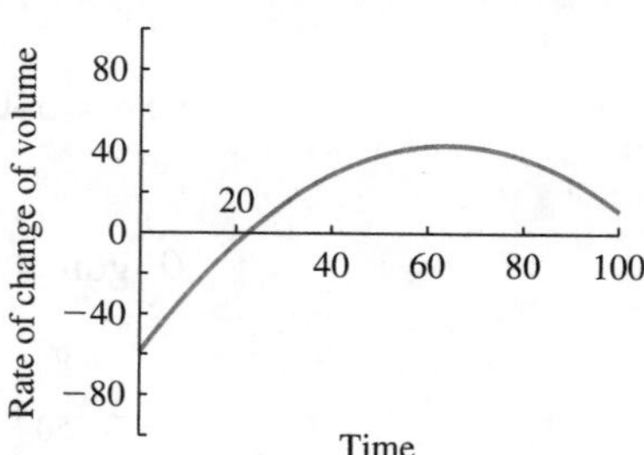

7–14 ▪ Find the indefinite integrals of the following functions.

7. $7x^2$

8. $10t^9 + 6t^5$

9. $72t + 5$

10. $y^4 + 5y^3$

11. $\frac{5}{x^3}$

12. $3z^{\frac{3}{7}}$

13. $\frac{2}{\sqrt[3]{t}} + 3$

14. $5z^{-1.2} - 1.2$

15–20 ▪ Use indefinite integrals to solve the following differential equations. Sketch a graph of the rate of change and the solution on the given domain.

15. $\frac{dV}{dt} = 2t^2 + 5$ with $V(1) = 19.0$. Sketch the rate of change and solution for $0 \le t \le 5$.

16. $\frac{dV}{dt} = 2t^2 + 5$ with $V(0) = 19.0$. Sketch the rate of change and solution for $0 \le t \le 5$.

17. $\frac{df}{dt} = 5t^3 + 5t$ with $f(0) = -12.0$. Sketch the rate of change and solution for $0 \le t \le 2$.

18. $\frac{dg}{dt} = -3t + t^2$ with $g(0) = 10.0$. Sketch the rate of change and solution for $0 \le t \le 5$.

19. $\frac{dM}{dt} = t^2 + \frac{1}{t^2}$ with $M(3) = 10.0$. Sketch the rate of change and solution for $0 \le t \le 3$.

20. $\frac{dp}{dt} = 5t^3 + \frac{5}{t^2}$ with $p(1) = 12.0$. Sketch the rate of change and solution for $1 \le t \le 3$.

21–22 ▪ There are no simple integral versions of product and quotient rules for derivatives. Use the given functions to show that the proposed rule does not work.

21. Use the functions $f(x) = x^2$ and $g(x) = x^3$ to show that the intergral of a product is *not* equal to the product of the integrals.

22. Use the functions $f(x) = x^2$ and $g(x) = x^3$ to show that

$$\int f(x)g(x)dx \ne g(x)\int f(x)dx + f(x)\int g(x)dx$$

Applications

23–24 ▪ Suppose a cell is taking water into two vacuoles. Let V_1 denote the volume of the first vacuole and V_2 the volume of the second. In each of the following cases:

a. Solve the given differential equations for $V_1(t)$ and $V_2(t)$.

b. Write a differential equation for $V = V_1 + V_2$, including the initial condition.

c. Show that the solution of the differential equation for V is the sum of the solutions for V_1 and V_2.

23.
$$\frac{dV_1}{dt} = 2.0t + 5.0$$
$$\frac{dV_2}{dt} = 5.0t + 2.0$$
with initial conditions $V_1(0) = V_2(0) = 10$.

24.
$$\frac{dV_1}{dt} = 3.6t^2 + 5.0t$$
$$\frac{dV_2}{dt} = 5.2t^3 + 2.0$$
with initial conditions $V_1(0) = 5.0$ and $V_2(0) = 10.0$.

25–26 ▪ Suppose organisms grow in mass according to the differential equation

$$\frac{dM}{dt} = \alpha t^n$$

where M is measured in grams and t is measured in days. For each of the following values for n and α:

a. Find the units of α.

b. Suppose that $M(0) = 5.0$ g. Find the solution.

c. Sketch a graph of the rate of change and the solution.

d. Describe your results in words.

25. $n = 1, \alpha = 2.0$

26. $n = -1/2, \alpha = 2.0$

27–30 ▪ In a new program, NASA sends unmanned expeditions to astronomical bodies. One of the more fascinating experiments involves having the robot release an object from a height $h = 100$ m with velocity $v = 5.0$ m/s (upward) to find its trajectory in the local gravitational field of strength a. For the following values of a:

a. Find the velocity and position of the object as functions of time.

b. How high will the object get?

c. How long will it take to pass the robot on the way down? How fast will it be moving?

d. How long will it take to hit the ground? How fast will it be moving? How fast is this in miles per hour?

e. Graph the velocity and position as functions of time.

27. A practice test on Earth, where $a = -9.8$ m/s^2.

28. On the moon, where $a = -1.62$ m/s^2.

29. On Jupiter, where $a = -22.88$ m/s^2.

30. On Mars's moon Deimos, where $a = 2.15 \times 10^{-3}$ m/s^2.

31–34 ▪ The velocities of four objects are measured at discrete times.

Time	Velocity of Object 1	Velocity of Object 2	Velocity of Object 3	Velocity of Object 4
0	1.0	9.0	25.0	1.0
1	3.0	7.0	16.0	3.0
2	5.0	5.0	9.0	6.0
3	7.0	3.0	4.0	10.0
4	9.0	1.0	1.0	15.0

Use Euler's method with $\Delta t = 1$ to estimate the position at $t = 4$ starting from the initial condition $p(0) = 10.0$. Next find a simple formula for the velocities, and use it to find the exact position at $t = 4$. Graph your results.

31. Object 1. To find the formula for the velocities, note that they increase linearly in time.

32. Object 2. To find the formula for the velocities, note that they decrease linearly in time.

33. Object 3. To find the formula for the velocities, compare them with the perfect square numbers.

34. Object 4. The velocities follow a quadratic equation of the form $v(t) = \frac{t^2}{2} + at + b$ for some values of a and b.

35–38 ▪ Consider again the velocities of four objects used in the previous set of problems. There is a more accurate variant of Euler's method that approximates the rate of change during a time interval as the average of the rate of change at the beginning of the interval and the rate of change at the end of the interval. For example, if $v(0) = 1.0$ and $v(1) = 3.0$, we approximate the rate of change for $0 \leq t \leq 1$ as 2.0. Use this variant of Euler's method with initial condition $p(0) = 10.0$ to estimate the position at $t = 4$ and compare your estimate with the exact position at $t = 4$. Graph your results.

35. Object 1.

36. Object 2.

37. Object 3.

38. Object 4.

4.3 Integration of Special Functions, Integration by Substitution, and Integration by Parts

We have seen how to solve any pure-time differential equation with the indefinite integral when the rate of change can be expressed as a polynomial or other combination of power functions. There are not too many other functions for which we can find the indefinite integral—and thus not too many pure-time differential equations that we can solve algebraically. In this section, we will learn first how to find integrals of exponential, logarithmic, and cosine functions. Using the chain rule for derivatives, we will derive the method of **substitution,** which is used to evaluate integrals involving parameters. Then, using the product rule for derivatives, we will derive the method of **integration by parts,** which adds a few more integrals to our arsenal.

Integrals of Special Functions

The derivatives of special functions help us to find a few more indefinite integrals. Recall that

$$\frac{d}{dx}[\ln(x)] = \frac{1}{x}$$

$$\frac{d}{dx}(e^x) = e^x$$

Because the indefinite integral, the antiderivative, undoes the action of the derivative,

$$\int \frac{1}{x}\,dx = \ln(|x|) + c \tag{4.3.1}$$

$$\int e^x\,dx = e^x + c \tag{4.3.2}$$

Try not to be confused by the absolute value bars inside the function $\ln(|x|) + c$ (Figure 4.3.20). The function $\frac{1}{x}$, unlike the natural logarithm, is defined for negative values of x. It must be the slope of some function. The graph of $\frac{1}{x}$ for negative x is the negative of the graph for positive x. The antiderivative for negative x must be the mirror image of the antiderivative for positive x. This integral fills in the $n = -1$ case for the power rule for integrals (Theorem 4.1).

Using the derivatives of sine and cosine,

$$\frac{d}{dx}[\sin(x)] = \cos(x)$$

$$\frac{d}{dx}[\cos(x)] = -\sin(x)$$

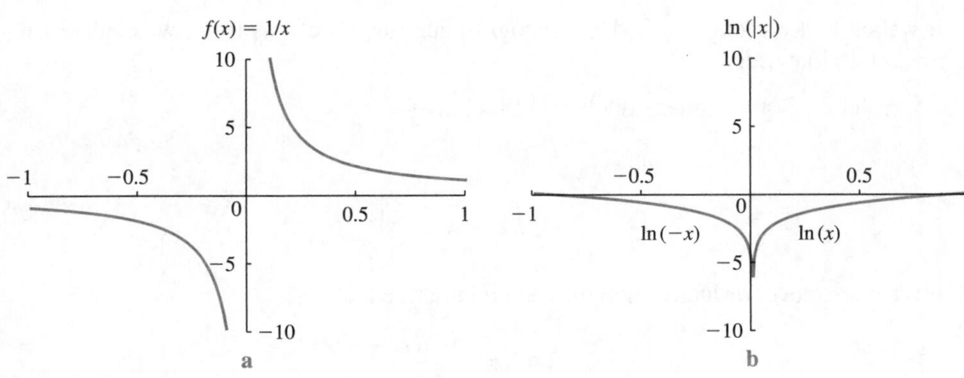

FIGURE 4.3.20
The integral of $1/x$

we see that

$$\int \cos(x)dx = \sin(x) + c \tag{4.3.3}$$

$$\int \sin(x)dx = -\cos(x) + c \tag{4.3.4}$$

Using the constant product and sum rules, we can integrate a few more complicated functions.

Example 4.3.1 Integrating a Complicated Function

We can compute

$$\int \left[\frac{1}{x} + 2e^x + 5\sin(x)\right]dx = \int \frac{1}{x}dx + 2\int e^x dx + 5\int \sin(x)dx$$
$$= \ln(|x|) + 2e^x - 5\cos(x) + c$$

according to the constant product rule (Theorem 4.2) and the sum rule (Theorem 4.3).

The sum rule, constant product rule, and the integrals of special functions form the basic building blocks of integration. The edifice that can be built from these blocks, even with several additional techniques, is rather paltry. Many perfectly reasonable functions cannot be integrated at all. Some sophisticated techniques are available to integrate a few additional functions and can be studied in a more advanced text (the method of **integration by partial fractions** is introduced in Section 5.4, Exercises 31–36). Only two are needed for the applications in this book: integration by substitution and integration by parts.

The Chain Rule and Integration by Substitution

The chain rule (Theorem 2.12) tells how to differentiate the compositions of functions. It states that

$$\frac{d(f \circ g)}{dx} = \frac{df}{dg}\frac{dg}{dx}$$

as expressed in differential notation. Integration by substitution is easier to understand in differential notation, and we will use it here. Because the indefinite integral, the antiderivative, undoes the action of the derivative,

$$\int \frac{df}{dg}\frac{dg}{dx}dx = (f \circ g)(x) + c$$

If we are lucky enough to find and recognize an integral of this form, we can use this method to integrate.

Example 4.3.2 Integrating a Complicated Function with a Lucky Guess

Suppose we are asked to find

$$\int 2xe^{x^2}dx$$

If we were clever or lucky enough, we might notice that

$$2xe^{x^2} = \frac{dg}{dx}\frac{df}{dg}$$

if $g(x) = x^2$ and $f(g) = e^g$. In other words,

$$\begin{aligned}\frac{d(f \circ g)}{dx} &= \frac{df}{dg}\frac{dg}{dx} \\ &= e^g \cdot 2x \\ &= 2xe^{x^2}\end{aligned}$$

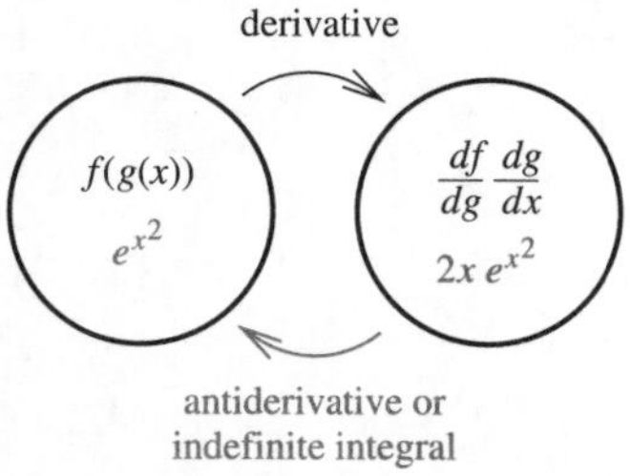

Therefore, because the indefinite integral undoes the action of the derivative,

$$\int 2xe^{x^2}dx = e^{x^2} + c$$

(Figure 4.3.21).

derivative

$f(g(x))$ e^{x^2} $\frac{df}{dg}\frac{dg}{dx}$ $2x\,e^{x^2}$

antiderivative or indefinite integral

FIGURE 4.3.21
The chain rule and the indefinite integral

Integration by substitution is a way to recognize these patterns, when they exist, without relying entirely on inspired guessing. There is, however, no guarantee that the technique will work.

Algorithm 4.2 Integration by Substitution

1. Define a new variable as some function of the old variable.
2. Take the derivative of the new variable with respect to the old variable.
3. Treat the derivative as a fraction and move the dx to the other side.
4. Put everything in the integral in terms of the new variable.
5. Try to integrate the expression in terms of the new variable.
6. After integrating, put everything back in terms of the old variable if possible.

Example 4.3.3 Integrating a Complicated Composition with Substitution

In Example 4.3.1, Algorithm 4.2 proceeds as follows:

1. Define a new variable to be the function of x most tangled up in the expression. In this case, x^2 is inside the exponential, so define y by

   $$y = x^2$$

   Our hope is to write everything in terms of the new variable y. The e^{x^2} term is now e^y, which we know how to integrate. However, there remains the piece $2xdx$.
2. Find the derivative of y with respect to x as

   $$\frac{dy}{dx} = 2x$$

3. This step looks weird but is legal. Multiply both sides by dx to find

   $$dy = 2xdx$$

4. By good luck, dy exactly matches the remaining piece $2x\,dx$. In terms of y, the integral is

$$\int 2xe^{x^2}dx = \int e^y dy$$

5. By more good luck, this is an expression we know how to integrate, finding

$$\int e^y dy = e^y + c$$

6. Put everything back in terms of x (using $y = x^2$), so

$$\int 2xe^{x^2}dx = e^{x^2} + c$$

▲

Example 4.3.4 Integrating a Complicated Composition with Clever Substitution

We will follow Algorithm 4.2 to evaluate

$$\int \frac{e^{2t}}{\left(1+e^{2t}\right)^2}dt$$

1. It is not obvious what to substitute. One good guess is to use the expression that is squared in the denominator,

$$u = 1 + e^{2t}$$

2. Take the derivative, finding

$$\frac{du}{dt} = 2e^{2t}$$

3. Solve for du:

$$du = 2e^{2t}dt$$

4. Put everything in terms of u. Note that $e^{2t}dt = du/2$, so

$$\int \frac{e^{2t}}{\left(1+e^{2t}\right)^2}dt = \int \frac{1}{u^2}\frac{du}{2}$$

5. We can attack the new integral with the constant product and power rules, finding

$$\begin{aligned}\int \frac{1}{u^2}\frac{du}{2} &= \frac{1}{2}\int u^{-2}du \\ &= \frac{1}{2}\left(-u^{-1}\right) + c = -\frac{1}{2u} + c\end{aligned}$$

6. Put everything back in terms of t, arriving at

$$\int \frac{e^{2t}}{\left(1+e^{2t}\right)^2}dt = -\frac{1}{2u} + c = -\frac{1}{2\left(1+e^{2t}\right)} + c$$

▲

Example 4.3.5 The Failure of Integration by Substitution

The problem with integration by substitution is that terms must match up exactly. Suppose we wanted to evaluate

$$\int 2x^2e^{x^2}dx$$

1. Try the substitution $y = x^2$ as before.

2. Then we get

$$\frac{dy}{dx} = 2x$$

3. We have $dy = 2x dx$.

4. Putting everything in terms of y is messy:

$$2x^2 dx = x \cdot 2x dx = x dy$$

To get rid of the remaining x, we have to solve for x in terms of y, finding $x = \sqrt{y}$. Substituting this value gives the new integral

$$\int \sqrt{y} e^y dy$$

5. We have no idea how to integrate this.

6. Give up.

In fact, there is no way to compute this indefinite integral in terms of basic functions.

Using Substitution to Eliminate Constants

Substitution is guaranteed to work in one case: when the integral would be possible if we could remove some excess constants. For example, the differential equation

$$\frac{dL}{dt} = 6.48e^{-0.09t} \tag{4.3.5}$$

can be used to describe the growth of a fish. If we could just get rid of the -0.09 in the exponent, there would be no problem finding the integral and solving the differential equation. Substitution can remove the excess constant. Alternatively, suppose we found that the rate of energy loss from an organism is proportional to the temperature above 36°C, so that the rate of change of energy reserves E obeys

$$\frac{dE}{dt} = 36.0 - P_d(t) = -0.8 - 0.3\cos[2\pi(t - 0.583)]$$

where we assumed that temperature follows the daily temperature cycle studied in "Describing Oscillations with the Cosine," Section 1.8. We would have no problem integrating and finding the total energy loss if we could make that $2\pi(t - 0.583)$ inside the cosine into a simple t. Again, substitution is guaranteed to work.

Example 4.3.6 Applying Substitution to Fish Growth

Suppose fish size begins at $L(0) = 0.0$ (measured from fertilization) and follows the differential equation

$$\frac{dL}{dt} = 6.48e^{-0.09t}$$

This equation expresses the fact that fish grow more and more slowly, but never stop growing, throughout their lives. Growth data for walleye in North Caribou Lake, Ontario, are consistent with this equation. To solve it, we need to find the indefinite integral of the rate of change $6.48e^{-0.09t}$ and then to compute the arbitrary constant. To find the integral, we follow Algorithm 4.2.

1. Define a new variable $z = -0.09t$.

2. $\frac{dz}{dt} = -0.09$.

3. $dz = -0.09dt$.

4. To get dt in terms of dz, solve to find

$$dt = -\frac{dz}{0.09}$$

and write

$$\int 6.48e^{-0.09t}dt = \int -6.48\frac{e^z}{0.09}dz = \int -72.0e^z dz$$

5. Integrate, finding

$$\int -72.0e^z dz = -72.0\int e^z dz = -72.0e^z + c$$

6. Put everything back in terms of t, arriving at

$$\int 6.48e^{-0.09t}dt = -72.0e^z + c = -72.0e^{-0.09t} + c \quad (4.3.6)$$

To finish solving the differential equation, we must find the arbitrary constant. The equation is

$$L(0) = 0.0 = -72.0e^{-0.09\cdot 0} + c = -72.0 + c$$

so $c = 72.0$. The solution is

$$L(t) = 72.0 - 72.0e^{-0.09t} = 72.0\left(1 - e^{-0.09t}\right) \quad (4.3.7)$$

This is called the **von Bertalanffy growth equation** (Figure 4.3.22). The size approaches a limit of 72.0 cm, although the fish never stops growing.

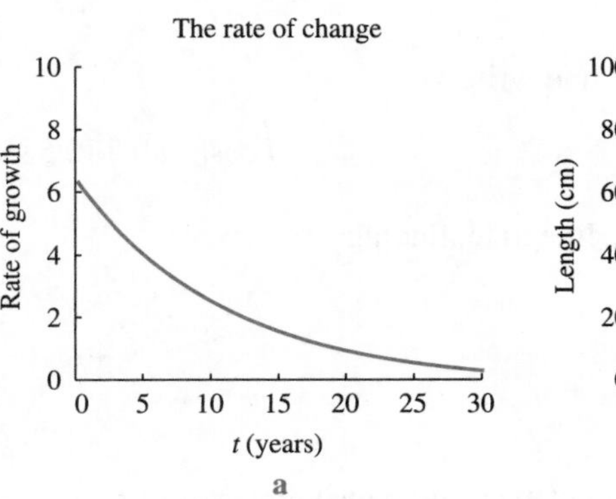

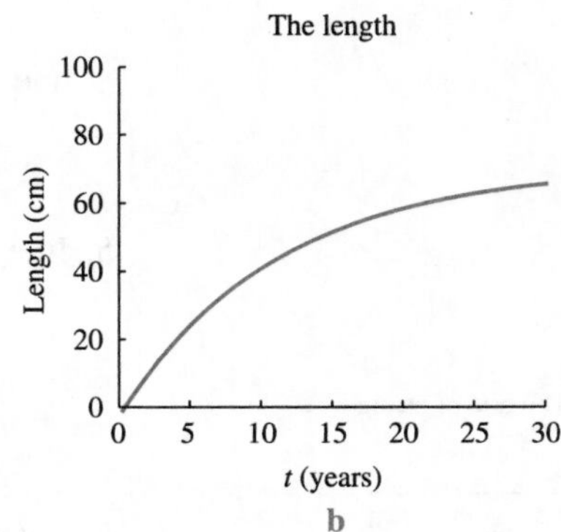

FIGURE 4.3.22
Growth of a fish

We can use this solution to find the age at which fish mature. Walleye begin to reproduce when they reach about 45 cm in length (but continue to grow after that). How long will it take this fish to mature?

Example 4.3.7 Finding the Age When a Fish Matures

We must solve

$$L(t) = 45$$

or

$$\begin{aligned}72.0\left(1 - e^{-0.09t}\right) &= 45.0\\ 1 - e^{-0.09t} &= \frac{45.0}{72.0} = 0.625\\ e^{-0.09t} &= 0.375\\ -0.09t &= \ln(0.375) = -0.98\\ t &= \frac{-0.98}{-0.09} = 10.9\end{aligned}$$

This fish will take about 11 years to mature (Figure 4.3.23).

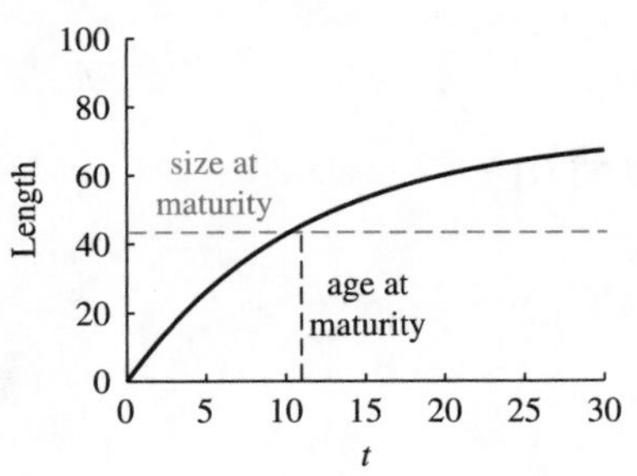

FIGURE 4.3.23
Finding the age of maturity of a walleye

Example 4.3.8 Applying Substitution to Energy Reserves

We can use substitution to find the total energy used in a day from the differential equation

$$\frac{dE}{dt} = 36.0 - P_d(t) = -0.8 - 0.3\cos[2\pi(t - 0.583)]$$

with initial condition $E(0) = 0$ because no energy has been used by time 0. To solve the equation, we must find the indefinite integral

$$E(t) = \int \{-0.8 - 0.3\cos[2\pi(t - 0.583)]\}\, dt$$

The hard term to deal with is $\cos[2\pi(t - 0.583)]$. We attack with the method of substitution.

1. Define a new variable $y = 2\pi(t - 0.583)$, the linear function of t inside the cosine.
2. $\frac{dy}{dt} = 2\pi$.
3. $dy = 2\pi dt$.
4. To write dt in terms of dy, solve to find
$$dt = \frac{dy}{2\pi}$$
and write
$$\int \cos[2\pi(t - 0.583)] = \int \cos(y)\frac{dy}{2\pi}$$
5. Integrate, finding
$$\int \cos(y)\frac{dy}{2\pi} = \frac{1}{2\pi}\int \cos(y)dy = \frac{1}{2\pi}\sin(y) + c$$
6. Put everything back in terms of t, arriving at
$$\int \cos[2\pi(t - 0.583)] = \frac{1}{2\pi}\sin[2\pi(t - 0.583)] + c$$

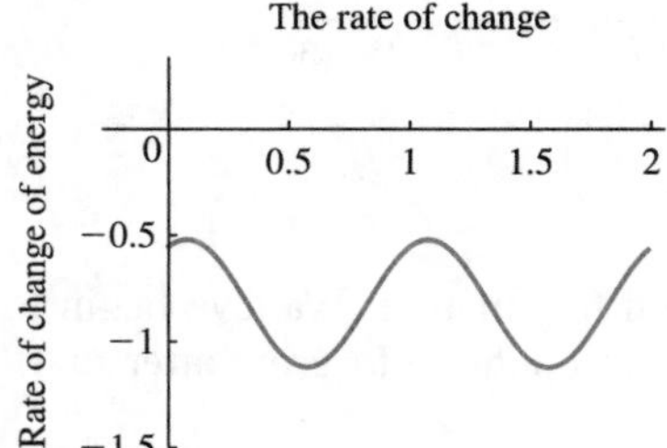

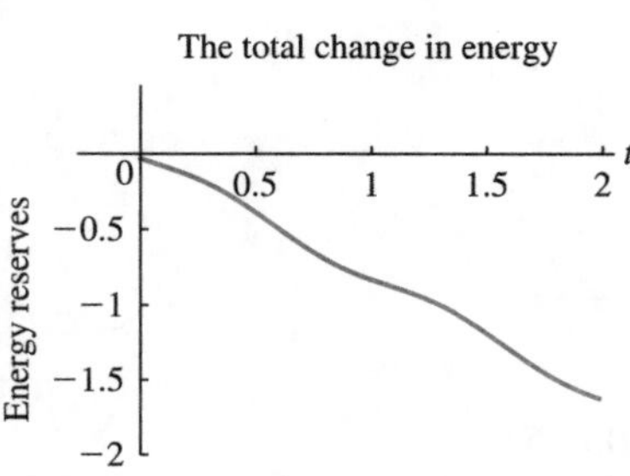

FIGURE 4.3.24
Loss of energy due to temperature

The solution of the whole equation is

$$E(t) = \int \{-0.8 - 0.3\cos[2\pi(t - 0.583)]\}dt = -0.8t - \frac{0.3}{2\pi}\sin[2\pi(t - 0.583)] + c \approx -0.8t - 0.048\sin[2\pi(t - 0.583)] + c$$

To find the constant c, we must solve

$$E(0) \approx 0 = -0.8 \cdot 0 - 0.048\sin[2\pi(0 - 0.583)] + c \approx -0.024 + c,$$

so $c \approx 0.024$. The solution is

$$E(t) = -0.8t - 0.048\sin[2\pi(t - 0.583)] + 0.024$$

(Figure 4.3.24).

Integration by Parts The sum rule and constant product rule for derivatives translate directly into similar rules for integrals. The chain rule for derivatives translates into integration by substitution, although finding the correct substitution can be difficult or impossible. The product rule for derivatives also leads to a corresponding method for integrals, called **integration by parts.** Like substitution, it provides a method that can sometimes transform unfamiliar integrals into familiar forms but is not guaranteed to work.

Recall the product rule for derivatives, written for the functions $u(x)$ and $v(x)$,

$$\frac{d[u(x)v(x)]}{dx} = u(x)\frac{dv}{dx} + v(x)\frac{du}{dx}$$

Solving for $u(x)\frac{dv}{dx}$ gives

$$u(x)\frac{dv}{dx} = \frac{d[u(x)v(x)]}{dx} - v(x)\frac{du}{dx}$$

Integrating both sides gives the formula for integration by parts:

$$\int u(x)\frac{dv}{dx}dx = \int \frac{d[u(x)v(x)]}{dx}dx - \int v(x)\frac{du}{dx}dx$$

$$\int u(x)\frac{dv}{dx}dx = u(x)v(x) - \int v(x)\frac{du}{dx}dx \tag{4.3.8}$$

The first term on the right-hand side simplifies because one indefinite integral of the derivative of $u(x)v(x)$ is the function $u(x)v(x)$ itself (from the definition of the antiderivative).

This may not look very useful. However, if we can *recognize* an integrand as a product

$$u(x)\frac{dv}{dx}$$

and be able to integrate $\frac{dv}{dx}$ to find $v(x)$ and recognize that

$$\int v(x)\frac{du}{dx}dx$$

is a familiar integral, then the method will work. Although the cases where these tricks work are not many, several are important.

Example 4.3.9 An Example of Integration by Parts

Suppose we wish to find the indefinite integral

$$\int xe^x dx$$

This is written as a product, so we can set $u(x) = x$ and $\frac{dv}{dx} = e^x$. Then

$$v(x) = \int e^x dx = e^x$$

(where we chose $c = 0$ for the arbitrary constant) and $\frac{du}{dx} = 1$. Substituting into the formula for integration by parts gives

$$\begin{aligned}\int u(x)\frac{dv}{dx}dx &= u(x)v(x) - \int v(x)\frac{du}{dx}dx \\ &= xe^x - \int e^x dx \\ &= xe^x - e^x + c\end{aligned}$$

Checking, we use the product rule to get

$$\frac{d}{dx}(xe^x - e^x + c) = e^x + xe^x - e^x = xe^x$$

▲

Example 4.3.10 Integration by Parts Applied to $\ln(x)$

We think of the integrand $\ln(x)$ as the product $\ln(x) \cdot 1$. Then let $u(x) = \ln(x)$ and $\frac{dv}{dx} = 1$. To use the formula, compute $v(x) = x$ (again picking $c = 0$ for the arbitrary constant) and $\frac{du}{dx} = \frac{1}{x}$, obtaining

$$\begin{aligned}\int u(x)\frac{dv}{dx}dx &= u(x)v(x) - \int v(x)\frac{du}{dx}dx \\ &= x\ln(x) - \int x\frac{1}{x}dx \\ &= x\ln(x) - \int 1dx \\ &= x\ln(x) - x + c\end{aligned}$$

Checking yields

$$\frac{d}{dx}(x\ln(x) - x + c) = \ln(x) + 1 - 1 = \ln(x)$$

Like integration by substitution, integration by parts can fail.

Example 4.3.11 Failure of Integration by Parts

Suppose we wish to find the indefinite integral

$$\int \frac{e^x}{x}dx$$

This can be thought of as the product of e^x and $\frac{1}{x}$. We could set $u(x) = \frac{1}{x}$ and $\frac{dv}{dx} = e^x$. Then $v(x) = \int e^x dx = e^x$ (as in Example 4.3.9) and $\frac{du}{dx} = -\frac{1}{x^2}$. Substituting, we get

$$\int \frac{e^x}{x}dx = \frac{e^x}{x} + \int \frac{e^x}{x^2}dx$$

The new integral is, if anything, worse than the one we started with.

Alternatively, we could set $u(x) = e^x$ and $\frac{dv}{dx} = \frac{1}{x}$. Then $v(x) = \int \frac{1}{x}dx = \ln(|x|)$ and $\frac{du}{dx} = e^x$. Substituting yields

$$\int \frac{e^x}{x}dx = e^x\ln(|x|) - \int \ln(|x|)e^x dx$$

Again, the new integral is no more familiar than the original one.

Like the function e^{x^2}, the function $\frac{e^x}{x}$ cannot be integrated in terms of the basic functions. This does not mean that the integral is not a reasonable function. By extending the Taylor polynomial found in Example 3.7.8. and integrating each term, we can find a Taylor polynomial for this function.

Summary On the basis of their derivatives, we found indefinite integrals of exponential, logarithmic, and trigonometric functions. To evaluate complicated integrals, we developed **integration by substitution,** the integral version of the chain rule of differentiation. This technique can be used to integrate a few complicated combinations of functions and can reliably eliminate excess constants from integrals. Finally, the method of **integration by parts,** the integral version of the product rule, can be used to compute a few additional integrals.

4.3 Exercises

Mathematical Techniques

1–6 ▪ Find the indefinite integrals of the following functions.

1. $\frac{3}{z^2}+\frac{z^2}{3}$
2. $3e^x+2x^3$
3. $e^x+\frac{1}{x}$
4. $\frac{2}{t}+\frac{t}{2}$
5. $2\sin(x)+3\cos(x)$
6. $x^2-20\sin(x)$

7–12 ▪ Use substitution, if needed, to find the indefinite integrals of the following functions. Check with the chain rule.

7. $3e^{\frac{x}{3}}$
8. $\cos[2\pi(x-2)]$
9. $\left(1+\frac{t}{2}\right)^4$
10. $(1+2t)^{-4}$
11. $\frac{1}{4+t}$
12. $\frac{1}{1+4t}$

13–20 ▪ Use substitution to find the indefinite integrals of the following functions.

13. $\frac{e^x}{1+e^x}$
14. $e^t\left(1+e^t\right)^4$
15. $2y\sqrt{1+y^2}$
16. $\cos(x)e^{\sin(x)}$
17. $\tan(\theta)$ (Write it as $\frac{\sin(\theta)}{\cos(\theta)}$ and use a substitution for the denominator.)
18. $\frac{t}{1+t}$
19. $\frac{1}{x\ln(x)}$
20. $\frac{\ln(x)}{x}$

21–24 ▪ Use integration by parts to evaluate the following. Check your answer by taking the derivative.

21. $\int xe^{2x}dx$
22. $\int x\cos(3x)dx$
23. $\int x^2e^xdx$ (You will need to integrate by parts twice.)
24. $\int x^2e^{-x}dx$ (You will need to integrate by parts twice.)

25–26 ▪ Integration by parts along with substitution can be used to integrate some of the inverse trigonometric functions.

25. The result of Section 2.10, Exercise 25 gives the derivative of $\tan^{-1}(x)$. Use integration by parts and a substitution to find $\int\tan^{-1}(x)dx$.
26. The result of Section 2.10, Exercise 23 gives the derivative of $\sin^{-1}(x)$. Use integration by parts and a substitution to find $\int\sin^{-1}(x)dx$.

27–28 ▪ In Examples 4.3.9 and 4.3.10, we chose the constant $c=0$ when finding $v(x)$. Follow the steps for integration by parts, but leave c as an arbitrary constant. Do you get the same answer?

27. Find the indefinite integral $\int xe^xdx$ as in Example 4.3.9.
28. Find the indefinite integral $\int\ln(x)dx$ as in Example 4.3.10.

29–30 ▪ Sometimes integrating by parts seems to lead in a circle, but the answer can still be found. Try the following.

29. Find the indefinite integral $e^x\sin(x)$ using integration by parts twice.
30. Find the indefinite integral $\frac{\ln(x)}{x}$ using integration by parts.

Applications

31–34 ▪ The following differential equations for the production of a chemical P share the properties that the rate of change at $t=0$ is 5.0 and the limit as $t\to\infty$ is 0. For each, find the solution starting from the initial condition $P(0)=0$, sketch the solution, and indicate what happens to $P(t)$ as $t\to\infty$. Compute $P(10)$ and $P(100)$. Why do some increase to infinity whereas others do not?

31. $\frac{dP}{dt}=\frac{5}{1+2.0t}$
32. $\frac{dP}{dt}=5.0e^{-0.2t}$
33. $\frac{dP}{dt}=2.5\left(\frac{1}{1+t}+e^{-t}\right)$
34. $\frac{dP}{dt}=\frac{5.0}{(1+t)^2}$

35–36 ▪ Use integration by parts to find solutions of the following differential equations.

35. Suppose the mass M of a toad grows according to the differential equation $\frac{dM}{dt}=(t+t^2)e^{-2t}$ with $M(0)=0$. When does this toad grow fastest? Find $M(1)$. How much larger would the toad be at time $t=1$ if it always grew at the maximum rate?
36. Suppose the mass W of a worm grows according to the differential equation $\frac{dW}{dt}=(4t-t^2)e^{-3t}$ with $W(0)=0$. When does this worm grow fastest? Find $W(2)$. How much larger would the worm be at $t=2$ if it always grew at the maximum rate?

37–38 ■ The following problems give the parameters for walleye in a variety of locations. For each location, the differential equation has the form $\frac{dL}{dt} = \alpha e^{-\beta t}$. Find:

a. Find the solution of the differential equation if $L(0) = 0$.

b. Find the limit of size as t approaches infinity.

c. Assume that all walleye mature at 45 cm in length. How old are these walleye when they mature?

d. Graph the size and compare with Ontario walleye (Figure 4.3.23).

37. In Texas, where $\alpha = 64.3$ and $\beta = 1.19$.

38. In Saskatchewan, where $\alpha = 6.48$ and $\beta = 0.06$.

39–42 ■ The population of lemmings $L(t)$ at the top of a cliff is increasing according to the formula given in each of the following problems. However, lemmings leap off the cliff at a rate equal to $0.1L$ and pile up at the bottom.

a. Write a pure-time differential equation for the number of lemmings $B(t)$ piled up at the bottom of the cliff.

b. Solve using the initial condition $B(0) = 0$.

c. Graph the number of lemmings at the top of the cliff and the number at the bottom.

d. Find the limit of the ratio $\frac{B(t)}{L(t)}$ at t approaches infinity.

39. $L(t) = 1000e^{0.2t}$

40. $L(t) = 1000e^{0.05t}$

41. $L(t) = 100t$

42. $L(t) = 100 + 100e^{0.5t}$

43–46 ■ Growth rates of insects depend on the temperature T. Suppose that the length of an insect L follows the differential equation

$$\frac{dL}{dt} = 0.001T(t)$$

with t measured in days starting from January 1 ($t = 0$) and temperature measured in °C. Insects hatch with an initial size of 0.1 cm. For each of the following equations for $T(t)$:

a. Sketch a graph of the temperature over the course of a year.

b. Suppose an insect starts growing on January 1. How big will it be after 30 days?

c. Suppose an insect starts growing on June 1 (day 151). How big will it be after 30 days?

43. $T(t) = 0.001t(365 - t)$

44. $T(t) = 40.0 - 5.0 \times 10^{-6}t^2(365 - t)$

45. $T(t) = 20.0 + 10.0\cos\left[\frac{2\pi(t - 190.0)}{365}\right]$

46. $T(t) = 20.0 + 10.0\cos\left[\frac{2\pi(t - 90.0)}{182.5}\right]$

Computer Exercises

47. Consider again the fish in Caribou Lake, growing according to

$$\frac{dL}{dt} = \alpha e^{-\beta t}$$

where $\alpha = 6.48$ and $\beta = 0.09$. However, suppose there is some variability among fish in the values of these two parameters.

a. Find the growth trajectories of five fish with values of α evenly spread from 10% below to 10% above 6.48.

b. Find the growth trajectories of five fish with values of β evenly spread from 10% below to 10% above 0.09.

c. Which parameter has a greater effect on the size of the fish?

48. Clever genetic engineers design a set of fish that grow according to the following equations.

$$\frac{dL_1}{dt} = 1$$

$$\frac{dL_2}{dt} = \frac{1}{1+\sqrt{t}}$$

$$\frac{dL_3}{dt} = \frac{1}{1+t}$$

$$\frac{dL_4}{dt} = \frac{1}{1+t^2}$$

$$\frac{dL_5}{dt} = \frac{1}{1+t^3}$$

$$\frac{dL_6}{dt} = e^{-t}$$

$$\frac{dL_7}{dt} = e^{-t^2}$$

Suppose they all start at size 0. Use your computer to sketch the growth of these fish for $0 \le t \le 5$. Then zoom in near $t = 0$. Could you tell which fish was which?

4.4 Integrals and Sums

When we cannot guess the answer or use one of the rules of integration to solve a pure-time differential equation, we can use Euler's method to approximate the solution. A graphical analysis of this method shows the link between integrals and sums. Using this link, we define the **definite integral** as the limit of **Riemann sums.** The definite integral represents the total amount of change during some period of time. This interpretation of the integral provides insight into a wide range of applications.

Approximating Integrals with Sums

Consider the pure-time differential equation for the volume V of water in a vessel,

$$\frac{dV}{dt} = t^2$$

where t is measured in seconds and V is measured in cubic centimeters. We are asked to find the total quantity of water that entered during the first second. We could solve the differential equation with the indefinite integral to find this quantity. Alternatively, we can take the limit of an approximation in the spirit of Euler's method.

Suppose we had measured the rate at which water was entering the vessel only every 0.2 s. For lack of knowledge of what happens between measurements, we assume that the rate is *constant* between measurements.

Time (s)	Rate (cm^3/s)
0.0	0.00
0.2	0.04
0.4	0.16
0.6	0.36
0.8	0.64
1.0	1.00

There are two ways to use this information to approximate the total amount of water entering during this second. In one, called the **left-hand estimate,** we pretend that the rate at which water enters between measurements is exactly equal to the value at the *beginning* of the interval (Figure 4.4.25a). In the other, the **right-hand estimate,** we pretend that the rate at which water enters between measurements is exactly equal to the value at the *end* of the interval (Figure 4.4.25b).

	Left-Hand Estimate			Right-Hand Estimate		
Time Interval	Rate During Interval	Influx During Interval	Net Influx	Rate During Interval	Influx During Interval	Net Influx
0.0–0.2	0.00	0.000	0.000	0.04	0.008	0.008
0.2–0.4	0.04	0.008	0.008	0.16	0.032	0.040
0.4–0.6	0.16	0.032	0.040	0.36	0.072	0.112
0.6–0.8	0.36	0.072	0.112	0.64	0.128	0.240
0.8–1.0	0.64	0.128	0.240	1.00	0.200	0.440

The estimate replaces the curve with a **step function,** a series of horizontal lines anchored on the actual function. Step functions are easy to deal with because rates are constant during each interval.

The computation of the net or total influx proceeds as follows. In the first time period, from $t = 0.0$ to $t = 0.2$, the left-hand estimate approximates the influx with the rate of flow at the beginning of the period, or 0.0. The influx is thus approximately 0.0

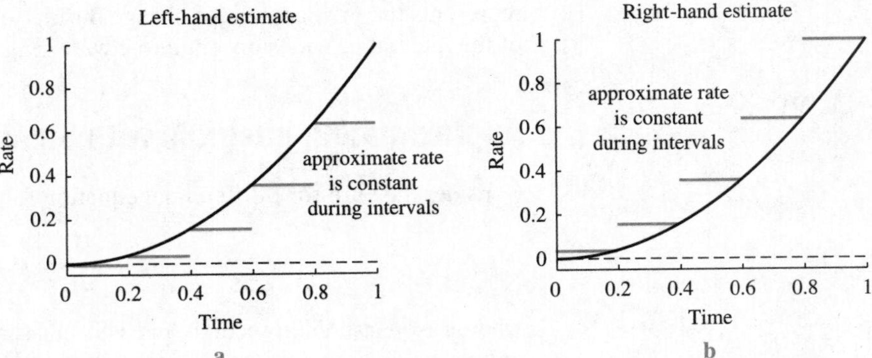

FIGURE 4.4.25
Left-hand and right-hand estimates of the integral

during this first interval. In the second period, from 0.2 to 0.4, the left-hand estimate approximates the rate of influx with 0.04, producing an influx of 0.008 (multiplying the rate by the time). Adding this to the 0.0 from the first interval gives a net of 0.008. Continuing in this way, we estimate a total influx of water of 0.24 cm^3 during the first second.

The right-hand estimate approximates the rate of influx during the first interval by 0.04, the rate at the end of the period. The total influx during this period is estimated as 0.008. During the second interval, the right-hand estimate approximates the rate of influx with 0.16, producing an influx of 0.032. Adding this to the 0.008 from the first interval gives a net of 0.040. Continuing in this way, we estimate a total influx of water of 0.44 cm^3.

We have computed two estimates of the total, a left-hand estimate of 0.24 and a right-hand estimate of 0.44. The two differ by quite a bit. Figure 4.4.25 tells us why. The step function associated with the left-hand estimate lies well below the exact measurement, whereas the step function associated with the right-hand estimate lies well above the exact measurement.

By using more measurements, we expect to get a more accurate answer. We can follow the same steps, assuming that we have measured every 0.1 s (Figure 4.4.26).

	Left-Hand Estimate			Right-Hand Estimate		
Time Interval	Rate During Interval	Influx During Interval	Net Influx	Rate During Interval	Influx During Interval	Net Influx
0.0–0.1	0.00	0.000	0.000	0.01	0.001	0.001
0.1–0.2	0.01	0.001	0.001	0.04	0.004	0.005
0.2–0.3	0.04	0.004	0.005	0.09	0.009	0.014
0.3–0.4	0.09	0.009	0.014	0.16	0.016	0.030
0.4–0.5	0.16	0.016	0.030	0.25	0.025	0.055
0.5–0.6	0.25	0.025	0.055	0.36	0.036	0.091
0.6–0.7	0.36	0.036	0.091	0.49	0.049	0.140
0.7–0.8	0.49	0.049	0.140	0.64	0.064	0.204
0.8–0.9	0.64	0.064	0.204	0.81	0.081	0.285
0.9–1.0	0.81	0.081	0.285	1.00	0.100	0.385

The two estimates are closer to each other.

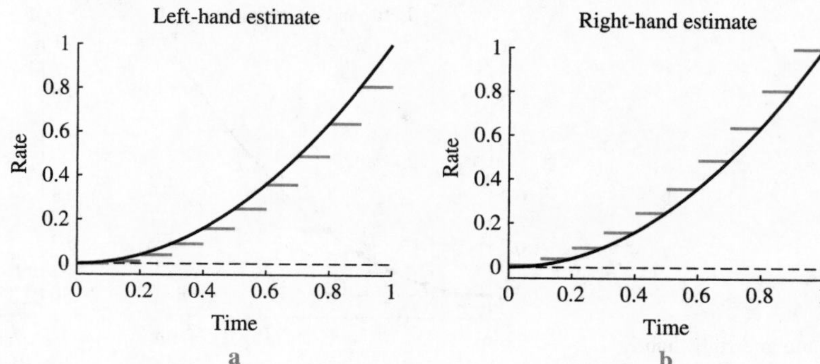

FIGURE 4.4.26
Left-hand and right-hand estimates of the integral: $n = 10$

Approximating Integrals in General

Our example was rather specific, working on a particular function (t^2) and two particular numbers of intervals (5 and 10). Now we will write out the estimates first for a general number of intervals n and for a general function f.

Generalizing this method of approximating integrals is easier if we use **summation notation** to write the expressions more compactly. As an example of the notation, we write

$$\sum_{i=1}^{3} x_i = x_1 + x_2 + x_3$$

The character Σ, the capital Greek letter sigma, stands for "sum." This expression is read "the sum, from i equals 1 to 3, of x sub i." This means that we add up x_i for i taking on values from 1 to 3. The letter i is the **index.** The values x_1, x_2, and x_3 are called **terms.**

Example 4.4.1 Summation Notation

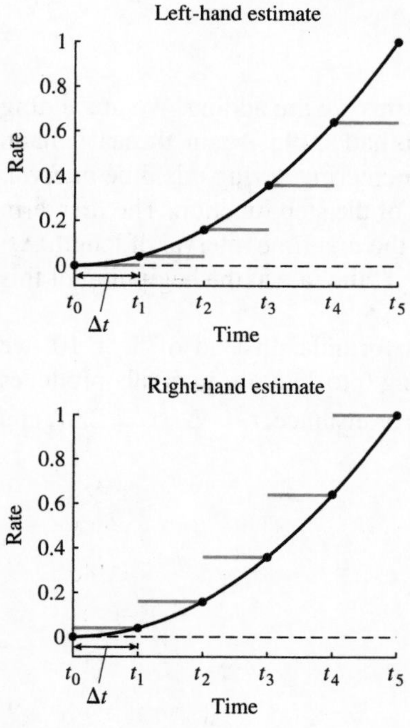

If $x_1 = 5$, $x_2 = 3$, and $x_3 = 1$, then

$$\sum_{i=1}^{3} x_i = x_1 + x_2 + x_3 = 5 + 3 + 1 = 9$$

Similarly,

$$\sum_{i=1}^{3} x_i^2 = x_1^2 + x_2^2 + x_3^2 = 5^2 + 3^2 + 1^2 = 35$$

To begin generalizing the method, let n denote the number of intervals to be used. Let t_i be the time at the end of the ith interval. With $n = 5$, we found that $t_1 = 0.2$, $t_2 = 0.4$, and so on. Set t_0 to be the time at the beginning, so $t_0 = 0.0$ in this case. Finally, set Δt to be the length of the intervals, or 0.2 when $n = 5$ (Figure 4.4.27). We can then write the left-hand and right-hand estimates of volume as sums:

$$\begin{aligned} I_l &= 0.0^2(0.2) + 0.2^2(0.2) + 0.4^2(0.2) + 0.6^2(0.2) + 0.8^2(0.2) \\ &= t_0^2\Delta t + t_1^2\Delta t + t_2^2\Delta t + t_3^2\Delta t + t_4^2\Delta t \end{aligned} \tag{4.4.1}$$

and

$$\begin{aligned} I_r &= 0.2^2(0.2) + 0.4^2(0.2) + 0.6^2(0.2) + 0.8^2(0.2) + 1.0^2(0.2) \\ &= t_1^2\Delta t + t_2^2\Delta t + t_3^2\Delta t + t_4^2\Delta t + t_5^2\Delta t \end{aligned} \tag{4.4.2}$$

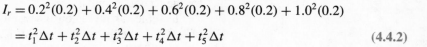

FIGURE 4.4.27
Writing the left-hand and right-hand estimates as sums: $n = 5$

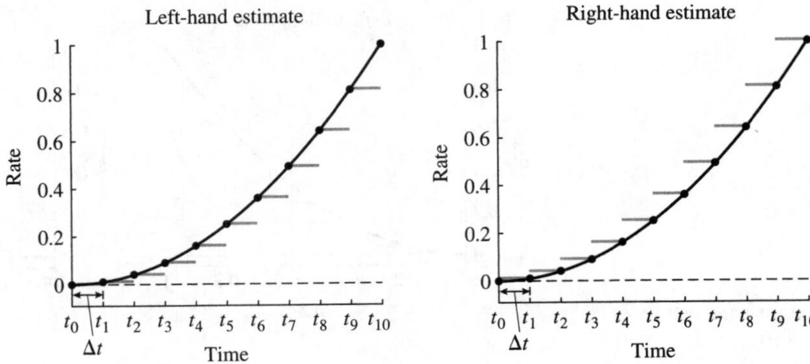

FIGURE 4.4.28
Writing the left-hand and right-hand estimates as sums: $n = 10$

We can use summation notation to rewrite our expressions for I_l and I_r as

$$I_l = \sum_{i=0}^{4} t_i^2 \Delta t$$

$$I_r = \sum_{i=1}^{5} t_i^2 \Delta t$$

These equations are a convenient shorthand for Equations 4.4.1 and 4.4.2 and are called **Riemann sums.**

With this notation, we can quickly write down what happens if we break the interval into ten pieces. The length Δt is 0.1, and $t_1 = 0.1$, $t_2 = 0.2$, up to $t_{10} = 1.0$ (Figure 4.4.28). We can write our estimates as

$$I_l = \sum_{i=0}^{9} t_i^2 \Delta t$$

$$I_r = \sum_{i=1}^{10} t_i^2 \Delta t$$

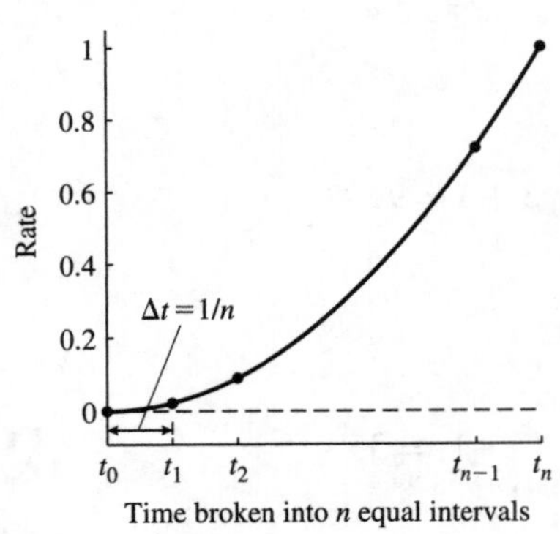

FIGURE 4.4.29
Writing the left-hand and right-hand estimates as sums: general case

The only thing that has changed is the number of terms we are adding. We are adding twice as many terms, but each is smaller because Δt is half as big. Again, these Riemann sums should approximate the total quantity of water entering during this time interval.

Each term in this sum corresponds to one piece of the step function. The first term is the approximate total amount that entered during the first time interval of length Δt. In the left-hand estimate, this term is the product of t_0^2, the rate at the beginning of this interval, times the width of the interval, Δt.

We are now ready to write down the general formula. Instead of 5 or 10, we substitute n into our formulas for I_l and I_r. Breaking 0 to 1 into n intervals produces intervals of length $\Delta t = \frac{1}{n}$. The times are $t_i = i\,\Delta t$. For instance, $t_1 = \Delta t$, $t_2 = 2\Delta t$, and so on, up to $t_n = 1.0$ (Figure 4.4.29). We can write

$$I_l = \sum_{i=0}^{n-1} t_i^2 \Delta t$$

$$I_r = \sum_{i=1}^{n} t_i^2 \Delta t$$

for the Riemann sums.

In Table 4.4.1 we show the results of computing these estimates for different values of n. The last column, denoted by I_a, is the average of I_l and I_r and converges rapidly to 0.333333 (Exercises 17–20). We call this the **averaged estimate.**

Table 4.4.1 Estimates of the Integral with Different n

n	Δt	I_l	I_r	I_a
5	0.200	0.240000	0.440000	0.340000
10	0.100	0.285000	0.385000	0.335000
20	0.050	0.308750	0.358750	0.333750
30	0.033	0.316852	0.350185	0.333519
40	0.025	0.320938	0.345938	0.333438
50	0.020	0.323400	0.343400	0.333400
100	0.010	0.328350	0.338350	0.333350
500	0.002	0.332334	0.334334	0.333334
1000	0.001	0.332833	0.333833	0.333333

Example 4.4.2 Finding Left-Hand, Right-Hand, and Averaged Estimates for an Exponential Function

Suppose we wish to find the amount of chemical P produced after 2.0 s in a reaction that obeys

$$\frac{dP}{dt} = e^{-t}$$

(Example 4.1.1). Using $n = 10$ steps, the interval from $t = 0$ to $t = 2$ breaks into intervals of width $\Delta t = 0.2$ (Figure 4.4.30).

	Left-Hand Estimate			Right-Hand Estimate		
Time Interval	Rate During Interval	Influx During Interval	Net Influx	Rate During Interval	Influx During Interval	Net Influx
0.0–0.2	1.000	0.200	0.200	0.819	0.164	0.164
0.2–0.4	0.819	0.164	0.364	0.670	0.134	0.298
0.4–0.6	0.670	0.134	0.498	0.549	0.110	0.408
0.6–0.8	0.549	0.110	0.608	0.449	0.090	0.497
0.8–1.0	0.449	0.090	0.697	0.368	0.074	0.571
1.0–1.2	0.368	0.074	0.771	0.301	0.060	0.631
1.2–1.4	0.301	0.060	0.831	0.247	0.049	0.681
1.4–1.6	0.247	0.049	0.881	0.202	0.040	0.721
1.6–1.8	0.202	0.040	0.921	0.165	0.033	0.754
1.8–2.0	0.165	0.033	0.954	0.135	0.027	0.781

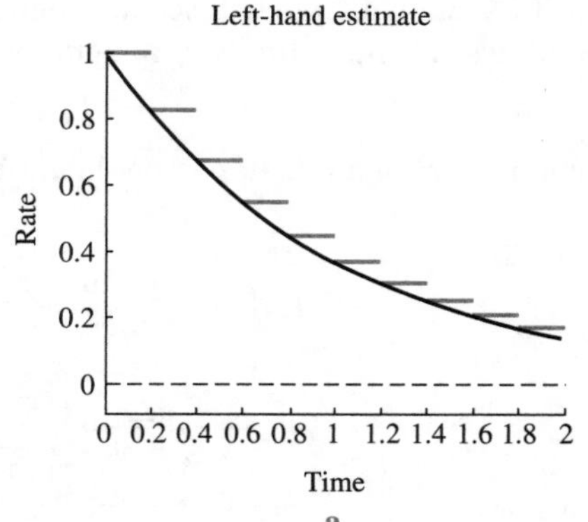

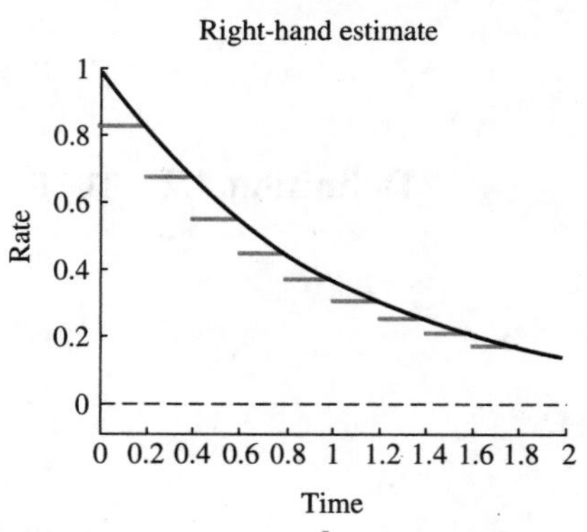

FIGURE 4.4.30

Left-hand and right-hand estimates of the integral

The Definite Integral

We have used sums to approximate the total volume that has been added according to the differential equation

$$\frac{dV}{dt} = t^2$$

during the time interval from $t = 0$ and $t = 1$. The general problem is to find the total change during the time interval from $t = a$ to $t = b$ when the state variable F obeys the pure-time differential equation

$$\frac{dF}{dt} = f(t)$$

Sums that approximate the integral of the function f are then

$$I_l = \sum_{i=0}^{n-1} f(t_i)\,\Delta t \tag{4.4.3}$$

and

$$I_r = \sum_{i=1}^{n} f(t_i)\,\Delta t \tag{4.4.4}$$

The **Riemann integral,** or **definite integral,** is defined as the *limit* of I_r or I_l as $n \to \infty$. It is denoted by $\int_a^b f(t)dt$. For example,

$$\int_0^1 t^2 dt = \lim_{n\to\infty} \sum_{i=0}^{n-1} t_i^2 \Delta t \tag{4.4.5}$$

$$= \lim_{n\to\infty} \sum_{i=1}^{n} t_i^2 \Delta t \tag{4.4.6}$$

(4.4.7)

where $\Delta t = (1 - 0)(n) = y_n$. The expression

$$\int_0^1 t^2 dt$$

is read "the integral from 0 to 1 of $t^2 dt$." The little numbers on the integral indicate the interval to be integrated over and are called the **limits of integration.** In this case, we are integrating (finding the total amount that entered) from time 0 to time 1. The dt in the integral can be thought of as the width of an infinitesimally small interval Δt. When limits of integration are present, the expression is called a **definite integral.** Remember that the definite integral is a number and the indefinite integral is a family of functions. In Section 4.5 we will see the connection between them.

In general, we substitute limits of integration from a to b and a function f.

Definition 4.2 The Riemann integral of a function f on the interval from a to b is

$$\int_a^b f(t)dt = \lim_{n\to\infty} \sum_{i=0}^{n-1} f(t_i)\Delta t$$

$$= \lim_{n\to\infty} \sum_{i=1}^{n} f(t_i)\Delta t$$

where the values $t_0, \ldots, t_n$ break the interval from a to b into n pieces, each of

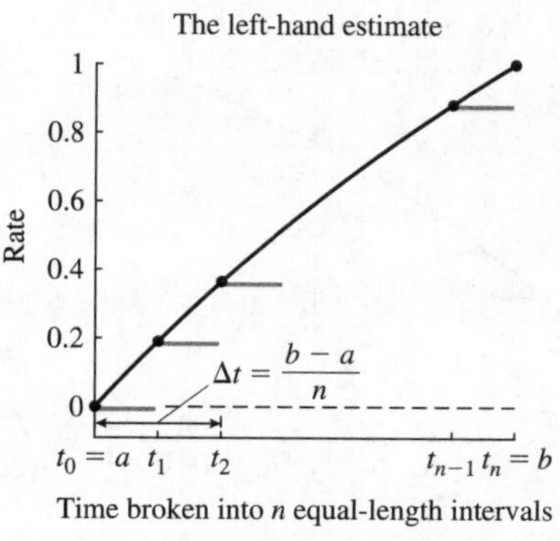

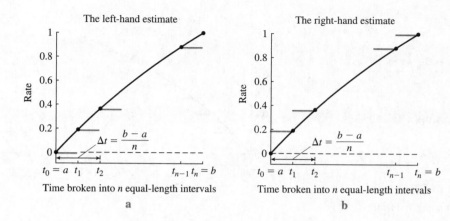

FIGURE 4.4.31
The Riemann integral in general

length

$$\Delta t = \frac{b-a}{n}$$

The elements of this definition are illustrated in Figure 4.4.31.

The steps to compute the Riemann sums that approximate the definite integral are given in the following algorithm.

Algorithm 4.3 Computing Riemann Sums

To evaluate the Riemann sums to approximate the integral $\int_a^b f(t)dt$ using n intervals:

1. Find the step size $\Delta t = \dfrac{b-a}{n}$.
2. Find the endpoints of the intervals as $t_0 = a$, $t_1 = a + \Delta t$, $t_2 = a + 2\Delta t$, and so on, up to $t_n = b$.
3. To evaluate the left-hand estimate, compute
$$I_l = \sum_{i=0}^{n-1} f(t_i)\Delta t$$
4. To evaluate the right-hand estimate, compute
$$I_r = \sum_{i=1}^{n} f(t_i)\Delta t$$

There are a couple of things that need to be proved regarding the definition of the Riemann integral. First, we should show that the Riemann sums really have limits as n approaches infinity. Second, we should show that the limits of the left-hand and right-hand Riemann sums are equal. For our purposes, we will believe these statements. The proofs are rather difficult and can be found in more advanced calculus texts. The Riemann integral works for functions that are continuous at all but a finite number of points. In fact, as long as the function f does not approach infinity at any point, it is difficult to find functions for which either of these statements is false.

Example 4.4.3 Using Riemann Sums to Approximate an Integral

Suppose we wish to evaluate

$$A = \int_1^3 \ln(t)dt$$

by breaking the interval from $t = 1.0$ to $t = 3.0$ into $n = 8$ pieces.

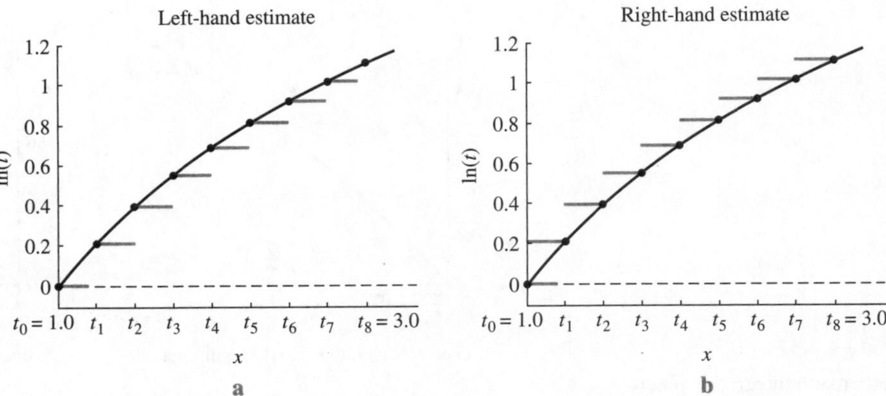

FIGURE 4.4.32
Approximating $\int_1^3 \ln(t)dt$

We must find the step size (width Δt of each interval), find the endpoints of the eight intervals, and evaluate the sum using the left-hand or right-hand estimate. The length of each piece is

$$\Delta t = \frac{3.0 - 1.0}{8} = 0.25$$

We next find the values $t_0, \ldots, t_8$ that break the interval into the eight equal pieces:

$$t_0 = 1.0,\ t_1 = 1.25,\ t_2 = 1.5,\ t_3 = 1.75,\ t_4 = 2.0,\ t_5 = 2.25,\ t_6 = 2.5,\ t_7 = 2.75,\ t_8 = 3.0$$

To use the left-hand estimate, we evaluate

$$\begin{aligned} I_l &= \sum_{i=0}^{7} \ln(t_i)\Delta t \\ &= \ln(1.0) \cdot 0.25 + \ln(1.25) \cdot 0.25 + \ln(1.5) \cdot 0.25 + \ln(1.75) \cdot 0.25 + \\ &\quad \ln(2.0) \cdot 0.25 + \ln(2.25) \cdot 0.25 + \ln(2.5) \cdot 0.25 + \ln(2.75) \cdot 0.25 \\ &= 1.1550 \end{aligned}$$

To use the right-hand estimate, we evaluate

$$\begin{aligned} I_l &= \sum_{i=1}^{8} \ln(t_i)\Delta t \\ &= \ln(1.25) \cdot 0.25 + \ln(1.5) \cdot 0.25 + \ln(1.75) \cdot 0.25 + \ln(2.0) \cdot 0.25 + \\ &\quad \ln(2.25) \cdot 0.25 + \ln(2.5) \cdot 0.25 + \ln(2.75) \cdot 0.25 + \ln(3.0) \cdot 0.25 \\ &= 1.4297 \end{aligned}$$

(Figure 4.4.32).

Summary We have approximated integrals with **Riemann sums,** expressing our results in **summation notation.** By making the sums correspond more and more closely to the function, we make the estimates get more and more accurate. The **definite integral** is defined as the limit of the Riemann sums between particular **limits of integration.**

4.4 Exercises

Mathematical Techniques

1–4 ▪ Evaluate the following sums.

1. $\sum_{i=1}^{5} x_i$, for $x_i = 1/i$

2. $\sum_{j=1}^{6} y_j$, for $y_j = 1/2^j$

3. $\sum_{i=1}^{5} x_i^2$, for $x_i = 1/i$

4. $\sum_{k=1}^{7} z_k$, for $z_k = 2^k$

5–8 ▪ Find the value of Δt and the values of $t_0, t_1, \ldots, t_n$ when the interval from $t = a$ to $t = b$ is broken into n equal-length intervals of width Δt.

5. $a = 0, b = 2, n = 5$
6. $a = 0, b = 2, n = 10$
7. $a = 2, b = 3, n = 5$
8. $a = 2, b = 3, n = 100$

9–12 ▪ Find the left- and right-hand estimates for the definite integrals of the following functions.

9. $f(t) = 2t$, limits of integration 0 to 1, $n = 5$.
10. $f(t) = 2t$, limits of integration 0 to 2, $n = 5$.
11. $f(t) = t^2$, limits of integration 0 to 2, $n = 5$.
12. $f(t) = 1 + t^3$, limits of integration 0 to 1, $n = 5$.

13–16 ▪ Write the left-hand and right-hand Riemann sums for the following cases using summation notation.

13. $f(t) = 2t$, limits of integration 0 to 1, $n = 5$ (as in Exercise 9).
14. $f(t) = 2t$, limits of integration 0 to 2, $n = 5$ (as in Exercise 10).
15. $f(t) = t^2$, limits of integration 0 to 2, $n = 5$ (as in Exercise 11).
16. $f(t) = 1 + t^3$, limits of integration 0 to 1, $n = 5$ (as in Exercise 12).

17–20 ▪ Another way to think about the column I_a in Table 4.4.1 is to think that the value of the function is approximated by the average of the values at the beginning and the end of the time interval. We pretend that the rate of change is $\frac{f(t_{i+1}) + f(t_i)}{2}$ during the interval from t_i to t_{i+1}. Use this method to estimate the following integrals. In each case:

a. Draw a graph illustrating the estimate.
b. Write an expression for I_a using summation notation.
c. Compute the sum.

17. $f(t) = 2t$, limits of integration 0 to 1, $n = 5$ (as in Exercise 9).
18. $f(t) = 2t$, limits of integration 0 to 2, $n = 5$ (as in Exercise 10).
19. $f(t) = t^2$, limits of integration 0 to 2, $n = 5$ (as in Exercise 11).
20. $f(t) = 1 + t^3$, limits of integration 0 to 1, $n = 5$ (as in Exercise 12).

21–24 ▪ One other estimate of the integral, called I_m, can be computed by pretending that the value during the interval from t_i to t_{i+1} is the value of the function at the midpoint, or $f[(t_{i+1} + t_i)/2]$. Use this method to estimate the following integrals. In each case:

a. Draw a graph illustrating this estimate for $n = 5$. Make sure you see the difference from I_a.
b. Write an expression for I_m using summation notation.
c. Compute the sum.

21. $f(t) = 2t$, limits of integration 0 to 1, $n = 5$ (as in Exercise 9).
22. $f(t) = 2t$, limits of integration 0 to 2, $n = 5$ (as in Exercise 10).
23. $f(t) = t^2$, limits of integration 0 to 2, $n = 5$ (as in Exercise 11).
24. $f(t) = 1 + t^3$, limits of integration 0 to 1, $n = 5$ (as in Exercise 12).

Applications

25–28 ▪ Use summation notation and find the total number of offspring for each of the following organisms.

25. The organism has 2 offspring in year 1, 3 offspring in year 2, 5 offspring in year 3, 4 offspring in year 4, and 1 offspring in year 5.
26. The organism has 0 offspring in year 1, 8 offspring in year 2, 15 offspring in year 3, 24 offspring in year 4, 31 offspring in year 5, 11 offspring in year 6, and 3 offspring in year 7.
27. The organism has $B_i = i(6 - i)$ offspring in years 0 through 6.
28. The organism has $B_i = \frac{i(i+1)}{2} + 4$ offspring in years 0 through 7.

29–32 ▪ Use Euler's method to estimate the solutions of the following differential equations with the following parameters. Suppose that $V(0) = 0$ in each case. Your answer should exactly match one of the estimates in Exercises 9–12. Can you explain why?

29. $\frac{dV}{dt} = 2t$, estimate $V(1)$ using $\Delta t = 0.2$ (as in Exercise 9).
30. $\frac{dV}{dt} = 2t$, estimate $V(2)$ using $\Delta t = 0.4$ (as in Exercise 10).
31. $\frac{dV}{dt} = t^2$, estimate $V(2)$ using $\Delta t = 0.4$ (as in Exercise 11).
32. $\frac{dV}{dt} = 1 + t^3$, estimate $V(1)$ using $\Delta t = 0.2$ (as in Exercise 12).

33–36 ▪ Suppose the speed of a bee is given in the following table.

Time (s)	Speed (cm/s)
0.0	127.0
1.0	122.0
2.0	118.0
3.0	115.0
4.0	113.0
5.0	112.0
6.0	112.0
7.0	113.0
8.0	116.0
9.0	120.0
10.0	125.0

33. Using the measurements on even-numbered seconds, find the left-hand and right-hand estimates for the distance the bee moved during the experiment.

34. Using all the measurements, find the left-hand and right-hand estimates for the distance the bee moved during the experiment.

35. Use the method of the last column of Table 4.4.1 (or Exercises 17–20) to estimate the distance moved (using all measurements).

36. Figure out a way to use the measurements on odd-numbered seconds to estimate the distance the bee moved during the experiment. Think about the method in Exercises 21–24.

37–40 ▪ Biologists measure the number of aspen that germinate in four sites over eight years but can measure only two sites per year. In the following table, NA indicates that no measurement was made in that year.

Year	Site 1	Site 2	Site 3	Site 4
1990	12	23	NA	NA
1991	NA	NA	34	10
1992	16	NA	NA	15
1993	17	21	NA	NA
1994	NA	NA	40	18
1995	NA	23	31	NA
1996	NA	27	NA	8
1997	13	NA	37	NA

The goal is to estimate the total number of aspen that germinated in each of the four sites during all eight years.

37. In site 1, estimate the total number of aspen using a modification of the left-hand estimate. How does this compare with finding the total number that germinated in the four years with measurements and multiplying by 2? Why are they different?

38. In site 2, estimate the total number of aspen using a modification of the left-hand estimate. How does this compare with finding the total number that germinated in the four years with measurements and multiplying by 2?

39. In site 3, estimate the total number of aspen using a modification of the right-hand estimate. How does this compare with finding the total number that germinated in the four years studied and multiplying by 2?

40. In site 4, the first and last years are both NA's. Come up with some variation on the left-hand or right-hand estimate to estimate the total number of aspen. Compare the result with finding the total number that germinated in the four years studied and multiplying by 2.

Computer Exercises

41. We will compare various methods used to estimate the solution of

$$\frac{dV}{dt} = t^2$$

with $V(0) = 0$. We wish to find $V(2)$.

a. Graph the rate of change as a function of t.

b. Use the right-hand estimate with $\Delta t = 0.2, 0.1,$ and 0.02.

c. Use the left-hand estimate with $\Delta t = 0.2,\ 0.1,$ and 0.02.

d. Find the average of these two estimates for each Δt.

42. We will compare various methods used to estimate the solution of

$$\frac{dp}{dt} = \ln(1 + \sqrt{t} - t^3)$$

with $p(0) = 0$. We wish to find $p(1)$.

a. Graph the rate of change as a function of t.

b. Use the right-hand estimate with $\Delta t = 0.2,\ 0.1,$ and 0.02.

c. Use the left-hand estimate with $\Delta t = 0.2,\ 0.1,$ and 0.02.

d. Try to figure out from your graph why the two estimates are the same.

4.5 Definite and Indefinite Integrals

We now have two types of integrals. The **indefinite integral** is a *function* that solves the pure-time differential equation

$$\frac{dF}{dt} = f(t)$$

We write

$$\int f(t)dt = F(t) + c$$

to indicate this solution, found by computing or guessing an antiderivative. This integral is **indefinite** because it includes an arbitrary constant c, which must be computed from the initial conditions of the differential equation.

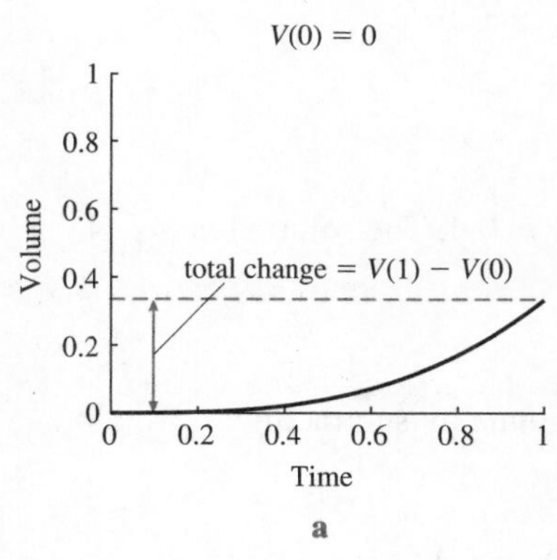

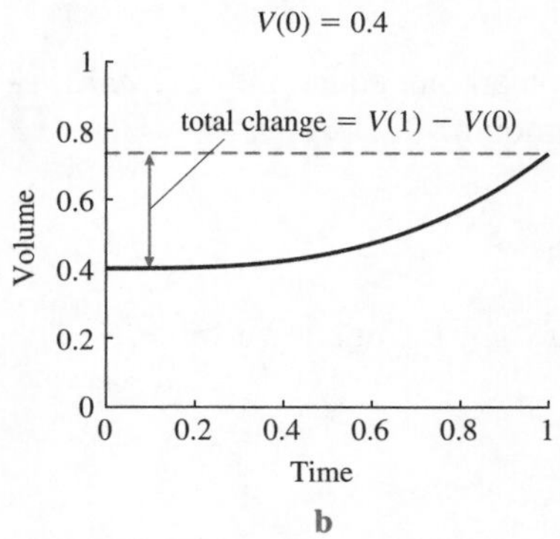

FIGURE 4.5.33

Total change with two different initial conditions

The **definite integral** is a *number*, the change in value between the two times represented by the limits of integration. If the rate of change is $f(t)$,

$$\text{the total change between } a \text{ and } b = \int_a^b f(t)dt$$

The definite integral is defined as the limit of **Riemann sums.** What is the relationship between these two mathematical approaches? In this section, we derive the connection, which is called the **Fundamental Theorem of Calculus.**

The Fundamental Theorem of Calculus: Computing Definite Integrals with Indefinite Integrals

Consider again the pure-time differential equation for volume,

$$\frac{dV}{dt} = t^2$$

The change between times 0 and 1 is given by the definite integral

$$(\text{change between } t = 0 \text{ and } t = 1) = \int_0^1 t^2 dt$$

We can use Riemann sums to approximate the definite integral, but the procedure requires a great deal of calculation.

If we think about the meaning of the differential equation, subtraction provides another way to express the change between the two times:

$$(\text{change between } t = 0 \text{ and } t = 1) = V(1) - V(0).$$

The total amount that entered between times 0 and 1 must equal the difference between the volumes at times 0 and 1 (Figure 4.5.33). Therefore, if V is a solution of the differential equation, then

$$\int_0^1 t^2 dt = V(1) - V(0)$$

We can thus compute the value of the definite integral without any Riemann sums if we can use the indefinite integral to compute the solution $V(t)$ and the value $V(1)$.

Example 4.5.1 Finding Total Change in Volume

Suppose that $V(0) = 0$. We solve the differential equation $\frac{dV}{dt} = t^2$ with the indefinite integral and the power rule, finding

$$V(t) = \int t^2 dt = \frac{t^3}{3} + c$$

With the initial condition $V(0) = 0$, so $c = 0$ and the solution is

$$V(t) = \frac{t^3}{3}$$

With this formula, we can find the total change during the first minute by subtracting:

$$\begin{aligned}\text{total change between times 0 and 1} &= V(1) - V(0)\\ &= \frac{1^3}{3} - \frac{0^3}{3} = \frac{1}{3} \approx 0.3333\end{aligned}$$

This closely matches the estimates we found using Riemann sums (Table 4.4.1), but took a lot less work. ▲

Example 4.5.2 Finding Total Change: Different Initial Condition

Suppose instead that $V(0) = 0.4$. Then

$$V(t) = \frac{t^3}{3} + c$$

as before, but with the initial condition $V(0) = 0.4$, $c = 0.4$. The solution is

$$V(t) = \frac{t^3}{3} + 0.4$$

We can again find the total change during the first minute by subtracting:

$$\begin{aligned}\text{total change between times 0 and 1} &= V(1) - V(0)\\ &= \left(\frac{1^3}{3} + 0.4\right) - \left(\frac{0^3}{3} + 0.4\right) = \frac{1}{3} \approx 0.3333\end{aligned}$$

Although the two solutions to the differential equation are not equal, they are *parallel* (Figure 4.5.33). Both increase by exactly the same amount.

Example 4.5.3 Finding Total Change: Irrelevance of Initial Condition

More generally, suppose we denote the volume at time 0 by the unknown value V_0. The solution of the differential equation is still

$$V(t) = \frac{t^3}{3} + c$$

but now the arbitrary constant c must satisfy

$$V(0) = V_0 = \frac{0^3}{3} + c = c$$

so $c = V_0$. The solution is

$$V(t) = \frac{t^3}{3} + V_0$$

and the change in volume is

$$\begin{aligned}V(1) - V(0) &= \left(\frac{1^3}{3} + V_0\right) - \left(\frac{0^3}{3} + V_0\right)\\ &= \frac{1}{3} \approx 0.3333\end{aligned}$$

The total change does not depend on the initial condition of the pure-time differential equation. The initial condition is required to answer a question such as "Where are you after driving 5 miles due north?" But the *change* in position is clear; you are 5 miles north of where you started.

This idea is the essence of the **Fundamental Theorem of Calculus.** A definite integral can be evaluated in two ways:

1. By evaluating Riemann sums and taking the limit
2. By solving the appropriate pure-time differential equation and subtracting.

When the differential equation can be solved with the indefinite integral, the second method is much simpler. However, when the indefinite integral is impossible, Riemann sums provide a guaranteed, if laborious, alternative.

It is convenient to write the Fundamental Theorem of Calculus with one bit of new notation. To represent the change in the value of $F(x)$ between $x = a$ and $x = b$, we use the shorthand

$$F(x)\big|_a^b = F(b) - F(a)$$

Instead of reading this notation in a new way, we say "$F(b)$ minus $F(a)$."

We can now state the theorem.

Theorem 4.4 The Fundamental Theorem of Calculus

If $f(x)$ is a continuous function with indefinite integral

$$F(x) = \int f(x)dx$$

Then

$$\int_a^b f(x)dx = F(b) - F(a) = F(x)\big|_a^b$$

The Fundamental Theorem applies to more than just continuous functions, including any function that you can graph (any function that is continuous at all but a finite number of points). This theorem is *fundamental* because it describes the relation between definite and indefinite integrals. In "Proof of the Fundamental Theorem of Calculus," later in Section 4.5, we sketch a proof in the case where the function $f(x)$ is continuous. First, we learn how to use this theorem.

Example 4.5.4 Using the Fundamental Theorem of Calculus

To find $\int_1^2 \frac{1}{x}dx$, we find any indefinite integral of $\frac{1}{x}$, valid for $1 \le x \le 2$, such as

$$\int \frac{1}{x}dx = \ln(x)$$

Then

$$\int_1^2 \frac{1}{x}dx = \ln(x)\big|_1^2 = \ln(2) - \ln(1) \approx 0.693$$

Example 4.5.5 Using the Fundamental Theorem of Calculus to Find How Far a Rock Falls

Suppose that the position of a rock $p(t)$ follows the differential equation

$$\frac{dp}{dt} = v(t) = -9.8t - 5.0$$

(as in "Solving Polynomial Differential Equations," Section 4.2) where t is measured in seconds and p is measured in meters (Figure 4.5.34). How far does the rock fall between $t = 1$ and $t = 3$? The total change in position is given by the definite integral of the rate of change of position,

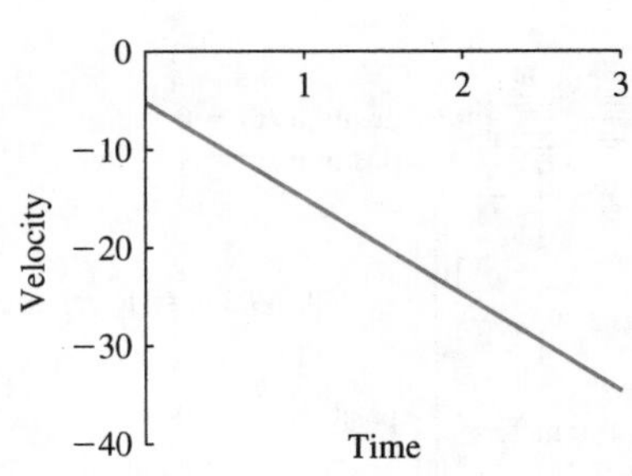

FIGURE 4.5.34
The velocity of a falling rock

$$\int_1^3 v(t)dt$$

According to the Fundamental Theorem of Calculus, we can compute this value by finding *any* indefinite integral of $v(t)$ and subtracting the values at $t = 1$ and $t = 3$. One indefinite integral is

$$\begin{aligned}\int v(t)dt &= \int(-9.8t - 5.0)dt \\ &= -9.8\frac{t^2}{2} - 5.0t \\ &= -4.9t^2 - 5.0t\end{aligned}$$

where we set the arbitrary constant to $c = 0$ for convenience. Then

$$\begin{aligned}\text{total change in position between } t = 1 \text{ and } t = 3 &= \left(-4.9t^2 - 5.0t\right)\Big|_1^3 \\ &= \left(-4.9 \cdot 3^2 - 5.0 \cdot 3\right) \\ &\quad -\left(-4.9 \cdot 1^2 - 5.0 \cdot 1\right) \\ &= -49.2\end{aligned}$$

The rock will have fallen 49.2 m during this time.

Example 4.5.6 Solving the Differential Equation to Find How Far a Rock Falls

The total distance fallen between times 1 and 3 can also be found by solving the differential equation with initial conditions. We can think of the position $p(t)$ as the change in position starting from $t = 1$. It follows the differential equation

$$\frac{dp}{dt} = v(t) = -9.8t - 5.0$$

as before, but with the initial condition $p(1) = 0$ indicating that the distance fallen at $t = 1$ is 0. Solving, we get

$$\begin{aligned}p(t) &= \int v(t)dt \\ &= \int(-9.8t - 5.0)dt \\ &= -9.8\frac{t^2}{2} - 5.0t + c \\ &= -4.9t^2 - 5.0t + c\end{aligned}$$

The constant c satisfies

$$\begin{aligned}p(1) = 0 &= -4.9 \cdot 1^2 - 5.0 \cdot 1 + c \\ c &= 4.9 \cdot 1^2 + 5.0 \cdot 1 = 9.9\end{aligned}$$

The solution is

$$p(t) = -4.9t^2 - 5.0t + 9.9$$

and the change in position by time $t = 3$ is

$$p(3) = -4.9 \cdot 3^2 - 5.0 \cdot 3 + 9.9 = -49.2$$

(Figure 4.5.35). The answer matches that in Example 4.5.5, but the approach using the Fundamental Theorem of Calculus is easier because we did not need to compute the arbitrary constant.

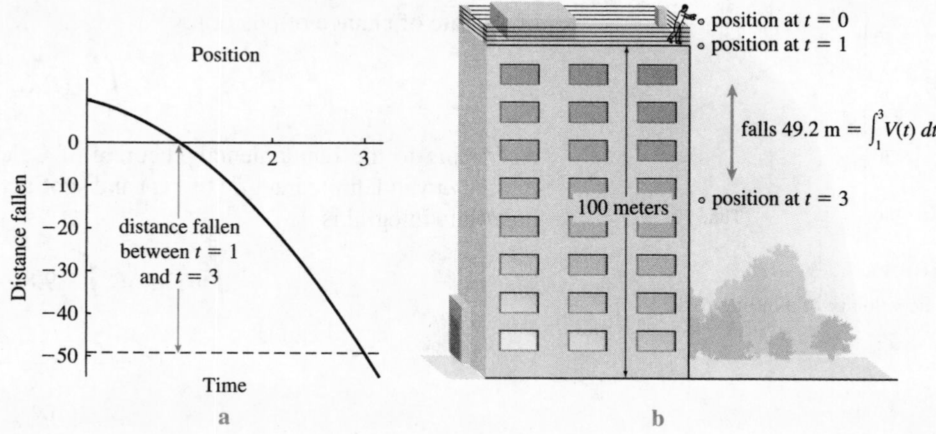

FIGURE 4.5.35
The position of a falling rock

Example 4.5.7 Using the Fundamental Theorem of Calculus to Find How Much a Fish Grows

Suppose the change in length of a fish follows the equation

$$\frac{dL}{dt} = 6.48e^{-0.09t}$$

(Example 4.3.6) with t measured as age in years and L measured in centimeters. How much does the fish grow between ages 2 and 5? The total change is

$$\int_2^5 6.48e^{-0.09t}\,dt$$

To evaluate, we find the indefinite integral

$$\int 6.48e^{-0.09t}\,dt = -72.0e^{-0.09t}$$

(the answer we found using substitution in Equation 4.3.6), but with the arbitrary constant set to 0 for convenience. The *change* in length is then

$$-72.0e^{-0.09t}\big|_2^5 = -72.0e^{-0.09\cdot 5} - (-72.0e^{-0.09\cdot 2}) \approx -45.9 - (-60.1) = 14.2$$

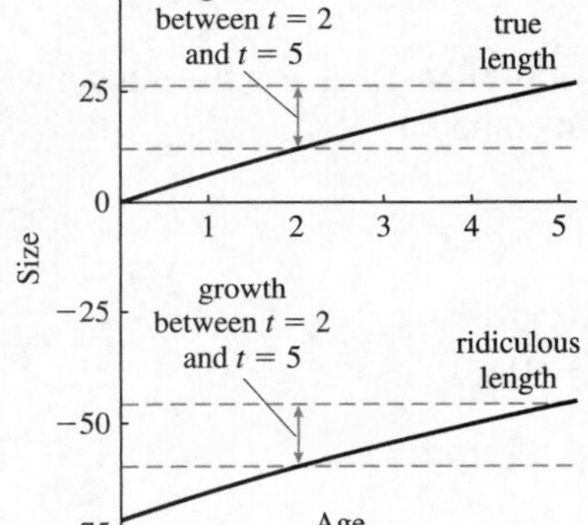

FIGURE 4.5.36
The growth of a walleye

Neither of the component terms (−45.9 and −60.1) makes biological sense. Their difference, however, gives the correct answer (Figure 4.5.36).

The solution using the realistic initial condition $L(0) = 0$ is

$$L(t) = 72.0 - 72.0e^{-0.09t} = 72.0\left(1 - e^{-0.09t}\right)$$

(Equation 4.3.7). The change is

$$\begin{aligned} L(t)\big|_2^5 &= L(5) - L(2) \\ &= 72.0\left(1 - e^{-0.09\cdot 5}\right) - 72.0\left(1 - e^{-0.09\cdot 2}\right) \\ &\approx 26.1 - 11.9 = 14.2 \end{aligned}$$

The difference 14.2 is now found by subtracting the actual lengths at ages 5 and 2 (Figure 4.5.36).

Integration by parts (Section 4.3) also works on definite integrals. In addition to carrying along the limits of integration, we must use the Fundamental Theorem of Calculus to include those limits in the term $u(x)v(x)$. The formula for definite integration by parts is

$$\int_a^b u(x)\frac{dv}{dx}dx = u(x)v(x)\big|_a^b - \int_a^b v(x)\frac{du}{dx}dx$$

Example 4.5.8 Definite Integration by Parts

Suppose the amount of chemical produced in a reaction obeys

$$\frac{dC}{dt} = te^{-t}$$

If there is no product at time 0, or $C(0) = 0$, how much will there be at time $t = 2$? The amount produced is the integral of the rate of production, or

$$C(2) = \int_0^2 te^{-t}dt$$

To integrate by parts, we set $u(t) = t$ and $\frac{dv}{dt} = e^{-t}$. Then $\frac{du}{dt} = 1$ and $v(t) = -e^{-t}$.

Therefore,

$$\begin{aligned}\int_0^2 te^{-t}dt &= -te^{-t}\big|_0^2 - \int_0^2 (-e^{-t})\,dt \\ &= -te^{-t}\big|_0^2 - e^{-t}\big|_0^2 \\ &= -\left(2e^{-2} - 0e^0\right) - \left(e^{-2} - e^0\right) = 1 - 3e^{-2} \approx 0.594\end{aligned}$$

The Summation Property of the Definite Integral

What happens if the function we want to integrate takes on both positive and negative values? If our function represents the rate at which water enters a vessel, a positive value means that water is entering, and a negative value means that water is leaving. Suppose

$$\frac{dV}{dt} = t^2 - t$$

where t is measured in seconds and V is measured in cubic centimeters. Water flows out during the first second when the rate is negative, and it flows in during the next second when the rate is positive (Figure 4.5.37a).

To find the total change in volume from time 0 until time 1, we use the indefinite integral and the Fundamental Theorem of Calculus to compute

$$\begin{aligned}\int_0^1 (t^2 - t)\,dt &= \left(\frac{t^3}{3} - \frac{t^2}{2}\right)\Big|_0^1 \\ &= \left(\frac{1}{3} - \frac{1}{2}\right) - (0 - 0) \\ &\approx -0.167\text{ cm}^3\end{aligned}$$

This means that 0.167 cm^3 of water *left* the vessel during the first second. During the next second, the change in volume is

$$\begin{aligned}\int_1^2 (t^2 - t)\,dt &= \left(\frac{t^3}{3} - \frac{t^2}{2}\right)\Big|_1^2 \\ &= \left(\frac{8}{3} - 2\right) - \left(\frac{1}{3} - \frac{1}{2}\right) \\ &\approx 0.833\text{ cm}^3\end{aligned}$$

This means that 0.833 cm^3 *entered* the vessel during the second second.

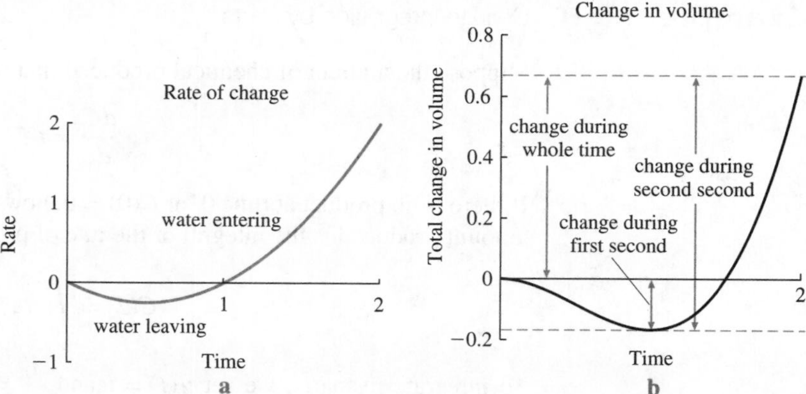

FIGURE 4.5.37
Positive and negative rates

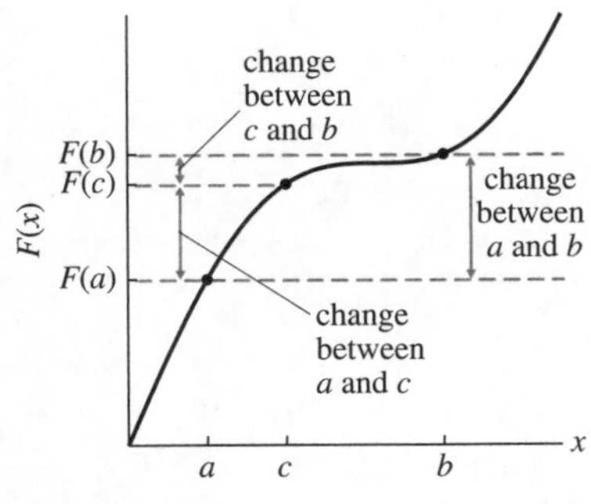

FIGURE 4.5.38

The summation property of the definite integral

What happens during the whole period between $t = 0$ and $t = 2$? Because $0.167\ \text{cm}^3$ left during the first second and $0.833\ \text{cm}^3$ entered during the second second,

$$\begin{aligned}(\text{change between } t = 0 \text{ and } t = 2) &= (\text{change between } t = 0 \text{ and } t = 1)\\ &\quad + (\text{change between } t = 1 \text{ and } t = 2)\\ &\approx -0.167 + 0.833 \approx 0.666\end{aligned}$$

Alternatively, evaluating the definite integral from $t = 0$ to $t = 2$, we get

$$\begin{aligned}\int_0^2 \left(t^2 - t\right)\, dt &= \left(\frac{t^3}{3} - \frac{t^2}{2}\right)\Bigg|_0^2\\ &= \left(\frac{8}{3} - 2\right) - (0 - 0) \approx 0.667\end{aligned}$$

This calculation points out an important property of the definite integral. The total change between times a and b is the change between a and some intermediate time c plus the change between time c and the final time b (Figure 4.5.38). This important and useful fact can be stated formally as a theorem.

Theorem 4.5 **Summation Property of the Definite Integral**

Suppose $f(x)$ is continuous on the interval from a to b and that $a \le c \le b$. Then

$$\int_a^b f(x)\, dx = \int_a^c f(x)\, dx + \int_c^b f(x)\, dx$$

The proof depends on a slightly more general definition of the Riemann integral based on breaking the interval from a to b into n intervals that need not be equal in length.

Example 4.5.9 The Summation Property Applied to a Falling Rock

If we wish to find how far the rock studied in Example 4.5.5 falls between $t = 1$ and $t = 3$, we can add the change of position between $t = 1$ and $t = 2$ to the change of position between $t = 2$ and $t = 3$. Between $t = 1$ and $t = 2$, the change of position is

$$\begin{aligned}\int_1^2 v(t)dt &= \int_1^2 (-9.8t - 5.0)dt\\ &= -4.9t^2 - 5.0t\Big|_1^2\\ &= \left(-4.9 \cdot 2^2 - 5.0 \cdot 2\right) - \left(-4.9 \cdot 1^2 - 5.0 \cdot 1\right) = -19.7\end{aligned}$$

and between $t = 2$ and $t = 3$, the change of position is

$$\begin{aligned}\int_2^3 v(t)dt &= \int_2^3 (-9.8t - 5.0)dt\\ &= \left(-4.9t^2 - 5.0t\right)\Big|_2^3\\ &= \left(-4.9 \cdot 3^2 - 5.0 \cdot 3\right) - \left(-4.9 \cdot 2^2 - 5.0 \cdot 2\right) = -29.5\end{aligned}$$

The total change of position, found earlier to be -49.2 m, is the sum of -19.7 m and -29.5 m (Figure 4.5.39).

Euler's Method and the Fundamental Theorem of Calculus

Riemann sums provide a way to estimate a definite integral, and Euler's method provides a way to estimate the numerical solution of a differential equation. First, we find the relationship between these two methods (examined in Section 4.4, Exercises 29–32). Then we show that the Fundamental Theorem provides a *proof* that using Euler's method with smaller and smaller step sizes is guaranteed to give an accurate approximation of the solution of a differential equation.

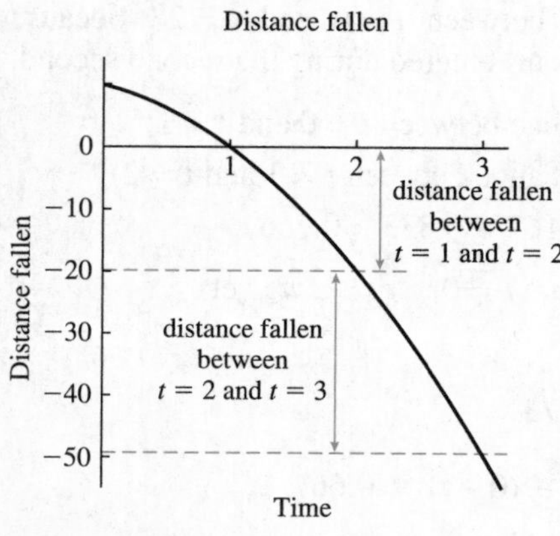

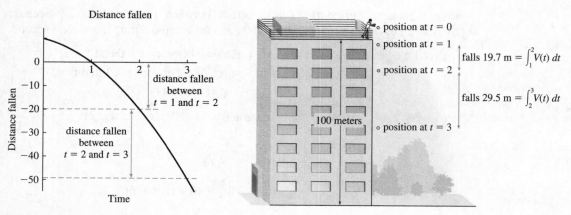

FIGURE 4.5.39
The summation property of distance traveled

Example 4.5.10 Riemann Sums and Euler's Method

Consider again finding a numerical solution to the differential equation

$$\frac{dP}{dt} = e^{-t}$$

with initial condition $P(0) = 0$ (from Example 4.1.8). To find $P(1)$, we can use Algorithm 4.1. If we choose a step size of $\Delta t = 0.2$, then we get the results shown in the following table.

t	$\hat{P}(t+\Delta t)$	$t+\Delta t$	$\hat{P}(t+\Delta t)$
0.0	$P(0) + P'(0)\Delta t = 0.0 + e^{-0} \cdot 0.2$	0.2	0.2
0.2	$\hat{P}(0.2) + P'(0.2)\Delta t = 0.2 + e^{-0.2} \cdot 0.2$	0.4	0.364
0.4	$\hat{P}(0.4) + P'(0.4)\Delta t = 0.364 + e^{-0.4} \cdot 0.2$	0.6	0.498
0.6	$\hat{P}(0.6) + P'(0.6)\Delta t = 0.498 + e^{-0.6} \cdot 0.2$	0.8	0.608
0.8	$\hat{P}(0.8) + P'(0.8)\Delta t = 0.608 + e^{-0.8} \cdot 0.2$	1.0	0.697

FIGURE 4.5.40
Euler's method applied to a pure-time differential equation matches the left-hand estimate

Euler's method corresponds to assuming that the rate of change is constant during each interval. As shown in Figure 4.5.40, this corresponds exactly to the approximation used in the left-hand Riemann sum. In this case, we can find the exact answer as follows:

$$P(1) = \int_0^1 e^{-t} dt = -e^{-t}\Big|_0^1 = 1 - e^{-1} \approx 0.63212.$$

Euler's method for pure-time differential equations is identical to the left-hand Riemann sum for integrals. The Fundamental Theorem of Calculus tells us that taking smaller and smaller steps in the Riemann sum gives an answer that converges to the antiderivative. Thus, for cases where the integration is impossible, we now have a proven numerical method for solving a differential equation.

Example 4.5.11 Euler's Method Converges to the Correct Answer

For the case in Example 4.5.10, choosing smaller and smaller step sizes gives the following results:

Δt	$\hat{P}(1)$
0.1	0.66425
0.01	0.63529
0.001	0.63244
0.0001	0.63215

As they must, the values converge toward the exact answer of $1 - e^{-1} \approx 0.63212$ as the step size becomes smaller.

Example 4.5.12 Solving the Impossible

Consider finding a numerical solution to the differential equation

$$\frac{dP}{dt} = e^{-t^2}$$

with initial condition $P(0) = 0$. Although this is similar to the differential equation in Example 4.5.10, it is impossible to evaluate the integral in terms of elementary functions and compute the exact answer. If we choose a step size of $\Delta t = 0.2$, then we get

t	$\hat{P}(t+\Delta t)$	$t+\Delta t$	$\hat{P}(t+\Delta t)$
0.0	$P(0) + P'(0)\Delta t = 0.0 + e^{-0^2} \cdot 0.2$	0.2	0.2
0.2	$\hat{P}(0.2) + P'(0.2)\Delta t = 0.2 + e^{-0.2^2} \cdot 0.2$	0.4	0.392
0.4	$\hat{P}(0.4) + P'(0.4)\Delta t = 0.392 + e^{-0.4^2} \cdot 0.2$	0.6	0.563
0.6	$\hat{P}(0.6) + P'(0.6)\Delta t = 0.563 + e^{-0.6^2} \cdot 0.2$	0.8	0.702
0.8	$\hat{P}(0.8) + P'(0.8)\Delta t = 0.702 + e^{-0.8^2} \cdot 0.2$	1.0	0.808

Choosing smaller and smaller step sizes gives the following results:

Δt	$\hat{P}(1)$
0.1	0.77782
0.01	0.74998
0.001	0.74714
0.0001	0.74686

Evaluation on an accurate computer gives an answer of 0.74682 to five decimal places.

Although the Fundamental Theorem of Calculus guarantees that Euler's method will converge to the correct answer, it tends to converge rather slowly. A project at the end of this chapter gives you a chance to explore some more advanced methods that combine the proven accuracy of Euler's method with much more rapid convergence.

Proof of the Fundamental Theorem of Calculus

Theorem 4.4 **The Fundamental Theorem of Calculus**

If $f(x)$ is a continuous function with indefinite integral

$$F(x) = \int f(x)dx$$

Then

$$\int_a^b f(x)dx = F(b) - F(a) = F(x)\Big|_a^b$$

Proof: First we show that the function

$$G(x) = \int_a^x f(s)ds$$

is an antiderivative of $f(x)$. The derivative of $G(x)$ is

$$\lim_{h\to 0} \frac{G(x+h)-G(x)}{h}$$

The quantity inside the limit can be simplified by using the Summation Property of the Definite Integral (Theorem 4.5).

$$\begin{aligned} \frac{G(x+h)-G(x)}{h} &= \frac{1}{h}\left(\int_a^{x+h} f(s)ds - \int_a^x f(s)ds\right) \\ &= \frac{1}{h}\int_x^{x+h} f(s)ds \end{aligned}$$

Because f is continuous, it takes on a minimum value (which we call $f_{\min}$) and a maximum value (which we call $f_{\max}$) on the interval between x and $x+h$. Then

$$f_{\min} \le \frac{1}{h}\int_x^{x+h} f(s)ds \le f_{\max}$$

because $f_{\min} \le f(s)$ and $f(s) \le f_{\max}$. As $h\to 0$, we know that $f_{\min} \to f(x)$ and $f_{\max} \to f(x)$ because $f(x)$ is continuous. Therefore,

$$\begin{aligned} \lim_{h\to 0} f_{\min} \le \lim_{h\to 0} &\frac{G(x+h)-G(x)}{h} \le \lim_{h\to 0} f_{\max} \\ f(x) \le\ &G'(x) \le f(x) \end{aligned}$$

which implies that $G'(x) = f(x)$. We have that $F'(x) = f(x)$ because $F(x)$ is an indefinite integral of $f(x)$. Therefore $F'(x) = G'(x)$, and the function $F(x) - G(x)$ has derivative equal to 0. The only functions with derivative equal to 0 are constants, so $F(x) = G(x) + c$ for some constant c. Therefore,

$$F(b) - F(a) = G(b) - G(a) = G(b) = \int_a^b f(x)dx$$

where we used the fact that $G(a) = 0$ (an integral over a domain of length zero is 0). This proves the theorem.

Summary The **Fundamental Theorem of Calculus** describes the connection between definite and indefinite integrals; the definite integral is equal to the difference between the values of the indefinite integral at the limits of integration. The Fundamental Theorem simplifies calculations of total change from pure-time differential equations by eliminating the need to solve for the arbitrary constant. The **Summation Property of Definite Integrals** states that the total change over two time intervals is the sum of the changes in each.

4.5 Exercises

Mathematical Techniques

1–4 ▪ Compute the following definite integrals and compare with your answer from the earlier problem.

1. $\int_0^1 2t\,dt$. Compare with Section 4.4, Exercises 9 and 17.
2. $\int_0^2 2t\,dt$. Compare with Section 4.4, Exercises 10 and 18.
3. $\int_0^2 t^2\,dt$. Compare with Section 4.4, Exercises 11 and 19.
4. $\int_0^1 (1+t^3)dt$. Compare with Section 4.4, Exercises 12 and 20.

5–24 ▪ Compute the following definite integrals.

5. $\int_0^1 7x^2\,dx$
6. $\int_0^1 (10t^9 + 6t^5)dt$
7. $\int_{-1}^2 (72t+5)dt$
8. $\int_{-2}^2 (y^4 + 5y^3)dy$
9. $\int_1^2 \frac{5}{x^3}\,dx$
10. $\int_1^4 3z^{\frac{3}{7}}dz$
11. $\int_1^8 \left(\frac{2}{\sqrt[3]{t}} + 3\right)dt$
12. $\int_{1.2}^{2.4} (5z^{-1.2} - 1.2)dz$

13. $\int_2^3 \left(\frac{3}{z^2} + \frac{z^2}{3}\right) dz$

14. $\int_0^1 (3e^x + 2x^3) dx$

15. $\int_1^4 \left(e^x + \frac{1}{x}\right) dx$

16. $\int_{-3}^{-1} \left(\frac{2}{t} + \frac{t}{2}\right) dt$

17. $\int_0^{\pi} (2\sin(x) + 3\cos(x)) dx$

18. $\int_{-\pi/2}^{\pi/2} [x^2 - 20\sin(x)] dx$

19. $\int_0^5 3e^{\frac{x}{5}} dx$

20. $\int_2^5 \cos(2\pi(x-2)) dx$

21. $\int_0^4 \left(1 + \frac{t}{2}\right)^4 dt$

22. $\int_1^{10} (1+2t)^{-4} dt$

23. $\int_{-3}^{0} \frac{1}{4+t} dt$

24. $\int_0^2 \frac{1}{1+4t} dt$

25–30 ▪ Compute the definite integrals of the following functions from $t = 1$ to $t = 2$, from $t = 2$ to $t = 3$, and finally from $t = 1$ to $t = 3$ to check the summation property of definite integrals.

25. $g(t) = t^2$

26. $h(t) = 1 + t^3$

27. $L(t) = \frac{5}{t^3}$

28. $B(t) = 3t^{\frac{3}{7}}$

29. $F(t) = e^t + \frac{1}{t}$

30. $G(t) = \frac{2}{t} + \frac{t}{2}$

31–34 ▪ Another way to write the Fundamental Theorem of Calculus (sometimes called the First Fundamental Theorem of Calculus) relates the definite integral and the derivative. It states that if we treat the definite integral $\int_a^x f(s)ds$ as a function of x, then

$$\frac{d}{dx}\left(\int_a^x f(s)\, ds\right) = f(x)$$

for any value of a. Check this in the following cases by computing the definite integral and then taking its derivative.

31. $f(x) = x^2$ with $a = 0$

32. $f(x) = 1 + x^3$ with $a = 1$

33. $f(x) = \left(1 + \frac{x}{2}\right)^4$ with $a = -1$

34. $f(x) = (1+2x)^{-4}$ with $a = 0$

Applications

35–40 ▪ Find the change in the state variable between the given times first by solving the differential equation with the given initial conditions and then by using the definite integral.

35. The change of position of a rock between times $t = 1$ and $t = 5$ with position following the differential equation $\frac{dp}{dt} = -9.8t - 5.0$ and initial condition $p(0) = 200$. Here t is measured in seconds and p in meters.

36. The amount a fish grows between ages $t = 1$ and $t = 5$ if it follows the differential equation $\frac{dL}{dt} = 6.48e^{-0.09t}$ with initial condition $L(0) = 5.0$. Here t is measured in years and L in centimeters.

37. The amount a fish grows between ages $t = 0.5$ and $t = 1.5$ if it follows the differential equation $\frac{dL}{dt} = 64.3e^{-1.19t}$ with initial condition $L(0) = 5.0$. Here t is measured in years and L in centimeters.

38. The number of new AIDS cases between 1985 and 1987 if the number of AIDS cases follows $\frac{dA}{dt} = 523.8(t - 1981)^2$ with initial condition $A(1981) = 13,400$. Here t is measured in years.

39. The amount of chemical produced between times $t = 5$ and $t = 10$ if the amount P follows $\frac{dP}{dt} = \frac{5}{1+2.0t}$ with initial condition $P(0.0) = 2.0$. Here t is measured in minutes and P in moles.

40. The amount of chemical produced between times $t = 5$ and $t = 10$ if the amount P follows $\frac{dP}{dt} = 5.0e^{-2.0t}$ with initial condition $P(0.0) = 2.0$. Here t is measured in minutes and P in moles.

41–46 ▪ Check the summation property for the solutions of the differential equations by showing that the change in value of the whole interval is equal to the change during the first half of the interval plus the change during the second half of the interval.

41. The position of a rock obeys the differential equation $\frac{dp}{dt} = -9.8t - 5.0$ with initial condition $p(0) = 200$ (as in Exercise 35.) Show that the distance moved between times $t = 1$ and $t = 5$ is equal to the sum of the distance moved between $t = 1$ and $t = 3$ and the distance moved between $t = 3$ and $t = 5$.

42. The growth of a fish obeys the differential equation $\frac{dL}{dt} = 6.48e^{-0.09t}$ with initial condition $L(0) = 5.0$ (as in Exercise 36.) Show that the growth between times $t = 1$ and $t = 5$ is equal to the sum of the growth between $t = 1$ and $t = 3$ and the growth between $t = 3$ and $t = 5$.

43. The growth of a fish obeys the differential equation $\frac{dL}{dt} = 64.3e^{-1.19t}$ with initial condition $L(0) = 5.0$ (as in Exercise 37.) Show that the growth between times $t = 0.5$ and $t = 1.5$ is equal to the sum of the growth between $t = 0.5$ and $t = 1.0$ and the growth between $t = 1.0$ and $t = 1.5$.

44. The number of AIDS cases obeys $\frac{dA}{dt} = 523.8(t - 1981)^2$ with initial condition $A(1981) = 13,400$ (as in Exercise 38.) Show that the number of new cases between times $t = 1985$ and $t = 1987$ is equal to the sum of the number of new cases between $t = 1985$ and $t = 1986$ and the number of new cases between $t = 1986$ and $t = 1987$.

45. The amount of chemical obeys $\frac{dP}{dt} = \frac{5}{1+2.0t}$ with initial condition $P(0) = 2.0$ (as in Exercise 39.) Show that the amount produced between times $t = 5$ and $t = 10$ is equal to the sum of the amount produced between $t = 5$ and $t = 7.5$ and the amount produced between $t = 7.5$ and $t = 10$.

46. The amount of chemical obeys $\frac{dP}{dt} = 5.0e^{-2.0t}$ with initial condition $P(0) = 2.0$ (as in Exercise 40.) Show that the amount produced between times $t = 5$ and $t = 10$ is equal to the sum of the amount produced between $t = 5$ and $t = 7.5$ and the amount produced between $t = 7.5$ and $t = 10$.

47–48 ▪ Two rockets are shot from the ground. Each has a different upward acceleration and a different amount of fuel. After the fuel runs out, each rocket falls with an acceleration of -9.8 m/s^2. For each rocket:

a. Write down and solve differential equations describing the velocity and position of the rocket while it still has fuel.

b. Find the velocity and height of the rocket when it runs out of fuel.

c. Write down and solve differential equations describing the velocity and position of the rocket after it has run out of fuel. What is the initial condition for each?

d. Find the maximum height reached by the rocket. Does it rise more while it has fuel or after the fuel has ran out? Why?

e. Find the velocity when it hits the ground.

47. The upward acceleration is 12.0 m/s^2 and it has 10 s worth of fuel.

48. The upward acceleration is 2.0 m/s^2 and it has 60 s worth of fuel.

Computer Exercises

49. Imagine that toward the end of the universe, acceleration due to gravity begins to break down. Suppose that

$$a = -9.8\frac{1}{1+t}$$

where time is measured in seconds after the beginning of the end. An object begins falling from 10.0 m above the ground.

a. Find the velocity at time t.

b. Find the position at time t.

c. Graph acceleration, velocity, and position on the same graph. Which of these measurements are integrals of each other?

d. When will this object hit the ground?

50. Suppose the volume of water in a vessel obeys the differential equation

$$\frac{dV}{dt} = f(t) = 1 + 3t + 3t^2$$

with $V(0) = 0$.

a. Graph the functions f and V for $t = 0$ to $t = 2$ and label the curves.

b. Find the volume at time $t = 10$. What is the definite integral that has the same value? Shade the area on your graph from part **a** and write the associated integral.

c. Define a function $A(T)$ that gives the **average** rate of change of volume as a function of time (the total volume added between times $t = 0$ and $t = T$ divided by the elapsed time). Graph this on the same graph as $f(t)$. Label the curves (and write the formula for $A(t)$ as a definite integral). Why is the average rate A greater than the instantaneous rate f?

d. Graph $f(t)$ between $t = 0$ and $t = 10$ and the constant function with rate equal to the average at time $T = 10$. What is the area under the line? Does it match what you found in part **b**? Why should it? Mark the point where the average and instantaneous rates are equal. Use your computer to solve for this point.

4.6 Applications of Integrals

In this section, we introduce several of the remarkable applications of the definite integral. First, we notice that the graph describing the Riemann sum can be interpreted geometrically as a way to approximate the **area under a curve.** In fact, geometric problems of this sort provided the motivation for Archimedes' near discovery of the integral about 2000 years ago, long before Newton introduced the study of differential equations. The idea of chopping quantities into small bits, adding them up with Riemann sums, and computing exact answers with the definite integral has many other applications, including finding the **average value** of a function and finding the total mass from a **density.**

Integrals and Areas

Suppose we want to find the area under the curve $f(x) = x^2$ between $x = 0$ and $x = 1$ (Figure 4.6.41). We can approximate the area with little rectangles, producing a picture identical to those used to find the left-hand Riemann sum (Figure 4.4.1). In particular,

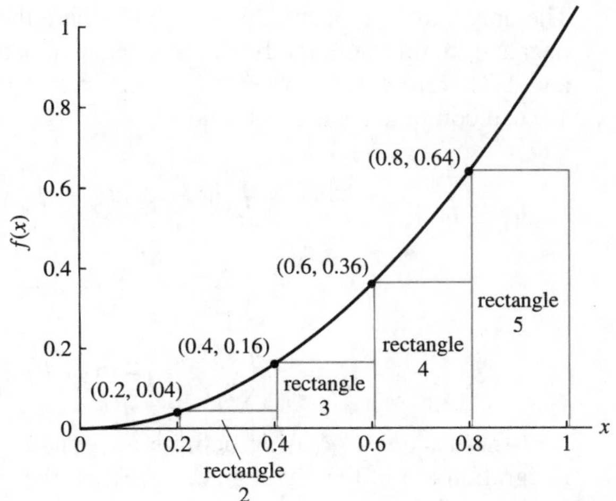

FIGURE 4.6.41
The area under $f(x) = x^2$

when we break the area into five rectangles as shown, their areas match the values found in computing the left-hand estimate.

Rectangle	Base	Height	Area	Total
1	0.2	0.0	0.0	0.0
2	0.2	0.04	0.008	0.008
3	0.2	0.16	0.032	0.040
4	0.2	0.36	0.072	0.112
5	0.2	0.64	0.128	0.240

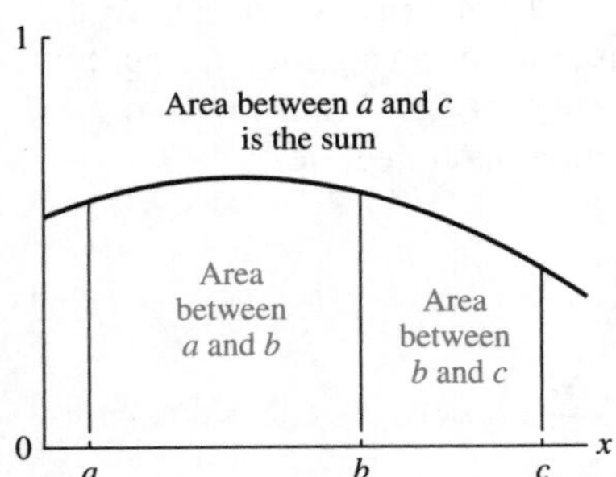

FIGURE 4.6.42
Areas and the summation property of definite integrals

Because the Riemann sums converge both to the area and to the definite integral,

$$\left(\text{area under } f(x) = x^2 \text{ between 0 and 1}\right) = \int_0^1 x^2 dx$$

We have already computed this integral several times, finding the pleasingly simple answer of $1/3$.

In general, we can find the area under the positive curve $f(x)$ from a to b by computing the definite integral between the limits of integration:

$$(\text{area under } f(x) \text{ between } a \text{ and } b) = \int_a^b f(x)\, dx \qquad (4.6.1)$$

The summation property of the definite integral (Theorem 4.5) also has a convenient geometric interpretation (Figure 4.6.42). The area between a and c is the sum of the area between a and b and the area between b and c.

Areas are positive, but definite integrals can give negative values. How are these interpreted?

Example 4.6.1 What to Do with a Negative Area

The integral

$$\int_0^2 \left(x^2 - x\right) dx$$

does not give the sum of the two shaded areas in Figure 4.6.43 but *subtracts* the area below the x-axis from the area above the x-axis.

To find the total shaded area, it is necessary to integrate the *absolute value* of the function, or

$$\int_0^2 |x^2 - x| dx$$

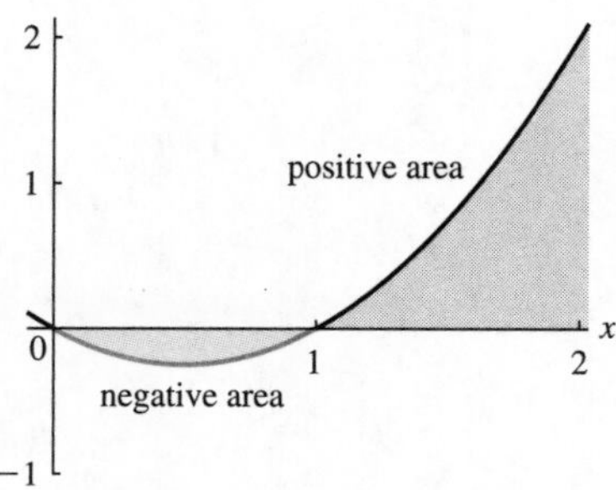

FIGURE 4.6.43
Positive and negative area

The only way to evaluate this is to find where the integrand is positive and where it is negative. In this case, the function is negative between 0 and 1 and positive between 1 and 2. Therefore, $|x^2 - x| = x - x^2$ for $0 \le x \le 1$ and $|x^2 - x| = x^2 - x$ for $1 \le x \le 2$. We can compute the area as follows:

$$\int_0^2 |x^2 - x| dx = \int_0^1 (x - x^2) dx + \int_1^2 (x^2 - x) dx$$
$$= \left(\frac{x^2}{2} - \frac{x^3}{3}\right)\Bigg|_0^1 + \left(\frac{x^3}{3} - \frac{x^2}{2}\right)\Bigg|_1^2$$
$$= \left(\frac{1}{2} - \frac{1}{3}\right) - (0 - 0) + \left(\frac{8}{3} - 2\right) - \left(\frac{1}{3} - \frac{1}{2}\right) = 1$$

Another quirk of using definite integrals to find areas arises when the limits of integration are in the "wrong" order: when the "lower" limit is a larger number than the "upper" limit.

Example 4.6.2 What to Do When the Limits of Integration Are in the Wrong Order

For example,

$$\int_1^0 t^2 dt = \frac{t^3}{3}\Big|_1^0 = 0 - \frac{1}{3} = -\frac{1}{3}$$

The answer is negative, because definite integrals treat left to right as the positive direction and models areas measured from right to left as being taken away. When computing areas, make sure that the limits of integration are in the right order.

When finding the indefinite integrals of complicated functions, we often use substitution. Substitution works for definite integrals but requires an additional step. Suppose we wish to find the area under the curve $f(t) = (1 + 2t)^2$ from $t = 0$ to $t = 1$ (Figure 4.6.44a). One way is to multiply out the function and integrate:

$$\int_0^1 (1 + 2t)^2 dt = \int_0^1 (1 + 4t + 4t^2) dt$$
$$= \left(t + 2t^2 + \frac{4t^3}{3}\right)\Bigg|_0^1$$
$$= 1 + 2 + \frac{4}{3} \approx 4.333$$

To use substitution, we employ a modified version of Algorithm 4.2.

Algorithm 4.4 Computing a Definite Integral with Substitution

1. Define a new variable as some function of the old variable.
2. Take the derivative of the new variable with respect to the old variable.

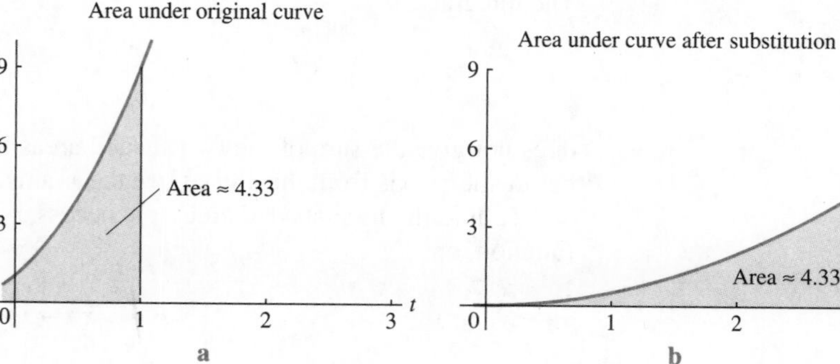

FIGURE 4.6.44
Computing an area with substitution

3. Treat the derivative as a fraction and move the dx to the other side.
4. Put everything in the integral in terms of the new variable.
5. Change the limits of integration into the new variable.
6. Try to integrate.

Example 4.6.3 Using Integration by Substitution to Compute an Area

In the example $\int_0^1 (1+2t)^2 dt$:

1. Set $u = 1 + 2t$
2. $\frac{du}{dt} = 2$
3. $du = 2dt$ or $dt = \frac{du}{2}$
4. Put the integrand in terms of u:

$$(1+2t)^2 dt = u^2 \frac{du}{2}$$

5. The new step is to *change the limits of integration.* The original limits are from $t = 0$ to $t = 1$. When $t = 0$, $u = 1 + 2 \cdot 0 = 1$, and when $t = 1$, $u = 1 + 2 \cdot 1 = 3$. The new integral, after substituting for every t, is

$$\int_1^3 \frac{u^2}{2} du$$

6. Work this out to find

$$\int_1^3 \frac{u^2}{2} du = \frac{u^3}{6}\Big|_1^3 = \frac{27}{6} - \frac{1}{6} \approx 4.333$$

We do not have to convert back to the old variable at the end because the answer is a number rather than a function. The area under the graph of this function is shown in Figure 4.6.44b. The height of the u curve is half that of the t curve, but its width has been doubled, thus preserving the area.

Integrals and Averages

Example 4.6.4 Finding an Average Rate

Suppose that water is flowing into a vessel at a rate of $(1 - e^{-t})$ cm^3/s for the 2 s between $t = 0.0$ and $t = 2.0$. What is the *average* rate at which water enters during this time? The average is the total amount of water that enters divided by the time, or

$$\text{average rate} = \frac{\text{total water entering}}{\text{total time}}$$

The total amount of water that enters is

$$\begin{aligned}\text{total water entering} &= \int_{0.0}^{2.0} (1 - e^{-t}) dt \\ &= (t + e^{-t})\Big|_{0.0}^{2.0} \\ &= 2.0 + e^{-2.0} - (0.0 + e^{-0.0}) \approx 1.135\end{aligned}$$

The average rate is

$$\text{average rate} \approx \frac{\text{total water entering}}{\text{total time}} = \frac{1.135}{2.0} \approx 0.568$$

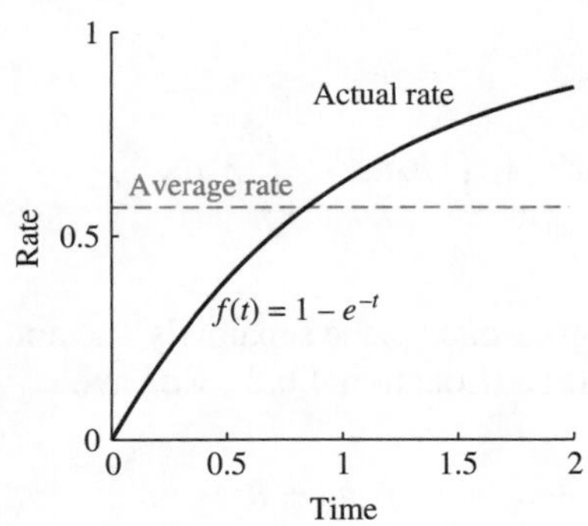

FIGURE 4.6.45
The average value of a rate

(Figure 4.6.45). If water enters at the constant rate of 0.568 cm^3/s for 2.0 s, then 1.135 cm^3 would enter, equal to the amount of water that entered at the variable rate $1 - e^{-t}$

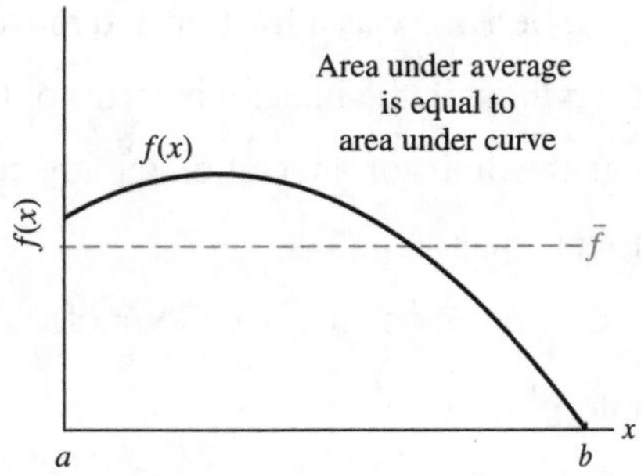

FIGURE 4.6.46
The average value in general

during those same 2.0 s. Geometrically, the area under the horizontal line at 0.568 is equal to the area under the curve $1 - e^{-t}$.

The general formula for the average value of a function f, often denoted by $\bar{f}$ on the interval from a to b, is

$$\text{average value of } f = \frac{1}{b-a}\int_a^b f(x)dx \tag{4.6.2}$$

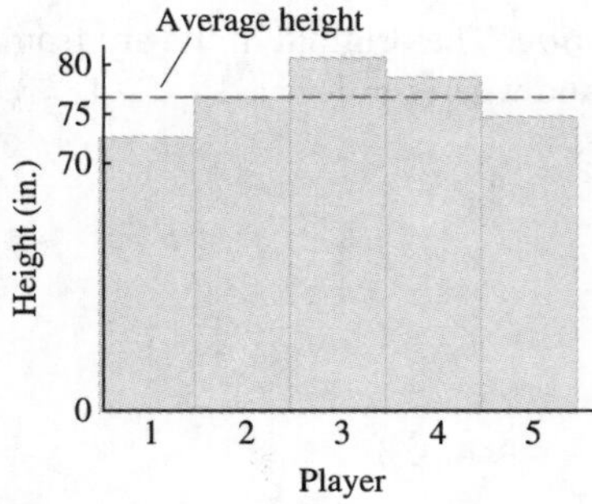

FIGURE 4.6.47
The average height of a starting basketball team

The area under the horizontal line representing the average is equal to the area under the curve (Figure 4.6.46).

How does this compare with the usual meaning of average? Suppose you wanted to find the average height of a starting basketball team. If h_i denotes the height of player i, the average $\bar{h}$ is ordinarily found by adding up the heights and dividing by 5 (the number of starters), or

$$\bar{h} = \frac{1}{5}\sum_{i=1}^{5} h_i$$

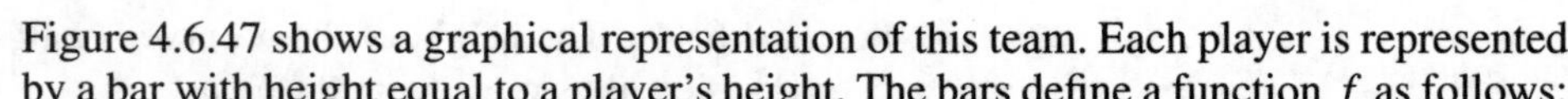

Figure 4.6.47 shows a graphical representation of this team. Each player is represented by a bar with height equal to a player's height. The bars define a function f as follows:

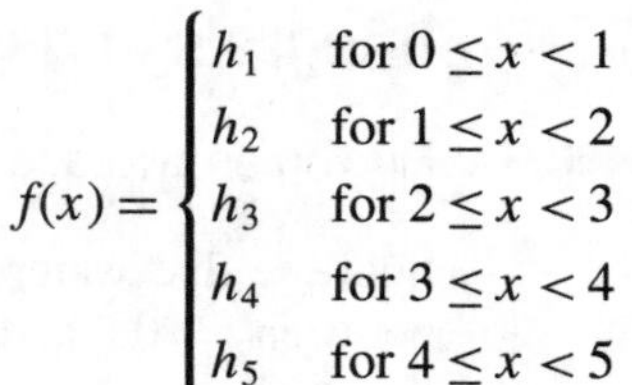

$$f(x) = \begin{cases} h_1 & \text{for } 0 \le x < 1 \\ h_2 & \text{for } 1 \le x < 2 \\ h_3 & \text{for } 2 \le x < 3 \\ h_4 & \text{for } 3 \le x < 4 \\ h_5 & \text{for } 4 \le x < 5 \end{cases}$$

From this graph, we can find the total height of the team as the integral

$$\begin{aligned} \text{total height} &= \int_0^5 f(x)dx \\ &= \int_0^1 h_1 dx + \int_1^2 h_2 dx + \int_2^3 h_3 dx + \int_3^4 h_4 dx + \int_4^5 h_5 dx \\ &= h_1 + h_2 + h_3 + h_4 + h_5 \end{aligned}$$

To integrate a function that is defined in pieces, integrate each piece separately and add up the results. Substituting the definition of the average (Equation 4.6.2), we have

$$\text{average height} = \frac{\text{total height}}{\text{total number}} = \frac{1}{5}(h_1 + h_2 + h_3 + h_4 + h_5)$$

matching the usual result.

Integrals and Mass

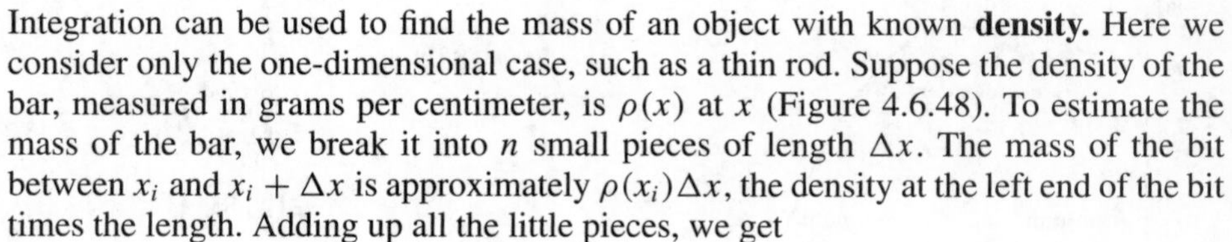

FIGURE 4.6.48
The mass of a bar

Integration can be used to find the mass of an object with known **density.** Here we consider only the one-dimensional case, such as a thin rod. Suppose the density of the bar, measured in grams per centimeter, is $\rho(x)$ at x (Figure 4.6.48). To estimate the mass of the bar, we break it into n small pieces of length Δx. The mass of the bit between x_i and $x_i + \Delta x$ is approximately $\rho(x_i)\Delta x$, the density at the left end of the bit times the length. Adding up all the little pieces, we get

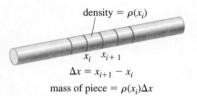

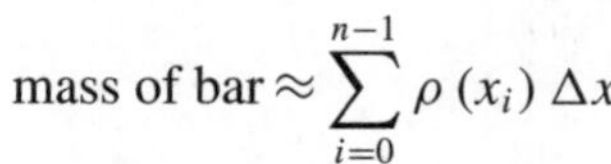

$$\text{mass of bar} \approx \sum_{i=0}^{n-1} \rho(x_i)\,\Delta x$$

This has the exact form of a Riemann sum. The limit as Δx approaches 0 and n approaches infinity is equal to the definite integral (Definition 4.2), so

$$\text{mass of bar} = \int_a^b \rho(x)dx \qquad \textbf{(4.6.3)}$$

Example 4.6.5 Finding the Mass of a Bar

Consider a 100-centimeter vertical bar composed of a substance that has settled and become denser near the ground. Let z denote the height above ground, and suppose that the density is given by

$$\rho(z) = e^{-0.01z}$$

in grams per centimeter. The mass is

$$\begin{aligned}\int_0^{100} e^{-0.01z}dz &= \frac{1}{-0.01}\left(e^{-0.01z}\right)\Big|_0^{100}\\ &= -100\left(e^{-0.01z}\right)\Big|_0^{100}\\ &= -100\left(e^{-0.01\cdot 100}\right) - \left[-100\left(e^{-0.01\cdot 0}\right)\right]\\ &= 100\left(1 - e^{-1.0}\right) \approx 63.21\end{aligned}$$

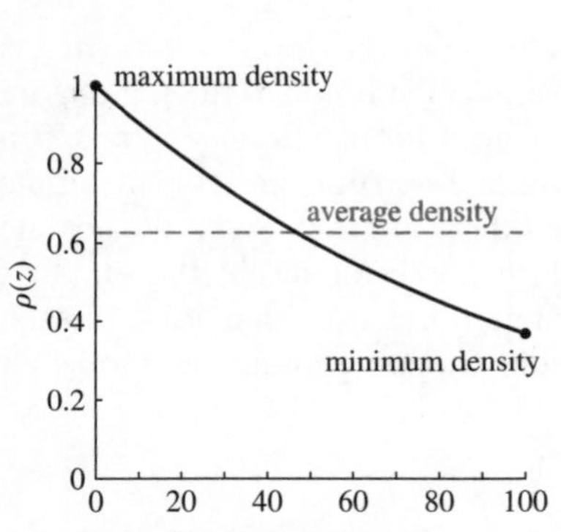

FIGURE 4.6.49
The average density of a bar

Does this result make sense? The density at the bottom of the bar is $\rho(0) = 1.0$ g/cm. If the entire bar had this maximum density, the mass would be 100 g. The density at the top of the bar is $\rho(100) = e^{-1} \approx 0.368$ g/cm, so the mass of the bar would be 36.8 g if the entire bar had this minimum density. Our result lies between these extremes. Furthermore,

$$\text{average density} = \frac{\text{total mass}}{\text{total length}} = \frac{\int_0^{100} \rho(x)dx}{100} \approx \frac{63.2}{100.0} = 0.632$$

The result lies between the minimum density of 0.368 and the maximum of 1.0 (Figure 4.6.49).

Example 4.6.6 Counting Otters with Integration

The same technique can be used to find totals when density is measured in other units. Suppose the density of otters along the coast of California is

$$f(x) = 3.0 \times 10^{-4}x(1000 - x)$$

in otters per mile, where x is measured in miles from the Mexican border and can take on values between 0 and 1000. The population density takes on a maximum value of 75 otters/mile halfway up the coast at $x = 500$ and a minimum value of 0 at $x = 0$ and $x = 1000$ (Figure 4.6.50).

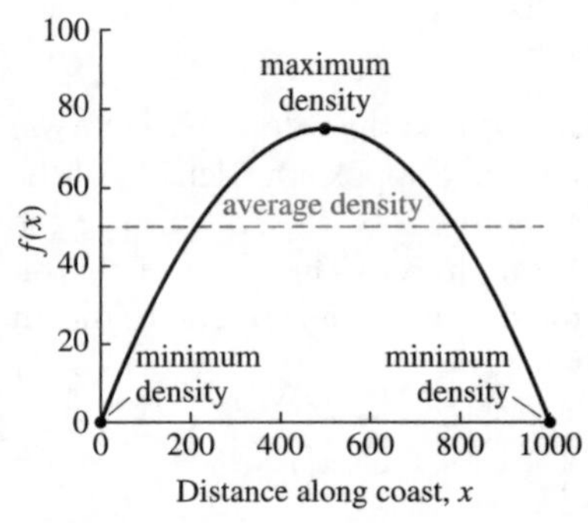

FIGURE 4.6.50
The average density of otters

The total number T is the definite integral of the density, or

$$
\begin{aligned}
T &= \int_0^{1000} 3.0 \times 10^{-4} x(1000 - x)dx \\
&= \int_0^{1000} (0.3x - 3.0 \times 10^{-4}x^2)dx \\
&= 0.15x^2\Big|_0^{1000} - 1.0 \times 10^{-4}x^3\Big|_0^{1000} \\
&= 1.5 \times 10^5 - 1.0 \times 10^5 \\
&= 0.5 \times 10^5 = 50,000 \text{ otters}
\end{aligned}
$$

The average density is

$$
\begin{aligned}
\text{average density} &= \frac{\text{total number}}{\text{total distance}} \\
&= \frac{50{,}000 \text{ otters}}{1000 \text{ miles}} \\
&= 50.0 \frac{\text{otters}}{\text{mile}}
\end{aligned}
$$

This value lies between the maximum density of 75 otters/mile and the minimum density of 0 otters/mile. The average value is *not* the average of these minimum and maximum values.

Summary The definite integral can be used to find the **area under a curve.** The area computed is negative if the value of the function itself is negative or if the limits of integration are in decreasing order. Integration by substitution, introduced for indefinite integrals, can be extended to definite integrals but requires the additional step of expressing the limits of integration in terms of the new variable. We used the definite integral to calculate **average** values of functions by dividing the integral (the total amount) by the length of the interval. Similarly, we computed masses or total numbers from **densities.** In each case, the underlying idea is that of the Riemann sum: chopping things up into small pieces and adding the results.

4.6 Exercises

Mathematical Techniques

1–6 ▪ Find the areas under the following curves. If you use substitution, draw a graph to compare the original area with that in transformed variables.

1. Area under $f(x) = 3x^3$ from $x = 0$ to $x = 3$.
2. Area under $g(x) = e^x$ from $x = 0$ to $x = \ln(2)$.
3. Area under $h(x) = e^{x/2}$ from $x = 0$ to $x = \ln(2)$.
4. Area under $f(t) = (1 + 3t)^3$ from $t = 0$ to $t = 2$.
5. Area under $G(y) = (3 + 4y)^{-2}$ from $y = 0$ to $y = 2$.
6. Area under $s(z) = \sin(z + \pi)$ from $z = 0$ to $z = \pi$.

7–12 ▪ The definite integral can be used to find the area between two curves. In each case:

a. Sketch the graphs of the two functions over the given range, and shade the area between the curves.

b. Sketch the graph of the difference between the two curves. The area *under* this curve matches the area *between* the original curves.

c. Find the area under the difference curve (remembering to use absolute value).

7. Find the area between $f(x) = 2x$ and $g(x) = x^2$ for $0 \le x \le 2$.
8. Find the area between $f(x) = e^x$ and $g(x) = x + 1$ for $-1 \le x \le 1$.
9. Find the area between $f(x) = 2x$ and $g(x) = x^2$ for $0 \le x \le 4$.
10. Find the area between $f(x) = x^2$ and $g(x) = x^3$ for $0 \le x \le 2$.
11. Find the area between $f(x) = e^x$ and $g(x) = \frac{e^{2x}}{2}$ for $0 \le x \le 1$.

12. Find the area between $f(x) = \sin(2x)$ and $g(x) = \cos(2x)$ for $0 \le x \le \pi$.

13–16 ▪ Find the average value of the following functions over the given range. Sketch a graph of the function along with a horizontal line at the average to make sure that your answer makes sense.

13. x^2 for $0 \le x \le 3$

14. $\frac{1}{x}$ for $0.5 \le x \le 2.0$

15. $x - x^3$ for $-1 \le x \le 1$

16. $\sin(2x)$ for $0 \le x \le \pi/2$

17–18 ▪ Use integration by parts to evaluate the following as definite integrals.

17. Find the area under the curve $g(x) = x\ln(x)$ for $1 \le x \le 2$. Sketch a graph to see whether your answer makes sense.

18. Find the area under the curve $g(x) = x\sin(2\pi x)$ for $0 \le x \le 2$. Sketch a graph to see whether your answer makes sense.

19–20 ▪ We have used little vertically oriented rectangles to compute areas. There is no reason why little horizontal rectangles cannot be used. Here are the steps to find the area under the curve $y = f(x)$ from $x = 0$ to $x = 1$ by using such horizontal rectangles.

a. Draw a picture with five horizontal rectangles, each of height 0.2, approximately filling the region to the right of the curve and to the left of the line $x = 1$.

b. Calculate an upper and a lower estimate of the length of each rectangle.

c. Use the areas of these rectangles to find upper and lower estimates of the area.

d. Think now of a very thin rectangle at height y. How long is the rectangle?

e. Write down a definite integral expression for the area.

f. Evaluate the integral and check that the answer is correct.

19. With $f(x) = x^2$.

20. With $f(x) = \sqrt{x}$.

21–22 ▪ Archimedes developed the basic idea of integration to find the areas of geometric figures. Often, this involves building regions out of small pieces with shapes more complicated than rectangles.

21. Use the fact that the perimeter of a circle of radius r is $2\pi r$ to find the area of a circle with radius 1. Think of the circular region as being built out of little rings with some small width Δr.

22. Use the fact that the area of a circle of radius r is πr^2 to find the volume of a cone of height 1 that has radius r at a height r. Think of the cone as being built of a stack of little circular disks with some small thickness Δr.

23–26 ▪ Some books define the natural log function with a definite integral:

$$l(a) = \int_1^a \frac{1}{x}\,dx$$

Using this definition, we can prove the laws of logarithms ("Laws of Exponents and Logs," Section 1.7).

23. Show that $l(6) - l(3) = l(2)$. (Use the summation property of the definite integral to write the difference as an integral, and then use the substitution $y = \frac{x}{3}$.)

24. Find the integral from a to $2a$ by following the same steps as in Exercise 23 (make the substitution $y = \frac{x}{a}$).

25. Show that $l(10^2) = 2 \cdot l(10)$. (Try the substitution $y = \sqrt{x}$ in $\int_1^{10^2} \frac{1}{x}dx$.)

26. Show that $l(a^b) = b \cdot l(a)$. (Try the substitution $y = \sqrt[b]{x}$ in $\int_1^{a^b} \frac{1}{x}dx$.)

Applications

27–28 ▪ The average of a step function computed with the definite integral matches the average computed in the usual way. Test this in the following situations by finding the average of the values, first directly and then as the integral of a step function.

27. Suppose a math class has four equally weighted tests. A student gets 60 on the first test, 70 on the second, 80 on the third, and 90 on the last.

28. A math class has 20 students. In a quiz worth 10 points, 4 students get 6 points, 7 students get 7, 5 students get 8, 3 students get 9, and 1 student gets 10.

29–32 ▪ Suppose water is entering a tank at a rate of $g(t) = 360t - 39t^2 + t^3$ where g is measured in liters per hour and t is measured in hours. The rate is 0 at times 0, 15, and 24.

29. Find the total amount of water entering during the first 15 h, from $t = 0$ to $t = 15$. Find the average rate at which water entered during this time.

30. Find the total amount and average rate from $t = 15$ to $t = 24$.

31. Find the total amount and average rate from $t = 0$ to $t = 24$.

32. Suppose that energy is produced at a rate of

$$E(t) = |g(t)|$$

in joules per hour. Find the total energy generated from $t = 0$ to $t = 24$. Find the average rate of energy production.

33–34 ▪ Several very skinny 2.0-m-long snakes are collected in the Amazon. Each has density of $\rho(x)$ given by the following formulas, where ρ is measured in grams per centimeter and x is measured in centimeters from the tip of the tail. For each snake:

a. Find the minimum and maximum density of the snake. Where does the maximum occur?

b. Find the total mass of the snake.

c. Find the average density of the snake. How does this compare with the minimum and maximum?

d. Graph the density and average.

33. $\rho(x) = 1.0 + 2.0 \times 10^{-8}x^2(300 - x)$

34. $\rho(x) = 1.0 + 2.0 \times 10^{-8}x^2(240 - x)$

35–36 ▪ A piece of *E. coli* DNA has about 4.7×10^6 nucleotides and is about 1.6×10^6 nm long. The genetic code consists of four nucleotides, called A, C, G, and T. For each of the following cases:

a. Use the given information to find the formula for the number of A's, C's, G's, and T's per thousand as a function of distance along the DNA strand.

b. Find the total number of A's, C's, G's, and T's in the DNA.

c. Find the mean number of A's, C's, G's, and T's in the DNA per thousand.

35. Suppose that the number of A's per thousand increases linearly from 150 at one end of the DNA strand to 300 at the other. The number of C's per thousand decreases linearly from 350 at one end to 200 at the other, and the number of G's per thousand increases linearly from 220 at one end to 320 at the other. The remainder is made up of T's.

36. Suppose that the number of A's per thousand increases linearly from 200 at one end of the DNA strand to 250 at the other. The number of C's per thousand increases linearly from 250 at one end to 300 at the other, and the number of G's per thousand decreases linearly from 300 at one end to 200 at the other. The remainder is made up of T's.

37–40 ▪ Suppose water is entering a series of vessels at the given rate. In each case, find the total amount of water entering during the first second and the average rate during that time. Compare the average rate with the rate at the "average time," at $t = 0.5$ halfway through the time period from 0 to 1. In which case is the average rate greater than the rate at the average time? Graph the flow rate function, and mark the flow rate at the average time. Can you guess what it is about the shape of the graph that determines how the average rate compares with the rate at the average time?

37. Water is entering at a rate of $t^3 \pm \text{cm}^3/\text{s}$.

38. Water is entering at a rate of $\sqrt{t}$ cm^3/s.

39. Water is entering at a rate of t cm^3/s.

40. Water is entering at a rate of $4t(1-t)$ cm^3/s.

Computer Exercise

41. Find the area between the two curves $f(x) = \cos(x)$ and $g(x) = 0.1x$ for $0 \le x \le 10$ (as in Exercises 7–12).

a. Graph the two functions. There should be three separate regions between them.

b. Have your computer find where each region begins and ends.

c. Integrate to find the area of each region.

d. Add the areas.

4.7 Improper Integrals

So far, we have considered only definite integrals of functions that do not approach infinity between finite limits of integration. Integrals of this sort are called **proper integrals. Improper integrals** are of two types: integrals with infinite limits of integration and integrals of functions that approach infinity somewhere within the limits of integration. We now learn how to compute and apply improper integrals.

Infinite Limits of Integration

"Infinite" measurements cannot crop up in biological experiments. Nonetheless, infinity is a useful mathematical abstraction of "very long" or "very far." Consider again the equation for chemical production with exponentially declining rate (Equation 4.1.2),

$$\frac{dP}{dt} = e^{-t}$$

in moles per second. The amount of product produced between $t = 0$ and $t = T$ is given by the definite integral

$$\text{production between 0 and } T = \int_0^T e^{-t}\,dt$$

The longer we wait, the more product has been produced. Let P_∞ denote the amount that would be produced if the experiment ran forever. We would like to write

$$P_\infty = \int_0^\infty e^{-t}\,dt$$

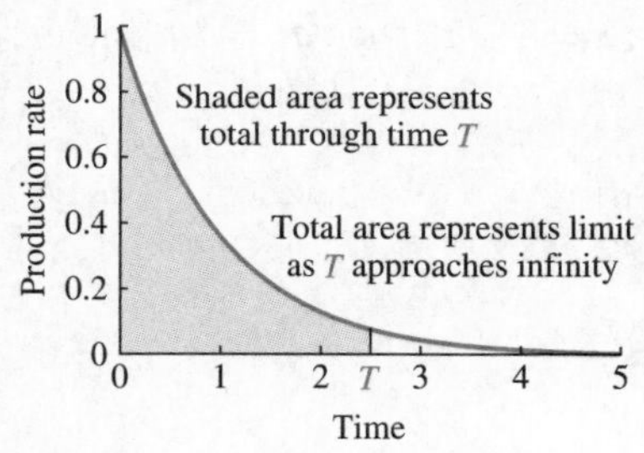

FIGURE 4.7.51

Computing an integral with infinite limits of integration

To be honest, however, we have never defined what this expression means. We *defined* the definite integral to be the limit of Riemann sums. Computing Riemann sums requires breaking the region between the limits of integration into n equally sized regions. But the infinite region from 0 to infinity cannot be broken into n finite regions of equal size. The Riemann sum approach never even gets started.

Instead, we can think of this **improper integral** as the *limit* of **proper integrals** with the formula

$$\int_0^{\infty} e^{-t}dt = \lim_{T\to\infty}\int_0^{T} e^{-t}dt$$

This formula captures the spirit of what we want. The proper integral gives the amount of production up to time T, and the limit enables us to make T "very large" (Figure 4.7.51). In this case,

$$\int_0^{T} e^{-t}dt = -e^{-t}\Big|_0^T = -e^{-T} + 1$$

Therefore,

$$\begin{aligned}\int_0^{\infty} e^{-t}dt &= \lim_{T\to\infty}\left(1 - e^{-T}\right)\\ &= \lim_{T\to\infty} 1 - \lim_{T\to\infty} e^{-T}\\ &= 1 - 0 = 1.0\end{aligned}$$

Exactly 1 mol of the product would be created after an infinite amount of time. If we wait for a "long time," such as 10 s, the exact amount is

$$1 - e^{-10.0} \approx 0.99995$$

quite close to the limit.

Formally, we define

Definition 4.3 The improper integral of the function f from a to ∞ is

$$\int_a^{\infty} f(t)dt = \lim_{T\to\infty}\int_a^{T} f(t)dt$$

Improper Integrals: Examples

Our definition does not guarantee that the limit is finite. Nothing mathematical prevents the definite integral from 0 to T from getting larger and larger as T approaches infinity. Consider a different chemical produced at the diminishing rate

$$\frac{dQ}{dt} = \frac{1}{1+t}$$

again in moles per second. This rate decreases to 0 more slowly than the exponential function (Section 3.6). How much product would this reaction produce after a long time?

The total product produced, Q_∞, is computed with the improper integral

$$\begin{aligned}Q_\infty &= \int_0^{\infty} \frac{1}{1+t}dt\\ &= \lim_{T\to\infty}\int_0^{T} \frac{1}{1+t}dt\end{aligned}$$

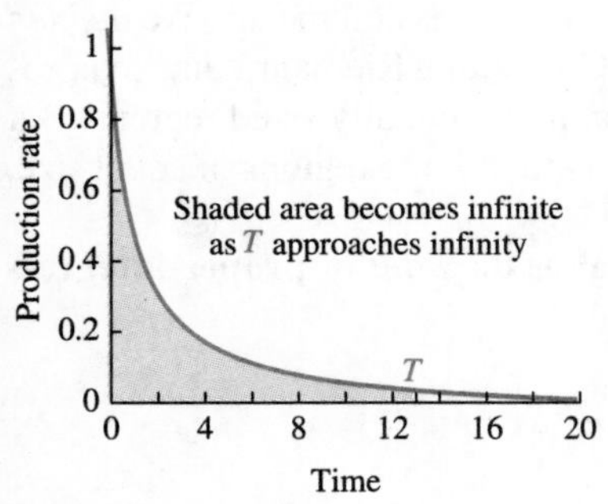

FIGURE 4.7.52

A divergent integral where the integrand decreases to 0 slowly

To compute this integral, we can use the substitution $u = 1 + t$. Then $dt = du$, and the limits of integration of $t = 0$ to $t = T$ become $u = 1$ to $u = 1 + T$. Then

$$\begin{aligned} Q_\infty &= \lim_{T\to\infty} \int_0^T \frac{1}{1+t} dt \\ &= \lim_{T\to\infty} \int_1^{T+1} \frac{1}{u} du \\ &= \lim_{T\to\infty} \ln(u)\Big|_1^{T+1} \\ &= \lim_{T\to\infty} \ln(T+1) - 0 \\ &= \infty \end{aligned}$$

If this rule were followed forever, the amount of product would be infinite (Figure 4.7.52). In this case, we say that the integral **diverges.** When the limit exists, we say that the integral **converges.** Such a result might seem absurd and irrelevant. But this very absurdity provides a valuable negative result N: no real system could follow this law indefinitely. Even though the rate gets smaller and smaller, the total production increases without bound.

What laws can be maintained indefinitely without producing an infinite amount of product? Any decreasing function that does not decrease to 0 has an infinite improper integral (Figure 4.7.53) because the total production gets larger and larger without bound. In terms of area, the region under the curve can be thought of as including a rectangle with positive height and an infinite length.

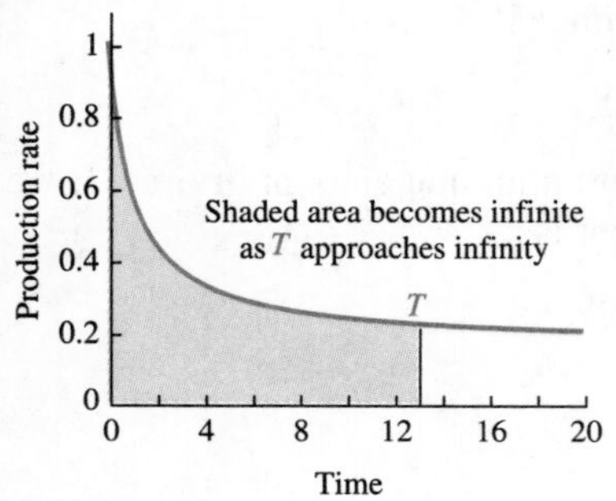

FIGURE 4.7.53

A divergent integral where the integrand does not decrease to 0

Of functions that decrease to 0 as their arguments approach infinity, we have learned to integrate those of the form $\frac{1}{t^p}$ for $p > 0$ and $e^{-\alpha t}$ for $\alpha > 0$. We can use the power rule to compute the integral of $\frac{1}{t^p}$ when $p \neq 1$. (We set the lower limit of integration to 1 to avoid the point $t = 0$ where the integrand approaches infinity.) When $p > 1$,

$$\begin{aligned} \int_1^\infty \frac{1}{t^p} dt &= \lim_{T\to\infty} \int_1^T \frac{1}{t^p} dt \\ &= \lim_{T\to\infty} \frac{t^{1-p}}{1-p}\Big|_1^T \\ &= \lim_{T\to\infty} \frac{T^{1-p}}{1-p} - \frac{1}{1-p} \end{aligned}$$

When $p > 1$, the power $1 - p$ is negative. Therefore, T^{1-p} approaches 0 as T approaches infinity. The improper integral is

$$\begin{aligned} \int_1^\infty \frac{1}{t^p} dt &= \lim_{T\to\infty} \frac{T^{1-p}}{1-p} - \frac{1}{1-p} \\ &= 0 - \frac{1}{1-p} \\ &= \frac{1}{p-1} \end{aligned}$$

This integral converges.

Example 4.7.1 Improper Integrals of Power Functions with $p > 1$

The integral of the function $\frac{1}{t^p}$ for $p = 1.2$ is

$$\int_1^\infty \frac{1}{t^{1.2}} dt = \frac{1}{1.2 - 1} = 5.0$$

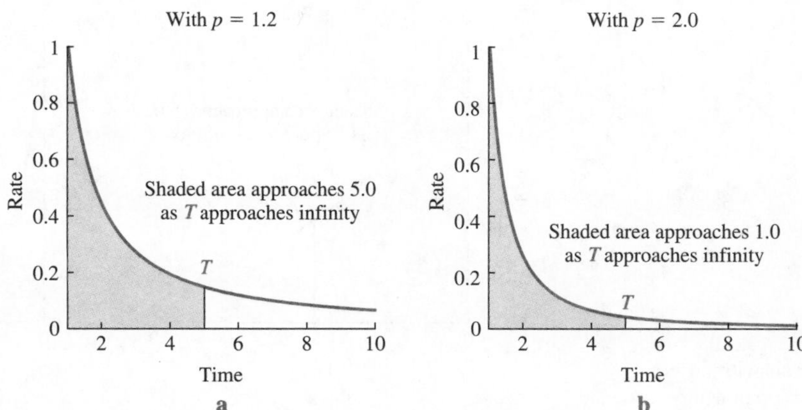

FIGURE 4.7.54
Power functions with $p > 1$

(Figure 4.7.54a). With the larger value $p = 2.0$,

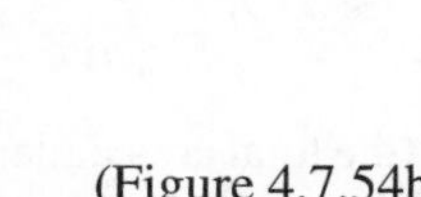

$$\int_1^{\infty} \frac{1}{t^{2.0}} dt = \frac{1}{2.0 - 1} = 1.0$$

(Figure 4.7.54b). The value of the improper integral (the total area under the curve, or the limiting amount of product produced) becomes smaller as the value of p becomes larger.

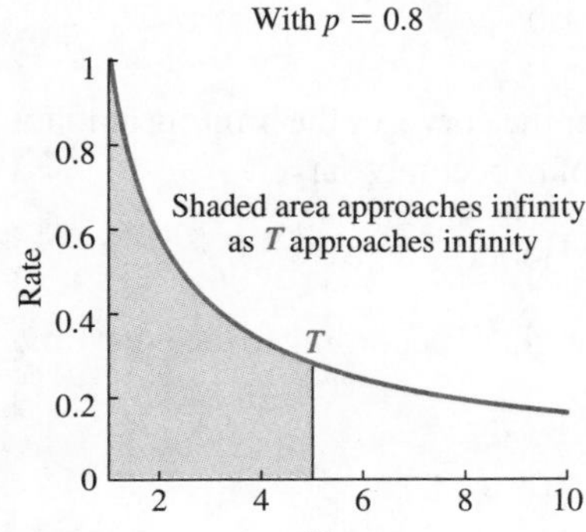

FIGURE 4.7.55
A power function with $p < 1$

With $p < 1$, the integration is the same. But when we take the limit, we find

$$\int_1^{\infty} \frac{1}{t^p} dt = \lim_{T \to \infty} \frac{T^{1-p}}{1-p} - \frac{1}{1-p}$$
$$= \infty$$

because T is taken to the *positive* power $1 - p$ when $p < 1$. This integral diverges. Recall that $\frac{1}{t^p}$ decreases to 0 faster for larger values of p. If the value of p is sufficiently large (greater than 1), the area under the curve is finite. When p is too small (less than 1), the function decreases to 0 more slowly and the area is infinite (Figure 4.7.55).

When the rate decreases exponentially with the formula $e^{-\alpha t}$, the improper integral is

$$\int_0^{\infty} e^{-\alpha t} dt = \lim_{T \to \infty} \int_0^T e^{-\alpha t} dt$$
$$= \lim_{T \to \infty} \int_0^{\alpha T} \frac{e^{-y}}{\alpha} dy$$
$$= \lim_{T \to \infty} -\frac{e^{-y}}{\alpha}\Big|_0^{\alpha T}$$
$$= \lim_{T \to \infty} -\frac{e^{-\alpha T}}{\alpha} + \frac{1}{\alpha}$$
$$= \frac{1}{\alpha}$$

where we used the substitution $y = \alpha t$. This exponential integral converges for every positive value of α, but the integral takes on a larger value for smaller α, as is consistent with the fact that $e^{-\alpha t}$ decreases to 0 more slowly when α is small (Figure 4.7.56).

Example 4.7.2 Improper Integrals of Exponential Functions

The integral of the function $e^{-0.2t}$ is

$$\int_0^{\infty} e^{-0.2t} dt = \frac{1}{0.2} = 5.0$$

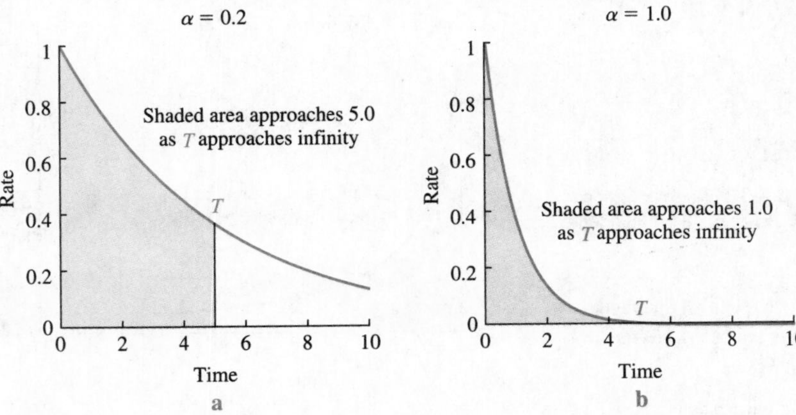

FIGURE 4.7.56
Improper integrals with different parameters in the exponent

With the larger value $\alpha = 1.0$,

$$\int_0^\infty e^{-1.0t}\,dt = \frac{1}{1.0} = 1.0$$

The value of the improper integral (the total area under the curve, or the limiting amount of product produced) becomes smaller as the value of α becomes larger.

Example 4.7.3 Checking Whether a Quantity Will Increase Without Bound

Suppose we wish to know whether a tree growing in height H according to the pure-time differential equation

$$\frac{dH}{dt} = \frac{1}{t^{3/4}}$$

with initial condition $H(1) = 5.0$ will reach arbitrarily large size. The height at time t is

$$H(t) = 5.0 + \int_1^t \frac{1}{s^{3/4}}\,ds$$

where the initial condition $H(0) = 5.0$ is added to the subsequent change. Because the power $3/4$ is less than 1, the integral

$$\int_1^\infty \frac{1}{s^{3/4}}\,ds$$

diverges. Therefore, $H(t)$ approaches a limit of infinity as t becomes large, and this tree would exceed any given height (if it lived long enough). We suspect, however, that it would be knocked over by a hurricane or would just collapse under its own weight if it became too tall.

Applying the Method of Leading Behavior to Improper Integrals The **method of leading behavior** (Section 3.6) can be used to analyze more complicated functions. The idea is that the behavior of the integral is determined by the leading behavior of the integrand, the piece that decreases to 0 most slowly. An alternative approach, called the **comparison test,** compares a given integrand with a known integrand directly.

Example 4.7.4 Using Leading Behavior to Establish that an Integral Diverges

Suppose we wish to know whether the integral

$$\int_1^\infty \left(\frac{1}{t} + \frac{1}{e^t}\right)dt$$

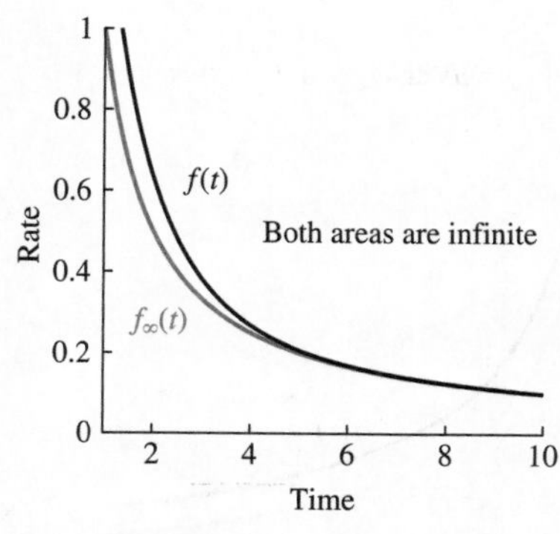

FIGURE 4.7.57
A divergent improper integral checked with the method of leading behavior

converges. The leading behavior of the integrand is the largest part, the part that decreases most slowly. Because power functions always grow more slowly than exponential functions, the leading behavior of $f(t) = \frac{1}{t} + \frac{1}{e^t}$ is

$$f_\infty(t) = \frac{1}{t}.$$

The original integral will converge if the integral of the leading behavior converges. In this case,

$$\int_1^\infty f_\infty(t)dt = \int_1^\infty \frac{1}{t}dt = \infty$$

(Figure 4.7.57). Therefore, the original integral also diverges.

Example 4.7.5 Using Leading Behavior to Establish that an Integral Converges

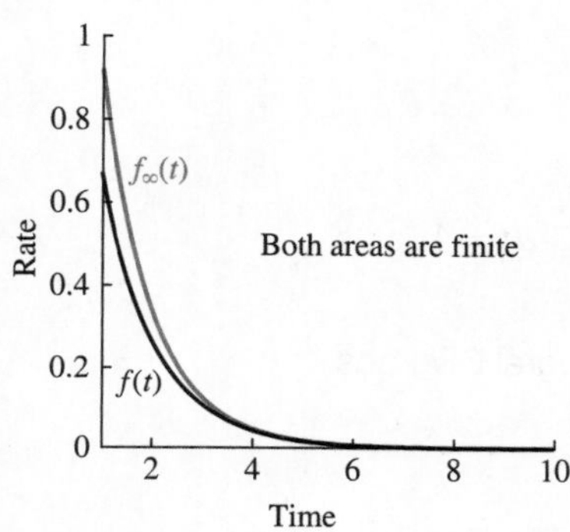

FIGURE 4.7.58
A convergent improper integral checked with the method of leading behavior

Now let's consider the similar-looking integral

$$\int_1^\infty \frac{1}{t + e^t}dt$$

The leading behavior of the integrand can be found by computing the leading behavior of the denominator $t + e^t$. Because the exponential is larger, we replace $t + e^t$ with e^t. The integral of the leading behavior is

$$\int_1^\infty \frac{1}{e^t}dt = \int_1^\infty e^{-t}dt$$

which converges (Figure 4.7.58). It is, however, impossible to compute the value

$$\int_1^\infty \frac{1}{t + e^t}dt$$

exactly without using numerical methods.

The **comparison test** provides an alternative method. If we can compare our function with a simple function, we can often establish that the integral converges or diverges.

The Comparison Test

1. **Proving convergence:** Suppose $0 \le f(x) < g(x)$ for all $x > a$. Then $\int_a^\infty f(x)dx$ converges if $\int_a^\infty g(x)dx$ converges.
2. **Proving divergence:** Suppose $f(x) > g(x) > 0$ for all $x > a$. Then $\int_a^\infty f(x)dx$ diverges if $\int_a^\infty g(x)dx$ diverges.

As shown in Figure 4.7.59a, if the positive function $f(x)$ lies below a positive function $g(x)$ that converges, then $f(x)$ also converges. Conversely, as shown in Figure 4.7.59b, if the positive function $f(x)$ lies above a positive function $g(x)$ that diverges, then $f(x)$ also diverges.

Example 4.7.6 Using the Comparison Test to Establish that an Integral Converges

Consider again the integral

$$\int_1^\infty \frac{1}{t + e^t}dt$$

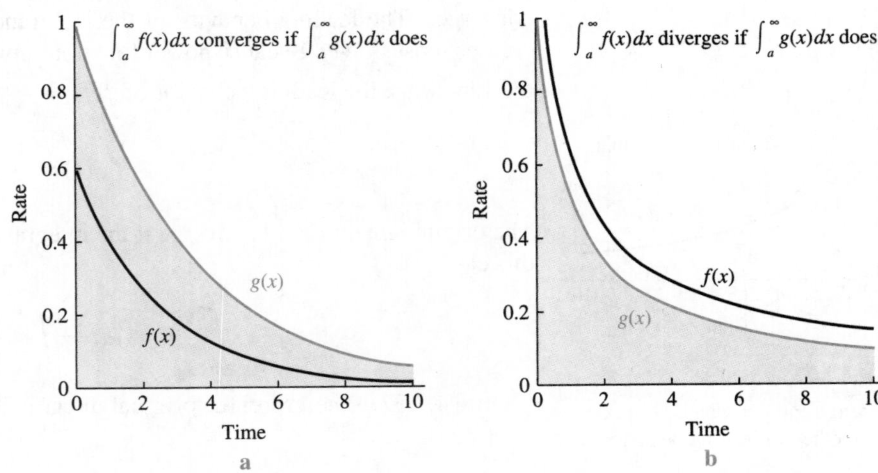

FIGURE 4.7.59
The comparison test with infinite limits of integration

from Example 4.7.5. Because $t > 0$ for all values of t,

$$0 < \frac{1}{t+e^t} < \frac{1}{e^t} = e^{-t}$$

Therefore,

$$0 < \int_1^\infty \frac{1}{t+e^t}dt < \int_1^\infty e^{-t}dt = 1$$

Example 4.7.7 Using the Comparison Test to Establish that an Integral Diverges

Consider evaluating

$$\int_1^\infty \frac{1}{t+\sqrt{t}}$$

For $t > 1$, $\sqrt{t} < t$, so

$$\frac{1}{t+\sqrt{t}} > \frac{1}{t+t} = \frac{1}{2t}$$

Since $\int_1^\infty \frac{1}{2t}dt$ diverges, the original integral diverges also.

Infinite Integrands

Although functions with infinite integrands crop up less frequently in biological problems, it is useful to be familiar with their behavior. Consider trying to find the area under the curve $f(x) = \frac{1}{\sqrt{x}}$ between $x = 0$ and $x = 1$ (Figure 4.7.60). This function approaches infinity at $x \to 0$.

Although one can, with some care, define this integral as a limit of right-hand Riemann sums, we instead use the limit to define and compute this second type of improper integral.

Definition 4.4 If the function f approaches infinity at $x \to 0$ but nowhere else between $x = 0$ and $x = a$, the improper integral of the function f from 0 to a is defined by

$$\int_0^a f(x)dx = \lim_{\epsilon \to 0^+} \int_\epsilon^a f(x)dx$$

The limit with the 0^+ indicates that ϵ approaches 0 from the right ("Limits of Functions," Section 2.2).

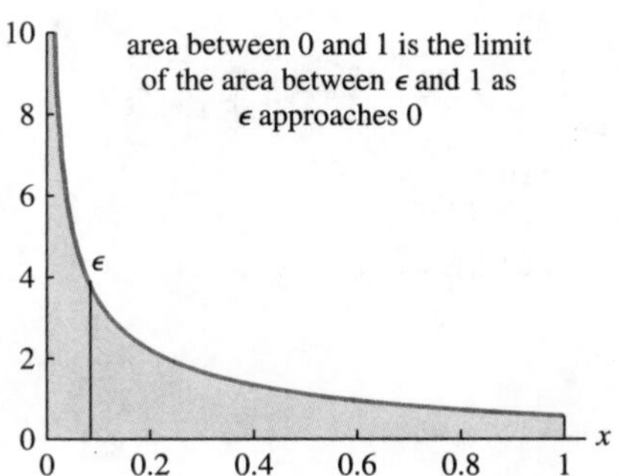

FIGURE 4.7.60
Computing an integral with an infinite integrand

Example 4.7.8 A Finite Area Even When a Function Approaches Infinity

With this definition, we have

$$\begin{aligned}\int_0^1 \frac{1}{\sqrt{x}}dx &= \lim_{\epsilon\to 0^+}\int_\epsilon^1 \frac{1}{\sqrt{x}}dx\\ &= \lim_{\epsilon\to 0^+} 2\sqrt{x}\Big|_\epsilon^1\\ &= \lim_{\epsilon\to 0^+} 2-2\sqrt{\epsilon}\\ &= 2\end{aligned}$$

Although the function is ill-behaved, the area is perfectly well defined.

Example 4.7.9 An Infinite Area Under a Function that Approaches Infinity

If $g(x)=\frac{1}{x^2}$, we have

$$\begin{aligned}\int_0^1 \frac{1}{x^2}dx &= \lim_{\epsilon\to 0^+}\int_\epsilon^1 \frac{1}{x^2}dx\\ &= \lim_{\epsilon\to 0^+} -\frac{1}{x}\Big|_\epsilon^1\\ &= \lim_{\epsilon\to 0^+} -1+\frac{1}{\epsilon}\\ &= \infty.\end{aligned}$$

For power functions of the form $\frac{1}{t^p}$ and $p\neq 1$, we can derive a general result for convergence over the interval from 0 to a.

$$\begin{aligned}\int_0^a \frac{1}{t^p}dt &= \lim_{\epsilon\to 0^+}\int_\epsilon^a \frac{1}{t^p}dt\\ &= \lim_{\epsilon\to 0^+} \frac{t^{1-p}}{1-p}\Big|_\epsilon^a\\ &= \lim_{\epsilon\to 0^+} \frac{a^{1-p}}{1-p}-\frac{\epsilon^{1-p}}{1-p}.\end{aligned}$$

If $p<1$, the integral converges, while if $p>1$, the limit is infinite and the integral diverges

Applying the Method of Leading Behavior to Improper Integrals As before, these rules can be extended with the method of leading behavior. The portion that counts is the part that increases most quickly.

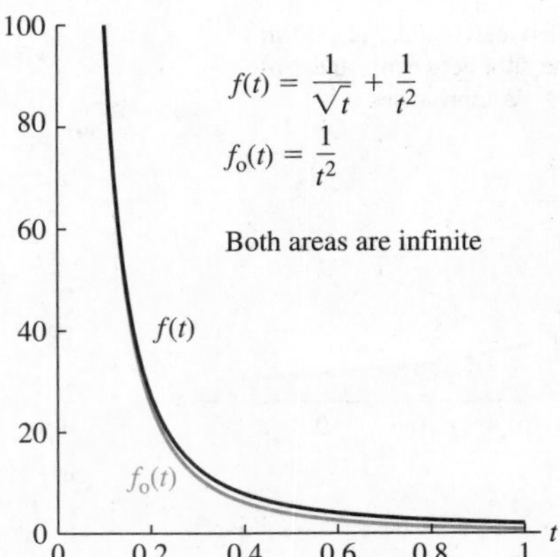

FIGURE 4.7.61

A divergent improper integral checked with the method of leading behavior

Example 4.7.10 Using the Method of Leading Behavior When the Integrand Approaches Infinity

The integrand of the integral

$$\int_0^1 \left(\frac{1}{\sqrt{t}} + \frac{1}{t^2}\right) dt$$

has two components, the larger of which is $\frac{1}{t^2}$. Therefore, the leading behavior is

$$\int_0^1 \frac{1}{t^2} dt = \infty$$

because the power is greater than 1, meaning that the original integral diverges (Figure 4.7.61).

Example 4.7.11 Using the Method of Leading Behavior When the Integrand Approaches Infinity

The leading behavior of the denominator of the integrand of

$$\int_0^1 \frac{1}{\sqrt{t} + t^2} dt$$

can be found by finding the leading behavior of the denominator. Both terms $\sqrt{t}$ and t^2 approach 0, but $\sqrt{t}$ approaches 0 more slowly, is larger, and is the leading behavior of the denominator. The integral of the leading behavior is

$$\int_0^1 \frac{1}{\sqrt{t}} dt$$

which converges because the power is less than 1 (Figure 4.7.62).

Example 4.7.12 Using the Comparison Test When the Integrand Approaches Infinity

Consider again

$$\int_0^1 \frac{1}{\sqrt{t} + t^2} dt$$

Because $t^2 < \sqrt{t}$ for $t < 1$, we have that

$$\frac{1}{\sqrt{t} + t^2} < \frac{1}{\sqrt{t} + \sqrt{t}} = \frac{1}{2\sqrt{t}}$$

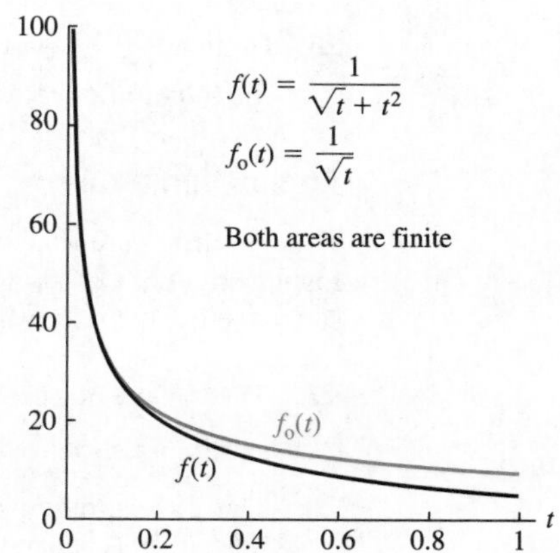

FIGURE 4.7.62
A convergent improper integral checked with the method of leading behavior

Therefore,

$$\int_0^1 \frac{1}{\sqrt{t + t^2}} dt < \int_0^1 \frac{1}{2\sqrt{t}} dt = \sqrt{t}\big|_0^1 = 1$$

Summary We have introduced **improper integrals** of two types: integrals with infinite limits of integration and integrals with infinite integrands. The former are defined as the limit when one limit of integration increases to infinity and the second as the limit when one limit of integration approaches a point where the function itself approaches infinity. If the limit exists, we say the integral **converges;** if not, we say the integral **diverges.** We found conditions for convergence or divergence of integrals of power and exponential functions and then extended these results with the method of leading behavior and the **comparison test.**

4.7 Exercises

Mathematical Techniques

1–4 ▪ Many improper integrals can be evaluated by comparing functions with the method of leading behavior. State which of the given pair of functions approaches its limit more quickly, and demonstrate the result with L'Hôpital's rule when needed.

1. Which function approaches 0 faster as x approaches infinity: e^{-x} or $\frac{1}{x}$?
2. Which function approaches 0 faster as x approaches infinity: $\frac{1}{1+x^2}$ or $\frac{1}{1+x}$?
3. Which function approaches infinity faster as x approaches 0: $\frac{1}{x^2}$ or $\frac{1}{x}$?
4. Which function approaches infinity faster as x approaches 0: $\frac{1}{x}$ or $\frac{1}{\sqrt{x}}$?

5–10 ▪ Evaluate the following improper integrals or explain why they don't converge.

5. $\int_0^\infty e^{-3t} dt$
6. $\int_0^\infty e^t dt$
7. $\int_1^\infty \frac{1}{\sqrt{x}} dx$
8. $\int_5^\infty \frac{1}{x^2} dx$
9. $\int_0^\infty \frac{1}{(1+3x)^{3/2}} dx$
10. $\int_0^\infty \frac{1}{(2+5x)^4} dx$

11–14 ▪ Evaluate the following improper integrals or explain why they don't converge.

11. $\int_0^1 \frac{1}{x} dx$
12. $\int_0^{.001} \frac{1}{x^2} dx$
13. $\int_0^{.001} \frac{1}{\sqrt[3]{x}} dx$
14. $\int_0^\infty \frac{1}{\sqrt[3]{x}} dx$

15–18 ▪ Use the method of leading behavior to deduce whether the following integrals converge.

15. $\int_0^1 \frac{1}{\sqrt[3]{x}+x^3}dx$

16. $\int_0^1 \frac{1}{x^2+e^x}dx$

17. $\int_1^\infty \frac{1}{\sqrt[3]{x}+x^3}dx$

18. $\int_1^\infty \frac{1}{\sqrt{x}+e^x}dx$

19–22 ▪ Use the comparison test to deduce whether the following integrals converge. If they do, find an upper bound on the value.

19. $\int_0^1 \frac{1}{\sqrt[3]{x}+x^3}dx$

20. $\int_0^1 \frac{1}{x^2+e^x}dx$

21. $\int_1^\infty \frac{1}{\sqrt[3]{x}+x^3}dx$

22. $\int_1^\infty \frac{1}{\sqrt{x}+e^x}dx$

23–26 ▪ There are many situations in which an infinite number of terms must be added called a *series* or *infinite series*. It is important in these cases to know whether the sum is finite (in which case it is said that the series **converges**) or infinite (in which case it is said that the series **diverges**). Compare the following series with the given integral to determine whether the sum approaches infinity.

23. Compare $\sum_{i=0}^{\infty} \frac{1}{2^i}$ with $\int_0^\infty \frac{2}{2^x}dx$.

24. Compare $\sum_{i=0}^{\infty} \frac{1}{3^i}$ with $\int_0^\infty \frac{1}{3^x}dx$.

25. Compare $\sum_{i=1}^{\infty} \frac{1}{i^2}$ with $\int_1^\infty \frac{1}{x^2}dx$.

26. Compare $\sum_{i=1}^{\infty} \frac{1}{i}$ with $\int_1^\infty \frac{1}{x}dx$. This is a famous series called the **harmonic series.**

Applications

27–30 ▪ Write pure-time differential equations to describe the following situations, find out what happens over the long term, and state whether the rule could be followed indefinitely.

27. The volume of a cell is increasing at a rate of $\frac{100}{(1+t)^2}$ $\mu m^3/s$, starting from a size of 500 μm^3.

28. The concentration of a toxin in a cell is increasing at a rate of $50e^{-2t}$ μmol/L/s, starting from a concentration of 10 μmol/L. If the cell is poisoned when the concentration exceeds 30 μmol/L, could this cell survive?

29. A population of bacteria is increasing at a rate of $\frac{1000}{(2+3t)^{0.75}}$ bacteria per hour, starting from a population of 10^6. Could this sort of growth be maintained indefinitely? When would the population reach 2.0×10^6? Would you say that this population is growing quickly?

30. A population of bacteria is increasing at a rate of $\frac{1000}{(2+3t)^{1.5}}$ bacteria per hour, starting from a population of 1000. Could this sort of growth be maintained indefinitely? Would the population reach 2000?

Computer Exercise

31. Use your computer to find the values of the integrals in Exercises 4.7.15–4.7.16 to 8 decimal places and compare with the integrals of the leading behavior.

Supplementary Problems

1. The voltage v of a neuron follows the differential equation

$$\frac{dv}{dt} = 1.0 + \frac{1}{1+0.02t} - e^{0.01t}$$

over the course of 100 ms, where t is measured in milliseconds and v in millivolts. We start at $v(0) = -70$ mV.

a. Sketch a graph of the rate of change. Indicate on your graph the times when the voltage reaches minima and maxima (you don't need to solve for the numerical values).

b. Sketch a graph of the voltage as a function of time.

c. What is the voltage after 100 ms?

2. Consider again the differential equation in the previous problem,

$$\frac{dv}{dt} = 1.0 + \frac{1}{1+0.02t} - e^{0.01t}$$

with $v(0) = -70$.

a. Use Euler's method to estimate the voltage after 1 ms and again 1 ms after that.

b. Estimate the voltage after 2 ms using left-hand and right-hand Riemann sums.

c. Which of your estimates matches Euler's method and why?

3. A neuron in your brain sends a charge down an 80-cm axon (a long skinny thing) toward your hand at a speed of 10 m/s. At the time when the charge reaches your elbow, the voltage in the axon is −70 mV, except on the 6-cm piece between 47 and 53 cm from your brain. On this piece, the voltage is

$$v(x) = -70.0 + 10.0\left[9.0 - (x-50.0)^2\right] \text{mV}$$

where $v(x)$ is the voltage at a distance of x cm from the brain.

a. How long will it take the information to get to your hand? How long did it take the information to reach your elbow?

b. Sketch a graph of the voltage along the whole axon.

c. Find the average voltage of the 6-cm piece.

d. Find the average voltage of the whole axon.

4. The charge in a dead neuron decays according to

$$\frac{dv}{dt} = \frac{1}{\sqrt{1+4t}} - \frac{2}{(1+4t)^{\frac{3}{2}}}$$

starting from $v(0) = -70$ mV at $t = 0$.

a. Is the voltage approaching 0 as $t \to \infty$? How do you know that it will eventually reach 0?

b. Write an equation (but don't solve it) for the time when the voltage reaches 0.

c. What is wrong with this model?

5. Consider the differential equations

$$\frac{db}{dt} = 2b$$

and

$$\frac{dB}{dt} = 1 + 2t$$

a. Which of these is a pure-time differential equation? Describe circumstances in which you might find each of these equations.

b. Suppose $b(0) = B(0) = 1$. Use Euler's method with $\Delta t = 0.1$ to find estimates for $b(0.1)$ and $B(0.1)$.

c. Use Euler's method with $\Delta t = 0.1$ to find estimates for $b(0.2)$ and $B(0.2)$.

6. Consider the differential equation

$$\frac{dp}{dt} = e^{-4t}$$

where $p(t)$ is product in moles at time t, and t is measured in seconds.

a. Explain in words what is going on.

b. Suppose $p(0) = 1$. Find $p(1)$.

7. Consider the differential equation

$$\frac{dV}{dt} = 4 - t^2$$

where $V(t)$ is volume in liters at time t, and t is measured in minutes.

a. Explain in words what is going on.

b. At what time is the volume a maximum?

c. Break the interval from $t = 0$ to $t = 3$ into three parts, and find the left-hand and right-hand estimates of the volume at $t = 3$ (assume $V(0) = 0$).

d. Write down the definite integral expressing volume at $t = 3$ and evaluate.

8. Find the area under the curve $f(x) = 3 + (1 + \frac{x}{3})^2$ between $x = 0$ and $x = 3$.

9. The population density of trout in a stream is

$$\rho(x) = |-x^2 + 5x + 50|$$

where ρ is measured in trout per mile and x is measured in miles. x runs from 0 to 20.

a. Graph $\rho(x)$ and find the minimum and maximum.

b. Find the total number of trout in the stream.

c. Find the average density of trout in the stream.

d. Indicate on your graph how you would find where the actual density is equal to the average density.

10. The amount of product is described by the differential equation

$$\frac{dp}{dt} = \frac{1}{\sqrt{1+3t}}$$

starting at time $t = 0$. Suppose p is measured in moles, t is measured in hours, and $p(0) = 0$.

a. Find the limiting amount of product.

b. Find the average rate at which product is produced on the interval from 0 to t, and compute the limit as $t \to \infty$.

c. Find the limit as $t \to 0$ of the average rate at which product is produced.

11. A student is hooked up to an EEG during a test, and her α brain wave power follows

$$A(t) = \frac{50}{2.0 + 0.3t} + 10e^{0.0125t}$$

where t runs from 0 to 120 min.

a. Convince yourself that brain wave power has a minimum value some time during the test. Sketch a graph of the function. Find the maximum.

b. Find the total brain wave energy (the integral of power) during the test.

c. Find the average brain wave power during the test. Sketch the corresponding line on your graph.

d. Estimate the minimum value from your average value.

e. Draw a graph showing how you would estimate the total brain wave energy using the right-hand approximation with $n = 6$. Write down the associated sum. Do you think your estimate is high or low?

12. Consider the function $G(h)$ giving the density of nutrients in a plant stem as a function of the height h,

$$G(h) = 5 + 3e^{-2h}$$

where G is measured in moles per meter and h is measured in meters.

a. Find the total amount of nutrient if the stem is 2.0 m tall.

b. Find the average density in the stem.

c. Find the exact and approximate amount between 1.0 and 1.01 m.

Projects

1. As noted in the text, Euler's method is not a very good way to solve differential equations numerically. In this project, you will compare Euler's method with the **midpoint** (or **second-order Runge-Kutta) method** and the **implicit Euler** method.

Suppose we know (or estimate) that the solution of the general differential equation

$$\frac{dy}{dt} = f(t, y)$$

takes on some value $y = y_0$ at time $t = t_0$. Our goal is to estimate the value of $y_1 = y(t_0 + h)$ with *step size h*.

We have seen that Euler's method uses the tangent line to estimate

$$y_1 = y(t_0) + hf(t_0, y_0)$$

This method has the drawback that it uses the derivative only at the beginning of the interval between times t_0 and $t_0 + h$. If the derivative changes significantly during this interval, the method can be very inaccurate.

An alternative called the midpoint method uses an estimate of the derivative at time $t_0 + \frac{h}{2}$ instead. The next step is

$$k = hf(t_0, y_0)$$

$$y_1 = y(t_0) + hf\left(t_0 + \frac{h}{2}, y_0 + \frac{k}{2}\right)$$

where k is the estimated change computed by Euler's method, and we use it to guess the value of y halfway through the interval. This method is more accurate than Euler's method.

Both Euler's method and the midpoint method are **unstable,** meaning that the approximate solutions they produce can fail to approach a stable equilibrium if the step size h is too large. The **implicit Euler scheme** is stable for linear equations. The idea is to use the derivative at the end of the interval instead of the beginning. That is,

$$y_1 = y(t_0) + hf(t_0 + h, y_1)$$

Because we do not know the value of y_1, we have to solve for it.

This project asks you to compare these three methods on four differential equations:

$$\frac{db}{dt} = b$$

$$\frac{dx}{dt} = -x$$

$$\frac{dV}{dt} = -e^{-t}$$

$$\frac{dy}{dt} = -e^{-t} + e^{-y}.$$

Suppose the state variable in each equation has the initial value of 1.0 at $t = 0$.

a. First, find the solution of each at $t = 1$. Try each method (if you can figure out how to get the implicit method to work on the last equation) with values of h ranging from 1.0 down to 0.001.

b. The equations for x and V should both approach 0 exponentially as t becomes large. Use large values of h (such as 10 or 100) in each of the three methods. How well do they do for large t?

c. The midpoint method is related to approximating the solution with a quadratic Taylor polynomial (Section 3.7). Develop an extension of Euler's method based on the quadratic approximation and compare with the midpoint method.

W. H. Press, S. A. Teukolsky, W. T. Vettering, and B. P. Flannery. *Numerical Recipes in FORTRAN: The Art of Scientific Computing,* 2nd Edition, Cambridge University Press, Cambridge, England, 1992.

2. In ancient times, the Greeks were fascinated by geometric problems such as finding the area of a circle. Archimedes, perhaps the greatest mathematician in the ancient world, came up with an idea closely related to the Riemann sum to solve this problem. Using some modern tools, we can apply his ideas to compute the value of π.

a. Break a circle of radius 1 into n wedges, each with angle $\theta = 2\pi/n$. Show that the area of a right triangle inside each wedge is $\sin(\theta)/2$. Be sure to draw a picture.

b. Approximate the area of a circle using $n = 8$. Look up (or remember) the half-angle formula giving $\sin(\theta/2)$ in terms of $\cos(\theta)$ to approximate the area with $n = 16$.

c. Continue in this way to approximate the area with $n = 32$ and so forth.

d. Use the same approach, but approximate each wedge with a right triangle that lies outside the circle. Show that the area of the triangle is $\tan(\theta)/2$.

e. Approximate the area of a circle using $n = 8$ (what happens when $n = 4$?). Look up (or remember) the half-angle formula giving $\tan(\theta/2)$ in terms of $\tan(\theta)$ to approximate the area with $n = 16$.

f. Continue in this way to approximate the area with $n = 32$ and so forth.

g. Can you think of a better method that Archimedes could have used to compute the value of π?

P. Beckmann. *A History of* π, 5th Edition, Golem Press, Boulder, Colo, 1977.

Chapter

5

Analysis of Autonomous Differential Equations

We have developed the indefinite integral and definite integral as tools to solve **pure-time differential equations** and have linked them with the Fundamental Theorem of Calculus. We will now use integrals and several graphical tools to study **autonomous differential equations,** where the rate of change is a **rule** relating change to the current state. In particular, we will use the **phase-line diagram** to find **equilibria** and their **stability,** much as we used cobwebbing to find equilibria and stability of discrete-time dynamical systems.

Because most biological systems involve several interacting measurements, we will extend our methods to address **systems of autonomous differential equations,** where the rate of change of each measurement depends on the value of the others. Generalization of the phase line to the **phase plane** makes possible the study of two-dimensional systems. We conclude with a careful study of a fundamental two-dimensional system of differential equations, called the **Fitzhugh-Nagumo equations,** that describe the firing of a neuron.

5.1 Basic Differential Equations

Temperature change, chemical exchange in the lung, and selection can be simply and accurately modeled with **autonomous differential equations.** In each case, the model describes the same biological situation as a related discrete-time dynamical system, but the equation usually looks completely different. After reviewing the terminology for autonomous differential equations, we will derive these fundamental equations from biological or physical laws.

Review of Autonomous Differential Equations

We have developed techniques to solve pure-time differential equations with the general form

$$\frac{dV}{dt} = f(t) \tag{5.1.1}$$

In these equations, the rate of change is a function of time and not of the state variable (volume in this case). Change is imposed from outside the system; consider the control of a lake level by the weather or by an engineer. In most biological systems, however, the rate of change depends on the current state of the system as well as on external factors. A lake that experienced increased evaporation at high lake levels would change as a function of the level itself, not just as a function of the weather or decisions of engineers.

The class of differential equations where the rate of change depends only on the state of the system and not on external circumstances is particularly important. These equations are called **autonomous differential equations** (Section 4.1). We have already studied one autonomous differential equation, which describes the growth of a bacterial population $b(t)$ as follows:

$$\frac{db}{dt} = 2b$$

(Example 4.1.3). The rate of change of the population size b depends only on the population size b and not on the time t.

The general autonomous differential equation for a measurement m is

$$\frac{dm}{dt} = g(m) \tag{5.1.2}$$

It differs from the general pure-time differential equation in that the rate of change $g(m)$ depends on m rather than t. Autonomous differential equations are slightly harder to solve than pure-time differential equations, but the techniques of solution are different and the solutions are often more interesting.

When the rate of change depends on both the state variable and the time, the equation is called a **nonautonomous differential equation.** The general form is

$$\frac{dm}{dt} = g(m, t) \tag{5.1.3}$$

These equations are generally much more difficult to solve than either pure-time or autonomous differential equations.

Although the *rate of change* in an autonomous differential equation does not depend explicitly on time, the *solution* does.

Example 5.1.1 The Autonomous Differential Equation for Population Growth

Suppose that a bacterial culture with 1.0×10^6 bacteria is refrigerated to prevent reproduction and then is warmed to room temperature at 9:00 A.M. and allowed to reproduce. The population $b(t)$ might follow the autonomous differential equation

$$\frac{db}{dt} = 2b$$

If $t = 0$ represents 9:00 A.M., the solution is

$$b(t) = 1.0 \times 10^6 \cdot e^{2t}$$

We check this solution by differentiating, finding that

$$\begin{aligned}\frac{db}{dt} &= \frac{d}{dt}\left(1.0 \times 10^6 \cdot e^{2t}\right)\\ &= 1.0 \times 10^6 \frac{d}{dt}\left(e^{2t}\right)\\ &= 1.0 \times 10^6 \cdot 2e^{2t}\\ &= 2 \cdot 1.0 \times 10^6 e^{2t}\\ &= 2b(t)\end{aligned}$$

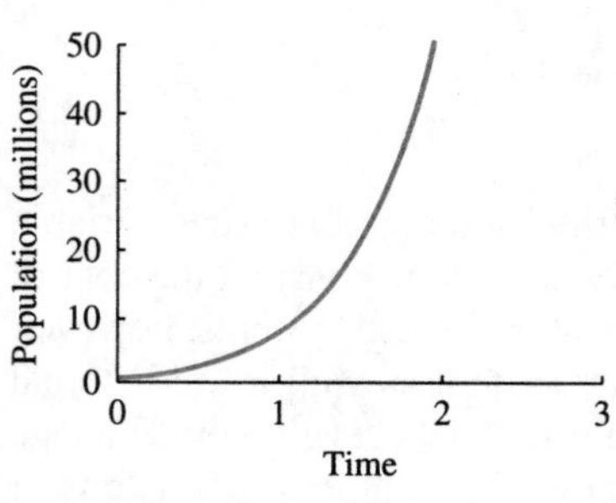

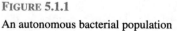

FIGURE 5.1.1
An autonomous bacterial population

Furthermore, $b(0) = 1.0 \times 10^6$ as required by the initial condition.

Although the *formula* for the rate of change always looks the same, the *value* of the rate of change (and the population size itself) become larger over time (Figure 5.1.1).

Euler's method (described for pure-time differential equations in Algorithm 4.1) extends directly to autonomous differential equations.

Algorithm 5.1 Euler's Method for Solving An Autonomous Differential Equation

Suppose a measurement m obeys the autonomous differential equation

$$\frac{dm}{dt} = f(m)$$

with initial condition $m(t_0) = m_0$.

1. Choose a **time step** Δt (the length of time between estimated values).
2. Use the initial condition and the differential equation to find the tangent line $\hat{m}(t)$ with base point $t = t_0$ and slope $f(m_0)$. Use it to compute $\hat{m}(t_0 + \Delta t)$.
3. Use the estimate $\hat{m}(t_0 + \Delta t)$ for $m(t_0 + \Delta t)$ and the differential equation to find the tangent line $\hat{m}(t)$ with base point $t_0 + \Delta t$ and estimate $\hat{m}(t_0 + 2\Delta t)$.
4. Repeat the method in the previous step to find $\hat{m}(t_0 + 3\Delta t)$ and so forth.

Example 5.1.2 Applying Euler's Method to a Differential Equation for Population Growth

Suppose we wish to apply Euler's method to the autonomous differential equation for population growth

$$\frac{db}{dt} = 2b$$

with initial condition $b(0) = 1.0$ to estimate $b(1)$.

1. Pick a time step of $\Delta t = 0.25$ (a smaller value should be more accurate).
2. The tangent line with base point $t = 0$ is

$$\begin{aligned} \hat{b}(0 + \Delta t) &= b(0) + b'(0)\Delta t && \text{equation for tangent line} \\ &= 1.0 + 2.0 \cdot \Delta t && b(0) = 1.0 \text{ (initial condition) and } b'(0) = 2b(0) = 2.0 \text{ (differential equation)} \end{aligned}$$

We therefore find that

$$\hat{b}(0.25) = 1.0 + 2.0 \cdot 0.25 = 1.5$$

3. For the next step, to find $\hat{b}(0.5)$, we compute

$$\begin{aligned} \hat{b}(0.25 + \Delta t) &= b(0.25) + b'(0.25)\Delta t && \text{equation for tangent line} \\ &\approx \hat{b}(0.25) + b'(0.25)\Delta t && \text{substitute } \hat{b}(0.25) \text{ for unknown } b(0.25) \\ &\approx \hat{b}(0.25) + 2\hat{b}(0.25)\Delta t && \text{substitute } 2\hat{b}(0.25) \text{ for unknown } b'(0.25) \\ &= 1.5 + 3.0\Delta t && \hat{b}(0.25) = 1.5 \end{aligned}$$

We therefore estimate that

$$\hat{b}(0.5) \approx 1.5 + 3.0 \cdot 0.25 = 2.25$$

4. To find $\hat{b}(0.75)$, we compute

$$\begin{aligned} \hat{b}(0.5 + \Delta t) &= b(0.5) + b'(0.5)\Delta t \\ &\approx \hat{b}(0.5) + 2\hat{b}(0.5)\Delta t \\ &= 2.25 + 4.5 \cdot \Delta t \\ \hat{b}(0.75) &= 2.25 + 4.5 \cdot 0.25 = 3.375 \end{aligned}$$

Finally, to find $\hat{b}(1.0)$, we compute

$$\begin{aligned} \hat{b}(0.75 + \Delta t) &= b(0.75) + b'(0.75)\Delta t \\ &\approx \hat{b}(0.75) + 2\hat{b}(0.75)\Delta t \\ &= 3.375 + 6.75 \cdot \Delta t \\ \hat{b}(1.0) &= 3.375 + 6.75 \cdot 0.25 = 5.0625 \end{aligned}$$

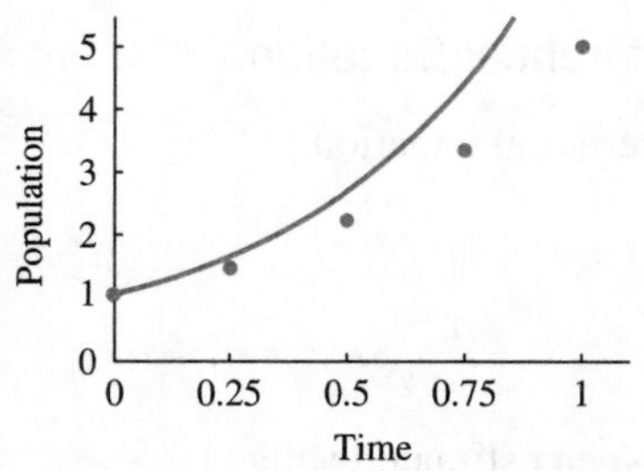

FIGURE 5.1.2
Euler's method applied to an autonomous differential equation

These values (and a comparison with the exact solution $b(t)=e^{2t}$) are plotted in Figure 5.1.2.

In this example, the approximation given by Euler's method falls further and further behind. Unlike the application of Euler's method to pure-time differential equations, where the rate of change is exact, both the value of the function and the rate of change are approximate when applied to an autonomous differential equation.

Newton's Law of Cooling

Both the concentration of a substance in a fluid and its temperature change continuously in time, making these appropriate quantities to model with differential equations. As we saw in our study of pure-time differential equations, it can be easier to measure the amount of fluid crossing a membrane than to measure the entire quantity of fluid inside. More important, the rules describing the movement of fluids and heat can be described compactly and intuitively with autonomous differential equations.

The basic idea is expressed by **Newton's law of cooling,** which states that

> the rate at which heat is lost from an object is proportional to the difference between the temperature of the object and the ambient temperature.

Denote the temperature of an object by H and the fixed ambient temperature by A. Newton's law of cooling can be written as the differential equation

$$\frac{dH}{dt}=\alpha(A-H) \tag{5.1.4}$$

where α is a positive constant with dimensions of $1/\text{time}$. This is an **autonomous differential equation** because it describes a *rule* and because the rate of change is a function of the state variable H and not of the time t. Remember that H is a function of time but that α and A are constants.

If the temperature of the object is higher than the ambient temperature ($H > A$), the rate of change of temperature is negative and the object cools. If the temperature of the object is lower than the ambient temperature ($H < A$), the rate of change of temperature is positive and the object warms up (Figure 5.1.3). If the temperature of the object is equal to the ambient temperature, the rate of change of temperature is zero, and the temperature of the object does not change.

The parameter α, with dimensions of 1/time, depends on the **specific heat** of the material and on its shape. Materials with high specific heat, such as water, retain heat for a long time, have low values of α, and experience small rates of heat change for a given temperature difference. Materials with low specific heat, such as metals, lose heat rapidly, have large values of α, and experience high rates of heat change for a given temperature difference. The parameter α also depends on the object's ratio of surface area to volume. An object with a large exposed surface relative to its volume will heat or cool rapidly, as a shallow puddle freezes quickly on a cold evening. An object with a relatively small surface area heats or cools more slowly.

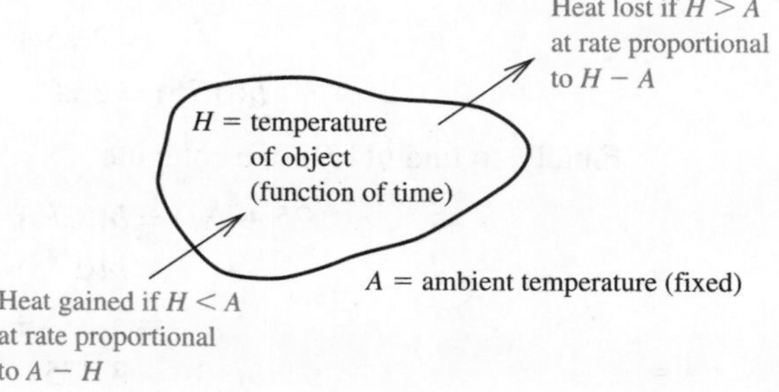

FIGURE 5.1.3
Newton's law of cooling

Although it is possible to guess the solution or solve the equation mathematically with the method of separation of variables (Section 5.4), we will first study Newton's law of cooling with Euler's method.

Example 5.1.3 Applying Euler's Method to Newton's Law of Cooling

First, suppose that α has the relatively small value of 0.1 per minute, that the ambient temperature A is 20°C, and that the initial condition is $H(0) = 40$°C. To study how the temperature changes over the first 10 min, we choose a time step of $\Delta t = 1$, as shown in the following table.

t	$\hat{H}(t+\Delta t)$	$t+\Delta t$	$\hat{H}(t+\Delta t)$
0	$H(0) + H'(0)\Delta t = 40.0 + 0.1(20 - 40)\Delta t$	1	38.0
1	$\hat{H}(1) + H'(1)\Delta t = 38.0 + 0.1(20 - 38.0)\Delta t$	2	36.2
2	$\hat{H}(2) + H'(2)\Delta t = 36.2 + 0.1(20 - 36.2)\Delta t$	3	34.6
3	$\hat{H}(3) + H'(3)\Delta t = 34.6 + 0.1(20 - 34.6)\Delta t$	4	33.1
4	$\hat{H}(4) + H'(4)\Delta t = 33.1 + 0.1(20 - 33.1)\Delta t$	5	31.8
5	$\hat{H}(5) + H'(5)\Delta t = 31.8 + 0.1(20 - 31.8)\Delta t$	6	30.6
6	$\hat{H}(6) + H'(6)\Delta t = 30.6 + 0.1(20 - 30.6)\Delta t$	7	29.6
7	$\hat{H}(7) + H'(7)\Delta t = 29.6 + 0.1(20 - 29.6)\Delta t$	8	28.6
8	$\hat{H}(8) + H'(8)\Delta t = 28.6 + 0.1(20 - 28.6)\Delta t$	9	27.7
9	$\hat{H}(9) + H'(9)\Delta t = 27.7 + 0.1(20 - 27.7)\Delta t$	10	27.0

If we start instead at $H(0) = 0$°C, we get the following data.

t	$\hat{H}(t+\Delta t)$	$t+\Delta t$	$\hat{H}(t+\Delta t)$
0	$H(0) + H'(0)\Delta t = 0.0 + 0.1(20 - 0.0)\Delta t$	1	2.0
1	$\hat{H}(1) + H'(1)\Delta t = 2.0 + 0.1(20 - 2.0)\Delta t$	2	3.8
2	$\hat{H}(2) + H'(2)\Delta t = 3.8 + 0.1(20 - 3.8)\Delta t$	3	5.4
3	$\hat{H}(3) + H'(3)\Delta t = 5.4 + 0.1(20 - 5.4)\Delta t$	4	6.9
4	$\hat{H}(4) + H'(4)\Delta t = 6.9 + 0.1(20 - 6.9)\Delta t$	5	8.2
5	$\hat{H}(5) + H'(5)\Delta t = 8.2 + 0.1(20 - 8.2)\Delta t$	6	9.4
6	$\hat{H}(6) + H'(6)\Delta t = 9.4 + 0.1(20 - 9.4)\Delta t$	7	10.4
7	$\hat{H}(7) + H'(7)\Delta t = 10.4 + 0.1(20 - 10.4)\Delta t$	8	11.4
8	$\hat{H}(8) + H'(8)\Delta t = 11.4 + 0.1(20 - 11.4)\Delta t$	9	12.3
9	$\hat{H}(9) + H'(9)\Delta t = 12.3 + 0.1(20 - 12.3)\Delta t$	10	13.0

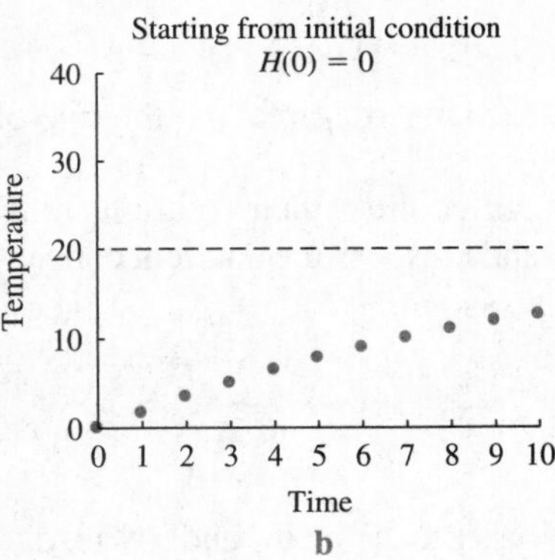

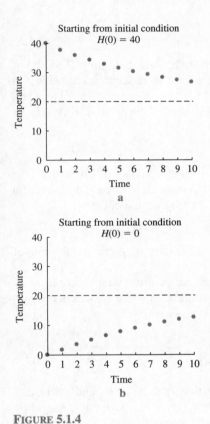

FIGURE 5.1.4

Newton's law of cooling approximated with Euler's method: small α

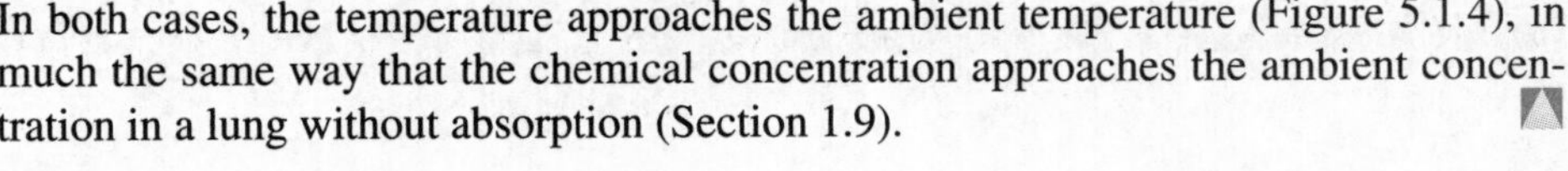

In both cases, the temperature approaches the ambient temperature (Figure 5.1.4), in much the same way that the chemical concentration approaches the ambient concentration in a lung without absorption (Section 1.9).

Diffusion Across a Membrane

The processes of heat exchange and chemical exchange have many parallels (which is remarkable, given that heat is not a substance, as once was thought). The underlying mechanism is that of **diffusion.** Substances leave the cell at a rate proportional to their concentration inside and enter the cell at a rate proportional to their concentration outside. The constants of proportionality depend on the properties of the substance and on the properties of the membrane separating the two regions (Figure 5.1.5).

Denote the concentration inside the cell by C, the concentration outside by Γ (the greek capital letter gamma), and the constant of proportionality by β. The rate at which

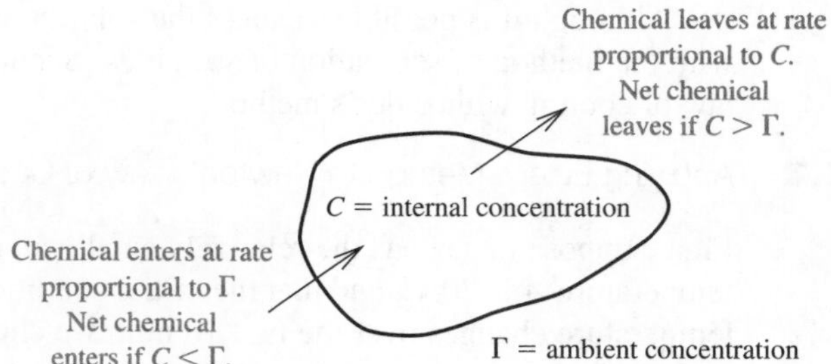

FIGURE 5.1.5
Passive diffusion between two regions

the chemical leaves the cell is βC, and the rate at which it enters is $\beta\Gamma$. Therefore,

$$\begin{aligned}\frac{dC}{dt} &= \text{rate at which chemical enters} - \text{rate at which chemical leaves}\\ &= \beta\Gamma - \beta C\\ &= \beta(\Gamma - C)\end{aligned} \tag{5.1.5}$$

Except for the letters, this is exactly the same as Newton's law of cooling! The rate of change of concentration is proportional to the difference in concentration inside and outside the cell.

This model looks completely different from the discrete-time dynamical system for the lung,

$$c_{t+1} = (1-q)c_t + q\gamma$$

(Equation 1.9.1), even though it describes a very similar situation. To be fair, the differential equation gives the rate of change of C, not the new value. The change in concentration for the lung described by the discrete-time dynamical system is

$$\Delta c = c_{t+1} - c_t = -qc_t + q\gamma = q\,(\gamma - c_t)$$

The two models now look similar, with the fraction exchanged, q, playing the role of the rate, β.

Because this model is identical to Newton's law of cooling, their solutions must match. The concentration of chemical will get closer and closer to the ambient concentration, just as it did with the discrete-time dynamical system.

A Continuous Time Model of Selection

Suppose we have two strains of bacteria, with population sizes denoted a and b, with rate of change proportional to population size (Equation 4.1.4). If the per capita production rate of strain a is μ and that of b is λ, they follow the equations

$$\frac{da}{dt} = \mu a$$

$$\frac{db}{dt} = \lambda b$$

If $\mu > \lambda$, type a has a higher per capita production rate than b, and we expect it to take over the population. However, we can often measure only the *fraction* of bacteria of type a and not the total number. We would like to write a differential equation for the fraction, and we can do so by following steps much like those used to find the discrete-time dynamical system for competing bacteria (Section 1.10).

The fraction p of type a is

$$p = \frac{a}{a+b}$$

Also,

$$1-p=\frac{b}{a+b}$$

because $1-p$ is the fraction of bacteria of type b.

We can use the quotient rule (Theorem 2.11) to compute the derivative of p, finding

$$\begin{aligned}
\frac{dp}{dt} &= \frac{d}{dt}\left(\frac{a}{a+b}\right) && \text{the derivative of } p\\
&= \frac{(a+b)\frac{da}{dt} - a\frac{d(a+b)}{dt}}{(a+b)^2} && \text{the quotient rule}\\
&= \frac{a\frac{da}{dt} + b\frac{da}{dt} - a\frac{da}{dt} - a\frac{db}{dt}}{(a+b)^2} && \text{the sum rule}\\
&= \frac{b\frac{da}{dt} - a\frac{db}{dt}}{(a+b)^2} && \text{cancel the } a\frac{da}{dt} \text{ terms}\\
&= \frac{\mu ab - \lambda ab}{(a+b)^2} && \text{plug in differential equations for } a \text{ and } b\\
&= \frac{(\mu-\lambda)ab}{(a+b)^2} && \text{factor}
\end{aligned}$$

We are not yet finished, however. To write this as an autonomous differential equation, we must express the derivative as a function of the state variable p, not of the unmeasurable total populations a and b. Then

$$\begin{aligned}
\frac{dp}{dt} &= \frac{(\mu-\lambda)ab}{(a+b)^2} && \text{previous equation}\\
\frac{dp}{dt} &= (\mu-\lambda)\left(\frac{a}{a+b}\right)\left(\frac{b}{a+b}\right) && \text{factor}\\
&= (\mu-\lambda)p(1-p) && \text{write in terms of } p \text{ and } 1-p
\end{aligned}$$

Although our derivation was similar, this differential equation looks nothing like the discrete-time dynamical system for this system,

$$p_{t+1}=\frac{sp_t}{sp_t+r(1-p_t)}$$

(Equation 1.10.7). This is a key point. Never try to make a discrete-time dynamical system into a differential equation by cheerfully changing the letters. It is safer to go back to the underlying mechanism. In addition, the parameters in the two equations have different meanings. The parameters s and r in the discrete-time dynamical system represent the *per capita production,* the number of bacteria produced per bacterium in one generation, whereas the parameters μ and λ in the differential equation represent the *per capita production rates,* the rates at which one bacterium produces new bacteria.

Like the discrete-time dynamical system describing this selection, this differential equation is **nonlinear** because the state variable p appears inside a nonlinear function, in this case a quadratic. As before, nonlinear equations are generally much more difficult to solve. In this case, however, the structure of the system makes it possible to find a solution. We begin by solving each of the differential equations for a and b. Suppose the initial number of type a bacteria is a_0 and the initial number of type b is b_0 (even though these values cannot be measured). The solutions are

$$a(t)=a_0e^{\mu t}$$
$$b(t)=b_0e^{\lambda t}$$

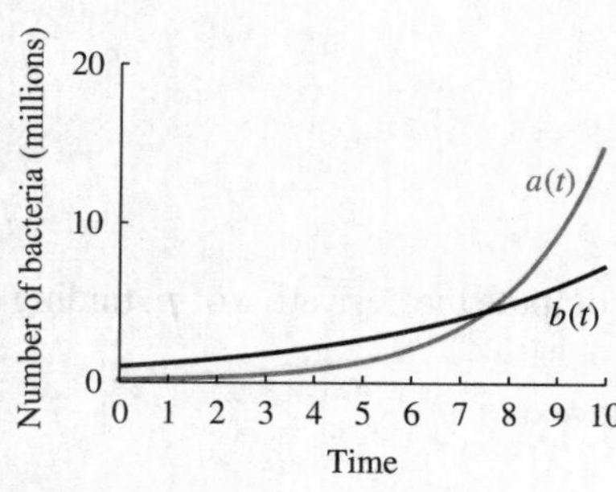

FIGURE 5.1.6
Exponential growth of two bacterial populations: $a_0 = 0.1$, $b_0 = 1.0$, $\mu = 0.5$, $\lambda = 0.2$

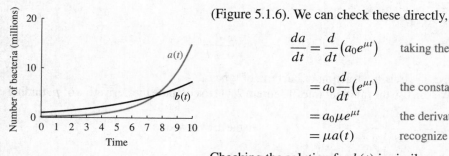

(Figure 5.1.6). We can check these directly,

$$\begin{aligned} \frac{da}{dt} &= \frac{d}{dt}(a_0 e^{\mu t}) && \text{taking the derivative} \\ &= a_0 \frac{d}{dt}(e^{\mu t}) && \text{the constant product rule} \\ &= a_0 \mu e^{\mu t} && \text{the derivative of an exponential function} \\ &= \mu a(t) && \text{recognize the formula for } a \end{aligned}$$

Checking the solution for $b(t)$ is similar.

We can now find the equation for the fraction p as a function of t as

$$\begin{aligned} p(t) &= \frac{a(t)}{a(t) + b(t)} \\ &= \frac{a_0 e^{\mu t}}{a_0 e^{\mu t} + b_0 e^{\lambda t}} \end{aligned}$$

Again, we are not quite finished. The initial conditions a_0 and b_0 cannot be measured; we can measure only the initial fraction $p(0) = p_0$. However, we do know that

$$p_0 = \frac{a_0}{a_0 + b_0}$$

Dividing the numerator and denominator of our expression for $p(t)$ by $a_0 + b_0$ yields

$$\begin{aligned} p(t) &= \frac{\frac{a_0}{a_0 + b_0} e^{\mu t}}{\frac{a_0}{a_0 + b_0} e^{\mu t} + \frac{b_0}{a_0 + b_0} e^{\lambda t}} \\ &= \frac{p_0 e^{\mu t}}{p_0 e^{\mu t} + (1 - p_0)\, e^{\lambda t}} \end{aligned} \qquad \textbf{(5.1.6)}$$

Checking this solution requires some algebraic gymnastics.

Example 5.1.4 Behavior of the Solution of the Selection Model

We can use the methods of reasoning about functions (Section 3.4) to study this solution. Suppose we use the parameter values $\mu = 0.5$ and $\lambda = 0.2$ and the initial condition

$$p_0 = \frac{a_0}{a_0 + b_0} = \frac{0.1}{0.1 + 1.0} \approx 0.091$$

(as in Figure 5.1.6). The solution is

$$\begin{aligned} p(t) &= \frac{0.091 e^{0.5t}}{0.091 e^{0.5t} + (1 - 0.091) e^{0.2t}} \\ &= \frac{0.091 e^{0.5t}}{0.091 e^{0.5t} + 0.909 e^{0.2t}} \end{aligned}$$

Because $0.5 > 0.2$, the leading behavior of the denominator for large values of t is the term $0.091e^{0.5t}$ (Section 3.6). Therefore, for large t

$$p(t) \approx \frac{0.091 e^{0.5t}}{0.091 e^{0.5t}} = 1$$

The fraction of type a does approach 1 as t approaches infinity (Figure 5.1.7). ▲

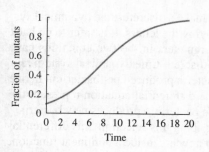

FIGURE 5.1.7
Solution for the fraction of type a bacteria

Summary The rate of change of an **autonomous differential equation** depends on the state variable and not on the time. The rate of change of a **nonautonomous differential equation** depends on both the state variable and the time. We have introduced autonomous differential equations describing three processes: cooling, diffusion, and selection, finding that the first two processes are governed by the same equation. The equation for selection, derived by returning to the underlying model, is a **nonlinear** equation, but it can be solved by combining the solutions for each separate population.

5.1 Exercises

Mathematical Techniques

1–4 ▪ Identify the following as pure-time, autonomous, or nonautonomous differential equations. In each case, identify the state variable.

1. $\dfrac{dF}{dt} = F^2 + kt.$

2. $\dfrac{dx}{dt} = \dfrac{x^2}{(x-\lambda)}.$

3. $\dfrac{dy}{dt} = \mu e^{-t} - 1.$

4. $\dfrac{dm}{dt} = \dfrac{e^{\alpha m} m^2}{(mt-\lambda)}.$

5–8 ▪ For the given time, value of the state variable, and values of the parameters, indicate whether the state variable is increasing, decreasing, or remaining unchanged.

5. $t=0$, $F=1$, and $k=1$ in the differential equation in Exercise 1.

6. $t=0$, $x=1$, and $\lambda=2$ in the differential equation in Exercise 2.

7. $t=1$, $y=1$, and $\mu=2$ in the differential equation in Exercise 3.

8. $t=2$, $m=0$, $\alpha=2$, and $\lambda=1$ in the differential equation in Exercise 4.

9–14 ▪ The following exercises compare the behavior of two similar-looking differential equations: the pure-time differential equation $\dfrac{dp}{dt} = t$ and the autonomous differential equation $\dfrac{db}{dt} = b$.

9. Use integration to solve the pure-time differential equation starting from the initial condition $p(0) = 1$, find $p(1)$, and sketch the solution.

10. Solve the pure-time differential equation starting from the initial condition $p(1) = 1$, find $p(2)$, and add the curve to your graph from Exercise 9.

11. Check that the solution of the autonomous differential equation starting from the initial condition $b(0) = 1$ is $b(t) = e^t$. Find $b(1)$ and sketch the solution.

12. Check that the solution of the autonomous differential equation starting from the initial condition $b(1) = 1$ is $b(t) = e^{t-1}$. Find $b(2)$ and add it to the sketch of the solution.

13. Exercises 9 and 10 give the value of p one time unit after it took on the value 1. Why don't the two answers match? (This behavior is typical of pure-time differential equations.)

14. Exercises 11 and 12 give the value of b one time unit after it took on the value 1. Why do the two answers match? (This behavior is typical of autonomous differential equations.)

15–18 ▪ Check the solution of the autonomous differential equation, making sure that it also matches the initial condition.

15. Check that $x(t) = -\frac{1}{2} + \frac{3}{2}e^{2t}$ is a solution of the differential equation $\dfrac{dx}{dt} = 1 + 2x$ with initial condition $x(0) = 1$.

16. Check that $b(t) = 10e^{3t}$ is a solution of the differential equation $\dfrac{db}{dt} = 3b$ with initial condition $b(0) = 10$.

17. Check that $G(t) = 1 + e^t$ is a solution of the differential equation $\dfrac{dG}{dt} = G - 1$ with initial condition $G(0) = 2$.

18. Check that $z(t) = 1 + \sqrt{1+2t}$ is a solution of the differential equation $\dfrac{dz}{dt} = \dfrac{1}{z-1}$ with initial condition $z(0) = 2$.

19–22 ▪ Use Euler's method to estimate the solution of the differential equation at the given time, and compare with the value given by the exact solution. Sketch a graph of the solution along with the lines predicted by Euler's method.

19. Estimate $x(2)$ if x obeys the differential equation $\dfrac{dx}{dt} = 1 + 2x$ with initial condition $x(0) = 1$. Use Euler's method with $\Delta t = 1$ for two steps. Compare with the exact answer in Exercise 15.

20. Estimate $b(1.0)$ if b obeys the differential equation $\dfrac{db}{dt} = 3b$ with initial condition $b(0) = 10$. Use Euler's method with $\Delta t = 0.5$ for two steps. Compare with the exact answer in Exercise 16.

21. Estimate $G(1.0)$ if G obeys the differential equation $\dfrac{dG}{dt} = G - 1$ with initial condition $G(0) = 2$. Use Euler's method with $\Delta t = 0.2$ for five steps. Compare with the exact answer in Exercise 17.

22. Estimate $z(4.0)$ if z obeys the differential equation $\dfrac{dz}{dt} = \dfrac{1}{z-1}$ with initial condition $z(0) = 2$. Use Euler's method with $\Delta t = 1.0$ for four steps. Compare with the exact answer in Exercise 18.

23–26 ▪ The derivation of the differential equation for p in the text requires combining two differential equations for a and b. Often, one can find a differential equation for a new variable derived from a single equation. In the following cases, use the chain rule to derive a new differential equation.

23. Suppose $\dfrac{dx}{dt} = 2x - 1$. Set $y = 2x - 1$ and find a differential equation for y. The end result should be simpler than the original equation.

24. Suppose $\dfrac{db}{dt} = 4b + 2$. Set $z = 4b + 2$ and find a differential equation for z. The end result should be simpler than the original equation.

25. Suppose $\frac{dx}{dt} = x + x^2$. Set $y = \frac{1}{x}$ and find a differential equation for y. This transformation changes a nonlinear differential equation for x into a linear differential equation for y (this is called a Bernoulli differential equation).

26. Suppose $\frac{dx}{dt} = 2x + \frac{1}{x}$. Set $y = x^2$ and find a differential equation for y. This is another example of a Bernoulli differential equation.

Applications

27–30 ▪ The simple model of bacterial growth assumes that the per capita production rate does not depend on population size. The following problems help you derive models of the form

$$\frac{db}{dt} = \lambda(b)b$$

where the per capita production rate λ is a function of the population size b.

27. One widely used nonlinear model of competition is the logistic model, where the per capita production rate is a linearly decreasing function of population size. Suppose that the per capita production rate has a maximum of $\lambda(0) = 1$ and that it decreases with a slope of -0.002. Find $\lambda(b)$ and the differential equation for b. Is $b(t)$ increasing when $b = 10$? Is $b(t)$ increasing when $b = 1000$?

28. Suppose that the per capita production rate decreases linearly from a maximum of $\lambda(0) = 4$ with slope -0.001. Find $\lambda(b)$ and the differential equation for b. Is $b(t)$ increasing when $b = 1000$? Is $b(t)$ increasing when $b = 5000$?

29. In some circumstances, individuals reproduce better when the population size is large and fail to reproduce when the population size is small (this is called the Allee effect). Suppose that the per capita production rate is an increasing linear function with $\lambda(0) = -2$ and a slope of 0.01. Find $\lambda(b)$ and the differential equation for b. Is $b(t)$ increasing when $b = 100$? Is $b(t)$ increasing when $b = 300$?

30. Suppose that the per capita production rate increases linearly with $\lambda(0) = -5$ and a slope of 0.001. Find $\lambda(b)$ and the differential equation for b. Is $b(t)$ increasing when $b = 1000$? Is $b(t)$ increasing when $b = 3000$?

31–36 ▪ The derivation of the movement of chemical assumed that chemical moved as easily into the cell as out of it. If the membrane can act as a filter, the rates at which chemical enters and leaves might differ or might depend on the concentration itself. In each of the following cases, draw a diagram illustrating the situation, and write the associated differential equation. Let C be the concentration inside the cell, Γ the concentration outside, and β the constant of proportionality relating the concentration and the rate.

31. Suppose that no chemical re-enters the cell. This should look like the differential equation for a population. What would be happening to the population?

32. Suppose that no chemical leaves the cell. What would happen to the concentration?

33. Suppose that the constant of proportionality governing the rate at which chemical enters the cell is three times as large as the constant governing the rate at which it leaves. Would the concentration inside the cell be increasing or decreasing if $C = \Gamma$? What would this mean for the cell?

34. Suppose that the constant of proportionality governing the rate at which chemical enters the cell is half as large as the constant governing the rate at which it leaves. Would the concentration inside the cell be increasing or decreasing if $C = \Gamma$? What would this mean for the cell?

35. Suppose that the constant of proportionality governing the rate at which chemical enters the cell is proportional to $1 + C$ (because the chemical helps to open special channels). Would the concentration inside the cell be increasing or decreasing if $C = \Gamma$? What would this mean for the cell?

36. Suppose that the constant of proportionality governing the rate at which chemical enters the cell is proportional to $1 - C$ (because the chemical helps to close special channels). Would the concentration inside the cell be increasing or decreasing if $C = \Gamma$? What would this mean for the cell?

37–38 ▪ The model of selection includes no interaction between bacterial types a and b (the per capita production rate of each type is a constant). Write a pair of differential equations for a and b with the following forms for the per capita production rate, and derive an equation for the fraction p of type a. Assume that the basic per capita production rate for type a is $\mu = 2$, and that for type b is $\lambda = 1.5$.

37. The per capital production rate of each type is reduced by a factor of $1 - p$ (so that the per capita production rate of type a is $2(1 - p)$). This is a case where a large proportion of type a reduces the production of both types. Will type a take over?

38. The per capital production rate of type a is reduced by a factor of $1 - p$, and the per capita production rate of type b is reduced by a factor of p. This is a case where a large proportion of type a reduces the production rate of type a, and a large proportion of type b reduces the production of type b. Do you think that type a will still take over?

39–40 ▪ We will find later (with separation of variables) that the solution for Newton's law of cooling with initial condition $H(0)$ is

$$H(t) = A + (H(0) - A)e^{-\alpha t}$$

For each set of given parameter values:

a. Write and check the solution.

b. Find the temperature at $t = 1$ and $t = 2$.

c. Sketch of graph of your solution. What happens as t approaches infinity?

39. Set $\alpha = 0.2/\text{min}$, $A = 10°\text{C}$, and $H(0) = 40°\text{C}$.

40. Set $\alpha = 0.02/\text{min}$, $A = 30°\text{C}$, and $H(0) = 40°\text{C}$.

41–42 ▪ Use Euler's method to estimate the temperature for the following cases of Newton's law of cooling. Compare with the exact answer.

41. $\alpha = 0.2/\text{min}$ and $A = 10°\text{C}$, and $H(0) = 40°\text{C}$. Estimate $H(1)$ and $H(2)$ using $\Delta t = 1$. Compare with Exercise 39.

42. $\alpha = 0.02/\text{min}$ and $A = 30°\text{C}$, and $H(0) = 40°\text{C}$. Estimate $H(1)$ and $H(2)$ using $\Delta t = 1$. Compare with Exercise 40. Why is the result so close?

43–44 ▪ Use the solution for Newton's law of cooling (Exercises 39 and 40) to find the solution expressing the concentration of chemical inside a cell as a function of time in the following examples. Find the concentration after 10 s, 20 s, and 60 s. Sketch your solutions for the first minute.

43. $\beta = 0.01/\text{s}$, $C(0) = 5.0\ \text{mmol/cm}^3$, and $\Gamma = 2.0\ \text{mmol/cm}^3$.

44. $\beta = 0.1/\text{s}$, $C(0) = 5.0\ \text{mmol/cm}^3$, and $\Gamma = 2.0\ \text{mmol/cm}^3$.

45–48 ▪ Recall that the solution of the discrete-time dynamical system $b_{t+1} = rb_t$ is $b_t = r^t b_0$. This is closely related to the differential equation $\frac{db}{dt} = \lambda b$.

45. For what values of b_0 and r does this solution match $b(t) = 1.0 \times 10^6 e^{2t}$ (the solution of the differential equation with $\lambda = 2$ and $b(0) = 1.0 \times 10^6$) for all integral values of t?

46. For what values of b_0 and r does this solution match $b(t) = 100e^{-3t}$ (the solution of the differential equation with $\lambda = -3$ and $b(0) = 100$) for all integral values of t?

47. For what values of λ do solutions of the differential equation grow? For what values of r do solutions of the discrete-time dynamical system grow?

48. What is the relation between r and λ? That is, what value of r produces the same growth as a given value of λ?

49–50 ▪ Use Euler's method to estimate the value of $p(t)$ from the selection differential equation for the given parameter values. Compare with the exact answer using the equation for the solution. Graph the solution, including the estimates from Euler's method.

49. Suppose $\mu = 2.0$, $\lambda = 1.0$, and $p(0) = 0.1$. Estimate the proportion after 2 min using a time step of $\Delta t = 0.5$.

50. Suppose $\mu = 2.5$, $\lambda = 3.0$, and $p(0) = 0.6$. Estimate the proportion after 1 min using a time step of $\Delta t = 0.25$.

51–52 ▪ The rate of change in the differential equation

$$\frac{dp}{dt} = (\mu - \lambda)p(1 - p)$$

is a measure of the strength of selection. For each value of λ, graph the rate of change as a function of p with $\mu = 2.0$. For what value of p is the rate of change greatest?

51. $\lambda = 1.0$

52. $\lambda = 0.1$

Computer Exercises

53. Suppose that the ambient temperature oscillates with period T according to

$$A(t) = 20.0 + \cos\left(\frac{2\pi t}{T}\right)$$

The differential equation is

$$\frac{dH}{dt} = \alpha(A(t) - H)$$

which has a solution with $A(0) = 20.0$ of

$$H(t) = 20.0 + \frac{\alpha^2 T^2 \cos\left(\frac{2\pi t}{T}\right) + 2\alpha\pi T \sin\left(\frac{2\pi t}{T}\right) - \alpha^2 T^2 e^{-\alpha t}}{\alpha^2 T^2 + 4\pi^2}$$

a. Use a computer algebra system to check that this answer works.

b. Plot $H(t)$ for five periods using values of T ranging from 0.1 to 10.0 when $\alpha = 1.0$. Compare $H(t)$ with $A(t)$. When does the temperature of the object most closely track the ambient temperature?

54. Apply Euler's method to solve the differential equation

$$\frac{db}{dt} = b + t$$

with the initial condition $b(0) = 1.0$. Compare with the sum of the results of

$$\frac{db_1}{dt} = b_1$$

and

$$\frac{db_2}{dt} = t$$

Do you think there is a sum rule for differential equations? Compare with Section 4.1, Exercise 33. If your computer has a method for solving differential equations, find the solution and compare with your approximate solution from Euler's method.

5.2 Equilibria and Display of Autonomous Differential Equations

Euler's method provides an algorithm for computing approximate solutions of autonomous differential equations. As with discrete-time dynamical systems, much can be deduced about the dynamics by algebraically solving for **equilibria** and plotting them on a graphical summary of the dynamics, here called a **phase-line diagram.**

Equilibria

One of the most important tools for analyzing discrete-time dynamical systems is the equilibrium, a state of the system that remains unchanged by the discrete-time

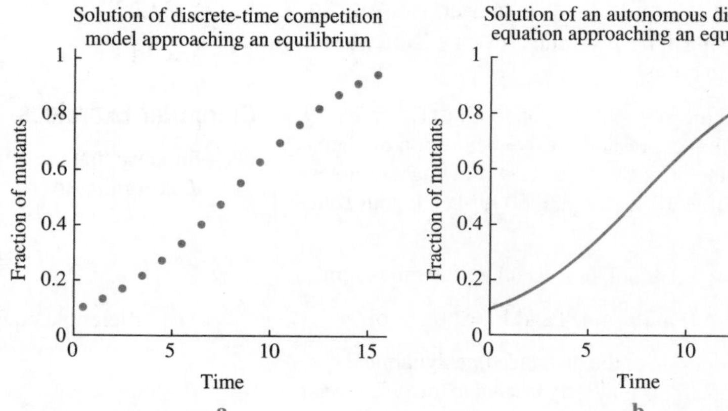

FIGURE 5.2.8

Solutions and equilibria: discrete-time dynamical systems and differential equations

dynamical system. Solutions starting from an equilibrium do not change over time. For example, solutions of the bacterial selection model (Equation 1.10.5) approach an equilibrium at $p = 1$ when the mutants are superior to the wild type whether the model is a discrete-time dynamical system (Figure 5.2.8a) or an autonomous differential equation (Figure 5.2.8b). In either case, if we started with all mutant bacteria, the population would never change.

Equilibria are as useful in analyzing autonomous differential equations as in analyzing discrete-time dynamical systems. As before, an equilibrium is a value of the state variable from which nothing happens.

Definition 5.1 A value m^* of the state variable is called an equilibrium of the autonomous differential equation

$$\frac{dm}{dt} = f(m)$$

if

$$f(m^*) = 0$$

At a point where $f(m^*) = 0$, the rate of change is 0. A rate of change of 0 indicates precisely that the value of the measurement remains the same.

The steps for finding equilibria closely resemble those for finding equilibria of a discrete-time dynamical system.

Algorithm 5.2 Finding Equilibria of an Autonomous Differential Equation

1. Make sure that the differential equation is autonomous.
2. Write the equation for the equilibria.
3. Factor.
4. Set each factor equal to 0 and solve for the equilibria.
5. Meditate upon the results.

Example 5.2.1 The Equilibria for the Bacterial Population Growth Model

The simplest autonomous differential equation we have considered is the equation for bacterial growth

$$\frac{db}{dt} = \lambda b$$

What are the equilibria of this differential equation? The rate of change depends only on b and not on the time t, so this equation is autonomous. The algebraic

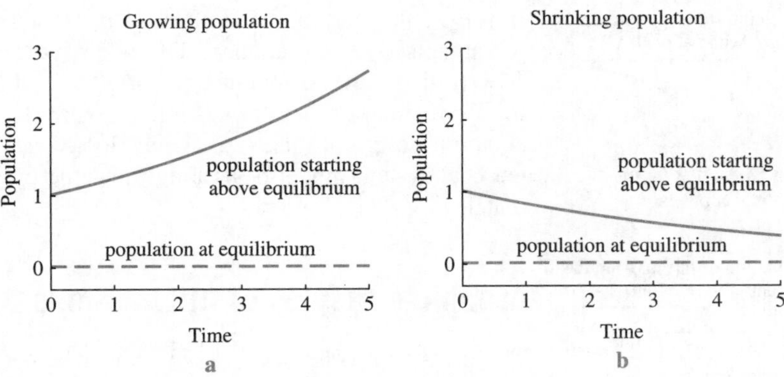

FIGURE 5.2.9
Solutions of the bacterial growth model

steps are

$$\lambda b^* = 0 \quad \text{the equation for the equilibrium}$$
$$\lambda = 0 \quad \text{or} \quad b^* = 0 \quad \text{set each factor equal to 0}$$

If $\lambda = 0$, every value of b is an equilibrium because the population does not change. This equilibrium corresponds to the case $r = 1$ of the related discrete-time dynamical system, $b_{t+1} = rb_t$. The other equilibrium at $b^* = 0$ indicates extinction, again matching the results for the discrete-time dynamical system. A solution starting from $b = 0$ remains there forever (Figure 5.2.9).

Example 5.2.2 The Equilibria for Newton's Law of Cooling

For Newton's law of cooling, the differential equation is

$$\frac{dH}{dt} = \alpha(A - H)$$

The rate of change depends only on H and not on the time t, so this equation is autonomous. To find the equilibria, we follow Algorithm 5.2.

$$\alpha(A - H^*) = 0 \quad \text{the equation for the equilibrium}$$
$$\alpha = 0 \quad \text{or} \quad A - H^* = 0 \quad \text{set each factor equal to 0}$$
$$\alpha = 0 \quad \text{or} \quad H^* = A \quad \text{solve each equation}$$

The solutions are $\alpha = 0$ and $H^* = A$. If $\alpha = 0$, no heat is exchanged with the outside world. Such an object is always at equilibrium. This corresponds to the case $q = 0$ of the lung model; a lung that exchanges no air with the outside world is at equilibrium. The other equilibrium is $H^* = A$. The object is in equilibrium when its temperature is equal to the ambient temperature. A solution with initial condition $H(0) = A$ remains there forever. This corresponds to the equilibrium $c^* = \gamma$ for the lung model (Section 1.9, p. 106), a lung that exchanges some air eventually comes to match the external environment.

Example 5.2.3 The Equilibria for Bacterial Selection Model

We follow the same algorithm to find the equilibria of the selection model

$$\frac{dp}{dt} = (\mu - \lambda)p(1 - p)$$

The equation is autonomous because the rate of change is not a function of t. The equation for the equilibria is

$$(\mu - \lambda)p^*(1 - p^*) = 0 \quad \text{the equation for the equilibrium}$$
$$\mu - \lambda = 0 \quad \text{or} \quad p^* = 0 \quad \text{or} \quad 1 - p^* = 0 \quad \text{set each factor equal to 0}$$
$$\mu = \lambda \quad \text{or} \quad p^* = 0 \quad \text{or} \quad p^* = 1 \quad \text{solve each equation}$$

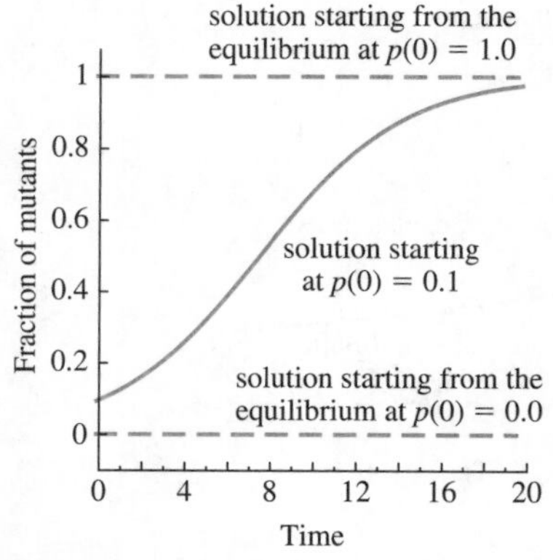

FIGURE 5.2.10

Three solutions of the bacterial selection equation

If $\mu = \lambda$, the per capita production rates of the two types match and the fraction of mutants does not change. The other two equilibria correspond to extinction. If $p^* = 0$, there are no mutants and if $p^* = 1$, there are no wild type. Solutions starting from either of these points remain there (Figure 5.2.10). Although the differential equation describing these dynamics looks very different from the discrete-time dynamical system model describing the same process (Equation 1.10.5), the equilibria match.

Graphical Display of Autonomous Differential Equations

The graphical technique of cobwebbing helped us sketch solutions of discrete-time dynamical systems with a minimum of algebra. A similarly useful graphical way to display autonomous differential equations is called the **phase-line diagram.** The diagram summarizes where the state variable is increasing, where it is decreasing, and where it is unchanged. According to the interpretation of the derivative, the state variable is increasing when the rate of change is positive, decreasing when the rate of change is negative, and unchanging when the rate of change is 0. By figuring out where the rate of change is positive, where it is negative, and where it is zero, we can get a good idea of how solutions behave.

The rate of change for Newton's law of cooling is graphed as a function of the state variable H (top of Figure 5.2.11). The rate of change is positive when $H < A$, is 0 at $H = A$, and is negative when $H > A$. The temperature is therefore increasing when $H < A$, is constant at the equilibrium $H = A$, and is decreasing when $H > A$.

This description can be translated into a one-dimensional drawing of the dynamics, the phase-line diagram, as shown at the bottom of Figure 5.2.11. The line represents the state variable, in this case the temperature, sometimes referred to as the **phase** of the system. To construct the diagram, draw rightward-pointing arrows at points where the temperature is increasing, leftward-pointing arrows at points where the temperature is decreasing, and big dots where the temperature is fixed. The directions of the arrows come from the values of the rate of change. When the rate of change is positive, the temperature is increasing and the arrow points to the right.

Solutions follow the arrows. Starting below the equilibrium, the arrows push the temperature up toward the equilibrium. Starting above the equilibrium, the arrows push the temperature down toward the equilibrium. Unlike the solutions of discrete-time dynamical systems, the temperature cannot overshoot the equilibrium.

More information can be encoded on the diagram by making the size of the arrows correspond to the magnitude of the rate of change. In Figure 5.2.11, the arrows are larger when H is farther from the equilibrium where the absolute value of the rate of

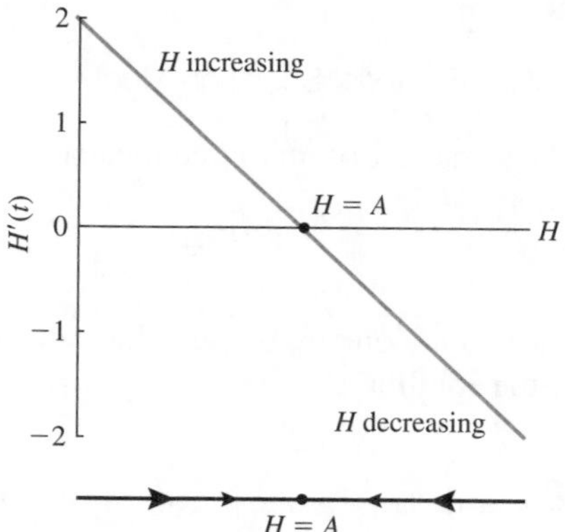

FIGURE 5.2.11

The rate of change and phase-line diagram for Newton's law of cooling

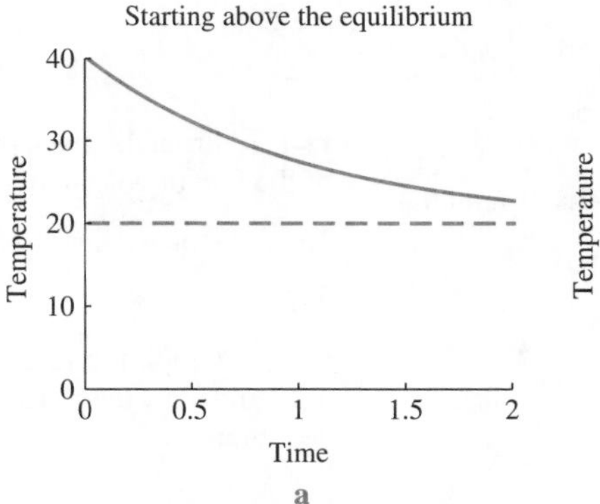

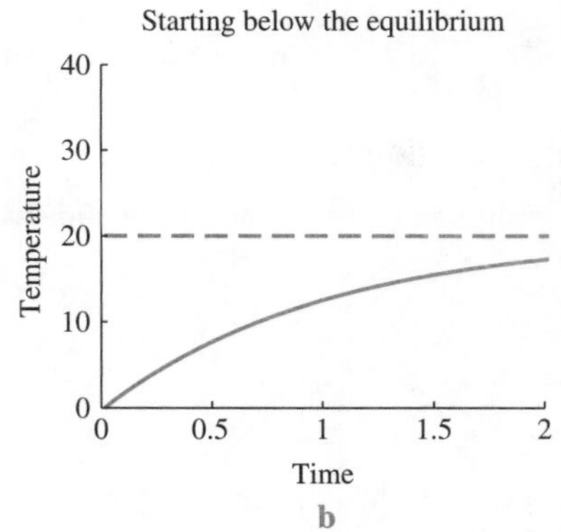

FIGURE 5.2.12
Two solutions of Newton's law of cooling

change of temperature is larger. The solutions (Figure 5.2.12) change rapidly far from the equilibrium A and more slowly near A.

Example 5.2.4 Phase-Line Diagram for the Selection Model: $\mu > \lambda$

The rate of change of the selection model

$$\frac{dp}{dt} = (\mu - \lambda)p(1 - p)$$

as a function of the state variable p in the case $\mu > \lambda$ is positive except at the equilibria (Figure 5.2.13). All the arrows on the phase-line diagram point to the right, pushing solutions toward the equilibrium at $p = 1$. The rate of change takes on its maximum value at $p = 0.5$, which means that the largest arrow is at $p = 0.5$ (Section 5.1,Exercises 51 and 52). A solution starting near $p = 0$ begins by increasing slowly, increases faster as it passes $p = 0.5$, and then slows down as it approaches $p = 1$ (Figure 5.2.10). Compared to the complicated algebra required to find a formula for this solution (Section 5.1, "A Continuous Time Model of Selection"), this method requires only the ability to graph and interpret a quadratic.

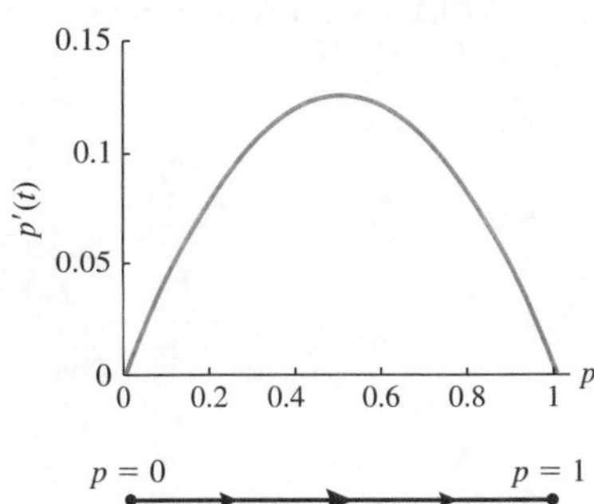

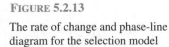

FIGURE 5.2.13
The rate of change and phase-line diagram for the selection model

The technique of phase-line diagrams is appropriate *only* for autonomous differential equations. Were we to try drawing arrows for a nonautonomous differential equation, the arrows would change with time. This is difficult to achieve in a drawing (although computers can do it through animation).

The phase-line diagram for the selection model (Figure 5.2.13) has two different kinds of equilibria. The arrows push the solution away from the equilibrium at $p = 0$ and toward the equilibrium at $p = 1$. We propose an informal definition of stable and unstable equilibria similar to that for discrete-time dynamical systems (Definition 1.16, p. 118).

Definition 5.2 An equilibrium of an autonomous differential equation is *stable* that if solutions that begin near the equilibrium approach the equilibrium. An equilibrium of an autonomous differential equation is *unstable* if solutions that begin near the equilibrium move away from the equilibrium.

Summary **Equilibria** of an autonomous differential equation are found by setting the rate of change equal to zero and solving for the state variable. By graphing the rate of change as a function of the state variable, we can identify values where the state variable is increasing or decreasing. This information can be translated into a **phase-line diagram** on which upward-pointing arrows indicate increasing solutions and downward-pointing arrows indicate decreasing solutions. This diagram can be used to sketch solutions by following the arrows.

5.2 Exercises

Mathematical Techniques

1–4 ▪ Find the equilibria of the following autonomous differential equations.

1. $\dfrac{dx}{dt} = 1 - x^2$

2. $\dfrac{dx}{dt} = 1 - e^x$

3. $\dfrac{dy}{dt} = y\cos(y)$

4. $\dfrac{dz}{dt} = \dfrac{1}{z} - 3$

5–8 ▪ Find the equilibria of the following autonomous differential equations that include parameters.

5. $\dfrac{dx}{dt} = 1 - ax$

6. $\dfrac{dx}{dt} = cx + x^2$

7. $\dfrac{dW}{dt} = \alpha e^{\beta W} - 1$

8. $\dfrac{dy}{dt} = ye^{-\beta y} - ay$

9–10 ▪ From the following graphs of the rate of change as a function of the state variable, draw the phase-line diagram.

9.

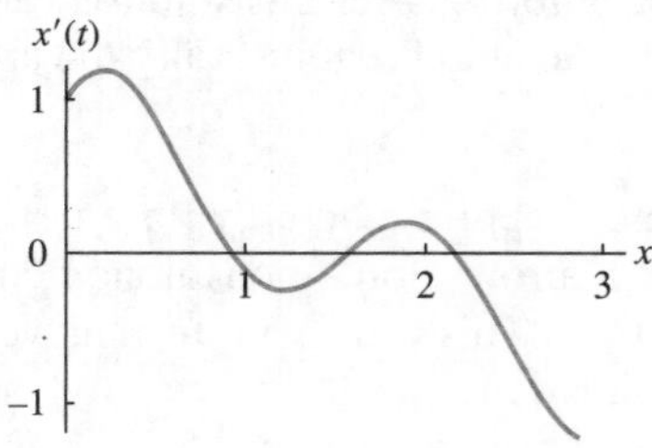

10.

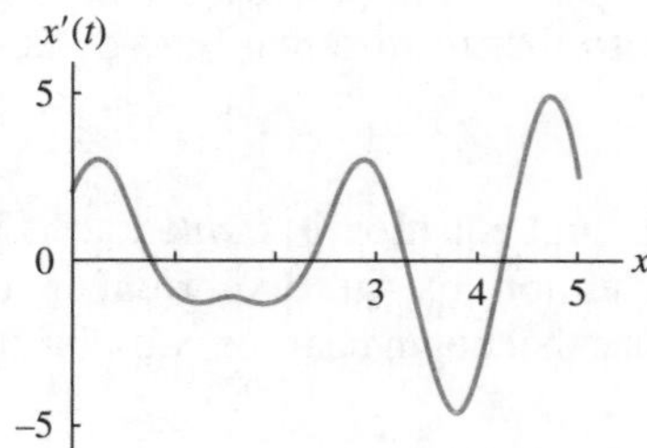

11–12 ▪ From the following phase-line diagrams, sketch a solution starting from the specified initial condition (at $x = 5$).

11. start here; $x = 2$, $x = 4$, $x = 8$

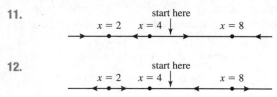

12. start here; $x = 2$, $x = 4$, $x = 8$

13–14 ▪ From the given phase-line diagram, sketch a possible graph of the rate of change of x as a function of x.

13. The phase line in Exercise 11.

14. The phase line in Exercise 12.

15–18 ▪ Graph the rate of change as a function of the state variable, and draw the phase-line diagram for the following differential equations.

15. $\dfrac{dx}{dt} = 1 - x^2$ (as in Exercise 1). Graph for $-2 \le x \le 2$.

16. $\dfrac{dx}{dt} = 1 - e^x$ (as in Exercise 2). Graph for $-2 \le x \le 2$.

17. $\dfrac{dy}{dt} = y\cos(y)$ (as in Exercise 3). Graph for $-2 \le y \le 2$.

18. $\dfrac{dz}{dt} = \dfrac{1}{z} - 3$ (as in Exercise 4). Graph for $0 < z \le 1$.

19–22 ▪ Try to find the "equilibria" of the following nonautonomous differential equations. What goes wrong? Graph the "equilibria" as functions of time for $0 \le t \le 5$.

19. $\dfrac{dx}{dt} = x - t$

20. $\dfrac{dx}{dt} = \ln(x) + t$

21. $\dfrac{dx}{dt} = x^2 - t + 1$

22. $\dfrac{dx}{dt} = x^2 - t^2$

Applications

23–24 ▪ Suppose that a population is growing at constant per capita production rate λ but that individuals are harvested at a rate of h. The differential equation describing such a population is

$$\frac{db}{dt} = \lambda b - h$$

For each of the following values of λ and h, find the equilibrium, draw the phase-line diagram, and sketch one solution with initial condition below the equilibrium and another with initial condition above the equilibrium. Explain your result in words.

23. $\lambda = 2.0$, $h = 1000$

24. $\lambda = 0.5$, $h = 1000$

25–28 ▪ Find the equilibria, graph the rate of change $\dfrac{db}{dt}$ as a function of b, and draw a phase-line diagram for the following models describing bacterial population growth.

25. The model in Section 5.1, Exercise 27. Check that your arrows are consistent with the behavior of $b(t)$ at $b = 10$ and $b = 1000$.

26. The model in Section 5.1, Exercise 28. Check that your arrows are consistent with the behavior of $b(t)$ at $b = 1000$ and $b = 5000$.

27. The model in Section 5.1, Exercise 29. Check that your arrows are consistent with the behavior of $b(t)$ at $b = 100$ and $b = 300$.

28. The model in Section 5.1, Exercise 30. Check that your arrows are consistent with the behavior of $b(t)$ at $b = 1000$ and $b = 3000$.

29–30 ▪ Find the equilibria, graph the rate of change $\frac{dC}{dt}$ as a function of C, and draw a phase-line diagram for the following models describing chemical diffusion.

29. The model in Section 5.1, Exercise 33. Check that the direction arrow is consistent with the behavior of $C(t)$ at $C = \Gamma$.

30. The model in Section 5.1, Exercise 34. Check that the direction arrow is consistent with the behavior of $C(t)$ at $C = \Gamma$.

31–32 ▪ Find the equilibria, graph the rate of change $\frac{dp}{dt}$ as a function of p, and draw a phase-line diagram for the following models describing selection.

31. The model in Section 5.1, Exercise 37. What happens to a solution starting from a small, but positive, value of p?

32. The model in Section 5.1, Exercise 38. What happens to a solution starting from a small, but positive, value of p?

33–40 ▪ Find the equilibria and draw the phase-line diagram for the following differential equations, in addition to answering the questions.

33. Suppose the population size of some species of organism follows the model

$$\frac{dN}{dt} = \frac{3N^2}{2 + N^2} - N$$

where N is measured in hundreds. Why might this population behave as it does at small values? This is another example of the Allee effect discussed in Section 5.1, Exercise 29.

34. Suppose the population size of some species of organism follows the model

$$\frac{dN}{dt} = \frac{5N^2}{1 + N^2} - 2N$$

where N is measured in hundreds. What is the critical value below which this population is doomed to extinction (as in Exercise 33)?

35. The drag on a falling object is proportional to the square of its speed. The differential equation is

$$\frac{dv}{dt} = a - Dv^2$$

where v is speed, a is acceleration, and D is drag. Suppose that $a = 9.8\ \text{m/s}^2$ and that $D = 0.0032$ per meter (values for a falling sky-diver). Check that the units in the differential equation are consistent. What does the equilibrium speed mean?

36. Consider the same situation as in Exercise 35 but for a sky-diver diving head down with her arms against her sides and her toes pointed, thus minimizing drag. The drag D is reduced to $D = 0.00048/\text{m}$. Find the equilibrium speed. How does it compare to the ordinary sky-diver?

37. According to Torricelli's law of draining, the rate at which a fluid flows out of a cylinder through a hole at the bottom is proportional to the square root of the depth of the water. Let y represent the depth of water in centimeters. The differential equation is

$$\frac{dy}{dt} = -c\sqrt{y}$$

where $c = 2.0\sqrt{\text{cm}}/\text{s}$. Show that the units are consistent. Use your phase-line diagram to sketch solutions starting from $y = 10.0$ and $y = 1.0$.

38. Write a differential equation describing the depth of water in a cylinder where water enters at a rate of 4.0 cm/s but drains out as in Exercise 37. Use your phase-line diagram to sketch solutions starting from $y = 10.0$ and $y = 1.0$.

39. One of the most important differential equations in chemistry uses the **Michaelis-Menton** or **Monod** equation. Suppose S is the concentration of a substrate that is being converted into a product. Then

$$\frac{dS}{dt} = -k_1 \frac{S}{k_2 + S}$$

describes how substrate is used. Set $k_1 = k_2 = 1$. How does this equation differ from Torricelli's law of draining (Exercise 37)?

40. Write a differential equation describing the amount of substrate if substrate is added at rate R but is converted into product as in Exercise 39. Find the equilibrium. Draw the phase-plane diagram and a representative solution with $R = 0.5$ and $R = 1.5$. Can you explain your results?

41–42 ▪ Small organisms such as bacteria take in food at rates proportional to their surface area but use energy at higher rates.

41. Suppose that energy is used at a rate proportional to the mass. In this case,

$$\frac{dV}{dt} = a_1 V^{2/3} - a_2 V$$

where V represents the volume in cubic centimeters and t is time measured in days. The first term says that surface area is proportional to volume to the 2/3 power. The constant a_1 gives the rate at which energy is taken in and has units of centimeters per day. a_2 is the rate at which energy is used and has units of per day. Check the units. Find the equilibrium. What happens to the equilibrium as a_1 becomes smaller? Does this make sense? What happens to the equilibrium as a_2 becomes smaller? Does this make sense?

42. Suppose that energy is used at a rate proportional to the mass to the 3/4 power (closer to what is observed). In this case,

$$\frac{dV}{dt} = a_1 V^{2/3} - a_2 V^{3/4}$$

Find the units of a_2 if V is measured in cubic centimeters and t is measured in days. (They should look rather strange.) Find the equilibrium. What happens to the equilibrium as a_1 becomes smaller? Does this make sense? What happens to the equilibrium as a_2 becomes smaller? Does this make sense?

Computer Exercises

43. Consider the differential equation

$$\frac{db}{dt} = -b^{-p}$$

for various positive values of the parameter p starting from $b(0) = 1.0$. For which values of p does the solution approach the equilibrium at $b = 0$ most quickly? Plot the solution on a semilog graph. When does the solution approach 0 faster than an exponential function?

44. In Section 5.1, Exercise 53 we considered the equation

$$\frac{dH}{dt} = \alpha(A(t) - H)$$

where

$$A(t) = 20.0 + \cos\left(\frac{2\pi t}{T}\right)$$

Using either the solution given in that problem or a computer system that can solve the equation, show that the solution always approaches the "equilibrium" at $H = A(t)$. Use the parameter values $\alpha = 1.0$ and values of T ranging from 0.1 to 10.0. For which value of T does the solution get closest to $A(t)$? Can you explain why?

5.3 Stable and Unstable Equilibria

Phase-line diagrams for autonomous differential equations have two types of equilibria: stable and unstable. Solutions starting near a stable equilibrium move closer to the equilibrium. The equilibrium of Newton's law of cooling (Figure 5.2.11) and the equilibrium at $p = 1$ of the selection equation with superior mutants (Figure 5.2.13) are stable in this sense. Solutions starting near an unstable equilibrium move farther from the equilibrium. The equilibrium at $p = 0$ of the selection equation (Figure 5.2.13) is unstable. By reasoning about the graph of the rate of change, we can find an algebraic way to recognize stable and unstable equilibria.

Recognizing Stable and Unstable Equilibria

Consider again Newton's law of cooling

$$\frac{dH}{dt} = \alpha(A - H)$$

(Figure 5.3.14). Our phase-line diagram and our intuition suggest that the equilibrium $H = A$ is stable. Arrows to the left of the equilibrium point right, pushing solutions up toward the equilibrium (a cool object warms up). Arrows to the right of the equilibrium point left, pushing solutions down toward the equilibrium (a hot object cools off). The equilibrium must be stable.

The rate of change is positive to the left of the equilibrium and negative to the right of a stable equilibrium. Therefore, the rate-of-change function must be **decreasing** at the equilibrium, implying that the **derivative** of the rate-of-change function is negative. An equilibrium is stable if the derivative of the rate of change *with respect to the state variable* is negative at the equilibrium. The right-hand equilibrium in Figure 5.3.15 satisfies this criterion.

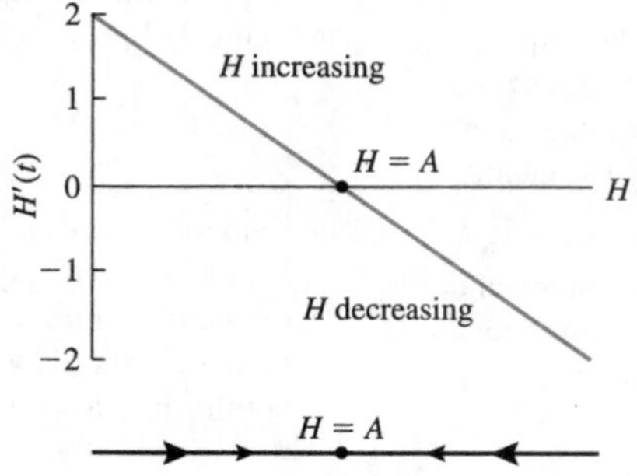

FIGURE 5.3.14

The rate of change and phase-line diagram for Newton's law of cooling revisited

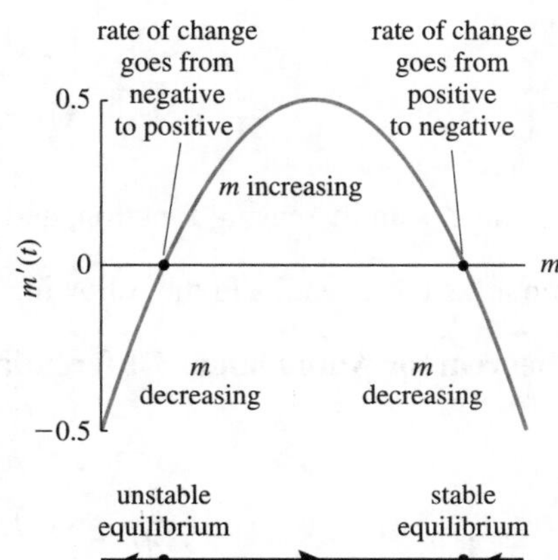

FIGURE 5.3.15

Behavior at equilibria with positive and negative derivatives

Example 5.3.1 The Derivative of the Rate-of-Change Function for Newton's Law of Cooling

The function $\alpha(A - H)$ gives the rate of change of H in Newton's law of cooling. If H is slightly larger than the equilibrium value A, the rate of change is negative. If H is slightly smaller than A, the rate of change is positive. To check stability with the derivative criterion, we compute the derivative of the rate of change with respect to the state variable H,

$$\frac{d}{dH}[\alpha(A - H)] = -\alpha < 0$$

The rate of change is a decreasing function at the equilibrium, and the equilibrium is therefore stable (Figure 5.3.14).

At an unstable equilibrium, the arrows push solutions away. Solutions starting above the equilibrium increase, and those starting below decrease. In terms of the rate of change, an equilibrium is unstable if the rate of change is negative below the equilibrium and positive above it. This implies that the rate of change function is increasing and that the derivative of the rate of change function is positive. An equilibrium is unstable if the derivative of the rate of change with respect to the state variable is positive at the equilibrium. The left-hand equilibrium in Figure 5.3.15 satisfies this criterion.

Example 5.3.2 The Rate of Change for a Perverse Version of Newton's Law of Cooling

Imagine a perverse version of Newton's law of cooling given by

$$\frac{dH}{dt} = \alpha(H - A)$$

with $\alpha > 0$. Objects cooler than A decrease in temperature, and objects warmer than A increase in temperature. The rate of change and the phase-line diagram are shown in Figure 5.3.16. The derivative of the rate of change with respect to H at

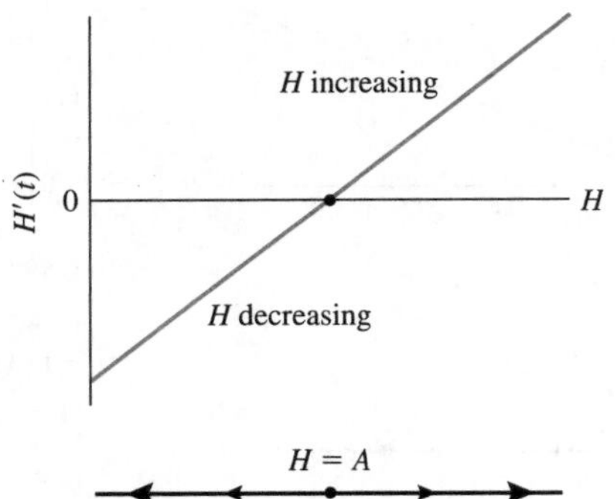

FIGURE 5.3.16

A perverse version of Newton's law of cooling

$H = A$ is

$$\frac{d}{dH}[\alpha(H - A)] = \alpha > 0$$

The rate of change is an increasing function, and the equilibrium is unstable.

We summarize these results in the following simple and powerful theorem.

Theorem 5.1 **Stability Theorem for Autonomous Differential Equations**

Suppose

$$\frac{dy}{dt} = f(y)$$

is an autonomous differential equation with an equilibrium at y^*. Let $f'(y)$ represent the derivative of f with respect to y. The equilibrium at y^* is stable if

$$f'(y^*) < 0$$

and is unstable if

$$f'(y^*) > 0$$

Applications of the Stability Theorem

We now apply the stability theorem for autonomous differential equations to our models of population growth and selection to check whether the phase-line diagrams are correct.

Example 5.3.3 Applying the Stability Theorem to Bacterial Population Dynamics

The equation for population growth is

$$\frac{db}{dt} = \lambda b$$

If $\lambda \neq 0$, the only equilibrium is $b^* = 0$. The derivative of the rate of change λb with respect to b is

$$\frac{d}{db}(\lambda b) = \lambda$$

According to the stability theorem for autonomous differential equations, the equilibrium is stable if the derivative is negative. If $\lambda > 0$, the equilibrium is unstable (Figure 5.3.17a) and if $\lambda < 0$ the equilibrium is stable (Figure 5.3.17b).

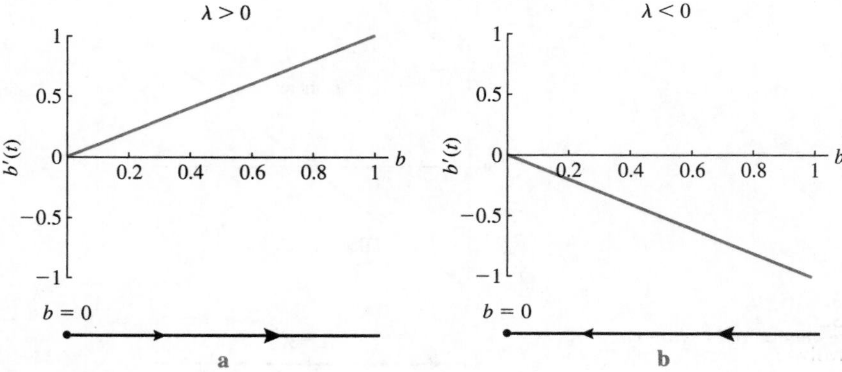

FIGURE 5.3.17
Phase-line diagrams for the bacterial growth model

On p. 420, we found the solution of the bacterial growth model by guessing. With initial condition $b(0) = b_0$, the solution is

$$b(t) = b_0 e^{\lambda t}$$

If $\lambda > 0$, the solution increases exponentially without bound from any positive initial condition, as is consistent with the instability of the equilibrium in this case (Figure 5.3.17a). If $\lambda < 0$, the solution decreases exponentially toward zero, as is consistent with the stability of the equilibrium in this case (Figure 5.3.17b).

There are two important differences between using the stability theorem for autonomous differential equations and solving the equation to figure out whether the equilibrium is stable. The stability theorem helps us recognize stable and unstable equilibria with a minimum of work; we solve for the equilibria and compute the derivative of the rate of change with respect to b. Finding what happens near an equilibrium by computing the solution requires more work: finding the solution and then evaluating its limit as t approaches infinity. We seem to have gotten something for nothing. In mathematics, as in life, this is rarely the case. The other difference between the two methods is that the simpler calculation based on the stability theorem gives less information about the solutions, telling us only what happens to solutions that start *near* the equilibrium.

Example 5.3.4 Applying the Stability Theorem to the Selection Equation

In cases where finding the exact solution is difficult or impossible, this **local information** about solutions near an equilibrium may be all we can find. Computing the solution of the selection equation

$$\frac{dp}{dt} = f(p) = (\mu - \lambda)p(1 - p)$$

is possible but tricky (Section 5.1, pp. 418–419). Finding the stability of the equilibria with the stability theorem is straightforward. The differential equation has equilibria at $p = 0$ and $p = 1$ (Section 5.2, pp. 425–426). The derivative of the rate of change $f(p)$ with respect to p is

$$f'(p) = \frac{d}{dp}[(\mu - \lambda)p(1 - p)] = (\mu - \lambda)(1 - 2p)$$

Then

$$f'(0) = \mu - \lambda$$
$$f'(1) = \lambda - \mu$$

If $\mu > \lambda$, the equilibrium $p = 0$ has a positive derivative and is unstable, and the equilibrium $p = 1$ has a negative derivative and is stable, matching Figure 5.3.18. These results make biological sense; the mutant is superior in this case. If $\mu < \lambda$, the mutant is at a disadvantage, and the $p = 0$ equilibrium is stable, and the $p = 1$ equilibrium is unstable.

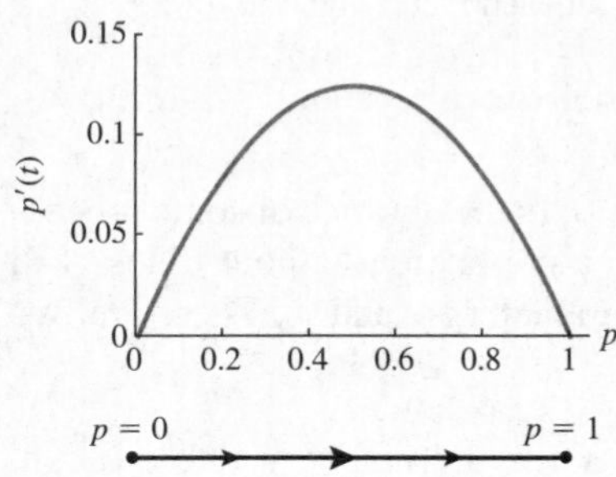

FIGURE 5.3.18
The rate of change and phase-line diagram for the selection model revisited with $\mu - \lambda = 0.5$

A Model of a Disease

Suppose a disease is circulating in a population. Individuals recover from this disease unharmed but are susceptible to reinfection. How many people will be sick at any given time? Is there any way that such a disease will die out? The factors affecting the dynamics are sketched in Figure 5.3.19.

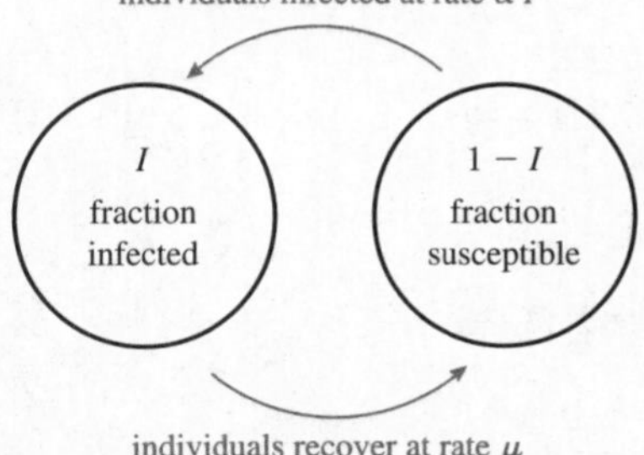

FIGURE 5.3.19
Factors involved in disease dynamics

Let I denote the fraction of infected individuals in the population. Each uninfected, or susceptible, individual has a chance of getting infected when she encounters an infectious individual (depending, perhaps, on whether she gets sneezed on). It seems plausible that a susceptible individual will run into infectious individuals at a rate proportional to the number of infectious individuals. Then

$$\text{per capita rate at which a susceptible individual is infected} = \alpha I$$

The parameter α combines the rate at which people are encountered and the probability that an encounter produces an infection.

What fraction of individuals are susceptible? Every individual is either infected or not, so a fraction $1 - I$ are susceptible. The overall rate at which new individuals are infected is the per capita rate times the fraction, or

$$\begin{aligned}&\text{rate at which susceptible individuals are infected}\\ &\quad = \text{per capita rate} \times \text{fraction of individuals}\\ &\quad = \alpha I(1 - I)\end{aligned}$$

Individuals recover from the disease at a rate proportional to the fraction of infected individuals, or

$$\text{rate at which infected individuals recover} = \mu I$$

Putting the two processes together by adding the rates, we have

$$\frac{dI}{dt} = \alpha I(1 - I) - \mu I \tag{5.3.1}$$

Suppose we start with a few infected individuals, a small value of I. Will the disease persist? The equilibria and their stability can provide the answer. To find the equilibria, we use Algorithm 5.2. Equation 5.3.1 is autonomous because the rate of change depends only on the state variable I and not on time.

$$\begin{aligned}\alpha I^*(1 - I^*) - \mu I^* &= 0 && \text{the equation for the equilibrium}\\ I^*[\alpha(1 - I^*) - \mu] &= 0 && \text{factor out } I^*\\ I^* = 0 \quad \text{or} \quad \alpha(1 - I^*) - \mu &= 0 && \text{set each factor equal to 0}\\ I^* = 0 \quad \text{or} \quad I^* &= 1 - \frac{\mu}{\alpha} && \text{solve each equation}\end{aligned}$$

Do these make sense? There are no sick people if $I = 0$. In the absence of some process bringing in infected people (migration, UFOs, etc.), a population without illness will remain so. The other equilibrium depends on the parameters α and μ. There are two cases, depending upon which parameter is larger.

Case 1: If $\alpha < \mu$, $1 - \frac{\mu}{\alpha} < 0$, which is nonsense. When the recovery rate is large, the only biologically plausible equilibrium is $I = 0$.

Case 2: If $\alpha > \mu$, $1 > 1 - \frac{\mu}{\alpha} > 0$, which is biologically possible. There are two equilibria if the infection rate is larger than the recovery rate.

To draw the phase-line diagrams for the two cases, we must compute the stability of the equilibria. The derivative of the rate of change with respect to the state variable I is

$$\frac{d}{dI}[\alpha I(1 - I) - \mu I] = \alpha - 2\alpha I - \mu \tag{5.3.2}$$

Case 1: If $\alpha < \mu$, the derivative at $I = 0$ is

$$\alpha - 2\alpha \cdot 0 - \mu = \alpha - \mu < 0$$

The single equilibrium is stable.

Case 2: If $\alpha > \mu$, the derivative at $I = 0$ is

$$\alpha - 2\alpha \cdot 0 - \mu = \alpha - \mu > 0$$

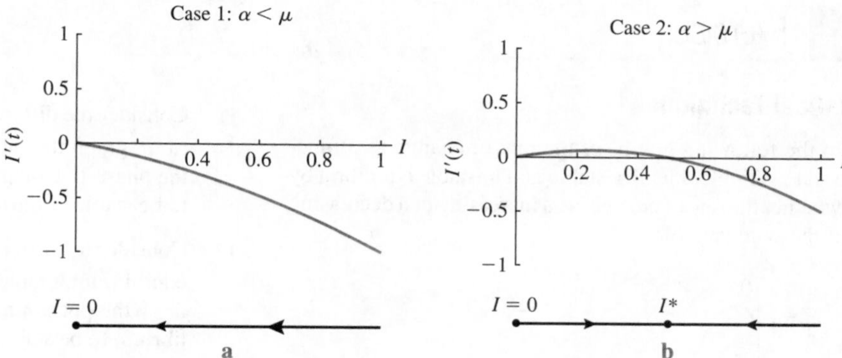

FIGURE 5.3.20

Phase-line diagrams for the disease model

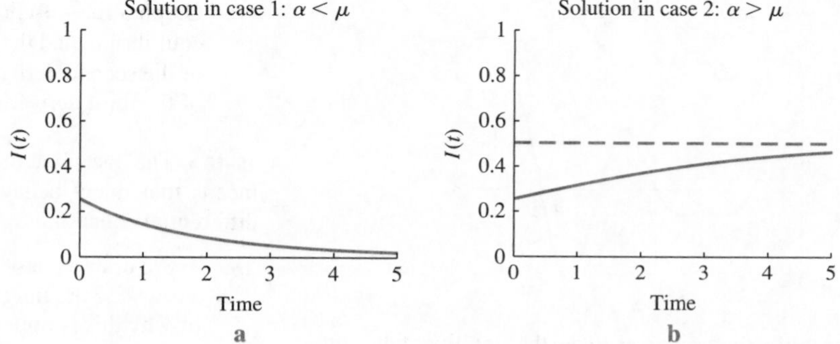

FIGURE 5.3.21

Solutions of the disease equation in two cases

and this equilibrium is unstable. At $I^* = 1 - \frac{\mu}{\alpha}$, the derivative of the rate of change is

$$\alpha - 2\alpha \cdot \left(1 - \frac{\mu}{\alpha}\right) - \mu = \mu - \alpha < 0$$

The positive equilibrium is stable. The phase-line diagrams for the two cases are drawn in Figure 5.3.20.

From our phase-line diagram, we can deduce the behavior of solutions. In case 1, with $\alpha < \mu$, all solutions converge to the equilibrium at $I = 0$ (Figure 5.3.21a). If control measures could be implemented to increase the recovery rate μ or reduce the transmission α, the disease could be completely eliminated from a population. The transmission α need not be reduced to zero to eliminate the disease. This is an example of the **threshold theorem**, an idea referred to in Section 1.1. In case 2, with $\mu < \alpha$, the equilibrium I^* is positive and stable. Solutions starting near 0 increase to I^* and the disease remains present in the population (Figure 5.3.21b). Such a disease is called **endemic.**

Summary By examining the phase-line diagram near an equilibrium, we found the stability theorem for autonomous differential equations. An equilibrium of an autonomous differential equation is stable if the derivative of the rate of change with respect to the state variable is negative and is unstable if this derivative is positive. Calculating stability in this way is easier than solving the equation but does not provide exact information about the behavior of solutions far from the equilibrium. We applied this method to several familiar models and to a model of a disease, showing that a disease could be eradicated without entirely stopping transmission.

5.3 Exercises

Mathematical Techniques

1–2 ▪ From the following graphs of the rate of change as a function of the state variable, identify stable and unstable equilibria by checking whether the rate of change is an increasing or a decreasing function of the state variable.

1. 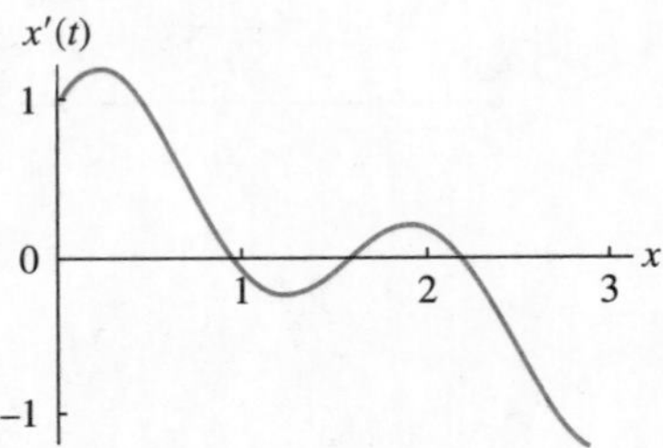

2. 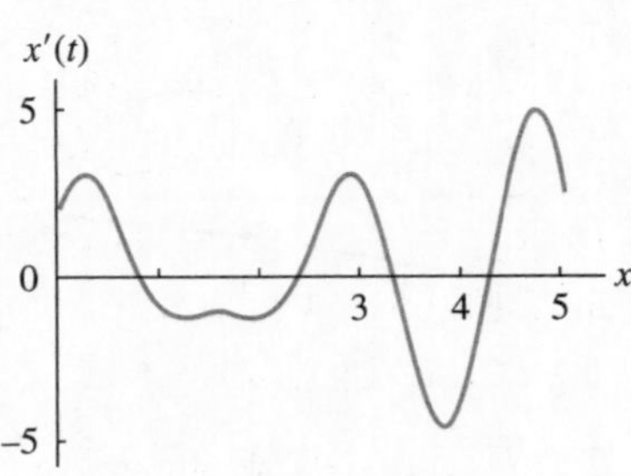

3–6 ▪ Use the stability theorem to evaluate the stability of the equilibria of the following autonomous differential equations.

3. $\frac{dx}{dt} = 1 - x^2$ (as in Section 5.2, Exercise 1). Compare your results with the phase line in Section 5.2, Exercise 15.

4. $\frac{dx}{dt} = 1 - e^x$ (as in Section 5.2, Exercise 2). Compare your results with the phase line in Section 5.2, Exercise 16.

5. $\frac{dy}{dt} = y\cos(y)$ (as in Section 5.2, Exercise 3). Compare your results with the phase line in Section 5.2, Exercise 17.

6. $\frac{dz}{dt} = \frac{1}{z} - 3$ (as in Section 5.2, Exercise 4). Compare your results with the phase line in Section 5.2, Exercise 18.

7–10 ▪ Find the stability of the equilibria of the following autonomous differential equations that include parameters.

7. $\frac{dx}{dt} = 1 - ax$ (as in Section 5.2, Exercise 5). Suppose that $a > 0$.

8. $\frac{dx}{dt} = cx + x^2$ (as in Section 5.2, Exercise 6). Suppose that $c > 0$.

9. $\frac{dW}{dt} = \alpha e^{\beta W} - 1$ (as in Section 5.2, Exercise 7). Suppose that $\alpha > 0$ and $\beta < 0$.

10. $\frac{dy}{dt} = ye^{-\beta y} - ay$ (as in Section 5.2, Exercise 8). Suppose that $\beta < 0$ and $a > 1$.

11–14 ▪ As with discrete-time dynamical systems, equilibria can act strangely when the slope of the rate of change function is exactly equal to the critical value of 0.

11. Consider the differential equation $\frac{dx}{dt} = x^2$. Find the equilibrium, graph the rate of change as a function of x, and draw the phase-line diagram. Would you consider the equilibrium to be stable or unstable?

12. Consider the differential equation $\frac{dx}{dt} = -(1-x)^4$. Find the equilibrium, graph the rate of change as a function of x, and draw the phase-line diagram. Would you consider the equilibrium to be stable or unstable?

13. Graph a rate-of-change function that has a slope of 0 at the equilibrium and the equilibrium is stable. What is the sign of the second derivative at the equilibrium? What is the sign of the third derivative at the equilibrium?

14. Graph a rate-of-change function that has a slope of 0 at the equilibrium and the equilibrium is unstable. What is the sign of the second derivative at the equilibrium? What is the sign of the third derivative at the equilibrium?

15–16 ▪ The fact that the rate-of-change function is continuous means that many behaviors are impossible for an autonomous differential equation.

15. Try to draw a phase-line diagram with two stable equilibria in a row. Use the Intermediate Value Theorem to sketch a proof of why this is impossible.

16. Why is it impossible for a solution of an autonomous differential equation to oscillate?

17–20 ▪ When parameter values change, the number and stability of equilibria sometimes change. Such changes are called bifurcations, and they play a central role in the study of differential equations. The following exercises illustrate several of the more important bifurcations. Graph the equilibria as functions of the parameter value, using a solid line when an equilibrium is stable and a dashed line when an equilibrium is unstable. This picture is called a **bifurcation diagram.**

17. Consider the equation
$$\frac{dx}{dt} = ax - x^2$$
for both positive and negative values of x. Find the equilibria as functions of a for values of a between -1 and 1. Draw a bifurcation diagram and describe in words what happens at $a = 0$. The change that occurs at $a = 0$ is called a **transcritical bifurcation.**

18. Consider the equation
$$\frac{dx}{dt} = a - x^2$$
for both positive and negative values of x. Find the equilibria as functions of a for values of a between -1 and 1. Draw a bifurcation diagram and describe in words what happens at $a = 0$. The change that occurs at $a = 0$ is called a **saddle-node bifurcation.**

19. Consider the equation

$$\frac{dx}{dt} = ax - x^3$$

for both positive and negative values of x. Find the equilibria as functions of a for values of a between -1 and 1. Draw a bifurcation diagram and describe in words what happens at $a = 0$. The change that occurs at $a = 0$ is called a **pitchfork bifurcation.**

20. Consider the equation

$$\frac{dx}{dt} = ax + x^3$$

for both positive and negative values of x. Find the equilibria as functions of a for values of a between -1 and 1. Draw a bifurcation diagram and describe in words what happens at $a = 0$. The change that occurs at $a = 0$ is a slightly different type of **pitchfork bifurcation** (Exercise 19) called a **subcritical bifurcation** (Exercise 19 is **supercritical**). How does your picture differ from a simple mirror image of that in Exercise 19?

Applications

21–24 ▪ Use the stability theorem to check the phase-line diagrams for the following models of bacterial population growth.

21. The model in Section 5.1, Exercise 27 and Section 5.2, Exercise 25.

22. The model in Section 5.1, Exercise 28 and Section 5.2, Exercise 26.

23. The model in Section 5.1, Exercise 29 and Section 5.2, Exercise 27.

24. The model in Section 5.1, Exercise 30 and Section 5.2, Exercise 28.

25–26 ▪ Use the stability theorem to check the phase-line diagrams for the following models of selection.

25. The model in Section 5.1, Exercise 37 and Section 5.2, Exercise 31.

26. The model in Section 5.1, Exercise 38 and Section 5.2, Exercise 32.

27–30 ▪ A **reaction-diffusion equation** describes how chemical concentration changes in response to two factors simultaneously, reaction and movement. A simple model has the form

$$\frac{dC}{dt} = \beta(\Gamma - C) + R(C)$$

The first term describes diffusion, and the second term $R(C)$ is the reaction, which could have a positive or a negative sign (depending on whether chemical is being created or destroyed). Suppose that $\beta = 1.0$/min and $\Gamma = 5.0$ mol/L. For each of the following forms of $R(C)$:

a. Describe how the reaction rate depends on the concentration.

b. Find the equilibria and their stability.

c. Describe how absorption changes the results.

27. $R(C) = -C$

28. $R(C) = 0.5C$

29. $R(C) = \dfrac{C}{2 + C}$

30. $R(C) = -\dfrac{C}{2 + C}$

31–40 ▪ Apply the stability theorem for autonomous differential equations to the following equations. Show that your results match what you found in your phase-line diagrams, and give a biological interpretation.

31. The equation in Section 5.2, Exercise 33.

32. The equation in Section 5.2, Exercise 34.

33. The equation in Section 5.2, Exercise 35.

34. The equation in Section 5.2, Exercise 36.

35. The equation in Section 5.2, Exercise 37.

36. The equation in Section 5.2, Exercise 38.

37. The equation in Section 5.2, Exercise 39.

38. The equation in Section 5.2, Exercise 40 with $R = 0.5$.

39. The equation in Section 5.2, Exercise 41.

40. The equation in Section 5.2, Exercise 42.

41–44 ▪ Exercises 17–20 show how the number and stability of equilibria can change when a parameter changes. Often, bifurcations have important biological applications, and bifurcation diagrams help in explaining how the dynamics of a system can suddenly change when a parameter changes only slightly. In each case, graph the equilibria against the parameter value, using a solid line when an equilibrium is stable and a dashed line when an equilibrium is unstable to draw the bifurcation diagram.

41. Consider the logistic differential equation (Section 5.1, Exercise 27) with harvesting proportional to population size, or $\frac{db}{dt} = b(1 - b - h)$ where h represents the fraction harvested. Graph the equilibria as functions of h for values of h between 0 and 2, using a solid line when an equilibrium is stable and a dashed line when an equilibrium is unstable. Even though they do not make biological sense, include negative values of the equilibria on your graph. You should find a *transcritical bifurcation* (Exercise 17) at $h = 1$.

42. Suppose $\mu = 1$ in the basic disease model $\frac{dI}{dt} = \alpha I(1 - I) - \mu I$. Graph the two equilibria as functions of α for values of α between 0 and 2, using a solid line when an equilibrium is stable and a dashed line when an equilibrium is unstable. Even though they do not make biological sense, include negative values of the equilibria on your graph. You should find a *transcritical bifurcation* (Exercise 17) at $\alpha = 1$.

43. Consider a version of the equation in Section 5.2, Exercise 33 that includes the parameter r,

$$\frac{dN}{dt} = \frac{rN^2}{1 + N^2} - N$$

Graph the equilibria as functions of r for values of r between 0 and 3, using a solid line when an equilibrium is stable and a dashed line when an equilibrium is unstable. The algebra for checking stability is messy, so it is necessary to check stability only at $r = 3$. You should find a *saddle-node bifurcation* (Exercise 18) at $r = 2$.

44. Consider a variant of the basic disease model given by

$$\frac{dI}{dt} = \alpha I^2(1 - I) - I$$

Graph the equilibria as functions of α for values of α between 0 and 5, using a solid line when an equilibrium is stable and a dashed line when an equilibrium is unstable. The algebra for checking stability is messy, so it is necessary to check stability only at $\alpha = 5$. You should find a *saddle-node bifurcation* (Exercise 18) at $\alpha = 4$.

45–46 ▪ Right at a bifurcation point, the stability theorem fails because the slope of the rate of change function at the equilibrium is exactly 0. In each of the following cases, check that the stability theorem fails, and then draw a phase-line diagram to find the stability of the equilibrium.

45. Analyze the stability of the positive equilibrium in the model from Exercise 44 when $\alpha = 4$, the point where the bifurcation occurs.

46. Analyze the stability of the disease model when $\alpha = \mu = 1$, the point where the bifurcation occurs in Exercise 42.

5.4 Solving Autonomous Differential Equations

The method of phase-line diagrams enables us to sketch solutions with a minimum of algebra. What if we want an exact formula for the solution? Guessing sometimes works, as with pure-time differential equations. For a more dependable method, we would like to transform the problem of solving an autonomous differential equation into an integration problem. The technique for doing this is called **separation of variables** and is among the most powerful techniques in applied mathematics.

Separation of Variables

Consider the autonomous differential equation for bacterial growth

$$\frac{db}{dt} = \lambda b \tag{5.4.1}$$

We cannot integrate to solve this as we could with a pure-time differential equation, because integrating the function λb requires knowing the solution $b(t)$.

The trick of separation of variables, as the name implies, is to separate the two variables: the b's and the t's. To separate variables, we divide both sides by b to get all the b's on the left-hand side and multiply by dt to get all the t's on the right-hand side, arriving at

$$\frac{db}{b} = \lambda\, dt$$

As with substitution, we can treat dt like the denominator of a fraction. The next step is to compute the indefinite integral of each side. The left-hand side has a db and can be integrated using b as the variable, or

$$\int \frac{1}{b}\, db = \ln(|b|) + c_1$$

The absolute value bars around b are unnecessary because b represents a population and must be positive. The right-hand side has a dt and can be integrated using t as the variable, or

$$\int \lambda\, dt = \lambda t + c_2$$

The idea of separation of variables is that if $\frac{db}{b} = \lambda dt$, the integrals must also be equal. Therefore,

$$\ln(b) + c_1 = \lambda t + c_2$$

Because c_1 and c_2 are arbitrary constants, we can combine the two constants into one by setting $c = c_2 - c_1$

$$\ln(b) = \lambda t + c$$

Finally, we solve for b in terms of t. In this case, we can do so by exponentiating both sides, finding

$$b = e^{\lambda t + c}$$

This solution might look strange because the arbitrary constant is inside the exponential function. It is often more convenient to move the constant outside. In particular, if we define the new constant

$$K = e^{c}$$

we find that

$$e^{\lambda t + c} = e^{\lambda t} e^{c} = K e^{\lambda t}$$

We find the constant K by substituting the initial condition.

Example 5.4.1 An Increasing Solution of the Bacterial Growth Equation

If $b(0) = 1000$, then

$$1000 = b(0) = K e^{\lambda \cdot 0} = K$$

The solution with $\lambda = 2$ and $b(0) = 1000$ is

$$b(t) = 1000e^{2t}$$

(Figure 5.4.22).

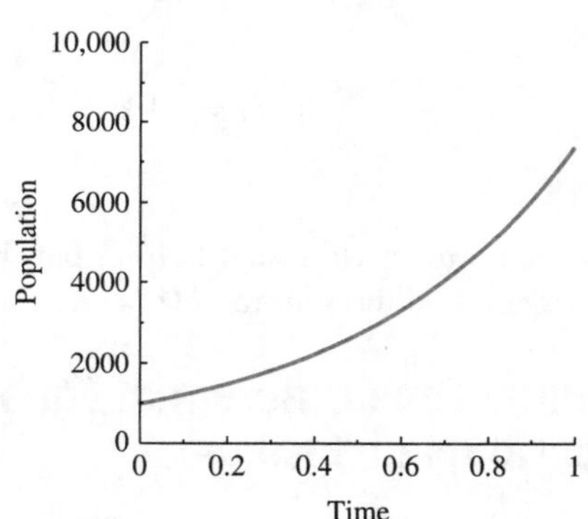

FIGURE 5.4.22
Solution of the bacterial growth equation: $b(0) = 1000$ and $\lambda = 2$

Example 5.4.2 A Decreasing Solution of the Bacterial Growth Equation

In contrast, if $b(0) = 9000$ and $\lambda = -1.5$, then

$$9000 = b(0) = K e^{\lambda \cdot 0} = K$$

The solution is

$$b(t) = 9000e^{-1.5t}$$

(Figure 5.4.23).

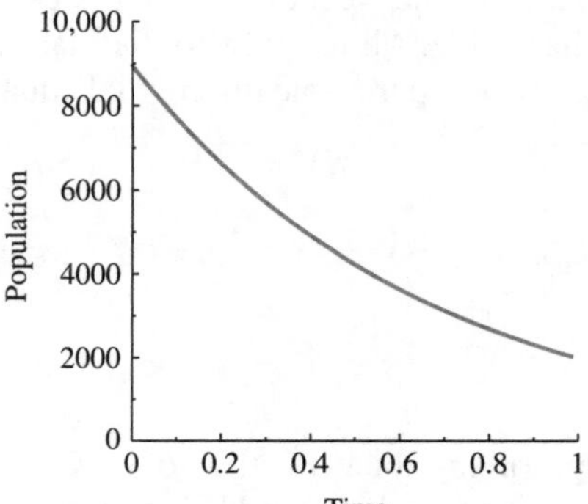

FIGURE 5.4.23
Solution of the bacterial growth equation: $b(0) = 9000$ and $\lambda = -1.5$

The following are the steps for **separation of variables.**

Algorithm 5.3 Separation of Variables

1. Move all instances of the state variable to the left-hand side and all instances of the time t to the right-hand side.
2. Integrate both sides.
3. Set the two integrals equal to each other.
4. Combine the two arbitrary constants into one.
5. Solve for the state variable in terms of the time t, possibly rewriting the constant in a more convenient form.
6. Solve for the constant with the initial conditions.

In our example, the first step of separating the state variable b from the time t could have been done differently had we chosen to move λ to the left-hand side:

$$\frac{db}{\lambda b} = dt$$

Following Algorithm 5.3, we find

$$\frac{1}{\lambda}\ln(b) + c_1 = t + c_2 \quad \text{integrating}$$

$$\frac{1}{\lambda}\ln(b) = t + c \quad \text{combining constants}$$

$$b = e^{\lambda t}e^{\lambda c} \quad \text{solving for } b$$

This has the same form we found before, but the constant looks different. If we set $K = e^{\lambda c}$, we again find the solution $b(t) = Ke^{\lambda t}$.

Solving Pure-Time Differential Equations with Separation of Variables

The technique of separation of variables is essentially the same method we used to solve pure-time differential equations.

Example 5.4.3 Separation of Variables Applied to a Pure-Time Differential Equation

Consider the pure-time differential equation for volume,

$$\frac{dV}{dt} = t^2$$

with initial condition $V(0) = 1.0\,\text{cm}^3$. We first solved this equation by finding the indefinite integral of t^2. The method of separation of variables requires computing the same integral. To begin, we multiply both sides by dt to move all instances of the time t to the right-hand side. All instances of the state variable V are already on the left-hand side because this is a pure-time differential equation. Following Algorithm 5.3, we get

$$dV = t^2 dt \quad \text{separating variables}$$

$$V + c_1 = \frac{t^3}{3} + c_2 \quad \text{integrating}$$

$$V = \frac{t^3}{3} + c \quad \text{combining constants}$$

The last step, solving for V in terms of t, is already done. Furthermore, the constant c appears in its traditional spot, added to an antiderivative. We find the constant c with the initial condition,

$$1.0 = V(0) = \frac{0^3}{3} + c = c$$

The solution of the equation is therefore $V = \frac{t^3}{3} + 1.0$.

Because the only V in this pure-time equation appears in dV, the left-hand side is easy to integrate. The function of t, however, might be difficult or impossible to integrate. In contrast, the only t in an autonomous differential equation appears as dt, making the t integral simple. The function of V might be difficult or impossible to integrate. With an autonomous differential equation, there is the additional difficult or impossible step of solving for the state variable. Exercises 19 and 20 give examples of autonomous differential equations for which this last step is impossible.

Applications of Separation of Variables

We can use separation of variables for Newton's law of cooling,

$$\frac{dH}{dt} = \alpha(A - H)$$

Following the algorithm, we find

$$\begin{aligned} \frac{dH}{A-H} &= \alpha dt && \text{separating variables} \\ -\ln(|A-H|) + c_1 &= \alpha t + c_2 && \text{integrating} \\ -\ln(|A-H|) &= \alpha t + c && \text{combining constants} \\ |A-H| &= e^{-\alpha t - c} && \text{solving for } |A-H| \\ |A-H| &= Ke^{-\alpha t} && \text{rewriting the constant as } K = e^{-c} \end{aligned}$$

To get rid of the absolute value bars, we consider two cases. If $H < A$, $|A - H| = A - H$ so

$$|A - H| = A - H = Ke^{-\alpha t}$$

We can now solve for H, finding

$$H(t) = A - Ke^{-\alpha t}$$

Example 5.4.4 A Solution of Newton's Law of Cooling

If $\alpha = 0.1/\text{min}$, $A = 40°\text{C}$, and $H(0) = 10°\text{C}$, the solution is

$$H(t) = 40 - Ke^{-0.1t}$$

We find the arbitrary constant K by substituting $t = 0$,

$$10 = H(0) = 40 - Ke^{-0.1 \cdot 0} = 40 - K$$

This has solution $K = 30$, so

$$H(t) = 40 - 30e^{-0.1t}$$

(Figure 5.4.24a). The solution approaches the ambient temperature 40°C because

$$\lim_{t \to \infty} \left(40 - 30e^{-0.1t}\right) = 40$$

as is consistent with our finding from the phase-line diagram that the equilibrium is stable. The solution gives more information by showing that the solution approaches the equilibrium exponentially.

If $H > A$, then $|A - H| = H - A$ and

$$|A - H| = H - A = Ke^{-\alpha t}$$

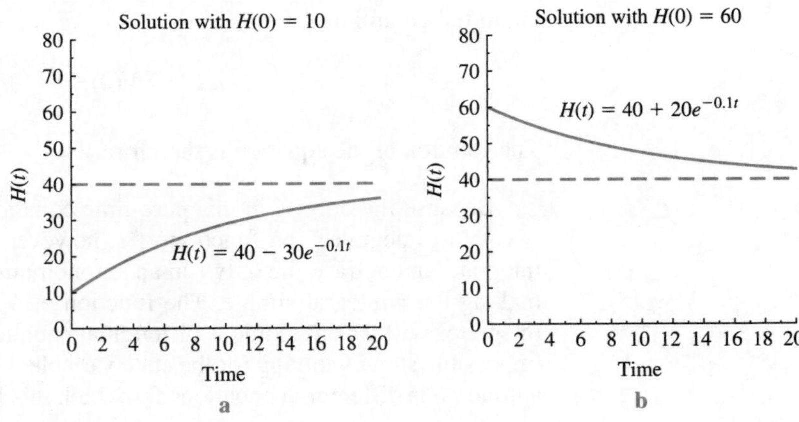

FIGURE 5.4.24
Solutions of Newton's law of cooling found with separation of variables

Next, we solve for H:

$$H(t) = A + Ke^{-\alpha t}$$

Example 5.4.5 The Solution with a Different Initial Condition

If $\alpha = 0.1$, $A = 40°\text{C}$, and $H(0) = 60°\text{C}$, the solution is

$$H(t) = 40 + Ke^{-0.1t}$$

We find the arbitrary constant K by substituting $t = 0$,

$$60 = H(0) = 40 + Ke^{-0.1 \cdot 0} = 40 + K$$

This has solution $K = 20$, so

$$H(t) = 40 + 20e^{-0.1t}$$

(Figure 5.4.24b). Again, the solution approaches the ambient temperature 40°C because

$$\lim_{t \to \infty} \left(40 + 20e^{-0.1t}\right) = 40$$

Example 5.4.6 A Population Explosion

As a more unusual example, suppose that the per capita production rate of some population with size b is

$$\text{per capita production rate} = b$$

This means that individuals reproduce more and more rapidly the more of them there are. We expect that this population will grow very quickly, and we can use separation of variables to compute how quickly. The differential equation for growth is

$$\begin{aligned}\frac{db}{dt} &= \text{per capita production rate} \cdot b \\ &= b \cdot b = b^2\end{aligned}$$

Separation of variables proceeds as follows:

$$\frac{db}{b^2} = dt \qquad \text{separating variables}$$

$$-\frac{1}{b} + c_1 = t + c_2 \qquad \text{integrating}$$

$$-\frac{1}{b} = t + c \qquad \text{combining constants}$$

$$b = \frac{-1}{t + c} \qquad \text{solving for } b$$

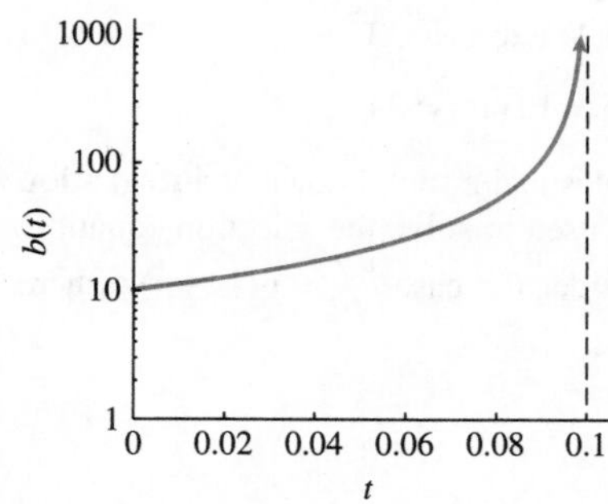

FIGURE 5.4.25

Semilog plot of a population with self-enhancing growth

The result looks dangerously negative. Proceeding anyway, suppose that $b(0) = 10$. We solve for c by substituting the initial conditions, finding

$$10 = b(0) = \frac{-1}{c}$$

so $c = -0.1$. Therefore,

$$b(t) = \frac{-1}{t - 0.1} = \frac{1}{0.1 - t}$$

(Figure 5.4.25). The population blasts off to infinity at time $t = 0.1$. What happens at $t = 0.11$? The solution does not exist. As far as this differential equation is concerned, the world comes to an end at $t = 0.1$. Models that include self-enhancing growth tend to have this sort of "chain reaction" property.

Summary We developed the method of **separation of variables** to solve autonomous differential equations. In this method, we isolate the state variable on the left-hand side and time on the right-hand side and then integrate to find a solution. Autonomous differential equations describing population growth and Newton's law of cooling can be solved with this technique. Solving pure-time differential equations with integration is a special case of separation of variables.

5.4 Exercises

Mathematical Techniques

1–6 ▪ Use separation of variables to solve the following autonomous differential equations. Check your answers by differentiating.

1. $\frac{db}{dt} = 0.01b,\ b(0) = 1000$

2. $\frac{db}{dt} = -3b,\ b(0) = 1.0 \times 10^6$

3. $\frac{dN}{dt} = 1 + N,\ N(0) = 1$

4. $\frac{dN}{dt} = 4 + 2N,\ N(0) = 1$

5. $\frac{db}{dt} = 1000 - b,\ b(0) = 500$

6. $\frac{db}{dt} = 1000 - b,\ b(0) = 1000$

7–10 ▪ Use separation of variables to solve the following pure-time differential equations. Check your answers by differentiating.

7. $\frac{dP}{dt} = \frac{5}{1 + 2t}$, with $P(0) = 0$

8. $\frac{dP}{dt} = 5e^{-2t}$, with $P(0) = 0$

9. $\frac{dL}{dt} = 1000e^{0.2t}$, with $L(0) = 1000$

10. $\frac{dL}{dt} = 64.3e^{-1.19t}$, with $L(0) = 0$

11–14 ▪ Separation of variables can help to solve some nonautonomous differential equations. For example, suppose that the per capita production rate is $\lambda(t)$, a function of time, so

$$\frac{db}{dt} = \lambda(t)b$$

This equation can be separated into parts depending only on b and on t by dividing both sides of the equation by b and multiplying by dt. For the following functions $\lambda(t)$, give an interpretation of the equation and solve the equation with the initial condition $b(0) = 10^6$. Sketch each solution. Check your answer by substituting into the differential equation.

11. $\lambda(t) = t$

12. $\lambda(t) = \frac{1}{1 + t}$

13. $\lambda(t) = \cos(t)$

14. $\lambda(t) = e^{-t}$

15–18 ▪ Find the solution of the differential equation $\frac{db}{dt} = b^p$ in the following cases. At what time does it approach infinity? Sketch a graph.

15. $p = 2$ (as in Example 5.4.6) and $b(0) = 100$

16. $p = 2$ and $b(0) = 0.1$

17. $p = 1.1$ and $b(0) = 100$

18. $p = 1.1$ and $b(0) = 0.1$

19–20 ▪ The following autonomous differential equations can be solved except for the step of finding x in terms of t. Use the steps to figure out how the solution behaves.

a. Solve the equation with separation of variables.

b. It is impossible to solve algebraically for x in terms of t. However, you can still find the arbitrary constant. Find it.

c. Although you cannot find x as a function of t, you can find t as a function of x. Graph this function for $1 \le x \le 10$.

d. Sketch the solution for x as a function of t.

19. The autonomous differential equation $\frac{dx}{dt} = \frac{x}{1+x}$ with $x(0) = 1$. This describes a population with a per capita production rate that decreases like $\frac{1}{1+x}$.

20. The autonomous differential equation $\frac{dx}{dt} = \frac{x}{1+x^2}$ with $x(0) = 1$. This describes a population with a per capita production rate that decreases like $\frac{1}{1+x^2}$. Describe in words how the solution differs from that in Exercise 19.

Applications

21–24 ▪ Using the method employed to find the solution derived for Newton's law of cooling, find the solution of the chemical diffusion equation $\frac{dC}{dt} = \beta(\Gamma - C)$ with the following parameter values and initial conditions. Find the concentration after 10 s. How long would it take for the concentration to get halfway to the equilibrium value?

21. $\beta = 0.01$/s, $C(0) = 5.0$ mmol/cm^3, and $\Gamma = 2.0$ mmol/cm^3.

22. $\beta = 0.01$/s, $C(0) = 1.0$ mmol/cm^3, and $\Gamma = 2.0$ mmol/cm^3. Why do you think the time matches that in Exercise 21?

23. $\beta = 0.1$/s, $C(0) = 5.0$ mmol/cm^3, and $\Gamma = 2.0$ mmol/cm^3.

24. $\beta = 0.1$/s, $C(0) = 1.0$ mmol/cm^3, and $\Gamma = 2.0$ mmol/cm^3.

25–26 ▪ Consider Torricelli's law of draining $\frac{dy}{dt} = -2\sqrt{y}$ (Section 5.2, Exercise 37) with the constant set to 2.

25. Suppose the initial condition is $y(0) = 4$. Find the solution with separation of variables, and graph the result. What really happens at time $t = 2$? And what happens after this time? How does this differ from the solution of the equation $\frac{dy}{dt} = -2y$?

26. Suppose the initial condition is $y(0) = 16$. Find the solution with separation of variables, and graph the result. When does the solution reach 0? What would the depth be at this time if draining followed the equation $\frac{dy}{dt} = -2y$?

27–28 ▪ Suppose that a population is growing at constant rate λ but that individuals are harvested at a rate of h, following the differential equation $\frac{db}{dt} = \lambda b - h$. For each of the following values of λ and h, use separation of variables to find the solution, and compare graphs of the solution with those found earlier from a phase-line diagram.

27. $\lambda = 2.0$, $h = 1000$ (as in Section 5.2, Exercise 23).

28. $\lambda = 0.5$, $h = 1000$ (as in Section 5.2, Exercise 24).

29–30 ▪ Use separation of variables to solve for C in the following models describing chemical diffusion, and find the solution starting from the initial condition $C = \Gamma$.

29. The model in Section 5.1, Exercise 33.

30. The model in Section 5.1, Exercise 34.

31–38 ▪ Separation of variables and a trick known as **integration by partial fractions** can be used to solve the selection equation. For simplicity, we will consider the case $\frac{dp}{dt} = p(1-p)$, where $\mu - \lambda = 1$.

31. Separate variables.

32. Show that

$$\frac{1}{p(1-p)} = \frac{1}{p} + \frac{1}{1-p}$$

and rewrite the left-hand side.

33. Integrate the rewritten left-hand side.

34. Combine the two natural log terms into one using a law of logs.

35. Write the equation for the solution with a single constant c.

36. Exponentiate both sides and solve for p.

37. Using the initial condition $p(0) = 0.01$, find the value of the constant. Evaluate the limit of the solution as t approaches infinity.

38. Using the initial condition $p(0) = 0.5$, find the value of the constant. Evaluate the limit of the solution as t approaches infinity.

39–42 ▪ There are many important differential equations for which separation of variables fails but that can be solved with other techniques. An important category involves Newton's law of cooling when the ambient temperature is changing. Consider, in particular, the case where $A(t) = e^{\beta t}$. Assume that the constant α is 1.0, so the differential equation is $\frac{dH}{dt} = -H + A(t)$. It is impossible to separate variables in this equation.

39. Create the new variable $y = e^t H$ and find a differential equation for y.

40. Identify the type of differential equation, and solve it with the initial condition $H(0) = 0$.

41. Graph your solution and the ambient temperature when β is small, say $\beta = 0.1$. Describe the result.

42. Graph your solution and the ambient temperature when β is large, say $\beta = 1.0$. Why are the two curves so much farther apart?

Computer Exercises

43. We have seen that solutions of the differential equation

$$\frac{db}{dt} = b^2$$

approach infinity in a finite amount of time. We will try to stop $b(t)$ from approaching infinity by multiplying the rate of change by a decreasing function of t in the nonautonomous equation

$$\frac{db}{dt} = g(t)b^2$$

Try the following three functions for $g(t)$:

$$g_1(t) = e^{-t}$$

$$g_2(t) = \frac{1}{1+t^2}$$

$$g_3(t) = \frac{1}{1+t}$$

a. Which of these functions decreases fastest and should best be able to stop $b(t)$ from approaching infinity?

b. Have your computer solve the equation in each case with initial conditions ranging from $b(0) = 0.1$ to $b(0) = 5.0$. Which solutions approach infinity?

c. Use separation of variables to try to find the solution in each of these cases (have your computer help with the integral of $g_2(t)$). Can you figure out when the solutions approach infinity? How well does this match your results from part **b**?

5.5 Two-Dimensional Differential Equations

We now begin the study of problems in two dimensions. The discrete-time dynamical systems and differential equations we have considered hitherto have described the dynamics of a single state variable: a population, a concentration, a fraction, and so forth. Most biological systems cannot be fully described without multiple measurements and multiple state variables. The tools for studying these systems, differential equations and discrete-time dynamical systems, remain the same, as does the goal of figuring out what will happen. The methods for getting from the problem to the answer, however, are more complicated. In this section we introduce two important equations for population dynamics and an extension of Newton's law of cooling that takes into account the changing temperature of the room. These are called **systems of autonomous differential equations** or **coupled autonomous differential equations.** Euler's method can be applied to find approximate solutions of these systems of equations.

Predator-Prey Dynamics

Our basic model of population growth followed a single species that existed undisturbed in isolation. Life is rarely so peaceful. Imagine a bacterial population disrupted by the arrival of a predator, perhaps some sort of amoeba. We expect the bacteria to do worse when more predatory amoebas are around. Conversely, we expect the amoebas to do better when more of their bacterial prey are around. We now translate these intuitions into differential equations.

Denote the population of bacteria at time t by $b(t)$ and the population of amoebas by $p(t)$ to represent predation. We can build the equations by considering the factors affecting the population of each type. Suppose that the bacteria would grow exponentially in the absence of predators according to

$$\frac{db}{dt} = \lambda b$$

How might predation affect the bacterial population? One ecologically naive but mathematically convenient approach is to assume that the organisms obey the principle of mass action.

> **The Principle of Mass Action:** Individual bacteria encounter amoebas at a rate proportional to the number of amoebas.

Doubling the number of predators therefore doubles the rate at which bacteria run into predators. If running into an amoeba spells doom, this doubles the rate at which each bacterium risks being eaten.

In equations,

$$\text{rate at which an individual bacterium is eaten} = \epsilon p$$

where ϵ is the constant of proportionality. Therefore,

$$\text{per capita growth rate of bacteria} = \lambda - \epsilon p$$

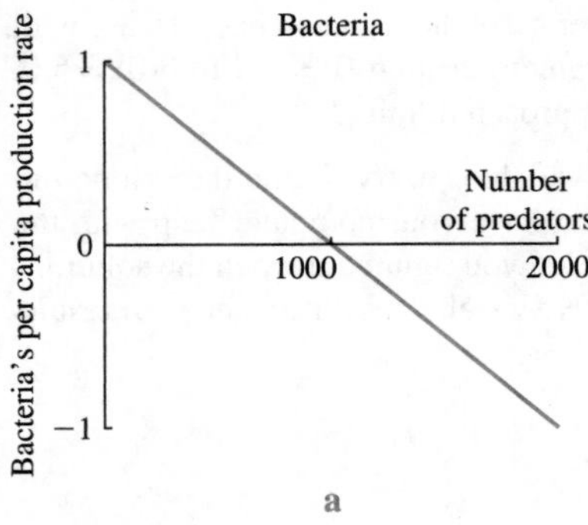

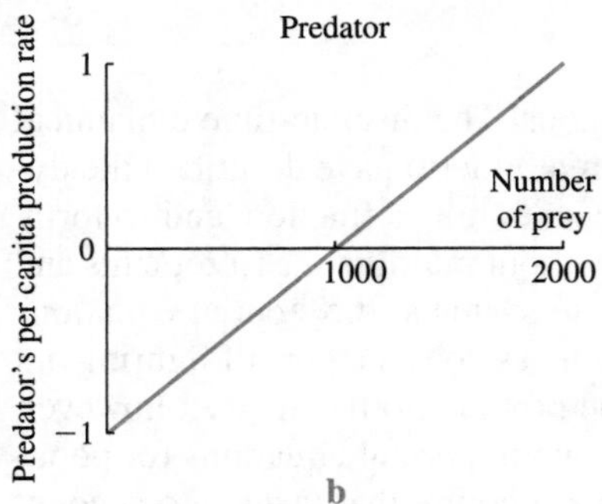

FIGURE 5.5.26
Per capita growth rates of prey and predator species

This separates the growth rate into the usual per capita production rate λ and the predation rate ϵp. This equation is illustrated with $\lambda = 1.0$ and $\epsilon = 0.001$ in Figure 5.5.26a. Because the growth rate of a population is the product of the per capita growth rate and the population size,

$$\begin{aligned}\frac{db}{dt} &= \text{per capita growth rate} \times \text{population size}\\ &= (\lambda - \epsilon p)b\end{aligned}$$

Suppose that the predators have a negative per capita rate of $-\delta$ in the absence of their prey, so

$$\frac{dp}{dt} = -\delta p$$

Solutions of this equation converge to 0. These predators must eat to live. How might predation affect the amoeba population? As above, we assume mass action: doubling the number of bacteria doubles the rate at which predators run into bacteria and thus doubles the rate at which they eat.

$$\text{rate at which an amoeba eats bacteria} = \eta b$$

(η is the Greek letter "eta," used to remind us of eating). If the per capita production rate is increased by the eating rate,

$$\text{per capita growth rate of predators} = -\delta + \eta b$$

These per capita growth rates are illustrated with $\delta = 1.0$ and $\eta = 0.001$ in Figure 5.5.26b. Multiplying the per capita growth rate of the amoebas by their population size gives

$$\begin{aligned}\frac{dp}{dt} &= \text{per capita growth rate} \times \text{population size}\\ &= (-\delta + \eta b)p\end{aligned}$$

We combine the differential equations into the **system of autonomous differential equations**

$$\begin{aligned}\frac{db}{dt} &= (\lambda - \epsilon p)b\\ \frac{dp}{dt} &= (-\delta + \eta b)p\end{aligned} \qquad (5.5.1)$$

These are also called **coupled autonomous differential equations** because the rate of change of the bacterial population depends on both their own population size and that of the amoebas, and the rate of change of the amoebas depends on both their own population and that of the bacteria. Two separate measurements are required to find the rate of change of either population. These equations are **autonomous** because neither rate of change depends explicitly on time.

Dynamics of Competition

We can use similar reasoning to describe the competitive interaction between two populations. Our basic model of selection is based on the *uncoupled* pair of differential equations

$$\begin{aligned}\frac{da}{dt} &= \mu a\\ \frac{db}{dt} &= \lambda b\end{aligned}$$

Although there are two measurements, the rate of change of each type does not depend on the population size of the other. This lack of interaction is an idealization. Two populations in a single vessel will probably interact. Suppose that the per capita growth rate of each type declines as a linear function of the total number $a + b$ according to

$$\text{per capita growth rate of type } a = \mu\left(1 - \frac{a+b}{K_a}\right)$$

$$\text{per capita growth rate of type } b = \lambda\left(1 - \frac{a+b}{K_b}\right)$$

We have written the growth rates in this form to separate out the maximum per capita production μ of type a and λ of type b. Growth of type a becomes negative when the total population exceeds K_a, and growth of type b becomes negative when the total population exceeds K_b. The values K_a and K_b are sometimes called the **carrying capacities** of types a and b, respectively.

Example 5.5.1 Per Capita Growth Rates with Particular Parameter Values

With $\mu = 2.0$, $\lambda = 2.0$, $K_a = 1000$, and $K_b = 500$,

$$\text{per capita growth rate of type } a = 2.0\left(1 - \frac{a+b}{1000}\right)$$

$$\text{per capita growth rate of type } b = 2.0\left(1 - \frac{a+b}{500}\right)$$

(Figure 5.5.27).

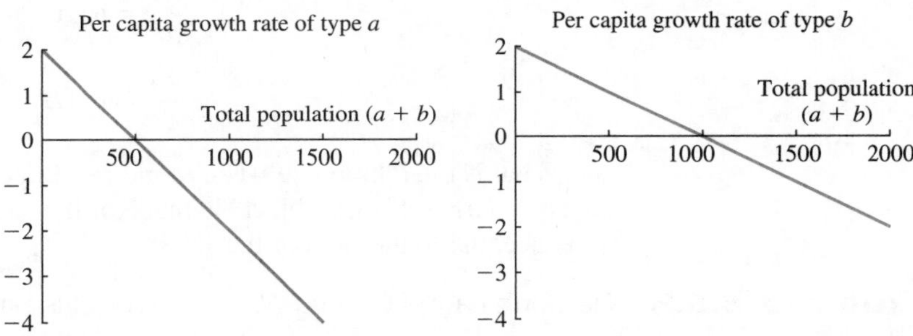

FIGURE 5.5.27
Per capita growth rates of competing species

We find the rates of change of the populations by multiplying the per capita growth rates by the population sizes, finding the coupled system of differential equations

$$\begin{aligned}\frac{da}{dt} &= \mu\left(1 - \frac{a+b}{K_a}\right)a \\ \frac{db}{dt} &= \lambda\left(1 - \frac{a+b}{K_b}\right)b\end{aligned} \tag{5.5.2}$$

The behavior of each population depends both on its own size and on that of the other species. Neither depends explicitly on time, so this system of equations is autonomous.

Example 5.5.2 Competition Model with Parameter Values

With $\mu = 2.0$, $\lambda = 2.0$, $K_a = 1000$, and $K_b = 500$ (as in Example 5.5.1), the model becomes

$$\frac{da}{dt} = 2.0a\left(1 - \frac{a+b}{1000}\right)$$

$$\frac{db}{dt} = 2.0b\left(1 - \frac{a+b}{500}\right)$$

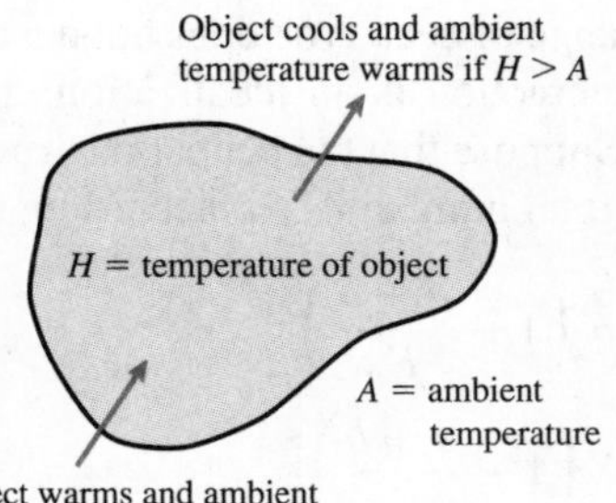
Object cools and ambient temperature warms if $H > A$
H = temperature of object
A = ambient temperature
Object warms and ambient temperature cools if $H < A$

FIGURE 5.5.28
Newton's law of cooling revisited

Newton's Law of Cooling

Both Newton's law of cooling and the model of chemical diffusion across a membrane ignored the fact that the ambient temperature or concentration might also change. A small hot object placed in a large room will have little effect on the room temperature, but a large hot object not only will cool off itself but will also heat up the room. We require a system of autonomous differential equations to describe both temperatures simultaneously (Figure 5.5.28). We will now derive the coupled differential equations that describe this situation.

Newton's law of cooling expresses the rate of change of the temperature, H, of an object as a function of the ambient temperature, A, by the equation

$$\frac{dH}{dt} = \alpha(A - H)$$

This equation is valid even if the ambient temperature A is itself changing. If $A < H$, heat is leaving the object and warming the room. The room follows the same law as the object itself, but we expect that the factor α, which depends on the size, shape, and material of the object, will be different from that of the object, or that

$$\frac{dA}{dt} = \alpha_2(H - A)$$

The rate of change of temperature of each object depends on the temperature of the other. Together, these equations give the following system of coupled autonomous differential equations:

$$\frac{dH}{dt} = \alpha(A - H)$$
$$\frac{dA}{dt} = \alpha_2(H - A)$$

What is the relation between α and α_2? In general, α_2 will be smaller as the room becomes larger. If the "object" is made of the same stuff as the "room," the ratio of α to α_2 is equal to the ratio of the sizes.

Example 5.5.3 Newton's Law of Cooling When the Object Is Smaller than the Room

If the room is three times as big as the object but is made of the same substance (such as a balloon of air), then

$$\alpha_2 = \frac{\alpha}{3}$$

(Figure 5.5.29).

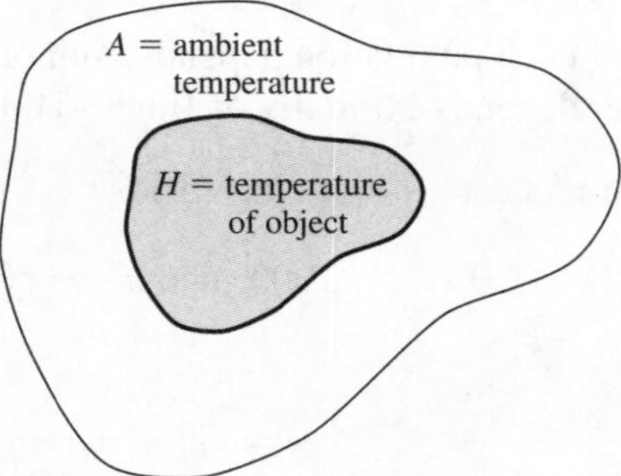
A = ambient temperature
H = temperature of object

FIGURE 5.5.29
Newton's law of cooling applied to objects of different sizes

If the ambient space is 3 times as large as object, the rate of change of the ambient temperature is one third smaller than that of the object

Example 5.5.4 Newton's Law of Cooling When the Object Cools More Rapidly than the Room

Suppose that the specific heat of the object in Example 5.5.3 is 10.0 times that of the object (meaning that a small amount of heat warms the room a great deal). Then α_2 is smaller by a factor of 3.0 because the room is larger, but larger by a factor of 10.0 because the specific heat is smaller. Thus

$$\alpha_2 = 10.0\frac{\alpha}{3} \approx 3.33\alpha$$

Applying Euler's Method to Systems of Autonomous Differential Equations

How do we find solutions of systems of autonomous differential equations? In general, this is a very difficult problem. In the next section, we will extend the method of equilibria and phase-line diagrams to sketch solutions. Surprisingly, perhaps, Euler's method for finding approximate solutions with the tangent line approximation works exactly the same way for systems as for single equations. We will apply the method to figure out how solutions behave for the systems describing predator-prey dynamics and competition.

Consider the predator-prey equations (Equation 5.5.1) with $\lambda = 1, \delta = 1, \epsilon = 0.001$, and $\eta = 0.001$:

$$\frac{db}{dt} = (1.0 - 0.001p)b$$

$$\frac{dp}{dt} = (-1.0 + 0.001b)p$$

Suppose the initial condition is $b(0) = 800$ and $p(0) = 200$. Initially, there are 800 prey and 200 predators. What will happen to these populations after 2.0 time units? We break this interval into 10 units of length $\Delta t = 0.2$. After one of these intervals, we can approximate each population with the tangent line by

$$\hat{b}(0 + \Delta t) = b(0) + b'(0)\Delta t \quad \text{equation for tangent line}$$

$$= 800 + (1.0 - 0.001 \cdot 200)800 \cdot \Delta t \quad b(0) = 800 \text{ (initial condition) and } b'(0) = (1.0 - 0.001p(0))b(0)$$

$$= 800 + 640 \cdot \Delta t \quad \text{compute that } b'(0) = 640$$

After a time $\Delta t = 0.2$, the approximate value of b is

$$\hat{b}(0.2) = 800 + 640 \cdot 0.2 = 928$$

At the same time, the value for p can be found with the tangent line approximation to be

$$\hat{p}(0 + \Delta t) = p(0) + p'(0)\Delta t \quad \text{equation for tangent line}$$

$$= 200 + (-1.0 + 0.001 \cdot 800)200 \cdot \Delta t \quad p(0) = 200 \text{ (initial condition) and } p'(0) = (-1.0 + 0.001b(0))p(0)$$

$$= 200 - 40 \cdot \Delta t \quad \text{compute that } p'(0) = -40$$

After a time $\Delta t = 0.2$, the approximate value of p is

$$\hat{p}(0.2) = 200 - 40 \cdot 0.2 = 192$$

(Figure 5.5.30).

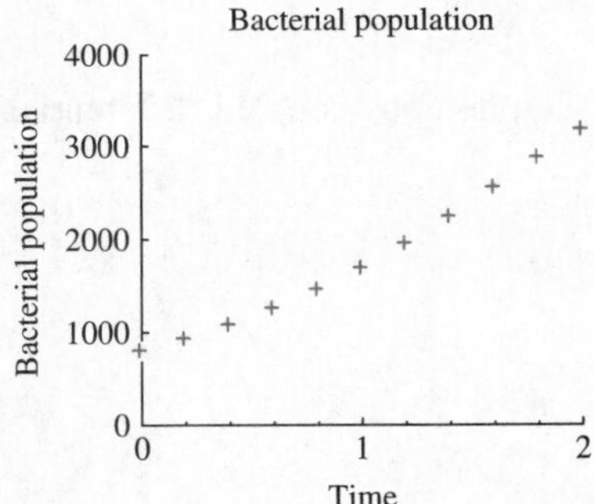

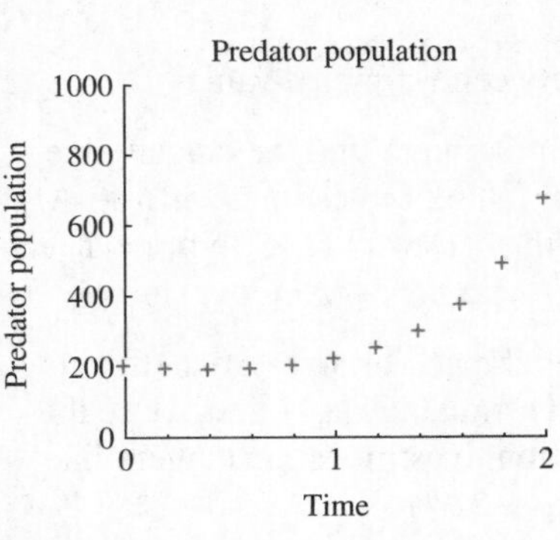

FIGURE 5.5.30

Euler's method applied to the predator-prey equations

The next step uses the same idea but requires the approximate values $\hat{b}(0.2)$ and $\hat{p}(0.2)$ found in the first step.

$$\hat{b}(0.2+\Delta t) \approx \hat{b}(0.2) + b'(0.2)\Delta t \qquad \text{equation for tangent line}$$

$$\approx 928 + (1.0 - 0.001 \cdot 192)928 \cdot \Delta t \qquad \hat{b}(0.2) = 928 \text{ and } b'(0.2) \approx (1.0 - 0.001\hat{p}(0.2))\hat{b}(0.2)$$

$$\approx 928 + 749.8 \cdot \Delta t \qquad \text{compute that } b'(0.2) \approx 749.8$$

Therefore,

$$\hat{b}(0.4) \approx 928 + 749.8 \cdot 0.2 \approx 1078.0$$

Things seem to be going pretty well for the prey. For the predators, we get

$$\hat{p}(0.2+\Delta t) \approx \hat{p}(0.2) + p'(0.2)\Delta t \qquad \text{equation for tangent line}$$

$$\approx 192 + (-1.0 + 0.001 \cdot 928)192 \cdot \Delta t \qquad \hat{p}(0.2) = 192 \text{ and } p'(0.2) = (-1.0 + 0.001\hat{b}(0.2))\hat{p}(0.2)$$

$$\approx 192 - 13.8 \cdot \Delta t \qquad \text{compute that } p'(0.2) \approx -13.8$$

Therefore,

$$\hat{p}(0.4) \approx 192 - 13.8 \cdot 0.2 = 189.2$$

The predator numbers are fading.

t	$\hat{b}$	$\hat{p}$
0.0	800.0	200.0
0.2	928.0	192.0
0.4	1078.0	189.2
0.6	1252.8	192.2
0.8	1455.2	201.9
1.0	1687.4	220.3
1.2	1950.6	250.6
1.4	2242.9	298.2
1.6	2557.8	372.3
1.8	2878.8	488.3
2.0	3173.4	671.8

We can continue following these steps to find the approximate solution at time $t = 2.0$. Continuing in this way we would see that the bacterial population eventually begins to decline.

The algorithm for Euler's method for coupled autonomous differential equations is an extension of that for a single autonomous differential equation (Algorithm 5.1).

Algorithm 5.4 Euler's Method for Solving Coupled Autonomous Differential Equations

Suppose a pair of measurements m and n obey the autonomous coupled differential equations

$$\frac{dm}{dt} = f(m,n)$$

$$\frac{dn}{dt} = g(m,n)$$

with initial condition $m(t_0) = m_0$, $n(t_0) = n_0$.

1. Choose a **time step** Δt (the length of time between estimated values).
2. Use the initial condition and the differential equation to find the tangent line $\hat{m}(t)$ with base point $t = t_0$ and slope $f(m_0, n_0)$. Use it to estimate $m(t_0+\Delta t)$ with $\hat{m}(t_0+\Delta t)$. Similarly, find the tangent line $\hat{n}(t)$ with base point $t = t_0$ and slope $g(m_0, n_0)$. Use it to estimate $n(t_0+\Delta t)$ with $\hat{n}(t_0+\Delta t)$.
3. Use the estimate $\hat{m}(t_0+\Delta t)$ and the differential equation to estimate the tangent line $\hat{m}(t)$ with base point $t_0+\Delta t$ and estimate $\hat{m}(t_0+2\Delta t)$. Use the estimate $\hat{n}(t_0+\Delta t)$ and the differential equation to estimate the tangent line $\hat{n}(t)$ with base point $t_0+\Delta t$ and estimate $\hat{n}(t_0+2\Delta t)$.
4. Repeat the method in the previous step to estimate $\hat{m}(t_0+3\Delta t)$ and $\hat{n}(t_0+3\Delta t)$ and so forth.

Example 5.5.5 Applying Euler's Method to the Coupled Differential Equations Describing Competition

Suppose we wish to apply Euler's method to the coupled differential equations for competition using the parameter values in Example 5.5.1,

$$\frac{da}{dt} = 2.0a\left(1 - \frac{a+b}{1000}\right)$$

$$\frac{db}{dt} = 2.0b\left(1 - \frac{a+b}{500}\right)$$

with initial condition $a(0) = 750$ and $b(0) = 750$ to estimate $a(0.3)$ and $b(0.3)$.

1. Pick a time step of $\Delta t = 0.1$ (a smaller value should be more accurate).
2. The tangent line with base point $t = 0$ is

$$\hat{a}(0+\Delta t) = a(0) + a'(0)\Delta t$$ equation for tangent line

$$= 750 + 2.0 \cdot 750\left(1 - \frac{750+750}{1000}\right)\Delta t$$ $a(0) = 750$ (initial condition) and $a'(0) = 2.0a(0)\left(1 - \frac{a(0)+b(0)}{1000}\right)$ (differential equation for a)

$$= 750 - 750\Delta t$$ substitute values

$$\hat{b}(0+\Delta t) = b(0) + b'(0)\Delta t$$ equation for tangent line

$$= 750 + 2.0 \cdot 750\left(1 - \frac{750+750}{500}\right)\Delta t$$ $b(0) = 750$ (initial condition) and $b'(0) = 2.0b(0)\left(1 - \frac{a(0)+b(0)}{500}\right)$ (differential equation for b)

$$= 750 - 3000\Delta t$$ substitute values

We therefore estimate $b(0.1)$ and $a(0.1)$ by

$$\hat{a}(0.1) = 750 - 750 \cdot 0.1 = 675$$

$$\hat{b}(0.1) = 750 - 3000 \cdot 0.1 = 450$$

3. For the next step, to find $\hat{a}(0.2)$ and $\hat{b}(0.2)$, we compute

$$\hat{a}(0.1+\Delta t) \approx \hat{a}(0.1) + a'(0.1)\Delta t$$ equation for tangent line

$$\approx 675 + 2.0 \cdot 675\left(1 - \frac{675+450}{1000}\right)\Delta t$$ $\hat{a}(0.1) = 675$ and $a'(0.1) \approx 2.0a(0.1)\left(1 - \frac{a(0.1)+b(0.1)}{1000}\right)$ (differential equation for a)

$$= 675 - 168.75\Delta t$$ substitute values

$$\hat{b}(0.1+\Delta t) \approx \hat{b}(0.1) + b'(0.1)\Delta t$$ equation for tangent line

$$\approx 450 + 2.0 \cdot 450\left(1 - \frac{675+450}{500}\right)\Delta t$$ $\hat{b}(0.1) = 450$ and $b'(0.1) \approx 2.0b(0.1)\left(1 - \frac{a(0.1)+b(0.1)}{500}\right)$ (differential equation for b)

$$= 450 - 1687.5\Delta t$$ substitute values

We therefore estimate that

$$\hat{a}(0.2) \approx 675 - 168.75 \cdot 0.1 = 658.125$$

$$\hat{b}(0.2) \approx 450 - 1687.5 \cdot 0.1 = 281.25.$$

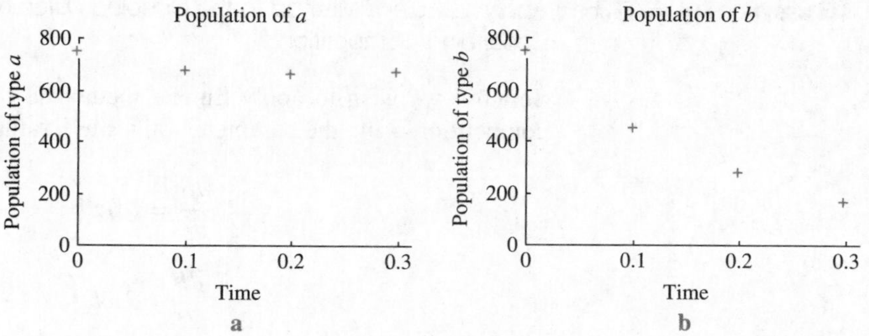

FIGURE 5.5.31
Euler's method applied to the competition equations

4. For the next step, to estimate $\hat{a}(0.3)$ and $\hat{b}(0.3)$, we compute

$$\hat{a}(0.2+\Delta t) \approx \hat{a}(0.2) + a'(0.2)\Delta t$$ equation for tangent line

$$\approx 658.125 + 2.0 \cdot 658.125\left(1 - \frac{658.125+281.25}{1000}\right)\Delta t$$ $\hat{a}(0.2) \approx 658.125$ and $a'(0.2) \approx 2.0a(0.2)\left(1 - \frac{a(0.2)+b(0.2)}{1000}\right)$

$$\approx 658.125 + 79.797\Delta t$$ substitute values

$$\hat{b}(0.2+\Delta t) \approx \hat{b}(0.2) + b'(0.2)\Delta t$$ equation for tangent line

$$\approx 281.25 + 2.0 \cdot 281.25\left(1 - \frac{658.125+281.25}{500}\right)\Delta t$$ $\hat{b}(0.2) \approx 281.25$ and $b'(0.2) \approx 2.0b(0.2)\left(1 - \frac{a(0.2)+b(0.2)}{500}\right)$

$$\approx 281.25 - 1156.6\Delta t$$ substitute values

We therefore estimate that

$$\hat{a}(0.3) \approx 658.125 + 79.797 \cdot 0.1 \approx 666.1$$
$$\hat{b}(0.3) = 281.25 - 1156.6 \cdot 0.1 = 165.6$$

These values are plotted in Figure 5.5.31.

Euler's method is an effective way to compute solutions but requires a great deal of numerical calculation. In the next section, we will begin to develop methods to predict how solutions will behave using graphical techniques.

Summary We have introduced three **coupled autonomous differential equations,** pairs of differential equations in which the rate of change of each state variable depends on its own value and on the value of the other state variable. We derived models of a predator and its prey, a competitive analogue of the system studied to describe selection, and a version of Newton's law of cooling that keeps track of the change in room temperature. Each system is **autonomous** because the rates of change depend only on the state variables and not on time. **Euler's method** can be used to compute approximate solutions of these equations using the tangent line approximation.

5.5 Exercises

Mathematical Techniques

1–4 ▪ Consider the following special cases of the predator-prey equations:

$$\frac{db}{dt} = (\lambda - \epsilon p)b \quad \text{and} \quad \frac{dp}{dt} = (-\delta + \eta b)p$$

Write the differential equations and tell what they mean.

1. $\epsilon = \eta = 0$

2. $\delta = 0$

3. $\eta = 0$

4. $\epsilon = 0$

5–6 ▪ If each state variable in a system of autonomous differential equations does not respond to changes in the value of the other, but depends only on a constant value, the two equations can be considered separately. For example, in the competition equation

$$\frac{da}{dt} = \mu\left(1 - \frac{a+b}{K_a}\right)a$$

we could treat b as a constant value. In each case, find the equilibrium and draw a phase-line diagram for a. Set the parameters to $\mu = 2$ and $K_a = 1000$.

5. Suppose that types a and b do not interact (equivalent to setting $b = 0$ in the differential equation for a).

6. Suppose that types a and b interact with a fixed population of 500 of the other (set $b = 500$ in the differential equation for a).

7–10 ▪ Apply Euler's method to the competition equations

$$\frac{da}{dt} = \mu\left(1 - \frac{a+b}{K_a}\right)a$$

$$\frac{db}{dt} = \lambda\left(1 - \frac{a+b}{K_b}\right)b$$

starting from the given initial conditions. Assume that $\mu = 2.0$, $\lambda = 2.0$, $K_a = 1000$, and $K_b = 500$.

7. Use $a(0) = 750$ and $b(0) = 500$. Take two steps, with a step length of $\Delta t = 0.1$.

8. Use $a(0) = 250$ and $b(0) = 500$. Take two steps, with a step length of $\Delta t = 0.1$.

9. Use $a(0) = 750$ and $b(0) = 500$. Take four steps, with a step length of $\Delta t = 0.05$. How do your results compare with those in Exercise 7?

10. Use $a(0) = 250$ and $b(0) = 500$. Take four steps, with a step length of $\Delta t = 0.05$. How do your results compare with those in Exercise 8?

11–14 ▪ Apply Euler's method to Newton's law of cooling

$$\frac{dH}{dt} = \alpha(A - H)$$

$$\frac{dA}{dt} = \alpha_2(H - A)$$

with the given parameter values and starting from the given initial conditions.

11. Suppose $\alpha = 0.3$ and $\alpha_2 = 0.1$. Use $H(0) = 60$ and $A = 20$. Take two steps, with a step length of $\Delta t = 0.1$.

12. Suppose $\alpha = 0.3$ and $\alpha_2 = 0.1$. Use $H(0) = 0$ and $A = 20$. Take two steps, with a step length of $\Delta t = 0.1$.

13. Suppose $\alpha = 3.0$ and $\alpha_2 = 1.0$. Use $H(0) = 60$ and $A = 20$. Take two steps, with a step length of $\Delta t = 0.25$. Do the results look reasonable?

14. Suppose $\alpha = 3.0$ and $\alpha_2 = 1.0$. Use $H(0) = 0$ and $A = 20$. Take two steps, with a step length of $\Delta t = 0.5$. Do the results look reasonable?

15–20 ▪ The spring equation or simple harmonic oscillator,

$$\frac{d^2x}{dt^2} = -x$$

which we studied in Section 2.10, "Applications, pp. 226–229," describes how acceleration (the second derivative of the position x) is equal to the negative of the position. The spring constant k has been set to 1 for simplicity. This one equation for the second derivative can be written as a system of two autonomous differential equations.

15. Write the velocity v in terms of the derivative of the position x, and the acceleration in terms of the derivative of the velocity v. Use the spring equation to write the derivative of the velocity in terms of the position x. Write the spring equation as a pair of equations for position and velocity.

16. Friction also creates acceleration proportional to the negative of the velocity (see Section 2.10, Exercise 39). A simple case obeys the equation

$$\frac{d^2x}{dt^2} = -2x - 2v$$

Write this as a pair of coupled differential equations for x and v.

17. We know that one solution of the basic spring equation in Exercise 15 is $x(t) = \cos(t)$. Find $v(t)$ and check that the solution matches the system of equations. What are the initial position and velocity?

18. One solution of the spring equation with friction in Exercise 16 is $x(t) = e^{-t}\cos(t)$. Find $v(t)$ and check that the solution matches the system of equations. What are the initial position and velocity?

19. Use Euler's method with $\Delta t = 0.2$ for five steps to estimate $x(1)$ and $v(1)$ for the model in Exercise 15 with initial position $x(0) = 1$ and initial velocity $v(0) = 0$. Compare with the results in Exercise 17.

20. Use Euler's method with $\Delta t = 0.2$ for five steps to estimate $x(1)$ and $v(1)$ for the model in Exercise 16 with initial position $x(0) = 1$ and initial velocity $v(0) = -1$. Compare with the results in Exercise 18.

Applications

21–24 ▪ Consider the following types of predator-prey interactions. Graph the per capita rates of change and write the associated system of autonomous differential equations.

21.

$$\text{per capita growth of prey} = 1.0 - 0.05p$$
$$\text{per capita growth of predators} = -1.0 + 0.02b$$

22.

$$\text{per capita growth of prey} = 2.0 - 0.01p$$
$$\text{per capita growth of predators} = 1.0 + 0.01b$$

How does this differ from the basic predator-prey system (Equation 5.5.1)?

23.
$$\text{per capita growth of prey} = 2.0 - 0.0001p^2$$
$$\text{per capita growth of predators} = -1.0 + 0.01b$$

24.
$$\text{per capita growth of prey} = 2.0 - 0.01p$$
$$\text{per capita growth of predators} = -1.0 + 0.0001b^2$$

25–28 ▪ Write systems of differential equations describing the following situations. Feel free to make up parameter values as needed.

25. Two predators that must eat each other to survive.

26. Two predators that must eat each other to survive, but with per capita growth rate of each reduced by competition with its own species.

27. Two competitors where the per capita growth rate of a is decreased by the total population, and the growth rate of b is decreased by the population of b.

28. Two competitors where the per capita growth rate of each type is affected only by the population size of the other type.

29–30 ▪ Follow these steps to derive the equations for chemical exchange between two adjacent cells of different size. Suppose the concentration in the first cell is designated by the variable C_1 and the concentration in the second cell is designated by the variable C_2. In each case:

a. Write an expression for the total amount of chemical A_1 in the first cell and of chemical A_2 in the second cell.

b. Suppose that the amount of chemical moving from the first cell to the second cell is β times C_1 and that the amount of chemical moving from the second cell to the first cell is β times C_2. Write equations for the rates of change of A_1 and A_2.

c. Divide by the volumes to find differential equations for C_1 and C_2.

d. In which cell is the concentration changing more rapidly?

29. Suppose that the size of the first cell is 2.0 μL and that the size of the second is 5.0 μL.

30. Suppose that the size of the first cell is 5.0 μL and that the size of the second is 12.0 μL.

31–32 ▪ Write systems of autonomous differential equations describing the temperature of an object and the temperature of the room in the following cases.

31. The size of the room is 10.0 times that of the object, but the specific heat of the room is 0.2 times that of the object (meaning that a small amount of heat produces a large change in the temperature of the room).

32. The size of the room is 5.0 times that of the object, but the specific heat of the room is 2.0 times that of the object (meaning that a large amount of heat produces only a small change in the temperature of the room).

33–38 ▪ There are many important extensions of the basic disease model (Equation 5.3.1) that include more categories of people and that model processes of birth, death, and immunity. The simplest two-dimensional model involves the same assumptions as the basic model but explicitly tracks the number of susceptible individuals (S) and the number of infected individuals (I) rather than the fraction. Individuals become infected (move from the S class into the I class) at a rate proportional to the product of the number of infected individuals with the number of susceptible people. Individuals recover (move from the I class into the S class) at a rate proportional to the number of infected individuals. Equations modeling this situation are

$$\frac{dI}{dt} = \alpha I S - \mu I$$
$$\frac{dS}{dt} = -\alpha I S + \mu I$$

33. Suppose that individuals who leave the infected class through recovery become permanently immune rather than becoming susceptible again. Write the differential equations, and compare your model with the predator-prey model (Equation 5.5.1).

34. Suppose that one-third of the individuals who leave the infected class through recovery become permanently immune and that the other two-thirds become susceptible again.

35. Suppose that all individuals become susceptible upon recovery (as in the basic model) but that there is a source of mortality, so both infected and susceptible individuals die at per capita rate k.

36. Suppose that all individuals become susceptible upon recovery (as in the basic model) but that there is a source of mortality, whereby susceptible individuals die at per capita rate k but infected individuals die at a per capita rate that is twice as large.

37. Suppose that all individuals become susceptible upon recovery (as in the basic model) but that all individuals give birth at rate b. The offspring of susceptible individuals are susceptible, and the offspring of infected individuals are infected.

38. Suppose that all individuals become susceptible upon recovery (as in the basic model) but that all individuals give birth at rate b and that all offspring are susceptible.

39–40 ▪ Write the following models of frequency-dependence as systems of autonomous differential equations for a and b.

39. The situation in Section 5.1, Exercise 37.

40. The situation in Section 5.1, Exercise 38.

Computer Exercises

41. Euler's method for systems of differential equations can be implemented as an updating system, a coupled pair of discrete-time dynamical systems. For example, with the predator-prey equations

$$\frac{db}{dt} = (1.0 - 0.001p)b$$
$$\frac{dp}{dt} = (-1.0 + 0.001b)p$$

Euler's method is

$$\begin{aligned}\hat{b}(t+\Delta t) &= \hat{b}(t) + b'(t)\Delta t \\ &= \hat{b}(t) + (1.0 - 0.001\hat{p}(t))\hat{b}(t)\Delta t \\ \hat{p}(t+\Delta t) &= \hat{p}(t) + p'(t)\Delta t \\ &= \hat{p}(t) + (-1.0 + 0.001\hat{b}(t))\hat{p}(t)\Delta t\end{aligned}$$

Starting from the initial condition $(b(0), p(0)) = (800, 200)$, follow this system until it loops around near its initial condition. Use the following values of Δt.

a. $\Delta t = 1.0$

b. $\Delta t = 0.2$

c. $\Delta t = 0.1$

d. $\Delta t = 0.01$

42. Follow the same steps as in the previous problem for the spring equations

$$\frac{dx}{dt} = v$$
$$\frac{dv}{dt} = -x$$

derived in Exercise 15. How close is your estimated solution to the exact solution? What happens if you keep running for many cycles?

5.6 The Phase Plane

Systems of autonomous differential equations are generally impossible to solve exactly. We have seen how to use Euler's method to find approximate solutions. As with autonomous differential equations and discrete-time dynamical systems, we can deduce a great deal about the behavior of solutions from an appropriate graphical display. For systems of autonomous differential equations, the tool is the **phase-plane** diagram, an extension of the phase-line diagram. Our goal is again to find **equilibria,** points where each of the state variables remains unchanged. Finding these points on the phase plane requires a new tool, the **nullcline,** a graph of the set of points where each state variable separately remains unchanged.

Equilibria and Nullclines: Predator-Prey Equations

A single autonomous differential equation has an equilibrium where the rate of change of the state variable is 0. An **equilibrium** of a two-dimensional system of autonomous differential equations is a point where the rate of change of *each* state variable is 0.

Consider again a predator and its prey described by the system of autonomous differential equations

$$\frac{db}{dt} = (1.0 - 0.001p)b$$
$$\frac{dp}{dt} = (-1.0 + 0.001b)p$$

(Equation 5.5.1 with $\lambda = 1.0$, $\delta = 1.0$, $\epsilon = 0.001$, and $\eta = 0.001$). The rates of change of both b and p are equal to 0 when the following hold simultaneously:

$$\frac{db}{dt} = (1.0 - 0.001p)b = 0$$
$$\frac{dp}{dt} = (-1.0 + 0.001b)p = 0$$

Solving **simultaneous equations** can be much harder than solving a single equation. Our technique is to break the problem down into pieces and use a graph to combine the results.

To begin, we review solving simpler linear simultaneous equations.

Example 5.6.1 Solving Linear Simultaneous Equations

To solve the equations

$$y = 3x - 1$$
$$y = 2x + 3$$

for x and y, we set the two expressions for y equal to each other. This gives the equation

$$3x - 1 = 2x + 3$$

which can be solved to give $x = 4$. Substituting into either equation then gives $y = 11$ (Figure 5.6.32).

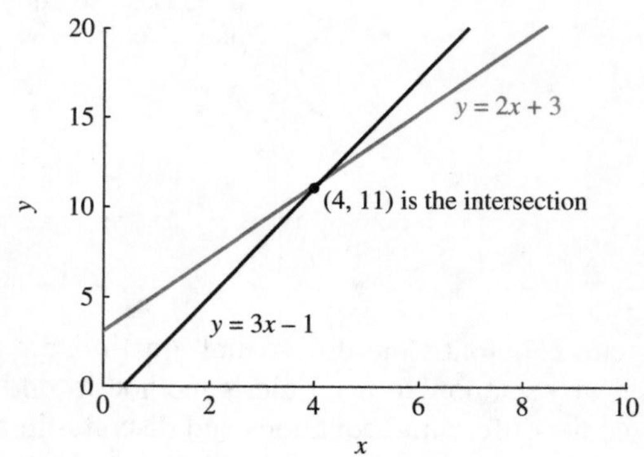

FIGURE 5.6.32
Two linear simultaneous equations

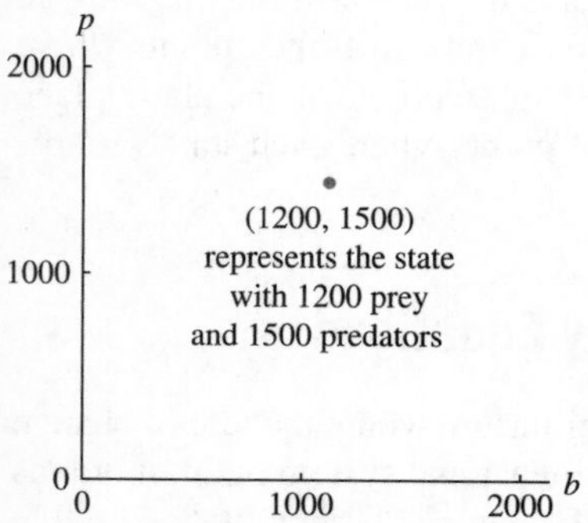

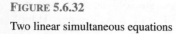

FIGURE 5.6.33
The phase plane with p on the vertical axis and b on the horizontal axis

How do we graph the solutions of an equation? We are used to graphing functions written in the form $y = f(x)$, placing x on the horizontal axis and y on the vertical axis. It is easy to graph because we have *solved* for y. To graph the solutions of

$$\frac{db}{dt} = (1.0 - 0.001p)b = 0$$

we must pick one of the variables b or p to place on the vertical axis like y. We can pick either one, and here we choose p. Our next step is to plot an empty graph with the vertical axis labeled p and the horizontal axis labeled b (Figure 5.6.33). This is a graph of the **phase plane.** Like the phase-line diagram, a phase-plane diagram is a picture of all possible values the state variables can take. For example, the point (1200, 1500) represents the system with 1200 prey and 1500 predators.

Now we can solve the equation

$$\frac{db}{dt} = (1.0 - 0.001p)b = 0$$

to find all values of b and p where the state variable b does not change. The first step in solving almost any equation is to factor and set each factor equal to 0. This equation, conveniently enough, is already factored as $1.0 - 0.001p$ times b. The two equations to solve are therefore

$$1.0 - 0.001p = 0 \quad \text{and} \quad b = 0$$

Solving means isolating p, the variable chosen as the vertical axis. On the first piece,

$$p = 1000$$

In the phase plane, the graph of this function is a horizontal line at $p = 1000$ (Figure 5.6.34a). The second piece, $b = 0$, does not include the variable p. This means that *any* value of p where $b = 0$ is a solution. The graph of this piece is a vertical line at $b = 0$ (Figure 5.6.34b).

These solutions represent the set of values where the rate of change of b is 0. This entire set is called the **b-nullcline** and is graphed in the phase plane in Figure 5.6.35.

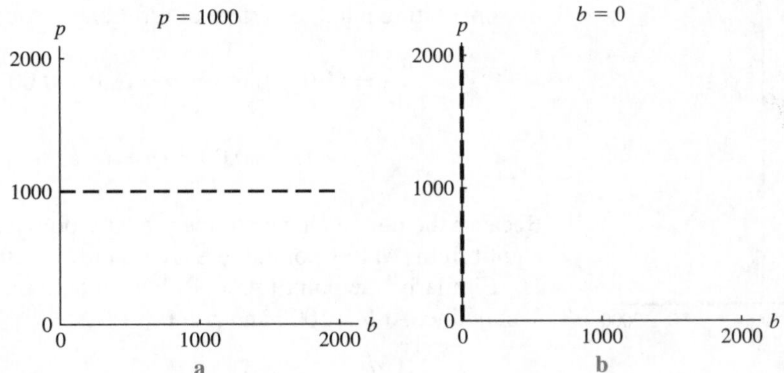

FIGURE 5.6.34

The two components of the b-nullcline

This might look like a strange graph, consisting as it does of two distinct pieces. Although no function could have a graph like this, it is typical of the behavior of nullclines.

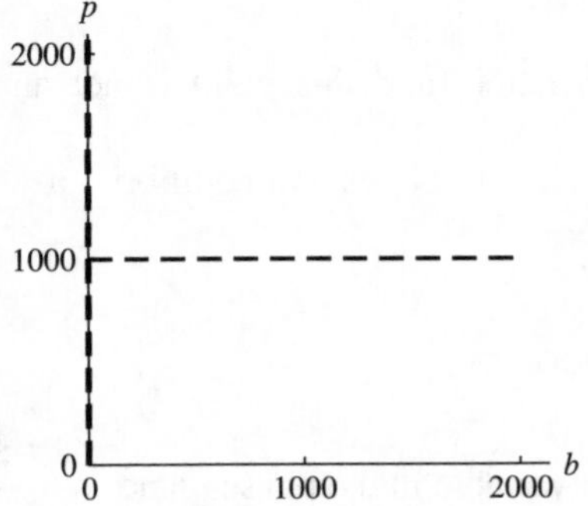

FIGURE 5.6.35

The b-nullcline: points in the phase-plane where b does not change

We use the same method to find the p-nullcline, the set of points where the rate of change of p is 0. The equation

$$\frac{dp}{dt} = (-1.0 + 0.001b)p = 0$$

has a solution where either of the factors is equal to 0. Because the equation is in factored form with factors $-1.0 + 0.001b$ and p, solutions occur where

$$-1.0 + 0.001b = 0 \quad \text{or} \quad p = 0$$

To graph them, we again solve for the vertical variable p. Remember to use the *same* vertical variable for both nullclines. The first piece lacks any occurrence of the vertical variable p to solve for. This indicates that the solution is a vertical line, found by solving for the horizontal variable. The solution of $-1.0 + 0.001b = 0$ is $b = 1000$, so the first piece of the p-nullcline is a vertical line at $b = 1000$ (Figure 5.6.36a). The second piece is the horizontal line $p = 0$. The entire p-nullcline is the combination of these two pieces (Figure 5.6.37).

The state variable b does not change on the b-nullcline. The state variable p does not change on the p-nullcline. Therefore, neither b nor p changes at any point where the two nullclines intersect. These intersections, therefore, are the equilibria. To find equilibria, plot both nullclines on the same graph, being careful to distinguish which piece belongs to which nullcline (Figure 5.6.38). There are two intersections of the nullclines, at (0, 0) and (1000, 1000). At the first equilibrium, both populations are extinct. At the second, both populations are positive and the system is balanced.

The points (0, 1000) and (1000, 0) are not equilibria because they do not lie at the intersection of the two nullclines. The point (0, 1000) lies on both pieces of the b-nullcline but not on the p-nullcline. We can check whether a point is an equilibrium

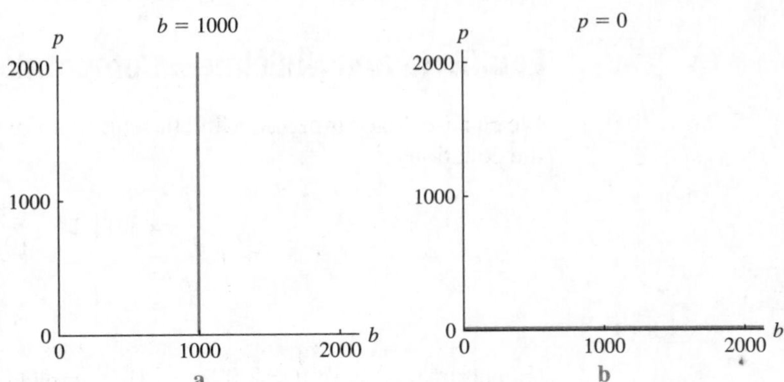

FIGURE 5.6.36

The two components of the p-nullcline

by substituting into the system of differential equations. At $b=0$ and $p=1000$,

$$\frac{db}{dt} = (1.0 - 0.001p)b = (1.0 - 0.001 \cdot 1000) \cdot 0 = 0$$

$$\frac{dp}{dt} = (-1.0 + 0.001b)p = (-1.0 + 0.001 \cdot 0) \cdot 1000 = -1000$$

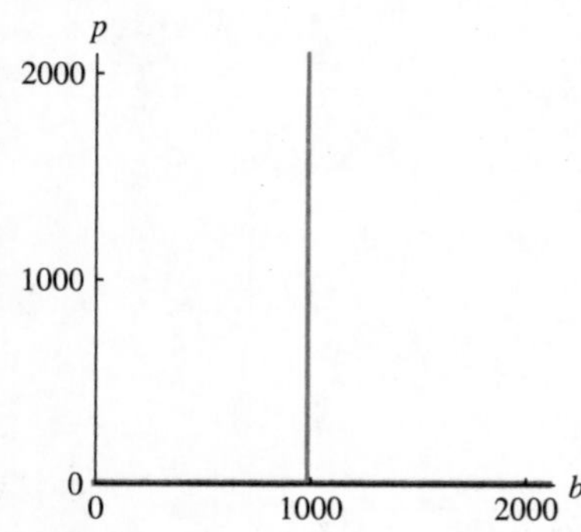

FIGURE 5.6.37

The p-nullcline: points in the phase-plane where p does not change

Because the rate of change of the predator population p is not equal to 0, this is not an equilibrium. At this point, there are no prey and the predator population declines.

Similarly, the point (1000, 0) lies on both pieces of the p-nullcline but not on the b-nullcline. At $b=1000$ and $p=0$,

$$\frac{db}{dt} = (1.0 - 0.001p)b = (1.0 - 0.001 \cdot 0) \cdot 1000 = 1000$$

$$\frac{dp}{dt} = (-1.0 + 0.001b)p = (-1.0 + 0.001 \cdot 1000) \cdot 0 = 0$$

Again, the rate of change of one state variable is not 0, and this point is not an equilibrium.

The following algorithm gives the steps to find the nullclines and equilibria of a system of autonomous differential equations.

▸▸ Algorithm 5.5 Finding the Nullclines and Equilibria of Coupled Autonomous Differential Equations

1. Pick one of the variables to act as the vertical variable in the phase plane.
2. Write the equation for the first nullcline by setting the rate of change of the first state variable equal to 0.
   (a) Factor.
   (b) Solve each factor for the vertical variable. If there is no vertical variable in the factor, solve for the horizontal variable.
   (c) Graph each solution in the phase plane. If the equation contains no vertical variable, the graph is a vertical line.
3. Follow the same steps to find the second nullcline, using the equation for the second state variable. Graph in the phase plane, using a different color or style.
4. Find the intersections, which are the equilibria of the system.

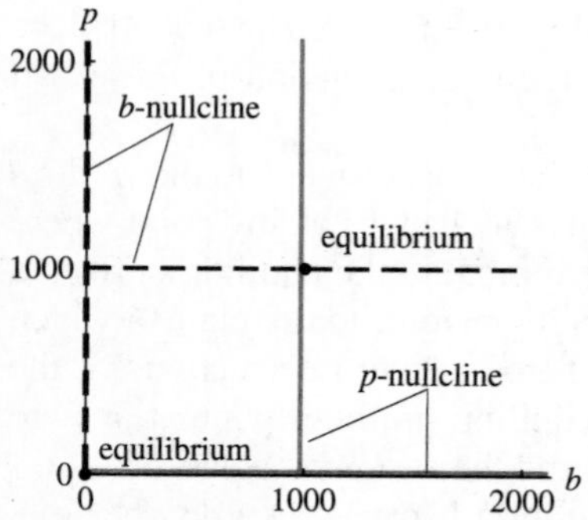

FIGURE 5.6.38

The nullclines of the predator-prey system

Solutions that begin at an equilibrium remain there. To figure out what other solutions do, we would need to assess the stability of our equilibria. The techniques to do this, extensions of the methods used in one dimension, involve *linear algebra,* a subject that lies just beyond the scope of this book. In the next section, however, we will learn to analyze at least some situations by drawing direction arrows on our phase-plane diagram.

Equilibria and Nullclines: Competition Equations

We can use Algorithm 5.5 to find the equilibria of competing bacterial types that follow the equations

$$\frac{da}{dt} = 2.0\left(1 - \frac{a+b}{1000}\right)a$$

$$\frac{db}{dt} = 2.0\left(1 - \frac{a+b}{500}\right)b$$

(Equation 5.5.2 with $\mu = 2.0$, $\lambda = 2.0$, $K_a = 1000$, and $K_b = 500$).

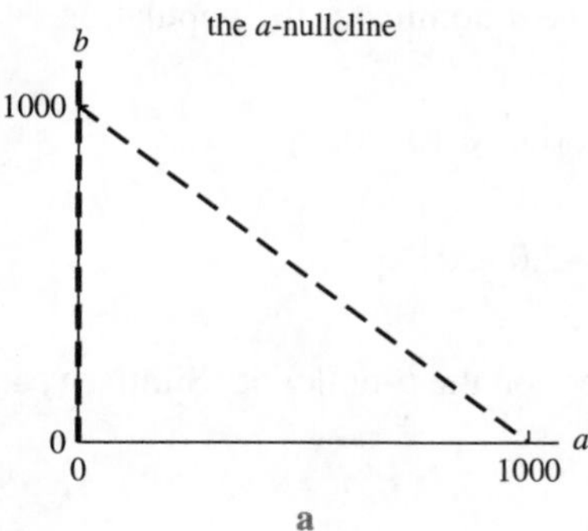

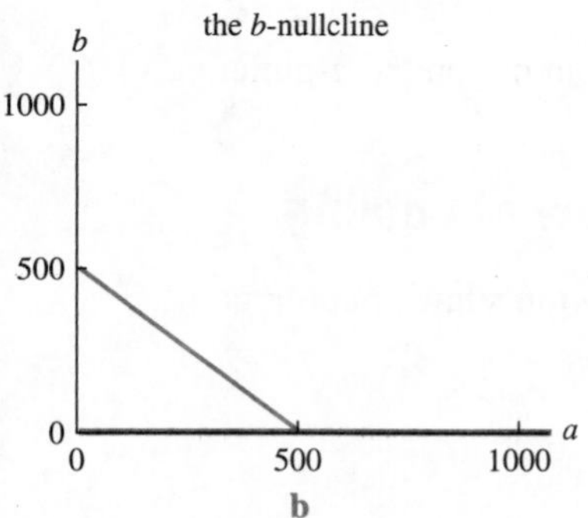

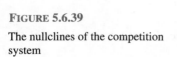

FIGURE 5.6.39
The nullclines of the competition system

1. We begin by choosing the vertical variable, picking b because it comes later in the alphabet.
2. To find the a-nullcline, we solve

$$\frac{da}{dt} = 2.0\left(1 - \frac{a+b}{1000}\right)a = 0$$

   (a) The factors are $2.0\left(1 - \frac{a+b}{1000}\right)$ and a

   (b) Solutions occur where

$$2.0\left(1 - \frac{a+b}{1000}\right) = 0 \quad \text{or} \quad a = 0$$

   We solve the first factor for b, the vertical variable, finding

$$\begin{aligned} 2.0\left(1 - \frac{a+b}{1000}\right) &= 0 \\ \left(1 - \frac{a+b}{1000}\right) &= 0 \\ \frac{a+b}{1000} &= 1 \\ a+b &= 1000 \\ b &= 1000 - a \end{aligned}$$

   The second factor has no vertical variable b and is therefore the vertical line at $a = 0$.

   (c) The graph is shown in Figure 5.6.39a.

3. To find the b-nullcline, we solve

$$\frac{db}{dt} = 2.0\left(1 - \frac{a+b}{500}\right)b$$

   (a) The factors are $2.0\left(1 - \frac{a+b}{500}\right)$ and b

   (b) Solutions occur where

$$2.0\left(1 - \frac{a+b}{500}\right) = 0 \quad \text{or} \quad b = 0$$

   We solve the first factor for the vertical variable, finding

$$\begin{aligned} 2.0\left(1 - \frac{a+b}{500}\right) &= 0 \\ \left(1 - \frac{a+b}{500}\right) &= 0 \\ \frac{a+b}{500} &= 1 \\ a+b &= 500 \\ b &= 500 - a \end{aligned}$$

   The second factor is a horizontal line at $b = 0$.

   (c) The graph is shown in Figure 5.6.39b.

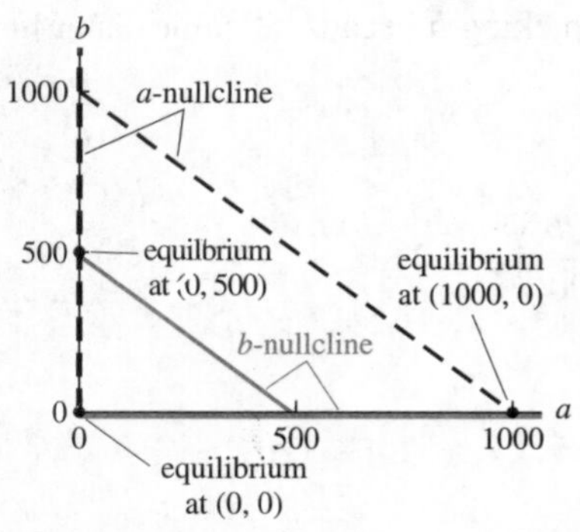

FIGURE 5.6.40
The nullclines and equilibria of the competition system

4. To find the equilibria, we plot both nullclines on the same graph of the phase plane (Figure 5.6.40). There are three intersections and thus three equilibria: at (0, 0), (1000, 0), and (0, 500). Both types are extinct at (0, 0), type b dominates the population at (1000, 0), and type a dominates the population at (0, 500).

The points (0, 1000) and (500, 0) are not equilibria. At (0, 1000),

$$\frac{db}{dt} = 2.0\left(1 - \frac{1000}{500}\right) = -2.0 < 0$$

The point lies on both pieces of the a-nullcline but not on the b-nullcline. Similarly, at (500, 0),

$$\frac{da}{dt} = 2.0\left(1 - \frac{500}{1000}\right) = 1.0 > 0$$

This point lies on both branches of the b-nullcline but not on the a-nullcline.

Equilibria and Nullclines: Newton's Law of Cooling

We use the same steps to find the equilibria for Newton's law of cooling:

$$\frac{dH}{dt} = \alpha(A - H)$$

$$\frac{dA}{dt} = \alpha_2(H - A)$$

1. To begin, we choose the temperature of the object H as the vertical variable.
2. The A-nullcline is the set of points where

$$\frac{dA}{dt} = \alpha_2(H - A) = 0$$

(a) This has only one component and does not need to be factored (unless $\alpha_2 = 0$).

(b) If $\alpha_2 > 0$, we solve for the vertical variable H,

$$H = A$$

If $\alpha_2 = 0$, all values of H and A lie on the nullcline because no heat is exchanged.

(c) The graph is shown in Figure 5.6.41a.

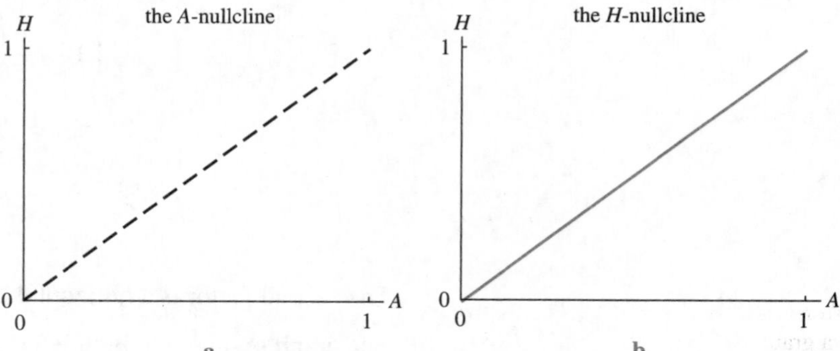

FIGURE 5.6.41
The nullclines of Newton's law of cooling

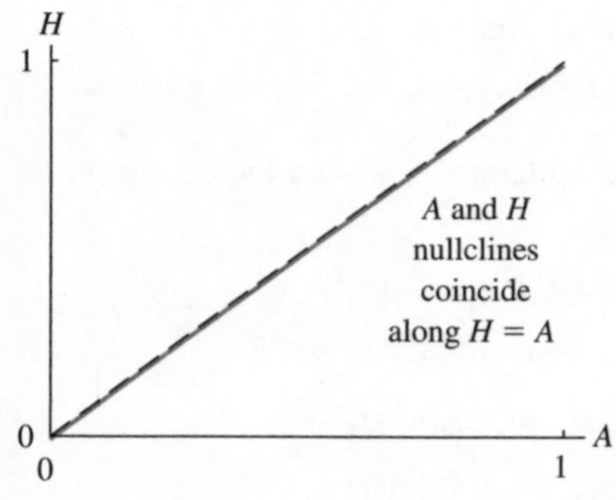

FIGURE 5.6.42
The nullclines and equilibria of Newton's law of cooling

3. The H-nullcline is the set of points where

$$\frac{dH}{dt} = \alpha(A - H) = 0$$

(a) This has only one component and does not need to be factored.

(b) Solving for the vertical variable H, we again find

$$H = A$$

(c) The graph is shown in Figure 5.6.41b.

4. The two nullclines exactly overlap. Because all points where the two nullclines intersect are equilibria, every point on the line $H = A$ is an equilibrium (Figure 5.6.42).

This peculiar result makes sense. When the two temperatures are the same, there is no further change in temperature by either the object or the room.

Summary We have introduced the **phase plane, nullclines,** and **equilibria** as tools to study autonomous systems of differential equations. Equilibria occur where the rate of change of each state variable is 0. They can be found on the phase plane (the Cartesian plane with axes labeled by the state variables) by graphing the two nullclines. The nullcline associated with a state variable is the set of values where it remains unchanged.

5.6 Exercises

Mathematical Techniques

1–4 ▪ Finding equilibria of coupled differential equations requires solving simultaneous equations. The following are linear equations, where the only possibilities are no solutions, one solution, or a whole line of solutions. For each of the following pairs, solve each equation for y in terms of x, set the two equations for y equal, and solve for x. Check that both equations give the same value for y. Sketch a graph with y on the vertical axis.

1.
$$-3 - y + 3x = 0$$
$$-2 + 2y - 4x = 0$$

2.
$$-6 + 3y + 3x = 0$$
$$-2 - 2y - 6x = 0$$

3.
$$3 - 3y + 3x = 0$$
$$-2 + 2y - 2x = 0$$

What goes wrong? Use your graph with y on the vertical axis to explain the problem.

4.
$$8 - 2y + 4x = 0$$
$$-2 + y - 2x = 0$$

What goes wrong? Use your graph with y on the vertical axis to explain the problem.

5–10 ▪ Finding equilibria of nonlinear coupled differential equations requires solving nonlinear simultaneous equations, which can have any number of solutions. For each of the following pairs, solve each equation for y in terms of x, set the two equations for y equal, and solve for x. Check that both equations give the same value for y. Sketch a graph with y on the vertical axis.

5.
$$-5 - y + 3x^2 + 2x = 0$$
$$-2 + 2y - 4x = 0$$

6.
$$-3 - y + 3x^2 + 2x = 0$$
$$-2 + 2y - 4x + 2x^2 = 0$$

7.
$$-y^2 + x^2 = 0$$
$$-2 + 2y - 4x = 0$$

Solving the first equation for y in terms of x does not give a function. Graph the relation and find the solutions.

8.
$$y(y - x^2) = 0$$
$$-6 + 2y - 4x = 0$$

Solving the first equation for y in terms of x does not give a function. Graph the relation and find the solutions.

9.
$$x(y - x) = 0$$
$$-6 + 2y - 4x = 0$$

Solving the first equation for y in terms of x includes a vertical section. Graph the relation and find the solutions.

10.
$$(x - 1)(y^2 - x^2) = 0$$
$$-2 + 2y - 6x = 0$$

Solving the first equation for y in terms of x does not give a function and includes a vertical section. Graph the relation and find the solutions.

11–16 ▪ Graph the nullclines in the phase plane and find the equilibria of the following.

11. Predator-prey model

$$\frac{db}{dt} = (\lambda - \epsilon p)b$$
$$\frac{dp}{dt} = (-\delta + \eta b)p$$

(Equation 5.5.1) with $\lambda = 1.0, \delta = 3.0, \epsilon = 0.002, \eta = 0.005$.

12. Predator-prey model with $\lambda = 1.0,\ \delta = 3.0,\ \epsilon = 0.005,\ \eta = 0.002$.

13. Newton's law of cooling

$$\frac{dH}{dt} = \alpha(A - H)$$
$$\frac{dA}{dt} = \alpha_2(H - A)$$

with $\alpha = 0.01$ and $\alpha_2 = 0.1$.

14. Newton's law of cooling with $\alpha = 0.1$ and $\alpha_2 = 0.5$.

15. Competition model

$$\frac{da}{dt} = \mu\left(1 - \frac{a+b}{K_a}\right)a$$
$$\frac{db}{dt} = \lambda\left(1 - \frac{a+b}{K_b}\right)b$$

(Equation 5.5.2) with $\lambda = 2.0, \mu = 1.0, K_a = 10^6, K_b = 10^7$.

16. Competition model with $\lambda = 1.0,\ \mu = 2.0,\ K_a = 10^6,\ K_b = 10^7$. How do the results compare with those in Exercise 15? Why?

17–20 ▪ Redraw the phase planes for the following problems, but make the other choice for the vertical variable. Check that you get the same equilibrium.

17. The equations in Exercise 11

18. The equations in Exercise 12

19. The equations in Exercise 15

20. The equations in Exercise 16

21–22 ▪ If each state variable in a system of autonomous differential equations does not respond to changes in the value of the other, but depends only on a constant value, the two equations can be considered separately. In this case, the phase plane is particularly simple. Find the nullclines and equilibria in the following cases.

21. The situation in Section 5.5, Exercise 5

22. The situation in Section 5.5, Exercise 6

Applications

23–26 ▪ Find the nullclines and equilibria for the following predator-prey models.

23. The model in Section 5.5, Exercise 21

24. The model in Section 5.5, Exercise 22

25. The model in Section 5.5, Exercise 23

26. The model in Section 5.5, Exercise 24

27–30 ▪ Find and graph the nullclines, and find the equilibria for the following models.

27. The model found in Section 5.5, Exercise 25

28. The model found in Section 5.5, Exercise 26

29. The model found in Section 5.5, Exercise 27

30. The model found in Section 5.5, Exercise 28

31–32 ▪ The models of diffusion derived in Section 5.5, Exercises 29 and 30 assume that the membrane between the vessels is equally permeable in both directions. Suppose instead that the constant of proportionality governing the rate at which chemical moves differs in the two directions. In each of the following cases:

a. Find the rate at which chemical moves from the smaller to the larger vessel.

b. Find the rate at which chemical moves from the larger to the smaller vessel.

c. Find the rate of change of the amount of chemical in each vessel.

d. Divide by the volumes V_1 and V_2 to find the rate of change of concentration.

e. Find and graph the nullclines.

f. What are the equilibria? Do they make sense?

31. The constant of proportionality governing the rate at which chemical enters the cell is three times as large as the constant governing the rate at which it leaves (as in Section 5.1, Exercise 33).

32. The constant of proportionality governing the rate at which chemical enters the cell is half as large as the constant governing the rate at which it leaves (as in Section 5.1, Exercise 34).

33–34 ▪ In our model of competition, the per capita growth rates of types a and b are functions only of the total population size. This means that reproduction is reduced just as much by an individual of type a as by an individual of type b. In many systems, each type interferes differently with type a than with type b. Check that the given set of equations matches the assumptions in each of the following cases, and find and graph the equilibria and nullclines.

33. Suppose that individuals of type b reduce the per capita growth rate of type a by half as much as individuals of type a, and that individuals of type a reduce the per capita growth rate of type b by twice as much as individuals of type b. The equations are

$$\frac{da}{dt} = \left(1 - \frac{a + b/2}{1000}\right)a$$
$$\frac{db}{dt} = \left(1 - \frac{2a + b}{1000}\right)b$$

34. Suppose that individuals of type b reduce the per capita growth rate of type a by half as much as individuals of type a, and that individuals of type a reduce the per capita growth rate of type b by half as much as individuals of type b. The equations are

$$\frac{da}{dt} = \left(1 - \frac{a + b/2}{1000}\right) a$$

$$\frac{db}{dt} = \left(1 - \frac{a/2 + b}{1000}\right) b$$

(There should be four equilibria).

35–40 ▪ Draw the nullclines and find equilibria of the following extensions of the basic disease model.

35. The model in Section 5.5, Exercise 33. Find the nullclines and equilibria of this model when $\alpha = 2.0$ and $\mu = 1.0$.

36. The model in Section 5.5, Exercise 34. Find the nullclines and equilibria of this model when $\alpha = 2.0$ and $\mu = 1.0$.

37. The model in Section 5.5, Exercise 35. Find the nullclines and equilibria of this model when $\alpha = 2.0$, $\mu = 1.0$, and $k = 0.5$.

38. The model in Section 5.5, Exercise 35. Find the nullclines and equilibria of this model when $\alpha = 2.0$, $\mu = 1.0$, and $k = 4.0$.

39. The model in Section 5.5, Exercise 37. Find the nullclines and equilibria of this model when $\alpha = 2.0$, $\mu = 1.0$, and $b = 2.0$.

40. The model in Section 5.5, Exercise 38. Find the nullclines and equilibria of this model when $\alpha = 2.0$, $\mu = 1.0$, and $b = 1.0$.

Computer Exercises

41. One complicated equation for chemical kinetics is the Schnakenberg reaction. Let A and B denote the concentrations of two chemicals A and B. A is added at constant rate k_1, B is added at constant rate k_4, A breaks down at rate k_2, and B is converted into A with an **autocatalytic reaction** (a reaction where the product increases the reaction rate). The equations are

$$\frac{dA}{dt} = k_1 - k_2 A + k_3 A^2 B$$

$$\frac{dB}{dt} = k_4 - k_3 A^2 B$$

The final term is somewhat like the term αIS in epidemic equations, but it differs in that the rate of the reaction becomes faster the larger the concentration of A. Suppose that $k_2 = k_3 = 1.0$.

a. Have your computer draw the nullclines and find the equilibria in the case $k_1 = 0.2$ and $k_4 = 2.0$.

b. Do the same with $k_1 = -0.2$ and $k_4 = 2.0$.

c. Try to explain your results.

42. A variant of the Schnakenberg reaction has the chemical A inhibiting its own production. In particular, assume that we replace $k_3 A^2 B$ with

$$k_3 \frac{AB}{1 + A}$$

Suppose that $k_2 = k_3 = 1.0$.

a. Write the equations describing this system.

b. Have your computer draw the nullclines and find the equilibria in the case $k_1 = 0.2$ and $k_4 = 2.0$.

c. Do the same with $k_1 = -0.2$ and $k_4 = 2.0$.

d. Try to explain your results.

5.7 Solutions in the Phase Plane

We have seen how to find nullclines and equilibria in the phase plane. Our real goal is to find *solutions,* descriptions of how the state variables change over time. We begin by graphing the results from Euler's method in the phase plane. To deduce the behavior of solutions without all the calculations necessary for Euler's method, we will add **direction arrows** to the phase-plane diagram. Like the arrows that appear in phase-line diagrams, they indicate where solutions are increasing or decreasing and can be used to sketch **phase-plane trajectories,** or solutions in the phase plane.

Euler's Method in the Phase Plane

We applied Euler's method to the predator-prey equations

$$\frac{db}{dt} = (1.0 - 0.001p)b$$

$$\frac{dp}{dt} = (-1.0 + 0.001b)p$$

in Section 5.5 and computed the values for ten steps of length $\Delta t = 0.2$ starting from the initial condition $b(0) = 800$ and $p(0) = 200$.

t	$\hat{b}$	$\hat{p}$
0.0	800.0	200.0
0.2	928.0	192.0
0.4	1078.0	189.2
0.6	1252.8	192.2
0.8	1455.2	201.9
1.0	1687.4	220.3
1.2	1950.6	250.6
1.4	2242.9	298.2
1.6	2557.8	372.3
1.8	2878.8	488.3
2.0	3173.5	671.8

We can plot these values in the phase plane (Figure 5.7.43). The value at $t = 0$ is plotted as the point (800, 200) in the phase plane, the value at $t = 0.2$ is plotted as (928, 192), and so forth. Following the points through time, we see that the prey population increases steadily and that the predator population begins by decreasing and then increases.

Euler's method does not provide an exact solution, however, and takes a lot of calculation. More precise techniques correct the errors produced by using the tangent line approximation and can be programmed on the computer to generate solutions accurate to any desired level. A solution generated with one such method (called the Runge-Kutta method) is plotted in Figure 5.7.44. The initial condition in this graph is $b(0) = 800$ and $p(0) = 200$. The solution consists of two curves, one for each of the state variables. At any time t, the values of b and p can be read from the graphs of b and p.

The populations oscillate, with the peak predator population occurring after the peak prey population. When prey are plentiful, the predators increase in number.

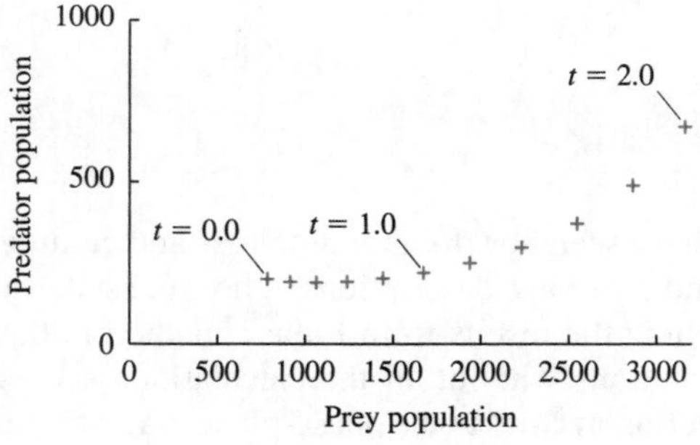

FIGURE 5.7.43
Results from Euler's method plotted in the phase plane

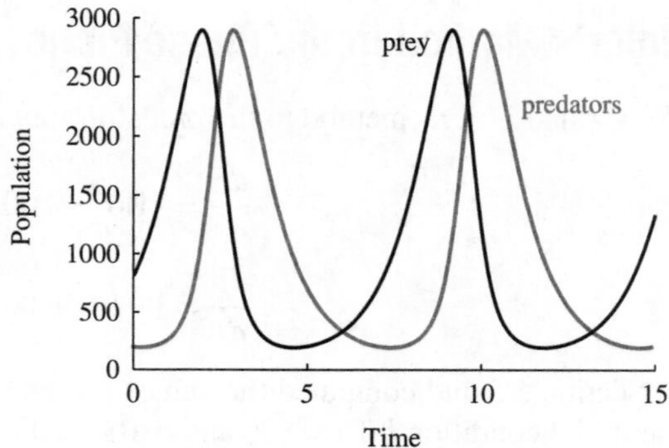

FIGURE 5.7.44
Solutions of the predator-prey system

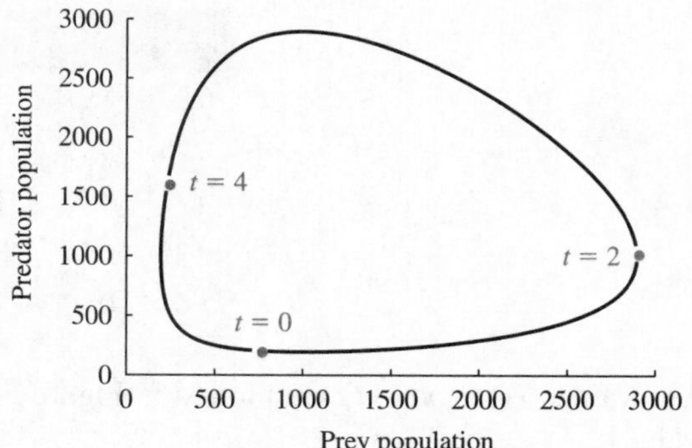

FIGURE 5.7.45
Solution of the predator-prey equations in the phase plane

They eat the prey, eventually decreasing the prey population. This reduces the predator food supply, which leads to an eventual reduction in the predator population. The prey can then increase, beginning the cycle again.

As with the results from Euler's method, we can graph these solutions in the phase plane as a **phase-plane trajectory** (Figure 5.7.45). The initial condition (800, 200) is plotted at the point (800, 200) (labeled $t = 0$). At $t = 2$, the population of prey is 2894 and the population of predators is 1051, so the point (2894, 1051) is plotted in the phase plane. Because time does not appear explicitly as part of a phase-plane trajectory, we have labeled several points with the time. The initial condition (b_0, p_0) is labeled with $t = 0$. We have graphed three things on one graph: the time, the prey population, and the predator population. This is called a **parametric graph.**

How can we translate back and forth between the solutions plotted as functions of time and the phase-plane trajectory? Starting from the solution, you can plot the number of predators against the number of prey at several times (such as $t = 0$, $t = 1$, and so forth) and connect the dots. Starting from the phase-plane trajectory, you can sketch the solutions by tracing along the graph at a constant speed. The horizontal location of your pencil gives the prey population, or the height of the graph of $b(t)$. The vertical location of your pencil gives the predator population, or the height of the graph of $p(t)$. In our example, we see that the prey population begins by increasing, reaches a maximum value of nearly 3000, and then decreases to a value of about 200 before beginning to increase again. The predator population decreases slightly below 200 before beginning an increase to nearly 3000. The predators reach their maximum after the prey and then decrease again.

Example 5.7.1 Graphing a Solution and a Phase-Plane Trajectory

Suppose that $x(t) = 1 - t$ and $y(t) = 1 + 2t$ are the solutions of two coupled differential equations for $0 \le t \le 1$. Both $x(t)$ and $y(t)$ are linear functions of time. We can plot $x(t)$ by computing $x(0) = 1$ and $x(1) = 0$ and connecting the points (0, 1) and (1, 0) with a line. Similarly, we can plot $y(t)$ by computing $y(0) = 1$ and $y(1) = 3$ and connecting the points (0, 1) and (1, 3) with a line (Figure 5.7.46a). To plot the phase-plane trajectory, we can make a chart of values.

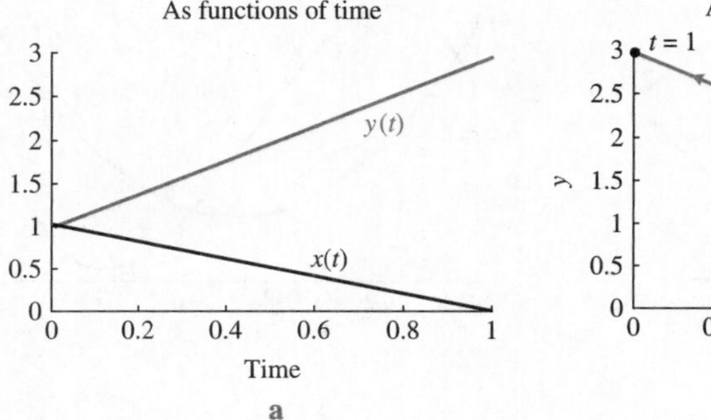

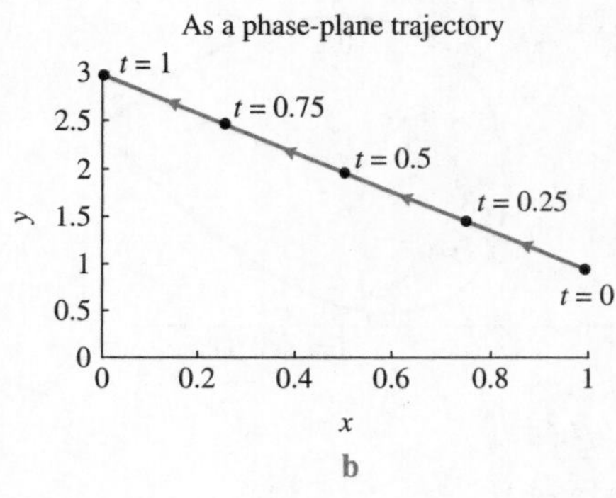

FIGURE 5.7.46
Graphing a solution and a phase-plane trajectory

t	$x(t)$	$y(t)$
0.0	1.0	1.0
0.25	0.75	1.5
0.5	0.5	2.0
0.75	0.25	2.5
1.0	0.0	3.0

The values $x(t)$ and $y(t)$ are plotted in Figure 5.7.46b, labeled by the corresponding value of t.

Example 5.7.2 Translating a Graph of a Solution into a Phase-Plane Trajectory

Suppose instead that we are given only the graph of a solution in Figure 5.7.47a. To plot the phase-plane trajectory, we identify the values of t for which the state variables

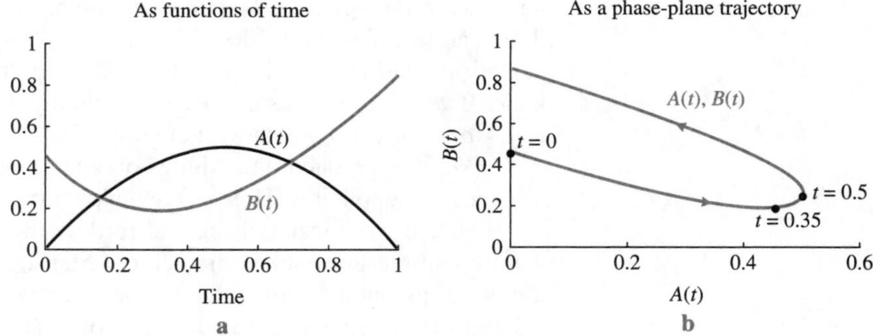

FIGURE 5.7.47

Translating a graph of a solution into a phase-plane trajectory

A and B are increasing and decreasing. From $t = 0$ until about $t = 0.35$, $A(t)$ is increasing and $B(t)$ is decreasing. From $t = 0.35$ until $t = 0.5$, $A(t)$ is increasing and $B(t)$ is increasing. From $t = 0.5$ on, $A(t)$ is decreasing and $B(t)$ is increasing.

t	Behavior of $A(t)$	Behavior of $B(t)$
0.0–0.35	Increasing	Decreasing
0.35–0.5	Increasing	Increasing
0.5–1.0	Decreasing	Increasing

Example 5.7.3 Translating a Phase-Plane Trajectory into a Graph of a Solution

Suppose instead that we are given only the graph of the phase-plane trajectory in Figure 5.7.48a. To plot the solution, we use the phase-plane trajectory to identify

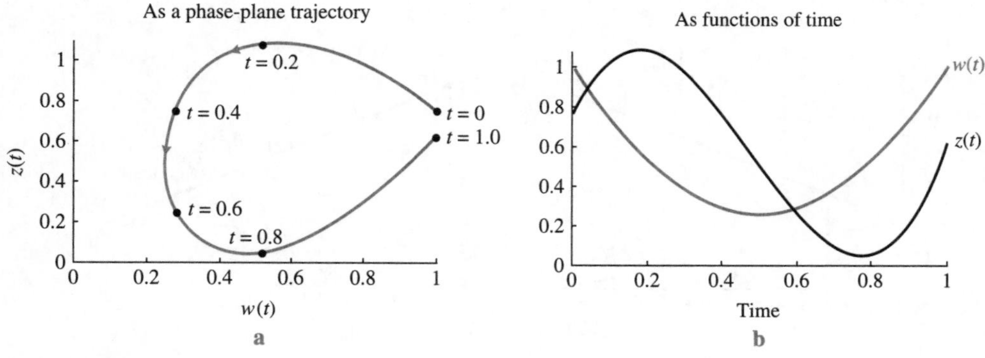

FIGURE 5.7.48

Translating a phase-plane trajectory into a graph of a solution values of t for which the state variables w and z are increasing and decreasing. From $t = 0$ until about $t = 0.2$, $w(t)$ is decreasing and $z(t)$ is increasing. From $t = 0.2$ until $t = 0.5$, $w(t)$ is decreasing and $z(t)$ is decreasing. From $t = 0.5$ until $t = 0.75$, $w(t)$ is increasing and $z(t)$ is decreasing. From $t = 0.75$ on, both $w(t)$ and $z(t)$ are increasing.

t	Behavior of $w(t)$	Behavior of $z(t)$
0.0–0.2	Decreasing	Increasing
0.2–0.5	Decreasing	Decreasing
0.5–0.75	Increasing	Decreasing
0.75–1.0	Increasing	Increasing

Direction Arrows: Predator-Prey Equations

The numerical solutions (Figures 5.7.44 and 5.7.45) give an accurate description of the dynamics. Our goal, however, is to understand the behavior of the populations without solving the equations. For one-dimensional systems, we sketched solutions from the direction arrows and equilibria on a phase-line diagram. We know how to draw nullclines and find equilibria on a phase-plane diagram. The next step is to figure out how to draw the direction arrows.

We have redrawn the nullclines and equilibria in the phase plane for the predator-prey system (Figure 5.7.49). The nullclines break the phase plane into four regions, labeled I, II, III, and IV. In each, we wish to determine whether the populations of predators and prey are increasing or decreasing.

There are three different approaches to finding this out.

- Method 1: Pick a pair of values (b, p) in the region and substitute into the differential equation. Check whether $\frac{db}{dt}$ and $\frac{dp}{dt}$ are positive or negative.
- Method 2: Algebraic manipulation of inequalities.
- Method 3: Reasoning about the equations.

Which method is best depends on the equations. We will apply all three to the predator-prey phase plane.

In region I, the predator population is below the b-nullcline $p = 1000$, and the prey population is below the p-nullcline $b = 1000$. Method I requires picking a pair of values in this region. One point in this region is (500, 500). We can substitute this into the differential equation to check whether the populations are increasing or decreasing. With these values,

$$\frac{db}{dt} = (1.0 - 0.001 \cdot 500) \cdot 500 = 250 > 0$$

$$\frac{dp}{dt} = (-1.0 + 0.001 \cdot 500) \cdot 500 = -250 < 0$$

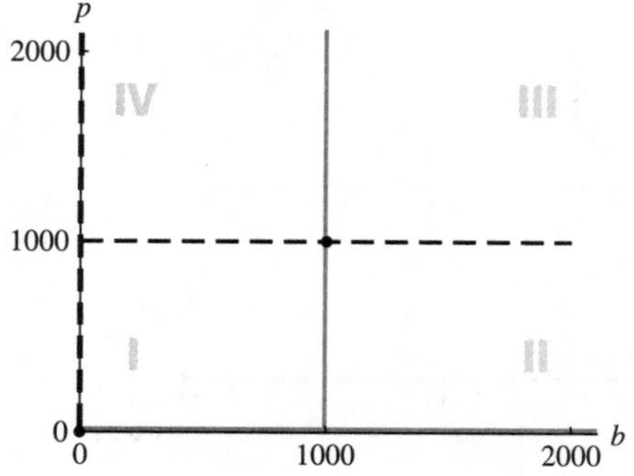

FIGURE 5.7.49

Regions of the phase plane for the predator-prey equations

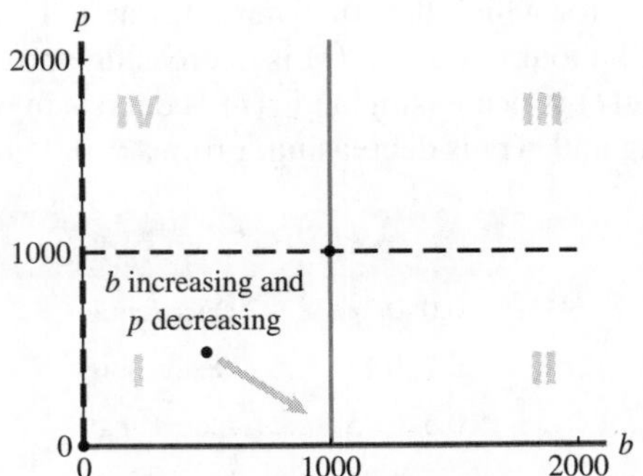

FIGURE 5.7.50
Direction arrow in region I of the predator-prey phase plane

The prey population is increasing because $\frac{db}{dt} > 0$, and the predator population is decreasing because $\frac{dp}{dt} < 0$. We indicate this by an arrow pointing toward larger values of the prey (to the right) and toward smaller values of the predator (down) (Figure 5.7.50). This is a **direction arrow.**

Method II is algebraic. If we are in region I, then

$$0 < b < 1000$$
$$0 < p < 1000$$

Then

$$\frac{db}{dt} = (1.0 - 0.001p)b > 0$$

because both $1.0 - 0.001p > 0$ and $b > 0$. The prey population increases in this region. Similarly,

$$\frac{dp}{dt} = (-1.0 + 0.001b)p < 0$$

because $-1.0 + 0.001b < 0$ and $p > 0$. The predator population decreases. Again, the direction arrow points to the right and down.

Method III uses reasoning about the equations. In region I, the prey and predator populations are both low. This means that the prey are happy (few predators to eat them) and the predators are sad (too few prey to eat). The prey population will increase and the predator population will decrease.

We can use any of the three methods to find the direction arrows in the three remaining regions (Figure 5.7.51). Using the reasoning method, in region II, we find that the prey population is large and the predator population is small. Both species should be happy and should increase, generating a direction arrow that points up and to the right. In region III, both populations are large. This is bad for the prey and good for the predators. The direction arrow therefore points toward lower values of prey

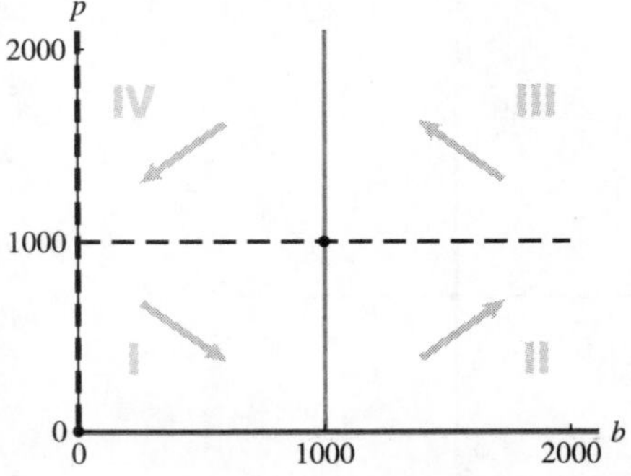

FIGURE 5.7.51
Direction arrows for the predator-prey equations

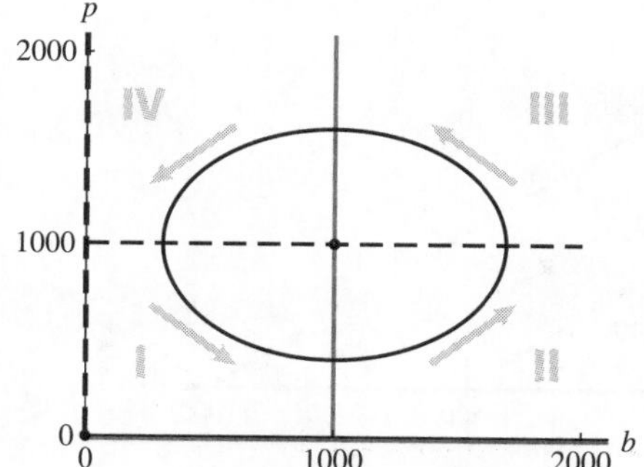

FIGURE 5.7.52
Direction arrows and solution for the predator-prey equations

(to the left) and larger values of predators (up). Finally, in region IV, the prey population is small and the predator population is large. Neither species does well under these circumstances, and the direction arrow points left and down.

As on a phase-line diagram, solutions follow the arrows (Figure 5.7.52). Starting in region I, where predator and prey populations are small, the arrow points down and to the right, pushing the solution into region II. Both populations then increase, following the arrows up and to the right into region III. The predators then increase while the prey decrease, moving the population into region IV, from which both populations decrease into region I. We cannot tell from this description whether the phase-plane trajectory circles around, spirals toward, or spirals away from the equilibrium.

What happens to direction arrows right on the nullclines? For example, what happens to a population with $b = 1000$ and $p < 1000$? This point lies on the p-nullcline, meaning that the population of predators remains unchanged. If an increasing predator population is associated with an upward-pointing arrow and a decreasing predator population is associated with a downward-pointing arrow, an unchanging predator population must be associated with an arrow that points neither up nor down. Such an arrow is horizontal. The population of prey, however, is changing. Because the number of predators is small, the prey population will increase and the arrow will point to the right (Figure 5.7.53). The other four direction arrows on nullclines can be found in a similar way.

Finding the direction arrows on the nullclines is useful for two reasons. First, it provides a useful check on the rest of the direction arrows. The directions can only change one at a time; when we move from region I to region II, the arrow switches from pointing down and to the right to pointing up and to the right. The only change was the vertical direction, and this change happens right at the nullcline where the arrow is horizontal. Second, these direction arrows can help in sketching more accurate phase-plane trajectories. Because solutions must follow the arrows, solutions must be horizontal when they cross the p-nullcline and vertical when they cross the b-nullcline. The solution sketched in Figure 5.7.52 satisfies these criteria.

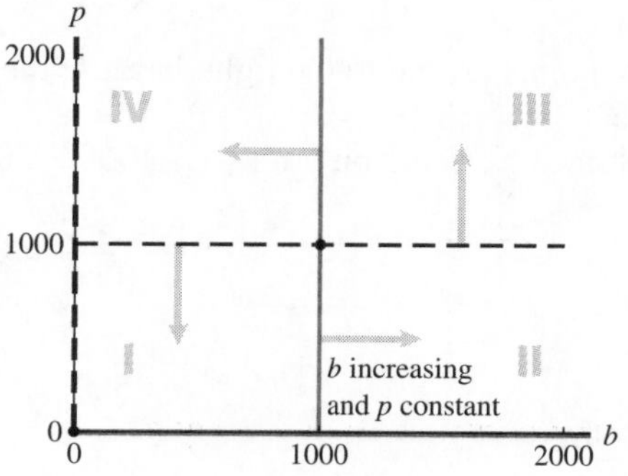

FIGURE 5.7.53
Direction arrows on nullclines

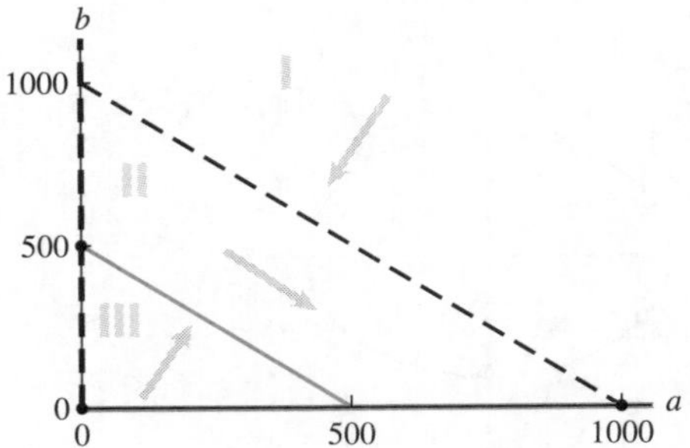

FIGURE 5.7.54
Direction arrows for the competition system

Direction Arrows: Competition Equations

For the competition model, the nullclines break the phase plane into three regions (Figure 5.7.54). We have again used the parameter values $K_a = 1000$ and $K_b = 500$, and we assume that μ and λ are positive. The a-nullcline lies above the b-nullcline. We can determine the direction arrows by using each of the three methods: substituting values, using algebra, and reasoning. With the first method, a point in region I is (1000, 1000). Then

$$\frac{da}{dt} = \mu\left(1 - \frac{1000 + 1000}{1000}\right) \cdot 1000 = -1000\mu < 0$$
$$\frac{db}{dt} = \lambda\left(1 - \frac{1000 + 1000}{500}\right) \cdot 1000 = -3000\lambda < 0$$

Because both derivatives are negative, both a and b are decreasing, meaning that the direction arrow points down and to the left. It is a bit harder to find a point in region II. This region is defined by

$$1000 > a + b > 500$$

so one point in the region is (400, 400). Then

$$\frac{da}{dt} = \mu\left(1 - \frac{400 + 400}{1000}\right) \cdot 400 = 80\mu > 0$$
$$\frac{db}{dt} = \lambda\left(1 - \frac{400 + 400}{500}\right) \cdot 400 = -240\lambda < 0$$

The direction arrow points down and to the right. The point (100, 100) lies in region III, where

$$\frac{da}{dt} = \mu\left(1 - \frac{100 + 100}{1000}\right) \cdot 100 = 80\mu > 0$$
$$\frac{db}{dt} = \lambda\left(1 - \frac{100 + 100}{500}\right) \cdot 100 = 60\lambda > 0$$

The arrow points up and to the right, because the rate of change of each state variable is positive.

Algebraically, in region I, $a + b > 1000 > 500$, so

$$1 - \frac{a+b}{1000} < 0$$
$$1 - \frac{a+b}{500} < 0$$

Therefore,

$$\frac{da}{dt} = \mu \left(1 - \frac{a+b}{1000}\right) a < 0$$
$$\frac{db}{dt} = \lambda \left(1 - \frac{a+b}{500}\right) b < 0$$

Both populations decrease, and the direction arrow points down and to the left. In region II, $500 < a + b < 1000$ and

$$\frac{da}{dt} = \mu \left(1 - \frac{a+b}{1000}\right) a > 0$$
$$\frac{db}{dt} = \lambda \left(1 - \frac{a+b}{500}\right) b < 0$$

The population of a increases, the population of b decreases, and the direction arrow points down and to the right. In region III, $a + b < 500 < 1000$, so

$$\frac{da}{dt} = \mu \left(1 - \frac{a+b}{1000}\right) a > 0$$
$$\frac{db}{dt} = \lambda \left(1 - \frac{a+b}{500}\right) b > 0$$

Both populations increase, and the direction arrow points up and to the right.

With the reasoning method, think of $K_a = 1000$ and $K_b = 500$ as the largest total populations that types a and b can tolerate. In region I, the total population exceeds both K_a and K_b. Both types suffer from overpopulation and have shrinking populations, generating a direction arrow that points down and to the left. In region II, the total population lies between 500 and 1000. Type b cannot withstand competition that type a can tolerate, producing a direction arrow that points down and to the right. In region III, the total population is less than both K_a and K_b. Both types can grow, generating a direction arrow pointing up and to the right.

The two phase-plane trajectories plotted in Figure 5.7.55a follow the arrows and are forced toward the equilibrium at (1000, 0) where type b has been driven extinct. This figure includes the direction arrows on the nullclines. On the a-nullcline, the population of b is decreasing because the total population is 1000, exceeding the tolerance of type b. The direction arrow therefore points straight down. On the b-nullcline, the population of a is increasing because the total population is 500, less than K_a for type a. The direction arrow points straight to the right. The solution starting in region III is plotted as a function of time in Figure 5.7.55b. Even though type b is doomed to extinction, it has an initial period of growth. The solution for b reaches a maximum when the trajectory crosses the b-nullcline.

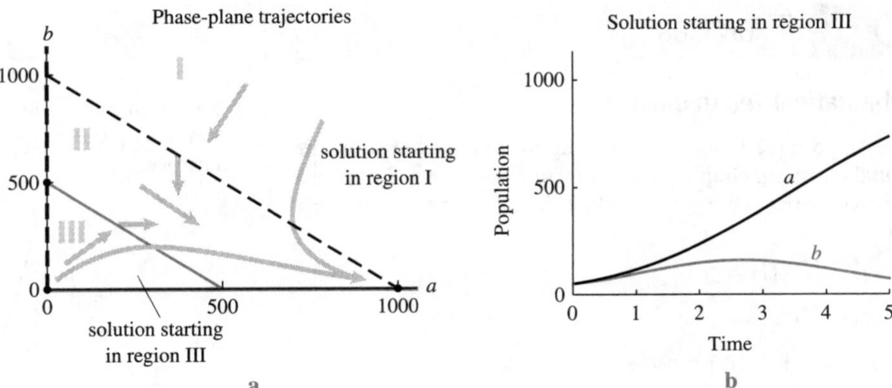

FIGURE 5.7.55
Solutions of the competition system

This model differs in several ways from the differential equations

$$\frac{da}{dt} = \mu a$$

$$\frac{db}{dt} = \lambda b$$

(which we reduced to a single equation for the fraction p of type a in Section 5.1). When $\lambda < \mu$, type b grows more slowly and goes extinct. In the competition model, the type better able to withstand competition (the one with the larger value of K) eventually wins out, even if its growth rate is lower.

Direction Arrows: Newton's Law of Cooling

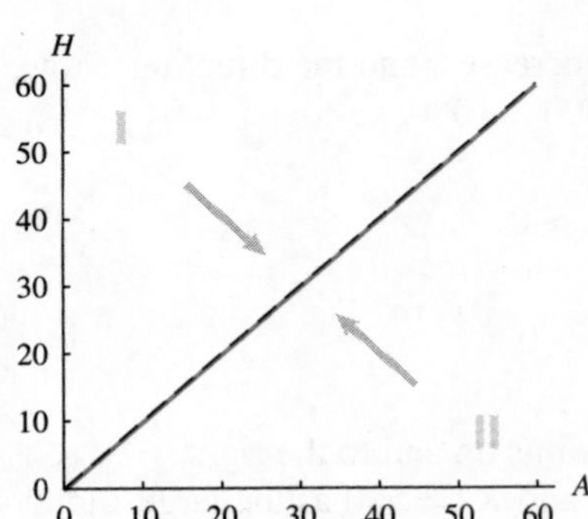

FIGURE 5.7.56

Direction arrows for Newton's law of cooling

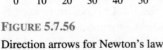

The direction arrows are simpler for Newton's law of cooling. The nullclines coincide and break the plane into only two regions (Figure 5.7.56). In region I, $H > A$. Therefore,

$$\frac{dH}{dt} = \alpha(A - H) < 0$$

$$\frac{dA}{dt} = \alpha_2(H - A) > 0$$

meaning that H decreases and A increases. The direction arrow points down and to the right. In region II, $H < A$. Therefore,

$$\frac{dH}{dt} = \alpha(A - H) > 0$$

$$\frac{dA}{dt} = \alpha_2(H - A) < 0$$

meaning that H increases and A decreases. The direction arrow points up and to the left. Solutions are pushed toward the line of equilibria. Physically, this means that the object and the room will tend to approach the same temperature.

Summary We have seen how to plot solutions of two-dimensional differential equations as functions of time and as **phase-plane trajectories.** The nullclines break the phase plane into regions, in each of which we can find a **direction arrow** indicating whether the state variables are increasing or decreasing. For additional information on the behavior of the phase-plane trajectories, we can draw vertical or horizontal direction arrows on the nullclines. Phase-plane trajectories follow the direction arrows.

5.7 Exercises

Mathematical Techniques

1–4 ▪ Suppose the following functions are solutions of some differential equation. Graph these as functions of time and as phase-plane trajectories for $0 \le t \le 2$. Mark the position at $t = 0$, $t = 1$, and $t = 2$.

1. $x(t) = t$, $y(t) = 3t$
2. $a(t) = 2e^{-t}$, $b(t) = e^{-2t}$
3. $f(t) = 1 + t$, $g(t) = e^{-t}$
4. $x(t) = 1 + t(t - 2)$, $y(t) = t(3 - t)$

5–6 ▪ From the following graphs of solutions of differential equations as functions of time, graph the matching phase-plane trajectory.

5.

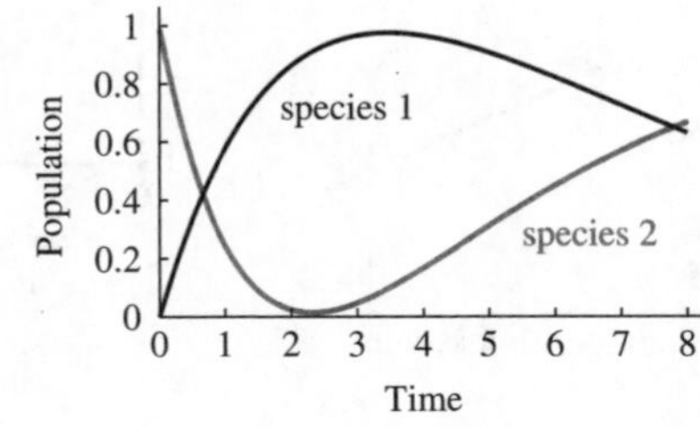

6.

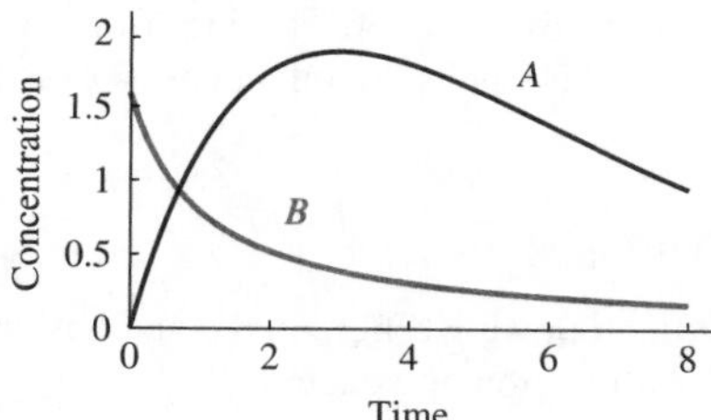

7–8 ▪ From the following graphs of phase-plane trajectories, graph the matching solutions of differential equations as functions of time.

7.

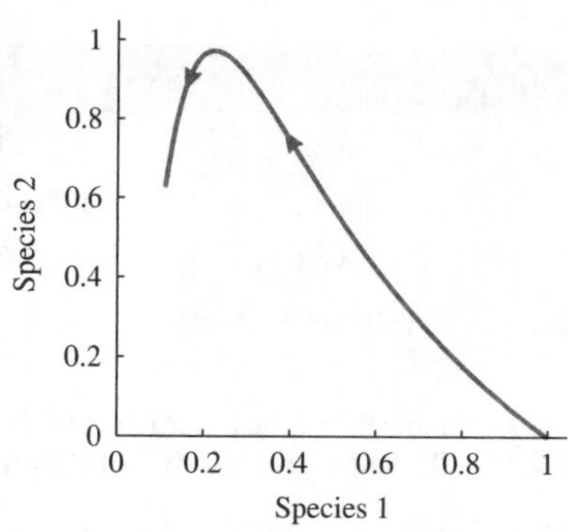

8.

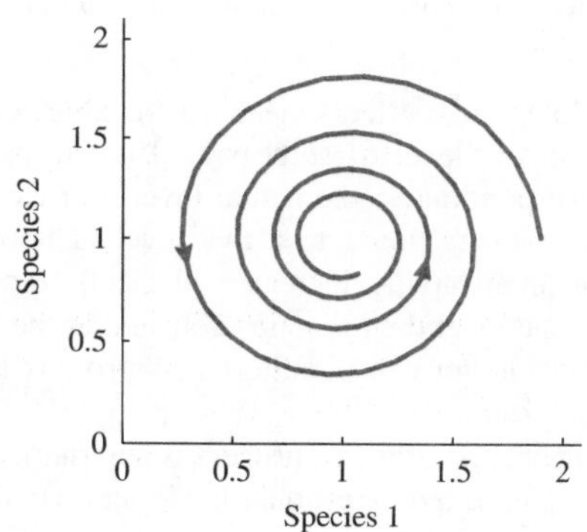

9–10 ▪ On the following phase-plane diagrams, use the direction arrows to sketch phase-plane trajectories starting from two different initial conditions.

9.

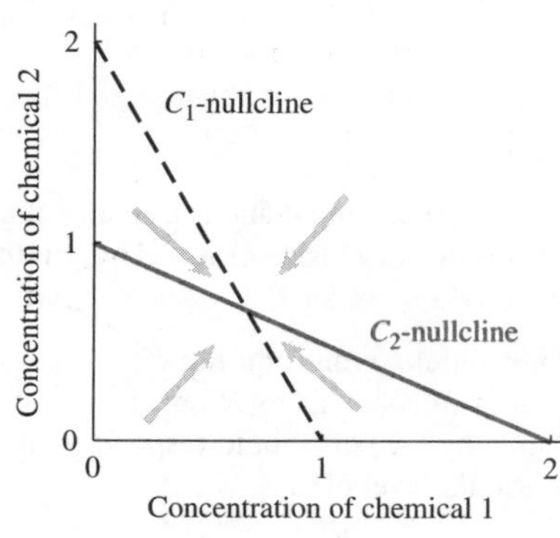

10.

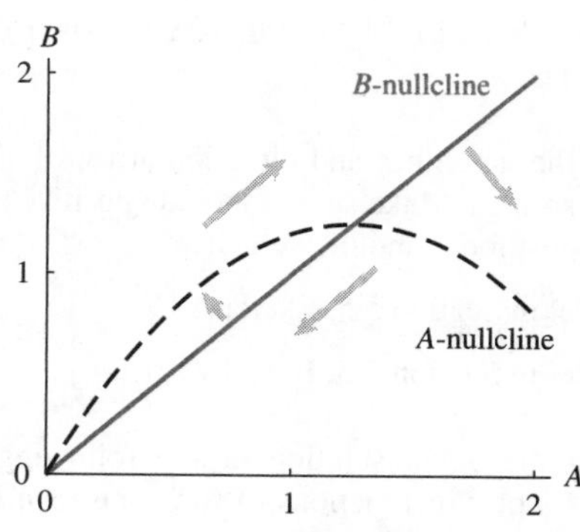

11–12 ▪ Use the information in the phase-plane diagram to draw direction arrows on the nullclines.

11. The diagram in Exercise 9

12. The diagram in Exercise 10

13–14 ▪ Compare solutions estimated with Euler's method with the phase-plane diagram and direction arrows found in the text for the competition equations (Figure 5.7.54)

$$\frac{da}{dt} = \mu\left(1 - \frac{a+b}{K_a}\right)a$$
$$\frac{db}{dt} = \lambda\left(1 - \frac{a+b}{K_b}\right)b$$

starting from the given initial conditions. Assume that $\mu = 2.0$, $\lambda = 2.0$, $K_a = 1000$, and $K_b = 500$.

13. Use $a(0) = 750$ and $b(0) = 500$. Take two steps, with a step length of $\Delta t = 0.1$, as in Section 5.5, Exercise 7.

14. Use $a(0) = 250$ and $b(0) = 500$. Take two steps, with a step length of $\Delta t = 0.1$, as in Section 5.5, Exercise 8.

15–18 ▪ Compare solutions estimated with Euler's method with the phase-plane diagram and direction arrows found in the text for Newton's law of cooling (Figure 5.7.56)

$$\frac{dH}{dt} = \alpha(A - H)$$
$$\frac{dA}{dt} = \alpha_2(H - A)$$

with the given parameter values and starting from the given initial conditions.

15. Suppose $\alpha = 0.3$ and $\alpha_2 = 0.1$. Use $H(0) = 60$ and $A(0) = 20$. Take two steps, with a step length of $\Delta t = 0.1$, as in Section 5.5, Exercise 11.

16. Suppose $\alpha = 0.3$ and $\alpha_2 = 0.1$. Use $H(0) = 0$ and $A(0) = 20$. Take two steps, with a step length of $\Delta t = 0.1$, as in Section 5.5, Exercise 12.

17. Suppose $\alpha = 3.0$ and $\alpha_2 = 1.0$. Use $H(0) = 60$ and $A(0) = 20$. Take two steps, with a step length of $\Delta t = 0.25$, as in Section 5.5, Exercise 13. Does this diagram help explain what went wrong?

18. Suppose $\alpha = 3.0$ and $\alpha_2 = 1.0$. Use $H(0) = 0$ and $A(0) = 20$. Take two steps, with a step length of $\Delta t = 0.5$, as in

Section 5.5, Exercise 14. Does this diagram help explain what went wrong?

19–20 ▪ Draw the nullclines and direction arrows for the following models of springs. Make sure to include positive and negative values for the position x and the velocity v.

19. The model in Section 5.5, Exercise 15.

20. The model in Section 5.5, Exercise 16.

21–22 ▪ Sketch the given solution of the following models of springs first as a pair of functions of time and then in the phase plane. Check that the solution follows the arrows.

21. The solution $x(t) = \cos(t)$ (Section 5.5, Exercise 17) of the spring equation in Exercise 19.

22. The solution $x(t) = e^{-t}\cos(t)$ (Section 5.5, Exercise 18) of the spring equation with friction in Exercise 20.

Applications

23–36 ▪ For the following problems, add direction arrows to the phase plane.

23. The model in Section 5.5, Exercise 21.

24. The model in Section 5.5, Exercise 22.

25. The model in Section 5.5, Exercise 25.

26. The model in Section 5.5, Exercise 26.

27. The model in Section 5.5, Exercise 27.

28. The model in Section 5.5, Exercise 28.

29. The model in Section 5.6, Exercise 33.

30. The model in Section 5.6, Exercise 34.

31. The model in Section 5.6, Exercise 35.

32. The model in Section 5.6, Exercise 36.

33. The model in Section 5.6, Exercise 37.

34. The model in Section 5.6, Exercise 38.

35. The model in Section 5.6, Exercise 39.

36. The model in Section 5.6, Exercise 40.

37–44 ▪ For the following problems, use the direction arrows on your phase plane to sketch a solution starting from the given initial condition.

37. The model in Exercise 25 starting from (1500, 200). Is there another path for the solution that is consistent with the direction arrows?

38. The model in Exercise 26 starting from (1500, 200).

39. The model in Exercise 27 starting from (200, 300).

40. The model in Exercise 28 starting from (200, 300).

41. The model in Exercise 31 starting from (0.5, 1).

42. The model in Exercise 32 starting from (0.5, 1).

43. The model in Exercise 35 starting from (0.5, 1).

44. The model in Exercise 36 starting from (0.5, 0.5). Can you be sure that the solution behaves exactly like your picture?

Computer Exercises

45. Consider the following differential equations describing diffusion and utilization of a chemical.

$$\frac{dC}{dt} = \alpha(\Gamma - C) - \frac{\delta C}{1 + C}$$

$$\frac{d\Gamma}{dt} = \frac{\alpha}{K}(C - \Gamma) + S$$

The parameters have the following meanings.

Name	Meaning	Values to Use
α	Diffusion rate	1.0
δ	Use efficiency	4.0 and 1.0
K	Ratio of volumes	2.0
S	Supplementation rate	1.0

a. Set $\delta = 4$ and the rest of the parameters to their designated values. Plot the nullclines and find the equilibrium.

b. Follow the same steps with $\delta = 1$. Is there an equilibrium? Can you say why not? (No math jargon allowed.) Sketch C and Γ as functions of time.

c. Try to figure out the critical value of δ where the behavior changes.

46. Many biological systems need to be able to respond to changes in the level of some signal (such as a hormone) without responding to the actual level. For example, a cell might have no response to a low level of hormone. If the hormone level rapidly increases, the cell responds. But if the hormone level then remains constant at the higher level, the cell again stops responding. This process is sometimes called *adaptation*.

One mechanism for this process is summarized in the following model. Internal response is a function of the fraction p of cell surface receptors that are bound by the hormone. This fraction increases when the hormone level, H, is high. However, hormone also dissociates from bound receptors. Assume this happens at a rate A but that this rate is controlled by the cell. One possible set of equations is

$$\frac{dp}{dt} = k_1 H(1 - p) - Ap$$

$$\frac{dA}{dt} = \epsilon(H - A)$$

Suppose that $k_1 = 0.5$ and that ϵ is a small value (such as 0.1 or 0.01). The value of H is determined by conditions external to the cell and does not have its own differential equation.

a. Find the nullclines and equilibria of this model assuming that H is a constant. Does H appear in your final results? Explain why the cell should respond in the same way to any constant level of H.

b. Use your computer to simulate the response when the level of H jumps quickly from $H = 1$ to $H = 10$. One way to do this is to solve the equations with $H = 10$, using as initial conditions the equilibrium values of p and A when $H = 1$. Draw graphs of p and A in the phase plane and as functions of time. Explain what is happening.

c. Do part **b** assuming that the level of H drops rapidly from $H = 10$ to $H = 1$.

5.8 The Dynamics of a Neuron

In Section 1.11, we studied a discrete-time dynamical system describing the heart, an important excitable system that responds to a periodic stimulus. To follow more precisely the response to a single stimulus, or to figure out mechanisms for *creating* a periodic stimulus, we need to use differential equations. In this section, we present a simplified (but venerable and valuable) model of a neuron.

A Mathematician's View of a Neuron

Some basic properties of a neuron are illustrated in Figure 5.8.57. The key measurements are of the concentrations of two ions, sodium and potassium. Like most cells, a resting neuron maintains an excess of potassium and a deficit of sodium. A neuron maintains a negative **resting potential,** meaning that there is an overall excess of negative charge inside the cell. Sodium and potassium ions are both positively charged. Because sodium concentrations are much higher than potassium concentrations, the deficit of these positive charges inside the cell contributes most of the negative charge of the cell. Cells use a significant amount of energy to run pumps to maintain this distribution of ions.

The neuron uses these gradients of sodium, potassium, and charge across the cell membrane to amplify and transmit information. The process depends on a set of **voltage-gated channels** for each ion. Such channels open and close in response to voltage (another name for potential) differences and are closed when the cell is at rest.

When a burst of positive charges enters the cell (and makes the potential of the cell less negative), voltage-gated sodium channels open (Figure 5.8.58). Because there is an excess of sodium outside the cell, more sodium ions enter, further increasing the potential of the cell until it actually becomes positive.

Two things then occur. One slower mechanism acts to block the voltage-gated sodium channels, and another slow mechanism begins to open voltage-gated potassium channels. Both of these processes act to diminish the build-up of positive charge in the cell. Blocking the sodium channels halts the entry of sodium, and opening potassium channels allows the exit of positively charged potassium. Neither process happens as fast as the opening of the sodium channels, and neither can halt the increase in potential immediately, just as a weak backward force applied to a heavy moving object only gradually slows it down and reverses its direction. When the potential of the cell has

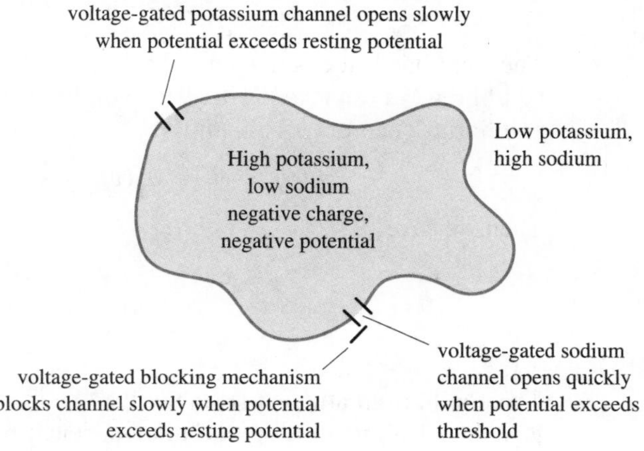

FIGURE 5.8.57
The basic elements of neural dynamics

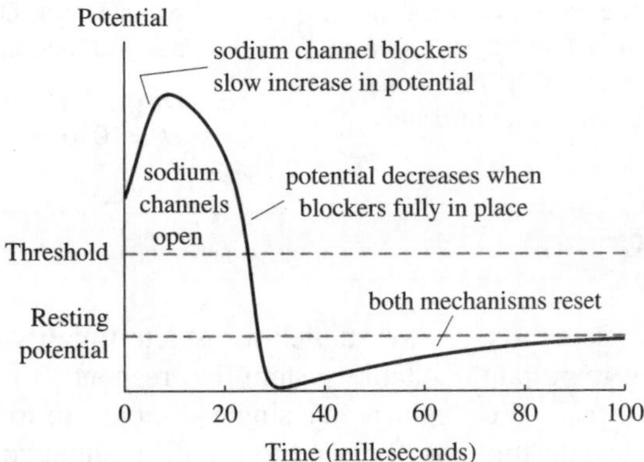

FIGURE 5.8.58
An action potential

again decreased to the resting potential or below, these mechanisms slowly turn off. Soon the cell is ready to begin the cycle again.

How does a neuron use this ability? This sharp peak of electrical excitation, called an **action potential,** can be transmitted precisely to other neurons. Action potentials are part of the language of the brain, like the 0s and 1s used by computers.

Our model is designed to study the structure of the interaction of two processes: a fast process with **positive feedback** (a slight increase in cell potential quickly induces sodium channels to open and increase the potential further) and a slow process with **negative feedback** (the increase in cell potential induces two mechanisms that halt the increase). Because this structure requires only the two mechanisms acting on sodium channels (fast opening and slow blocking), we concentrate on these. Cells without functioning potassium channels produce action potentials that are less sharp.

The Mathematics of Sodium Channels

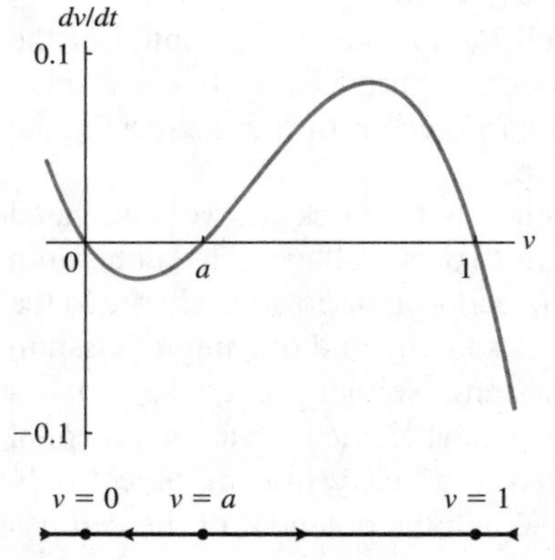

FIGURE 5.8.59
The phase-line diagram without the slow mechanism for blocking sodium channels

The potential in a cell can be scaled to more convenient mathematical values. Denoting the scaled potential by v, we set

$$\begin{cases} v = 0 & \text{resting potential} \\ v = a & \text{the threshold above which the neuron fires} \\ v = 1 & \text{potential with sodium channels completely open} \end{cases} \tag{5.8.1}$$

Small deviations above resting potential are not amplified, and the potential returns to rest. However, if the cell potential is raised above the threshold a, the cell moves toward the higher potential found when the sodium channels are open. A phase-line diagram for cell potential following this description is shown in Figure 5.8.59.

One convenient equation consistent with this diagram is

$$\frac{dv}{dt} = -v(v-a)(v-1) = f(v) \tag{5.8.2}$$

The right-hand side is in factored form, and the values $v = 0$, $v = a$, and $v = 1$ are all equilibria. We can take the derivative of the rate of change to check the stability of the equilibria (Theorem 5.1), finding

$$f'(v) = -(v-a)(v-1) - v(v-1) - v(v-a)$$

Then we have

$$f'(0) = -a < 0$$
$$f'(a) = a(1-a) > 0$$
$$f'(1) = -(1-a) < 0$$

The equilibrium at $v = 0$ is stable, the one at $v = a$ is unstable, and the one at $v = 1$ is stable. The graph of f and the associated phase-line diagram are consistent with

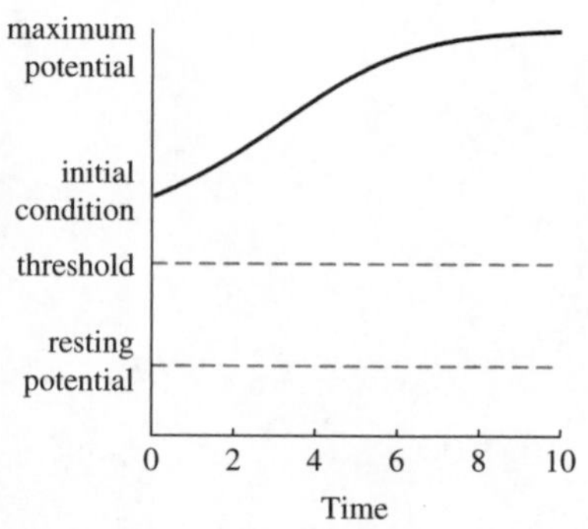

FIGURE 5.8.60

Solution without the slow mechanism for blocking sodium channels

our biological assumptions (Figure 5.8.59). This cubic (Equation 5.8.2) is the simplest equation describing the basic rules of sodium dynamics, and we use it to illustrate the behavior of the system.

Suppose a cell at resting potential receives an influx of positive charges from another neuron that raises its potential slightly above the threshold a. The solution moves upward, amplifying the signal, the first task of a functioning neuron. However, this neuron gets stuck at the higher equilibrium $v = 1$ (Figure 5.8.60). The neuron cannot be restimulated.

The Mathematics of Sodium Channel Blocking

Without the slow mechanism for blocking sodium channels, a neuron could respond only to a single stimulus. How does blocking the sodium channels help the neuron function?

Let w represent the strength of the blocking mechanism. At $v = 0$, this mechanism is turned off, so $w = 0$. As v gets closer to 1, the mechanism becomes stronger and stronger, so w takes on larger and larger values. A simple equation that *seems* to model this behavior is

$$\frac{dw}{dt} = \epsilon v$$

for positive ϵ. However, if v remains positive (above resting potential) for a long time, w might approach infinity. There must be an upper bound on the strength of the blocking mechanism.

To incorporate the requirement that the blocking mechanism have a maximum possible strength, we use an equation resembling Newton's law of cooling,

$$\frac{dw}{dt} = \epsilon(v - \gamma w) \tag{5.8.3}$$

For every fixed value of v, this equation has an equilibrium at

$$w = \frac{v}{\gamma}$$

If $v = 0$, w approaches 0 and the mechanism does not operate. If, however, $v = 1$, w increases to an equilibrium value of $\frac{1}{\gamma}$. This represents the maximum possible strength of the blocking mechanism. A smaller γ produces a larger equilibrium value. If $\gamma = 1.0$ and $v = 1$, the equilibrium is $w = 1.0$. If $\gamma = 10.0$ and $v = 1$, the equilibrium is $w = 0.1$ (Figure 5.8.61).

The parameter ϵ does not affect the equilibrium level. It instead changes the rate at which the equilibrium is approached. A small value of ϵ produces a small rate of change and a slow response of w. Because the blocking mechanism is slow, ϵ has a fairly small value.

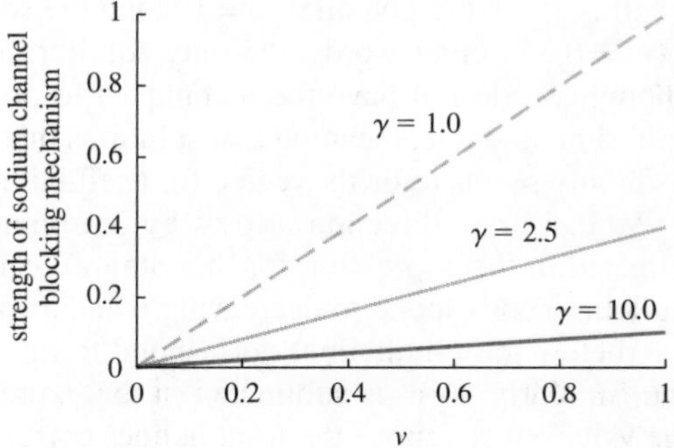

FIGURE 5.8.61

Equilibrium strength of blocking mechanism for fixed voltage

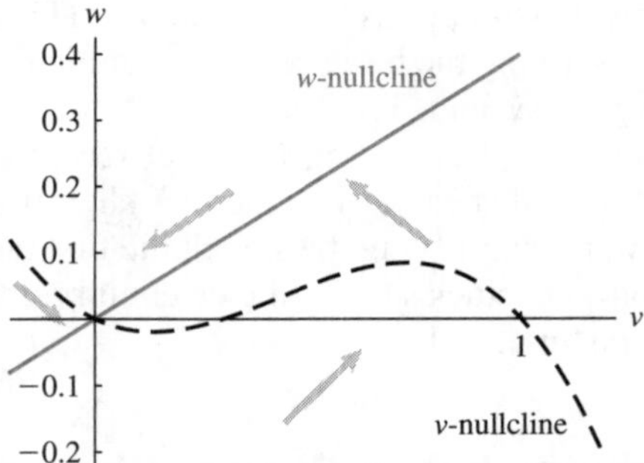

FIGURE 5.8.62
The nullclines and direction arrows for the Fitzhugh-Nagumo equations

The Fitzhugh-Nagumo Equations

How does the blocking mechanism modify the rate of change of the potential v? In other words, how do we couple the dynamics of v to the value of w? When w is large, the sodium channels have been blocked, stopping the entry of more sodium ions. The cell then tends to return to its resting potential. For convenience, we assume that the rate at which the potential decreases toward the resting potential is proportional to w. This gives the coupled system of equations

$$\frac{dv}{dt} = -v(v-a)(v-1) - w \tag{5.8.4}$$

$$\frac{dw}{dt} = \epsilon(v - \gamma w) \tag{5.8.5}$$

These are called the **Fitzhugh-Nagumo** equations. Can they reproduce the firing behavior of the neuron?

Figure 5.8.62 shows the nullclines and direction arrows for the Fitzhugh-Nagumo equation with $\gamma = 2.5$ and $a = 0.3$, where we have chosen w as the vertical variable. The v-nullcline can be found by solving

$$\frac{dv}{dt} = -v(v-a)(v-1) - w = 0$$

for w, with solution

$$w = -v(v-a)(v-1)$$

The w-nullcline is found by solving

$$\frac{dw}{dt} = \epsilon(v - \gamma w) = 0$$

for w, with solution

$$w = \frac{v}{\gamma}$$

In the case shown, the nullclines intersect only at the point $(0, 0)$. At this equilibrium, the cell is at resting potential ($v = 0$), and the sodium channel blocking mechanism is off ($w = 0$). In other words, the only equilibrium describes a cell completely at rest. Although we do not have the techniques to prove it (linear algebra is needed), this equilibrium is stable, meaning that solutions that start nearby return to the equilibrium. This hardly seems to be the recipe for useful dynamics.

We can draw direction arrows by reasoning about the equations. Because w is subtracted in the expression for the rate of change of v, large values of w (above the v-nullcline) correspond to decreasing v and arrows that point to the left. Small values of w (below the v-nullcline) correspond to increasing v and arrows that point to the right. Similarly, $\epsilon\gamma w$ is subtracted in the expression for the rate of change of w, so large values of w (above the w-nullcline) correspond to decreasing w and arrows that

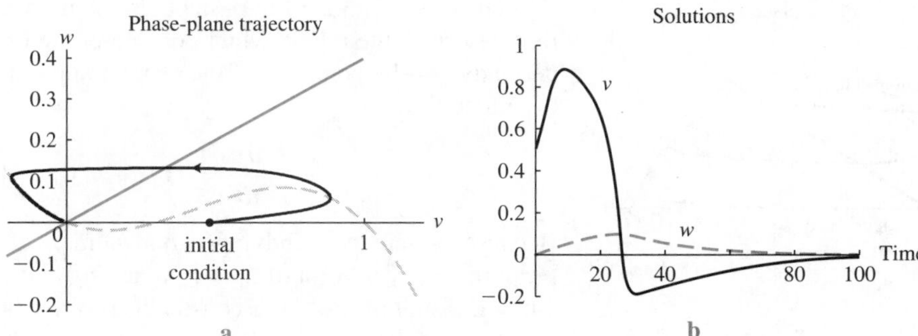

FIGURE 5.8.63

Results of perturbing above resting potential

point down. Small values of w (below the w-nullcline) correspond to increasing w and arrows that point up (Figure 5.8.62).

What happens when the potential of the cell is raised above the threshold a? Mathematically, this corresponds to initial conditions $(v_0, 0)$ with $v_0 > a$. With the equation for sodium channels opening alone (Equation 5.8.2), the potential moves up to the equilibrium at $v = 1$ and remains there, leaving the cell paralyzed and useless.

The results of this same experiment with the slow mechanism for blocking sodium channels are quite different. Initially, the potential of the cell increases (the phase-plane trajectory moves to the right) due to the rapid opening of the sodium channels (Figure 5.8.63). Slowly, however, the blocking mechanism kicks in (the trajectory moves toward larger values of w). When the trajectory crosses the v-nullcline, the potential begins to decrease (the trajectory moves to the left), and when it crosses the w-nullcline, the blocking mechanism begins to turn off (the trajectory heads down). The trajectory undershoots $v = 0$ before the sodium channel blocking mechanism returns to 0. This system has the basic properties of a neuron: the ability to amplify a signal quickly and return to a state of readiness for the next signal. In addition, the mathematical analysis predicts an unexpected (but real) phenomenon, the undershoot of the potential. This undershoot results from the slowness of the mechanism for blocking the sodium channels.

If the perturbation of the cell is insufficient to open the sodium channels ($v_0 < a$), the cell does not amplify the signal. In this way, the cell acts as a filter that can ignore small stimuli (Exercise 6).

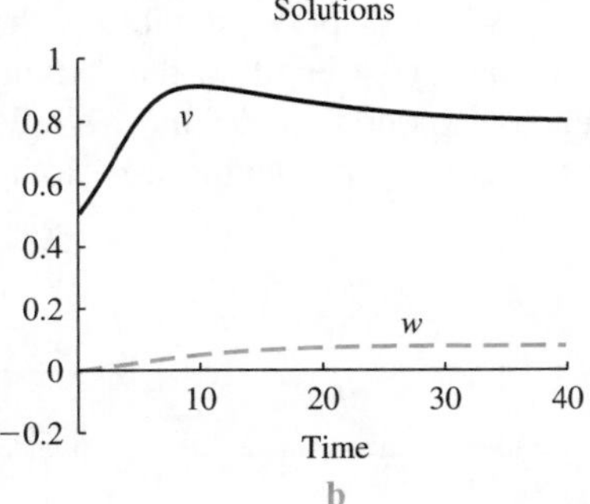

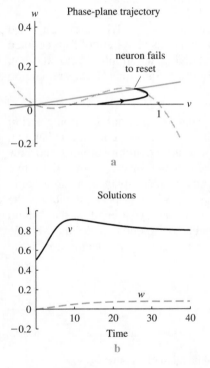

FIGURE 5.8.64

Dynamics with weak sodium channel blocking response

Weak Channel Blocking Mechanism

The larger the value of γ, the smaller the response of the sodium channel blocking mechanism. A cell without this mechanism (Equation 5.8.2) could respond only to a single stimulus. What happens if this mechanism is weak?

When the value of γ is large, the w-nullcline swings down to intersect the v-nullclines in three places (Figure 5.8.64). Although we cannot prove it without linear algebra, the central equilibrium is unstable and the outer two are stable. If we stimulate the cell by raising the potential of the cell above the threshold a, the potential rises further as the sodium channels open. However, the blocking mechanism cannot overcome the opening, and the trajectory is trapped at the upper equilibrium (Figure 5.8.64).

Once the w-nullcline lowers enough to cross the v-nullcline, the neuron stops firing. Further increases in γ change where the potential gets stuck but not the *qualitative* behavior of the cell. In effect, a cell with a weak blocking mechanism acts like a cell with no blocking mechanism at all.

The Effects of Constant Applied Current

We have imagined a resting cell receiving a single pulse of positively charged ions. One interesting experiment alters this situation by giving the cell a constant input of positive ions. Can the cell convert a constant input into a usable output?

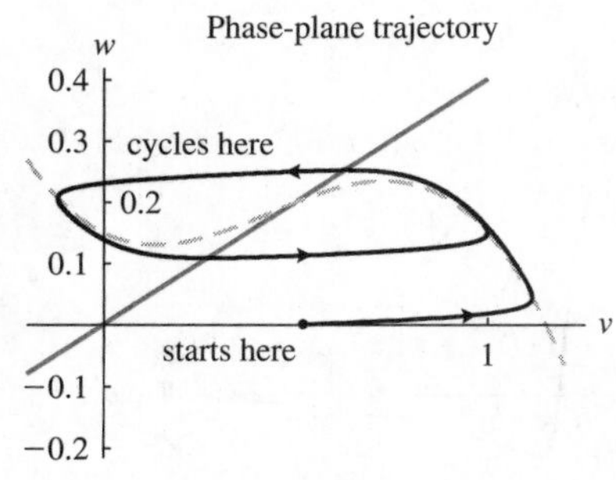

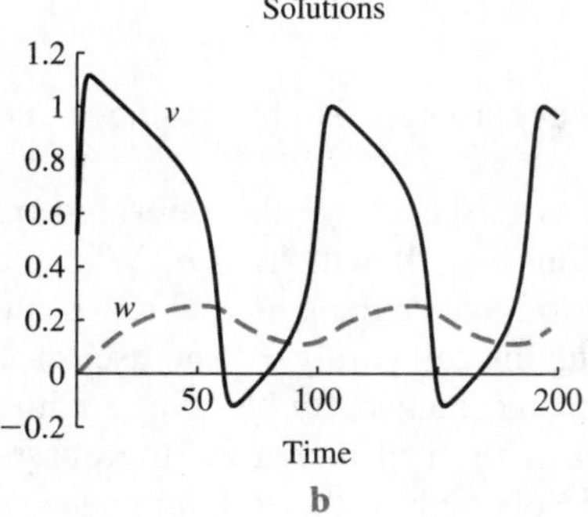

FIGURE 5.8.65
Dynamics with a constant applied current

The modification of the Fitzhugh-Nagumo equations is not complicated. The current describes the rate at which ions enter the cell and is therefore proportional to the derivative of the potential. If the current applied is I_a, we add I_a to the rate of change of potential, finding

$$\frac{dv}{dt} = -v(v-a)(v-1) - w + I_a \tag{5.8.6}$$

Because we are not studying actual numerical values, we have set the constant of proportionality in front of I_a to 1, assuming that 1 unit of current raises the potential by 1 unit in 1 unit of time. The constant is positive because current increases the potential.

The v-nullcline is

$$w = -v(v-a)(v-1) + I_a$$

and the w-nullcline is unchanged (Figure 5.8.65a). As in the original case (Figure 5.8.62), the nullclines intersect at only a single point. In this case, however, the equilibrium is unstable (we would again need linear algebra to prove it). A phase-plane trajectory and the corresponding values of v and w as functions of time are shown in Figure 5.8.65.

The neuron shows a periodic "bursting" behavior. Real neurons also produce periodic spikes when subjected to a constant current. This periodic output translates a current, an analogue input, into periodic bursts, a digital output, and can be used by the body as a pacemaker for a periodic process.

A cautionary note is in order. The equations we have been studying are a simplified version of the *four-dimensional* Hodgkin-Huxley equations (a system of four coupled autonomous differential equations). The value of studying this simplified model lies in its ability to mimic qualitatively more complicated and accurate models while remaining easy to understand with phase-plane techniques.

Summary We used some basic facts about sodium channels to derive equations describing **action potentials,** the firing of neurons. In particular, we have seen how one mechanism that opens **voltage-gated sodium channels** can amplify an incoming stimulus and how a slower voltage-gated mechanism can block those channels. We combined these two processes into the **Fitzhugh-Nagumo equations** and used phase-plane analysis to study these equations in several circumstances. The basic equations display excitability, the ability to temporarily amplify a signal and reset. Reducing the strength of the sodium channel blocking mechanism can make the cell unable to respond to more than a single stimulus. An excitable cell responds to a constant stimulus by producing a periodic sequence of action potentials.

5.8 Exercises

1. Give an equation like Equation 5.8.2 describing a system with two thresholds. The system has a stable equilibrium at a resting potential at 0, but it will be pushed to a higher positive equilibrium if the potential is raised above a particular positive threshold, and to a negative equilibrium if the potential is dropped below a particular negative threshold. Draw a phase-line diagram and check that your equations match it.

2. Draw phase-line diagrams for Equation 5.8.2 in the following cases.

   a. $a = 0.01$. How might this neuron malfunction?

   b. $a = 0.5$

   c. $a = 0.99$. Why might this neuron work poorly?

3. Use the method of separation of variables to solve

$$\frac{dw}{dt} = \epsilon(v - \gamma w)$$

(Equation 5.8.3) assuming that v is constant. Show how the dynamics are slowed when ϵ is small but that ϵ does not affect the equilibrium.

4. Assuming that w is constant (perhaps the sodium channel blocking mechanism is jammed in a particular state) and $a = 0.3$, figure out the dynamics of

$$\frac{dv}{dt} = -v(v-a)(v-1) - w$$

(Equation 5.8.4) thought of as a one-dimensional differential equation. Try it with $w = 0.01$, $w = 0.05$, and $w = 0.1$.

5. Draw direction arrows on the nullclines for the Fitzhugh-Nagumo equations.

6. Sketch the phase-plane trajectory and solutions of the Fitzhugh-Nagumo equations when the initial stimulus is less than the threshold.

7. Sketch the phase-plane diagram and solution for the Fitzhugh-Nagumo equations for the following values of ϵ. (Think of changing ϵ as changing the direction arrows: the arrows are nearly horizontal when ϵ is small because w, the vertical variable, changes slowly.)
   a. ϵ very small
   b. ϵ rather large

8. With positive applied current there could be three intersections of the nullclines (as in Figure 5.8.64). Draw a phase-plane diagram illustrating this scenario, and take a guess at the dynamics. Try to make sense of the results biologically.

9. There could also be a single intersection with positive applied current, but on the rightmost decreasing part of the v-nullcline. Draw such a phase plane. Assuming that this equilibrium is stable, sketch the dynamics. Why might this cell also be thought of as excitable?

10. What happens to the phase plane and the cell if the applied current is negative? Can the cell lose its ability to respond if the applied current is negative and large?

11. Suppose that a higher applied current I_a in Equation 5.8.6 produces faster bursting. How might the body use this ability to translate signal strength into response speed?

Computer Exercises

12. Use a computer to study a cell that is forced by an external current I_a that oscillates. Try different periods and amplitudes of the oscillation. What happens? Do you see any strange behaviors?

13. The behaviors observed in the previous problem can occur when an object that naturally oscillates at one frequency is **forced** at a different frequency. For example, a spring following the equation

$$\frac{d^2x}{dt^2} = -x$$

naturally oscillates with period 2π. Forcing can be added with the modified equation

$$\frac{d^2x}{dt^2} = -x + A\cos\left(\frac{2\pi t}{T}\right)$$

Study this equation with the following values of T, trying a range of values of A from 0.1 to 10.0.
   a. $T = 2\pi$
   b. $T = \frac{\pi}{2}$
   c. $T = 4\pi$
   d. $T = 3.0$
   e. $T = 4.0$
   f. $T = 3.14$

Supplementary Problems

1. Consider the differential equation

$$\frac{dC}{dt} = 3(\Gamma - C) + 1$$

where C is the concentration of some chemical in a cell, measured in moles per liter, and Γ is a constant.
   a. What kind of differential equation is this? Explain the terms in the equation.
   b. Draw the phase-line diagram.
   c. Verify the stability of the equilibrium by using the derivative.
   d. Sketch solutions as functions of time starting from two initial conditions: $C(0) = 0$ and $C(0) = \Gamma + 1$.

2. Consider the differential equation

$$\frac{dC}{dt} = 3(\Gamma - C) + 1$$

where Γ is a constant.
   a. Solve the equation when $C(0) = 0$.
   b. Check your answer.
   c. Find $C(0.4)$.
   d. After what time will the solution be within 5% of its limit?

3. Consider the system of equations

$$\frac{d\Gamma}{dt} = (C - \Gamma) - \frac{\Gamma^2}{3}$$

$$\frac{dC}{dt} = 3(\Gamma - C) + 1$$

where C is the internal concentration of a chemical and Γ is the external concentration.
   a. Describe in words the two processes affecting concentration in the external environment. How big is the external environment relative to the cell?
   b. Draw a phase plane replete with nullclines, equilibria, and direction arrows. *Hint:* It is easier to put C on the vertical axis.

4. Give conditions wherein you might observe population growth described by the following.
   a. One-dimensional autonomous differential equation.
   b. One-dimensional nonautonomous differential equation.
   c. One-dimensional pure-time differential equation.
   d. Two-dimensional autonomous differential equation.

5. Consider the differential equation

$$\frac{dV}{dt} = 12 - t^2$$

where $V(t)$ is volume in liters at time t, and t is measured in seconds.
   a. What kind of differential equation is this?
   b. Graph the rate of change and use it to sketch a graph of the solution.
   c. At what time does V take on its maximum?
   d. Suppose $V(0) = 0$. Use Euler's method to estimate $V(0.1)$.
   e. Suppose $V(0) = 0$. Find the time T when $V(t)$ is 0 again.
   f. What is the average volume between 0 and T?

6. Consider the differential equation

$$\frac{dx}{dt} = 3x(x-1)^2$$

   a. Draw the phase-line diagram of this equation.
   b. Find the stability of the equilibria using the derivative.
   c. Sketch trajectories of x as a function of time for initial conditions $x(0) = -0.5$, $x(0) = 0.5$, and $x(0) = 1.5$.

7. Suppose the per capita production rate of a bacterial population is given by

$$\text{per capita production rate} = \frac{1}{\sqrt{b}}$$

where $b(t)$ is the population size at time t, and t is measured in hours.
   a. Find the differential equation describing this population.
   b. Solve the equation and check your answer.
   c. What is the population after 2 h if the population starts at $b(0) = 10000$?
   d. Does this population grow faster or slower than one growing exponentially? Why?

8. Differential equations to describe an epidemic are sometimes given as

$$\frac{dS}{dt} = \beta(S+I) - cSI$$

$$\frac{dI}{dt} = cSI - \delta I$$

where S measures the number of susceptible people and I the number of infected people.
   a. Compare these equations with the predator-prey equations. What is different in these equations? What biological process does each term on the right-hand side describe?
   b. Sketch the nullclines and find the equilibria if $\beta = 1$ and $c = \delta = 2$. (Draw only the parts where S and I are positive.)
   c. Sketch direction arrows on your phase-plane diagram.

9. Consider the following differential equation, which describes the concentration of sodium ions in a cell following consumption of a bag of Doritos at time $t = 0$ s.

$$\frac{dN}{dt} = 2 - 10t$$

Suppose $N(0) = 50$ mmol/cm^3.
   a. What kind of differential equation is this?
   b. Sketch a graph of the rate of change as a function of time.
   c. Sketch a graph of the concentration as a function of time.
   d. Use Euler's method to estimate $N(0.1)$.
   e. Find $N(1)$ exactly.
   f. At what times is $N(t) = 50$?

10. Consider the following differential equation, which describes the concentration of sodium ions in a cell.

$$\frac{dN}{dt} = 2(N-50) - (N-50)^2$$

Assume this equation works only for $45 \le N \le 55$.
   a. What kind of differential equation is this? What does each term mean?
   b. Sketch a graph of the rate of change as a function of concentration.
   c. Draw the phase-line diagram.
   d. Sketch solutions starting from $N(0) = 48$, $N(0) = 51$, and $N(0) = 54$.
   e. Suppose $N(0) = 51$. Estimate $N(0.1)$.
   f. What method would you use to solve this equation?

11. Two types of bacteria with populations a and b are living in a culture. Suppose

$$\frac{da}{dt} = 2a\left(1 - \frac{a}{500} - \frac{b}{200}\right)$$

$$\frac{db}{dt} = 3b\left(1 + \frac{a}{1000} - \frac{b}{100}\right)$$

   a. What kind of differential equation is this? Explain the terms.
   b. Draw the phase plane, including nullclines, equilibria, and direction arrows.

12. Suppose the scaled potential v and level of sodium channel blocking w in a neuron are described by

$$\frac{dv}{dt} = v(1 - v) - w$$

$$\frac{dw}{dt} = v - 2w$$

a. Draw a phase line for v assuming that w is fixed at 0.

b. Draw the phase plane for the full system, including equilibria, nullclines, and direction arrows.

13. The density of sugar in a hummingbird's 20-mm tongue is

$$s(x) = \frac{1.2}{1.0 + 0.2x}$$

where x is measured in millimeters from the end of the tongue and s is measured in moles per meter.

a. Find the total amount of sugar in the hummingbird's tongue.

b. Find the average density of sugar in the tongue.

c. Compare the average with the minimum and maximum density. Does your answer make sense?

14. The length L of a microtubule is found to follow the differential equation

$$\frac{dL}{dt} = -L(2 - L)(1 - L)$$

where L is measured in microns and t is measured in seconds.

a. Draw the phase-line diagram.

b. Check the stability of the equilibria using the derivative.

c. Sketch trajectories starting from $L(0) = 0.5$, $L(0) = 1.5$, and $L(0) = 2.5$.

15. A lab finds that

$$\frac{dL}{dt} = -2.0L + 5.4LE$$

$$\frac{dE}{dt} = 3.5 - LE$$

where E is the level of some component of the microtubules and L is the length of the microtubule.

a. Explain the terms in these equations.

b. Draw the phase-plane diagram, including nullclines, equilibria, and direction arrows.

16. Consider the differential equation describing a population of mathematically sophisticated bacteria,

$$\frac{db}{dt} = b \ln\left(\frac{2b + 1}{2 + b}\right)$$

a. What kind of differential equation is this?

b. Draw the derivative as a function of the state variable, and draw the phase-line diagram.

c. Sketch trajectories starting from $b(0) = 0.8$ and $b(0) = 1.2$.

d. Check the stability of the equilibrium at $b = 0$ by taking the derivative of the rate of change.

e. Use Euler's method to estimate $b(0.01)$ if $b(0) = 0.5$.

Projects

1. Computer Exercise 46 in Section 5.7 presents one possible model of adaptation. This project studies a simpler, alternative model (proposed by H. G. Othmer). Because this model is so simple, we can compare the results of phase-plane analysis with actual solutions of the equations.

Consider the equations

$$\frac{dp}{dt} = k(H - A - p)$$

$$\frac{dA}{dt} = \epsilon(H - A)$$

where p represents the response of the cell and H the external condition driving the response. The variable A describes some internal state of the cell. First, suppose that H is constant.

a. Find the nullclines and equilibria and draw the phase plane, including direction arrows.

b. The equation for A is the same as Newton's law of cooling. Write down the solution for A with an arbitrary initial condition.

c. Substitute this solution into the equation for p. There is a clever way to solve the resulting nonautonomous equation. Make up a new variable $q(t) = e^{kt} p(t)$. With a bit of manipulation, you can write a pure-time differential equation for q. Solve this equation and find the solution for $p(t)$.

d. Plot this solution as a phase-plane trajectory for several different initial conditions. Are the results consistent with the phase plane?

Using these results, we can study what happens when H changes. Suppose first that the cell is at equilibrium with $H = 1$ and then that H jumps up to 10. Set $k = 1$ and $\epsilon = 0.1$.

e. How long will it take before A has roughly reached its new equilibrium value?

f. What is the value of p at this time? How long will it take p to nearly reach its equilibrium value again?

g. Suppose now that $H = 1$ for a time T, jumps to $H = 10$ for a time T, jumps back to 1, and so forth. Experiment with different values of T. How large must T be before the cell produces a healthy response to each change? What happens when T is much smaller than this value? What might the cell do to be able to respond more quickly?

2. Consider an interaction between two mutually inhibiting proteins with concentrations x and y, given by the differential equations

$$\frac{dx}{dt} = f(y) - x$$

$$\frac{dy}{dt} = g(x) - y$$

Both $f(y)$ and $g(x)$ are decreasing functions.

a. Explain each of the terms in these equations.

b. Try to imagine a biological situation they might describe.

c. Sketch the nullclines (remember that both f and g are decreasing).

d. Show that equilibria occur where $f[g(x)] = x$. What discrete-time dynamical system shares the equilibria of the system of differential equations?

Next try the following steps for functions of three different forms:

$$\text{Case 1:} \quad f(y) = \frac{1}{1+\alpha y}, \quad g(x) = \frac{1}{1+\alpha x}$$

$$\text{Case 2:} \quad f(y) = e^{-\alpha y}, \quad g(x) = e^{-\alpha x}$$

$$\text{Case 3:} \quad f(y) = \frac{1}{1+\alpha y^2}, \quad g(x) = \frac{1}{1+\alpha x^2}$$

Experiment with different values of α.

e. Find the function $f[g(x)]$ and graph it on a cobwebbing diagram. Does the equilibrium look stable?

f. Draw the nullclines and direction arrows for the differential equation. Is the equilibrium stable?

g. Why does the stability you "found" in **e** match that in **f**?

h. Try to figure out whether it is possible to have three equilibria (it is possible in Cases 2 and 3).

Why might it be important for a biological system to have three equilibria? How could it operate as a switch?

J. L. Cherry and F. R. Adler 2000. How to Make a Biological Switch. *Journal of Theoretical Biology* 203: 117–133.

Index

Rules of Differentiation

Suppose $f(x)$ and $g(x)$ are differentiable functions and c is a constant.

Rule	Function	Derivative
Sum rule	$f(x)+g(x)$	$f'(x)+g'(x)$
Constant sum rule	$f(x)+c$	$f'(x)$
Power rule	x^n	nx^{n-1}
Product rule	$f(x)g(x)$	$f(x)g'(x)+g(x)f'(x)$
Constant product rule	$cf(x)$	$cf'(x)$
Quotient rule	$\frac{f(x)}{g(x)}$	$\frac{f'(x)g(x)-g'(x)f(x)}{(g(x))^2}$
Chain rule	$f(g(x))$	$f'(g(x))g'(x)$
Exponential	e^x	e^x
Natural logarithm	$\ln(x)$	$\frac{1}{x}$
Sine	$\sin(x)$	$\cos(x)$
Cosine	$\cos(x)$	$-\sin(x)$

Basic Indefinite Integrals

$$\int x^n dx = \frac{x^{n+1}}{n+1} + c \quad \text{if } n \neq -1$$

$$\int \sin(\alpha x)dx = -\frac{\cos(\alpha x)}{\alpha} + c \quad \text{if } \alpha \neq 0$$

$$\int \frac{1}{x} dx = \ln(|x|) + c$$

$$\int \cos(\alpha x)dx = \frac{\sin(\alpha x)}{\alpha} + c \quad \text{if } \alpha \neq 0$$

$$\int e^{\alpha x} dx = \frac{e^{\alpha x}}{\alpha} + c \quad \text{if } \alpha \neq 0$$

Definitions in Probability Theory

Conditional Probability: The probability of event A conditional on event B is $\Pr(A \mid B) = \Pr(A \cap B)/(\Pr(B))$ if $\Pr(B) \neq 0$.

Independence: Event A is **independent** of event B if $\Pr(A \mid B) = \Pr(A)$.

Expectation: The mean of a random variable is the sum of the values weighted by their probabilities.

Median: The value of a random variable that is exceeded by 50% of the measurements.

Mode: The most probable value of a random variable.

Variance: A measure of the spread of a random variable equal to the mean squared deviation from the mean.

Standard Deviation: The square root of the variance.

Theorems of Probability

Law of Total Probability: Suppose that $E_1, E_2, \ldots, E_n$ form a set of mutually exclusive and collectively exhaustive events. Then for any event A, $\Pr(A) = \sum_{i=1}^{n} \Pr(A \mid E_i)\Pr(E_i)$.

Bayes' Theorem: For any events A and B where $\Pr(A) \neq 0$,

$$\Pr(B \mid A) = \frac{\Pr(A \mid B)\Pr(B)}{\Pr(A)}.$$

Multiplication Rule for Independent Events: Suppose A and B are any two independent events. Then $\Pr(A \cap B) = \Pr(A)\Pr(B)$.

Expectation of the Sum of Random Variables: The expectation of the sum of random variables is equal to the sum of the expectations.

Variance of the Sum of Independent Random Variables: The variance of the sum of independent random variables is equal to the sum of the variances.

Central Limit Theorem: The sum of sufficiently many independent, identically distributed random variables with finite mean and variance has approximately a normal distribution.

Probability Distributions

Distribution	Type of Random Variable	When to Use	Formula	Expectation	Variance
Binomial	Discrete	Number of successes N in n trials each with probability p	$\Pr(N=k)=b(k:n,p) = \binom{n}{k}p^k(1-p)^{n-k}$	np	$np(1-p)$
Poisson	Discrete	Number of events N in time t at rate λ	$\Pr(N=k)=p(k;\lambda t)=\frac{e^{-\lambda t}(\lambda t)^k}{k!}$	λt	λt
Geometric	Discrete	Time T before a success in a series of trials each with probability q	$\Pr(T=t)=g_t=q(1-q)^{t-1}$	$\frac{1}{q}$	$\frac{1-q}{q^2}$
Exponential	Continuous	Waiting time T for an event that occurs at rate λ	p.d.f. $=\lambda e^{-\lambda t}$	$\frac{1}{\lambda}$	$\frac{1}{\lambda^2}$
Normal	Continuous	Value X of many continuous measurements	p.d.f. $=\frac{1}{\sqrt{2\pi}\sigma}e^{-\frac{(x-\mu)^2}{2\sigma^2}}$	μ	σ^2

Exponentials and Logarithms

Laws of Exponents for Any Base $a > 0$		Laws of Logarithms for Base e	
Law 1	$a^x \cdot a^y = a^{x+y}$	Law 1	$\ln(xy) = \ln x + \ln y$
Law 2	$(a^x)^y = a^{xy}$	Law 2	$\ln(x^y) = y \ln x$
Law 3	$a^{-x} = 1/a^x$	Law 3	$\ln(1/x) = -\ln x$
Law 4	$a^y/a^x = a^{y-x}$	Law 4	$\ln(x/y) = \ln x - \ln y$
Law 5	$a^1 = a$	Law 5	$\ln(e) = 1$
Law 6	$a^0 = 1$	Law 6	$\ln(1) = 0$

Areas under the Standard Normal Curve

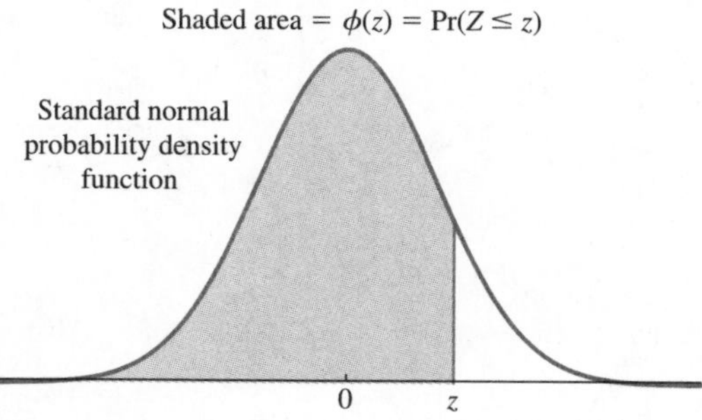

z	$\Phi(z)$	z	$\Phi(z)$	z	$\Phi(z)$	z	$\Phi(z)$
−4.0	0.00003	−2.0	0.02275	0.0	0.50000	2.0	0.97725
−3.9	0.00005	−1.9	0.02872	0.1	0.53986	2.1	0.98214
−3.8	0.00007	−1.8	0.03593	0.2	0.57926	2.2	0.98610
−3.7	0.00011	−1.7	0.04457	0.3	0.61791	2.3	0.98928
−3.6	0.00016	−1.6	0.05480	0.4	0.65542	2.4	0.99180
−3.5	0.00023	−1.5	0.06681	0.5	0.69146	2.5	0.99379
−3.4	0.00034	−1.4	0.08076	0.6	0.72575	2.6	0.99534
−3.3	0.00048	−1.3	0.09680	0.7	0.75804	2.7	0.99653
−3.2	0.00069	−1.2	0.11507	0.8	0.78814	2.8	0.99744
−3.1	0.00097	−1.1	0.13567	0.9	0.81594	2.9	0.99813
−3.0	0.00135	−1.0	0.15865	1.0	0.84134	3.0	0.99865
−2.9	0.00187	−0.9	0.18406	1.1	0.86433	3.1	0.99903
−2.8	0.00256	−0.8	0.21185	1.2	0.88493	3.2	0.99931
−2.7	0.00347	−0.7	0.24196	1.3	0.90320	3.3	0.99952
−2.6	0.00466	−0.6	0.27425	1.4	0.91924	3.4	0.99966
−2.5	0.00621	−0.5	0.30854	1.5	0.93319	3.5	0.99977
−2.4	0.00820	−0.4	0.34458	1.6	0.94520	3.6	0.99984
−2.3	0.01072	−0.3	0.38209	1.7	0.95543	3.7	0.99989
−2.2	0.01390	−0.2	0.42074	1.8	0.96407	3.8	0.99993
−2.1	0.01786	−0.1	0.46017	1.9	0.97128	3.9	0.99995

Critical values of the *t* distribution

Degrees of Freedom	95% Confidence Limit	99% Confidence Limit
1	12.71	63.66
2	4.303	9.925
3	3.182	5.841
4	2.776	4.604
5	2.571	4.032
6	2.447	3.707
7	2.365	3.499
8	2.306	3.355
9	2.262	3.250
10	2.228	3.169
11	2.201	3.106
12	2.179	3.055
13	2.160	3.012
14	2.145	2.977
15	2.131	2.947
16	2.120	2.921
17	2.110	2.898
18	2.101	2.878
19	2.093	2.861
20	2.086	2.845
21	2.080	2.831
22	2.074	2.819
23	2.069	2.807
24	2.064	2.797
25	2.060	2.787
26	2.056	2.779
27	2.052	2.771
28	2.048	2.763
29	2.045	2.756
30	2.042	2.750

Letters of the Greek Alphabet Used in the Text

Capital Letter	Lowercase Letter	Pronunciation	Capital Letter	Lowercase Letter	Pronunciation
	α	Alpha		μ	Mu
	β	Beta		ν	Nu
Γ	γ	Gamma	Π	π	Pi
Δ	δ	Delta		ρ	Rho
	ϵ	Epsilon	Σ	σ	Sigma
	η	Eta		τ	Tau
Θ	θ	Theta	Φ	ϕ	Phi
Λ	λ	Lambda		χ	Chi